797,885 Books
are available to read at

Forgotten Books

www.ForgottenBooks.com

Forgotten Books' App
Available for mobile, tablet & eReader

ISBN 978-1-331-50038-4
PIBN 10198525

This book is a reproduction of an important historical work. Forgotten Books uses state-of-the-art technology to digitally reconstruct the work, preserving the original format whilst repairing imperfections present in the aged copy. In rare cases, an imperfection in the original, such as a blemish or missing page, may be replicated in our edition. We do, however, repair the vast majority of imperfections successfully; any imperfections that remain are intentionally left to preserve the state of such historical works.

Forgotten Books is a registered trademark of FB &c Ltd.
Copyright © 2017 FB &c Ltd.
FB &c Ltd, Dalton House, 60 Windsor Avenue, London, SW19 2RR.
Company number 08720141. Registered in England and Wales.

For support please visit www.forgottenbooks.com

1 MONTH OF FREE READING

at

www.ForgottenBooks.com

By purchasing this book you are eligible for one month membership to ForgottenBooks.com, giving you unlimited access to our entire collection of over 700,000 titles via our web site and mobile apps.

To claim your free month visit: www.forgottenbooks.com/free198525

* Offer is valid for 45 days from date of purchase. Terms and conditions apply.

English
Français
Deutsche
Italiano
Español
Português

www.forgottenbooks.com

Mythology Photography **Fiction**
Fishing Christianity **Art** Cooking
Essays Buddhism Freemasonry
Medicine **Biology** Music **Ancient Egypt** Evolution Carpentry Physics
Dance Geology **Mathematics** Fitness
Shakespeare **Folklore** Yoga Marketing
Confidence Immortality Biographies
Poetry **Psychology** Witchcraft
Electronics Chemistry History **Law**
Accounting **Philosophy** Anthropology
Alchemy Drama Quantum Mechanics
Atheism Sexual Health **Ancient History**
Entrepreneurship Languages Sport
Paleontology Needlework Islam
Metaphysics Investment Archaeology
Parenting Statistics Criminology
Motivational

AGRICULTURE APPROPRIATION BILL, 1920

HOUSE REPORT. No. 980

AND

HEARINGS

BEFORE THE

COMMITTEE ON AGRICULTURE

HOUSE OF REPRESENTATIVES

SIXTY-FIFTH CONGRESS
THIRD SESSION

ON THE

AGRICULTURE APPROPRIATION BILL

WASHINGTON
GOVERNMENT PRINTING OFFICE
1919

AGRICULTURE APPROPRIATION BILL, 1920

HOUSE REPORT No. 980

AND

HEARINGS

BEFORE THE

COMMITTEE ON AGRICULTURE

HOUSE OF REPRESENTATIVES

SIXTY-FIFTH CONGRESS
THIRD SESSION

ON THE

AGRICULTURE APPROPRIATION BILL

WASHINGTON
GOVERNMENT PRINTING OFFICE
1919

the Secretary of Agriculture, the regular and supplemental estimates submitted by the Department of Agriculture to the committee, the amount carried in this bill, the increases and decreases of the bill, as compared with the estimates submitted by the department, and the increases and decreases of the bill, as compared with the appropriation for the present fiscal year:

Appropriations, 1920, United States Department of Agriculture.

Bureau or office.	Appropriation in agricultural act, 1919.	Bureau or office estimates, 1920.	Department estimates, 1920.	Reported by House committee.	Increase (+) over or decrease (−) below department estimates.	Increase (+) over or decrease (−) below 1919 appropriations.
Office of Secretary	$462,000	$513,930 [1] 30,870	$491,720 [1] 30,870	$501,020	− $21,570	+ $39,020
Office of Farm Management	305,090	305,030 [1] 120 [2] 162,00	305,090 [1] 120 [2] 162,000	305,090	− 162,120	....
Weather Bureau	1,912,930	1,912,930 [1] 24,900	1,906,850 [1] 24,900	1,880,210	− 51,540	− 32,720
Bureau of Animal Industry	4,079,588	4,389,228 [1] 23,180	4,080,468 [1] 23,180	5,127,033	+1,023,385	+1,047,445
Bureau of Plant Industry	3,137,038	3,500,088 [1] 37,900	3,294,138 [1] 37,900	3,251,398	− 80,640	+ 114,360
Forest Service	5,731,555	6,024,829 [1] 33,900	6,026,629 [1] 33,900	5,966,869	− 93,660	+ 735,314
Bureau of Chemistry	1,243,391	[3]1,838,091 [1] 18,600	[3]1,611,571 [1] 18,600	1,381,571	− 248,600	+ 138,180
Bureau of Soils	491,235	511,235 [1] 3,130	509,895 [1] 3,130	491,235	− 21,790	....
Bureau of Entomology	986,680	[4]1,035,810 − 14,460	[4]1,035,960 − [1] 4,460	1,031,360	− 140	+ 44,680
Bureau of Biological Survey	586,350	988,870 [1] 900	710,870 [1] 900	662,170	− 49,600	+ 75,820
Division of Accounts and Disbursements	44,920	44,620 −[1] 120	44,920 −[1] 120	44,620	− 180	− 300
Division of Publications	214,740	248,720 [1] 36,710	223,190 [1] 36,710	239,690	− 20,210	+ 24,950
Bureau of Crop Estimates	346,232	414,701 [1] 24,650	389,901 [1] 24,650	371,102	− 43,449	+ 24,870
Library	50,160	59,660 [1] 8,100	50,160 [1] 8,100	50,160	− 8,100	....
Miscellaneous expenses, Department of Agriculture	142,500	142,500	142,500	142,500	....	....
Rent in the District of Columbia	158,689	158,689	158,689	158,689	....	....
States Relations Service	3,150,820	3,246,160 [1] 2,640 [5]4,473,680	3,245,820 [1] 2,640 [5]4,473,680	4,705,820	−3,016,320	+1,555,000
Bureau of Public Roads	593,540	642,860 [1] 3,480	642,820 [1] 3,480	594,320	− 51,980	+ 780
Bureau of Markets	2,023,255	3,723,275 [1] 10,660	3,131,455 [1] 10,660	2,689,365	− 452,750	+ 666,110
Insecticide and Fungicide Board	[2]21,240	125,240 [1] 3,820	122,740 [1] 3,820	123,940	− 2,620	+ 2,700
Federal Horticultural Board	74,800	79,000 [1] 240 [6] 50,000	79,000 [1] 240 [6] 50,000	129,000	− 240	+ 54,200
Total, Department of Agriculture, for routine and ordinary work	25,856,753	34,850,366	33,149,286	29,847,162	−3,302,124	+3,990,409
MISCELLANEOUS APPROPRIATIONS.						
Demonstrations on reclamation projects	48,600	48,600	48,600	48,600	....	....
Cooperative fire protection of forested watersheds of navigable streams	100,000	100,000	100,000	100,000	....	....

[1] Supplementary estimates, statutory salaries.
[2] Supplemental estimate, farm labor.
[3] Includes $250,000 for drying vegetables, fruits, etc., transferred from miscellaneous section of the bill.
[4] Includes $20,000 for eradication of sweet-potato weevil transferred from miscellaneous section of the bill.
[5] Supplemental estimate, farmers' cooperative demonstrations.
[6] Supplemental estimate, European potato-wart disease.

Appropriations, 1920, United States Department of Agriculture—Continued.

Bureau or office.	Appropriation in agricultural act, 1919.	Bureau or office estimates, 1920.	Department estimates, 1920.	Reported by House committee.	Increase (+) over or decrease (−) below department estimates.	Increase (+) over or decrease (−) below 1919 appropriations.
MISCELLANEOUS APPROPRIATIONS—continued.						
Experiments and demonstrations in live-stock production in the cane-sugar and cotton districts of the United States...	$60,000	$60,000	$60,000	$60,000		
Experiments in dairying and live-stock production in semi-arid and irrigated districts of the western United States......	40,000	40,000	40,000	40,000		
Eradication of the foot-and-mouth and other contagious diseases of animals.............	1,000,000	1,000,000	1,000,000	1,000,000		
Eradication of pink bollworm....	500,000	595,800	595,800	595,800		+ $95,800
Drying vegetables, fruits, etc.....	1 250,000					− 250,000
Eradication of sweet-potato weevil.................	2 20,000					− 20,000
Grand total, Department of Agriculture.............	27,875,353	36,694,766	34,993,686	31,691,562	−$3,302,124	+3,816,209

[1] Transferred to the Bureau of Chemistry.   [2] Transferred to the Bureau of Entomology.

REVENUES.

In considering the above table it should be borne in mind that the appropriations of the Department of Agriculture are offset to some extent by certain revenues resulting from or incident to its activities. These revenues during the fiscal year 1918 amounted to $8,802,836.62, and were covered into the Treasury as miscellaneous receipts. They include the following items:

Receipts from national forests, $3,574,930.07.—The receipts from the national forests were derived from the following sources, and represent an increase of $117,901.66 over the year 1917:

(a) Timber, $1,621,697.16: Sales of all classes of stumpage on the national forests, payments for timber destroyed on rights of way or other uses, payments for timber cut or removed without previous permit, and damages assessed against persons setting fire to forest areas.

(b) Grazing, $1,725,821.94: Payments for grazing privileges on national forest ranges for cattle, horses, swine, sheep, and goats, and for unauthorized use of grazing areas.

(c) Special uses, $227,410.97: Payments for use of forest lands for various purposes, such as residences, camps, cabins, hotels, rights of way, agriculture, wharves, water power, telegraph and telephone lines, reservoirs, conduits, etc., and use of forest areas for turpentine extraction.

Benefits derived by States from receipts from national forests.—Under existing law 10 per cent of the forest receipts is expended by the Secretary of Agriculture in the construction of roads and trails, and 25 per cent of the forest receipts is paid to the States by the Federal Government for the benefit of county schools and roads. The amounts expended in or paid to each State during the fiscal year 1918 are shown below:

State.	School and road moneys payable to States.	Road and trail moneys expendable by Secretary of Agriculture.
Alabama	$32.48	$12.99
Alaska	24,141.95	9,656.78
Arizona	92,586.32	37,034.52
Arkansas	9,491.35	3,796.54
California	108,603.36	43,441.35
Colorado	89,103.82	35,641.53
Florida	2,310.94	924.38
Georgia	431.25	172.50
Idaho	107,177.43	42,870.98
Maine	287.07	114.83
Michigan	90.28	36.11
Minnesota	8,035.21	3,214.08
Montana	76,597.56	30,639.02
Nebraska	2,308.66	923.46
Nevada	21,675.52	8,670.22
New Hampshire	3,169.62	1,267.85
New Mexico	68,572.15	27,428.86
North Carolina	1,574.58	629.83
Oklahoma	1,509.60	603.84
Oregon	95,187.20	38,074.87
South Carolina	96.63	38.65
South Dakota	15,300.89	6,120.36
Tennessee	1,224.45	489.78
Utah	57,306.75	22,922.70
Virginia	5,730.72	2,292.29
Washington	42,457.38	16,982.96
West Virginia	735.54	294.21
Wyoming	40,595.68	16,238.26
Total	876,334.39	350,533.75

Additional benefits derived by Arizona and New Mexico from receipts from national forests.—The States of Arizona and New Mexico received additional shares of national-forest receipts for their school funds on account of school lands included within national forests, as follows: Arizona, $48,656.12; New Mexico, $20,936.47.

Telegrams over Government lines, $4,763.30.—These receipts are derived through the transmission of private messages over Weather Bureau telegraph lines in isolated regions where commercial lines are not yet available.

Sale of cotton standards, $2,360.60.—These receipts are derived through the sale of practical forms of the official cotton standards prepared by the department to the various exchanges, spot-market dealers, merchants, cotton mills, agricultural colleges, and textile schools.

Cost of cotton-futures disputes, $1,227.70.—These receipts are derived through the settlement of disputes referred to the department from time to time by either party to a contract of sale of cotton for future delivery, for determination as to the quality, grade, or length of staple of the cotton, in accordance with the provisions of the United States cotton-futures act.

Sale of loose cotton, $33,578.66.—In the preparation of practical forms of the official cotton standards it is necessary for the department to purchase in the open market considerable quantities of cotton in order to match the various types and classes of cotton. A large quantity of the cotton thus purchased is found unsuitable for use in making copies of the official cotton standards and this is disposed of to dealers at the best price obtainable.

Cost of grain-standards appeals, $1,458.48.—These receipts represent charges made for the settlement of appeals from the grading of grain by licensed inspectors; also disputes as to the correct grade of grain entering into interstate commerce between noninspection points referred to the Department of Agriculture in accordance with the provisions of the United States grain-standards act.

Sale of photo prints, lanterns slides, etc., $675.58.—These receipts are derived through the sale of photo prints, lantern slides, transparencies, blue prints, and motion-pictures films to State institutions, publishers, and individuals for use in lecture work and in connection with the preparation of publications bearing on agriculture and related subjects.

Sale of hearings, $58.10.—These receipts are derived through the sale of hearings conducted by the department from time to time in connection with the enforcement of regulatory acts, particularly the food and drugs act and the insecticide and fungicide act. These hearings are sold to corporations, firms, and individuals desiring them at the rate of 10 cents per folio to cover the cost of preparing them.

Sale of card indexes, $26.31.—These receipts are derived through the sale of card indexes of experiment station literature to various agricultural colleges, experiment stations, educational instututions, and libraries throughout the country.

Sale of other miscellaneous property, $62,031.60.—This covers the sale of unserviceable property owned by the department which has been passed upon and condemned by a board of survey appointed by the Secretary of Agriculture. It also covers the proceeds derived through the sale of farm products obtained at the various experiment stations of the department, other than the insular experiment stations; animals and animal products no longer needed in the work of the department; forest maps and maps and publications of the Weather Bureau; pathological and zoological specimens; samples of pure sugars and naval stores; microscopical specimens, etc.

Sale of products, agricultural stations, Alaska, Hawaii, Porto Rico, and Guam, $2,825.85.—These receipts are derived through the sale of agricultural products obtained on the land belonging to the agricultural experiment stations in Alaska, Hawaii, Porto Rico, and the Island of Guam.

Sale of seeds to farmers, $1,490,173.96.—These receipts are derived through the sale of seeds to farmers for cash, at cost, in sections where, on account of drought or other unfavorable conditions, such assistance was needed. Such sales are specifically provided for in the food production act.

Sale of nitrate of soda to farmers, $3,628,726.41.—These receipts are derived through sale of nitrate of soda to farmers for cash, at cost, in sections where a special need for such assistance existed. Such sales are specifically provided for in the food control act.

In the following pages the reasons for all increases in appropriations are given, and all changes in amounts in the statutory rolls are indicated.

AGRICULTURE APPROPRIATION BILL.

OFFICE OF THE SECRETARY.

STATUTORY SALARIES.

(P. 2, line 3.)

The statutory roll of the Office of the Secretary carries an apparent increase of $39,020, but there is an actual increase of $18,700, as indicated in detail in the following table:

Promotions:		
Private secretary to the Secretary of Agriculture, $2,500 to $3,000.	$500	
1 inspector, $2,750 to $3,000	250	
		$750
New places:		
1 Assistant Secretary of Agriculture	5,000	
1 attorney	3,500	
1 attorney	3,250	
		11,750
Transfer from extra-labor roll of Secretary's Office, which fund has not been correspondingly reduced: 1 mechanical assistant	1,400	
For extra labor and emergency employments, increase of	8,000	
	21,900	
Places dropped: 2 law clerks, at $1,600 each	3,200	
Actual increase		18,700

Transfers from funds of other bureaus, which funds have been correspondingly reduced.

1 clerk, class 3, from statutory roll, Bureau of Chemistry	$1,600
2 clerks, class 2, from marketing and distributing farm products and grain standards act, Bureau of Markets	2,800
1 clerk, class 1, from statutory roll, Division of Publications	1,200
2 clerks, at $1,100 each, from meat inspection, Bureau of Animal Industry	2,200
5 clerks, at $900 each, 1 from meat inspection and 2 from statutory roll, Bureau of Animal Industry; 1 from statutory roll, Bureau of Plant Industry; and 1 from statutory roll, Bureau of Chemistry	4,500
1 mechanical assistant, from statutory roll, Bureau of Markets	1,380
1 assistant engineer, from meat inspection, Bureau of Animal Industry	1,200
1 instrument maker, from statutory roll, Bureau of Animal Industry	1,200
1 electrical wireman, from collecting and distributing market information, Bureau of Markets	1,100
4 watchmen, at $720 each, 1 from general administrative expenses, Bureau of Entomology, and 1 each from marketing and distributing farm products, rural cooperation, and administration of warehouse act, Bureau of Markets	2,880
1 skilled laborer, from statutory roll, Bureau of Animal Industry	900
1 skilled laborer, from statutory roll, Bureau of Public Roads	720
1 messenger boy, from meat inspection, Bureau of Animal Industry	600
1 laborer, from food habits of birds and mammals, Bureau of Biological Survey	480
1 charwoman, from statutory roll, Bureau of Crop Estimates	360
	23,120

Transfers to rolls of other bureaus and the Secretary's roll correspondingly reduced.

2 clerks, class 2, 1 each to statutory rolls of Bureau of Chemistry and Division of Publications	2,800	
		20,320
Apparent increase		39,020

The following proviso has been inserted in the statutory roll:

That hereafter the position of attorney in the Department of Agriculture shall be and remain in the competitive classified civil service, anything in the law or in the civil-service rules and regulations to the contrary notwithstanding, and the law clerks now in said department who may be appointed or promoted to said positions of attorney shall retain all the rights of competitive employees, and the Secretary of Agriculture may detail said attorneys for service in or out of the District of Columbia.

OFFICE OF FARM MANAGEMENT.

STATUTORY SALARIES.

(P. 5, line 1.)

The statutory roll of the Office of Farm Management carries an apparent increase of $3,500, but there is no actual increase, as indicated in detail in the following table:

Transfers from lump fund of this office, which fund has been correspondingly reduced.

2 clerks, class 1, from general expenses	$2,400
1 draftsman, from general expenses	1,100
Apparent increase	3,500

GENERAL EXPENSES.

Farm management and farm practice investigations (p. 5, line 15).—There is an apparent decrease in this item of $3,500, but, as that amount has been transferred to the statutory roll, there is actually no change. A proviso has been inserted authorizing the expenditure of $23,873 for ascertaining the cost of production of the principal staple agricultural products.

WEATHER BUREAU.

STATUTORY SALARIES.

(P. 6, line 2.)

The statutory roll of the Weather Bureau carries an apparent increase of $13,940, but an actual decrease of $720, as indicated in detail in the following table:

Place dropped: 1 skilled mechanic	$720
Actual decrease	720

Transfers from lump funds of this bureau, which funds have been correspondingly reduced.

4 clerks, at $1,000 each, from aerological stations	$4,000	
1 skilled mechanic, from aerological stations	1,300	
1 repairman, from station salaries	960	
10 laborers, at $720 each, from aerological stations	7,200	
2 laborers, at $600 each, from aerological stations	1,200	
		14,660
Apparent increase		13,940

AGRICULTURE APPROPRIATION BILL.

GENERAL EXPENSES.

Expenses outside of Washington (p. 9, line 11).—There is an apparent decrease in this item of $7,960, but as $960 has been transferred to the statutory roll there is an actual decrease of $7,000.

Aerological investigations (p. 9, line 20).—There is an apparent decrease in this item of $13,700, but as that amount has been transferred to the stautory roll there is actually no change.

Repairs to telegraph and cable lines.—The appropriation act for 1919 carries an item of $25,000 for repairing and renewing the seacoast telegraph cable lines. This item has been omitted from the present bill, as the purpose for which the appropriation was made will be accomplished during the current fiscal year.

BUREAU OF ANIMAL INDUSTRY.

STATUTORY SALARIES.

(P. 10, line 2.)

The statutory roll of the Bureau of Animal Industry carries an apparent increase of $73,440, but an actual decrease of $5,500, as indicated in detail in the following table:

Place dropped: 1 assistant in live-stock investigations		$1,600
Transfers to statutory roll, Secretary's office:		
2 clerks, at $900 each	$1,800	
1 instrument maker	1,200	
1 skilled laborer	900	
		3,900
Actual decrease		5,500

Transfers from lump funds of this bureau, which funds have been correspondingly reduced.

1 executive clerk, from eradicating cattle ticks	$2,000
1 clerk, class 4, from tuberculosis eradication	1,800
1 clerk, from meat inspection	1,500
8 clerks, class 2, 2 from inspection and quarantine, 2 from dairy industry, 1 from animal husbandry, 1 from eradicating hog cholera, 1 from control of viruses, serums, and toxins, and 1 from meat inspection	11,200
27 clerks, class 1, 3 from inspection and quarantine, 3 from tuberculosis eradication, 2 from eradicating cattle ticks, 7 from dairy industry, 2 from animal husbandry, 2 from poultry feeding and breeding, 1 from eradicating hog cholera, 1 from control of viruses, serums, and toxins, 1 from eradicating dourine, and 5 from meat inspection	32,400
3 clerks, at $1,100 each, 1 from eradicating cattle ticks, 1 from animal husbandry, and 1 from eradicating hog cholera	3,300
5 clerks, at $1,080 each, 1 from inspection and quarantine, 1 from tuberculosis eradication, 1 from eradicating cattle ticks, 1 from dairy industry, and 1 from control of viruses, serums, and toxins	5,400
1 clerk, from dairy industry	1,020
12 clerks, at $960 each, from meat inspection	11,520
1 laboratory mechanician, from meat inspection	1,440
1 skilled laborer, from animal husbandry	1,000
1 skilled laborer, from inspection and quarantine	900
1 laborer, from military horse breeding	900
5 laborers, at $720 each, 2 unskilled from eradicating cattle ticks, 1 unskilled from dairy industry, and 2 skilled from hog-cholera research	3,600
2 charwomen, at $480 each, from meat inspection	960
	78,940
Apparent increase	73,440

GENERAL EXPENSES.

Inspection and quarantine (p. 13, line 3).—There is an apparent decrease in this item of $8,380, but, as that amount has been transferred to the statutory roll, there is actually no change.

Tuberculosis of animals (p. 13, line 13).—There is an apparent increase in this item of $493,520, but, as $6,480 has been transferred to the statutory roll, there is an actual increase of $500,000.

This sum is needed for the more effective prosecution of the campaign against tuberculosis which the department has actively under way, in cooperation with the authorities in the various States, and especially to provide for the payment of the Federal Government's share of the indemnities authorized by the paragraph.

The language of the paragraph has been changed by the substitution of the words "condemnation" and "condemned" for "destruction" and "destroyed." Under the present wording of the item, the animals actually must be destroyed in the same State, county, or municipality where found diseased. If the change recommended is made, the movement of diseased animals to recognized slaughtering centers in other States for slaughter would be permitted.

Tick eradication (p. 15, line 22).—There is an apparent decrease in this item of $8,020, but, as that amount has been transferred to the statutory roll, there is actually no change.

Dairy investigations (p. 16, line 11).—There is an apparent decrease in this item of $14,020, but, as that amount has been transferred to the statutory roll, there is actually no change.

Animal husbandry investigations (p. 16, line 15).—There is an apparent decrease in this item of $1,000, but as $9,200 has been transferred to the statutory roll, there is an actual increase of $8,200. This sum will be used for the extension of farm sheep investigations.

Hog cholera (p. 17, line 20).—There is an apparent increase in this item of $194,145, but, as $8,820 has been transferred to the statutory roll, there is an actual increase of $202,965. This merely represents a transfer from the food production act.

Dourine eradication (p. 18, line 10).—There is an apparent decrease in this item of $9,000, but, as $1,200 has been transferred to the statutory roll, there is an actual decrease of $7,800.

MEAT INSPECTION.

(P. 18, line 18.)

There is an apparent increase in this item of $326,760, but, as $27,720 has been transferred to statutory rolls, there is an actual increase of $354,480. This sum will be used for increasing the salaries of 2,932 employees of the meat-inspection service by $120 per annum each and of 11 employees of said service by $240 per annum each.

AGRICULTURE APPROPRIATION BILL.

BUREAU OF PLANT INDUSTRY.

STATUTORY SALARIES.

(P. 19, line 9.)

The statutory roll of the Bureau of Plant Industry carries an apparent increase of $51,260, but an actual decrease of $300, as indicated in detail in the following table:

New places:		
1 map tracer or laboratory aid	$900	
1 blacksmith	1,200	
		$2,100
Places dropped:		
1 map tracer	$600	
1 blacksmith	900	
		1,500
Transfer to statutory roll of Secretary's office: 1 clerk	900	
		2,400
Actual decrease		300

Transfers from lump funds of this bureau, which funds have been correspondingly reduced.

1 executive clerk, from administrative expenses	$1,980	
2 clerks, class 4, from foreign seed and plant introduction and purchase and distribution of valuable seeds	3,600	
2 clerks, class 3, from crop acclimatization and pomological investigations	3,200	
1 clerk, from crop acclimatization	1,500	
2 clerks, class 2, from citrus canker eradication and blister rust control	2,800	
3 clerks, at $1,320 each, 1 from forest pathology and 2 from blister rust control	3,960	
15 clerks, class 1, 1 from citrus canker eradication, 2 from blister rust control, 6 from cereal investigations, 1 from soil fertility, 2 from foreign seed and plant introduction, 1 from forage crops, 1 from new and rare seeds, and 1 from purchase and distribution of valuable seeds	18,000	
1 draftsman, from horticultural investigations	1,200	
2 clerks, at $1,100 each, from blister rust control	2,200	
3 clerks, at $1,080 each, from citrus canker eradication, blister rust control, and cereal investigations	3,240	
5 clerks, at $1,000 each, 1 each from dry-land agriculture, horticultural investigations, and new and rare seeds, and 2 from foreign seed and plant introduction	5,000	
1 laborer, from cereal investigations	720	
1 artist, from economic and systematic botany	900	
1 skilled laborer, from foreign seed and plant introduction	1,100	
4 messenger boys, at $480 each, 1 from pomological investigations and 3 from foreign seed and plant introduction	1,920	
1 charwoman, from bacteriology and nutrition	240	
		51,560
Apparent increase		51,260

GENERAL EXPENSES.

Citrus canker (p. 22, line 1).—There is an apparent decrease in this item of $53,680, but, as $3,680 has been transferred to the statutory roll, there is an actual decrease of $50,000

Forest pathology (p. 22, line 19).—There is an apparent decrease in this item of $1,320, but, as that amount has been transferred to the statutory roll, there is actually no change.

White-pine blister rust (p. 23, line 1).—There is an apparent decrease in this item of $9,720, but, as that amount has been transferred to the statutory roll, there is actually no change.

Soil bacteriology investigations (p. 23, line 21).—There is an apparent decrease in this item of $240, but, as that amount has been transferred to the statutory roll, there is actually no change.

Soil-fertility investigations (p. 24, line 3).—There is an apparent decrease in this item of $1,200, but, as that amount has been transferred to the statutory roll, there is actually no change.

Crop acclimatization and fiber plant investigations (p. 24, line 8).—There is an apparent decrease in this item of $3,100, but, as that amount has been transferred to the statutory roll, there is actually no change.

The language of the first proviso has been changed by the substitution of the word "may" for "shall."

Cereal investigations (p. 25, line 15).—There is an apparent decrease in this item of $9,000, but, as that amount has been transferred to the statutory roll, there is actually no change. The immediately available clause in the proviso setting aside $150,000 for the destruction of vegetation from which rust spores originate has been omitted.

Sugar-plant investigations (p. 26, line 14).—There is an apparent increase in this item of $30,000, which represents a transfer from the food-production act. This sum will be used as follows: (a) $10,000 for sugar-beet nematode work, and (b) $20,000 for the control of a new sugar-cane disease in Porto Rico.

Economic and systematic botany (p. 27, line 3).—There is an apparent decrease in this item of $900, but, as that amount has been transferred to the statutory roll, there is actually no change.

Dry-land agriculture investigations (p. 27, line 6).—There is an apparent decrease in this item of $1,000, but, as that item has been transferred to the statutory roll, there is actually no change.

The proviso removing the limitation as to the cost of buildings, so far as it applies to this paragraph, has been omitted.

Pomological investigations (p. 27, line 21).—There is an apparent decrease in this item of $2,080, but, as that amount has been transferred to the statutory roll, there is actually no change.

Horticultural investigations (p. 28, line 12).—There is an apparent increase in this item of $12,800, but, as $2,200 has been transferred to the statutory roll, there is an actual increase of $15,000. This sum will be used in connection with the location and improvement of seed stocks, and represents a transfer from the food production act.

Foreign seed and plant introduction (p. 29, line 1).—There is an apparent decrease in this item of $8,740, but, as that amount has been transferred to the statutory roll, there is actually no change.

New and rare seeds; forage-crop investigations (p. 29, line 7).—There is an apparent decrease in this item of $3,400, but, as that amount has been transferred to the statutory roll, there is actually no change.

Administrative expenses (p. 29, line 16).—There is an apparent decrease in this item of $1,980, but, as that amount has been transferred to the statutory roll, there is actually no change.

Administration expenses (p. 29, line 16).—There is an apparent decrease in this item of $1,980, but, as that amount has been transferred to the statutory roll, there is actually no change.

PURCHASE AND DISTRIBUTION OF VALUABLE SEEDS.

(P. 29, line 23.)

There is an apparent increase in this item of $116,660, but, as $3,000 has been transferred to the statutory roll, there is an actual increase of $119,660.

FOREST SERVICE.

STATUTORY SALARIES.

(P. 32, line 15.)

There is an apparent increase in the statutory roll of $2,040, but an actual increase of $240, as indicated in detail in the following table:

Promotion: 1 forest supervisor, $2,800 to $3,040..........................	$240
Actual increase..	$240
Transfer from lump fund of this bureau, which fund has been correspondingly reduced: 1 surveyor, from survey of lands...............................	1,800
Apparent increase...	2,040

GENERAL EXPENSES.

Introductory paragraph (p. 35, line 3).—The limitation on the cost of any building erected on the national forests has been increased from $650 to $800.

National forests and general administration (p. 44, line 1).—There is an increase in this item of $266,074, which will be used as follows: (a) $225,568 for additional fire protection on a number of the national forests; (b) $5,000 for the maintenance of Government stock; (c) $22,002 for the employment of additional forest assistants and scalers and for brush burning and other expenses incident to the increased timber sale business; (d) $5,304 for the administration of grazing on certain forests; (e) $3,500 for the administration and protection of land added to the Colorado national forest by presidential proclamation; and (f) $4,700 for general administrative expenses on certain forests.

Land classification and entry surveys (p. 44, line 10).—The item for land classification and the item for entry surveys have been combined in one paragraph. They show an apparent decrease in the total appropriation of $12,800, but as $1,800 has been transferred to the statutory roll, there is an actual decrease of $11,000. The proviso in the item for entry surveys has been omitted.

Tree planting on national forests (p. 45, line 15).—A proviso has been added to authorize the purchase, at a cost of not to exceed $200, of land now used as a forest nursery site for the Michigan national forest.

Reconnaissance of forest resources (p. 46, line 4).—There is a reduction in this item of $20,000.

BUREAU OF CHEMISTRY.

STATUTORY SALARIES.

(P. 47, line 24.)

There is an apparent increase in the statutory roll of $17,760, but an actual decrease of $1,100, as indicated in detail in the following table:

Transfers from lump fund for food and drugs act of this bureau, which fund has been correspondingly reduced.

1 administrative assistant	$2,500
1 clerk, class 3	1,600
9 clerks, class 1	10,800
2 multigraph operators, at $1,000 each	2,000
1 mechanic	1,000
4 charwomen, at $240 each	960
	18,860

Transfers to statutory roll, Secretary's office.

1 clerk, class 3	$1,600	
1 clerk	900	
		2,500

Transfer from statutory roll, Secretary's office.

1 clerk, class 2	$1,400
Actual decrease	1,100
Apparent increase	17,760

GENERAL EXPENSES.

Poultry and egg investigations (p. 50, line 12).—There is an increase in this item of $5,000. This sum will be used for extending the work relating to the conservation of poultry.

Fish and oyster investigations (p. 50, line 18).—The item relating to fish investigations and the item relating to oyster and shellfish investigations have been combined in one paragraph. There is an increase in the combined items of $1,000, which will be used in extending the work in connection with fish investigations.

Color investigations (p. 51, line 6).—There is an increase in this item of $29,280. This sum will be used to complete the equipment of the experimental laboratory at Arlington Farm and to provide additional assistance to carry on the necessary experimental work.

Sirup investigations (p. 51, line 12).—There is an increase in this item of $5,000, which merely represents the transfer from the food production act of the item for the manufacture of sweet sirups by the utilization of new agricultural sources. The necessary changes have been made in the language to provide for this work.

Enforcement of the food and drugs act (p. 51, line 16).—There is an apparent increase in this item of $11,140, but as $18,860 has been transferred to the statutory roll, there is an actual increase of $30,000. This sum is needed to meet the increased cost of travel incidental to the enforcement of the food and drugs act and to purchase chemicals and chemical apparatus entering into laboratory work, as well as more effectively to inspect the interstate and import shipments of foods and drugs.

Dehydration investigations (p. 52, line 18).—There is a decrease in this item, which has been transferred from the miscellaneous sections of the bill, of $200,000, and the language has been changed so as to provide "for the study and improvement of methods of dehydrating materials used for food, in cooperation with such persons, associations, or corporations as may be found necessary, and to disseminate information as to the value and suitability of such products for food."

Manufacture of new and rare chemicals (p. 52, line 23).—This is a new item. It provides $10,000 for experiments in the manufacture of rare chemicals for use in chemical research, and authorizes the Secretary of Agriculture to furnish, upon application, samples of them to investigators for research work, charging a price to cover the cost thereof.

Utilization of wool-scouring wastes (p. 53, line 7).—This item carries an appropriation of $9,000 and represents a transfer from the food-production act.

BUREAU OF SOILS.

STATUTORY SALARIES.

(P. 53, line 12.)

There is no change in the amount of the statutory roll of the Bureau of Soils.

GENERAL EXPENSES.

Classification of lands in national forests (p. 55, line 7).—The language of this paragraph has been amended so as to authorize the Bureau of Soils to cooperate with other bureaus of the department and other departments of the Government in the classification of agricultural lands.

BUREAU OF ENTOMOLOGY.

STATUTORY SALARIES.

(P. 55, line 23.)

There is an apparent increase in the statutory roll of $8,680, but an actual decrease of $4,600, as indicated in detail in the following table:

Promotion: 1 chief of bureau, $4,500 to $5,000		$500
New places:		
3 clerks, class 2	4,200	
5 clerks, class 1	6,000	
		$10,700
Places dropped:		
5 clerks, at $900 each	4,500	
2 clerks, at $840 each	1,680	
4 foremen, at $1,080 each	4,320	
1 messenger boy	360	
1 mechanic	1,080	
1 mechanic	900	
1 mechanic	840	
1 gardener	600	
1 laborer	600	
1 laborer	420	
		15,300
Actual decrease		4,600

Transfers from lump funds of this bureau, which funds have been correspondingly reduced.

1 clerk, class 3, from general administrative expenses	$1,600
1 clerk, class 2, from truck crop and stored product insects	1,400
3 clerks, class 1, 1 each from deciduous fruit insects, southern field crop insects, and general administrative expenses	3,600
1 insect delineator, from southern field crop insects	1,600
2 insect delineators, at $1,400 each, 1 each from deciduous fruit insects and truck crop and stored product insects	2,800
1 photographer, from southern field crop insects	1,200
1 laborer, from forest insects	1,080
	$13,280
Apparent increase	8,680

GENERAL EXPENSES.

Deciduous fruit insect investigations (p. 57, line 3).—There is an apparent increase in this item of $2,400, but, as $2,600 has been transferred to the statutory roll, there is an actual increase of $5,000. This sum will be used in connection with the campaign against the Japanese beetle, a dangerous insect pest of orchard and other fruits, recently imported from Japan.

Cereal and forage insect investigations (p. 57, line 7).—There is an increase in this item of $25,000, of which $10,000 is to be made immediately available. This sum will be used for investigations looking to the control of the European corn borer.

Southern field crop insect investigations (p. 57, line 11).—There is an apparent decrease in this item of $4,000, but, as that amount has been transferred to the statutory roll, there is actually no change.

Forest-insect investigations (p. 57, line 15).—There is an apparent decrease in this item of $1,080, but, as that amount has been transferred to the statutory roll, there is actually no change.

Truck-crop and stored-products insect investigations (p. 57, line 16).—There is an apparent increase in this item of $17,200, but as $2,800 has been transferred to the statutory roll there is an actual increase of $20,000. This sum merely represents the transfer of the item for the control of the sweet-potato weevil from the miscellaneous section of the bill.

Administrative expenses (p. 58, line 9).—There is an apparent decrease in this item of $3,520, but as that amount has been transferred to statutory rolls there is actually no change.

BUREAU OF BIOLOGICAL SURVEY.

STATUTORY SALARIES.

(P. 59, line 11.)

There is an apparent increase in the statutory roll of $7,800, but an actual increase of $500, as indicated in detail in the following table:

Promotion: 1 chief of bureau, $3,500 to $4,000	$500
Actual increase	$500

18   AGRICULTURE APPROPRIATION BILL.

Transfers from lump funds of this bureau, which funds have been correspondingly reduced.

1 clerk, class 2, from food habits of birds and mammals	$1,400
4 clerks, class 1, from food habits of birds and mammals, destroying noxious animals, biological investigations, and maintenance of mammal and bird reservations	4,800
1 clerk, from food habits of birds and mammals	1,100
	$7,300
Apparent increase	7,800

GENERAL EXPENSES.

Enforcement of the Lacey Act (p. 61, line 14).—This item has been combined with the item for the enforcement of the migratory bird treaty act.

Maintenance of mammal and bird reservations (p. 60, line 3).—There is an apparent decrease in this item of $400, but, as $1,200 has been transferred to the statutory roll, there is an actual increase of $800. This sum will be used for the construction of a fenced roadway in the game preserve in the Sully's Hill National Park, N. Dak.

Food habits of birds and mammals (p. 60, line 16).—There is an apparent decrease in this item of $5,380, but, as that amount has been transferred to statutory rolls, there is actually no change.

Biological investigations (p. 61, line 10).—There is an apparent decrease in this item of $1,200, but, as that amount has been transferred to the statutory roll, there is actually no change.

Enforcement of the migratory bird treaty act (p. 61, line 14).—There is an apparent increase in this item of $97,000, but, as the item for the enforcement of the Lacey Act, carrying an appropriation of $22,000, has been transferred to it, there is an actual increase of $75,000. This sum is needed for the effective enforcement of the migratory bird treaty act.

DIVISION OF ACCOUNTS AND DISBURSEMENTS.

STATUTORY SALARIES.

(P. 62, line 11.)

There is a decrease in this item of $300, as indicated in the following table:

New places: 2 clerks, class 1	$2,400
Places dropped: 3 clerks, at $900 each	2,700
Actual decrease	300

DIVISION OF PUBLICATIONS.

STATUTORY SALARIES.

(P. 62, line 22.)

There is an increase in the statutory roll of $16,700, as indicated in detail in the following table:

New places:
1 chief editor	$3,000
1 superintendent of distribution	2,500
5 machine operators, at $1,200 each	6,000

AGRICULTURE APPROPRIATION BILL. 19

```
New places—Continued.
    5 skilled laborers, at $1,000 each..............................  $5,000
    1 messenger or laborer...........................................     900
                                                                          ——————  $17,400
Places dropped: 1 assistant photographer...............................     900
                                                                                   16,500
              Transfer from statutory roll, Secretary's office.
1 clerk, class 2......................................................  $1,400
1 clerk, class 1......................................................   1,200
                                                                          ——————     200
     Actual increase..................................................            16,700
```

GENERAL EXPENSES.

Labor-saving machinery (p. 64, line 8).—There is an increase in this item of $1,500, which will be used for the purchase of additional labor-saving machinery and necessary supplies.

Photographic equipment (p. 64, line 12).—There is an increase in this item of $5,000, which is necessary to meet the increased cost of photographic materials.

Communication and transportation service (p. 64, line 22).—There is an increase in this item of $250 to cover necessary telephone, telegraph, freight, and express charges.

Vehicles (p. 64, line 24).—There is an increase in this item of $500 for the purchase of supplies for trucks and wagons and for necessary replacements.

Miscellaneous expenses (p. 65, line 1).—There is an increase in this item of $1,000 to meet the additional expenses necessitated by the normal growth of the work of the Division of Publications.

BUREAU OF CROP ESTIMATES.

STATUTORY SALARIES.

(P. 65, line 9.)

There is a decrease in this item of $1,380, as indicated in the following table:

```
New place: 1 messenger boy................................................   $660
Places dropped: 2 messengers, at $840 each............................  $1,680
Transfer to statutory roll, Secretary's office: 1 charwoman............     360
                                                                          ——————  2,040
     Actual decrease.....................................................          1,380
```

GENERAL EXPENSES.

Administrative expenses (p. 65, line 24).—There is an apparent increase in this item of $1,250, of which $250 will be used for increasing the compensation of the assistant chief of the bureau, and $1,000 for the purchase of stationery, furniture, typewriters, and other necessary office equipment and supplies.

Field investigations (p. 66, line 3).—There is an increase in this item of $25,000 which will be used for extending the work and facilities of the Bureau of Crop Estimates in the field.

MISCELLANEOUS EXPENSES.

Miscellaneous expenses, Department of Agriculture (p. 67, line 2).—The proviso making $5,000 immediately available has been omitted.

STATES RELATIONS SERVICE.

STATUTORY SALARIES.

(P. 67, line 24.)

There is an apparent increase in the statutory roll of $22,860, but no actual increase, as is indicated in detail in the following table:

Transfers from lump funds of this bureau, which funds have been correspondingly reduced.

1 clerk or chief accountant, from general administrative expenses	$2,400
1 clerk, from farmers' cooperative demonstrations in South	1,980
3 clerks, class 3, from general administrative expenses, colleges and stations, and farmers' cooperative demonstrations in North and West	4,800
1 clerk, class 2, from general administrative expenses	1,400
2 clerks, at $1,320 each, from home economics	2,640
5 clerks, class 1, 1 from colleges and stations, 2 from farmers' cooperative demonstrations in North and West, 2 from farmers' cooperative demonstrations in South, and 1 from home economics	6,000
2 clerks, at $1,100 each, from colleges and stations and general administrative expenses	2,200
2 laborers, at $720 each, from farmers' cooperative demonstrations in North and West and farmers' cooperative demonstrations in South	1,440
Apparent increase	22,860

GENERAL EXPENSES.

Administration of Hatch, Adams, and agricultural extension acts (p. 69, line 7).—There is an apparent increase in this item of $1,100, but, as $3,900 has been transferred to the statutory roll, there is an actual increase of $5,000. This sum will be used in connection with the administration of the agricultural extension act.

Farmers' cooperative demonstrations outside of the cotton belt (p. 70, line 4).—There is an apparent decrease in this item of $3,520, but, as that amount has been transferred to the statutory roll, there is actually no change.

Farmers' cooperative demonstrations in the South (p. 70, line 8).—There is an apparent increase in this item of $5,100, but, as that amount has been transferred to the statutory roll, there is actually no change.

Cooperative agricultural extension work (p. 70, line 20).—This is a new item. It appropriates $1,500,000, to be allotted, paid, and expended in the same manner, upon the same terms and conditions, and under the same supervision as the additional appropriations made by the act of May 8, 1914, commonly known as the cooperative agricultural extension act. Its purpose is to anticipate the appropriations that will be available under the items of the act when it reaches its full development in 1922. The food-production act of November 21, 1918, carries an appropriation of $6,100,000 for extension work, in addition to the funds provided by the agricultural extension act. The present item, therefore, represents a reduction of $4,600,000 below the total amount available during the current fiscal year.

Insular experiment stations (p. 71, line 22).—There is an increase in this item of $25,000, which will be used as follows: (*a*) $10,000 for the Alaska stations; (*b*) $5,000 for the Hawaii station; (*c*) $5,000 for the Porto Rico station; (*d*) $5,000 for the Guam station.

The language of the paragraph has been changed so as to make immediately available the increases recommended for the Alaska and Guam stations, and to authorize the erection of barns, the purchase of breeding live stock, and other expenses connected with the stock-breeding experiments on the island of Kodiak and at the Matanuska station in Alaska; and also to repair the damage done by a typhoon on the island of Guam. The first proviso has been amended so as to permit the use of not to exceed $10,000 for extension work in Hawaii. A new proviso has been added, granting to permanent employees of the department on the Virgin Islands the same privileges as to annual leave as is now conferred on employees assigned to Alaska, Porto Rico, Hawaii, and Guam, and permitting the permanent employees at all these stations to accumulate and use at one time annual leave accruing within a period of four years.

Home economics investigations (p. 73, line 9).—There is an apparent increase in this item of $16,160, but, as $3,840 has been transferred to the statutory roll, there is an actual increase of $20,000. This sum will be used for extending the home economics investigations.

Administrative expenses (p. 73, line 18).—There is an apparent decrease in this item of $1,500, but as $6,500 has been transferred to the statutory roll, there is an actual increase of $5,000. This sum will provide for increased administrative expenses incident to the enlarged activities of the States Relations Service.

BUREAU OF PUBLIC ROADS.

STATUTORY SALARIES.

(P. 74, line 2.)

There is an apparent increase in this item of $9,620, but an actual increase of $780, as indicated in the following table:

Promotion: 1 chief of bureau, $4,500 to $6,000	$1,500
Transfer to statutory roll, office of the Secretary: 1 skilled laborer	720
Actual increase	780

Transfers from lump funds of this bureau, which funds have been correspondingly reduced.

1 instrument maker, from road material	$1,800	
1 clerk, class 4, from road management	1,800	
1 clerk, from road building and maintenance	1,100	
1 mechanic, from road building and maintenance	1,500	
2 laborers, at $900 each, from road material	1,800	
1 laborer, from road material	600	
1 charwoman, from road building and maintenance	240	
		8,840
Apparent increase		9,620

GENERAL EXPENSES.

Road management investigations (p. 75, line 20).—There is an apparent decrease in this item of $1,800, but, as that amount has been transferred to the statutory roll, there is actually no change.

Road building and maintenance investigations (p. 76, line 1).—There is an apparent decrease in this item of $2,840, but, as that amount has been transferred to the statutory roll, there is actually no change.

Road material investigations (p. 76, line 5).—There is an apparent decrease in this item of $4,200, but, as that amount has been transferred to the statutory roll, there is actually no change.

BUREAU OF MARKETS.

STATUTORY SALARIES.

(P. 78, line 9.)

There is an apparent increase in the statutory roll of $283,960, but an actual increase of $168,400, as indicated in detail in the following table:

Promotion: 1 chief of bureau, $4,500 to $5,000	$500	
New places: 4 telegraph operators, at $1,600 each	6,400	
		$6,900
Places dropped:		
6 laboratory aids, at $720 each	4,320	
6 telegraph operators, at $1,080 each	6,480	
1 telegraph operator	1,020	
1 telephone operator	600	
1 map tracer	480	
11 messenger boys, at $420 each	4,620	
1 messenger boy	360	
		17,880
		10,980

Transfers from emergency fund of this bureau for stimulating agriculture (market distribution and food survey work), which fund has been correspondingly reduced.

Market news service on fruits and vegetables:		
2 clerks, class 2	$2,800	
12 clerks, class 1	14,400	
10 clerks, at $1,100 each	11,000	
7 clerks, at $1,080 each	7,560	
20 telephone operators, at $1,400 each	28,000	
2 multigraph operators, at $1,200 each	2,400	
1 machine operator (mimeograph operator)	1,200	
1 machine operator (multigraph operator)	1,100	
1 chauffeur	900	
2 laborers, at $720 each	1,440	
1 laborer	600	
3 messenger boys, at $540 each	1,620	
		73,020
Market news service on live stock and meats:		
1 clerk, class 3	1,600	
1 clerk, class 2	1,400	
11 clerks, class 1	13,200	
11 clerks, at $1,100 each	12,100	
16 telegraph operators, at $1,400 each	22,400	
1 telephone operator	900	
1 telephone operator	840	
1 machine operator (multigraph operator)	1,100	
1 laborer	840	
1 messenger	720	
1 laborer	600	
1 messenger boy	540	
		56,240

AGRICULTURE APPROPRIATION BILL.

Market news service on dairy and poultry products:
7 clerks, class 1	$8,400	
4 clerks, at $1,000 each	4,000	
3 telegraph operators, at $1,400 each	4,200	
1 telegraph operator	1,200	
1 machine operator (mimeograph operator)	1,200	
1 machine operator (graphotype operator)	1,000	
1 laborer	600	
		$20,600

Market news service on grain, hay, and milled feeds:
5 clerks, class 1	6,000	
1 clerk	1,100	
1 laborer	720	
3 messenger boys, at $540 each	1,620	
		9,440

Seed reporting service:
5 clerks, class 1	6,000	
5 clerks, at $1,100 each	5,500	
1 messenger boy	540	
		12,040

Market inspection of perishable foods:
1 clerk, class 1	1,200	
1 clerk	1,100	
		2,300

City market service:
1 clerk	1,320	
3 clerks, class 1	3,600	
2 clerks, at $1,100 each	2,200	
		7,120

	180,760	
Transfer to statutory roll, Secretary's office: 1 mechanical assistant	1,380	
		$179,380

Actual increase 168,400

Transfers from lump funds of this bureau in the Agricultural act, which funds have been correspondingly reduced.

1 administrative assistant, from administrative expenses	$3,000
2 executive clerks, at $2,000 each, from collecting and distributing market information and warehouse act	4,000
1 clerk, from market reports on live stock and meats	2,000
1 executive assistant, from grain standards act	1,980
4 clerks, class 4, from marketing and distributing farm products, collecting and distributing market information, cotton-futures act, and grain standardization	7,200
1 clerk, from grain standards act	1,740
3 clerks, class 3, from collecting and distributing market information, market reports on live stock and meats, and grain standards act	4,800
6 clerks, class 2, 1 from marketing and distributing farm products, 1 from market reports on live stock and meats and 4 from grain standards act	8,400
3 clerks, at $1,320 each, 2 from market reports on live stock and meats, and 1 from grain standards act	3,960
28 clerks, class 1, 5 from marketing and distributing farm products, 2 from collecting and distributing market information, 5 from market inspection of perishable foods, 3 from grain standardization, 1 from standard container act, 11 from grain standards act, and 1 from warehouse act	33,600
7 clerks, at $1,100 each, 1 from marketing and distributing farm products, 2 from collecting and distributing market information, 2 from market inspection of perishable foods, 1 from cotton-futures act, and 1 from grain standards act	7,700
9 clerks, at $1,000 each, 2 from marketing and distributing farm products, 2 from collecting and distributing market information, 1 from market inspection of perishable foods, 1 from rural cooperation, 1 from grain standardization, and 2 from grain standards act	9,000

AGRICULTURE APPROPRIATION BILL.

1 clerk, from grain standards act	$1,080
1 clerk, from State cooperation in marketing work	960
1 superintendent of telegraph, from collecting and distributing market information	2,000
1 telegraph operator, from collecting and distributing market information	1,600
7 telegraph operators, at $1,400 each, 6 from collecting and distributing market information, and 1 from market reports on live stock and meats	9,800
1 telegraph operator, from collecting and distributing market information	1,320
1 telephone operator, from collecting and distributing market information	900
1 draftsman, from marketing and distributing farm products	1,400
1 draftsman, from grain standards act	1,200
2 chauffeurs, at $900 each, from cotton-futures act	1,800
1 laborer, from collecting and distributing market information	840
1 laborer, from cotton futures act	720
2 messenger boys, at $540 each, from market inspection of perishable foods, and grain standards act	1,080
1 laborer, from cotton-futures act	600
1 messenger boy, from grain standards act	480
1 messenger boy, from rural cooperation	480
1 charwoman, from cotton-futures act	480
4 charwomen, at $300 each, from rural cooperation, grain standardization, cotton-futures act, and grain standards act	1,200
1 charwoman, from warehouse act	240
	$115,560
Apparent increase	283,960

GENERAL EXPENSES.

Marketing and distribution (p. 80, line 4).—There is an apparent increase in this item of $25,280, but, as $15,820 has been transferred to statutory rolls, there is an actual increase of $41,100. Of this amount, $27,000 represents a transfer from the food production act, so that the net actual increase is $14,100. The increase of $41,100 will be used as follows: (a) $15,000 for cooperative purchasing and marketing activities; (b) $12,000 for foreign marketing investigations; and (c) $14,100 for cotton handling and marketing work.

Market news service on fruits and vegetables (p. 80, line 12).—There is an apparent increase in this item of $53,340, but, as $118,780 ($28,160 from the regular appropriation and $90,620 from the food production act) has been transferred to statutory rolls, there is an actual increase of $172,120. This sum will be used for the market news service on fruits and vegetables. The food production act of November 21, 1918, carries an additional appropriation of $500,000 for this purpose during the present fiscal year. The amount provided in this present bill thereforere presents an actual reduction of $327,880 below the amount available during 1919.

Market news service on live stock and meats (p. 80, line 16).—There is an apparent increase in this item of $47,400, but, as $52,600 ($9,040 from the regular appropriation and $43,560 from the food production act) has been transferred to the statutory roll, there is an actual increase of $100,000. This sum will be used for the market news service on live stock and meats. The food production act of November 21, 1918, carries an additional appropriation for this purpose of $300,000, so that the amount provided in the present bill represents an actual reduction of $200,000 below the amount available during 1919.

Market news service on dairy and poultry products (p. 81, line 9).—This is a new item, carrying, with transfers to the statutory roll aggregating $29,400, an appropriation of $110,000. This sum will be used for the market news service on dairy and poultry products. The food production act of November 21, 1918, carries an appropriation of $164,000 for this purpose, so that the amount provided by the present bill represents an actual reduction of $54,000 below the amount available during 1919.

Market news service on grain, hay, feeds, and seeds (p. 81, line 13).—This is a new item, carrying, with transfers to the statutory roll aggregating $14,880, an appropriation of $64,880. This sum will be used for the market news service on grain, hay, feeds, and seeds. The food production act of November 21, 1918, carries an appropriation of $150,000 for this purpose, so that the amount provided by the present bill represents an actual reduction of $85,120 below the amount available during 1919.

Food supply investigations (p. 81, line 17).—The word "production" has been omitted.

Food products inspection service (p. 81, line 24).—There is an apparent increase in this item of $37,000, but as $12,040 (including $9,740 from the regular appropriation and $2,300 from the food production act) has been transferred to the statutory roll, there is an actual increase of $49,040. The food production act of November 21, 1918, carries an additional appropriation of $51,000 for the "market inspection of perishable foods." This amount is being used in connection with the food products inspection service conducted under the regular appropriation. The amount provided in the present bill, therefore, will be $1,960 less than the amount available for this purpose during 1919.

The language of the paragraph has been amended so as to limit the inspections to products entering into interstate commerce. It has also been amended by the insertion of the words "poultry, butter, and hay" and the elimination of the words "and other perishable farm products." The effect of the latter change is to confine the inspections under this paragraph to fruits, vegetables, poultry, butter, and hay.

Rural cooperation (p. 82, line 20).—There is an apparent decrease in this item of $12,500, but, as $2,500 has been transferred to statutory rolls, there is an actual decrease of $10,000. The language of the paragraph has been amended by the elimination of the following language: "in matters of rural credits and of other forms of cooperation in rural communities."

State cooperation in marketing work (p. 83, line 3).—There is an apparent increase in this item of $16,250, but, as $960 has been transferred to the statutory roll, there is an actual increase of $17,210. This sum will be used for expanding the work in States where it is now conducted and for extending it to additional States.

Grain standardization investigations (p. 83, line 8).—There is an apparent decrease in this item of $6,700, but, as that amount has been transferred to the statutory roll, there is actually no change.

Enforcement of standard container act (p. 83, line 11).—There is an apparent decrease in this item of $1,200, but, as that amount has been transferred to the statutory roll, there is actually no change.

Experimental flour mill.—This item, carrying $50,000, has been omitted.

Administrative expenses (p. 83, line 11).—There is an apparent increase in this item of $1,000, but, as $3,000 has been transferred to the statutory roll, there is an actual increase of $4,000. This sum will provide for increased administrative expenses incident to the enlarged activities of the bureau.

ENFORCEMENT OF THE COTTON FUTURES ACT.

(P. 83, line 23.)

There is an apparent increase in this item of $18,200, but, as $6,800 has been transferred to the statutory roll, there is an actual increase of $25,000. This amount is needed to meet the increased expenses in connection with the administration of the act, and especially for the purchase of cotton required in the preparation of standards for Sea Island and American-Egyptian cotton and of types showing length of staple.

ENFORCEMENT OF THE GRAIN STANDARDS ACT.

(P. 84, line 7.)

There is an apparent increase in this item of $142,020, but, as $33,540 has been transferred to the statutory roll, there is an actual increase of $175,560. This sum is needed in order to enable the department to conduct the work necessary to enforce the present standards for wheat and corn in an adequate and satisfactory way, to promulgate standards for rice and oats and to enforce them, and to render increased service to the grain trade by passing informally on the character and grade of grain not handled under regular appeals. A proviso has been inserted amending section 6 of the grain standards act by striking out of the last sentence the words "made after the parties in interest have had opportunity to be heard."

ADMINISTRATION OF THE WAREHOUSE ACT.

(P. 84, line 17.)

There is an apparent decrease in this item of $18,540, but, as $4,160 has been transferred to statutory rolls, there is an actual decrease of $14,380.

AUTHORITY TO ADMINISTER OATHS, EXAMINE WITNESSES, ETC.

(P. 85, line 1.)

The language of this item has been changed so as to make it applicable to the fiscal year 1920.

ENFORCEMENT OF THE INSECTICIDE ACT.

STATUTORY SALARIES.

(P. 85, line 16.)

There is an apparent increase in the statutory roll of $2,400, but an actual increase of $1,200, as indicated in the following table:

New place: 1 clerk, class 1	$1,200
Actual increase	1,200

AGRICULTURE APPROPRIATION BILL.

Transfer from lump fund of this office, which fund has been correspondingly reduced.

clerk, class 1, from general expenses	$1,200
Apparent increase	2,400

GENERAL EXPENSES.

Enforcement of the insecticide act (p. 86, line 8).—There is an apparent increase in this item of $300, but, as $1,200 has been transferred to the statutory roll, there is an actual increase of $1,500. This sum is needed to meet the increased cost of travel and of samples of insecticides and fungicides collected under the provisions of the insecticide act.

FEDERAL HORTICULTURAL BOARD.

STATUTORY SALARIES.

(P. 86, line 16.)

There is an apparent increase in the statutory roll of $4,800, but no actual increase, as indicated in the following table:

New places:		
1 clerk	$1,980	
5 clerks, class 1	6,000	
		$7,980
Places dropped:		
1 clerk	1,080	
6 clerks, at $1,000 each	6,000	
1 clerk	900	
		7,980

Transfers from lump funds of this board, which funds have been correspondingly reduced.

1 clerk, from eradication of pink bollworm	$1,560
1 clerk, from eradication of pink bollworm	1,440
1 clerk, class 1, from eradication of pink bollworm	1,200
1 messenger boy, from general expenses	600
Apparent increase	4,800

GENERAL EXPENSES.

Enforcement of the plant-quarantine act (p. 87, line 4).—There is an apparent decrease in this item of $600, but, as that amount has been transferred to the statutory roll, there is actually no increase.

Eradication of the potato wart (p. 87, line 12).—This is a new item. It appropriates $50,000, to be immediately available, to enable the Secretary of Agriculture to meet the emergency caused by the establishment of the potato wart in eastern Pennsylvania and to provide means for the extermination of this pest in Pennsylvania or elsewhere in he United States, in cooperation with the State or States concerned.

Plant quarantine in the District of Columbia (p. 87, line 22).—This is a new item. Its purpose is to give the Secretary of Agriculture authority to regulate the movement of plants and plant products, including nursery stock, from or into the District of Columbia, and power to control injurious plant diseases and insect pests within the District.

MISCELLANEOUS.

PASSENGER-CARRYING VEHICLES.

(P. 92, line 18.)

This paragraph carries no appropriation. The amount authorized to be expended for the purchase, maintenance, repair, and operation of passenger-carrying vehicles outside of the District of Columbia has been increased by $12,000. This amount will be required properly to provide for the maintenance, repair, and operation of vehicles now owned by the department and for the purchase, maintenance, repair, and operation of new vehicles necessary to the effective prosecution of its activities.

ERADICATION OF FOOT-AND-MOUTH DISEASE AND OTHER DISEASES OF ANIMALS.

(P. 93, line 9.)

There is no change in the amounts carried by this paragraph. The language has been amended so as to continue the availability of the unexpended balance of the appropriation of $3,500,000 included in the appropriation act for the fiscal year 1916.

PINK BOLLWORM OF COTTON.

(P. 94, line 23.)

There is an apparent increase in this item of $95,800, but as $4,200 has been transferred to the statutory roll, there is an actual increase of $100,000.

This sum is needed to cover the cost of materials and supplies required in the disinfection, in specially constructed fumigation houses on the Texas-Mexican border, of freight, express, baggage, and other materials entering the United States from Mexico. It is estimated that the fees charged for disinfection, which will be deposited in the Treasury, will fully cover the cost of the materials and supplies so purchased. The language of the paragraph has been amended so as to make immediately available the appropriation for this work.

LOAN OR EXCHANGE OF AMERICAN BISON.

(P. 96, line 16.)

This is a new item. It authorizes the Secretary of Agriculture, in his discretion, and under such conditions as he may prescribe, to supply any municipality or public institution not more than one American bison from any surplus which may exist in any herd under the control of the department, and also to loan or exchange animals with other owners of American bison.

MILEAGE RATE FOR MOTOR VEHICLES.

(P. 97, line 1.)

This paragraph has been amended so as to authorize the Secretary of Agriculture to pay not to exceed 2½ cents per mile for a motor cycle and 7 cents per mile for an automobile when used for necessary travel on official business. The proviso has been omitted.

COOPERATION.

(P. 97, line 8.)

This is a new item. It provides that hereafter, in carrying on the activities of the Department of Agriculture involving cooperation with State, county, and municipal agencies, associations of farmers, individual farmers, universities, colleges, boards of trade, chambers of commerce, or other local associations of business men, business organizations, and individuals within the State, Territory, district, or insular possession in which such activities are to be carried on, moneys contributed from such outside sources, except in the case of the authorized activities of the Forest Service, shall be paid only through the Secretary of Agriculture or through State, county, or municipal agencies, or local farm bureaus or like organizations cooperating for the purpose with the Secretary of Agriculture. It also provides that the officials and employees of the Department of Agriculture engaged in the activities described and paid in whole or in part out of funds contributed as provided therein, and the persons, corporations, or associations making such contributions shall not be subject to the proviso contained in the legislative, executive, and judicial act of March 3, 1917, and that no official or employee engaged in the cooperative activities of the Forest Service, or the persons, corporations, or associations contributing to such activities shall be subject to the said proviso.

AGRICULTURE APPROPRIATION BILL.

COMMITTEE ON AGRICULTURE,
HOUSE OF REPRESENTATIVES,
Friday, January 3, 1919.

The committee met at 10.30 o'clock a. m., Hon. A. F. Lever (chairman) presiding.

The CHAIRMAN. The committee will come to order. Gentlemen, we will take up this morning the estimates and hear the representatives of the department on various items of the bill. I would like to say that I would be very glad indeed if members would attend the meetings promptly at 10.30 in the morning, because it is the desire of everybody to hasten the consideration of this bill and get it reported to the House. And to these gentlemen who represent the department I would like to say that I wish they would correct their notes as quickly as possible and get them back to the clerk of the committee, so when we come to consider the bill on the floor of the House we will have the testimony before us. It is my hope, if all of us will work together, to be able to complete this bill by the latter part of next week; if so, I think we will be able to take it up immediately after the conclusion of the consideration of the legislative bill, which, I understand, comes next.

SUMMARY OF ESTIMATES.

STATEMENT OF MR. FLOYD R. HARRISON, ASSISTANT TO THE SECRETARY, UNITED STATES DEPARTMENT OF AGRICULTURE.

Mr. HARRISON. Mr. Chairman, I have prepared a brief statement, a copy of which has been furnished to each member of the committee, which indicates just what the estimates involve and the policy followed in preparing them. I will insert it in the record if you so desire.

The CHAIRMAN. Without objection, we will insert that in the record.

(The statement referred to follows:)

MEMORANDUM.

The estimates of the Department of Agriculture for the fiscal year 1920, as submitted by the bureaus, aggregated $31,749,866, an increase of $3,874,513 over the appropriation for the present fiscal year. The total amount approved by the Secretary was $30,308,006, an increase of $2,432,653 over the fiscal year 1919. Of the latter amount, $849,960 represents transfers from the food production act, so that the net actual increase is only $1,582,693. The main items of increase are as follows:

Animal husbandry investigations _____ $17,480
Investigations of commercial fertilizer _____ 125,000
Fire suppression in the national forests _____ 226,568

Forest-products investigations	$35,000
Silvicultural investigations	25,000
Color investigations	29,280
Enforcement of the food and drugs act	50,000
Investigations of rare chemicals	10,000
Control of the European corn borer	25,000
Protection of migratory birds	125,000
Crop reporting and estimating	42,279
Insular experiment stations	25,000
Home-economics investigations	50,000
Farm-machinery investigations	50,000
Marketing and distribution	14,100
Food products inspection service	50,000
State cooperation in marketing work	34,420
Milling and baking investigations	35,000
Enforcement of the United States cotton-futures act	25,000
Enforcement of the United States grain-standards act	175,560
Administration of the United States warehouse act	20,600
Eradication of the pink bollworm of cotton	100,000

The items transferred from the food-production act are as follows:

Plant-disease survey (transferred to item " Investigations in plant pathology ")	$23,000
Sugar-beet nematode work (transferred to item " Sugar-plant investigations ")	10,000
Control of a new sugar-cane disease (transferred to item " Sugar-plant investigations ")	20,000
Location of Irish-potato seed stocks (transferred to item " Horticultural investigations ")	30,000
Preparation of sweet sirups (transferred to item " Sirup investigations ")	5,000
Utilization of wool-scouring wastes (new item under Bureau of Chemistry)	9,000
Special marketing activities (transferred to item " Marketing and distribution ")	27,000
Market news service on fruits and vegetables (transferred to item " Market reports on fruits and vegetables ")	244,800
Market news service on live stock and meats (transferred to item " Market reports on live stock and meats ")	170,000
Market news service on butter, cheese, eggs, and poultry (new item under Bureau of Markets)	110,000
Market news service on grain, hay, feeds, and seeds (two new items under Bureau of Markets as follows):	
(a) Market reports on grain, hay, and feeds	53,160
(b) Seed-reporting service	47,000
City market service (new item under Bureau of Markets)	50,000
Market inspection of perishable foods (transferred to item " Food-products inspection service ")	51,000
Total	849,960

The law requires that the estimates be submitted to the Secretary of the Treasury on or before October 15. It was decided to follow the plan adopted last year, and to make provision in the regular estimates only for the normal activities of the department without special reference to war conditions. The conclusion was reached also, after discussion between the heads of the various departments, that no changes in the statutory rolls, except those involved in transfers from lump funds, would be suggested. It was agreed, however, that all recommendations for promotions, new places, changes in title, and the like would be submitted to the Secretary of the Treasury in the form of supplemental estimates. This was done, and the supplemental estimates have been incorporated in the committee print. These supplemental estimates involve a net increase of $259,220. Of this sum, however, $184,030 represents the amount required to carry out the recommendations regarding minimum salaries for certain positions.

When the regular estimates were prepared, the United States was actively at war. It was contemplated at the time that estimates to cover the emergency appropriations would be submitted at a later date. The signing of the

AGRICULTURE APPROPRIATION BILL. 33

armistice and the cessation of hostilities brought about a change in the situation. Nevertheless, the question naturally arises whether it would not be in the national interest to make provisions for the continuance of at least a part of the emergency work after the end of this fiscal year. Certain items, as I have indicated, already have been transferred, in whole or in part, to the regular bill. As the Secretary points out in his annual report, the Nation is now engaged, under the act of May 8, 1914, in developing the agricultural extension service, and, in his opinion, it would be wise to anticipate the amount that would accrue under this measure by the end of the period 1922, and to make such further provision as may be necessary for the continuance of agents of proven efficiency on the rolls, as well as to continue the intensive work for the more speedy control and eradication of tuberculosis, hog cholera, and the cattle tick, and perhaps other important lines of effort. The Secretary believes that expenditures for these activities are investments and that it is simply a question how rapidly the Nation wishes the work to proceed. If the finances of the Nation permit it, he thinks, of course, that adequate provision should be continued, and so recommends. Indications from every point of the Union are that the efforts of the agricultural colleges and the department in emergency directions have been fruitful and are appreciated by the great masses of the farmers.

It is not the Secretary's intention at this time to submit formal recommendations for the continuation of the emergency activities, other than the extension work conducted in cooperation with the agricultural colleges and the farm-labor work during the next fiscal year. Definite suggestions regarding the extension and farm-labor work will be placed before the committee in a few days. Chiefs of bureaus, as they appear before the committee, will be glad, of course, to explain the emergency work conducted under their direction and to indicate the results that have been secured. The committee will then be in a position to determine whether, in the light of the financial situation confronting the Nation, the projects authorized by the food production act should be continued next year, either on their present basis or on a reduced scale.

A summary of the regular estimates for 1920 has been prepared and it will be inserted in the record if the committee so desires.

Mr. HARRISON. We have also prepared the usual detailed statement, which will give the committee a bird's-eye view of the estimates. It includes all the changes suggested in the estimates. You will recall that we inserted a similar statement in the record last year.

The CHAIRMAN. Without objection, that will be inserted in the record.

(The statement referred to follows:)

Estimates, 1920, United States Department of Agriculture.

Appropriations.	Increase.	
	Apparent.	Actual.
Statutory salaries (including new $90,000 lump-fund item for salaries of mechanical employees)	$856,900	$259,220
Lump-fund appropriations	1,575,753	2,173,433
Total	[1] 2,432,653	[1] 2,432,653

Appropriation, 1919	$27,875,353
Estimates, 1920, as submitted by bureaus	31,749,866
Increase, 1920, as submitted by bureaus	[2] 3,874,513
Estimates, 1920, as approved by the Secretary	30,308,006
Increase, 1920, as approved by the Secretary	[3] 2,432,653

[1] Includes supplemental estimates providing for changes in the statutory rolls.
[2] Includes $1,584,070 to be transferred from food production act.
[3] Includes $849,960 to be transferred from food production act.

AGRICULTURE APPROPRIATION BILL.

Statement showing proposed changes in the salary rolls of the Department of Agriculture for the fiscal year ending June 30, 1920.

SUMMARY.

	Number.	Increase.	Total.
Promotions	2,395	$312,040	
New places	545	482,870	
Lump-fund appropriation for salaries of mechanical employees		90,000	+$884,910
Places dropped	743		−625,690
Actual increase			[1] 259,220
Transfers from lump funds with corresponding reduction:			
Agricultural appropriation act	320	355,320	
Food production act	207	240,960	
			596,280
Transfer from lump fund without corresponding reduction	1		1,400
Apparent increase			856,900

[1] Of this amount, $184,030 represents the increase required to effect the minimum salary scale recommended in the supplemental estimates of the department.

NOTE.—On July 1, 1918, there was a total of 25,239 employees in the Department of Agriculture, of whom 4,545 were carried on statutory rolls and 20,694 on lump funds.

NOTE.—In accordance with a general understanding among the executive departments no increases or other changes were recommended in the statutory rolls of the Department of Agriculture in the estimates of appropriations for the fiscal year 1920, except transfers from lump-fund rolls in accordance with the provision of law requiring such transfers, and in all such cases the lump-fund rolls were correspondingly reduced. A number of promotions and other changes were, however, under consideration at that time and were subsequently submitted as a supplemental estimate to the Secretary of the Treasury under date of November 25, 1918: The supplemental estimate of each bureau will be found immediately after the statutory roll of that bureau in the committee Book of Estimates, and the reasons for each change are fully set forth.

In addition to the promotions based solely on meritorious service a number of promotions and other changes affecting certain clerical and subclerical employees are recommended in order that the salaries of such positions may conform to a minimum scale, as follows:

Clerks	$1,000	Elevator conductors	$840
Clerks (minor)	900	Telephone operators	840
Repairmen	1,000	Repairmen	1,000
Skilled laborers	1,000	Gardeners	1,000
Gardeners	1,000	Cabinetmakers or carpenters	1,200
Messengers or laborers	900	Electricians	1,200
Messenger boys	480	Painters	1,200
Laboratory helpers	900	Plumbers	1,200
Watchmen	900	Blacksmiths	1,200
Firemen	1,000	Mechanics	1,200

This action is necessary in order to enable the department to meet the ever increasing difficulty of securing and retaining competent clerks, mechanics, and subclerical employees. The large number of resignations in these grades has interfered seriously with the efficient conduct of the work of the department, and it is highly urgent and necessary that the present low salary scale be increased as recommended.

PROMOTIONS.

Office of the Secretary:
    1 inspector, $2,750 to $3,250.... $500
    1 inspector, $2,250 to $2,500..... 250
    1 assistant chief clerk and captain of the watch, $1,800 to $2,250.. 450

AGRICULTURE APPROPRIATION BILL.

Office of the Secretary—Continued.
1 assistant in exhibits, $2,000 to $2,400	$400	
1 clerk, class 4, to 1 executive clerk, $2,000	200	
16 clerks, $900 to $1,000 each	1,600	
2 clerks, $840 to $1,000 each	320	
4 messengers or laborers, at $840 each, to 4 skilled laborers, at $1,000 each	640	
10 messengers or laborers, $840 to $900 each	600	
12 assistant messengers, laborers, or messenger boys, at $720 each, to 12 messengers or laborers, at $900 each	2,160	
1 messenger or laborer, $660 to $900	240	
73 watchmen, $720 to $900 each	13,140	
14 assistant messengers, messenger boys, or laborers, at $600 each, to 14 messengers or laborers, at $900 each	4,200	
8 laborers or messenger boys, at $480 each, to 8 messengers or laborers, at $900 each	3,360	
1 skilled laborer, $960 to $1,080	120	
1 skilled laborer, $960 to $1,000	40	
1 skilled laborer, $840 to $1,000	160	
1 skilled laborer, $720, to 1 watchman, $900	180	
1 skilled laborer, $720, to 1 telephone operator, $840	120	
1 janitor, $900 to $1,000	100	
1 messenger or messenger boy, $360, to 1 messenger boy, $480	120	$28,900

Office of Farm Management:
1 library assistant, $900 to $1,100	200	
1 messenger or laborer, $720 to $900	180	380

Weather Bureau:
1 chief clerk, $2,500 to $3,000	500
3 lithographers, $1,200 to $1,350 each	450
1 pressman, $1,200 to $1,350	150
6 printers or compositors, $1,080 to $1,200 each	720
5 printers or compositors, $1,000 to $1,200 each	1,000
4 folders and feeders, at $720 each, to 4 press feeders, at $840 each	480
3 instrument makers, $1,300 to $1,440 each	420
1 instrument maker, $1,260 to $1,440	180
3 skilled mechanics, at $1,200 each, to 3 mechanics, at $1,320 each	360
6 skilled artisans, at $840 each, to 6 laborers, at $900 each	360
1 skilled mechanic, $840, to 1 mechanic, $1,200	360
5 skilled mechanics, at $1,000 each, to 5 mechanics, at $1,200 each	1,000

Weather Bureau—Continued.
1 engineer, $1,300 to $1,500	$200	
1 fireman and steamfitter, $840, to 1 mechanic, $1,200	360	
4 firemen, $720 to $1,000 each	1,120	
1 repairman, $960 to $1,200	240	
4 repairmen, $840 to $1,000 each	640	
4 repairmen, $720 to $1,000 each	1,120	
4 watchmen, $720 to $900 each	720	
28 messengers, messenger boys, or laborers, at $720 each, to 28 messengers or laborers, at $900 each	5,040	
6 messengers, messenger boys, or laborers, at $660 each, to 6 messengers or laborers, at $900 each	1,440	
22 messengers, messenger boys, or laborers, at $600 each, to 22 messengers or laborers, at $900 each	6,600	$23,460

Bureau of Animal Industry:
14 clerks, $960 to $1,000 each	560	
52 clerks, $900 to $1,000 each	5,200	
2 laboratory helpers, $840 to $900 each	120	
1 laboratory helper, $720 to $900	180	
2 laboratory helpers, $600 to $900 each	600	
1 carpenter, $1,140 to $1,200	60	
2 carpenters, $1,000 to $1,200 each	400	
10 skilled laborers, $900 to $1,000 each	1,000	
1 painter, $900 to $1,200	300	
8 messengers, skilled laborers, or laborers, at $840 each, to 8 messengers or laborers, at $900 each	480	
1 messenger, skilled laborer, or laborer, $840, to 1 skilled laborer, $1,000	160	
3 laborers, at $780 each, to 3 messengers or laborers, at $900 each	360	
26 messengers, skilled laborers, or laborers, at $720 each, to 26 messengers or laborers, at $900 each	4,680	
3 messengers, skilled laborers, or laborers, at $720 each, to 3 skilled laborers, at $1,000 each	840	
4 laborers, $660 to $900 each	960	
24 laborers, $600 to $900 each	7,200	
12 laborers, $540 to $900 each	4,320	
10 laborers, $480 to $900 each	4,200	
8 messenger boys, $360 to $480 each	960	32,580

Bureau of Plant Industry:
1 artist, $1,620 to $1,800	180	
1 clerk or artist, $1,400 to $1,600	200	
1 clerk or artist, $1,200 to $1,600	400	
1 laborer, $780 to $900	120	
42 messengers or laborers, $720 to $900 each	7,560	
4 laboratory aids, $840 to $900 each	240	

AGRICULTURE APPROPRIATION BILL.

Bureau of Plant Industry—Contd.
  15 gardeners, $900 to $1,000 each. $1,500
  19 gardeners, $780 to $1,000 each. 4,180
  1 skilled laborer, $960 to $1,000.. 40
  2 skilled laborers, $900 to $1,000 each. 200
  3 skilled laborers, $840 to $1,000 each. 480
  1 mechanician, $1,080 to $1,200.. 120
  1 carpenter, $900 to $1,000. 300
  1 painter, $900 to $1,200. 300
  1 teamster, $840, to 1 laborer, $900 60
  1 teamster, $600, to 1 laborer, $900. 300
                                                                $16,180

Forest Service:
  1 chief of office of accounts and fiscal agent, $2,500 to $2,760... 260
  Forest supervisors and assistant forest supervisors—
    1, $2,800 to $3,180. 380
    1, $2,700 to $2,760. 60
    5, $2,400 to $2,760. 1,800
    3, $2,400 to $2,640. 720
    6, $2,200 to $2,640. 2,640
    12, $2,200 to $2,520. 3,840
    2, $2,200 to $2,400. 400
    18, $2,000 to $2,400. 7,200
    31, $2,000 to $2,280. 8,680
    5, $1,800 to $2,280. 2,400
    48, $1,800 to $2,040. 11,520
    2, $1,700 to $1,800. 200
    20, $1,600 to $1,680. 1,600
    13, $1,600 to $1,620. 260
    12, $1,500 to $1,620. 1,440
  Forest rangers—
    11, $1,500 to $1,620. 1,320
    7, $1,400 to $1,620. 1,540
    16, $1,400 to $1,500. 1,600
    9, $1,300 to $1,500. 1,800
    69, $1,300 to $1,380. 5,520
    6, $1,200 to $1,380. 1,080
    100, $1,200 to $1,320. 12,000
    318, $1,100 to $1,200. 31,800
    242, $1,100 to $1,140. 9,680
  Forest guards—
    55, $1,100 to $1,140 (six months' service). 1,100
    40, $1,100 to $1,140 (three months' service). 400
  Clerks—
    21, $1,600 to $1,620. 420
    3, $1,500 to $1,620. 360
    25, $1,400 to $1,500. 2,500
    7, $1,300 to $1,500. 1,400
    2, $1,300 to $1,380. 160
    38, $1,200 to $1,380. 6,840
    45, $1,200 to $1,320. 5,400
    25, $1,100 to $1,200. 2,500
    70, $1,100 to $1,140. 2,800
    10, $1,020 to $1,140. 1,200
    44, $1,020 to $1,080. 2,640
    16, $960 to $1,080. 1,920
    14, $960 to $1,020. 840
    31, $900 to $1,020. 3,720
    73, $900 to $1,000. 7,300
    1, $600 to $900. 300

Forest Service—Continued.
  Surveyors, draftsmen, artists, photographers, map-colorists, blue-printers, compilers, or compositors—
    1, $2,000 to $2,040............ $40
    4, $1,600 to $1,800............ 800
    5, $1,600 to $1,620............ 100
    4, $1,500 to $1,620............ 480
    3, $1,400 to $1,500............ 300
    13, $1,400 to $1,440........... 520
    1, $1,300 to $1,440............ 140
    3, $1,300 to $1,320............ 60
    5, $1,200 to $1,320............ 600
    1, $1,100 to $1,200............ 100
    2, $1,100 to $1,140............ 80
    3, $1,020 to $1,140............ 360
    1, $1,000 to $1,140............ 140
    1, $1,000 to $1,020............ 20
    1, $960 to $1,020............. 60
    7, $900 to $1,020............. 840
  Machinists, carpenters, or electricians—
    1, $1,260 to $1,500............ 240
    1, $1,200 to $1,320............ 120
    1, $1,020 to $1,200............ 180
    3, $1,000 to $1,200............ 600
    1, $960 to $1,200............. 240
  Laboratory aids or engineers—
    1, $1,000 to $1,200............ 200
    4, $900 to $1,200............. 1,200
    1, $900 to $1,080............. 180
    4, $900 to $1,020............. 480
    2, $800 to $1,020............. 440
  Telephone operators—
    2, $800 to $840............... 480
  Watchmen, laboratory helpers, packers, messengers, or laborers—
    1, $1,000 to $1,020............ 20
    2, $960 to $1,020............. 120
    3, $900 to $1,020............. 360
    2, $840 to $1,020............. 360
    2, $840 to $960............... 240
    4, $840 to $900............... 240
    4, $780 to $900............... 480
    6, $720 to $900............... 1,080
    6, $660 to $900............... 1,440
    1, $600 to $900............... 300
  Messenger boys, 2, $420 to $480... 120
                                          ——— $165,300
Bureau of Chemistry:
  1 executive clerk, $2,000 to $2,280........................ 280
  1 laboratory helper, $1,200, to 1 laboratory assistant, $1,400..... 200
  1 clerk, $960 to $1,000........... 40
  11 clerks, $900 to $1,000 each..... 1,100
  9 laboratory helpers, messenger boys, or laborers, at $720 each, to 9 messengers or laborers, at $900 each....................... 1,620
  2 laboratory helpers, messenger boys, or laborers, at $600 each, to 2 messengers or laborers, at $900 each....................... 600

AGRICULTURE APPROPRIATION BILL.

Bureau of Chemistry—Continued.
 2 messengers, at $840 each, to 2 messengers or laborers, at $900 each.......................... $120
 1 skilled laborer, $840 to $1,000... 160
           $4,120

Bureau of Soils:
 1 chief clerk, $2,000 to $2,500.... 500
 1 clerk, class 4, to 1 editor, $2,100. 300
 3 laboratory helpers, $840 to $900 each............................ 180
 1 messenger, $840 to $900........ 60
 1 messenger, messenger boy, or laborer, $480, to 1 laborer, $900.. 420
 2 laborers, at $600 each, to 2 skilled laborers, at $1,000 each. 800
 1 laborer, $600 to $900............ 300
 1 laborer, $300 to $450............ 150
 1 charwoman or laborer, $480, to 1 laborer, $900.................... 420
           3,130

Bureau of Entomology:
 1 entomologist, who shall be chief of bureau, $4,500 to $5,000..... 500
 1 entomological draftsman, $1,080 to $1,200...................... 120
 4 entomological preparators, $840 to $1,000 each................... 640
 8 entomological preparators, $720 to $900 each.................... 1,440
 1 messenger or laborer, $840 to $900............................. 60
           2,760

Bureau of Biological Survey:
 3 clerks, $900 to $1,000 each...... 300
 1 messenger, $720 to $900........ 180
 1 messenger boy, $360 to $480..... 120
 1 laborer, $600 to $900............ 300
           900

Division of Accounts and Disbursements:
 1 messenger, $720 to $900................. 180

Division of Publications:
 2 draftsmen or photographers, $1,600 to $1,800 each............ 400
 2 draftsmen or photographers, $1,200 to $1,400 each............ 400
 1 lantern-slide colorist, $840 to $900............................. 60
 1 laboratory aid, $720 to $900.... 180
 1 assistant in document section, $1,400, to 1 assistant, $1,600.... 200
 36 clerks, $900 to $1,000 each.... 3,600
 2 skilled laborers, $900 to $1,000 each.............................. 200
 7 skilled laborers, $840 to $1,000 each.............................. 1,120
 4 skilled laborers, $780 to $1,000 each.............................. 880
 13 skilled laborers, messengers, or messenger boys, at $720 each, to 13 skilled laborers, at $1,000 each.............................. 3,640
 1 skilled laborer, $720 to $1,000.. 280
 1 folder, $1,000 to $1,400......... 400
 2 messengers, $840 to $900 each... 120

Division of Publications—Continued.
1 laborer, $840 to $900............	$60	
2 laborers, $600 to $900 each.....	600	
2 messengers or messenger boys, at $420 each, to 2 messenger boys, at $480 each..................	120	
2 messengers or messenger boys, at $360 each, to 2 messenger boys, at $480 each..................	240	
		$12,500

Bureau of Crop Estimates:
1 chief clerk, $1,800 to $2,250....	450	
1 messenger, $840, to 1 messenger or laborer, $900...............	60	
3 messengers or laborers, $720 to $900 each......................	540	
1 charwoman, messenger boy, or laborer, $360, to 1 charwoman, $480.........................	120	
		1,170

Library:
1 librarian, $2,000 to $2,500.....	500	
1 junior library assistant, messenger, or messenger boy, $720, to 1 messenger, $900..............	180	
		680

States Relations Service:
1 chief clerk, $2,000 to $2,400....	400	
1 clerk, $900, to 1 clerk or addressograph operator, $1,000........	100	
5 clerks, $900 to $1,000 each.....	500	
1 clerk or lantern-slide colorist, $900, to 1 clerk, $1,000........	100	
5 messengers, messenger boys, or laborers, at $720 each, to 5 messengers or laborers, at $900 each.	900	
1 messenger, messenger boy, or laborer, $480, to 1 messenger or laborer, $900.................	420	
1 skilled laborer, $900 to $1,000..	100	
		2,520

Bureau of Public Roads:
1 director, who shall be a scientist, and have charge of all scientific and technical work, $4,500 to $5,000.......................	500	
1 clerk or draftsman, $900 to $1,000.......................	100	
1 clerk, $1,100 to $1,140.........	40	
4 clerks, $900 to $1,000 each.....	400	
1 messenger, laborer, or laboratory helper, $840 to $900............	60	
1 messenger or laborer, $840 to $900........................	60	
2 messengers, laborers, or laboratory helpers, $720 to $900 each.	360	
2 messengers or laborers, $660 to $900 each......................	480	
2 messengers, laborers, or laboratory helpers, $720 to $900 each..	360	
2 messengers or laborers, $660 to $900 each......................	480	
4 messengers, laborers, or messenger boys, at $600 each, to 4 messengers or laborers, at $900 each.	1,200	
1 fireman, $720 to $1,000........	280	
		3,480

AGRICULTURE APPROPRIATION BILL.

Bureau of Markets:
1 chief of bureau, $4,500 to $5,000.	$500	
2 clerks, $960 to $1,000 each	80	
24 clerks, $900 to $1,000 each	2,400	
3 clerks, $840 to $1,000 each	480	
2 clerks, $720 to $1,000 each	560	
1 laboratory aid, $840 to $900	60	
1 laboratory aid, $720 to $900	180	
1 map tracer, $720 to $900	180	
1 map tracer, $600 to $900	300	
2 skilled laborers, $900 to $1,000 each	200	
2 laborers, at $840 each, to 2 skilled laborers, at $1,000 each	320	
1 laborer, $840, to 1 messenger or laborer, $900	60	
2 laborers, at $720 each, to 2 skilled laborers, at $1,000 each	560	
4 laborers, at $720 each, to 4 messengers or laborers, at $900 each	720	
1 laborer, $660, to 1 skilled laborer, $1,000	340	
3 laborers, at $660 each, to 3 messengers or laborers, at $900 each	720	
1 messenger, $720, to 1 messenger or laborer, $900	180	
1 messenger boy or laborer, $600, to 1 skilled laborer, $1,000	400	
5 messenger boys or laborers, at $600 each, to 5 messengers or laborers, at $900 each	1,500	
2 messenger boys or laborers, at $540 each, to 2 messengers or laborers, at $900 each	720	
3 messenger boys, $420 to $480 each	180	
1 messenger boy, $360 to $480	120	
1 messenger boy, $300 to $480	180	$10,940
Enforcement of the Insecticide Act:		
1 executive assistant, $2,000 to $2,280	280 280	
1 clerk, class 1, to 1 clerk, class 2	200	
1 clerk, $1,140, to 1 insecticide and fungicide inspector, $1,400	260	
2 insecticide and fungicide inspectors, $1,600 to $1,800 each	400	
1 laboratory helper, $840 to $1,000	160	
1 laboratory helper, $720 to $900	180	
1 laboratory helper, $600 to $900	300	
1 unskilled laborer, $600, to 1 laborer, $900	300	
1 unskilled laborer, $480, to 1 laborer, $900	420	
1 messenger boy, $360 to $480	120	2,620
Federal Horticultural Board:		
2 messenger boys, $360 to $480 each	240	
Total for promotions		$312,040

NEW PLACES.

Office of the Secretary:		
1 attorney	$3,500	
1 attorney	3,250	
6 attorneys, at $2,500 each	15,000	$21,750

AGRICULTURE APPROPRIATION BILL.

Office of Farm Management:
2 clerks, class 2	$2,800	
4 clerks, at $1,100 each	4,400	
17 clerks, at $1,000 each	17,000	
1 draftsman	1,100	
		$25,300

Weather Bureau:
2 clerks, class 4	3,600	
1 clerk, class 3	1,600	
1 clerk, class 2	1,400	
5 clerks, class 1	6,000	
		12,600

Bureau of Animal Industry:
14 messengers of laborers, at $900 each		12,600

Bureau of Plant Industry:
1 seed warehouseman	1,000	
11 clerks, at $1,500 each	16,500	
16 clerks, class 2	22,400	
8 clerks, class 1	9,600	
9 laboratory aids, at $900 each	8,100	
1 map tracer or laboratory aid	900	
52 messengers or laborers, at $900 each	46,800	
1 blacksmith	1,200	
16 messenger boys or charwomen, at $480 each	7,680	
		114,180

Forest Service:
162 forest guards, at $1,140 each (three months' service)	46,170	
15 watchmen, laboratory helpers, packers, messengers, or laborers, at $900 each	13,500	
		59,670

Bureau of Chemistry:
15 laboratory helpers, at $900 each	13,500	
4 mechanics, at $1,200 each	4,800	
38 messengers or laborers, at $900 each	34,200	
		52,500

Bureau of Entomology:
2 executive clerks, at $1,980 each	3,960	
3 clerks, class 2	4,200	
5 clerks, class 1	6,000	
5 messengers or laborers, at $900 each	4,500	
		18,660

Bureau of Biological Survey:
1 clerk		1,560

Division of Accounts and Disbursements:
2 clerks, class 1		2,400

Division of Publications:
1 chief editor	2,750	
1 superintendent of distribution	2,500	
3 clerks, class 3	4,800	
3 clerks, class 2	4,200	
8 clerks, class 1	9,600	
7 clerks, at $1,000 each	7,000	
5 machine operators, at $1,200 each	6,000	
5 skilled laborers, at $1,000 each	5,000	
1 laborer	900	
		42,750

Bureau of Crop Estimates:
5 clerks, class 4	$9,000	
5 clerks, class 3	8,000	
3 clerks, class 2	4,200	
16 clerks, class 1	19,200	
7 clerks, at $1,000 each	7,000	
1 messenger boy	660	
		$48,060

Library:
1 assistant librarian	2,000	
3 library assistants, at $1,800 each	5,400	
4 library assistants, at $1,440 each	5,760	
3 library assistants, at $1,320 each	3,960	
3 clerks, class 1	3,600	
		20,720

States Relations Service:
12 clerks, class 2	16,800	
2 clerks, class 1	2,400	
3 messengers or laborers, at $900 each	2,700	
2 messenger boys, at $720 each	1,440	
		23,340

Bureau of Markets:
8 clerks, class 2	11,200	
4 telegraph operators, at $1,600 each	6,400	
		17,600

Enforcement of the Insecticide Act:
1 clerk, class 1		1,200

Federal Horticultural Board:
5 clerks, class 1	6,000	
1 clerk	1,980	
		7,980
Total, new places		$482,870

LUMP-FUND APPROPRIATION FOR SALARIES.

Office of the Secretary:
Lump-fund appropriation for salaries of employees of the mechanical shops	90,000	
		$884,910

PLACES DROPPED.

Office of the Secretary:
6 law clerks, at $2,250 each	$13,500
2 law clerks, at $1,600 each	3,200
1 mechanical superintendent	2,500
1 mechanical assistant	1,800
1 mechanical assistant	1,400
1 mechanical assistant	1,380
1 engineer	1,400
1 electrical engineer and draftsman	1,200
2 assistant engineers, at $1,200 each	2,400
2 assistant engineers, at $1,000 each	2,000
1 fireman	840
8 firemen, at $720 each	5,760
1 chief elevator conductor	840
16 elevator conductors, at $720 each	11,520
3 elevator conductors, at $600 each	1,800
1 superintendent of shops	1,400
1 cabinet-shop foreman	1,200
5 cabinetmakers or carpenters, at $1,200 each	6,000
3 cabinetmakers or carpenters, at $1,100 each	3,300

Office of the Secretary—Continued:
9 cabinetmakers or carpenters, at $1,020 each	$9,180	
3 cabinetmakers or carpenters, at $900 each	2,700	
1 instrument maker	1,200	
1 electrician	1,100	
2 electrical wiremen, at $1,100 each	2,200	
1 electrical wireman	1,000	
1 electrical wireman	900	
1 electrician's helper	840	
3 electrician's helpers, at $720 each	2,160	
1 painter	1,020	
1 painter	1,000	
5 painters, at $900 each	4,500	
5 plumbers or steamfitters, at $1,020 each	5,100	
2 plumber's helpers, at $840 each	1,680	
2 plumber's helpers, at $720 each	1,440	
1 blacksmith	900	
1 elevator machinist	900	
1 tinner or sheet-metal worker	1,100	
1 tinner's helper	720	
4 mechanics, at $1,200 each	4,800	
1 mechanic	1,000	
1 skilled laborer	900	
		$109,78?

Office of Farm Management:
4 clerks, at $1,080 each	4,320	
18 clerks, at $900 each	16,200	
6 clerks or map tracers, at $840 each	5,040	
		25,560

Weather Bureau:
10 clerks, at $900 each	9,000	
1 skilled mechanic	720	
2 repairmen, at $720 each	1,440	
		11,160

Bureau of Animal Industry:
20 laborers, at $540 each	10,800	
20 laborers, at $480 each	9,600	
1 assistant in live-stock investigations	1,600	
		22,000

Bureau of Plant Industry:
43 clerks, at $900 each	38,700	
1 clerk or draftsman	900	
11 clerks, at $840 each	9,240	
1 seed warehouseman	840	
7 laboratory aids, at $720 each	5,040	
1 laboratory apprentice	720	
1 map tracer	600	
1 blacksmith	900	
16 messenger boys, at $360 each	5,760	
1 photographer	840	
6 messengers, messenger boys, or laborers, at $660 each	3,960	
16 messengers, messenger boys, or laborers, at $600 each	9,600	
21 laborers, at $540 each	11,340	
4 laborers, messengers, or messenger boys, at $480 each	1,920	
5 laborers or messenger boys, at $420 each	2,100	
		92,460

Forest Service:
2 deputy forest supervisors, at $1,700 each	3,400	
19 deputy forest supervisors, at $1,500 each	28,500	
18 deputy forest supervisors, at $1,400 each	25,200	

AGRICULTURE APPROPRIATION BILL.

Forest Service—Continued.
70 forest rangers, at $1,100 each	$77,000	
45 forest guards, at $1,100 each (for six months' service)	24,750	
18 clerks, at $900 each	16,200	
2 clerks, at $840 each	1,680	
6 draftsmen or map colorists, at $900 each	5,400	
1 lithographer's helper	780	
1 blue-printer	720	
3 messenger boys or laborers, at $600 each	1,800	
1 messenger boy or laborer	540	
1 messenger boy or laborer	420	
13 messenger boys or laborers, at $360 each	4,680	
		$191,070

Bureau of Chemistry:
7 laboratory helpers, at $840 each	5,880	
2 laboratory helpers, at $780 each	1,560	
14 laboratory helpers, messenger boys, or laborers, at $720 each	10,080	
22 laboratory helpers, messenger boys, or laborers, at $600 each	13,200	
1 mechanic	1,020	
1 mechanic	1,000	
1 mechanic	960	
1 mechanic	900	
3 messenger boys or laborers, at $480 each	1,440	
3 messenger boys or laborers, at $420 each	1,260	
2 messenger boys or laborers, at $360 each	720	
		38,020

Bureau of Entomology:
2 clerks, class 3	3,200	
5 clerks, at $900 each	4,500	
2 clerks, at $840 each	1,680	
4 foremen, at $1,080 each	4,320	
7 entomological preparators, at $600 each	4,200	
3 messengers or laborers, at $720 each	2,160	
1 messenger boy	360	
1 mechanic	1,080	
1 mechanic	900	
1 mechanic	840	
1 gardener	600	
1 laborer	600	
1 laborer	540	
1 laborer	480	
1 laborer	420	
		25,880

Bureau of Biological Survey:
1 clerk	840	
1 clerk	720	
		1,560

Division of Accounts and Disbursements:
3 clerks, at $900 each		2,700

Division of Publications:
21 clerks, at $840 each	$17,640	
1 assistant photographer	900	
		18,540

Bureau of Crop Estimates:
1 clerk	1,300	
24 clerks, at $900 each	21,600	
2 messengers, at $840 each	1,680	
		24,580

Library:
3 clerks, at $1,020 each	3,060	
4 clerks, at $1,000 each	4,000	
6 clerks, at $900 each	5,400	
1 clerk	840	
		13,300

46 AGRICULTURE APPROPRIATION BILL.

States Relations Service:		
20 clerks, at $900 each	$18,000	
1 messenger, messenger boy, or laborer	360	
3 messengers, messenger boys, or laborers, at $300 each	900	
3 clerks, at $840 each	2,520	
2 clerks, at $720 each	1,440	
		$23,220
Bureau of Markets:		
6 telegraph operators, at $1,080 each	6,480	
1 telegraph operator	1,020	
6 laboratory aids, at $720 each	4,320	
1 telephone operator	600	
1 map tracer	480	
11 messenger boys, at $420 each	4,620	
1 messenger boy	360	
		17,880
Federal Horticultural Board:		
1 clerk	1,080	
6 clerks, at $1,000 each	6,000	
1 clerk	900	
		7,980
Total, places dropped		$625,690
Actual increase		$259,220

TRANSFERS FROM LUMP FUNDS TO STATUTORY ROLLS WITH CORRESPONDING REDUCTION IN THE LUMP-FUND APPROPRIATIONS.

(a) AGRICULTURAL ACT.

Office of Farm Management:		
2 clerks, class 1	$2,400	
1 draftsman	1,100	
		$3,500
Weather Bureau:		
4 clerks, at $1,000 each	4,000	
1 skilled mechanic	1,300	
1 repairman	960	
10 laborers, at $720 each	7,200	
2 laborers, at $600 each	1,200	
		14,660
Bureau of Animal Industry:		
To statutory roll of Bureau of Animal Industry—		
1 executive clerk ... $2,000		
1 clerk, class 4 ... 1,800		
1 clerk ... 1,500		
8 clerks, class 2 ... 11,200		
27 clerks, class 1 ... 32,400		
3 clerks, at $1,100 each ... 3,300		
5 clerks, at $1,080 each ... 5,400		
1 clerk ... 1,020		
12 clerks, at $960 each ... 11,520		
1 laboratory mechanician ... 1,440		
1 skilled laborer ... 1,000		
1 skilled laborer ... 900		
1 laborer ... 900		
5 laborers, at $720 each ... 3,600		
2 charwomen, at $480 each ... 960		
	78,940	
To statutory roll of Office of the Secretary—		
2 clerks, at $1,100 each ... 2,200		
1 clerk ... 900		
1 assistant engineer ... 1,200		
1 messenger boy ... 600		
	4,900	
		83,840

AGRICULTURE APPROPRIATION BILL.

Bureau of Plant Industry:
1 executive clerk	$1,980	
2 clerks, class 4	3,600	
2 clerks, class 3	3,200	
1 clerk	1,500	
2 clerks, class 2	2,800	
3 clerks, at $1,320 each	3,960	
15 clerks, class 1	18,000	
1 draftsman	1,200	
2 clerks, at $1,100 each	2,200	
3 clerks, at $1,080 each	3,240	
5 clerks, at $1,000 each	5,000	
1 laborer	720	
1 artist	900	
1 skilled laborer	1,100	
4 messenger boys, at $480 each	1,920	
1 charwoman	240	
		$51,560

Forest Service:
1 surveyor		1,800

Bureau of Chemistry:
1 administrative assistant	2,500	
1 clerk, class 3	1,600	
9 clerks, class 1	10,800	
2 multigraph operators, at $1,000 each	2,000	
1 mechanic	1,000	
4 charwomen, at $240 each	960	
		18,860

Bureau of Entomology:
To statutory roll of Bureau of Entomology—			
1 clerk, class 3	$1,600		
1 clerk, class 2	1,400		
3 clerks, class 1	3,600		
1 insect delineator	1,600		
2 insect delineators, at $1,400 each	2,800		
1 photographer	1,200		
1 laborer	1,080		
		13,280	
To statutory roll of Office of the Secretary—			
1 watchman		720	
			14,000

Bureau of Biological Survey:
To statutory roll of Bureau of Biological Survey—			
1 clerk, class 2	$1,400		
4 clerks, class 1	4,800		
1 clerk	1,100		
		7,300	
To statutory roll of Office of the Secretary—			
1 laborer		480	
			7,780

States Relations Service:
1 clerk or chief accountant	2,400	
1 clerk	1,980	
3 clerks, class 3	4,800	
1 clerk, class 2	1,400	
2 clerks, at $1,320 each	2,640	
5 clerks, class 1	6,000	
2 clerks, at $1,100 each	2,200	
2 laborers, at $720 each	1,440	
		22,860

Bureau of Public Roads:
1 instrument maker	1,800	
1 clerk, class 4	1,800	

Bureau of Public Roads—Continued.
1 clerk	$1,100	
1 mechanic	1,500	
2 laborers, at $900 each	1,800	
1 laborer	600	
1 charwoman	240	
		$8,840

Bureau of Markets:
To statutory roll of Bureau of Markets—
1 administrative assistant	$3,000	
2 executive clerks, at $2,000 each	4,000	
1 clerk	2,000	
1 executive assistant	1,980	
4 clerks, class 4	7,200	
1 clerk	1,740	
3 clerks, class 3	4,800	
6 clerks, class 2	8,400	
3 clerks, at $1,320 each	3,960	
28 clerks, class 1	33,600	
7 clerks, at $1,100 each	7,700	
9 clerks, at $1,000 each	9,000	
1 clerk	1,080	
1 clerk	960	
1 superintendent of telegraph	2,000	
1 telegraph operator	1,600	
7 telegraph operators, at $1,400 each	9,800	
1 telegraph operator	1,320	
1 telephone operator	900	
1 draftsman	1,400	
1 draftsman	1,200	
2 chauffeurs, at $900 each	1,800	
1 laborer	840	
1 laborer	720	
2 messenger boys, at $540 each	1,080	
1 laborer	600	
1 messenger boy	480	
1 messenger boy	480	
1 charwoman	480	
4 charwomen, at $300 each	1,200	
1 charwoman	240	
		115,560

To statutory roll of Office of the Secretary:
2 clerks, class 2	2,800	
1 electrical wireman	1,100	
3 watchmen, at $720 each	2,160	
		6,060
		121,620

Enforcement of the Insecticide Act:
1 clerk, class 1		1,200

Federal Horticultural Board:
1 clerk	1,560	
1 clerk	1,440	
1 clerk, class 1	1,200	
1 messenger boy	600	
		4,800

Total, agricultural act................................ $355,320

(b) FOOD PRODUCTION ACT.

Bureau of Plant Industry:
From plant-disease survey—
1 clerk, class 2	$1,400	
1 clerk, class 1	1,200	
1 clerk	1,100	
		$3,700

AGRICULTURE APPROPRIATION BILL. 49

Bureau of Markets:
  From market news service on fruits and vegetables—
2 clerks, class 2	$2,800
15 clerks, class 1	18,000
10 clerks, at $1,100 each	11,000
7 clerks, at $1,080 each	7,560
7 clerks, at $1,000 each	7,000
30 telegraph operators, at $1,400 each	42,000
1 telegraph operator	1,320
1 telegraph operator	1,300
7 telegraph operators, at $1,200 each	8,400
2 multigraph operators, at $1,200 each	2,400
1 machine operator	1,200
1 machine operator	1,100
1 chauffeur	900
2 laborers, at $720 each	1,440
1 laborer	600
3 messenger boys, at $540 each	1,620

  From market news service on live stock and meats—
1 clerk, class 3	1,600
1 clerk, class 2	1,400
1 clerk	1,320
11 clerks, class 1	13,200
11 clerks, at $1,100 each	12,100
5 clerks, at $1,000 each	5,000
16 telegraph operators, at $1,400 each	22,400
3 telegraph operators, at $1,200 each	3,600
1 telephone operator	900
1 telephone operator	840
1 machine operator	1,100
1 laborer	840
1 messenger	720
1 laborer	600
1 messenger boy	540

  From market news service on butter, cheese, eggs, and poultry—
7 clerks, class 1	8,400
8 clerks, at $1,100 each	8,800
4 clerks, at $1,000 each	4,000
3 telegraph operators, at $1,400 each	4,200
1 telegraph operator	1,200
1 machine operator	1,200
1 machine operator	1,000
1 laborer	600

  From market news service on grain, hay, feeds, and seeds—
10 clerks, class 1	12,000
6 clerks, at $1,100 each	6,600
2 clerks, at $1,080 each	2,160
1 laborer	720
4 messenger boys, at $540 each	2,160

  From market inspection of perishable foods—
1 clerk, class 1	1,200
1 clerk	1,100

  From city market service—
1 clerk	1,320
3 clerks, class 1	3,600
2 clerks, at $1,100 each	2,200

                                                                         $237,260

Total, food production act $240,960
                                                                                 $596,280

AGRICULTURE APPROPRIATION BILL.

TRANSFER FROM LUMP FUND TO STATUTORY ROLL WITHOUT CORRESPONDING REDUCTION IN LUMP-FUND APPROPRIATION.

Office of the Secretary:
 From extra labor roll of Office of the Secretary—
  1 mechanical assistant... $1,400

   Apparent increase.. 856,900

TRANSFERS BETWEEN STATUTORY ROLLS OF DIFFERENT BRANCHES OF THE DEPARTMENT.

Office of the Secretary:
 To Bureau of Chemistry, 1 clerk, class 2.............................. $1,400
 To Division of Publications, 1 clerk, class 2........................... 1,400

Bureau of Animal Industry, Office of the Secretary:
 2 clerks, at $900 each... 1,800
 1 instrument maker... 1,200
 1 skilled laborer... 900
                   3,900

Bureau of Plant Industry, to Office of the Secretary, 1 clerk............. 900

Bureau of Chemistry, to Office of the Secretary:
 1 clerk, class 3.. 1,600
 1 clerk.. 900
                   2,500
Division of Publications, to Office of the Secretary, 1 clerk, class 1...... 1,200
Bureau of Crop Estimates, to Office of the Secretary, 1 charwoman....... 360
Bureau of Public Roads, to Office of the Secretary, 1 skilled laborer..... 720
Bureau of Markets, to Office of the Secretary, 1 mechanical assistant.... 1,380

CHANGES IN TITLE.

Office of the Secretary:
 1 law clerk, $3,250, to 1 attorney, $3,250.
 2 law clerks, at $3,000 each, to 2 attorneys, at $3,000 each.
 2 law clerks, at $2,750 each, to 2 attorneys, at $2,750 each.
 4 law clerks, at $2,500 each, to 4 attorneys, at $2,500 each.
 2 law clerks, at $2,250 each, to 2 attorneys, at $2,250 each.
 1 law clerk, $2,200, to 1 attorney, $2,200.
 5 law clerks, at $2,000 each, to 5 attorneys, at $2,000 each.
 1 skilled laborer, $840, to 1 telephone operator, $840.
 8 assistant messengers, messenger boys, or laborers, at $600 each, to 8 messenger boys, at $600 each.
 16 laborers or messenger boys, at $480 each, to 16 messenger boys, at $480 each.
Office of Farm Management:
 1 messenger, messenger boy, or laborer, $660, to 1 messenger boy, $660.
 3 messengers, messenger boys, or laborers, at $480 each, to 3 messenger boys, at $480 each.
 1 messenger, messenger boy, or laborer, $480, to 1 charwoman, $480.
Weather Bureau:
 1 skilled mechanic, $1,300, to 1 mechanic, $1,300.
 11 messengers, messenger boys, or laborers, at $600 each, to 11 messenger boys, at $600 each.
 99 messengers, messenger boys, or laborers, at $480 each, to 99 messenger boys, at $480 each.
Bureau of Animal Industry:
 1 editor and compiler, $2,250, to 1 executive clerk, $2,250.
 1 laboratory helper, $480, to 1 charwoman, $480.
Bureau of Plant Industry:
 1 seed warehouseman, $1,400, to 1 clerk, class 2.
 5 messengers, messenger boys, or laborers, at $660 each, to 5 messenger boys, at $660 each.

AGRICULTURE APPROPRIATION BILL. 51

Bureau of Plant Industry—Continued.
  14 messengers, messenger boys, or laborers, at $600 each, to 14 messenger boys, at $600 each.
  31 laborers, messengers, or messenger boys, at $480 each, to 31 messenger boys, at $480 each.
  4 laborers, messengers, or messenger boys, at $480 each, to 4 charwomen, at $480 each.
  4 laborers or charwomen, at $480 each, to 4 charwomen, at $480 each.
Bureau of Chemistry:
  1 laboratory helper, messenger boy, or laborer, $720, to 1 messenger boy, $720.
  2 laboratory helpers, messenger boy, or laborers, at $660 each, to 2 messenger boys, at $660 each.
  10 laboratory helpers, messenger boys, or laborers, at $600 each, to 10 messenger boys, at $600 each.
  3 messenger boys or laborers, at $540 each, to 3 messenger boys, at $540 each.
  10 messenger boys or laborers, at $480 each, to 10 messenger boys or charwomen, at $480 each.
Bureau of Soils:
  2 messengers, messenger boys, or laborers, at $480 each, to 2 messenger boys, at $480 each.
Bureau of Entomology:
  1 chief clerk and executive assistant, $2,250, to 1 chief clerk, $2,250.
  1 administrative assistant, $2,250, to 1 executive clerk, $2,250.
Bureau of Biological Survey:
  2 messengers, messenger boys, or laborers, at $480 each, to 2 messenger boys, at $480 each.
Division of Accounts and Disbursements:
  1 messenger, or messenger boy, $600, to 1 messenger boy, $600.
Division of Publications:
  1 assistant in charge of document section, $2,000, to 1 assistant, $2,000.
  1 assistant in document section, $1,800, to 1 assistant, $1,800.
  1 draftsman or photographer, $1,200, to 1 laboratory aid, $1,200.
  7 skilled laborers, messengers, or messenger boys, at $720 each, to 7 messenger boys, at $720 each.
  3 messengers or messenger boys, at $600 each, to 3 messenger boys, at $600 each.
  2 messengers or messenger boys, at $480 each, to 2 messenger boys, at $480 each.
Bureau of Crop Estimates:
  2 messengers, messenger boys, or laborers, at $660 each, to 2 messenger boys, at $660 each.
  1 messenger, messenger boy, or laborer, $480, to 1 messenger boy, $480.
  1 charwoman, messenger, or laborer, $540, to 1 charwoman, $540.
Library:
  1 messenger, messenger boy, or laborer, $480, to 1 messenger boy, $480.
States Relations Service:
  1 financial clerk, $2,000, to 1 executive clerk, $2,000.
  5 messengers, messenger boys, or laborers, at $600 each, to 5 messenger boys or charwomen, at $600 each.
  15 messengers, messenger boys, or laborers, at $480 each, to 15 messenger boys or charwomen, at $480 each.
  4 laborers or charwomen, at $480 each, to 4 charwomen, at $480 each.
  11 laborers or charwomen, at $240 each, to 11 charwomen, at $240 each.
Bureau of Public Roads:
  1 model maker, $1,800, to 1 model maker or clerk, $1,800.
  1 draftsman, $1,320, to 1 draftsmen or clerk, $1,320.
  1 mechanician, $1,680, to 1 mechanician or clerk, $1,680.
  1 lantern-slide colorist, $1,320, to 1 lantern-slide colorist or clerk, $1,320.
  1 mechanic. $1,200, to 1 mechanic or skilled laborer, $1,200.
  1 skilled laborer, $1,200, to 1 skilled laborer or clerk, $1,200.
  2 laborers, at $900 each, to 2 messengers, laborers, or laboratory helpers, at $900 each.
  1 mechanic, $1,500, to 1 mechanic or clerk, $1,500.
  3 messengers, laborers, or messenger boys, at $600 each, to 3 messenger boys, at $600 each.

52   AGRICULTURE APPROPRIATION BILL.

Bureau of Public Roads—Continued.
  8 laborers, messenger boys, or charwomen, at $480 each, to 8 messenger boys, at $480 each.
Bureau of Markets:
  1 clerk in charge of supplies and accounts, $2,250, to 1 executive clerk, $2,250.
  1 clerk, $2,000, to 1 executive clerk, $2,000.
  1 executive assistant, $1,980, to 1 executive clerk, $1,980.
  1 administrative assistant, $1,980, to 1 executive clerk, $1,980.
  5 messenger boys or laborers, at $600 each, to 5 messenger boys, at $600 each.
  10 messengers, at $540 each, to 10 messenger boys, at $540 each.
  5 messenger boys or laborers, at $540 each, to 5 messenger boys, at $540 each.
  21 messenger boys or laborers, at $480 each, to 21 messenger boys, at $480 each.
  1 messenger, $480, to 1 messenger boy, $480.
Enforcement of the Insecticide Act:
  2 messenger boys or laborers, at $480 each, to 2 messenger boys, at $480 each.

NEW LANGUAGE—OFFICE OF THE SECRETARY.

(a) After the item "Two law clerks, at $1,600 each," the following new language has been added:
"*Provided*, That hereafter the position of attorney in the Department of Agriculture shall be and remain in the competitive classified civil service, anything in the law or in the civil-service rules and regulations to the contrary notwithstanding, and the law clerks now in said department who may be appointed or promoted to said positions of attorney shall retain all the rights of competitive employees, and the Secretary of Agriculture may detail said attorneys for service in or out of the District of Columbia."

The object of this provision is to preserve the classified civil-service status of the positions of attorney and of the persons who may be appointed or promoted to those positions. Without such a proviso, the attorneyships would fall within the exception in the civil-service rules and could be filled without compliance with the civil-service rules applicable to positions in the competitive classified civil service.

(b) The following new language has been inserted after the item "Fifteen charwomen, at $240 each":
"For salaries and compensation of necessary employees in the mechanical shops and power plant of the Department of Agriculture, $90,000: *Provided*, That hereafter the Secretary of Agriculture may, by transfer settlement through the Treasury, reimburse any appropriation made for the salaries and compensation of employees in the mechanical shops of the department from the appropriation made for the bureau, office, or division for which any work in said shops is performed, and such reimbursement shall be at the actual cost of such work for supervision and labor."

The entire mechanical-shop force of the department has been underpaid for some years. All places on the shop roll are statutory, and promotions have been comparatively infrequent.

The present roll does not afford sufficient flexibility in filling vacancies with the class of employees most needed at a given time.

The rates of pay also are lower than those obtainable under commercial employment and are not up to the standard in other branches of the Government. On this account it has been impossible to obtain the high-grade service which the special work of the Department of Agriculture demands. A lump-sum appropriation for the salaries and compensation of the mechanical employees would overcome these difficulties, salary adjustments could be made from time to time to suit the varying labor conditions, and a contented and efficient working force could always be secured. The creation of this new lump fund of $90,000 contemplates the elimination of the present statutory places occupied by the employees of the mechanical shops, which now aggregate $93,080. The apparent saving by such a change would be $3,080. But, inasmuch as the plan proposes that the various bureaus, offices, and divisions of the department for whom mechanical work is done shall be required to make reimbursement from their lump-sum appropriations for all services performed by the mechanical shops, the actual result would be that the cost of all the mechanical work of the department except that performed for the Office of the Secretary would

AGRICULTURE APPROPRIATION BILL. 53

ultimately be met from the lump-fund appropriations of such bureaus, offices, and divisions through the transfer settlement provided for under this new arrangement. The actual saving, therefore, would be considerable.

Statement showing proposed changes in lump-fund appropriations of the Department of Agriculture for the fiscal year ending June 30, 1920.

SUMMARY.

Items.	Increase. Apparent.	Increase. Actual.	Decrease. Apparent.	Decrease. Actual.
Office of the Secretary:				
Extra labor and emergency employments	$8,000	$9,400		
Office of Farm Management:				
Farm-management investigations			$3,500	
Weather Bureau:				
Expenses outside of Washington	17,960	18,920		
Establishment and maintenance of aerological stations			13,700	
Repair of cable and telegraph lines			25,000	$25,000
Bureau of Animal Industry:				
Inspection and quarantine			8,380	
Tuberculosis investigation and eradication			6,480	
Tick eradication			8,020	
Dairy investigations			14,020	
Animal husbandry investigations	8,280	17,480		
Hog-cholera investigation and eradication			8,820	
Dourine investigation and eradication			9,000	7,800
Meat inspection			27,720	
Bureau of Plant Industry:				
Investigations in plant pathology	19,300	1 23,000		
Eradication of citrus canker			53,680	50,000
Investigations in forest pathology			1,320	
Eradication of white-pine blister rust			9,720	
Soil-bacteriology and plant-nutrition investigations			240	
Soil-fertility investigations			1,200	
Crop-acclimatization and fiber-plant investigations			3,100	
Cereal investigations			9,000	
Sugar-plant investigations	30,000	1 30,000		
Investigations in economic and systematic botany			900	
Dry-land agriculture investigations			1,000	
Pomological investigations			2,080	
Horticultural investigations	27,800	1 30,000		
Foreign seed and plant introduction			8,740	
Purchase and distribution of new and rare seeds, and forage-crop investigations			3,400	
Investigations of commercial fertilizers (new)	125,000	125,000		
Administrative expenses			1,980	
Purchase and distribution of valuable seeds			3,000	
Forest Service:				
National forests	266,074	266,074		
Land classification and entry surveys 2			12,800	11,000
Forest-products investigations	35,000	35,000		
Silvicultural investigations	25,000	25,000		
Reconnoissance of forest resources			20,000	20,000
Bureau of Chemistry:				
Poultry and egg investigations	10,000	10,000		
Fish investigations	6,000	6,000		
Color investigations	29,280	29,280		
Sirup investigations	5,000	1 5,000		
Enforcement of the food and drugs act	31,140	50,000		
Investigations of rare chemicals (new)	10,000	10,000		
Utilization of wool-scouring waste	9,000	1 9,000		
Bureau of Soils:				
Investigations of fertilizer resources	18,660	18,660		
Bureau of Entomology:				
Deciduous-fruit insect investigations	2,400	5,000		
Cereal and forage insect investigations	25,000	25,000		
Southern field-crop insect investigations			4,000	
Forest insect investigations			1,080	
Truck-crop and stored-product insect investigations			3 2,800	
Administrative expenses			3,520	
Bureau of Biological Survey:				
Maintenance of mammal and bird reservations			1,200	
Economic investigations (food habits of birds and mammals, etc.)			5,380	
Biological investigations			1,200	
Protection of migratory birds	4 125,000	4 125,000		

1 Transferred from food production act.
2 Combination of items (1) land classification and (2) entry surveys.
3 Exclusive of $20,000 for eradication of sweet-potato weevil, transferred from miscellaneous section of bill.
4 Exclusive of $22,000 for enforcement of the Lacey Act, transferred to this item.

AGRICULTURE APPROPRIATION BILL.

Statement showing proposed changes in lump-fund appropriations of the Department of Agriculture for the fiscal year ending June 30, 1920—Continued.

Items.	Increase.		Decrease.	
	Apparent.	Actual.	Apparent.	Actual.
Division of Publications:				
Labor-saving machinery and supplies	$1,500	$1,500		
Photographic equipment and materials	5,000	5,000		
Communication and transportation service	250	250		
Purchase and maintenance of vehicles	500	500		
Miscellaneous expenses	1,000	1,000		
Bureau of Crop Estimates:				
Administrative expenses	1,750	1,750		
Field investigations	42,279	42,279		
States Relations Service:				
Administration of the Hatch, Adams, and Smith-Lever Acts, and administration of insular experiment stations	6,100	10,000		
Extension work in the Northern and Western States			$3,520	
Extension work in the Southern States			5,100	
Insular experiment stations	25,000	25,000		
Home-economics investigations	46,160	50,000		
Administrative expenses	3,500	10,000		
Bureau of Public Roads:				
Road management			1,800	
Road building and maintenance			2,840	
Road-material investigations			4,200	
Rural-engineering investigations	50,000	50,000		
Bureau of Markets:				
Marketing and distribution	25,280	[1] 41,100		
Market reports on fruits and vegetables	108,000	[2] 244,800		
Market reports on live stock and meats	94,800	[2] 170,000		
Market reports on dairy and poultry products (new)	80,600	[2] 110,000		
Market reports on grain, hay, and feeds (new)	41,560	[2] 53,160		
Seed reporting service (new)	34,960	[2] 47,000		
City market service (new)	42,880	[2] 50,000		
Food products inspection service	88,960	[3] 101,000		
Studies of rural cooperation			2,500	
State cooperation in marketing work	33,460	34,420		
Grain-standardization investigations			6,700	
Enforcement of the standard-container act			1,200	
Milling and baking investigations	35,000	35,000		
Administrative expenses	5,000	8,000		
Enforcement of the cotton-futures act	18,200	25,000		
Enforcement of the grain-standards act	142,020	175,560		
Administration of the warehouse act	16,440	20,600		
Enforcement of the Insecticide Act	300	1,500		
Federal Horticultural Board:				
Enforcement of the plant-quarantine act			600	
Miscellaneous:				
Eradication of pink bollworm	95,800	100,000		
Net	1,880,193 / 1,575,753	2,287,233 / 2,173,433	304,440	$113,800

[1] $27,000 of this amount transferred from food production act.
[2] Transferred from food production act.
[3] $51,000 of this amount transferred from food production act.

OFFICE OF THE SECRETARY.

Extra labor and emergency employments.—Apparent increase, $8,000; actual increase, $9,400.

Under this appropriation provision is made for the temporary employment of clerks, laborers, watchmen, mechanics, etc. The continued growth of the department and the higher wage scale of mechanics and laborers selected for temporary employment necessitates an increase in this fund.

WEATHER BUREAU.

Expenses outside of Washington.—Apparent increase, $17,960; actual increase, $18,920.

The agricultural act for 1919 provides the sum of $5,000 for frost-protection investigations and $2,000 for storm-warning equipment on the Pacific coast. Inasmuch as neither of these items will be carried in the act for 1920, the actual increase in Weather Bureau funds for expenses outside of Washington is $25,920. This amount is desired for the purpose of increasing the compensation of field employees. The salaries of the technical force of the Weather Bureau are considerably lower than those paid by other branches of the Government for comparable services.. These employees are charged with the responsibility of the maintenance of important offices having close relations with civic, commercial, and other Government organizations, and an improvement in their salary status, especially in view of present living conditions, is essential.

Repairs to telegraph and cable lines.—Apparent and actual decrease, $25,000.
The purpose of this appropriation will be accomplished during the present fiscal year. The item therefore has been omitted.

BUREAU OF ANIMAL INDUSTRY.

Animal husbandry investigations.—Apparent increase, $8,280; actual increase, $17,480.
It is planned to develop further the farm-sheep investigations, especially in the South and East, and also the range-sheep investigations in the West. This work will contribute to the stabilizing of the sheep industry and aim to foster and maintain the increased development resulting from the stimulation of production under war conditions.

Dourine investigation and eradication.—Apparent decrease, $9,000; actual decrease, $7,800.
It is expected that by the beginning of the fiscal year 1920 this work will have diminished to some extent, so that it can be carried on satisfactorily with a reduced appropriation.

BUREAU OF PLANT INDUSTRY.

Investigations in plant pathology.—Apparent increase, $19,300; actual increase, $23,000.
This increase represents the transfer of the item under the food production act for enlarging the plant-disease survey, the object being to place this activity on an adequate permanent basis. The work was not fully organized until the present year, when its rapid development was made possible by the use of emergency funds. Its value as a complement to both research and extension activities already has been amply demonstrated, and its usefulness is constantly increasing with the development of a better organization throughout the country for collecting disease data through cooperation with pathological workers in the various States.

Eradication of citrus canker.—Apparent decrease, $53,680; actual decrease, $50,000.
The progress of the citrus-canker eradication campaign has been so satisfactory that it has been possible to discontinue the work in Georgia and South Carolina. It is believed that the work can be effectively carried on in the remaining infested territory during the next fiscal year with a reduced appropriation.

Sugar-plant investigations.—Apparent and actual increase, $30,000.
This increase represents the transfer of the item of $10,000 for sugar-beet nematode work and the item of $20,000 for the control of a new sugar-cane disease in Porto Rico from the food production act. Both these lines of work involve the study of diseases of sugar-producing plants which will undoubtedly require several years' investigation for their solution and for the development of adequate remedial measures. They are responsible for very large losses in sugar production, and it is believed that every effort should be made to control them.

Horticultural investigations.—Apparent increase, $27,800; actual increase, $30,000.
The food production act for the current fiscal year includes an item of $30,000 for "locating Irish-potato seed stocks." It is proposed to transfer this amount to the agricultural appropriation bill, as the work will necessarily require several years for its completion. There is urgent need for the production of a sufficiently large second crop of Irish potatoes in the South to fully supply the normal demands in that region. If this need were met by the southern growers it would obviate the necessity for long-distance shipments of potatoes from the North and West during the winter season, thereby releasing for more urgent purposes a large number of freight cars. The present practices of the growers

of second-crop seed in the South are responsible in large measure for the inadequacy of the crop produced. It is believed that the work proposed, conducted in cooperation with State experiment stations at various points in Arkansas, Oklahoma, Louisiana, Texas, Alabama, and Florida, will serve to demonstrate the possibility of materially increasing the production of second-crop potatoes. Sufficient study has been given to the problem to make it possible to outline the work in such a way as almost certainly to meet and solve some of the difficulties that heretofore have stood in the way of a larger production of late potatoes in this section.

Investigations of commercial fertilizers.—New item, $125,000.
There is need to undertake experiments in cooperation with State agricultural experiment stations, agricultural colleges, and other agencies in regions where the use of fertilizers now amounts annually to a large expenditure and in those regions where the increased use of fertilizers is expected to develop rapidly. Many valuable experiments have been conducted throughout those regions by the State colleges and experiment stations, but the extreme diversity of plan in developing the experimental tests and the absence of any correlation between experimental work in different sections have led to much confusion in the results obtained. Undoubtedly very effective correlation of existing activities will be possible if the department can aid in developing more consistent plans for conducting these experiments.

FOREST SERVICE.

National forests.—Apparent and actual increase. $266,074.
In a number of the national forests the normal protective force is insufficient to meet the fire situation. Large areas in these forests are far removed from settlements, and when fires occur it is difficult, owing to inadequate means of transportation and long distances, to secure emergency fire fighters promptly. In order to remedy this situation and to have available an adequate fire-fighting force at the time of greatest need, it is believed advisable to place the regular protective short-term organization on a four-months basis, instead of two or three months as at present. Additional sums are also needed to cover the increased cost of maintaining Government stock, for the employment of additional forest assistants and scalers, and for brush burning and other expenses incident to increased timber-sale business, and for expenses incident to the administration of grazing on several of the forests; for the administration and protection of 470,394 acres added to the Colorado National Forest by presidential proclamation; and for general administrative expenses in connection with certain national forests, including new forests comprised in the areas purchased under the Weeks law.

Land classification and entry surveys.—Apparent decrease, $12,800; actual decrease, $11,000.
This represents a combination of the two items "Classification of lands for homestead settlement" and "Survey of lands chiefly valuable for agriculture." A decrease in the appropriation is made possible by the completion of land classification in a number of localities and a consequent reduction in the number of field parties engaged in this work.

Forest-products investigations.—Apparent and actual increase, $35,000.
The Forest Products Laboratory at Madison, Wis., has been cooperating with the War and Navy Departments in many ways, the requirements of this work being covered by special allotment from the departments concerned. There are, in addition, increasing demands upon the organization by the wood-using industries for assistance in connection with the production of many materials required to meet the conditions growing out of the war, which service must be financed from the regular Forest Service appropriations.

Silvicultural investigations.—Apparent and actual increase, $25,000.
The department is studying certain phases of the lumber industry, with special references to supplies, production, and distribution of lumber and other economic facts and conditions essential to the Government in securing materials. The work will follow logically that already done by the Forest Service in cooperation with the Federal Trade Commission. The rapidly growing demands upon the Forest Service for information can be met only through an increase in appropriations beyond the funds now provided.

Reconnoissance of forest resources.—Apparent and actual decrease, $20,000.
It is believed that $80,000 will be adequate under present labor conditions to provide for such timber-cruising parties as can be assembled for valuation of

national-forest timber resources and also for the appraisal of grazing and other resources of the forest, especially as, due to the loss of several of the most efficient grazing examiners of the Forest Service, it may not be possible to carry out in full the plans originally contemplated for this work during the fiscal year 1920. When normal conditions are restored, however, it will be desirable to continue the work on the present basis if the requisite personnel can be secured.

BUREAU OF CHEMISTRY.

Poultry and egg investigations.—Apparent and actual increase, $10,000.

The extension of the work on the conservation of poultry is especially necessary in order to supplement the supply of beef, mutton, and pork. This investigation will provide the fundamental information and the means for its dissemination looking to the more general prevention of waste and decay. The study of the utilization for poultry fleshing of feeds now wholly or largely wasted would mean the cheap and quick production of millions of pounds of chicken flesh. Great losses during transportation can be prevented or reduced by the extension of this work.

Fish investigations.—Apparent and actual increase, $6,000.

There is an immense annual loss from spoilage of fish because of a lack of knowledge as to the best methods of handling and shipment. The work already done by the department has shown that great improvement can be effected in these methods. The continuation and extension of these studies will undoubtedly contribute materially to the conservation of the meat supply by increasing the use of fish as food, especially at interior points where fresh fish can not now be obtained in quantity.

Color investigations.—Apparent and actual increase, $29,280.

The color investigations already have produced very valuable results. New chemical processes for the manufacture of some of the most important compounds used in the production of dyes have been devised and are now being tested on a large commercial scale. The increased appropriation, if granted, will be used to complete the equipment and for the employment of additional scientists required for the proper conduct of the experimental work under way.

Sirup investigations.—Apparent and actual increase, $5,000.

This increase represents the transfer of the item under the food production act for "Preparation of sweet sirups." The work on sweet sirups is important in its bearing on the sugar supply and will probably require several years' investigation for its proper development.

Enforcement of the food and drugs act.—Apparent increase, $31,140; actual increase, $50,000.

This sum is needed to cover the increased cost of travel and for the purchase of chemicals and apparatus. Because of the scarcity of certain foods and many drugs, some manufacturers are tempted to put out spurious products. This requires increased vigilance on the part of inspectors and necessitates expert chemical and bacteriological investigations. In addition to the regular work, the War and Navy Departments are calling upon the Bureau of Chemistry for assistance in insuring that foods and drugs for the use of the Army and Navy are wholesome and of the quality represented.

Investigations of rare chemicals.—New item, $10,000.

Certain rare chemicals necessary in research work are not now manufactured in the United States. It is not profitable to produce them commercially because the quantity required is small and the demand very variable. In order that the chemical industry may be developed to the fullest extent possible, it is highly important that investigators be able to obtain any rare chemicals needed to carry on research. It is proposed to manufacture in the laboratories of the Bureau of Chemistry only such rare chemicals as are not otherwise obtainable in this country.

Utilization of wool-scouring waste.—New item, $9,000.

This new item merely represents the transfer of the appropriation under the food production act for "Utilization of wool-scouring wastes." The development of methods for utilizing such wastes probably will require several years' investigation, and it is therefore believed desirable to have the item included in the agricultural act.

BUREAU OF SOILS.

Investigations of fertilizer resources.—Apparent and actual increase, $18,660.
The several lines of investigational work in connection with the development of fertilizer resources have expanded very materially during the past year and a half. The War Department is interested especially in the experiments of the Bureau of Soils on nitrogen fixation and has detailed a number of chemists to this department to assist in undertaking cooperative work in this direction. Without this assistance it would have been impossible to develop the work to its present stage. Inasmuch as the War Department may withdraw its chemists at any time, it is believed desirable that the Department of Agriculture should be in a position to continue the work without outside assistance.

BUREAU OF ENTOMOLOGY.

Deciduous-fruit insect investigations.—Apparent increase, $2,400; actual increase, $5,000.
In order to carry out effectively the work of eradication and prevention of the spread of the Japanese beetle, an increased appropriation will be necessary. Surveys during the present season have shown the insect to be more or less abundant over some 10,000 acres, as compared with the known infestation of 600 or 700 acres last fall. The beetles have also been found in sparse numbers over an area of approximately 25,000 acres. This pest is very destructive to orchard and other fruits, and every effort should be put forth to eradicate it.

Cereal and forage insect investigations.—Apparent and actual increase, $25,000.
An increase of $25,000 ($10,000 to be immediately available) is needed for use in combating the European corn borer, the most dangerous insect enemy of corn which has ever appeared in this country. In Hungary it has been found to take one-fourth of the entire crop in a single season. At the present time the pest is confined to an area of about 300 square miles in the vicinity of Boston, where it has caused serious injury to the sweet-corn industry. The insect attacks many plants besides corn, including hops, hemp, garden crops, and native grasses and weeds. Strong efforts should be made to prevent its further spread and to effect its extermination, if possible.

BUREAU OF BIOLOGICAL SURVEY.

Protection of migratory birds.—Apparent and actual increase, $125,000.
In order to administer the migratory-bird treaty act of July 3, 1918, over the entire United States and Alaska, a very material increase in the present appropriation will be necessary. At present in many of the States there is no Federal representative to enforce this law. Reports from 43 States indicate a substantial increase in migratory wild fowl and insectivorous birds even under the operation of the former imperfect migratory-bird law. Under the present act, with its added powers, it is believed that with sufficient funds to give a fairly effective administration of the law a very great increase can be secured in the migratory game birds as well as in the useful insectivorous species of the country.

DIVISION OF PUBLICATIONS.

Labor-saving machinery and supplies.—Apparent and actual increase, $1,500.
The addressograph system has recently been installed in the division to replace a slower and more or less antiquated system of addressing envelopes. The expansion of the addressograph system will require the purchase of more machinery and supplies in order to properly take care of the work. Additional funds are also needed for the purchase of general supplies required in connection with the duplicating work.

Photographic equipment and materials.—Apparent and actual increase, $5,000.
The cost of all sorts of photographic equipment and materials has increased greatly during the past year. Additional funds will be needed in order to meet this cost and to adequately provide for the large increase in the motion-picture and general photographic laboratory work.

Communication and transportation service.—Apparent and actual increase, $250.

A small increase in this item is recommended in order to provide for the increased cost of freight and express service, including the shipment of motion-picture films.

Purchase and maintenance of vehicles.—Apparent and actual increase, $500.

The present appropriation of $500 is insufficient for the purchase of necessary supplies for trucks and wagons, including tires and gasoline and the replacing of parts of the trucks when necessary.

Miscellaneous expenses.—Apparent and actual increase, $1,000.

Many articles not provided for by other items must be purchased from this appropriation, including a large number of line engravings and half-tone cuts. The present appropriation is not adequate to meet these requirements.

BUREAU OF CROP ESTIMATES.

Administrative expenses.—Apparent and actual increase, $1,750.

Provision is made under this item for the promotion of three of the administrative officers of the bureau and for additional funds for the purchase of stationery, furniture, typewriters, and other necessary office equipment and supplies.

Field investigations.—Apparent and actual increase, $42,279.

This sum is needed to strengthen and extend the work of the department in estimating the production of truck and fruit crops and to make more effective the routine work involved in estimating and reporting general farm crops. It is proposed to use this amount as follows: $240 for the promotion of the chief of the field force; $3,600 for the employment of two additional assistant truck-crop specialists; $5,000 for traveling expenses of these two specialists; $18,450 for additional traveling expenses of 41 field agents; $900 for traveling expenses of one fruit-crop specialist and two assistants; $1,300 for inspection trips of administrative officers of the bureau; $4,500 for stationery; $4,000 for equipment and material required by field agents; $1,058 for rental of office quarters, including water, heat, light, and janitor service; $1,500 for telegraph, telephone, and postage charges; and $1,731 for miscellaneous items.

STATES RELATIONS SERVICE.

Administration of the Hatch, Adams, and Smith-Lever Acts and administration of insular experiment stations.—Apparent increase, $6,100; actual increase, $10,000.

An increase is recommended in the allotment for the administration of the Smith-Lever funds, which will be increased by $1,000,000 during the fiscal year 1920.

Insular experiment stations.—Apparent and actual increase, $25,000.

Experiment stations are now maintained by the department in Alaska, Hawaii, Porto Rico, Guam, and the Virgin Islands. These stations are rendering valuable assistance in the solution of local agricultural problems. Additional funds are needed for the more effective prosecution of the work at these places. The increase will be apportioned as follows: $10,000 to the Alaska stations, for the erection of suitable sanitary cattle barns on the island of Kodiak, and for the construction of a stock barn, clearing land for pasture, and purchase of breeding stock necessary to undertake investigations in dairying and pig raising at the Matanuska station, this sum to be immediately available; $5,000 to the Hawaii station, to provide for the further development of the demonstration and extension work; $5,000 to the Porto Rico station, to be used for the stimulation of the increased local production of many foods now largely imported from the mainland; and $5,000 to the Guam station, to repair the damages caused by a serious typhoon which visited the island in July last, this amount to be immediately available.

Home-economic investigations.—Apparent increase, $46,160; actual increase, $50,000.

The Department of Agriculture is the only organization specifically authorized to conduct investigations covering the field of home economics. Its work, however, has been greatly handicapped because of a lack of adequate appropriations. The broad and urgent demand for information along home-economic lines has made it necessary for the department to use the services of its small staff very largely in collating and writing up material gathered from various sources. If the department is to maintain leadership as a research agency in this field, it must be in position to conduct original studies under such conditions as will enable it to make frequent contributions to the knowledge of the subject.

Administrative expenses.—Apparent increase, $3,500; actual increase, $10,000.

Although the personnel and volume of work of the States Relations Service has greatly increased during the past three or four years, there has been no proportionate increase in the appropriation for administrative expenses. The additional sum requested will provide for the normal growth of the business connected with personnel records, the better handling of supplies, the employment of temporary assistance, and numerous other necessary expenses.

BUREAU OF PUBLIC ROADS.

Rural-engineering investigations.—Apparent and actual increase, $50,000.

The importance of farm machinery in connection with crop production is obvious. The maximum of efficiency in the utilization of such machinery can be obtained only through the development of simple, standardized, and highly efficient types. Because of its relative importance, the tractor is receiving particular attention at this time. The increase requested will make it possible to install a testing plant at the Arlington Farm and to employ the requisite personnel for undertaking a thorough investigation along this line.

BUREAU OF MARKETS.

Marketing and distribution.—Apparent increase, $25,280; actual increase, $41,100.

Of this amount, $27,000 represents a transfer from the item for "Special marketing activities" under the food production act, of which $15,000 will be used for cooperative purchasing and marketing investigations and $12,000 for foreign marketing investigations, with a view to placing these activities on an adequate permanent basis. The balance of the increase recommended ($14,100) will provide for the extension of the investigations relating to the handling and marketing of cotton, which up to the present time, owing to a lack of sufficient funds, has necessarily been limited to three or four of the cotton-producing States.

Market reports on fruits and vegetables.—Apparent increase, $108,000; actual increase, $244,800.

This increase represents the transfer of a similar amount from the item for "Market news service on fruits and vegetables" under the food production act. When the appropriation was so largely expended under war conditions, the work was enlarged in the only possible way, the bureau pushing through in a single year arrangements for a service which, under normal conditions, might not have been so expanded for three or four years. On account of the very nature of the work, a permanent, not a temporary, machine necessarily was built up. Unless the proposed transfer of funds is effected, a large portion of the work will have to be discontinued upon the withdrawal of the emergency appropriations.

Market reports on live stock and meats.—Apparent increase, $94,800; actual increase, $170,000.

This increase represents the transfer of a similar amount from the item for "Market news service on live stock and meats" under the food production act. As in the case of the market news service on fruits and vegetables, this service was expanded within a year to a point which ordinarily would not have been reached in two or three years. A temporary interruption of the service on account of the discontinuance of emergency funds would react very unfavorably on the live-stock industry. The appropriations now provided under the agricultural act are not sufficient to maintain even the six original offices, established before emergency funds became available, if the reports which are now being released are to be continued and are to be transmitted over the leased wires.

Market reports on dairy and poultry products.—Apparent increase, $80,600; actual increase $110,000.

This is a new item and represents the transfer of a similar amount from the item for "Market news service on butter, cheese, eggs, and poultry" under the food production act. Under emergency appropriations it has been possible to institute a service on these commodities which has been received with much appreciation by the producers and handlers of dairy products, this field hitherto having been very poorly supplied with accurate and dependable market information. It is felt, therefore, that even a temporary discontinuance of the work would have serious effects in taking from the industries concerned valuable market information at the very time when it will be needed most.

Market reports on grain, hay, and feeds.—Apparent increase, $41,560; actual increase, $53,160.

This is a new item and represents the transfer of a similar amount from the item for "Market news service on grain, hay, feeds, and seeds" under the food production act. It is believed that the transfer of funds recommended should be effected in order to provide producers of grain, hay, and feeds with accurate market information. Exceedingly useful work in several emergencies has been conducted during the past winter, particularly in connection with the soft-corn and Texas drought situations. Representatives of the bureau are now assisting to locate and distribute hay, grain, and feed for the farmers and cattlemen in the drought-stricken areas. Basic questions involved in hay marketing should receive careful consideration. The crop is probably the third in value in the country, and its handling has resulted in many abuses, particularly in methods of weighing and grading and in its sale at country and terminal markets.

Seed reporting service.—Apparent increase, $34,960; actual increase, $47,000.

This is a new item and represents the transfer of a similar amount from the item for "Market news service on grain, hay, feed, and seeds" under the food production act. During the short time in which the seed reporting service has been in operation those engaged in the seed business of the country have come to depend upon it for information needed by them. For some time it has been apparent that it would be extremely desirable to have reliable and disinterested seed crop and market information available for general use. The little information then available was not always dependable. The National Agricultural Advisory Committee of the Department of Agriculture and the Food Administration has adopted resolutions indorsing the seed reporting and other market news services, and recommending that they be made a permanent feature of the work of the department, and many representatives of the seed trade and other interested agencies have expressed their appreciation of the value of this service and their desire for its continuation.

City market service.—Apparent increase, $42,880; actual increase, $50,000.

This is a new item and represents the transfer of a similar amount from the item for "City market service" under the food production act. With these funds it will be possible to establish a permanent local market-reporting service in 18 or 20 of the large cities of the country. This service covers an entirely new field, and its discontinuance would leave a large number of truck growers, consumers, and fruit and produce tradesmen in cities without information which has proved to be very valuable to them. So far as known, no agencies, unless it be certain individual commission merchants, have ever attempted to furnish local truck growers with reliable market reports dealing primarily with "home-grown" fruits and vegetables. So far as accurate and intelligible market information to consumers is concerned, the work of the Bureau of Markets during the past year marks the first comprehensive effort of this nature. The little work of this kind that has been done by private agencies has been, on the whole, very unreliable.

Food products inspection service.—Apparent increase, $88,960; actual increase, $101,000.

Of this amount $51,000 represents a transfer from the item for "Market inspection of perishable foods" under the food production act. The actual increase for carrying on this work, therefore, is only $50,000. This amount will be required in order to inaugurate an inspection service for butter, cheese, eggs, and poultry. The appropriation of $113,000 carried in the agricultural act for the current fiscal year, together with the $51,000 provided under the food production act, will enable the department to place the inspection service for fruits and vegetables upon a permanent basis and make it thoroughly effective and operative at all the points where it is most urgently needed. There seems to be no good reason why these appropriations should not be combined; as this work, although of peculiar usefulness at the present time, is of permanent value and is a necessary and logical development of the activities of the Bureau of Markets. An inspection service on butter, cheese, eggs, and poultry established upon a national basis has been desired by producers and distributors for many years. With the $50,000 requested it is estimated that a modest service could be conducted at five or six of the most important markets. It is proposed to start work of this character during the current fiscal year, though, necessarily, with the funds in hand, only a small beginning can be made.

State cooperation in marketing work.—Apparent increase, $33,460; actual increase, $34,420.

With the present appropriation cooperative work in marketing has been actively under way in 25 States. The increased amount requested will permit the expansion of the work in these States and the extension of the cooperation to six additional States in which it is proposed to inaugurate work before the close of the present fiscal year. The heavy demand for assistance made upon the department by State institutions and by individuals necessitates more adequate provision for this work in the States in which field agents have been placed than has been possible heretofore.

Milling and baking investigations.—Apparent and actual increases, $35,000.

In the agricultural appropriation act for the current fiscal year the Congress authorized the installation of an experimental flour mill and baking and other apparatus, in order to investigate the milling and baking qualities of wheat and other grains, and made an appropriation for this purpose of $50,000. In connection with the enforcement of the grain-standards act the necessity for having the Government standards for grains established upon a basis of absolute accuracy is imperative. It is therefore essential that the studies in milling and baking that are being conducted during the current year should be materially extended. In view of the advisability of constructing a special building for conducting these investigations and because of the prevailing high cost of labor and materials an increase in the present appropriation is essential.

Administrative expenses.—Apparent increase, $5,000; actual increase, $8,000.

The present appropriation will be insufficient to defray expenses properly chargeable against it during the fiscal year 1920. Additional funds are needed to meet emergency requirements for special assistants and for travel, supplies, office equipment, furniture, etc.

Enforcement of the cotton-futures act.—Apparent increase, $18,200; actual increase, $25,000.

This additional sum is required for the purchase of cotton for the preparation of standards for Sea Island and American-Egyptian cotton and of types showing length of staple. The price of cotton and all materials entering into the preparation of the standards has greatly increased. It is also necessary to pay higher salaries to new appointees, and the expenses for traveling and freight are much greater than heretofore.

Enforcement of the grain-standards act.—Apparent increase, $142,020; actual increase, $175,560.

Increased funds are necessary in order to enable the department to conduct the work necessary to enforce the present standards for wheat and corn in an adequate and satisfactory way, to promulgate standards for rice and oats and to enforce them, and to render increased services to tne grain trade by passing informally on the correct grade of grain not handled under regular appeals. In enforcing the present standards more adequately it is imperative to secure greater uniformity of inspection between markets, to handle effectively the increasing number of appeals received from the trade, and to investigate in a prompt and thorough manner complaints regarding the work of licensed inspectors. In enforcing the standards for rice and oats it will be necessary to employ additional assistants, provide for supplies and equipment, and make increased expenditures for rent.

Administration of the warehouse act.—Apparent increase, $16,440; actual increase, $20,600.

The present force of inspectors is insufficient for the proper administration of this law. Additional men are needed to inspect warehouses applying for licenses and to conduct other field work.

ENFORCEMENT OF THE INSECTICIDE ACT.

Enforcement of the insecticide act.—Apparent increase, $300; actual increase, $1,500.

A small increase in this item is recommended in order to provide for additional traveling expenses, due to advance in railroad fares, and to meet the increased cost of insecticide and fungicide samples.

MISCELLANEOUS.

Control of pink bollworm of cotton.—Apparent increase, $95,800; actual increase, $100,000.

The pink bollworm, now prevalent in several localities in Mexico, is the most destructive insect enemy of cotton. Every effort should be made to prevent its entrance and establishment in this country. One of the means for its exclusion is the inspection, cleaning, and disinfection of railway cars and other vehicles, and freight, express, baggage, and other materials from Mexico. Additional funds for the purchase of chemicals and other materials and for labor are needed in order to do this work in the most effective manner.

CHANGES IN PHRASEOLOGY.

OFFICE OF THE SECRETARY.

Salaries, Office of the Secretary.—A proviso has been added having for its purpose the preservation of the classified civil-service status of the positions of attorney. New language also has been inserted providing for the payment of the salaries of employees in the mechanical shops of the department from a lump-fund appropriation.

WEATHER BUREAU.

Introductory paragraph, general expenses.—This paragraph has been amended by substituting for "folders and feeders" the term "press feeders," as the latter designation better describes the character of work performed by these employees.

BUREAU OF ANIMAL INDUSTRY.

Tuberculosis investigation and eradication.—The words "condemnation" and "condemned" have been substituted for "destruction" and "destroyed." Under the present wording of the law, tuberculous animals actually must be destroyed in the same State, county, or municipality where found diseased. The proposed change in language would permit the movement of diseased animals to recognized slaughtering centers in other States for slaughter.

Meat inspection.—A proviso relating to overtime work performed by meat-inspection employees has been added to this paragraph. The meat-inspection service has suffered deterioration and its efficiency has been impaired through the loss of many of its trained and experienced employees. Many employees have resigned to accept places outside the department at higher salaries, where they also receive pay for overtime work. The demand upon official establishments to supply meats and products is very great, and inspection incident to overtime operations must be furnished whenever possible. This has resulted in many instances in imposing excessive hours of service on bureau employees, without any corresponding increase in pay. Under this proviso the Secretary of Agriculture would have authority to pay employees of the Bureau of Animal Industry for overtime service in connection with the inspection of meat and to accept from establishments operating under the meat-inspection law reimbursement for any sums paid out by him for such overtime work.

BUREAU OF PLANT INDUSTRY.

Cereal investigations.—The clause making immediately available the $150,000 set aside under this subappropriation for the destruction of vegetation from which the spores of black rust and stripe rust originate has been omitted.

FOREST SERVICE.

Introductory paragraph, general expenses.—The provision relative to the erection of buildings on the national forests has been amended so as to raise the limitation on the cost of buildings from $650 to $1,500. A clause also has been inserted to provide payment of rewards for information leading to arrest and conviction for violation of the laws and regulations relating to fires in or near national forests and for the unlawful taking of or injury to Government property.

National forests.—A number of minor changes indicating the consolidation of certain forests have been made.

Nebraska National Forest.—The proviso relating to the cost of buildings at nurseries has been omitted, in view of the recommendation that the limitation on the cost of buildings to be erected on the national forests be increased to $1,500.

Land classification and entry surveys.—The items for "Classification of lands for homestead settlement" and "Survey of lands chiefly valuable for agriculture" have been combined, and minor changes in phraseology have been made. The lines of work are so similar and the training and qualifications of the men employed are so nearly identical that it is difficult to distinguish between the two. Because of the increased elasticity that will result from this combination, the special proviso continuing the unexpended balance of the entry-survey fund has been omitted.

Tree planting on national forests.—A proviso has been added to this paragraph authorizing the purchase of a small tract of land now used as a nursery site for the Michigan National Forest.

Use of national forest timber by other Government departments.—The paragraph authorizing the War Department or any other department, board, or commission of the Government to take from the national forests such timber as may be needed in the prosecution of the war has been omitted, as it is continuing legislation during the period of the war.

Mileage rates for hire of motor vehicles.—This paragraph has been transferred to the "Miscellaneous" section of the bill.

BUREAU OF CHEMISTRY.

Sirup investigations.—New language has been added to this item in order to provide for the work on the preparation of sweet sirups, transferred from the food production act.

Detail of medical officers from the Public Health Service.—The paragraph authorizing the detail of medical officers from the Public Health Service to the Department of Agriculture for cooperative assistance in the administration of the food and drugs act has been omitted, as it is a permanent legislation.

BUREAU OF SOILS.

Soil-survey investigations.—The language of this paragraph has been amended by adding to it the item for "Classification of agricultural lands in forest reserves," with a view to the more efficient administration and direction of these two lines of work.

BUREAU OF ENTOMOLOGY.

Introductory paragraph, general expenses.—New language has been added to this paragraph for the purpose of providing specific authority to demonstrate the results of the investigations and experiments conducted under the several general expense items of the bureau.

Cereal and forage insect investigations.—A clause has been added to this paragraph making $10,000 immediately available upon the passage of the act. This sum is needed in order to promptly institute investigations looking to the control of the European corn borer.

BUREAU OF BIOLOGICAL SURVEY.

Protection of migratory birds.—The language of this paragraph has been amended so as to make its provisions applicable to the migratory-bird treaty act of July 3, 1918, between the United States and Great Britain, which supersedes the migratory-bird law of March 4, 1913. There has also been incorporated in this paragraph the item for the enforcement of the Lacey Act, much of the work heretofore carried on under the latter act being now provided for by the migratory-bird treaty act; and assistants under the game-preservation appropriation will hereafter devote a considerable portion of their time to the enforcement of the migratory-bird treaty act.

STATES RELATIONS SERVICE.

Colleges and stations.—The second and third provisos under this paragraph, directing payment to the Georgia experiment station of appropriations authorized under the Hatch and Adams acts, have been omitted, this being permanent legislation.

Insular experiment stations.—Clauses have been inserted in this paragraph making immediately available (a) $10,000 for the erection of barns, purchase of breeding stock, and other expenses connected with the stock-breeding experiments on the island of Kodiak and at the Matanuska Station, in Alaska; and (b) $5,000 for the repair of damages caused by a typhoon to the property of the station in Guam.

BUREAU OF MARKETS.

Milling and baking investigations.—The language of this paragraph has been broadened so as to authorize the purchase of property necessary for an experimental flour mill and to construct, equip, and operate such mill and baking and other apparatus, for the purpose of investigating the milling and baking qualities of wheat and other grains.

Enforcement of the United States grain-standards act.—A proviso has been added to this item amending section 6 of the United States grain-standards act of August 11, 1916, so as to remove certain limitations which have prevented the Secretary of Agriculture from entertaining jurisdiction in many appeals, which might otherwise have been heard, from inspections made by licensed inspectors, and generally to simplify the procedure in taking and hearing appeals under the act.

Authority to administer oaths, summon witnesses, etc.—A minor change in phraseology has been made extending the authority of the Secretary of Agriculture to administer oaths, examine witnesses, and call for the production of books and papers, in connection with the administration or enforcement acts relating to the Department of Agriculture, to cover the fiscal year 1920.

MISCELLANEOUS.

Eradication of foot-and-mouth and other contagious diseases of animals.—Minor changes have been made in this paragraph in order to make available for expenditure during the fiscal year 1920 any unexpended balance of an appropriation of $2,500,000 carried in the agricultural act for the fiscal year 1916.

Eradication of pink bollworm.—A clause has been added making $148,560 immediately available for carrying out the work of inspecting and disinfecting freight, express, baggage, and other materials entering the United States from Mexico.

Receipts from sale of nitrate of soda.—The paragraph appropriating and making immediately available as a revolving fund any moneys received from the sale of nitrate of soda pursuant to section 27 of the act of August 10, 1917 (food control act), is continuing legislation until the date of the termination of the war as proclaimed by the President and therefore has been omitted.

Dehydration of vegetables, fruits, and other perishable edible products.—This item has been transferred to the Bureau of Chemistry section of the bill. The clause making the appropriation immediately available has been omitted.

Control of the sweet-potato weevil.—This paragraph has been omitted as a separate appropriation and the funds transferred to the item for truck-crop and stored-product insect investigations under the Bureau of Entomology.

Amendment to the oleomargarine law.—These paragraphs are omitted as the legislation is permanent.

Transfer of bison to municipalities and public institutions.—A new item, carrying no appropriation, has been inserted which authorizes the Secretary of Agriculture to supply to any municipality or public institution bison from any surplus which may exist in any herd under the control of the Department of Agriculture; and, in order to aid in the propagation of the species, to loan animals to or exchange them with other owners of American bison.

Mileage rates for hire of motor vehicles.—This paragraph, transferred from the Forest Service section of the bill, under its present terms authorizes the Secretary of Agriculture to pay not to exceed 2 cents per mile for a motorcycle or 6 cents per mile for an automobile used for necessary travel on official business whenever during the fiscal year 1919, he shall find that the expenses of travel can be reduced thereby. It has been amended so as to make the legislation permanent and to remove the limitations as to rates of reimbursement per mile for the use of such motor vehicles, leaving the fixing of rates discretionary with the Secretary.

Contributions from outside sources to the salary of employees of the Department of Agriculture.—A new paragraph has been added designed to remove the restrictions contained in the legislative, executive, and judicial appropriation act for the fiscal year ending June 30, 1918, relative to the payment by agencies other than Federal, State, county, or municipal governments of any part of the salary of any Government official or employee for services rendered in the peformance of his duties as such official or employee, in so far as these provisions apply to officials and employees of the Department of Agrculture.

The CHAIRMAN. The first item of estimate is the statutory roll of the Secretary's office. Who presents that, Mr. Harrison?

Mr. HARRISON. Mr. Reese.

The CHAIRMAN. All right.

Mr. HARRISON. In preparing the regular estimates, after discussion with the heads of departments, it was decided not to include any changes in the statutory rolls other than those involving transfers from the lump-fund roll at the same salaries. It was agreed, however, that we would submit recommendations for promotions, changes in title, new places, and the like, in the form of supplemental estimates, to the Secretary of the Treasury. That was done, and you will find these supplemental estimates at the end of the statutory roll in each bureau. It really is not necessary, therefore, for the committee to consider the first part of the statutory roll because it involves nothing but transfers from lump funds at the same salary.

The CHAIRMAN. Let me make this statement. It will save us a good deal of time. I had a conference with Mr. Byrns of Tennessee yesterday, chairman of the subcommittee on the legislative bill, and he informs me that that committee has unanimously agreed upon the proposition touching salaries that is now the law—the $120 a year raise, or whatever it is—so that I imagine this committee would feel disposed to follow the appropriation committee on that proposition. If there is any inclination to adopt a different policy I think we ought to know it in the beginning of the hearings on this bill.

Mr. HARRISON. Most of our emergency employees were paid from the appropriations made by the food production act, and, of course, we have not provided for their transfer to the regular bill, except in the case of those employed on work which we are suggesting should be made a part of the regular activities of the department. Those employed on the regular lump funds have been transferred in these estimates at their same salaries.

Mr. ANDERSON. Do I understand you, Mr. Harrison, that the employees and the activities covered by the emergency stimulation act are not carried in these estimates?

Mr. HARRISON. Except in the case of a few items, which are enumerated in the statements you have before you.

Mr. ANDERSON. Was it the intention to bring in supplemental estimates covering the same activities as are carried in this appropriation bill?

Mr. HARRISON. When these estimates were prepared we were actively at war. It was contemplated at the time that we would later submit estimates to cover the emergency appropriations, but, of course, the signing of the armistice and the cessation of hostilities brought about a change in the situation. Nevertheless, the Secretary feels that the question ought to be considered as to whether it would not be desirable to continue some of these appropriations, especially those for the extension work, the market news services, the farm labor work, the eradication of animal diseases, and perhaps some other important activities. The indications are that valuable results have been secured from the prosecution of these activities, and we are getting many demands for their continuation; but it is not the Secretary's intention at this time to submit any formal recommendations for the continuation of the emergency work in addition to those already included in the regular estimates, with the exception of the extension work and of the farm-labor work. We will send up some definite suggestions in a few days with reference to these two items. As to the others, the chiefs of bureaus, as they appear before the committee, will, if the committee desires, explain the emergency work that has been conducted under their direction and indicate the results that have been accomplished. The Secretary feels that the committee will then be in a position to determine, in the light of the financial situation, whether these projects should be continued on their present basis or on a reduced scale.

Mr. ANDERSON. It seems to me we ought to have the whole picture before us, and we ought to know now when we consider these estimates whether we are going to be called upon later to consider an entirely new set of estimates, involving to some extent the same activities, and to some extent new activities. We can not pass upon these estimates, and then later pass upon an entirely new set of estimates. We have got to have some basis. We have got to keep these estimates within something like reason.

Mr. HARRISON. As I have just said, we do not expect to transmit any formal suggestions for the continuation of the emergency activities, in addition to the items already included in the regular estimates, except in the case of extension work and the farm-labor work. We will send recommendations to the committee regarding these two items in a few days.

Mr. ANDERSON. I understand you to intimate you intend to "pass the buck," so far as the estimates in the stimulation bill were concerned, up to us.

Mr. HARRISON. I don't look at it just that way. The Secretary does not feel that he ought to recommend—specifically recommend—the continuation of all the emergency activities in the light of the financial situation. He feels that valuable results have been secured; but, in view of all of the circumstances, he does not feel justified in specifically recommending the continuance of all the emergency items which, as you know, were authorized originally as war measures.

Mr. ANDERSON. Well, then, with the exception of these two instances, can we feel certain what we have before us now, these estimates, represent, so far as can be known at the moment, the judgment of the Secretary as to what ought to be appropriated for the next fiscal year?

Mr. HARRISON. The items already included in the regular estimates and the suggestions we propose to submit in a few days regarding the extension and farm-labor work indicate naturally what the Secretary has in mind at this time. This does not mean, of course, that appropriations for the continuation of other phases of the emergency work could not be effectively used or that valuable results would not be secured from such expenditures. But, as I have stated, the Secretary does not feel justified at this time in submitting any additional suggestions.

Mr. HAUGEN. No emergency bill will be asked for this year?

Mr. HARRISON. We are not contemplating the submission of any emergency list, except with reference to the two items I have mentioned.

Mr. LESHER. For those two items, have you submitted the estimates in this bill?

Mr. HARRISON. We will submit them in a few days. They will come before the committee before we reach the items in the bill.

The CHAIRMAN. Anything further along that line? Mr. Harrison, let me ask you as to this statutory roll for the Secretary's office. You make the statement that all this year's increases here are nothing more nor less than increases by way of transfers?

Mr. HARRISON. That is true of the main statutory roll. You will find recommendations for new places, promotions, changes of title, and the like, in the form of supplemental estimates, at the end of each statutory roll. Under the Secretary's office, however, we have a special item, No. 102, on page 12, for extra labor and emergency employments.

The CHAIRMAN. If the committee adopts the policy of the Appropriations Committee, you won't consider this at all.

Mr. HARRISON. Unless the committee is willing to consider individual increases; and I assume that, even if it does follow the policy adopted by the Appropriations Committee, you will wish to consider those above $2,500.

The CHAIRMAN. Of course.

Mr. HARRISON. As the note on page 14 explains, we are suggesting certain changes throughout the estimates with a view to establish minimum salaries for certain positions, which are indicated there. All the other departments have made similar suggestions, although their minimum salaries are somewhat higher than those we recommend.

The CHAIRMAN. My understanding, after this conference with Mr. Byrns yesterday, is that they propose to continue the present salary raise of $120, up to $2,500, and to ask for the creation of a joint commission, consisting of five Senators and five Members of the House, to study the whole salary proposition and submit their recommendations to the next Congress. In view of that statement and the unanimous report of their subcommittee, it seems to me this committee would not desire to take up much time in the consideration of salaries except those individual cases above $2,500. What is the judgment of the committee?

Mr. HAUGEN. I would like to ask how the salaries of those transferred from the lump-fund roll to the statutory roll compare with the salaries of those on the statutory roll?

Mr. HARRISON. They are about the same, Mr. Haugen. Of course, you know the great difficulty that has been experienced in getting stenographers and typewriters, and that the salary scale for stenographers and typewriters has increased to some extent during the war.

Mr. HAUGEN. And the salaries fixed here are on the present scale, or war scale?

Mr. HARRISON. The employees are transferred at their present salaries.

Mr. HAUGEN. Then they really are increased salaries?

The CHAIRMAN. I don't think you understand it.

Mr. HAUGEN. They are fixed on the present scale.

Mr. HARRISON. Mr. Haugen apparently is speaking of the people appointed in the last year. We have appointed a number of stenographers and typewriters at $1,200. Some were appointed at $900 or $1,000. All these have been transferred to the statutory roll at their present salaries as a matter of course.

Mr. HAUGEN. At an increased salary over normal conditions?

Mr. HARRISON. Certainly it is greater than it used to bo.

Mr. HAUGEN. Let us be fair about it. Let us get exactly where we are at. We want to treat them all alike. We don't want to carry somebody at $900 and somebody at $1,100 because they came in later.

Mr. HARRISON. We have suggested the elimination in the bill of all $900 places for stenographers and typewriters and clerks, and have recommended a minimum salary of $1,000.

Mr. HAUGEN. I am more interested in treating everybody fairly. I want to see everybody treated alike, according to the merits, of course.

Mr. HARRISON. Would you suggest a reduction of those——

Mr. HAUGEN. I am simply asking the question, how the salaries compare with those previously appointed, or those carried on the statutory roll.

Mr. HARRISON. As I indicated, Mr. Haugen, we had to be governed by conditions and to appoint these people at salaries at which they were certified by the Civil Service Commission and at which we could get them.

Mr. HAUGEN. Then, the fact remains that they have been appointed at a higher salary than those previously appointed?

Mr. HARRISON. That is true to a certain extent.

Mr. HAUGEN. That is what I asked.

Mr. HARRISON. That has been the situation right along. For the past 10 or 15 years salaries have been increasing. When I entered the department we had stenographers and typewriters at $40 a month.

Mr. HAUGEN. How do you propose to adjust these matters? Put them all on an equality?

Mr. HARRISON. We are not proposing to make any adjustments, except to create certain minimum grades and to make certain individual promotions. Some stenographers and typewriters and some clerks have been appointed at $1,000, some at $900, whenever we could get them. We appointed people at the salaries at which we could secure them. We have necessarily been bound by the regulations of the Civil Service Commission. If they certify to us a person as eligible for appointment at $1,200, we have it pay that salary. We have no alternative.

Mr. HAUGEN. The fact of it is, the Civil Service Commission is practically a dead letter. That has been evaded and whipped around so much, there has not been much left of it.

Mr. HARRISON. That has not been true in our department.

Mr. HAUGEN. It is practically true everywhere else. What I am interested in is having everybody treated alike. As I understand you the recent employees have come in at an increased salary. How are you going to adjust the matter, so as to give them all a square deal? My contention is the new people that have come in and served only a month or two, or a year, are not entitled to any more consideration than those who have faithfully served the Government for a number of years.

Mr. HARRISON. That has been an unfortunate condition in all the departments for many years. The reason for it is that the salaries generally have been increasing right along, but when we have suggested readjustments in statutory salaries, they have usually been eliminated. Nearly every year we recommended certain increases in statutory salaries but they have not been approved.

Mr. HAUGEN. Yes; and the committee has made increases without the recommendations of the department. A number of the increases wouldn't have been made for the department if it had not been for this committee. It is this committee that took the matter in hand, cut out the small salaries, and gave the increase.

Mr. HARRISON. I don't want you to misunderstand me. I am not criticising the action of the committee in the slightest degree. I am merely stating the reason for this condition.

Mr. HAUGEN. I am not criticising. I want to get at the facts. I would like to see the adjustment made along lines that will be absolutely fair to all of them. I don't want to see any discrimination. Perchance some of them have come in and evaded the civil-service laws, and possibly there might be some inclination to favoritism, but that is not what I call a square deal; that is, for the employees. I would prefer to see them all treated alike.

The CHAIRMAN. What would be your suggestion? How would you get at it, Mr. Haugen? Would you reduce those who have recently come in to $900, or increase those appointed before the war from $900 to $1,200? What would be the best adjustment?

Mr. HAUGEN. When we have all the facts we can determine how to deal with it. What I was trying to get at, if there has been any discrimination, and if things need repairing.

Mr. HARRISON. As I indicated, Mr. Haugen, we have been compelled every year, in many instances, to pay new people higher salaries than those received by some of the older employees of the department.

Mr. HAUGEN. As I understand, though, there is no plan, but here you have two sets of clerks—one appointed at a certain time at a certain scale; another set appointed at a higher salary. Now, to my mind it ought to be adjusted. You will either have to lower or raise it—cut the thing in two or in some way; dispose of it and try to make it as fair to all if possible.

Mr. HARRISON. If we decrease the salaries of those we have appointed, of course we will lose them, because some of the other departments and outside agencies are paying somewhat higher salaries than we are.

Mr. YOUNG of Texas. Let me see if I get the point at issue. Take the census. In the old prewar times we had a lot at probably $1,000 a year.

Mr. HARRISON. Yes, sir.

Mr. YOUNG of Texas. Now, since the war is on we have had to take on additional forces down there. These have been certified to you by the Civil Service Commission, and you probably have had to pay those $1,200 a year.

Mr. HARRISON. Many of them.

Mr. YOUNG of Texas. If I get Mr. Haugen's idea, there seems to be an injustice that will prevail. If these war employees certified on this list at $1,200 per year get that amount and the older employees doing a like service getting $1,000 per year, it would be in the nature of a discrimination for all those serving the longest to draw the lowest salary and to be carried at that salary, whereas the new man is being carried at the higher salary. Is that the condition that we are going to find to exist?

Mr. HARRISON. Undoubtedly; that exists in every branch of the Government service. We can not remedy it. We can not transfer the old employees to the lump-fund roll, because Congress has passed laws that prohibit such action unless there is a distinct change in the duties and responsibilities.

Mr. YOUNG of Texas. Will we find in your department that the $1,000 man I have indicated is doing exactly the same kind of work as the $1,200 new man?

Mr. HARRISON. You will perhaps find many of those cases.

Mr. YOUNG of Texas. Is there no way to avoid that?

Mr. HARRISON. The same question was raised here last year. The committee discussed the matter, but decided to do nothing about it.

Mr. YOUNG of Texas. That is up to us, I guess. We will have to do something.

Mr. HARRISON. Of course, one way to remedy the situation is to increase the salaries of the old employees of the department who are rendering the same kind of service as the new employees.

The CHAIRMAN. Have you more clerks than you need?

Mr. HARRISON. We will have to let many go; we have already separated some. Many of our employees are now returning from the military or naval service, and our policy is, of course, to reinstate them in their old positions so far as it can possibly be done.

Mr. YOUNG of Texas. Take a young man that has been let out of a thousand-dollar job when he went into the war service, does he go back to his old thousand-dollar position?

Mr. HARRISON. He goes back to his old thousand-dollar position, unless in the meantime vacancies have occurred in a higher grade to which he would have been entitled if he had remained in the service. In such circumstances, depending, of course, upon the merits of the case in the light of all the facts, he gets the higher position and the people promoted temporarily during the war are demoted to their old positions.

Mr. LEE. That seems fair.

Mr. HARRISON. We are doing everything possible to see that justice is done to those who entered the military or naval service.

Mr. LEE. I understand you have a difficult situation to deal with.

Mr. HARRISON. An especially difficult situation. It has puzzled all of us, and we have been doing our best to handle it. I may say that the Departments of Labor, Justice, and the Treasury have recommended a minimum salary of $1,200 for clerks.

Mr. RUBEY. What is your policy of letting out those that it may be necessary to let out? Let out those in the service the shortest length of time?

Mr. HARRISON. The memorandum issued by the Secretary says that the most recently appointed and least efficient employees will be furloughed. We furlough them rather than terminate their appointments, and we require the appointment clerk to keep a list of these people. Whenever the bureaus need any additional employees on account of vacancies, instead of going to the Civil Service Commission, the appointment clerk certifies to the bureaus the names of those who have been furloughed who seem to have the requisite qualifications. We are doing everything in our power to take care of them so far as it is feasible.

The CHAIRMAN. I think that is a very good plan.

Mr. HARRISON. In addition, the Civil Service Commission has established what is known as a reemployment register to take care of the employees of the different departments who are separated from the service on account of a reduction in the force.

Mr. YOUNG of Texas. What do I understand by "furlough?"

Mr. HARRISON. It simply means "without pay."

Mr. YOUNG of Texas. That is, when a new man has come on and you don't need his services any more, he goes off the pay roll?

Mr. HARRISON. He goes off the pay roll.

Mr. RUBEY. It is a reserve list?

Mr. HARRISON. It is a reserve list.

Mr. YOUNG of Texas. It is up to him if he wants to get back. It is simply a list——

Mr. HARRISON (interposing). It is simply a list. The appointment clerk will try to keep track of these people so as to give them every opportunity for reemployment as the need for additional employees arises.

Mr. LESHER. Can you hold them longer than for one year?

Mr. HARRISON. I doubt whether we can under the civil-service regulations, but the commission may make a special dispensation on account of the unusual situation.

Mr. LESHER. I thought you might be able to hold them on the eligible list for a longer period than one year.

Mr. HARRISON. Under the regulations of the Civil Service Commission we are not supposed to hold anyone on furlough for longer than the year; otherwise the reinstatement rule would be defeated. But, in any event, the President has issued an order which permits employees who entered the military or naval service to be reinstated within five years after their separation.

The CHAIRMAN. Anything further on that point, gentlemen? If not, Mr. Reese will take up the Secretary's roll in so far as increases above $2,500 are concerned.

Mr. HAUGEN. I would like to know something about these disbursements. I am not satisfied with this arrangement. I don't believe we can submit to anything of that kind. We ought to have a little string on those salaries, to know something about what is going on.

The CHAIRMAN. All right.

Mr. HAUGEN. I mean about those transfers.

The CHAIRMAN. Go ahead and ask questions.

Mr. HAUGEN. Let us find out about those transfers, when the employees are appointed, at what salary, who authorized the salary, and how the salaries compare with those authorized by the committee.

AGRICULTURE APPROPRIATION BILL.

Office of the Secretary.

STATEMENT OF MR. R. M. REESE, CHIEF CLERK, UNITED STATES DEPARTMENT OF AGRICULTURE.

Mr. REESE. I speak for the Secretary's roll only. If you will look at page 13, you will find there a list of "transfers from funds of other bureaus, which have been correspondingly reduced."

The CHAIRMAN. All right, Mr. Reese, see if you can further enlighten us.

Mr. HAUGEN. Those are transfers from lump funds of other bureaus?

Mr. REESE. Yes.

Mr. HAUGEN. We want to know something about the salaries. How are the salaries fixed?

Mr. REESE. You want to know about transfers from the lump fund to the statutory roll?

Mr. HAUGEN. Yes; those who go from the lump fund to the statutory roll or into some other bureau.

The CHAIRMAN. Let us take the first item, "1 clerk, class 3, from statutory roll, Bureau of Chemistry." That transfer, I take it, was at the same salary he was getting?

Mr. REESE. That was the same salary he got in the Bureau of Chemistry.

Mr. HAUGEN. Is that the present scale or the old scale?

Mr. REESE. That is the regular scale for a clerk of that class, class 3.

Mr. HAUGEN. Present time or normal time?

Mr. REESE. Present time; all time.

Mr. HAUGEN. Not all time?

Mr. REESE. I mean for several years past.

Mr. HARRISON. That employee, if I remember right, has been in the department for six or seven years.

Mr. HAUGEN. All right; we will pass him.

Mr. REESE. There are 11 clerks there, the highest salary being $1,600, and running down to as low as $900. This is the usual procedure every year. When we borrow clerks from the bureaus for the use in any branch of the Secretary's office, we transfer them in the estimates to the Secretary's roll, and reduce the lump-fund appropriations accordingly.

Mr. ANDERSON. Well, in those cases, do the heads of the bureaus who have lost those employees in the next year ask for enough so they can hire a man that is taken away from them?

Mr. REESE. Sometimes, no doubt.

Mr. ANDERSON. So that, after all, this is a sort of a continuous circle?

Mr. REESE. I think it is, Mr. Anderson; but the department is growing all the time.

Mr. HARRISON. We show in every instance when employees are transferred from the lump-fund roll. Assuming, for example, that we desire to recommend an increase of $5,000 in an appropriation and that an employee at $1,200 is being transferred from this appropriation to the statutory roll, the apparent increase in the lump fund will be only $3,800, while the actual increase, considering the transfer to the statutory roll, is $5,000.

The CHAIRMAN. You use two words to describe your increase, "apparent" and "actual," all through the bill.

Mr. ANDERSON. I understand that perfectly, as far as the money transaction is concerned; but what I am wondering is where Congress ge s any command of this proposition at all. You hire a man out of at lump-sum appropriation; you fix his salary; subsequently he is borrowed from the bureau which had that lump-sum appropriation by the Secretary's office or some other office, and he is transferred to that office at the salary which you have fixed. Those transfers go through these estimates and go into the appropriations. We haven't any control over them at all.

The CHAIRMAN. There are certain classes of employees whose salaries are fixed by law. The salaries of all these clerks, for instance, are fixed by law. In the case of certain other clerks, watchmen, and so on, their salaries are fixed by law. We can keep a perfect check on them. As for the technical men on the lump-sum roll we have no control of their salaries, except to fix a maximum of $4,500.

Mr. ANDERSON. Are they fixed by law?

The CHAIRMAN. They are all fixed by law.

Mr. REESE. Clerks of class 1, $1,200; class 2, $1,400; class 4, $1,800. But for many years we have had a number of clerks who have passed first-grade examinations paid less than $1,200.

Mr. ANDERSON. It is not the matter of salary at which each man is taken in, because I don't see any possibility, so far as certain clerks and employees are concerned, of their getting more than is coming to them. The only thing that I am raising any question about at all is this: That there is no control over the number of employees that are constantly being placed on the statutory roll.

The CHAIRMAN. The only control is to refuse to transfer them.

Mr. ANDERSON. If this thing goes like it is, we don't have any control at all.

The CHAIRMAN. It seems to me we are the final arbiters of the matter. "One clerk, class 3, from statutory roll, Bureau of Chemistry." We can simply say we refuse to make that transfer or that we will reduce it to $1,000. That is our privilege, it seems to me.

Let me ask this question, Mr. Reese. In making your appointments, on the lump-fund appropriations, of a clerk, for instance, of class 3, are you compelled by the law to make that appointment at a $1,600 salary?

Mr. REESE. If appointed as a clerk of class 3, $1,600 is the salary fixed for that class.

The CHAIRMAN. No matter what the chief of the bureau——

Mr. REESE. We may fix the salary at anything less than that if we choose.

The CHAIRMAN. Can you fix the salary on a lump-fund roll of a clerk at any higher salary than the class——

Mr. REESE. You can if a clerk were appointed to do a specified line of work.

Mr. HARRISON. Mr. Lever, if I may say it, we are bound to a certain extent by the regulations of the Civil Service Commission in this matter. A vacancy occurs. We want a certain class of clerk to fill that vacancy. We ask the Civil Service Commission for a certification, stating generally the qualifications required to fill the place, and indicate what we think the work ought to pay. The commission then certifies the names of three eligibles to us. If they certify a man who is eligible for $1,600, the department has to appoint him at that figure. If they certify him for $1,800, we have to pay that amount.

The CHAIRMAN. And you couldn't pay him anything more?

Mr. HARRISON. We couldn't pay him anything more without the approval of the Civil Service Commission.

Mr. RUBEY. You couldn't pay him anything less.

Mr. WASON. Couldn't Congress change it?

Mr. HAUGEN. Isn't it in the power of the department to appoint all of them at $1,800, or at $1,100, or $1,300, or at any salary it chooses?

Mr. HARRISON. Different clerks have different qualifications. Generally speaking, the entrance salary for first-class stenographers and typewriters within the last two years has been $1,200.

Mr. HAUGEN. How are the special qualifications of the $1,800 clerks different from those of the $1,200?

Mr. HARRISON. They are men having longer experience, especially in executive capacities, in auditing and accounting work, and matters of that sort.

Mr. HAUGEN. Do you wish to be understood that the Civil Service Commission fixes the salaries for the department?

Mr. HARRISON. No.

Mr. HAUGEN. I want to know who is fixing it.

Mr. HARRISON. The Civil Service Commission keeps certain registers and places on those registers the names of the eligibles, the percentages obtained by them in the examinations, and like information, and it certifies these eligibles for appointment at certain salaries upon the request of the department. When the commission certifies a man as eligible for $1,200 we have to pay him $1,200. We could not pay him $1,400 because the commission would say that would be an injustice to other people who have passed higher in the examination and who are more entitled to $1,400 than the particular man certified for $1,200.

The CHAIRMAN. Is that true in all the departments?

Mr. HARRISON. Yes.

Mr. HAUGEN. That is not exactly the information I get from the Civil Service Commission. My information is that the department indicates the salary it is willing to pay and the commission certifies accordingly.

Mr. HARRISON. I said, Mr. Haugen, that we indicated what we thought the job was worth and the qualifications we thought the man ought to have to fill it.

Mr. HAUGEN. Recently I have had a number of suggestions that eligibles can change their declaration, and lower it from, say, $1,200 to $1,100, and the Civil Service Commission advises me that the departments are not offering to pay high salaries at the present moment; that would indicate the department was fixing the salaries.

Mr. HARRISON. Yes. I have tried to indicate the procedure followed in the department. We are not appointing all clerks at $1,200. We are appointing some at $1,100.

Mr. HAUGEN. The question is, is it not in the power of the department to fix its own salaries for clerks at $1,600 or $1,800?

Mr. HARRISON. Yes, on lump funds, of course.

Mr. HAUGEN. And if the committee, or Congress, appropriates so much money, the department might use every dollar of it for $1,800 salaries?

Mr. HARRISON. That is true.

Mr. HAUGEN. Well, then, it is the department that fixes the salary?

Mr. REESE. It seems to me, Mr. Chairman, that the commission to which you referred is the very body to consider these points that Mr. Haugen has raised.

Mr. McLAUGHLIN. The Civil Service?

Mr. REESE. The commission the chairman spoke of.

The CHAIRMAN. The Appropriations Committee is recommending a joint commission.

Mr. HAUGEN. Just a minute, Mr. Chairman. Now, I think that every member of this committee has confidence in the department. I think our action in the past would warrant that statement. We have confidence, but, after all, I think it is due that this committee and that Congress should have detailed information, so that we may be able to answer questions on the floor about these transfers. There has been a good deal said about abuse in fixing salaries, and we might just as well be frank with each other and get at the things that we think may give the information. I think it is due the committee, and I think it is due Congress.

Mr. HARRISON. We will be glad to give you any information you want, Mr. Haugen.

Mr. HAUGEN. I have been trying to get it for half an hour and we finally get down to this—that the department fixes the salary.

The CHAIRMAN. Go ahead and ask your questions. We don't know what you are driving at.

Mr. REESE. Would it meet your question to furnish, as far as this list is concerned [referring to list on page 13 of the Book of Estimates], a statement showing length of service, when appointed, etc. I can furnish you with that.

Mr. HAUGEN. If you will do that, we will have something to work on.

The CHAIRMAN. How long will it take to get that up, Mr. Reese?

Mr. REESE. Several days.

Mr. RUBEY. How large would the statement be if it included everyone?

Mr. REESE. It would be very large indeed.

Mr. HAUGEN. I don't think it would be so very large.

The CHAIRMAN. He might give some of those so as to indicate just the method of the procedure in the department.

Mr. REESE. Probably one statement covering this list would be sufficient to give you an exact line on the general practice. It is the same throughout the department. We will be glad to furnish the committee with such a statement.

The CHAIRMAN. Could you give us a detailed statement, Mr. Reese, of the number of employees you have transferred from the food production act to the statutory rolls in these estimates?

Mr. HARRISON. The statement which I inserted in the record contains this information. It indicates that there are 207 employees transferred from the food production act, involving a total of $240,960. These transfers are made necessary, of course, by the transfer from the food production act of those items which the Secretary thinks ought to be made a part of the permanent work of the department. These items also are listed in the statement you have before you.

The CHAIRMAN. So we have that information before the committee now?

Mr. HARRISON. The total number of employees transferred from regular lump sums to the statutory roll is 320.

Mr. YOUNG of Texas. This seems to be taken from this war legislation we have had—emergency legislation—and incorporated into the permanent scale of rates. Personally, before we go into the individual items of transfers from this war legislation—emergency legislation—so that it becomes a fixed and permanent legislation, before discussing each individual item, I would like to have a statement made by somebody as to the scope of this emergency legislation that is sought to be incorporated into the permanent legislation.

Mr. HARRISON. That is incorporated in the statement to which I referred. On page 2 there is a list of the items suggested for transfer. They are "Plant-disease survey work, sugar-beet nematode work, control of a new sugar-cane disease, location of Irish potato seed stocks, preparation of sweet sirups, utilization of wool-scouring wastes, special marketing activities, market news service on fruits and vegetables, market news service on live stock and meats, market news service on butter, cheese, eggs, and poultry; market news on grain, hay, feeds, and seeds; city market service, and market inspection of perishable foods. These items total $849,960. I may add that wherever we have transferred an employee from the food production act to the regular bill we have so indicated it.

Mr. YOUNG of Texas. My own mind is yet to be made up about that policy. Now, personally I have got this idea about all war legislation: I think the quicker we can dispense with this expense account, where it can be dispensed with without doing injury, that we ought to do it, and not fasten a permanent appropriation upon the people of the Nation who have to pay the taxes. I want to do everything necessary.

Mr. HARRISON. As I explained to Mr. Anderson a short time ago, the Secretary does not intend, aside from the items already included in the regular estimates—you know we have to submit them to the Secretary of the Treasury on October 15—to submit any formal recommendation for the continuation of the emergency activities, except in the case of the extension work and the farm-labor work. This does not mean that the Secretary does not think that work is valuable or desirable or that it has not produced good results. If the financial situation permits, he thinks it would be highly desirable to continue many of these activities, and he so recommends; but, realizing the financial situation confronting the Nation, he does not feel justified in submitting formal recommendations for their continuance.

Mr. McLaughlin. You say you propose to transfer and continue the war work only as it relates to these diseases of animals and so on, and the extension work; but on page 2 you transfer a number of matters from the food-production act. Now, the food-production proposition was all war-time work, and we are taking work that costs nearly a million dollars from the food production act.

Mr. Harrison. These items may be said to be developmental in character, and they would have been suggested in normal times as a part of the regular work. It seemed to the Secretary, in considering the estimates, which, as I have said, had to be presented to the Secretary of the Treasury by October 15, that it would be desirable to make permanent provision for these lines of work to the extent indicated. Now that the armistice has been signed and hostilities have ceased, the Secretary does not feel justified in recommending the continuation of the other emergency activities, except in the case of extension work and the farm-labor work.

The Chairman. Let me see if I understand you. In other words, where they come to the various items here like "Plant-disease survey," you recommend the elimination of that?

Mr. Harrison. No. In preparing the regular estimates, we regarded the lines of work listed on page 2 of the statement in the nature of permanent activities which ought to be continued irrespective of the war.

Mr. Young of Texas. That is this list?

Mr. Harrison. Yes. We contemplated submitting at a later date estimates to cover the emergency appropriations, and we expected, of course, to eliminate from such estimates the items included in the list before you. Then the armistice was signed and hostilities ceased. We had to reconsider the whole matter, and the Secretary does not now feel justified in submitting formal recommendations for the continuance of the emergency activities, other than those indicated in the list, except the extension work and the farm-labor work. You see the situation has changed and we have had to adjust our plans accordingly.

Mr. McLaughlin. Now, in order to carry out this plan outlined on page 2, the items transferred from the food-production act, etc., involve an expenditure of about $850,000. That would make necessary the transfer of a large number of clerks.

Mr. Harrison. As I have indicated, 207.

Mr. McLaughlin. Two hundred and seven. Now, as each transfer is made from the food-production pay roll, temporary employment during emergency, the transfer is made to the permanent statutory roll, and in each case at the salary the employee was receiving for the emergency work?

Mr. Harrison. Yes: that is true, Mr. McLaughlin.

Mr. McLaughlin. I don't want to do an injustice to the food production people, but in some lines of that work the salaries would seem to be large, larger than were necessary, larger certainly than would be paid during normal times, and it would seem to me that when you transfer those clerks at the old salaries, you would be employing some of them at more than they are worth and more than they ought to receive, and besides you would be doing great injustice to employees under them. Have you in every case transferred these employees at the salaries they were receiving for this emergency war work?

Mr. HARRISON. In every case.

Mr. MCLAUGHLIN. Have you made no effort to reduce any of those salaries?

Mr. HARRISON. No, sir. Those people were and are eligible for appointment at their present salaries.

The CHAIRMAN. Anything further on this salary business, gentlemen?

Mr. WASON. On page 13, the second item says, "two clerks, class 2, from marketing and distributing farm products and grain standards act, Bureau of Markets, $2,800." Further down, " two clerks, class 2, one each to statutory rolls of Bureau of Chemistry and Division of Publications, $2,800." Now, you take two out of the Secretary's office and put two in?

Mr. REESE. Yes, sir.

Mr. WASON. For the same kind of work?

Mr. REESE. No; both clerks are in the same class.

Mr. WASON. What is that transfer——

Mr. REESE. The transfers were probably not made at the same time.

Mr. WASON. Why were they made at all?

Mr. REESE. First, because of the necessities of the work in the Secretary's office.

Mr. WASON. What necessity required taking two out of the Bureau of Markets and sending two out; incompetency or inefficiency?

Mr. REESE. No.

Mr. WASON. What were the conditions?

Mr. REESE. I can not tell you without going back to the record. I can do that in full detail with the records before me.

Mr. RUBEY. Perhaps those are several months apart.

Mr. WASON. I don't care if they were a year apart. Some man may have wanted to send those two there for his own reasons, outside of the efficiency of the service.

Mr. HARRISON. The Secretary has authority, under general law, to detail employees to and from his office.

Mr. WASON. I am asking the reason for this particular case.

Mr. HARRISON. I don't know just what this particular case involved. These changes occur through the course of a year, and it is difficult, of course, to keep track of them in your memory. We have to have additional help, for instance, in preparing the estimates and the numerous reports we have to send to Congress. When we say " Office of the Secretary," it does not necessarily mean the Secretary's immediate office; it includes the supply division, the office of inspection, the office of the solicitor, the office of information, and the offices of the three Assistant Secretaries. These adjustments, as I have said, are made through the year by detail, for which the Secretary has authority under the law.

Mr. WASON. I know, but there must be a reason for taking competent men away from work in which they are efficient and putting in men of the same class that have not had experience.

Mr. HARRISON. I think all these men were experienced employees of several years' service.

Mr. ANDERSON. In these cases of detail, do you know whether there would be any transfer to the statutory roll, back and forth, as is contemplated in these items?

Mr. HARRISON. That depends. If it is considered desirable to continue it as a permanent thing, we make the transfer in the next estimates, in accordance with the committee's desire. If it is a mere temporary affair, it would not be presented in the estimates at all.

Mr. ANDERSON. You have been suggesting it was a temporary affair in explanation of something that appears here in the record as permanent.

Mr. HARRISON. I did not intend to create that impression, Mr. Anderson. I said we detail these people to or from the Secretary's office as their services are needed. If the arrangement is likely to be permanent, we include it in the next estimates; if it is merely temporary, it will not appear in the estimates at all.

Mr. OVERMYER. Supposing it was found that a man was qualified to do work in another department, it would be better policy to get him over there.

Mr. HARRISON. Yes. Mr. Reese will be able to give you the detailed information about those people.

Mr. WASON. All right, if you will.

(The statement referred to follows:)

EXPLANATION OF CERTAIN TRANSFERS TO AND FROM THE ROLL OF THE SECRETARY'S OFFICE AT $1,400.

The two clerks at $1,400 transferred in the estimates from funds of other bureaus to the statutory roll, office of the Secretary, are:

One stenographer and typewriter, first appointed at $1,400 on the miscellaneous roll, Bureau of Markets, December 19, 1917; detailed to the office of the Secretary for duty as stenographer to the chief editor, Division of Manuscripts; transferred in estimates at same salary, it being apparent that the services of the employee will be permanently needed in the Secretary's office.

One clerk, first appointed at $700 per annum, November 14, 1906; promoted through the various grades until, after 12 years of service, she reached the $1,400 grade on miscellaneuos roll, Bureau of Markets; detailed July 1, 1918, to the office of the Secretary for duty in the transportation section of the Office of Inspection; transferred in estimates at same salary. This is an experienced financial clerk whose services are needed in the examination of transportation accounts.

The two clerks at $1,400 transferred in the estimates from the office of the Secretary to statutory rolls of other bureaus are:

One clerk first appointed as messenger at $360, April 15, 1901; promoted through the various grades until, after 17 years of service, he reached the $1,400 grade by promotion to a $1,400 vacancy on the statutory roll, Office of the Secretary; detailed to Division of Publications, where his duties consist of keeping records, auditing accounts, making purchase requisitions, and caring for supplies and property; transferred in estimates to statutory roll, Division of Publications, at same salary.

One clerk transferred from Navy Department at $1,100 per annum, May 1, 1915; resigned September 15, 1915, and was reinstated at $1,100 August 21, 1916; promoted to $1,200 May 4, 1917, to $1,400 January 16, 1918, and detailed to Bureau of Chemistry to take charge of that bureau's file room; transferred in estimates to statutory roll, Bureau of Chemistry, at same salary.

The two clerks transferred to the statutory roll of the Secretary's office are women; the two transferred from the same roll are men. All four possess different qualifications. They were detailed from and to the Secretary's office at different times as the needs of the work required, such details being authorized by law. As it becomes apparent that these employees will be permanently needed in the places to which they have been on detail, adjustment of the rolls is provided for by transferring the places. The record of the transaction is shown in the estimates, although, so far as these four clerks are concerned, no change in the total amount of the Secretary's roll is involved.

AGRICULTURE APPROPRIATION BILL. 81

Mr. HAUGEN. I understand you to say, Mr. Harrison, that had it not been for the food-production act a number of items carried there would have been estimated and inserted in the permanent legislation.

Mr. HARRISON. I did not intend to say that. I said that we were considering the regular estimates before the war was over, and that it seemed to the Secretary then that the items listed on page 2 of this memorandum, and some additional provision for the extension work and the farm-labor work, ought to be carried in the regular bill as a part of the permanent work of the department.

Mr. HAUGEN. Before the war——

Mr. HARRISON. They represent merely developments of existing activities—developments for which we would have recommended appropriations irrespective of the war. We had it in mind at that time that we would later submit estimates to cover the remainder of the emergency appropriations. In those estimates the items listed in the memorandum would not have been included.

Mr. HAUGEN. Yes; but you estimated a number of increases here. Why estimate a few or a number of them and not all of them?

Mr. HARRISON. We have estimates for or will estimate for all those we propose to recommend.

Mr. HAUGEN. My understanding has been all the time that what was carried in the present bill was sufficient to take care of the activities of the department under normal conditions.

Mr. HARRISON. That was true to a certain extent. The emergency activities have been developed during the war, and the results secured seemed to the Secretary to justify the transfer of certain items to the regular bill in whole or in part.

The CHAIRMAN. In other words, if there had been no war you would have made these same estimates anyhow?

Mr. HARRISON. Yes.

Mr. HAUGEN. That is not in accord with the testimony before the committee before or the action taken by the committee. It was clearly understood that the bill was intended to take care of the regular work and that the emergency proposition should stand on its own bottom and be treated as a separate proposition.

Mr. HARRISON. It can be.

The CHAIRMAN. Take your first propostion, "Plant-disease survey, $23,000." The department says it has been transferred to item "Investigations in plant pathology." If the war had never been on at all, as I understand it, the department this year, 1919, or 1918, would have recommended that, notwithstanding?

Mr. HARRISON. Yes; in all probability.

The CHAIRMAN. Just as we have increased appropriations every year, in war or out of war. The only mistake Mr. Harrison has made is in saying that this has been transferred from the food production act. It is a direct recommendation.

Mr. HARRISON. Yes; it is a direct recommendation.

Mr. YOUNG of Texas. This work has been developed under the food-production act.

Mr. ANDERSON. I want to know whether or not those items on page 2 of this recommendation are now included in these estimates in addition to the regular estimates?

Mr. HARRISON. They are all included in the committee print you have before you.

Mr. ANDERSON. This is a segregation of the items as they appear?

Mr. HARRISON. Yes; I just listed them for the convenience of the committee to show the items that were transferred.

Mr. RUBEY. The Secretary, in other words, recommends that this work be continued?

Mr. HARRISON. Yes.

Mr. RUBEY. It is the duty of the committee, after investigating the facts, to decide whether or not this work should be done.

Mr. HARRISON. Yes.

Mr. WASON. Right on that second page. I have footed it up and found that $752,960 of that relates to different forms of your market bureau. In other words, less than $100,000 is for other activities in your market department. Is that right, Mr. Harrison?

Mr. HARRISON. I have not figured it out in just that way. I have no doubt the figures you give are correct.

Mr. WASON. I took for the first item "Market news service on fruits and vegetables."

Mr. HARRISON. You will have to go back to "Special marketing activities."

Mr. WASON. Yes; $27,000. From that down.

Mr. HARRISON. From that item down to the end is for the Bureau of Markets.

Mr. WASON. $753,000, practically, for the Bureau of Markets. At some time before the hearing closes I wish you would have one of your men testify here as to the particular value of that service.

Mr. HARRISON. Mr. Brand will appear before the committee and he will give the committee the full information.

The CHAIRMAN. Anything further on this salary matter? We are anticipating a lot of things we can talk over again. Is there any statements you want to make, Mr. Reese, about the statutory roll?

Mr. REESE. Not at present. I should like to revert, before we pass it, to item 102, on page 12, which, I think, we skipped.

The CHAIRMAN. Yes; the extra labor and emergency fund.

Mr. REESE. The appropriation for "extra labor and emergency employments" has been fixed at $12,000 for the last three years. As I have endeavored to state in the note there, it is always inadequate. It is intended for emergency employment, just as it states, when we need additional help for a temporary period, such as a few additional clerks, watchmen, or other employees. I have estimated here an apparent increase in that fund of $8,000, but an actual increase of $9,400, because there is a transfer from that lump fund to the statutory roll, without reduction. I hope the committee will see its way to consider that favorably. The appropriation is always inadequate. That is one of the reasons why we have to be constantly calling upon the bureaus of the department to carry help for the Secretary's office.

Mr. ANDERSON. I was just getting to that. If we increase this item here for temporary employment, would there be a reduction in the transfers from the other bureaus?

Mr. REESE. There would.

Mr. WASON. Who has the final say about this?

Mr. REESE. The Secretary of Agriculture. All I can do is to recommend. The note sets forth, I think, as fully as I can do it before the committee, why the increase is requested.

Mr. THOMPSON. Are there any increases of salaries for any clerks in the Secretary's office—on the Secretary's roll, as I call it?

Mr. REESE. Yes; I was coming to that next. Turn to page 14. An increase is recommended there for only one man whose salary is above the $2,500 limit—the inspector at $2,750. This man has been in the employ of the department for 23 years, and is a most excellent and serviceable man. During the war he has had a good deal to do with looking into suspected cases of disloyalty throughout the department, and regularly his work is to investigate personnel cases, involving derelictions of duty, and to review all personnel cases presented by the bureaus to the Secretary for consideration. The work has grown very much.

Mr. THOMPSON. That is, during the war, wasn't it? The war is over now.

Mr. REESE. Yes; but I am afraid derelictions of duty won't cease with the termination of the war.

Mr. HAUGEN. Haven't you a gentleman that makes reports? Don't the employees make reports to the heads of the bureaus?

Mr. REESE. Yes; the cases are apt to come up first from some report to the head of a bureau. Under our procedure, if we are satisfied that the dereliction is trifling, the head of the bureau may dispose of it himself. If we desire further information, the office of inspection goes into it thoroughly.

Mr. HAUGEN. What is the clerk getting now for that class of service?

Mr. REESE. $2,750.

The CHAIRMAN. How long has he been getting that salary?

Mr. REESE. Since July 1, 1912. He has had no promotion for six years.

The CHAIRMAN. How old a man is he?

Mr. REESE. About 45. He does other work besides this, too. He directs the fiscal accounting work for the Office of the Secretary. That is to say, he gives the first administrative examination of the accounts involving appropriations in the Office of the Secretary.

Mr. HARRISON. He makes periodical inspections also of the accounting work in the various bureaus, to see whether it is up to date and, in general, how it is being carried out.

The CHAIRMAN. His title does not indicate all the work he does.

Mr. MCLAUGHLIN. What was the increase of salary in 1912?

Mr. REESE. $250.

Mr. MCLAUGHLIN. Was it often that anyone was guilty of lack of loyalty?

Mr. REESE. There were relatively few considering the size of the force. We got rid of some of them.

Mr. MCLAUGHLIN. How many?

Mr. REESE. Ten were dismissed. Approximately 1,500 cases were investigated.

Mr. HAUGEN. Can you state the salary paid for secret service and detective work?

Mr. REESE. I can not without looking it up.

Mr. MCLAUGHLIN. Isn't it about $5 a day?

Mr. REESE. I don't know. I think a man in a supervisory position such as this should have a higher salary than——
Mr. MCLAUGHLIN. How many supervisors have you over there?
Mr. REESE. In the office of inspection, just one.
Mr. MCLAUGHLIN. I understood you had a division in the department that checks up accounts and audits accounts?
Mr. REESE. The law requires the administrative examination of accounts to be made in the bureaus.
Mr. HAUGEN. How much is asked for the Office of Secretary? What is the total amount?
Mr. REESE. If you turn to page 3, Mr. Haugen——
Mr. HAUGEN. You have estimated for the Secretary's office $796,810?
Mr. REESE. Not on the statutory roll. On page 3, statutory salaries, Secretary's office, this present fiscal year, $462,000; estimates for 1920, $491,720. That is right at the top of page 3.
Mr. HAUGEN. Statutory salaries, Secretary's office, $491,000?
Mr. REESE. Yes; there is an actual increase in estimates of 1920 over 1919 of $29,720.
Mr. HAUGEN. How much money are you handling in the Secretary's office? How many accounts are audited?
Mr. REESE. The accounts involve all accounts from miscellaneous expenses of $142,500, and also all accounts for the item of rent in the District of Columbia. The same office prepares letters of authorization to all the bureaus.
Mr. HAUGEN. How much money is handled in the office? How many accounts are audited?
Mr. Reese. On page 197 of the appropriation measure is $142,500 for miscellaneous expenses. They handle all the accounts under that. The appropriation for rents is $158,000. They handle all the accounts under those two, and accounts under the appropriation for stimulating agriculture, miscellaneous items.
Mr. HAUGEN. At any rate, less than a million dollars?
Mr. REESE. Yes.
Mr. HAUGEN. Don't you think $2,750 is pretty good pay for that work, with all the other experts you have?
Mr. REESE. I am frank to say I think $3,250 is not too much for an officer charged with the responsibilities of this man.
Mr. HAUGEN. Responsibility? His activity is largely given, 1 understand, to detective work?
Mr. REESE. Not entirely. He has under him two auditors and two other clerks, who handle those accounts; one other account I forgot to mention, the telegraph account, a large and complicated one.
The CHAIRMAN. How long has this system been going on in the department, Mr. Reese?
Mr. REESE. Since 1914.
The CHAIRMAN. You have had this inspector since 1914?
Mr. REESE. We had the office of inspector before that. But the change whereby the administrative examination of accounts was all placed in the respective branches of the department was made in 1914. No increase in salary was given this officer when this additional work was placed upon him.
The CHAIRMAN. Take up your next case—104.

Mr. REESE. That refers to the principal assistant to the inspector under Item 103.

The CHAIRMAN. When did he get his last raise?

Mr. REESE. He got his last raise in 1914 and has been eight years in the department. This gentleman is a lawyer by training and an excellent man in investigating and collecting evidence in connection with these personnel cases.

Mr. HAUGEN. What personnel cases?

Mr. REESE. Those cases I spoke of—investigating cases of dereliction on the part of the employees, loyalty, and so on.

Mr. LEE. What was his increase?

Mr. REESE. His last increase was $250.

Mr. THOMPSON. How many cases of derelictions does this man report on each year?

Mr. REESE. There might be 200, perhaps more, of various degrees of importance. Some of them were of minor importance; others serious.

Mr. THOMPSON. Were there any of very serious importance that you can recall which took any length of time to make a report on?

Mr. REESE. Speaking now from recollection and subject to correction, I recall a case in the meat-inspection service, where it was necessary to investigate the loyalty of an employee. That involved a trip to the place, interviewing many witnesses, collecting all the evidence.

Mr. THOMPSON. The loyalty matter is over now that the war is over?

Mr. REESE. It is difficult to say; I hope so.

Mr. THOMPSON. It will be simply derelictions on the part of employees of the department?

Mr. REESE. Principally, perhaps, but I can not say.

Mr. THOMPSON. And those cases, I take it, mostly happen here in Washington, don't they?

Mr. REESE. No; I can say that in the length——

Mr. HARRISON (interposing). The great majority of them occur in the field.

Mr. THOMPSON. Do you send a man out from Washington in each instance to make that investigation?

Mr. REESE. Only when the case is serious enough.

Mr. THOMPSON. You don't send him out in each of those 200 cases you mentioned?

Mr. REESE. Only in the most important cases.

Mr. THOMPSON. Will you get up a statement showing the number of cases where men have actually gone out and made investigations?

Mr. REESE. I shall be very glad to do so.

Mr. THOMPSON. The armistice cut the loyalty out. That won't be a feature in future, will it?

Mr. REESE. I can not tell. There is a strong probability of loyalty investigations being necessary, in my judgment.

Mr. OVERMYER. You say a man does not have to be loyal now?

Mr. THOMPSON. There is no question of loyalty, I think.

Mr. YOUNG of Texas. I think we ought to be pretty careful about putting men on the pay roll in the future.

Mr. HARRISON. We are still requiring evidence of loyalty, so far as it can be gotten.

Mr. THOMPSON. I understand you will get up a statement showing the number of dereliction cases during the last year and the number of cases where the man had to go out from Washington to make the investigation?

Mr. REESE. Yes.

Mr. THOMPSON. And the number of days they worked at that.

(The statement referred to follows:)

STATEMENT RELATIVE TO THE WORK OF THE OFFICE OF INSPECTION, UNITED STATES DEPARTMENT OF AGRICULTURE.

On May 1, 1914, the Office of Inspection, which at that time was already conducting the personnel work of the department, was charged with the additional duty of supervising the fiscal work in connection with the appropriations to the office of the Secretary, and the departmental transportation and telegraph accounting work were brought together and placed in the same office.

All the bureau recommendations to the Secretary involving disciplinary action in the department's personnel are reviewed in this office, and, wherever discrepancies in evidence or statements have appeared, available field officials either of the bureau concerned or of some other bureau have been directed by this office to secure such additional information as might be needed to enable the Secretary to arrive at a fair judgment in each case. In this work at times material assistance has been given by the Department of Justice and the Bureau of Military Intelligence. During 1918, 483 bureau cases were thus reviewed, digested, and summarized for consideration by the Secretary, in addition to which 104 original investigations have been undertaken by the Office of Inspection on its own initiative in Washington. In view of the volume of this work, it has not been possible, except in comparatively few cases, for the inspectors of the office personally to conduct investigations in the field. During 1918 one trip involving two days was made to Philadelphia, and one involving three days to Baltimore by employees of the office. Other cases which necessitated the detail of representatives from the Washington office were one in Missouri, involving approximately 10 days; one in New York City, 10 days; and one trip to New Mexico and El Paso, Tex., which required the inspector's absence from Washington for several weeks.

In connection with the bureau cases reviewed by the Office of Inspection and the original investigations initiated by it, the office has, at the direction of the Secretary, drafted formal charges for his signature against 30 employees of the department, has considered the answers to these charges when submitted by the employees involved, and has transmitted the complete files to the Secretary with recommendations of appropriate final action in the premises. The recommendations in such cases have varied from acquittals to dismissals.

The work of the Office of Inspection, however, is not confined to the consideration of personnel matters. Its fiscal section audits the vouchers and keeps a record of the liabilities and expenditures under the appropriations for miscellaneous expenses, rent of buildings, stimulating agriculture (miscellaneous items), statutory salaries (Office of the Secretary), and salaries (extra labor). During the year 4,209 vouchers were audited (administratively examined) and passed for payment under the above-named appropriations. In addition the section has prepared an dissued under the Secretary's direction 654 letters of authorization for travel and miscellaneous expenditures. It reviewed and prepared for the Secretary's signature of approval approximately 3,500 authorizations and requisitions originating in the several bureaus of the department. It has reviewed approximately 3,000 letters and other documents relating to fiscal matters requiring approval or other action by the head of the department. It has prepared the annual report of expenditures and the report of expenditures from the contingent funds of the department, has assisted in the preparation of the annual report of travel, and prepared approximately 2,500 letters of inquiry in connection with claims against the department for materials, equipment, and the like.

The transportation section of the office has procured and distributed to the various bureaus and offices of the department approximately 276,000 transportation requests, and has kept a record of the same. It has audited and passed for payment 298 railroad vouchers for passenger transportation; 150 accounts have been handled that required correspondence to adjust. The section has supplied several hundred itineraries for officers an demployees. It has checked on approximately 1,200 vouchers for cash fares paid by employees. It has endeavored to keep in touch with the orders of the. Railroad Administration, and has kept the bureau accounting offices and employees generally apprised, thereof. It has audited and passed for payment 120 freight vouchers; has furnished, upon application of the several bureaus. more than 1,000 freight rates; has, upon bureau resquests, routed approximately 300 freight shipments; and has advised the bureaus generally as to proper freight classifications and rates to be used by the bureaus in setting up liabilities in advance of actual shipments. In the field of express it has audited and paid 241 vouchers and has supplied the bureaus with many express rates, classifications, and routings. It has audited and transmitted to the disbursing officer for payment 60 telegraph vouchers. This number is not impressive without the additional information that one of these accounts now represents as many as 12,000 telegrams. The section has also handled many claims for loss, damage, and overcharge in connection with freight and express shipments, and has adjusted many accounts involving purchased and unused railroad tickets. There is maintained in the section quite a complete file of passenger, freight, and express tariffs, in order that the bureaus may be correctly advised at all times regarding current rates. The maintenance of these files during the past year, when rates of all the sorts indicated have changed so materially, has entailed a considerable increase of effort.

The CHAIRMAN. Item 105, on page 15, would not be involved here. It is a $1,800 place. No. 106 would not be involved; 107 would not be; 108 would not be; 109 would not be; and 110 would not be. Where is your next one?

Mr. McLAUGHLIN. That is, on the theory that we are going to abide by and be satisfied with the $120 increase?

The CHAIRMAN. Yes.

Mr. HAUGEN. With that understanding we cut out all these increases.

The CHAIRMAN. Yes; that is, people below $2,500.

Mr. THOMPSON. All the rest of those would go out?

The CHAIRMAN. Except page 16, one attorney, $3,500. That is a new place.

Mr. REESE. Mr. Chairman, the items from 124 to 135, inclusive, relate to the changes in the solicitor's office, and with your permission I will give place to the solicitor to speak regarding them.

Mr. LEVER. All right, Mr. Williams.

STATEMENT OF MR. W. M. WILLIAMS, SOLICITOR, UNITED STATES DEPARTMENT OF AGRICULTURE.

Mr. WILLIAMS. Mr. Chairman and gentleman, I very much regret that apparently you have reached the conclusion not to consider any increases below $2,500. The plan I had worked out required an increased appropriation of only $5,050. With that sum I had hoped to help 22 very deserving, and I think underpaid, old employees of the department. If you have definitely reached that conclusion, it will, of course, be useless for me to speak of the general plan which I had in mind, and which appears on pages 16, 17, and 18 of the "estimates," where it is shown that we are asking for one new place at $3,500, another at $3,250, and six at $2,500 each, with permission to drop six law clerk places at $2,250 and two at $1,600, the net result being the same number of statutory places, and a total increase of $5,050.

The CHAIRMAN. Mr. Williams, take your law clerk at $1,600. To what salary do you propose to promote him?

Mr. WILLIAMS. The man I have in that place would go into an $1,800 place, and the $1,600 place would be dropped.

The CHAIRMAN. In other words, you increase his salary $200?

Mr. WILLIAMS. $200.

The CHAIRMAN. What increase would he get under this present law?

Mr. WILLIAMS. $120.

The CHAIRMAN. So it will be a difference of $80 of salary?

Mr. WILLIAMS. Yes.

Mr. THOMPSON. If he went to $1,800, he would get $120 upon top of that?

Mr. WILLIAMS. If he were permitted to receive the temporary increase. Even if that were the case and he received the $120 increase, he would still be underpaid, and that is true of every man involved. I am not asking anything for myself. It is merely for these "law clerks." They are underpaid. They are good lawyers. If you will let me, I would like to discuss the matter a little with you.

Mr. McLAUGHLIN. Which item covers your case, Mr. Williams?

Mr. HARRISON. Beginning with item 124 on page 16, Mr. McLaughlin.

Mr. McLAUGHLIN. His individual case.

The CHAIRMAN. Page 8.

Mr. WILLIAMS. I have no individual case. I am asking nothing for myself.

Mr. McLAUGHLIN. You are No. 3 there, $5,000?

Mr. WILLIAMS. That is my salary.

Mr. McLAUGHLIN. How long have you been employed?

Mr. WILLIAMS. Eighteen months.

The CHAIRMAN. He took Mr. Caffey's place.

Mr. WILLIAMS. Yes, sir.

The CHAIRMAN. All right, Mr. Williams; proceed.

Mr. WILLIAMS. It is hardly necessary for me to call your attention to the fact that the cost of living has increased very much, and will probably remain at its present high rate for an indefinite period. I approach you in this matter merely in order that justice may be done to these men, and at the same time preserve in the Department of Agriculture an efficient legal organization. With that $5,050 I could help 22 deserving men who have been in the service, most of them, a long time, the oldest 28 years, and the last man who would receive a promotion has been in the service, I believe, two years. The greatest increase would be $250, ranging down to $50. In several instances these men, especially the assistants in the West, in the Forest Service, on July 1, 1919, will not have had an increase for six years; several others for five years; some for four; some for three; some for two, and, I believe, two for one year. Under ordinary conditions probably it might not be right to ask for an increase for a man who received a promotion a year ago, but such increases, only two, would necessarily come about by the promotions that I would make in order to take care of the others; and, besides, in both instances

·they would be entitled to the increases which they would receive under that plan.

Mr. ANDERSON. May I ask you one question, Mr. Williams?

Mr. WILLIAMS. Yes.

Mr. ANDERSON. Are any men in your force employed outside of Washington?

Mr. WILLIAMS. Yes.

Mr. ANDERSON. How many?

Mr. WILLIAMS. I have six in the West. They do the work for the national forest. I have a man at each of the so-called forestry headquarters. There are 146 national forests. They comprise more than 200,000,000 acres of land. Those forests have connected with them many administrative officials. In the course of the year a great deal of litigation arises. A great many contracts and legal papers have to be prepared. These men are there on the ground where they can give first hand the necessary legal advice. They serve the officers of the national forest in the capacity of counsel, and all the other lawyers in the solicitor's office perform a similar service for the other bureaus and offices in the department. If the administrative officers have a difficult problem, they come and talk it over. They receive advice from a trained man, unbiased and unprejudiced.

Last year my assistants in the field and my office here in Washington handled 549 land claims. You gentlemen, of course, understand that these are contested land entries under the homestead laws. The part of those cases that were decided in favor of the Government during the past fiscal year resulted in retaining in the national forest timber of approximately the value of $350,000. All of the work in handling those cases was done by the solicitor's office. The handling of such a case as that consists in filing a contest in the local land office, appearing at the hearing, attending to the taking of testimony, and arguing the legal questions before the register. If the case is decided against the Government an appeal is taken here to Washington to the commissioner, where we attend to it, filing the necessary papers, preparing the briefs, and making the arguments. If the commissioner's decision is adverse to the Government, the case is appealed to the Secretary of the Interior, and we prepare and submit the necessary briefs, etc.

Mr. THOMPSON. Will it disturb you if I ask you a question?

Mr. WILLIAMS. Not at all.

Mr. THOMPSON. Out there in the local land office, where these contests are filed, that is largely a clerical matter, isn't it?

Mr. WILLIAMS. Well, no. It involves the preparation of a legal paper. Of course, the preparation of almost any paper is in a way clerical; but in order to properly prepare it, you must know the law, and then there comes the hearing, where you must take the testimony, and then comes the argument on the law, and the application of the law to the facts.

Mr. OVERMYER. Are these clerks outside of Washington furnished anything in the way of a library, or expenses?

Mr. WILLIAMS. They are furnished office rent, where they are not in the building occupied by the forest service, and they have a few law books.

Mr. OVERMYER. Furnished by the Government?

Mr. WLILIAMS. Furnished by the Government.

The CHAIRMAN. All right, Mr. Williams, it is now 12 o'clock. Can you finish your statement in five minutes?

Mr. WILLIAMS. If you gentlemen can listen to me longer, I would like to have you do so, because I feel that justice really requires that I should say something to you about these men. I don't want to tire you, but I desire to do full justice to them.

(Thereupon, at 12 o'clock noon, the committee took a recess until 1.30 p. m.)

AFTER RECESS.

The committee met at 1.30 p. m., pursuant to the taking of recess.
The CHAIRMAN. The committee will come to order.

STATEMENT OF MR. W. M. WILLIAMS, SOLICITOR, UNITED STATES DEPARTMENT OF AGRICULTURE—Continued.

The CHAIRMAN. Mr. Williams, you may proceed with your statement. If you can complete what you have to say within 10 or 15 minutes we will appreciate it, as the committee must hurry along.

Mr. WILLIAMS. I will hurry. The duties and activities of the solicitor's office are so varied and cover such a broad field that it would take a long time to furnish you the details necessary for a comprehensive view. I shall only endeavor to give you a general idea of the situation. I will furnish you some facts on which if you should feel inclined you could approve the general plan I outlined at the morning session, or, failing in that, you could give us the $3,500 place and the $3,250 place and cut off two $1,600 places.

Proceeding according to the latter plan, you would be in line with the recommendation of the Committee on Appropriations.

There have been assigned to the Department of Agriculture more than 30 statutes, most of which are regulatory in their nature and carry penal provisions. During the past fiscal year the solicitor's office has handled 3,084 cases arising under those statutes. It has prepared 3,314 contracts, leases, and bonds. It has furnished 1,292 written opinions, which are in addition to the informal conferences and informal opinions that are from time to time given the different administrative officers. Under the Federal aid road act we have examined and passed on 663 project statements. These project statements in each instance constitute a different case, involving a separate construction of the statute, including an examination into the legality of the resolution as passed by the county board of revenue making the appropriation. We have reviewed 216 project agreements under which the work is done. These agreements provide the method for doing the work, and also include the plans and specifications therefor. These project agreements involved the expenditure of more than $14,000,000. We also prepared, examined, and reviewed 49 contracts and cooperative agreements for road construction under section 8 of the Federal road act.

I have heretofore referred to the 549 land claims handled for the Forest Service.

Under the Weeks law we have examined the titles to and recommended for purchase and condemnation 137,728 acres of land, completed the contracts for the purchase of 65,561 acres, and completed, in conjunction with the Department of Justice, the condemnation proceedings for 109,278 acres. Prior to 1917, the petitions for condemnation were prepared in the Department of Justice. It was thought that much time and labor could be saved if they were prepared in the solicitor's office. So that procedure was adopted and has proved very beneficial.

In addition to preparing the regulations for the warehouse act, which is comparatively a recent statute, the office assisted in the preparation of proclamations of the President to license the ammonia, fertilizer, and farm equipment industries and stockyard operators and others handling or dealing in live stock in connection with stockyards. This office prepared, either in whole or in part, the regulations of the President governing operations of licensees under the aforesaid proclamations, the regulations for the administration of the so-called food-products inspection law, various legal forms in connection with the licenses required under the several proclamations, the schedules and orders for making the food surveys conducted under section 2 of the food-production act, and forms of contracts, applications, and other papers in connection with the distribution of nitrate of soda under the food-control act; and also various standards under the several statutes authorizing the Secretary to establish standards.

We reviewed the records in 1,458 appeals under the United States grain standards act. We gave assistance to the Bureau of Markets in the consideration of 146 disputes under the United States cotton-futures act, involving 6,895 bales of cotton. We also handled with the Patent Office 49 applications for letters patent on the part of different employees of the department, to be dedicated to the Government and the public. Some of those applications were contested, and we followed them all the way through.

You are familiar with the assistance that the solicitor's office gives in the matter of the preparation of committee reports. Also, with the assistance that it gives in the matter of drafting legislation, which is very responsible and important work. During the past year we have drafted several bills in addition to the numerous appropriation items. In all we have drafted and have had referred to us for suggestion, comment, and amendment 65 bills touching the Department of Agriculture.

While the fines under these regulatory laws are small in individual cases, yet it is interesting to note, even if we look at them from a financial standpoint, that——

Mr. THOMPSON (interposing). Mr. Williams, will it interfere with your argument if I ask you a question there?

Mr. WILLIAMS. No, sir.

Mr. THOMPSON. I just came in while you were reciting the activities of your office.

The CHAIRMAN. Mr. Thompson, suppose you let Mr. Williams conclude the statement he had begun and then propound your questions.

Mr. THOMPSON. Very well.

Mr. WILLIAMS. I was talking about the fines. It is interesting to note the fines and recoveries under the various statutes administered by the department. The fines are small in individual cases, but the total during the year is a large sum. In the year 1918 the amount was $175,003.79; for 1917 they aggregated $247,155; and in 1916 the sum was $116,430; in 1915, $134,496; in 1914, $107,846; in 1913, $131,710; and in 1912, $122,098. During the year 1918 the fines and recoveries represented 3,084 violations. I have a statement here segregating the cases under the various classes of violations, and if I may insert it in the record you will have the matter in more comprehensive form.

The CHAIRMAN. You may just hand the paper to the official stenographer and he will make it a part of the record.

(The paper referred to follows:)

Statement showing fines imposed and revenues collected for violations of statutes administered by the Department of Agriculture during the fiscal year 1918.

Statutes.	Number of violations.	Amount of fines and recoveries.
Laws for the protection of national forests	444	$71,404.54
Food and drugs act	797	19,407.00
28-hour law	1,168	64,925.00
Animal quarantine act	385	12,750.00
Meat inspection	29	758.25
Lacey Act	38	2,873.00
Bird reservation trespass law	27	45.00
Virus act	3	
Insecticide act	123	2,446.00
Plant quarantine act	11	95.00
Miscellaneous	59	300.00
Total	3,084	175,003.79

Mr. WILLIAMS. This morning Mr. Anderson was asking about the work of our assistants in the West, and I called attention to their handling land claims. In order to give you a little more definite idea of the class of law which these men handle, I might call your attention to the case of the United States *v.* The Great Northern Railway Co. That was a fire trespass. It was a negligence case. You gentlemen know that to prepare a case of importance it requires ability. In that case the Government recovered $53,793.50.

Mr. ANDERSON. You are not suggesting that we should pay these attorneys on the basis of what was allowed at Hog Island?

Mr. WILLIAMS. Oh, no, Mr. Anderson. I am merely calling attention to the size of these matters in order to impress their importance upon the committee.

In the case of the Utah Power & Light Co. *v.* United States (243 U. S., 389)——

Mr. THOMPSON (interposing). I was called out of the room for a moment and did not hear that. What was that proposition?

Mr. WILLIAMS. I was just calling attention to some reported cases in order to give the committee an idea of the class of law questions these assistants have to deal with.

In that case the Utah Power & Light Co. entered the public lands of the United States and built their power houses, reservoirs, and so forth. They insisted that they had a right to stay there regardless of any regulations on the part of the Secretary of Agriculture and without the consent, and regardless of any regulations, of the Secretary of the Interior. We filed a bill praying for an injunction to restrain the use of these lands and asking for an accounting. There were many difficult law questions involved, such as conflict of State and Federal jurisdiction, power of Congress with reference to delegating authority to administrative officers in the matter of regulations, validity of such regulations, and so forth. We were successful not only in securing an injunction but an accounting, under which the Government recovered in that one case $39,201. And, further, as the result of that case the Colorado Power Co. paid $5,815.55 damages in a similar suit against it, and the Government recovered $5,403.67 in another case which was settled on account of the decision in the Utah Power & Light Co. suit.

Mr. THOMPSON. Where was that suit filed?

Mr. WILLIAMS. In the District Court of the United States for Utah.

Mr. THOMPSON. Were you assisted by the district attorney there?

Mr. WILLIAMS. I will explain that: With reference to practically all the litigation arising in the Forest Service the work is done by my office. I will say practically all of it. These assistants attend every session of the court. The United States attorneys have absolute confidence in them and practically turn the work over to them. While the United States attorney is there to assist, yet they——

Mr. THOMPSON (interposing). In this particular case were you not also assisted by the Solicitor for the Interior Department; I mean in the case of the Utah Power & Light Co.?

Mr. WILLIAMS. No; that is not my understanding. This case arose before I came here. It is my recollection, though I am not sure, that we were not assisted by the Solicitor for the Interior Department. We were assisted by the United States attorney for that district, but, as I explained——

Mr. THOMPSON (interposing). As a matter of fact did not the United States attorney present the case in the trial court? Isn't that always the case, and your man who is edtailed to go out there simply assists him?

Mr. WILLIAMS. Not always; not in the West.

Mr. THOMPSON. I am speaking of the West because that is where I come from and that is what I know about.

Mr. WILLIAMS. Well, as I understand those cases in the West with reference to Forest Service matters the work is practically all done by the assistants to the solicitor. The United States attorney is there, but our assistant really does the work.

Now, when this particular case (Utah Power & Light Co. v. United States) went to the Court of Appeals one of my assistants argued it with the United States attorney.

I might cite another case to illustrate the character of the legal questions with which these assistants have to deal, Chicago, Milwaukee & St. Paul Railway Co. v. United States (244 U. S., 351). In that case the question arose as to the conditions under which a railroad might acquire a right of way through the public lands. Several interesting legal questions were involved by reason of the fact that the Secretary of the Interior made the land in question a temporary reservation which afterwards was made permanent by the President's proclamation, the railroad in the interim having filed its plans and specifications under the law of 1875. After the company filed its first plans and specifications it filed other plans and specifications making a material divergence in its original route. They insisted that they had the right to stay in the forest regardless of any action on the part of the Secretary of Agriculture or the Secretary of the Interior, and they cut about 9,000,000 feet of timber in connection with the change in the right of way. A bill for injunction was filed in that case, and an accounting asked for. The injunction was granted, and an accounting allowed, resulting in a judgment in favor of the United States for about $89,000.

As further illustrative of the legal questions handled by the office, I might mention the cases of United States *v.* Forty Barrels and Twenty Kegs Coca-Cola (241 U. S., 265) (known as the "Coca-Cola" case); United States *v.* Lexington Mill & Elevator Co. (232 U. S., 399) (known as the "Bleached Flour" case); United States *v.* Johnson (221 U. S., 488); United States *v.* The Antikamnia Chemical Co. (231 U. S., 654); Eckman Alterative *v.* United States (239 U. S., 510); United States *v.* Four hundred and forty-three Cans Frozen Egg Product (226 U. S., 172); Hipolite Egg Co. *v.* United States (220 U. S., 45); Oscar J. Weeks *v.* United States (245 U. S., 618); St. Louis Independent Packing Co. *v.* David F. Houston, et al. (215 Fed., 553) (pending in Supreme Court); Pittsburg Melting Co. *v.* United States (October term, 1918, United States Supreme Court); Brougham et al. *v.* Blanton Manufacturing Co. (243 Fed., 503) (pending in Supreme Court); Lewis et al. *v.* United States (235 U. S., 282); Armor & Co. *v.* United States (222 Fed., 233); Baltimore & Ohio Southwestern Railroad Co. (220 U. S., 94); United States *v.* Sioux City Stock Yards (162 Fed., 556); United States *v.* Pere Marquette Railway (171 Fed., 586); Grand Trunk *v.* United States (248 Fed., 905); Grand Trunk *v.* United States (191 Fed., 803); and United States *v.* Southern Pacific (157 Fed., 459).

In the administration of statutes by the Bureau of Markets, most of which are recent, a multitude of interesting and difficult legal questions arise. The following list fairly illustrates that work:

Legal discussion of meaning and scope of antitrust laws, particularly the Clayton amendment, in connection with the cooperative projects of the Bureau of Markets.

Opinion concerning proposed agreement between the Maine sardine packers, involving a legal discussion of cooperation by manufacturers as affected by antitrust laws of United States and State of Maine.

Legal discussion of patronage dividends in farmers' cooperative organizations.

Discussion of proposed cooperative law of the State of Oregon, particularly as affected by section 6 of the Clayton Act.

Legality of provision for liquidated damages in by-laws of farmers' cooperative association under State and Federal antitrust laws.

Brief on constitutionality of bill H. R. 4630, subsequently enacted and known as the food-control act.

Views on constitutionality of three bills dealing with cotton-future exchanges, one of which was enacted and is known as United States cotton-futures act.

Constitutionality of United States warehouse act.

Applicability of grain-standards act to contracts entered into prior to promulgation of standards.

Effect of grain-standards act upon activities of State grain inspection officials.

Authority to establish standards of quality for commodities under the weights and measures clause of the United States Constitution.

Discriminations against farmers' organizations by fertilizer companies under food-control act.

Right of seller to tender cotton according to his own classification without regard to that of the exchange under a contract entered into on cotton exchange, subject to section 5 of the United States cotton-futures act.

Extent to which findings of the Secretary of Agriculture under the United States cotton-futures act are binding on the parties to disputes under that act.

Elements involved in the ascertainment of "cost" of seed sold to farmers under the food-production act.

Extent of authority of President to guarantee a price to producers of wheat of the crop of 1918 pursuant to the food-control act.

Interpretation of the exemption of retailers under section 5 of the food-control act as applied to dealers in farm equipment.

Opinion as to what constitutes a "sale by grade" for purposes of United States grain-standards act.

Mr. ANDERSON. You have been solicitor for about 18 months?

Mr. WILLIAMS. Yes.

Mr. ANDERSON. During that time how many new men have been added to your force? I do not mean how many new places have been created but how many new men have come in?

Mr. WILLIAMS. Well, I have lost a good many men and have taken in some new ones. I lost one man to the Department of Justice; two to administrative bureaus; one to Armour & Co., and four who returned to private practice. And I lost these men because I could not pay them more money.

Mr. ANDERSON. Have you had any difficulty in filling these places at the salaries established by law?

Mr. WILLIAMS. Yes: it is practically impossible to get men of the ability and experience requisite for the work for $1,600.

Mr. ANDERSON. Well, were all the men that you took in taken in at the $1,600 rate?

Mr. WILLIAMS. Yes; they were all taken in at $1,600.

Mr. ANDERSON. And the places left vacant by resignation were filled by men in the office by promotion?

Mr. WILLIAMS. Yes; but that does not mean that every man below the one resigning would be promoted. A day or two ago I secured a man by transfer, or at least I expect to secure him, in a $1,600 place, and I have three $1,600 vacancies now although I have tried to fill them. I might say that during the war two of these $1,600 places were filled by young men who came to Washington to try to do something for the Government. They were just above the draft age, and said they did not feel like remaining at home during war.

Mr. THOMPSON. What draft age? The original draft age of 21 to 31?

Mr. WILLIAMS. Yes; the original draft age, 21 to 31. You, of course, understand that I have to get all these men from the civil-service list. These two men were not on the civil-service list, but the Civil Service Commission made a ruling that if a man would volunteer his services at, say, one-half of what his income had been in private practice they would let him take what is called the nonassembled examination.

Mr. McLAUGHLIN. What kind of examination?

Mr. WILLIAMS. The nonassembled examination. Those two young men came within that class. But they have left since the armistice was signed.

Mr. ANDERSON. Have you had any resignations in the classes carrying salaries above $1,600?

Mr. WILLIAMS. Yes.

Mr. ANDERSON. In those cases is it the practice of your bureau to promote men already in the service or to bring men in from the outside to fill the vacancies?

Mr. WILLIAMS. To promote men in the service.

Mr. ANDERSON. To what extent has that been done within the last 18 months?

Mr. WILLIAMS. Wherever I have had a resignation of a man above the $1,600 class the man next in line was promoted.

Mr. ANDERSON. So that if this new scheme of yours is carried out some of these men will receive a second promotion under it?

Mr. WILLIAMS. Well, I will show you: If that scheme is carried out two men who, on July 1, 1919, will not have been promoted in 6 years will be assisted; another who has had no promotion in 5½ years; three others, 3 years and 11 months; another, 3 years and 5 months; and so on down to two men, one year. The two last-mentioned men have been in the solicitor's office for 7 and 4½ years, respectively. During the past year one of them received a promotion of $200 and the other of $50.

Mr. ANDERSON. Well, then, the plan which you propose substantially is this, as I understand it: You have salaries now in your office ranging as high as $3,000, and you propose to create a place with a salary of $3,250, and——

Mr. WILLIAMS (interposing). No; I want to create one place paying $3,500, and I want that place for the first assistant to the solicitor, who acts as solicitor in the absence of the solicitor; and I want another place paying $3,250.

Mr. ANDERSON. I do not find anything in the estimates of appropriations for the Department of Agriculture with reference to $3,500.

Mr. WILLIAMS. It is in there.

The CHAIRMAN. Mr. Anderson, you will find it on page 16, under the subhead "New places," with a note:

NEW PLACES.

(124) 1 attorney_____ $3,500
    (This place and 1 attorney, $3,250, and 6 attorneys, at $2,500 each, are recommended in lieu of 6 law clerks, at $2,250 each, and 2 law clerks, at $1,600 each, dropped, as below.
    If these changes are approved, it will make possible increases in the salaries of 22 lawyers in the solicitor's office. Several of the most efficient and valuable lawyers in the department have had no promotion for 6 years, and in other cases no promotion has been received for from 3 to 4 years. At a time when private enterprises are offering unusually high salaries for various services, including legal, it is difficult to retain men in the department at the small salaries they are now receiving. Recently one of the solicitor's assistants resigned to accept, at a much higher salary than the department was paying, a position with a large commercial corporation in Chicago. Similar opportunities are presented to other lawyers of the departemnt.)
(125) 1 attorney (see preceding note)_____ 3,250
(126) 6 attorneys, at $2,500 each (see preceding note)_____ 15,000

PLACES DROPPED.

(127) 6 law clerks, at $2,250 each (see preceding note)_____ 13,500
(128) 2 law clerks, at $1,600 each (see preceding note)_____ 3,200

Mr. ANDERSON. I see, now.

Mr. MCLAUGHLIN. What is that amount now?

Mr. WILLIAMS. $3,500.

Mr. ANDERSON. Substantially you propose to create a place up at the top and to move the others up?

Mr. WILLIAMS. That is it.

Mr. MCLAUGHLIN. When you consider a man like this, who is exceedingly capable and deserving and doing more work than he is being paid for, you put the matter up to the committee, and if the committee agrees with you and makes the recommendation to Congress and Congress approves it and increases that man's salary, and then suppose the committee looks over the others and finds that they are now being properly compensated, action as to the one and not as to the others could be taken by the committee, could it not?

Mr. WILLIAMS. Oh, yes; such action could be taken by the committee.

Mr. MCLAUGHLIN. But under this recommendation if we should find that one man is exceptionally capable and deserving and recommend that his salary should be increased to $3,500, by that very action we will be promoting everybody below him $250 or $500, as the case may be?

Mr. WILLIAMS. No; unfortunately that is not the case.

Mr. MCLAUGHLIN. In answering the question that Mr. Anderson asked you you so stated?

Mr. ANDERSON. No; he thereby increases the man at the top.

Mr. MCLAUGHLIN. By giving him an increase of $250?

Mr. ANDERSON. Well, that depends on what he gets. But if you want to do what you stated, Mr. McLaughlin, you will have to increase all of the salaries $250 all the way down.

Mr. MCLAUGHLIN. Suppose the committee is impressed with the recommendation that this man should have more money, but is not impressed with the idea of giving more money to the men below him, the giving to this man an increase automatically increases all the men below him, although the committee might not think they deserve it?

Mr. WILLIAMS. If you got that impression from my answer to Mr. Anderson, you got an erroneous impression.

Mr. ANDERSON. I did not get that impression.

Mr. HAUGEN. That is, if you leave the number the same, there is no opportunity for promotion.

Mr. WILLIAMS. It depends upon the classes. You have to consider them in classes and have to take all of one class before you go to another class.

Mr. MCLAUGHLIN. Here is a man receiving $3,250?

Mr. WILLIAMS. Yes.

Mr. MCLAUGHLIN. If Congress should determine that that man is worth $3,500 and provide that salary for him, and if the same kind of argument you make as to the salary of the others did not appeal to the committee or to Congress at all and it were not provided, yet if we allow this man to have the $3,500 it does move up everyone below him?

Mr. WILLIAMS. No, sir; unfortunately it does not so result.

Mr. MCLAUGHLIN. "Unfortunately," you say. If you create this new place and attach the increased salary to it, then these men go up; the same result is reached if we decide to increase this man's salary?

Mr. WILLIAMS. No.

Mr. McLAUGHLIN. Another man takes the place he occupies now?

Mr. WILLIAMS. No; not if his salary were merely increased and no new place created.

Mr. McLAUGHLIN. Suppose the Congress, in its wisdom or otherwise, should determine that the men getting $2,250 were properly paid, yet under your plan if you increase the salary of the first man on the list it will make one vacancy all the way up, and one of those eight men would get the increased pay?

Mr. WILLIAMS. No; that would not be true. We would not reach the $2,250 class.

Mr. HAUGEN. You would reach only one?

Mr. WILLIAMS. Yes; the one man whose salary was increased.

Mr. HAUGEN. But if you reduce the number of men in the class which he is in then that stops the promotion?

Mr. WILLIAMS. If you give us this new $3,500 place we could assist nine men. If you merely increase the present $3,250 place to $3,500, only the man occupying that place will be helped. If you give us two new places, one at $3,500 and another at $3,250, and drop two $1,600 places, we can assist 16 men, at a total increase of only $3,550 in the appropriation.

The CHAIRMAN. Who is the employee for whom the $3,500 place is intended?

Mr. WILLIAMS. That is Mr. R. W. Williams, the first assistant to the solicitor. You will observe his name is "Williams," but he is not related to the solicitor.

The CHAIRMAN. What is Mr. Quiggle's salary now?

Mr. WILLIAMS. Mr. Quiggle is one of the men I want to promote, and he gets $3,000.

The CHAIRMAN. I do not hesitate to say that he deserves it.

Mr. WILLIAMS. He deserves it and a great deal more.

Now, gentlemen of the committee, let me say that I make this appeal not for myself, for I have no axe to grind; I am not asking for any increase for the solicitor, but it is asked for others, with whose services and needs I am well acquainted. I ask it as a matter of simple justice. It is in the interest of the Government service to secure and maintain an efficient organization. I want to keep these men together, but we can not do it unless you increase their salaries.

The CHAIRMAN. Mr. Williams, how do you happen to hold a man like Mr. Quiggle? I think he is one of the brightest and most active and efficient young men I have ever seen.

Mr. WILLIAMS. I do not know how we do hold him, unless it is that Mr. Quiggle is very modest and perhaps does not realize his own ability.

The CHAIRMAN. Well, that may account for it.

Mr. WILLIAMS. He has one of the best minds I have ever come in contact with. He is worth $5,000 of any good law firm's money.

Mr. ANDERSON. Mr. Williams, I would like to ask you whether you have made any investigation into how the salaries which you propose for the assistant solicitors, etc., compare with salaries paid for assistant solicitors in other departments?

Mr. WILLIAMS. With reference to that matter I regret that I can not speak definitely of my own knowledge, but I am under the impression that the lawyers in the solicitor's office of the Department of Agriculture suffer by comparison with lawyers in some of the other departments, considering the salary and work of relatively the same importance and responsibility. And I know that they suffer by comparison with administrative employees in our own department. I have here a list of attorneys in the other departments——

Mr. McLaughlin. Do they suffer by comparison in ability?

Mr. Williams. I say in amounts.

Mr. McLaughlin. You mean in the amount of their salaries?

Mr. Williams. In the salaries received. I am under the impression that my men have equally responsible work, although they are paid less than lawyers in other departments. I want to qualify that statement by saying that I can not make it of my own knowledge, but some of you gentlemen will remember that when Mr. Caffey appeared before you in 1916 in reference to this matter he pointed out several instances that he knew of himself. When Mr. Caffey appeared before you, he had been here three years and a half. He had had opportunity to go around in the departments and know what the men were doing. I have been here only 18 months and I can not give you of my own personal knowledge the information that would be desirable. However, if you are sufficiently interested, I wish you would refer to his statement made before you on December 5, 1916.

Mr. Anderson. I was under the impression that such a statement had been filed, and that was one reason why I asked the question.

Mr. Williams. I would like to introduce a comparative statement on the subject so that you may have it before you.

The Chairman. Without objection it will be put into the record.

(The statement referred to follows:)

Statement showing statutory salaries of lawyers in Government departments other than the Department of Agriculture.

DEPARTMENT OF JUSTICE.		DEPARTMENT OF JUSTICE—continued.	
1 Assistant to the Attorney General	$9,000	2 attorneys, each	$2,750
6 Assistant Attorneys General, each	7,500	5 attorneys, each	2,500
1 Solicitor for Department of Interior	5,000	1 attorney	2,400
1 Solicitor for the Post Office	5,000	1 chief law clerk, Office of Solicitor of the Treasury	2,250
1 Solicitor of Internal Revenue	5,000	4 attorneys, each	2,000
1 Solicitor for State Department	5,000	1 assistant examiner of titles	2,000
1 Solicitor of the Treasury	5,000	3 law clerks, each	2,000
1 Solicitor of Commerce	5,000	2 law clerks, each	1,800
1 Solicitor of Labor	5,000	1 attorney in charge of pardons	3,000
4 attorneys, each	5,000		
1 attorney	4,500	FEDERAL TRADE COMMISSION.	
1 attorney	3,750	11 attorneys, examiners, and special examiners, each	4,000
4 attorneys, each	3,500	19 attorneys, special attorneys, examiners, and special agents, each	3,600
1 attorney	3,250		
14 attorneys, each	3,000	5 attorneys, examiners, and special agents, each	3,300
1 Assistant Solicitor of the Treasury	3,000	29 special attorneys, examiners, and special agents, each	3,000
1 Assistant Solicitor of Commerce	3,000		

FEDERAL TRADE COMMISSION—continued.

9 attorneys and examiners, each	$2,800
12 attorneys, special examiners, special agents, and examiners, each	2,500
48 attorneys, special attorneys, special agents and examiners, each	2,400
3 special attorneys, examiners, and clerks, each	2,280
22 attorneys, special agents, examiners and clerks, each	2,100

INTERSTATE COMMERCE COMMISSION.

1 chief counsel	10,000
1 solicitor	7,500
2 assistant counsel, each	5,000
1 chief of bureau and attorney	5,000
10 attorney examiners, each	5,000
5 valuation attorneys, each	4,200
3 attorneys, each	4,200
1 chief attorney	4,000
5 attorneys, each	3,600
3 attorneys, each	3,300
16 attorneys, each	3,000
15 attorneys, each	2,640
2 attorneys, each	2,520
1 assistant valuation attorney	2,520
7 attorneys, each	2,400
1 law clerk	2,400
3 assistant attorneys, each	2,100
1 assistant attorney	1,980
5 assistant attorneys, each	1,200

DEPARTMENT OF THE INTERIOR.

Office of the solicitor:	
3 attorneys (board of appeals), each	4,000
1 assistant attorney	3,000
2 assistant attorneys, each	2,750

DEPARTMENT OF THE INTERIOR—contd.

Office of the solicitor—Continued.	
4 assistant attorneys, each	$2,500
7 assistant attorneys, each	2,250
11 assistant attorneys, each	2,000
General Land Office:	
1 chief law clerk	2,500
2 law clerks, each	2,200
17 law examiners, each	2,000
10 law examiners, each	1,800
18 law examiners, each	1,600
Indian Office: 1 law clerk	2,000
Pension Office: 1 law clerk	2,250
Patent Office: 5 law examiners, each	2,750

POST OFFICE DEPARTMENT.

1 assistant attorney	2,750
1 assistant attorney	2,500
3 assistant attorneys	2,000
1 law clerk	1,800

NAVY DEPARTMENT.

Office of the solicitor:	
1 solicitor	4,000
1 law clerk	2,500
1 law clerk	2,250
2 law clerks, each	2,000
Office of Judge Advocate General:	
1 chief law clerk	2,250
1 law clerk	2,200
1 law clerk	1,600

WAR DEPARTMENT.

Office of Judge Advocate General:	
1 solicitor	2,500
1 law clerk	2,400
1 law clerk	2,000
Office of Surgeon General: 1 law clerk	2,000
Bureau of Insular Affairs: 1 law officer	4,500

Mr. THOMPSON. You say you receive $5,000 a year?

Mr. WILLIAMS. Yes.

Mr. THOMPSON. And your first assistant receives how much?

Mr. WILLIAMS. $3,250.

Mr. THOMPSON. The attorney general of my State receives $4,000 a year and his first assistant $2,750 and the others $2,500.

Mr. WILLIAMS. Yes.

Mr. THOMPSON. They are amongst the best lawyers in the State, and I do not hear any complaint from them.

Mr. WILLIAMS. Well, of course, I do not know anything about their work. I do know something about the work of the attorney general of Alabama and know that he is absolutely underpaid, and I know that you can not get the most desirable lawyers to accept the place.

Mr. THOMPSON. The attorney general of Alabama gets how much?

Mr. WILLIAMS. $2,500.

Mr. THOMPSON. And yet lawyers run for that office.

Mr. WILLIAMS. Oh, you can always get somebody to run for the office.

Mr. THOMPSON. Don't they have pretty good lawyers run for that office?

Mr. WILLIAMS. They do not have the lawyers they ought to have.

Mr. THOMPSON. Do not the lawyers who occupy the office of attorney general of Alabama sometimes go to the supreme court of the State and occupy other high offices in the State?

Mr. WILLIAMS. I can recall right now but one man who has been attorney general and afterwards went on the supreme bench.

Mr. THOMPSON. In my State the attorney general receives $4,000, and the men occupying that position usually become governor or judges on the supreme bench.

Now, Mr. Williams, if I read correctly this memorandum that you gave me you have had 3,084 cases of violations——

The CHAIRMAN. Mr. Thompson, before you get to that let me ask a question or two on this point: Mr. Williams, these men in the States who run for various legal positions, such as attorney general, usually have some political ambition in mind and accept these positions somewhat as stepping stones to attain the higher and more lucrative positions, do they not?

Mr. WILLIAMS. They all have political ambition, either for Congress or for governor or for the supreme court.

The CHAIRMAN. For instance, the attorney general in my State only gets $1,900 a year, and the governor receives only $3,000 a year. Everybody admits that these men are underpaid; yet you can always find somebody who wants to run for governor and for attorney general. The honor connected with the offices amounts to something. But these men whom you have here—Mr. Quiggle, for instance, are absolutely unknown to the world.

Mr. WILLIAMS. They have little chance to become known to the outside world. They are simply stuck out there in the department doing their best in their efforts to advance the interests of the Government. They have been there—the most of them—for years; experts in their line, and serving the people earnestly and diligently but unostentatiously.

As an illustration of about the only opportunity to become known, we might take a patent medicine case. If it is a difficult case, by arrangement with the Department of Justice, we send a man out to help try it. And we usually go up against the very best legal talent that can be gotten, because losing the case on the part of the person charged with some violation means much more than the loss of a few thousands of dollars. To the patent medicine concern it means the loss and destruction of its business. These men are pitted against the very best legal talent in the country, but they do not take the leading part.

Mr. THOMPSON. The man you send out is given all the time he needs to prepare his case?

Mr. WILLIAMS. All the time he can get.

Mr. THOMPSON. All he asks for, isn't he given?

Mr. WILLIAMS. Well, I will tell you; all of us work overtime in the solicitor's office.

Mr. Thompson. He is permitted to have all the assistance in working up the case that he asks for?

Mr. Williams. All that we can give him; yes, sir.

Mr. Thompson. And if he goes out and makes an exceptionally brilliant presentation he is offered a very fine salary from private interests.

Mr. Williams. Sometimes a man may be offered a much better compensation. But in the management of these food and drugs cases, of course, the United States attorney has the opportunity and does take the leading part. An assistant sent from my office furnishes the United States attorney with the law, with the facts, and with the technical knowledge that the assistant must have in order that he may properly handle that kind of a case.

The Chairman. All right, Mr. Thompson. I do not want to cut off any proper and necessary inquiry, but it seems to me you have gone into that matter pretty thoroughly, and we must get along.

Mr. Thompson. I wish to ask a few questions with reference to this memorandum which I secured from Mr. Williams.

Mr. Williams, if I get this memorandum read correctly, you had 3,084 cases of violations in 1918?

Mr. Williams. Yes.

Mr. Thompson. During the past year?

Mr. Williams. Yes.

Mr. Thompson. What do I understand was done about these 3,084 cases?

Mr. Williams. You will understand just this, which I explained before you came in: There are entrusted to the Department of Agriculture for administration more than 30 statutes, a majority of which are regulatory in their nature and carry penal provisions. The cases to which you refer arose under these statutes, involving violations thereof. We will take, for instance, a food and drugs case: An inspector of the Bureau of Chemistry will find an article that is deleterious to health; perhaps an article of food that is adulterated, or perhaps of a putrid character. That fact will be reported to the Bureau of Chemistry for an investigation. In the investigation they have the assistance of the solicitor's office, and the case is worked up, just like one of you lawyers would work up a case in your private practice. Of course, not with the idea of putting anything over, but with the idea of doing absolute justice. And——

Mr. Thompson (interposing). With this difference, that the lawyer in private practice would either have to work the case up himself or hire some one to go out and work up the facts for him. Whereas in these cases the Government furnishes the solicitor with an expert to work up everything, and it is brought to and laid down before the Solicitor of the Department of Agriculture or one of his assistants simply for consultation.

Mr. Wililiams. Well, I do not believe that you could say that is precisely the procedure, because you will find that while men may be called experts, yet when it comes to the preparation of a case for court you need and must have the assistance of a well-balanced lawyer. He can be ever so expert in technical matters but he must have the assistance of a lawyer. Take these cases of——

Mr. THOMPSON (interposing). The solicitor does not get up the facts at all, does he?

Mr. WILLIAMS. He does not actually go out and get the facts, no. But, for instance, they will bring over a case and say, "Here are the facts." Some one in the solicitor's office will go over those facts, and he will indicate how and in what manner the record should be supplemented.

Mr. THOMPSON. It is largely like the solicitor for a railroad company who has a damage case filed against his company. When the claim agent comes in the railroad attorney says, "Go yonder and get such and such a statement," or that particular form of deposition, and sends out to get the deposition or statement. Isn't that about the situation?

Mr. WILLIAMS. Not exactly, but very similar perhaps.

Mr. THOMPSON. It is largely routine, isn't it, Mr. Williams?

Mr. WILLIAMS. Oh, yes; I guess you may say it is largely routine, but a very essential part of the work. It is different, though, from the railroad claim agent preparing a negligence case. It is the matter of preparing a case involving technical knowledge of chemistry as well as applying the law to these questions. The question of negligence, so far as railroads are concerned, is not a difficult matter when you know how to get the facts, for, after all, negligence is the failure to exercise common sense in the circumstances.

Mr. THOMPSON. They present quite a different state of facts in each case?

Mr. WILLIAMS. Oh, yes; every case is different.

Mr. THOMPSON. You say 3,314 contracts, leases, and bonds. I presume that you mean you drew contracts in that number of cases?

Mr. WILLIAMS. No; not in that number of cases.

Mr. THOMPSON. That many different leases, contracts, and bonds?

Mr. WILLIAMS. Yes.

Mr. THOMPSON. You drew that many different leases, contracts, and bonds?

Mr. WILLIAMS. Yes.

Mr. THOMPSON. Of course, that is altogether routine, is it not?

Mr. WILLIAMS. Yes, sir; it is routine, but——

Mr. THOMPSON (interposing). Those are all forms, aren't they? The leases, bonds, and contracts are practically all prescribed forms?

Mr. WILLIAMS. Well, to a great degree they are forms, but there are many instances where there are special covenants which have to be inserted, and these contracts are all contracts of importance. For instance, you take the national forest again: Under the national forest laws the department may sell all dead timber and matured timber. But you come from the West and probably know what a timber contract means?

Mr. THOMPSON. Very well.

Mr. WILLIAMS. You know that you would not want any inexperienced or incompetent man to prepare for you a timber contract. If you were a timberman I know that you would not want to entrust such a matter to an inexperienced man.

Mr. THOMPSON. Well, it is not a particularly difficult contract, especially when you have a form.

Mr. WILLIAMS. Oh, no; not a particularly difficult contract to draw, but yet an important one. You would not want an inexperienced or incompetent man to prepare a contract involving valuable timber. Under such contracts during the last year we——

Mr. THOMPSON (interposing). It is like acquiring a right of way for a railroad. You would not want an inexperienced man to acquire right of way for a railroad?

Mr. WILLIAMS. No.

Mr. THOMPSON. But it is a matter of routine after a man becomes acquainted with the work?

Mr. WILLIAMS. I would not call it exactly routine, because there are special covenants to be embodied in them. Then there are contracts with reference to construction work. Sometimes appropriation items give us authority to construct buildings. The contracts of the department are important. For instance, last year you appropriated $10,000,000 to buy nitrate of soda for farmers. We attempted to buy that nitrate, and conducted long negotiations for it. Finally we reached a preliminary agreement with the importers of nitrate and they presented to the department an old Spanish form of contract which they said was customarily used on the Valparaiso exchange, in Chile, and their attitude was to the effect that "If you don't have the Secretary to sign that contract you can not get your nitrate." That contract contained many provisions which were absolutely illegal when measured by the laws passed by Congress. For instance, there was one feature which required every dispute to be arbitrated on the Valparaiso exchange under a lot of rules which appeared to me to be foolish. It required payment for a part of the nitrate before it was delivered, and contained several other provisions which we could not pass. Ten million dollars were involved. We drafted for them a contract and they practically refused to sign it. They thought I was very technical and grew impatient. They insisted that other departments had signed such contracts, and could not see why I should not recommend to the Secretary that he should sign it. Our draft of the contract was finally executed, and later one of the nitrate men, having promptly received his money from the Department of Agriculture, expressed himself as much pleased with the fact that we had insisted on what he at one time had termed mere "technicalities," and stated that up to that time he had not been able to collect under the other contracts.

Mr. THOMPSON. That was because of the unusual situation growing out of the war.

Mr. WILLIAMS. It was an unusual situation.

Mr. THOMPSON. We are talking about conditions after the war is over and your employees during peace times.

Mr. WILLIAMS. Yes.

Mr. THOMPSON. That would not occur again during the succeeding years, would it?

Mr. WILLIAMS. The $10,000,000 appropriation has been carried forward into the present appropriation act as a revolving fund. Referring to forestry contracts again, the receipts under those last year were over $1,000,000.

Mr. THOMPSON. That would not signify the number of contracts that were signed, because some might be very large and some very small?

Mr. WILLIAMS. Yes; but I was citing that to show the importance of them.

Mr. THOMPSON. In my own State there might well be one contract to run over a million dollars?

Mr. WILLIAMS. Yes. I will take another important feature—the Federal aid road act. Under the law and regulations, the State highway departments have to present to the Secretary what they call a project statement. That statement describes the road proposed to be improved, the cost per mile, and contains a resolution which has been passed by the county board of revenue appropriating the county's part of the money. The validity of that resolution has to be looked into, and then the question has to be determined whether or not the road which they propose to improve is a "post road" within the meaning of the statute. Each one of these project statements involves a separate case, and we have had a great deal of difficulty in construing the law.

Mr. THOMPSON. In the first place—and I am very well acquainted with these cases—you refer them to the Post Office Department?

Mr. WILLIAMS. No.

Mr. THOMPSON. It comes to you from the Post Office Department?

Mr. WILLIAMS. No.

Mr. THOMPSON. Your statement comes from the Post Office Department showing whether or not it is a post road?

Mr. WILLIAMS. No; I do not get that from the Post Office Department. We get it all from the State highway department.

Mr. THOMPSON. It is a matter of routine, because you do get the information?

Mr. WILLIAMS. A part of it is routine.

Mr. THOMPSON. So far as its being a postal highway is concerned it is a matter of routine?

Mr. WILLIAMS. No; I do not consider any case a matter of routine, because it——

Mr. THOMPSON (interposing). You have nothing to do with designating it as a postal highway?

Mr. WILLIAMS. No; but we have to take the particular facts and determine whether under the law it is a "post road." I do not believe that you could say it is a matter of routine when every case presented involves a definite construction of the statute.

Mr. THOMPSON. If the mail is carried over the road it is a postal highway, isn't it?

Mr. WILLIAMS. Yes.

Mr. HARRISON. The act says "are or may be" used for mail transportation.

Mr. THOMPSON. You have not passed any applications that "may be" postal highways, have you?

Mr. WILLIAMS. Yes.

Mr. THOMPSON. You have passed some in that way?

Mr. WILLIAMS. Yes.

Mr. THOMPSON. That is different from what you have applied to Oklahoma?

Mr. WILLIAMS. I do not remember all the Oklahoma cases, but we have applied the same rule to Oklahoma as to other States.

Mr. THOMPSON. In one case the road between Oklahoma City and Lawton, on which we had to build a bridge over the Canadian River at a cost to my county of $250,000, you refused to pass upon it until the Post Office Department had established a post road over it?

Mr. WILLIAMS. I do not have that particular one in mind just now, but I assume that the evidence in the folder or in the record was not sufficient to lead to a reasonable conclusion that the road intended to be improved would, within a reasonable time after construction, be used as a " post road." When the evidence fails to show that fact we do, in some instances, apply to the Post Office Department for information. But if the statement contains the necessary evidence to show that in event the road were improved a post route would be put upon it, we go ahead and improve it. But if the facts do not show that we feel that it would be in violation of the law to approve the project.

Mr. THOMPSON. After all, it would not require a lawyer to pass upon that, would it?

Mr. WILLIAMS. Yes.

Mr. THOMPSON. It would?

Mr. WILLIAMS. Yes.

Mr. THOMPSON. On a question of fact like that?

Mr. WILLIAMS. Well, I do not know that.

Mr. THOMPSON. It is absolutely a question of fact?

Mr. WILLIAMS. It is a mixed question of fact and law.

Mr. THOMPSON. How do you make a mixed question of fact and law out of a question of that kind?

Mr. WILLIAMS. I would make it like this: There is a statute which reads in a certain way. The facts are presented which it is hoped will tend to show a certain conclusion. The facts are not definite. Therefore your conclusion must be by inferences. The man who determines both questions, the construction of the statute and the application of the law to the indefinite data presented, is one and the same man. I would call it a mixed question of law and fact.

Mr. THOMPSON. I would not agree with you there.

Mr. WILLIAMS. That is my opinion. Of course, where there is a post route on the entire road sought to be improved, the matter is easy enough; but in the majority of instances there are gaps in or sections of the road over which the mails are not carried, and in some instances no part of the road is used for carrying the mails.

Mr. THOMPSON. You say you prepared 1,292 written opinions?

Mr. WILLIAMS. Yes.

Mr. THOMPSON. How many solicitors have you in your department? I mean assistants, attorneys, clerks, etc.

Mr. WILLIAMS. They are all called "law clerks." Under my supervision as solicitor there are at the present, I believe, 42.

Mr. THOMPSON. There are 42?

Mr. WILLIAMS. Yes.

The CHAIRMAN. They are all shown here in the estimates.

Mr. WILLIAMS. I am talking about some who do title work. They are employed under the Weeks forestry law, under the National Forest Reservation Commission. There are several who do nothing but examine titles, but they come under my supervision. I am responsible for them. They examine titles in the several States under the Weeks law.

Mr. THOMPSON. There are 42 men who do work under your office?

Mr. WILLIAMS. Yes.

Mr. THOMPSON. To do the work which you have outlined in your memorandum that I have?

Mr. WILLIAMS. Yes. It is divided up.

Mr. THOMPSON. You have had only four to resign during the last year?

Mr. WILLIAMS. No; its is my recollection that I stated more than that. I detailed them a moment ago.

Mr. THOMPSON. I understood that one accepted private employment?

Mr. WILLIAMS. Let me go over it again: One went to the Department of Justice; one went to Armour & Co.——.

Mr. THOMPSON (interposing). I am not asking about those going to other departments, but who went back to private life.

Mr. WILLIAMS. I lost, I believe, four to private life.

Mr. THOMPSON. That is what I understood.

Mr. WILLIAMS. Yes.

Mr. THOMPSON. Those who went into other departments, did they receive larger salaries, increased salaries?

Mr. WILLIAMS. I have two cases in mind. It is my recollection that when the administrative officer asked for these two men I talked to the Secretary about letting them go. The solicitor's office has been shot to pieces from year to year, and we discussed the matter. The Secretary consented that they should go·on the same salary that was being paid them in the solicitor's office; but they felt even then that they would have better opportunity in administrative work than in law work, and they were willing to give up all the years they spent in academic training, in college, and in their professional course. That is the condition that confronts them, one and all.

Mr. THOMPSON. Well, they do not hesitate to resign when they are offered better salaries in private life, I mean while they are in the public service?

Mr. WILLIAMS. Well, so far as my own personal observation is concerned there has only been one instance where one of these men was offered a contract of employment in private life. That was the man who was taken by Armour & Co. during the past year. He merely wrote me that he could not stay with us on the salary that he was getting and that he had an offer from Armour & Co. and was going to accept it. The men who have gone into private practice felt that they could do better.

Mr. McLAUGHLIN. Do you know how much the man received who went to Armour & Co.?

Mr. WILLIAMS. No; I do not.

Mr. THOMPSON. Of course, you do not want to convey the impression to the committee nor to the public that the Government of the United States ought to compete with private interests in so far as fixing salaries is concerned, do you?

Mr. WILLIAMS. Well, no. Still, I think we can not help being affected by that situation, and justice demands that we pay better salaries to our men.

Mr. THOMPSON. If you took that view a large number of the justices of the supreme court, not only of the United States but of practically all the States, would resign. Practically all of the justices of the Supreme Court of the United States, as well as the justices of the supreme courts of the several States, gave up a practice that paid them more money than the salaries they are receiving in order to accept these positions.

Mr. WILLIAMS. That is true, but they occupy positions of honor, as well as of emolument.

Mr. THOMPSON. Aren't these positions of honor?

Mr. WILLIAMS. They are honorable positions, but carry very little "honor" with them.

The CHAIRMAN. That is a very good distinction.

Mr. THOMPSON. I do not agree with you on that. I can not get your idea?

Mr. WILLIAMS. Well, it is just this: It is very honorable to work for the Government, but these men over in the department are little known, and there is very little opportunity for them to become known, and if a man is sought for employment on the outside it is almost by chance. He hasn't got the same hope of advancement that the outside man has. For instance, I think that the man who is clerk of your committee has a better prospect of advancement. The man in the department can not entertain the same kind of hope for promotion in the department or for honors in the political world. You take a man who is made a member of the supreme court of his State; he is occupying a position which carries a great deal of honor with it. Take a man who is appointed by the President to be a Federal judge, at $6,000 a year, and he has a very honorable position, a very desirable position. All the time that judge can hope that some day he will be put on the Court of Appeals, and if he has the right kind of ambition he will have his eye on the Supreme Court of the United States. We can not compare such positions with positions like these in the department.

Mr. THOMPSON. I do not agree with that statement. Of course, if I could agree with that statement, that all these Federal judges could have their eyes on the Supreme Court of the United States, you and I could be in harmony in our views. But I venture the assertion that there is not 1 in every 25 of them—and I think we have less than 150 Federal judges—with his eye on the Supreme Court of the United States.

The CHAIRMAN. Gentlemen, I think we are drawing this investigation out into quite a lengthy hearing.

Mr. THOMPSON. I think this is an important matter.

The CHAIRMAN. We covered all this in 1916 in great detail when Col. Caffey was before the committee.

Mr. WILLIAMS. The conditions are practically the same now, though somewhat accentuated.

The CHAIRMAN. I do not want to cut anybody off, but we must make better headway with the hearings.

Mr. THOMPSON. I would like to ask a few additional questions, Mr. Chairman.

Mr. Williams, you and I can not agree on the proposition that all these Federal and State supreme court judges may hope to become judges of the Supreme Court of the United States. In fact, I do not think that one in 25 ever hopes to be. Down in my State we have a vacancy, which has just been filled to-day, and the best lawyers of Oklahoma have come up here besieging the delegation from Oklahoma, Senators and Representatives, urging us to support their friends. Men who are now attorneys for oil companies and other big corporations, on salaries from $20,000 to $25,000 a year, are anxious to be appointed to this $6,000 job; none of whom I suspect, and I think I may safely assert it, ever hopes to attain a higher judicial position than that. But they are anxious to accept that $6,000 job. There is quite a difference between an assured salary from the Government——

Mr. WILLIAMS (interposing). Yes; a good paymaster is always desirable.

Mr. THOMPSON (continuing). And a position as a practicing lawyer, where you have to pay your office expenses, stenographers, clerks, and so forth, and work up your own evidence, and take all the chances of a law practice. Therefore you would not assert, would you, Mr. Williams, that the Government ought to enter into competition with private concerns in paying salaries to its employees?

Mr. WILLIAMS. No; I wouldn't go that far. But as I stated before, I think that the Government must be influenced by outside conditions. While there may be a little lower scale in Government salaries, because of the honor and because of the sure pay, I do not think, as a matter of common justice, that the salaries ought to be too low. If you get them too low I do not believe you can maintain the efficiency of the Government service.

Mr. THOMPSON. My observation has been that we have very satisfactory service in the Government.

Mr. WILLIAMS. Yes; very satisfactory, but——

Mr. THOMPSON (interposing). These lawyers are very competent to look after the Government business?

Mr. WILLIAMS. Yes; and the first thing that struck me, when I came to Washington, was their competency on the one hand, and their low pay on the other.

Mr. THOMPSON. For all of these positions that become vacant, there is an abundance of applications from men of character and ability?

Mr. WILLIAMS. Well, I can not say that. I have had a right hard time getting lawyers for my office.

Mr. THOMPSON. Perhaps so, during the war, when questions were involved that would not be involved in peace times.

Mr. WILLIAMS. Well, Mr. Caffey told me that he has had a good deal of trouble. I talked to him about getting lawyers to fill the $1,600 places, and he said he had had a good deal of trouble. Now, you doubtless realize that all these salaries were fixed years ago; since then conditions have changed, and we can not live on the same money now that we did then. Neither can you gentlemen of Congress. You know that your expenses are much greater here in Washington than was the case a year or two ago. These men down in the Department of Agriculture feel the increased cost of living quite keenly, just as all of you feel it. We have the same condition all around us; it is not one man's cry, but it is the cry of all. I know the situation existing in the Solicitor's office, and I feel that it is but just and right that the salaries of these men should be increased. And I feel that if we do not increase their salaries that these men will be compelled to seek employment elsewhere and then you are not going to have the efficiency in the department that you now have and that you ought to have, for it will be just as hard to get new men to come in at these salaries as it will be to retain the experienced men we now have. And I feel, too, that there has never been a time in the history of the Government when more efficiency was demanded than will be during the reconstruction period.

Mr. THOMPSON. You must take into consideration also in this connection, Mr. Williams, that when these salaries are once fixed, it does not make any difference how much the cost of living is reduced or how much the work may be reduced, salaries do not go down with the reduction in the volume of work or in the cost of living.

Mr. WILLIAMS. That is true; but the volume of work is not going to be reduced, so far as I can see, in the Solicitor's office. And we have all worked overtime during the war. Gentlemen of the committee, let me say to you that there has not been a holiday and but very few Sundays, while I have been in Washington, that I have not worked. I worked New Year's day; and I only refer to this as illustrative of the demands upon and the service rendered by the men under me. That is the situation in the Solicitor's office to-day, and, I dare say, will continue to be the situation for an indefinite period in the future. If you do not help these men, I feel that it will be an injustice not only to them but to the Government as well. Now, just one word as to these men who have been designated "law clerks." They have always been so designated in the law. I wish that you might see fit to change that designation to "attorneys." It is not fair for men to spend four years in college, two or three years in a law school, and then serve as a lawyer in the Government service for from two to sixteen years and be called merely "law clerks." That designation hurts their dignity. Perhaps, it is more a matter of fine feeling than otherwise, but it means something to them. I do not believe that lawyers doing such responsible work should be called law clerks, and I sincerely urge you to favor the change that we recommend.

Now, in conclusion, let me say that I hope you will grant the first plan I have outlined to you. I really believe that it would be no more than a fair and reasonable recognition of services required and rendered, and that it would insure the efficient conduct of the Government's business. In event you think you can not grant that plan, I hope you will not fail to give me the $3,500 place and the $3,250 place, cutting out two $1,600 places. Under the first plan I will then have the same number of assistants with a total increased appropriation of $5,050, and under the second plan there would be no increase in the number of assistants, and the increased appropriation would be only $3,550, which is asking but little, gentlemen, considering all the work that is done in the Solicitor's office. I could not detail it to you in two hours. No; it would take me three or four hours to detail all the work required of my office. It is very voluminous indeed, and everybody who looks at the report of the Solicitor for the Department of Agriculture is surprised at the character and amount of work. There is hardly a subject of the law that does not pass through my office—constitutional questions, the law of contracts, torts, real estate, patent law, criminal law, questions arising under the various State laws relating to condemnation of lands, the laws relating to the public lands, the various State statutes in connection with the Federal aid road act, and the regulatory acts administered by the department, and the law of procedure, including the Rules in Admiralty under the food and drugs act. I do not believe that there is a law office in any branch of the Government where the duties are so varied as they are in the office of the Solicitor of Agriculture. I am very earnest in the making of these recommendations.

The CHAIRMAN. Mr. Thompson, do you wish to ask anything more?

Mr. THOMPSON. I believe not, Mr. Chairman.

The CHAIRMAN. Does any other member of the committee wish to ask Mr. Williams any questions?

Mr. HAUGEN. I would like to ask a question or two.

The CHAIRMAN. You may proceed, Mr. Haugen.

Mr. HAUGEN. Mr. Williams, how are these law positions filled; by young men fresh from college, or by drawing men from the ranks of practitioners?

Mr. WILLIAMS. I will tell you how we try to get these men, but we can not always do it. I think it very desirable to take young men who have had three or four years experience in actual practice; men who have had not only a high-school, college, and law-school education, but a few years actual experience in the practice of their profession. If we can get a man along about 26 or 27 years of age, with the education and experience I have mentioned, he makes a very valuable man, starting in in one of the lower grades.

Mr. HAUGEN. You prefer to take men from the ranks of practitioners?

Mr. WILLIAMS. Yes.

Mr. HAUGEN. As a general thing aren't they appointed fresh from college?

Mr. WILLIAMS. No; we try to get those who have had some practice.

Mr. HAUGEN. But do you succeed in that effort?

Mr. WILLIAMS. Well, I haven't been very successful in that effort in filling these $1,600 places.

Mr. HAUGEN. You spoke of one of your men going to Armour & Co.; what was he doing?

Mr. WILLIAMS. He was in the Forest Service.

Mr. HAHGEN. That is all I wish to ask.

The CHAIRMAN. Mr. Williams, this item 139 simply provides that attorneys, in the event we change the title from law clerks to attorneys, shall be kept in the classified civil service, where they are now?

(139) After the item "two law clerks, at $1,600 each," insert:
"*Provided*, That hereafter the position of attorney in the Department of Agriculture shall be and remain in the competitive classified civil service, anything in the law or in the civil-service rules and regulations to the contrary notwithstanding, and the law clerks now in said department who may be appointed or promoted to said positions of attorney shall retain all the rights of competitive employees, and the Secretary of Agriculture may detail said attorneys for service in or out of the District of Columbia."

(This proviso is added in order to preserve the classified civil-service status of the positions of attorney and of the persons who may be appointed or promoted to those positions. Without such a proviso the attorneyships would fall within the exception in the civil-service rules and could be filled without compliance with the civil-service rules applicable to positions in the competitive classified civil service.)

Mr. WILLIAMS. Yes; if we did not change the title in the law they would not remain in the classified civil service.

The CHAIRMAN. Is there anything further you wish to say, Mr. Williams?

Mr. WILLIAMS. No; except that I will put in a statement showing the present statutory law-clerk roll in my office and what is proposed under the first plan.

(The statement referred to follows:)

Personnel of office of solicitor, United States Department of Agriculture.

1919		1920	
1 law clerk, at $3,250	$3,250	1 attorney, at $3,500	$3,500
2 law clerks, at $3,000	6,000	2 attorneys, at $3,250	6,500
2 law clerks, at $2,750	5,500	2 attorneys, at $3,000	6,000
4 law clerks, at $2,500	10,000	2 attorneys, at $2,750	5,500
8 law clerks, at $2,250	18,000	10 attorneys, at $2,500	25,000
1 law clerk, at $2,200	2,200	2 attorneys, at $2,250	4,500
5 law clerks, at $2,000	10,000	1 attorney, at $2,200	2,200
3 law clerks, at $1,800	5,400	5 attorneys, at $2,000	10,000
4 law clerks, at $1,600	6,400	3 attorneys, at $1,800	5,400
		2 law clerks, at $1,600	3,200
30 Total	66,750	30 Total	71,800
			66,750
		Net increase	5,050

The CHAIRMAN. Now we will resume with Mr. Reese.

STATEMENT OF MR. R. M. REESE, CHIEF CLERK, UNITED STATES DEPARTMENT OF AGRICULTURE—Continued.

The CHAIRMAN. I wish you would explain items 140 and 141, which appear in the Book of Estimates as follows:

(140) For salaries and compensation of necessary employees in the mechanical shops and power plant of the Department of Agriculture, $90 000: *Provided*, That hereafter the Secretary of Agriculture may, by transfer settlement through the Treasury, reimburse any appropriation made for the salaries and compensation of employees in the mechanical shops of the department from the appropriation made for the bureau, office, or division for which any work in said shops is performed, and such reimbursement shall be at the actual cost of such work for supervision and labor.

(141) The following places, aggregating $93,080, should be omitted from the statutory roll of the Office of the Secretary:

1 mechanical superintendent	$2,500	1 cabinet-shop foreman	$1,200
1 mechanical assistant	1,800	5 cabinetmakers or carpenters, at $1,200 each	6,000
1 mechanical assistant	1,400	3 cabinetmakers or carpenters, at $1,100 each	3,300
1 mechanical assistant	1,380	9 cabinetmakers or carpenters, at $1,020 each	9,180
1 engineer	1,400	3 cabinetmakers or carpenters, at $900 each	2,700
1 electrical engineer and draftsman	1,200	1 instrument maker	1,200
2 assistant engineers, at $1,200 each	2,400	1 electrician	1,100
2 assistant engineers, at $1,000 each	2,000	2 electrical wiremen, at $1,100 each	2,200
1 fireman	840	1 electrical wireman	1,000
8 firemen, at $720 each	5,760	1 electrical wireman	900
1 chief elevator conductor	840	1 electricians' helper	840
16 elevator conductors, at $720 each	11,520	3 electrician's helpers, at $720 each	2,160
3 elevator conductors, at $600 each	1,800	1 painter	1,020
1 superintendent of shops	1,400		

AGRICULTURE APPROPRIATION BILL. 113

1 painter	$1,000	1 tinner or sheet-metal worker	$1,100
5 painters, at $900 each	4,500	1 tinner's helper	720
5 plumbers or steamfitters, at $1,020 each	5,100	4 mechanics, at $1,200 each	4,800
2 plumber's helpers, at $840 each	1,680	1 mechanic	1,000
2 plumber's helpers, at $720 each	1,440	1 skilled laborer	900
1 blacksmith	900		93,080
1 elevator machinist	900	A net increase of $30,870.	

The entire mechanical-shop force of the department has been underpaid for some years. All places on the shop roll are statutory, and promotions have been slow and comparatively infrequent.

It is believed that as long as a statutory roll for mechanics and other employees in the shops and power plant is retained, the situation will be unsatisfactory for the following reasons:

(1) The statutory roll is not flexible. There may be a large amount of outstanding work in the cabinet shop with simultaneously a small amount of work in the plumbing shop. Yet a vacancy in the plumbing shop occurring at this time would have to be filled with a plumber and could not be used to obtain a cabinetmaker, though the services of a cabinetmaker rather than a plumber might be required.

(2) The force can not be readily changed to suit the volume of work. This makes it necessary for the bureaus to carry on their lump-sum funds extra mechanics to meet the increasing volume of work. These extra men, though often not so good mechanics as the regular force, have to be paid the prevailing rate. This naturally causes much dissatisfaction among the regular men who receive lower compensation for doing a better class of work.

(3) It is impossible to get good mechanics to accept the low entrance salaries. Hence the loss of efficiency to the department and the increased difficulty of getting men who can do the high-class work required on the department's special work.

(4) Rates of pay do not follow commercial rates. The Government Printing Office, the Bureau of Engraving and Printing, and the Washington Navy Yard carry their mechanical force on lump-sum rolls on a per diem basis. These departments have increased the rates of pay of their mechanical force as the demand for labor has increased during the past two years, while the rates paid the Department of Agriculture's force have remained stationary, although small increases have been asked in the estimates each year.

(5) Under the present statutory-roll arrangement the particular project desiring mechanical work can not be charged for labor performed in the manufacture of scientific apparatus, equipment, etc. Hence the tendency is to increase the amount of work performed by the mechanical shops over what would be required if the cost were charged against the appropriation of the particular project requesting the work.

The new provision designed to carry this plan into effect has been prepared in consultation with the solicitor of the department and is believed to be adequate for the purpose in view. It has a twofold object:

(A) To provide a lump-sum appropriation of $90,000 in lieu of the present statutory and lump-sum places aggregating $93,080.

(B) To authorize reimbursement of this $90,000 lump sum from bureau lump funds at the actual cost of the labor performed by the shop force for bureau needs.

The plan proposed would have the following advantages:

(1) Each shop's relations with the bureaus would be on a business basis. Each bureau would pay by reimbursement monthly for all work performed on its projects. Hence funds would be automatically provided for the expansion of the mechanical force as necessary to provide for increased volume of work desired by the bureaus.

(2) Each project would be charged for the actual work done on the design and construction of scientific apparatus and equipment. Hence reports of expenditures on these projects would more nearly show the actual money expended.

(3) The number and kind of mechanics could be varied to exactly suit the requirements of the work.

(4) The salaries of the mechanical force could be changed from time to time to suit the varying labor conditions, and a contented and efficient working force could be always secured.

The total in salaries now paid this force is $93,080, and the proposed readjustment will result in a total salary roll of $119,760, or an increase of $26,680. The difference between the $119,760 and the $90,000 provided by this paragraph will be made up by reimbursement for labor performed for bureaus by transfer settlement, the cost of each job to be accurately computed.

A comparison of the salaries paid the various classes of mechanics on the present statutory roll of this department with the salaries paid for similar services in the Bureau of Engraving and Printing, the Washington Navy Yard, and the Government Printing Office shows that the rates paid the latter employees are much in excess of those prevailing in the Department of Agriculture.

If the lump-fund appropriation of $90,000 is allowed, all the mechanical-shop and power-plant employees now carried on the statutory roll (with salaries aggregating $93,080) will be transferred to this new item.

Mr. REESE. That suggests new language, the effect of which is to provide a lump-sum appropriation for the employees in the mechanical shops and power plant in lieu of the statutory places which are listed in item 141. There are 97 such places, with aggregate salaries of $93,080. The argument for the change is set forth in some detail in the note. I might say that we have found great difficulty in retaining mechanics in the shops in these low-salaried statutory places. We have lost some 16 mechanics to the outside world since July 1, 1917, and several firemen.

The CHAIRMAN. What do you propose to do?

Mr. REESE. To drop the statutory roll for mechanics and adopt a lump-sum appropriation, with this idea in view, that in performing shopwork for a bureau we will be able to secure reimbursement not only for the material used under the authority we now have but for the labor required on any given job. That, I think, is desirable, because it is a fair way to do business.

Mr. McLAUGHLIN. What do you mean by that?

Mr. REESE. When you do work for a bureau that bureau will pay for it. We now have authority under the law to secure reimbursement for all material used when performing a job of work for one of the bureaus, and this will also give us authority to charge that bureau for the labor required in performing that job.

Mr. WASON. But the money comes out of the Treasury of the United States.

Mr. McLAUGHLIN. Yes; as it were, taking it from one pocket and putting it into another.

Mr. HAUGEN. It is a more a matter of bookkeeping it seems to me.

The CHAIRMAN. Would it increase the bookkeeping?

Mr. REESE. No. A voucher would be prepared monthly covering the labor and materially actually used on work done for each bureau.

The CHAIRMAN. You simply send a man at this time from the mechanical shops to a bureau, say, the Bureau of Animal Industry, to do the work?

Mr. REESE. Yes; or do the work at the shops.

The CHAIRMAN. If you charge the Bureau of Animal Industry, say, for the labor and material required in performing that work, then the Bureau of Animal Industry, in order to protect itself, must set up another accounting system?

Mr. REESE. It involves just one monthly voucher covering the number of hours of labor and the amount of material used on work performed for the bureau.

The CHAIRMAN. The Bureau of Animal Industry will hardly permit you to make a charge against its funds unless you allow it to keep account of what you charge against it.

Mr. REESE. Yes; they would keep an account.

The CHAIRMAN. Would not that entail some extra work?

Mr. REESE. Not very much.

The CHAIRMAN. But it would entail some?

Mr. REESE. Not a great deal; little more than the examination of one voucher a month.

The CHAIRMAN. What is the idea of the change?

Mr. REESE. One idea of this change from the statutory to a lump-sum appropriation is that it will make the shop force more flexible. We find ourselves in this situation: That we may have a vacancy among the plumbers and are not at the moment in need of a plumber to fill the vacancy, but do need another carpenter. Under the statutory roll we can not put into the plumber vacancy a carpenter, but if we had a lum-sum roll we can appoint any kind of mechanic for two or three weeks or months, as the necessity arises.

The CHAIRMAN. Why wouldn't it be better to provide language in the law which would permit that flexibility of action rather than provide this complicated method?

Mr. REESE. That is what we are trying to do in item 140.

The CHAIRMAN. The difficulty in this proposition is that you are taking out of the eyes of Congress all these statutory places, amounting to $93,080, and creating a lump-sum fund, which is absolutely against the idea of the Congress.

Mr. REESE. That is a matter for the committee to decide.

The CHAIRMAN. Isn't there sufficient ingenuity in the department to work out that proposition in order to give you the flexibility that you desire?

Mr. REESE. I do not see how it is possible under the statutory roll.

The CHAIRMAN. Why wouldn't it be possible to say that in the mechanical force of the Department of Agriculture these substitutions may be made without regard to civil service or whatever is needed?

Mr. REESE. If that could be done, it would be all right, but the Civil Service Commission would never consent to the certification of a carpenter for appointment to the statutory place of a plumber.

Mr. HARRISON. The main purpose of this recommendation, as I understand it, is to adjust the salaries of mechanics without increasing the total amount of the appropriation. The total amount asked for under the lump-sum appropriation is $90,000, whereas the total of the statutory roll for the positions affected is $93,080. Under this plan, however, it is believed the matter may be so adjusted as to have the smaller sum cover the requirements. As you all know, the scale of wages for mechanics has gone up, and it is impossible to handle the matter satisfactorily under the present arrangement.

The CHAIRMAN. Illustrate that proposition.

Mr. HARRISON. Mr. Reese has the figures.

Mr. REESE. I have figures showing maximum and minimum wages paid to mechanics by Government establishments—the District government, union and nonunion establishments, and the union rate.

(The statement referred to follows:)

Comparative statement of wages paid mechanics by Government establishments and by private employers.

Occupation.	Government.		District of Columbia.		Nonunion establishments.		Union rate.	Union establishments.	
	Minimum.	Maximum.	Minimum.	Maximum.	Minimum.	Maximum.	Minimum.	Minimum.	Maximum.
Blacksmiths	$900	$1,000			$1,565		$1,670	$1,670	$1,716
Carpenters	720	1,500	$1,602	$1,802	1,095	$1,878	1,716	1,716	2,002
Electricians	720	1,500	1,400	1,752	1,252	2,080	1,716	1,716	2,288
Electricians' helpers								984	1,373
Elevator conductors	480	1,200			522	1,040	(1)	(1)	(1)
Engineers	840	1,800	1,252	1,802	1,080	2,400	1,830		
Engineers, chief	1,320	2,160				2,607			
Engineers, assistant	720	1,800				1,565			
Firemen	660	840	840	1,252	840	1,409	1,252		
Skilled laborers	600	1,590	1,001	1,565	1,017	1,565			
Laborers	400	1,000	782	1,017	828	960	915	915	
Machinists	840	1,800	1,652	1,802	1,252	1,817	1,716	1,602	1,716
Messengers	720	960	600				(1)	(1)	(1)
Messengers, chief	1,000	1,100					(1)	(1)	(1)
Messengers, assistant	480	600					(1)	(1)	(1)
Messenger boys	240	420							
Painters	900	1,200	1,592	1,752	1,095	1,300	1,716		
Plumbers	720	1,565	1,752	1,802	936	1,486	1,716	1,716	2,288
Plumbers, foremen									2,997
Plumbers' helpers								858	915

[1] Not organized.

Mr. HAUGEN. The real object is to enable you to increase your salaries, is it not?

Mr. REESE. That is one idea we have in mind.

Mr. HAUGEN. To enable you to go out on the street and compete with private enterprises and contractors, and to pay $100 a week, if necessary?

Mr. REESE. We want to raise the salaries of these shop men, but have in mind no figure approaching $100 a week.

Mr. HAUGEN. That does not seem to me to be fair, for us to go out in competition with those contractors and others who are temporarily paying large salaries and wages, perhaps $100 a week in some cases, while in permanent work under different and normal working conditions you are paying men $1,100 a year, and, I dare say, soon if not now any number can be had for such permanent work under normal conditions at that salary?

Mr. REESE. If the general wage scale for outside employment were to go down rapidly that would possibly be the case.

Mr. HAUGEN. It seems to me the idea is to put everybody under the present scale of wages and continue them under normal conditions. On the other hand my way of doing things would be to meet the emergency in a proper way but not to saddle any of these people on the Government at double wages or salaries, and it would amount to about that when we return to normal conditions.

Mr. REESE. I might say that under this lump-sum appropriation plan we would have the power not only to increase but to reduce.

Mr. HAUGEN. I understand, but to reduce salaries is not the Government's practice in past years when salaries or wages have once been fixed.

The CHAIRMAN. Under this lump-sum appropriation you could pay one of the mechanics $4,500 a year, couldn't you?

Mr. REESE. No.

The CHAIRMAN. Why not? Under your proposed plan the salaries of mechanics would not be fixed by law.

Mr. REESE. We could never secure a certification from the Civil Service Commission on any such salary basis as that.

The CHAIRMAN. Well, it might be that we would have some little hold on you there.

Mr. HAUGEN. You spoke of temporary appointments, for two or three weeks or months; the Civil Service Commission has nothing to do with them?

Mr. REESE. Yes, sir; it does. If we wish to make a temporary appointment of any kind of mechanic we must first ask the Civil Service Commission for a certification. If the commission happens to have no eligible list of the particular kind of mechanic wanted, we can secure permission to put one on "pending certification," provided we can find one willing to accept the salary we have to offer. During the past year and a half this has frequently been very difficult to do.

Mr. WASON. I would like to know what the Civil Service Commission would do in the case of appointments made under this lump-sum roll?

Mr. REESE. The Civil Service Commission would probably permit us to put in mechanics at something like the outside salaries paid for such services. Carpenters, for example, in the employ of the District of Columbia, are getting from $1,602 to $1,802. Non-union establishments are paying from $1,095 to $1,878. I submit here a copy of an agreement dated July, 1918, between the Builders' and Manufacturers' Exchange, the Master Builders' Association, the Builders' League, and the Carpenters' District Council, of Washington, D. C., and vicinity, which fixes a minimum rate of wages of 75 cents an hour for 44 hours a week, with time and one-half for overtime, etc. The agreement provides for eight hours a day, five days a week, and four hours on Saturday. At 75 cents an hour these carpenters would make $33 a week. Assuming that they took four weeks off during the year and worked 48 weeks, their annual earnings (without overtime) would be $1,584. The highest paid carpenters or cabinet makers in the Department of Agriculture receive $1,200 per annum, and the salaries range downward from that figure to $900.

(The paper submitted is as follows:)

[Carpenters' District Council of the U. B. of C. and J. of A., Washington, D. C., and vicinity.]

JULY, 1918.

An agreement entered into July 1, 1918, by the Builders' and Manufacturers' Exchange, the Master Builders' Association, the Builders' League, and the Carpenters' District Council of Washington, D. C., and vicinity.

The minimum rate of wages to be 75 cents per hour.

Eight hours to constitute a day's work for the first five days of the week and four hours on Saturday.

Time to be made between 7 a. m. and 4 p. m., the first five days of the week, and between 7 a. m. and 11.30 a. m. on Saturday, making 44 hours per week.

All overtime, except Sundays and holidays, to be paid for at the rate of time and one-half.

All time made on Sundays and holidays shall be paid for at the rate of double time.

Should any work be permitted by the District Council on Saturday in excess of the four hours, this time to be paid for at the rate of double time.

The contractor shall provide a good tool shed, equipped with a first-class lock, for carpenters' tools, clothing, etc.

And on all large building operations the contractor shall provide weather-proof and heated quarters for keeping of clothing and eating lunches; the quarters to be provided with not less an one sash for every 120 feet of floor space.

Free transportation in excess of fare within the District of Columbia shall be proivded to and from the place of employment.

Carpenters required to work outside the District of Columbia, and do not return home at night, shall be furnished with free lodging.

Should it be necessary for temporary quarters to be built, they shall be weather tight, properly partitioned off, and heated; not more than five persons shall sleep in any one compartment; beds not to be in tiers, and to be provided with ample bed clothes; linen to be renewed every week and otherwise kept in a clean and sanitary condition; one movable window to be provided to each compartment of not less than 7 square feet to each window.

Kitchen and dining hall to be of ample size and in charge of a competent cook. Ample light to be furnished during the evening for reading, writing, and other recreation. Sleeping quarters, kitchen, and dining hall to be screened in season.

Ample toilet facilities, properly partitioned off, to be provided for in all cases, and must be kept in the best possible sanitary condition and thoroughly screened.

NOTE.—The question of board is still pending.

The above agreement to be in force until December 31, 1918, and that a conference shall take place not later than November 1, 1918, between the builders of Washington, D. C., and vicinity, and the District Council, to take up the matter of readjustment of the above wage scale.

R. H. BURDETTE, *President.*
THOS. W. WOLTZ, *Secretary.*

The CHAIRMAN. It is costing from $1.25 to $2 per hundred pounds to pick cotton in South Carolina now, but it is hardly fair to suppose that under normal conditions with normal prices for cotton such prices can continue to be paid to cotton pickers.

Mr. REESE. That is the way it is at present. But if outside wages go down we could, with a lump-sum appropriation, reduce wages.

The CHAIRMAN. How many resignations have you had from your force of mechanics during the year?

Mr. REESE. Sixteen from the mechanical force.

The CHAIRMAN. What is your entire force?

Mr. REESE. Ninety odd.

The CHAIRMAN. That is a pretty heavy percentage.

Mr. REESE. They have sometimes left us flat. On one day five plumbers in the department left us and went to outside work.

The CHAIRMAN. You said you desired flexibility. You now say you want to increase their salaries?

Mr. REESE. Both, as expressly stated in the note appended to the item in the Book of Estimates. We need flexibility and to increase the salaries of the men in order to get them and to keep them.

The CHAIRMAN. What suggestion have you to make in regard to increasing salaries?

Mr. REESE. Not as high at all as that salary scale that I began to read, and which I have put into the record for your information.

The CHAIRMAN. Have you a concrete proposition to offer in the matter of increasing salaries?

Mr. REESE. We have. Turn to page 21 of the estimates of appropriations and you will find a concrete proposition showing about what we want to pay these men on a statutory-salary basis if your committee does not want to adopt a lump-sum plan:

(142) If the recommendation for a lump fund of $90,000 to provide for the salaries of employees of the mechanical shops is not favorably acted upon by the committee, the following additional changes affecting these employees, and involving an increase of $26,680, should be made in the statutory roll, in order to bring their salaries up to the minimum scale for such positions as set forth in the general note regarding minimum salaries, making a total net increase in the statutory roll of of the office of the Secretary of $61,370:

(143)	1 mechanical assistant, $1,800 to $2,000	$200
(144)	1 mechanical assistant, $1,400 to $1,600	200
(145)	1 mechanical assistant, $1,380 to $1,600	220
(146)	1 engineer, $1,400 to $1,800	400
(147)	1 electrical engineer and draftsman, $1,200 to $1,500	300
(148)	2 assistant engineers, $1,200 to $1,500 each	600
(149)	2 assistant engineers, $1,000 to $1,200 each	400
(150)	1 fireman, $840, to 1 oiler, $1,000	160
(151)	8 firemen, $720 to $1,000 each	2,240
(152)	1 chief elevator conductor, $840 to $960	120
(153)	16 elevator conductors, $720 to $840 each	1,920
(154)	3 elevator conductors, $600 to $840 each	720
(155)	1 superintendent of shops, $1,400, to 1 mechanical assistant, $1,600	200
(156)	1 cabinet shop foreman, $1,200, to 1 cabinetmaker or carpenter $1,500	300
(157)	5 cabinetmakers or carpenters, $1,200 to $1,500 each	1,500
(158)	3 cabinetmakers or carpenters, $1,100 to $1,500 each	1,200
(159)	9 cabinetmakers or carpenters, $1,020 to $1,400 each	3,420
(160)	3 cabinetmakers or carpenters. $900 to $1,200 each	900
(161)	1 electrician, $1,100, to 1 mechanic, $1,500	400
(162)	2 electrical wiremen, at $1,100 each, to 2 mechanics at $1,500 each	800
(163)	1 electrician or wireman, $1,000, to 1 mechanic, $1,400	400
(164)	1 electrical wireman, $900, to 1 mechanic, $1,200	300
(165)	1 electrician's helper, $840 to $960	120
(166)	3 electrician's helpers, $720 to $960 each	720
(167)	1 painter, $1,020 to $1,400	380
(168)	1 painter, $1,000 to $1,400	400
(169)	5 painters, $900 to $1,200 each	1,500
(170)	5 plumbers or steamfitters, at $1,020 each, to 5 mechanics, at $1,500 each	2,400
(171)	2 plumber's helpers, $840 to $960 each	240
(172)	2 plumber's helpers, $720 to $960 each	480
(173)	1 blacksmith, $900, to 1 mechanic, $1,400	500
(174)	1 elevator machinist, $900, to 1 mechanic, $1,400	500
(175)	1 tinner or sheet-metal worker, $1,100 to $1,400	300
(176)	1 tinner's helper. $720 to $960	240
(177)	1 mechanic, $1,200, to 1 mechanical assistant, $1,500	300
(178)	3 mechanics, $1,200 to $1,500 each	900
(179)	1 instrument maker, $1,200 to 1 mechanic, $1500	300
(180)	1 mechanic $1,000 to $1,400	400
(181)	1 skilled laborer, $900 to $1,000	100
	Total	26,680

The CHAIRMAN. This would be what you would do if you had a lump-sum appropriation?

Mr. REESE. Yes.

Mr. ANDERSON. Are you asking enough increase in the lump-sum appropriation for a statutory roll covering these figures?

Mr. REESE. It can not be covered except by the project I have mentioned of allowing reimbursement from the bureaus. That, of course, plainly means an increased appropriation. If you give us $90,000 in a lump sum, then when we do a job of work for a bureau and secure reimbursement for the total amount, labor, and material, of course we would have more than $90,000.

The CHAIRMAN. The proposition of the reimbursement by the bureau seems to me to be a very bothersome proposition. There is a difference of about how much?

Mr. REESE. Between the present statutory roll and the proposed lump sum of $90,000 there is a difference of about $3,000.

The CHAIRMAN. Wouldn't the matter of the bookkeeping and the organization required by this extra trouble amount to more than $3,000?

Mr. REESE. I doubt it. There would only be a few vouchers to prepare, one for each bureau for which work was done——

The CHAIRMAN (interposing). That would mean a clerk for each bureau?

Mr. REESE. Oh, no; the present clerical force could handle it all.

Mr. HARRISON. We can determine the cost of every piece of work done at the shops, and we can examine the cost to see if it is reasonable. But the greatest advantage is that it puts a check on the bureaus. If they have to pay for the work from their own funds, they will be more careful.

The CHAIRMAN. In other words, the hog would rather eat your corn than his own?

Mr. HARRISON. That is it; it puts it on a businesslike basis.

Mr. HAUGEN. How much are those mechanics underpaid, compared to people outside?

Mr. REESE. Underpaid?

Mr. HAUGEN. Yes. Here is a man at $1,800.

Mr. REESE. That is an assistant; the man next to the head.

Mr. HAUGEN. And this man $1,400.

Mr. REESE. Which one are you referring to—No. 144?

Mr. HAUGEN. Yes.

Mr. REESE. That man is a foreman of a small plumbing force we have. In the statement which I am inserting regarding wages paid mechanics outside the Department of Agriculture a foreman in a union establishment is listed at $2,900.

Mr. HAUGEN. Is that for the scale per hour? Let us drop to these others then.

Mr. REESE. Let us drop to the plain plumbers.

Mr. HAUGEN. Yes; to plain people.

Mr. REESE. In the District of Columbia?

Mr. HAUGEN. Which one have you now?

Mr. REESE. I am speaking of 144.

Mr. HAUGEN. You said he was a foreman.

Mr. REESE. Yes, sir. Let us drop to another man.

Mr. HAUGEN. There is some difference between a foreman having hundreds of people under him and one with only a few.

Mr. REESE. Drop to 170.

Mr. HAUGEN. One hundred and seventy?

Mr. REESE. Yes, sir; those now paid $1,020.

Mr. HAUGEN. Well, are all those people high class—above the average?

Mr. REESE. They are all good workmen.

Mr. HAUGEN. They are all supposed to be good workmen, aren't they, whether in private employment or not?
Mr. REESE. They are supposed to be good workmen.
Mr. HAUGEN. Are all those people superintendents and foremen?
Mr. REESE. Oh, no.
Mr. HAUGEN. What are these people at $1,200—assistant engineer, for instance, $1,200?
Mr. REESE. That is the watch engineers. We have a power house which requires 24 hours a day attention.
Mr. HAUGEN. The chief engineer doesn't work 24 hours?
Mr. REESE. He works eight hours and then shifts after that.
Mr. HAUGEN. And then it takes three shifts?
Mr. REESE. Three shifts.
Mr. HAUGEN. But he shouldn't have three credits; let us get at the comparison. How does it compare with the engineer's pay outside? How does it compare, per hour?
Mr. REESE. I have it per annum, not per hour; for nonunion chief engineer, $2,607, and assistant engineers, from $1,560——
Mr. HAUGEN (interposing). Get down to your hour schedule, so we can get at it.
Mr. REESE. I haven't got an hour schedule.
Mr. HAUGEN. You had it a minute ago. You gave us the carpenter's schedule.
Mr. REESE. That is the 75 cents an hour minimum rate in the agreement between the Carpenters' District Council and the builders' associations.
Mr. HAUGEN. Do you accept that statement?
Mr. REESE. Yes, sir.
Mr. HAUGEN. Seventy-five cents an hour?
Mr. REESE. Yes, sir.
Mr. HAUGEN. Your carpenters, how much are they paid?
Mr. REESE. One thousand two hundred dollars is the highest, and down to $900.
Mr. HAUGEN. How much are they underpaid, according to that schedule?
Mr. REESE. The difference of between $1,200 and about $1,800.
Mr. HAUGEN. How many hours do they work?
Mr. REESE. Seven and one-half hours.
Mr. HAUGEN. At 75 cents an hour that is about $5.62 per day. How many days of leave?
Mr. REESE. They are entitled under the law to 30 days annual leave and 30 days sick leave. They do not always get it all.
Mr. HAUGEN. Seventy-two days?
Mr. REESE. Sixty days.
Mr. HAUGEN. And then they have holidays?
Mr. REESE. Seven holidays.
Mr. HAUGEN. And 52 Sundays, and Saturday afternoons at times?
Mr. REESE. Yes, sir.
Mr. HAUGEN. They are being paid from $1,200 to $1,800 salary and $120 bonus. If they take all the leave and holidays they work seven and one-half hours for about 240 days a year, which would amount to about $1,350 at 75 cents per hour.
Mr. REESE. We are asking $1,200 to $1,500.

Mr. HAUGEN. Now, then, they are getting $1,200 to $1,500, besides annual and sick leave. They are overpaid now.

Mr. REESE. No, sir; I don't think so.

Mr. HAUGEN. They are probably not $1,200 men, but I am speaking of the $1,500 men.

Mr. REESE. The solicitor in his remarks mentioned something that is absolutely true—the increase in the cost of living.

Mr. HAUGEN. But we are discussing the wages paid by this department and the others; let us stick to that. We all have to pay the high cost of living, and I presume this scale is fixed upon the present cost of living.

Mr. REESE. These statutory salaries have been in existence for years; this scale here of $6 per day——

Mr. HAUGEN (interposing). What is the present scale? I understood you to say this was the present scale.

Mr. REESE. It is the scale for carpenters according to an agreement between the carpenters and their employers covering the period July 1, 1918, to December 31, 1918.

Mr. HAUGEN. It is quite recent then?

Mr. REESE. Yes, sir.

Mr. HAUGEN. According to your figures the $1,200 men would be underpaid about $30 and the $1,500 men overpaid $180.

Mr. REESE. We are trying to get these men up to what looks to us to be a fairly living wage.

Mr. HAUGEN. And we are trying to do justice to the employees and the Government; that is our sworn duty. We are not trying to be unfair to the individual or with Congress. I think when a man comes and says that anybody is underpaid he should be able to verify that with the facts. You have fallen down in that.

Mr. REESE. In what respect, sir?

Mr. HAUGEN. I asked you for a comparison of the wages paid outside or in any department.

Mr. REESE. And I endeavor to show that these men I mentioned made more.

Mr. HAUGEN. They work eight hours a day and get paid for what they do; and if you apply the same wage, the same scale, to those in the department, they would in most cases get more.

Mr. REESE. How about the comparison with the mechanics in the Department of Agriculture and other governmental establishments?

Mr. HAUGEN. Oh, well, we can't keep up this competition; we have had competition between these departments and I can't see the justice in that. All we can do is to do justice to our employees, and if other committees do not do it we are not to blame.

The CHAIRMAN. Is there anything further? We can sit here and talk about this until doomsday and not get anywhere. Is there anything further, Mr. Reese?

MISCELLANEOUS EXPENSES.

Mr. REESE. I would like to speak a moment of the miscellaneous expenses on page 197.

The CHAIRMAN. All right.

Mr. REESE. There is no change in the verbiage or amount.

RENT IN THE DISTRICT OF COLUMBIA.

Mr. REESE. The next page, 198, the item of rent in the District of Columbia, the same statement applies—no change in the language and no change in the amount.

Mr. McLAUGHLIN. What did you do with the Atlantic Building?

Mr. REESE. We still have it.

Mr. McLAUGHLIN. At what rate?

Mr. REESE. The department agreed to pay $4,500 increase.

Mr. McLAUGHLIN. Which makes a total of $22,500.

Mr. REESE. Yes, sir; they asked an increase of $16,000 which the department absolutely refused.

Mr. HAUGEN. What is the policy of the department as to future rents?

Mr. REESE. The policy is that we will not rent if we can get the free space we expect from the War Department; we have, in fact, a promise to-day of space, with a tentative promise of more space when available.

Mr. HAUGEN. I presume there is much vacant space already.

Mr. REESE. There is not as much vacant as we expected, for the reason that the War Department finds itself in need of space still to accommodate offices which are now in rented buildings, and also, I am told, they have to provide storage for all the records of the draft boards in the United States, which will be sent to Washington and housed here; and that is a big proposition.

Mr. HAUGEN. Our understanding is that thousands of clerks are being dismissed every day and that ought to make room.

Mr. THOMPSON. Where did you get that understanding, Mr. Haugen?

Mr. HAUGEN. That is general talk.

Mr. THOMPSON. I have never heard it. I have heard it, but I mean I have never heard it verified.

The CHAIRMAN. Can you give the committee any statement of the emergency clerks who have left the department since the armistice was signed?

Mr. REESE. As a matter of fact, the force in Washington has been decreasing without any special separations or dismissals.

The CHAIRMAN. I can see how there would be few separations on account of the work caused by the food-stimulation act.

Mr. McLAUGHLIN. Can you give us the number separated from the service since the armistice was signed?

Mr. HARRISON. We can get the number and insert it in the record.

(The statement referred to follows:)

Statement showing appointments to and separations from the Department of Agriculture in Washington, D. C., since the signing of the armistice on Nov. 11, 1918.

	Appointed.	Separated.		Appointed.	Separated.
Nov. 11 to 16	113	64	Dec. 15 to 21	49	67
Nov. 17 to 23	77	105	Dec. 22 to 28	53	51
Nov. 24 to 30	82	113	Dec. 29 to Jan. 4	27	23
Dec. 1 to 7	80	81			
Dec. 8 to 14	41	49	Total	522	553

Net decrease in number of employees, 31.

Mr. HAUGEN. When may we look for the War Department to vacate these buildings and make the space available for the Department of Agriculture?

Mr. REESE. They have been vacating some, but apparently they are shifting their own units into the quarters.

Mr. HAUGEN. How much did you ask for?

Mr. REESE. The same amount; in view of the uncertainty as to vacated buildings, it seemed wise to estimate for the amount now provided.

Mr. HAUGEN. If there is any uncertainty I think we should make it certain.

Mr. HARRISON. Mr. Haugen, the Secretary of War, at the request of the President, has designated Mr. Dorr to consider the whole situation with reference to the use of these emergency buildings, and we have had the matter up constantly with him. In the meantime, the Secretary is refusing to spend the $25,000 that was provided in the food production act for rental. I understand we have a promise of space in one of the buildings on the Mall in the near future.

Mr. HAUGEN. If there is any question about it I think it should be made certain.

Mr. HARRISON. We are not going to spend the money if we can get these other buildings.

Mr. HAUGEN. That is not the question. Are we going to spend $158,000 for rent?

Mr. HARRISON. No, sir; we are not going to spend it if we get the other buildings.

Mr. HAUGEN. Is there any question about it?

Mr. HARRISON. Yes, sir; there is a question. The Secretary has been active in trying to get this space. We tried to get the building at Fourteenth and B Streets NW., which was built for the War Industries Board, and we found that the Secretary of the Treasury was trying to get space in it for one of his bureaus, I think, the Internal Revenue; and the Secretary of Commerce is also seeking a very large building for his force for the next census; they have begun to organize their force for that. Now, the War Department is going to take a long time to discontinue some of its activities and they are moving some of their offices into the new buildings. We have taken the matter up with the President and the Secretary of War and every other official we could think of.

Mr. HAUGEN. The Food Administration building, is that being made vacant now?

Mr. HARRISON. One of their buildings is. We have had under consideration the possibility of using this building, but, as it involves the payment of ground rent, we could not take it over.

Mr. WASON. Is there any question about the Fuel Administration building being made vacant?

Mr. HARRISON. I do not know. The whole matter is in the hands of Mr. Dorr, and we have laid our situation before him.

Mr. WASON. The United States Government owns the land?

Mr. HARRISON. No; the Food Administration rented the land.

Mr. REESE. I think I may answer Mr. Wason's question by the statement that the Fuel Administration building stands on the same general tract of land that the Food Administration does, namely, north of B Street, and therefore on private property and not on Government property at all.

Mr. HAUGEN. I think this item of $158,000 is worth going into; the matter of rent that is paid when these other buildings are becoming vacant.

Mr. THOMPSON. Was there any extra appropriation in 1919 over 1918?

Mr. REESE. Yes, sir.

Mr. THOMPSON. How much?

Mr. REESE. Fifteen thousand dollars.

Mr. THOMPSON. And you are asking $15,000 for 1920 again?

Mr. REESE. Yes, sir.

Mr. THOMPSON. Then you didn't take into consideration that you are to get any space out of these vacated buildings?

Mr. REESE. At the time these estimates were made up and submitted the country was still at war and no consideration could be given to space in vacated buildings because the possibility of securing such space had not arisen. It has come only since the armistice was signed, November 11, 1918. Even at this date what we may get in the matter of space in vacated buildings is uncertain.

Mr. THOMPSON. And you did not take into consideration the reduction of the force of the Department of Agriculture by reason of the cessation of the war?

Mr. REESE. No; and for the same reason. When these estimates were made the war was still on. That, too, as I see it, is still a matter of uncertainty; we don't know yet what we have to do.

The CHAIRMAN. There will be some reduction, without doubt?

Mr. REESE. I think there will. But it is impossible at this time to say how much.

The CHAIRMAN. Was the $15,000 which was given you due to the war emergency?

Mr. REESE. We had $15,000 provided in the emergency act for rents, and we rented buildings out of it. We couldn't tell when it would come to an end; if it had come to an end and left us without money for rent it would have interfered with the work. We secured $15,000 for that reason.

The CHAIRMAN. As a matter of fact, you have to carry out the provisions of the food production act this present year?

Mr. REESE. Yes, sir.

The CHAIRMAN. And you have $15,000 for rent?

Mr. REESE. Yes; but we will not expend it for rent unless we have to.

Mr. HARRISON. We have canceled some options that we had.

The CHAIRMAN. When the $15,000 was asked for did the department anticipate a large increase in the force on account of the war?

Mr. REESE. That is true, but we also wanted to make sure that we could have the buildings we had rented and that we wouldn't be left high and dry without money.

The CHAIRMAN. Doesn't it stand to reason that the department may be able to get a good deal of space in these buildings about to be vacated?

Mr. REESE. As Mr. Harrison has explained, we have not been able to get anything definitely. They promised us 13,000 square feet with some more in the future.

The CHAIRMAN. How much would that cost you?

Mr. REESE. It all depends on what part of the city it is in. Uptown it would cost 80 cents a square foot, and that is very moderate rent.

The CHAIRMAN. That is $10,000 or $12,000. Suppose it is a dollar a square foot, could we reduce this provision $10,000 or $15,000?

Mr. REESE. I would not like to see it done.

The CHAIRMAN. I wish you would look into that very carefully and let us know how much you can reduce this appropriation.

Mr. LEE. If you should get a definite promise of space you could afford to cut this amount?

Mr. REESE. Perhaps, but, considering the uncertainty as to what we may get in any vacated buildings and the department's continued need for space for regular projects, I strongly deprecate reducing this appropriation for rent.

The CHAIRMAN. If you are sure that you will get 13,000 square feet of space you could reduce this $13,000 at least.

Mr. REESE. I wouldn't want to state that definitely, Mr. Chairman, without going into the matter very carefully.

Mr. HAUGEN. All these years we have been having this Maltby Building standing idle, a building 50 per cent superior to the fire traps hired by the Department of Agriculture. It is a disgrace that these people are put into the buildings we have. I understand they are now painting this building and moving in there.

Mr. HARRISON. They were repairing it a year and a half ago.

Mr. HAUGEN. They are repairing it now and some people are moving in there.

Mr. HARRISON. The objection we had to it was that it was not structurally sound.

Mr. HAUGEN. It is sound now?

Mr. HARRISON. They apparently spent a considerable sum in fixing it up.

Mr. HAUGEN. Yes, I went through it myself.

The CHAIRMAN. Is there anything else? If not the Weather Bureau comes next, page 27. We will hear Prof. Marvin.

AGRICULTURE APPROPRIATION BILL.

COMMITTEE ON AGRICULTURE,
HOUSE OF REPRESENTATIVES,
Monday, January 6, 1919.

OFFICE OF FARM MANAGEMENT.

The CHAIRMAN. Turn to page 22, the Office of Farm Management. Mr. Christie, the Assistant Secretary, will present the estimates.

STATEMENT OF MR. G. I. CHRISTIE, ASSISTANT SECRETARY, UNITED STATES DEPARTMENT OF AGRICULTURE.

The CHAIRMAN. Mr. Christie, the statutory roll involves no increase in salaries above $2,500.

Mr. CHRISTIE. I think not, Mr. Chairman.

The CHAIRMAN. Is that true, Mr. Harrison?

Mr. HARRISON. Yes; there are no increases in the statutory roll above $2,500.

The CHAIRMAN. Then we will take up the lump-sum appropriation on page 25.

Mr. MCLAUGHLIN. Were those transfers from the lump sum made at the same salaries?

Mr. HARRISON. They were made at the same salaries in every instance.

The CHAIRMAN. Throughout the entire department?

Mr. HARRISON. Yes.

Mr. MCLAUGHLIN. There comes up the question again that a lot of these men were employed at emergency salaries for temporary work.

The CHAIRMAN. We have already covered that very fully.

Mr. MCLAUGHLIN. This just emphasizes it—the repetition of it.

The CHAIRMAN. Mr. Christie, I understand there is a proposition in the department to thoroughly reorganize the Office of Farm Management. The committee would be very glad if you would tell us something about the plans you have in mind for that work for the next fiscal year.

Mr. CHRISTIE. The work in farm management, which includes that of agricultural economics, is perhaps one of the most important lines of agricultural work that we have at the present time. The Secretary has, perhaps, given as much thought to agricultural economics and to farm management as to any other one subject that we have before us in the Department of Agriculture. When he came to the Department of Agriculture he was especially interested in two big things, marketing and economics, because of his training, because of his direct interest in these subjects, because of his connection with the agricultural college, and because of his interest in the broader aspects of agriculture itself. He has been able to establish a large and efficient Bureau of Markets, and I think this committee is familiar with the very excellent work that is being carried on. He has attempted to develop an Office of Farm Management that would carry out in some measure his views along that line. The farm-management work originally was under the Bureau of Plant Industry, but it was agreed that it should stand more definitely apart from any one bureau and so the Office of Farm Management was transferred to the Secretary's Office.

Mr. ANDERSON. When?

Mr. CHRISTIE. July 1, 1915. Dr. Spillman was placed in charge of this, and in the work the study of farm practice, farm business, and farm organization has been taken up. One phase of the work to which the Office of Farm Management gave some time was the study of the cost of production of various farm products. After this work had been going on for some time, the Secretary of Agriculture, hearing criticisms of the studies from several sources, conferred with Dr. Spillman and expressed his views and ideas of the best means of conducting such lines of investigations. The Secretary suggested that the methods and plan of procedure should be modified.

Little attention seems to have been given to the suggestions, for the same loose and unsatisfactory methods continued.

We have not been able to get exactly what we wanted out of these studies for the reason that they have been carried on by the department too much alone. I find in making a study of the work that there has been little agreement between the Department of Agriculture and the agricultural colleges in making studies along farm-management lines. The Office of Farm Management is cooperating with three institutions—New York, Minnesota, and Wisconsin. These institutions are conducting the work largely according to their own individual ideas. Now, it is the idea of the Secretary that, if this work is to go forward, it should be unified—it should be placed on one basis; and so he has asked us to give some attention to that point.

Recently we invited to the department representatives of the agricultural colleges, of the departments of agricultural economics and divisions of farm management. With these men we have conferred on the way to proceed to outline the farm-management work. We then, at their suggestion, have secured Prof. Adams, head of the farm-management work of California University; Prof. Falconer, head of agricultural economics of the Ohio University; Prof. Taylor, head of agricultural economics of the University of Wisconsin; and other leaders to come to Washington to collaborate with us and help us place this work on a solid foundation. These men are now at work and are attempting to outline the projects in such a way that they will be satisfactory not only to the agricultural-economics and farm-management people of the Department of Agriculture, but will also be satisfactory to the agricultural-economics and farm-management people and related interests in the colleges. We will have the full cooperation of the colleges in this movement. Several of the men have been here and have conferred with us and advised with us, and we are getting the plans to a point where we hope to reach an early agreement on them.

When we do that along these lines and get down to a working basis, I think we will have made a big move for fundamental farm-management study. It is a work that must be carried on in a big way. There are many lines of farm-management work that are regional in character; it is not possible to take them up by States and investigate them and complete them as individual State problems. They are really Federal problems, since they are regional in scope, and can not be confined to State lines. For this reason there must be the very closest cooperation between the farm-management departments of the agricultural colleges of the States and the Federal Government in the work which we propose to carry on.

Also in the study of farm practice and in the study of methods and farm organization we propose to establish that same relationship. It is also the idea of the Secretary that, since agricultural economics is a fundamental part of farm management, some of the best agricultural-economics people who can be had should be brought into the department and associated here in the work.

The projects of the Office of Farm Management now carried on along the lines of farm practice, farm organization, and special problems, such as the preparation of an atlas of American agriculture, are desirable, and through these the department is furnishing large and valuable aid to farmers. It is proposed to continue this work with such changes and modifications as will strengthen it and make it of even greater value. It is not the plan to lessen our efforts along farm-management and farm-economics lines, but to enlarge the work and render the largest possible assistance.

This gives you, in a general way, the plans we have at this time.

Mr. ANDERSON. I gathered from a statement made by the Secretary some time ago, in response to a Senate resolution, that the work that has heretofore been done by the Office of Farm Management, so far as it related to the cost of production, at least, was practically worthless. Do you agree to that?

Mr. CHRISTIE. I agree to that to a certain degree and to certain lines of work that were mentioned. The line of work in question, in the letter of the Secretary, was the cost of wheat production.

Mr. ANDERSON. And the same methods, I take it, were pursued in respect to ascertaining the cost of other products, were they not?

Mr. CHRISTIE. To a certain extent, except this, that when a man gathers data on sugar beets on one method from 1,025 sugar-beet farmers, he has data that you would value a great deal more than you would data obtained by the same method from 158 farmers in the wheat belt taken up on a hurry-up trip.

Mr. ANDERSON. What, specifically, is the difficulty with the Spillman method of determining the cost of production of wheat?

Mr. CHRISTIE. The criticism of the methods of determining the cost of production of wheat was that the workers did not gather data on the cost of production of wheat. For instance, an elaborate questionnaire on the items covering the cost of production of wheat was outlined. Then two men were sent into several of the States east of the Rocky Mountains and two other men into Pacific-coast States, with this questionnaire in hand to gather data on cost of production. The men selected an area in Kansas, another one in Missouri, one in Illinois, one in Oklahoma, and one in Indiana. The representatives of the Office of Farm Management then visited in these States 158 farmers. They found the farmer very busy; so they sat down and talked to him a little while, and, instead of filling in the questionnaire, they many times took notes in a book. They asked 8 or 10 questions of farmer A, questions 10 to 14 of farmer B, and then questions 18 to 35 of farmer C. After interviewing 25 farmers in the district in this manner and 30 in another and 10 in another, those men came back, and with some general data they had in the office and some basic data from cost-accounting records they prepared a manuscript on the cost of production of wheat in the States east of the Rocky Mountains. Now, when this came to the Secretary's attention, he questioned, of course, the reliability of such data on the actual cost of the production of wheat.

Mr. ANDERSON. Would there be anywhere that you would find farmers who were keeping sufficiently accurate records so that they could answer a questionnaire of this character?

Mr. CHRISTIE. Perhaps not; but if you say you secured data from the farmer and you did not get it, then there is room for a question.

Mr. ANDERSON. I assume that the first step in securing the data on the cost of production of any article would be the use by somebody producing that article of a system of accounting that would give you that data. You have told us what you consider the deficiencies of the Spillman method. Have you worked out a method you intend to pursue?

Mr. CHRISTIE. That is a matter that is partially worked out at this moment. It will be carried Wednesday to Baltimore, when the National Farm Management Association meets, and we will confer with their members and modify it according to their suggestions, and then we will submit it to the agricultural colleges and farm-management men, when we hope to have it in such shape that it can be used.

Mr. ANDERSON. I am interested in knowing how, without any concrete plan to proceed with, you are able to estimate now what the expense of carrying out that plan will be?

Mr. CHRISTIE. Of course, we have the projects that were outlined for the department for this coming year. These will continue on practically the same basis. I am concerned with the reorganization of the methods and the practices to be followed.

Mr. ANDERSON. I may be mistaken about it, but it occurs to me the character of the organization you set up and the methods you pursue in ascertaining costs or any other investigation you make will have a very important bearing upon the cost of the service; and if you have a plan of procedure from which you can determine the cost of the service, I really am interested in knowing what it is.

Mr. HARRISON. Those things are being worked out now. The gentlemen mentioned by Mr. Christie came here only a few days ago, and they are working as rapidly as possible. It must be remembered that these estimates were submitted in October. The Secretary, in a recent statement to the agricultural editors, said that he hoped to present at a future time projects for an enlarged Office of Farm Management. This shows very clearly that he does not contemplate any curtailment of the work. On the contrary, he thinks it should be further developed and strengthened; and it involves not only studies of cost of production but matters of general farm practice and business management. That he recognizes the importance of farm economies and farm management is indicated by the fact that he has discussed these problems in his annual report on several occasions, as well as in public addresses.

Mr. ANDERSON. So far as this item is concerned now it is absolutely blind; it is not based on any known system of reorganization of farm-management work.

Mr. HARRISON. I would not say that because, as Mr. Christie has indicated, we expect to continue, generally speaking, the same lines of work that have been under way. It is more a question of methods than anything else.

Mr. CHRISTIE. It is more a question of methods than disbanding an organization and discarding what has been done and trying to establish a new department.

Mr. ANDERSON. It seems to me the committee ought to be in this position, whether it is or not: We have just made a discovery after we have spent some hundreds of thousands of dollars, that the work heretofore done under this bureau was practically without value, largely due to the fact that the organization and methods and ascertainment of results were faulty. Now, before we proceed to appropriate $218,000 and, as Mr. Harrison suggests, perhaps a larger amount, it seems to me the committee ought to be satisfied that the method of organization which is going to be followed in the future and the policies which are going to be followed in the future are likely, at least, to secure results that will have value.

Mr. CHRISTIE. I do not like the statement, Mr. Anderson, that the work of this bureau has all been worthless or faulty. The Office of Farm Management has done a lot of valuable and helpful work and is now doing a large amount of helpful work. There has been this one line which has been prominent, because the matter of fixing prices has been before the country. This has attracted some attention and has called forth some criticism. But I would not agree with the statement that all of the work of the Office of Farm Management has been bad or that the money has been wasted, for it has not.

The CHAIRMAN. Do you happen to know how long the department has been studying the cost of production of farm products? Is not that rather a recent work?

Mr. CHRISTIE. On any extensive basis it is recent, and the amount of money put into it is not large. We have other projects; farm practices being followed in the Southern States; farm practices being followed in the Pacific-coast States in the production of wheat; farm practices being followed in sugar-beet production, beef production, etc. Those are the projects that have consumed the money, and I think you will find from the publications of the Department of Agriculture that they have given results worth while. We should not allow one item to cloud the issue.

Mr. ANDERSON. Of course, I do not mean to suggest there was absolutely nothing of any value done by this bureau. My only impression has been, as to the information given before the committee here before, that this work on cost of production has been of a rather doubtful character, and exceedingly vague, and much of it absolutely absurd. Now, it may be that I expect too much, but as far as I am personally concerned, I would like to know something about the methods to be followed in the future, in respect to this particular proposition.

Mr. CHRISTIE. We can give you the three items.

Mr. ANDERSON. If you have not got it now, we would like to have it later on.

Mr. CHRISTIE. We have it near enough, I think. to answer the question now. To determine the cost of production it is fundamental that cost-accounting work shall be conducted. I do not think we can get along without it. And that is one fundamental principle we are establishing now. The cost-accounting work, as you state, is work that is somewhat expensive; it requires time, must be carefully done, and must be done not only in one State but in several States along one line. It is the aim to establish relations with the State agricultural colleges and to do the work in a thorough, satisfactory way.

Now, to supplement that, there is the survey method that has been used pretty largely by the department and is used largely by many institutions. This reaches out in an extensive way and touches large numbers of farmers. The survey method should be limited to a few factors on which we can get fairly accurate information in a ready manner. Then the cost accounting would furnish us the basic data for the relation of labor, the relation of fertilizer, and the relation of the feed of live stock to the production of crops, production of milk, etc., and such other factors as will be of value in the different studies.

Mr. ANDERSON. Let me be sure I understand what you have in mind when you say cost accounting, because I am a little bit of a crank on that subject myself. Is it the intention, then, to find a number of farmers who will be at least typical of the region who will keep a set of books on the basis of cost accounting in accordance with the uniform method in which you expect to get these data?

Mr. CHRISTIE. That is the general idea at the present time.

Mr. ANDERSON. Then you anticipate, I presume, that you will have to keep a sufficient supervisory force to see that those books are kept up and to supervise the people who are carrying out the project?

Mr. CHRISTIE. We will keep this on a farm basis. There is a method of cost accounting followed now where, in the case of beef production, the study covers only beef production. It fails to consider the production of the crops, the utilization of labor at all times of the year, and a number of other factors that really ought to be studied. So in future cost-accounting work it is our desire to study the whole farm.

The CHAIRMAN. And out of the study of the whole farm you will get the cost of the individual thing you study?

Mr. CHRISTIE. Its relative cost.

Mr. ANDERSON. The principles of cost accounting are the same, I take it, without reference to what business they are applied to. I assume you have to have some special method, perhaps, with respect to agriculture. But you must have a sound basis of the principles of cost accounting on which to proceed in the first instance. Has anybody in your bureau made any study of the question of cost accounting as it is used in commercial establishments?

Mr. CHRISTIE. Prof. Adams, of California University, has been connected with that work for some time. He has been in commercial work and knows something of it as he has been close to it. Then Prof. Falconer, who is an eastern man and a graduate of Wisconsin University, also is well versed and has a good grasp of the subject.

The CHAIRMAN. I have thought a good deal about this cost-of-production business myself. Take North Dakota, for instance, where some portions of the State produce wheat some years at the rate of 4 bushels to the acre and some years at the rate of 14 bushels to the acre; or, here you have two farmers side by side, one a thoroughly good farmer and a man of brains and intelligence, who knows how to handle machinery, and here you have another one who is ignorant, slovenly in his methods, who may not be so energetic, certainly not so sensible. What are you going to do in a case of that kind? It seems to me you would have to have a standard of intelligence by which to measure the whole thing from time to time. To my mind, I do not see that it is possible to get at the cost of production.

Mr. CHRISTIE. You must take into consideration in the case of the 4-bushel man the methods used.

The CHAIRMAN. In other words, your conclusion would be based upon the proposition of the general average of farm methods?

Mr. CHRISTIE. It must be. Of course, we have become confused in this matter this year because we have been talking of prices. Our work really should be on the basis of cost of production. The cost of production is one thing and the price is another. These figures that have been given to Congress have relation to the price, and they have been beyond cost, because it was claimed that it was necessary to stimulate production; it was necessary to encourage the farmers to use high-priced labor; it was necessary to have him gamble with the seasons, high seed, and high fertilizer. So the prices we have come to speak of are something different from the question of costs we are trying to determine. I think when we get that established in the farmer's mind it will be helpful.

Mr. HAUGEN. Do you think there is ever any possibility of working out any plan that will enable you to give information of any value whatever as to the cost of production of wheat?

Mr. CHRISTIE. Yes; I think we will have information that will be of great value. I would not say that we will have information that would alone be sufficient for Congress to fix one price that will cover the cost of production on all the different farms in all the different regions under all the different conditions.

Mr. HAUGEN. Then of what value is it?

Mr. CHRISTIE. It is of value to the individual farmer; it is of value to the community; it is of value to the State.

Mr. HAUGEN. The cost varies with every farm?

Mr. CHRISTIE. Yes.

Mr. HAUGEN. And on a productive farm you can produce wheat at a less cost than on an unproductive farm; and land costing $10 an acre will produce wheat sometimes just as well as land costing $100 an acre; and sometimes it costs less to produce wheat on land costing $10 an acre than it does on land costing $100 an acre. The chairman has called your attention to the different methods of farming, and all of those things will have to be taken into consideration, and the result will be that you will find the cost varies according to the number of farms. And then what value could that information be? Spillman kept books for 137 farmers in Pennsylvania, and he gave the information on those 137 farms in Pennsylvania. That child has been declared faulty and laughed out of court.

Mr. HEFLIN. What is the information he gave?

Mr. HAUGEN. It is in the book. He gave the average for 137 farms, and he showed the growing of oats was more productive than wheat. And, as we all know who have had any experience in farming, oats might do very well in one year, the yield is large, and the price is up, and there would be more profit then in oats than there would be in wheat. Now, the climate and the method of farming have all to do with it.

Mr. HEFLIN. Do you recall now the average cost of production in that region that he mentioned?

Mr. HAUGEN. No; I do not. But it is in the record. I want to know if there can be any hope of getting any information along this line that is of any value whatever? We are asked here to appropriate $218,000; yet, as I said, the child has been laughed out of court. There is not a thing in the bill that has been criticised and ridiculed as much as this proposition; and I took it from a lot of stuff that had gone into the record that the department had dropped it.

Mr. CHRISTIE. There is no question but what we are able to get data of great value to agriculture in regions and in States and communities so that the farmers will know more definitely what it is costing them to produce these various products.

Mr. HAUGEN. You speak of information—a lot of information—but the farmer wants information of value; he does not want information that will mislead him.

Mr. CHRISTIE. But the right kind of investigation should get accurate information.

Mr. HEFLIN. Would it help you if, through publication, you would suggest to the wheat growers whom you are going to ask for this information and to try to get them to keep accounts?

Mr. CHRISTIE. More farmers each year, as a result of farm-management demonstrations, are keeping books. There have been distributed more than 150,000 farm account books to farmers, who have agreed to keep an accurate and careful account of their farm business and give us the figures for the advice and assistance we have given them in return. Out of these records we get a lot of information which should pave the way, as you suggest, for an accurate, careful cost-accounting system.

Mr. HAUGEN. Oh, well, 150,000 is not much out of seven million.

Mr. CHRISTIE. The records from this number of farms should be of great value.

Mr. HAUGEN. It is just a question of how much it will cost to get these books in the hands of the farmers. And they have been keeping books. Spillman prepared books for them and he kept the books and gave them the results. But, after all, you had nothing to do with that. But those are the facts in the case, and the whole thing has been ridiculed, and here we are asked to appropriate $218,000 again.

The CHAIRMAN. You don't want to be understood as saying that this total appropriation is to be used in studies of the cost of production?

Mr. CHRISTIE. We must have this understood, that only a part of the funds is to go into specific work of that kind.

The CHAIRMAN. And you would like to be distinctly understood that this specific work which we have been discussing will take up only a small proportion of this appropriation?

Mr. CHRISTIE. Yes, sir.

Mr. HAUGEN. What is this money to be used for—what projects?

Mr. CHRISTIE. The projects, with proposed expenditures, are as follows:

General administration:
    Planning and directing farm-management investigations and the business and clerical routine incident thereto _____ $5, 200
Farm economics:
    Detailed studies of crop and live-stock enterprises, involving labor requirements, rotations, the farm business, best methods of farm practice, approved practices in feeding and handling live stock, etc _____ 38, 460
Farm organization:
    Regional investigations of the practices, organization, and administration of individual farms, and studies of types and systems of farming, with a view to enable farmers to improve their systems of farm management; study of farm equipment; cooperative farm-management investigations, etc _____ 124, 900
Cost-of-production studies:
    Determination by farm-management surveys, cost accounting, and other approved methods, unit elements of production in crop and live-stock enterprises _____ 23, 800
Special farm-management problems:
    Correlation of statistical data covering the relation of geographic factors to farm enterprises; the relation of farm practice to crop yields; practical systems of farm bookkeeping for farmers' use__ 25, 800
                                                                      218, 160

Mr. HAUGEN. Where do these county agents come in?

Mr. CHRISTIE. County agents are not investigators. County agents are men who take information that has been collected and carry it to farmers.

Mr. HAUGEN. They are sort of ornaments?

Mr. CHRISTIE. No; they are hardly that.

Mr. HAUGEN. I have been trying to find out what are the functions of the county agents?

Mr. CHRISTIE. They are supposed to give information to the farmers and as far as possible secure its application.

The CHAIRMAN. The county agent was never intended as an investigator, but a disseminator—a " walking teacher."

Mr. CHRISTIE. He is the man who gets in close touch with the farmers and gives them needed valuable help.

Mr. HAUGEN. What are you going to do with this?

Mr. CHRISTIE. We have the work on the agricultural geography, and then we have projects on farm practices, farm economics, and farm organization. For instance, we will study the practice to be followed in the production of meat, production of wheat, sugar beets. farm organization, etc.

Mr. HAUGEN. Go into that a little more in detail. What have you in mind in that?

Mr. CHRISTIE. In the corn belt the practice of wintering beef cows is a big question. We send men who study the practices on twenty, thirty, fifty, or a hundred farms in Missouri or Iowa, and from that we show the general and most desirable practices that are being followed, and out of that study we are able to make recommendations to the farmers as to the best practices to follow.

Mr. HAUGEN. What would you say about the wintering of cows in Iowa or any other State? Have you given that much study?

Mr. CHRISTIE. The Office of Farm Management has done some work in Iowa and has secured much helpful information for the farmers on this subject.

Mr. HAUGEN. The thought was this, Why duplicate the work?

Mr. CHRISTIE. We are cooperating with the colleges, and then the same practice in Iowa really extends into Illinois or into Missouri or over into Indiana. Our work is to unify these methods and extend the work from one State to the other.

Mr. HAUGEN. What I am afraid of is that investigations will be carried on by one State and they will be duplicated by the Federal Government, and in the end we will not know where we are at all.

Mr. CHRISTIE. We are not duplicating in that work.

The CHAIRMAN. Anything further?

Mr. HAUGEN. Only this: You say you are going to use for ascertaining the cost of production a part of this $218,000?

Mr. CHRISTIE. We will use a part of this fund.

Mr. HAUGEN. Some things a scientist thinks a great deal of and a practical farmer can't figure it out that way. I beg to agree with them in a great many ways, but when it comes to the practical side of it I have had a little experience.

Mr. CHRISTIE. I want to say that the heads of the Kansas, Minnesota, South Dakota, Wisconsin, and Indiana State Colleges are all asking for this cooperative help.

FARM LABOR.

The CHAIRMAN. Suppose you tell us about the labor item of the emergency bill, carrying an appropriation of $162,000.

Mr. CHRISTIE. The idea of the Secretary is simply to continue the organization that we now have in the various States and render assistance to farmers in securing farm help. It is our feeling, from what study we have made, that the need for this work will be nearly as great this coming year as it was this past year. We gave to the Army and to the military forces nearly a million men from the farms. For every man that went off the farm to the military forces there was about a man and a half, or a million and one-half, that went into industries.

The CHAIRMAN. That makes two and one-half million farmers.

Mr. CHRISTIE. Two and one-half million men have gone off the farms, and that will account for the farm-labor shortage that exists at this time and has existed this past season.

The CHAIRMAN. Let me ask you two questions: First, what is your opinion as to the return of the farm boys to the farms—to their old vocations? What has been Canada's experience in that direction?

Mr. CHRISTIE. Up to this time no large percentage of them has gone back. I am speaking of those men who have returned up to this time. Of course, we are expecting that our men, who have not been away as long as Canada's men, will return in larger numbers. A large number of the Canadian men have been away since 1914, and the longer they are away from the farms the more they are weaned from the farms.

The CHAIRMAN. Do you think there will be 90 per cent?

Mr. CHRISTIE. That is pretty high.

Mr. HAUGEN. Don't you think that is very largely due to the high wages paid to farmers——

The CHAIRMAN. I was going to ask that question. What percentage of this million and one-half men who have gone into the industries will, when conditions become more or less normal, return to the farms?

Mr. CHRISTIE. That is going to depend entirely on the conditions we create on the farms before they return.

The CHAIRMAN. It is largely a wage condition, is it not?

Mr. CHRISTIE. It is wages and homes—a chance to live. A great number of those men are married. If we can put homes on the farms where these married men can live with their families, rear their children, and have a place for a cow and garden, I have no fear of getting those men back to the farms.

The CHAIRMAN. I had a great experience in my office here not long ago. A boy came in and said, "There is a colored man out there waiting for you. He says you knew him well." I said, "Show him in." He proved to be a farmer that lived near our plantation and owned a farm of 140 acres. His father used to belong to my grandfather. He was a very successful farmer. I said, "What are you doing here, Henry?" He said, "I am down here at Hopewell, Va., working at the munition factory." I asked him what he was making a day, and he said $8. There he was; he had come 500 miles. I imagine as soon as that munition factory closes and this old darkey don't get an $8-a-day job there or around here, he is going back to his farm, but I imagine that it is going to be a slow process to get these men back to the farm.

Mr. CHRISTIE. There will have to be some inducements for them to go back to the farms, and I think the good farms will offer those inducements. We have just made a study of the question, "How I keep help on my farm," and have some interesting stories. It is a common every-day illustration of people in agricultural communities to show how much a farmer gives to his help. He gives them good wages, gives them their garden, a cow, a couple of pigs, all the chickens they want to raise; many times he furnishes them with their meat; he usually keeps a horse and buggy, and many farmers furnish him an automobile and his fuel. About the only thing that man has to buy is some sugar and a few groceries and some clothes. When a man has an opportunity like that there is no great trouble in keeping him on the farm. There is a shortage of homes for that class of men; we don't have them on our farms. We usually have one house on the farm, and the help lives with the farmer's family. The women are rebelling and calling for help. The farms are not only short on men, but I think we will agree on this: They are in need of women. They can't hire girls as easily as they can hire men. When they have a tenant, his wife will be out there and will assist with the washing and the housework. The children grow up rapidly and will do many chores. When you take one married man you are many times getting additional help.

The CHAIRMAN. That is all very interesting, but that is outside of this $162,000. What are you going to use that for?

Mr. CHRISTIE. We have placed a man known as a farm-help specialist in each State. This man works through the agricultural college, and has been locating sources of supply of labor and has been helping get men to the farms that need them. One of the big things he did this past summer, when he found he could not get regular laborers, was to tell business men of the great needs of the farmers and to organize thousands of those men of the cities to help the farmers harvest their crops.

Another thing we are doing is to show the farmer how they can use better equipment and thus in a material way reduce the amount of labor. One man I know has lost three men off the farm to the war—one right after another. He had a herd of 30 milch cows. When he was about to call a sale I advised him to get a milking machine. He milks his cows now in less time than he and his hired man could milk them before. Farmers are using self-feeders in connection with hogs and cattle. They are using sulky plows where one man will drive four, five, or six horses where before they drove two horses with a walking plow.

In one community last year I was able myself to get five farmers to cooperate in harvesting their wheat. They went to one farm and with two binders cut the grain and had three men shock it. They then went to a second farm, and so on.

A farm-help specialist is able to render a big service.

The CHAIRMAN. What is the Employment Service doing along this line?

Mr. CHRISTIE. The Employment Service establishes offices in cities. They have a man who wants a job and they have a man who wants help. It is the aim of the Employment Service to bring the two together. It is found, however, that where a farmer wants a man he applies to the county agent. The county agents this year have placed directly farm hands on over 100,000 farms.

The CHAIRMAN. I am glad to hear you make this statement, because I had some doubt about that last year.

Mr. HAUGEN. How much are you asking for the support of that work?

Mr. CHRISTIE. $162,000.

Mr. HAUGEN. For farm help?

Mr. CHRISTIE. Yes.

Mr. HAUGEN. That is for getting farm labor for the farm?

Mr. CHRISTIE. Yes; to do this work of which I am speaking.

The CHAIRMAN. You say your county agents placed over 100,000 last year?

Mr. CHRISTIE. Yes.

The CHAIRMAN. Do you have any record of how many men were placed by these farm-help specialists of yours?

Mr. CHRISTIE. The farm-help specialist is working in connection with the county agents.

Mr. ANDERSON. The experience we have had up in our country was that the county agent was never able to catch the labor specialist with any men on his list?

Mr. CHRISTIE. Of course, that is unfortunate; with a large labor shortage it is hard to find loose men.

The CHAIRMAN. The best way to get farm labor in my country is to enforce the vagrancy law in the cities and towns.

Mr. HAUGEN. I have made special inquiry and I haven't been able to find one man that a farm-help specialist has placed on the farm.

Mr. CHRISTIE. Out in your country the farm-help specialist organized the movement to have city people aid the farmers.

Mr. HAUGEN. Not in our country. That system is over 50 years old there.

The CHAIRMAN. Mr. Christie, if there is nothing else and no further questions, we are very much obliged to you.

(Thereupon, at 5.20 o'clock p. m., the committee took a recess until 10.30 a. m., Tuesday, January 7, 1919.)

AGRICULTURE APPROPRIATION BILL.

Committee on Agriculture,
House of Representatives,
Friday, January 3, 1919.

WEATHER BUREAU.

STATEMENT OF MR. CHARLES F. MARVIN, CHIEF OF THE WEATHER BUREAU, UNITED STATES DEPARTMENT OF AGRICULTURE.

The CHAIRMAN. You have no changes in your statutory roll except by way of transfers?

Mr. MARVIN. That is all, Mr. Chairman, under the general plan.

The CHAIRMAN. And all those transfers are made at the same salaries?

Mr. MARVIN. They are all made at the same salaries. I heard some of the statements this morning concerning transfers from lump funds to statutory rolls. These transfers come about in this way: We have a lump-sum appropriation for aerological work. We hire additional employees, some of whom should be carried on the statutory roll. We take these in during the year and in the next estimates have their places transferred to the statutory roll; the lump-sum roll is reduced accordingly. On page 28, at the bottom, is an apparent increase of $14,660. Now, the salaries there are mostly low salaries—mechanics and laborers only. The transaction is in no sense a means of increasing, as is perhaps suspected, either the salary of employees or the number carried on the statutory roll.

The CHAIRMAN. Any questions on that, gentlemen?

Mr. THOMPSON. You don't ask for any promotions or increases in salaries at all in your department, then?

The CHAIRMAN. On page 29, Mr. Thompson.

Mr. MARVIN. On the roll as submitted here there is no increase asked for; however, on the plan for the whole department, the changes that should be made are covered in this supplemental estimate, beginning on page 29.

Mr. THOMPSON. Now, I notice in your supplemental estimate your increases are of the high-paid fellows; they are the men who receive the high salaries and not of the men who receive less than $1,000 a year; you haven't any between $1,000 and $1,800.

Mr. HARRISON. It runs to page 32.

Mr. THOMPSON. I understand; and I don't see on any of those that there are any recommendation for increases where the salaries are between $1,000 and $1,800.

The CHAIRMAN. Turn to page 30, No. 50; the mechanics are increased from $1,200 to $1,350, and No. 58, an engineer from $1,300 to $1,500; there are a number of them.

Mr. THOMPSON. There may be a few, but a large proportion of the employees are between $1,000 and $1,800.

Mr. MARVIN. Yes, sir.

Mr. THOMPSON. About what per cent, could you say, Doctor?

Mr. MARVIN. I couldn't give you that in percentage.

Mr. THOMPSON. Could you give us an idea as to the percentage?

Mr. MARVIN. About 60 per cent would be a rough guess.

Mr. THOMPSON. All the employees in all the bureaus——

Mr. MARVIN (interposing). I am speaking for the Weather Bureau.

Mr. THOMPSON. And you don't know about the others?

Mr. MARVIN. No, sir.

Mr. THOMPSON. Sixty per cent; can you tell us what per cent of the recommendations for increases are between $1,000 and $1,800?

Mr. MARVIN. The percentage there would be very small. I could look up the actual record. I should say 10 or 15 per cent.

Mr. THOMPSON. Will you look up the record and give the committee the number of employees in your bureau who receive salaries between $1,000 and $1,800 in comparison with the number who receive salaries of less than $1,000 and more than $1,800, and then also give the committee the number of recommendations in percentages between $1,000 and $1,800 as compared with those above $1,800.

Mr. MARVIN. I would be glad to do so.

(The statement referred to follows:)

Statement showing Weather Bureau employees on the statutory roll receiving less than $1,000 or more than $1,800 per annum.

Grades.[1]	Present number of employees.[1]	Recommendations in estimates.	
		Number of promotions recommended.	Promotion percentage.
Above $1,800	8	1	12
$1,000 to $1,800, inclusive	155	28	18
Below $1,000	212	85	40
Entire roll	375	114	30

[1] Including transfers from miscellaneous roll.

This table indicates the small percentage of persons above $1,800 recommended for promotion. Of 375 persons on the entire roll, only 2 per cent receive salaries in excess of $1,800, whereas 41 per cent of the force receive salaries from $1,000 to $1,800, inclusive, and 57 per cent receive less than $1,000.

The table shows 114 persons recommended in the estimates for promotion. Twenty-five per cent of these are in grades between $1,000 and $1,800, inclusive, 75 per cent are in grades of less than $1,000, and only one individual (less than 1 per cent) receives more than $1,800.

Mr. THOMPSON. Now, as I understand you, you and the rest of the bureaus in the department make your recommendations on the ground of the high cost of living. Doesn't the high cost of living apply to those people who receive between $1,000 and $1,800 as well as those above?

Mr. MARVIN. Yes, sir. I think the answer to that question is this, Mr. Thompson: The Secretary submits in these estimates certain increases which I have recommended and believe are just and necessary to the efficiency of the service. As administrative officers, the Secretary and myself are just as solicitous to bring about an equality of the pay of the men as anybody can be; all we desire is a reasonable uniformity in the pay of the men in the Weather Bureau. Now, we are inevitably obliged to take in new men; we must take in new men as time goes on. We can't get new men at the rate of pay at which men were formerly employed; we have to pay a higher rate in many cases. So far as this whole supplemental estimate is concerned, I can say conscientiously that it is an effort to adjust and equalize the rate of pay and eliminate the injustice that exists at the present time, because we must take in new and less experienced people at higher rates than the older employees can now receive.

Mr. THOMPSON. Well, that would apply between $1,000 and $1,800 as well as above.

Mr. MARVIN. This supplemental estimate covers many under $1,800.

Mr. THOMPSON. I am excluding those. It would apply to those below as well as to those above.

Mr. MARVIN. I am not asking for increases in salaries of those above $1,800 except in one case.

Mr. THOMPSON. You are not, in your department?

Mr. MARVIN. Not on the statutory roll; I am speaking of that as distinguished from the lump-sum roll.

Mr. THOMPSON. There is only the one?

Mr. MARVIN. There is only one in the bureau who receives more than $1,800 for whom we asked an increase.

The CHAIRMAN. Will you tell us about that and give us the page?

Mr. MARVIN. Page 29, item 49; he is the chief clerk of the Weather Bureau; we are asking that his salary be increased from $2,500 to $3,000. This is not really an increase, but is a restoration. It was reduced by congressional action and it should be restored.

The CHAIRMAN. The committee allowed this increase last year.

Mr. MARVIN. No, sir; the question was not submitted, Mr. Chairman.

The CHAIRMAN. Wasn't it submitted some time ago?

Mr. MARVIN. No, sir; this increase has never been submitted by the Secretary; it has been requested by the bureau, but has not been submitted to Congress.

The CHAIRMAN. How long has it been since he has had an increase?

Mr. MARVIN. Not for 10 years or more. He has been a department employee for 27 years. He has done actual station work in the field and is acquainted with all lines of work of the service. He acted for a time as secretary to the Secretary of Agriculture in Mr. Morton's administration. He was transferred at that time from the Weather Bureau. At one time he was in charge of the Division of Accounts and Disbursements and received a salary of $2,750.

The CHAIRMAN. How old a man is he?

Mr. MARVIN. He is between 46 and 50. He has been in the service nearly 28 years.

Mr. McLAUGHLIN. Twenty-seven of those years assistant?

Mr. MARVIN. Yes, sir.

The CHAIRMAN. Anything further on that item?

Mr. THOMPSON. You say he was reduced from $3,000 by the Senate?

Mr. MARVIN. No, sir; the circumstances connected with that were these: Before the war he was solicited to go into private business with his brother-in-law. He concluded to accept that offer and go into private business, and the war came on and he desired to be reinstated in the Weather Bureau because of his affection for the work in the bureau, and because of his liking for the general line of work in the bureau, and he was reinstated, but not at his former salary.

Mr. THOMPSON. Reinstated at $2,500?

Mr. MARVIN. Yes, sir.

Mr. THOMPSON. He made application and accepted that out of private life?

Mr. MARVIN. The other position had been filled at that time.

Mr. THOMPSON. He wanted that place and came back at that salary?

Mr. MARVIN. Yes, sir; that was four years ago.

Mr. HAUGEN. Then he has been in the service only a few months?

Mr. MARVIN. He has been with us 27 years.

Mr. HAUGEN. Before he resigned; he gave that up.

Mr. MARVIN. We count the length of a man's service the time he spends in the service. It is not continuous service in this case, but it is from the time he was originally appointed, with the exception of less than a year.

The CHAIRMAN. All right. Turn to page 33 and take up the general-expense paragraph. Doctor, I see you have cut out the words "folders and feeders" and substituted the words "press feeders."

Mr. MARVIN. May I have just a little time before we leave this other matter to speak about the new places on page 32? It involves salary increases, but I don't wish to ask it if the committee considers it useless.

The CHAIRMAN. If it involves salary increases, it is.

Mr. MARVIN. It does.

The CHAIRMAN. This change of language, I suppose, is made in order to comply with civil-service rules?

Mr. MARVIN. It is made "press feeders" to describe the work these men do.

The CHAIRMAN. Is that change absolutely necessary; couldn't that run along with the same language?

Mr. MARVIN. That change there is because there is included on page——

The CHAIRMAN (interposing). You suggested a similar change in your statutory roll.

Mr. MARVIN. On page 30; it is in the statutory roll at the top of page 30. We desire to change the title there to "press feeders," with the change of salary; it comes in in that same change.

The CHAIRMAN. That is not absolutely necessary to the running of the bureau, is it?

The CHAIRMAN. It wouldn't do the bureau any good to make the change?

Mr. MARVIN. Not absolutely necessary.

Mr. MARVIN. It is a consistent change to make. Formerly we folded a good deal by hand, but we don't do it any more, and this change simply describes the nature of the work.

Mr. LESHER. Isn't it possible to get along with a few less messengers?

Mr. MARVIN. These messengers are mostly at the 200 stations throughout the country. These messengers are distributed to the outlying stations, that is the reason for so many messengers.

Mr. HAUGEN. How many messengers have you in the office here?

Mr. MARVIN. Sixteen. These come under the title of "messengers and laborers." At the present time we have 16 laborers and 13 messengers.

Mr. THOMPSON. And you have about how many messengers in all—60?

Mr. MARVIN. One hundred or more messengers; the total number is 100 or more. We have 200 stations.

Mr. THOMPSON. You don't have a messenger at each one of those stations?

Mr. MARVIN. No sir; not each one, but we have messengers at a considerable number of stations to distribute maps and bulletins and such things; each city has its office and employees.

Mr. HAUGEN. How many employees have you in these stations; the smaller stations?

Mr. MARVIN. There are about twenty-five one-man stations; the majority of them have from two to five men.

Mr. HAUGEN. How many of the two?

Mr. MARVIN. I couldn't give you the exact number offhand. The largest stations have not to exceed 10 or 15 men, possibly.

The CHAIRMAN. Anything further on that, gentlemen? If not, turn to the general expense items, beginning on page 34.

Mr. MARVIN. There is no change in the language there.

The CHAIRMAN. Expenses in the city of Washington; there is no change in that?

Mr. MARVIN. No, sir; no change in that.

Mr. MCLAUGHLIN. Let me ask a question on 82. After the estimates were prepared it was suggested that the word "volcanology" be added, and it was added to take care of the Hawaiian experimental station or the work in connection with that, and $10,000 of that is for that purpose; can you tell us how that was spent?

Mr. MARVIN. It has not been spent. That is to be arranged for now. In the first place it became available October 1, and the arrangements were made for the transfer of the activities and matters are not consummated yet, but in a highly advanced stage, and I think activities will begin in the near future.

Mr. MCLAUGHLIN. What does that mean, "transfer of activities"?

Mr. MARVIN. The proper legal transfer of activities to the bureau from the Hawaiian Volcano Research Association. The transfer of all the records and the control of them and the taking over of the personnel and the program of observation.

Mr. MCLAUGHLIN. The association out there have offered to transfer the title to the Government, have they not?

Mr. MARVIN. They are willing to do that. The form in which that can be done is a matter that involves some technical legal questions; and in the first place——

Mr. McLAUGHLIN (interposing). Is there some obligation that the Government might assume to carry on the work in the future? Is that where the difficulty lies?

Mr. MARVIN. For instance, the tract of ground is in a national park; the title to the ground is not in the Hawaiian Volcano Research Association; they are lessees of the tract, and the effort of the bureau and the association to transfer the properties to the Government and permit the Government to occupy the properties and conduct the work has to be put in the proper legal form. That is the matter that is being adjusted at the present time.

Mr. McLAUGHLIN. I think many who have seen that place and have learned by their visits the kind of work that is being done and who have met those who are carrying on the work have been impressed with the importance of it, and I would like to see it in the hands of the Federal Government; and there are some men who are employed there that impress those who meet them as being very learned and very capable men, and men who ought to be better taken care of in the matter of salaries than they are now; and I simply voice quite a general sentiment of those who have studied this question when I ask for this increase and putting it in as it is. I was expressing my own opinion all the time, but a great many feel as I do, so I say I was voicing their sentiment, and I had hoped and they hoped that a part of this money would be paid to the men out there. A very able and distinguished man is working for next to nothing. If the Government is interested in this work, as I believe it is and ought to be, it ought to provide something better for him. I was hoping that you would say some of this money has reached him.

Mr. MARVIN. The matter of an appropriate salary to be paid is to be adjusted.

Mr. McLAUGHLIN. He has had none of it?

Mr. MARVIN. That whole work is under the supervision of the Hawaiian Volcano Research Association, and I understand he is receiving $4,000 a year.

The CHAIRMAN. Isn't he receiving a salary from a Boston society?

Mr. McLAUGHLIN. There was a society that did pay some money, but for some years the money has not been forthcoming and the money has not been coming to him, and this man has not been receiving a very liberal salary, and he has been working for much less than he ought to work and getting less than he ought to have. And it was hoped that the Government would supplement it a little bit.

Mr. MARVIN. That is a state of affairs that has not been known to us as you represent it; because, in the first place, this gentleman you refer to——

Mr. McLAUGHLIN. Dr. Jaggar.

Mr. MARVIN. He inaugurated the work. He went there for the Massachusetts Institute of Technology. I don't know just when he went there; they terminated their work, I believe, in June, 1916; subsequent to that time the work was continued by the Hawaiian Volcano Research Association, who financed all the work; and it has been represented to us that the salary of that man was paid as director.

Mr. HAUGEN. Four thousand dollars?
Mr. MARVIN. Four thousand dollars.
Mr. HAUGEN. What is your source of information as to that?
Mr. MARVIN. Our official in charge of the station in Hawaii at Honolulu was instructed to collect all this information from the Hawaiian Volcano Research Association in regard to the salaries paid to these employees at the Volcano Association house, and those are the figures.
Mr. HAUGEN. And your representatives report that salary paid?
Mr. MARVIN. Yes, sir.
Mr. MCLAUGHLIN. Up to this time?
Mr. MARVIN. That was in the summer of 1918. We will take that over just as quickly as we can make the arrangements; the Secretary is asking for some reports which I am just ready to make.
Mr. MCLAUGHLIN. This total amount of $109,250, how much of that will be used for that kind of work?
Mr. MARVIN. None of that sum. The work comes out of the field expenditures.
The CHAIRMAN. Item 84?
Mr. MARVIN. Yes; it comes out of the total in that sum.
Mr. MCLAUGHLIN. How much of that will be used for that?
Mr. MARVIN. $10,000 was the amount appropriated; this year we will not be able to use that much, but the next year it is contemplated we will need that much money.
Mr. MCLAUGHLIN. This will be for the fiscal year 1920?
Mr. MARVIN. Yes, sir.
Mr. MCLAUGHLIN. Now, is it your intention to do any building out there?
Mr. MARVIN. No, sir; the present arrangement contemplates taking over the scientific activities and investigations there, utilizing the equipment and building of the Hawaiian Volcano Research Association, supplementing the equipment with such as we supply; but no buildings; we would have to come to you for that.
Mr. MCLAUGHLIN. The buildings are not suitable, it seems to me. The invaluable instruments and records that are made there and are being made all the time ought to be in fireproof buildings, whereas that is just a wooden shell.
Mr. MARVIN. I understand there is a part of a building there that is somewhat durable.
Mr. MCLAUGHLIN. Some of the instruments are set in a sort of a cement cellar, but not what it ought to be.
Mr. MARVIN. It has been my hope to get over there and see the situation, but thus far we have got all our information from the representative at the station and the Hawaiian Volcano Research Association.
Mr. MCLAUGHLIN. Mr. Chairman, there has been some question as to the value of this work; as to whether there was any practical good in it. I have been told, and the Doctor can say whether or not there is anything in it, that by means of the instruments used in seismology and aerology and other methods, that it was possible during this last war to calculate and find the exact location of German guns; do you know whether that is true?
Mr. MARVIN. I think it is true that by means of sounds communicated through the air it has been possible to locate large pieces of

artillery by sounding devices—sound ranging, as it is called in military circles. I am not personally advised as to the details of the work, but that methods of that kind were employed is unquestioned; how successful they were I am unable to say, but it is theoretically possible by noting the time of arrival of sound waves at different stations to work out the source, or locate or fix the source by noting the time of the arrival of earth waves in the same way. I understand sound ranging has been more successful than seismological apparatus.

Mr. McLaughlin. I understand some of that work has been done with seismological apparatus.

Mr. Marvin. Yes; they may use very sensitive seismographs for that.

The Chairman. Anything further? Take up item 83; any change in that?

Mr. Marvin. No, sir.

The Chairman. Has there been any change in the character of the work?

Mr. Marvin. No, sir. That is a continuation of the work as conducted for a number of years.

The Chairman. Take up item 84.

Mr. Marvin. There is an actual increase in that item of $18,920. We are proposing to drop the frost-protection investigations (for which $5,000 is allotted this year), and $2,000 which we are expending for storm-warning equipment on the Pacific coast will also be released; so that we will have an actual increase in Weather Bureau funds under this item of $25,920. We are asking for this amount for the purpose and with the hope of making a better provision for lump-sum employees.

The Chairman. Now, let us see; you say you have an actual increase of $18,000?

Mr. Marvin. An actual increase of $18,920.

The Chairman. Assuming that the committee should disallow that, you could work out a readjustment of the other figures in this item?

Mr. Marvin. We could work it out on the other allowances; yes, sir.

The Chairman. This is to go for salaries?

Mr. Marvin. This is for salaries of the field men.

The Chairman. These field men whose salaries you propose to increase are all receiving less than $2,500?

Mr. Marvin. It is impossible to make a correct list showing how the apportionment would be made, but the increases would go chiefly to the men in the grades between $1,400 and $2,500.

The Chairman. Have you any above the grade of $2,500 that you would increase?

Mr. Marvin. No, sir.

The Chairman. So there is no use to discuss that proposition.

Mr. Anderson. Is this increase for the lump-sum salaries intended for those whose salaries are in the statutory roll, or is it an independent proposition?

Mr. Marvin. It is independent; it has no connection with the statutory roll at all; it is intended to remove the disparity of pay to Weather Bureau men in the field.

Mr. Anderson. So, whether the increase is allowed in the statutory roll or not, you think this should be allowed?

Mr. MARVIN. Yes, sir; I can't say enough about the justification for this. All salaries have been very low and increases have not been made, and it is partly to remove the difficulty and the disparity for the field men in the Weather Bureau; that is recognized by the Secretary, and, irrespective of any other increases, I think this that is asked for is fully justified.

The CHAIRMAN. I notice that you increase for work in connection with frost-protection investigation on the Pacific coast, for which there was an appropriation of $5,000. What results did you get?

Mr. MARVIN. We are continuing that investigation. We had originally $10,000 for the work, which was started before the war conditions became unfavorable and it proved an inopportune time to pursue the work as successfully as might be. We cut down the appropriation to $5,000. This year we hope to complete the work. The work was carried on in the California citrus region and in Oregon and Salt Lake, and in Florida to some extent. The results have not been worked out fully as yet, but we hope by our investigations to demonstrate the proper method of protecting orchards. Some investigations we could not work out on account of the cost of fuel oil, etc., but we will complete the work this year. The $5,000 now in the bill we hope to have you continue in the next appropriation for the next year to use for salary purposes.

The CHAIRMAN. Now, have you anything new or interesting to tell us that you have discovered during the past year? If so, tell us briefly.

Mr. MARVIN. I think the most important work might be the work in connection with aerological investigation.

The CHAIRMAN. That is the next item?

Mr. HAUGEN. The heating of orchards, is that being done now?

Mr. MARVIN. Yes, sir.

Mr. HAUGEN. Is there anything new about that?

Mr. MARVIN. I don't know that there is anything new. The most serious trouble is the high cost of fuel oil used for that purpose, and that makes it almost prohibitive and hard to employ the artificial heating methods that could be formerly done. It is an economic question.

Mr. HAUGEN. Have you any hopes of overcoming that?

Mr. MARVIN. It is not exactly our problem to overcome that or to find substitutes for oil for heating purposes. There may be other methods but we don't know of any better material than oil, although some other methods are being investigated and I would not want to make any statement that oil heating is the only method practicable.

Mr. HAUGEN. How much money are you asking for the investigation of heating orchards?

Mr. MARVIN. Five thousand dollars in the present appropriation; nothing in the present estimate.

Mr. McLAUGHLIN. This shows conclusively that the orchards can be protected by lamps and stoves; the only question is whether one can afford to buy the material and fuel; what scientific question is involved?

Mr. MARVIN. The question we have investigated and are investigating is, if we burn 100,000 gallons of oil how much does it heat the air over what it would have been if we had not burned the oil; that is the question.

Mr. McLaughlin. Have you been trying to lay down rules as to how many stoves a man must have, etc.?

Mr. Marvin. That is part of it. Suppose we see from the charts that the thermometer is to drop to 18°; if we know there is to be a fall to 18° it may be useless for an orchardist to spend several hundred dollars, perhaps, and still have the temperature fall low enough to kill his fruit.

Mr. McLaughlin. How do you determine that?

Mr. Marvin. That it is going to 18°?

Mr. McLanghlin. That it is useless to spend the money?

Mr. Marvin. That is the question. We put men in the orchards and they read the temperature both in orchards which are heated and those not heated. Our investigation aims to determine how much the artificial heating checks the fall of temperature.

Mr. McLaughlin. It falls in one place and in the next place it does not fall; you can't have any rules for that, can you?

Mr. Marvin. Yes, sir; that is our business. We attempt to tell definitely whether the orchardist should fire. There are two problems: The first, whether it is going to need fire; and, second, whether it is going to be so cold as not to be profitable.

Mr. McLaughlin. We ride through the country and we see one farm that is hit and one that is not.

Mr. Marvin. That is a part of the problem.

Mr. McLaughlin. How can you determine definitely that you will give notice to A that he had better light his fires, and to B that his farm is not to be hit?

Mr. Marvin. It is not so haphazard as you might imagine; there are questions of topography, and the experts in the field know the probability of the frost hitting A or B, or missing one or both.

Mr. McLaughlin. It seems to me sending out so many notices to reach any considerable number that you couldn't afford to do it.

Mr. Marvin. It is not so difficult as you suppose, and our men in the field are actually doing it, and those are the men that we want to have a little more pay for.

Mr. Wason. Where are you doing that?

Mr. Marvin. At Medford, Oreg., is one place, and a number of places in California, and in Florida; there is scarcely any horticultural district in the country that we do not get information to them to determine whether artificial measures should be employed.

Mr. Wason. Any in New England?

Mr. Marvin. Yes, sir; and especially in the cranberry district.

Mr. Haugen. Do you contend that it is possible for your department to determine just what part of the farm of a man is to be struck?

Mr. Marvin. To a certain extent we are doing that.

Mr. Haugen. To what extent, might I ask?

Mr. Marvin. In the orchards in Oregon——

Mr. Haugen (interposing). We are speaking about a farm; here is a farm as flat as this table.

Mr. Marvin. I doubt whether you will find a farm as flat as this table where artificial heat would be used.

Mr. Haugen. An elevation, say, of 10 feet to a mile.

Mr. MARVIN. In a case of that kind it is a question in my mind whether there is place where frost kills in one place and not in another.

Mr. HAUGEN. I can tell from experience; I had that happen on my farm in 1916.

Mr. MARVIN. If we had been there and studied the situation, I think we could have told you.

Mr. HAUGEN. Do you say you can tell in Washington?

Mr. MARVIN. It is not done in Washington; the men are in the field. For instance, we give general forecast for a district in Florida. The section director at Jacksonville has that instruction about the general situation in Florida and he applies the forecasts to his district. He knows the local situation and can tell pretty accurately. It is not done here in Washington.

Mr. HAUGEN. Well, I doubt whether a farmer can know.

Mr. MARVIN. We have testimonials from these people who have benefited by the service.

Mr. HAUGEN. To what degree can your forecast be relied upon as to the rise in temperature?

Mr. MARVIN. We consider the general forecasts are verified to the extent of about 88 to 90 per cent.

Mr. HAUGEN. Now, how much of an area does that cover? Can you forecast what the weather is going to be in Washington or within 10 miles of Washintgton?

Mr. MARVIN. The forecast is for a State or for the District of Columbia, say.

Mr. HAUGEN. Say a radius of 500 miles; if it rains within 500 miles you have made good, is that the idea?

Mr. MARVIN. No, sir; the forecast is for the State of Pennsylvania, or New Jersey, for instance, and the verifier examines the conditions for that State and if fair weather is forecast and it rains over half of the State it is a half verification, and if it rains over the whole State it is a failure.

Mr. HAUGEN. As we understand, that is 88 to 90 per cent verification?

Mr. MARVIN. Yes, sir.

Mr. HAUGEN. How does it happen that we miss more than we hit on the forecasts printed and hung in the elevators here, for instance?

Mr. MARVIN. I don't know that I can answer that. It is, perhaps, a difference in judgment or a difference in fact. Our impartial verifications show that we miss only about 12 times in 100.

Mr. HAUGEN. Take inauguration day, when we were promised good weather, and it rained and snowed all day?

Mr. MARVIN. As I told you, we miss 12 times out of 100; and we miss because the area over which the rain is expected to come is not quite that over which it falls; some areas, however, do have rain, and some do not have it, and so there is a difference of judgment there, but we do not judge the forecast on a condition that we personally may experience at one locality, but we look at the map and see what the conditions were over the region of eastern Pennsylvania or western Pennsylvania, or whatever the area may be, and we compare the forecast and the condition as a whole and see what the verification is.

Mr. LEE. Occasionally you have a flareback, don't you?

Mr. MARVIN. Occasionally we make mistakes.

Mr. HAUGEN. If you make a prediction that it is to rain I think you would hit it 20 times out of 30 in March, or in the spring; but that does not help us if it is tested in a 500-mile area, as I understand, and it is tested in that area.

Mr. MARVIN. As a rule, it is a forecast for States; those are the natural areas and the conditions may be expected to be the same over the whole State. If the eastern half is to have one condition and the western half some other condition that would be specified in the forecast.

Mr. HAUGEN. It hardly ever happens that it rains all over a State.

Mr. MARVIN. My dear sir, in the last few days we have had rain all over the eastern half of the United States; the whole eastern half of the United States has been flooded with rain. If you look at the weather map you will see by the shaded areas on the map that it has been an enormous rain.

Mr. HAUGEN. How many people does it take to handle this heating proposition?

Mr. MARVIN. We have nothing to do with that; we give the information to the farmer and he does the work.

Mr. HAUGEN. But you tell him when to heat?

Mr. MARVIN. Yes, sir.

Mr. HAUGEN. He has to be familiar with the local conditions?

Mr. MARVIN. No; he goes on our advice. If we tell him in the morning that it is liable to frost at night he has to get his force of men and get the pots all ready to light. He places them and gets ready for his fire.

Mr. HAUGEN. But he must know which portion of his orchard to light.

Mr. MARVIN. It is not so complex as that; it is for the whole orchard, usually.

Mr. HAUGEN. Wouldn't it be a waste of oil to use it on the whole orchard if a part of the orchard was struck and a portion not?

Mr. MARVIN. It would. That is what our opinion is good for. We strive to tell him the best thing to do.

Mr. HAUGEN. I assume that it would require an examination by an expert to be absolutely sure that you would hit the right spot.

Mr. MARVIN. The frost is not so selective as that; our observations are that when the temperature falls to say, 28, it is apt to go to 28 over a large region, unless there are marked changes in topography. One man has to burn more oil to protect his orchard if the others do not come in and help in that section.

Mr. WASON. Have you ever pursued the investigation of what is called the smoke protection?

Mr. MARVIN. That is included; it is impossible to heat without more or less smoke, and the smoke is a contributing factor.

Mr. WASON. You don't get it in oil?

Mr. MARVIN. Yes; in some types of oil stoves you don't get so much but you can't get rid of smoke to some extent.

The CHAIRMAN. Anything further? If not, take up Item 85, covering your traveling expenses.

Mr. MARVIN. That is exactly the same; no change in that.

The CHAIRMAN. Do you usually spend all of that?

Mr. MARVIN. I think this year, Mr. Chairman, we will not spend all of that, but next year the sum will be necessary. The reason we have not spent the money this year was because we did not have the men; we could only employ men at the town to take the places of the men on furlough, whereas, ordinarily we have to transfer men to maintain the service.

The CHAIRMAN. What is the nature of this travel?

Mr. MARVIN. This travel is for the maintenance of the service at our 200 stations, and for inspection. We can't let the stations go without inspection. The bureau, in addition to the 200 stations, has four or five thousand cooperative stations and the Section Directors in the section must travel to the cooperative stations clearing up the records, and so on, and maintaining the efficiency of the service by adequate inspection.

The CHAIRMAN. Do you pay the traveling expenses in all cases where a man is transferred from one station to another?

Mr. MARVIN. When the man is a regular employee we must.

The CHAIRMAN. What part of this is out of the Washington office?

Mr. MARVIN. Not much of it. An inspector may go to a number of stations in the east part of the country, but that is all.

Mr. McLAUGHLIN. No part of this is for transportation about Washington or in any other city?

Mr. MARVIN. A very small part.

Mr. HAUGEN. Do you supply the Bureau of Crop Estimates now as to the condition of the crops?

Mr. MARVIN. No, sir; we give them the weather conditions, the meteorological conditions but the crop conditions are determined by their own employees or reporters.

Mr. HAUGEN. You did furnish them with some information on that?

Mr. MARVIN. No, sir; I think not with crop information.

Mr. HAUGEN. Are all the reporters under your bureau?

Mr. MARVIN. They are under the Bureau of Crop Estimates.

Mr. HAUGEN. You have none in your bureau?

Mr. MARVIN. We have observers who report the weather conditions and the effect of the weather on crops, many of them unpaid; all the cooperative reporters are unpaid.

Mr. HAUGEN. That is, you have the same reporters; they report to the Bureau of Crop Estimates and to yourself at the same time?

Mr. MARVIN. No, sir; I think there is no case in which our men make reports to the Bureau of Crop Estimates.

Mr. HAUGEN. They make reports to you?

Mr. MARVIN. Yes, sir.

Mr. HAUGEN. And to the Bureau of Crop Estimates?

Mr. MARVIN. No, sir; none of our observers report directly to the Bureau of Crop Estimates.

Mr. HAUGEN. They have been doing it in my county, and I understood that was the arrangement.

Mr. MARVIN. I think there must be a misunderstanding as to the kind of reporters we are speaking of. The kind I speak of are weather observers who have thermometers and observe the rainfall and make measurements, and so on. I don't understand they report to the Bureau of Crop Estimates directly.

Mr. HAUGEN. Some of them do; I don't know that it is arranged for by your bureau.

Mr. MARVIN. It is not an arrangement. My understanding is that the Bureau of Crop Estimates does not obtain reports from the men who are observing the climatological conditions.

Mr. HAUGEN. They might be the same men.

Mr. MARVIN. They might be.

The CHAIRMAN. Anything else?

Now, Doctor, take the item 86, on page 37, " For the establishment and maintenance by the Weather Bureau of additional aerological stations, for observing, measuring, and investigating atmospheric phenomena in the aid of aeronautics, including salaries, travel, and other expenses in the city of Washington and elsewhere, $85,040." That was put in the bill as a new item last year. Tell us something about the work.

Mr. MARVIN. That is for the purpose of increasing the number of stations in which we observe free air conditions and became necessary because of the development of aviation; I mentioned that a moment ago, and its development, with reference to forecasting conditions in the free air. We have five stations and had originally another, making six. About 20 secondary stations are maintained by the Army at the Army posts and training schools. At these six stations of the bureau we send up kites and sounding balloons and devices for determining the conditions in the free air. At the 15 or 20 stations maintained by the military authorities at the aviation camps and training schools they send up small balloons which are watched by means of a theodolite for the purpose of determining the currents of air in the different layers, and those results are telegraphed to Washington and we furnish a report to the Postmaster General and to the sections of the Army and state the probable progress and weather conditions for the aerial mail service, and whether it is to be good for flights in one direction or another, and the conditions in the free air with reference to the use of the free air for aviation.

The CHAIRMAN. Was any work of this character done in Europe during the war?

Mr. MARVIN. Yes, sir; three or four times a day these small rubber balloons were relieved and ascended slowly and their flight was watched; the flight of the balloon gives an idea of the currents of air in the different strata.

The CHAIRMAN. Did you have any men over there?

Mr. MARVIN. Yes, sir; 190 of our men went into military service. The leaders and many others in this work overseas were Weather Bureau men.

The CHAIRMAN. I mean in this work.

Mr. MCLAUGHLIN. They were separated from your service?

Mr. MARVIN. They were separated from the service. The number of men in this exact work I can't say, but the leader of the aerological work is over there yet; he is a weather man and has with him a large number of soldiers and privates, some taken from among the bureau men and some from private life and assigned to this duty; they are doing their work over there and were during the war, and this work we are doing is in connection with the work at the posts and with the Aerial Mail Service in the United States.

Mr. ANDERSON. Have the places of these men been filled?
Mr. MARVIN. Yes, sir; every place that was made vacant by the military service has been filled.
Mr. ANDERSON. What do you expect to do with these men when they come back?
Mr. MARVIN. Take them back; the arrangements are fully prepared for taking these men back by letting out men who have been temporarily employed and otherwise. The vacancies automatically occur all the time; many of these men come in to fill these automatic vacancies, but the regulations the Secretary has drawn up for reinstating the men on military furlough contemplates the greatest justice to the men who have been in temporary employment and those who have been in military service.
The CHAIRMAN. Doctor, you say you have six stations; where are they located?
Mr. MARVIN. The original station is at Drexel, Nebr., and one north of that at Ellendale, N. Dak.; and south of that we have two, one in Oklahoma and one in Texas, and two farther east, one in Indiana and one in Georgia.
The CHAIRMAN. And you say 15 or 20 other——
Mr. MARVIN (interposing). Observing points at military posts; I can't give you the list at the moment.
The CHAIRMAN. Does the War Department have an appropriation for this at all?
Mr. MARVIN. No, sir; there is no specific appropriation for this. At the beginning of the war, when the United States entered the war, it was very necessary to organize what was known as the meteorological unit in the Signal Corps, and the men assigned in that unit were drawn in the draft and some of them were taken from the Weather Bureau.
The CHAIRMAN. Does the Post Office Department have a fund?
Mr. MARVIN. No, sir.
The CHAIRMAN. Then, there is no duplication for this purpose?
Mr. MARVIN. No, sir; unless you call the employment of the soldiers a duplication; and in connection with that we are preparing to take this over as fast as the Army will release them. I would like to say right there, you see the impossibility of the Weather Bureau maintaining this aerological service in a military post. A civilian in a military post is out of place. The Army makes the observations at the post and we make them at the civil stations.
The CHAIRMAN. This work will very likely develop, will it not, Doctor?
Mr. MARVIN. I don't see how it is possible for it not to develop, unless we think of aviation going out of existence; but this work should be continued and become a permanent feature of the service. It is already a permanent feature of the European service, and you can't think of the proper navigation of the air without a proper examination of the free air currents to determine the cloudiness and all that; it is inseparably connected with that.
The CHAIRMAN. Without opening up the discussion as to Mount Weather, do you still have that station or have you disposed of it?
Mr. MARVIN. I am sorry to say that we have not disposed of it in spite of promising possibilities. We have had the matter up with the

Surgeon General of the Army and every branch of the Government that might possibly use it during the war times and it has been examined several times, but so far nobody has been willing to establish activities there.

Mr. LEE. The best chance would be to sell it to somebody for a summer resort.

Mr. MARVIN. Possibly.

Mr. HAUGEN. What was the object of locating these stations, so many of them in the Southern States?

Mr. MARVIN. There are three in the northern tier and three in the southern tier of States; there is one in Indiana. I would like to have one farther east in the northern part of the country.

Mr. HAUGEN. What was the object in placing so many down South, in the Southern States?

Mr. MARVIN. There is one at Groesbeck, Tex., and one at Leesburg, Ga., that is two; then there is one at Broken Arrow, Okla.; that is an intermediate point.

Mr. HAUGEN. At any rate you haven't any in the North except in South Dakota.

Mr. MARVIN. In North Dakota.

Mr. McLAUGHLIN. They are located in connection with the flying fields.

Mr. MARVIN. Let me say one object was to get them close to the flying fields, but the primary object also was to get two or three lines across the country across which storm movements will take place, so that observations could be made in different parts of the storms as they move across the country.

Mr. HAUGEN. There are storms in the North as well as in the South?

Mr. MARVIN. They come from the West and move East and from the North and move South. Now, the line from Groesbeck, Tex., to Ellendale, N. Dak., is a track across which they usually go. Now we go east to Royal Center, in Indiana, and south to Leesburg, Ga., is another line from North to South.

Mr. HAUGEN. Occasionally we have a storm up North; I happened to be in one not long ago.

Mr. MARVIN. There are few storms that do not cross Royal Center, Ind.

Mr. HAUGEN. How about New York and Ohio?

Mr. MARVIN. The storms in New York cross the western part of the country before they get to New York.

Mr. HAUGEN. But here you have the one corner, I should judge one-third of the whole country, that is not covered at all.

Mr. MARVIN. We would be glad to put a station in there; I grant you there is need of a station in there and we would be glad to do it if we had the funds.

Mr. HAUGEN. You have none on the Lakes.

Mr. MARVIN. The one in Indiana is in that region.

Mr. HAUGEN. Whereabouts in Indiana?

Mr. MARVIN. A little to the east and south of Chicago, and representative of that region.

Mr. HAUGEN. How far?

Mr. MARVIN. About one-third of the way down the State line.

Mr. McLaughlin. About one-third of the way down the Indiana line?

Mr. Marvin. Yes, sir; I can't tell you the exact location. We would be glad to have an additional station.

Mr. Haugen. I wanted to know why it was you put them down there; I suppose there was a good reason for it.

Mr. Marvin. We have to have a good open country where we can put these stations to fly kites; that is a consideration in the selection of the site.

Mr. Haugen. Is it on practically level land?

Mr. Marvin. Yes, sir.

Mr. Haugen. There is some level land in Michigan and up North.

Mr. Marvin. Yes, sir. We can locate additional stations if we had additional money.

The Chairman. Do you really need additional stations, or do you want to accommodate somebody?

Mr. Marvin. We would be glad to have a station in the central district—central Pennsylvania and the Northern States—and possibily one in New England would be a good addition to this line, but I am not pushing it.

The Chairman. You abandoned the Mount Weather Station on account of the great difficulty of maintaining it?

Mr. Marvin. The trouble in getting supplies to it; that is the principal reason, I think. The roads are not good; the 6 miles to cover between the railroad terminal and the station are not good roads and it is not economical to establish activities there that do not require that kind of locality.

The Chairman. How far is it between the stations at Drexel and Ellendale?

Mr. Marvin. Ellendale and Drexel are about 200 or 300 miles apart.

Mr. Haugen. If Ellendale is in North Dakota, I think the distance of Ellendale from Drexel would be close to a thousand miles.

Mr. Marvin. It is on the line, as I remember it.

The Chairman. You need those stations located so as to catch the storms as they come from the west?

Mr. Marvin. Yes, sir; that is the object.

The Chairman. And a thousand miles is a pretty big gap?

Mr. Marvin. But a storm is a pretty big thing. What we mean by a storm is the general condition and distribution of atmospheric pressure.

The Chairman. Is there anything further you wish to say, Mr. Marvin?

Mr. Marvin. I think not.

The Chairman. I see you have omitted the item for repairing, renewing, and improving the sea coast telegraph and cable line.

Mr. Marvin. The purposes for which that was appropriated will be accomplished during this year.

The Chairman. Is there anything further?

Mr. Marvin. No, sir.

The Chairman. Then we will take up the Bureau of Animal Industry and will hear Dr. Mohler.

AGRICULTURE APPROPRIATION BILL.

COMMITTEE ON AGRICULTURE,
HOUSE OF REPRESENTATIVES,
Friday, January 3, 1919.

BUREAU OF ANIMAL INDUSTRY.

STATEMENT OF DR. JOHN R. MOHLER, CHIEF OF THE BUREAU OF ANIMAL INDUSTRY, UNITED STATES DEPARTMENT OF AGRICULTURE.

The CHAIRMAN. On page 39, take up the statutory salaries, Doctor. You have a number of increases there. I presume they are transfers.

Dr. MOHLER. Yes, Mr. Chairman; the increases are to cover the positions which have been transferred at the same salary to the statutory from the lump-sum roll.

The CHAIRMAN. You mean they go from the lump-sum to the statutory roll at the same salary?

Dr. MOHLER. At the same salary.

The CHAIRMAN. Have you any new places?

Dr. MOHLER. No, sir.

The CHAIRMAN. Have you any increases in salaries above $2,500?

Dr. MOHLER. There are none above $1,000. You will find that itemized in the supplemental estimate beginning on page 42.

The CHAIRMAN. Any further questions? Doctor, your general expenses begin on page 45.

Dr. MOHLER. Before we reach there I would like to state that the department has recommended a change in items 84 and 85, so that the nomenclature would agree with the work performed by those individuals concerned.

The CHAIRMAN. Is that absolutely essential?

Dr. MOHLER. It is not essential to the service.

The CHAIRMAN. Then we will disallow it, I will tell you now. There is no use going on the floor of the House with a matter about which a lot of questions will be asked if it is not essential to the service.

In your next item, on page 45, there is no change.

Dr. MOHLER. No change whatever.

The CHAIRMAN. Your next is on page 46, for quarantine work; there is no change.

Dr. MOHLER. No, sir; the total has been decreased on account of several clerks having been transferred to the statutory roll.

The CHAIRMAN. Now, have you anything new to report, or is it the same class of work as heretofore?

Dr. MOHLER. It is the same class of work that we have been conducting for a number of years. I would like to report that on April 15 last we took the Federal quarantine off the remaining territory for cattle scabies and off all but 24 counties in 3 States for sheep scabies.. This shows the progress we have been making in eradicating those diseases.

The CHAIRMAN. You couldn't make any reduction in this fund on that account?

Dr. MOHLER. No, sir; because of the fact that the State forces have been decreased on account of the war and we are apt to have recurrences. We have just heard from New York, Iowa, and Michigan and several other points that have recently become infested with sheep scabies because of the shortage of experienced veterinarians. The scab work is only a part of this big item, you understand, which takes in the inspection of southern cattle, the enforcement of the 28-hour law, the supervision of the transportation of live stock, the establishment and maintenance of quarantine stations at ports of entry, the inspection and quarantine of imported animals, and the inspection work relative to the existence of contagious diseases and the mallein testing of animals. Therefore the scabies work consumes only a part of the appropriation for inspection and quarantine work.

The CHAIRMAN. Do you recall just how much the item for sheep scabies was?

Dr. MOHLER. It is about $120,000 for sheep scabies.

The CHAIRMAN. You have lifted the quarantine; do you mean that you have control of the disease?

Dr. MOHLER. We believe we have control of the disease, so that from now the States should be able to keep it from ever becoming a menace again. We have removed the quarantine this last year from over 239,000 square miles of previously infested territory, with the idea that the States will be able to hold any local areas of infestation under their control.

The CHAIRMAN. Now, having done that and having discovered only a few small outbreaks, it seems to me $120,000 would be a pretty big sum.

Mr. MCLAUGHLIN. I got a different idea. I understood that having it under control it would require more supervision.

Dr. MOHLER. We have to keep our inspectors ever on the alert as an insurance measure, the same as we do in the foot-and-mouth disease, in order that the first cases of this disease may be detected. In Chicago, Omaha, and all other market centers we have inspectors present who are constantly on the watch for animals affected with scabies, and it would not be advisable to take them off and have no supervision over this disease. The success or failure in the sheep business is often involved in this one disease. Sheep scabies ruins the wool and reduces the flesh of the sheep. This is the only fund we have for this line of work.

Mr. MCLAUGHLIN. This fund, then, will be used for watching the scab situation?

Dr. MOHLER. Yes, sir; that is the idea.

Mr. MCLAUGHLIN. And it is an insurance fund?

Dr. MOHLER. Yes, sir; this fund covers all the work done on sheep scab throughout the entire country. When we get a shipment at a market center that is found infested we go back to the point of origin and dip all the infested and also the exposed sheep. Thus at the present time there are counties in Idaho that have recently become infested. There has been a little controversy out there. The dry farmers and the sheepmen have been squabbling, and the sheepmen have only recently developed sufficient power to get the necessary regulations enacted to compel the dipping of exposed as well as infested sheep. In the meantime the scabies has got the start of them, and we will supervise the dipping of probably 1,000,000 sheep in that section of Idaho this spring.

Mr. McLaughlin. Is there any possibility or probability of getting rid of this disease?

Dr. Mohler. Yes, sir; there is. It is getting less all the time.

Mr. McLaughlin. But you still must watch it, especially at the market centers?

Dr. Mohler. We must watch it at the market centers; that is imperative.

The Chairman. Is there anything further? If not, we will take up the next item on page 47. You have a little decrease there. I suppose that is on account of transfers.

Dr. Mohler. Yes, sir; the decrease applies to the clerks that have been taken off the lump sum and put on the statutory roll at the same salaries.

The Chairman. Then, you have a change in language near the bottom of the page. You strike out the word "destruction" and insert the word "condemnation."

Dr. Mohler. Yes, sir; and a similar change on page 48, where "destroyed" is recommended to be changed to "condemned."

Mr. McLaughlin. I think that change is good.

The Chairman. Let us find out why you do it.

Dr. Mohler. The solicitor has ruled that under the present law we are unable to indemnify owners of reacting cattle if these animals are shipped out of the State for slaughter. For instance, an owner of tuberculous cattle in eastern Iowa may decide to ship them for slaughter to St. Joe as a matter of convenience. The present language of the law would prohibit him from obtaining any Federal indemnity for these cattle. The change of language recommended will rectify this, as the animals will be "condemned" by the tuberculin test in Iowa; and if they are then "destroyed" in Missouri, we still will be able to pay an indemnity to the Iowa farmer. In many cases stockmen live nearer to an abattoir in an adjacent State than they do to one in their own State.

This condition was recently brought to my attention by farmers in southern Washington; their cattle are slaughtered as a rule in Portland, Oreg. Now, if they are "destroyed" in Portland, the owner can not be reimbursed in the State of Washington. In southern New Jersey the cattle go to Philadelphia—at least the most of them go there. In eastern North Dakota they go to St. Paul, but under the present law when they leave the State the owner can not be indemnified.

Mr. Haugen. Doesn't this give you the power to condemn the cattle, a power which you did not have before? Your could not destroy them without some mutual agreement with the owner.

Dr. MOHLER. This particular feature is merely relating to indemnity. An owner living in the eastern part of your State can not be remunerated if his tuberculous animal is slaughtered in St. Joe.

Mr. HAUGEN. Haven't you the power to condemn now?

Dr. MOHLER. Yes, sir; but we can not indemnify the owner if the animal is taken out of the State where found diseased.

Mr. ANDERSON. That does not comply with the law. That is not my understanding of it. You say "under the present wording of the law the animals must actually be destroyed in the same State, county, or municipality where found diseased."

Dr. MOHLER. Yes, sir; that is right if indemnity is to be allowed. Under the existing law animals must be destroyed in the State where they were found diseased if the owner is to be remunerated.

Mr. ANDERSON. Here is a bunch of cattle shipped from some point in Iowa to St. Joe, as you state; they are found to be diseased when they arrive at St. Joe.

Dr. MOHLER. No; right there is where we misunderstand each other. These animals to which I refer are all found to be tuberculous by the tuberculin test in Iowa and are shipped to St. Joe for slaughter as a convenient point, but at present the owner can not be reimbursed for any loss, although if he had shipped them to some point in Iowa for slaughter he would receive Federal indemnity. In a case like the one you mention, where Iowa cattle are not found diseased until they are slaughtered in an abattoir at St. Joe, the law itself wisely prohibits reimbursement.

The CHAIRMAN. There was a conflict of ideas there.

Dr. MOHLER. I believe the committee tried to have the farmers indemnified whether their cattle were slaughtered by a packer or not.

Mr. ANDERSON. What I understood the committee was trying to do was to prevent the payment of indemnity to the packers.

Dr. MOHLER. Yes, sir; and you will do that if you change these words as recommended. That was the idea—not to pay the packer. If the cattle are condemned in Iowa on the farm and then shipped and destroyed in St. Joe or Omaha, the indemnity could still go to the farmer and not to the packer.

The CHAIRMAN. In other words, if they come from Iowa to Swift & Co. in Chicago and are destroyed you can't indemnify the owner?

Dr. MOHLER. No, sir.

The CHAIRMAN. Although you have condemned them before shipping them?

Dr. MOHLER. Yes, sir.

The CHAIRMAN. And now if you adopt this language you will remedy that?

Dr. MOHLER. Yes, sir; we will still pay the owner but not Swift & Co. We will pay the farmer but not the packer.

Mr. MCLAUGHLIN. If you hadn't had that language in at all you might have gone into the stockyards and if you hadn't had that language in you would have paid Swift & Co.?

Dr. MOHLER. Yes, sir.

Mr. MCLAUGHLIN. And this was put in to prevent that?

Dr. MOHLER. Yes, sir.

Mr. MCLAUGHLIN. Yet the doctor says that the comptroller has ruled under that language he is not able to pay the farmer from whose farm they came from Iowa or Minnesota. I suppose that this is the way it works: If a man's herd of animals is tested and found to be tubercular they can still be good enough for food.

Dr. MOHLER. Yes, sir.

Mr. MCLAUGHLIN. And he decides to sell them to the stockyards, and they are tested and found tubercular and shipped away to the stockyard and there destroyed but the owner can't get paid.

Dr. MOHLER. If he ships them out of his State he can get paid by the packer the amount they are considered to be worth, but according to the language here the Government can't pay him any indemnity. You have permitted the owner to make an interstate shipment of his cattle but you have stopped the indemnity feature by using the words "destroy" and "destruction" and we believe it adivsable to remedy this.

Mr. HAUGEN. You pay the difference between the value of a small animal and the condemned value?

Dr. MOHLER. We pay only one-third of the difference between the salvage and the appraised value, the State pays the second one-third and the owner loses the other third.

Mr. HAUGEN. Does this give you power to pay the packer also?

Dr. MOHLER. No, sir; neither here nor under the meat-inspection act.

Mr. ANDERSON. I do not agree with that construction at all.

Dr. MOHLER. There is another change recommended since these estimates went to press that I would like to suggest: After the word "State" insert the word "territory" so it will read "State, territory, or county."

The CHAIRMAN. What line is that on, doctor?

Dr. MOHLER. It should appear at three different points in lines 8, 17, and 25, on page 47, and in the first line on page 48. This addition is recommended because Hawaii has expressed a desire to take up accredited herd work. Hawaii being a territory we can't cooperate with her without having this provision made in the bill.

Mr. WASON. I am not quite satisfied with the changing of this word here. Now, doctor, you pay in connection with the State?

Dr. MOHLER. Yes, sir.

Mr. WASON. Of course, any legislation that we may pass or any ruling the comptroller may make does not affect the payment by the State in any particular. But if it has been shipped to the stockyards in Chicago, is the State going to allow its money to be paid out for property not destroyed in the State? Now, under the present wording and under the comptroller's ruling, why can't the title to that animal pass from the owner in the State and then be shipped and he be given his pay?

Dr. MOHLER. I will tell you the reason; it is this: According to the law we pay only one-third the difference between the salvage and the appraised value of the animal; we have to get figures from the packers to find out what the salvage is. Some carcasses are used only for fertilizers and some for food purposes.

Mr. WASON. Why can't you get the animal and pay him the difference?

Dr. MOHLER. Because the law does not allow that. You will see that it gives the Secretary no discretion in the matter. Payment by the Government can be made only after the State has paid its share; the word "supplementary" appears here.

Mr. WASON. Suppose you get up against some State authorities who won't pay for animals slaughtered outside of the State.

Dr. MOHLER. We couldn't pay anything then, because the law says we can't pay anything until the State has paid its share.

Mr. MCLAUGHLIN. We are helping the States to take care of their people. If they don't cooperate, we can't go over their heads if they are not interested enough to pay a part of the money.

Mr. WASON. But he has to lose it if the State does not pay and if the animal can't be slaughtered.

Dr. MOHLER. If it is slaughtered outside of the State at present, he would receive neither Federal nor State indemnity in the case you mention.

Mr. MCLAUGHLIN. He puts in here that they can be.

Mr. ANDERSON. The word "condemnation" does not refer to what we ordinarily understand as legal condemnation.

Dr. MOHLER. No, sir.

Mr. ANDERSON. It refers to the fact that the animal is tubercular and destroyed?

Dr. MOHLER. The term is not used in the legal sense at all, but in a medical sense, and means that the animal has tuberculosis.

Mr. ANDERSON. I don't think that is clear.

Dr. MOHLER. It is clear in tuberculosis phraseology.

The CHAIRMAN. You have the same language in the meat-inspection act?

Dr. MOHLER. Yes, sir.

The CHAIRMAN. So I think it is pretty clear.

Dr. MOHLER. As you know, Mr. Chairman, some of the State legislatures are in session or about to go into session. We are cooperating with about 40 States and some of those which have no indemnity measures are arranging to change their laws to correspond with the Federal act.

Mr. MCLAUGHLIN. You have how many?

Dr. MOHLER. We have an indemnity agreement in about 17 States; some other States are not ready to indemnify yet, some haven't the money, and some have no law. But a great many of the latter have this question before them.

Mr. MCLAUGHLIN. How about the others? Are they States that have tuberculosis? Are they excused?

Dr. MOHLER. None should be excused.

Mr. MCLAUGHLIN. Can you name the eight States that have not done anything?

Dr. MOHLER. I can give you the States we are cooperating with and you can eliminate them from the others and tell by that. New York, Georgia, Alabama, Maine, Massachusetts, Rhode Island, New Hampshire, Connecticut, Illinois, South Carolina, Colorado, Wyoming, Iowa, Pennsylvania, Indiana, Wisconsin, Kentucky, Ohio, Mississippi, Kansas, Michigan, Tennessee, Louisiana, Nebraska, Oregon, Washington, Virginia, North Carolina, Vermont, Minnesota, Montana, North Dakota, South Dakota, Utah, Idaho, Florida, New Jersey, Delaware, and the District of Columbia; so the States I have not named are the ones we are not cooperating with.

The CHAIRMAN. What does that statement show in addition to that?

Dr. MOHLER. It shows the number of herds tested, the number of cattle in each herd, the number reacting, the number slaughtered, the increase in number tested over the previous month's work, and the number of bureau employees in addition to the State employees.

The CHAIRMAN. I think that is an interesting statement to go into the record.

(The statement referred to follows:)

Summary of tuberculosis-eradication work in cooperation with the various States, month of November, 1918.

Station.	States.	Number of lots.	Number of cattle tested.	Number reacted.	Number slaughtered.	Increase in number tested over previous month.	Bureau.	State.	Inspector in charge.
Albany, N. Y	New York	11	398	5	21	78	1	1	Dr. H. B. Leonard.
Atlanta, Ga	Georgia	15	789	21	14	256	2	1	Dr. W. M. MacKellar.
Birmingham	Alabama	313	1,396	25	2	17	7	1	Dr. R. E. Jackson.
Boston, Mass	Maine	31	340	6	6		2	2	Dr. E. A. Crossman.
	Massachusetts	11	386	16	28		3		
	Rhode Island	1	2	2			1		
	New Hampshire	4	81	3			1		
	Connecticut	8	187	23	11	148	1		
Chicago, Ill	Illinois	59	1,250	81	98	40	5	2	Dr. J. J. Lintner.
Columbia, S. C	South Carolina	10	253	8	37		1	1	Dr. W. K. Lewis.
Denver, Colo	Colorado	2	10	3					Dr. W. E. Howe.
	Wyoming	529	2,944	11		2,858	1	1	
Des Moines, Iowa	Iowa	12	502	34	4	248	3	2	Dr. F. H. Thompson.
Harrisburg, Pa	Pennsylvania	27	233	8	2		1	2	Dr. P. E. Quinn.
Indianapolis, Ind	Indiana	22	702	11	20	32	9	5	Dr. J. E. Gibson.
	Wisconsin	13	428	4		126	2	5	
	Kentucky	24	431	11	2	198	4	3	
	Ohio	33	376	26	8		5	5	
Jackson, Miss	Mississippi	77	706	12	16	254	3		Dr. J. A. Barger.
Kansas City, Kans	Kansas	22	1,061	80		980			Dr. T. J. Eagle.
Lansing, Mich	Michigan	19	606	24	14		4	1	Dr. T. S. Rich.
Nashville, Tenn	Tennessee	26	1,109	33	20	519	4	1	Dr. W. B. Lincoln.
New Orleans, La	Louisiana	22	586	33	15	386	2		Dr. R. W. Tuck.
Omaha, Nebr	Nebraska	7	105		16		4	1	Dr. H. Busman.
Portland, Oreg	Oregon	14	223	6			1	1	Dr. S. B. Foster.
	Washington	6	803	5	2	654	1	3	
Richmond, Va	Virginia	60	1,293	31	31	10	7	1	Dr. R. E. Brookbank.
	North Carolina	21	349	1	2		2	1	
St. Albans, Vt	Vermont	56	1,575	197	141	844	6	3	Dr. A. J. DeFosset.
St. Paul, Minn	Minnesota	29	1,164	26			10	4	Dr. W. J. Fretz.
	....do	54	1,043	99					
	Montana	28	689	17			2	4	
	North Dakota	50	636	19		14	2	5	
	South Dakota	16	440	14		110	1	2	
Salt Lake City, Utah	Utah	25	252	5			4	2	Dr. F. E. Murray.
	Idaho	6	223	2		176	1		
Tallahassee, Fla	Florida	9	201	1	1	14	3	1	Dr. J. G. Fish.
Trenton, N. J	New Jersey	3	393	3	3	290	1		Dr. W. G. Middleton.
	Delaware	8	308	10		243			
Washington, D. C	District of Columbia	12	98	3	3	41	1		Dr. J. A. Kiernan.
	Maryland	33	401	114	94		5		
	Miscellaneous	13	32				1		
Total		1,739	24,994	1,033	611		115	61	

NOTE.—The first line of Minnesota is accredited herds; the second, area work.

The CHAIRMAN. If there is no further question on this word "condemnation," you might indicate in a general way what progress you have been making. It is now manifest you are making progress.

Dr. MOHLER. You will remember, Mr. Chairman, the bill only passed on the 1st of October, 1918.

The CHAIRMAN. Yes.

Dr. MOHLER. But the original food-production act contained about $150,000 for the investigation and eradication of tuberculosis, abortion, and several other diseases. It was with an allotment from this fund that we began these tuberculosis projects. At the present time, as I stated a while ago, we have 40 States in which we are working, and we have 120 inspectors; the States have about 70, but they are gradually increasing the number. The idea is to have one State inspector to every Federal inspector. There are over 6,000 herds at the present time under supervision; 296 herds of cattle are fully accredited under the project we call tuberculosis-free accredited herds. These herds are accredited because they have been found free of tuberculosis in the last two tests. In addition, there are 1,462 herds that have passed one successful test. We have started circumscribed-area work in certain counties in Alabama, Tennessee, Minnesota, Pennsylvania, and Ohio. In Sumter County, S. C., we have a circumscribed area where there has been very little tuberculosis found.

Mr. ANDERSON. Do you have anything to do with the system of accredited herds, as you call it?

Dr. MOHLER. Yes, sir; that is the project I spoke about. We have accredited 296 herds; 1,462 additional herds have passed one test, and in six months we will have many more.

The CHAIRMAN. Have you arrived at any theory except the two methods you have mentioned?

Dr. MOHLER. No, Mr. Chairman; we are going along the line of least resistance. We have met with less resistance and more support along the line of the accredited-herd system than any other method we have ever undertaken. The work is developing so fast that we have not the men to carry it out. There are more demands than we can supply. We will not be able to extend this work much more, as the plan already outlined is going to occupy all our time. The circumscribed-area work is going to be more "up and down" than the accredited-herd work. At the time I was here last year I thought the State would get Waukesha County lined up for area work. They had a vote on whether the farmers wanted it, and the majority of the farmers voted in favor of it and the tuberculin test. They started, and then the war took their men, with the result that there was little further done. In my opinion the circumscribed-area work will not go so fast as the accredited-herd work.

Mr. ANDERSON. The accredited herd naturally produces results in a community?

Dr. MOHLER. Yes, sir; it should.

Mr. ANDERSON. In other words, where you have a number of accredited herds it becomes naturally easier to do the work?

Dr. MOHLER. Yes, sir; quite so. It becomes a matter of pride. And these accredited herds are mostly pure-bred herds and are the fountain head of the grade herds. So we are doing more good with this system than with any other.

The CHAIRMAN. You have no doubt that you will eventually control this situation?

Dr. MOHLER. There is no reason to doubt that we will control it. Some day we may recommend a quarantine around the worst infected States, where these States are not preventing the spread of the disease.

Mr. MCLAUGHLIN. Doctor, do they not forbid now the shipping of an animal from one State to another for breeding purposes until they have been tuberculin tested?

Dr. MOHLER. They do have laws or regulations of that kind, but all States do not enforce them.

Mr. MCLAUGHLIN. All States have it?

Dr. MOHLER. Yes, sir; but all States do not enforce them.

Mr. HAUGEN. Do you say all States have it?

Dr. MOHLER. Yes, sir. Even where they try to enforce it there is a method of "plugging" the cattle which tends to nullify the test. The best thing I know of to circumvent this is the 60-day retest. In those States which have adopted this feature, the plugging system has become valueless.

Mr. MCLAUGHLIN. Do these 40 States you speak of have laws for the contribution of indemnity or compensation?

Dr. MOHLER. No, sir; not all of them do.

Mr. MCLAUGHLIN. In the States where they have it I suppose it is varied very much?

Dr. MOHLER. Very much. In Connecticut and New York they are paying $125, against our $50, for pure-bred cattle. And each State has its own method of indemnifying its live-stock owners. This makes it very hard for us to work with the various States on account of the variation of their laws. As you know, in your State of South Carolina, Mr. Chairman, the law says there shall be no compensation for animals having contagious diseases, but yet each year the State legislature appropriates the money sufficient to pay for cattle destroyed the preceding year. However, in a case like this, we will have to wait until the State appropriates the money before we can pay the stock owner.

Mr. MCLAUGHLIN. Have you gone far enough to know whether the amounts we provided the Government should pay for grade animals and the pure-bred animals are right, or are too much or are too small?

Dr. MOHLER. They are far from being right.

Mr. MCLAUGHLIN. In what way?

Dr. MOHLER. They are entirely too small; that is the main thing that has been criticized by the stockmen about this tuberculosis act—the small amount that is allowed for grade and pure-bred cattle. We pay only one-third the appraisal, and 3 times 25 is $75 for a grade; and 3 times 50 is $150 for a pure bred.

Mr. MCLAUGHLIN. Isn't $75 a large price for a grade animal?

Dr. MOHLER. No, sir; they are getting almost that for bolognas with a good framework.

Mr. MCLAUGHLIN. But some animals have tuberculosis to the extent they should be slaughtered?

Dr. MOHLER. That is very true, sir.

Mr. MCLAUGHLIN. Do they estimate the value of that animal on the physically perfect basis?

Dr. MOHLER. To a certain extent, they make that comparison, basing the appraisal on what the animal was worth immediately before the tuberculin test. The biggest difference of values is in the pure bred; that is where the greatest variation occurs between our appraisal value and the worth of the animal to the owner.

Mr. McLAUGHLIN. What is it in a pure bred?

Dr. MOHLER. $50.

Mr. McLAUGHLIN. Do you recommend an increase in one or both?

Dr. MOHLER. In both.

Mr. McLAUGHLIN. How much?

Dr. MOHLER. As was stated in a letter from the Secretary to this committee last year, this first figure of $25 should be doubled. That does not mean that we should pay that sum on all grade cattle condemned, but it would permit us to give more than $25 if these cattle are worth more.

Mr. McLAUGHLIN. On the pure breds?

Dr. MOHLER. No; the grades I am speaking of now.

Mr. McLAUGHLIN. What on the pure breds?

Dr. MOHLER. That I would like to have left with the Secretary, but it should at least be doubled. It was not long ago a little Holstein bull calf sold for $106,000.

Mr. HAUGEN. Do you believe we should pay one-third of $106,000?

Dr. MOHLER. No, sir; but I think it should be left discretionary with the Secretary of Agriculture as to how much to pay, since the law prohibits the Government paying more than the State.

Mr. McLAUGHLIN. I don't think it should be left discretionary for the Secretary to pay one-third of $106,000.

Dr. MOHLER. I don't think there would be any possibility of such an occurrence.

Mr. McLAUGHLIN. Isn't it dangerous to have these amounts too high? Wouldn't the farmers be careless about caring for their animals?

Dr. MOHLER. Yes, they might. In fact, in the old days of pleuropneumonia some unscrupulous dealers exposed their stock in order to get paid for them and have them buried.

Mr. McLAUGHLIN. I thought at the time these amounts were not quite high enough but I did not have an idea they should be what you say—$50 for a grade animal, and an unlimited amount for pure bred. Haven't you some recommendation?

Dr. MOHLER. My recommendation is that the grade be made $50 and the value of the pure bred be left discretionary with the Secretary of Agriculture, because there are such wide variations in values and so many things to be considered that the man on the ground is better able to judge. In no case could we pay more than the State pays.

Mr. McLAUGHLIN. Do you know of any State law that allows pay without limit?

Dr. MOHLER. Yes, sir.

Mr. McLAUGHLIN. What States?

Dr. MOHLER. Kansas is one, and we are working in cooperation with that State. Some States allow $150, others $200, while Montana allows full assessed value not to exceed $500.

Mr. McLAUGHLIN. That is the total value, or the State to pay up to $200.

Dr. MOHLER. Up to $200.

Mr. MCLAUGHLIN. Then if the State paid up to $200 and we paid $50, that is $250.

Dr. MOHLER. Yes, sir.

Mr. MCLAUGHLIN. Which is a pretty good price?

Dr. MOHLER. All the States are not doing that. Vermont has recently raised her limit. We had a fine herd of Ayrshires that were found tubercular and this increased appraisal permitted the owner to get off fairly well. They were not badly affected, as the local practitioner had been testing them for years.

Mr. MCLAUGHLIN. And the salvage, of course?

Dr. MOHLER. The salvage is practically the same for a grade as for a pure bred, of course.

The CHAIRMAN. Have you any State in mind that leaves the question of value for pure breds to the discretion of a State officer?

Dr. MOHLER. Yes, sir. Kansas and Oklahoma have fixed no limit. I have all that information in my office; we had it collected during the foot-and-mouth disease outbreak.

The CHAIRMAN. Don't you think, if we left it to the Secretary of Agriculture, there would be a revolution in the country in about 10 years because we did not go high enough?

Dr. MOHLER. Possibly.

Mr. WASON. These prices that the doctor states for animals are the prices paid by gentlemen farmers that make their money on wheat in Chicago?

Dr. MOHLER. A well-known dairy concern on the Pacific coast paid the $106,000 for the bull I spoke of.

Mr. ANDERSON. That is for advertising purposes?

Mr. MCLAUGHLIN. This amount we are speaking of will naturally grow; more money will be needed as time goes on. What do you think of this amount for next year, being your second year in the work, paying all your inspectors and overhead expenses, and will you have money enough left for your contributions out of that?

Dr. MOHLER. Gentlemen, you will remember last year when this item was before the House Committee it was for $250,000 without indemnity; then the Senate increased it to $500,000 and added the indemnity feature. We will need all of this amount for the year's work now in sight.

Mr. MCLAUGHLIN. You will need all the $500,000 then from the 1st of October to the 1st of July?

Dr. MOHLER. Yes, sir; the demands for tuberculin tests and correlated work have been coming in very fast and if we meet all the requests we will need more money. We could expend judiciously twice the amount that is in this item with the indemnity feature the way it is now.

Mr. MCLAUGHLIN. Would your suggestion for that increase have the approval of the Secretary of Agriculture?

Dr. MOHLER. If the committee so decided, I do not believe there would be any objection on the part of the Secretary. He did not feel disposed to ask for any increase in this item himself. But there is no objection, certainly, to the committee increasing it in its wisdom to that amount.

Mr. MCLAUGHLIN. And you could use it?

Dr. MOHLER. Yes, sir; judging from the way this work has increased in the last six weeks and the way the various States are taking a steady and growing interest in it.

Mr. ANDERSON. Right at that point, if I may inquire, have you any statement from which you could compile a synopsis of the amount being expended in different States for this purpose?

Dr. MOHLER. Yes, sir.

Mr. ANDERSON. I would like to have such a statement.

Dr. MOHLER. Your State of Minnesota has the greatest number of accredited herds. They have been working on this for several years, and have an appropriation of $40,000. The amounts appropriated by some of the other States are as follows:

Connecticut, $50,000 (biennial) ; Georgia, $50,000 (annual) ; Kentucky, $15,000 (annual) ; Maine, $40,000 (annual) ; Maryland, $7,000 (annual) ; Massachusetts, $43,000 (annual) ; New Jersey, $25,600 (annual) ; New York, $150,000 (annual) ; North Dakota, $30,000 (biennial) ; Ohio, $100,000 (annual) ; Pennsylvania, $100,000 (annual) ; Rhode Island, $7,374 (annual) ; South Dakota, $15,000 (biennial) ; Vermont, $65,000 (annual) ; Wisconsin, $25,000 (annual); Wyoming, $6,000 (biennial).

Quite a number of additional States have some funds that can be used for cooperative tuberculosis eradication, and we are now cooperating with these States to some extent in this work. Of course we can not take part in indemnifying owners for tuberculous cattle except where provision for indemnity has been made by the State.

Mr. HAUGEN. Are these tests made without expense to the owner of the herd?

Dr. MOHLER. The only expense to him is to meet the man at the station and sometimes to put him up overnight and give him his meals.

Mr. HAUGEN. The States are cooperating with you?

Dr. MOHLER. Yes, sir; tests are made.

Mr. HAUGEN. And all without expense?

Dr. MOHLER. Yes, sir; all cooperative between the officials.

Mr. HAUGEN. And all without expense?

Dr. MOHLER. Yes, sir.

Mr. HAUGEN. Now, isn't it a fact that $75, and the salvage, pays for the animal?

Dr. MOHLER. No, sir; I wouldn't say that. Some of these animals are so slightly affected they are good for food, and if they are of twelve or fourteen hundred pounds weight the salvage is high.

Mr. HAUGEN. For salvage—how much is that?

Dr. MOHLER. If they are condemned they are worth their hide; the owner may get $10 or $12 or $14 for the salvage of a tank carcass.

Mr. HAUGEN. For a tank carcass?

Dr. MOHLER. Yes; a certain portion is entirely lost to the owner in this case.

Mr. HAUGEN. In nearly every shipment some animals are tagged or condemned, and in many instances they bring more than they would if sold to the packers or the scalpers. The hide alone brings considerable.

Dr. MOHLER. Yes; 22 cents a pound.

Mr. HAUGEN. And 100 pounds?

Dr. MOHLER. They don't weigh 100 pounds; some may weigh 60 pounds, but they average below that.

Mr. HAUGEN. Were you describing all grade steers, were you, or heavy steers?

Dr. MOHLER. Oh, steers; we have not gone into steer testing at all; we are testing breeding and dairy animals. The steer question is a different proposition, but we haven't started on that.

Mr. McLAUGHLIN. Isn't it true that tuberculosis is found more in dairy cattle, resulting from their being kept in barns and confined?

Dr. MOHLER. Yes, sir; that is true.

Mr. McLAUGHLIN. And the dairy cattle are not the heavy cattle whose carcasses are as heavy as the others?

Dr. MOHLER. No, sir.

Mr. HAUGEN. The average cow to-day does not sell for $100.

Dr. MOHLER. I can't buy them for $100. I am in the market to-day and will give $200 for good grade cattle.

Mr. HAUGEN. In my country we sold hundreds of them at sales this fall and very few of them brought $100. At the stock yards you can get a fair cow for $100.

Dr. MOHLER. The French High Commission is now trying to buy grade cattle to take back to France and they have had some offers of $250; they do not want to pay more than $175 to $200 and they can't get them.

Mr. HAUGEN. According to the quotations to-day you can get them for that.

Dr. MOHLER. The average price of cattle on the market in Chicago does not represent the average for the dairy breed. They are the culls and discards that you see in the Chicago quotations of the papers here, if that is what you go by.

Mr. HAUGEN. No; I spent a day over there. I sold dairy cattle for $100 and was at sales, and in our section of the country very few are selling for $100, and they are good, average cows—not the high graded or registered cows.

Dr. MOHLER. That is different from the information we have in this vicinity. At Annapolis we are buying for the Government herd and we can not get them at that price. We can buy an ordinary cow that gives about 10 quarts of milk, when she is fresh, for that money.

Mr. HAUGEN. I sold a dairy cow giving about 12 quarts of milk for $107. How many animals were condemned or destroyed under this act?

Dr. MOHLER. I couldn't tell you; it has been in effect only since the 1st of October, 1918, and the records for the past two months are just coming in. Thus far indemnity has been paid in but one or two instances.

Mr. HAUGEN. This compensation is along the line of the policy as adopted for the foot-and-mouth disease?

Dr. MOHLER. Somewhat similar, although that was a 50-50 proposition; 50 by the State and 50 by the Federal Government.

Mr. HAUGEN. What was the limitation?

Dr. MOHLER. No limitation, except in the case of a few States.

The CHAIRMAN. It was an appraisal proposition?

Dr. MOHLER. It was an appraisal proposition, the State and Federal Government each paying half.

The CHAIRMAN. Have you anything further to present on this item?

Dr. MOHLER. I think not.

Mr. MCLAUGHLIN. I would like to leave this matter open and get something from the joint conference of the Secretary of Agriculture and Dr. Mohler, so that there will not be any doubt in our minds what is recommended; some recommendations from them as to the amounts to be put in; some amount to be put in if any change is to be made, and the amount of the total. Dr. Mohler says the matter has been talked over by him and the Secretary and he thinks a much larger amount could be used.

The CHAIRMAN. I understood from Mr. Harrison this morning that the Secretary was considering some supplemental estimate.

Mr. HARRISON. The only supplemental estimates in mind at present are those for extension work and for farm-labor work. Of course, all these activities are productive of good results, and it is merely a question as to how much Congress wants to spend on them.

Dr. MOHLER. This committee last year recommended $250,000 without any indemnity, and the Senate increased it to $500,000 but added the indemnity feature. We are going to spend more than $250,000 on indemnifying owners.

The CHAIRMAN. Some one may ask how much will be spent for indemnification and how much for the other work; have you reached a conclusion on that?

Dr. MOHLER. No; I have not, except in a general way. The indemnity feature is just since the 1st of October and only about 17 States are now ready to conform to the requirements.

The CHAIRMAN. Do you have an idea that a great many more States during the winter through their legislatures will conform?

Dr. MOHLER. Yes, sir; I know that will be the case because of the letters we have received from the governors and officials asking our opinion on the phraseology of their proposed laws.

The CHAIRMAN. As I understood you, 17 States are now conforming?

Dr. MOHLER. Yes, sir.

The CHAIRMAN. Do you believe there will be that many more?

Dr. MOHLER. I believe all States that take any action at all will conform to this present act. That is the opinion I have, based on conferences which I attended when in Chicago at the live-stock show. I saw a great many live-stock men and they were much interested in this item.

The CHAIRMAN. If the department desires to make any further suggestions as to this item, I think it should come in the way of supplemental estimate, because this committee has been fearfully abused in the past because we have allowed appropriations on requests rather than those coming through the regular channels. If you want to submit anything further, we would like to have it come through the regular channel.

The next item, No. 89, is the southern cattle-tick proposition.

Dr. MOHLER. Yes, sir; that is the item covering the eradication of southern cattle-ticks and will be decreased because of the transfer of these clerks to the statutory roll.

The CHAIRMAN. Briefly, what progress are you making in this matter?

Dr. MOHLER. During the past year we released from quarantine the greatest area of any period during the history of our work; 79,600 square miles were released, including the State of South Carolina, at one time on December 1, 1918; and 67,000 square miles, including the State of Mississippi, were released on December 1, 1917.

The CHAIRMAN. That leaves you how much still under quarantine?

Dr. MOHLER. That leaves us 37 per cent under quarantine; we have freed 63 per cent of the territory.

The CHAIRMAN. At the rate you have gone this year, how long will it be before you conclude this work?

Dr. MOHLER. By 1923.

The CHAIRMAN. Will you still have to maintain some skeleton organization after this tick is cleaned up?

Dr. MOHLER. For some years. If the work goes well we hope to take Louisiana out next year, and all but six counties of Arkansas.

The CHAIRMAN. All the States that are cooperating with you are helping?

Dr. MOHLER. Yes; they are really doing more than the Federal Government. I would like to give you the number of inspectors that are being used in this work in the various counties and States. The number of bureau inspectors is 288; the number of State inspectors is 223, and the number of county inspectors is 1,076, so that we have a small proportion of the entire personnel of the force that is working in eradicating the tick in these sections.

Mr. ANDERSON. In what proportion of the counties are you doing work? In all of them?

Dr. MOHLER. No, sir; in Texas we are working about 65 counties; we are starting in the first of this year to make a systematic effort to dip all the cattle in Zone I, according to the provisions of the State-wide tick-eradication law. The counties in Zone II will be worked in 1920, and those in Zone III during 1922.

Mr. ANDERSON. Has the area in which you are actually working increased from year to year

Dr. MOHLER. Yes, sir.

Mr. ANDERSON. You will be working in more territory next year than this year?

Dr. MOHLER. Yes, sir; up to a certain point.

Mr. McLAUGHLIN. Do you find any recurrences?

Dr. MOHLER. Yes; occasionally we find recurrences the same as you do in influenza and other diseases.

The State of Alabama, in addition, expects to pass a State-wide tick-eradication law at this session of her legislature, and if she does so, it will go in effect in April, and we will clean up Alabama this year.

The CHAIRMAN. So, on the whole, you feel that you are making good progress?

Dr. MOHLER. Yes, sir.

The CHAIRMAN. And you are holding out the hope that in 1923 you can have that tick eradicated?

Dr. MOHLER. Yes, sir.

The CHAIRMAN. Doctor, if you want to extend your remarks at length in the record on any subject you are at liberty to do so.

(Thereupon, at 5.30 p. m., the committee took a recess until Saturday, January 5, 1919, at 10.30 o'clock.)

HOUSE OF REPRESENTATIVES,
COMMITTEE ON AGRICULTURE,
Saturday, January 4, 1919.

The committee met at 10:30 o'clock a. m., Hon. Asbury F. Lever chairman), presiding

BUREAU OF ANIMAL INDUSTRY—Continued.

STATEMENT OF MR. B. H. RAWL, CHIEF OF THE DAIRY DIVISION, BUREAU OF ANIMAL INDUSTRY, UNITED STATES DEPARTMENT OF AGRICULTURE.

The CHAIRMAN. The next item, gentlemen, is No. 90, on page 51, "For all necessary expenses for the investigations and experiments in dairy industry," etc. Mr. Rawl, Chief of the Dairy Division, is here and will discuss the work.

Mr. RAWL. Mr. Chairman and gentlemen, there are no changes proposed for this work, and I do not know how much time you wish to give to a review of the dairy problems.

The CHAIRMAN. Suppose you make a general statement of about 5 or 10 minutes on the various lines of work you are conducting; refer to any changes you have to suggest, and any progress you have made.

Mr. RAWL. Perhaps you would be interested in the export and import situation. In 1913, the balance of trade, reducing everything to pounds of milk, was about 400,000,000 pounds against us. In 1914, it was approximately 700,000,000 pounds against us. In 1915, the balance of trade swung over in our favor, and has increased every year since until in 1918 the balance in our favor amounted to approximately 1,900,000,000 pounds. This means a change from 700,000,000 pounds against us in 1915 to 1,900,000,000 in our favor for the year 1918, or a change of about 2,600,000,000 pounds of milk, or its equivalent.

Mr. MCLAUGHLIN. When that balance of trade was against us, during 1913 and 1914, from what parts of the world did it come, and of what did it consist, largely?

Mr. RAWL. You understand what I mean when speaking in terms of pounds of milk; instead of referring to so many pounds of butter, cheese, condensed milk, etc., I am giving the pounds of milk required to make the quantities of these products that constituted the balance of trade mentioned.

That balance of trade in 1913 and 1914 consisted largely of cheese, most of which came from Switzerland, Italy, Holland, and England. A little butter, in excess of what we exported, was also received. This chart [indicating another chart] shows the amount of butter, cheese, and condensed milk. You see, what has happened to the condensed-milk industry, we exported about 18,000,000 pounds prior to the war, last year we exported practically 500,000,000 pounds.

Mr. LESHER. Are we going to be able to keep this up after the war?

Mr. RAWL. Not likely. However, that will, of course, depend upon the ability of foreign countries to supply their own needs. We may retain some of it, if we compete with them in quality and other things.

Mr. YOUNG of Texas. That butter industry has been very largely reduced, if I am correctly informed?

Mr. RAWL. In some localities it has; in some it has not.

Mr. THOMPSON. So far as the depletion in stock itself is concerned, it looked to me in Italy and France like every farmer had an abundance of cattle on his farm at the time I was there, during July and August of this year.

Mr. MCLAUGHLIN. Did you get into Italy?

Mr. THOMPSON. Yes.

The CHAIRMAN. What was their condition?

Mr. THOMPSON. They were in as fine condition as they could be.

Mr. RAWL. I might say we have been following the situation as closely as possible so as to put out such information as this. You can see at a glance we have built up a war condensed milk industry of considerable size. We could not possibly jump from 18,000,000 pounds a year export to 500,000,000 without a very materially enlarged equipment. The permanency of this enlargement is going to depend on the manufacturers' ability to find markets and to meet the competition which they will have after the war.

Mr. THOMPSON. Don't you think even without the demand from the foreign countries, there is an enormous market in this country for cheese?

The CHAIRMAN. If the people are taught to use it. They never have used much of it in this country, have they?

Mr. RAWL. We consume only about four pounds of cheese per person per year.

The CHAIRMAN. That is an unusually small amount.

Mr. RAWL. Very small, and that is an important question in developing the home markets for dairy products. It is also very important in developing in a large way the dairying of the country. By getting out this information from time to time, we have hoped to keep the industry posted as to just what the conditions were. We believe that this is the most useful way to help them to take care of themselves under the shifting conditions that are likely coming now.

Mr. YOUNG of Texas. Before you pass from that, I am curious to know what effect the war has had on the large dairy herds over the country; have they been reduced to any extent?

Mr. RAWL. Last January's reports showed a slight increase in cattle and a material increase in calves.

Mr. MCLAUGHLIN. January, 1917?

Mr. RAWL. 1918; just a year ago now. Another report will come out shortly, but we have not that as yet. During the year there has been some discouragement and in some places the conditions have perhaps shifted somewhat. From the information we have been able to gather from various sources, our herds have not decreased during the past year.

The CHAIRMAN. Was this large increase in exportation at the expense of consumption in this country, or did our normal consumption keep up?

Mr. RAWL. No; our total production of milk is only about 84,000,000,000 pounds. The change in the balance of trade has been almost 8,000,000,000 pounds. It is improbable that we have had any such increase as that, so that part of the export is due to decreased consumption at home.

The CHAIRMAN. Exactly. What is the normal consumption of cheese and the like of that expressed in terms of pounds of milk, in England, France, and so on, as compared to the average in this country? What I am trying to bring out is whether or not we can find a market for our own dairy products here if we taught our people their proper and full use.

Mr. RAWL. Yes, we have possiblities for very greatly enlarging our home market. Our per capita consumption of fluid milk is about one pint per day, which includes the farm families. In recent years investigations have indicated that proper nutrition, particularly in growing children, is to such a large extent dependent upon milk that we regard the knowledge about the use of milk in the cities and in the country as of enormous importance to our general public health and welfare.

Mr. THOMPSON. You did not answer the question as to the consumption in this country as compared with foreign markets.

Mr. RAWL. Of some products our consumption is lower. This is probably not the case with milk; some of the foreign countries are probably suffering in their cities as much from the small consumption of milk as we are. The consumption of cheese in most foreign countries is greater than here. For example, in the United Kingdom it is 10.2 pounds; in Denmark. 12.3 pounds; and in Switzerland much more, as against 4 pounds here at home.

The CHAIRMAN. Of course, that would not be a fair comparison, because Switzerland is a cheese country.

Mr. RAWL. It is so simply because they have developed it; it is no more of a natural cheese country than is this country. We have been working for a number of years on the methods of making Swiss cheese. We are convinced we can make the same grade of cheese that is made in Switzerland. Why the great Rocky Mountain valleys, with their cool climate and water and their rich grasses, can not, I think, be surpassed for natural advantages for cheese production.

The CHAIRMAN. The committee would be very glad to have you tell them about that.

Mr. RAWL. Of course, everyone is familiar with the Swiss cheese characteristics, the holes, flavor, etc. Some years ago we undertook to get from the Swiss people their process of manufacture, but we found they did not have exact knowledge of the factors involved. We started a study of the problems some years ago, and have carried on the work systematically ever since. There is in Wisconsin quite an amount of Swiss cheese made, but it is not regarded as equal in quality to the imported. It has been found that a starter made of imported Swiss cheese and used in connection with a pure culture gives good results. During the past year an organism has been isolated which appears to be essential. Experiments are being carried on in two factories at the present time and the results are very favorable. We feel confident now, with the information at hand, while it is not entirely complete, that the processes can be controlled in a way to give a product that is as good as the imported.

Some of the regions in this country, such, for example, as the one mentioned for natural advantages, can not be surpassed anywhere in the world. And I may say that one concern on the Pacific coast has now undertaken the manufacture of this variety in a large way.

Mr. McLaughlin. What has been the success in the manufacture of these different kinds of cheeses known as foreign cheeses, commercially in this country? I know you have done it very successfully, and you feel that your experiments have been satisfactory; but how about it being done on a commercial scale?

Mr. Rawl. This particular variety is being manufactured to a considerable extent on a commercial scale, but it is often sold at a disadvantage. A good deal of it is not equal in quality to the foreign cheese—the bulk of it is not. That which does approach the foreign in quality is sold as such. Hence the reputation of our domestic is really not as good as it should be. One concern on the Pacific coast is now undertaking the manufacture of Swiss cheese on a large scale, and it has, in fact, employed one of our men to take charge of its factory. It has been operating for six months and so far very successfully. We think the manufacture of Swiss cheese can go forward now on a perfectly safe basis commercially.

Mr. McLaughlin. There are some factories, however, that are not turning out the product entirely satisfactorily, aren't there?

Mr. Rawl. Very few.

Mr. McLaughlin. You spoke of some considerable production that lacked the proper flavor or quality. Are there some that are entirely satisfactory?

Mr. Rawl. Until recently, I doubt if any factory ever turned out a product that was uniformly equal to the foreign product.

Mr. McLaughlin. In order for them to reach the place where it will be a success, does it involve any added expense?

Mr. Rawl. Yes, sir; it involves some added expense. It involves skill in dealing with these refined processes that the elementary cheese man is hardly able to deal with. As we get into these more complicated processes, it requires a skill that the ordinary cheaper type of cheese does not require. It so happens under the natural conditions of certain places in Europe, where certain varieties originated, that great skill is not required. Roquefort, for instance, originated in France under the most favorable conditions possible for its production. And when we reproduce this variety of cheese under somewhat different conditions, it requires skill and added expense.

Mr. McLaughlin. In your judgment, though, they are making progress that promises they will be able to make it satisfactory commercially?

Mr. Rawl. I think there is no question now that the methods of making both Swiss and Roquefort are so well established that where the factories are able to carry out these methods they can succeed.

Mr. McLaughlin. Some of these imported cheeses are sold at a pretty high price?

Mr. Rawl. Very high prices.

Mr. McLaughlin. What prices have been charged at home here as compared to the other?

Mr. Rawl. With imported Swiss selling at 75–80 cents a pound, our domestic will sell well up toward that price. Of course, supplies of foreign cheeses have fallen off now, and that is one reason for the change in the balance of trade, because that 60,000,000 pounds we used to get probably has largely stopped.

Now, it is exceedingly important, it seems to me, that we should do what we can to utilize all the means we have for producing cheese of all sorts.

The CHAIRMAN. What are you doing along that line; what methods are you pursuing?

Mr. RAWL. We have some cheese men in the field; not very many, however. I spoke a moment ago of the Rocky Mountain conditions for cheese making. So far they have not, with the exception of the California plant mentioned, taken up these more complicated varieties, but are adhering to the ordinary American type.

Mr. McLAUGHLIN. Haven't they in Wisconsin?

Mr. RAWL. Yes; Wisconsin makes a large part of the Swiss cheese that is made in this country.

Mr. HAUGEN. They have been making it for many years, haven't they?

Mr. RAWL. Yes; for quite a while.

Mr. HAUGEN. For 50 years?

Mr. RAWL. I do not know. The Swiss people have been making it probably since their arrival.

Mr. HAUGEN. I know they were making it 40 years ago in large quantities.

Mr. RAWL. We have several people working in the Rocky Mountain States. There the settlements are compact and with the cool weather and cold water the conditions are peculiarly favorable. There is a lot of territory in that region where it would be possible to run a cheese factory on a section of land. The work there is coming along fairly well, and it would be a good thing if we could do a little more.

The work in the southern mountains has been of the same type. You may remember the beginning was made in North Carolina. The first two factories made less than $3,000 worth of cheese the first year. That was in 1914. And this mountain region in the Blue Ridge, including parts of North Carolina, Virginia, West Virginia, and Tennessee, this past year sold nearly half a million dollars worth of cheese. North Carolina alone has 30 factories, back in the mountains, some 50 miles away from the railroads.

Mr. McLAUGHLIN. Are they following your methods?

Mr. RAWL. Yes, sir. I say ours, but I am speaking also of the colleges and extension departments with whom we are cooperating to the very fullest extent; but because it is a highly specialized business the extension departments down there are not in shape to deal with it alone, because they have not developed the dairy-manufacturing business. That has been one of the most interesting pieces of work we have had anything to do with. The mountain boys and girls, too, are the cheese makers. We are maintaining half a dozen men in that region. The States are bearing approximately half the expenses.

Mr. THOMPSON. Where do they get their milk supply; from cattle or goats?

Mr. RAWL. From cattle entirely.

Mr. THOMPSON. In Europe they get a large milk supply from goats, you know?

Mr. RAWL. Some work has been done by the bureau here in connection with the utilization of goat milk. But our people have not gotten used to the idea of milking goats.

Mr. THOMPSON. Just one other question. Mr. Lever asked you a few moments ago to compare the amount of cheese used in this country—that is, to go back to its final analysis, the amount of milk in this country as compared with Europe. You did not do that. I presume it would be impossible to give any accurate figures during the period of the war, but have you those figures prior to the war?

Mr. RAWL. Yes, sir; I think we have.

Mr. THOMPSON. Would you mind putting those in the record if you have them?

(The statement referred to follows:)

Amount of cheese used per capita by various countries.

	Pounds.
United States	3.8
Italy	4.8
Norway	7.1
Netherlands	8.0
France	8.1
United Kingdom	10.2
Denmark	12.3

Mr. THOMPSON. Another question. Do you know whether or not the European records would disclose the amount of milk from goats?

Mr. RAWL. Our bureau has no record of the amount of milk produced by goats in Europe.

Mr. THOMPSON. In northern France, when the war was on, and in the mountains particularly of Italy, France, and Switzerland, a large part of the milk comes from the goat. You know the method of handling the goat proposition. They do not milk the goats and carry it around the country as we do, but they bring the goats in themselves and let the housewife milk the goat right in front of the premises.

Mr. RAWL. Yes.

Mr. THOMPSON. Would that be included in the reports you have?

Mr. RAWL. I do not think it would be.

Mr. THOMPSON. In a large part of Italy, France, and Switzerland—those are the countries I visited—a majority of the milk used at that particular time—I do not know whether it prevails in peace times—a large part of the goat milk is milked by the housewives themselves right in front of their homes every morning.

Mr. RAWL. The most attractive opportunity to my mind for the use of goats in this country is around the small villages and towns where a garden is maintained, but where there isn't enough space to keep a cow a goat might be kept.

Mr. THOMPSON. Over there they bring the herds in from the country. The herder brings them in with a whistle.

Mr. RAWL. The practice of drawing milk in the public streets is open to question; such surroundings are not sanitary.

Mr. THOMPSON. They do it over there.

Mr. RAWL. Yes; but their sanitary control over milk is often not very good in Europe. It is not as good as ours.

Mr. MCLAUGHLIN. Does this goat milk and the milk from cows mix readily?

Mr. RAWL. Yes.

Mr. McLAUGHLIN. Can they be used as a mixture in the production of these things you speak of?

Mr. RAWL. Not always.

Mr. McLAUGHLIN. How about butter?

Mr. RAWL. I have never seen butter made from goat milk. Goat milk is slightly different in flavor. It is also slightly different chemically, but in the main it has the same properties as cow milk. One of our problems in making Roquefort cheese is to make it from cow milk, whereas in France it is made from sheep milk.

Mr. HAUGEN. To what extent is Roquefort cheese manufactured in this country?

Mr. RAWL. Not at all that I know of.

Mr. HAUGEN. We are buying it every day.

Mr. RAWL. Then, you are probably buying imported Roquefort.

Mr. HAUGEN. Oh, no; it does not require an expert to tell the difference between imported and domestic Roquefort cheese.

Mr. RAWL. I do not know of any domestic Roquefort. We are going to start the production of it commercially very soon.

Mr. HAUGEN. Aren't the climatic conditions against you?

Mr. RAWL. Yes; they are entirely if you would have to rely entirely upon natural conditions. Take the question of humidity; you can not produce Roquefort cheese unless you maintain a high humidity. Our humidity, even on the Atlantic coast, varies very widely, but by the use of a little spray of water the proper humidity can be maintained. We have not the French cave, the natural humidity of which is just the thing for Roquefort; neither have we natural refrigeration to take care of fruits, meats, and other things. We will have to control temperature and humidity largely, but that is what you have to do even in the manufacture of butter and, to some extent, a great many of our dairy products.

Mr. HAUGEN. You have been experimenting with it?

Mr. RAWL. Yes.

Mr. HAUGEN. What are the results?

Mr. RAWL. In our laboratory, where we have a small box just 6 or 8 feet square, we do control temperature and humidity without any trouble and virtually reproduce the French cave. But we have not done this commercially right along through the year.

Mr. HAUGEN. You haven't brought it up to the standard of the imported Roquefort, have you?

Mr. RAWL. We think so. We have had a great many people compare it.

Mr. HAUGEN. What is on the market is not of the standard. I buy it from the dealers.

Mr. RAWL. There has been a certain amount coming in. For instance, it is very remarkable, but we are still bringing in condensed milk from Europe. That seems remarkable, when we have increased our exports from 18,000,000 pounds to 530,000,000 pounds. But almost the normal amount is still coming in.

Mr. HAUGEN. That shows the importance of a protective tariff; and as a result of our policy our dairy cows are going to the block.

Mr. RAWL. Are you sure you are not confusing some of the other types of cheese that resemble Roquefort?

Mr. HAUGEN. Oh, no; you go down to the stores here and they will tell you some of it is American and some of it is imported.

Mr. RAWL. I know of none that is made in this country.

Mr. HAUGEN. It is certainly inferior to the imported.

Mr. THOMPSON. All Roquefort is not of the same grade, even the imported, recently?

Mr. RAWL. There are different grades.

Mr. HAUGEN. I have been told there is a private factory running up here in New York.

Mr. RAWL. I do not know about it.

Mr. HAUGEN. I have been told about it.

The CHAIRMAN. We will find out about it at some other time.

Mr. RAWL. We are not ready to advise the manufacturer of Roquefort until the commercial experiments are made; we have advised the Swiss cheese makers to use the methods we have developed.

Mr. HAUGEN. They have been going ahead with the manufacture of Swiss cheese for the last 40 years.

Mr. RAWL. But they have not produced the quality.

Mr. HAUGEN. They have been making it ever since the department was organized, and long before.

Mr. RAWL. And they have sold it for less than the foreign cheese.

Mr. HAUGEN. It has been a pretty good bit of the time.

Mr. RAWL. It has been pretty good, but it has not been equal.

Mr. HAUGEN. I suppose the climatic conditions and, as you say, the milk has something to do with it.

Mr. RAWL. We do believe they can go ahead and make a Swiss cheese now that will compete with the imported; there is enough known about it at the present time. But as for Roquefort we have not said that, because we wanted to make commercial experiments first. On account of the war this work has been delayed.

The CHAIRMAN. Explain, briefly, some of your other experiments.

Mr. RAWL. Our laboratory has done some interesting work during the year, with casein glue. That was a war problem, the requirements for casein of a certain standard to make glue to be used in the production of aeroplanes became an important problem, and for a time we put our laboratories almost entirely on that question with, I think, excellent results. A casein that seems to have met their requirements better than anything before used has been made, and we hope it is going to lead to the extended use of casein of domestic production.

Mr. MCLAUGHLIN. Do you know anything about the kind of glue that was used in putting veneered woods together to use in aeroplanes? In my district, there was a factory using some patented process, some new kind of glue, that was very strong and would resist water and they make boats with it.

Mr. RAWL. It probably was casein glue, but I am not sure.

Mr. HARRISON. The forestry people would know about that, Mr. McLaughlin. They have been doing a lot of work in the laboratory.

Mr. RAWL. In fact, our work has been done in cooperation with the forestry people.

Mr. MCLAUGHLIN. I think this factory has a new process. They use the word "Haskelite," and, I think, that is the name of the man who invented it. It is evidently a wonderful product, and it fastens veneered wood together so that it is just like one solid piece.

The CHAIRMAN. All right, doctor, take up your next item.

Mr. RAWL. We have attempted to keep our research work relative to dairy production going. The study of the effect of mineral salts upon milk production has gone forward, although it has been curtailed somewhat, showing decidedly interesting results. A most interesting thing is that some dairy cows secrete in the milk more of certain minerals per day than is contained in the feed they consume.

Generally speaking, the dairy industry is holding up quite well. About 100 cow-testing associations were stopped last year, because they were unable to get enough men for the work. Women have been used to some extent, I believe, about 27 are run by women now. The prevailing higher prices for cattle have greatly stimulated interest in the bull clubs. While the number of those organizations has not increased so much during the year, the time seems to be ripe now for getting the farmers to take interest in breeding cows systematically to good bulls and on a community cooperative basis. And certainly to the extent we can help crystallize that feeling, it will be of great advantage not only to the welfare of our own breeders and farmers, but in supplying the needs of cattle for other countries as well. Just what these needs will be we do not know, but there is a greater interest in better cattle, caused by the higher prices of feed, labor, and dairy products and the higher prices for cattle, all of these contribute to the greater need for cattle that produce well, and the bull club gives the means to the man with only one cow and the man with three cows or five cows in a neighborhood to use a meritorious bull. It is a business proposition, and I wish we could get every banker, every county agent, and every school in the rural districts of the nation aroused as to this means of getting good bulls, because there is no longer any question that a good bull will often double the production of the cows in a community in one or two generations.

Mr. McLAUGHLIN. You spoke of sending out men to advise commercially in the production of cheese: How is that expense met?

Mr. RAWL. It is met under our general expenses.

Mr. McLAUGHLIN. Where a company or individual, with plenty of money, wishes your help and you send a man across the country to give him advice, do you pay all of that expense?

Mr. RAWL. In some cases we do not, in others we do. Often we have a new method that we want to put into practice and this offers the opportunity.

Mr. McLAUGHLIN. It is to their interest to put it into effect?

Mr. RAWL. It is to their interest to put it into effect, but it is also to the interest of the community at large, and often times we seek to interest them in applying this so as to establish it. There is a limit to which that sort of work can go, I agree; but where you have these methods that must pass from the experimental stage to the commercial stage, there is a certain amount of uncertainty and risk involved. We sent a man to the Pacific Coast recently, because a factory there agreed to make the cheese at their expense, to use our pure cultures, and to determine at their own risk whether or not these cultures were reliable commercially. If we had undertaken to safeguard them (you know a Swiss cheese weighs 150 to 220 pounds), it would mean quite an expense. Then there are many small factories that need help. When visits are made to a factory for no other purpose than to help that factory out of trouble, such visits are made, as a rule, only by some one in the vicinity. Men are not sent long distances for such purposes.

Mr. McLAUGHLIN. At your laboratory you have all the varieties and are adding to the processes. Do any of these individuals or companies that wish to engage in the work come to you and look them over, and let it go at that, or do you go and seek them out all the time?

Mr. RAWL. A great many come to us.

Mr. McLAUGHLIN. About this condensed milk proposition: During the war there was a large increase in the number of condensed milk factories and they paid more for milk than the creameries had been paying, or were able to pay, and the result was that as the condensed milk factories increased in number and capacity, the number of the creameries was reduced and many of them have had to go out of business. Now if there is a falling off in the condensed milk business, if the manufacture of it was stopped, and the creameries having gone out of business, it would leave a very bad situation. What do you learn about that?

Mr. RAWL. Well, in some places the situation has been not so good, and some of the condenseries are going to fail unless they keep up this foreign trade indefinitely, which is improbable. These condenseries are either compelled to establish markets at home or make something else for which they can get markets either at home or abroad. A good many of those factories have no home markets; they were built and operated entirely for supplying foreign markets.

Mr. McLAUGHLIN. Do you look for a continued large production and demand for condensed milk?

Mr. RAWL. I do, yes, sir; but I think there will be a gradual reduction in it. On the other hand, there is a very large demand for butter. For instance, in normal times Russia exports 180,000,000 pounds per year. Then, too, butter production in Europe is necessarily short. So that while the demand for condensed milk from Europe may decrease, and likely will, the demand for butter apparently is very good.

Mr. HAUGEN. Right there, you speak of that demand for butter. Isn't it a fact that the demand is not all the time? The demand is much less than it was before?

Mr. RAWL. You mean in this country or abroad?

Mr. HAUGEN. Yes. Isn't it a fact that all the soldiers and a large percentage of the population have been fed on something other than butter?

Mr. RAWL. The soldiers, I understand, have received oleomargarine and butter. I don't know the proportions.

Mr. HAUGEN. Do you know any soldiers who have been fed wholly on butter?

Mr. RAWL. No. But we are told that a certain amount of butter is used. It may be very litle in some cases.

Mr. McLAUGHLIN. Is it in a mixture?

Mr. RAWL. I do not know.

Mr. HAUGEN. Can you make oleomargarine without mixing cream or butter? That is what gives it the flavor, isn't it?

Mr. RAWL. Yes; but much of the oleomargarine has no butter in it.

Mr. HAUGEN. The falling off in the creameries is due to the low price paid for butter and the demand for butter is less, isn't it?

Mr. RAWL. No, sir; I think not. The price of butter has not been low, but the price of other things has been higher. We never can have butter produced in competition with whole milk. The cities must have whole milk, and it is logical to draw that milk from the adjacent territory; therefore the milk that comes to New York City must come not from the Middle West or other distant sections, but from the territory around New York City. The condenseries, because of the very great demand for condensed milk, out of proportion to the demand for cheese and butter, have been able to go right into the cities' milk territory and buy milk, which is economically wrong in normal times.

Mr. HAUGEN. That is due to the abnormal demand?

Mr. RAWL. Yes. The kind of competition which can succeed in the market-milk territory, of course, is even more successful in the butter territory.

Mr. HAUGEN. I come from a section of the country where practically all the milk is consumed by the creameries for the manufacture of butter of the highest character, and we find now that because of the condenseries the creameries in a number of cases have fallen off; and there has been a good reason why, because the price of butter was low as compared with the price of feed and labor.

Mr. RAWL. There has not been a very wide margin in butter production; the price of feed and labor are high. I think those conditions will gradually adjust themselves. And speaking of the market for the condensery, the condensery must be able to shift its business to meet the new conditions, or it may have to go out of business.

Mr. HAUGEN. The condensery is on a par with the munition manufactuers of this country; it was created to supply a demand for export, due to the emergency.

Mr. RAWL. To be sure.

Mr. HAUGEN. Of course, when the war is over and that foreign demand is over, that is the end of the condensery just the same as it is the end of the munitions manufacturer?

Mr. RAWL. Some of the old creameries adopted the condensing business, and a good many of them can shift back and will shift back to butter production.

Mr. WASON. I understood you to say that the condenseries had put many creameries out of business. I presume it follows there has been a lessened production by reason of those creameries going out of existence?

Mr. RAWL. In cases there has been reduced production.

Mr. WASON. Hasn't there been a reduced consumption of butter and an increase in the consumption of butter substitutes in the last few years?

Mr. RAWL. Of course, there has been a large increase in the production of substitutes, part of which has been consumed at home.

Mr. WASON. Can you tell us what percentage of increase in substitutes for butter there has been?

Mr. RAWL. No, sir; I can not.

Mr. WASON. Do you keep the reports of the monthly or quarterly production?

Mr. RAWL. The Internal Revenue Bureau keeps all that.

Mr. Wason. You do not keep track of it?
Mr. Rawl. We do not keep track of it.
Mr. Wason. Has anybody in your bureau ascertained whether the mixture of oleo and butter finds its way on the market, country wide, practically, at substantially the same price pure butter is? Right here in Washington you will find it.
Mr. Rawl. That is the business of the Bureau of Internal Revenue.
Mr. Wason. Do you know there are a couple of so-called butter factories in New York that paid, last year, their ordinary 13 per cent dividend and declared a 33 per cent increase, and that the principal part of that is due to substitutes mixed in with butter flooded on the market? That does not come under your bureau?
Mr. Rawl. No, sir; oleomargarine made from animal fats must be inspected by our bureau where the plants are inspected under the meat-inspection act.
Mr. Wason. Supposed to be.
Mr. Rawl. The prevention of the sale of oleomargarine as butter is a matter for the Internal-Revenue Bureau.
Mr. Wason. In straight creamery butter factories, supposed to be manufacturing straight butter, do any of your men inspect those at any intervals?
Mr. Rawl. Not in a regulatory capacity.
Mr. Wason. For instance, I have known of this case that happened some years ago, that a respectable creamery factory with a good reputation in the community manufactured quite a product yearly and sold it to New England. A prosecution was instituted against a consumer, who happened to be a hotel man, for using something other than pure butter on his table. The attorneys who defended him traced it to this creamery and found that over 30 per cent of the oil of oleo was mixed right in with the cream and made into butter. And it is needless to say that the fellow had to suffer, although he paid for straight butter. And we traced it from my city to Boston and from Boston to the factory.
Mr. Rawl. Yes.
The Chairman. Your bureau has nothing to do with those cases?
Mr. Rawl. Our bureau has nothing to do with those cases.
Mr. Wason. What bureau does?
Mr. Rawl. The Internal-Revenue Bureau. Of course, under the law that product would be oleomargarine and subject to tax.
Mr. Wason. That was some 20 years ago, and it has been increasing instead of decreasing. You are interested in dairying, and let me ask you this question, whether you know where a man can buy straight butter in Washington?
Mr. Rawl. Yes. The Washington markets are not the very best for finest butter, not equal of course to Philadelphia, New York, or Boston. There are several brands of butter here in Washington that while not the very best in quality are a good quality.
Mr. Haugen. Aren't they selling creamery butter here?
Mr. Rawl. Oh, yes.
Mr. Haugen. Where do they get their butter from?
Mr. Rawl. They sell quite a lot of creamery butter here; but the Washington market for butter is not comparable with Philadelphia,

New York, or Boston markets. We do not have the great volume of choice creamery butter here.

Mr. HAUGEN. Is not all creamery butter straight butter?

Mr. RAWL. Yes; if it is creamery butter it is, of course.

Mr. HAUGEN. I want to know.

Mr. RAWL. The case he speaks of——

Mr. HAUGEN. He is speaking of oleomargarine; they changed the label. They were selling oleomargarine instead of butter and selling it under a false label.

Mr. RAWL. They were. As to what per cent of factories do that I can not say. I do not think it is great.

Mr. HAUGEN. There are dishonest men in every line of work, and you can not get away from it; but is creamery butter straight butter, or is it a substitute?

Mr. RAWL. It could not be a substitute if it is creamery butter.

Mr. HAUGEN. We are speaking of butter now. Is there a substitute for butter?

Mr. RAWL. Well, that is getting off into a technical question. Of course, there is a substitute for butter; if a man has been using a pound of butter a day and buys something else in place of it he regards that as a substitute.

Mr. HAUGEN. That is a dishonorable practice; we do not have to deal with them. We hope there are many honest people in this country engaged in a legitimate and honorable business.

Mr. RAWL. I think the butter people are as honest as any other class.

Mr. HAUGEN. Only some of them are dishonest?

Mr. RAWL. I do not think any more of them are practicing dishonest methods than is the case in any other business.

Mr. HAUGEN. What is butter, anyway? If creamery butter isn't, what is?

Mr. RAWL. I think I do not understand you.

The CHAIRMAN. The straight answer to it is that butter is butter, and it can not be anything else.

Mr. HAUGEN. Do you consider creamery butter straight butter?

Mr. RAWL. If it is creamery butter it is straight butter.

Mr. HAUGEN. I do not think there is any difference of opinion as to that. Now, then, what are they selling in Washington?

Mr. RAWL. As far as I know, they are selling quite a considerable volume of creamery butter. But, as I stated a moment ago, the volume of the choicest creamery butter in Washington is not very great.

Mr. HAUGEN. The volume of creamery butter sold in Washington is not great?

Mr. RAWL. No. They are selling a large volume of creamery butter in the city, but the volume of the choicest creamery butter in the city of Washington is not very great.

Mr. HAUGEN. That is all.

The CHAIRMAN. Is there anything further, Doctor?

Mr. RAWL. I might say a word or two on a matter that is not quite relevant. We have no money for the cottage-cheese work in the estimates and do not ask for any, but would you like to have a word or two about what was accomplished last year?

The CHAIRMAN. I would be very glad to have it.

Mr. RAWL. That work, I think, has been badly misunderstood. I believe if you will confer with your own people, your own State-extension people and food-administration workers, that you will find that the work done to stimulate the use of cottage cheese last year was very successful. A gentleman from a western State told me this morning that the efforts made in connection with the utilization of cottage cheese had brought in more food than a similar amount of money spent on anything else during the time the work was in progress. That work has been subject to a lot of criticism, because cottage cheese is an old product, not very much used generally. Never before has this product constituted a very substantial part of the food supply of any community.

Mr. HAUGEN. It never did and never will, will it?

Mr. RAWL. Yes, sir.

Mr. HAUGEN. It is just a question of labor, that is all.

Mr. RAWL. No, sir; it is just a question of knowledge and taste.

Mr. HAUGEN. It always tasted good to me, but I could not get anybody to make it?

Mr. RAWL. Why couldn't you?

Mr. HAUGEN. Because they did not seem to take very kindly to it.

Mr. RAWL. It is very easy to make.

The CHAIRMAN. I can take an old cheesecloth and make the finest in the world.

Mr. RAWL. Yes. But you will find the situation Mr. Haugen speaks of. In your city of Des Moines, for instance, where prior to a week's work there was used only about 100 pounds. And this is not our own work, it is work done with the Des Moines Chamber of Commerce and the extension people of Iowa, the county agent, and one person from our office. We had a woman who worked in that region to help stimulate this, and in one week's time the amount of cottage cheese increased from 100 to 700 pounds a day in the city of Des Moines. And there are quite a number of cases similar to that. For instance, eight factories in New York that had made none, with a little help (I do not know exactly how much, possibly two or three days or a week), made an average of 1,000 pounds a day during last summer.

Mr. HAUGEN. Can you tell me why it is hardly ever sold under its right name, but is labeled something else?

Mr. RAWL. I did not know that was the case.

Mr. HAUGEN. For instance, at the hotel it is a Philadelphia cheese, and in some of the stores it goes under some other name.

Mr. RAWL. Philadelphia cream cheese is very similar to cottage cheese, except it has more fat in it.

Mr. HAUGEN. What they serve here as Philadelphia cream cheese is not a very excellent cottage cheese, at that.

Mr. RAWL. It is not a very excellent cottage cheese?

Mr. HAUGEN. No; there is very little, if any, cream in that.

Mr. RAWL. That may be the case. But generally speaking, the food law will catch them if it is misbranded.

Mr. HAUGEN. I do not know that it is misbranded, but it goes under some other name—Philadelphia cheese, although it is really cottage cheese.

Mr. RAWL. Cottage cheese is becoming very popular in many places and will often be found now in public eating places.

I want to cite a few more cases. We had a small group of men who worked with the factories last year and cost about $28,000. The factories they worked with utilized in making this product last summer approximately 26,000,000 pounds of skimmed milk, for which they had no other use. The city of Detroit became overstocked with cottage cheese and in a little while accumulated 60,000 or 70,000 pounds. Two or three women with the home demonstration work of the States Relations Service went to Detroit and in a very short period, 10 days or 2 weeks, they had entirely opened the market for the product, because they had shown the consumers the various ways of using it and making it palatable. The factories we got reports from last summer used on the average 384,000 pounds of skimmed milk a day in making this product. Many we have not heard from. The results of all such work radiates out so that you can not accurattely measure it.

A number of similar cases could be cited. One dealer in San Francisco, who had never handled a pound of it, was handling 800 pounds a day and said he could have handled a thousand pounds more if he could have gotten the product of the highest grade. One company in Wilmington, Del., made a large quantity of it. In Portland, Oreg., one firm manufactured during the flush season last year 10,000 pounds of milk a day and found ready sale for it; but not until our people had gone there and put on a little campaign of four or five days or a week making demonstrations and getting the people interested.

So that taking the whole thing through, the general comments from the country over have been very favorable. The question of using it as a food is the question of getting people to appreciate and know how to prepare it, to make it into desserts, various salads, and the like, in ways that the older people never used it, and making it by improved methods. This is a line of work that in many States will go forward, whether they are given any help or not. And I feel, on the whole, you would regard the money as well spent, not only as a war measure, but a measure of much economic value at any time.

The CHAIRMAN. You say you have no allotment for cottage-cheese work under this appropriation?

Mr. RAWL. This work was done as an emergency act which is not involved here.

The CHAIRMAN. Do you think that work ought to continue as a peace proposition?

Mr. RAWL. I think it ought to continue as a peace proposition on an enlarged scale. I forgot here in this connection our work with the farmers. We got cards from 38,000 farmers saying they were making cottage cheese because of the demonstrations and are making it a part of their regular diet. I believe if there are 38,000 farmers who would go to the trouble to write that, there are many more who have not said anything. I believe this work should be enlarged.

The CHAIRMAN. How much are you spending on it this year?

Mr. RAWL. We spent on it last year—1918—out of the emergency fund, $23,066 on the factory work, $38,167 on the farm work, and $3,907 on the city work, making all-told $65,141. What I think should be done, since you have asked the question, is that we should enlarge this work to cover the whole field of the utilization of milk and milk products on the farm and in the cities. There is no question about it; the utilization of the milk on the farms the country over, and in the cities as well, is badly misunderstood. On the farms we do not produce anything like the milk we should for home use, both from the standpoint of economy and from the standpoint of proper nutrition. I believe it would be of great value if we could broaden our work to cover the whole field of the utilization of milk for the benefit and improvement of the farm table, and the city table as well. It is well established that the lack of milk in some places is causing serious trouble. Pellagra is atributable by the investigations of the Public Health Service to insufficient quantities of milk and meats combined. What I should like to see done is that a sufficient amount of money be made available, so that we could start this work in a comprehensive way.

Mr. HAUGEN. Isn't it safe to leave that to the several county agents?

Mr. RAWL. The county agent can not start these new specialized things. The county agent has such a great multitude of things to do you can not expect him to initiate these new undertakings. And I feel the great field of the dairy division is to initiate things which are desirable and useful and to inaugurate them and then gradually work them into the extension system. And that is the function I am speaking of.

Mr. LESHER. What is the difference between this Philadelphia cheese and cottage cheese?

Mr. RAWL. Philadelphia cream cheese is made of whole milk with a little cream added: it is supposed to be made of milk with about 6 per cent of fat. I believe. Cottage cheese may have no fat or it may have a little added to make it more palatable. Essentially, the processes are the same.

Mr. LESHER. What I thought was, they can store that Philadelphia cheese and probably it would be better for the farmers to make that instead of cottage cheese.

Mr. RAWL. We are carrying on some experiments in storing cottage cheese, too, and I think there is no doubt we can store it; but the question never came up until this summer and we are working on the temperatures required and the length of time, etc.

Mr. WASON. When you began to speak about this, you spoke about the extension workers, the war workers of the State. Have you heard except from this 38.000 population?

Mr. RAWL. No. sir. Of course, we have had an occasional letter from a private individual.

Mr. WASON. From what part of the country did these 38,000 letters to the department come, generally speaking? I do not mean in detail. A good many from New England and New York?

Mr. RAWL. I have them right here. We got 3.900 from Maine, New Hampshire, Massachusetts. Rhode Island. Connecticut. New York, New Jersey, Delaware, and Ohio.

Mr. WASON. How many from New Hampshire?

Mr. RAWL. We got 438.

Mr. WASON. From New Hampshire farmers?

Mr. RAWL. I would not say they are all farmers, but from people who are in a position to produce their own milk or to get milk from which to make cottage cheese. Of course, we did not distinguish between farmers and others who could get milk. From the Middle West, Illinois, Indiana, Missouri, and Kansas, Michigan, North Dakota, South Dakota, and Wisconsin, we got 5,217.

Mr. WASON. I guess if you will investigate those inquiries from New Hampshire you will find they came from the cities; but I do not believe there is a farmer's wife in the State, unless it is somebody that has gone out from the city, made their money in some way and bought a place in the country, but what knows how to make cottage cheese.

Mr. RAWL. That may be.

Mr. McLAUGHLIN. But they do not do it; they do not make it.

Mr. WASON. They make it for home use, most of them.

Mr. RAWL. But they do not use it to any extent.

Mr. WASON. Oh, there is lots of it used there. I have made cottage cheese for 40 years and never bought any of it on the market.

Mr. RAWL. Have you ever seen cottage-cheese pie?

Mr. WASON. No.

Mr. RAWL. It is fine. Did you ever eat cottage-cheese pudding?

Mr. WASON. No, I never ate cottage cheese pudding, and I never ate pumpkin pie, for a great many years made out of sweet potatoes.

Mr. HAUGEN. You spoke about the little cards and letters you received.

Mr. RAWL. Little cards, asking them to report.

Mr. HAUGEN. You said voluntarily. They were solicited, weren't they?

Mr. RAWL. Yes.

Mr. HAUGEN. Of course, if you have people around the country peddling cards and asking people to send them in, you ought to get 38,000 out of a hundred million.

The CHAIRMAN. This is all very interesting, but there is not a dollar in here for cottage-cheese work, and it is taking the time of the committee.

Mr. WASON. Mr. Chairman, I do not want to be misunderstood about that part of it. My questions were directed particularly to Mr. Rawl on the cards to the fact that all his news that came from the extension agents in the field is not exactly from the country people. Now, I favor advocating and encouraging the cottage cheese; it is absolutely essential to our population, and I think a limited sum spent on that propaganda in a judicious way is wise.

Mr. RAWL. Let me add one word more. The Woman's Club of one State wrote in protesting against this cottage-cheese work, and one of our workers went to see this club and made a demonstration of making it and using it in the various ways and the economic side of it, and those women immediately withdrew their protest and said, "We want to change our record on this matter." And we have had a lot of individual letters like that. I wanted to mention that, because that does come from a representative organization, and was, of course, unsolicited.

The CHAIRMAN. It is merely another proof of the value of good advertising.

Mr. THOMPSON. How much would you suggest could be used on this cottage-cheese work?

Mr. RAWL. We could use to great advantage $75,000 a year.
Mr. WASON. How much could you do with, say, $25,000?
Mr. RAWL. We could do quite a bit with that.
Mr. WASON. Couldn't you get in touch with the different State organizations?
Mr. RAWL. Not with all of them with that amount; I think we could use more than $75,000 to advantage—we could do quite a bit of work with $25,000 and could deal with the matter fairly well with $75,000.

I think also that the bull club can earn millions of dollars for the dairymen if the circumstances warrant our pushing it. I am not asking funds for that, but mention it because of its very vital importance to a big fundamental industry. The spending of $100,000, or even much more, on bull club work for the improvement of dairy cattle would be a very desirable thing to do and very profitable. And I simply mention these things for your information; we have nothing new in the estimates for this purpose.

Mr. McLAUGHLIN. I agree with you entirely as to both these lines of work as to the importance of them; but after all, as to this bull club work, it will largely have to be carried out by the extension service.

Mr. RAWL. Yes.

Mr. McLAUGHLIN. And any money you would use sending men into the field seems to me would be a duplication of work, and we have to be careful about that.

Mr. RAWL. No, sir; our effort is directed at assisting the county agent and the extension departments in taking up that work.

Mr. McLAUGHLIN. The county agent is connected with the extension work, and if you connect yourself with him, you will likely duplicate the work the extension department is doing.

Mr. RAWL. No; our relation with the county agent comes only through the State extension department. We would not go to the county agent direct; we would only go to the county agent in accordance with the agreement or request from the State extension director.

Mr. HAUGEN. To what extent have you advertised certain herds?

Mr. RAWL. Certain breeds?

Mr. HAUGEN. Well, herds. For instance, your men go out and advocate the purchase of a pure-bred bull, and naturally the question is asked, Where can one be bought?

Mr. RAWL. We have to deal with that with a good deal of caution. Our answer to that question will always be frank and based on this plan: Get the bull whose ancestors have produced the most pounds of butter fat, and who is the best individual.

Mr. HAUGEN. Oh, yes; but you are up in the pictures.

Mr. RAWL. No, sir.

Mr. HAUGEN. The South Carolina farmer will not pay $106,000 for a bull, will he?

Mr. RAWL. A South Carolina farmer got a bull for $1,000 a few days ago.

Mr. HAUGEN. But a South Carolina farmer did not get a $106,000 bull, did he?

Mr. RAWL. That is something of an advertisement, I think.

Mr. HAUGEN. But how can you answer the question? It would take you from now until next New Years to get a pedigree such as you suggest.

Mr. RAWL. No, sir; all you have to do is to look up the records.

Mr. HAUGEN. I appreciate it is a difficult proposition, and how do you handle it?

Mr. RAWL. Well, say you are offered five bulls; I would take the bull whose ancestors have produced the most, according to official records, provided he is a good individual. That is just what I would say to anybody regarding any breed.

Mr. HAUGEN. That cuts you down; you see, there are only two or three of them. That narrows the whole proposition down to one or two breeders, or three or four or half a dozen.

Mr. RAWL. Oh, no, sir. There are hundreds of herds making records.

Mr. HAUGEN. Oh, yes; but, then, as I told you, there are several volumes, and you can not go through all these volumes every time the question is asked.

Mr. RAWL. If you were considering the purchase of a bull and wanted information, we could go to the records and tell you what the record is.

Mr. HAUGEN. If they wanted to buy such and such a bull. But those people do not know any bull by name or by number.

Mr. RAWL. They would have offers, and any man could tell if he had an offer.

Mr. HAUGEN. After they had the offer, it wouldn't be necessary to go down and tell them or ask them?

Mr. RAWL. No; but it would be necessary to determine which of those offers was best. And what we do is to tell them just how to select the one that is best.

Mr. HAUGEN. If a farmer wants a bull he sends out and gets offers and comes down here and you tell him?

Mr. RAWL. No, sir.

Mr. HAUGEN. How is it done?

Mr. RAWL. If he is a beginner and needs help, the extension people in charge of the dairy work in any community will help him, or he can send to us for information and we will tell him how to proceed to buy a bull. Or if he has certain ones in mind, we will give him information regarding those. No matter what breed it is, if he gets an offer we can tell him of some one who can help him personally.

Mr. HAUGEN. Do you go with the farmer or purchaser and help him to make the selection?

Mr. RAWL. In rare cases we do.

Mr. HAUGEN. In rare cases? How many cases?

Mr. RAWL. That depends on circumstances; for instance, in some of the Western States at times they have asked for our men to come back into a dairy State to help pick out a whole trainload of cattle. That is preliminary work, and in the beginning we allowed our men to go at the expense of the purchaser and assist in selecting the cattle; but he is not to have anything to do with the business transaction. In other words, he helps to get the right sort of animals.

Mr. HAUGEN. You talk of a trainload of cattle; but there is nobody who ever buys a trainload of cattle, is there?

Mr. RAWL. They do in some cases.

Mr. HAUGEN. You mean one purchaser?

Mr. RAWL. No; the whole community gets together; this man wants one, that man wants three or four, and another half a dozen. I say a trainload. This, of course, is an exceptional case; but often several carloads are bought in this way.

Mr. HAUGEN. There is always a charge of partiality?

Mr. RAWL. No, sir.

Mr. HAUGEN. Have you had any trouble along that line?

Mr. RAWL. We have not had any; we have been doing work along that line occasionally for seven or eight years and have not had any trouble that I know of.

Mr. HAUGEN. I know, but I think you would have difficulty and probably a great deal.

Mr. RAWL. The community knows what it wants to do and what it wants to breed.

Mr. HAUGEN. Do you keep a list of the individual names of breeders?

Mr. RAWL. We have the published lists.

Mr. HAUGEN. Have you published them in the department?

Mr. RAWL. No; we do not publish them; the breed associations publish them.

Mr. McLAUGHLIN. I have two pure-bred Holstein bulls on my farm and really am in doubt about which one to keep. If I could send you the names and numbers, can you advise me which would be the best for my herd?

Mr. RAWL. You have doubtless all the information we could give you. What we would do would be to compare the production records of the ancestors of the two, and the individual type of the two and take the one that was best in both respects.

STATEMENT OF MR. GEORGE M. ROMMEL, CHIEF OF THE DIVISION OF ANIMAL HUSBANDRY, BUREAU OF ANIMAL INDUSTRY, UNITED STATES DEPARTMENT OF AGRICULTURE.

The CHAIRMAN. Dr. Rommel, I notice in item 91, page 53, you have a slight increase there of $17,480. Could you tell the committee briefly just what you propose to do with that increase?

Mr. ROMMEL. That increase, Mr. Chairman, is covered by two of the projects in our work in sheep investigations, the increase of $8,200 for farm sheep investigations and the increase of $9,280 for our range sheep investigations. The experimental work in farm sheep investigations is carried on at the experimental farm in Addison County, Vt., and at the experimental farm in Prince Georges County, Md.

The problems we are studying are those pertaining to the farm sheep industry, studies of methods of management, production, feeding, breeding, the economic phases of the situation, and so forth. Among the principal features that we have been attending to in these farm sheep investigations is the study of the reduction of the grain requirement for the farm flock of sheep and a study of the possibility of increasing the length of the fiber with, at the same time, a retention of the mutton carcass. That work has been progressing very satisfactorily and the data obtained is made available through the extension forces. One project which we have under way at the experimental farm at Beltsville is a study of the wool from the various flocks that we have, based on actual net yield of wool.

Unfortunately that work had to be suspended during the war because the man who had laid out the equipment went into the Army, but he is back now and we hope to resume it. We have the apparatus there which he originated, by which all the extraneous matter, the grease, dirt, etc., is extracted by the usual processes, but the apparatus itself uses accurately weighed quantities of wool and makes possible individual tests. We hope to have in time a mass of material pertaining to the inheritance of wool production and the correlation between wool production and mutton production which will be the best information of its kind available in the world. There is very little such information now available, if any. We are starting into a new field. The principle, however, which we are trying to get at in our farm sheep demonstrations is to determine the possibility of farm sheep production in the United States. In England they have about as many sheep per population as we have hogs in the United States. In other words, about 1 sheep to every 2 people in Great Britain. In this country we have about 1 pig to every 2 people.

The CHAIRMAN. And how many sheep?

Mr. ROMMEL. About 1 to 2. The number of pigs is more than 1 to 2; the number of sheep is just about an even 1 to 2. There are about 70,000,000 hogs and 50,000,000 sheep, roughly. But, of course, there is one condition here which is important in this connection and that is that the great majority of our sheep are in the range States; they are not farm sheep. If we take strictly the farm sheep we would have a much smaller ratio. The sheep of Great Britain are principally farm sheep; you do not find many there that run under range conditions, except in the highlands and in the border counties.

That in a general way gives the work of the farm sheep project.

The CHAIRMAN. You started that only a year ago?

Mr. ROMMEL. While that was started a year ago, we have been doing farm-sheep work for nearly 10 years.

The CHAIRMAN. But you have not been doing farm-demonstration work?

Mr. ROMMEL. I am not speaking of farm-sheep demonstration work; that was started only about a year ago.

The CHAIRMAN. What progress are you making?

Mr. ROMMEL. Excellent as far as we find it possible to get men competent to serve in this capacity. We have men in Connecticut, Georgia, Illinois, Indiana, Iowa, Kansas, Louisiana, Maine, Massachusetts, Michigan, Mississippi, Missouri, New Hampshire, New York, North Carolina, South Dakota, Tennessee, Texas, Vermont, and West Virgina.

The CHAIRMAN. The question in my mind as it has always been is whether the South was not possibly a sheep country on account of its climate and mountain States. What do you say as to that proposition?

Mr. ROMMEL. It is an open question and one for study. One of the points we had in mind in asking for this increase for farm-sheep investigations was to begin experimental work at some point in the South and to go right into that point you mention. Sheep prevail to a considerable extent throughout the South and you will find them clear down into the peninsula of Florida, in considerable flocks. It is also a fact that apparently these sheep in the far South are seriously infested with parasitic diseases of various kinds. At any rate, we know that northern sheep coming in contact with them suffer badly from stomach worm and similar troubles. There is a good deal of interest in the subject. We have a good man in North Carolina, and in Louisiana, and we are just putting a man in Georgia.

Mr. HAUGEN. How do you expect to make sheep production or to stimulate sheep production outside of making it attractive or a paying proposition?

Mr. ROMMEL. I do not know that I just get your question. This item is not a question of stimulating sheep production.

Mr. HAUGEN. Sheep has not been paying very well, except up to right now, when wool is high and mutton is high.

Mr. ROMMEL. Yes; wool and mutton are high right now. One of the reasons in our opinion for the fact the number of sheep in the United States has been showing a tendency to decline is that they have been handled from a false viewpoint. In the first place, it does not pay to raise sheep for wool alone on the farms.

Mr. HAUGEN. It has been a losing proposition?

Mr. ROMMEL. Exactly. In the second place, you can not feed a sheep for the meat he produces and expect him to compete with the dairy cow or the pig. Therefore, the place of the sheep on farms is as a dual-purpose animal, for the production both of wool and meat and, consequently, he must consume products which can not be marketed to better advantage by using some other animals. In other words, you have to keep the amount of grain you feed sheep to the minimum. Now, while I do not want to give the committee the impression farmers should keep sheep as scavengers—that is a mistake, because any scavenger is an outcast and is going to be neglected. You can not neglect sheep; sheep need to be carefully handled, and the man who handles them must know them. However, if you will travel around the country you will find that ordinarily the fields that have sheep on them are clean fields, and the farm that has sheep on it is a clean farm. Sheep eat more weeds than any other animal, and not only that but a smaller percentage of seed goes through the sheep without losing the germinating power than with any other animal. So, for instance, if you have a weedy farm, such for instance as the rocky pastures of the North Atlantic States and New England, there is no better way to clean that farm than by using sheep. This is being demonstrated at the Morgan horse farm in Vermont. The weed known as paintbrush is one of the most noxious weeds of the north, but sheep seem to have a peculiar appetite for paintbrush and dandelion. At the Morgan horse farm the only field free from dandelions is the permanent sheep pasture. In another field we had a little patch of paintbrush; we turned the sheep out on it, and in three weeks time there was no paintbrush left. That is just one factor. If you combine with that peculiar habit of the sheep a sufficient amount of intelligence on the part of the farmer, he is going to find sheep raising a profitable venture.

Mr. HAUGEN. At present; but it wasn't before the war.

Mr. ROMMEL. Oh, yes; it was before the war, undoubtedly.

Mr. HAUGEN. Do you contend a farmer, with a farm valued at $125 or $150 an acre, can compete with the range? I mean at the prices we had a few years ago?

Mr. ROMMEL. It depends on what you are doing, entirely.

Mr. HAUGEN. You spoke about the weeds; you find the farm clean from weeds, but you found lean hogs and fat sheep, because the sheep get the grain?

Mr. ROMMEL. If you let the sheep into the cornfield and keep the hogs out, I expect it would work that way.

Mr. HAUGEN. And ninety times out of a hundred—of course a lot depends on the question of open fences, but as a general thing you will find the sheep getting the corn, and he is the first one on the job.

Mr. ROMMEL. Let me make this very clear, that I do not claim as a meat producer the sheep can compete with the hog. He can not. It is impossible. Neither can he compete with the dairy cow.

Mr. HAUGEN. That all depends on the price you get.

Mr. ROMMEL. The dairy cow will return in milk about 18 pounds of milk, of human food, for every hundred pounds of feed. The hog returns about 15 pounds, and the sheep will return 2.8 pounds. Therefore, the hog is about five times as profitable, as a human food producer, as the sheep, and the dairy cow about six. So if you are going to raise sheep on the farm, the sheep has to eat something the hog can not eat or the dairy cow can not eat, and there is plenty of stuff all over these United States that the sheep can use which no other animal will turn into a profit.

Mr. LESHER. Just about the same thing as keeping 200 chickens on a farm to pick up things that will go to waste.

Mr. ROMMEL. Very much the same way; and if you take those 200 chickens and handle them with skill and intelligence, you are going to find an additional source of income from the farm; and if you are inclined to let them get lousy and get wet and so on, you are going to find it a losing proposition.

Mr. HAUGEN. How about stimulating; that is what I want to get at.

Mr. ROMMEL. The first thing we have to do is to get facts that can be depended upon as giving the proper rôle of the sheep on the farms. That is the first thing, and we are going to get information on that.

Mr. HAUGEN. You have reached no conclusion as yet?

Mr. ROMMEL. Oh, yes; indeed. I have been giving you conclusions. My discussion has been based on what we have already worked out.

Mr. HAUGEN. On returns; you have reached conclusions as to the returns as proof of the value?

Mr. ROMMEL. We did not work that out. That was worked out long years ago. That is one of the fundamental facts of agriculture; worked out 50 years ago. The conclusions we have reached are these I have just mentioned, that the sheep has this rôle of utilizing feed that other animals on the farm do not utilize and we find where the lambs are raised as largely as possible on temporary pasture crops and mother's milk, that it is possible to fatten those lambs with very little grain.

Mr. HAUGEN. There is nothing new about that; we all know that and have known that for a long time. How are you going to stimulate production except you increase the price and make it a paying proposition to the farmer?

Mr. ROMMEL. Increased price is the very best stimulator there is.

Mr. HAUGEN. But when you stimulate production, the market goes down; that has been our trouble. We have tried to raise sheep up in our country and we could not make it pay. Of course, it is paying now, the same as everything else.

Mr. ROMMEL. There is a reason for that. The most profitable animal in Iowa is the pig.

Mr. HAUGEN. Well, we are not all confined to hog raising.

Mr. ROMMEL. There are more pigs in Iowa than anywhere else.

The CHAIRMAN. Is there anything further on this particular proposition? If not, take up your other increase.

Mr. ROMMEL. The next increase is largely a bookkeeping increase, Mr. Chairman. At the sheep experiment station in Fremont County, Idaho, to which we moved a little over a year ago, we are carrying approximately a thousand sheep. We have plans which will run that flock up to 2,000, so that it will be a flock which will compare in all respects with other range flocks in the neighborhood. The income from that flock last year was about $10,000. As time goes on we will find that it will be very nearly, if not quite, self-supporting. But we can not use any of these funds we get from the sale of animals or wool for the direct maintenance of this experimental work. In order to enable us to meet the increased costs at that station, we are asking for this increase of about $10,000. One reason for requesting the increase is the increase in the cost of supplies of all kinds, labor and everything else.

You might be interested to know that one of the rams from this flock was sold at the sale at Salt Lake City in September for $525. We are selling the surplus stock we do not need for breeding purposes.

The CHAIRMAN. That is a cross between the Corriedale and range sheep?

Mr. ROMMEL. No; that was a pure-bred Corriedale, Mr. Chairman. The cross-bred sheep we do not sell; only the pure bred.

Mr. HAUGEN. What are you going to use your ten thousand for?

Mr. ROMMEL. To meet the increased expense of the station. The flock runs now about a thousand head, and we want to run it up to 2,000 head.

Mr. HAUGEN. The expense of the purchase of sheep?

Mr. ROMMEL. The maintenance of the sheep.

Mr. HAUGEN. Oh, maintenance?

Mr. ROMMEL. Labor expenses and things of that kind. We are buying comparatively few sheep.

The CHAIRMAN. Your experiments in that direction on crossing the Corriedale with the range sheep is showing pretty good results?

Mr. ROMMEL. Oh, yes. The Corriedale is showing up very well, indeed. It has a future in the United States unquestionably. A number of private individuals, following the Government's lead, went to New Zealand for Corriedales and more will go now. As you may remember, this importation was made in 1914. In fact, our man sailed from Vancouver the day the war was declared, and it has been very difficult to get them out, although they have been bringing a few into this country.

Mr. McLaughlin. What do they add particularly to the home sheep, the native sheep?

Mr. Rommel. The Corriedale attracted attention first because it was thought to be a better combined wool and mutton breed than anything known on the western range. It was brought in not so much as a farm sheep but for the range. They shear heavily in wool and still retain their mutton carcass. They have a better mutton carcass than other white-faced sheep.

Mr. McLaughlin. Is the quality of the meat and wool of a high grade?

Mr. Rommel. Very. The wool is graded as three-eighths combing which is largely used to manufacture the clothese we wear. The meat is excellent.

Mr. McLaughlin. Are you asking for money now to import more of those?

Mr. Rommel. No, sir. We have our flock established. We do not have to worry about that condition for the present, certainly. This increase is to provide for the increase in the flock at the sheep experiment station.

Mr. McLaughlin. How many were imported?

Mr. Rommel. We imported 65 head.

Mr. McLaughlin. What sex?

Mr. Rommel. Both.

Mr. McLaughlin. And how many different places have those been to?

Mr. Rommel. They are at the sheep experiment station in Fremont County, Idaho. We have not distributed them except by sale. We have sold them at public sale.

Mr. McLaughlin. As you produce the pure-bred male and female, I suppose you are collecting and distributing them?

Mr. Rommel. Yes, sir. I might say, Mr. Chairman, we are making an individual study of the entire flock, the only one of the kind that is being made anywhere. This includes taking a weighed sample of the wool at each shearing, which samples are sent on here to Washington to be used in the laboratory at Beltsville. Then each sheep at the time of shearing is graded, you might say, or scored, by a very simple score-card system, not on the percentage basis but on a simple basis of grades, so that we have a record of each of the individuals. This, of course, entails additional work.

Mr. Wason. I do not know anything about these sheep, but about what does, say, one fleece weigh when it is sheared?

Mr. Rommel. You mean the Corriedale?

Mr. Wason. Yes.

Mr. Rommel. One hundred head of ewes kept on the range averaged 10¾ pounds of wool in 1918.

Mr. Wason. About what will they weigh live and dressed?

Mr. Rommel. The live weight runs around 125 or 130 pounds. The lambs, of course, go on the market just as other lambs do. The best lambs will weigh around 70 or 80 pounds.

Mr. Wason. Live weight?

Mr. Rommel. Yes.

Mr. WASON. They are about the same size sheep, then, of the Shropshire?

Mr. ROMMEL. Just about, and except for the wool on the Shropshire's face they look something like the Shropshire. It is a little different character of wool. They were developed by crossing the Lincoln and Merino with some Leicester blood.

Mr. WASON. There is some Lincoln blood in them?

Mr. ROMMEL. Yes; and there is Merino and a little Leicester.

Mr. McLAUGHLIN. This item 91 carries the old wording permitting the use of $8,000 for a building at Fremont County, Idaho. Is there still use of money for building there?

Mr. ROMMEL. Yes, sir; there is. I may say, Mr. Chairman, that one of the undeterminable factors in the equipment of that station, in addition to the rise in all sorts of supplies, material, and labor, is the matter of a water supply. We found the well we had put in there was extremely expensive, and we need the funds provided here—not an increase but simply a continuation of that amount for the equipment of that station. We have now a cottage for the superintendent and sheds and things of that sort.

The CHAIRMAN. The construction work you speak of will be the erection of sheds and things of that sort, will it not?

Mr. ROMMEL. Yes; largely sheds and fences and things of that kind.

Mr. HAUGEN. How many sheep have you there?

Mr. ROMMEL. We have a thousand head.

Mr. HAUGEN. And how much have you invested in buildings?

Mr. ROMMEL. I can not answer that exactly. We have had this item of $8,000 now for two years. But that has not all gone into buildings, by any means.

Mr. HAUGEN. And you are asking for $8,000 more?

Mr. ROMMEL. We are asking for a continuation of the appropriation.

Mr. HAUGEN. Being about $24 per head for buildings. It would take a pretty good profit, wouldn't it, to make that pay?

Mr. ROMMEL. We were not figuring that way at all, sir. We do not figure on the basis of the head of sheep. But as a matter of fact, there will be 2,000 sheep there in two years.

Mr. HAUGEN. And $24,000 for buildings will be——

Mr. ROMMEL. A great deal of equipment necessarily should be charged as the natural equipment of an experiment station, which naturally will run it up higher than if you were running a commercial venture.

Mr. HAUGEN. What does that consist of?

Mr. ROMMEL. We need, for example, a cottage for the superintendent. That cottage has been built. It cost about $3,000. He has his office in one room of that building. We have sheds for horses; we need sheds for the lambs, particularly, and sheds for the sheep. That is one of the most important things. It is absolutely necessary to have suitable, commodious, and warm sheds for use in lambing time.

Mr. HAUGEN. Yes; that is true.

Mr. ROMMEL. And then we will need a bunk house and quarters for the men employed.

Mr. HAUGEN. How many men do you employ now to take care of them?

Mr. ROMMEL. My recollection now is that there are two; only two, in addition to the superintendent.

Mr. HAUGEN. A bunk for two men would not cost very much?

Mr. ROMMEL. There will be more than two men when we get 2,000 sheep.

Mr. HAUGEN. How many men will you need when you get 2,000 sheep?

Mr. ROMMEL. We will probably need one or two more, and we will need quarters, of course, for the men who come at shearing time. As I said awhile ago, one of the biggest items of expense was drilling the well for our water supply. Nobody could tell us what it would cost, and nobody was willing to undertake it, and we were not at all sure how deep we would have to go to get a water supply.

The CHAIRMAN. How deep did you have to go?

Mr. ROMMEL. We had to go down 740 feet.

The CHAIRMAN. Is it a flowing well?

Mr. ROMMEL. No; it is run with gasoline power. You see, it is out in the dry country, in the lava beds, and a country of which we have not a great deal of information on the geological formation.

Mr. HAUGEN. Are your sheep running at large, or are they fenced?

Mr. ROMMEL. We have not gotten any fences yet because we have not had the money to fence the fields.

Mr. HAUGEN. How are these sheep cared for—by herders?

Mr. ROMMEL. Part of them by herders, and as we get the money for fencing we intend to put up fences to take care of the herd.

Mr. HAUGEN. I was curious to know what five men were doing with only a thousand sheep.

Mr. ROMMEL. One of them is the superintendent.

Mr. HAUGEN. Superintendent of the men?

Mr. ROMMEL. Superintendent of the station, to collect the data.

Mr. HAUGEN. He is a bookkeeper?

Mr. ROMMEL. No, sir; he is a scientist. If you run an experiment station, you have to have a large amount of records kept, and if those records are going to be of any value, they must be kept absolutely according to scientific method and with the very greatest accuracy. If a man should make a mistake in entering a record and the mistake is not detected, the entire record may be thrown out throughout an entire series of experiments. The value of scientific work is in direct proportion to the care that is spent in obtaining it.

Mr. HAUGEN. That is bookkeeping.

Mr. ROMMEL. I beg your pardon, sir; that is not.

Mr. HAUGEN. The record is.

Mr. ROMMEL. Very well, sir, the record is; but the man in charge of that work, if he is a valuable man, is a great deal more than a bookkeeper.

Mr. HAUGEN. Who keeps the books, then? Is that the superintendent?

Mr. ROMMEL. We have had a clerk there part of the time, and we have had an assistant clerk there part of the time. And the superintendent has been chief cook and bottle washer part of the time.

Mr. HAUGEN. What do these other men do?

Mr. ROMMEL. The next man we had regularly there was a clerk, until he went into the Army. He did not wait for the United States to go into the war; he was too old, nearly 50 years old, and he went into Canada and enlisted. He is now in France, I believe. The next man—there were two men, one was a teamster and one was a herder to look after the sheep.

Mr. HAUGEN. You have a superintendent, a herder, a clerk, and a teamster; what else?

Mr. ROMMEL. I believe that is all.

Mr. HAUGEN. What does the teamster do?

Mr. ROMMEL. Drives horses.

Mr. HAUGEN. Are you cultivating land out there?

Mr. ROMMEL. Not very much. We will probably have some dry farming carried on. We are in a dry-farming country; there are lots of dry farms around there, and one of the things we can work out to advantage is to determine whether sheep will be profitable under dry-farming conditions. If that is the case, we will want to have some dry farming done right there on the farm, and a man can be used on that.

Mr. HAUGEN. Did you put up your own hay?

Mr. ROMMEL. No; we did not put up our own hay, I am sorry to say.

Mr. HAUGEN. You have to buy your hay?

Mr. ROMMEL. We have to buy our hay.

Mr. HAUGEN. And to haul it from town?

Mr. ROMMEL. We buy it from near-by farms, too. If we find some from whom we can buy in the near vicinity, we buy it and move the sheep to it.

Mr. HAUGEN. How many tons of hay would you have to buy for feed?

Mr. ROMMEL. Well, our feed bill—I would prefer to give that.

Mr. HAUGEN. I was trying to find out what this teamster does. you say it is driving and hauling; what does he haul?

Mr. ROMMEL. Feed, largely.

Mr. HAUGEN. Only feed? How much feed do you need in a year?

Mr. ROMMEL. At the station it is usually necessary to feed 100 days in winter. With the present flock and for work stock and stud rams, we use about 500 tons of hay and 30 tons of grain feed. More will be required as the flock grows, and it would be economy to secure land near by that can be irrigated and raise our own feed.

Mr. HAUGEN. You really think there is work for one man hauling feed?

Mr. ROMMEL. That is only one of the things he does.

Mr. HAUGEN. What other things does he do?

Mr. ROMMEL. There is a great deal of it. He hauls supplies of all sorts. We are 6 miles from town, from the railroad station, and the supplies have to be brought out from town. During the past summer this man broke and fallowed 30 acres of land. Next season we will see whether this land can produce any of our winter feed.

Mr. HAUGEN. What are the supplies, for instance?

Mr. ROMMEL. Gasoline, for instance, to run the well and pump. And take, for example, at the time of shearing, the supplies for the men who do the shearing, and supplies and everything of that kind. And the wool has to be hauled back to town.

Mr. HAUGEN. There would be two or three loads of wool, wouldn't there?

Mr. ROMMEL. I should hope it would be all of that.

Mr. HAUGEN. You say they shear 8 pounds, which would be 8,000 pounds?

Mr. ROMMEL. Is the idea that the man is not being kept occupied all the time; is that your idea?

Mr. HAUGEN. I had an idea he wasn't. I was trying to find out.

Mr. ROMMEL. We manage to keep them busy at all times.

Mr. HAUGEN. Many run a thousand sheep as a little side line; we do not hire any extra help.

Mr. ROMMEL. Mr. Haugen, I beg your pardon. I may be extremely dense, but there is a very decided difference between a flock of sheep that is managed purely for the money one can make out of it, where he has to eliminate absolutely every unnecessary expense——

Mr. HAUGEN. There is no difference whether——

Mr. ROMMEL (continuing). And the flock of sheep that is run as a source of scientific information. The matter of the revenue from the scientific standpoint can only be regarded as incidental. If the man in charge of a scientific project can show he is meeting the outgo with an equal income, he is showing more than almost any other experiment station would show. We last year had revenues of $10,000 from this station and eventually we will be able almost, if not quite, to meet the expenses at that point.

Mr. HAUGEN. Your contention, then, is that a teamster must be an expert bookkeeper?

Mr. ROMMEL. No, sir; nothing of the kind, sir.

Mr. HAUGEN. Then, point out where this hauling of 8,000 pounds of wool from an experiment station differs from hauling from a farm?

Mr. ROMMEL. Not at all.

Mr. HAUGEN. Of course, I appreciate there is additional work in keeping records, but it seems to me you are piling up a pretty big expense here in taking care of a thousand sheep on the desert, which require the services of four or five men; whereas a boy of 14 can do most of it on the farm.

Mr. MCLAUGHLIN. Is this land of such quality and its location such that you have reason to expect soon to be able to raise hay and other stuff that the animals will need?

Mr. ROMMEL. No, sir. Unfortunately, the land is only suitable for grazing. We will never to able to raise hay there, so far as we know.

The CHAIRMAN. You located it there for that very reason, didn't you, Doctor, because it was a grazing proposition?

Mr. ROMMEL. That it was a grazing proposition pure and simple, right there in the grazing country. There were very few settlers in that country.

Mr. HAUGEN. How many acres have you there?

Mr. ROMMEL. Twenty-eight thousand acres.

Mr. WASON. Was any part of it ever irrigated?

Mr. ROMMEL. No, sir.

Mr. WASON. Can it be?

Mr. ROMMEL. I do not think so. I have not myself been on the property and the man in my division most familiar with it has been sick with the influenza and not available for testimony, so that I can not give you a picture of it; I am quite certain none of it is irrigable.

Mr. WASON. You spoke of buying hay and some other products from near-by ranch men. It seems to me unfortunate in this very large area you selected that you have not selected any that can be irrigated and have to buy all your own products or the products used there in order to maintain that station.

Mr. ROMMEL. We could only get irrigated land by purchase and we have never had an appropriation to purchase land for this purpose.

The CHAIRMAN. My understanding of this work is that when we first imported the Corriedale sheep the purpose was to see whether or not these sheep could be crossed with range sheep, and also to find out whether or not the Corriedale would thrive under range conditions. The purpose was not to make investigations of the Corriedale under farm conditions. Is that not the case?

Mr. ROMMEL. Quite so.

The CHAIRMAN. So that your selection is not a bad selection?

Mr. ROMMEL. This must be a range proposition. Its use to the western range men will be nil unless those sheep are handled under range conditions.

Mr. MCLAUGHLIN. Something was said in a previous hearing about the ownership of that land. How did we acquire it?

Mr. ROMMEL. By Executive order. It was public land set aside by Executive order.

The CHAIRMAN. Those sheep had previously been located at another point?

Mr. MCLAUGHLIN. Previous to obtaining this place, those sheep were on a rented place?

Mr. ROMMEL. They were running with another flock.

Mr. HAUGEN. They were first in Wyoming?

Mr. ROMMEL. Yes.

Mr. HAUGEN. Where are they now?

Mr. ROMMEL. In Fremont County, Idaho.

Mr. MCLAUGHLIN. Where is that?

Mr. ROMMEL. That is north of Pocatello, on the line running from Pocatello to Butte. The station is Dubois.

The CHAIRMAN. I would like to ask you about this horse breeding for military purposes. Are you going to continue that work? Do you think it is necessary to continue it?

Mr. ROMMEL. Yes; I do.

The CHAIRMAN. How many stallions have you now; you had about 40 last year?

Mr. ROMMEL. The same number; we are not increasing. We got a slight increase last year, but it was absorbed by the increase in feed.

The CHAIRMAN. Is there anything further, Dr. Rommel, that you would like to discuss?

Mr. MCLAUGHLIN. Have you any mares of the same breed?

Mr. ROMMEL. We simply stand the stallions.

Mr. McLAUGHLIN. Have you an arrangement by which to buy the colts?

Mr. ROMMEL. The War Department has an arrangement to buy the colts. The War Department bought the first considerable number of colts last spring.

Mr. HAUGEN. At what age do they buy them?

Mr. ROMMEL. Three years old.

Mr. HAUGEN. You keep them until they are three years old on the farm?

Mr. ROMMEL. On the farm.

Mr. HAUGEN. And agree to deliver at a certain price?

Mr. ROMMEL. The War Department agrees to pay $150 a head.

Mr. McLAUGHLIN. How have the colts turned out; have you had any reports on them?

Mr. ROMMEL. Yes; we have quite a number of reports on them. They vary somewhat. The reports indicate that they get a better grade of horses than the average run of horses of that kind that they find in a community. I am inclined to think that if the work is continued and broadened out to make it extensive and important, that the Government should buy the horses at 5 years of age instead of 3.

Mr. McLAUGHLIN. Do you get any reports from the War Department? Do you get anything like a systematic and regular report, or is all your information as to the quality of the horses and how they turn out just casual observations or hearsay?

Mr. ROMMEL. We had our men with the War Department when they were buying last spring; they followed with the War Department officers right through. Last year was the first year any considerable number of the horses were bought for the military service. Before that there was only a small number each year; a dozen or so.

Mr. McLAUGHLIN. Does not the War Department report to you whether they are successful or not?

Mr. ROMMEL. They were 3 years old last spring, and they will not be in actual service until next winter or the following spring.

Mr. McLAUGHLIN. The War Department buys them before they need them?

Mr. ROMMEL. That is what the War Department has been doing with the colts bought as 3-year-olds, and developing them so that they will be finished horses at the time they are turned over to the troops.

Mr. HAUGEN. They pay $150, regardless of quality?

Mr. ROMMEL. Oh, not at all.

Mr. HAUGEN. You say they were buying them?

Mr. ROMMEL. They pay $150 for the ones they accept.

Mr. HAUGEN. They accept, just the same as they do with any other colt?

Mr. ROMMEL. Yes.

Mr. HAUGEN. There is nothing gained by that?

Mr. ROMMEL. They do not accept all the colts that are offered.

Mr. HAUGEN. They do just the same as when they buy any other horse?

Mr. ROMMEL. Yes.

Mr. HAUGEN. At what expense is this service maintained?

Mr. ROMMEL. The item this year is $37,840.
Mr. HAUGEN. What is the net?
Mr. ROMMEL. The net cost per head?
Mr. HAUGEN. No; the whole service?
Mr. ROMMEL. $37,840.
Mr. HAUGEN. And out of that there are no receipts; that is the net cost to the Government, and nothing is turned in to the Government?
Mr. ROMMEL. Oh, no; there is no return to the Government. What the Government gets out of it is a horse bred for a specific purpose.
Mr. HAUGEN. The Government does not get the horses.
Mr. ROMMEL. The Government gets the horses when the Army buys them.
Mr. HAUGEN. They pay for them.
Mr. MCLAUGHLIN. Do you use the stallions; is there a charge for the service fee where it is understood the Army is not to buy the colt?
Mr. ROMMEL. If a farmer wants to cancel the contract with the Government, he can cancel at any time by paying the service fee.
Mr. WASON. How much is that?
Mr. ROMMEL. $25. If he wants to keep the colt, he can pay the service fee.
Mr. MCLAUGHLIN. Have you receipts from that source?
Mr. ROMMEL. Yes, sir.
Mr. MCLAUGHLIN. How much does it amount to?
Mr. ROMMEL. Not very much.
Mr. HAUGEN. If you want to make that deduction, you deduct that amount?
Mr. ROMMEL. That is, the net?
Mr. HAUGEN. Yes. If you want to get at the net, how much should we deduct?
Mr. ROMMEL. I can not give you the figures.
Mr. HAUGEN. Approximately?
Mr. ROMMEL. The receipts from service fees for calendar year 1919 was $700.
Mr. HAUGEN. You say it cost the Government $37,840, and the colts are sold just the same way as any other colt, and the farmer gets the $150 colt by paying the service fee. Can you estimate the number of colts that the service fee has been paid on any retained by the farmer?
Mr. ROMMEL. The number that has been retained by the farmer? It is a small number; it is not more than 15 or 20 a year. The number retained by farmers in 1917 by payment of service fees was 28.
Mr. HAUGEN. Fifteen or twenty a year, and you have 40 stallions?
Mr. ROMMEL. Yes.
Mr. HAUGEN. You serve how many mares?
Mr. ROMMEL. The number of mares served in 1917 was over 2,000; approximately 2,500. The number of mares served in 1918 was considerably less. The falling off in horse breeding last year was very large all over the country.
Mr. HAUGEN. And how many per cent of colts?
Mr. ROMMEL. Those stallions get about 50 per cent.
Mr. HAUGEN. About 50 per cent?
Mr. ROMMEL. About 50 per cent.
Mr. HAUGEN. And you served 2,000, you say?

Mr. ROMMEL. About that.

Mr. HAUGEN. And about 15 service fees paid out of a thousand, or 15 retained by the farmers for every thousand colts?

Mr. ROMMEL. Approximately that.

Mr. HAUGEN. For a thousand mares served and getting a thousand colts, there are about 15 retained by the farmers.

Mr. ROMMEL. If the committee wishes, I would be very glad to file a tabulated statement along those lines, giving all those points.

The CHAIRMAN. We have the figures in the hearings of last year, except that they are not brought up to date.

(The statement referred to follows:)

Statement regarding military horse-breeding work for the calendar year 1917.

Number of stallions in service	35
Number of mares bred	1,594
Average number of mares bred per stallion	45
Number of colts retained by farmers by payment of service fee	28

Mr. MCLAUGHLIN. How many acres have you?

Mr. ROMMEL. We use no land in this connection.

Mr. MCLAUGHLIN. Where do you keep your stallions?

Mr. ROMMEL. We keep them in rented quarters.

Mr. MCLAUGHLIN. I was thinking you kept them at this place in Vermont?

Mr. ROMMEL. No; the place in Vermont is run independently of this. We use some of the stallions bred at the Morgan horse farm, and quarter all the stallions used in New England at the farm outside of the breeding seasons. The other stallions are kept in rented quarters.

Mr. HAUGEN. The expense is approximately a thousand dollars a horse?

Mr. ROMMEL. It is approximately a thousand dollars a stallion.

Mr. HAUGEN. It would exceed that?

Mr. ROMMEL. It is a little less than that.

Mr. HAUGEN. You have your overhead charges there; you have 40 stallions, and, I take it, there are other charges and other items that go into that expense?

Mr. ROMMEL. $37,840 includes all the expenses chargeable to this item, sir. Our system of bookkeeping is such we see to it that all items properly chargeable to this item are included in the $37,840.

Mr. HAUGEN. How much of that $38,000 includes overhead charges of your office here, for instance? I mean your office; you are at the head of it.

Mr. ROMMEL. The overhead charges are not over $5,000.

Mr. HAUGEN. Is that included in that $38,000?

Mr. ROMMEL. Yes, sir.

The CHAIRMAN. We are very much obliged to you, Doctor.

(Thereupon, at 12.45 o'clock p. m., a recess was taken until 2 p. m.)

AFTER RECESS.

The committee reconvened, pursuant to the taking of recess, at 2.10 o'clock p. m.

STATEMENT OF DR. JOHN R. MOHLER, CHIEF OF THE BUREAU OF ANIMAL INDUSTRY, UNITED STATES DEPARTMENT OF AGRICULTURE—Continued.

The CHAIRMAN. The next item will be found on page 56, item 92, for necessary expenses for scientific investigation of diseases of animals, and so on. Dr. Mohler, will you tell us something about that?

Dr. MOHLER. Mr. Chairman, there is no change recommended in this particular item.

The CHAIRMAN. Is there anything you would like particularly to call to the committee's attention?

Dr. MOHLER. There is nothing special to speak of in this connection. The item covers principally the various scientific investigations that are being conducted on animal diseases; and that is one of the places where the bureau was hit hardest as a result of the war. We lost a great many of our laboratory men who were taken by the War Department for laboratory research work in the Surgeon General's office.

Mr. WASON. Doctor, I have in my pocket a letter signed by you relating to an inquiry I made of your bureau last summer about bovo-vaccine.

Dr. MOHLER. Yes, sir.

Mr. WASON. In that letter—perhaps it would be better for you to just look at it and refresh your memory—you say that you can not direct me where it can be obtained. It says that the use of bovo-vaccine and similar preparations has been studied by this bureau and several States, but the results have not been satisfactory as a whole. What do you mean by that statement?

Dr. MOHLER. Gentlemen, this bovovaccine is a German preparation which consists of desiccated human tubercle bacilli. It is injected into the veins of cattle to immunize them against tuberculosis. The Pennsylvania livestock sanitary board, the Maryland Agricultural College, as well as several other colleges and the Bureau of Animal Industry, have studied this bovovaccine and find it contains live organisms of the human tuberculosis type. The injections of this bovovaccine in a number of cases have caused localized lesions of tuberculosis in inoculated animals that were supposed to be immunized by such injections. The lesions produced by this bovovaccine were found to be located in various portions and tissues of the body, particularly in the lungs, kidneys, udders, brains, or knees of the cattle. In one herd I saw five or six bovovaccinated cattle with large swellings on the knees, and when the tuberculin test was applied they all reacted, and the lesions were found to be localized tuberculosis of the human type involving these joints.

In 1913, as you will remember, there was a serum toxin act passed by Congress, and since that time no biological product of this class could be imported into this country without a permit. And that was the reason why I stated in this letter to you that there is no bovo-vaccine in this country that could be obtained, because there has been no permit granted for bringing in bovovaccine.

Mr. Wason. I particularly had reference to that portion of your letter relating to the result of the slight investigations or of such investigations as had been made that you were aware of.

Dr. Mohler. This subject of bovovaccination was carried out on a very large scale by the State Livestock Sanitary Board of Pennsylvania, by Dr. Pearson and his coworkers, and they found that some of those animals inoculated with the human type of tubercle bacilli had lesions in the lung, udder, wind pipe and in various other localities. And the result of all the work on bovovaccine that has been reported on by European investigators, as well as by experts in this country, would indicate that while considerable immunity is conferred there is great danger of spreading human tubercle bacilli to human beings through raw milk from these inoculated cattle.

There is another point with reference to the germs becoming localized. Theobald Smith, of Harvard, now with the Rockefeller Institute in New Jersey, inoculated a number of cattle with this type of material and he found that the germs became localized in the lung and udder, and at times in the brain, producing nervous symptoms. A post mortem examination showed the meninges contained these little tubercles.

Our own work was published in a circular several years ago, and I believe I sent you a copy of this circular, No. 190, which contained the information.

Mr. Wason. You did not send it; you said you would.

Dr. Mohler. I shall do so. That contains the results of the investigations by the Bureau of Animal Industry.

Mr. Wason. Now, Doctor, the reason of my request to your bureau was an inquiry from a man in my congressional district who has managed a large herd of dairy cattle for more than 20 years, and they have used that constantly in the herd, and he is without that and he desires it. Have you any information in your department about the results of its use in the State of New Hampshire.

Dr. Mohler. No, sir.

Mr. Wason. Or in the State of Maine?

Dr. Mohler. I know in the State of Maine they have been doing some work with vaccine for tuberculosis, but I have not heard of any of the results, nor have I seen any such data in the Maine reports.

Mr. Wason. Have you ever read the testimonial of the Board of Agriculture, I think they call it, for Maine, strongly indorsing it to farmers?

Dr. Mohler. This bovovaccine?

Mr. Wason. Yes.

Dr. Mohler. No, sir; I have not.

Mr. Wason. Have you seen the statistics of the number of herds that had been treated with it and the result of those statistics?

Dr. Mohler. I have seen a certain amount of statistics in certain publications. I know the firm that acted as United States agent for this product, the Bishoff Co., of New York City, and I am very well acquainted with the man who acted as their salesman, Dr. Newcomb, of Massachusetts. But I have not seen any very lasting results as a consequence of the use of bovovaccine.

Mr. Wason. There are a number of herds in New Hampshire that it has been tried out in for a number of years, and except with isolated cases no results such as you earlier described have appeared.

Dr. MOHLER. How many years ago, Mr. Wason?

Mr. WASON. I should say they began to use it—this is from my recollection; I thought I had my data at hand, but I could not find it this morning—I should say they began to use it beginning in 1896 or in 1897.

Dr. MOHLER. That must be a different product, Mr. Wason, because this product has not been on the market in this country much before 1906. It was worked out by Von Behring, at Marburg, Germany, with the assistance of Römer. The Argentine Government was so enthusiastic about the possibilities of bovovaccine that they employed Römer to come to Buenos Aires, about 1907 or 1908, and he stayed there several years for the purpose of testing out this bovovaccine. He is not there to-day, and, I understand, they are not using any of this bovovaccine in Argentina. Prof. Lignieres, of Buenos Aires, has reported that the germs introduced by vaccination remain alive and active in the bodies of the animals for two years. This study of immunization against tuberculosis did not begin until about 1901, but it has been under investigation in almost every country since then.

Mr. WASON. The indorsement, I speak of, from the State of Maine, if my recollection is right, was in 1907; and there were many herds that had been treated with it in Maine, in New Hampshire, in Massachusetts, and some in Vermont. My purpose of making the inquiry is this, that I think instead of spending so much money in observing and destroying animals affected by it, you ought to spend the money in research work along this line.

Dr. MOHLER. That is being done, gentlemen, as you know, under this very item. I do not know who conducted the experiments in New Hampshire or in Maine; but I understand they have been going on in Maine recently. I do know that men like Theobald Smith, now of the Rockefeller Institutue, men like Leonard Pearson, Gilliland, and like Dr. Buckley, of the Maryland Agricultural College, all tried out this product in various ways and their results were practically the same.

There is a herd to-day, not more than 45 miles outside of the city, that had this treatment successively for a number of years, and I have been present at the post-mortem examinations of some of those animals, at the Baltimore abattoirs, where the lesions were very apparent on animals that were supposed to have been immunized. And the great danger is the possibility of spreading the human tubercle bacilli from the inoculated bovine animals to human beings.

Mr. WASON. You speak of these lesions. Were they active lesions?

Dr. MOHLER. Yes, sir; they were active lesions of the human type; they were not of the cattle type. They were of the type of the disease which was injected into the cattle to protect them against bovine tuberculosis. This was proved by laboratory experiments.

Mr. LESHER. And could be transmitted from the animal to the human being again?

Dr. MOHLER. We never have made an experiment of that kind; but, by analogy, there would not be any reason why they could not be transmitted to human beings. These germs in the bovovaccine are of the human type of the tuberculosis organism.

Mr. WASON. How does the germ of the animal tuberculosis differ from the human type of tuberculosis?

Dr. MOHLER. The bovine germ is a very short, stubby, evenly-stained, rod-like organism, which is much more virulent than the human type. The human organism is very long and narrow and beaded in appearance and it is not so pathogenic. You can not inoculate rabbits with the human germs with any degree of satisfaction; but with the bovine germ you can infect rabbits without any difficulty. That is one way of differentiating it. It is more difficult to infect cattle with human tubercle bacilli, but it is very easy to infect them with the bovine germ of tuberculosis.

Mr. WASON. Is it easy to infect human beings with bovine tuberculosis?

Dr. MOHLER. We have never attempted that. I do not know whether it would be easy or not, but there are a number of recorded cases where the human being under natural conditions has developed lesions which have been caused by the bovine germ.

Mr. WASON. If the scientist does not think that the germ of bovine tuberculosis is likely to infect human beings, why is this United States-wide propaganda to watch the dairy herds and particularly the milk carried out?

Dr. MOHLER. Gentlemen, we certainly do think there is a possibility and quite a considerable possibility of the bovine germ infecting especially children and invalids, but we are not making that point here. We are trying to eradicate bovine tuberculosis purely from the economic side of the question. We believe it is to the interest of the farmer to get rid of tubercular cattle, whether those tubercular cattle are going to spread the disease to human beings or not. We are trying to put our stress on the economic side of the eradication of the tuberculosis for the farmer's own sake.

Mr. WASON. I appreciate that, but I have been taught—and supposed it was a fact, although not a scientist on tuberculosis, but I have seen a great deal of it—that the use of milk from infected animals, dairy animals, by human beings, was dangerous to the human health. Is that not a fact?

Dr. MOHLER. Yes, sir. I would not want to drink any milk from a tubercular animal. I believe it is a dangerous proposition to advocate, and I believe the only safe way of protecting public health from bovine tuberculosis under present conditions is by pasteurization of milk which is to be consumed by human beings. That is an easy proposition for the protection of public health. You do not have to get rid of tubercular cattle to protect public health. But that is a problem of the Public Health Service, and it is not at this time a problem *per se* of the Bureau of Animal Industry. It is quite easy of solution by pasteurizing the milk from these tubercular animals. However, we are emphasizing at present the value of getting rid of tuberculosis from a purely business standpoint.

Mr. WASON. Following your answer a step further, an animal, to the eye in perfect health, in good flesh, and wholesome in every appearance, upon slaughtering or upon test discloses the presence of the germ of tuberculosis in his system. That animal is ready for beef, and when slaughtered, unless the bovine germ is a menace to public health, why shouldn't that animal be used as human food?

Dr. MOHLER. Such an animal is used for human food, under the meat-inspection regulations, provided the extent of the lesions is not sufficient to warrant other action.

Mr. WASON. Then, coming back to the product of the dairy cow, if the lesions on the cow are in the lungs or in the throat and not in the mammary glands or on the udder, the milk would be perfectly safe?

Dr. MOHLER. Yes, sir; very often the milk is entirely safe. We do not find tuberculosis germs in the milk except in the advanced stages, but you can not tell the stage of the disease by looking at the exterior of the animal.

Mr. WASON. That is true. Then the reason why your department, before you had charge of it and now, have discouraged the use of this bovovaccine, is because it anticipated or feared by the use of that germ it would spread from the animal to the human being?

Dr. MOHLER. Yes, sir; that is one of the principal reasons.

Mr. WASON. Have you any instances where these lesions appeared in the udder of the vaccinated animal?

Dr. MOHLER. Yes, sir. Just as I have stated, the experiments conducted at Boston by Theobald Smith, of Harvard University, as well as by Weber, Titze, Hutyra, Pearson, and others, showed a number of such cases where vaccinated animals, developed localized lesions in the udder, and usually in the left hind quarter. Whether that is merely a coincidence or not, I do not know, but the majority of those cases showed the lesions were localized in the left hind quarter of the udder.

Mr. WASON. You know, probably, this bovovaccine that was discovered about 1890, by this German, Von Behring, has been used quite extensively in that empire?

Dr. MOHLER. Yes, sir.

Mr. WASON. With comparatively good success?

Dr. MOHLER. No; I would not care to admit that by any means.

Mr. WASON. More than 50 per cent of the cases they felt were immune?

Dr. MOHLER. That is not the record, Mr. Wason, of the most recent literature in Germany. My information is that the more or less satisfactory results were obtained only where hygienic and prophylactic measures, effective in themselves, were instituted at the same time. Moreover, the immunity is of short duration, being considerably reduced in 12 months and disappearing entirely six months later. Prof. Heyman, of Belgium, came to this country to demonstrate the Belgian method of tuberculosis immunization by injecting under the skin of the cattle a little reed capsule (something like the capsule in which you buy quinine), filled with human tubercle bacilli. He inserted those capsules in a number of cattle at our experiment station, at our request, with the idea of protecting them against tuberculosis. We slaughtered those animals after a given time and found the lesions had spread from these capsules to adjacent lymph glands, and to the lungs. Still this method was reported by Heyman as being very efficient in Belgium. That was in 1908, at the time the International Tuberculosis Congress was held in Washington. It was quite extensively used in Belgium at that time, but since then you have heard very little about it. I am speaking of before the war. Of course, since the war there has been no activity along that line. The Belgian method of protecting cattle against tuberculosis seems to have fallen flat, and it is the same thing with this bovovaccine in Argentina and the so-called Friedmann turtle vaccine for human tuberculosis exploited in this country several years ago. Certainly bovovaccine has not decreased the percentage of tuberculosis among the cattle of Germany, judging by statistics available before the war.

I would like very much to see a report of the beneficial effects you spoke about in New Hampshire, because I have not seen any figures showing such results.

Mr. WASON. As soon as I can put my hands on them, I will be glad to take them up with you.

Dr. MOHLER. But as a general proposition it is more or less hazardous to inject any living organism into cattle to protect them against that disease, especially when the animals may contract the disease inoculated and transmit it to human beings. At best the immunity is of short duration and at present it must be considered as a means to protect livestock by endangering public health.

Mr. WASON. Is not the same thing tried on human beings?

Dr. MOHLER. I do not know of any living bacilli of any disease that are injected into human beings to protect them against that disease.

Mr. WASON. I guess most of us were vaccinated in our childhood to protect us against smallpox?

Dr. MOHLER. Yes. sir; but we were not vaccinated with the germs of smallpox. We were inoculated with lymph taken from a very mild disease of cattle called vaccinia or cow pox, which is quite a different proposition. This vaccine could never produce smallpox. Then there are several other vaccines, one against typhoid, another against pneumonia, and another against paratyphoid infection. But all the germs which are used to make these vaccines are killed before they are inoculated into human beings.

Mr. WASON. And at the present time there is a vaccine for the "flu?"

Dr. MOHLER. Yes, sir; but this vaccine contains only dead germs; there are no living germs in any of those vaccines which I have seen used in this city.

Mr. WASON. Perhaps by studying the germ of the animal, your scientists in time may get a vaccine?

Dr. MOHLER. That is very true; that may be.

Mr. WASON. And if you could, you would make the animals immune, instead of having to have an army of men traveling over the country destroying animals of different ages.

Dr. MOHLER. And it would be an excellent idea if we could vaccinate cattle so that they would not contract tuberculosis, but it is not being successfully done by any community, State, or government with which I am familiar. It has been tried on a large scale in some foreign countries, but the last word from those foreign countries indicates it has not proved satisfactory.

Mr. WASON. You will admit, possibly, that as a basic proposition, with the cattle of New England, unless the place where they are kept in the winter months is well ventilated, etc., it would be the place where the germ would thrive best?

Dr. MOHLER. Yes.

Mr. WASON. And if we could find herds there that are apparently protected by this, it would be worth consideration?

Dr. MOHLER. It certainly would.

Mr. WASON. I think we can furnish you with that information.

Dr. MOHLER. I shall be very glad to get it, I am sure.

Mr. HAUGEN. You are suggesting pasteurizing the milk to protect human beings. Does this pasteurized milk retain the same flavor and nutrition of raw milk?

Dr. MOHLER. If it is properly pasteurized at 145° for 20 or 30 minutes, it does not affect the chemical composition of the milk at all; but if you go higher, it does change the chemical composition and affects the taste. We recommend that it be pasteurized at a temperature of 145° for 30 minutes.

Mr. HAUGEN. And the same thing applies to cream?

Dr. MOHLER. Yes, sir; the cream that is made into butter, also.

Mr. WASON. I think it improves it.

Dr. MOHLER. That solves the public-health question, so far as tuberculosis arising from milk is concerned, because that temperature will kill the tubercle bacilli.

Mr. WASON. We have proved that in our State institutions.

Mr. HAUGEN. Some of the State laws require that.

The CHAIRMAN. Page 57, item 93, the hog-cholera item.

Dr. MOHLER. The next item refers to the control and eradication of hog cholera. We have been working strenuously on this subject this last year, both with the general appropriation fund as well as with the appropriation under the food-production act. As a result of this double fund, we have been conducting the work in 34 different States, with the result that the death rate in hogs has been reduced from 120 per thousand in 1914 to 42 per thousand last year. This death rate is lower than it has been for 35 years. The figures we have would indicate that the disease has been reduced about 60 per cent.

There was an item in one of the agricultural papers several weeks ago which showed that in Iowa alone the loss of hogs had been reduced from 2,700,000 in 1913 to 189,000 in 1917. And the report of the committee on swine diseases that is connected with the United States Livestock Sanitary Board would indicate that the extent of the disease in 1918 was even less than it was in 1917.

Mr. HAUGEN. Will you tell us just what you are doing to prevent the spread? What do you do in Iowa, and how many cases have you discovered in Iowa?

Dr. MOHLER. We have 17 men in Iowa, who are cooperating with the State extension leader and the State regulatory authorities. As soon as we hear of an outbreak of hog cholera the men are immediately sent to the farm to confirm the diagnosis by post-mortem examination. If it proves to be hog cholera, they supervise and assist in vaccinating the animals on that farm; the farmer is advised as to the necessity of burying the animals that have died and disinfecting the premises. In certain cases the farm is quarantined by the State, but not by the Federal Government, of course. Our men hold meetings in that community and advise what precautions the farmers in adjacent territory should take in order to prevent the spread from that infected farm to the adjacent farms.

Mr. LESHER. Don't you believe that the quarantine system is doing about as much good as anything else?

Dr. MOHLER. It is. It is of the greatest assistance in controlling it. When you have a disease so widespread as influenza or hog cholera, good results are always obtained by quarantine.

Mr. HAUGEN. That is very good, but how many cases did you discover in Iowa last year?

Dr. MOHLER. I could not say offhand, but we have the report.

Mr. HAUGEN. Any considerable number?

Dr. MOHLER. It has been under control fairly well in Iowa. There have been very few secondary centers of infection spread from the original centers.

Mr. HAUGEN. In fact, has there been any?

Dr. MOHLER. Oh, yes. Yes, indeed, there have been a number of cases, especially in western Iowa. I can not give you the exact number, because I haven't it here, by counties, but I can give you in the record the precise number of outbreaks, the number of hogs on the farms infected, and the number of meetings held in your State and any other State.

Mr. HAUGEN. The visiting and meetings do not get very far in preventing the spread.

Dr. MOHLER. We supervised the injection of over 5,000,000 hogs last year, and a certain proportion of those were in Iowa. We are working in 34 States, and have 17 men in your State.

Mr. HAUGEN. Does that include the stockyards?

Dr. MOHLER. No, sir; that is entirely different. These are hogs on the farms. At the stockyards we vaccinated in October, November, and December of 1917 about 250,000 stocker hogs; but during this last fall there were not so many feeders and stockers, as you know.

Mr. HAUGEN. Of course, the State law requires that, but that is outside of your bureau?

Dr. MOHLER. Not if they are public stockyards. We did considerable vaccinating at all the public stockyards like Omaha, Kansas City, St. Louis, Chicago, Indianapolis, Louisville, etc.

Mr. HAUGEN. Are they included in this 5,000,000?

Dr. MOHLER. No, sir; the latter were on the farms. In addition to those, in 1917, in connection with the program to increase hog production, we vaccinated 250,000 stock hogs in the stockyards at St. Paul, East St. Louis, St. Joe, Omaha, Chicago, Indianapolis, etc.

Mr. HAUGEN. I have inquired of a number of people throughout the State, and I have not been able to find a single case of hog cholera in Iowa, but we are told last year there were a considerable number in the western part of the State, and I am very much interested to know about that.

Dr. MOHLER. I would be glad to give you the number of farms and the number of animals affected.

Mr. HAUGEN. Can you name the counties?

Dr. MOHLER. No. As I say, I shall be very glad to put that in the record.

The CHAIRMAN. Suppose you put that in the record for Iowa.

Mr. MOHLER. I shall be glad to.

(The statement referred to follows:)

AGRICULTURE APPROPRIATION BILL.

Outbreaks of hog cholera in Iowa for the period May to October, 1918, inclusive.

County.	Number of outbreaks.	Number of hogs on farm.	Number sick treated.	Apparently well treated.	Number died before treatment.	Too sick to be treated.
Humboldt	21	1,674	300	1,373	56	23
Polk	32	2,758	1,065	1,614	26	30
Madison	37	3,131	580	1,769	90	64
Jefferson	56	3,524	970	2,191	76	28
Sac	3	240	38	201	8	1
Adams	13	1,146	409	508	22	8
Kossuth	45	3,844	891	2,534	139	605
Buchanan	27	1,350	144	1,027	88	168
Johnson	22	2,617	756	1,513	70	130
Fremont	35	3,629	511	1,936	186	22
Sioux	17	1,733	453	1,032	67	39
Mahaska	29	1,935	352	1,346	32	31
Warren	5	510	60	465	20	
Louisa	1	160	5	155	2	
Cass	92	7,001	1,029	5,232	521	411
Wright	33	2,376	279	2,002	156	58
Delaware	7	562	110	415	27	36
Benton	40	4,001	553	3,152	184	94
Taylor	4	188	147	30	22	8
Plymouth	11	1,310	194	966	98	10
Clayton	1	52	10	42	12	
Hancock	2	133	56	45	9	12
Bremer	1	25	2	21		2
Chickasaw	1	19	2	17	30	1
Appanoose	4	186	56	130	15	
Buena Vista	2	120	46	44	4	30
Audubon	5	725	154	527	128	44
Floyd	8	150	55	95	8	
Greene	17	2,116	288	896	56	4
O'Brien	13	948	321	470	98	103
Keokuk	3	312	9	293	3	
Hardin	9	591	73	432	57	64
Hamilton	38	3,164	625	2,337	120	57
Clinton	3	180	70	112	23	
Dubuque	2	87	31	10	7	46
Osceola	4	546	71	232	13	18
Des Moines	1	30	10	20		
Winnebago	6	396	51	338	33	9
Crawford	7	912	203	460	128	18
Calhoun	22	1,237	491	698	31	46
Van Buren	1	47	20	27	13	
Decatur	2	132	6	126	7	
Jasper	33	2,395	552	1,516	173	115
Jackson	7	840	64	245	17	26
Adair	20	1,371	350	882	28	10
Poweshiek	10	752	148	...	56	38
Guthrie	27	2,160	271	1,635	36	21
Webster	11	1,161	151	722	61	147
Lucas	3	160	47	101	5	11
Monroe	6	698	78	319	6	
Clarke	2	93	58	35	9	
Iowa	5	498	85	321	26	8
Grundy	12	1,143	183	862	11	1
Wayne	4	271	86	168	4	
Palo Alto	5	474	70	280	24	24
Harrison	7	596	90	464	25	
Franklin	8	524	104	369	36	15
Boone	4	194	53	141	5	
Mills	25	3,493	281	2,734	160	58
Lyon	11	1,508	316	964	165	26
Montgomery	22	2,171	427	1,603	137	48
Page	21	1,790	174	1,016	120	111
Shelby	34	2,351	356	1,382	169	219
Cherokee	20	1,930	356	1,360	87	251
Wapello	25	1,293	229	864	36	12
Dallas	114	8,204	5,749	6,194	133	72
Black Hawk	18	1,379	268	958	60	5
Tama	28	2,732	574	1,877	116	128
Carroll	13	1,118	217	620	39	40
Butler	4	226	69	149	5	3
Marion	11	923	154	728	77	11
Pocahontas	9	680	152	393	17	7
Woodbury	16	1,872	593	1,118	88	25
Ringgold	3	280	40	210	5	20
Taylor	31	1,940	493	1,034	58	199
Union	9	475	97	362	24	5
Story	5	179	42	237	3	
Clay	1	14	1	13	11	

Outbreaks of hog cholera in Iowa for the period May to October, 1918, inclusive—Continued.

County.	Number of outbreaks.	Number of hogs on farm.	Number sick treated.	Apparently well treated.	Number died before treatment.	Too sick to be treated.
Monona	5	434	161	186	34	85
Emmet	16	1,036	288	747	37	51
Marshall	7	454	199	254	7	1
Henry	3	119	31	77	17	6
Washington	9	1,059	247	480	64	51
Muscatine	4	251	121	102	43	28
Linn	15	1,769	190	598	21	6
Pottawattamie	38	3,592	721	2,645	286	32
Total	1,288	114,947	26,416	73,292	5,236	4,136

Mr. HAUGEN. How much are you asking for this year?

Dr. MOHLER. The same amount as was included in last year's act. The entire amount for the three projects mentioned here is $438,080, and out of that amount there is $163,000 which is used for the enforcement of the virus-serum act and $30,000 for the investigation of hog diseases, particularly hog cholera. That leaves about $244,000 for hog-cholera control work in the field.

Mr. HAUGEN. How is that progressing; are they making as much serum as they were?

Dr. MOHLER. The hog-cholera serum?

Mr. HAUGEN. Yes.

Dr. MOHLER. More than ever. During the fiscal year 1917 there were about 238,000,000 c. c. made. In the fiscal year 1918 there were 271,000,000 c. c. made. For this last calendar year, 1918, we have not the full records yet, but it will approximate 350,000,000 c. c. And of that number the inspectors of the different plants condemned over 2,000,000 c. c. as being contaminated or impotent, which otherwise might have been put on the market without the control or supervision of the bureau.

Mr. HAUGEN. A considerable amount is being sold and used?

Dr. MOHLER. Yes, sir.

Mr. HAUGEN. And more than ever?

Dr. MOHLER. Yes, indeed. I think that accounts to a large extent for the smaller number of hogs which have died in the past year. There has been so much more vaccine immunization against hog cholera that it has resulted in greatly reducing the losses.

Mr. HAUGEN. How did you prevent the spread of it; what was done in preventing the spread of hog cholera?

Dr. MOHLER. Wherever we heard in these 34 States that hog cholera existed, we immediately went directly to the farm and supervised the vaccination of the remaining hogs on that farm and we buried the hogs or saw that they were buried, disinfected the premises and stopped the source of infection right there. And then we were cooperating with the county agents and other leaders, holding meetings to explain to farmers the nature of the disease and what should be done to eradicate it. They were informed that John Jones, in a certain county, had the disease, and it was necessary for them to take precautions and that they ought not to visit that farm. If necessary, if they had been over there recently, we recommended that their herds be vaccinated. And in that way we controlled the spread of the disease. All those States are organized; in your State, as in other States, we have a number of men. The State is divided into districts, so that one man will cover probably three or four counties, and he will hear from various sources where an outbreak occurs. We are also cooperating with the State veterinarians through our meat-inspection service. In the case of every hog that shows hog cholera on the killing floor we try to ascertain the name of the owner and trace it back to the farm where it originated. We then write a letter to the State regulatory people and also write a letter to our inspector in charge of hog-cholera work in the State where this hog originated. So that by taking these measures I speak of, we prevent adjacent herds from becoming infected.

Mr. HAUGEN. You have certain counties where vaccinated hogs are kept under your observation. How does the loss in those counties compare with counties where that is not done?

Dr. MOHLER. We are covering almost all of the counties in the State of Iowa and in some other of these 34 States.

Mr. HAUGEN. But they are giving special attention to certain counties. I think Delaware County, in our State, was one and there are two or three others. Are the losses in those counties any less than they are in counties outside, where there is no supervision of your men?

Dr. MOHLER. Yes, sir; there is a decrease in hog cholera in the counties where our men are at work. And there is a great decrease of hog cholera in the States where our men work, as compared with States where they are not working.

Mr. HAUGEN. For instance, in my own county, we haven't had any hog cholera, and there are no specialists on hog cholera there.

Dr. MOHLER. That is true. This committee I spoke about a few minutes ago, in a report a week ago to the Chicago convention, state as follows: The information obtained from all the States of the Union indicates that the loss from hog cholera was less than the previous year, except in New York, Pennsylvania, and Washington.

Mr. HAUGEN. It travels all the time?

Dr. MOHLER. Yes; but they are three of the States where we are not cooperating, and in those three States hog cholera has not been reduced. You can draw your own inference whether it is because our men are not operating there or whether it is because it travels in cycles.

But now is the time to keep the disease under control. It is much easier to push a disease downhill than it is to get it under control when it is going uphill; and hog cholera is certainly on the decline, as the statistics indicate. The loss of 42 hogs per thousand is very, very slight, as compared with the great losses four years ago, when the mortality was 120 per thousand. And those figures are the lowest that have been recorded in the last 35 years.

Mr. HAUGEN. Do the climatic conditions have anything to do with it?

Dr. MOHLER. No, sir; not at all.

Mr. HAUGEN. It starts at certain times of the year?

Dr. MOHLER. Yes.

Mr. HAUGEN. In the fall generally?

Dr. MOHLER. In the fall very often.

Mr. HAUGEN. After they begin the feeding of soft corn?

Dr. MOHLER. Yes. There is no virus of hog cholera conveyed in soft corn, however; that is merely a coincidence.

Mr. HAUGEN. In these losses that are charged up to hog cholera, is it not a fact that most of the losses are due to other things?

Dr. MOHLER. I would not say most of the losses are chargeable to other things. I think hog cholera destroys more hogs than all other diseases put together; but there are several diseases of hogs which the bureau is now studying, which must be held responsible for a certain amount of the losses.

Mr. HAUGEN. You hold post-mortem examinations to ascertain what the cause was?

Dr. MOHLER. In every case. When a farm is visited, after a report has been received to the effect that hogs have died supposedly of hog cholera, the remaining hogs are never vaccinated until the result of a post mortem confirms the suspicions of the farmer.

Mr. HAUGEN. What have you found in your investigations—that it is due principally to hog cholera, or to other diseases?

Dr. MOHLER. As I say, in the vast majority of cases the losses were caused by what we call the filterable virus—that is, were due to hog cholera—but in certain other cases they were caused by necrotic enteritis and by another infection called swine plague. However, these diseases all combined do not produce the amount of losses that hog cholera produces.

Mr. LEE. Have you found any way of cheapening the virus?

Dr. MOHLER. No, sir.

Mr. LEE. The expense of inoculation seems to be the great trouble in my country.

Dr. MOHLER. With hogs selling at the price they are now and with labor so high and everything going into the preparation of the serum being so much higher than several years ago, I do not see any possibility of a reduction in the price. As a rule, it sells for $1\frac{1}{2}$ cents a cubic centimeter, and in some cases 2 cents a cubic centimeter. But mostly it sells for $1\frac{1}{4}$ cents.

Mr. HAUGEN. What was the price when hogs were cheaper?

Dr. MOHLER. I have known of serum selling for 75 cents a hundred cubic centimeters.

Mr. HAUGEN. It is just about double in price now, and hogs have doubled.

Dr. MOHLER. That serum was a little lower in price than normal. It used to sell from a cent to a cent and a quarter, and it has gone up that much.

The CHAIRMAN. Item 94, for all necessary expenses for investigation and treatment and eradication of dourine. I notice in the note you think this will be completed during the coming fiscal year.

Dr. MOHLER. The work is nearing completion, both in North Dakota and in Wyoming. In North Dakota we had only 23 reactions last year and in Wyoming only 2. The situation in Montana and South Dakota is also improved. But our greatest trouble with dourine will be, as it has been in the last year or two, on the Indian reservations in New Mexico and Arizona, as I explained a year ago.

It is very hard to get the Indians to round up their animals and keep them under control while the tests are being made.

The CHAIRMAN. You have to have a small appropriation here?

Dr. MOHLER. Yes; we recommend a reduction of $8,700.

The CHAIRMAN. You could not recommend a reduction of a little more than that?

Dr. MOHLER. I think not, because of the indemnity feature, which permits us to buy and destroy those horses that are condemned. We need more than we otherwise would on account of the indemnity.

Mr. HAUGEN. My recollection is we started in with about $100,000?

Dr. MOHLER. Yes, sir.

Mr. HAUGEN. The contention at that time was that we should make the amount a hundred thousand, instead of a smaller amount, so that the work might be concluded; and it has been running along for several years.

Dr. MOHLER. Yes, for three or four years. The amount appropriated at that time was on account of the discovery of this imported disease in Montana horses, and the more we worked the more evidence we found that it had spread over to Wyoming, North Dakota, and to the upper portion of South Dakota. And then the Indian ponies down on the Navajo Reservation and the Apache Reservation, as well as some of the animals that belonged to the neighboring ranchmen proved to be infected, and we have now a worse outbreak in Arizona and New Mexico than we had in the original centers in Montana and North Dakota.

Mr. HAUGEN. Is it confined to those two States?

Dr. MOHLER. To those six States——

Mr. HAUGEN. Is there any in Iowa?

Dr. MOHLER. No; Iowa has been clean for about four or five years. There was a small outbreak in 1913 or 1914, but Iowa, Nebraska, and Illinois, which were formerly infected, have been cleaned up. There were only two cases in Wyoming last year, and this year we think there won't be any. And there were only 23 found last year in North Dakota. We tested 45,000 horses and we found 1,010 that were infected, which is about 2.2 per cent. A year ago it was about 2.5 per cent, so it is gradually being wiped out. It is something like syphilis in man and is frequently called equine syphilis. The disease runs a very chronic course and there is no way of telling when it has disappeared except by puncturing the jugular vein of the horse and making a test of the blood, the same way as we test the blood of a man for syphilis.

Mr. HAUGEN. Do you test a whole herd?

Dr. MOKLER. Yes, sir; we test all the animals that are exposed.

Mr. HAUGEN. You test those that are exposed?

Dr. MOHLER. Yes, sir.

The CHAIRMAN. The next item, No. 95, on page 60, is for general administration expenses. There is no change in that, so we will not discuss it. The next is on page 61, item 96, proposing an increase in the appropriation for meat inspection. You have some new language there authorizing the Secretary of Agriculture to pay employees for overtime service.

Dr. MOHLER. This added paragraph has been recommended to cover overtime work performed by our meat-inspection employees in order that they could be reimbursed for overtime in the same manner as the butchers are being paid overtime by their employers. The men now are working from 7 o'clock in the morning until 6, 7, or 8 o'clock at night, and it is impossible under existing law to pay them for such overtime. This provision permits the Secretary to accept from the establishments where this overtime work is performed an appropriate reimbursement, and the Government will then pay this overtime money to the meat-inspection employees. It is the same proposition that now obtains in Canada, and in talking with the Canadian authorities they assured us that it has worked very satisfactorily. The owners of inspected establishments pay the Ottawa Government, and then the latter sends the money to the various employees who have worked overtime. That is the proposition we have here.

The CHAIRMAN. Why not pay the employees direct? As you pay them their regular salary, why not pay direct for overtime? Wouldn't that be a better system than to have to go through an intermediate process?

Dr. MOHLER. That would be satisfactory if we had sufficient funds. One reason this method was suggested was because it involved no additional appropriation of funds. The way the law reads now, Mr. Chairman, it prohibits the packers from giving any money to inspectors or inspectors receiving any money from the packers.

The CHAIRMAN. That is true, and I think that is a very wise provision.

Mr. HAUGEN. That is the one thing we had in mind particularly, that they should be independent from the packers. We did not want any partnership between the packers and the inspectors.

Dr. MOHLER. But we do not consider there would be any such partnership if the department charged the various establishments for the overtime and then reimbursed the inspectors. In this manner the department would always know what was going on.

The CHAIRMAN. I do not know that I quite catch the full meaning of this proposition; but, as I understand your statement, this proviso allows the packers to pay overtime and then you reimburse the packers?

Dr. MOHLER. No; we charge the packer for overtime of our employees, and when the packer sends in the money we will pay our inspectors the money the packer has paid to us. In that way we know exactly what is being done, and there is no connection between the employee in the establishment and the packer. The packer pays the Washington office the amount of overtime pay, and then we in turn send it to our inspectors in Chicago, for instance.

The CHAIRMAN. The packer does not pay the permanent appropriation of $3,000,000?

Dr. MOHLER. No, sir; this is entirely a new feature. The packer will send the money to us and we will send it to the inspectors. We are asking the privilege of charging the packer for overtime work. Our men are working from 7 o'clock in the morning until 7 and 8 o'clock at night, and they are working on Sundays and holidays, Thanksgiving, Christmas, and New Year's, without additional remuneration, while the butchers are being paid time and a half for overtime on week days and double time for Sundays and holidays.

The CHAIRMAN. On what theory would you justify the Government paying the normal salary and the packers paying the overtime salary? Haven't you an inconsistent theory in the two propositions?

Dr. MOHLER. We feel that an eight-hour day is about what the Government is expecting from its employees; and if for the benefit and accommodation of the business of the packer in a commercial way it is necessary for our men to work overtime, it seems to me the packer ought to be willing to pay for the overtime service that is necessary to care for his increased business.

The CHAIRMAN. I am not interested in whether the packer is willing to do it or not.

Mr. HARRISON. It is an accommodation to the packer, Mr. Chairman.

Mr. HAUGEN. Isn't the packer benefited by the regular day's work just as much as by the overtime?

The CHAIRMAN. Exactly. And won't you run into this difficulty— I am not objecting to the proposition, but I am objecting to the way you propose doing it—won't you in a measure lose control of your inspection force and permit the packers probably to overwork these men by giving them the privilege of paying those inspectors through this plan of reimbursement?

Dr. MOHLER. Mr. Chairman, it has worked just the opposite in the only other country I know of where they are doing it, and that is in Canada. The head of the Canadian meat-inspection force has told me that instead of doing that it has resulted in the opposite effect. The packers are not making the Government inspectors stay those long hours when they have to pay for that overtime; they are hurrying up their killing so that they will get through quicker. Instead of finishing at 8 or 9 o'clock at night they are very often through at six in the evening, and with very little Sunday work. I assume that will be the result here.

The CHAIRMAN. But the Government has a right to say how much overtime work those men shall perform?

Dr. MOHLER. Entirely so; we do that now.

The CHAIRMAN. Can't you speed up the killing and things like that?

Dr. MOHLER. They are killing now from 850 to 900 an hour, and you can not speed it up much faster than that. A man's eye and hand can work just so fast, and when 900 hogs go by every hour it is about the limit for an 8-hour day, let alone a 10 or 12 hour day. Some time could be saved by avoiding unnecessary delays, etc.

The CHAIRMAN. I have seen them work; it is wonderful the way they do it.

Dr. MOHLER. They have speeded up under present conditions to the maximum.

The CHAIRMAN. Of course under the present conditions, but you do not expect those conditions to continue; there will be a slowing down at some time.

Dr. MOHLER. I hope so. But with the unprecedented number of animals in the country they are working overtime in all the establishments, and the butchers working for the packers are being paid very often twice as much as the inspectors are receiving.

The CHAIRMAN. I have always been opposed to making any concern which the Government regulates pay the freight. We have a system of that kind down in South Carolina in the regulation of the railroads. On that proposition I was opposed, when I first became a member of this committee, to having the packers pay the bill. I think the Federal Government ought to do it. I feel the same way about this proposition; I think the Government ought to pay for the whole proposition. However, that is a matter the committee will decide for itself.

Mr. HAUGEN. How much does this overtime amount to in dollars and cents; what would be the cost?

Dr. MOHLER. That would depend entirely on the rate per hour that we would ask the establishments to pay for the overtime.

Mr. HAUGEN. Suppose you pay them for all overtime.

Dr. MOHLER. Some of these men are now working eight hours on Sundays, and other men are working from 7 o'clock in the morning until 7 and 8 at night.

Mr. HAUGEN. There are some of them, but not a considerable number?

Dr. MOHLER. They are all doing that at the big packing houses, and very often working Sundays. We get telegrams on Saturday afternoon asking permission to have the men work the following day. The packers are not allowed to work our men overtime, especially on Sundays and holidays, without permission.

Mr. HAUGEN. Do we understand those inspectors have been working all the time from 7 o'clock in the morning to 7 and 8 at night?

Dr. MOHLER. From 7 to 6 or even later, and very often all day Sunday and on holidays.

Mr. LESHER. Does that continue the whole year around?

Dr. MOHLER. No; but it has continued since September and will continue this way right through until April, without any doubt.

Mr. HAUGEN. Do you mean they work that number of hours on the killing floor?

Dr. MOHLER. Yes, sir.

Mr. HAUGEN. Do the packers start to kill at 7 o'clock in the morning?

Dr. MOHLER. Yes, sir; they start to kill at 7 in the morning, and our men are there 20 minutes ahead of that to get their clothes changed and be on the job when the knocker starts to work.

Mr. HAUGEN. That has been during the war, but not in normal times?

Dr. MOHLER. That has been the condition in the big packing concerns every winter for the last five or six years, and we haven't enough men at present on account of the war conditions to give relief to those men. In former years we have been able to have three men to fill in two men's places when there was overtime work.

Mr. HAUGEN. And they haven't been paid for the overtime?

Dr. MOHLER. Not a penny.

Mr. HAUGEN. They have been required to work for 12 hours a day instead of 8 hours, without any overtime pay?

Dr. MOHLER. Yes, indeed; and Sundays besides. At Jersey City, 10 of our inspectors work practically every Sunday the year round.

Mr. HAUGEN. How many are there of them that are working overtime?

Dr. MOHLER. We have 2,700 employees in the meat-inspection division.

Mr. HAUGEN. In the meat inspection?

Dr. MOHLER. In the meat-inspection division.

Mr. HAUGEN. That does not include the yards outside?

Dr. MOHLER. No; only meat inspection. And more than 50 per cent of those employees have been working from 10 to 12 hours right along since last September.

Mr. HAUGEN. But what do they do in normal times?

Dr. MOHLER. In normal times, they do the same thing they do now, only they do not have such excessive hours. They go on at 7 or 8 o'clock in the morning and are through at 5 in the afternoon.

Mr. HAUGEN. I take it all we expect of anybody is to work eight hours a day.

Dr. MOHLER. That is what we are trying to provide for now.

Mr. HAUGEN. How many of them work overtime?

Dr. MOHLER. Over 50 per cent of those men are working overtime right now, and have been working overtime all fall.

Mr. HAUGEN. But taking it the year through, I take it there are many days when they do not work at all. There are a good many packing establishments that only kill on certain days in the week.

Dr. MOHLER. Yes; but yet our men are there when the place opens in the morning, whether they are killing or not. They may kill to-day and cut and cure to-morrow and make sausage the third day; but our men are there all the time the place is open.

Mr. HAUGEN. Can you estimate what it will cost to take care of this overtime?

Dr. MOHLER. Yes, sir; I can; but this overtime, the way it reads here, is to be paid by the owners of the inspected establishments.

Mr. HAUGEN. Do you remember our quarrel over this matter some years ago, and it was distinctly understood at that time there should be no partnership between the packers and the inspectors, but the two should be absolutely separate and they should have absolutely not a thing to do with each other. And we didn't want the packers to hand out extra time or anything of the kind, and the proposition then was that our Government ought to pay every cent of it or prevent the packer paying the expense. And so we made the permanent annual appropriation of $3,000,000 and since that we have increased it. And it seems to me that policy has proven most excellent and I think it ought to be continued. So far as paying the little expense of this overtime, that is only a drop in the bucket, but I take it it would be necessary to get an estimate of the amount required.

Dr. MOHLER. This amount for overtime would not be so little as you might think. The way it has worked in Canada, where they have had a similar measure in effect for some time, a number of the men take home thirty or forty dollars extra each month, which is paid to them by the Canadian Government who received it from the packers. And I imagine it would be that way here.

Mr. HAUGEN. Can you give us an estimate and add it to the estimates you have submitted?

Dr. MOHLER. It is difficult to forecast accurately what sum of money would be paid by the packers to the department should this paragraph become a law. From reports of work at the various meat-inspection stations throughout the country it is roughly estimated that the yearly total would be $345,275, provided the requirements at the present time continue. This sum is arrived at by estimating as closely as possible the unusual hours bureau employees have put in during the past year and by allowing for this unusual time on the basis ordinarily used in computing overtime, Sunday, and holiday pay in commercial establishments, including the packing establishments under consideration.

The CHAIRMAN. It will be a matter of policy for the committee to determine what action it should take.

Dr. MOHLER. In this connection, I would like to state that since these estimates were prepared the Secretary has indicated his desire to submit a supplemental estimate asking for a specific amount to promote some of these men I have been talking about. So that you may expect a supplemental recommendation covering the promotion of some of these men, not as a substitute paragraph, but as an additional provision.

(The estimate referred to follows:)

JANUARY 9, 1919.

Hon. A. F. LEVER,
   House of Representatives.

DEAR MR. LEVER: I desire to recommend, for the consideration of the Committee on Agriculture, that the item "Meat inspection" in the Agricultural appropriation bill for the fiscal year 1920, be increased from $449,480, the amount suggested in the estimates, to $673,140, in order that the salaries of employees of the meat-inspection service of the Bureau of Animal Industry may be increased. If this recommendation is approved, it is proposed to use the additional sum for the promotion of the following employees in the manner indicated:

662 lay inspectors from $1,200 to $1,380, $180 each	$119,160
495 veterinary inspectors from $1,500 to $1,620, $120 each	59,400
28 veterinary inspectors from $1,600 to $1,800, $200 each	5,600
25 veterinary inspectors from $1,620 to $1,800, $180 each	4,500
175 veterinary inspectors from $1,800 to $2,000, $200 each	35,000
1385: Total	223,660

Only a very few of these employees have been promoted within three years and in many instances, a much longer time has elapsed since their last promotion. As a result of the patriotic action of the farmers and of the work of the department and of its great allies, the agricultural colleges in the various States, the number of food animals in the United States has very greatly increased. This increase has been reflected in the extension of the activities of the packing houses subject to the meat-inspection law, where receipts of animals have been unprecedented and where plants, in order to dispose of the animals, have been compelled to operate overtime, nights, Sundays, and holidays.

Large numbers of the best and most experienced men on the meat-inspection force, which now totals 2,700, have been drawn into the military or naval service. Many others have resigned to take advantage of the opportunities offered for higher pay in commercial activities. This has made necessary the employment of inexperienced, temporary inspectors, and also, it has thrown on the old employees to an unusual degree increased responsibility and a greater volume of work. I think it may be truthfully said that practically all the older employees who have remained with the department have accepted this greater burden faithfully and without complaint. Their hours necessarily have been lengthened and often it has been necessary for them to work on Sundays and holidays. They have seen the compensation of the packing-house employees, side by side with whom they work, increased until the packing-house scale is now considerably higher than that of the Government. In many instances unskilled laborers in commercial employment are receiving greater compensation than the old and experienced men in the Government service who have been especially trained for the important work to which they are assigned.

It is impossible, with the existing funds, for the department to remedy this situation. I earnestly hope, therefore, that the committee will give favorable consideration to this recommendation.

Very truly, yours,

                                            D. F. HOUSTON, *Secretary.*

Mr. HAUGEN. These estimates, though, are based upon the service rendered now, taking the overtime into consideration?

Dr. MOHLER. Yes. This present proposition is based on our desire to promote 662 inspectors in grade 2, who have not been promoted for three years, and some of these 662 men have not been promoted for seven years. We have considered $1,200 as being the maximum salary for the average grade 2 inspector. Now they are working alongside of butchers making 75 and 80 cents an hour, with that one and a half for overtime when they work beyond eight hours and double time for Sundays. I have seen the records which show that some of those butchers have been making $50, $60, and up to $115 a week as a result of the overtime pay plus the ordinary pay. We have recently been getting a number of petitions from our employees on account of the small amount of pay they are getting in contrast with even the unskilled laborers, to whom the packers are paying so much more.

Mr. HAUGEN. Right there, the butchers' increase is largely due to the abnormal conditions, isn't it, and salaries are to be fixed for all time to come?

Dr. MOHLER. The packers have been paying higher wages to the butchers as a result of the decision of the mediation committee that President Wilson appointed. The common laborer, the negroes, Mexicans, Polacks, and Russians, are now getting 40 cents an hour, and the skilled butchers are paid a rate up to 75 and 80 cents an hour. And Judge Alshuler, of Chicago, at the present time has under consideration the question of increasing that per-hour rate again. That makes a very bad contrast with our bureau salaries, and the situation is really serious. Our men are all exercised about the amount of work they are asked to do for such small wages, as compared with these unskilled laborers.

Mr. HAUGEN. But that scale is fixed on account of the present emergency, and when we fix the salaries of the inspectors they are fixed for all future time. Of course, they can be changed, but salaries are never reduced.

Dr. MOHLER. Don't you think these 662 inspectors who have not been promoted for from three to five to seven years, and who are only getting $1,200, are entitled to an increased compensation on account of efficiency and long experience?

Mr. HAUGEN. They should be promoted, of course, on merit and efficiency. I do not care about the number and length of time, but if they are deserving of promotion they should have it.

Dr. MOHLER. It is not a question entirely of the high cost of living, because that affects us all, nor of sentiment or pride; but it is one of common justice and absolute necessity.

Mr. HAUGEN. I believe the salaries of many of those inspectors should be increased, but I would like to see it done wherever merit warrants an increase.

Dr. MOHLER. We have been receiving many petitions from these men; the American Federation of Labor has started to write in about these employees. In order to present the most urgent cases that need immediate relief, I have put down here these 662 lay inspectors, grade 2, who represent at the present time the largest number of our men who are underpaid.

Mr. HAUGEN. What are lay inspectors?
Dr. MOHLER. Our grade 2 men are experts who have educated and trained senses of sight and smell, who do the work in the pickling, salting, smoking, curing, processing, and oleo and lard departments.
Mr. HAUGEN. And what are they getting?
Dr. MOHLER. $1,200 to-day.
Mr. HAUGEN. And what is recommended?
Dr. MOHLER. $1,380. The next group contains 495 veterinary inspectors now getting $1,500.
Mr. HAUGEN. And what do you recommend?
Dr. MOHLER. We recommend that they get $1,620.
Mr. HAUGEN. What are they doing?
Dr. MOHLER. They are doing the post-mortem work, picking out the abnormal conditions and diseases in the various carcasses of the animals slaughtered. These are the veterinarians who have been in the service not less than three years, but who have not gained the experience to be put in charge of an individual plant or a city. Then there are 25 veterinary inspectors at $1,620 who have been in over five years, and 28 veterinary inspectors at $1,600 who have been in about the same length of time. We recommend that they all be promoted to $1,800.
Mr. HAUGEN. What do they do?
Dr. MOHLER. They are a little higher grade men and have had more experience than those $1,500 veterinary inspectors, but they also do the post-mortem work. Then there are 175 veterinary inspectors who are now getting $1,800. We heretofore have considered that this was the maximum for general veterinary inspection, but under present conditions it is entirely too low and we recommend that those 175 men be promoted to $2,000. All these veterinary inspectors are college graduates who have passed the civil service examination. The course is now four years——
Mr. HAUGEN. What do they do; they are men of more skill?
Dr. MOHLER. They are men of more skill, longer experience, and better judgment. They have charge of a department, and some of them have charge of an entire plant. We have men in charge of big plants like Wilson, Armour, or Swift's making $1,800. I had a conference with some of our men in Chicago, and they are very much wrought up about the meager salaries they are getting as compared with the butchers. I found one man there getting $1,900 in charge of one of the biggest plants in Chicago, and a very capable supervisor, having been in the service more than eight years with but one promotion.
Mr. HAUGEN. He is in charge of your force?
Dr. MOHLER. Yes, sir; he is the supervisor at that plant in Chicago.
Mr. HAUGEN. How many have you there?
Dr. MOHLER. We have between four and five hundred men in Chicago. At Omaha we have one of these supervising inspectors whose salary is $1,680 and who has been promoted but once in five years.
Mr. ASON. Do these salaries all come under the Byrnes resolution? W
The CHAIRMAN. Yes; I think they do.
Mr. HAUGEN. They get $120 bonus?
Dr. MOHLER. They get $120 bonus, but the question now, however, is to raise the basic salaries. Men who have not received any increase

in seven years, it seems to me, ought to receive some consideration different from the rank and file of employees.

Mr. HAUGEN. We can not do that under the resolution.

The CHAIRMAN. We will have to consider that. Let him complete his statement, so that we will have it in the record. What does that total now?

Dr. MOHLER. The total is $223,660.

The CHAIRMAN. About the overtime proposition—what is the basis of estimating the overtime? I mean to say by that, is it a percentage of full time, or what?

Dr. MOHLER. In Canada they charge 50 cents per hour for these lay inspectors for each hour overtime, and 75 cents per hour for veterinary inspectors.

The CHAIRMAN. I asked that question because there is absolutely no limit here as to the amount you might pay for overtime. You might pay $2 a minute for overtime if you wanted to do it. Of course, we know you would not do that.

Dr. MOHLER. My idea would be that it should be in direct relation to the salaries they are drawing at the present time.

The CHAIRMAN. I should think so, too. I think Congress ought to keep its hand on the proposition, if they are going to grant it at all.

Mr. WASON. If I understand that proposition, it means if their salary is $1,200 for a year's work, at 8 hours a day, and they work 10 hours a day for the year, there would be a 25 per cent increase in the pay. There would be two hours out of the eight; that would be a fourth. Is that right?

The CHAIRMAN. My own idea is that, instead of 25 per cent, you might double it.

Dr. MOHLER. I think we should follow the general practice of one-and-a-half time on week days, just as in commercial lines, and double time for Sundays and holidays.

Mr. HAUGEN. In Canada you say they pay 50 cents?

Dr. MOHLER. 50 cents an hour in Canada to the lay inspectors; and 75 cents an hour to the veterinary inspectors. But I think in this country it would be better to follow the lines adopted for paying mechanics all over the country—one and a half for more than eight hours, and double time for holidays and Sundays.

The CHAIRMAN. Don't you think we ought to guard against the danger of opening this too far in this act?

Dr. MOHLER. I do. I think it would be very advisable.

I do not desire to take up the time of the committee in presenting a lengthy statement regarding the loyalty of our employees, their high qualifications as measured by the examination they must pass, and the unpleasant and sometimes dangerous environment in which they are forced to pursue their duties. These subjects have been very fully covered in previous hearings, especially on the Lobeck bill. However, I would like to call your attention to the present changed conditions.

Due to the department's effective campaign for increased production, the demand for the inspection of meat and meat food products has vastly increased. Receipts of animals have been unprecedented. Plants have been forced to operate at maximum capacity overtime, nights, holidays, and Sundays, to dispose of the animals brought in.

Owing to the hundreds of separations from the service for military duty, and resignations of old employees to accept higher salaries elsewhere, it has been necessary to employ inexperienced temporary inspectors, thus throwing increased responsibility and a greater volume of work upon the old employees who have remained. All our older employees who have remained have been working faithfully and without complaint, long hours, holidays, nights, and Sundays. Moreover, they have been working with no hope of pay for overtime, side by side with the employees of the packing houses, all of whom draw extra pay for every minute they put in over the regular working hours. Not only do our inspectors get nothing for extra time in glaring contrast with the packing-house employees, but the scale of salaries paid to the latter has greatly risen until they are considerably higher than those the bureau pays. In many instances even unskilled laborers now receive more than our experienced and scientifically trained men. In order to relieve the situation which confronts us, it is urgently desired to promote these outstanding employees to whom I have referred. In most cases, these employees at this date have not been promoted for three years, and in many cases, the time is very much longer.

Mr. WASON. I would like to make a suggestion on that, Mr. Chairman. The doctor makes quite a point of having the packers advance to the Government the cost of the overtime work, on the theory it will lessen the hours of overtime. Now, if we give the men the same rate per hour for overtime that they receive for the day, that will not encourage the overtime; but if we give them three hours for two hours work, the tendency will be they would like the overtime. While I think they ought to have relief, it seems to me if we do not give them any inducement to encourage overtime, it might have a tendency to lessen the overtime.

The CHAIRMAN. This situation with reference to your meat inspectors is a rather serious matter, isn't it?

Dr. MOHLER. It is extremely serious; it certainly is. It was bad enough in October, at which time we thought this overtime pay would probably relieve the situation. But since that time, it has become more serious, and for this reason, I have come before you to-day to present, with the consent of the Secretary, a plea for a supplemental appropriation to the meat-inspection item, in addition to the provision already included in this Book of Estimates, for permitting the department to collect overtime pay from the packers for our employees. With these two provisions adopted, our force will be better satisfied and will do even better work, and the meat-inspection duties will prove more attractive to others whom we may wish to employ than it does to-day. Our men have been loyal and efficient, but recently one or two misguided employees have shown a somewhat surprising tendency which I will discuss more fully later.

If the committee pleases, I would like to read this letter from the grade 2 lay inspectors at one of our stations, Sioux City, Iowa, addressed to the Secretary of Agriculture and the Secretary of Labor. We have received many others of similar tenor.

(Reading:)

Hon. D. F. HOUSTON,
SIOUX CITY, IOWA, *December 21, 1918.*
Secretary of Agriculture.

SIR: We, the undersigned lay inspectors, grade 2, formerly meat inspectors in the Bureau of Animal Industry, do hereby appeal to you in the name of justice to help us in our endeavor to secure a living wage.

We entered the service as meat inspectors in 1906 at $1,000 per year, and after six years' service were promoted to $1,200. We served five years at $1,200, and in 1917 received an increase of 5 per cent—$60—for one year. July 1, 1918, we received an increase of $120 for one year only, taking the place of the 5 per cent increase, both granted by Congress. We are at present receiving $1,320 per year, an increase of $320 in 12 years.

We are a class of scientifically trained men on meat inspection, with years of experience. Men working for the packers in the same capacity are now receiving $1,600 to $1,800 per year, with their case for higher wages now before Judge Alshuler. For some reason, unknown to us, our wages remain at a standstill while the cost of living soars. Common labor is now receiving at packing plants better wages than Government inspectors.

We are not allowed to resign, without prejudice, unless we wait until the bureau is able to fill our places. We are not allowed compensation for overtime, Sunday, or holiday work. We are working 8 to 12 hours per day with packinghouse employees who receive extra compensation for overtime and double time for Sundays and holidays.

Trusting you will give due consideration to a just request, we remain faithful to our duties, etc.

And here is a similar letter, which is somewhat fuller and which represents the views of our inspectors at Kansas City. One of the grade 2 inspectors came to Washington and presented this in person, addressed to the Secretary of Agriculture. You will note that he has taken a very broad view of the situation and recommends promotions for the other classes of employees as well as for those in his own group.

WASHINGTON, D. C., *December 11, 1918.*
Hon. DAVID FRANKLIN HOUSTON,
Secretary of Agriculture, Washington, D. C.

HONORABLE SIR: Having been selected by the lay inspectors, grade 2, to come to Washington, D. C., and present for your consideration an increase in salary, I beg leave to submit the following: When the grade 2 lay inspectors entered the service as meat inspectors in 1906 the entrance salary was $1,000. Since that time they have been promoted to a basic salary of $1,200. In 1906 the grade 1 lay inspectors entered the service at a salary of $720, and since then have been promoted to $1,140. In the same year—1906—the veterinarians entered the service at $1,200, and since then have been promoted to $1,800. So that in the matter of promotions the grade 2 men feel that they have been overlooked or neglected.

I do not feel that I would be doing my duty if I failed to present to you at this time conditions as they now prevail with reference to all B. A. I. employees. Take, for instance, the cattle and hog butchers; their weekly wage for the weeks ending 10/12, 10/19, 10/26, 11/2, 11/9, 11/16, and 11/23 amounted to $63, $62, $63, $60, $62, $59, and $62 each; in addition to wages many of those men received a bonus amounting, in some instances, to several hundred dollars. The above wage is an average of what is being paid to what is known as skilled labor, and includes floormen, rumpers, backers, fell cutters, splitters, hide droppers, and chuck splitters; in many instances these men are uneducated, and when you compare their wages with the salary of the veterinarian who has spent the best of his young days in school and college to educate and prepare himself for his life's work—namely, the preservation of the health of humanity in the preparation of meat-food products—you will very readily see that even under normal conditions these gentlemen are very poorly paid, and extremely so at this time, considering the increased cost of living, rentals, clothing, provisions, etc. They were better paid in 1906 at $1,200 than they are to-day at $1,800, and as the figures given above are true and correct, and can be corroborated by going over the pay rolls of the packers, it is only fair and just to these gentlemen that the entrance salary should not be less than $2,000 per annum, with a maximum of $3,000.

This may appear high to you, but kindly let me submit the following table of wages paid to beef boners for the weeks ending the same as above, respectively: Loin, rib, chuck, and plate boners averaged $50 to $101, $50 to $105, $50 to $103, $37 to $70, $47 to $104, $50 to $80, and $50 to $120. In view of the figures respectfully submitted for your consideration, unless these gentlemen receive a substantial increase commensurate with their responsibilities and the duties they owe the American public in the production of pure meat food products along with the education of sanitation and ventilation, not overlooking by any means the eradication of disease among cattle; saving millions of dollars annually to the American farmer, I say that unless these gentlemen receive a substantial increase that it would look as though our Government considers what is known as uneducated skilled labor worth more to the American people than the educated.

Now, with reference to the grade 2 lay inspectors, these gentlemen successfully passed a competitive examination in 1906 and as stated above received a salary of $1,000 on entering the service and have since been promoted to $1,200. A short time ago a very small per cent of them were promoted to $1,380 and those who failed to receive said promotion feel that they were entitled to the same consideration, and respectfully ask you, honorable sir, for the same promotion in a group. The basic salary they now receive does not equal the purchasing power of $600 at time of entry in 1906.

I would also submit the following facts and figures, and respectfully ask that the entrance salary of lay inspectors be raised to $1,500 per annum, with promotions when recommended by the inspector in charge to a maximum of $1,800 per annum.

Common laborers in the beef cutting, who as a class are composed of uneducated negroes, Mexicans, Russians, Polacks, and Austrians, receive weekly wages from $25 to $38, same class of labor in dry salt curing cellars receive $28 to $40, and in the sweet-pickle curing cellars from $30 to $45. Foremen and assistant foremen in these departments, whose duties are not more arduous than ours and who at all times have advantages for promotion, receive from $40 to $65 per week, and it can be truly stated that there is not a lay inspector who has not got the educational and executive ability to manage the various departments.

In view of these facts we feel that our services to the American public should at least be compensated on an equality with the uneducated foreigner who in many instances is even unable to speak the English language and is American only to the extent of earning dollars and cents.

Trusting for your indulgence and consideration of the above facts and figures and sincerely hoping that you will grant the small increase prayed for in the very near future, I beg to remain,

Very obediently, yours,

THOMAS NOONE,
Lay Inspector, Grade 2.

You understand we are not anywhere near that maximum in these salaries we are now proposing.

The CHAIRMAN. It is a curious thing that the tendency now is to pay unskilled labor more than skilled labor. A man who has had a college education now does not get as much as a bricklayer.

Dr. Mohler, does that complete your statement, sir?

Dr. MOHLER. Yes, sir; with the exception of the foot-and-mouth disease item, which appears on page 274 of the Book of Estimates. All we request is a continuation of this item so that, in case anything of this kind comes up, we can use these funds to eradicate it. The only change is in substituting 1920 for 1919, the remainder of the item being a continuation of the same phraseology that we had in 1916, 1917, and 1918.

The CHAIRMAN. Anything else?

Dr. MOHLER. No, sir.

AGRICULTURE APPROPRIATION BILL.

COMMITTEE ON AGRICULTURE,
HOUSE OF REPRESENTATIVES,
Tuesday, January 14, 1919.

The committee met at 10.30 o'clock a. m., Hon. Asbury F. Lever (chairman) presiding.

SALARIES OF MEAT INSPECTORS.

The CHAIRMAN. We have met this morning, gentlemen, to consider the item found on page 61, for additional expenses for carrying out the meat-inspection act. We have gentlemen here representing the meat-inspection force and, inasmuch as Mr. Rainey, of our committee, is familiar with this whole matter and has taken a very active interest in it, I will ask him to take charge of the hearing.

STATEMENT OF HON. JOHN W. RAINEY, REPRESENTATIVE IN CONGRESS FROM THE STATE OF ILLINOIS.

Mr. RAINEY. Mr. Chairman and gentlemen, it will not be necessary for me to consume much time. There are men here, not directly connected with the Bureau of Animal Industry, but who come in contact with the men engaged in the work of this bureau, and I thought it advisable, with your permission, to have them come here and suggest to you, as all of you who are familiar with this bureau know, the importance at this time of recognizing the worth of the men associated with that bureau.

I propose, gentlemen, to offer an amendment to item 96, on page 61, where the amount requested is $499,480, and insert $1,029,790. The Secretary has forwarded a letter to the chairman of this committee in which he suggests an increase of $233,660. The regular appropriation was $449,480. He did that in order to care for increases for men engaged in this important work. In his suggestion, if this amount was given him, he had in mind increasing the salaries of 1,385 members of the department. My proposal is to go farther and to take care of 2,950 men in the Bureau of Animal Industry, including the lay inspectors of grade 1 and grade 2, and all veterinarians.

There are at this time employed by the United States Department of Agriculture approximately 1,700 veterinarians, whose duties are to inspect live stock which are used for meat purposes and to aid live-stock owners and State live-stock sanitary officials in the control and eradication of contagious, infectious, and communicable diseases of animals.

The meat-inspection service, in which bureau veterinarians are employed, consists in the examination of cattle, sheep, swine, and goats from the moment they are received at public stockyards, where they are unloaded from stock cars, through the commission merchants' pens, into the packing houses, where they are slaughtered; thence to the innumerable sections of packing houses where the meat is prepared in various ways for human consumption. In other words, these servants of the Government inspect and are charged with the responsibility of seeing that only wholesome meat food products enter into commerce for interstate shipment, as well as meats which are consumed within the States, and other meat products which may be exported.

As testimony of the efficiency of the Government meat-inspection service, not one valid complaint has been sustained against the service since the outbreak of the great world's war in 1914, notwithstanding that these products which have been labeled with the stamp of Government approval have been sent to every corner of the world. From several sources complaints have been received and upon investigation have been confirmed of shipments of meat to Army camps from plants where Government inspection is not maintained.

This work was inaugurated many years ago, but the principal meat-inspection act under which the work is now being carried out did not become effective until 1906.

A corps of veterinarians are employed in the control and eradication of diseases of live stock, such as hog cholera, tuberculosis, the eradication of the cattle tick, the eradication of scabies of sheep and cattle, the eradication of glanders from horses, and several other maladies which live stock may contract.

Twenty years ago the sheep industry of the United States was rather a precarious one on account of the excessive existence of scabies. At that time there was really no true type of sheep in the United States. Sheep developed much like wolves and coyotes; they multiplied, but without any appreciable upbreeding. It was a case of "survival of the fittest." Oregon sheep were long legged and thin and could be recognized in contrast with Montana sheep. Texas sheep were different from those raised in California, and the sheep from the plains of New Mexico were unlike those from Utah and Idaho. The disease known as scabies, which is caused by a parasite not visible to the naked eye and which causes scabs to appear upon the hides and also causes the shedding of the wool, existed in practically every State, and not very much attention was paid to it. It was spreading so rapidly that, if no effort had been made to control it, is it not reasonable to suppose that the industry would have been so seriously handicapped that it would have proved entirely unprofitable?

The United States Department of Agriculture took up the question of the controlling of this disease with State live-stock sanitary officials and the sheep owners, experiments were conducted by treating the sheep with disinfectant to kill the bug which was the cause of the trouble. From those experiments evolved a very practical method of freeing the sheep from the disease by a process of dipping them in a solution of lime and sulphur. Dipping vats were constructed on the sheep ranges and at all of the public stockyards, and whenever a band of sheep were found diseased they were prohibited from being shipped into the country unless they were properly disinfected under supervision. This work developed very rapidly because it proved of vital benefit to the sheep owners.

In the course of 10 or 12 years this disease was practically exterminated and the quarantine under which many of the States had been placed was removed, thus permitting the free traffic anywhere in the United States. Veterinarians were removed from the work to be placed on work of greater emergency at that time, and in consequence the disease began to spread again and it became necessary, and, in fact, the sheepmen demanded, that the inspectors be returned to the field to direct the eradication work.

Sheep scabies exists to but a moderate degree in the United States to-day, and out of the hazardous business which was despised by most live-stock men 20 years ago, there has developed one of the most lucrative and interesting branches of the live-stock industry. There has been developed in the United States true types of sheep. Sheepmen are progressing along definite, well-planned lines, and they are not handicapped now by a disease which but a few years ago threatened them with bankruptcy, for it is impossible for sheep to thrive that are affected with scabies and other parasitic diseases.

In 1906 the bureau veterinarians were sent in the Southern States, to aid the farmers in the boll-weevil stricken areas, in the eradication of the cattle tick. It has been proven beyond a peradventure that a profitable cattle industry could not be developed where the cattle tick existed. It has been found by the Bureau of Animal Industry that this parasite which transmits the organism which causes a fatal disease known as Texas fever could be eradicated by dipping the cattle which harbored the pest. This work has proven one of the most popular and successful pieces of live-stock sanitary work ever undertaken in any part of the world. More than 70 per cent of the original area quarantined on account of the Texas fever has been freed of the tick, and in the freed counties and States there has been developed, and will continue to be developed, a high-class of cattle husbandry. Cattle, which in 1906 were valued at about $10 per head in the tick-infested area, are now worth $40 per head, and the increased valuation is not entirely due to the high price of cattle everywhere, but these animals are worth more, because they are in better condition to be used for beef; that is, while the animals are covered with ticks the parasites suck the blood, and, in consequence, the host always remains in an unthrifty condition, unsuited for beef purposes. This work will be carried on until there are no cattle ticks left in the United States. This one piece of live stock sanitation is worth at least $50,000,000 in the additional beef that the Nation conserves thereby.

Other veterinarians in the Bureau of Animal Industry are engaged in the eradication of hog cholera, a disease which, a few years ago, was the cause of an annual loss to the Nation of $100,000,000. It was discovered by the Bureau of Animal Industry that swine could be immunized against the infection of cholera. This immunization consists of injecting the hogs with a serum obtained from swine, which through treatment have become highly immunized against the disease. Millions of hogs are treated annually by veterinarians of the bureau, and thereby the losses have been reduced to a very large degree.

Another field in which veterinarians are engaged is in the eradication of tuberculosis. It was absolutely necessary that some agency inaugurate a campaign to check the ravages of this insidious disease. It was spreading from State to State and from herd to herd, as may be judged from the amount of infected animals found in the abattoirs in 1918, where Government inspection was demanded. Out of 35,000,000 swine slaughtered in those establishments, practically 3,500,000 animals were found tuberculous to some extent. Likewise with the cattle which were killed; more than 200,000 cattle were found to be infected with tuberculosis in those abattoirs. The owners of live stock from every section of the United States demanded that this work of controlling the eradication of this disease be taken up by the Federal Government. While the campaign has been in existence only a little more than a year, there is sufficient evidence to show that it is making satisfactory progress, and is proving to be a very popular work with the farmers.

The Bureau of Animal Industry has in its organization a pathological division, in which veterinarians are engaged in scientific investigations dealing with live-stock diseases. Every year thousands of samples of diseased specimens are forwarded to the bureau, where they are examined microscopically and by animal inoculation, so as to determine the exact nature of the malady.

There are a number of other branches of the live-stock industry to which the veterinarians of the bureau are assigned, such as the supervision of the manufacture by private concerns of hog-cholera serum, virus, and other biological products, such as black-leg vaccine, tetanus antitoxin, tuberculin, mallein, etc.

The entrance salary of the veterinarians in the Bureau of Animal Industry is $1,500 per annum, and, of course, with this parsimonious stipend, the bureau is having great difficulty in obtaining the services of professionally trained veterinarians. The future opportunities for veterinarians in the Bureau of Animal Industry is anything but attractive to an earnest, competent, and energetic employee. Of course, the lack of appreciation of the Federal Government for this class of employees has caused hundreds of them to resign every year to take up positions which enable them to support their families and bring them up in a true American way. The average veterinarian in the Bureau of Animal Industry does not receive sufficient compensation to properly feed and clothe the average-sized family.

Many of the best posted live-stock owners and other persons interested in that industry have grave apprehensions as to how their immense industry is going to be properly protected in the future. Veterinary colleges are closing their doors because young men are not attracted to the profession, simply because there is no opportunity for them to gain a respectable livelihood in it. During the past 12 months four veterinary colleges in the United States terminated their careers. These institutions were known as the George Washington Veterinary College, Washington, D. C., the Kansas City Veterinary College, the San Francisco Veterinary College, and the Terre Haute Veterinary College. It is believed that it will be necessary within the next 12 months for other schools to discontinue.

A veterinarian to-day is a trained man who receives an education of the same completeness as a medical man receives at colleges for physicians. The veterinarian is required to be a high-school graduate, and his course in the veterinary college is fixed at four years of nine months each. Can you imagine a vigorous, intelligent, ambitious high-school graduate being attracted to take up the veterinary profession when the best prospects that he has in sight as an employee of the Federal Government is $1,500 per annum? Such men will spurn any such proffer for a lifetime career. They need not complete a high-school course or a grammar-school course to become a butcher, which trade will give them $60 to $90 per week; or a puddler in a steel factory, which will pay them $100 a month, or any other line of industry. The Federal Government, if it does appreciate the services of its employees, should have enough business acumen to see that the efficiency of the whole structure of the Nation will be greatly diminished unless efficiency is recognized and equitable compensations made. Unless the Government is aspiring to inefficiency and failure it must be willing to at least go part of the way in increasing compensations to its employees as the merchants and manufacturers and every other person, firm, and corporation throughout the length and breadth of the land have done in recognizing the services of the employee.

The veterinarian is the agency which the live-stock industry of the Nation, valued at $10,000,000,000 must place its faith in to preserve that gigantic business from the ravages of disease. What would it profit this country to go on building up the cattle, swine, and sheep industry if at the foundation of the industry it was rotten with disease. We are coming to an era now where European countries and South American countries will be seeking for breeding cattle, swine, and sheep. If they come to our land and buy these animals, and later they are found to be diseased, our reputation and industry along that line is ruined for all time to come; whereas, if we sell them the right kind of live stock, free from disease, the Nation will build up a reputation throughout the world that will assure for all time a prosperous industry.

The grade lay inspectors are men who through years of practical experience have gained a wide knowledge of the meat industry. They are men who are qualified to serve the United States Government in the capacity of inspectors, or as foremen of various branches of the packing-house industries. A great many of this class of employees have left the Government service to fill positions of more lucrative nature with the meat-packing concerns.

Some time ago I took up with Secretary Houston, and also suggested to his assistant, Mr. Harrison, the imperative need of a substantial increase for the lay inspectors and veterinarians in the Bureau of Animal Industry. The Secretary has been kind enough to suggest an increase for about half of the employees. His hesitancy in suggesting the majority was responsible, I presume, on account of the great difficulty in getting increased appropriations from this committee.

I desire to urge upon you the imperative need of increasing the salaries of these employees. I know something of their work. I have the distinction to represent in Congress the fourth congressional district of Chicago, Ill., in which are located all of the great packing industries. I know that these men report at their post of duty long before 7 o'clock each working-day; that they work from 9 to 12 hours, and, during the busy season, often work both Sundays and holidays.

I know that the veterinarians are responsible for all the work in the enforcement of the regulations pertaining to the meat-inspection laws, that they are directly responsible for all the work performed by the inspectors under their supervision, and that they are responsible for the enforcement of all the sanitary regulations at the packing houses.

I know that the receipts of animals of recent months have been unprecedented.

I know that many employees have resigned to take up work in commercial fields where the compensation is considerably greater. This has necessitated greater responsibility on the older employees. I know that a great number of them have not been advanced for several years, and I also know that by comparing the salaries of the Bureau of Animal Industry employees with the packing-house employees, that the employees of the packing industries receive from 50 to 100 per cent more than do the Government employees for equal responsibilities.

Safeguarding the health of the consumer of packing-house products is of greatest importance, and I feel that I am extremely conservative in my amendment in urging that the sum I request be appropriated for the fiscal year 1920.

I want to thank the chairman and the members of this committee for their indulgence and the courtesy extended by making possible this hearing.

I have present a number of gentlemen, representing many different States, who are not members of the Bureau of Animal Industry, but who come in contact with the work of this department, and they are here voluntarily to suggest to the members of this committee their appreciation of the work that the members of this department are doing, and I am sure they will be glad to answer any questions you gentlemen may desire to ask.

I have also a Mr. Hughes, from New York, whom I am sure will give some interesting facts relative to the pay received by lay inspectors and also that given to common laborers in the packing houses.

And let me offer this suggestion with reference to lay inspectors as against some of the employees in the Chicago packing houses. Take, for instance, the cattle and hog butchers, their weekly wages for the weeks ending, respectively, October 12, 19, 26, November 2, 9, 16, and 23, 1918, amounted to $63, $62, $63, $60, $62, $59, and $62 each. In addition to the wages many of these men received a bonus amounting, in some instances, from $200 to $300.

The above wage is an average of what is being paid to what is known as skilled labor and includes floor men, rumpers, packers, fell cutters, splitters, hide droppers, and chuck splitters. In many instances these men are uneducated, and when you compare their wages with the salary of the Government inspector who has spent the best part of his young days in educating and preparing himself for his life's work, namely, the preservation of the health of humanity in the preparation of meat-food products, you will readily see, even under normal conditions, these inspectors are very poorly paid and extremely so at this time, considering the increased cost of living.

Let me further submit the following table of wages paid to beef boners for the same weeks suggested heretofore: Loin, rib, chuck, and plate boners, average, $50 to $100, $50 to $105, $50 to $103, $37 to $70, $47 to $104, $50 to $80, and $50 to $120.

Common laborers in the beef cutting who as a class are men composed of uneducated Mexicans and the like, receive weekly wages from $25 to $38. The same class of laborers in dry salt curing cellars receive from $28 to $40, and in the sweet pickle curing cellars from $30 to $45. Foremen and assistant foremen in these departments, whose duties are not more arduous than inspectors, and who at all times have advantages for promotion, receive from $40 to $65 per week, and it can easily be said that the lay inspectors in educational and executive ability measure up to the standards of these foremen.

The award made by Judge Alschuler in the arbitration between the packers and their employees convinces me that the Government employees are the lowest paid men in the packing industry, and they are the men that the public holds responsible for the condition of every piece of meat and all meat products that leave the packing house.

I think, gentlemen, that the amendment I offer is very conservative, considering at the present time, as we must take into consideration, the high cost of living and the unusual expenses that are necessary for a man to attempt to care for a family as every American, gentlemen, would like to do. I know that these lay inspectors and veterinarians have given to the Government the best that is in them. I know that the packing industries in Chicago employ men to supervise the work of the veterinarians and the lay inspectors. I know, for instance, a gentleman, I think Dr. Neil, in charge of the office in Chicago, who receives a salary of somewhere about $3,500 a year for the work he performs; and several of the packing houses have men who sort of supervise his work and the work of his assistants, and they pay them a much higher salary per year for the same kind of work.

Now, if the Government desires to encourage the work of Dr. Neil, if they want to put him on a par with the other employees of the packing industries, I think they should offer him some encouragement by a stipend commensurate with the great work he is doing out there.

I am not going to take up any more of your time, but will call on these gentlemen who have kindly joined us here this morning, to suggest to you their intimacy with the work of the Bureau of Animal Industry, and I believe they will corroborate me when I say, once more, that the men engaged in this line of work should receive a very substantial increase in salary in the coming year.

The CHAIRMAN. In this prepared matter which you will submit for the record, do you show in detail the amount of increases proposed in the various grades?

Mr. RAINEY. I do. I set out here, following the suggestion of the Secretary of Agriculture, the number that are to be promoted and the amounts they are receiving now—the amount we expect to have them receive, and the increase.

Proposed increase of salaries for Bureau of Animal Industry employees engaged in the meat-inspection service.

	Number.	Present salary.	Proposed salary.	Increase.	Total increase.
Lay inspectors, grade 1	812	$1,080	$1,200	$120	$97,440
Do	96	1,140	1,200	60	5,760
Lay inspectors, grade 2	999	1,200	1,380	180	179,820
Do	25	1,320	1,440	120	3,000
Do	81	1,380	1,560	180	14,580
Do	4	1,400	1,560	160	640
Do	20	1,560	1,680	120	2,400
Do	3	1,600	1,740	140	420
Veterinary inspectors	476	1,500	1,680	180	105,680
Do	40	1,600	1,780	180	7,200
Do	46	1,620	1,780	160	7,360
Do	1	1,680	1,880	200	200
Do	34	1,740	1,940	200	6,800
Do	170	1,800	2,000	200	34,000
Do	32	1,900	2,080	180	5,760
Do	18	1,920	2,040	160	2,880
Do	18	1,980	2,130	150	3,700
Do	14	2,000	2,130	130	1,820
Do	14	2,040	2,160	180	2,520
Do	1	2,100	2,220	120	120
Do	16	2,220	2,400	180	2,880
Do	3	2,250	2,400	150	450
Do	11	2,400	2,600	200	2,100
Do	1	2,460	2,630	170	170
Do	4	2,500	2,680	180	720
Do	3	2,750	3,060	310	930
Do	2	2,760	3,060	300	600
Do	4	3,000	3,300	300	1,200
Do	1	3,300	3,680	300	300
Do	1	3,500	3,750	250	250
Total					491,700

STATEMENT OF DR. W. HORACE HOSKINS, DEAN OF THE VETERINARY COLLEGE, NEW YORK UNIVERSITY.

Dr. HOSKINS. Mr. Chairman and members of the committee, why I came down here this morning is rather in the nature of a protest against the bad faith of the Government for a long period of time. We, who have charge of veterinary schools, have been persuading men to come into this service because it was a very needful service, and among other inducements we laid before them was the fact they might enter the bureau service at a salary of $1,500 a year and every two years they would have an increase of salary of about $200 a year, and it was ultimately possible for them to reach a salary of $4,000 or $5,000 a year. For a matter of six or seven years, the Government has not kept faith with those men; the Government has not kept faith with the Civil Service Commission, which has sent out continually its notice inviting veterinarians to enter this service.

Now, it is not necessary for me to go into the increased cost of living and the warrant for the Government paying these men for the service they render, at least to give them an increase of 50 per cent in their salaries, if they are going to live as they have been in the habit of living or as they would like to live, and to rear their families. I think we all realize the great world problem to-day is one of hunger, and it is hunger for food, and in this Nation we have got to supply a very large part of that food for the entire world, if we are going to stay the spirit of unrest that is abroad everywhere, not alone in foreign nations, but in our own country. I realize that when this country has been losing more than $200,000,000 a year from infectious and contagious diseases because of not enlarging this service and not offering a substantial compensation for men to go in and carry out this service to the fullest measure we are going very materially to spread the unrest all over the world and among our own people.

The CHAIRMAN. I do not quite follow your reasoning there. What influence does the meat-inspection force of the Bureau of Animal Industry have on the disease of animals out in the field?

Dr. HOSKINS. The Bureau of Animal Industry not only has the meat-inspection service, but has control of all contagious and infectious diseases, and I want to say it has reduced from $100,000,000 a year the losses from hog cholera, down to $40,000,000 and then to $25,000,000 a year, to give you a conception of the service these men have been rendering. I want to say that in over 400,000 square miles of territory in the South they got rid of the cattle tick, where we now hope to grow a larger number of cattle and supply the deficiency in the food supply. They have done a world service there.

The CHAIRMAN. That is very true, but that service is not paid for out of this appropriation. We have an appropriation of $750,000 for that work, and we have a large appropriation for the hog cholera work, and $500,000 for animal tuberculosis. This item has only to do with the meat-inspection service.

Dr. HOSKINS. I would like to bring to your mind an understanding of the breadth of this service and how absolutely essential it is. Apparently, if you control these animal diseases, you are going to conserve a large amount of the food that goes into the rendering tanks every year from those diseases.

The CHAIRMAN. That is very true, but you do not catch my point. We have separate items in this bill for that class of work, and I believe it would be better for you to address yourself to the proposition of increasing the salaries of the meat-inspection force.

Dr. HOSKINS. No; I would like to address myself to increasing the salaries of all the men, because this is a mobile service, and those men to-day may be in meat inspection and to-morrow hog cholera control, and the next day tick eradication.

The CHAIRMAN. Not under this item.

Dr. HOSKINS. They may be transferred to the meat-inspection service from either one of those fields. Is not that true, Dr. Mohler, that this is a mobile service?

Dr. MOHLER. That is true, and, as I understood Congressman Rainey, he was providing for an increase for the field service as well as the meat-inspection service.

The CHAIRMAN. The amendment does not do anything except increase the fund available under item 96. It is a proposition to increase the salaries of the meat-inspection service.

Dr. HOSKINS. If that would be true, then you will help demoralize the service by simply increasing one branch, because you will find the larger number of men will want to go into the service which pays the larger salary. If you do not make this apply to all the men in the bureau service it will absolutely fail.

The CHAIRMAN. If you wanted to increase the salaries of your field men, doctor, you would have to increase your lump-fund appropriation for cattle tick eradication, hog cholera, and all other lines of field activity?

Dr. MOHLER. That is very true, beyond certain limits. As I understood Mr. Rainey, he was proposing a provision to take care of men in the other divisions, as well as the meat-inspection division. That was the understanding I obtained from his statement.

The CHAIRMAN. He would have to change the language of this amendment.

Mr. RAINEY. My idea was to take care of the veterinarians throughout the entire service.

Dr. HOSKINS. Now, our schools have gone on regardless of the lack of inducements on the part of the Federal Government for this absolutely essential service for the well being of everybody, and have continued to increase the requirements for all the men entering the veterinary schools. From the reading, writing, and arithmetic, they have gone on to require now that every man entering the schools shall have had a high-school education and then four years of instruction; and during that period of time, if these men are to enter the Bureau of Animal Industry service, we must conform to their requirements as to a certain number of hours of instruction in particular subjects on which the bureau is working, in order for these men to be eligible to these positions. And then to be offered a salary of $1,500 a year, and sometimes to remain at that salary for five, six, or seven years without any increase, it is very difficult to persuade young men to go into a service of this kind that offers no greater inducements, and particularly when the cost of living has gone on apace from what it was five years ago, with no increase in salaries.

The CHAIRMAN. Do you happen to know what salary the average school-teacher of the country is receiving?

Dr. HOSKINS. Yes; and the teachers to-day have all too little money. We have teachers in the service who are practically starving to death. We have got to get away from that, and have got to get into a line of action for the well-being of all the people.

Mr. THOMPSON. How about the farmer?

Dr. HOSKINS. Up to a few years ago, he was——

Mr. THOMPSON. He was getting 20 cents for cotton, 70 cents for corn, and 70 cents for wheat, to which figures it is bound to go back after this war.

Dr. HOSKINS. Yes, sir.

Mr. THOMPSON. What about him? He does not make an average of $400 a year—the ordinary farmer.

Dr. HOSKINS. That may be true, that he does not make more than that, but he always has this assurance, there is the assurance of a good living. I am just as strong for the farmers as you, because I realize in New York alone we have 15,000,000 acres of idle land, and there is something wrong about the economic situation that works against the men staying on the farms and tends to increase the number of idle acres; and to my mind we have gotten down to the bottom to-day in the spirit of unrest, not only in our own land but we have gotten down to the bottom of the spirit of unrest in every land on the face of the earth. And you can not correct these economic conditions until you take away the perils of animal industry, and you have to have veterinarians to take away the perils of animal industry. You have got to go into the work in all the abattoirs and on the farms and take care of tuberculosis in animals, and especially of these lines of large milk producers in the various breeds, lines which ought to be preserved. And when you do that, we will reach not by legislation but reach by the true way some of the things you have been trying to reach here in dealing with the great companies that have been making millions of dollars even during all this period of stress in the world to-day.

Mr. HAUGEN. You said the farmer gets a good living. According to Dr. Spillman, he gets $240 for fuel, rent, and clothing, and $162 in cash for the services of 4.6 people?

Dr. HOSKINS. Yes.

Mr. HAUGEN. Do you consider that a good living?

Dr. HOSKINS. No; I do not consider that a good living.

Mr. HAUGEN. Then you had better revise your remarks.

Dr. HOSKINS. I do not consider that a good living.

Mr. HAUGEN. That is what he gets, if you accept Dr. Spillman's estimates.

Dr. HOSKINS. But I want to say this, that he has what the average man in the large city does not have, in constantly increasing numbers in our own land, the fear of where to-morrow's food is going to come from. He does not have that fear before him. And it is that fear to-day in the large cities that is creating the spirit of unrest, and we are trying to correct it by increasing the Military Establishments and increasing the constabulary and things of that kind.

Mr. HAUGEN. But you will concede that the farmer, in part, contributes to the food supply of the United States?

Dr. HOSKINS. Yes; absolutely. We are dependent upon him.

Mr. HAUGEN. But we are not absolutely dependent on the services of the veterinarians?

Dr. HOSKINS. The food of the world is so largely contributed by animals we must increase the animals; and to increase the animals you must take away the perils of the animals and thereby producing better animal industry. And, apparently, if you are going to get men to do that kind of work, you have to offer them as fair compensation as they can go out in like service and obtain.

Mr. WASON. Would not the research work in discovering a preventive for these diseases you are talking about be of far greater value to the average farmer and the average community than paying a lot of veterinarians and railroad and traveling expenses to go through the country and destroy animals?

Dr. HOSKINS. We have the research work done, sir.

Mr. WASON. Then there is an antitoxin for tuberculosis?

Dr. HOSKINS. No, sir; but community herds would help solve that, and the proposition now of accredited herds, where a man can go with safety and buy his animals free from disease, is a remedy for that. And because we have neglected the application of those remedies that have been at our hand for the last 10 or 12 years, we ought not to cry about it now.

Mr. WASON. But wouldn't it be getting at the root of the evil by making the animals immune instead of spending millions of dollars in the other direction?

Dr. HOSKINS. Some day we may reach that, sir; but we have not done so up to the present time. Medical science has not been able to make immune to tuberculosis the human race, nor have we been able to make stock immune to tuberculosis; and 60 per cent of our children, the greater portion of whose diet is milk, are dying from some form of tuberculosis or suffering from it.

Mr. WASON. And I judge from your answer that the disease in the little children all comes from the product of the dairy?

Dr. HOSKINS. I do not say that; but I will say that this is the milk-consuming age, and a large preponderance of all those cases develop in the digestive tract, and it is pretty conclusive how they get it— that it is carried into their systems through the digestive tract. And you have to induce men to go out into this service to-day and to offer them sufficient compensation to do that work; and there is nothing to-day that will increase the farmer's income like taking away the perils of animal industry; because you can not have successful agriculture that is not linked up with animal industry.

Mr. HAUGEN. What do you estimate the decrease in the loss of hogs from hog cholera to be?

Dr. HOSKINS. We have lost as much as $100,000,000 a year from hog cholera in this country; you have lost in Iowa as much as $20,000,000. And I think the loss from that disease to-day is from $25,000,000 to $30,000,000 in this country. Is that not true, Dr. Mohler?

Dr. MOHLER. Data compiled by the department show losses of $75,000,000 in 1914, and about $32,000,000 for the year ending March 31, 1918. So far as our records show, we have never had the loss as high as $100,000,000.

Mr. HAUGEN. On an average, what are the hogs worth that die from hog cholera?

Dr. HOSKINS. They vary in value from year to year.

Mr. HAUGEN. I know they do; but what is the average? Take, for instance, 1913 and 1914?

Dr. HOSKINS. I am not going to answer you in statistics, as to just what the value is, but I do know this, that as you decrease the losses you thereby enable the large masses of the people in the great centers to buy larger quantities of meat, and in so doing make them less vulnerable to and more immune from disease. And when you get 70-cent bacon, like they have to-day in the city of New York, you have a mighty serious problem.

Mr. HAUGEN. I call attention to Farmers' Bulletin No. 834. The estimate of losses in 1913 was $6,064,470. In 1914, it was $6,304,320, and a loss of 522,000 hogs, or about half a million. It seems to me you are getting your estimates up in the pictures.

Dr. HOSKINS. Oh, no; 9.5 per cent of all the hogs slaughtered——

Mr. HAUGEN. Here we have the Government bulletin; let us confine ourselves to that. What was the value of 522,000 hogs lost in 1913 and 1914?

Dr. HOSKINS. I do not know the value of them, sir.

Mr. HAUGEN. You assert there has been a saving of so much.

Dr. HOSKINS. Yes; the reduction of losses I have talked about.

Mr. HAUGEN. I presumed you were familiar with the facts to sustain your contention.

Dr. HOSKINS. The reduction of losses I am talking about.

AGRICULTURE APPROPRIATION BILL. 243

Mr. HAUGEN. That on 522,000 you have saved $30,000,000 or $100,000,00?

Dr. HOSKINS. That this country has lost, in a single year, as high as $100,000,000.

Mr. HAUGEN. That is about $200 a hog, isn't it?

Dr. HOSKINS. No.

The CHAIRMAN. If you will multiply the average cost of hogs in 1914 by 522,000, it will give you what you are after.

Dr. HOSKINS. There are more losses than that of hogs in this country, because the losses have ranged from 400,000 to 500,000. They lost 400,000 a year ago.

Mr. HAUGEN. That is half a million?

Dr. HOSKINS. That is about half a million.

Mr. HAUGEN. Placing the loss at $100,000,000, that is $200 a hog?

Dr. HOSKINS. Yes.

Mr. HAUGEN. Do you contend hogs are worth $200 a head?

Dr. HOSKINS. Bear in mind those were only hogs condemned by the bureau that went through the Federal meat-inspection service to be inspected for food. I am not talking about the hogs on the farm, because I do not think we have it complete.

Mr. HAUGEN. This says estimated number of hogs in each State from January 1, 1913, losses from hog cholera, through March 31, 1917. These are the estimates.

Dr. HOSKINS. That is not for the bureau; that is only the losses they come in contact with in the meat-inspection service.

Mr. HAUGEN. I will ask Dr. Mohler if these are not the hogs you come in contact with?

Dr. MOHLER. I think Dr. Hoskins is referring to the number of carcasses found infected in meat-inspection work, while the table you are referring to shows the hog-cholera losses on farms, which amounted to about 3,000,000 animals in 1917. The figures never reached $100,000,000. We estimated from $67,000,000 to $75,000,000 in 1914, and we know in 1917 it had been reduced to $32,000,000. That is already in the record.

Mr. LEE. Isn't there at least 25 or 50 per cent that die that you never hear of?

Dr. MOHLER. No; no such percentage as that.

Mr. LEE. There is a great percentage. I know in my county hundreds and hundreds of hogs die, and I have no idea the Government ever hears of it.

Dr. MOHLER. These figures are all obtained by the crop correspondents, and are collected by the Bureau of Crop Estimates; so that the man who figures out the acreage of wheat and corn in a county or district is the man who figures out the losses from hog cholera.

Mr. HAUGEN. What were the losses in 1917?

Dr. MOHLER. $32,000,000.

Mr. HAUGEN. That is about $30 a hog. Now is it not a fact that the hogs that die are small hogs—the shoats?

Dr. MOHLER. Not entirely.

Mr. HAUGEN. But generally?

Dr. MOHLER. The pig is immune until it is 6 weeks old.

Mr. HAUGEN. Oh, well, a 6-week-old hog doesn't weigh very much.

Dr. MOHLER. Those are the figures of the Bureau of Crop Estimates, and the loss per hog was figured at approximately $11. We are standing on $32,000,000 of losses from hog cholera for 1917. as figured by the Bureau of Crop Estimates.

Mr. HAUGEN. I am giving the numbers, quoting from the bulletin.

Dr. HOSKINS. For very many years the man who had hog cholera was not disposed to let it be known, as long as they had no remedy for it, and to accurately estimate the loss is impossible.

Dr. MOHLER. According to those very figures of 3,000,000 hogs lost, the price would only have to be $11 a hog.

Mr. HAUGEN. For the year 1917?

Dr. MOHLER. Yes.

Mr. HAUGEN. It is 4,057,000 hogs the year before.

Dr. MOHLER. I am speaking of 1917 here in this table. There were 2,959,322, practically 3,000,000, hogs which died of hog cholera, and the loss was $32,000,000.

Mr. HAUGEN. And 4,000,000 the year before?

Dr. MOHLER. Four million hogs in 1916.

Mr. HAUGEN. Which leaves you 1,000,000.

Dr. MOHLER. I do not see how you figure it.

Mr. HAUGEN. It says the losses for 1916 were 4,087,000.

Dr. MOHLER. Yes, sir; and 3,000,000 for 1917.

Mr. HAUGEN. Yes.

Dr. MOHLER. Why subtract the 1917 losses from those of 1916 to get the annual loss. If those figures show anything, they show that we saved 1,000,000 more hogs in 1917 than in 1916.

Mr. HAUGEN. You lost more that year than you did before.

Dr. MOHLER. We lost a million hogs more in 1916 than in 1917. This table is not intended as a comparative table of values. It shows the numerical loss of hogs, but does not show the monetary loss.

Mr. HAUGEN. I thought you were talking about a comparison by years.

Dr. MOHLER. No; there is no comparison of values shown in the table.

STATEMENT OF MR. E. S. BAYARD, EDITOR NATIONAL STOCKMAN AND FARMER, PITTSBURGH, PA.

Mr. BAYARD. Mr. Chairman and gentlemen, I will not detain you very long. I want to say I am not concerned in this matter from the standpoint of the veterinarians. I suppose if they do not get this salary increase they will have to scuffle along the best way they can the same as everybody else. I am not here to plead for them. What I am concerned in is animal industry and the wholesomeness of our meat. It does not appear to me we can afford to put in charge of our great animal industry anybody but good men, and we can not afford to put meat inspection in the hands of anybody but good men, competent men, skilled men. I am not willing to eat meat that is passed by just anybody, and neither are you. None of you wants a fairly good egg; you want a good egg. Of course, that is off the subject, but that is what we want, and that illustrates the point. And the only way I have found to keep good men in any service is to pay the wages that will keep them there.

The CHAIRMAN. How much do you pay your farm labor now, Mr. Bayard? I am asking you for information.

Mr. BAYARD. I have just got one man now and I do not know. I have not made any arrangement for this year. He will be paid more than last year, but he has a house and a cow and other things. I wish I could tell you exactly what it would amount to, but I do not know. But I shall have to pay him a good deal more than I used to.

Mr. LESHER. You mean to say you can not tell what you are paying your men?

Mr. BAYARD. No; I can tell what I am paying that man now on the farm. But I want to say this to you, that I have only one man, and I could use more, but we have not been able to get them at all in our country.

Mr. THOMPSON. You know what you are paying him, outside of these additional considerations you mention?

Mr. BAYARD. Yes; I know what I am paying per diem.

Mr. THOMPSON. What is that?

Mr. BAYARD. I am paying him a dollar and a half a day and furnishing him with those other things—various things. I do not know just how much it will be, but I think it will be more this year. That was last year. And I think he is better off, too, at the end of the year, with all these things, than some of the rest of us. But I would not want you to take that as an example of farm wages, because it is not. This man, I think, is rather an exception; he is really a friend of the family in regard to other things, and that is only part of his wages. But that is off the question. The question is whether we are going to pay enough in our Government service to keep good men in it, or whether we are going to let them get away and go somewhere else.

I hold in our animal-industry service we ought to keep the best men at work, not only in the packing houses and in that sort of work, but elsewhere—everywhere. And I do not see how some of those men who live in the great cities can get along, and you must remember that the most of those men have to live in the great cities, in the packing-house centers of this country, because they are in the great cities. And they are not being paid according to the country's standard of wages. They are not living on the scale of the man in the country; their food, supplies, and rents are on the scale of the great city, and their wages must be, if they remain in this work, on the city scale. And I do not really think we can make any comparison with farmers or anything else; we have to take the facts as they are.

Mr. YOUNG of Texas. Is not this true, that from year to year the farm is being depopulated by people going to these great cities, because they figure the wages are better there than they can get on the farm, and for that reason they are leaving the farm, and as the constant demand of living in the cities is higher as the years go by and therefore they must increase the city wages, which is an inducement for the farmer to leave the farm and go to the city and thereby depopulate the farm?

Mr. BAYARD. I think you are correct. But at the same time we are talking here about professional men, men who have taken a four years' college course, and the man who will go to college and take a four years' college course is going to leave the farm, anyhow, and the people who have taken these courses have come from the farm and have made good.

Mr. HAUGEN. Do you understand that those who engage in the hog-cholera work live in the large cities?

Mr. BAYARD. No, sir; those engaged in the hog-cholera work do not live in the large cities, but I understood the chairman to say we ought to limit our remarks to this inspection business.

The CHAIRMAN. Unless you broaden the item it will be necessary to confine your statement to it.

Mr. HAUGEN. Would you want to differentiate between inspectors—between those who operate in the cities and have to live in the cities and those who operate in the country?

Mr. BAYARD. Gentlemen, I do not want to dictate, to differentiate, or anything; I want simply to impress upon your mind that if we are going to keep competent men and inspectors in this business we have to pay a wage that will keep them there.

Mr. HAUGEN. The contention is the men in the service are underpaid and the salaries shall be increased. We assume all of the men in the service are efficient men and that the same people are to be employed, and it seems to me we are getting away from the subject entirely; that we ought to make some comparison of the salaries paid to these people and the salaries paid to others, so that we might ascertain the worth of all of those people in the service. The proposition is not to dismiss those people; the same people are to continue and the service to be identical as it has been and performed by the same people.

Mr. BAYARD. Yes; and if these people are to continue in this service, I want to say they will have to have a living wage; that is, a wage that will allow them to live, and you can not figure any other way. It is not a matter of comparison.

Mr. WILSON. How can we pay a living wage if we feed Europe?

Mr. BAYARD. Gentlemen, I want to say to you here if we had not had in this country the veterinarians—now, there used to be a kind of veterinarian, you might say; that is, the veterinarians I knew in my boyhood days, but they were not the class of men we have now; they were "horse doctors," and when they went to give the horse something potable it was a question whether they got it or the horse got it—if it was drinkable. But to-day the veterinarian is a man who has to take a four-year college course. He is a college man, and I challenge you to go into any of their meetings or discussions and compare them with the discussions in the meetings of the medical profession or any other profession. Now, if we are going to get that kind of men, we are going to have to pay them something. And regarding Europe, I want to say just a few years ago the medical profession, the Bureau of Animal Industry, and these same men saved this country from a condition that would have prevented us from feeding Europe and from feeding our own people, and that was the foot-and-mouth disease. I went through the mill, and I know something about it. I have been through two attacks of it. Dr. Hoskins told you the truth when he told you about the cattle tick and the fever ticks, but that is not the question. It is just a question of allowing these men to live and to continue to do this work.

The CHAIRMAN. In the cattle-tick work you do not require a veterinarian to give instructions and supervise the work, do you?

Mr. BAYARD. Yes; but who discovered that and who put it into commission and who put it into effect? And the same thing with the foot-and-mouth disease and other things that we have been guarded against and will continue to be guarded against, and the same thing with tuberculosis and hog cholera.

Now, then, I say another thing: You can not keep these men at work in your Government service in the future, because they are going to find opportunities outside of it. I have been getting calls for veterinarians, and I do not know where to find them.

Mr. LESHER. Why don't you take some of these men?

Mr. BAYARD. They are all busy; there is not a man who hasn't a good practice.

Mr. THOMPSON. According to the statement of Mr. Rainey, four colleges went out of business.

Mr. BAYARD. Yes.

Mr. THOMPSON. How is it, if there is such a great demand for them, that these colleges quit?

Mr. BAYARD. I say this demand is coming. I may be a prophet or a false prophet, or I may not be, but I say this demand is coming, and I am already getting demands for veterinarians. And here is why it is coming: Our live stock is getting to be too valuable to monkey with, and when a man has an animal that is sick, he wants a man right there on the job, and the difficulty is going to be in the future to take those men away from this work and put them into the country. And I can place one or two of them right now. A man in Pittsburgh, in the stockyards, his clerk made a mistake of $46 in the price of one hog—$46 in the price of one hog.

Mr. HAUGEN. Who did that?

Mr. BAYARD. The clerk of a commission man made a mistake of $46 in the price of one hog.

Mr. HAUGEN. What did that hog sell for?

Mr. BAYARD. Thirty cents a pound, and the clerk wrote it at 18 cents and thereby made a mistake. That shows what he is worth. And take cattle: I bought cattle this fall, and it cost over $100 a head to feed them, and we are not going to lose those animals for lack of service if we can help it. The stockmen are going to take these men away from the official work, and if you people do not pay them enough they are going into the country where they can live.

Mr. YOUNG of Texas. There are a lot of veterinarians to-day who have a practice out in the country, just like the physician.

Mr. BAYARD. Yes, sir.

Mr. YOUNG of Texas. And a man who locates in a town of three or four thousand people, about what can he make at general practice?

Mr. BAYARD. I do not know; but it is evident he is getting more than the Federal veterinarian or he would try to get a Federal job. And that is about the last thing he is trying to do, isn't it, Dr. Mohler?

Dr. MOHLER. Under present conditions, it is.

Mr. BAYARD. These matters are all matters for your consideration.

I merely want to bring before you a few points. Until recent years we have never fully appreciated the value of prevention of disease and medical treatment for our farm animals. Up until two years ago the State of Iowa could not even quarantine to stop the hog cholera—that great live-stock State of Iowa.

Mr. HAUGEN. My understanding is nobody questions the efficiency of these men and the value of their services. I do not think that is a question to be discussed here.

The CHAIRMAN. I think you are entirely right.

Mr. HAUGEN. But we ought to know something about these salaries. I think every member of this committee has the highest regard for the services of the men employed in the service; I do not think anybody questions their efficiency.

Mr. BAYARD. I do feel most of us do not realize this, that if we do not pay salaries commensurate with the services and commensurate with the abilities of the men, you can not expect, and I do not think anybody ought to expect, to keep anybody but the best men in the service.

The CHAIRMAN. We admit that; and the issue here is what those men ought to be paid. If you will confine yourselves to that, we will save time.

Mr. HAUGEN. We are just wasting the time of the committee.

Mr. BAYARD. I do not want to waste any of your time. But I can not give you any figures, because I do not know. I can not go into details, as Dr. Mohler and these other men will do. But I want to say this, that for the right kind of men you want to take the ground the Kentucky man did when he said " you might put up the price of a drink of whisky, but you can not get any more than what it is worth."

Mr. RAINEY. I now wish to introduce Dr. Peter F. Bahnsen, State veterinarian, Atlanta, Ga., and also a dairy man.

STATEMENT OF DR. PETER F. BAHNSEN, STATE VETERINARIAN, ATLANTA, GA.

Dr. BAHNSEN. I think we have been getting away from the proposition entirely. We have been comparing veterinarians with farm labor. You might just as well compare officers, lieutenants, and captains of the Army, with privates, and certainly the Government makes a difference between the private and the officer. And that is exactly the position of the veterinarian; the veterinarian is not a farm laborer, and therefore we can not compare him with the farm laborer, and we can not compare his services with the services of the farm laborer.

The CHAIRMAN. You can compare the veterinarian in private practice and what he makes with the salary of the veterinarian in the Government service.

Dr. BAHNSEN. That is right. That is fine, and just speaking from the Georgia viewpoint, now, the average Georgia practitioner, that is the man engaged in private practice and devoting all his time to it, will make anywhere from as little as $2,000 up to as much as $5,000 or $6,000, depending on his location and his pushability. Some men haven't any push, and you have some of those people in your official life the same as in private life. But if your man has really got the push and he is a progressive veterinarian, he can make perhaps from $5,000 to $6,000 a year in private practice.

The day has been when the lucrative practice was in the city, but that is a thing of the past. The man who does anything now in the veterinary practice, has to go and get into an active agricultural community. And the man with little ability or the man with little aggressiveness; that is, just the ordinary man, can easily make $2,000.

And that is over and above his expenses, his actual expenses incurred in his practice.

And I would like to say in reference to the bureau veterinarians, we have been intimately associated with them and I can recall quite a number of the best men who were in the service to my personal knowledge, and I do not know, Mr. Lee, but that probably you can recall Mr. Fred Moore, who was engaged in the tick eradication in Walker County. The Government paid him $1,600. He wanted an increase to $1,800 (he wanted to stick) and they would not give it to him. He had been some three or four years without an increase in salary and he quit the service and started with a hog-cholera concern at an initial salary of $2,500, and it is my understanding he is making between four and five thousand dollars at present. And there was another man connected with the hog cholera work in the State of Georgia who was getting $1,600 a year and we offered him $1,800, but he did not want to quit the service with the bureau; he had been to college and had big hopes he would be advanced in the bureau service. I wrote to Dr. Mohler that I did not want to hurt the service by taking away the men under him, and they changed his location and gave him $1,800—a man worth easily $2,500 and who could make $4,000 if he would get out and try to practice for himself. And I can recall any number of instances. Of course, some men in the bureau service are not very active and aggressive, and some men, unless you start them, can not move at all. And you can hardly blame them; that is what you are paying them for; you are paying for the men you have to start up every morning and you are not paying for the man who wants to do things and who is capable of doing things. And that is the position we take, that the Government can only afford to hire the best men, the men who can get up and do something.

Mr. LESHER. You say you are not getting that class of men?

Dr. BAHNSEN. I say you are not paying for that class of men.

Mr. LESHER. You said we were not getting them?

Dr. BAHNSEN. You are not retaining the best of them.

Mr. LESHER. And we are not getting them, either?

Dr. BAHNSEN. Not always; that is right. In many instances you are getting inferior material for the simple reason the salary paid by the bureau really calls for that class of men, the people with a lack of aggressiveness, people that are attracted to it because there is a fixed salary given by the Government and they hope to advance and hope to do better later on. But the people with real push in them, you can not get them at the salaries you offer; and I take it the Government is really wasting money, and if you offer the salaries that will attract the best men, you will then get the best men, and it would be economy if you did get them.

Mr. HAUGEN. Are the communities pretty well supplied with veterinarians throughout the country?

Dr. BAHNSEN. I can only speak, of course, for the territory in Georgia. I am not familiar with any of the other States. I understand possibly the Middle Western States have quite a number of veterinarians. But in Georgia and through the South we could use a limited number of good veterinarians. There are many counties that are very anxious to get good veterinarians, and they will patronize the right kind of men.

Mr. HAUGEN. I take it, if the community is progressive, the demand for veterinarians will increase?

Dr. BAHNSEN. That is right.

Mr. HAUGEN. And that the greatest need of the supply and greatest demand is from the country.

Dr. BAHNSEN. To give you a fair idea, about 10 years ago we had only six graduate veterinarians in the State of Georgia. To-day there are 136 licensed by the State board of veterinary examiners. That shows you something of the increase of the veterinarians. And they are all doing reasonably well.

Mr. HAUGEN. The reason I ask you is this: The Army is retaining them by the thousands, probably by the hundred thousands, for all I know. The horses have been disposed of, and I haven't seen a sick horse since they entered the service—none within hundreds of miles—and why those people are retained in the Army I do not know. I understand there are several thousand right now within a few miles of Washington.

Dr. BAHNSEN. I assure you, the majority of them do not want to be retained.

Mr. HAUGEN. I am trying to get a few of them out, because they are needed in the country. People are asking and petitioning for them to come home and help in the communities.

Dr. BAHNSEN. I assure you the Army officials, they have a slow sort of way of getting rid of them again; there is a great deal of official red tape in getting them disbanded, I understand. I know we need the men all right.

STATEMENT OF DR. V. A. MOORE, DEAN OF THE VETERINARY COLLEGE, CORNELL UNIVERSITY, ITHACA, N. Y.

Dr. MOORE. Mr. Chairman and gentlemen of the committee, there are one or two points that I wish to emphasize. In the first place, I wish to emphasize the fact, which has already been brought out, that the veterinary profession to-day is a different proposition from what it was not so many years ago.

The CHAIRMAN. Of course, we would be interested to have you go into the history of that, but this committee is fairly well familiar with that. Some of the men have been on this committee for 20 years. What we want to do is to try to get a salary comparison.

Dr. MOORE. I will try to get at this point, that in this change I referred to, it has brought about a tremendous increase in the requirements of the men. Years ago a man could go to the veterinary college from the farm or shop, and would be prepared, after studying for two years, of six months each, to go out as a full-fledged veterinarian. Now he has to go through four years of high school and then four years in the professional school, and that is very expensive to him. Consequently, we have a professional type of man, in the true sense.

Now, we have in the work of this country, in maintaining the live stock interests, we have to have a differentiation of men. The veterinary profession is one of those differentiations. These men have for their purpose the protection of live stock from disease—the treating of the sick, as best they can, in saving life, and, in public life, the protection of our meat inspection, the protection of our populace against diseased meat, and the various other activities of the tuberculosis and hog-cholera work referred to here. And this requires a professional man.

As to the matter of salary, men go out into any part of the country that I know anything about, and they make, it is constantly said, from $2,000 to $10,000 or $15,000 a year, according to their pushability, as the doctor referred to. There are very few practitioners that are recognized in the profession who are making less than $2,000 a year. The majority of them are making from $3,000 to $6,000 and $8,000 a year.

Now, there are men who have gone into the bureau work with the same spirit of patriotism that the veterinarians went into the Army. There is a need of the country, in serving our people, to have this work well done and to have the best service, and there are many men who have push and energy, who have an ambition to serve the people in doing this work; but after they have been in the service for a number of years they are met with the fact that their salary does not permit them to raise a family and to protect and care for it as their classmates in college, for example, who are in practice can do. And these men are leaving the service.

Now, there are conditions, sir, in regard to the meat inspection, to which you wish this point addressed, that are peculiar. These men are temporary men in the community; they can not become citizens of the town; they can not own their little home and have their family. Many, many men whom I have known, who have been stationed at a place for a few years and have thought probably they would be kept there, have invested what little they might have saved in a home, only to be ordered across the continent or hundreds of miles away when they had hardly become established. And these men are transients, living under considerable expense, and that takes the heart out of life to a considerable extent.

The CHAIRMAN. It seems to me, in the great cities like Chicago and Kansas City, where they must have these men, the department ought to adopt the policy of retaining them there permanently, which would tend to efficiency.

Dr. MOHLER. That is being done wherever it is possible to do so. We have men who have been in some cities for 15 or 20 years.

The CHAIRMAN. These transfers, then, are exceptional cases?

Dr. MOHLER. They are more or less exceptional cases. Of course, we can not guarantee that a man is going to be stationed at one city for any length of time, because the exigencies of the service must be met. If we had an outbreak of foot-and-mouth disease, or if some other exigency occurred, our service is sufficiently mobile to permit the transfer of our inspectors from the city to the field, or vice versa. But wherever it is possible we try to keep the men at their home stations.

Mr. THOMPSON. Otherwise the transfers are only upon application, are they not?

Dr. MOHLER. A large majority of them are upon application.

Mr. HAUGEN. And some for cause?

Dr. MOHLER. Some few for cause.

Dr. MOORE. The efficiency of the service demands it, because some men are more competent to do certain things that have to be met.

The next point of difference of these men from the private practitioner is the conditions under which they have to work. Those men have to go into the packing houses and have to associate during their working hours largely with the butchers and an uneducated class of men. They have to work under environments that are exceedingly disagreeable. They have to go from the steam of the killing floor into the cooling refrigerators, and back, off and on, and it is an exceedingly unpleasant environment under which they live, and a good many men leave the service because of that condition; not many like to stay in.

In addition to that, it is a service which is injurious to the health, and they are exposed to infection and many men have been infected in the service.

And, taking all those conditions into account, if we are going to have an efficient veterinary inspection, we have to offer these men some inducement over that in private life.

When it comes back to the student, a number of years ago, before there was this call for veterinarians in the country, which has come about because of the high price of live stock, those in the older class to which I refer were instructed in connection with the horse. Now that business has changed and the value of food-producing animals has increased until the veterinary profession is to look after the food-producing animals of the country. And the modern schools are oriented in that direction. Now, these men do not care to go into this environment and into a class of work that pays them, at best, less than the minimum which a good wide-awake practitioner can make in any of these agricultural communities where there is live stock. Now that is the gist of the thing. And then take it with the student. Twenty years ago the men in the veterinary colleges, many of them, came there with the explicit purpose of going into the bureau work, into this inspection work. In those days they did not have the responsibility that they do now in regard to sanitary conditions of the packing houses. But as time has gone on the men say "no," and to-day it is only, as Dr. Bahnsen said, the man that lacks the "push-ability" in him, who thinks of going into the service. The good man, the live man, does not do it; and the good men, the live men, the men with red blood in their veins who are in the service are looking for places outside. I have had, within the last month, three good men of the Bureau of Animal Industry ask me about locations to practice. They are tired of these conditions; they have been promised promotions and have not received them, and they are thinking of leaving.

Now, sir, how is our live-stock business, how is the great meat industry going to stand in the eye of Europe if you do not have in this service as good men as can be had? And if the salaries are right you can get good men. Now, that is the whole thing.

Mr. HAUGEN. How do the salaries paid by the Federal Government compare with the salaries paid by the States? The States employ veterinarians, do they not?

Mr. MOORE. Yes, sir. I am not in a position to answer that. I have not a State position, and our men in New York State are started in at $1,800 or more and they go up, I think, to $2,700.

Dr. HOSKINS. To three thousand.

Dr. MOORE. Some of them, I know, are getting three thousand.

Mr. HAUGEN. Can you state about other States?

Dr. MOORE. Dr. Munce is here and I think he can state for Pennsylvania.

Dr. MUNCE. We start them at $1,800.

The CHAIRMAN. What is the maximum?

Dr. MUNCE. Our highest paid man is three thousand; that is, excluding the State veterinarian; $4,000 for State veterinarians.

Mr. HAUGEN. How about Iowa, Dr. Koen?

Dr. KOEN. The dean of the veterinary college, I understand, receives $5,000.

Mr. HAUGEN. I mean those employed by the State.

Dr. KOEN. They are per diem. They have no regular yearly employees.

Mr. HAUGEN. How much is that per diem?

Dr. KOEN. That is $5 a day, but not a one of them is willing to accept unless forced into it.

Mr. RAINEY. What do they make in practice?

Dr. KOEN. If I may give a comparison, in Iowa the practitioners are receiving, that is, the lowest ones, $2,000 above their living, and from that up to $2,500 and $3,000. Those are the mediocre practitioners. Then there are many what you might call the successful practitioners who are getting from $3,000 to $4,000 above expenses. And there are some, Dr. Thompson, of Armstrong, a man who is said to be making from $7,000 to $10,000 a year in private practice.

Mr. HAUGEN. But they maintain automobiles and have other expenses?

Dr. KOEN. Yes; but it is in addition to that. Now, one of my men who is getting $1,500, plus the $120, making $1,620, is leaving the service on the 20th of this month to engage in practice with one of the men in his district, at a salary to begin with of $2,120. Another of my men is wishing to resign this morning to enter private practice, feeling that as he is a single man he can no longer exist on $135 a month which he is getting now. And there are men like Dr. McFarland, receiving $2,000, who after 15 or 18 years of service immediately stepped into a salary of $3,500 and I think now is getting $5,000. One of his assistants left the service last fall, who was getting $1,800 for a number of years in the bureau service, and he is now getting $2,400 with a commission. Dr. Hough, who was engaged in our work when we first started in Dallas County, Iowa, was getting $1,600, and now he is earning $3,000 and better in his own work. I am sorry I am not so fortunate. Dr. Talbert, a practitioner whom we persuaded to come with us last spring for $1,500 we were able to hold only a few months and now he is making better than $2,500 in private practice.

We are unable to get competent men to serve in our work of the bureau in Iowa. We are getting the failures in practice and we are getting the men just out of school who are broke and must have ready money. And as soon as they get on their feet and get squared away again, they are leaving. We were getting some good ones during the war, who felt they could render more service to their country in our service than in the Army service. And they were willing to come for the duration of the war and during the reconstruction or conservation period afterwards, and then we will lose them again. And then there are those who entered the serivce when the salary was $1,600 and who are not getting more than $200 above that to-day, who have stayed on hoping that some day the promises of the Government would be fulfilled and they are still hoping; but many of them are leaving and we will lose more of them unless the conditions of the service are remedied. And it is for the welfare of the service and for the efficiency of the service that it be maintained and be not demoralized that we come before you, asking not for anything unreasonable but that we may have something like a similar opportunity in the Government service to that which is offered in other fields to which we can turn our attention.

Dr. MUNCE. Does the statement I offered as to Pennsylvania appear in this hearing?

The CHAIRMAN. Yes.

Dr. MUNCE. Then I would like to qualify it. I said our men—the veterinarians—are started at $1,800 a year. The State veterinarian receives $4,000 a year, the minimum, and the administration has indicated there will be an increase all along the line.

STATEMENT OF MR. H. H. HALLADAY, CHAIRMAN LIVE-STOCK SANITARY BOARD, LANSING, MICH.

Mr. HALLADAY. Mr. Chairman and gentlemen of the committee, I shall be very brief in my statements here this morning. I have been in the live-stock business all of my life; in fact, I was raised on the farm and now operate a farm.

Michigan is now going into the live-stock industry and we are trying to push it. We believe we have the greatest opportunities to build up the live-stock industry in Michigan that there are in any State of the Union. And we are demanding that we have assistance from the Bureau of Animal Industry, and we are making our requests quite generally and freely and asking that they be sent to us whenever we get in trouble, which has been frequently. And we only want such men as are capable of carrying on the work. And we believe, in looking over the schedule of prices, that they are entirely too low.

If I may be permitted, Mr. Chairman, I am speaking from the standpoint of the inspector in the field more generally than the inspector in the packing house, because I come in touch with those men more than anything else. One thing that has not been brought out here, I think, is that the inspectors are subjected to considerable hardship which you do not realize. The inspector in tuberculosis eradication is necessarily taken away from his family. If he has a station that permits him to be with his family at the week end he is perhaps taken across the State, and especially in this tuberculosis eradication work, which is commendable, and in which we are very much interested in Michigan and which is gaining popularity very fast. We also have the hog-cholera work, which is being done in cooperation with the Bureau of Animal Industry, and which has materially reduced our losses in the past.

We appreciate all those things, but times have changed, and we realize your inspectors are not being paid according to the rise in prices which has been spoken of this morning. You know about those things without my speaking about them. But we feel, in starting this great work in Michigan, that we want the very best men you can send us, and the best practitioners in the State can not be induced to take hold of this proposition at the present time unless you increase the salaries. At the present time we have a serious outbreak of scabies in the State of Michigan that was brought in through our efforts to increase the population of the sheep in the State of Michigan. And, unfortunately, at the beginning we were faced with a serious outbreak of scabies. Immediately we made an appeal to the Bureau of Animal Industry to assist us. They have one man in the State who may be considered an expert along that line, and I want to say to you that he is doing more to assist us than any two men we could put in there, because he is an expert along his line, and should be paid for his services commensurate to the service he has rendered.

The CHAIRMAN. What is his salary?

Dr. MOHLER. He gets $1,200 a year as a lay inspector, grade 2.

Mr. HALLADAY. This man I know from personal experience is worth more to the State of Michigan to-day than any two men, because he is an expert along his line. He is going into the matter and he is working in the northern part of the State of Michigan in snow up to his knees dipping sheep, and under the most adverse circumstances, and you are paying him $1,200 a year. I say it is ridiculous to pay men of that type that salary.

The CHAIRMAN. Have you authority to pay that man more money?

Dr. MOHLER. He has been recommended for more money, and I hope it will be made effective on the 1st of January.

The CHAIRMAN. He is not on the statutory roll?

Dr. MOHLER. No, sir; he is on the lump-sum roll.

The CHAIRMAN. How much are you going to pay him?

Dr. MOHLER. He has been recommended for $1,380, which, plus the $120, will give him $1,500.

Mr. HAUGEN. Does it require any skill to dip sheep?

Dr. MOHLER. No; it does not require much skill to dip sheep, but it does require a great deal of skill to detect the presence of scabies in sheep and to know whether you should or should not dip them.

Mr. HALLADAY. The future of the live-stock industry in Michigan depends upon how well we can establish the business, and one of the many facts we have to contend with is that these animals are coming into the State and are necessarily animals of commerce, and we must watch the health or else we lose production.

Mr. MCLAUGHLIN. The large bunches of sheep which are evidently brought into Michigan are almost exclusively placed in the isolated areas and there is not much danger, is there, of the spread of this disease to the old sections of the State where sheep have been kept on the farms of Michigan?

Mr. HALLADAY. I am glad the Congressman from my State has brought that point out, because he knows the conditions. But the conditions are a little different than he states, from the fact that in the principal part of the State of Michigan the farmers who have 6 or 8 or 10 sheep are anxious to go in the sheep business on a large scale and in this particular instance have brought the scabies-infected stock until now it has spread over two counties in nearly every flock in those counties because they purchased from those areas. They were purchased before the scabies was known to exist in these flocks.

Mr. McLaughlin. Isn't there a law providing for the inspection of animals before they are brought from one State to another, in order to determine whether they are free from disease?

Mr. Halladay. Yes, sir.

Mr. McLaughlin. Wasn't that done in Michigan?

Mr. Halladay. Yes; that was done in Michigan, but that outbreak has developed since, through exposure, or probably due to the fact they were a hand-picked bunch which would not show the disease at the time they were shipped in.

STATEMENT OF MR. J. F. HUGHES, NEW YORK, REPRESENTING THE LAY INSPECTORS.

Mr. Hughes. Mr. Chairman and gentlemen, I will be very brief here in my remarks. As I understand, the committee would like to get the basic of pay paid by the packers and the basic of pay paid by the Federal Government. In the schedule of wages of the packinghouse employees at New York the foreman on the killing floor receives $60 a week plus bonuses. This bonus is given to them twice a year. The butchers on the killing floor receive from $45 to $75 a week; the laborers on the killing floor receive from $30 to $35 a week. The foreman of the food department receives $75 a week, plus bonuses. The elevator man receives $35 a week. The beef loggers receive $35 a week. The storeroom keepers receive $25 a week, plus bonuses. Salesmen—of course, those are high-priced men—receive from $100 to $150 a week, plus bonuses. Beef boners $30 a week, plus bonuses. All laborers receive time and a half for overtime and double time for Sundays and holidays. Eight hours constitutes a day's work, and the laborers receive time and a half for all overtime.

Mr. McLaughlin. What are beef boners you speak of?

Mr. Hughes. Beef boners are the men who bone the beef.

Mr. McLaughlin. You speak of bonuses.

Mr. Hughes. That is a salary given by the packers to their superintendents, storeroom keepers, and so forth, twice a year.

Mr. McLaughlin. A percentage of their salary?

Mr. Hughes. I presume it is a percentage of their salary. It is given to them twice a year.

Mr. McLaughlin. Is that large or small; can you tell us?

Mr. Hughes. Some of them receive as high as $240 every six months; others have received as high as $500.

Mr. Lesher. What do they receive this bonus for?

Mr. Hughes. It is a gift, I presume, from the packer for faithful service.

Mr. Haugen. Exception is taken to a comparison made with farm labor, and I take it this comparison should compare with those in the profession. I do not take it the man working on the killing floor is in connection with the profession?

Mr. Rainey. Mr. Hughes does not represent the veterinarian as a professional man; he represents the lay inspectors that are also being considered, grade 1 and grade 2, lay inspectors. He is offering to show here that as against the stipend of $1,200, which the lay inspectors receive, that the elevator men, the boners and butchers, and others who assist in the packing industry in a way as common labor are receiving these larger salaries.

Mr. HAUGEN. I take it we do not get anywhere in comparing those salaries with the packers' employees who receive profits of several hundred dollars from the packers, who have made several hundred million dollars during the war, in spite of competition. Those are emergency wages and they are not the normal wages paid. Of course, we are not computing three or four concerns making several hundred million dollars a year excess profits or war profits. That is pretty stiff competition, and I do not think that is a fair comparison. If you make that comparison you will have to make the comparison made here a little while ago with the wages paid to the farmer, and all along the line. I should think the proper thing to do would be to compare with the men in the professions who require some skill, education, and training.

Mr. HUGHES. You take the meat butcher, what we call the head dresser on the floor; in one establishment in New York the head dresser gets $70.

Mr. HAUGEN. He is not a veterinarian?

Mr. HUGHES. No, sir; he is nothing but a common laborer, a butcher by trade.

Mr. HAUGEN. Objection is made to comparing their salaries with the salary of common laborers or the farmer.

Mr. LESHER. How many years has he received $70 a week? That is the point you are getting at.

Mr. HAUGEN. I do not think it is; those are abnormal conditions.

Mr. RAINEY. Previous to the war, can you suggest what those butchers and others you have just enumerated received, approximately, in salary?

Mr. HUGHES. On the average, $50 a week.

The CHAIRMAN. That was before the war?

Mr. HUGHES. Yes, sir. I have seen sheep butchers in New York City getting for their weekly salary $72 a week.

Mr. THOMPSON. He has to be an expert, doesn't he, a man who butchers sheep? He can not be anything else or any other kind of butcher?

Mr. HUGHES. That is a trade, nothing more.

Mr. HAUGEN. An expert will kill a hundred sheep where the other fellow kills half a dozen; it is all in the skill.

Mr. HUGHES. They work piecework in New York.

Mr. HAUGEN. For instance, take the man who sticks the hogs, or those making $10 or $20 a day; they are experts.

Mr. RAINEY. Isn't it true the lay inspectors are also experts?

Mr. HUGHES. Yes, sir; they are scientific men. The packers are paying men doing similar work anywhere from $1,600 to $1,800 a year. There are a great many meat inspectors, lay inspectors, who have resigned from the bureau in order to become packing-house employees, while those of us who have remained faithful to the bureau are not looked up to with the respect the position calls for on account of the low salaries paid.

Mr. HAUGEN. They have met that situation by providing for the bonuses. I understand you are now contending for an increase and that that increase be made permanently?

Mr. HUGHES. Permanently; yes, sir.

Mr. HAUGEN. You would not suggest that we fix the permanent salaries to meet the prices paid at the present time on an emergency?

Mr. HUGHES. I did not get that.

Mr. HAUGEN. You would not contend that Congress should fix the permanent salaries to meet the wages paid during the emergency—equivalent to the wages paid now?

Mr. HUGHES. The men would like to get some immediate relief to get away from the conditions we are up against at the present time.

Mr. HAUGEN. I agree with you. I think you are entitled to some relief, but we are trying to get at what it should be.

Mr. RAINEY. In other words, you would be perfectly satisfied and the other men associated with you in the lay inspection work if Congress would fix salaries now commensurate with the salaries received by employees of the packing industries before the abnormal conditions. You suggested the butchers were getting $50 a week. You would be perfectly satisfied if Congress saw fit to arrange the salaries of the lay inspectors on a par with those lay butchers or other laborers of the packing industry?

Mr. HUGHES. I would.

Mr. RAINEY. I want to ask Dr. Hoskins, who is familiar probably with the questions asked by some of the gentlemen here, whether or not he could inform us as to the income of veterinarians in private practice as against the veterinarians employed by the Government? Approximately, Doctor, if you can?

Dr. HOSKINS. We have 100 practitioners in the city of Philadelphia. I practiced there for 36 years. Their practices range from $2,500 a year up as high as $15,000. I enjoyed a practice in the city of Philadelphia for 30 years of $10,000 a year. I turned it over to my son, and he wrote me a letter a few days ago and said he had done $10,000; and he said the State had offered him $1,800 to aid them, and afterwards he was offered by a firm in the State of Michigan $3,000 to come down and do like work in the State of Michigan. He was away three weeks, about, and he added $500 more to his salary. That shows you how private firms appreciate a man in the profession. We have men in the city of New York who have done as high as $35,000, and men in Chicago who have done as high as $40,000, and they had to keep one, two, three, and four assistants.

The CHAIRMAN. Those are exceptional men. Some lawyers make $150,000 a year.

Dr. HOSKINS. Yes. But you bear in mind our animals; they have a fixed value, and that is not like it is with the human being and in the practice of medicine or law, because our animals always have a definite value, so that the practice must always be limited. The average practice of the men throughout the country to-day will run from $2,000 up to $5,000 in all the rural districts.

The CHAIRMAN. That is a better statement for the committee.

Dr. HOSKINS. And they can go out to-day and do that; and this work, bear in mind, for the Government prohibits them from doing outside work. In my State the men who get $1,800 and $2,000 a year, they are permitted to go outside and practice, whereas the Federal Government forbids its employees from going outside and practicing.

Mr. McLaughlin. Is that entirely true? Has the Government official, during his spare time, no opportunity to make a spare dollar outside?

Dr. Hoskins. No, sir; they won't let him come down and teach in the school of which I am dean.

Mr. McLaughlin. That is regular work.

Dr. Hoskins. No, sir; he only has to teach a few hours a week. But we are able to get men to teach there, because they are men employed by the packers, and we bring them down there for teaching. The Government starts every man on the Army service at $1,700, and not only that, but they are provided with pensions and retirements after a few years, and they can go up to $4,000 in the service in the Army. And it seems to me the lowest these men ought to be started should be $1,700, the same as they start them in the Army veterinary service who have no pensions.

STATEMENT OF MR. CHARLES F. NAGL, OF CHICAGO.

Mr. Nagl. All I have to say is this, that the requirements made at the present time between the packers and the employees of the different packing-house industries is not a temporary affair; it is a permanent affair. We have had hearings for the last few weeks and the wages established now they are going to maintain. I want to say that nearly half of the force of the meat-inspection service in Chicago have recently taken positions in the packing-house industry, some of them even as laborers. Some of the common laborers in the United States are getting $20 and $30 more a month than the meat inspectors. And I would like to be permitted to file a schedule of the wages paid by the packers and the Bureau of Animal Industry, certified to by Judge Alschuler, that will give you the actual facts. In the packing-house industries out West the wages paid have been established by Judge Alschuler; that is, by agreement between the packers and the employees, and they have agreed to it, and that has been in force now and will be in force in the future.

Mr. Haugen. Mr. Rainey, does the proposed amendment fix a definite salary, or does it leave it to the discretion of the Secretary?

Mr. Rainey. No; it is discretionary with the Secretary.

Mr. Haugen. It does not fix the salaries; your amendment is simply to increase the appropriation, leaving the question of salaries to the discretion of the Secretary?

Mr. Rainey. Leaving it to the discretion of the Secretary.

STATEMENT OF DR. CASSIUS WAY, CHIEF VETERINARIAN OF BORDEN'S FARM PRODUCTS CO.

Mr. Way. The Borden's Condensed Milk Co. employs 13 veterinarians. A few years ago the minimum salary in starting the service was $2,000 to $2,100 per annum. At the present time we are obliged, in order to get good men, to start them at $2,250 to $2,500. The maximum salary depends on the ability of the individual and ranges from $3,000 to $3,500.

The nature of the work is milk inspection, dairy sanitation in the control of the milk supply for large cities, and for manufacture in condensed and other milk products.

(The committee thereupon went into executive session.)

AGRICULTURE APPROPRIATION BILL.

COMMITTEE ON AGRICULTURE,
HOUSE OF REPRESENTATIVES,
Saturday, January 3, 1919.

BUREAU OF PLANT INDUSTRY.

STATEMENT OF DR. WILLIAM A. TAYLOR, CHIEF OF THE BUREAU OF PLANT INDUSTRY, UNITED STATES DEPARTMENT OF AGRICULTURE.

The CHAIRMAN. We will not discuss your statutory rolls unless you have some promotions suggested there above the $2,500 limit. Have you any such suggestions?

Dr. TAYLOR. I think not.

The CHAIRMAN. Have you any new places, Doctor?

Dr. TAYLOR. None except transfers from lump to the statutory roll; such cases, for example, as item 8, on page 64, " three executive clerks at $1,980, increase of one by transfer from the lump fund for administrative expenses."

The CHAIRMAN. As a matter of fact, there are no new places except by transfer.

Dr. TAYLOR. No, sir; I think that is the case throughout.

The CHAIRMAN. You do not recommend any increases in your general force?

Dr. TAYLOR. No, sir.

Mr. HAUGEN. How long has this person been in that service, item 8?

Dr. TAYLOR. I think about nine months. You see automatically we transfer in the next estimates submitted after the appointment is made.

Mr. HAUGEN. He was appointed under the Civil Service Commission?

Dr. TAYLOR. Yes, sir.

Mr. HAUGEN. At what salary?

Dr. TAYLOR. $1,980.

Mr. HAUGEN. That is quite above the ordinary salary, isn't it?

Dr. TAYLOR. Yes, sir; we transfer automatically at the same salary in the next estimates which are submitted.

Mr. HAUGEN. He is a person of some special training, isn't he?

Dr. TAYLOR. A high-grade clerk. I think in this case it was a woman. That is my recollection.

Mr. HAUGEN. Then she was certified to you at $1,980?

Dr. TAYLOR. Either certified from the Civil Service Commission or secured by transfer.

Mr. HAUGEN. What is the rule about transfers from one service to the other? Is it done at an increase in salary?

Dr. TAYLOR. In some cases; yes, sir. Cases where a clerk possessing a particular qualification is transferred from one bureau to another, or from one department to another, at an increase of salary. We have lost from the Bureau of Plant Industry a large number of experienced clerks in this way during the past two years, and particularly the last year, to the other departments of the Government.

Mr. HAUGEN. It seems to be a disposition to prohibit a transfer from one department to another department of the Government.

Mr. TAYLOR. I think not, sir. There is a provision against the transfer from one department to another until after a certain length of service, and the head of each department has authority to decline to release a clerk from his department to another department, even though an advanced salary is offered to the clerk in that case.

Mr. HAUGEN. Is that the present law?

Dr. TAYLOR. I think so, sir, in so far as a transfer is concerned. I think the head of the department can decline to consent to a transfer.

Mr. HAUGEN. But can they be transferred within a year, or do they have to stay the year before they can transfer?

Dr. TAYLOR. That is my understanding now. I don't think that has been changed.

The CHAIRMAN. What is the law with reference to that, Mr. Harrison?

Mr. HARRISON. They must serve three years before they can be transferred.

Mr. HAUGEN. They can't be transferred.

Mr. HARRISON. The law prohibits it.

Mr. HAUGEN. At any rate, they have to serve three years before they may be transferred from one department to another?

Mr. HARRISON. Yes, sir. Of course, these new employees can resign and have their names restored to the eligible register of the Civil Service on what is known as the reemployment register.

Mr. HAUGEN. But those are war workers?

Mr. HARRISON. Yes, sir; they are people who came here during the war.

Mr. HAUGEN. How long does that take to change their status?

Mr. HARRISON. They are out of the service, and it is simply a question of reemployment or reinstatement. They can be reinstated within a year.

Mr. HAUGEN. But they take the chance with the others on the rolls?

Mr. HARRISON. Yes, sir; a transfer means a transfer from one department to another.

Mr. WASON. Then, there was an Executive order about that, wasn't there?

Mr. HARRISON. With reference to those people who went into the military service the President extended the period of reinstatement to five years.

Mr. WASON. I mean transfers.

Mr. HARRISON. Yes; the President prohibited the transfer of anybody from one department to another unless the head of the department in which the person was serving certified that the employee, in his opinion, could render better service for the Government in the department to which he wished to be transferred than in his present position.

Mr. WASON. Then your certificate followed?

Mr. HARRISON. Yes, sir; if we could conscientiously make it. We have been compelled to refuse to make a number in the department.

Mr. WASON. Is that still in force?

Mr. HARRISON. Yes, sir. It has made it difficult for the employees in many cases; nevertheless, we had to consider the work of the department.

Mr. HAUGEN. We are frequently asked about these transfers. As I understand it now they can't be transferred unless they serve three years.

Mr. HARRISON. Yes, sir.

Mr. HAUGEN. I am safe in making that statement?

Mr. HARRISON. Yes, sir; three years.

Mr. THOMPSON. On pages 69 and 70 you have a number of new places.

The CHAIRMAN. We are not considering those at all.

Mr. THOMPSON. No; I understand that you are not where there is an increase in salary below $2,500.

The CHAIRMAN. We are not considering this supplemental estimate at all.

Your first general expense item is on page 73, No. 119, for investigations of plant diseases. You have an increase there, Doctor, of $23,000. Briefly explain to the committee what you want with that.

Dr. TAYLOR. This increase is for the plant-disease survey work, and it is a recommendation that there be provided in the regular appropriation for the continuance of the enlarged plant-disease survey work that has been prosecuted under the food-production act. This $23,000 is the amount that has been used for the plant-disease survey under the food-production act, supplementing a small amount—$9,000, I think—carried by the regular appropriation this year.

The CHAIRMAN. $9,000 carried by the bill at present.

Dr. TAYLOR. $10,000 in the project carried by the present bill. Plant-disease survey work is, as its name indicates, a continuing activity, through which it is attempted to keep track of the occurrence and damage done by plant diseases throughout the country. It is largely done in cooperation with the pathologists of the State experiment stations and agricultural colleges, and amounts in effect to a correlation of the information regarding plant-disease outbreaks while it is fresh and the dissemination of that information immediately to the plant-disease workers of the country. There has been, as you know, a gradual development in every State of plant pathological work, particularly during the past 10 years. The workers have been largely working separately and often without knowledge of what was going on in the adjacent States or in other States with regard to the same diseases or other diseases affecting the same crop. Through this plant-disease survey it has been found possible very greatly to increase the efficiency of the pathological workers of the department, and also of the pathological workers of the States. It is an instrumentality through which, you may say, the plant-disease work of the country is being unified in a practical way. It is an instrument which is useful to all of them and which they have very strongly urged that the department enlarge and continue. We think that the experience of the past year, during which this enlarged activity has been in action, fully justifies its continuance as an aid to our peace crop production program.

The CHAIRMAN. Doctor, how many people have you working on this item?

Dr. TAYLOR. Twenty.

The CHAIRMAN. And you have an estimated appropriation for this work for the next year of $33,000?

Dr. TAYLOR. Yes, sir.

The CHAIRMAN. And the balance of that $81,000 will be used in the regular work?

Dr. TAYLOR. That is the regular investigational work of the pathological laboratory, most of which relates to bacterial diseases of plants.

Mr. HAGUEN. What plants especially have been given attention under this appropriation?

Dr. TAYLOR. Particularly a bacterial disease of wheat which was mentioned, I think, a year ago as occurring in the Middle West, a disease which was new. Whether it would become serious or not was not clear. It was felt that it would be better to attack before it became serious. The investigational work is still in its relatively early stages.

I have a statement of some of the important investigations being conducted under this item, which I shall be glad to insert in the record if the committee so desires.

(The statement referred to follows:)

OUTLINE OF IMPORTANT ACTIVITIES UNDER WAY IN THE PATHOLOGICAL LABORATORY OF THE BUREAU OF PLANT INDUSTRY.

An important work occupying a considerable part of the laboratory time has been the investigation of a bacterial disease of wheat which has appeared in the Middle West. The causal organism has been isolated and many experiments have proved that it attacks the vegetative parts of the plants as well as the wheat berry. It tends to destroy the leaves, to shorten the heads, and to shrivel the wheat kernels, thus reducing the yield. The department's experiments have shown that it is carried over on the seed. This year field studies were again made from Texas northward to learn as much as possible of its distribution. The disease has not been reported east of Illinois and Wisconsin, and it occurs east of the Mississippi only to a very limited extent. The disease was most prevalent this year in Iowa, but occurred in all the wheat-growing States west of the Mississippi. It is a disease capable of doing great damage in favorable seasons. Studies of the organism have been continued, and much time has been put on the discovery of a proper treatment of the seed wheat with good prospect of ultimate success, because it has been found that the organism causing the disease is very sensitive to a dry heat and to various germicides, such as copper sulphate, mercuric chloride, and formaldehyde.

The cause of the bacterial wilt of cucurbits was isolated and determined in this laboratory, and practically all knowledge of it depends on this work. Investigations on the disease have been continued, and a manuscript is now ready for publication entitled, "Further Studies of Bacterial Wilt of Cucurbits." This covers work on summer and winter transmission of the disease, relation of the wilt bacteria to cucumber beetles, studies on the relative virulence of a large number of isolations from different hosts and localities, host relations, and distribution and control.

An extensive seed-transmission test was carried out in connection with the investigations on bacterial wilt of corn using seed purchased in the open market from widely separated parts of the country, as well as many seed transmission experiments from inoculated plants and seeds. Soil transmission tests were also made. Observations were made relative to distributio and amount of damage in southern New York State, New Jersey, Delaware, Maryland, southern Pennsylvania, Virginia, Tennessee, Kentucky, Ohio, Missouri, Iowa, Minnesota, and Wisconsin. These observations were supported by cultures of the causal organism made from material collected.

A paper has been published this year dealing with three bacterial diseases of lettuce, all original work. Two of these are diseases which occurred destructively in two large commercial lettuce-growing sections of the South. Suggestions for control were given in each case.

A manuscript on a bacterial disease of oats is nearly ready for publication.

Investigations on the wheat disease will be continued. The studies on crown gall will be continued. Studies will be continued on various bacterial diseases of tomatoes and potatoes.

Much work of high importance remains to be done on a variety of destructive bacterial diseases as opportunity offers.

Further studies will be made of the morphology and cultural characters of weak versus virulent isolations of the cucurbit wilt organism (Bacillus tracheiphilus); relation between insects and the causal organisms and host relations, with the idea of more clearly approaching some of the fundamental biological relations between host and parasite and the transmitting insect. With a thorough understanding of these principles the question of control becomes much simplified.

The work on corn wilt will include further tests on seed and soil transmission and observations on distribution, amount of damage done, and also experiments relative to control, such as seed disinfection, search for other modes of transmission, determining in what part of the seed the bacteria find lodgment for transmission from season to season, search for varietal differences in resistance as a possible method of control, and cultural and morphological studies of the causal organism.

Mr. HAUGEN. What other lines of work are you conducting under this item?

Dr. TAYLOR. In connection with the plant-disease survey an entirely unexpected development occurred which illustrates the importance of having such an organization, such an organized piece of human machinery for dealing with plant diseases. A wheat-damaging nematode was discovered in the Shenandoah Valley of Virginia, the previous existence of which in this country, I think, had not been suspected. The pest is transmissible through seed, and if it should become at all widely distributed would be an exceedingly damaging trouble.

Similarly, the case of the newly-discovered wart disease of the potato. The wart disease of the potato, so far as in this country is concerned, was first found last summer in certain of the mill villages of Pennsylvania, where imported potatoes from Europe had been brought in, about 1912, before the plant quarantine act was passed and used as seed. It was in a year of a relatively small American potato crop when potato imports were very heavy. Some of these imported diseased potatoes were used for seed in the gardens in those mill-villages. It is now found there is considerable territory in which the garden soils are already infected with this destructive organism which renders the growth of our American type of potatoes almost impossible, a trouble which we must exercise every effort to clean out of our potato country. It is a trouble which in England has been found so destructive to this important crop that the government is buying and furnishing to the potato growers seed of certain immune varieties and prohibiting them from planting the susceptible varieties in the infested soil.

The CHAIRMAN. We will have to shorten up on the discussion, as you understand this is a short session. Your next item is No. 120, for the investigation of diseases of orchard fruits. There is no change in that, I believe, as far as the amount is concerned.

Dr. TAYLOR. There is no change in this appropriation. Would the committee desire a running comment on that work?

The CHAIRMAN. Just briefly.

Dr. TAYLOR. The more special features of this work during the past year have been the concentration upon distinctive war features under the food production act, particularly the organization and maintenance of a pathological inspection service covering fruits that were in process of transportation and marketing; a service advisory to the Bureau of Markets perishable inspection work, which we feel has rendered very large returns for the expenditure made upon it. It has made possible the placing of that perishable inspection service upon a basis scientifically sound, and of articulating back into the field of production promptly and effectively as it must do if we are permanently to reduce these very heavy losses in the transportation of our fruit and vegetables. That work is costing $18,000 this year.

There is, however, no money carried by this appropriation for the continuance of that work beyond the present fiscal year, as that must necessarily——

The CHAIRMAN. Do you intend to divert some of this present appropriation for that work?

Dr. TAYLOR. We could not without serious obstruction of the investigational work which it is important to continue.

Mr. HAUGEN. How much of this stimulating bill is to be merged into this regular appropriation? In the aggregate, how much is it?

Dr. TAYLOR. In so far as the Bureau of Plant Industry is concerned the food production items included in these estimates total $83,000.

Mr. HAUGEN. How much was the appropriation for that under the appropriation bill?

Dr. TAYLOR. Each of these items that it is proposed to transfer is transferred at the same amount carried by the food-production act.

Mr. HAUGEN. So the whole thing is to be swallowed up by this bill?

Dr. TAYLOR. In the case of these four items—plant-disease survey; sugar-cane disease, which is being worked upon in Porto Rico; sugar-beet- nematode, which is being worked upon in our Western States; and the seed-potato improvement work. The total of the plant-industry items is——

Mr. HAUGEN (interrupting). Of the amount appropriated for research work, how much goes into this?

Dr. TAYLOR. Merely this $83,000.

Mr. HAUGEN. How much was appropriated in the bill?

Dr. TAYLOR. The total for plant-industry work was nearly $460,000.

Mr. HAUGEN. $83,000 of $460,000?

Dr. TAYLOR. About that.

The CHAIRMAN. Your citrus-canker item, 121, page 74, is the next. How long will it take to complete that work, Doctor?

Dr. TAYLOR. Dr. Kellerman is familiar with that, and I will ask him to answer that question.

STATEMENT OF DR. KARL F. KELLERMAN, ASSOCIATE CHIEF OF THE BUREAU OF PLANT INDUSTRY, UNITED STATES DEPARTMENT OF AGRICULTURE.

Dr. KELLERMAN. The work has proceeded so favorably that we have discontinued work in South Carolina and Georgia. The work is in very favorable condition in all the other States. We have just received telegraphic report of a serious outbreak in the Rio Grande section of Texas. That is the only recent outbreak of canker of serious proportions that we have had. The work now consists of locating the occasional dormant infection chiefly on stunted trees, and therefore hard to find, that are scattered through the citrus district.

The CHAIRMAN. How many men have you now employed in this work, Doctor?

Dr. KELLERMAN. We have at the present time 189 men, as compared with close to 500 when we had the largest number of men in the work.

The CHAIRMAN. The States are still cooperating with you?

Dr. KELLERMAN. The States are still cooperating with us on the dollar-for-dollar basis. Florida will probably spend more than we do during the present and next year.

The CHAIRMAN. In view of your statement that we have had only one serious outbreak, don't you think we could reduce the amount of this appropriation without danger?

Dr. KELLERMAN. Not without danger. The cost per inspector on scattered inspections is greater, because the men must be moved more than when they are all working in badly infected regions. In addition, I feel it is absolutely necessary to have a few thousand dollars as a reserve fund. We will plan to hold some $20,000 of this appropriation for occurrences such as this one which has just broken out in Texas, where an isolated planting of citrus trees which had not been discovered——

The CHAIRMAN. Did you use your total appropriation this year?

Dr. KELLERMAN. We came very close to it; I can't tell you exactly; we had only a few thousand dollars return.

The CHAIRMAN. Do you think, with the progress you are making, that you are in position to say that in the course or a year or two you will practically have rid the country of citrus canker and that it will only be necessary to maintain a force sufficient to keep the disease in check?

Dr. KELLERMAN. I think that is possible. Within two or three years we will complete the heavy work, and after that we will do nothing beyond scouting, and if the work goes on as favorably as before, we hope that much of that work can be turned over to the States. I am hoping that in three years we can eliminate this entirely.

Mr. HAUGEN. When this item was first inserted in the bill, two or three hundred thousand dollars, if I remember right, it was done with a view that the work might be completed in two or three years; I think the work was expected to be completed in two or three years.

Dr. KELLERMAN. I think not, Mr. Haugen. I think if you will look up the Secretary's report when he first asked for the appropriation I think you will find the suggestion made in the Secretary's letter that approximately $4,000,000 would in all probability be required to eradicate this disease and it would take a series of years to completely eradicate it; that not only prompt work of a large number of trained men was necessary to carry out the work, but several years would be required to remove the last traces of infection. I think you will find that even in our first statement the total cost is pretty accurately set forth.

Mr. HAUGEN. I remember the committee taking the view of it that we had better make a large appropriation to begin with and get through with it.

Dr. KELLERMAN. Yes; I think we are doing that.

Mr. HAUGEN. You are now asking for $198,000?

Dr. KELLERMAN. Practically that; yes, sir.

Mr. HAUGEN. You think all that amount is necessary?

Dr. KELLERMAN. I think we will spent about $170,000. I think the rest of it we will not spend unless we have some sudden outbreak that I hope will not occur.

Mr. HAUGEN. You feel you are making good progress?

Dr. KELLERMAN. We are making very good progress.

Mr. HAUGEN. How about Florida; has it been entirely exterminated?

Dr. KELLERMAN. Not entirely; but there has been very little loss this year from canker.

Mr. HAUGEN (interposing). How far west did it ever extend?

Dr. KELLERMAN. To Laredo, Tex. It never got to the Pacific coast.

STATEMENT OF DR. WILLIAM A. TAYLOR, CHIEF OF THE BUREAU OF PLANT INDUSTRY, UNITED STATES DEPARTMENT OF AGRICULTURE—Continued.

The CHAIRMAN. Dr. Taylor, your next item is 122, on page 76, for the investigation of diseases of forest and ornamental trees and shrubs, and so on. There is no change in that?

Dr. TAYLOR. No change in that.

The CHAIRMAN. Does anybody desire to ask any questions about that? If not, we will take your next item, which is 123. This has to do with the white-pine blister eradication work.

Dr. TAYLOR. I would like to say with regard to item 122, as a matter of distinct interest and importance, that after 10 years of careful search in connection with the investigation of the chestnut tree bark disease certain apparently highly resistant native chestnut trees have been located, trees which appear to have been attacked by the disease and have thrown it off, that is, to have substantially outgrown the disease in the midst of infection in one of the earliest infected localities in the country where this very destructive disease got a foothold. It appears to afford at least a basis for a constructive breeding program looking forward to the reconstitution of our native chestnut.

You may recall that we have had under way for several years certain hybridizing work, using the resistant Chinese chestnut and our native. The Chinese chestnut, however, while yielding a good nut, does not produce a timber tree. It is relatively a small tree. This appears to give at least a basis for a breeding program and the only one that seems promising in the direction of overcoming the disease.

Mr. LESHER. You are referring to the chestnut blight?

Dr. TAYLOR. Yes, sir.

Mr. LESHER. I think we ought to make an appropriation and let them go ahead with that work.

Dr. TAYLOR. That is being done under the investigational paragraph.

Mr. HAUGEN. Have you given up all hope of its eradication?

Dr. TAYLOR. Yes, sir; of its eradication. We have not for two years past been doing any eradication work.

Mr. WASON. Does chestnut blight work in my section of the country, New England?

Dr. TAYLOR. Yes, sir; very destructive in Connecticut and Massachusetts and in the southern part of New Hampshire.

Mr. WASON. You say you have discovered so we can get trees?

Dr. TAYLOR. Not yet trees. We have merely located and secured nuts and scions from the trees that have endured and come through.

Mr. WASON. So you think there will be an opportunity for us so we can get a reforestation?

Dr. TAYLOR. Yes; I don't wish to raise overoptimistic hopes or expectations of immediate replacement of our native chestnut, but eventually.

Mr. HAUGEN. This $82,315 is for the control of it?

Dr. TAYLOR. No, sir; that is for the investigation of all forest tree diseases, and under this paragraph——

Mr. HAUGEN (interposing). How much do you use for this chestnut blight?

Dr. TAYLOR. I couldn't say exactly without referring to our books.

Mr. HAUGEN. One-half of it, a quarter of it, or a third of it?

Dr. TAYLOR. About $3,500 is used for chestnut blight investigation. Under this paragraph it was necessary to divert a considerable proportion of our force temporarily to special timber inspection service on the Pacific Coast, where the question of detection of weak streaks and spots in the spruce that was being cut for airplanes was found practicable through expert pathological inspection.

Mr. HAUGEN. How do you expect to control this blight? By the destruction of the trees?

Dr. TAYLOR. The chestnut blight?

Mr. HAUGEN. Yes.

Dr. TAYLOR. No; that can only come through the development and propagation of resistant trees. That is, a tree that will be able to resist the disease sufficiently to survive and thrive when attacked, without being materially damaged.

Mr. HAUGEN. Is it a spray?

Dr. TAYLOR. No, sir.

The CHAIRMAN. The next is your white-pine blister work. Briefly, how are you getting along with that work and what hopes can you hold out to us?

Dr. TAYLOR. That work has proceeded during the year under great difficulties, because of our heavy losses of men to the Army and of the difficulty of replacing men with sufficient rapidity. In so far as the territory of the five leaf pine county of the West is concerned, where the largest body of pine timber of high value is located, the scouting has not revealed yet any cases of the disease. We are not entirely sure yet, however, that the West is, in fact, free from the disease. In the East, that is, in New England and in New York, the disease will probably have to be controlled in the future through systematic eradication of the ribes (that is, the currants and the gooseberries) on which the disease passes its intermediate stage. We are confident as a result of the work so far done that practical control methods that are economically possible in white pine production in New England and New York will be established. Further West, in Wisconsin and Minnesota, in what is now the most critical section, we were rather discouraged during the last 8 or 10 weeks to learn of a larger infection in Wisconsin than had previously been located. An infection which will require much larger expenditure and harder work than we have previously anticipated. Minnesota, which is the western outpost of the disease at the present time, is in relatively good shape. We are not recommending any increase of the appropriation, but feel that the appropriation should be continued at its present figure for the next fiscal year along substantially the lines followed this year.

The CHAIRMAN. Any questions? If not, take the next item, No. 124, on page 124, for the investigation of diseases of cotton, potatoes, truck crops, forest crops, drug and related plants. There is no change in your appropriation there?

Dr. TAYLOR. There is no change in the appropriation. The most conspicuous features of the work connected with this paragraph this year have been those upon which we have concentrated much of our available force, both regular and emergency. One feature of this is service work with the Bureau of Markets on the pathological inspection of vegetables in the process of transportation and shipment. The other consists of extension work done cooperatively with a number of the States through which we have placed in those States technical extension pathologists to advise the county agents and assist them promptly to undertake control work on the diseases of these crops. For that work which has been done under the food production act no funds are provided by these estimates.

The CHAIRMAN. Is this the item in which a lot of these pathological people are interested? They had a convention here recently.

Dr. TAYLOR. I presume so. The pathologists of the country have shown much interest in both the fruit pathological inspection service work and the vegetable pathological inspection and extension work.

The CHAIRMAN. A committee called on me the other day from the experiment stations and pleaded very strongly for a continuance of the emergency appropriation for this character of work. I think it was this work.

Dr. TAYLOR. That would be the work they have in mind.

The CHAIRMAN. Did they have a meeting in Baltimore a few days ago?

Dr. TAYLOR. Yes, sir. The larger part of the work that I have mentioned has been under the food production act. Under the food production act we have spent about $88,720; for the inspection work, about $28,550, and for the pathological extension work, about $60,170.

The CHAIRMAN. Anything further on that item, Doctor?

Dr. TAYLOR. No, sir; except to say we have no provision for the continuance of that very important work in this estimate.

The CHAIRMAN. Page 79, item 126, for soil bacteriology and plant-nutrition investigation, and so on. There doesn't seem to be any change in that.

Dr. TAYLOR. I think not.

The CHAIRMAN. The next is on page 80, item 127, for soil-fertility investigation. There seems to be no change in that.

Dr. TAYLOR. No, sir; the same character of work has been continued.

The CHAIRMAN. Any questions, gentlemen? The next item is, 128, on page 80, for acclimatization and adaptation investigations of cotton, corn, and other crops introduced from tropical regions, and for the improvement of cotton and other fiber plants by cultural methods, breeding, and selection. Is there any change in that, Doctor?

Dr. TAYLOR. No, sir; not in that work.

The CHAIRMAN. May I ask you about that New Zealand flax proposition?

Dr. TAYLOR. The $3,000 for that item became available in October, and we have not actually begun operations under that yet. We are now endeavoring to find a suitable man to carry it forward. It will necessarily involve considerable time as there is practically no New Zealand flax being grown in this country. One of the first things to be done is to determine the quality of fiber that can be produced under American conditions in California and perhaps Florida.

The CHAIRMAN. But you haven't done that yet?

Dr. TAYLOR. No, sir.

Mr. HAUGEN. But this appropriation is for experimenting in the production of flax.

Dr. TAYLOR. For experimenting in the production of New Zealand flax. We have not made any plantings of New Zealand flax.

Mr. HAUGEN (interposing). Are there any plants in the United States?

Dr. TAYLOR. Yes, sir; a few scattering small plantings in southern California, and I understand there is a planting in Florida.

Mr. HAUGEN. Seed can be procured here in the United States?

Dr. TAYLOR. I think not. I think seed can be brought from New Zealand.

Mr. HAUGEN. Is there any prohibition against the importation of them?

Dr. TAYLOR. There is prohibition against diseased plants, but not against the seed.

Mr. HAUGEN. Then any quantity that they have here could be tested out?

Dr. TAYLOR. In a small way.

Mr. HAUGEN. Does it require any extensive experimenting to ascertain——

Dr. TAYLOR (interposing). Not after the plants have attained sufficient age to determine their fiber yield and the quality.

Mr. HAUGEN. What do you mean by age; the age of the plant?

Dr. TAYLOR. Yes; my recollection is it requires five years from seed to yield leaves that are mature enough for a harvest of the fiber.

Mr. HAUGEN. The International Harvester Co. imported some of these plants, didn't it, and carried on an experiment?

Dr. TAYLOR. I understood that they made a shipment of plants which were found diseased and were destroyed. I think none of their importations actually got into the ground to grow.

Mr. HAUGEN. According to that you will have to wait five years or you will have to go to New Zealand?

Dr. TAYLOR. We are hoping to connect up with these small scattered patches and save time in the preliminaries in that way. If necessary we will bring in the seed from——

The CHAIRMAN. This item was put in the bill last year by the committee and not by the department, was it not?

Dr. TAYLOR. That is my recollection.

The CHAIRMAN. We had a very full discussion at that time.

Dr. TAYLOR. Yes, sir; but the money did not become available until October.

The CHAIRMAN. You haven't been able to do anything so far except to look around to get a man?

Dr. TAYLOR. No, sir.

The CHAIRMAN. Item 129, page 82, for the investigation, testing, and improvement of plants yielding drugs, spices, poisons, oils, and related products and by-products, and for general physiological and fermentation investigation. Is there any change in that?

Dr. TAYLOR. No, sir.

The CHAIRMAN. The next is on page 83, item 130, for crop technological investigations, including the study of plant-infesting nematodes. There are no changes in that?

Dr. TAYLOR. No, sir; the work at present is chiefly upon the plant-infesting nematodes. The work is continuing satisfactorily along the lines previously reported.

The CHAIRMAN. The next item is on page 83, item 131, for biophysical investigations in connection with the various lines of work herein authorized. Anything new on that?

Dr. TAYLOR. No, sir.

The CHAIRMAN. Your next item is on page 84. No. 132, for studying and testing commercial seeds, and so on. Anything new on that?

Dr. TAYLOR. This work has demonstrated its very great importance during the last year, in particular due to the scrutiny that has been kept of the importations of field seed, especially clover and grass seeds through which there have been kept out of the country considerable quantities of dead seed that otherwise would have gone as they formerly did, to the farmers, mixed with live seed, at live-seed prices. We feel that the operation of the import seed law is proving distinctively advantageous to the farmers in protecting them against dead and impure seed.

The CHAIRMAN. The next item is 133, for the investigation and improvement of cereals and methods of cereal production, and the study of cereal diseases. There is an apparent decrease in the item of $9,000.

Dr. TAYLOR. That is only apparent.

Mr. HAUGEN. These are new items that were introduced in the last bill. Have you any report to make on this?

Dr. TAYLOR. The corn root and stalk disease item and the barberry item were new last year. I will ask Dr. Kellerman if he will discuss these as he has had direct supervision of them.

FURTHER STATEMENT OF DR. KARL F. KELLERMAN, ASSOCIATE CHIEF OF THE BUREAU OF PLANT INDUSTRY, UNITED STATES DEPARTMENT OF AGRICULTURE.

Dr. KELLERMAN. The investigation of the seedling and root disease has been progressing very satisfactorily. It is found to be rather widespread, more widespread than we had hoped originally and the methods for control are just being developed. We are just learning what the symptoms of the disease are, and what causes it. It may be caused by several different fungi. The fungus that causes wheat scab will cause this corn-root rot.

Mr. HAUGEN. Can it be overcome by a selection of seed?

Dr. KELLERMAN. It can be very largely reduced by a selection of seed, that is, we believe so. It is not improbable that developing methods for diagnosing this trouble in the ear corn may make it possible to eliminate a diseased ear and in that way avoid the spreading of the disease.

Mr. HAUGEN (interposing). Would the selection of the seed require examination of an expert or a microscopical examination?

Dr. KELLERMAN. It will now. You can detect it in a good many severe cases with the naked eye.

Mr. HAUGEN. Have you gotten far enough along with your investigation that you can make any recommendation?

Dr. KELLERMAN. I think not yet. About as far as we could go now would be to say that the standard methods of selecting seed corn from healthy looking plants are going to eliminate a great deal of the disease. They won't eliminate all.

Mr. HAUGEN. But we find also that those making a specialty of the careful selection of seed find these weak stalks.

Dr. KELLERMAN. Yes, sir. We have a peculiar disease to deal with, probably three or four diseases, and the complications of the symptoms of these different diseases makes the development of a method of diagnosis difficult.

Mr. HAUGEN. You think it is well worth continuing?

Dr. KELLERMAN. No doubt about it, I think. I think we will develop not only a way of recognizing the diseased ears when they come from the field but will develop rotations to check the trouble, and furthermore we may be able to develop methods of seed treatment.

Mr. LEE. You think that would be the best way of doing it in the end?

Dr. KELLERMAN. In the end I think the question of seed selection and the development of disease-resistant corn is going to be the important thing.

Mr. LEE. You treat wheat with the smut——

Dr. KELLERMAN (interposing). Yes; we think the seed treatment may be possible, but it is very difficult to treat seed for bacterial diseases.

Mr. HAUGEN. You have no suggestion on the seed treatment at the present time?

Dr. KELLERMAN. No, sir.

Mr. HAUGEN. How about the others, oats and barberry?

Dr. KELLERMAN. The barberry eradication work is very successful. In earlier years there has been a great deal of skepticism as to the responsibility of barberry for the epidemics of wheat rust. Barberries were found much more widely distributed in the wheat-growing regions than anybody realized. Furthermore, a close association of barberry plants and the fields that have suffered continuously from rust has been established. This was not a bad rust year so it is difficult to say to what extent the barberry campaign has reduced wheat rust this year. Climatic factors did not favor rust.

Mr. HAUGEN. That had much to do with it this year, the climatic factors?

Dr. KELLERMAN. Undoubtedly.

Mr. HAUGEN. Very often we don't have the black rust at all. This year the wheat matured before the hot winds. Hasn't that been true?

Dr. KELLERMAN. That has been true; but, in addition to these very destructive epidemics that damage large areas and which occur only if the weather favors rust, there have been small areas that have lost more or less from rust every year.

Mr. HAUGEN. But you think that the barberry is the cause of the black rust, or you think that the eradication of the barberry bush will eradicate the black rust?

Dr. KELLERMAN. I think we can prevent these very large destructive epidemics. There may be an occasional epidemic of black rust, because when you get in regions farther south the winters are not cold enough to kill the red spores of the rust.

Mr. HAUGEN. The barberry bush is the only host in the earlier stages, I believe it is claimed?

Dr. KELLERMAN. No; the barberry bush is the necessary host in starting off the very resistant winter spores in the spring. Those won't affect the wheat, but the so-called summer spores which can live on the native grass all winter in southern wheat areas can start epidemics of rust in the wheat.

Mr. HAUGEN. How much time does it require to develop a spore?

Dr. KELLERMAN. Just a few days; it depends on the weather.

The CHAIRMAN. How long have you had this appropriation?

Dr. KELLERMAN. This work is handled under the $100,000 appropriation for black and stripe rust and the $150,000 appropriation for eradication of barberry.

The CHAIRMAN. You could not do much in the past two months except to organize your campaign. What is your method of doing that?

Dr. KELLERMAN. This work has been carried on since the beginning of last spring, very early last spring. As soon as there seemed to be a practical certainty of the department's having funds to start this work, the educational campaign which is evidenced by that poster (indicating) was immediately started.

The CHAIRMAN. And you propose to keep up that line of work next year?

Dr. KELLERMAN. We feel it is necessary. Without going into a long discussion I would suggest that I put into the record a statement showing the distribution of the barberry and the progress of our work.

Mr. HAUGEN. Do you find any black rust outside the barberry-infected places?

Dr. KELLERMAN. In many places people would say, "there is no barberry in this region, but we have wheat rust." In those regions we found in sheltered places, especially where birds roost or where seed may have been carried accidently, little barberry plants thoroughly rusted and ready to carry the infection back to the field.

The CHAIRMAN. Do you actually do the digging up or merely induce it?

Dr. KELLERMAN. We induce it. I think none of the work of actually digging up has been carried on by our men.

The CHAIRMAN. In this publicity campaign are you using the forces of the States Relations Service?

Dr. KELLERMAN. To the fullest extent.

Mr. HAUGEN. So far as the publicity and what the States have been doing, in the States that have taken hold of it, very little has been done outside of that?

Dr. KELLERMAN. I think we do about as much as could be done. The campaign has been very successful.

Mr. HAUGEN. Have you investigated the number of States that have adequate laws to meet the situation, that require the destruction of the barberry bush?

Dr. KELLERMAN. There isn't very much in the late enactments. North Dakota has had a law prohibiting the common barberry for about a year and a half.

Mr. HAUGEN. What about Wisconsin?

Dr. KELLERMAN. They have authority under their nursery-inspection law to condemn infected bushes and the State entomologist has ordered the destruction of infected barberry bushes. The order does not require the destruction of all bushes; to that extent the law is defective.

Mr. HAUGEN. Are you contemplating calling their attention to that?

Dr. KELLERMAN. That has been called to their attention by the nurserymen in all these States. I would like to add that the nurserymen in this work have responded very helpfully.

Mr. HAUGEN. Do they meet with any resistance in going into a man's front yard to dig out a barberry bush that he has spent a good deal of money on in fertilizing it and cultivating it?

Dr. KELLERMAN. There have been very few cases of friction. I think in every case it was the result of over enthusiasm of a little squad of eradicators that started in to urge the destruction of bushes without sufficient explanation of why they were doing it. There has been no permanent objection, and I don't think there were altogether more than a dozen people that objected. Their objections have been very satisfactorily met, and they have been perfectly willing as soon as they thoroughly understood what the campaign was heading for.

Mr. HAUGEN. You discussed it in public meetings?

Dr. KELLERMAN. Yes, sir. That is the main activity in getting a large number of people to understand it.

Mr. HAUGEN. You are going to prosecute the work vigorously from now on?

Dr. KELLERMAN. Yes, sir.

Mr. HAUGEN. Use every dollar you can get?

Dr. KELLERMAN. Yes, indeed.

THE BARBERRY ERADICATION CAMPAIGN.

The barberry eradication campaign was carried on by the Bureau of Plant Industry with the cooperation of the States Relations Service and State officials of Ohio, Michigan, Illinois, Indiana, Wisconsin, Minnesota, Iowa, Nebraska, South Dakota, North Dakota, Montana, Wyoming, and Colorado. Since the campaign could not be developed to its full effectiveness until the early spring, since it had to be supported by incidental expenditures from general cereal investigations, it was concentrated on the States of Wisconsin, Minnesota, North Dakota, South Dakota, Iowa, and Nebraska, where the presence of the barberry has been the cause of the most heavy losses.

Legal authority for the eradication of barberry bushes existed only in North Dakota, and South Dakota. In Colorado, the State entomologist has authority under the terms of the crop pest law to require the destruction of the common barberry. This regulation was promulgated and is being effectively inforced. In Wisconsin, the State entomologist has authority, under the nursery inspection law, to condemn all barberry bushes infected. In Michigan, the State entomologist has similar authority, and has taken similar action. Practically the same authority and similar action exists in Indiana. In Illinois, the State director of agriculture issued an order requiring the destruction of all infected barberry bushes. Soon after the beginning of the campaign, the Public Safety Commission of Minnesota issued Order No. 28 requiring the eradication of all common barberries. The State Council of Defense of Nebraska issued an order very similar to the Minnesota order.

All of the States interested in the campaign has issued quarantines prohibiting the importation of common barberries from other States.

The Treasury Department issued an order to custodians of all Federal buildings in the States in the barberry eradication campaign requiring the immediate removal of all common barberries.

An appeal was made to railroads, and many of them, including the Pennsylvania, the Baltimore and Ohio, and others, took steps to secure the removal of all common barberry bushes from railroad property in the interested States.

The National Nurserymen's Association in their meeting at Chicago, June 30, 1918, passed the following resolution:

"In view of the information given us by pathologists regarding the dissemination of black rust of grains, be it resolved that it be the sense of this assembly that the propagation and dissemination of Berberis vulgaris and purpurea be discontinued, and we appeal to all loyal and patriotic members of this organization to support us in this position."

Practically every nursery of any consequence whatever in the barberry eradication area has destroyed all of the bushes growing on its premises. The Minnesota Nurserymen destroyed 598,549. At least as many, if not more, were destroyed by Wisconsin nurserymen. One nurseryman in Iowa destroyed over 50,000 bushes, and many nurserymen throughout Illinois, Michigan, Minnesota, and Wisconsin destroyed as many or more. Over 23,000 bushes were destroyed in Cedar Rapids, Iowa. Practically all of the bushes which have been located by the scouts have been destroyed.

An appeal was sent to the members of the National Landscape Gardeners' Association, urging them to omit common barberry from future plantings. Replies were received from about 50, and all indicated their intention to comply with the request.

Results of the campaign.—From the above it is quite evident that strong sentiment for the eradication of the barberry has been aroused.

It bcame evident early in the campaign that there were more barberry bushes in the upper half of the United States than anyone had ever suspected. Many bushes were removed by nurserymen and private citizens before any of the State or Department of Agriculture agents had a chance to record them. Yet some idea of the number may be gained from the following facts:

In Colorado one man working for one month located over 2,000 bushes. In Illinois over 40,000 bushes were located in the northern quarter of the State, north of latitude 41°. In this part of the State it is estimated that there was no area 10 miles square which did not contain barberry bushes. In South Dakota one man located over 21,000 common barberry bushes. In Wisconsin 95,000 bushes were located on private and public grounds. In addition thousands had already been destroyed by nurserymen and thousands more were found escaped from cultivation. There were between 10,000 to 15,000 bushes on the property of the University of Wisconsin. Along the Park and Pleasure Association Drives near Madison, Wis., there were at least 25,000. In Minnesota there were about 600,000 bushes in nurseries and 50,000 others were located on private and public grounds. Barberry bushes were found in every county in Wisconsin with two exceptions. These counties in which none were found were in the northern undeveloped portions of the State. In Grand Rapids, Mich., 35 plantings containing 202 bushes were located in one day, after the city had been scouted a few months previously, of these 146 were dug immediately. In Bay City, Mich., a 5-acre neglected barberry plantation, 50 or 60 years old, contained about 1,500 clumps of bushes. In addition there were about 30,000 bushes in the city. It was soon found that there were more bushes in the country than had been generally supposed. In South Dakota, for instance, where scarcely any bushes were supposed to occur in the country, a hedge half mile long on both sides of the road was located in the midst of an important wheat-growing region. In northern Nebraska there was a hedge in the country over a mile long. Equally large hedges were found in the country in Wisconsin, Michigan, Ohio, and northern Illinois.

The following is a typical statement from a barberry scout:

"The work goes on well here, but I am more and more bewildered by the universal presence of the barberry. Hedges and hedges, bushes and bushes confront me everywhere I go, even on farms, and all are rusted. The whole wheat section, so far as I have seen it, is full of barberries."

It was known that the barberry had escaped from cultivation in the New England States, but it was not generally believed that they had escaped in the grain-growing regions of the Middle West. However, although no careful survey has been made of country districts, barberry was found to have escaped from cultivation in at least 12 places in Wisconsin, in about the same number of places in Michigan, and at several places in Illinois and in Iowa. In Minnesota, fairly extensive areas of wild barberries were found along the Mississippi River and at various other places in the grain-growing districts of the State. Between Anoka and Elk River, Minn., barberries have escaped extensively for 20 miles along the Mississippi River. At Trempealeau, Wis., and Winona, Minn., the bushes have escaped to the bluffs along the Mississippi River and are present in large numbers. The significance of the escape of the barberry from cultivation is perfectly obvious.

While the berries are not eaten by many birds and then only when other food is scarce, they are scattered somewhat in this way.

One of the arguments advanced by a great many conservative people against barberry eradication was that rust epidemics occurred in the upper Mississippi Valley before barberry bushes were grown. Definite records obtained show very clearly that this is not true. These records show that barberry seeds or bushes were brought into new regions by the first settlers from New England and Canada. In Wisconsin, for instance, it has been shown very clearly that large numbers of barberries were planted as early as the decade between 1840 and 1850. In the same way it has been shown that the earliest settlers in Michigan brought barberry bushes with them. In Minnesota many living bushes 50 or 60 years old have been found and a few of them are as much as 70 years old. The situation in Ohio, Indiana, Illinois, Nebraska, and Iowa is the same.

In these early times the barberry was cultivated to a certain extent as a fruit bush. The berries were used particularly for preserves, jelly, and wine making. Barberry bushes were, therefore, planted in considerable numbers around the first log cabins in the Middle West. It is from these early plantings that many of the scattered bushes have escaped.

It soon became evident that barberries rusted much more universally and over a wider area than had ever been supposed. It had been supposed that the bushes did not rust much south of the southern boundary of Iowa. However, the bushes rust heavily in Nebraska, Colorado, in northern Missouri, and quite far south in Illinois. It was stated by eminent botanists that the bushes never rusted in Illinois. However, it was found that the entire northern quarter of the State, the only part which was carefully surveyed, was full of rusted barberry bushes. In the same way, it was generally thought that the bushes rusted very infrequently in Nebraska. Some of the heaviest infection found in any place, however, was found in the southwestern and southern counties of that State. The same is true of Ohio. Infected bushes were found even at an altitude of over 6,000 feet in Wyoming. In Wisconsin practically every barberry bush located was rusted except in the centers of the largest cities. The same is true of Michigan, Minnesota, North Dakota, South Dakota, and Iowa. Infected bushes were found as far south as Jackson and Knoxville, Tenn. The bushes rusted very early in the spring.

Heavily infected bushes were found by May 10 in Iowa, Minnesota, and Wisconsin. At that time no stem rust whatever could be found away from barberry bushes. This is especially significant because the records of rusted bushes are very incomplete. Tremendous numbers of the bushes had been removed before they were seen by scouts. Again, many districts in several States were not carefully scouted at all, and undoubtedly large numbers of rusted barberry bushes occurred.

Enough evidence has been obtained to convince the most skeptical that the barberry is the most important factor in the spread of rust north of the northern boundary of Missouri. The situation south of this line is not so well known. About May 25 the grasses and grains near rusted barberries became heavily infected and the rust soon spread from these centers of infection to other grains and grasses until it became quite general throughout the entire region. A few typical examples will show what effect the rusted bushes have on the surrounding grains and grasses. At Lake Preston, S. Dak., a hedge one-half mile long was heavily rusted, and wheat for a distance of over 3 miles also was heavily attacked. The amount of rust was inversely proportional to the distance from the barberry bushes, indicating very clearly that the bushes had served as centers of infection and that the rust had spread directly from them.

In Minnesota five farmers in Lyon County had discontinued growing wheat because it was always destroyed by rust. Examination of the locality by the county agent showed that there were a great many wild barberry bushes in an old hog pasture in the center of this rust area. At Lake Minnetonka, Minn., a farmer had been unable to grow grain for 10 years because it had always been destroyed by rust. This year, however, a barberry hedge on his farm was removed and his oats yielded 60 bushels per acre—the first successful crop in 10 years.

In Montana all stem rust found could be traced directly to barberry bushes. In Wisconsin practically every serious outbreak of stem rust was traced directly to infected barberry bushes. Affidavits were secured from several farmers or groups of farmers showing very clearly that the evidence was so conclusive that they themselves took the initiative in calling it to the attention of Federal or State authorities and requested these authorities to do everything within their power to secure eradication of the barberry bushes.

It is especially significant that some of these most striking cases occurred in Ohio, Indiana, and Montana, States in which the barberry was not thought to be a prime factor in the spread of rust.

Coupled with the results of the rust overwintering studies, which showed that the stem rust, at least in the winter of 1917-18, did not live through in the red stage, and the further fact that the rust appeared near infected barberry bushes in the Northern States quite as soon as it began to appear in the Gulf States, the evidence against the common barberry was absolutely conclusive.

Cooperation of Canada.—Canadian pathologists, at a meeting in Guelph, Ontario, December 6-7, adopted resolutions requesting Provincial and Dominion authorities to take all legitimate means for eradicating the common barberry entirely from Canada. Since Manitoba and Saskatchewan have already eradicated most of the bushes from those Provinces, and since the barberry is known to be extremely important in Ontario and other Provinces in eastern Canada, it is quite likely that much will be accomplished in the Dominion. The closest cooperation between Canada and United States is quite essential, as the barberry rust does not respect boundaries, particularly when these boundaries are imaginary lines. It would be futile for Canada to eradicate barberries unless the United States succeeded in completely eradicating them from the several States. In the same way if the bushes are eradicated from the United States and they remain in Canada those remaining in Canada would be a constant menace to the grain crops of the States.

There is every reason to believe that the present campaign will not fizzle as many previous barberry campaigns have done. Sentiment is thoroughly aroused and public-spirited citizens are demanding that the barberry menace be removed. Pathologists are cooperating in the campaign in a way in which they have never cooperated before. It is to be hoped, therefore, that the Federal and State authorities will continue to take a very definite and firm stand in regard to the complete eradication of the barberry.

CEREAL-SMUT ERADICATION.

The campaign for the prevention of cereal smuts by seed treatment was somewhat similar in character to the campaign for the prevention of rust epidemics of cereals by barberry eradication. The smut campaign, however, was conducted as an emergency activity under the food-stimulation bill.

The following brief statement regarding the campaign for the prevention of cereal smuts beginning in September, 1917, indicates what results have been accomplished, and also estimates the annual losses resulting from wheat, oat, and barley smuts.

(1) Twenty-five per cent more farmers treated seed in 1917-18 seeding season than in 1916-17. (Based on survey and on increased demand for formaldehyde and copper sulphate in rural communities.)

(2) Number of farmers personally advised on their farms regarding smuts and smut prevention, 21,500.

(3) Number of farmers and others receiving instruction through seed-treatment demonstrations and personal instruction average 2,630 per State in 43 States, or a total of 113,090.

(4) Assuming that the smut campaign has resulted in a 25 per cent increase in acreage planted to treated seed (a fairly conservative estimate) the saving in wheat will amount to 5,000,000 bushels, oats 27,000,000 bushels, and barley 1,000,000 bushels.

(5) Estimated national loss due to wheat smuts in 1918 crop, 25,500,000 bushels.

(6) Estimated national loss due to oat smuts in 1918 crop, 110,000,000 bushels.

(7) Estimated national loss due to barley smuts in 1918 crop, 6,000,000 bushels.

(8) Minnesota and Nebraska together lost this year over 8,000,000 bushels of wheat from stinking smut alone. Practically all of this could have been prevented.

STATEMENT OF DR. WILLIAM A. TAYLOR, CHIEF OF THE BUREAU OF PLANT INDUSTRY, UNITED STATES DEPARTMENT OF AGRICULTURE—Continued.

The CHAIRMAN. Take your next item, 134, on page 87, Dr. Taylor, for the investigation and improvement of tobacco and the methods of tobacco production and handling.

Dr. TAYLOR. That work has proceeded substantially along the lines heretofore followed.

The CHAIRMAN. Any questions on that? If not, we will take up item No. 135, on page 88, for testing and breeding fibrous plants, including the testing of flax straw and hemp, in cooperation with the North Dakota Agricultural College, which may be used for paper making. There is no change in that item?

Dr. TAYLOR. No, sir.

Mr. HAUGEN. How much are you spending on this flax straw?

Dr. TAYLOR. The total in that item is $16,000 and odd; I can not answer exactly as to flax. The flax-straw work this last year has been the major feature of that work. The work has reached a stage where it appears almost certain that out of the flax straw qualities of paper can be made which during the present shortage of linen rags (which is world-wide, as is the shortage of new linen) will be suitable not only for high-grade bond paper, and so on, but for currency paper. This activity is now working very actively in cooperation with the Bureau of Engraving and Printing at their request in an effort to produce a paper that will be suitable for currency.

Mr. HAUGEN. But I think the thing that the department had in mind at the time was for developing its utility for binding twine.

Dr. TAYLOR. No, sir; this work has aimed at the production of paper and binder board from the start.

Mr. HAUGEN. You have abandoned the idea entirely of making twine?

Dr. TAYLOR. We have not prosecuted that; we have not undertaken that.

Mr. HAUGEN. It was given a thorough trial by the International Harvester Co. and abandoned.

Dr. TAYLOR. Yes, sir; and our understanding was that they did not succeed.

Mr. HAUGEN. I think the thought was that some new ideas might be introduced along by the side of it.

The CHAIRMAN. Take the next item, Doctor, No. 136, on page 88, for breeding and physiological study of alkali-resistant and drought-resistant crops.

Dr. TAYLOR. The work under this item has continued as during the last two years.

Mr. HAUGEN. What can you tell us about alkali? That is a very interesting question.

Dr. TAYLOR. Under this paragraph there are being developed crops that resist alkali to a greater or less extent. There have been developed varieties of cotton that made possible the production of Egyption cotton in the Southwest—California and Arizona.

Mr. HAUGEN. Do you know of anything that can be grown in our country, in Iowa alkaline land?

Dr. TAYLOR. No; not on land strongly alkaline. In fact, cotton will not grow in land that is strongly alkaline.

Mr. HAUGEN. In fact, nothing will grow in land that is alkaline?

Dr. TAYLOR. Nothing that is useful.

The CHAIRMAN. The next item is 137, on page 88, for sugar-plant investigations, including studies of diseases and the improvement of the beet and beet seed, etc. There you have an increase, Doctor, of $10,000.

Dr. TAYLOR. We have a total increase there, Mr. Chairman, of $30,000 in two items, and both of these are transfers of investigational items from the the food-production act. The first one is for $10,000 for sugar-beet nematode work. The sugar-beet nematode has been found in certain of the irrigated districts in California, Utah, Idaho, and Colorado to an extent that is peculiarly harmful to this crop for this reason: That the production of beets annually must be made within an economical haul of the sugar factory.

If the land is permitted to become infested with a destructive organism such as the sugar-beet nematode to the extent that it cuts the sugar beet out of profitable growth, the production of the factory is necessarily reduced, because new land for beets can only be secured at a distance entirely beyond the economical hauling range. The work so far has been devoted chiefly to the location of the actually infested farms and soils and the determination of what crop-rotation methods are most promising to clean out the infested fields. This work requires vigorous, continuous prosecution if we are to maintain the sugar production in certain of those irrigated districts.

The CHAIRMAN. What is the total amount that you propose to use for this sugar-beet nematode work?

Dr. TAYLOR. $10,000.

The CHAIRMAN. You haven't done any work on this line before?

Dr. TAYLOR. No, sir.

Mr. HAUGEN. The disease is quite general?

Dr. TAYLOR. No, sir. It is restricted to certain of the irrigated sugar-beet fields of California, Utah, Colorado, and Idaho.

Mr. HAUGEN. Are the yields falling off in those sections?

Dr. TAYLOR. On the farms infested, yes, sir; and this necessarily will continue until it is corrected.

The CHAIRMAN. Doctor, the hookworm of the human being seems to thrive most in a hot and humid country. I wonder if the nematode has the same characteristic?

Dr. TAYLOR. When we say "nematode," we mean almost a million organisms.

The CHAIRMAN. I was struck by the fact that this is indicated only in those irrigated sections where they have water.

Dr. TAYLOR. The common and most widespread plant-infesting nematode, that which causes the root knot of plants in our southern States, is worse in soil that does not freeze in winter. The sugar-beet nematode, however, stands freezing. It came to this country, so far as known, from Germany. It has been troublesome there in the beet industry, and it has a more northern range than the common root knot nematode.

The CHAIRMAN. This $20,000 is to be used how?

Dr. TAYLOR. The $20,000 item is to continue the work on the relatively newly discovered mottling disease of sugar cane, which about a year ago became evident was quite widely distributed and distinctive in Porto Rico. The work upon that has been well begun and it is necessary to continue it. Also to ascertain definitely whether the suspicion is correct that the disease is already upon our mainland. We have got to begin at the beginning of the next growing season a very thorough investigation of this.

The CHAIRMAN. The next item is on page 90, item 138, for investigations in economic and systematic botany. There is no change in that?

Dr. TAYLOR. No, sir; no change in that.

Mr. HAUGEN. What is this, for the utilization of wild plants and grasses and so on?

Dr. TAYLOR. The work under that covers such features as the cultural improvement of the blueberry, for instance, which is coming forward in a very gratifying way. The grazing work is an advisory study of the plant flora of the forest ranges, in cooperation with the Forest Service. We do the technical botanical work for the Forestry Service. They control the ranges of the forest reservations, and our work in that field under this paragraph is devoted to the technical and taxonomic work that they require.

Mr. HAUGEN. Then it has reference to the selection of seed most adaptable to cut-over land?

Dr. TAYLOR. No, sir; we have not gone into that. The Forest Service has been handling that, but the determination of the identity of the many species that are found in the range flora which they are dealing with.

Mr. HAUGEN. How many new varieties have been introduced—what progress have you made?

Dr. TAYLOR. We have not worked on the line of introduction. It is the study of the existing flora.

Mr. WASON. Is it used for grazing purposes?

Dr. TAYLOR. Yes, sir.

Mr. WASON. What benefit is it to the American farmer to spend time on that?

Dr. TAYLOR. The work as it stands here is almost wholly with respect to the technical identification of the plants that the Forest Service needs to have done in connection with its studies and experiments in the actual management and administration of the ranges——

Mr. WASON (interposing). This will take, covering a series of years, several appropriations from the Treasury to bring about what you have in mind or what you have described, will it not?

Dr. TAYLOR. Yes, sir. What it represents is the time that is spent in that sort of work. This is on page 90, paragraph 138.

Mr. WASON. $22,000.

Dr. TAYLOR. For all the investigations in economic and systematic botany and the improvement and utilization of wild plants and grazing lands.

Mr. WASON. Is it of any benefit outside of that particular area where it is scattered that you are studying?

Dr. TAYLOR. This improvement of the blueberry has reached a stage where commercial blueberry culture has begun in New Jersey and I think in Minnesota. I am not sure but that it has in New Hampshire.

Mr. WASON. They have been doing that for half a century.

Dr. TAYLOR. This is cultural work.

Mr. WASON. I know a farmer who lives 20 miles from my home that has spent one thousand or fifteen hundred dollars a year on 100 acres outside of his farm, in his pasture. He looks after it as carefully as anybody does his orchard.

Dr. TAYLOR. That type of work has been going on for quite a while, but in this work varieties are being bred which yield fruit much superior to the wild blueberry in size and quality, which are considered to be promising for commercial planting.

Mr. WASON. Have you got any samples of that fruit that you speak of?

Dr. TAYLOR. We have in preserving solution. I will be very glad if you could come over to Mr. Coville's laboratory and see what he has accomplished. We feel that after a century of effort to improve and to domesticate the blueberry success is at last in sight; methods of propagating, transplanting, and improvement through breeding have been perfected that are now being put into commercial application. It points toward a profitable utilization of much of our eastern acid-soil territory from New Jersey to Maine and westward through the Lakes region that has not previously been profitable.

Mr. WASON. That is an acid soil?

Dr. TAYLOR. The blueberry is an acid-soil crop. It does not thrive in our good garden soils, which are alkaline.

Mr. WASON. I hope you will improve the blueberry as well as they have improved the domestic strawberry over the wild. They have never done that.

The CHAIRMAN. Take your next item, No. 139, on page 91; there is no change in that amount?

Dr. TAYLOR. No, sir; that work is being continued as it has been going on practically since it was started.

Mr. THOMPSON. How long has that work been going on?

Dr. TAYLOR. Dry farming?

Mr. THOMPSON. Yes, sir.

Dr. TAYLOR. Perhaps 13 years.

Mr. THOMPSON. What progress have you made in improving production on land of that character?

Dr. TAYLOR. Distinct progress has been made with respect to certain phases of this——

Mr. THOMPSON (interposing). This takes in the Mandan farm?

Dr. TAYLOR. Yes, sir; this takes in the whole dry-farming tillage investigation work. The field stations are all in the Great Plains territory, reaching from North Dakota to Texas. Suppose I furnish a summary that would outline what has been done.

Mr. THOMPSON. I would be glad if you would do that. We have some of that land in Oklahoma, semiarid.

Dr. TAYLOR. We have a field station at Woodward, Okla.

Mr. THOMPSON. And the State has a station beyond that in the Panhandle.

The CHAIRMAN. I want to make this suggestion: All of this was covered very fully last year in the hearings. If you gentlemen would take those hearings and run over them at night, I think you would find in most instances these very things you speak of, and in most cases the bureau issued a report.

Dr. TAYLOR. I think in this instance we could help the committee by preparing a short summary that would help you.

(The statement referred to follows:)

STATEMENT OUTLINING RESULTS OF THE WORK OF THE BUREAU OF PLANT INDUSTRY IN CONNECTION WITH DRY-LAND AGRICULTURE INVESTIGATIONS.

The Office of Dry-Land Agriculture of the Bureau of Plant Industry was created July 1, 1905. Thirteen years ago the information on the possibilities of agriculture in the semiarid sections of the country was meager and chaotic. The uncertain crop production, sometimes abundant and sometimes a failure, resulting from an uncertain or fluctuating rainfall, made the vast plains of fertile soil in this area either an attractive or a forbidding field to the prospective farmer, depending upon the experience and objective of the one from whom he obtained his information. Nowhere was there accurate authentic information by which the settler could be protected from the unscrupulous or from enthusiastic but unsound exploitation, or by which endeavor could be directed along safe and productive lines.

The section of the country to which each crop is adapted and the best and most profitable methods of producing spring wheat, oats, corn, barley, kafir, milo, and winter wheat have been determined and published in Department of Agriculture Bulletins 214, 218, 219, 222, 242, 268, 595; and Farmer's Bulletin 895. While certain crops in well-defined areas have shown profitable response to intensive cultural methods, the largest net profits have usually been obtained from crops raised by cultural methods involving a low cost of production rather than from high yields obtained from methods involving a high cost of production. In other words, extensive instead of intensive systems of farming should be followed. From results under known conditions in the past years the average results of a series of years in any section can now be foretold with a reasonable degree of certainty, but nowhere in the Great Plains can the results of a single season be forecast.

It has been found that the relative value of early and late fall plowing and of spring plowing is determined by the amount and distribution of rain and snow before and after plowing. The subject is discussed in detail in Department of Agriculture Bulletin 253.

By a long-continued series of experiments covering a wide range of soils and climatic conditions, it has been conclusively proven that subsoiling does not increase average yields and does not afford any protection against drought. Neither is amelioration of dry-farming conditions to be obtained through deep tilling with dynamite or special plows. The results of these experiments have been published in detail in Vol XIV, No. 11, of the Journal of Agricultural Research.

Soil-moisture determinations have been productive of information of fundamental importance to dry-land agriculture. These are now being prepared for publication.

From the information obtained in these and closely related investigations it is now possible within certain limits to interpret soil and climatic conditions in terms of crop-production possibilities. This has been of great value in assisting the United States Geological Survey in the classification of lands under the act providing for 640-acre stock-raising homesteads. Results of the work in their respective States have been published in 11 bulletins by cooperating State experiment stations.

At the Mandan field station five years' results have been obtained in investigation of the methods of growth of garden vegetables. These results are now in manuscript form for publication.

Test and breeding to secure hardy horticultural plants is making satisfactory progress. Two severe winters in succession have forwarded this work by eliminating unadapted material. In cooperative shelter-belt work in the northern Great Plains active cooperation is now maintained with 507 farmers, who were furnished and planted stock in 1916, 201 who planted in 1917, and 392 who are on application for future planting. In 1916, 701,911, and in 1917, 357,700 trees were placed with such cooperating farmers. In 1916 the percentage of growth was 80, and in 1917 it was 81.2.

Valuable and far-reaching results of fundamental importance have already been obtained, but they increase in value with the accumulation of data from year to year. In such a section, where climatic conditions fluctuate from year to year or in cycles of unknown or uncertain length, it has been recognized from the beginning that reliable results can only be obtained from experiments that cover a long period of years. The work has, therefore, been planned as continuing long-time experiments. The increasing value of the results with the increase in the length of time they cover fully pustifies the wisdom of this procedure. While important and valuable results have already been obtained, they are small in comparison with those now in sight from the carefully coordinated work of 24 field stations operated either independently or in cooperation with the State experiment stations.

The establishment of the fact that in some sections of the Great Plains cultural methods alone are not sufficient to overcome unfavorable conditions, but that a sound agriculture must be based on the growth of feed and the production of live stock, has resulted in the establishment of cooperative work with the Division of Animal Husbandry and the Dairy Division of the Bureau of Animal Industry, through which the possibilities and methods of beef, pork, and dairy production will be determined. This work has been started at Ardmore, S. Dak., and at Huntley, Mont. Its establishment at other points has been delayed by the exigencies arising from war conditions. This work, which is supported by special appropriation, is conducted in connection with the work in dry-land agriculture on stations already established.

Mr. THOMPSON. This has been going on for about 15 years. Has the amount of the appropriation been about the same all the 15 years?

Dr. TAYLOR. No, sir; the beginning was made in a very small way. I do not recall what the amount was.

Mr. THOMPSON. Is it contemplated that this appropriation should be continued indefinitely?

Dr. TAYLOR. I would not say indefinitely. It should be continued as a nucleus for much other work which the Bureau of Plant Industry and the State experiment stations are doing which is connected with this, utilizing the facilities at the field stations for plant breeding and other work in the dry-farming territory. At certain of the stations live-stock work is being undertaken by the Bureau of Animal Industry. It constitutes what may be said to be the only extensive coordinated series of field experiments that are under way in this country at this time, and it is very important.

Mr. HAUGEN. Could you approximate the expense on the Mandan farm?

Dr. TAYLOR. I couldn't offhand.

Mr. HAUGEN. How many stations have you outside of that?

Dr. KELLERMAN. Twenty-three, including those in which the States cooperate.

Mr. HAUGEN. Is this the only appropriation made for these stations?

Dr. TAYLOR. Yes, sir.

Mr. HAUGEN. Does this include the two in Nebraska?

Dr. TAYLOR. The dry-farming stations; yes, sir.

The CHAIRMAN. Take your next item on page 92, item 140, for investigations in connection with western irrigation agriculture, the utilization of lands reclaimed under the reclamation act. There is no change in that item?

Dr. TAYLOR. No, sir. That work is continuing; that is on the reclamation projects.

Mr. HAUGEN. What work are you doing on those reclamation projects? I believe there has been a good deal of pressure brought to bear for an increase by the people out there.

The CHAIRMAN. No; this isn't the item. The item for which they asked an increase is under the Bureau of Roads.

Item 141, improvement of fruits, and so on. There is no change in that?

Dr. TAYLOR. No change in that.

The CHAIRMAN. And the character of your work is about the same as heretofore, I suppose, Doctor?

Dr. TAYLOR. Substantially; yes, sir.

The CHAIRMAN. Any questions, gentlemen? If not, take the next item on page 94, item 142, to cultivate and care for the gardens and grounds of the Department of Agriculture, in the city of Washington.

Dr. TAYLOR. This is to maintain the out-door activities on the department grounds, including the greenhouse facilities.

The CHAIRMAN. Any questions on that? If not, take the next item, 143, for horticultural investigations. You seem to have an increase there, Doctor.

Dr. TAYLOR. In this case there is an increase in the estimate by transfer from the food-production act of an item of $30,000 for seed-potato improvement. It is to carry forward systematically the improvement and maintenance of seed-potato types suitable to the important commercial potato-growing sections of the country, both North and South. It has a distinct bearing on the southern commercial potato production, the supplies of seed for which come almost entirely from the Northern States, such as Maine, Wisconsin, Michigan, Minnesota, and New York. It has almost equally important bearing upon the western commercial potato-producing regions of both the dry and irrigated territories.

The CHAIRMAN. Just what do you do, very briefly? Do you locate these seed stocks?

Dr. TAYLOR. In the first place to locate disease-free, productive strains of commercially useful varieties and to develop methods for maintaining those disease-free and productive against the constant tendency that has been in evidence for many years to plant indiscriminately selected commercial seed which the grower finds, as he expresses it, "has run out."

The CHAIRMAN. This doesn't conflict with that item you were discussing awhile ago, does it?

Dr. TAYLOR. No, sir; this is a commercial seed-potato development and maintenance activity.

The CHAIRMAN. When you have found those thing, who do you do further?

Dr. TAYLOR. In every way practical it is expected—what is needed most now is actual determination of those best strains through experimental-demonstration planting. That is what the potato men of the country feed is essentially necessary. That is particularly the view of Mr. Sweet who, I think, perhaps, has been before the committee in years past, the Colorado potato grower, and what is desired is, first, to determine and then to demonstrate and then to encourage the general adoption by farmers of methods that will permit them to secure stock that is free from disease. I could submit a more clearly expressed statement, a more comprehensive statement.

The CHAIRMAN. Suppose you do that.

(The statement referred to follows:)

SEED-POTATO IMPROVEMENT WORKS.

During the season of 1918, two new lines of work were undertaken by the Bureau of Plant Industry. One of these projects which is designated "Seed-Potato Improvement" was rendered necessary because of the shortage of seed in 1917, which brought about the use of mixed, low-grade, and ill-adapted varieties in many sections. In order that the seed for the 1918 crop might be the best available, it was necessary to carry on field and bin inspection of the 1917 crop for the purpose of locating the growers who had seed of those varieties adapted to the sections and of a purity and grade suitable for seed purposes. It was felt that a failure to do this would result in a falling off in grade and quality of the commercial crop which would be difficult to overcome. The general good quality of the crop of 1918 indicates that efforts to insure it against such depreciation were successful.

In normal times, this work will be taken care of through the farm-seed potato plot, which is being strongly advocated, the basis being the hill which produces the largest proportion of desirable merchantable potatoes of the variety best adapted to the locality; the purity and grade of the product of this plot to be maintained at the highest possible point through continuous field rogueing and bin inspection. Such a seed plot on each farm of a size sufficient to meet the needs of that farm for seed for the commercial crop is the aim in this work.

The other line of work which has been undertaken on a larger scale than heretofore is that of developing high-grade seed potatoes for the benefit of the industry in the several important commercial potato-producing regions. This work is based on the best available seed, either certified or otherwise, which can be secured in the region. Samples are obtained from the growers who have a reputation for producing the highest grade and quality of potatoes. These samples are grown side by side for the purpose of determining their purity and trueness to name, as well as productive qualities. After the best strain has been secured from the grower's stock, the product from this sample is used as a basis of a more extensive planting to form the nucleus for a supply of seed to be distributed, through the State experiment station in cooperation with which the work may be carried on, to the growers of the region.

This work is already under way in Maine, Wisconsin, and Minnesota, and it is proposed to extend it during the coming year to New York and Michigan among eastern producing States, and Iowa, Oregon, and Washington in the western group. The work will not only cover those varieties which form the basis of the commercial crop in the regions immediately adjacent to the location of the field station but will also include the varieties generally used for the planting of the southern crop, which is so extensively produced for the early market. Special attention will be given to varieties for southern planting along the Atlantic coast in Maine, and to the varieties used in the southern Mississippi Valley and adjacent regions in Wisconsin and Minnesota, the region from which this territory draws its supply of seed.

Already cooperative tests are under way in Louisiana, Texas, Oklahoma, and Arkansas to determine the reaction of seed stock of the Triumph, the most important early variety grown in the southern Mississippi Valley and adjacent territory, the seed having been obtained in Nebraska, Wisconsin, Minnesota, Michigan, and Maine. In addition to these usual sources of seed supply, Colorado seed is being tested out in Oklahoma. As rapidly as promising seed can be developed in accordance with the plans above outlined, field tests will be carried on in all the regions to which the seed is adapted for the purpose of determining the relative commercial value of high-grade seed of this character in comparison with the usual grade of commercial seed used heretofore in these territories. It is confidently believed that a considerable increase in yield will result from these activities because of the elimination of unproductive hills or of plants which do not mature with the variety.

In connection with this work, it is also the purpose to determine the comparative value of a number of exceedingly promising seedling varieties which have been developed in the breeding work carried on by the department, but which, for lack of adequate facilities for testing under controlled conditions, have not yet been widely tried out. It is not the purpose to make a distribution of any of these sorts until they have proven their superiority to commercial sorts already in use.

(Thereupon, at 5.30 p. m., the committee adjourned, to meet again on Monday, January 6, 1919, at 10.30 a. m.)

HOUSE OF REPRESENTATIVES,
COMMITTEE ON AGRICULTURE,
Monday, January 6, 1919.

The committee met at 10.30 o'clock a. m., Hon. A. F. Lever (chairman) presiding.

BUREAU OF PLANT INDUSTRY—Continued.

STATEMENT OF DR. WILLIAM A. TAYLOR, CHIEF OF THE BUREAU OF PLANT INDUSTRY, UNITED STATES DEPARTMENT OF AGRICULTURE—Continued.

The CHAIRMAN. The committee will come to order.. The next item under the Bureau of Plant Industry is on page 95, item 144, I think, Dr. Taylor.

Dr. TAYLOR. One hundred and forty-four; yes, sir.

The CHAIRMAN. That is the item for the upkeep of the Arlington farm.

Dr. TAYLOR. There is no change in this item. It covers the maintenance and operation of Arlington, the experimental farm of the department across the river.

The CHAIRMAN. Any questions on that? If not, take up the next item, No. 145, on page 96, " Investigations in foreign seed and plant introduction." There seems to be no change in that.

Dr. TAYLOR. There is no change in that item.

The CHAIRMAN. Any statement you desire to make about that, Doctor?

Dr. TAYLOR. The work continues to be of distinct and growing importance, especially since the enforcement of the plant-quarantine act necessarily reduces the importation of seeds and plants from foreign countries by private agencies, because of the risk of bringing in diseases. A much larger proportion of the country's inflow of experimental plant material is through the department now than ever before. In a way this safeguards our agriculture against the introduction of plant diseases, because of the reduction of the number of channels. An organization has been perfected through which the most careful inspection for diseases and insects is possible, which very greatly reduces the previous risk. Because of the restriction of commercial importations of plants and nursery stock likely to carry injurious diseases and insects, greatly increased activity in this work will be necessary during the next year to assist in the development of home production of such stock.

Mr. McLAUGHLIN. Some years ago the introduction of foreign seeds for sugar beets was new, and I suppose was included in this item, or along the lines of activity set forth here. It has become an old matter, but since the beginning of the war it has taken on added interest. Have you explained about that before in this hearing?

Dr. TAYLOR. I think not, Mr. McLaughlin. I may say——

Mr. McLAUGHLIN. Will that come in another item?

Dr. TAYLOR. That should have been discussed in connection with our sugar-plant item. I can say here, however, that the result of the combined activity of the beet-sugar industry and the department has been the production of more than 6,000,000 pounds of sugar beet seed in this country this year. This is about half of our 1919 requirement for normal acreage of sugar beets. The present prospect is that the plantings to be made next spring of beets grown and now held specifically for seed production will increase the acreage for seed in 1919 about 20 per cent more. So that, in combination with more economical methods of use of seed in planting and better preparation of the soil for the planting, the supply of seed is regarded as adequate for a normal acreage of sugar beets in 1919.

Mr. McLAUGHLIN. What do you mean by the more economical use of seed in planting?

Dr. TAYLOR. In particular, the development of equipment suitable for hill planting in contradistinction to row planting, which requires more than double the seed required for hill planting and which involves also increased hand labor—that is, hoe labor—in the blocking out for the thinning of the beets.

Mr. McLaughlin. I infer, then, your opinion is that too much seed has been used?

Dr. Taylor. More seed has been used than is necessary with the improved planting devices. With seed at low prices—say 7 cents a pound, as it was obtainable in Germany in prewar times—the seed cost item was so small in contrast with other items that there was extravagant use of seed—the whole tendency was in that direction—20 to 25 pounds per acre. This year the crop on the average probably has not been seeded at heavier rates than 12 to 15 pounds. The experimental work that has been in progress this last year indicates that the quantity per acre can be materially cut by these hill-planting devices, which have only recently been perfected. They are adaptations of the bean planter and corn planter and drop the seeds in small bunches at regular intervals instead of scattering them throughout the row.

Mr. McLaughlin. Then the hill planting not only saves seed, but it results in such planting as to make unnecessary so much of the thinning?

Dr. Taylor. Yes. It should reduce the labor cost of thinning. It is not entirely perfected yet, and that is one of the features whcih in our sugar-beet work we are giving special attention to this year. At present the greatest uncertainty as to the seed supply is with regard to the year 1920 rather than the year 1919.

Mr. McLaughlin. There was a time——

Dr. Taylor (interposing). If you will pardon me this further statement: There has been available up to now some Russian seed. In fact, there is understood to be still some Russian seed at Vladivostok on its way here. There is some also at Archangel—some owned by Americans; some owned by Russians. There is some in this country that has been carried over from last year's importations.

Mr. McLaughlin. From——

Dr. Taylor. From Russia, which has been the only foreign source of supply for the past two years.

Mr. McLaughlin. There was a time when the growers in this country thought there was no good seed outside of Germany or that could be had outside of Germany. How have they found the Russian seed as compared with the German seed that they formerly had?

Dr. Taylor. We have found that it is the same seed to a very large extent; that the seed which we bought from Germany was in fact grown in Russia, by Russian labor, but under German direction, from mother beets grown in Germany and sent to Russia for seed production. The results of the last two seasons, during which largely increasing quantities of American-grown beet seed have been used in the fields, indicate that we are getting fully as high sugar content and in every way as satisfactory seed out of our own production as we formerly got through German and Austrian grown, and to quite an extent Russian-grown seed.

Mr. McLaughlin. Now, if the American seed is just as good, if we have found a way to raise it, we will ultimately at least be able to rely on our own home-grown seed altogether.

Dr. Taylor. There is every present indication——

Mr. McLaughlin (interposing). But what you say indicates that we are still dependent to some extent on foreign-grown seed.

Dr. TAYLOR. In the year 1920 we shall still have to use considerable foreign-grown seed.

Mr. McLAUGHLIN. Then the work of growing it in this country is going along slowly; so slowly that it can not be developed so as to supply a sufficient quantity for the next year—that is, for 1920?

Dr. TAYLOR. It is growing rapidly, I should say, Mr. McLaughlin, taking into account the difficulties attendant upon such an enterprise. Sugar-beet seed is a two-year crop, the roots for which must be specially grown the first year, and then dug and buried and held through the winter until the spring, planted out for growing the seed crop that year.

Mr. McLAUGHLIN. The German method of growing sugar beet was very elaborate—long continued and very elaborate. It is a most interesting story, and I have wondered if it was necessary to go through all that, if it was found to be necessary, or whether it was found that some other plan could be carried on in this country more expeditiously, or without so much lapse of time, had been worked out.

Dr. TAYLOR. It is not entirely clear yet that the elaborateness with which they conducted their breeding work was not desirable. This, of course, should be remembered, that we started with their best. We secured as good as they had, so that the beet seed industry in America as it has developed during the war has developed from the basis of the best that they had when the war began.

Mr. McLAUGHLIN. I know when the European war began, the sugar-beet growers in this country were very much discouraged; they thought at that time that there was no source of supply like the German source.

The CHAIRMAN. Anything further?

Mr. McLAUGHLIN. I am glad to hear you say about the development of the industry of growing seed in this country, you think it promises very soon to supply our entire need in this country.

Dr. TAYLOR. We feel confident that it does. There is every reason to expect that we can be independent.

Mr. McLAUGHLIN. Of course that means it is just as good in sugar content, and has every other quality present?

Dr. TAYLOR. Yes, sir.

The CHAIRMAN. What about your clover-seed proposition? Are you making progress in getting clover seed for which you used to depend on Russia?

Dr. TAYLOR. The clover-seed situation at present is in rather critical condition. The Russian supply has been almost entirely cut off, although we had information as recently as two weeks ago that there was some quantity of Russian and Siberian seed at Vladivostok likely to come this way, but no large quantity. It may interest the committee to know that the department has now two men in Europe investigating that specific question of stocks of clover seed, and world requirements for clover seed. We have been able in the past to get considerable quantities of Italian clover seed in some years; but the Italian seed is not suitable for the northern portions of the country, which are the most important clover territory.

The CHAIRMAN. Why can not we grow our own clover seed?

Dr. TAYLOR. We do grow a large proportion of it, but the winter damage a year ago to clover in the northern corn belt and northwestern clover country, coupled with the drought damage of last spring and summer, reduced our home crop of clover seed very materially. We are making a special inquiry now into the stocks—the Bureau of Markets—into the stocks of seeds, and the Bureau of Plant Industry into the seed requirements.

Mr. McLaughlin. You spoke of getting clover seed from Russia and Siberia and Italy. From what other parts of Europe have you been getting the seed?

Dr. Taylor. Those have been in the past our principal initial sources of clover seed. Quite a good deal of the Russian seed before the war reached us through Germany and through German merchants through the port of Hamburg, and sometimes was known as German seed.

Mr. McLaughlin. To what extent has it been necessary for us to rely on foreign grown clover seed?

Dr. Taylor. We have had to rely on—I can not give the percentage, but we have had to import considerable quantities of red clover seed and white clover seed from European countries. Two years ago a considerable quantity of red clover seed came in from Chile and it is of a very desirable type, winter hardy and excellent; but, unfortunately, much of the Chilean seed has been contaminated with dodder, and under our import seed law dodder-contaminated seed is properly excluded.

Mr. McLaughlin. We don't need any more dodder in this country than we have now?

Dr. Taylor. No, sir.

Mr. McLaughlin. That is all.

The Chairman. Anything further? Then take up item 146, on page 97, "for the purchase, propagation, testing, and distribution of new and rare seeds," and so on.

Dr. Taylor. The clover-seed discussion would properly come here.

The Chairman. Any further questions about that?

Mr. Thompson. What about alfalfa seed?

Dr. Taylor. Alfalfa seed is in relatively good supply. The most acute situation with respect to forage crop seeds is with respect to red clover, and it is a world question. It is a question regarding which we are endeavoring to ascertain world stocks and world requirements, as there is practically sure to come considerable demand for clover seed from the war-damaged countries, particularly from France and Belgium, as they get their agricultural reconstruction program under way.

The Chairman. All right. Anything further? If not, your next item is on page 98, item 147, which is a new item, reading "For the investigation of the use of commercial fertilizers and other materials proposed for stimulating or increasing crop growth, $125,000." I wish you would tell us about that, Doctor, as briefly as you can, and yet in some detail.

Dr. Taylor. This is a new item, as the note indicates, and the general purpose of it is, I think, well outlined in the explanatory note.

As Dr. Kellerman has given special attention to this item, I will ask you to allow him to outline it in further detail.

The Chairman. All right, Dr. Kellerman.

FURTHER STATEMENT OF DR. KARL F. KELLERMAN, ASSOCIATE CHIEF OF THE BUREAU OF PLANT INDUSTRY, UNITED STATES DEPARTMENT OF AGRICULTURE.

Dr. KELLERMAN. The fertilizer question has always been an important one. It has proved of unusual importance during the war period, and presumably will continue so during the reconstruction period that will follow the war. In the older regions, the agriculturally older regions, of the country the use of fertilizers has developed to very considerable proportions. I think it is true that the local stations, the State experiment stations in each State, the fertilizer companies themselves, and individual experimenters have assembled a great deal of reliable information.

Comparatively little of this work has been carried on in relation to the soil types of the country, and also, unfortunately, comparatively little of the work has been carried on in connection with the standard cropping systems. That is, the experiments have been based on the result of a single crop, or one or two standard rotations continued through a long series of years, and the evidence that has been secured from these experiments has not been such that it could be applied through wide regions. Also the plan of experimentation in the different States has been so diverse that there was practically no method of comparing the results of one experiment with those of another. Very little general facts could be deduced accordingly. And it has been practically impossible to develop any consistent plan of fertilizer device, either in the States or from the standpoint of wide geographic regions. The probability that the Middle West, and the West, too, for that matter, will be the scene of active sales campaigns for fertilizer, and the fact that the farmers in these regions are becoming somewhat interested in the use of fertilizer is another reason why we feel that it is especially important that we collect more reliable information, and collect it on such a comprehensive plan that we can speak with more authority than from the unrelated experiments that we have had.

The CHAIRMAN. Just what is your plan here, Doctor, in working out these experiments? Will you take plots of ground representing different types of soil, under different climatic conditions, and all that sort of thing?

Dr. KELLERMAN. That is exactly the plan, the foundation of our plan.

The CHAIRMAN. Field experiments rather than laboratory experiments?

Dr. KELLERMAN. It will be field experiments, conducted on the major soil types in the big agricultural regions. I think we will—parenthetically I would perhaps better say, that the plans will be worked out in cooperation with the State institutions, and, accordingly, we are as yet unable to say just how the final details may work out—but we will probably have seven or eight general districts, with one or more field stations in each district run in cooperation with the States of that region. Each general region will cover some general type of agriculture, also some one of the major soil types of the country.

The CHAIRMAN. Then you would also have to make experiments on that same soil type with reference to the principal crops grown there that use fertilizer?

Dr. KELLERMAN. Yes.

The CHAIRMAN. I imagine the effect of fertilizer on corn is one thing, its effect on cotton another, and on watermelons, cabbage, and lettuce still other propositions.

Dr. KELLERMAN. That is quite true; furthermore, the problem of what the relationship of these crops should be to each other and to the fertilizer campaigns——

The CHAIRMAN (interposing). You would also, I should think, have to work out a proposition of how much fertilizers can be economically and wisely used for these various soil types and for these various crops?

Dr. KELLERMAN. That will necessarily come in.

The CHAIRMAN. In the last two or three years there has been a tremendous increase in the use of nitrate of soda. In fact, its value has been discussed to any extent only during the past four or five years.

Dr. KELLERMAN. Its use in general farming has been comparatively recent. Of course, it has been a standard fertilizer for many years in this country, especially in trucking.

The CHAIRMAN. Doctor, can you tell the committee what the total expenditure for commercial fertilizers in this country at the present time is? My recollection is that it is something like $100,000,000. Is that right?

Dr. KELLERMAN. It is at least that. I think it runs over $150,000,000.

The CHAIRMAN. My recollection is that it is something like $3,000,000 a year in South Carolina alone.

Dr. KELLERMAN. Yes; that is one of the heavy fertilizer States.

The CHAIRMAN. Doctor, what do you have to say to the committee as to the indiscriminate and unwise use of commercial fertilizer, as it is practiced in America now? If you do not catch my meaning, let me make this statement: My belief is that fully one-half of the commercial fertilizer used in this country is thrown away.

Dr. KELLERMAN. Well, I think your guess is probably correct.

The CHAIRMAN. It is only my guess.

Dr. KELLERMAN. It would be a guess on the part of anyone. I think no one is in a position to say with any finality what the waste or overuse of fertilizers, or in using the wrong fertilizers, in this country is. It is enormous; we are certain of that. The sale of fertilizers probably depends on the salesmanship of the fertilizer man more than any other one thing. There is practically no evidence, beyond the general fact that fertilizers will increase the crops, and the special facts that in some sections particular crops will be increased by certain definite applications. We have this further interesting fact that bears out your statement on the waste of fertilizers. The use of fertilizers, of course, has been very materially changed during the war. Potash was cut off, and in many regions where people thought that it was absolutely essential to have liberal applications of potash to grow crops, crops substantially the same have been grown with fertilizers without potash.

The CHAIRMAN. It has always been considered that you could not grow Irish potatoes without potash.

Dr. KELLERMAN. That has been the general belief in the regions where fertilizer is used.

The CHAIRMAN. Has the yield per acre for potatoes fallen off?

Dr. KELLERMAN. In some regions; but that is a reaction that has been shown to be definitely tied up with soil conditions and soil types. There are certain soil types where the yield of potatoes has gone down very much, and the quality of the potatoes also, through lack of potash. In other regions there has been comparatively little or no reduction in the yield from the lack of the use of potash. Heretofore, however, the potash was used over all of these areas in the same quantity. The same is true of cotton in many—I think in most of the cotton-growing regions of the East. Along the Atlantic coast the belief has been, I think, very general that liberal applications of potash were necessary for the successful cotton crop.

The CHAIRMAN. Light sandy soils?

Dr. KELLERMAN. Yes; cotton may rust badly on that soil if it does not have potash; but we know that it is only a relatively small proportion of the land that seriously needed potash.

The CHAIRMAN. Do certain types of soil carry potash naturally?

Dr. KELLERMAN. Yes.

The CHAIRMAN. The Secretary, gentlemen, is very much interested in this subject, and in his report he says:

> I am convinced that there is much indiscriminate use of commercial fertilizers in this country, and therefore much waste of money. This arises from the lack of available satisfactory data. Soils require careful treatment just as does the human body. A number of States have conducted fertilizer experiments over a long period and have obtained and disseminated valuable information. Because of the importance of this matter for the whole Union, I believe that the Federal Government should participate in this work, and that an adequate sum should be made available to the department for cooperative experiments with State institutions.

Doctor, in your summary here of the manner in which this money has been expended, I note that $38,000 of it is to be for salaries and $22,000 for wages. What do you mean by wages as contradistinguished from salaries?

Dr. KELLERMAN. We are distinguishing there between the scientific employee and the floating employee—the man we hire to take care of the crop, the plowing, the planting, and harvesting. All the labor that can be hired as floating labor we class as wages, as distinguished from the technical men necessary for planning the experiments, for supervising them, and for doing the accurate recording of the weights of the different yields of the different fertilizer plots. The work of all the technical men is carried in the salary list.

The CHAIRMAN. Now, your next expenditure there is for traveling expenses—$12,000. That would be for your scientific men, I take it?

Dr. KELLERMAN. Entirely for the scientific men.

The CHAIRMAN. Then, you have there "equipment and material, $46,000." What equipment and what materials are required?

Dr. KELLERMAN. The equipment would be almost entirely the farm machinery, the plows, harrows, and the reapers, and other necessary implements. The materials would include fertilizers, seed, and other materials that would be necessary in running an experimental farm, or, for that matter, would be necessary in running any farm; that is, would be substantially the same as a farm, except that we have a much higher overhead resulting from the cost of the technical men.

The CHAIRMAN. You speak of farm machinery, and so on. How large are these plots to be?

Dr. KELLERMAN. The plots will probably have to vary a good deal, depending upon how much land the State institutions will be able to find that they can use satisfactorily. The plot of an individual fertilizer experiment may be anywhere from one-thirtieth of an acre up to half an acre. It is not likely to be larger than half an acre, nor smaller than one-twentieth of an acre.

The CHAIRMAN. It occurs to me, Doctor, except where the Government has land of its own, or the States have lands of their own (my State, I believe, does not have over 5,000 acres of public land), if you have to work this in cooperation with the individual farmer, you have to get his land?

Mr. LEE. Machinery, too.

The CHAIRMAN. And the machinery. It seems to me you would not need very much machinery or material, because you will find some progressive farmer, living on a soil type with which you want to experiment, would be very pleased to do the work for you, no doubt.

Dr. KELLERMAN. That would be true of short-time experiments. If we were experimenting only for a few years we probably would not want any other machinery, and our materials would consist probably of nothing but fertilizer. I think though the experiments will become more valuable to the country at large, as well as to the region in which the work of the individual experimental farm may be located from year to year—I think that work of this character will be more valuable during the second decade than the first. That makes it very difficult to cooperate on an informal basis with the individual farmer.

The CHAIRMAN. I had an idea that this would be a short-time experiment, covering probably four or five years. This is to be a perpetual-motion proposition, is it?

Dr. KELLERMAN. No; but that is a thing that I think should not be decided now. It depends on whether the work will clearly justify itself before the country. After a five-year period I think the decision as to whether it should be continued or not can best be made. My own opinion is that after it has run five years the farmers who are beginning to get more authoritative results, more accurate and helpful recommendations from work of this character, will be exceedingly loath to have it stopped. I think that the experience of our long-time work has shown that although certain problems may be pretty well solved in a few years, problems still more important come up that need continued attention; and these experiment farms probably will become exceedingly valuable, because of the detailed history that has been collected during a period of years, that you can not get from any individual farm. The experiment station at Rothamstead, England, that has been operated for fertilizer experiments for 70 years, is now perhaps more valuable to the entire world than any other fertilizer station; yet the difference of the

American and English soils and climates precludes our depending entirely on the Rothamstead work.

Mr. ANDERSON. Is it your intention, Doctor, to establish experiment farms for the purpose of carrying out this work all over the country?

Dr. KELLERMAN. Not all over the country, but there will necessarily be several experiment farms that will be established.

Mr. ANDERSON. Then you are going to buy the land and build the buildings, and all that sort of thing?

Dr. KELLERMAN. I think in no case will it be necessary to buy land. I think it will be necessary to lease land in some cases. Probably in most cases, the station will have land that can be devoted to purposes of that sort without any expenditure at all. Where the station is in the type of soil not generally distributed throughout a region, then it might be necessary to actually lease land.

Mr. ANDERSON. What good is a station of that sort anywhere?

Dr. KELLERMAN. An agricultural station?

Mr. ANDERSON. A station which does not conform to the general type of soil of the region can not be of much value any place.

Dr. KELLERMAN. It can aid in many ways, but not in fertilizer experiments. One of the curious things, however, Mr. Anderson, is that the State agricultural experiment stations of this country are very frequently on soil types that are very minor in extent, and unusual, so that the soil experiments carried on at the State agricultural stations often have very little significance, as a whole.

The CHAIRMAN. Unfortunately, in many States the location of the experiment station has been fixed by the State legislature. Take my own State, for instance. It was fixed by the will of Clemson, a son-in-law, I believe, of John C. Calhoun, and it is in a section of the State not representative of the soil of that State. Their experiments with fertilizers practically amount to nothing, so far as the State is concerned.

Mr. LEE. Take the State of Georgia, extending from the mountains to the sea coast. It is impossible to locate a station near every type of soil we have.

The CHAIRMAN. And the location is made by the legislature and not by the scientists.

Mr. MCLAUGHLIN. Your note says that the experiments have been numerous and extensive, but they have not been correlated, whatever that means. Now, can not these experiment stations continue their experiments with some suggestions from you as to how it should be done, and how the records are kept, and all that?

Dr. KELLERMAN. It is not a question merely of keeping records in work of this character.

Mr. MCLAUGHLIN. Can they be planned after your suggestion? You have control over the experiment stations to that extent, to a large extent. Couldn't you include that?

Dr. KELLERMAN. I would not like to be understood as criticizing the State work, except from a large regional standpoint. I think in most cases, if not in all cases, the work that has been carried on at a State station has had value, and very practical value, to the agriculture of that State. As a general rule, however, the work conducted in one State has had little and perhaps no significance beyond the borders of that State. For example, the experiments planned in Minnesota and South Dakota may be so different that they will not be mutually helpful. To reconstruct them so that they will be mutually helpful may mean that some work will be done by Minnesota that is not of major importance to Minnesota, and the same would be true in all the interrelations of the different States.

Partly for that reason I feel that it is necessary for the department to carry a distinct financial interest in the work, to make it possible for the department to finance those portions of the work that are of broad regional interest rather than local or State interest, and make it possible, without undue hardship on the States, to enlarge the work at particular points, or in some States to originate a plan of work, so that there is a community of plan that will give us the fundamental results we need.

Mr. McLAUGHLIN. It would seem to me that results would naturally be different. The soil is different in different States; the climate is different, and all that. Experiments made in Minnesota naturally would not be helpful to the farmers of South Carolina.

Dr. KELLERMAN. Perhaps not, but they should be helpful to Michigan.

Mr. McLAUGHLIN. Well, there is a difference between Minnesota and Michigan as to soil and climate, and it would seem to me that these experiment stations ought to carry out these experiments, changing their plan to meet your views, and the best kind of work can be done by the local plan in the local communities, or by the people of a State.

Dr. KELLERMAN. That is the reason that this plan of cooperative activity is believed to be the best. Each State has the local point of view most clearly in mind.

Mr. McLAUGHLIN. Isn't that natural, and isn't it proper?

Dr. KELLERMAN. It is natural and proper, but probably, without Federal aid in developing cooperative work, each State will have to work out its own method of fertilizer application, starting at the very bottom. It will not be possible for them to develop substantial, general conclusions as to fertilizer practice that will apply not only to a State alone, but apply to the geographic regions that are not bounded by State boundaries.

Mr. McLAUGHLIN. Is it true that these experiment stations must start from the beginning? Your note says that for a long time they have been making these experiments very extensively, but there is fault in their method. That is the effect of your note there—what may be fathered from it. Now, each State receives a large amount of money. Why can not these experiments be carried on by the stations under your direction, or under local conditions, and learn what fertilizers will do in those localities? It seems to be, at first sight, unnecessary for you to have a very large amount of money to go into these States and work independently of the stations. It would seem to me those stations are the ones to carry on this work. If they are not doing it quite right, if what work they have done don't produce results satisfactory, or you can not find out what the results are, suggest some change of method to them, so that the results will be known and will be valuable.

The CHAIRMAN. Let me ask Dr. Kellerman this question, which may clear up this proposition in both our minds: Just what control does the Federal Government have over the State stations in the way of compelling them to apply certain plans worked out by the Department of Agriculture?

Dr. KELLERMAN. Aside from the requirement that the department must approve the investigational projects taken up under the Adams fund, I think there is no control at all of the State experiment stations.

Mr. MCLAUGHLIN. Under that fund it is necessary for an experiment station to submit to the Secretary of Agriculture each year its projects?

Dr. KELLERMAN. Only of the Adams fund.

Mr. MCLAUGHLIN. Under that fund, why isn't it incumbent upon the Secretary of Agriculture to suggest to them, or approve or disapprove their plans, so it could include something of this kind, that have been doing the work, and, as you say, that have been doing it extensively for a long time, but not quite as you think it ought to be done? Why can not it be done as you think it should be done?

Dr. KELLERMAN. I think the history of the fertilizer experiments, which is very voluminous, is about the only answer to that. Something of that general plan has been attempted through the informal discussion of results, the attempt to develop plans, and it has not been possible to examine results that have been secured from isolated stations and work out a panacea for the fertilizer business.

Mr. MCLAUGHLIN. You will have to have a plan if you are going into this work.

Dr. KELLERMAN. Yes.

Mr. MCLAUGHLIN. You will have to have different plans in different plants and different States. Why can not you suggest your plan to the experiment stations which have all the machinery and all the land and the methods of keeping records?

Dr. KELLERMAN. That can all be done, and still it will not be a coherent plan, because it will be impossible for any one group of people to keep in touch with the different phases of the work and to make the plan develop uniformly. It is the conviction of the people who have been thinking over this question of fertilizers that only by continuous study of the experiments in different regions as they are going on, by having these different developments followed by a single group of scientists, so that they will be aware instantly of any important results that are being secured, that in that way only is it going to be possible to make rapid progress. Progress can be made in the old way, but very, very slowly.

Mr. MCLAUGHLIN. It does not strike me favorably now to have the department going into the States of the Union, and perhaps in the several different parts of each State, and buy or lease land and buy agricultural equipment for each of those places, hire a lot of men to prepare the soil, cultivate it and harvest the crop, and keep the records in general of these separate places, when we already have experiment stations, one or more in each State, more or less under control of the Government, established for the very purpose of doing that particular thing.

Dr. KELLERMAN. Mr. McLaughlin, since early Roman times they have been using fertilizers. It would seem that farmers in these centuries should have learned the fertilizer business, but they have not. I think the only way we can put this question up clearly is this: Enormous amounts of money are being wasted annually through the unscientific application of fertilizers. In conferences with fertilizer men, in conferences with State experimenters, we have come to the conclusion that through a development of substantially this type of cooperative organization we can collect information more reliably, more satisfactorily, and much more rapidly than by any of the methods tried up to the present time. We believe that the expenditure of this sum, which looks somewhat large, is but a very small fraction of the loss that occurs to the American farmers annually. Take your own region, where the question of whether acid phosphate is to be used for the production of wheat—that is one of the big questions for the immediate future. It is found to be successful in Ohio. The State experiment station and the farmers have worked that out.

Mr. McLaughlin. I have read of that.

Dr. Kellerman. Now, the fertilizer companies, with the excessive production of sulphuric acid that came during war time, with the discovery of great deposits of phosphate in the Northwest, are expecting to develop energetic campaigns for stimulating the use of acid phosphate throughout the northern wheat regions. Minnesota has conducted some very important work on the use of acid phosphate. There has been more or less of a controversy up in Minnesota on the question of how the fertilizer developments are best worked out to the interest of the farmers. Dr. Alway, of the Minnesota State station, is convinced, as the men of the Atlantic seaboard are convinced, that the magnitude of the problems, the urgency of their solution, requires some combination for securing a pooling of interests for obtaining the best results. The State agencies will do everything in their power, I think, to model their work on plans that we suggest, to change their plans, if necessary, to put in extra men, extra work, extra land. If the Federal action in this matter indicates a serious intention to require progress, I think the States can be counted on without question to do all of this, but there is still a great deal that must be done in the development of a rapid solution of these great fertilizer problems.

Mr. Anderson. May I ask a question?

The Chairman. Yes.

Mr. Anderson. I think we see the nose of the camel coming under the tent in this item. As far as I am concerned, I want to see the camel. The first question, it seems to me, is this: Is this work to be done on land furnished by the Federal Government, or is it to be done on land furnished by the States?

Dr. Kellerman. Preferably on land furnished by the States.

Mr. Anderson. That does not answer the question. I want to know what the plan is.

Dr. Kellerman. The plan is to have it done on land furnished by the States, unless such land can not be secured. I would think it a mistake to limit the securing of land entirely to the States because no State in a particular geographic division might be able to supply the kind of land that was necessary, without very cumbersome procedures, or the purchase of land through acts of legislatures, where I think we would be able to lease land at very small cost.

Mr. Anderson. How large a tract of land would be required under normal conditions for the carrying on of one of these experiments or a series of experiments such as you have in mind in a particular locality?

Dr. KELLERMAN. That, I think, would vary somewhat with the different sections of the country, but between 150 and 200 acres I think would be the most satisfactory size of an experiment farm for this purpose.

Mr. ANDERSON. Would the ordinary farm buildings you would find on a farm of that size be suitable for your purpose, or would you have to construct new buildings?

Dr. KELLERMAN. It would be desirable for us to have an office or laboratory building in addition to the ordinary farm building.

The CHAIRMAN. In your opening statement I got the impression that you would use very small areas of land for these experiments?

Dr. KELLERMAN. I meant, Mr. Chairman, the plot where the individual fertilizer treatment is used. When you consider the number of crops in a region, fertilizer applications are complicated.

The CHAIRMAN. Let us see about that. Take my own section, because I am more familiar with it. Go into Sumter County, in my district. We grow about three principal crops there, corn, oats, and cotton. You might want to experiment with cowpeas. Very little wheat is grown there. It would not be necessary to make an experiment in that region, for instance, with the growing of wheat.

Dr. KELLERMAN. No.

The CHAIRMAN. Or cabbage?

Dr. KELLERMAN. No.

The CHAIRMAN. Or sugar beets?

Dr. KELLERMAN. No crop that was useless to the region.

The CHAIRMAN. So, it seems to me, instead of having a farm of 150 acres, you could easily conduct your experiment on the main crops, with an area of 6, 8, or 10 acres, or 15 acres at the very most. If you went into a sugar-beet area you certainly would not need 150 acres to develop the proper application of the proper kind of fertilizer for sugar beets. You could do that on an acre. My own thought was you could find in almost every county—I think in every county—some farmers who would be delighted to have the experiment going on on his farm. It would make his farm a kind of show place. I don't think this note here gives you the authority to buy land, in the first place.

Dr. KELLERMAN. We have no authority to buy land.

The CHAIRMAN. I doubt whether that gives you the authority to lease land. The trouble about the States furnishing the land is that many of the States have no land at all in these soil types, and they would have to get through legislative action authority to furnish the land. I thought when the matter first was brought to my attention that it would be largely one of cooperation with the State experiment station and there the individual farmer would be glad to give you his farm.

Dr. KELLERMAN. It is easy to get farmers to give land for the purpose of demonstration after the experimental stage is passed, but at first it is necessary to run experiments that result in decrease as well as experiments that result in increase, in order that we may establish the principles that we are working for.

The CHAIRMAN. I recognize that difficulty; of course, I can see that.

Dr. KELLERMAN. Without having what is substantially a farm it is really impossible to develop what would be a real farm practice in the use of fertilizer, testing various combinations of materials on good rotations. I have mentioned only standard types of fertilizers. There is one other question in connection with the fertilizers which might be called scientific freaks. It requires some additional land if we are going to test these types of fertilizers, widely advertised and usually based on some new scientific theory as yet untested and whose worth is completely unknown.

Many of those fertilizers, I think, are frauds. Perhaps that is too harsh a word to use; perhaps they are not, from the standpoint of the manufacturer; the manufacturer may be perfectly honest in the belief that some new theory is suitable for commercial exploitation. But we have there one of the losses that is beginning to increase annually to the farmers.

Mr. ANDERSON. That brings up the question of policy. Is it going to be the policy in regard to these experiments to develop the proper kind of fertilizers, or is it going to be the policy to test out the different varieties of commercial fertilizers to determine whether they have any basis of intrinsic merit?

Dr. KELLERMAN. We have in mind the development of fertilizers for the different regions and different crops, but as a side issue the value of new materials must be tested, for the sources of fertilizer materials is continually changing.

Mr. ANDERSON. How many of these stations will be established as now contemplated?

Dr. KELLERMAN. We can divide the country into seven or eight major geographic districts, with one station in each district.

Mr. ANDERSON. Do you regard the proposition as one likely to continue in its present size, so far as Federal appropriations are concerned, or likely to grow as the experiments develop?

Dr. KELLERMAN. I said a while ago that I thought this would be likely to continue for a number of years, possibly two or three decades.

Mr. ANDERSON. It has been my experience that these new propositions not only continue, but that they grow in annual expenditures of a continuously increasing amount. I wanted to know whether you regarded this proposition as one which would run along with the contemplated expenditure of the sum you estimate here, or would it increase in size and the amount of estimated expenditure?

Dr. KELLERMAN. Since the department is counting on a cooperative undertaking with the expectation that part of the work will be done by the States, I think it is fair to say that this expenditure will be maintained for the next five years. I am not a prophet— I think it is unfair for me to attempt to say what is in the future, at least beyond that five-year period.

I would be willing to stake my reputation on the immediate financial returns that will be secured through the expenditure of this much annually for the next five years.

Mr. ANDERSON. I have not yet quite clearly in my mind what sort of cooperation you expect from the State. It struck me from what you said that this would be in reality practically a Federal experiment; that these stations will be run as United States experimental stations, and if there is any cooperation from the States it is going to be very limited, except in so far as they may run their own stations upon their own theories.

Dr. KELLERMAN. I think during the first year the Federal expenditures might be greater than the State expenditures. From the first year I expect that the State expenditures will equal or be greater than the Federal expenditures in each of the regions in which we may be working.

Mr. ANDERSON. Let us see about that. I am not opposing this proposition, but I want to know what it is, because I anticipate it is going to last a long while and cost considerable money.

Mr. ANDERSON. If I understand you correctly, you propose in some instances to lease the land; you propose to erect the necessary buildings; you propose to furnish scientific men; you propose to pay the wages of the men who do the actual work; you propose to keep the books; you propose to furnish the farm equipment, the seed, and the fertilizer. If you do that, what is the State going to furnish?

Dr. KELLERMAN. I would say in all those cases we are furnishing a part of those things, because I do not think we will be furnishing more than half of them except in the case of the technical men, and even there it is uncertain whether we will be furnishing more technical men.

Mr. McLAUGHLIN. How will the State be furnishing anything if you have selected a piece of land far removed from the State experiment stations?

Dr. KELLERMAN. We would expect from the State cooperation in conducting the experiments on that isolated tract if it were necessary to secure such a one; we would expect from the State the facilities of its laboratories and the aid of its men at the laboratories. We would expect from the State the undertaking of the special, more or less local problems that developed in connection with these more comprehensive problems.

Mr. ANDERSON. But this cooperation on the part of the State is to be conducted upon its own ground, in its own laboratories, and not in the stations you are establishing; is that correct?

Dr. KELLERMAN. No; in our stations as well as its own. Our hope is that this is to be a genuine cooperative activity. We want our men to work together with the State men on the same ground.

The question of our leasing ground is a question, as the chairman made very clear a few minutes ago, only of leasing ground in a State where the State is not in a position to furnish the type of ground that really would be desirable. In such cases, rather than have that section of the country neglected, I think it is preferable for us to lease the land. But I think it will never be necessary for us to lease land generally, and that in but few instances is it likely that we will lease land. Nor is it likely that we will lease land at anything except nominal rates.

Mr. ANDERSON. I do not agree with you about that at all. My own guess is that you will have to lease land in practically every instance if your experiments are going to be worth anything.

Dr. KELLERMAN. Mr. Anderson, I think we have a precedent in this matter. In our work in the Great Plains we lease some land, but we also had land from the stations. We pay hardly anything for any of the land we have in that region, although we are leasing some of it. In many cases the State is providing the land. I do not see why we can not do about the same thing in the case of the fertilizer work.

Mr. ANDERSON. I want you to understand I am not hostile to the proposition, but I want to understand the proposition and know what it is.

As far as I am concerned, I am not willing to simply stick up a fund of $125,000, to be continued, or to be increased indefinitely, without knowing in advance more concretely at least what the plan is going to be. That is exactly my position.

Dr. KELLERMAN. Have I not made the plan clear?

Mr. ANDERSON. I think you have, except that it is entirely indefinite so far as the matter of State cooperation is concerned, and it is indefinite there, absolutely, except insofar as you say you hope to be able to get State cooperation.

Dr. KELLERMAN. I have said that for this reason: This plan has been taken up informally and discussed with several of the State people. In every case there has been enthusiastic indorsement of the general idea, and I think we have very good reason to believe that the same feeling exists at the different stations.

We have not taken up with the stations the detailed plans, since the matter of arranging plans for work of this character is one of considerable expense. It seems useless to take up detailed plans in regard to cooperation until it is possible to say we are going to proceed.

If we can go to a station and say, "We are ready for a comprehensive undertaking; can land be secured, or can it not," I think in most cases land can be secured.

Mr. ANDERSON. You mean State land can be secured; that the State can get land and place it at your disposal?

Dr. KELLERMAN. I think in most cases that will be possible.

Mr. ANDERSON. It is your intention to go ahead irrespective of whether the State furnishes the land or does not furnish it?

Dr. KELLERMAN. No; we would prefer to have the State furnish the land. If, in a particular geographic soil type one State could furnish land and another State could not, the station would be located in the region where the land would be available.

The CHAIRMAN. Suppose neither one did that?

Dr. KELLERMAN. Then, I think it would be necessary for us to lease land rather than neglect that part of the country.

Mr. McLAUGHLIN. I am not as familiar with other States as I am with my own, but in our State there are all kinds of land, from the highest quality down to pretty light soil, of very little agricultural value. You talk about a piece of land being typical of the State: I doubt very much if you can find in any State land that would be typical of the State.

The CHAIRMAN. I did not understand Dr. Kellerman to say that.

Dr. KELLERMAN. We want to disregard State lines and try to follow the lines of the big-soil types.

Mr. McLAUGHLIN. The more you disregard State lines the more difficult it will be to carry on an experiment at one point that would be of value in other places. You say you have conferred with State officials and have found them enthusiastic. Do you not find that enthusiasm everywhere when it is suggested that Federal money be used in a State?

Dr. KELLERMAN. No, I think not. The difficulty with the fertilizer experiment has been the question of reputation that the fertilizer experiment has gradually gotten into. Many stations are somewhat averse to conducting fertilizer experiments because a good deal of money has been expended in fertilizer testing without getting very comprehensive results.

It is more a question of the department shouldering the responsibility than it is a question of the department shouldering the financial burden in this matter. As I say, I confidently expect that eventually the States will spend very much more than the Federal Government in this work. But the responsibility of the work, the burden of proof, the objection if the work is not successful, will fall mainly on the department. I think that is the main item.

Mr. ANDERSON. You say the States will spend more money than the Federal Government. They are spending it now?

Dr. KELLERMAN. They are in some States.

Mr. ANDERSON. You mean money in addition to what they are spending now?

Dr. KELLERMAN. Yes.

Mr. HAUGEN. To what extent are these experiments carried on; in how many States?

Dr. KELLERMAN. The States conducting experiments of considerable size are probably Rhode Island, Massachusetts, Pennsylvania, New Jersey, Ohio, I think both North and South Carolina, Tennessee, Mississippi, Minnesota, Wisconsin, Indiana, and Illinois. There are other States, but I believe the States I mentioned probably have made the larger expenditures.

Mr. HAUGEN. Probably about half the States are carrying on experiments?

Dr. KELLERMAN. I think so.

Mr. HAUGEN. So that after all there is not much interest in it?

Dr. KELLERMAN. You must remember, Mr. Haugen, that the States of the middle West and West have supposed until recently that the fertilizer question was one that would never touch them, and so there has been very little work carried on there.

Mr. HAUGEN. But you have it in your power to dictate what shall be done when any particular project is submitted to you, and you can dictate to each station—when I say you can dictate I mean the department—and prescribe just what that money shall be used for?

Dr. KELLERMAN. I believe we have no power——

Mr. HAUGEN (interposing). Unless the department approves the project, they can not spend a dollar.

Dr. KELLERMAN. That is in connection with the Adams fund.

Mr. HAUGEN. In connection with the Adams fund.

Dr. KELLERMAN. The Adams fund will not cover the expenditure on all the research projects in many States.

Mr. HAUGEN. Well, I know; if this is of importance, and I take it this is the main source of success to the farmer, yet so far half the States have absolutely ignored that proposition, and the department has overlooked it.

Dr. KELLERMAN. Frankly, Mr. Haugen, I think the department should have been investigating fertilizer use more than it has in the past. And I think the States should have. But one of the difficulties in the expansion of the State work on fertilizers is the fact that the fertilizer experiment has not a particularly good reputation at the present time.

Mr. HAUGEN. If it is of enough importance, why not say to the stations that they should conduct this type of very important investigations, with the view of giving the results desired, and getting what we hope to accomplish under this provision?

Dr. KELLERMAN. That can be done more easily if we can show evidence of our own real conviction that this is an important work.

Mr. HAUGEN. But I understood you to say that the experiments had been carried on by the States. Are we to infer that the findings of the various stations can not be relied upon?

Dr. KELLERMAN. I do not believe I quite understand your question.

Mr. HAUGEN. The experiments carried on, as I understand it, are of very little value at present.

Dr. KELLERMAN. I think that is a little bit more sweeping than I would like to agree to. The experiments are too diverse in plan and many have not been of as much value as they should be.

Mr. HAUGEN. Can they be improved upon through the experiment stations? This appears to me in this way, that it is a continuance of this untiring effort to build up the dual system in this country. We have our State experiment stations and there seems to be a determined effort on the part of the department to build up a dual system, and it seems that the department is endeavoring to get into every State and run the State affairs. It seems to me that with one station in each State, and having them under one control, the department ought to be at the head of it, it ought to supervise the issuing of bulletins and giving them information, but we should not go into these States and interfere with the organizations that are there.

Dr. KELLERMAN. I want to emphasize the point you raised, that the plan of experimentation here outlined is an attempt to bring the department in closer cooperation with the State station, and not to develop an independent station.

Mr. HAUGEN. But the department is in as close relations with the stations as it can be, if it controls every dollar that can be expended under the Adams Act so far as the Adams Act goes.

Dr. KELLERMAN. But this is the point. If, for example, a State is equipped for investigating the returns from protein feeding in cattle, it is proper to approve a project for that purpose, and such projects may exhaust the Adams fund.

Mr. HAUGEN. But you have the right to dictate to the State what it should be used for.

Mr. KELLERMAN. From the Adams fund?

Mr. HAUGEN. But if this is of enough importance to say that the Adams fund has to be used for this particular project, it is placed in the power of the department.

I have been trying to find out what is the function of the experiment station and the States Relation Service. It seems to me they have been reduced to an ornamental proposition, that there is nothing left for them to do, and when you talk about this proposition in connection with fertilizers, that is going to the limit. It seems to me, so far as the scientists are concerned, whom you speak of in connection with the spreading of fertilizer and the keeping of accounts, as to what you use and the results obtained, it seems to me that is going to the limit. I should suppose that almost anyone employed in the States Relations Service would be able to supervise the work of spreading manure over a field and harvesting it, keeping account of the grain harvested.

Dr. KELLERMAN. A few years ago potash was used in large quantities in the south. The conviction of farmers in that region was that it was necessary. The war has shown that in much of that region it was not necessary. There has been a lot of money wasted in that way, more money than this would amount to in a hundred years.

Mr. HAUGEN. The only question is how can the results desired be best obtained. Do you think they can be best obtained through the experiment stations, or through the department?

Dr. KELLERMAN. I think through both.

Mr. HAUGEN. Should we set up here separate machinery and build up a dual opposition and then in the end not know where we are, whether we are simply interfering with the arrangements which have been made and which I think have worked out fairly satisfactorily. I know it has in our State. I believe those people are capable of doing the few things that are necessary in connection with the spreading of fertilizer and harvesting a crop on a half-acre tract.

Dr. KELLERMAN. The fertilizer history is such a troublesome one that the conviction of the State people, so far as I have talked with them, and the conviction of our own people is that it will take a combination of about the best people we can get together, working enthusiastically together, to get prompt results that are reliable and lasting.

Mr. HAUGEN. You have the talent in Washington and that is the proper place for it, but it is not necessary for the department to send people traveling all over the country with the machinery available in the States. You have probably 5,200 county agents traveling over the country, and they ought to be of some service. You have in many of the States two stations. They started with one and I take it this is an effort to put in a few more.

A few years ago we appropriated $10,000 for sheep and now we have $24,000 in buildings, $10,000 for sheep, and $24,000 for buildings.

Are we going to start in on these lands and build buildings? If we are, the first thing we know we will have two or three stations in every State, when only one is required. We have been cutting out these stations, and nearly every locality which has one comes in and wants an extra station. It seems to me this is an effort to get these extra stations. In my section of the country the experiment stations cooperate with the counties and the counties will meet them half way, and give them the use of the land and appropriate money to carry on these experiments, and I venture to say that any county would be willing to put up half of the money, and you would accomplish the same results.

Dr. KELLERMAN. I hope that would be possible in practically every case.

Mr. HAUGEN. One hundred and twenty-five thousand dollars to start with is quite a large amount, on top of the $60,000,000 carried in the bill. That is quite a large amount at this time, especially at a time when you ought to give your attention to economy.

Dr. KELLERMAN. I think there are two kinds of economy. I think if we allow fertilizer to be used unwisely we might lose millions, where we might save by spending hundreds.

Mr. HAUGEN. We do not want to allow it to be used unwisely.

Dr. KELLERMAN. It is only on that basis that I think it is proper to urge this comparatively large appropriation for initial work. I think if this work is worth doing, and I think it is undoubtedly worth doing. it is worth starting on a scale of such magnitude that it will have a chance of good results. That is the only defense possible, or necessary, for the large expenditure.

Mr. MCLAUGHLIN. Have you considered whether or not this could be done reasonably, satisfactorily through county agents?

Dr. KELLERMAN. It can not be done at all through the county agents. If we had something we knew would work we could tell the county agents what combination of fertilizers should be used. But to tell the county agents, in addition to their other duties, to establish some experiments to find out what kind of fertilizer is the best, would be unwise.

Mr. HAUGEN. You are speaking about the other duties of the county agents. It seems to me that special agents are sent from each bureau to do special work and there is nothing left for the county agent to do.

Dr. KELLERMAN. We find that the county agents are very busy, and our special agents merely take the time to tell them some new thing that they can use to advantage.

Mr. HAUGEN. I suppose if an agent is sent out he ought to know something about fertilizer; that is really the source of the farmer's success, and I presumed that was one of the functions he was expected to perform—to enlighten the people as to the use of it, and the department might be able through the experiment station and through cooperation with the station to furnish him with the necessary information.

Dr. KELLERMAN. It is the lack of that information that makes this item desirable, I believe. You can not tell the county agent much about the fertilizers he ought to advise.

STATEMENT OF DR. WILLIAM A. TAYLOR, CHIEF OF THE BUREAU OF PLANT INDUSTRY, UNITED STATES DEPARTMENT OF AGRICULTURE—Continued.

Dr. TAYLOR. I would like to leave this thought in the minds of the committee, that this proposition, inherently, is for the constructive unification of the investigations of fertilizer use in the country instead of leaving it in its present scattered, diverse, and in many respects unsatisfactory condition.

Mr. ANDERSON. May I suggest, Dr. Taylor, that this language, on its face, does not contemplate any cooperation at all.

Dr. TAYLOR. It does not specifically provide for cooperation, although the consideration of the matter by the department has been upon that basis, as Dr. Kellerman has said.

Mr. ANDERSON. Is it your judgment that this language would permit cooperative expenditure or cooperative use of equipment?

Dr. TAYLOR. Yes, sir; it is comparable with that in practically all of the investigational items in the Bureau of Plant Industry. The initial paragraph of the bureau appropriation gives the broad, blanket authority for cooperation.

Mr. ANDERSON. Many of these cooperative projects involve joint expenditure on the part of the Federal Government and the State government for the same purpose. For instance, you pay part of the salary of a man and the State government pays part of the salary. Is that spirit of cooperation contemplated under this item?

Dr. TAYLOR. Yes, sir. You will find on page 72 the initial paragraph which covers the whole authority to expend that money, under " Expenses in the investigation of fruit and fruit trees, etc., " in cooperation with other branches of the department and State experiment stations and practical farmers."

Mr. ANDERSON. That language is construed to be broad enough to cover the payment of a part of the salary of a man in cooperation with the State?

Dr. TAYLOR. Yes, sir. That is the blanket authority under which we operate and operate cooperatively under most of these paragraphs—in fact, under every paragraph where that method of prosecution appears advisable.

Mr. MCLAUGHLIN. Then, if the wording carries all through this with reference to all these different items, the other portions of that same paragraph would carry all through in the same way, including the words, " for the erection of necessary farm buildings," and that would permit you in any of the places you select to spend any portion of the money you think you ought to expend for farm buildings?

Dr. TAYLOR. That would follow the application of that authority. That is the broad, basic authority of the initial paragraph.

The CHAIRMAN. Take your next item, No. 148, on page 98, for general administrative expenses. There is no change in that item?

Dr. TAYLOR. No, sir; that paragraph is a continuing general paragraph.

The CHAIRMAN. The next item, No. 149, " for purchase, propagation, testing, and congressional distribution of valuable seeds, bulbs, trees, shrubs, vines, cuttings, and plants," and so forth, is the same as last year. There is no change in that?

Dr. TAYLOR. No, sir.

Mr. HAUGEN. How many packages will you be able to furnish under this appropriation?

Dr. TAYLOR. The quotas this year are 14,000 vegetable and 1,000 flower.

Mr. HAUGEN. That is for the current year?

Dr. TAYLOR. Yes.

Mr. HAUGEN. What do you estimate for next year under this appropriation?

Dr. TAYLOR. We have no basis for forecasting the prices of seed for next year.

Mr. HAUGEN. You have no estimates?

Dr. TAYLOR. No; but we anticipate that the peak of the seed prices has been passed. Much will depend, however, on what foreign demand develops in the reconstruction of the agriculture of Europe. The vegetable seed production in this country this year has been much in excess of the year before, except in respect to a few seeds such as cabbage, turnips, and rutabagas, and there the world's supply is apparently short. We are looking into that now.

Mr. HAUGEN. If the question was asked as to the number of packages, what might be the answer?

Dr. TAYLOR. Subject to——

Mr. HAUGEN (interposing). About the same as the current year?

Dr. TAYLOR. We have not yet opened our bids for growing contracts for this year. Late in January we receive our bids for furnishing seeds under the growing contracts; the method under which we commonly secure a considerable portion of these seeds. Those bids will come along about the last of this month, and that is as early as we can expect to have any definite indication of the price for next year's supply.

Mr. HAUGEN. Bids will be opened in about three weeks?

Dr. TAYLOR. About the last of January.

Mr. HAUGEN. Then you will know definitely?

Dr. TAYLOR. Then we will know the basis upon which we can have the seeds grown this summer—those to be secured under this appropriation for next year's distribution.

Mr. HAUGEN. The answer would be about the same number as last year?

Dr. TAYLOR. About the same number, with the chances favoring an enlargement because we feel that the top price has passed.

The CHAIRMAN. There is a great deal of complaint on account of the size of the package of cotton seed. I believe you send out a quart package, and the average farmer will not plant them because it is not enough to plant.

Dr. TAYLOR. The plan under which we are working is to send the quart package for an initial test. In cases where the lint sent in by the farmer from that initial test is found satisfactory, as determined by examination here, we furnish the next year a quantity sufficient, under good cultural conditions, to grow a bale of cotton, so that a commercial test can be made.

Mr. HAUGEN. Just a word as to the distribution of other seeds. They are in small packages and each farmer is limited to one package.

Dr. TAYLOR. To a quantity sufficient for a field test.

Mr. HAUGEN. The trouble is when these are sent out promiscuously if they could get a larger quantity that would give them a fair test, especially in the matter of alfalfa, of which, I believe, the size of the packages is 4 pounds.

Dr. TAYLOR. Four pounds of alfalfa is enough for about a quarter of an acre.

Mr. HAUGEN. That is not enough to give them a real test.

Dr. TAYLOR. It is not enough to give an acreage test. However, it does give the farmer a chance to make a comparison of that with any other alfalfa that he has. For instance, if he has the common alfalfa and is sent the Grimm, he can make an exact comparison of hardiness on a scale sufficient to be very instructive to him with regard to that. He would be glad to have enough for an acre, or in many cases for 5 acres.

Mr. HAUGEN. I do not think it is necessary for him to have enough for 5 acres.

Dr. TAYLOR. We have felt that, in fairness to all the farmers and in the effort to make the fund available accomplish as much as possible, we should do it in that way.

Mr. HAUGEN. It occurred to me that the farmer who would really give it a thorough test might be entitled to two packages, or enough to sow an acre. Farmers who farm a couple hundred acres do not like to spend any time with a quarter of an acre.

The CHAIRMAN. How much does seed for an acre of alfalfa cost?

Mr. HAUGEN. Dr. Taylor says 4 pounds makes a quarter of an acre.

Mr. McLAUGHLIN. What is the market price of Grimm alfalfa seed now?

Dr. TAYLOR. My recollection is that it is around 35 cents a pound wholesale.

(Thereupon, at 12.15 o'clock p. m., a recess was taken until 1.30 p. m.)

AGRICULTURE APPROPRIATION BILL

HEARINGS

BEFORE THE

COMMITTEE ON AGRICULTURE

HOUSE OF REPRESENTATIVES

SIXTY-FIFTH CONGRESS

THIRD SESSION

ON THE

AGRICULTURE APPROPRIATION BILL

OFFICE OF FARM MANAGEMENT

MONDAY, JANUARY 6, 1919

WASHINGTON
GOVERNMENT PRINTING OFFICE
1919

AGRICULTURE APPROPRIATION BILL.

Committee on Agriculture,
House of Representatives,
Monday, January 6, 1919.

Office of Farm Management.

The Chairman. Turn to page 22, the Office of Farm Management. Mr. Christie, the Assistant Secretary, will present the estimates.

STATEMENT OF MR. G. I. CHRISTIE, ASSISTANT SECRETARY, UNITED STATES DEPARTMENT OF AGRICULTURE.

The Chairman. Mr. Christie, the statutory roll involves no increase in salaries above $2,500.

Mr. Christie. I think not, Mr. Chairman.

The Chairman. Is that true, Mr. Harrison?

Mr. Harrison. Yes; there are no increases in the statutory roll above $2,500.

The Chairman. Then we will take up the lump-sum appropriation on page 25.

Mr. McLaughlin. Were those transfers from the lump sum made at the same salaries?

Mr. Harrison. They were made at the same salaries in every instance.

The Chairman. Throughout the entire department?

Mr. Harrison. Yes.

Mr. McLaughlin. There comes up the question again that a lot of these men were employed at emergency salaries for temporary work.

The Chairman. We have already covered that very fully.

Mr. McLaughlin. This just emphasizes it—the repetition of it.

The Chairman. Mr. Christie, I understand there is a proposition in the department to thoroughly reorganize the Office of Farm Management. The committee would be very glad if you would tell us something about the plans you have in mind for that work for the next fiscal year.

Mr. Christie. The work in Farm Management, which includes that of Agricultural Economics, is perhaps one of the most important lines of agricultural work that we have at the present time. The Secretary has, perhaps, given as much thought to agricultural economics and to farm management as to any other one subject that we have before us in the Department of Agriculture. When he came to the Department of Agriculture he was especially interested in two big things, marketing and economics, because of his training, because of his direct interest in these subjects, because of his connection with the agricultural college, and because of his interest in the broader aspects of agriculture itself. He has been able to establish a large and efficient Bureau of Markets, and I think this committee is familiar with the very excellent work that is being carried on. He has attempted to develop an Office of Farm Management that would carry out in some measure his views along that line. The farm management work originally was under the Bureau of Plant Industry, but it was agreed that it should stand more definitely apart from any one bureau and so the Office of Farm Managament was transferred to the Secretary's Office.

Mr. ANDERSON. When?

Mr. CHRISTIE. July 1, 1915. Dr. Spillman was placed in charge of this and in the work the study of farm practice, farm business, and farm organization has been taken up. One phase of the work to which the Office of Farm Management gave some time was the study of the cost of production of various farm products. After this work had been going on for some time, the Secretary of Agriculture hearing criticisms on the studies from several sources, conferred with Dr. Spillman and expressed his views and ideas of the best means of conducting such lines of investigations. The Secretary suggested that the methods and plan of procedure should be modified.

Little attention seems to have been given to the suggestions for the same loose and unsatisfactory methods continued.

We have not been able to get exactly what we wanted out of these studies for the reason they have been carried on by the department too much alone. I find in making a study of the work that there has been little agreement between the Department of Agriculture and the agricultural colleges in making studies along farm-management lines. The Office of Farm Management is cooperating with three institutions—New York, Minnesota, and Wisconsin. These institutions are conducting the work largely according to their own individual ideas. Now, it is the idea of the Secretary that, if this work is to go forward, it should be unified, it should be placed on one basis, and so he has asked us to give some attention to that point.

Recently we invited to the department representatives of the agricultural colleges, of the departments of agricultural economics, and divisions of farm management. With these men we have conferred on the way to proceed to outline the farm-management work. We then, at their suggestion, have secured Prof. Adams, head of the farm management of California University; Prof. Falconer, head of agricultural economics of the Ohio University; Prof. Taylor, head of agricultural economics of the University of Wisconsin; and other leaders to come to Washington to work with us and help us in placing this on a solid foundation. These men are now at work and are attempting to outline the projects in a way that they will be satisfactory not only to the agricultural economics and farm-management people of the Department of Agriculture, but will also be satisfactory to the agricultural economics and farm-management people and related interests in the colleges. We will have the full cooperation of the colleges in this movement. Several of the men have been here and have conferred with us and advised with us and we are getting the plans to a point where we hope to get an early agreement on them.

When we do that along these lines, get down to a working basis, I think we have made a big move for fundamental farm-management study. It is a work that must be carried on in a big way. There are many lines of farm-management work that are regional in character; it is not possible to take them up by States and investigate them and complete them as a State. They are really Federal problems, since they are regional problems, and can not be confined to State lines. For this reason there must be the very closest cooperation between the farm-management departments of the agricultural colleges of the States and the Federal Government in the work which we propose to carry on.

Also in the study of farm practice and in the study of the methods and farm organization we propose to establish that same relationship. It is also the idea of the secretary that, since agricultural economics is a fundamental part of farm management, some of the best agricultural economics people who can be had should be brought into the department and associated here in the work.

The projects of the Office of Farm Management now carried on along the lines of farm practice, farm organization, and special problems, such as the preparation of an atlas of American agriculture, are desirable, and through these the department is furnishing large and valuable aid to farmers. It is proposed to continue this work with such changes and modifications as will strengthen it and make it of even greater value. It is not the plan to lessen our efforts along farm management and farm economics lines, but to enlarge the work and render the largest possible assistance.

This gives you, in a general way, the plans we have at this time.

Mr. ANDERSON. I gathered from a statement made by the secretary some time ago, in response to a Senate resolution, that the work that has heretofore been done by the Bureau of Farm Management, so far as it related to the cost of production, at least, was practically worthless. Do you agree to that?

Mr. CHRISTIE. I agree to that to a certain degree and to certain lines of work that were mentioned. The line of work in question, in the letter of the secretary, was the cost of wheat production.

Mr. ANDERSON. And the same methods, I take it, were pursued in respect to ascertaining the cost of other products, were they not

Mr. CHRISTIE. To a certain extent, except this, that when a man gathers data on sugar beets on one method from 1,025 sugar-beet farmers, he has data that you would value a great deal more than by the same method obtaining data from 158 farmers in the wheat belt taken on a hurry-up trip.

Mr. ANDERSON. What, specifically, is the difficulty with the Spillman method of determining the cost of production of wheat?

Mr. CHRISTIE. The criticism on the methods of determining the cost of production of wheat was that the workers did not gather data on the cost of production of wheat. For instance, an elaborate questionnaire on the items covering the cost of production of wheat was outlined. Then two men were sent into several of the States east of the Rocky Mountains and two other men into Pacific Coast States, with this questionnaire in hand to gather data on cost of production. The men selected an area in Kansas, another one in Missouri, one in Illinois, one in Oklahoma, and one in Indiana. The representatives of the Office of Farm Management then visited in these States 158 farmers. They found the farmer very busy, so they sat down and talked to him a little while, and instead of filling in the questionnaire, they many times took notes in a book. They asked 8 or 10 questions of farmer A, questions 10 to 14 of farmer B, and then questions 18 to 35 of farmer C. After interviewing 25 farmers in this district in that manner and 30 in another and 10 in another, then those men came back and with some general data they had in the office and some basic data from cost-accounting records they prepared a manuscript on the cost of production of wheat in the States east of the Rocky Mountains. Now, when this came to the Secretary's attention, he questioned, of course, the reliability of such data on the actual cost of the production of wheat.

Mr. ANDERSON. Would there be anywhere that you would find farmers who were keeping sufficiently accurate records so that they could answer a questionnaire of this character?

Mr. CHRISTIE. Perhaps not; but if you say you secured data from the farmer and you did not get it, then there is room for a question.

Mr. ANDERSON. I assume that the first step in securing the data on the cost of production of any article would be the use by somebody producing that article of a system of accounting that would give you that data. You have told us what you consider the deficiencies of the Spillman method. Have you worked out a method you intend to pursue?

Mr. CHRISTIE. That is a matter that is partially worked out at this moment. It will be carried Wednesday to Baltimore, when the National Farm Management Association meets, and we will confer with their members and modify it according to their suggestions, and then we will submit it to the agricultural colleges and farm-management men, when we will hope to have it in such shape that it can be used.

Mr. ANDERSON. I am interested in knowing how without any concrete plan to proceed you are able to estimate now what the expense of carrying out that plan will be?

Mr. CHRISTIE. Of course, we have the projects that were outlined for the department for this coming year. These will continue on practically the same basis. I am concerned with the reorganization of the methods and the practices to be followed.

Mr. ANDERSON. I may be mistaken about it, but it occurs to me the character of the organization you set up and methods you pursue in ascertaining costs or any other investigation you make will have a very important bearing upon the cost of the service; and if you have a plan of procedure from which you can determine the cost of the service I really am interested in knowing what it is.

Mr. HARRISON. Those things are being worked out now. The gentlemen mentioned by Mr. Christie came here only a few days ago, and they are working as rapidly as possible. It must be remembered that these estimates were submitted in October. The Secretary, in a recent statement to the agricultural editors, said that he hoped to present at a future time projects for an enlarged Office of Farm Management. This shows very clearly that he does not contemplate any curtailment of the work. On the contrary, he thinks it should be further developed and strengthened; and it involves not only studies of cost of production but matters of general farm practice and business management. That he recognizes the importance of farm economies and farm management is indicated by the fact that he has discussed these problems in his annual report on several occasions, as well as in public addresses.

Mr. ANDERSON. So far as this item is concerned now it is absolutely blind; it is not based on any known system of reorganization of farm management work?

Mr. HARRISON. I would not say that because, as Mr. Christie has indicated, we expect to continue, generally speaking, the same lines of work that have been under way. It is more a question of methods than anything else.

Mr. CHRISTIE. It is more a question of methods than disbanding an organization and discarding what has been done and trying to establish a new department.

Mr. ANDERSON. It seems to me the committee ought to be in this position, whether it is or not: We have just made a discovery after we have spent some hundreds of thousands of dollars, that the work heretofore done under this bureau was practically without value, largely due to the fact that the organization and methods and ascertainment of results were faulty. Now, before we proceed to appropriate $218,000 and, as Mr. Harrison suggests, perhaps a larger amount, it seems to me the committee ought to be satisfied that the method of organization which is going to be followed in the future and the policies which are going to be followed in the future are likely, at least, to secure results that will have value.

Mr. CHRISTIE. I do not like the statement, Mr. Anderson, that the work of this bureau has all been worthless or faulty. The Office of Farm Management has done a lot of valuable and helpful work and is now doing a large amount of helpful work. There has been this one line which has been prominent, because the matter of fixing prices has been before the country. This has called forth some attention and has called forth some criticism. But I would not agree with the statement that all of the work of the Office of Farm Management has been bad or that the money has been wasted, for it has not.

The CHAIRMAN. Do you happen to know how long the department has been studying the cost of production of farm products? Is not that rather a recent work?

Mr. CHRISTIE. On any extensive basis it is recent, and the amount of money put into it is not large. We have other projects; farm practices being followed in the Southern States; farm practices being followed in the Pacific Coast States in the production of wheat; farm practices being followed in sugar-beet production, beef production, etc. Those are the projects that have consumed the money and I think you will find from the publications of the Department of Agriculture they have given results worth while. We should not allow one item to cloud the issue.

Mr. ANDERSON. Of course, I do not mean to suggest there was absolutely nothing of any value done by this bureau. My only impression has been, as to the information given before the committee here before, that this work on cost of the production has been of a rather doubtful character, and exceedingly vague, and much of it absolutely absurd. Now, it may be I expect too much, but as far as I am personally concerned, I would like to know something about the methods to be followed in the future, in respect to this particular proposition.

Mr. CHRISTIE. We can give you the three items.

Mr. ANDERSON. If you have not got it now, we would like to have it later on.

Mr. CHRISTIE. We have it near enough I think now to answer the question. To determine the cost of production it is fundamental that cost-accounting work shall be conducted. I do not think we can get along without it. And that is one fundamental principle we are establishing now. The cost-accounting work, as you state, is work that is somewhat expensive, and it requires time and it must be carefully done and it must be done not only in one State but in several States along one line. It is the aim to establish relations with the State agricultural colleges and to do the work in a thorough, satisfactory way.

Now, to supplement that, then there is the survey method that has been used pretty largely by the department and is used largely by many institutions. This reaches out in an extensive way and touches large numbers of farmers. The survey method should be limited to a few factors on which we can get fairly accurate information in a ready manner. Then the cost accounting would furnish us the basic data for the relation of labor, the relation of fertilizer, and the relation of the feed of live stock to the production of crops, production of milk, etc., and such other factors as will be of value in the different studies.

Mr. ANDERSON. Let me be sure I understand what you have in mind when you say cost accounting, because I am a little bit of a crank on that subject myself. Is it the intention, then, to find a number of farmers who will be at least typical of the region who will keep a set of books on the basis of cost accounting in accordance with the uniform method in which you expect to get this data?

Mr. CHRISTIE. That is the general idea at the present time.

Mr. ANDERSON. Then you anticipate, I presume, you will have to keep a sufficient supervisory force to see that those books are kept up and to supervise the people who are carrying out the project?

Mr. CHRISTIE. We will keep this on a farm basis. There is a method of cost accounting followed now where, in the case of beef production, the study covers only beef production. It fails to consider the production of the crops and the utilization of labor at all times of the year and a number of other factors that really ought to be studied. So in future cost-accounting work it is our desire to study the whole farm.

The CHAIRMAN. And out of the study of the whole farm you get the cost of the individual thing you study?

Mr. CHRISTIE. Its relative cost.

Mr. ANDERSON. The principles of cost accounting are the same, I take it, without reference to what business they are applied to. I assume you have to have some special method perhaps with respect to agriculture. But you must first have a sound basis of the principles of cost accounting on which to proceed in the first instance. Has anybody in your bureau made any study of the question of cost accounting as it is used in commercial establishments?

Mr. CHRISTIE. Prof. Adams, of California University, has been connected with that work for some time, and he has been in commercial work, and he knows something of it and has been close to it; and then Prof. Falconer, who is an eastern man and a graduate of Wisconsin University, also is well versed and has a good grasp of the subject.

The CHAIRMAN. I have thought a good deal about this cost-of-production business myself. You take in North Dakota, for instance, where some portions of it produce wheat some years at the rate of 4 bushels to the acre and some years at the rate of 14 bushels to the acre; or, here you have two farmers side by side, one a thoroughly good farmer and a man of brains and intelligence, who knows how to handle machinery, and here you have another one who is ignorant, slovenly in his methods, who may be not so energetic, certainly not so sensible. What are you going to do in a case of that kind; how are you going to produce it? It seems to me you would have to have a standard of intelligence by which to measure the whole thing from time to time. To my mind, I do not see it is possible to get the cost of production.

Mr. CHRISTIE. Except you must take into consideration in the case of the 4-bushel man the methods used.

The CHAIRMAN. In other words, your conclusion would be based upon the proposition of the general average of farm methods?

Mr. CHRISTIE. It must be. Of course, we have become confused in this matter this year because we have been talking of prices. Our work really should be on the basis of cost of production. The cost of production is one thing and the price is another. These figures that have been given to Congress have relation to the price, and they have been beyond cost, because it was claimed it was necessary to stimulate production; it was necessary to encourage the farmers to use high-priced labor; it was necessary to have him gamble with the seasons, high seed, and high fertilizer. So the prices we have come to speak of are something different from the question of costs we are trying to determine. I think when we get that established in the farmer's mind it will be helpful.

Mr. HAUGEN. Do you think there is ever any possibility of working out any plan that will enable you to ascertain the cost of giving information of any value whatever as to the cost of production of wheat?

Mr. CHRISTIE. Yes; I think we will have information that will be of great value. I would not say that we will have information that would alone be sufficient for Congress to fix one price that will cover the cost of production on all the different farms in all the different regions under all the different conditions.

Mr. HAUGEN. Then of what value is it?

Mr. CHRISTIE. It is of value to the individual farmer; it is of value to the community; it is of value to the State.

Mr. HAUGEN. The cost varies with every farm?

Mr. CHRISTIE. Yes.

Mr. HAUGEN. And on the productive farm you can produce wheat at a less cost than on an unproductive farm; and land costing $10 and acre will produce wheat sometimes just as well as land costing $100 an acre; and it costs less to produce wheat on land costing $10 an acre than it does on land costing $100 an acre. The chairman has called your attention to the different methods of farming, and all of those things will have to be taken into consideration, and the result will be you will find the cost varies according to the number of farms. And then what value could that information be? Spillman kept books for 137 farmers in Pennsylvania, and he gave the information on that 137 farms in Pennsylvania. That child has been declared faulty and laughed out of court.

Mr. HEFLIN. What is the information he gave?

Mr. HAUGEN. It is in the book. He gave the average of 137 farms, and he showed the growing of oats was more productive than wheat. And as we all know who have had any experience in farming, oats might do very well in one year, the yield is large, and the price is up, and more profit then would be in oats then than there would be in wheat. Now, the climate and the method of farming has all to do with it.

Mr. HEFLIN. Do you recall now the average cost of production in that region that he mentioned?

Mr. HAUGEN. No; I do not. But it is in the record. I want to know if there can be any hopes of getting any information along this line that is of any value whatever? We are asked here to appropriate $218,000; yet, as he said, the child has been laughed out of court. There is not a thing in the bill that has been criticised and ridiculed as much as this proposition; and I took it from a lot of stuff that had gone into the record that the department had dropped it.

Mr. CHRISTIE. There is no question but what we are able to get data of great value to agriculture in regions and in States and in communities so that the farmers will know more definitely what it is costing them to produce these various products.

Mr. HAUGEN. You speak of information—a lot of information—but the farmer wants information of value; he does not want information that would mislead him.

Mr. CHRISTIE. But the right kind of investigation should get accurate information.

Mr. HEFLIN. Would it help you if, through publication, you would suggest to the wheat growers you are going to ask for this information and to try to get them to keep accounts?

Mr. CHRISTIE. More farmers each year, as a result of farm management demonstrations, are keeping books. There have been distributed more than 150,000 farm account books to farmers, who have agreed to keep an accurate and careful account of their farm business, and give us the figures for the advice and assistance we have given them in turn. Out of these records we get a lot of information which should pave the way, as you suggest, for an accurate, careful cost-accounting system.

Mr. HAUGEN. Oh, well, fifty thousand is not much out of seven million.

Mr. CHRISTIE. The records from this number of farms should be of great value

Mr. HAUGEN. It is just a question of how much it will cost to get these books in the hands of the farmers. And they have been keeping books. Spillman prepared books for them and he kept the books and gave them the results. But, after all, you had nothing to do with that. But those are the facts in the case, and the whole thing has been ridiculed, and here we are asked to carry on $218,000 again.

The CHAIRMAN. You don't want to be understood as saying that this total appropriation is to be used in studies of the cost of production?

Mr. CHRISTIE. We must have this understood, that only a part of the funds is to go into specific work of that kind.

The CHAIRMAN. And you would like to be distinctly understood that this specific work which we have been discussing will take up only a small proportion of this appropriation?

Mr. CHRISTIE. Yes, sir.

Mr. HAUGEN. What is this money to be used for—what projects?

Mr. CHRISTIE. The projects, with proposed expenditures, are as follows:

General administration:
    Planning and directing farm-management investigations and the business and clerical routine incident thereto_____ $5,200
Farm economics:
    Detailed studies of crop and live-stock enterprises, involving labor requirements, rotations, the farm business, best methods of farm practice, approved practices in feeding and handling live stock, etc _____ 38,460
Farm organization:
    Regional investigations of the practices, organization, and administration of individual farms, and studies of types and systems of farming, with a view to enable farmers to improve their systems of farm management; study of farm equipment; cooperative farm-management investigations, etc_____ 124,900
Cost-of-production studies:
    Determination by farm-management surveys, cost accounting, and other approved methods, unit elements of production in crop and live-stock enterprises _____ 23,800
Special farm-management problems:
    Correlation of statistical data covering the relation of geographic factors to farm enterprises; the relation of farm practice to crop yields; practical systems of farm bookkeeping for farmers' use__ 25,800

                                                                          218,160

Mr. HAUGEN. Where do these county agents come in?

Mr. CHRISTIE. County agents are not investigators. County agents are men who take information that has been collected and carry it to farmers.

Mr. HAUGEN. They are sort of ornaments?

Mr. CHRISTIE. No; they are hardly that.

Mr. HAUGEN. I have been trying to find out what are the functions of the county agents?

Mr. CHRISTIE. They are supposed to give information to the farmers and as far as possible secure its application.

The CHAIRMAN. The county agent was never intended as an investigator, but a disseminator—a "walking teacher."

Mr. CHRISTIE. He is the man who gets in close touch with the farmers and gives them needed valuable help.

Mr. HAUGEN. What are you going to do with this?

Mr. CHRISTIE. We have the work on the agricultural geography, and then we have projects on farm practices, farm economics, and farm organization. For instance, we will study the practice to be followed in the production of meat, production of wheat, sugar beets farm organization, etc.

Mr. HAUGEN. Go into that a little more detailed. What have you in mind in that?

Mr. CHRISTIE. In the corn belt the practice of wintering beef cows is a big question. We send men who study the practices on twenty, thirty, fifty, or a hundred farms in Missouri or Iowa, and from that we show the general and most desirable practice that is being followed, and out of that study we are able to make recommendations to the farmers as to the best practice to follow.

Mr. HAUGEN. What would you say about the wintering of cows in Iowa or any other State? Have you given that much study?

Mr. CHRISTIE. The Office of Farm Management has done some work in Iowa and has secured much helpful information for the farmers on this subject.

Mr. HAUGEN. The thought was this, Why duplicate the work?

Mr. CHRISTIE. We are coperating with the colleges, and then the same practice in Iowa really extends into Illinois or into Missouri or over into Indiana. Our work is to unify these methods and extend the work from one State to the other.

Mr. HAUGEN. What I am afraid of, we are getting in here; we will carry on investigations by one State and they are duplicated by the Federal Government, and in the end we will not know where we are at all.

Mr. CHRISTIE. We are not duplicating in that work.

The CHAIRMAN. Anything further?

Mr. HAUGEN. Only this: You say you are going to use for ascertaining the cost of this part of this $218,000?

Mr. CHRISTIE. We will use a part of this fund.

Mr. HAUGEN. Some things a scientist thinks a great deal of and a practical farmer can't figure it out that way. I beg to agree with them in a great many ways, but when it comes to the practical side of it I have had a little experience.

Mr. CHRISTIE. I want to say the head of the Kansas State College, the head of the Minnesota State College, South Dakota, Wisconsin, and Indiana are all asking for this cooperative help.

FARM LABOR.

The CHAIRMAN. Suppose you tell us about the labor item of the emergency bill, carrying an appropriation of $162,000.

Mr. CHRISTIE. The idea of the Secretary is simply to continue the organization that we now have in the various States and render assistance to farmers in securing farm help. It is our feeling, from what study we have made, that the need for this work will be nearly as great this coming year as it was this past year. We gave to the Army and to the military forces nearly a million men from the farms. For every man that went off the farm to the military forces there was about a man and a half, or a million and one-half, that went into industries.

The CHAIRMAN. That makes two and one-half million farmers.

Mr. CHRISTIE. Two and one-half million men have gone off the farms, and that will account for the farm-labor shortage that exists at this time and has existed this past season.

The CHAIRMAN. Let me ask you two questions: First, what is your opinion as to the return of the farm boys to the farms—to their old vocations? What has been Canada's experience in that direction?

Mr. CHRISTIE. Up to this time no large per cent of them are going back. I am speaking of those men that have returned up to this time. Of course, we are expecting that our men who have not been away as long as Canada's men will return in larger numbers. A large number of the Canadian men have been away since 1914, and the longer they are away from the farms the more they are weaned from the farms.

The CHAIRMAN. Do you think there will be 90 per cent?

Mr. CHRISTIE. That is pretty high.

Mr. HAUGEN. Don't you think that is very largely due to the high wages paid to farmers——

The CHAIRMAN. I was going to ask that question. What per cent of this million and one-half men who have gone into the industries will, when conditions become more or less normal, return to the farms?

Mr. CHRISTIE. That is going to depend entirely on conditions we create on the farms before they return.

The CHAIRMAN. It is largely a wage condition, is it not?

Mr. CHRISTIE. It is wages and homes, a chance to live. A great number of those men are married. If we can put homes on the farms where these married men can live with their families, their children, and have a place for a cow and garden, I have no fear of taking those men back to the farms.

The CHAIRMAN. I had a great experience in my office here not long ago. A boy came in and said, "There is a colored man out there waiting for you. He says you knew him well." I said, "Show him in." He proved to be a farmer that lived near our plantation, owned a farm of 140 acres. His father used to belong to my grandfather. He was a very successful farmer. I said, "What are you doing here, Henry?" He said, "I am down here at Hopewell, Va., working at the munition factory." I asked him what he was making a day, and he said $8. There he was; he had come 500 miles. I imagine as soon as that munition factory closes and this old darkey don't get an $8-a-day job there or around here, he is going back to his farm, but I imagine that it is going to be a slow process to get these men back to the farm.

Mr. CHRISTIE. There will have to be some inducements for them to go back to the farms, and I think the good farms will offer those inducements. We have just made a study of the question, "How I keep help on my farm," and have some interesting stories. It is a common every-day illustration of people in agricultural communities to show how much a farmer gives to his help. He gives them good wages, gives them their garden, he gives them a cow, a couple of pigs, all the chickens they want to raise; he furnishes them many times their meat; he usually keeps a horse and buggy, and many farmers furnish him an automobile and his fuel. About the only thing that man has to buy is some sugar and a few groceries and some clothes. When a man has an opportunity like that there is not any great trouble in keeping him on the farm. There is a shortage of homes for that class of men—we don't have them on our farms. We usually have one house on the farm, and the help lives with the farmer's family. The women are rebelling and calling for help. The farms are not only short men on the farm, but I think we will agree on this: They are in need of women. They can't hire girls as easily as they can hire men. When they have a tenant, his wife will be out there and will assist with the washing and the housework. The children grow up rapidly and will do many chores. When you take one married man you are many times getting additional help.

The CHAIRMAN. That is all very interesting, but that is outside of this $162,000. What are you going to use that for?

Mr. CHRISTIE. We have placed a man that is known as a farm-help specialist in each State. This man works through the agricultural college, and has been locating sources of supply of labor and has been helping get those men to the farms that need them. One of the big works that he did this past summer, when he found he could not get regular laborers, was to tell business men of the great needs of the farmers and organize thousands of those men of the cities to help the farmers harvest their crops.

Another thing we are doing is to show the farmer how they can use better equipment and thus in a material way reduce the amount of labor. One man I know has lost three men off the farm to the war—one right after another. He had a herd of 30 milch cows. When he was about to call a sale I advised him to get a milking machine. He milks his cows now in less time than he and his hired man could milk them before. Farmers are using self-feeders in connection with hogs and cattle. They are using sulky plows where one man will drive four, five, and six horses where before they drove two horses with a walking plow.

In one community last year I was able myself to get five farmers to cooperate in harvesting their wheat. They went to one farm and with two binders cut the grain and had three men to shock it. They then went to a second farm, and so on.

A farm-help specialist is able to render a big service.

The CHAIRMAN. What is the Employment Service doing along this line?

Mr. CHRISTIE. The Employment Service establishes offices in cities. They have a man that wants a job and they have a man who wants help. It is the aim of the Employment Service to bring them together. It is found, however, that where a farmer wants a man he applies to the county agent. The county agents this year have placed directly farm hands on over 100,000 farms.

The CHAIRMAN. I am glad to hear you make this statement, because I had some doubt about that last year.

Mr. HAUGEN. How much are you asking for that?

Mr. CHRISTIE. $162,000.

Mr. HAUGEN. For farm help; just itself?

Mr. CHRISTIE. Yes.

Mr. HAUGEN. That is for getting farm labor for the farm?

Mr. CHRISTIE. Yes; to do this work of which I am speaking.

The CHAIRMAN. You say your county agents placed over 100,000 last year?

Mr. CHRISTIE. Yes.

The CHAIRMAN. Do you have any record of how many men were placed by these men of yours?

Mr. CHRISTIE. The farm-help specialist is working in connection with the county agents.

Mr. ANDERSON. The experience we have had up in our country was that the county agent was never able to catch the labor specialist with any men on his list?

Mr. CHRISTIE. Of course, that is unfortunate; with a large labor shortage it is hard to find loose men.

The CHAIRMAN. The best way to get farm labor in my country is to enforce the vagrancy law in the cities and towns.

Mr. HAUGEN. I have made special inquiry and I haven't been able to find one man that a farm-help specialist has placed on the farm.

Mr. CHRISTIE. Out in your country the farm-help specialist organized the movement to have city people aid the farmers.

Mr. HAUGEN. Not in our country. It is over 50 years old there.

The CHAIRMAN. Mr. Christie, if there is nothing else and no further questions, we are very much obliged to you.

(Thereupon, at 5.20 o'clock p. m., the committee took a recess until 10.30 a. m., Tuesday, January 7, 1919.)

AGRICULTURE APPROPRIATION BILL.

Committee on Agriculture,.
House of Representatives,
Tuesday, January 7, 1919.

The committee met at 10.30 o'clock a. m., Hon. A. F. Lever (chairman) presiding.

The CHAIRMAN. The committee will come to order. Turn to page 102 of the Book of Estimates, and we will take up this morning the Forest Service. Prof. Graves is with us.

Forest Service.

STATEMENT OF MR. HENRY S. GRAVES, FORESTER AND CHIEF, FOREST SERVICE, UNITED STATES DEPARTMENT OF AGRICULTURE.

The CHAIRMAN. Doctor, in the statutory roll, have you any recommendations for an increase of salary above the $2,500 limit?

Mr. GRAVES. Yes, sir. We have the same problem as every other bureau and department of the Government has with reference to maximum salaries and low-grade salaries for clerks and others. We have also the very serious problem of our forest supervisors and assistants, the salaries of a number of them running over $2,500.

The CHAIRMAN. Have you made any recommendation for their increase?

Mr. GRAVES. Yes, sir; we made up a supplemental estimate.

The CHAIRMAN. The committee has decided not to consider that supplemental estimate at all. In your regular statutory roll, have you made any recommendations?

Mr. GRAVES. The first roll was submitted without any recommendation of any kind, with the idea that the supplemental estimate would take care of all the promotions.

The CHAIRMAN. Then we won't discuss the statutory roll at all. Turn to page 113, gentlemen. I notice there, Doctor, you have a recommendation for changing the limit of the cost of buildings from $650 to $1,500. There is some additional language there. I wish you would explain to the committee the reason for that.

Mr. GRAVES. The committee a number of years ago placed a limitation of $650 on the cost of buildings that might be erected by the Forest Service. We have found it to be impossible to erect buildings suitable as headquarters for our rangers for $650. Last year we requested the Office of Public Roads, through its rural engineering division, to make us plans for ranger stations on the basis of the present statutory limitation. They declined to do it on the ground that it could not be done. They recommended an increase of limitation to $1,500. It sometimes happens that a building burns down.

Our ranger stations are at isolated points, often a long distance from railroads and from centers of supplies. Occasionally buildings are burned or become unserviceable that were erected at a time when the cost of construction, cost of materials, and cost of labor were such as to permit us to erect buildings at $650. We simply can not replace them under present conditions within this limitation. I have in mind a specific instance on the Tonto National Forest, in Arizona, where a ranger station situated 117 miles from the railroad was burned down. We simply could not replace it within the statutory limitations. Since then the forest ranger and his wife have been living in a tent under pretty hard conditions.

The CHAIRMAN. What is the character of this building, Doctor? It can not be much of a building for $650.

Mr. LEE. In other words, tell us what this building is made of—lumber or logs?

Mr. GRAVES. The national forests are still so undeveloped that in order to place our rangers at points where they can render the best service in the protection of the forests and taking care of the local business we must erect headquarters for them. This is specifically authorized in the general language of the statute.

Mr. MCKINLEY. Are they built of logs?

Mr. GRAVES. Sometimes of logs and sometimes of lumber. The cost of a log house is about the same as of lumber.

Mr. LEE. Not if you haul the lumber 117 miles.

Mr. GRAVES. There are certain things you would have to haul—nails and other materials—and then there is the difficulty of getting labor that distance.

Mr. THOMPSON. You don't build them all that far from the railroad?

Mr. GRAVES. That was an extreme case that occurred during the war, at a time when we were not building any new buildings, and it simply illustrates a rather extreme case, where we simply could not build any kind of a suitable building for our forest officers.

The CHAIRMAN. How many rooms are in these buildings?

Mr. GRAVES. The ranger stations have usually three or four small rooms.

The CHAIRMAN. Do you build the stables for the horses at the stations?

Mr. GRAVES. We also have a barn for the horses, and sometimes sheds and other buildings.

Mr. MCKINLEY. You are limited to $650 for a building. You could build four buildings, couldn't you, at that price for each?

Mr. GRAVES. We can not build one building suitable for a ranger and his family for $650.

Mr. MCKINLEY. Can not you build two for $650 each? That is the way Mr. Roosevelt built the Agricultural Department down here.

Mr. GRAVES. Wouldn't it be better to recognize the situation and provide for one building, frankly, as a ranger station, rather than try to get around it by building two buildings?

The CHAIRMAN. I think so. It would be a great deal better.

Mr. GRAVES. Our program does not call for a large number of buildings, but we do have these occasional cases where we have to replace our buildings already erected, and from time to time we have to build new buildings.

The CHAIRMAN. It will not be your purpose to use any of this to rebuild existing structures?

Mr. GRAVES. Only as they reach a point where they have to be rebuilt. It is a matter of good economy to build a house that will last more than two or three years.

Mr. RUBEY. Where do you buy your lumber?

Mr. GRAVES. At the nearest possible mills.

Mr. RUBEY. Do you buy it from private stores?

Mr. GRAVES. Yes; the nearest place we can find.

Mr. RUBEY. You don't use this forestry lumber in the building of these houses?

Mr. GRAVES. If there is a mill near by, we do.

The CHAIRMAN. Explain this language—this new language as follows: "Including the payment of rewards under regulations of the Secretary of Agriculture for information leading to arrest and conviction for violation of the laws and regulations relating to fires in or near national forests, or for the unlawful taking of, or injury to, Government property." Are you having difficulty in getting testimony?

Mr. GRAVES. We always have a certain amount of incendiarism. It is not as large as one might expect, but frequently there are as many as 10 per cent of our fires set purposely. The incendiarism has not been so much from malice—I think it is seldom that—as from the desire to get rid of the forest cover, with the idea or purpose of clearing the undergrowth, so the stock can have more grass, prospecting be simpler, and so on. But we must recognize that there is a certain amount of incendiarism, forest fires set purposely. We have posted the forests offering a reward for anyone found setting fires, for information leading to their arrest and conviction. The posting of the forests with these notices has had a salutary effect; a few convictions go farther under such conditions than any amount of general education, though, of course, we are carrying that on at the same time. We have been informed by our solicitor that there is a question whether the department has legal authority to pay these rewards directly. We have taken the matter up with the Department of Justice. They concur in that idea, and concur also in the plan which we have presented here, feeling that it is much better to have these rewards offered and paid by the Secretary of Agriculture rather than to put the whole burden on the Department of Justice. Therefore we are asking for authority to enable us to offer these rewards and pay them. It will be a matter that may amount to several hundred dollars a year, not very much, but even the occasional case will help us very much in preventing incendiarism.

The CHAIRMAN. If there is no other question on that proposition, we will take up the matter of "Salaries and field and station expenses," pages 114 to 121. They are summarized on page 121. I notice you have an increase there of $266,074.

Mr. GRAVES. May I in this connection speak of the receipts from the national forests?

The CHAIRMAN. Yes. Do that first, and then tell us about this increase.

Mr. GRAVES. The Forest Service, in the handling of the national forests, is receiving income from the use of its various resources, the grazing, the sale of timber, use of waterpower, and other uses. Nine years ago, in the fiscal year 1909, the receipts were $1,766,088.

Mr. LEE. From all sources?

Mr. GRAVES. From all sources. This last year, that is, the fiscal year ending June 30, 1918, the receipts were $3,574,930.

The CHAIRMAN. What was it in 1917?

Mr. GRAVES. $3,457,028. There was a small increase that year. We are completing the readjustment of the grazing fees, which in 1916 it was announced would be increased during a period of three years, so that we estimate that during the current year, that is, the fiscal year in which we are now operating, we will receive an increase of from eight to nine hundred thousand dollars, bringing the receipts up to approximately $4,400,000 and possibly more if our timber-sale business picks up.

Mr. ANDERSON. Those timber sales include spruce for airplane purposes, or anything of that sort?

Mr. GRAVES. We made several small sales of Sitka spruce for airplanes, but most of the airplane timber which was accessible was privately owned, and most of the Government-owned airplane spruce was remote.

Mr. ANDERSON. I was trying to get at whether such increase as your figures showed was likely to be a permanent one, or arose out of conditions due to the war.

Mr. GRAVES. It will be a permanent one. This last year we had more live stock in the national forests under temporary permit as a war measure. I am not certain whether we can continue to graze the present number, but that will be more than offset by the increase in grazing fees. Undoubtedly our timber business in the course of a year or two will pick up so there will be a substantial increase in that also.

Mr. LEE. On the method of bookkeeping: You furnished crossties for Alaska, you say, and you furnished airplane stock to the Government, whatever they wanted. Does the Forest Service get credit for that?

Mr. GRAVES. So far, there has been relatively little timber given away to other departments of the Government.

Mr. LEE. Well, ought there to be any given away?

Mr. GRAVES. Yes; I think so, but I do think our books should show the value as a credit return.

Mr. LEE. I think so myself. You might be very short on receipts from the forests, and yet the Government is getting the benefit of that, and the Forest Service should get credit for whatever goes out from the forests, I should think.

Mr. GRAVES. So far the values have merely been mentioned in our reports, and there has not been a formal credit.

Mr. LEE. Why shouldn't it be given credit?

Mr. GRAVES. I think it would be desirable, sir.

Mr. LEE. The Government might take half of what we have, and we never get credit for it.

The CHAIRMAN. Doctor, will you itemize those receipts, so much in grazing fees, so much the sale of timber, and other uses?

Mr. GRAVES. I have it for the year 1918. For 1919 it would merely be an estimate.

The CHAIRMAN. Let that go in the record.

(The statement referred to follows:)

National forest receipts for the fiscal year ending June 30, 1918.

Disposal of timber	$1,633,649.42
Grazing	1,726,118.36
Special use	121,185.94
Water power	93,976.35
Total	$3,574,930.07

Mr. RUBEY. Have you also a statement of the expenditures this year, and the expenditures nine years ago?

Mr. GRAVES. I have that and can insert that in the record.

(The statement referred to follows:)

National forest receipts and appropriations for the fiscal years 1909 to 1919, inclusive.[1]

Fiscal year.	Receipts.	Appropriations.	Fiscal year.	Receipts.	Appropriations.
1909	$1,766,088.46	$3,896,200.00	1915	$2,481,469.35	$5,548,256.00
1910	2,041,181.22	4,646,200.00	1916	2,823,540.71	5,553,256.00
1911	1,968,993.42	5,008,100.00	1917	3,457,028.41	5,549,735.00
1912	2,109,256.91	5,533,100.00	1918	3,574,930.07	5,712,275.00
1913	2,391,920.85	5,343,040.00	1919	[2] 4,400,000.00	5,731,555.00
1914	2,437,710.21	5,399,679.00			

[1] In the year 1914, $75,000, and in the years 1915 to 1919, inclusive, $100,000 for each year were appropriated to aid States in fire protection on the watersheds of navigable streams.
[2] Estimated.

Deficits were incurred to meet extraordinary fire emergencies in the following years:

Fiscal year:	Amount.
1911	$900,000
1915	349,243
1916	57,300
1918	775,000
	2,081,543

The emergency item for fighting and preventing forest fires carried in the regular appropriations was supplemented by a second emergency fund which made available $1,000,000 in 1912, $200,000 in 1913, $200,000 in 1914, and $100,000 in 1915, additional to the sums listed above. Of the $1,000,000 item less than $40,000 was spent.

Mr. RUBEY. The point I wanted to make is this: You gave the receipts nine years ago and the receipts last year, and I would like to know what the expenses were nine years ago and the expenditures last year, so we can get an idea how we are getting along and how the receipts compare with expenditures.

Mr. GRAVES. The receipts now practically cover the current operating expenses of the national forests. They do not yet cover the research work, the permanent improvements, and other expenses that are not properly chargeable to operation.

Mr. RUBEY. The annual question we ask is, how long is it going to be until the recipts will cover the expenditures?

Mr. GRAVES. Well, the receipts this year are covering the operating expenditures of the business of the National Forests.

Mr. Rubey. Just about reached that point?

Mr. Graves They have reached that point, if we don't include permanent improvements, like road building and research work, and similar items.

Mr. McKinley. Just to put it right so people can read it, the receipts are $4,400,000?

Mr. Graves. Our receipts this year will be approximately $4,400,000.

Mr. McKinley. And your expenses $6,000,000?

Mr. Graves. Our expenses for everything, about $6,000,000.

The Chairman. But your operating expenses?

Mr. Graves. About four and one-fourth million dollars.

Mr. Lee. The rest goes into permanent improvements?

Mr. Graves. Permanent improvements, research, planting, and settlement of land question, surveys for settlers, and things of that sort, which, from a business standpoint, are hardly chargeable to operating expenses.

Mr. Lee. Roads and buildings.

Mr. Graves. Of course we have not yet covered all the expenses of the Forest Service by something like a million and a half dollars, but we have reached the point of covering that one phase of it, the current operating costs of the National Forests.

Mr. McKinley. Then, don't the States, or the people living in the States, say you monopolize a great deal of grazing lands the State would get taxes from if you didn't keep them?

Mr. Graves. Congress appropriated 25 per cent of the receipts from the National Forests direct to the States for the use of schools, school fund, and for roads, and in most cases those receipts, together with the additional amount the Government has appropriated for road building is equal, or will eventually equal, what they could have secured in taxes. This will be a permanent and increasing fund.

Mr. McKinley. Then when you say you have received $4,400,000, is it not a fact you are actually only receiving $3,300,000 net?

Mr. Graves. I regard the 25 per cent given the States as a separate appropriation which Congress has made, a disposition of the funds which have been received.

Mr. McKinley. It costs $6,000,000 to run the department, and you get net back $3,300,000?

Mr. Graves. Approximately, that is what is left.

The Chairman. Any further statement, Doctor, on that subject? Do you desire to make any other general statement before we go to these various lines of work?

Mr. Graves. Not connected with the immediate subject.

Mr. Anderson. I would like to make an inquiry, which is, perhaps, a general inquiry.

The Chairman. Go ahead.

Mr. Anderson. I gathered from something I saw in the newspapers the other day that the Forest Service had under consideration the use of airplanes for ranger work. Is there anything you can say on that subject?

Mr. Graves. The question has been raised by some of the Army officers as to the possibility of having forest protection as one of the civil uses of airplanes. We have furnished information regarding the practicability of their use, as far as we could see it, in the national forests and elsewhere, as a means of scouting for and locating fires. I feel personally that it is a possible, a very practical, use of the airplane. From the standpoint of the national-forest funds, it would be an expensive undertaking. But if the Army made that one of the civil uses of airplanes, in connection with the training of aviators and in the development of the art and science of building and using airplanes, I think it would be an exceedingly valuable thing. From the standpoint of the forests, it would result in a great deal of saving.

Mr. ANDERSON. From the standpoint of the economical use of money which is appropriated in this bill for forestry purposes, you don't think that the use of airplanes is feasible?

Mr. GRAVES. I don't think it is within the limits of what I could ask for in our regular appropriation bill. A system of aircraft patrol would be, I fancy, a pretty expensive thing. If it were adopted it would have to be combined with the Army use of airplanes. If the Army is going to have airplanes, this might be one more practical civil use which would give an added value besides merely the training of men for warfare; but there is no question that the use of airplanes for scouting for fires would be practical and would save lots of timber, enabling us to do some things we can not do now.

The CHAIRMAN. Anything further, Mr. Anderson? All right, Doctor, your next item is on page 124, item 353, where you have combined two items.

Mr. GRAVES. There are some changes in the individual forest appropriations.

The CHAIRMAN. In the individual forest appropriations?

Mr. GRAVES. I will insert in the record a statement showing the changes in individual forest appropriations.

(The statement referred to follows:)

STATEMENT SHOWING THE PROPOSED CHANGES IN THE APPROPRIATIONS FOR THE INDIVIDUAL NATIONAL FORESTS.

Item No. 203, Beartooth National Forest.—The amount now provided for the Beartooth National Forest, $4.313, is changed to $5,437, an increase of $1,124. It is necessary to place the regular protective short-term organization on a four-months' basis, which will require an estimated increase of $1,124. The present protective organization is based on two to three months' employment for lookouts, smoke chasers, and patrolmen. This is the actual period of the season of fire hazard, and does not provide a period of instruction, training, and preparation prior to entering upon the protection work, which is the key to any efficient organization and is fully recognized by our Army. The experience of the past has brought home very forcibly that these inexperienced employees require some training and preparation to render them effective. Further, the period of two or three months is not attractive enough to secure the character of men required. Four months of this work would place the Forest Service protective work on a par with other woods and field activities, and tend to draw the type of men needed to build an efficient fire organization.

Item No. 206, Bitterroot National Forest.—The amount now provided for the Bitterroot National Forest, $10,367, is changed to $17,189, an increase of $6,822. Of this increase, $250 is needed to cover increased cost of maintaining Government stock now assigned to and needed on this National Forest. It is necessary to maintain a pack train and also two teams for protective and administrative purposes. Forage and the necessary shoeing, etc., of Government horses have increased steadily the past two years, and further advances may be expected.

The Bitterroot National Forest is a heavily timbered Forest of 1,155,868 acres supporting a stand of timber consisting of approximately 5,000,000,000 feet board measure. A large part of this national forest is far removed from settlements, and when fires occur it is difficult, owing to inadequate means of transportation and long distance, to secure emergency fire fighters promptly. Lightning-caused fires are particularly numerous some seasons and often several days will elapse before a fire crew can be conveyed to the scene of the fire, thus allowing the fire to gain great headway. It has been found that the normal protective force which has been provided in the past is inadequate to meet the situation, and it is proposed to increase the summer force by 10 men for four months each, which would cost $5,000. It is also necessary to place the regular protective organization for the Bitterroot National Forest on a four-months' basis instead of, as at present, two to three months. This will require an estimated increase of $1,572. The records show that during every severe fire season during the last 10 years, the Bitterroot National Forest has suffered materially; that in 1910 25,000,000 feet board measure were burned; and in 1917 13,383,000 feet board measure. The cost of emergency fire suppression, in addition to the regular administrative and protective force, was, in 1910, $18,177, and in 1917 $23,090.

Item No. 207, Blackfeet National Forest.—The amount now provided for the Blackfeet National Forest, $12,969, is changed to $19,888, an increase of $6,919. Of this increase $500 is needed to cover increased cost of maintaining Government stock now assigned to and needed on this National Forest. It is necessary to maintain a team and several pack trains—in all 21 head—for protective and administrative purposes. The Blackfeet National Forest is a heavily timbered forest of 1,067,090 acres supporting a stand of timber consisting of approximately 2,398,000,000 feet b. m. A large part of this National Forest is far removed from settlements and when fires occur, it is difficult, owing to inadequate means of transportation and long distances, to secure emergency fire fighters promptly. It has been found that the normal protective force which has been provided in the past is inadequate to meet the situation, and it is proposed to increase this force by five men, costing $2,500. It is also necessary to place the regular protective organization for the Blackfeet National Forest on a four-months' basis which will require an estimated increase of $3,919. The records show that during every severe fire season during the last 10 years, the Blackfeet National Forest has suffered materially; that in 1910, 110,000,000 feet b. m. were burned; in 1914, 10,115,000 feet b. m.; and in 1917, 38,568,000 feet b. m. The cost of emergency fire suppression in addition to the regular administrative and protection force was, in 1910, $63,358; in 1914, $13,716; and in 1917, $51,780.

Item No. 211, Cabinet National Forest.—The amount now provided for the Cabinet National Forest, $9,133, is changed to $16,806, an increase of $7,673. The Cabinet National Forest is a heavily timbered forest of 1,026,550 acres supporting a stand of timber consisting of approximately 958,000,000 feet b. m. A large part of this National Forest is far removed from settlements and when fires occur, it is difficult, owing to inadequate means of transportation and long distances, to secure emergency fire fighters promptly. It has been found that the normal protective force which has been provided in the past is inadequate to meet the situation, and it is proposed to increase this force by 10 men, costing $5,000. It is also necessary to place the regular protective organization of the Cabinet National Forest on a four-months' basis, which will require an estimated increase of $2,673. The present protective organization is based on two to three months' employment for lookouts, smoke chasers, and patrolmen. The records show that during every severe fire season during the last 10 years, the Cabinet National Forest has suffered materially; that in 1910, 700,000,000 feet b. m. were burned; in 1914, 3,064,000 feet b. m.; and in 1917, 5,303,000 feet b. m. The cost of emergency fire suppression in addition to the regular administrative and protective force was in 1910, $78,045; in 1914, $28,135; and in 1917, $54,282.

Item No. 220, Clearwater National Forest.—The amount now provided for the Clearwater National Forest, $12,665, is changed to $38,201, an increase of $25,536. Of this increase, $1,500 is needed to cover the increased cost of maintaining Government stock now assigned to and needed on this national forest. It is necessary to maintain a team and several pack trains—in all 49 head—for protective and administrative purposes. The Clearwater National Forest is a heavily timbered forest of 907,846 acres, supporting a stand of timber consisting of approximately 5,000,000,000 feet b. m. A large part of this national forest is far removed from settlements and when fires occur it is difficult, owing to inadequate means of transportation and long distances, to secure emergency fire fighters promptly. Lightning-caused fires are particularly numerous some seasons and often several days will elapse before a fire crew can be conveyed to the scene of the fire, thus allowing the fire to gain great headway. It has been found that the normal protective force which has been provided in the past is inadequate to meet the situation, and it is proposed to increase this force by one fire chief whose duty will be responsibility for year-long attention to fire protection and its problems and the coordination of ranger districts in fire-protection plans and through field work, to perfect the forest-protection plan to the point where it will be sure of execution. The salary of this employee will be $1,800, and an estimated amount of $300 will be provided for necessary travel. It is also proposed to employ two assistants at $1,300 each, whose duties will be to act as foremen of the fire-protection crews and to be employed primarily on fire-protection and suppression work and to assist the district rangers in such work on their ranger districts. It is also proposed to add to the protective force 30 men for four months, costing $15,000.

If mobilized in crews, these men will be employed in improving and constructing trails at such times during the four-month periods as they are not actively engaged in fire detection or fire-suppression work. It is also necessary to place the regular protective organization for the Clearwater National Forest on a four-months' basis, which will require an estimated increase of $4,336. The present protective organization is based on two to three months' employment for lookouts, smoke chasers, and patrolmen. This is the actual period of the season of fire hazard, and does not provide a period of instruction training and preparation prior to entering upon the protective work, which is the key to any efficient organization and is fully recognized by our Army. The experience of the past has brought home very forcibly that these inexperienced employees require some training and preparation to render them effective. Further, the period of two or three months is not attractive enough to secure men of the character required. Four months of this work would place the forest service protective work on a par with other woods and field activities, and tend to draw the type of men needed to build an efficient fire organization. The records show that during every severe fire season during the last 10 years the Clearwater National Forest has suffered materially; that in 1910, 1,350,000,000 feet b. m. were burned; in 1914, 29,699,000 feet b. m.; and in 1917, 1,811,000 feet b. m. The cost of emergency fire suppression, in addition to the regular administrative and protective force, was, in 1910, $81,718; in 1914, $102,571; and in 1917, $12,974.

Item No. 223, Coconino National Forest.—The amount now provided for the Coconino National Forest, $16,386, is changed to $21,673, an increase of $5,305. For the fiscal year 1917, the Coconino National Forest collected $150,254.34 for the sale of timber, grazing of stock, and from other sources, while the operating cost for that national forest was only $43,453.45. During the fiscal year 1918, timber-sale business decreased on account of labor disturbances and market conditions, so that the total receipts amounted to $138,557.03, while the operating expenses were $44,018.94. Market conditions are now improving so that the cut for 1919 will probably exceed that for either 1917 or 1918, and, in addition to this, there is an application for an additional large timber sale near Stoneman Lake which, if consummated, will result in an entirely new enterprise. It has developed that a careful study of grazing privileges must be made on the Coconino National Forest. While the regulations provide for the distribution of grazing resources so as to benefit the greatest number of owners, it has been brought to the attention of the local forest officers that the spirit of the grazing regulations can not be rigidly enforced without the collection of data as to the number of stock belonging to corporations and in excess of the permitted number which should be removed from the ranges so as to provide grazing privileges for those entitled to and needing them. The $5,305 increase over the appropriation will provide for the employment of two scalers at $1,400, one grazing examiner at $1,600, with $905 for necessary travel and incidental expenses for the three.

Item No. 224, Coeur d'Alene National Forest.—The amount now provided for the Coeur d'Alene National Forest, $36,717, is changed to $53,290, an increase of $16,573. The Coeur d'Alene National Forest is a heavily timbered forest of 790,234 acres, supporting a stand of timber consisting of approximately 4,100,000 000 feet b. m. A large part of this national forest is far removed from settlements, and when fires occur it is difficult, owing to inadequate means of transportation and long distances, to secure emergency fire fighters promptly. It is proposed to increase the protective force by one fire chief, whose duty will be responsibility for year-long attention to fire protection and its problems, and the coordination of ranger districts in fire-protection plans and through field work to perfect the forest-protection plan to the point where it will be sure of execution. The salary of this employee will be $1,500, and an estimated amount of $300 will be provided for necessary travel. It is also proposed to employ two assistants at $1,300 each whose duties will be to act as foremen of the fire-protection crews and to be employed primarily on fire-protection and suppression work, and to assist the district rangers in such work on their ranger districts. It is also proposed to add to the protective force 15 men, costing $7,500. It is also necessary to place the regular protective organization for the Coeur d'Alene National Forest on a four months' basis, which will require an estimated increase of $4,673. The records show that during every severe fire season during the last 10 years, the Coeur d'Alene National Forest has suffered materially; that in 1910, 2,000,000,000 feet b. m. were burned; in 1914, 590,000 feet b. m.; and in 1917, 537,000 feet b. m. The cost of emergency fire suppression in addition to the regular administrative and protective force was in 1910 $154,114; in 1914, $10,099 ;and in 1917, $23,586.

Item No. 225, Colorado National Forest.—The amount now provided for the Colorado National Forest, $3,959, is changed to $7,459, an increase of $3,500. This increase is necessary on account of the large addition of 470.394 acres by presidential proclamation of June 27, 1917, under congressional authority as provided in the act of September 8, 1916 (39 Stat., 850), entitled "An act authorizing the addition of certain lands to the Colorado and Pike National Forests, Colorado." The administration and protection of this additional area require the services of two additional rangers and four summer guards at a salary of $75 per month for a period of four months each. On account of the increased territory and largely increased timber-sale business, it will be necessary also to employ a forest examiner at a salary of $1,300. Travel and other expenses incident to this addition to the forest amount to $1,000, making a net increase in expenditures for salaries and expenses of approximately $3,500. no increased appropriation for the Colorado National Forest having been made since the additional area was included.

Item No. 227, Colville National Forest.—The amount now provided for the Colville National Forest, $6,883, is changed to $11,183, an increase of $4,300. The Colville National Forest is a heavily timbered forest of 816,000 acres supporting a stand of timber consisting of approximately 2,847,000,000 feet b. m. It is proposed to increase the protective force by one fire chief, whose duty will be responsibility for year-long attention to fire protection and its problems and the coordination of ranger districts in fire-protection plans and through field work to perfect the forest-protection plan to the point where it will be sure of execution. The salary of this employee will be $1,500, and an estimated amount of $300 will be provided for necessary travel. It is also proposed to add to the protective force five men to be assigned to strategic points on the forest and either to be mobilized in crews capable of quick transport to the location of fires or scattered throughout the forest as fire patrolmen and smoke chasers. This will cost $2,500. The records show that during every severe fire season during the last 10 years the Colville National Forest has suffered materially; that in 1910, 22,000,000 feet b. m. were burned; in 1914, 880,000 feet b. m.; and in 1917, 1,737,000 feet b. m. The cost of emergency fire suppression in addition to the regular administrative and protective force was in 1910, $18,046; in 1914, $14,874; and in 1917, $14,437.

Item No. 228, Coronado National Forest.—The amount now provided for the Coronado National Forest, $9,044, is changed to $11,050, an increase of $2,006. Constantly increasing intensive use of the various divisions of the Coronado National Forest will necessitate providing salary and expenses for an additional forest examiner to handle timber sales, the leasing of residence sites, and the survey of lands in connection with applications from settlers and near-by residents for permits of varying character. The threatened practical destruction by fire of national-forest resources on the entire Chiricahua division of the Coronado National Forest in 1917 has prompted a careful study of protection plans and shows the necessity of placing additional fire patrolmen on that division as well as the Santa Catalina division. The topography of these areas is so irregular as to make it impossible for fire guards to travel the great distances possible on some other national forests, and until additional trails are built it will be necessary to continue this additional expense in protection. The increase of $2,006 will provide for the salary and travel of one forest examiner, year long, and two fire guards for two months, each at a salary of from $75 to $80 per month. The words "and New Mexico" are added, since 129,152 acres of the Coronado National Forest are located in New Mexico. This portion of the Coronado National Forest was formerly a part of the Chiricahua National Forest, which was consolidated with the Coronado National Forest on July 1, 1917, and inadvertently the addition of the words "and New Mexico" was omitted from the Coronado National Forest subappropriation in the appropriation bill for the fiscal year 1919.

Item No. 229, Crater National Forest.—The amount now provided for the Crater National Forest, $19,288, is changed to $22,688, an increase of $3,400. The Crater National Forest is a heavily timbered forest of 1,079,325 acres, supporting a stand of timber consisting of approximately 8,847,000,000 feet b. m. It has been found that the normal protective force which has been provided in the past is inadequate to meet the forest-fire situation, and it is proposed to increase this force by one-half the time of one fire chief whose duty will be responsibility for attention to fire protection and its problems and the coordination of ranger districts in fire-protection plans and through field work, to perfect the forest-protection plan to the point where it will be sure of execution. The salary of this employee for six months will be $750, and an estimated amount of $150 will be provided for necessary travel. The remainder of his salary and travel will be chargeable to the Umpqua National Forest which adjoins the Crater National Forest on the north. It is also proposed to add to the protective force five men for four months costing $2,500, to be assigned to strategic points on the forest and either to be mobilized in crews capable of quick transport to the location of fires or scattered throughout the forest as fire patrolmen and smoke chasers. The Crater National Forest has suffered materially during every severe fire season during the last 10 years; in 1910, 290,491,000 feet b. m. were burned, and in 1917, 21,584,000 feet b. m. The cost of emergency fire suppression in addition to the regular administrative and protective force was in 1910, $40,804; in 1914, $6,677; and in 1917, $41,632.

Item No. 232, Datil National Forest.—The amount now provided for the Datil National Forest, $11,009, is changed to $13,950, an increase of $2,941. The receipts from the grazing of stock, sale of timber, and other uses on the Datil National Forest amounted for the fiscal year 1918 to $54,044.67, an increase of $5,015.60 over the fiscal year 1917. This national forest has an acreage of 2,672,016.69 acres, all of which is intensively used for the grazing of stock. In order to formulate a definite plan of management for the economic use of the forage crop without injury and also to provide for equitable distribution of the range between the hundreds of permittees, it is necessary to employ a grazing examiner. The great influx of settlers from Texas, Oklahoma, and Missouri has resulted in much land which has hitherto been used for grazing alone being cultivated and converted into homes and farms. This has resulted in the forest supervisor being called upon to have more surveys and land examinations than hitherto, and requires the assignment of a national forest examiner to this forest. The $2,941 increase will provide for one grazing examiner at $1,300 and one national forest examiner at $1,500, and $141 for incidental expenses.

Item No. 240, Flathead National Forest.—The amount now provided for the Flathead National Forest, $25,900, is changed to $51,826, an increase of $25,926. Of this increase, $1,250 is needed to cover increased cost of maintaining Government stock now assigned to and needed on this national forest. It is necessary to maintain a team and several pack trains—in all 48 head—for protective and administrative purposes. Forage and the necessry shoeing, etc., of Government horses have increased steadily the past two years, and further advances may be expected. Figures are now at hand showing a general increase in horse feed caused by failure of local crops and the fact that large areas formerly devoted to hay raising have been put into grain and other crops. To meet this increase in cost, $1,250 additional will be needed to provide for Government stock. The Flathead National Forest is a heavily timbered forest of 2,088,720 acres, supporting a stand of timber consisting of approximately 5,800,000,000 feet b. m. A large part of this national forest is far removed from settlements and when fires occur it is difficult, owing to inadequate means of transportation and long distances, to secure emergency fire fighters promptly.

The normal protective force which has been provided in the past is inadequate to meet the situation, and it is proposed to increase this force by one fire chief, whose duty will be responsibility for yearlong attention to fire protection and its problems and the coordination of ranger districts in fire protection plans and through field work to perfect the forest-protection plan to the point where it will be sure of execution. The salary of this employee will be $1,800, and an estimated amount of $300 will be provided for travel. It is also proposed to employ two assistants at $1,300 each, whose duties will be to act as foremen of the fire-protection crews and to be employed primarily on fire-protection and suppression work and to assist the district rangers in such work on their ranger districts. It is also proposed to add to the protective force 30 men for four months, to be assigned to strategic points on the forest and either to be mobilized in crews capable of quick transport to the location of fires or scattered throughout the forest as fire patrolmen and smoke chasers. This item will cost $15,000. If mobilized in crews, these men will be employed in improving and constructing trails at such times during the four-month periods as they are not actively engaged in fire detection or fire suppression work. It is also necessary to place the regular protective organization for the Flathead National Forest on a four-months' basis, which will require an estimated increase of $4,976. The records show that during every severe fire season during the last 10 years the Flathead National Forest has suffered materially; that in 1910 146,962,000 feet b. m. were burned; in 1914 13,400,000 feet b. m.; and in 1917 21,049,000 feet b. m. The cost of emergency fire suppression in addition to the regular administrative and protective force was, in 1910, $38,095; in 1914 $64,297; and in 1917 $50,015.

Item No. 244, Gila National Forest.—The amount now provided for the Gila National Forest—$8,907—is changed to $10,847, an increase of $1,940. On account of a number of saw-timber sales on various ranger districts of the Gila National Forest it will be necessary to assign a forest assistant to this forest, whose duties will be the marking of all the timber which is to be cut on the various sales and the making of periodic checks of the scaling done by the forest rangers, who, on account of numerous personnel changes, are inexperienced along many lines of work, and particularly so in connection with the application of national forest rules and policy covering the cutting and scaling of timber. On account of the increase in wages at near-by mine centers it has been found impossible to procure competent fire guards at the former rates of pay, and accordingly a higher scale of wages must be adopted for the Gila National Forest. The $1,940 increase will provide for one forest assistant, yearlong, with necessary traveling expenses, and $240 for increase of pay from $60 to $70 for eight fireguards for three months each.

Item No. 250, Humboldt National Forest.—The amount now provided for the Humboldt National Forest, $5,780, is changed to $6,330, an increase of $550. This national forest, containing 1,301,073 acres of land and supporting 59,600 head of cattle and horses and 364,000 head of sheep, consists of three widely separated units with 643 miles of exterior boundary. The curtailment of the open unreserved public range outside the forest is causing increasing congestion of stock along the forest boundary to such an extent that the present force of eight rangers is no longer able to properly control the numbers of stock entering the forest, regulate the use of the range, or give proper protection to owners of live stock permitted to occupy the national forest. An additional patrolman is needed for five months during the field season. His salary and travel expenses will amount to the $550 increase requested.

Item No. 251, Idaho National Forest.—The amount now provided for the Idaho National Forest, $11,585, is changed to $18,385, an increase of $6,800. The Idaho National Forest is a heavily timbered forest of 1,209,280 acres, supporting a stand of timber consisting of approximately 3,813,000,000 feet b. m. It is far removed from settlements, and when fires occur it is difficult, owing to inadequate means of transportation and long distances, to secure emergency fire fighters promptly. It is proposed to increase this force by one fire chief, whose duty will be responsibility for year-long attention to fire protection and its problems and the coordination of ranger districts in fire-protection plans and through field work to perfect the forest-protection plan to the point where it will be sure of execution. The salary of this employee will be $1,500, and an estimated amount of $300 will be provided for necessary travel.

It is also proposed to add to the protective force 10 men for four months, to be assigned to strategic points on the forest and either to be mobilized in crews capable of quick transport to the location of fires or scattered throughout the forest as fire patrolmen and smoke chasers. This will cost $5,000. The records show that during every severe fire season during the last 10 years the

Idaho National Forest has suffered materially; that in 1910, 70,000,000 feet b. m. were burned; in 1914, 60,000,000 feet b. m.; and in 1917, 39,696,000 feet b. m. The cost of emergency fire suppression in addition to the regular administrative and protective force was in 1910, $5,778; in 1914, $4,019; and in 1917, $51,295.

Item No. 253, Jefferson National Forest.—The amount now provided for the Jefferson National Forest, $5,064, is changed to $8,430, an increase of $3,366. The Jefferson National is a heavily timbered forest of 1,175,685 acres, supporting a stand of timber consisting of approximately 923,000,000 feet b. m. It has been found that the normal protective force which has been provided in the past is inadequate to meet the forest-fire situation, and it is proposed to increase this force by five men for four months, to be assigned to strategic points on the forest and either to be mobilized in crews capable of quick transport to the location of fires or scattered throughout the forest as fire patrolmen and smoke chasers. This will cost $2,500. It is also necessary to place the regular protective organization for the Jefferson National Forest on a four-months' basis, which will require an estimated increase of $866. The cost of emergency fire suppression in addition to the regular administrative and protective force was in 1910, $11,634; in 1914, $1,020; and in 1917, $4,415.

Item No. 255, Kaniksu National Forest.—The amount now provided for the Kaniksu National Forest, $25,146, is changed to $34,943, an increase of $9,797. The Kaniksu National Forest is a heavily timbered forest of 835,740 acres, supporting a stand of timber consisting of approximately 1,571,000,000 feet b. m. The greater portion of this national forest is far removed from settlements and when fires occur it is difficult, owing to inadequate means of transportation and long distances, to secure emergency fire fighters promptly. The normal protective force, which has been provided in the past, is inadequate to meet the situation, and it is proposed to increase this force by one fire chief, whose duty will be responsibility for yearlong attention to fire protection and its problems and the coordination of ranger districts in fire-protection plans and through fieldwork, to perfect the forest-protection plan to the point where it will be sure of execution. The salary of this employee will be $1,300. It is also proposed to add to the protective force 10 men for four months, costing $5,000. It is also necessary to place the regular protective organization for the Kaniksu National Forest on a four-months' basis, which will require an estimated increase of $3,497. The records show that during every severe fire season during the last 10 years, the Kaniksu National Forest has suffered materially; that in 1910, 90,000,000 feet b. m. were burned; and, in 1917, 2,685,000 feet b. m. The cost of emergency fire suppression, in addition to the regular administrative and protective force was, in 1910, $39,998; and in 1917, $11,572.

Item No. 257, Kootenai National Forest.—The amount now provided for the Kootenai National Forest, $17,861, is changed to $26,102, an increase of $8,241. The Kootenai National Forest is a heavily timbered forest of 1,623,340 acres, supporting a stand of timber consisting of approximately 3,500,000,000 feet b. m. It is far removed from settlements and, when fires occur, it is difficult, owing to inadequate means of transportation and long distances, to secure emergency fire fighters promptly. It has been found that the normal protective force, which has been provided in the past, is inadequate to meet the situation, and it is propsed to increase the protective force by 10 men for four months, costing $5,000. It is also necessary to place the regular protective organization for the Kootenai National Forest on a four-months' basis, which will require an estimated increase of $3,241. The records show that during every severe fire season during the last 10 years, the Kootenai National Forest has suffered materially; that in 1910, 50,000,000 feet b. m. were burned; and, in 1917, 18,068,000 feet b. m. The cost of emergency fire suppression, in addition to the regular administrative and protective force was, in 1910, $82,515; and, in 1917, $56,661.

Item No. 262 Lewis and Clark National Forest.—The amount now provided for the Lewis and Clark National Forest, $5,914, is changed to $10,626, an increase of $4,711. The Lewis and Clark National Forest is a heavily timbered forest of 1,826,360 acres, supporting a stand of timber consisting of approximately 305,000,000 feet b. m. It has been found that the normal protective force, which has been provided in the past, is inadequate to meet the forest-fire situation, and it is proposed to increase this force by five men for four months, costing $2,500. It is also necessary to place the regular protective organization for the Lewis and Clark National Forest on a four-months' basis, which will require an estimated increase of $2,211. The records show that during every severe fire season, during the last 10 years, the Lewis and Clark

National Forest has suffered materially; that in 1910, 141,000,000 feet b. m. were burned; in 1914, 1,000,000 feet b. m.; and, in 1917, 5,000,000 feet b. m. The cost of emergency fire suppression, in addition to the regular administrative and protective force, was, in 1910, $18,856; in 1914, $15,680; and, in 1917, $16,241.

Item No. 263, Lincoln National Forest.—The amount now provided for the Lincoln National Forest, $9,984, is changed to $11,178, an increase of $1,194. The timber-sale work on this national forest has become sufficient to warrant the employment of a forest assistant to mark all the timber for cutting on the various sales, including the Sacramento Lumber Co. sale, which requires the continual time of one scaler, and to correlate the management of the various smaller sales handled by the district rangers. The $1,194 increase requested will allow the employment of a forest assistant, at $1,100, with $94 for incidental expenses.

Item No. 264, Lolo National Forest.—The amount now provided for the Lolo National Forest, $11,939, is changed to $26,652, an increase of $14,713. The Lolo National Forest is a heavily timbered forest of 1,181,018 acres supporting a stand of timber consisting of approximately 1,913,000,000 feet b. m. A large part of this national forest is far removed from settlements, and when fires occur it is difficult, owing to inadequate means of transportation and long distances, to secure emergency fire fighters promptly. It is proposed to increase this protective force by one fire chief whose duty will be responsibility for year-long attention to fire protection and its problems, and the coordination of ranger districts in fire-protection plans and through field work, to perfect the forest-protection plan to the point where it will be sure of execution. The salary of this employee will be $1,500, and an estimated amount of $300 will be provided for necessary travel.

It is also proposed to employ one assistant, at $1,300, whose duty will be to act as foreman of the fire-protection crews and to be employed primarily on fire protection and suppression work, and to assist the district rangers in such work on their ranger districts. It is also proposed to add to the protective force 15 men for 4 months, costing $7,500. It is also necessary to place the regular protective organization for the Lolo National Forest on a four-months' basis, which will require an estimated increase of $4,113. The records show that during every severe fire season during the last 10 years the Lolo National Forest has suffered materially; that in 1910, 382,000,000 feet b. m. were burned; in 1914, 1,991,000 feet b. m.; and in 1917, 18,068,000 feet b. m. The cost of emergency fire suppression in addition to the regular administrative and protective force was, in 1910, $77,773; in 1914, $13,561; and in 1917, $63,948.

Item No. 268, Manti National Forest.—The amount now provided for the Manti National Forest, $5,090, is changed to $6,090, an increase of $1,000. This national forest is the most intensively used from a grazing standpoint of any national forest in Utah, and the grazing problems are unusually complicated, which will necessitate an unusual amount of travel by the 10 forest officers who constitute the permanent year-long organization. The increase of $1,000 is required on account of this increased travel and the marked increase in the cost of travel and supplies.

Item No. 275, Missoula National Forest.—The amount now provided for the Missoula National Forest, $9,380, is changed to $15,212, an increase of $5,832. The Missoula National Forest is a heavily timbered forest of 1,368,191 acres supporting a stand of timber consisting of approximately 3,575,000,000 feet b. m. It has been found that the normal protective force which has been provided in the past is inadequate to meet the forest-fire situation, and it is proposed to increase this force by one fire chief whose duty will be responsibility for yearlong attention to fire protection and its problems and the coordination of ranger districts in fire-protection plans and through field work, to perfect the forest-protection plan to the point where it will be sure of execution. The salary of this employee will be $1,300. It is also proposed to add to the protective force five men for four months, costing $2,500. It is also necessary to place the regular protective organization for the Missoula National Forest on a four months basis, which will require an estimated increase of $2,032. The present protective organization is based on two to three months' employment for lookouts, smoke chasers, and patrolmen. The records show that during every severe fire season during the last 10 years the Missoula National Forest has suffered materially; that in 1910, 40,000,000 feet b. m. were burned; and in 1917 28,496,000 feet b. m. The cost of emergency fire suppression in addition to the regular administrative and protective force was, in 1910, $24,205; and in 1917, $58,767.

Item No. 282, Nezperce National Forest.—The amount now provided for the Nezperce National Forest, $12,620, is changed to $25,690, an increase of $13,070. Of this increase $500 is needed to cover increased cost of maintaining Government stock now assigned to and needed on this national forest. It is necessary to maintain a team and several pack trains—in all 24 head—for protective and administrative purposes. Forage and the necessary shoeing, etc., of Government horses have increased steadily the past two years, and further advances may be expected. To meet this increase in cost $750 additional will be needed to provide for Government stock. The Nezperce National Forest is a heavily timbered forest of 1,666,079 acres supporting a stand of timber consisting of approximately 3,500,000,000 feet b. m. A large part of this national forest is far removed from settlements and when fires occur it is difficult, owing to inadequate means of transportation and long distances, to secure emergency fire fighters promptly. Lightning-caused fires are particularly numerous some seasons and often several days will elapse before a fire crew can be conveyed to the scene of the fire, thus allowing the fire to gain great headway. It has been found that the normal protective force which has been provided in the past is inadequate to meet the situation, and it is proposed to increase this force by one fire chief whose duty will be responsibility for yearlong attention to fire protection and its problems and the coordination of ranger districts in fire-protection plans and through field work, to perfect the forest-protection plan to the point where it will be sure of execution. The salary of this employee will be $1,500, and an estimated amount of $300 will be provided for necessary travel.

It is also proposed to employ one assistant at $1,300 whose duty will be to act as foreman of the fire-protection crews to be employed primarily on fire protection and suppression work and to assist the district rangers in such work on their ranger districts. It is also proposed to add to the protective force 10 men for four months, costing $5,000. It is also necessary to place the regular protective organization for the Nezperce National Forest on a four months' basis, which will require an estimated increase of $4,470. The present protective organization is based on two to three months' employment for lookouts, smoke chasers, and patrolmen. This is the actual period of the season of fire hazard, and does not provide a period of instruction training and preparation prior to entering upon the protective work, which is the key to any efficient organization. The experience of the past has brought home very forcibly that these inexperienced employees require some training and preparation to render them effective. The records show that during every severe fire season during the last 10 years the Nezperce National Forest has suffered materially; that in 1910, 90,000,000 feet b. m. were burned; in 1914, 2,000,000 feet b. m. were burned; and in 1917, 17,568,000 feet b. m. The cost of emergency fire suppression in addition to the regular administrative and protective force was in 1910 $15,278, in 1914 $10,021, and in 1917 $35,114.

Item No. 284, Okanogan National Forest.—The amount now provided for the Okanogan National Forest, $8,964, is changed to $11,464, an increase of $2,500. The Okanogan National Forest is a heavily timbered forest of 1,541,000 acres supporting a stand of timber consisting of approximately 3,642,000,000 feet b. m. It is far removed from settlements and when fires occur, it is difficult, owing to inadequate means of transportation and long distances, to secure emergency fire fighters promptly. It has been found that the normal protective force which has been provided in the past is inadequate to meet the forest fire situation, and it is proposed to increase this force by five men for four months, costing $2,500, to be assigned to strategic points on the forest and either to be mobilized in crews capable of quick transport to the location of fires or scattered throughout the forest as fire patrolmen and smoke chasers. The records show that during every severe fire season during the last 10 years the Okanogan National Forest has suffered materially; that in 1910, 13,000,000 feet b. m. were burned; in 1914, 7,233,000 feet b. m. were burned; and in 1917, 16,008,000 feet b. m. The cost of emergency fire suppression in addition to the regular administrative and protective force was in 1910 $9,973, in 1914 $1,992, and in 1917 $17,233.

Item No. 286, Oregon National Forest.—The amount now provided for the Oregon National Forest, $16,009, is changed to $20,409, an increase of $4,400. The Oregon National Forest is a heavily timbered forest of 1,140,920 acres supporting a stand of timber consisting of approximately 12,177,000,000 feet b. m. Large portions are far removed from settlements and when fires occur, it is difficult, owing to inadequate means of transportation and long distances, to secure emergency fire fighters promptly. Lightning-caused fires are often numerous and much time will elapse before a fire crew can be conveyed to the scene of the fire, thus allowing the fire to gain great headway. It has been found that the normal protective force which has been provided in the past is inadequate to meet the situation, and it is proposed to increase this force by one fire chief whose duty will be responsibility for yearlong attention to fire protection and its problems and the coordination of ranger districts in fire protection plans and through field work, to perfect the forest protection plan to the point where it will be sure of execution. The salary of this employee is estimated at $1,400. It is also proposed to add to the protective force six men for four months, costing $3,000, to be assigned to strategic points on the forest and either to be mobilized in crews capable of quick transport to the location of fires or scattered throughout the forest as fire patrolmen and smoke chasers. The records show that during every severe fire season during the last 10 years the Oregon National Forest has suffered materially; that in 1910, 10,275,000 feet b. m. were burned; in 1914, 15,555,000 feet b. m. were burned; and in 1917, 35,049,000 feet b. m. The cost of emergency fire suppression in addition to the regular administrative and protective force was in 1910 $5,078, in 1914 $17,961, and in 1917 $12,390.

Item No. 289, Pend Oreille National Forest.—The amount now provided for the Pend Oreille National Forest, $12,020, is changed to $20,074, an increase of $8,054. The Pend Oreille National Forest is a heavily timbered forest of 874,738 acres, supporting a stand of timber consisting of approximately 1,222,000,000 feet b. m. It has been found that the normal protective force which has been provided in the past is inadequate to meet the situation, and it is proposed to increase this force by 10 men for four months, costing $5,000. It is also necessary to place the regular protective organization for the Pend Oreille National Forest on a four months' basis, which will require an estimated increase of $3,054. The records show that during every severe fire season during the last 10 years the Pend Oreille National Forest has suffered materially; that in 1910, 273,300,000 feet b. m. were burned; in 1914, 590,000 feet b. m. were burned; and in 1917, 1,337,000 feet b. m. The cost of emergency fire suppression, in addition to the regular administrative and protective force, was in 1910, $46,213; in 1914, $6,733; and in 1917, $44,287.

Item No. 297, Saint Joe National Forest.—The amount now provided for the Saint Joe National Forest, $15,830, is changed to $32,026, an increase of $16,196. The Saint Joe National Forest is a heavily timbered forest of 975,668 acres, supporting a stand of timber consisting of approximately 2,165,000,000 feet b. m. It has been found that the normal protective force which has been provided in the past is not adequate to meet the situation, and it is proposed to increase this force by one fire chief whose duty will be responsibility for yearlong attention to fire protection and its problems and the coordination of ranger districts in fire-protection plans, and through field work to perfect the forest-protection plan to the point where it will be sure of execution. The salary of this employee will be $1,500 and an estimated amount of $300 will be provided for necessary travel. It is also proposed to employ two assistants at $1,300 each, whose duties will be to act as foremen of the fire-protection crews and to be employed primarily on fire protection and suppression work and to assist the district rangers in such work on their ranger districts. It is also proposed to add to the protective force 15 men for four months, costing $7,500. It is also necessary to place the regular protective organization for the Saint Joe National Forest on a four months' basis, which will require an estimated increase of $4,296. The present protective organization is based on two to three months' employment for lookouts, smoke chasers, and patrolmen. The records show that during every severe fire season during the last 10 years the Saint Joe National Forest has suffered materially; that in 1914, 1,098,000 feet b. m. were burned, and in 1917, 573,000 feet b. m. The cost of emergency fire suppression, in addition to the regular administrative and protective force, was, in 1914, $27,205, and in 1917, $48,230.

Item No. 298, Salmon National Forest.—The amount now provided for the Salmon National Forest, $5,377, is changed to $6,177, an increase of $800. Approximately half of this increase is occasioned by the necessity of having to pay short-term forest guards increased wages. Formerly the short-term men have been paid at the rate of $1,100 per annum. On the Salmon National Forest it is now necessary to pay $110 per month or go without the men, and this national forest, on account of its isolation, rough topography, and heavy stand of timber, presents one of the greatest fire hazards in central Idaho.

The balance of the increase requested is on account of increased cost of travel and supplies. These costs have been rising gradually during the past two years, but up to the present time they have been offset by savings effected on the Salmon National Forest. The increased costs have now reached a point where either an increase in appropriation must be secured or a curtailment made in necessary protection.

Item No. 302, Santa Fe National Forest.—The amount now provided for the Santa Fe National Forest, $14,673, is changed to $17,040, an increase of $2,367. A large timber sale has been made to the New Mexico Lumber Co., on the Jemez division of the Santa Fe National Forest. At the present time one scaler is assigned to handle the sale, but as soon as operations get well under way the entire time of two competent men will be required to handle the work satisfactorily. In addition to this, there are a number of smaller sales on the Pecos division which have been handled hitherto by the various district rangers, but it has recently developed that an additional scaler is needed to travel from one district to another to assist the district rangers, particularly in marking the timber for cutting. The $2,367 increase will supply one scaler at $1,200 and one at $1,100, together with $67 for incidental expenses.

Item No. 305, Selway National Forest.—The amount now provided for the Selway National Forest, $17,112, is changed to $47,367, an increase of $30,255. Of this increase, $1,000 is needed to cover increased cost of maintaining Government stock now assigned to and needed on this national forest. It is necessary to maintain a team and several pack trains—in all 52 head—for protective and administrative purposes. Forage and the necessary shoeing, etc., of Government horses have increased steadily the past two years, and further advances may be expected. Figures are now at hand showing a general increase in horse feed, caused by failure of local crops and the fact that large areas formerly devoted to hay raising have been put into grain and other crops. To meet this increase in cost $1,000 will be needed to provide for Government stock. The Selway National Forest is a heavily timbered forest of 1,802,000 acres, supporting a stand of timber consisting of approximately 6,673,000,000 feet b. m. A large part of this national forest is far removed from settlements, and when fires occur it is difficult, owing to inadequate means of transportation and long distances, to secure emergency fire fighters promptly. Lightning-caused fires are particularly numerous some seasons and often several days will elapse before a fire crew can be conveyed to the scene of the fire, thus allowing the fire to gain great headway. It has been found that the normal protective force which has been provided in the past is inadequate to meet the situation, and it is proposed to increase this force by one fire chief, whose duty will be responsibility for year-long attention to fire protection and its problems and the coordination of ranger districts in fire-protection plans and through field work, to perfect the forest-protection plans to the point where it will be sure of execution. The salary of this employee will be $1,800, and an estimated amount of $300 will be provided for necessary travel. It is also proposed to employ three assistants at $1,300 each, whose duties will be to act as foremen of the fire-protection crews and to be employed primarily on fire protection and suppression work and to assist the district rangers in such work on their ranger districts. It is also proposed to add to the protective force 30 men for four months, costing $15,000. It is also necessary to place the regular protective organization for the Selway National Forest on a four-months' basis, which will require an estimated increase of $8,255. The present protective organization is based on two to three months' employment for lookouts, smoke chasers, and patrolmen. The records show that during every severe fire season during the last 10 years the Selway National Forest has suffered materially; that in 1914, 30,915,000 feet b. m. were burned; and in 1917, 59,174,000 feet b. m. The cost of emergency fire suppression, in addition to the regular administrative and protective fire force, was in 1914, $93,316, and in 1917, $70,028.

Item No. 315, Snoqualmie National Forest.—The amount now provided for the Snoqualmie National Forest, $12,366, is changed to $13,566, an increase of $1,200. This increase is necessary on account of many new timber sales on this national forest, which will require the services of an additional scaler at $1,200.

Item No. 324, Tonto National Forest.—The amount now provided for the Tonto national Forest, $6,972, is changed to $7,685, an increase of $713. The communication system of the Tonto National Forest, Ariz., has been extended from both Globe and Phoenix to Roosevelt and from Roosevelt north to Payson, where it branches into four separate lines leading to various communities and ranger stations. It is necessary to install a small central system at the town of Payson, at which point an operator will be employed. The increased number of sheep passed over the Heber-Reno trail and the resultant possibility for congestion will necessitate the employment of additional sheep guards from time to time during the spring and fall. The $713 increase will provide for the salary of the telephone operator, yearlong, at $25 per month, $300, and two sheep guards at $85 per month for a period of about two and one-half months each.

Item No. 329, *Umpqua National Forest.*—The amount now provided for the Umpqua National Forest, $10,109, is changed to $13,509, an increase of $3,400. The Umpqua National Forest is a heavily timbered forest of 1,221,391 acres, supporting a stand of timber consisting of approximately 23,500,000,000 feet b. m. A large part of this national forest is far removed from settlements, and when fires occur it is difficult, owing to inadequate means of transportation and long distances, to secure emergency fire fighters promptly. The normal protective force which has been provided in the past is inadequate to meet the situation, and it is proposed to increase this force by one-half the time of one fire chief, whose duty will be responsibility for attention to fire protection and its problems and the coordination of ranger· districts in fire-protection plans and through field work to perfect the forest-protection plan to the point where it will be sure of execution. The salary of this employee for six months will be $750, and an estimated amount of $150 will be provided for necessary travel. The remainder of his salary and travel will be chargeable to the Crater National Forest, which adjoins the Umpqua National Forest on the south (see Item No. 229). It is also proposed to add to the protective force five men for four months, costing $2,500, to be assigned to strategic points on the forest and either to be mobilized in crews capable of quick transport to the location of fires or scattered throughout the forest as fire patrolmen and smoke chasers. The records show that during every severe fire season during the last 10 years the Umpqua National Forest has suffered materially; that in 1910, 179,293,000 feet b. m. were burned; in 1914, 4,300,000 feet b. m. were burned; and in 1917, 41,704,000 feet b. m. The cost of emergency fire suppression, in addition to the regular administrative and protective force, was, in 1910, $14,538; in 1914, $3,103; and in 1917, $38,625.

Item No. 339, *Whitman National Forest.*—The amount now provided for the Whitman National Forest, $17,425, is changed to $18,725, an increase of $1,300. This increase is necessary on account of the constantly increasing timber-sale business on this national forest, which will require the services of an additional scaler at $1,300.

Item No. 342, *Additional national forests created, or to be created, under section 11 of the act of March 1, 1911.*—The amount now provided for additional national forests created, or to be created, under section 11 of the act of March 1, 1911, $65,200, is changed to $76,850, an increase of $11,650. The following tabulation shows the area, amount appropriated for the administration and protection, and the receipts from the new forests for the fiscal years 1915 to 1918, inclusive:

Fiscal year.	Area acquired.	Appropriation.	Receipts.
	Acres.		
1915	348,275	$67,000	$3,977.60
1916	706,974	67,000	9,595.13
1917	947,197	[1] 66,000	22,153.94
1918	1,078,510	[1] 65,200	53,129.00

[1] Reductions due to transfers to statutory roll.

The great increase in area and the increased activity on the new forests, as indicated by the receipts, makes an increase of $11,650 necessary, as follows:

Item 1. In lieu of salaries paid from fund for acquisition of lands	$2,500
Item 2. One forest examiner, White Mountain Forest; salary, $1,600; travel, $400	2,000
Item 3. One forest examiner, Shenandoah and Natural Bridge forests, $1,800; travel, $400	2,200
Item 4. One forest examiner, White Top and Unaka forests, $1,400; travel, $400	1,800
Item 5. Three assistant forest rangers, White Mountain and Shenandoah forests, $2,700; travel, $450	3,150
Total	11,650

The area of the purchased forests has grown nearly 300 per cent in the past four years and the receipts have increased approximately 1,700 per cent. A normal but rapid growth in the receipts may be expected from year to year with the diminished supply of timber on private lands. Some of the forests having the greatest amount of mature timber are still backward in sales business because of inaccessibility, but this condition is rapidly changing. The need for additional funds is due almost entirely to increasing timber-sales business. The following is an explanation of the need for each item:

No. 1.—Work on the purchased forests has had to do with purchase of lands and their administration when acquired. For this reason supervisors in charge of the forests have been paid in part from " General expenses, Forest Service," and in part from " Weeks-law " acquisition funds. The work on many of the units has now progressed to the point where the officer in charge must give more time to administrative work, and the amount which is properly payable from acquisition funds is accordingly less. The same condition also exists with respect to forest clerks.

No. 2.—The sales business on the White Mountain National Forest requires an experienced forest examiner to assist in the appraisal and sale of timber. The receipts on the White Mountain Forest for the fiscal year 1918 amounted to $13,826.76.

No. 3.—A capable forest examiner is needed on the Shenandoah and Natural Bridge National forests. The receipts from these national forests exceeded $20,000 during the fiscal year 1918, and business is on the increase.

No. 4.—There are very desirable sales to be made on the White Top forest, and the work has been handicapped, due to insufficient force. A forest examiner is needed to assist for the White Top and Unaka forests.

No. 5.—The increase in the sales business and other activities requires the services of three assistant forest rangers, one on the White Mountain National Forest and two on the Shenandoah National Forest. The time of these men will be devoted almost entirely to scaling timber.

SUMMARY.

Of the $225,568 necessary for additional fire protection, $225,008 are required for the national forests in the States of Montana, Idaho, Oregon, and Washington. The greater number of the national forests in these States, especially west of the Continental Divide, consists of vast, inaccessible, heavily timbered, mountainous areas, where, with the present fire-protection organization, it often takes days to reach a fire even after it has been detected by a lookout man. This delay allows fires in these forests to gain great headway, with a consequent large loss in Government timber and the ultimate high cost in the final suppression or control of the fires. Many of these mountain areas are extremely susceptible to lightning-caused fires, and oftentimes several such fires will be started along the same mountain range, necessitating the securing of large numbers of fire fighters from distant cities, and by the time the fire fighters arrive the fires have assumed large proportions. With the proper number of men on the ground, the bulk of these fires could be suppressed in their incipiency. The estimated stand of timber on the national forests in these four States is 301,442,840,000 feet b. m., which is over 50 per cent of the total stand on all national forests. The records show that during every severe fire season during the last 10 years the national forests in Montana, Idaho, Oregon, and Washington have suffered severely. In 1910, the loss was 6,333,773,000 feet b. m., valued at $14,561,657, the cost of emergency fire suppression being $1,011,766, as compared with a total loss on all the national forests of 6,508,369,000 feet b. m., valued at $14,889,724, the total cost of emergency suppression being $1,150,119; in 1914, the loss was 290,297,000 feet b. m., valued at $270,903, the cost of emergency fire suppression being $596,137, as compared with 339,430,000 feet b. m., valued at $307,303 for all national forests, the total cost of fire suppression being $746,677; in 1917, the loss was 488,517,000 feet b. m., valued at $663,737, the emergency suppression being $900,753, as compared with 523,800,000 feet b. m., valued at $718,684 for all the national forests, the total cost of emergency fire suppression being $1,121,450.

During the past summer season, the first part of which was exceedingly dry, the fire-suppression costs in these four States reached $636,288. It will thus be seen that the greatest loss of timber has occurred in Montana, Idaho, Oregon, and Washington, and that the greater portion of fire-suppression costs have also been confined to these States. It is now proposed to remedy this situation by increased fire protection through placing the regular protective organization on a four-months' basis instead of a two or three months' employment, in order to train and prepare inexperienced employees so that they will be able to do effective fire-suppression work and also in order to be able to secure and hold experienced men of the character required. Four-months' employment will place the Forest Service protective work on a par with other woods and field activities and tend to draw the type of men needed to build up an efficient fire organization. When not actually needed in fire detection and suppression work these men will be profitably employed in clearing out, improving, and constructing trails and other improvements directly contributory to more efficient fire protection. It is also proposed to add to the present protective organization 26 so-called fire chiefs and their assistants at salaries ranging from $1,300 to $1,800, who will be solely responsible for year-long attention to fire protection and its numerous problems and the coordination of ranger districts and adjacent national forests and, through field work, to bring the forest plan to the point where it will be practicable and sure of execution. It is also proposed to increase the protective force by 236 four-months' men at a monthly salary which, with subsistence, will be approximately $125 per month. These men will be assigned to the national forests of greatest fire hazard and either mobilized in crews capable of quick transportation to the location of the fires or scattered throughout the national forests as fire patrolmen and smoke chasers. When mobilized in crews, they will be employed in improving and constructing trails and other improvements directly contributory to more efficient fire protection at such times during the four-months' period as they are not actually engaged in fire-detection or fire-suppression work. On such national forests where these men are scattered and assigned as patrolmen and smoke chasers, they will also be required to spend their time profitably on improvement work when not engaged in fire suppression or fire detection.

Under present conditions it must be assumed that men can not be hired for a less period than four months and at a salary, including subsistence, of not less than $125. Even with this salary, the attraction in this class of work proves the means of securing men, since in outstanding work there is still greater compensation. The individual national forest needs, as determined by the forest fire chiefs, will decide whether such men will be mobilized in crews or scattered out as patrolmen and smoke chasers. Under the present system on these national forests of high fire hazard, an annual outlay is required which experience has shown to be inadequate for proper protection. This has resulted in a large annual outlay for fire-suppression crews during the drier seasons, and also the slow attrition of the national resources which can not be accurately estimated. The proposed new system will make the protection force an investment rather than an outlay, as such a force will accomplish a large amount of improvement and maintenance work annually, especially in a subnormal season. The proposed system will train specialized fire overhead men and crews which can be mobilized immediately at any great danger point, be that danger point on the specific national forest or some near-by national forest. It will obtain labor all during the season instead of the nondescript kind now obtainable in an emergency. It will prevent stagnation in the ranger force by giving increased responsibility, and will try out and train replacement members for this force. It will tend to do away with the annual disruption of the administrative work in the offices of the district foresters and forest supervisors. With the proposed increase in the protective force under the proposed new system, it is believed that the loss of Government stumpage on the national forests of high fire hazard in the Northwest can be reduced to a minimum, and also the cost of emergency fire suppression. Five hundred and sixty dollars of the requested increase for additional fire protection is needed on the Coronado the Gila National Forests in Arizona and New Mexico, as explained in detail in items 228 and 244.

Of the proposed increase requested, $5,000 is necessary for the maintenance of Government stock, consisting of horse and mule teams, pack horses and pack mules. There has been a marked increase in the cost of forage, amounting to approximately 21 per cent, throughout the West during the last year, and it is expected that especially in Idaho and Montana the cost will continue to advance during the fiscal year 1920. There are maintained on the national forests of Idaho and Montana 371 Government-owned animals, and the $5,000 increase will allow approximately for the increase of 33⅓ per cent in the cost of maintaining this Government stock. Figures are now at hand showing a general increase in horse feed, caused to some extent by the failure of local crops and the fact that large areas formerly devoted to hay raising have been put into grain and other crops so that the grass crop can be discontinued to a large extent until present conditions are relieved. The $5,000 increase is therefore urgently needed to properly maintain the Government stock necessary for efficient protection and administration of the national forests in Idaho and Montana.

Twenty-two thousand and two dollars of the increase is necessary for handling timber-sale work on the national forests as listed above. This amount will be used for additional forest assistants and scalers and for brush burning and other expense needed for carrying on the increasing timber-sale business on the Coconino, Coronado, Gila, Lincoln, Santa Fe, Snoqualmie, Whitman, and the Appalachian Forests, which can not be properly handled by the force provided by the present appropriation.

Five thousand three hundred and four dollars of the increase is needed for a more thorough administration of the grazing business on the Coconino, Datil, Humboldt, Manti, and Tonto National Forests, as explained in detail in items 223, 232, 250, 268, and 324.

Four thousand seven hundred dollars of the increase is needed for increased cost of general administration on the Datil, Salmon, Tonto, and Appalachian Forests, as explained in detail in items 232, 298, 324, and 342.

Three thousand five hundred dollars of the increase is needed for the administration of the addition of 470,394 acres which were added to the Colorado National Forest by presidential proclamation of June 12, 1917, under congressional authority as provided by the act of September 8, 1916 (39 Stat., 850), entitled "An act authorizing the addition of certain lands to the Colorado and Pike National Forests, Colo."

The CHAIRMAN. You have an increase on page 121 of $266,074.

Mr. GRAVES. The principal part of this increase is an aggregate of $225,568, for increases on 26 forests for increased fire-protection work. This last summer we had another bad season. We narrowly escaped a catastrophe. We have made a careful analysis of the whole situation to see where our difficulties are in fire protection and how to prevent the losses that still recur. We find that we have gotten control of the situation on about 65 per cent of the area of the national forests; that is to say, with the ordinary appropriations which we secure we can safeguard these portions of the forests from fire. But on the heavily timbered forests in Oregon, Washington, northern Idaho, and northwestern Montana we have a situation which is requiring us to spend too much money in fighting fires after they have already started. In bad years 80 per cent of the total fire costs have been spent in fighting fires in the forests of these four States. We are are losing more timber by destruction from fires than we ought. We are asking for an increased appropriation on these 26 forests to enable us to reduce the large expenditure for fighting fires that have several times involved large deficits, and to save the loss in timber that is occurring in these special districts. These forests are still in the condition of a wilderness, with very dense timber, very meager development of roads and trails; and in dry seasons there are a great many fires from lightning.

Mr. McLAUGHLIN. From what?

Mr. GRAVES. Lightning. Fifty per cent of the fires which occurred in Montana and Idaho this last summer, where we had so much trouble, were from lightning. They frequently start fires in these remote sections, in the heart of the wilderness, and it often takes us a week to cut our way into the fire with the men and equipment to fight it, during which time it has gained such headway that it takes many men to put it out. It then means great outlay of money for labor, equipment, transportation, etc., and the loss of large quantities of timber.

The CHAIRMAN. Now, what is your plan of handling the situation?

Mr. GRAVES. Our plan is to put more money on preventive work in order to save money in fighting fires. Our general proposition is, in the first place, to increase the time of employment of our regular summer protective force by from two to four weeks each summer; that where we have a protective force of from two to three months we increase it to from three to four months. That will mean some additional cost.

Mr. McLAUGHLIN. It begins when now, and ends when?

Mr. GRAVES. We usually get our force on early in July. This last summer our fires started the middle of June and caught us unprepared, and we lost a lot of timber for that reason. We will put our force on by early June, or by the middle of June, and get the men trained in, organized, and keep them on altogether for three or four months, according to the season and locality.

Mr. McLAUGHLIN. At the present time you have been keeping your men late enough, but you didn't begin early enough?

Mr. GRAVES. We haven't had our men early enough, and in several instances we have laid them off too early in the fall. The fire season would close and open up again, and we had not kept them on long enough. That will cost a little more money. The main increase, however, is to have a larger number of men, and my plan is to put an aggregate of 262 more men than we now have on these 26 forests for fire-preventive work.

The CHAIRMAN. How many have you now? What will be the total?

Mr. GRAVES. The total will be 1,719. We propose to organize these men in fire-fighting crews, and when the fire season is not bad to have them build trails and do improvement work, and have them in the woods there for this improvement work, the patrol work, and fighting the fires that occur in the backwoods. By having these men scattered through the woods we will be able to put out most of these fires before they get under headway.

The CHAIRMAN. These men would not be forest rangers. They would be short-time men?

Mr. GRAVES. Short-time men.

Mr. McLAUGHLIN. Over what time would their employment extend?

Mr. GRAVES. It would vary. From three to four months, ordinarily.

Mr. McLAUGHLIN. You said you would have these men scattered through the woods. You could hardly do any improvement work systematically.

Mr. GRAVES. I should not have said "scattered" through the woods. I should have said "located in crews of varying sizes in different parts of the woods," so that there would be in these remote sections men who could reach the fires quickly and who, when there wasn't great danger, would be putting in their time building trails.

Mr. McLAUGHLIN. How much longer time would they be employed then than the ordinary fire watchers or fire fighters are employed?

Mr. GRAVES. In those sections from two to four weeks longer than the watchers. Fire fighters are hired as needed—extra labor; often for only a few days or even hours.

The CHAIRMAN. What salaries do you pay these men ordinarily, Doctor?

Mr. GRAVES. That varies from $75 to $125 a month, including subsistence. The total cost is $125 per month where you have to hire a man and give him subsistence, too.

Mr. McLAUGHLIN. Do you have any difficulty in getting men for that short time?

Mr. GRAVES. We have been successful in getting men for that short time, even in the heart of the inland empire, where they have had a great deal of difficulty from labor, and from the I. W. W.

Mr. McLAUGHLIN. Who are they, homesteaders?

Mr. GRAVES. No, sir; they are mostly of the lumberjack type; men who are accustomed to the woods.

Mr. McLAUGHLIN. What do they do the rest of the time?

Mr. GRAVES. They are often men who do not remain in any one class of employment very long. They work in the sawmills part of the year; they work in the lumber mills part of the year. In some cases, when the industrial conditions are not very brisk, we are able to get a very high class of men, of the woods foreman type.

Mr. McLAUGHLIN. Do you find that entirely satisfactory, or just have to put up with the best you can get?

Mr. GRAVES. We have a great many difficulties, and often have to put up with the best we can get. Where we have a very serious fire season, and it is a question of getting men by the hundreds, or even thousands, we have to go into the general labor market, to places like Spokane, for instance, and hire practically anybody we can get.

Mr. McLAUGHLIN. Have you put into the record a statement showing the loss by fire this year as compared with other years?

The CHAIRMAN. That is included in your annual report, is it not, Doctor?

Mr. GRAVES. Yes. About 80 per cent of our fire-fighting money goes into this northwestern region, and mostly on these 26 forests.

Mr. McLAUGHLIN. In making these roads you speak of: You need little besides trails; you don't take in any apparatus?

Mr. GRAVES. We must have trails to take in supplies, and my idea is that the use of these special men when not on actual fire work would be almost wholly on trail work. In some of these remote sections roads may take us up to within 15 to 25 miles of a fire, and and then the balance of that would have to be over trails.

The CHAIRMAN. Any further questions, gentlemen, on that? If not, Dr. Graves, tell us about this $5,000 for the maintenance of Government stock. I didn't know you had any Government stock.

Mr. GRAVES. We have some pack trains in the remote forests, such as I am just speaking of. We have found it an economy to own our pack horses and mules, because of there being very few roads and most of the supplies for work on the forests having to be transported by pack animals. We own in the four Northwestern States—Oregon, Washington, Idaho, and Montana—375 pack animals. The requested increase is to meet the increased cost of forage.

The CHAIRMAN. This is absolutely new to me. I didn't know you owned any horses and mules.

Mr. GRAVES. Yes; I think it has been brought up in connection with our hearings from time to time that we have them on certain forests.

Then, of course, we have also teams in connection with our nursery work, tree planting, and other improvement work on the forests.

The CHAIRMAN. Can you put into the record the entire number of horses the Forest Service owns?

Mr. GRAVES. Seven hundred and twelve animals altogether for all purposes in all of the national forests.

The CHAIRMAN. That includes——

Mr. GRAVES. Horses, mules, and burros.

The CHAIRMAN. Any questions on that, gentlemen?

Mr. McLAUGHLIN. You keep them all the year round, do you?

Mr. GRAVES. Yes.

The CHAIRMAN. Take up you next item, No. 353, on page 124, where you have combined two items, with a decrease of something like $10,000. Was it your purpose in making that combination to save bookkeeping, or what?

Mr. GRAVES. It is entirely in the interest of simplicity. The work of land classification, searching out land suitable for agriculture, and permanently classifying the land, and the work of surveying the homesteads which have been opened up for entry on behalf of the homesteaders are so similar that we have to employ the same class of men; and in general the same men do one class of work part of the time and part of the time the other. It seems that the two funds might perfectly well be combined. It enables us to drop certain language and to have a simpler item.

The CHAIRMAN. That seems to me to be a more sensible arrangement. I don't know why it was not combined to begin with.

Mr. GRAVES. We have had, for instance, language which carried over the appropriation from one year to another to enable us to expend the second year the unexpended balance of the previous year. It was a little confusing, being different from the ordinary language in the bill.

Mr. McLAUGHLIN. In classifying this land, are you still cooperating with the Bureau of Soils?

Mr. GRAVES. Yes.

Mr. McLAUGHLIN. Do you find that necessary? What is your opinion? Is that necessary? Haven't your men experience enough now, when they see the different kinds of lands, to know what they are?

Mr. GRAVES. We have men who are very expert. At the same time there are always questions coming up on which we would like to have the advice of the Bureau of Soils.

Mr. McLAUGHLIN. For example?

Mr. GRAVES. As to possibilities of production, suitability for farming especially, when you get to the border line between what is suitable for agriculture and what is not. I think, too, the assistance of the Bureau of Soils increases the public confidence in our classification—getting the best judgment not only of the men in the Forest Service, but also of an organization like the Bureau of Soils.

The CHAIRMAN. Anything further on that, gentlemen? If not, turn to page 126, item 354, "For fighting and preventing forest fires, and for other unforeseen emergencies." There is no change in that item, which explains itself, unless you want to make some general statement about it.

Mr. GRAVES. We have used sometimes the unexpended balances of money not used in fighting fires, during years when there was a great deal of rain, in fighting insects, under the authority of "unforeseen emergencies." I merely want to call attention to the fact that we have a very serious insect problem in the national forests. It is one that is likely to break out at different points at almost any time. We have an infestation now in California, which we estimate is destroying something like $275,000 worth of timber a year.

The CHAIRMAN. What kind of insect is it?

Mr. GRAVES. It is a bark beetle; it works in the inner bark and girdles the trees.

The CHAIRMAN. How do you fight it?

Mr. GRAVES. We control it by cutting down in the early spring trees which contain the broods. There may be thousands of insects breeding in a single tree. By cutting such trees down and destroying the insect broods, one reduces the number of insects. By carrying that process out to a certain point it is possible to check the invasion. Within a few weeks I have had word from southern Colorado that there is a serious infestation starting there which is likely to destroy a large quantity of Government timber, as well as private timber, and which I think should be handled promptly. It was my original thought to ask for a small sum as a specific item to fight insects. The Secretary felt, when that was brought to his attention, the war not having stopped at that time, that we ought not to ask for any new items but that we should just take a chance with the insects. I did wish, however, to call the attention of the committee to the situation, and that there is danger in it.

The CHAIRMAN. Of course, I think you have the authority here to do that kind of work, but I doubt that it was the intention of the committee that you should do that kind of work under this item.

Mr. GRAVES. I suppose that ordinarily the amount spent out of that was about $10,000. Usually the fund is used up in fire fighting. There isn't any left after the fire season for the next spring, so we couldn't carry on, anyway, any systematic work year after year.

The CHAIRMAN. If you feel that the problem is important enough to have a separate appropriation and will suggest an item to cover the work, I will lay it before the committee and have it considered.

Mr. GRAVES. We suggested $25,000. I just heard of this very serious infestation in southern Colorado, and I think $5,000 ought to be spent on that next spring.

The CHAIRMAN. I think the committee would much prefer to have your insect fighting work in a separate item rather than to have it covered here in the words "other unforeseen emergencies."

Mr. GRAVES. We would much prefer it, because it stands out clearly, and it will enable us to get a great deal of cooperation from lumbermen. They are very much interested in that phase of it, as they are in fires.

Mr. McLAUGHLIN. Is this infestation in Colorado something new?

Mr. GRAVES. It has been working slowly and is just coming to the point of invasion; that is where it is going to break out and destroy a lot of timber. Often it may take several years for an infestation to come to that point.

Mr. McLaughlin. Is it a new insect pest or something you understand how to control?

Mr. Graves. It is one of the bark beetles which is constantly present in the woods, but which, under ordinary circumstances, the natural enemies keep down to damage to scattering trees. Occasionally there is a multiplication of the insects to the point where they get ahead of their natural enemies and destroy a great deal of timber. The item which I presented to the Secretary was as follows:

> For preventing and combating infestations of insects injurious to forest trees on and near the national forests, independently or in cooperation with other branches of the Federal Government, with States, counties, municipalities, or with private owners, $25,000.

Mr. McLaughlin. I would like to ask another question in regard to these large emergency appropriations. I am not fully informed as to the authority of the Secretary of Agriculture to transfer one appropriation to another, or take money appropriated for one use and use it for another purpose. There is a sort of a 10 per cent transfer authorized by the Secretary of Agriculture. Suppose you make one of these very large emergency appropriations, like for fighting fires, and you don't have to use it, is there authority to take 10 per cent of that and use it for some entirely different purpose?

Mr. Graves. We never have used this fire-fighting emergency fund for anything except fires and insects.

Mr. McLaughlin. The Secretary has the power to do it?

Mr. Graves. I think there would be authority to do it under the 10 per cent item, but we never have done that.

Mr. McLaughlin. That would be a very important matter, it seems to me. If a very large amount should be appropriated, as has been the case, for an emergency, and the Secretary was authorized to use 10 per cent of that for hiring forest rangers, or traveling expenditures, or for buildings or stationery. You say that has not been done?

Mr. Graves. Of course we have transferred between items under the 10 per cent authority, particularly in the forests, where there is great need of the 10 per cent authority, because the seasons vary, the business varies, and a transfer is frequently necessary, but we don't transfer between the forest appropriations and our special items in the way that you suggest. Where we have to incur a deficit, that is under a different authority. That is under the general authority to protect the public property. We then go to Congress and ask for a deficiency.

The Chairman. Take up your next item. Mr. Graves. No. 356, "For investigations of methods for wood-distillation and for the preservative treatment of timber," etc. There seems to be an increase there of $35,000. Tell us about the increase, Doctor.

Mr. Graves. This is necessary for the work at the Madison laboratory.

Mr. Wilson. What laboratory?

Mr. Graves. The Madison (Wis.) laboratory, where we conduct studies of wood products. During the war our entire force at the laboratory was devoted to war purposes. The Army and the Navy, Shipping Board, War Trade Board, and various other organizations called on us for a great deal of information in connection with the use of wood. They required more information than we already had. They requested many special studies. These departments made allotments of $352,000 to increase our work, so that we could get the information necessary for them. I might say, if I am permitted to speak of this just a moment longer, that one single item of work which we did for the Army saved them over $5,000,000.

Mr. McLAUGHLIN. What was that?

Mr. GRAVES. Our work in connection with the development of plywood.

Mr. WILSON. Development of what?

Mr. GRAVES. Development of plywood. Plywood is made up of two or more layers of veneer, and is used in the various parts of airplanes and for other purposes. They are using it now even in the covering of the body of the car, for the frame, and, for instance, in the wing ribs—pieces that support the wings—and in various other parts.

Mr. McLAUGHLIN. Saved $5,000,000?

Mr. GRAVES. Yes.

Mr. McLAUGHLIN. How do you know?

Mr. GRAVE. Because the officers of the Army told me so, sir. The art of making plywood suitable for airplanes was very little developed. There was a lack of waterproof glues, for one thing. Only a limited number of concerns knew how to manufacture it at all. Very few kinds of wood were known to be satisfactory. The result of our work in developing new glues, demonstrating the suitability of several woods, and in showing methods of control of manufacturing and of using the wood resulted in reducing the price of plywood from 50 cents to less than 20 cents per square foot. Inasmuch as they used about 20,000,000 square feet, as I was told by one of the officers of the Bureau of Aircraft Production, there was a saving of about $6,000,000 as the result of this work.

Mr. WILSON. Do you know what became of the $6,000,000?

Mr. McKINLEY. They didn't tell you, Doctor, it cost $1,000,000 for every American plane they got over to France, did they?

The CHAIRMAN. Anything further?

Mr. GRAVES. In connection with that work, we had a great many requests from the industries which were doing work for the War Department, those who were building planes, those building Army vehicles and other Army equipment, information regarding methods of treating, methods of handling wood, information regarding supplies of raw materials, and so on. This increase is asked primarily to enable us to meet the requests for assistance from the industries. That is the chief purpose for which we would like to spend this money.

The CHAIRMAN. If you will pardon me, I was wondering whether you had not asked this increase on account of the state of war at the time these estimates were made up.

Mr. GRAVES. When I made up this estimate we were at war. I find, however, that the requests for industrial help has continued, and from all indications will greatly increase. For example, take our work in connection with boxes. That was one of the lines of work conducted both during the war and previous to that. We are getting a great many requests from box manufacturers for advice as well as for special tests. We are getting many requests from vehicle manufacturers connected with the seasoning of wood.

Mr. ANDERSON. Are you doing any work now on kiln processes?

Mr. GRAVES. Yes. We are anxious to get the information to the industry.

The CHAIRMAN. I might say I have a good many letters from box factories very strongly commending your work in that regard.

Mr. GRAVES. I think our greatest weakness, Mr. Chairman, is that we are not getting the information we are obtaining at the laboratory into direct use in the industries, and we need to send men out to give advice with regard to the use of the different processes we work out, as well as to take up certain necessary investigative work for them.

The CHAIRMAN. Any further question on that item? This is an old item and pretty well understood. Your next is on page 158, item 357, "For experiments and investigations of range conditions within national forests, $35,000." There is no change in that item?

Mr. GRAVES. No, sir.

The CHAIRMAN. You might make a brief statement of the progress you have made in that work.

Mr. GRAVES. Mr. Barnes has charge of our grazing. I think he could make, perhaps, a little clearer statement as to the specific advantages of this investigative work than I could.

The CHAIRMAN. All right, Mr. Barnes, give us a brief summary.

STATEMENT OF MR. WILL C. BARNES, ASSISTANT FORESTER IN CHARGE OF GRAZING, FOREST SERVICE, UNITED STATES DEPARTMENT OF AGRICULTURE.

Mr. BARNES. One of the principal losses in grazing is from poisonous plants. We have been carrying on a study of that for several years, until we have arrived at the best method of exterminating them. We want to put that into direct effect. It seems to be a big job. The loss from larkspur in the national forests, by actual count, is almost 5,000 cattle every year. We found we could locate the larkspur in small areas, and by going in with a crew of men and grubbing it out we have reduced these losses greatly; and shown that we can practically eradicate the larkspur. Take the Fishlake National Forest, in Utah, where we have had heavy losses year after year—$15,000 or $20,000 worth of stock on an average every year—we have almost wiped out those losses by grubbing out the plants. Where we put up the money to pay for the food, and furnish the tools, the stockmen furnish the labor. In that way we want to go over the ranges, and eventually we will eliminate the larkspur. I suppose you gentlemen know something of the effect of the loco weed on stock. Stockmen say, "Why can't you clean up the loco?" because the losses from that are very severe, and have been for years past. We want to use some of this money, first, in the study of methods to get rid of the loco. We believe it could be chopped off just the same as the larkspur. We want to put some of the money into practical use. We want to take areas and grub it out, a hundred acres, and see whether it comes back, how soon, whether it has to be grubbed deep or shallow. The studies that tell how to do this in practice are the principal uses to which we put this money.

The CHAIRMAN. That gives the committee some idea of this character of work.

Mr. HAUGEN. Now, after it is all done, what do the stockmen do to compensate the Government for fixing up the land for them and saving their stock?

Mr. BARNES. They are paying good fees now; they will after this year. We have raised the fees.

Mr. HAUGEN. How much are they paying now?

Mr. BARNES. Eighty cents a year is the lowest.

Mr. HAUGEN. What is the highest?

Mr. BARNES. One dollar and fifty cents.

Mr. HAUGEN. For what?

Mr. BARNES. For the year's grazing for one cow.

Mr. HAUGEN. What is it for sheep?

Mr. BARNES. One-fourth of that.

Mr. HAUGEN. For horses?

Mr. BARNES. Twenty-five per cent higher.

Mr. HAUGEN. The maximum is $1.50?

Mr. BARNES. For cattle. That is the unit rate. Sheep are 25 per cent of the cattle rate, and horses are 25 per cent higher than the cattle rate. The rates are increased really about 60 per cent over 1918, practically increased 60 per cent.

Mr. HAUGEN. Were you giving the current rates or the future rates?

Mr. BARNES. The future rates.

Mr. HAUGEN. Up to the present time they were less than half of that?

Mr. BARNES. Yes, sir.

Mr. HAUGEN. How many acres does it take, on an average? How many acres do you give for an animal?

Mr. BARNES. Roughly considered, about 20 acres to a cow; some forests, 14 acres to the cow, some 12, some 40.

Mr. HAUGEN. You get about 6 cents an acre?

Mr. BARNES. Yes; just roughly. We feel that the Nation's needs are——

Mr. HAUGEN. How much are you spending? Getting 6 cents, you can not do much improving at 6 cents an acre, can you?

Mr. BARNES. No; not if we have to do it for every acre.

Mr. HAUGEN. Don't you think that $1.50 for 20 acres of grazing for an animal for a whole year is rather reasonable?

Mr. BARNES. Yes; we do.

Mr. HAUGEN. Why don't you get more?

Mr. BARNES. Well, we thought we would put it up. We went at it from a commercial basis. We estimated the charges based on what the stockmen were paying for like areas of equal grazing value in that vicinity. Then we discounted that, considering that the Government requires certain things of the stockmen. For instance, we say to them, "We will give you a grazing permit for this piece of range, provided we don't have to close it up, if we need to do so, to protect the timber reproduction or a watershed." There are certain things that the Government requires that a private owner who leases land would not. We discounted that about one-third. For instance, in Arizona the stockmen pay $2.40 a head for grazing on the Apache

Indian Reservation; but they get absolute control; they are not bothered with any conditions as to watershed or taking care of timber reproduction, or anything of that kind.

Mr. McLaughlin. Who fixes the prices of grazing on the Indian Reservation you speak of?

Mr. Barnes. It is all let out on public bid.

Mr. McLaughlin. It is public bidding that fixes the rate?

Mr. Barnes. Yes; the Commissioner of Indian Affairs settles it. He advertises that the grazing on the Apache Indian Reservation, for example, in Arizona, will be leased at a certain time; that sealed bids will be received, and the highest bidder gets it.

Mr. McLauglin. And under that plan one-third more is obtained than you will obtain under your plan?

Mr. Barnes. And lately we——

Mr. McLaughlin. Had it occurred to you you might use the same plan?

Mr. Barnes. Yes; if it is done, it——

Mr. Haugen (interposing). Is yours open to competitive bids?

Mr. Barnes. No.

Mr. Haugen. Can you tell us why? There is a good deal of complaint about this leasing business. I don't know whether it is well founded or not, but I'd like to know. The complaint is that the small fellows are excluded and the big fellows hog it all. That is the charge. I don't know whether the change is well founded or not.

Mr. Barnes. It is not. Over 60 per cent of our permittees are small men, grazing less than 40 head of cattle. We are doing all we can to help the little man. He gets free grazing for 10 head of his work and milch stock. No permit is required and this is open to everybody—every little settler and homesteader. This policy began from the first, and we believe it a wise one. It gives the new settler a boost—furnishes him a chance to graze his work horses or oxen, his milch cows, a pig or two, or even his goats, free of charge, and thus maintain his family.

Mr. Lee. If you put it to the highest bidder, it would protect the big men.

Mr. Barnes. Yes; we don't think it would be a wise public policy.

Mr. Haugen. Not at all. You could sublet it, under small contracts. We were promised this service would be made self-supporting, and that that is the object of the service. I should think you would be interested in getting the highest sum.

Mr. McLaughlin. Do you think the advertising plan would shut out the small ones?

Mr. Barnes. Yes; unquestionably.

Mr. McLaughlin. Tell us why.

Mr. Barnes. Because, naturally, they tend to deal with the big man.

Mr. McLaughlin. Who does?

Mr. Barnes. The Government, or anybody finds it simpler to deal with one man that grazes 5,000 head than 50 men that graze 100 head. Out on the Apache Indian Reservation it has shut out the little man entirely.

Mr. McLaughlin. Suppose the Government officials did not have that disposition? That part of it eliminated, what other reasons are there?

Mr. Barnes. For not leasing them by public auction?

Mr. McLaughlin. No; the other reason for believing that putting it up at public auction would shut out the small ones.

The Chairman. That is sufficient, isn't it?

Mr. Graves. The big ones could naturally afford to pay more.

Mr. Heflin. If I understood you, you said that out in Arizona they advertised for bids and received sealed bids?

Mr. Barnes. Yes; on the Indian reservations.

Mr. Heflin. And the one who bid the highest got, for instance, a 20,000-acre field to use for his purpose?

Mr. Barnes. Yes.

Mr. Heflin. And the others were turned down?

Mr. Barnes. Yes.

Mr. Heflin. Then, he could let them graze or not, as he saw fit?

Mr. Barnes. He could; yes, sir.

Mr. Heflin. And that is why you say the little man would be shut out if you would lease to the highest bidder?

Mr. Barnes. It would prevent a permanence in the business. Take a forest where the country contiguous is interested in stock raising and farming. These little men have a permanence. If you put their permits up at auction every few years, they would be all upset. On the Indian reservation they lease the land every three years, and there is a great overturning.

Mr. McLaughlin. How do the small ones have a permanency?

Mr. Barnes. We say to them, "As long as you comply with the regulations and continue to pay your grazing fees, your permits will be renewed." It is practically a guaranty, as long as they wish to use the ranges. Many of them go from year to year and have no doubt of their permanency. In fact the Secretary has authorized the issue of permits for five years, which are guaranteed against any reductions or changes, except for nonpayment of fees or violations of the regulations.

Mr. McLaughlin. An actual settler is permitted to graze his own stock?

Mr. Barnes. Yes. There are so many complications in handling it by putting it up at public auction that it would not be a wise public policy, and it would put out the little fellow, unquestionably.

Mr. Haugen. Unquestionably. Explain that. That does not go with the public.

Mr. Barnes. Unless Congress passed a law and provided for a limitation as to the number of acres any one man could graze.

Mr. Haugen. You don't have to pass any law to make a limitation as to the contracts. You say that 60 per cent of them are now small contracts?

Mr. Barnes. Yes.

Mr. Haugen. It is in your power to lease a thousand acres, or 10 acres, or a hundred acres. It is just up to the Forest Service whatever course to pursue?

Mr. Graves. May I interject a statement there? You see the small men are small settlers living in and near the forests.

Mr. Haugen. And it is the small men that are complaining.

Mr. Graves. These are the men we have been trying to take care of and have been giving the preference to.

Mr. Haugen. And these are the fellows who claim they have been excluded.

Mr. GRAVES. Of course, there is always a limit to the number of stock that can be gra ed on a given forest.

Mr. HAUGEN. Certainly.

Mr. GRAVES. Our purpose is not merely to make money out of the grazing. Our first object is to protect the forests and the watersheds, and this other, the use of the grazing, is a secondary use, and I think that most of the complaints come from men who perhaps are new settlers who come in and find the forests all filled up.

Mr. HAUGEN. Do you contend that a large ranch is more destructive than a small one?

Mr. GRAVES. No, sir.

Mr. HAUGEN. Then, where does that come in?

Mr. GRAVES. The point I was making was that these ranchers are men who are living near the forests. Grazing stock on the national forests becomes a part of their enterprise. We feel we ought not to put them in competition perhaps with outsiders, often from a distance. They should be charged a reasonable market rate rather than have a rate forced out of them by competition.

Mr. HAUGEN. But they are the ones that are complaining that they are excluded. They are the ones who would like to have it open to competition.

The CHAIRMAN. To whom are they complaining? I have not seen any complaints.

Mr. HAUGEN. I receive complaints every session of Congress.

The CHAIRMAN. I have not had a complaint.

Mr. HAUGEN. It is not law.

Mr. GRAVES. It is perfectly true that the national forests in some portions of the West have not sufficient range to accommodate all the people who would like to get on.

Mr. HAUGEN. Yes; but then there are some of them accommodated with thousands of head, and others don't get in. That's the trouble. What are the largest contracts you have?

Mr. GRAVES. I think that in some remote sections where there is very little settlement—what is the largest contract you have (speaking to Mr. Barnes)?

Mr. BARNES. We have, I believe, one or two for over 10,000 head.

Mr. HAUGEN. On all the forests? In the largest forests haven't you contracts running up to 50,000?

Mr. BARNES. No, sir. I think the largest is on one New Mexico forest, which is a big forest, where we have never turned down a little man; there is vacant range there for small men, and very few applications. In the Sawtooth Forest in Idaho we have several permittees who have large bands of sheep, but it is not a country that little men can operate in, due to the character of the country, long distance from the railroad, and the necessity of running large outfits.

Mr. HAUGEN. Do I understand you to say that no syndicate or individual or corporation or company is granted a grazing permit to exceed 10,000?

Mr. BARNES. We have very few over 5,000.

Mr. HAUGEN. What is the maximum number? It may be I am misinformed.

Mr. BARNES. The maximum is between 8,000 and 12,000.

Mr. HAUGEN. No more than that? You are positive of that?

Mr. BARNES. You are speaking of cattle?

Mr. HAUGEN. Yes.

Mr. BARNES. I am positive it will not exceed the number given.

Mr. HAUGEN. How many of sheep?

Mr. BARNES. We have one or two outfits in the Northwest that run as high as 35,000. We have one in the Southwest that runs about 45,000 head all told, but using more of their own land than of national-forest land, which takes care of no more than 16,000 of their total. They own tremendous holdings of land. Their land investment runs up to $300,000 or $400,000. We have reduced some of the large men to let the little fellows in; we have reduced some over 50 per cent in their holdings. We reduced them very heavily. We get quite as much criticism from the large men as from the small men.

Mr. HAUGEN. I think that will satisfy the chairman that there is some criticism.

The CHAIRMAN. I said I hadn't gotten any.

Mr. BARNES. As Mr. Graves has said, we can not take care of all the men—that is impossible—but the criticism comes mostly from the men turned down for want of room.

Mr. GRAVES. The number of small stockmen on the forests has been steadily increasing.

Mr. HAUGEN. All criticism is not well founded, and I was not bringing this up here to criticize the Forest Service; but I think it is due the committee that we should know, in order that we may answer these questions intelligently; and I shall answer the question that no permittee will be permitted to exceed 10,000 head of cattle.

Mr. GRAVES. We will get the exact number and insert it in the record.

(The statement referred to follows:)

Grazing permits.

The maximum number of head of cattle and sheep for which individual grazing permits have been issued by the Forest Service are as follows:

	Head.
Cattle	8,215
Sheep	65,960

The CHAIRMAN. On page 129, item 358, there is no change except that you have added a proviso setting aside $200 for the purchase of a nursery site.

Mr. ANDERSON. Was not this item proposed last year?

Mr. GRAVES. I was not here myself last year; I don't know.

Mr. ANDERSON. I am quite certain it was.

Mr. GRAVES. It may have been.

The CHAIRMAN. I don't think it was. I do not recall it myself.

Mr. GRAVES. The request is for authority to spend $200 for land which we have in connection with our nursery on the Michigan National Forest.

The CHAIRMAN. Haven't you any land of your own there now?

Mr. GRAVES. There is very little suitable land for a nursery. We have got to have water and good soil and reasonable accessibility. This was land we leased near our headquarters in a very suitable place, and the lessor did not want to lease it any more but wanted to sell it. So our supervisor stepped in and bought it personally at $175 to protect the Government's interests.

Mr. McLaughlin. You say "the additional $25 will be barely sufficient to cover the cost of survey, taxes, preparation of deed, etc." The Government doesn't have to pay taxes, does it?

Mr. Graves. That would be for expenses the supervisor incurred. He paid $175 for it, and since then he has been paying taxes on it. I think it would be fair to cover his actual expenses.

Mr. McLaughlin. How large is it?

Mr. McKinley. Isn't it a fact the man bought it for $175, and proposes to sell it for $200?

Mr. Graves. We would pay him exactly what it cost him, and no more. There are some expenses that he incurred in connection with acquiring title to the land, which I think it would be fair for us to pay, but I don't think the whole thing would exceed $200. There would be no profit in it for him.

Mr. McKinley. Tell us about the tree planting.

Mr. Graves. We are making progress in the tree planting on all of the national forests, one of the greatest items of progress being the learning of how to do it. The planting in Michigan and Minnesota is comparatively simple compared with some parts of the West, particularly in the dry regions like the Rocky Mountains. It has taken some years in experiments to learn how to plant trees in the drier climates. I feel that the tree-planting work is of importance, not only in forests like the Michigan forests, where the trees have been practically all killed by cutting and fires, and in the Nebraska sand hills, where new forests are being very successfully established, but it is important in certain regions of the other portions of the national-forest regions to build up forests on important watersheds, and also as an education.

The Chairman. I wish you would put in the record, for the use of the committee, the cost per acre, and so on, and some detailed facts about it.

(The statement referred to follows:)

NATIONAL-FOREST NURSERIES.

During the last year the Forest Service planted 6,085 acres on the national forests. This is a smaller acreage than usual because of the reduction of $20,000 in the appropriation for this work and because of the high cost of labor. Of course, when wages increase 50 per cent or more, it is impossible to hire as many laborers to plant trees as could be done previously. The cost per acre varies widely with conditions. In Michigan the plantations cost the department about $5 per acre last year, and this cost can be reduced somewhat as the work is conducted on a larger scale. In the Northwest the plantations cost $8 to $10 per acre; and in the drier regions in the Rocky Mountains, where the work is largely on an experimental scale, the costs averaged from $15 to $20 per acre. In dry regions like the Rocky Mountain country or Nebraska it is necessary to plant many more trees per acre than in other regions, where the rainfall is abundant and it is assured that practically every tree that is planted will grow.

Mr. McLaughlin. Is this nursery in Michigan adjoining or connected in any way with the areas where you are doing planting work?

Mr. Graves. Yes; it is very close.

Mr. McLaughlin. How large an area there are you planting?

Mr. Graves. I am sorry I haven't got the figures in mind now as to the exact progress in Michigan.

The Chairman. Anything further, Mr. McLaughlin?

Mr. McLaughlin. No.

The CHAIRMAN. The next item is on page 130, No. 353. An increase of $25,000 is asked. Tell us about the increase, Doctor?

Mr. GRAVES. The purpose of this increase is to extend our work in the study of the lumber industry, and in the economic questions in connection with the forests all over the country. We have been carrying on studies of production, markets, supplies, and other, economic problems connected with the lumber industry during the war at the request of the War Industries Board, War Trade Board, and some of the other organizations. The question of supplies is at points already getting pretty serious. The question of supplies in connection with our paper industry is at points a serious one. While we have been, during the war, making studies especially of supplies of vehicle stock, locust for tree nails, material for ships, and other special requirements for war purposes, we wish to continue that same kind of work in connection with these same and other industries, whose supplies, at least locally, are becoming scarce. In Wisconsin, for instance, some paper manufacturers are even looking to the Rocky Mountains for possible supplies to send materials east to the Wisconsin mills.

The CHAIRMAN. Was this increase estimated on the basis of the war situation?

Mr. GRAVES. The first increase was estimated during the war. It was not, however, on a basis of what the War Department—the military departments—could properly allot money for. They asked for information which we ought to be in a position to supply from our regular studies. But I think it is just as important, Mr. Chairman, to continue that work now, in peace times, and even more important during the period of rehabilitation of industries.

The CHAIRMAN. In other words, when you did work for the War Department, the War Department made an allotment?

Mr. GRAVES. The War Department made an allotment, except where it was work which properly we could and should do, and when it was rather questionable whether they could do it, then we used our own funds. I feel that we ought to be prepared with information in regard to not only forest supplies but in regard to the industry itself, the questions of production and distribution of lumber, and the multitude of questions which are coming up and about which information is constantly being asked of us by the Federal Trade Commission, Department of Commerce, and other organizations which have to do with wood. The Tariff Board frequently asks us questions regarding the industry in matters pertaining to tariff questions, wood-pulp problems, shingle problems, and so on. We endeavor to keep in touch with the industries and the economic and industrial problems, but we haven't been able to do as much as I think we should do. The work would be really very useful to the industries themselves, aside from information furnished the Government departments.

Mr. MCLAUGHLIN. Do you find that as years go by kinds of wood heretofore thought to be unsuitable for making paper and pulp are now used for that purpose?

Mr. GRAVES. Yes, sir.

Mr. MCLAUGHLIN. And found to be entirely satisfactory?

Mr. GRAVES. Yes; there is prospect of opening the use of other woods, too. Of course the technical phases of that are being studied at the Madison laboratory. The forest industry we are studying under this item under discussion.

Mr. McLaughlin. You say studying. With what result? Do you not find that woods heretofore thought unsuitable for making paper are now found to be entirely suitable?

Mr. Graves. Hemlock, for example. Hemlock is now being used for paper practically as a result of studies at the Madison laboratory, and various pines are suitable. We hope before we get through to find ways of using other woods in large amounts for news print.

Mr. McLaughlin. You say the Wisconsin paper manufacturers have found it necessary to go to the Rocky Mountains?

Mr. Graves. Some have inquired of us about national-forest timber. I can not answer that question specifically. They are concerned as to future supplies and are making inquiries as to future supplies after their present supplies are gone. It is a very urgent question for them.

Mr. Candler. Is any white pine left in the United States to amount to anything?

Mr. Graves. The eastern white pine is very much depleted, but the western white pine of Idaho is very rapidly coming into the market. The remaining virgin stands of white pine in the Lake States are mainly in Minnesota. Those of Michigan and Wiscinson have been very largely cut over. The best estimates available indicate that the total of both white and Norway pine for the Lake States is from twelve to fifteen billion feet.

In the Eastern States the stands are almost entirely second growth and yield lumber suitable for little else than boxes. There is about thirteen billion feet of this second growth, mostly in New England and very largely in small tracts.

Mr. Candler. There is lots of it in the West?

Mr. Graves. The western white pine is a different species, closely allied, and not quite so good.

The Chairman. Your next item is 360, " for estimating and appraising timber "; you have a decrease there of $20,000.

Mr. Graves. That is a war decrease, Mr. Chairman. Our personnel was very much reduced. We lost during the first year of the war about 1,000 persons from the Forest Service. About half of these went into the military service and the others resigned. Our forces were much depleted, and the industrial demands were falling off, so we felt that we ought not to ask for $100,000 during the war. The war is over. This item provides money which is expended to build up our timber sale business, to cruise timber, and make our sales. I anticipate that by the next fiscal year the demand for timber will be sufficient to make it desirable to have the entire $100,000. I would like very much if the committee would have that restored to the sum of last year.

The Chairman. We will consider that, Doctor.

Mr. Harrison. I would like to say that Mr. Graves has discussed the matter with the Secretary and that the suggestion meets with his approval.

The Chairman. All right, gentlemen, page 131, item 361, " Other miscellaneous forest investigations, $31,280." There is no change in that?

Mr. Graves. No.

The CHAIRMAN. That is the same kind of work you have been doing?

Mr. GRAVES. Same thing year after year.

The CHAIRMAN. Your next item is No. 362, "For the construction and maintenance of roads, trails, bridges," etc., $450,000; there is no change in that item?

Mr. GRAVES. This is another item for which I originally suggested an increase to the Secretary. There is a demand for the eradication of larkspur and for building drift fences, and other grazing improvements in the national forests. The stockmen are asking us to do more than heretofore. We are going to have an increase in receipts of about $850,000 this year by the increase of the grazing fees, and the stockmen are asking the Government to do more work in the eradication of poisonous plants and other improvements for the benefit of the range. During the war, when this matter came up, the Secretary felt we ought not to ask for that during that period, especially the time when wire could not be obtained, labor could not be obtained, etc. The stockmen are anxious to have us do this work, and it would be a matter for the committee to consider an increase.

Mr. HAUGEN. How much money are you spending for fences?

Mr. GRAVES. I am sorry I haven't that data.

Mr. HAUGEN. Is it any considerable amount?

Mr. GRAVES. Not a very great amount. I think it was $20,000 last year, but I would not be certain.

Mr. HAUGEN. Well, are many of these ranges inclosed?

Mr. GRAVES. They are not inclosed. They are drift fences.

Mr. HAUGEN. They are not fencing the ranges, simply inclosing them.

Mr. GRAVES. I recall an estimate of one of my grazing experts that the expenditure of $20,000 would enable us to increase the number of stock on the forests, through the drift fences which regulated the movement of the stock, so that the grazing would pay for the improvements in two years. Thus the cost of building of the drift fences is soon paid back.

Mr. HAUGEN. How do you account for that? How do you figure that out? The drift fences would not increase the growth of the the grass, would they?

Mr. GRAVES. No; but it enables the control of the stock, so that you could put more on the range because of the better distribution. If you don't control the stock, they are apt to congregate in a few places and destroy the range so you get poor results, whereas if you distribute them right you can get a greater number of stock on the range.

Mr. HAUGEN. You are not inclosing any of the ranges?

Mr. GRAVES. Except here and there pastures, which are leased as a special use, and for which a special charge is made; but we are not inclosing the range in the old way.

Mr. HAUGEN. You add to the rate indicated here a while ago wherever you fence it?

Mr. GRAVES. If there is a pasture that is handled separately and used exclusively by an individual permittee.

Mr. HAUGEN. You charge more than $1.50?

Mr. GRAVES. A special charge is made for the use of such individual pastures.

Mr. HAUGEN. About how much?

Mr. BARNES. Ten cents an acre, on an average. It should be understood that these individual pastures are fenced at his own cost by the stockman using them, for the purpose only of holding saddle and work horses and beef animals being gathered for shipment. The pasture is incidental to the use of the range. There is no fencing of individual ranges allowed. They are used in common for cattle, the drift fences merely separating the large range areas into what may be called community units.

The CHAIRMAN. Mr. Graves, in that connection, I wish you would put into the record the number of miles of road you built during the past year, the trails and fences, and so on, and the average cost of each, and also give the total.

Mr. HAUGEN. It is given in the notes.

The CHAIRMAN. You had better put it in the record.

Mr. GRAVES. I can insert a brief statement of it.

(The statement referred to follows:)

STATEMENT RELATIVE TO IMPROVEMENTS ON THE NATIONAL FORESTS.

Fiscal year 1918.

Classes.	Amount.	Average unit cost.	Total cost.
Roads...........miles..	56	$554	$31,033
Trails...........do....	696	54	37,644
Telephone lines...........do....	1,044	51	53,244
Fire breaks...........do....	33	71	2,343
Fences...........do....	367	135	49,545
Lookout towers and buildings.	54	135	7,290
Dwellings (includes 1-room cabins).	96	463	44,248
Barns.	72	210	15,120
Other buildings.	304	52	15,808
Corrals.	10	49	490
Bridges.	19	369	7,011
Water improvements.	238	77	18,326
Miscellaneous improvements.			19,360
Total construction.			301,462
Maintenance of existing improvements (33 per cent).			148,538
Total.			450,000

Fiscal year 1919.

Classes.	Approximate amount.	Approximate average unit cost.	Approximate total cost.
Trails...........miles..	596	$96	$57,216
Telephone lines...........do....	433	79	34,207
Firebreaks...........do....	6	130	780
Fences...........do....	121	180	21,780
Lookout towers and buildings.	35	278	9,730
Dwellings.	16	650	10,400
Barns.	22	260	5,720
Other buildings.	194	81	15,714
Corrals.	4	88	352
Bridges.	8	720	5,760
Water improvements.	285	131	27,335
Stock driveways...........miles..	93	47	4,371
Clearing pastures...........acres..	138	13	1,794
Larkspur eradication.			8,558
Miscellaneous improvements.			47,484
Approximate total construction.			251,201
Approximate total, maintenance of existing improvements (44 per cent).			198,799
Total.			450,000

The CHAIRMAN. On page 133, item 365, you have the administrative expenses under the Weeks act, $21,770. There is no change in that?

Mr. GRAVES. No, sir; that is simply authority to use the money for that purpose.

The CHAIRMAN. It is really not an appropriation. Now, gentlemen, turn to page 265. That provides for the cooperative fire-fighting force under the Weeks act. There is no change in that?

COOPERATIVE FIRE PROTECTION.

Mr. GRAVES. It authorizes cooperation with the States. Of course, with the increased cost of labor we can do less with $100,000 than we have heretofore. The increased cost of fire protection is about 25 per cent since we originally asked for this item, so we are doing about 25 per cent less effective work than before.

The CHAIRMAN. How many States are cooperating with you, Doctor; do you recall?

Mr. GRAVES. It is 22. We have found, Mr. Chairman, that this item has been productive of a great deal of good, because the States have been very eager to cooperate with us, and oftentimes a very small allotment to a State has resulted in their spending several times that amount. It is very educational. I think it is one of the best things for the awakening of interest in fire protection among private owners, and in awakening an interest in the States for fire-protective legislation.

The CHAIRMAN. On page 279 are two items; item 12, " That hereafter the Secretary of Agriculture may, in his discretion and under such conditions as he may prescribe, supply to any municipality or public institution not more than one American bison "——

Mr. ANDERSON (interposing). We can not cover these two items before recess. I would like to know something about this motorcycle and automobile item. I suppose Mr. Graves is going to take that up.

Mr. GRAVES. Yes, sir.

The CHAIRMAN. The committee will stand in recess until half past one.

(Thereupon, at 12.05 o'clock p. m., the committee took a recess until 1.30 p. m.)

AFTER RECESS.

The committee reassembled at 1.30 o'clock p. m., pursuant to the taking of recess.

TRANSFER OF BISON TO MUNICIPALITIES AND PUBLIC INSTITUTIONS.

STATEMENT OF MR. HENRY S. GRAVES, FORESTER AND CHIEF, FOREST SERVICE, UNITED STATES DEPARTMENT OF AGRICULTURE—Continued.

The CHAIRMAN. Mr. Graves, at the time we took recess you were just about to discuss item No. 12, on page 279—

That hereafter the Secretary of Agriculture may, in his discretion and under such conditions as he may prescribe, supply to any municipality or public institution not more than one American bison from any surplus which may exist in any herd under the control of the Department of Agriculture; and, in order to aid in the propagation of the species, animals may be loaned to or exchanged with other owners of American bison.

Mr. Graves. Some of the herds of American bison under the control of the department already contain a surplus of bulls. The purpose of this proposed legislation is to provide an opportunity for municipalities and parks to secure without charge a specimen of historic and educational value and to enable the Government, municipalities, public parks, and other owners of American bison to improve the strain of their herds and to avoid inbreeding, through the loan or exchange of animals.

We are cooperating with cities and other organizations in game culture. We have on one of our national forests a herd of bison which we are handling with such assistance as we need from the biological survey, and there are problems which arise in connection with the handling of a herd of animals like that where it may be desirable to reduce the number of bulls. It frequently happens that a city or municipal park may desire a loan of a bull, and this is to give us a little wider authority in such cooperation.

Mileage Rates for Motor Vehicles.

The Chairman. The next item is No. 13, on page 279—

Whenever hereafter the Secretary of Agriculture shall find that the expenses of travel can be reduced thereby, he may, in lieu of actual traveling expenses, under such regulations as he may prescribe, authorize the payment of such rates per mile for motorcycles and automobiles used for necessary travel on official business of the Department of Agriculture as he shall determine to be necessary to reimburse the owner of such motorcycle or automobile for the operating expenses thereof.

Mr. Graves. This is a question of limitation on the amount of mileage that we will allow to forest officers so far as it concerns the Forest Service for the use of their personal cars on official business.

The language of the provision as contained in the act for 1919 limits its operation to that year, but, as the method of reimbursing employees for the use of personally owned motorcycles and automobiles in conducting the field work of the department has proven to be expedient and distinctly economical, in that the Government secures the full use of the vehicles without the initial outlay for their purchase and subsequent expenditures for repairs and replacement, to say nothing of depreciation, it is highly desirable that the authority be continued. Therefore, in order to obviate the necessity of repeating the language from year to year, it is recommended that the words " during the fiscal year ending June 30, 1919 " be omitted, and the word " hereafter " be substituted.

It is also recommended that the specific rates per mile for motorcycles and automobiles, viz, 2 and 6 cents, respectively, be omitted, and language substituted which will allow the Secretary of Agriculture more latitude in fixing mileage rates. The rates established for the present fiscal year were recommended by the department a year ago, at which time it was believed that they would be entirely adequate to cover actual operating expenses. Conditions, however, have completely changed during the past year and the rates authorized in the present provision will not reimburse employees for such expenses.

The records of the department indicate that the cost of operating Government-owned automobiles varies from 6 to 12 cents per mile for light cars, and from 8 to 16 cents per mile for heavier cars.

These variations in rates are due almost entirely to local factors, such as the difference in the cost of supplies in the various sections of the country and road conditions in the locality where the car is being used.

Many employees of the department feel unable to pay from their personal funds the difference between the established rates and the actual cost of operation, and for this reason a number have disposed of their cars, while others are not inclined to continue to use their vehicles in official work. Unless this condition is remedied the field work of the department will be greatly impeded, and it is, therefore, urgently recommended that the language of the paragraph as submitted be enacted into law.

The proviso prohibiting the payment of mileage for the use of motorcycles and automobiles furnished or owned by or maintained by the Government is recommended omitted, as such payments are prohibited by existing law.

As I say, the experience we have had has shown that 6 cents does not cover the cost. We have in the Forest Service 471 privately owned cars which the forest officers use in connection with official business. Most of these are light cars, the only kind that officers of the Forest Service can afford, and it unquestionably has saved the Government a good deal of money to have the forest officer use his own car.

We have not encouraged the idea of purchasing from Government funds passenger cars for use in the national forests. We feel that a certain number of Government-owned trucks are an economy in fire fighting, where otherwise we would have to hire machines to get the materials, equipment, and men to the fires. But we have not felt that it would be desirable to furnish officers of the Forest Service with cars. Ordinarily the man who owns his own car takes much better care of it than he does of a Government-owned car. That is our experience, and I think it is the universal experience of business men. I know that is true in the case of the Army.

I understand that certain large concerns whose employees use cars on company business have taken the same position in regard to having their men use the cars of the firm or corporation, but have encouraged their men to own their own cars, and then give them mileage rather than furnish them with cars.

I do feel, however, that it is proper, where a forest officer has a car which he uses for official business, that the proportionate expense of the running of the car, covering the mileage where it is used for official purposes, should be met by the Government.

Six cents is less than the actual cost, and that is best demonstrated by the fact that a good many forest officers have given up their cars because they could not afford to run them for official business. They were paying out of their own pockets more than the cost of running the car when they used them for official business.

The actual cost of the running of these cars varies for the light cars up to nearly 12 cents. We had, I believe, one year during which a Ford car which we had in connection with the land-classification work cost approximately 12 cents a mile.

Mr. ANDERSON. Did that include depreciation?

Mr. GRAVES. That included depreciation and a good many repairs that year. The average cost of the average light car is considerably less than 12 cents.

We had a good many figures sent in to us from different forest officers which show that the cost of the Ford car, varying under conditions of roads and cost for gasoline at the distance from the railroad to the point where they have to buy the gasoline, and so on, runs all the way from 6 cents to 9 cents and a fraction. The average for the Ford car would be less than 9 cents.

For the different cars the actual cost of operation, not including depreciation, taxes, license fees, insurance, and all that sort of thing—the average for the private cars in the Forest Service is as follows:

District No. 1, 8.5 cents; district No. 2, 8 cents; district No. 3, 10.5 cents; district No. 4, 7.5 cents; district No. 5, 9.5 cents; district No. 6, 9 cents; and district No. 7, 7.5 cents.

The CHAIRMAN. What is the average?

Mr. GRAVES. It is 8.6 cents. That includes some other cars than the Ford. It includes Dodges, and some Buicks, some Chevrolets. some Studebakers, some Dorts, and some Overlands; probably 80 per cent of them would be light cars.

Mr. HARRISON. We inserted this item in the estimates originally, Mr. Chairman, on October 15, 1917, the date when the estimates were furnished to the Treasury Department. The present maximum amounts, therefore, were suggested more than a year ago, and the cost of everything connected with the upkeep of an automobile has increased very greatly since that time. The provision did not become effective until the 1st of October last, and many of the bureaus have advised the Secretary's office that they can not operate under it, except to a very limited extent, on account of the low rates.

Mr. GRAVES. If there were language accepted such as is proposed I should vary the rates in the different forests. From the past experience we have had I would not permit more than 6½ or 7 cents per mile for a Ford where there are pretty good roads, as there are in southern California. We have very low costs there—I think a little over 6 cents for the Ford cars. It is obvious that they can be operated there for that amount. Back in the mountains a Ford car would cost 8 or possibly 9 cents a mile, and if you included depreciation it would cost more than that.

The CHAIRMAN. That is the reason you suggested discretionary language?

Mr. GRAVES. Yes; because it varies, and the present 6 cents is certainly too low. I think we are defeating our own ends by making it as low as that, because we are in that way discouraging the private owners, and that is going to bring pressure for Government cars. I think we should stick primarily to the purchase from Government funds of trucks where there is trucking needed, and purchase passenger cars only in exceptional circumstances.

Mr. HARRISON. The Bureau of Animal Industry, for example, insists that it can not operate under the 6-cent rate.

Mr. ANDERSON. I have a strong impression that where it costs more than 8 cents a mile to run a Ford, either the operator of the machine is very inexpert or his machine is in very bad condition or the circumstances must be very exceptional. If it costs more than that to run a

Ford it would certainly be cheaper to junk it and get one that costs less than that to keep it.

Mr. GRAVES. Of course that would include tires, and the kind of roads we run our cars over in the mountains is very hard on tires. That is where the cost would run up. It would make a tremendous difference whether we run over a stony and rough road in the mountains or run over the smoother roads below. The wear and tear on a machine running over the mountain roads is terrific, and at the very best, under careful running, the cost is considerable. That is what brings up the cost with us; and, in addition, there is the occasional situation where the nearest place to purchase gasoline is pretty far out in the mountains, where the cost of gasoline is very high and it has to be hauled in a long distance.

Mr. ANDERSON. Are you of the opinion that any maximum at all in this provision would greatly interfere with your operating under this provision?

Mr. GRAVES. I think 6 cents is too low, and I think the uncertainties of costs from year to year would make it much better to leave it to administrative discretion.

Mr. ANDERSON. We have already left so much to administrative discretion that we have not very much left.

Mr. GRAVES. The very limitation on the appropriation itself is a limitation. We could not possibly authorize an extravagant mileage and run very many miles.

Mr. ANDERSON. I suppose that is true.

Mr. GRAVES. I doubt myself whether there would be many cases where we would want to authorize more than 10 cents.

Mr. ANDERSON. I notice that in the statement or the estimate of the amount you have allowed for maintenance and repair and upkeep of the Government-owned machines you allow amounts running from $450 to $600. I do not know what mileage that is based on, but I would assume that if you get anything like maximum efficiency out of these machines it must be based on 1,000 miles a month, or 12,000 miles a year; and if that is true, your basis there is much lower than the basis here.

Mr. GRAVES. That includes motorcycles and speeders.

Mr. ANDERSON. Taking the automobiles in the service generally, the maintenance charge runs from $450 to $600, and perhaps in some cases slightly larger. That is a maximum basis on something like 5 cents a mile.

Mr. BRONSON. The mileage for the Forest Service automobiles is estimated at 6,000 miles each per year for the three Forest Service automobiles. Two of them are very old; one was bought in 1913, and the second one about two years later.

Mr. GRAVES. Does not that figure include motorcycles and speeders?

Mr. BRONSON. Motorcycles and speeders are in separate items.

The CHAIRMAN. What about your motorcycle item? You have a 2-cent limitation in the present bill.

Mr. GRAVES. We have not had the same complaint about motorcycles as we have had about automobiles.

The CHAIRMAN. If you put a limitation on this for automobiles, you would say about 10 cents a mile?

Mr. GRAVES. I would feel that it ought not to be less than that. I think, from an administration standpoint, the average in our work would be about 8 cents. That would make it run from 6 to 10 cents, with the average about 8 cents. The thing I have in mind is to take care of those cases in the mountains where the cost is high, and not with the idea of allowing an extravagant amount.

The CHAIRMAN. What do you say about the relative wisdom of this flat limitation and the discretionary authority you confer upon the Secretary in this item?

Mr. GRAVES. I feel that the discretionary authority, from our standpoint, is the most businesslike, because I know the way the matters are handled we have to make a very strong showing to the Secretary in connection with our administrative limitations, and I like the idea of sufficient elasticity to take care of the practical conditions.

Mr. ANDERSON. I have an impression that your costs are very high. I have run an automobile for a good many years and kept tab of the cost.

Mr. GRAVES. I think it might be interesting, Mr. Anderson, to look over some of the reports we have had come in. They are in considerable detail, and they run, in the types of cars, all the way from a Buick car to a Ford, and I think these reports throw some light on that point.

AUTHORITY TO MAKE ARRESTS FOR VIOLATIONS OF GAME-RESERVE REGULATIONS.

Mr. GRAVES. I have one other matter, Mr. Chairman, which has come up very recently. The matter which I now desire to speak of concerns the handling of the game on the Pisgah Game Preserve. You will recall that the State of North Carolina authorized the Federal Government to handle game on the Pisgah Game Preserve or such other areas as the President might proclaim to be national game preserves.

Mr. McLAUGHLIN. In that State?

Mr. GRAVES. In that State. The President has proclaimed the Pisgah National Forest also as a national game preserve.

Mr. McLAUGHLIN. What is the area of it?

Mr. LEE. It is about 89,000 acres, is it not?

Mr. GRAVES. Yes, sir.

Mr. McLAUGHLIN. Formerly State land?

Mr. GRAVES. Formerly owned by private owners and purchased from private owners, the largest single purchase being from the Vanderbilt estate.

It is very well stocked with a number of game animals, and we are introducing other animals, like the elk and bison.

We find that our forest officers have not the authority to make arrests for violations on this preserve. They have to go through such a roundabout procedure in going to the marshal and getting a warrant sworn out that the game is suffering. There is a great deal of poaching, a great deal of killing of animals, and we are losing ground.

You may recall that under the act of February 6, 1905, the forest officers are given authority to make arrests for the violation of the laws and regulations relating to forest reserves.

Mr. McLAUGHLIN. Without papers?

Mr. GRAVES. Without warrants. They have authority to search and make arrests and take a man in to the commissioner.

Mr. MCLAUGHLIN. Where are the courts located before which the party arrested is to be taken?

Mr. GRAVES. He is brought before the United States commissioner and then bound over and brought before the Federal courts. But the point is that in order to reach this problem of stopping the poachers, the forest ranger must have authority when he catches a man with a deer or otherwise violating the Secretary's regulations to take him down to the commissioner.

Mr. MCLAUGHLIN. Generally speaking, one who is caught with the goods, as the saying goes, is subject to arrest without the formal issuing of papers, the papers being in the possession of the one arresting him. Do you think your men have not had that authority?

Mr. GRAVES. The solicitor of the department says our men not only have no authority to arrest a man who has a deer in his possession, but they have no authority to search him as to whether or not he has a gun or a deer, in case he is driving in a covered vehicle of some sort, and the solicitor says our men have no authority to take away the deer if they find it.

Mr. MCLAUGHLIN. And now it is proposed to insert language to give authority without any complaint or warrant, or anything of that kind?

Mr. GRAVES. I would propose to extend to the forest officers in the Mount Pisgah Game Preserve the same authority which has already been granted by Congress under the act of February 6, 1905, by some very simple wording, such as the following——

Mr. MCLAUGHLIN (interposing). Will you read the act of February 6, 1905, first, so that we will know what you are proposing to do?

Mr. GRAVES. It is a very short act, and I will read it entire. [Reading:]

Act of February 6, 1905 (33 Stat., 700):

"That all persons employed in the forest reserve and national park service of the United States shall have authority to make arrests for the violation of the laws and regulations relating to the forest reserves and national parks, and any person so arrested shall be taken before the nearest United States commissioner, within whose jurisdiction the reservation or national park is located, for trial; and upon sworn information by any competent person any United States commissioner in the proper jurisdiction shall issue process for the arrest of any person charged with the violation of said laws and regulations; but nothing herein contained shall be construed as preventing the arrest by any officer of the United States, without process, of any person taken in the act of violating said laws and regulations."

This wording has been approved by the solicitor:

That hereafter the authority to make arrests conferred by the act of February 6, 1905 (33 Stat., p. 700), is hereby extended to persons employed by the United States in the enforcement of laws and regulations for the protection of any game or bird reservations created by or under any act of Congress or Executive order.

Mr. LEE. Does that cover poaching?

Mr. GRAVES. It says "for the protection of any game or bird reservation," and that would cover poaching. It is simply extending to this one particular situation the authority we have elsewhere, and if we have that we can stop the poaching, and if we do not have it we are not going to be able to meet the situation. It is game preservation which has been authorized by Congress.

Mr. LEE. I thought you had a plan by which the State of North Carolina would confer the right on you?

Mr. GRAVES. They have conferred the authority and also have conferred the responsibility.

Mr. LEE. I thought under that you could do that?

Mr. GRAVES. We could do that; if the State still retained that authority they could delegate certain authority to us, but they have turned the whole thing over to us.

Mr. MCLAUGHLIN. The act you have read and the language you propose says arrests may be made for the violation of the laws and regulations. Everyone is presumed to know the law, but is everyone presumed to know the regulations? I would like to ask in that connection what you do by way of publishing your regulations so that those who frequent that place or may possibly be subject to arrest can be reasonably held to have knowledge of those regulations?

Mr. GRAVES. Here is a small pamphlet on the Pisgah National Game Preserve, containing the regulations. It is very widely advertised locally, and I venture to say there is not a local settler in that vicinity, or a lumberjack or anyone else working in the woods, who does not know that this is a game preserve and that hunting is prohibited, except in conformity with the regulations.

Mr. MCLAUGHLIN. You say these are very widely circulated. How circulated, and how widely?

Mr. GRAVES. In the first place, our local forest officers know personally and are circulating around among the settlers, and the city of Asheville is very close to this game preserve and every hotel man and every boarding-house keeper is cognizant of the rgulations which pertain to the Pisgah Game Preserve.

Mr. MCLAUGHLIN. How do you know they are? Are notices published in these hotels and boarding houses?

Mr. GRAVES. Yes.

Mr. LEE. Do you not have posters on the trees?

Mr. GRAVES. Yes.

Mr. MCLAUGHLIN. You do have posters?

Mr. GRAVES. Yes; they are posted on the land. We are having a good deal of trouble with the lumberjacks who are operating there. We purchased this land subject to an existing contract that is still running, and a good many hundred men are working on the area, and we have an arrangement with the foreman to dismiss anyone who is caught poaching, but that does not always meet the situation. They are able to cover it over. Our local forest officers feel very strongly that unless they have somewhat further authority there will be a general impression created in that country that the Federal Government is powerless to protect the game.

Mr. MCLAUGHLIN. How large is this preserve?

Mr. GRAVES. It contains something over 88,000 acres approved for purchase, of which about 78,500 acres have been actually acquired.

Mr. LEE. The original purchase was 89,000 acres?

Mr. GRAVES. I believe it was offered as 89,000 acres, but did not come to that. Other purchases have been authorized since.

Mr. MCLAUGHLIN. That is about 5 miles square. I have no objection to this provision being added, but when one is made subject to the penalty of arrest and punishment for violation of a regulation he ought to be informed of what the regulations are, and they ought to be circulated so that they can be known.

Mr. GRAVES. I think we have the preserve pretty well posted. There is not an entrance that has not got the posters on it.

Mr. MCLAUGHLIN. Is it inclosed?

Mr. GRAVES. No; it is not inclosed, but there are entrances by the main roads. There are certain roads and trails that go through the area, and we post the roads and trails. It is exactly the same situation as the violation of the Secretary's regulations in other matters in the national forests. We reach that by posting the regulations and distributing our book of regulations.

Mr. MCLAUGHLIN. What I have said in regard to this would apply to all areas where those regulations are in force, and I think some extra pains should be taken to advise the people as to the existence of those regulations, because it is a little unusual, if one is liable to punishment for violating a regulation. It is on limited areas that these regulations are in force, and those who live there all the time may know them, but others going in there for the first time may not know them. I think some extra effort ought to be made by your department to advise the people as to those regulations, and that violation of them would make one liable to arrest and punishment.

Mr. GRAVES. I think that is absolutely sound.

Mr. LEE. It is the same regulation you have, and the same method of advising people you have, at the Yellowstone National Park, is it not?

Mr. GRAVES. Of course, we have not jurisdiction of the Yellowstone National Park in our forest regulations. We have thoroughly posted the reservations and use different ways, locally, of acquainting people with them, and I think we have been pretty successful in getting this practice known and in the reasonable handling of trespass cases, as shown by the great reduction in the number of trespass cases after the regulations become known, and after it is known that we are going to follow that up and carry it through.

Mr. MCLAUGHLIN. I would like to ask a question in the matter of paying mileage for automobiles. There was a provision in the old law that no mileage should be paid for the use of a Government-owned automobile. It is suggested that that language be left out. The explanation is that it is already law. Where will you find that?

Mr. HARRISON. That is a part of the general law. The solicitor of the department and the Comptroller of the Treasury, as I understand it, have both held that we can not reimburse any one for operating a Government-owned machine. We pay, of course, the operating expenses of our own machines.

Mr. MCLAUGHLIN. It is not strange, but no one on the floor of the House knew that, and that amendment was demanded on the floor before this could go through.

Mr. HARRISON. There is no real reason why it should not be retained. . We merely suggested the elimination of what we regarded as useless language—language which does not have any effect—but if the committee wants to retain it, there is absolutely no objection on our part.

Mr. McLaughlin. It is a ruling; you can not point to a specific law for it.

The Chairman. Except the law of common sense. Why should the Government pay itself for operating its own machines?

Mr. McLaughlin. If it is a law, it is a proper law, I think; but if it is something which is merely the opinion of somebody, some official, he might change his opinion.

Mr. Harrison. There is no specific law on the subject. But, on the general principles of accounting law, the solicitor has said, I know, and I understand the comptroller has also said, that we can not pay anyone a mileage for operating Government-owned machines.

AGRICULTURE APPROPRIATION BILL.

COMMITTEE ON AGRICULTURE,
HOUSE OF REPRESENTATIVES,
Tuesday, January 7, 1919.

BUREAU OF CHEMISTRY.

STATEMENT OF DR. CARL L. ALSBERG, CHIEF OF THE BUREAU OF CHEMISTRY, UNITED STATES DEPARTMENT OF AGRICULTURE.

The CHAIRMAN. Dr. Alsberg, you have no increase in the statutory salary roll above $2,500?

Dr. ALSBERG. No, sir.

The CHAIRMAN. Then we will go to page 140 and ask you about item 84, "For conducting the investigations contemplated by the act of May 15, 1862, relating to the application of chemistry to agriculture, $42,400." There is no change in that?

Dr. ALSBERG. No change in that.

The CHAIRMAN. Are you conducting the same lines of work as in previous years?

Dr. ALSBERG. There are one or two lines of work that we have been conducting which are not exactly new, but which have increased in volume owing to the war.

We had before the war among others a project on the development of simple methods for mildew and water proofing fabrics, methods sufficiently simple to be used by the farmer in lengthening the life of canvas covers for machinery and the like. At the beginning of the war the same problem arose in relation to tentage and other articles of military accoutrement. This made it necessary to extend this particular line of work. We have furnished the War Department with practically all of their formulæ and methods for water and mildew proofing fabrics, and we have done a great deal of work for them in the inspection of material, so that this particular project has been conducted on a more extensive scale than hitherto, owing to the demands of the War Department.

The CHAIRMAN. The next item, No. 85, is, "For collaboration with other departments of the Government desiring chemical investigations and whose heads request the Secretary of Agriculture for such assistance, and for other miscellaneous work, $14,000." There is no change in that?

Dr. ALSBERG. No change in that. There is only this to be said, that the situation during this year has been such that the demands on the Bureau of Chemistry for work of this type have been tremendous. We ordinarily carry on this allotment the cost of work which is asked for by other departments of the Government requiring the kind of chemical work that the Bureau of Chemistry is better equipped to handle than they are. There has not been for some years a checking up of the cost of this kind of work. I have had it checked up recently. If we were to combine the salaries of the men who have been at work on war problems it would amount to a very large sum. Even in normal times the appropriation as it stands is not adequate for the demands made upon us, but we have not asked for an increase, because we have only realized recently that such is the case.

Mr. McLAUGHLIN. Have you had any allotment from any other department or any other fund?

Dr. ALSBERG. No. We have, I figure, expended in time of the men that do this work—and that is what it chiefly amounts to—about $125,000. Of this sum but little represents purchase of equipment and chemicals. It represents, in the main, the time of men already in our employ taken from their regular work. The Quartermaster's Department of the War Department, the Post Office Department, the Department of Justice, and pretty nearly every other department of the Government has made enormous demands on us. The Quartermaster Corps, the Bureau of Aircraft Production, the Medical Corps, and the Chemical Warfare Service have detailed a few drafted and commissioned chemists to the bureau.

The CHAIRMAN. How does the Post Office Department get into this?

Dr. ALSBERG. It is with this fund that we carry on most of the work that we do for the Post Office Department in relation to the suppression of the fraudulent use of the mails. For instance, there are lots of patent medicines, prescription fakes, fraudulent articles or devices of one kind or another which have to be examined chemically. The Post Office Department asks us to make such examinations, and when the cases are tried in court our analysts are very frequently the principal Government experts in court.

Last year we had two men who attended court for about six weeks in the Sargol case, an alleged tonic sold at an exorbitant price. We could not get at it under the food and drugs act because it did not carry a fraudulent label. So the Post Office Department got after it and won the case. It was put out of business and a fine of some $30,000 imposed. As we did the analytical work, our experts attended court as witnesses. There has been particularly great activity of that kind on the part of the Post Office Department in the past year.

We have also carried on with this fund a part of that work which we have been doing in cooperation with the Bureau of Mines on thresher and mill-dust explosions, on which I think I reported last year.

It may be interesting to you for me to give some of the data on the result of the thresher-explosions work. When this started in the Pacific Northwest in 1914 there were thresher explosions which destroyed thrashing machines and grain estimated to be valued at about $1,000,000. There were some 300 such occurrences. We made a survey at that time and in 1915 started work to determine what preventive measures should be used. The damage that year was only about $300,000 or $400,000. The season was not so dry as in 1914.

In 1916, after the protective devices which we developed had been pretty well introduced, the losses were only about $75,000, and last year there were only 20 explosions and fires which happened in threshers that had not been protected by the devices we recommended. The total losses were between $10,000 and $15,000, with no destruction of grain to amount to anything.

Mr. McLaughlin. As to those experiments, you have finished them and found out the cause?

Dr. Alsberg. That particular project is closed.

Mr. McLaughlin. You are not asking any money for continuing that?

Dr. Alsberg. Not that particular part of the work. There is another part of the work which we have in part paid for out of this appropriation, and in part out of some of the emergency appropriations; this deals with the prevention of fires in mills and elevators.

We have had, let us say, good luck with this work. We have not had, since the work was undertaken under the food production act—from which the Secretary allotted some additional money for this campaign—a large mill or elevator explosion. How much of this is due to the campaign we put on and how much to luck, nobody can say. But there is the fact.

The work we have done in that connection was an educational campaign. We divided the country into districts. We held meetings in each district at which we called together all of the managers of mills and elevators and their workmen and explained how important it was to take all possible precautions. Then we visited all of the large plants and called the workmen together and got out a pledge card, by signing which the workman pledged himself not to do certain things, such as smoking, and the mill superintendent pledged himself to keep the plant clean and to observe the necessary precautions. I have some of that literature here. We issued a small circular which sets out what the dangers in that kind of a plant are, and we got out a poster which was conspicuously posted around the plants.

Mr. Lee. It is largely a question of ventilation, is it not?

Dr. Alsberg. It is not entirely a matter of ventilation. Three or four different factors are involved. In the first place, you want to keep dust out of the plant. If you get dust suspended in the air and bring it in contact with a flame, if the dust and air are in the proper proportion, the dust will burn so fast that it explodes like gasoline. If you have no dust you eliminate that danger. Then you must avoid open flames, matches, and smoking. Moreover, you want to prevent elevator " choke-ups."

One of the common causes is that the elevator leg chokes. The pulley over which the belt runs keeps on going, and of course the belt does not move. That creates friction, and the friction will ultimately generate enough heat so that the belt catches fire. The belt will burn through, and then the belt which has been burnt through will drop to the bottom of the elevator leg and send up a cloud of dust. The cloud of dust will explode, and the explosion may travel along the conveyor system until it reaches an empty bin, explode the dust cloud in the bin, and perhaps tear off the roof or the side of the building.

Here in this poster is an illustration of how such explosions run. Here is a mill in which the whole side of the building was blown out. There was a man in the building who, fortunately, was blown out into the river and was not killed.

Mr. McLaughlin. How much of the emergency fund was transferred for that work?

Dr. Alsberg. On all of this work to prevent dust explosions there was a total allotment of $51,000. We have had a large force in the field. That amount went practically all for salaries and traveling expenses.

Mr. McLaughlin. In what act was the money carried in which this transfer was made?

Dr. Alsberg. In the food production act.

Mr. McLaughlin. What provision of that act?

Dr. Alsberg. In the first food production act there was no specific provision, but an allotment was made under the appropriation for miscellaneous items. But in the second food production act there was a specific provision of $75,000 for the prevention of plant explosions and fires. Under the authority he had in the original act the Secretary made an allotment to the Bureau of Chemistry for that work.

Of course you can never tell whether this campaign, in which we had a large proportion of the operators in the mills and elevators in the country sign a pledge not to do any of these things, and in which we got superintendents to make changes in the plants and keep the plants free from dust, accomplished anything; but the fact is that there has not been any appreciable loss of grain from this cause this year, whereas in other years often there have been losses mounting into the millions of dollars. The fire in the Dow elevator in Brooklyn represented a loss of $8,000,000. We are now going into the dry winter season, when the danger is greatest. Of course we like to think that we had something to do with saving a considerable amount of wheat.

A small portion of the funds assigned by the Secretary of Agriculture for this work were used to investigate complaints received from the Southwest, particularly from Texas and Oklahoma, that the growers and ginners of cotton were suffering great losses from fires and explosions. Investigations that have been made indicate that the majority of these disastrous fires which destroy a great deal of property are due to static electricty. During this season a number of gins were so wired as to ground them and remove any static electricty that would be generated by the friction of the dry cotton fiber passing through the machinery and conveyors. These gins that were wired under the supervision of members of the Bureau of Chemistry went through this season without difficulty, and there were but two small fires during this season, which can probably be attributed to other causes than to static electricity. While these gins were operating without interruption and without loss, many of the gins in the surrounding neighborhood, operating under exactly the same conditions, had serious fires, and some of them were destroyed.

The continuance of this work would probably result in the prevention of many hundred thousands of dollars of loss annually in the South and Southwest. Inasmuch as this work is being carried on under funds assigned to it from the food-production act, it can not be continued after this fiscal year.

The CHAIRMAN. Item 86, on page 141, is "For investigating the character of the chemical and physical tests which are applied to American food products in foreign countries," and so on. There is no change in that item?

Dr. ALSBERG. There is nothing new to be said about that. It involves merely testing of goods for export.

The CHAIRMAN. The next item, No. 87, "For investigating the preparation for market, handling, grading, packing, freezing, drying, storing, transportation, and preservation of poultry and eggs." You are asking for an increase of $10,000 in that item?

Dr. ALSBERG. There is an increase of $10,000 in that item. The extension of the work on the conservation of poultry is especially necessary, in order to supplement the supply of beef, mutton, and pork. This investigation will provide the fundamental information and the means for its dissemination looking to the more general prevention of waste and decay. The study of the utilization for poultry fleshing of feeds now wholly or largely wasted would mean the cheap and quick production of millions of pounds of chicken flesh. Great losses in transportation can be prevented or reduced by the extension of this work. The increased cost of travel and of supplies of all kinds makes additional funds necessary.

That increase, Mr. Chairman, is asked for in the main because of the general increased cost of operations of all kinds. This appropriation involves considerable travel and considerable field work. It involves the employment of people, especially trained and skilled, who can not be gotten at the same salaries at which we formerly employed them. The travel and demonstration work can not be carried on for the same sum for which it formerly could be carried on.

It is desired to enlarge the work a little, but in the main the increase is for the purpose of enabling us to continue on about the same scale as in the past.

The CHAIRMAN. You did not base this estimate on the fact that the country was engaged in war?

Dr. ALSBERG. No, sir; because the Secretary had set aside for a similar purpose a sum for doing emergency work to increase poultry production by conservation.

Mr. MCLAUGHLIN. Why is this matter of keeping poultry in the Bureau of Chemistry?

Dr. ALSBERG. A good many things are placed where they are as a matter of expediency. The feeding which we are doing here is an outgrowth of the work done on the packing and shipping of poultry. The Bureau of Animal Industry handles the matter of breeding and raising poultry on the farms. The Bureau of Chemistry got into this line of work originally because of certain questions which arose with reference to the application of the food and drugs act to cold-storage problems. The question arose whether the birds should be drawn before being put into cold storage. Out of such cold-storage problems developed this work. Such studies were not at that time being made anywhere else. It might have been done elsewhere, and we are now planning to transfer that part of it which bears on marketing to the Bureau of Markets, the experimental laboratory work remaining where it is.

The demands for the work on feeding arose in this way: We found that it is the custom for the small packers to take the birds as they come from the farm and put them in cages, or batteries as they are termed in the trade, where they are fed intensively and fattened. Nobody has ever made a study to learn how to do this in the most efficient way. We have such studies in regard to the fattening of steers but not of poultry. There has not been anything of that kind done.

It would be perfectly logical for the Bureau of Animal Industry to do this work if they had established relations with the small poultry packing houses all over the South and the Middle West, but they have not the relations that we have with them. We were cooperating with them on the chilling and freezing of the birds, and it seems logical, therefore, for us to take this up on the side.

The feeding of poultry is now being done in a very wasteful manner. We have been developing methods which will give us the most efficacious results. The fleshing of birds can not be done by the farmer economically, because the bird shrinks too much in the transporting from the farm to the slaughterhouse. The shrinkage on a small animal or bird is very great. So it is best to fatten the bird immediately before slaughter. If you have to transport it between the time of fattening and the time of slaughtering, you are apt to lose most of what you have gained in fattening.

Mr. McLaughlin. It strikes me if you continued that work you would overlap the work of the Bureau of Animal Industry and the Bureau of Markets.

Dr. Alsberg. I do not think we are overlapping the work of the Bureau of Animal Industry, because they are not doing just this sort of thing. We have, in a sense, been doing marketing work under this appropriation, but the work was started before the Bureau of Markets was in existence, and we are now in a process of transferring the marketing feature to the Bureau of Markets.

Mr. McLaughlin. Then that will take off some of the work from your bureau; but you are asking for an increased appropriation.

Dr. Alsberg. These estimates were made before that transfer was being arranged, and there is no provision in the estimate for the Bureau of Markets to take care of this work when it is transferred. It will have to be made in next year's estimate.

The Chairman. The next item is No. 88. "For investigating the handling, grading, packing, canning, freezing, storing, and transportation of fish." You are asking for an increase of $6,000 in that item?

Dr. Alsberg. Yes, sir. An increase of $6,000 is recommended in this appropriation. There is an immense annual loss from spoilage of fish because of the lack of knowledge of methods of handling and shipping these products. The work already done by the department has shown that great improvement can be effected in these methods. The continuation and extension will greatly contribute to the conservation of the meat supply by increasing the use of fish as food, especially at interior points where fresh fish can not now be secured in quantities. The increase in cost of travel and supplies makes additional funds necessary.

We ask for the increase for two reasons. Among the things we have done under this appropriation is to inaugurate what might be called a special service for the shipping of fish into middle western territory from the Gulf. There is an immense fish supply available in the Gulf of Mexico which is not being used and which should be used in the Middle West. No machinery existed for the transportation and the handling of the fish. We did not know how best to pack, to handle, or to store the fish. Under this investigation we have determined the best methods of handling.

With the information thus obtained it was possible to contribute directly to the country's food supply by the establishment of a service by which fish were shipped from points in Florida through to such points as Nashville, Louisville, and Indianapolis.

The railroad connections were bad and the railroad accommodations were bad, but when the Railroad Administration came into being we made arrangements by which the fish could be shipped promptly to those points, and we supervised the shipments. Assisted by the Food Administration an educational campaign was conducted in these centers, so that at the present time they are receiving each week carload shipments of fish which are being sold at a relatively cheap price, where these varieties of fish were never known before. We have popularized a lot of varieties which were absolutely unknown in that section of the country. My understanding is that there is a carload going each week into these localities. In this manner the food supply of the country was added to materially. At the same time we are cooperating with fish canners in Florida and in California, in determining the best methods of canning fish that had never been canned before or had not been canned successfully.

The CHAIRMAN. Do you mean methods that had never been used before, or kinds of fish that had never been canned before?

Dr. ALSBERG. Kinds of fish that had never been canned before. We have been endeavoring to assist in the establishment of new industries, in producing new food products from fish that have not been marketed before. That was chiefly in Florida and California. It may interest you to know that there is a development which we have endeavored to encourage, in southern California, in the matter of the canning of fish. There has been a great development in southern California of the canning of fish in the last three years, particularly of sardines. Three or four years ago there were only a few sardines packed in an experimental way; but this year the pack is about 2,000,000 cases, with either 48 or 100 cans to a case.

The CHAIRMAN. And they are mighty fine sardines.

Dr. ALSBERG. They are genuine sardines. We have been packing so-called American sardines in Maine, and the pack there has been about 2,000,000 cases a year. What we are packing in California is equivalent to what we are packing in Maine. In Maine the sardine is not a sardine in the European sense of the word, but a young herring.

The CHAIRMAN. What is a genuine sardine? How does it differ from the herring?

Dr. ALSBERG. It is a different species of fish.

The CHAIRMAN. How will it compare with the French sardine?

Dr. ALSBERG. The Pacific coast fish is the same species. There is no reason why California should not pack an article of very high quality. They have the same fish. It simply means handling them in the proper way.

The CHAIRMAN. They have the olive oil?

Dr. ALSBERG. They have the olive oil, but they have not enough for their requirements. This year the War Trade Board put an embargo on the importation of olive oil, which made it necessary for the Californians to pack a great deal of their sardines in other oils.

The CHAIRMAN. Cottonseed oil is just as good.

Dr. ALSBERG. They pack them in cottonseed as well as olive oil, and they have also developed a new oil industry. They are pressing oil from peach and apricot pits. They crack the stones and take out the kernel and press out the oil, and it makes a very satisfactory oil.

Before the war they used to ship the kernels to Hamburg, where the oil was pressed out. Some of it came back to this country as apricot oil, but now they are pressing the oil out in California from the peach and apricot pits for use in the canning of sardines. They did not have enough olive oil to go around. We do not press out much olive oil in this country because it pays better to market the oil in the form of ripe olives, and it does not make any difference, as far as feeding the people is concerned, whether they get the olive oil with the sardines or eat the ripe olive.

Mr. McLAUGHLIN. Are the people in Maine permitted to put up and put on the market herring and call them sardines?

Dr. ALSBERG. Technically speaking, I suppose it is a misbranding, but it is a misbranding that has existed for 30 or 40 years before the food and drug act was passed. It has been held that the words "American sardines" are words with which everybody was familiar. It was held that the term "American sardine" had acquired a secondary meaning, just as the word "currant" is a corruption of the name of the city of Corinth, which is the place these small raisins used to be shipped from, though they are now shipped from Patras. Everybody recognizes that the term "American sardine" has acquired a secondary meaning. They are not, strictly speaking, sardines, and no one felt that the name which had not been objected to for 40 years should be objected to if they were labeled American sardines with the name of the place where they were packed put on the label.

Mr. HAUGEN. Have you investigated sufficiently to satisfy yourself that the American sardine is equal in quality to the imported?

Dr. ALSBERG. The best quality put up in California to-day, in olive oil, is equal, in my judgment, to the best imported.

Mr. HAUGEN. Is there a difference in quality in the sardines?

Dr. ALSBERG. The California sardine is the same species, identical with the European sardine.

The CHAIRMAN. It seems to be bigger.

Dr. ALSBERG. It runs in various sizes. Some of the California sardines are very much larger. But size is not a sign of variety in fish as in most other animals. Take, for instance, the ordinary brook trout, which rarely runs over 3 or 4 pounds in the United States, whereas in the rivers of New Zealand, I understand, they catch them weighing up to 15 and 20 pounds. Fish seem to be something like a tree—they can keep on growing for quite a while. Apparently the California sardines do. But the large sizes are not canned. One of the things we have done under this appropriation is to show the people of California how they can handle the large sardines.

Mr. HAUGEN. Has not the climate something to do with the quality.

Dr. ALSBERG. When it comes to fish we do not know about that.

It may interest you to know, in that connection, that one of the Members of the Senate introduced a bill with reference to the fish industry, and we brought to the hearing a selection of fish of various kinds which have been put under our supervision. Various gentlemen tasted them, and the majority of them thought that the best grade of California sardines were entirely satisfactory.

The CHAIRMAN. The next item is item No. 89, "For investigating the packing, handling, storing, and shipping of oysters and other shellfish." There is no change in that item?

Dr. ALSBERG. There is nothing new about that. We are cooperating with the Public Health Service in helping them to supervise the oyster industry of the country. The essential purpose of this investigation is to gather information to prevent the sale and shipment of bad oysters and oysters that have been adulterated in fresh water, which causes them to swell so that 3 quarts of oysters may look as big as 5.

The CHAIRMAN. The next item is No. 90, "For the biological investigations of food and drug products." There is no change in that?

Dr. ALSBERG. There is no change in that. I can report some of the results.

This is research in regard to the food value, from the chemical standpoint, of a good many foods and feeds. This year we have investigated the protein and nitrogenous material in the velvet bean, which is a relatively new crop. We have been able to make recommendations on the best method of using the velvet bean in a feed and experiments on the use of the velvet bean mixed with other feeds are now going on, based on this investigation of ours.

We have also been investigating the coconut, which, while not an American product, has assumed tremendous importance in this country. The shipping situation was such that the copra, which is the trade name for dry coconut meat, was accumulating on the wharves all through the South Sea Islands. It could not be shipped to Hamburg or Liverpool or Marseille, where it ordinarily goes.

Our people were able to buy it in large quantities, and a great many of the oil-crushing establishments have been piecing out their season by crushing copra and getting coconut oil. The pressed cake has come on the market in quantity in the last year as a feed. In Europe it is recognized as a very valuable dairy feed. Not much experience was available in this country on its value. We have made an investigtion in which we have convinced ourselves that copra press-cakes is one of the most valuable feeds. The chemical investigation has advanced so far that intelligent, practical feed experiments can now be made.

Coconut oil, in the manufacture of which the press-cake is a by-product, has been going into various so-called nut margarines and into the soap industry. The soap industry could not get an abundance of the oils it used to get, so it has been using coconut oil. It is an oil at the temperature of the Tropics, but in our climate coconut oil is somewhat solid and can therefore be used instead of stearine in margarines to give hardness or substance to cottonseed or peanut oil to make the mixture of the right consistency.

We are also at work on experiments to show how such materials as wheat and corn, which are in themselves not adequate feeds, can be best supplemented by more valuable materials like peanuts or copra.

Mr. LEE. Have you not developed the soy bean for human food?

Dr. ALSBERG. That is a project which we have carried on partly under the appropriation for agricultural chemistry. We have been studying its preparation for human food. We have not had much success with it yet, so far as introducing its use as human food is concerned.

My own feeling is that the soy bean will have to be used in this country in the same manner in which it is used in the Orient. Nobody uses the soy bean in the Orient, in China and Japan, as we use the navy bean. It has a beany taste and a consistency that does not make it as palatable when baked as our navy bean. The way they use the soy bean in the Orient is this: They take the soy bean and soak it and then mix it with water and grind it on a regular old-fashioned burrstone mill that grinds up the soy bean very fine. This procedure yields a liquid that looks like milk. This is strained through a cloth to remove the hulls. It is then coagulated by heating and adding salt. The curd is collected by straining through a coarse cloth. It looks not unlike cottage cheese, though its texture is denser and its color grayer. In this form the curd is sold throughout the villages and towns of China. It is one of the foods of the poor people. It has this advantage: It has almost no taste and no flavor, and it is a wonderful stretcher of flavors. You can mix this material with 5 per cent of ham and fry it and get a product that you can hardly tell from a meat ball made entirely of ham.

In the same way you can work it into soups and stews and get an enormous increase in their nitrogenous food value without affecting the flavor; it is a means of adding to the food value of almost anything that you want to use without affecting the flavor, because it has no more flavor than so much chalk. In my judgment, if we are going to use it for human food, we have got to use it in some such manner. We can't expect, as in China, to develop little plants in every town for this purpose. But what we can do is to put it in cans with meat and other highly flavored foods to produce fairly cheap highly nutritious products, but we have not been able to interest anybody as yet in the commercial marketing of such products.

Mr. LEE. Plenty of people are growing them now?

Dr. ALSBERG. Yes; but not for human food. because people don't like them very well when they are baked or boiled. To increase our bean crop, and the Army has taken an enormous quantity of beans, pinto and pink beans are being grown in Colorado and New Mexico. Large quantities of them are coming on the market and people like them for cooking and baking. People do not like the soy bean as well because it is apt to be soggy and heavy.

Mr. LEE. They are a very rich food.

Dr. ALSBERG. Yes, sir; but we have to use them with other food.

Mr. MCLAUGHLIN. Have you anything to do with poi?

Dr. ALSBERG. No; poi, as I recall it, comes from the Hawaiian Islands and is made from the cassava root, I think.

The CHAIRMAN. Any other questions? If not, take up the next item, No. 91.

Mr. HAUGEN. Just a minute; there seems to be a number of salaries boosted here. In item 90 I see you have dropped one; you have one you didn't have last year. You jump him from $3,000 to $3,240.

Dr. ALSBERG. That represents a promotion for one of the ablest men we have in the bureau, a chemist.

Mr. HAUGEN. You propose to jump him up to $3,240 from $3,000?

Dr. ALSBERG. Yes, sir; that is Dr. Johns, who has charge of this investigation.

Mr. MCLAUGHLIN. When you make a promotion like that that carries a larger salary is that a new position and does it create a vacancy in the place the man formerly held?

Dr. ALSBERG. No, sir; it does not create any new position.

Mr. HAUGEN. On page 144 you jump one from $3,250 to $3,500.

Dr. ALSBERG. That is a promotion for the man in charge of that line of work. That promotion has been made.

Mr. HAUGEN. Under the lump sum that the committee has no knowledge of?

Dr. ALSBERG. Yes, sir. You gentlemen should realize that the Bureau of Chemistry during the last two or three years has had a pretty rough time so far as personnel is concerned. There is hardly a competent man in the bureau that has not had an opportunity to leave the service at better pay.

Mr. HAUGEN. These notes here should call these matters to the attention of the committee. I haven't looked it over very closely, but I take it that these promotions should not be made without some explanation.

The CHAIRMAN. In these cases the promotion has been made on the lump-sum funds.

Dr. ALSBERG. No promotions have been proposed——

The CHAIRMAN (interposing). Except as they are sent out in these cases?

Dr. ALSBERG. Yes, sir.

Mr. THOMPSON. They are put on the permanent roll now?

Dr. ALSBERG. No, sir; these are lump-sum positions.

Mr. HAUGEN. And in this case you drop one——

Dr. ALSBERG (interposing). The man in charge of this work received in 1918 a salary of $3,000. He is promoted to a salary of $3,240, and there is no other appointment at $3,000.

Mr. HAUGEN. You drop that, and then you advance the other way.

Mr. MCLAUGHLIN. These are statutory positions?

Dr. ALSBERG. No; these are not statutory positions. We may have a man who has been in the bureau for many years, who came in at a low salary and whose salary is now $3,500. Such a man may die or resign, and his place will not be filled at all. His work may be divided up in two lines and two men put in at lower salaries, or it may be filled by a promotion of a man to that salary, according to what seems to be the best interest of the service.

Mr. MCLAUGHLIN. I like to see good salaries and promotions to worthy men, and like to see them get an increase, but I have thought the plan was open to abuse if by putting a man at the top in a higher salary they really create a new position and a vacancy in the place he did occupy and gave opportunity for the moving up of everybody below him, whether worthy of increase in salary or not.

Dr. ALSBERG. That is not done.

Mr. HARRISON. That is what the statutory roll does; that is what we avoid on the lump sum, Mr. McLaughlin.

Mr. MCLAUGHLIN. Is it proper under the statutory roll?

Mr. HARRISON. It is not proper if the people below are not entitled to promotion.

Mr. HAUGEN. Here is the way it is done: On page 144 you add one at $3,500 and drop one at $3,250. I don't think that that was intended when this committee passed on this appropriation; it was never intended that we should turn over this matter of promotions and the fixing of salaries to the department, and that we should have nothing to say about it. I think we are entitled to know something about it and we should know why these promotions are made; if they are made on merit we are all for it, and if not that is a different thing. I take it they are made on merit, and yet I take it the committee should have something to say about it. As it is, we have nothing to say about it; we have nothing to say about the promotions and we have no knowledge of many of them.

Mr. MCLAUGHLIN. Right in that connection, suppose the committee, for a good reason or otherwise—suppose the committee should determine that that promotion should not be made, is there any way to prevent it?

Mr. HAUGEN. Not after you give the authority; and that gives it.

The CHAIRMAN. How long have you had this authority?

Dr. ALSBERG. There isn't any authority that the Bureau of Chemistry has, but the Secretary of Agriculture has authority to fix the salaries of these employees who are on the lump-sum fund and that are not on the statutory roll.

The CHAIRMAN. How long has that authority existed?

Dr. ALSBERG. I don't know, but I think from the beginning of the department.

Mr. HARRISON. That is true, so far as I know. Certainly it has existed for 12 or 15 years.

Mr. HAUGEN. It is a question with the committee whether it wants to continue it.

The CHAIRMAN. Five years ago, I think, the whole proposition as to whether or not the lump-sum employees should be put on the statutory roll was fought out on the floor of the House. The fight was made by Mr. Page, and the House itself took the position that the committee has taken for 16 years, ever since I have been on the committee.

Mr. HAUGEN. I take it the committee should have information and report to Congress.

The CHAIRMAN. We fix the salaries on the statutory roll, of course.

Mr. HAUGEN. No; not even that, because they are always transferred at salaries fixed by the department.

The CHAIRMAN. We fix them as far as we are able.

Mr. HAUGEN. No; I beg pardon; we never did. I think the committee ought to, because it is their duty.

The CHAIRMAN. What plan do you suggest?

Mr. HAUGEN. I would inquire as to the merit of these promotions and then determine whether it should be made.

The CHAIRMAN. We went over the estimates and the inquiry has been made.

Mr. HAUGEN. We have for several years inquired and have never made any headway.

Mr. HARRISON. These are not suggested promotions for next year.

Mr. HAUGEN. They are transfers. We know what is done, and what is the use beating around the bush?

Mr. HARRISON. If there are promotions in the cases to which Mr. Haugen refers, they have already been made and are not proposed promotions.

Mr. HAUGEN. Didn't I understand that this is a promotion from $3,250 to $3,500?

Mr. ALSBERG. Yes; that has been made.

Mr. HARRISON. The man is now receiving $3,500.

The CHAIRMAN. The horse is already out of the stable, and how are we going to prevent it?

Mr. HAUGEN. We can prevent it, if the committee will do its duty.

The CHAIRMAN. How? This has been passed on.

Mr. HAUGEN. We can limit these salaries.

Mr. HARRISON. This statement shows the amount the man is now receiving, $3,500.

Mr. HAUGEN. The doctor says it is a promotion, and if you turn to page 144 you will see that it is clearly indicated that the salary is——

The CHAIRMAN (interposing). You don't get the point; the point is, this represents what is already done.

Mr. HAUGEN. No; this represents what is to be done.

The CHAIRMAN. No; I don't understand it that way.

Mr. HAUGEN. Here you have one at $3,250 and it goes up to $3,500, and the doctor says that is a promotion, and this bill goes into effect July 1; it is in the future and not what has happened; it is to be and shows what is to take place.

Mr. HARRISON. As I stated before, Mr. Haugen, one column reports the expenditures for 1918 and the other column the estimates for 1920. In other words, we necessarily skip the present fiscal year, because only four months have elapsed when we submit our estimates. My recollection is that this man was promoted from $3,250 to $3,500 on July 1, 1918.

Mr. HAUGEN. I take the doctor's word for it. Your statements are not consistent.

The CHAIRMAN. What about that?

Dr. ALSBERG. Our statements are not inconsistent. This represents a promotion which this man got on the 1st of July last.

The CHAIRMAN. And you propose to continue that salary?

Dr. ALSBERG. We propose to continue that salary. He is getting that and he will get that for next year.

Mr. HAUGEN. I asked the question, if it was a promotion?

Dr. ALSBERG. What I meant was that it is a promotion that has been made.

Mr. HAUGEN. Why don't you set out the 1919 salaries?

Mr. HARRISON. This is a form prescribed by the Treasury Department; we set it out according to its direction.

Mr. HAUGEN. I can't understand why they keep the committees in the dark.

Mr. HARRISON. We have to make our estimates on the 15th of October for the next year—that is the practice.

Mr. HAUGEN. I don't approve of the practice.

Mr. HARRISON. That is the form prescribed by the Treasury Department.

Mr. HAUGEN. The form can be changed. It is a question whether we want to change or whether we want to go on in this way. According to that, we might as well turn over the Public Treasury and have nothing further to say about it.

The CHAIRMAN. Anything further on that? If not, take up the next item, No. 91. There is no change in that?

Dr. ALSBERG. No change in that.

The CHAIRMAN. Is there anything unusual to report?

Dr. ALSBERG. We have completed the work on the manufacture——

Mr. HAUGEN (interposing). Would it be asking too much for these gentlemen to say something about these promotions?

The CHAIRMAN. They have been saying it for the last half hour.

Mr. HAUGEN. I, for my part, would like to know something about it.

The CHAIRMAN. Go on and take the witness.

Mr. HAUGEN. Just explain these promotions, and whether made on merit or not. It is not necessary to take up much time, but enough so we can get an idea.

Dr. ALSBERG. Which one?

Mr. HAUGEN. All the promotions.

Dr. ALSBERG. I have got to go over them, as we come to them, because I haven't prepared any special data.

Mr. HAUGEN. I think the better way would be to handle them all at one time; I think it would take less time, and then we would have it all before us.

Dr. ALSBERG. Would I have an opportunity to tabulate it and bring it here? I can't give the data about every man offhand.

The CHAIRMAN. Suppose you tell him what you want, Mr. Haugen.

Mr. HAUGEN. What we want to know is about these promotions and why the promotions were made, and say something about the nature of the service.

Dr. ALSBERG. How low down in salary do you want to go?

Mr. HAUGEN. We are not dealing with any salaries below $2,500.

Mr. HARRISON. Doctor, perhaps Mr. Haugen wants a general statement about our general procedure with reference to lump-sum promotions?

Mr. HAUGEN. No; I know all about that.

Dr. ALSBERG. I would be very glad, if you will give me time to get the figures together, to give you a little statement of every man that was promoted above $2,500 during the year 1918. Would that be satisfactory?

Mr. THOMPSON. Better get them all—those below $2,500 as well—when it come to the lump sum.

The CHAIRMAN. Now, let us see whether we understand what you want; tell us what you want.

Mr. HAUGEN. A brief statement giving the reasons for the promotions.

The CHAIRMAN. In each case?

Mr. HAUGEN. Yes. It might not be practical in each case, in each event.

The CHAIRMAN. He can't give you something if he doesn't know what you want.

Mr. HAUGEN. What I want is information; the number of years the clerk has served and then the reason for the promotion; the salary he received in the past, the salary you propose to pay for the coming year, and the salary he is receiving the current year.

Dr. ALSBERG. You understand this does not refer to clerks; these are technically trained men.

Mr. HAUGEN. Mr. Thompson suggests we ought to have it below $2,500; I think it should go down the line.

Dr. ALSBERG. I shall be glad to give you a statement of what you wish.

Mr. HAUGEN. How much of a task would it be?

Dr. ALSBERG. I think we could do that, if we put one of our clerks at work, in a few hours; if it is not what you want and you will let me know, I will then revise it.

Mr. HAUGEN. If it only involves a few hours' work in each bureau we ought to have it for the whole department.

Dr. ALSBERG. Of course, we are a relatively small bureau; we have a total force of in the neighborhood of 600. It may take longer in some bureaus.

Mr. HAUGEN. You are not asking for many promotions?

Dr. ALSBERG. Hardly any in the clerical force; they are all transfers. Of course, we do make every six months a certain number of promotions of our technically trained men who are on the miscellaneous roll. Now all these figures we are discussing here are for technically trained men. This man here is an instance. He was promoted on last July from $3,000 to $3,250. That is Dr. Johns. He is a man about 45 or 46 years old—somewhere along there—and he came to the Bureau of Chemistry about five years ago from Yale, where he was associate professor of chemistry. He came to the bureau at $2,500, as I recall, which was about the same salary he was getting as associate professor at Yale. He has done excellent work in research and he is the man to whom I have delegated all matters of finding men for chemical work, because of his academic connections. He has been doing that for the last year and doing it exceedingly well, in addition to his research work.

Mr. HAUGEN. Now that is real information, and all that is necessary. Just do it in your way.

Dr. ALSBERG. We will get something together, and if it is not what you want I will try to get what you would like. We will try to make it satisfactory.

Mr. HAUGEN. It is embarrassing to stand on the floor and acknowledge that we don't know anything about it; we have been doing that for years and to me it is exceedingly humiliating. I am not criticizing you, but I am criticizing the procedure. I think it is due the House that the House should have some information. On that proposition this committee has certainly been very lame.

The CHAIRMAN. Not any more than any other committee. It has been done with every other committee. It may be that the whole procedure in the House is weak, but I don't think it can be charged against this committee any more than against the Appropriations Committee.

Mr. HAUGEN. That may be.

Dr. ALSBERG. When it comes to fixing the salaries for the technical men, that is a question of policy, in fact, of what is the best policy. When you fix salaries, the exceptional men can't be promoted unless somebody leaves or resigns. You make it exceedingly hard to keep the best technical men. We have had trouble in keeping them as it it. I haven't the figures, but if I recall them correctly, we lost sixty or more chemists during the last few years, and we lost more to industry than to the Army. I have in mind a man——

Mr. HAUGEN (interposing). I think we all agree that you are the proper man to pass on the salaries of these men; but if we are not asking too much, I think we ought to say: Give us the information that is necessary to explain to the House; this man is a very excellent man, and deserving of promotion suggested; we have increased his salary from time to time, and we propose to do it again. It doesn't seem to me that is asking too much, and that is all we are asking.

Dr. ALSBERG. I would be very glad to get it for you for the Bureau of Chemistry if you will give me 48 hours to get it up.

The CHAIRMAN. Take up item 91, Doctor.

Dr. ALSBERG. The work on this has progressed. The development of the manufacture of citric acid has been worked out and is now in successful use. We have made progress in the production of lemon and orange oil, but we have not yet completed the work on that subject. We have also fostered the manufacture of candied products from cull lemons and oranges. Before the war we, in the main, imported this material from the other side, and we are now producing a lot of it in California that we formerly imported from Spain and France. We have assisted in the establishment of these industries. The big problem that remains to be solved is the manufacture of lemon oil. Lemon oil is easy to manufacture, but it is hard to manufacture it so cheaply that you can compete with the cheap labor of Sicily.

Mr. LEE. For what is it used?

Dr. ALSBERG. It is used for flavoring. It is quite a valuable product; it fluctuates with the market from $3 to $5.50 a pound. We should make it in California, but in order to do so we have to invent machinery to do what is done by hand in Sicily, and we have not yet perfected the invention of such machinery.

The CHAIRMAN. Anything further? Take the next item, "For investigation and experiments in the utilization, for coloring purposes, of raw materials grown or produced in the United States, in cooperation with such persons, associations, or corporations as may be found necessary." You are asking an increase there of $29,280, Doctor.

Dr. ALSBERG. We are asking for a material increase to purchase some additional equipment and to extend the work. We feel that this particular work of the bureau has been of great value to the dye industry, and is bound to be of very much greater value in the future. We have, during the past year, not done quite so much in this connection as we had planned, on account of the war. The force of this laboratory has been at work on problems relating to the war to a large extent. For example, the Medical Corps needed a dye called "vital red"; it was necessary for the Medical Corps to study the blood of men who were engaged in flying at high altitudes. The dye had hitherto been used only in a small way for laboratory experiments and was imported from Europe. The Surgeon General asked us to produce the dye. It was not necessary for us to manufacture it; but it was necessary for us to develop methods of purifying the dye, so that it could be used on the human subject.

And then this laboratory has practically directed the chemical research work of the Research Division of the Bureau of Aircraft Production. There were a lot of important problems involved. There was need of a material called acetone, which is a solvent for the varnish that is used on the wings of airplanes. This laboratory was of great assistance in developing a new process of manufacturing acetone, which so far as we can see now bids fair to be a profitable industry, and we would have produced large quantities had the armistice not made it unnecessary to develop it further. You all know that the photographic plate consists of a gelatin film in which are suspended fine particles of bromide of silver which turn black when the light strikes it; or at any rate when certain rays of light strike it. Now, when you have to photograph late in the evening when there is only a red light in the atmosphere, or early in the morning, or under similar adverse atmospheric conditions you can't take a good photograph, because the kind of light that blackens the silver is not present in sufficient quantities. However, you can take a photograph if you have dyed your plate with a dye which absorbs the rays of light that are present; for instance, if you dye a plate red with a certain dye that will absorb the red rays, then you can photograph objects that can not be photographed with an undyed plate.

Now, these dyes were all made in Europe and it was necessary for us to produce them here. The processes were largely secret, and one of the things this laboratory did was to develop methods for the production of these dyes. The work was practically completed so that the Bureau of Aircraft Production could have gone ahead and manufactured them had it been necessary to do so. Up to that time we bought photographic plates in England where they did not have all the dyes desirable.

The CHAIRMAN. That is all good work, Doctor, and very interesting; but what are you going to do with this appropriation?

Dr. ALSBERG. With this appropriation we want to carry on the work that we have been carrying on, as well as to increase it, and purchase certain material for the plant at Arlington. This plant came in very handy this year because it was loaned to the Nitrate Division of the Bureau of Ordnance to develop some work on nitrogen fixation, and probably saved the War Department three or four months' time.

The CHAIRMAN. I notice that in 1918 you spent for equipment and material $7,737.79, and you propose for the fiscal year 1920 to expend $51,000 for that purpose.

Dr. ALSBERG. Yes; we find it necessary in our work to put in a number of stills and process kettles and also a small refrigerating plant; that will have to be built very largely out of copper; the price of copper has gone up enormously, so that in order to get all the equipment we should have will take quite a sum. This will be for the equipment.

The CHAIRMAN. I notice for miscellaneous items you spent in 1918 $579.76, and you propose for the next fiscal year to spend $10,000. What do those miscellaneous items consist of, in a general way?

Dr. ALSBERG. Hitherto we have been operating, in the main, on a laboratory scale, on a small scale, and now we have begun to operate on a larger scale, as we must if we are to make this work count. We have loaned this plant to Ordnance, which is now using it. Now, when we come to operate it on a semicommercial scale, which we want to do, because we can't work out processes except on that scale, it will be necessary for us to buy raw materials. We have need, for instance, of sulphuric acid; we have been buying it in pounds, and we will have to buy it in carboys; the same is true of napthalene. We will need that in quantities.

The CHAIRMAN. You distinguish between those items of raw material and the copper and that kind of stuff?

Dr. ALSBERG. Yes, sir; there is a difference between those two items.

Mr. McLAUGHLIN. Is this the item that was put in two or three years ago over the objection of those who wished this work done entirely by the Bureau of Standards?

Dr. ALSBERG. Yes, sir.

The CHAIRMAN. I intended to ask you, Dr. Alsberg (I am glad you brought it up, Mr. McLaughlin), whether there is any duplication between this work and that of the Bureau of Standards?

Dr. ALSBERG. There is no duplication with the Bureau of Standards that I am aware of. There was in the war a slight duplication, to this extent: That the War Department asked the two bureaus, without either bureau knowing that the other bureau had been asked, to develop the sensitizing dyes for the photographer that I have just discussed. We got to work on it, and perhaps the Bureau of Standards did. So far as I know, the Bureau of Standards did not get to the point of producing the dyes, and we did.

Mr. HAUGEN. Isn't the Bureau of Standards doing any of this kind of work?

Dr. ALSBERG. Not so far as I know.

Mr. HAUGEN. What progress have you made in this way? As I understand, a number of our dyes are not up to the foreign dyes?

Dr. ALSBERG. We are producing in tonnage the quantity of dyes we used before the war.

Mr. HAUGEN. Are they inferior in quality?

Dr. ALSBERG. No; they are equal in quality to the same dyes that were imported. The difference in the situation to-day and five years ago is that five years ago we used to use several hundred dyes; to-day we are using a smaller number, because we are not yet producing all kinds. We are making a tonnage equivalent to what we used to need, but a smaller assortment, and for many purposes we haven't got the dyes we used to use.

Mr. HAUGEN. The general impression throughout the country is, and every merchant discusses that, that the general standard is not up to the imported dyes.

Dr. ALSBERG. I think that impression prevails; as for the dyes we are producing, the quality is equal to the same dyes that were imported, but we are not producing enough variety to satisfy the manufacturers' needs.

Mr. HAUGEN. Is it your belief that all of the dyes in the United States can be brought up to the same standard?

Dr. ALSBERG. Unquestionably.

Mr. HAUGEN. All of them?

Dr. ALSBERG. All of them; there isn't any question but that we can produce anything that was produced in Germany.

Mr. HAUGEN. Then, is it due to the processes, or what is it due to?

Dr. ALSBERG. The difference is we have not been producing dyes extensively; we have been producing dyes extensively for only a few years, and the Germans have been producing dyes for a long time and have been accumulating a lot of secret information which is not contained in their patents. The patents are written to deceive. You can hardly ever work a German patent. They are written to deceive; they are written with that intent. They have been accumulating a mass of secret knowledge which we haven't got.

Mr. McLAUGHLIN. Then the remedy is in discovering the secrets?

Dr. ALSBERG. That is the point and that is the exact thing we have been trying to do with this appropriation. Take the substance which is not in itself a dye, but is used in producing dyes, phthalic anhydride, concerning which I reported last year. That substance could not be produced in the United States at anything like the figure at which the Germans were making it and importing it into this country, because we did not know their processes. Our people working under this appropriation have developed a method, so far as I know it is new—it may be a rediscovery of something the Germans have known but never talked about, although I don't think so—of developing the raw material much more cheaply than the Germans have ever imported it. At the present time it is being produced in two plants and is a regular merchantable article which you can buy. The price has come down for the raw material from $7.50 to $3.50.

Mr. McLAHGHLIN. Your processes will be patented?

Dr. ALSBERG. Yes, sir.

Mr. McLAUGHLIN. Will they be available for anybody to use?

Dr. ALSBERG. It is a service patent; the man who has done the work on Government time can not patent it; but it is a service patent, which is assigned to the Secretary of Agriculture, and is available for everybody.

Mr. McLAUGHLIN. Suppose you prepare a process and it turns out to be similar to a German formula or patent—I mean a formula on which the Germans have a patent—will you be permitted to use it?

Dr. ALSBERG. Well, as long as the war continues we would be permitted to use it; after the war, of course, it would be an interference with the German patent.

Mr. HAUGEN: But if they are not patented?

Dr. ALSBERG. If they are not patented, of course, it would not interfere.

Mr. McLaughlin. Suppose, as you say, the German patents do not give a proper description of the processes, and all that; suppose your patent does give an exact and proper formula and process, and all that, won't the lack of detail in the German application showing everything that goes into a patent and that a patent should contain—won't that protect you, or will you still be violating their patent?

Dr. Alsberg. I understand not. My understanding is—I am not a patent attorney—but my understanding is a man must disclose his invention in the patent. If he does not disclose his invention in the patent, his patent is not valid.

The Chairman. Is there anything further?

Mr. Haugen. The contention is that clothing fades more rapidly than when imported dyes were used. Can that be prevented?

Dr. Alsberg. That can be prevented.

Mr. Haugen. It has not been prevented yet?

Dr. Alsberg. That depends on what colors you are dealing with. If you are dealing with standard shades, ours are as good as any German dyes; but if you are dealing with certain shades, then our clothing may fade faster. But there isn't any reason why we can't produce better dyes than we brought over. It is a question for research. There is no reason why in the course of a few years we should not have just as good dyes as were ever imported.

Mr. Haugen. Could you conveniently give a list of dyes that are up to the standard?

Dr. Alsberg. I can send you such a list.

The Chairman. Can you put them in the record, Doctor?

Dr. Alsberg. Yes, sir; I can.

(The statement referred to follows:)

STATEMENT REGARDING THE DYESTUFFS SITUATION IN THE UNITED STATES.

Before discussing the kinds of dyes of American manufacture now available, it seems necessary to point out that there exists in the mind of the public a misunderstanding concerning what quality in dyes signifies. The satisfaction which a dyed fabric will give to the consumer depends upon quite a number of factors, such as the suitability of the dye selected by the dyer, the manner in which the dyer uses it, and the shade which is produced. When one speaks of the quality of the dye substance itself it is not as though one speaks of the quality of a complex material. Most dye substances are largely distinct chemical individuals and, if prepared free from admixture of other materials, must always be of the same quality, since they are the same chemical substance. One can, therefore, not speak of any single European dye, say indigo, as being of better quality than American indigo. If the two materials are both indigo they will be identical, provided they are both reasonably free from adventitious material and assuming that they have been placed on the market in equal dilution. It is as though one should say that pure European lead is superior to pure American lead. If they are both pure lead there is no difference between them, since lead is the same no matter where fabricated. Of course, to give the desired effects the proper dyes must be mixed in the proper proportions, and great skill is required in this work.

The individual dyes now being produced in the United States have been, on the whole, pure dyes and exactly identical with the dyes purporting to be the same substances produced in Europe. One can not speak of their being inferior in quality, since they are the same substance. The difficulty in the situation at the present time is merely that dyes are not being produced in this country in as large an assortment and variety as formerly imported from abroad and they are not being properly used.

The dyes produced in the United States in the largest tonnage are the so-called sulphur dyes, which include the black shades in hosiery dyes and the olive-drab and khaki shades. They also include a number of other colors. There has been a not inconsiderable exportation of this class of dyes. Their production in such volume is due in part to the ease with which they can be produced, but in the main to the fact that the raw materials required have been obtainable in abundance.

Among the dyes being produced to-day in the United States are the blues of the indigo series and a very large variety of wool and cotton dyes of all colors of what is technically known as the azo series. The indigoes are excellent and many of the azo dyes are giving excellent results for a wide variety of uses. Others of this type are not fast and do not stand light and washing well. This is not characteristic of the American product but is equally true of the same product produced abroad. Certain of them in some shades, whether produced here or abroad, are not as fast when exposed to light or washing as is desired. They are not intended for use in draperies, curtains, and dress goods, where the light and washing requirements are drastic. They have been used unwisely for these purposes and, as might have been predicted, have not given satisfaction. This was, however, not due to the fact that these particular dyes or mixtures were inferior to the European product but to the fact that they should not have been used for these purposes. The fault here has been that the dyer has used the wrong dye, often against the advice of the manufacturer of the dye.

A large number of dyes of the triphenylmethane series, which are mostly brilliant blues, greens, and reds, are being produced, but we still lack a considerable number, particularly certain brilliant blues which are necessary for the satisfactory production of what are known as taupe shades. We still lack certain other important fast dyes, particularly in the reds and in the violets and blue, which belong to what are technically known as the anthraquinone series. We are, for example, producing only a limited amount and variety of alizarin dyes. The very important dye, turkey red, is a member of the alizarin group.

It is impossible to furnish more than the general statement just given, since to give a list mentioning by name each individual dye substance now being produced would have but little value, because it would be out of date before it could be printed. The dye manufacturers are constantly adding new dyes to their output and substituting for dyes which they have been manufacturing other dyes which have definite and more desirable qualities. Since, as is evident from what has just been stated, there is hardly a series of dyes which does not contain individuals covering almost the whole range of color, it is impossible to prepare a list by shades. It would be far easier to classify dyes by uses, whether they are used for the dyeing of wool, silk, cotton, paper, leather, fur, and the like.

The point that can not be too much emphasized is that any American dye substances compared with the same European product is of the same quality. The misunderstanding that prevails has resulted in part from lack of skill in the manufacture in the earlier days of the great war, but, in the main, from the fact that we have not produced all necessary dyes and that we have mixed and used such dyes as we did produce, because they were all that were procurable, for purposes to which they were not well adapted. However, the dyes themselves are and have been in most cases exactly of the same quality as the same dye produced abroad. Furthermore, it is a fact that we are now producing certain new and very superior dyes which, so far as known, have never been manufactured before anywhere.

Incidentally it may be noted that the situation from now on will mend very rapidly, because the production of certain dyes in this country was not undertaken on a sufficient scale owing to the fact that the raw materials necessary were required for the manufacture of explosives. This is especially true in the triphenylmethane series, in the production of which toluene is necessary. From toluene is produced trinitrotoluene, known popularly as T. N. T., one of the most successful explosives used in military operations.

Mr. McLaughlin. This item has been attacked each time on the ground that it provides for a duplication of work and that the work could be more properly done by the Bureau of Standards. There are gentlemen on the floor who are very much enamored with that bureau and insist that everything that can be done there should be done there. Have we all the information now that we need to defend this item, showing that it is not a duplication and that the work is properly done here?

Dr. ALSBERG. This, Mr. McLaughlin, is a study in organic chemistry; the Bureau of Standards has no corps of organic chemists, so far as I know, on its staff. We divide chemists into a number of classes, inorganic and organic, etc. Organic chemists are the ones who deal with the chemistry of carbon; carbon is a material that is fundamentally found in all products of life. Dyestuffs are such products because they are made from coal which originally was plants. Now, the Bureau of Standards has no corps of chemists of this kind. For a number of years we have been dealing with dyestuffs because they are used in food materials. The Bureau of Standards has no special facilities for such work, while the Bureau of Chemistry has been doing such work for a long time.

Mr. McLAUGHLIN. You know what the Bureau of Standards has been doing and you can tell us that the work of that bureau and yours is no duplication?

Dr. ALSBERG. My understanding is that in general the work of the Bureau of Standards is to study how to measure color; how to measure intensity, to find its shade; that is, standardize it. We do none of that. It is physics rather than chemistry.

Mr. HAUGEN. I was going to ask you if the work done by the Bureau of Standards of measuring colors, which has been done for a number of years, do you consider that a duplication?

Dr. ALSBERG. No; we have nothing to do with that.

Mr. HAUGEN. That is on a different line?

Dr. ALSBERG. That is a physical proposition; there is no chemistry to that at all. It consists of taking a color, making a solution of it, and then letting the light fall through it under standard conditions and measuring the intensity with which light passes through it. It is a matter of physics, and hasn't anything to do with chemistry.

Mr. McLAUGHLIN. Are we right in defending this in the bill when we say that the Secretary of Agriculture and the Bureau of Standards officials have agreed that this appropriation should be contained in the Department of Agriculture bill and not be given to the Bureau of Standards?

Dr. ALSBERG. That is correct. As I recall it, I have a letter in which Dr. Stratton takes that position.

Mr. HARRISON. Yes; I think you wrote to Dr. Stratton at the time and explained it to him.

The CHAIRMAN. Item 92, "For the investigation and development of methods for the manufacture of table sirup," and then this new language, "and of methods for the manufacture of sweet sirups by the utilization of new agricultural sources." Tell us briefly about that. There is a $5,000 increase there.

Dr. ALSBERG. This work, I think, I reported on pretty fully last year. The question of making a sirup—that is, the method of making a sirup that will not crystalize, that you can boil down to any thickness—has been solved. The work that is being done under this appropriation at the present time—under this $7,000 of the present appropriation—is in the nature of demonstration work to demonstrate among the producers of southern Georgia, Florida, and Alabama the methods which the bureau has developed. It also involves improvements in the methods of decolorizing sirup. One of the things that prevents the marketing of sirups all over the United States is that sometimes it is as black as your hat and the next time it is light.

Mr. McLaughlin. Of the same product?

Dr. Alsberg. It is made just like sorghum.

Mr. McLaughlin. Does the material made by the same process, the same material, have one color one time and another color another time?

Dr. Alsberg. Yes, sir; because sometimes you burn it and sometimes you do not. It is a question of skill in boiling it, the same as in two maple sirups, one will be light and the other dark.

Mr. McLaughlin. If you work out a process, you can hardly stand by and see that the fellow does not burn his stuff.

Dr. Alsberg. No; but what we are after is to treat it afterwards; we are working out a method of treating it afterwards.

Mr. McLaughlin. You let him be careless and you correct his mistakes?

Dr. Alsberg. It is pretty difficult to be careful in boiling in the open kettle over a wood fire; you can't expect the ordinary man to do it just so. The method we are developing and have about succeeded in developing is to use a charcoal to take the color out and by this method the sirup will get a different color according to the treatment by the charcoal method.

Mr. McLaughlin. There is another item that Mr. Park, of Georgia, took up at one time.

Dr. Alsberg. This is it.

Mr. Haugen. When this was ushered in it was thought it would stand on its own pegs; it seems to grow.

Dr. Alsberg. The sirup proposition will stand on its own pegs very shortly, but we have not solved entirely the second part of the problem.

The Chairman. What is that?

Dr. Alsberg. Producing a uniform sirup. We have solved the problem of keeping it from sugaring off; that is solved. We have not solved as yet the problem of getting a uniformly colored sirup.

The Chairman. What are these other new agricultural sources which you expect to use?

Dr. Alsberg. Such things as sorghum, grapes, and fruit products of that kind.

Mr. McLaughlin. That solves the prohibition problem in California?

Dr. Alsberg. At the present time they are making a certain amount of such sirup there. This involves grapes and other fruit products, as well as better methods of producing sorghum sirup.

Mr. McLaughlin. I had an inquiry the other day about making sirup out of apples.

Dr. Alsberg. That can be done and is done on a large scale. You can make very nice sirup out of apples and a number of other fruits.

Mr. Haugen. Do you consider that a wholesome article?

Dr. Alsberg. Entirely a wholesome article. Of course, the nicest sirup is not made by a boiling process but by taking the apple juice, freezing the water out of it, thus you get an article which makes a very nice sirup.

Mr. McLaughlin. Have you any printed matter on that subject that you can send to me?

Dr. Alsberg. I think so.

Mr. HAUGEN. In your opinion how long do you think it will take to finish up this work?

Dr. ALSBERG. That depends on whether you want to stop it with the production of a good cane sirup in the South or extend it to other sirups produced elsewhere.

Mr. HAUGEN. But this is not cane sirup; this is table sirup.

Dr. ALSBERG. I was coming to that, Mr. Haugen. We have confined our work up to this time to cane sirup, because that is the most important. Under this new language we want to expand it to sorghum sirup to see if a satisfactory and uniform sirup can not be made out of sorghum. At the present time sorghum sirup is often unpalatable except to the people who used it in childhood. It does not find a ready market. Now, it is a question whether we stop with the cane or go on to the sorghum. I think we can be through with the cane in perhaps two or three years. It depends on how much demonstration you want us to do. Our method is to go into a community and teach the people. We have only two men at the present time.

Mr. HAUGEN. And you are making good progress?

Dr. ALSBERG. Good progress.

Mr. HAUGEN. Satisfactory, are you, Dr. Alsberg?

Dr. ALSBERG. Satisfactory to me. For example, we operated in eastern Texas a part of last year, and in consequence the acreage of cane which will go into that particular neighborhood where we operated is much greater, because the men learned how to make a satisfactory sirup and got a price for it which induces them to increase their acreage in that section. That is the sort of thing we are doing in various places. It is largely demonstration work through the crushing season.

Mr. HAUGEN. During the war did you use this to some extent?

Dr. ALSBERG. The shortage of sugar increased the demand for all sirups, and all sirups went up in price. One handicap we have had in demonstration is that a man could sell anything last year, so that he has not been so keen to make good stuff.

The CHAIRMAN. Take the next item, on page 145, No. 94. There is an increase there; tell us how you propose to use it.

Dr. ALSBERG. It is not proposed with this increase to start anything new or to open up any new lines of work. We have under the enforcement of the food and drugs act, we find, had a task much more expensive than usual. There are two reasons for it. The main reason is that it costs more to do everything. Our inspectors, of whom we have 45, keep circulating around, and our witnesses have to travel to court. They have to live in the field. We have to buy samples of suspected goods and pay for them, and prices are up. The general cost of operating is greater than it used to be. At the present moment there is more work to do under the food and drugs act than there was before the war, because the war has brought about a certain laxness in the attitude of the manufacturers toward their product because of the high price of material. Thus there is an extra inducement to adulterate. Some of the practices which have grown up during the war it has been difficult to suppress because of the abnormal conditions, and they will require vigorous action.

The CHAIRMAN. Let us see about that. On page 146 the traveling expenses for 1918 were $66,488.52. You propose to spend next year $70,900; that is about $4,900 increase. And then the next item is "Equipment and material"; in 1918 it was $92,828.38, and in the next fiscal year you propose to spend $103,321, or about $11,000 increase; making a total increase of those two itmes of about $15,000. Now, your telegraph and telephone service is a little less for 1920 than for 1918; and the miscellaneous item is a little less. What has become of the $35,000?

Dr. ALSBERG. That leaves a balance of $35,000?

The CHAIRMAN. Just about $35,000.

Dr. ALSBERG. Well, one thing you must take into consideration here is that during the past year our force was at a very low ebb. We couldn't get enough force to go around, and our expeditures were considerably less. I think we turned in some money at the end of the year and will have to turn some more money into the Treasury at the end of this year, because our forces were depleted.

The CHAIRMAN. You have a number of transfers there, haven't you, Doctor?

Dr. ALSBERG. Yes, sir.

The CHAIRMAN. The note says:

There is an apparent increase of $31,140, but taking into consideration transfers to the statutory roll, amounting to $18,860, the actual increase is $50,000.

Dr. ALSBERG. Of which $15,000 is to cover traveling and equipment and material.

Mr. MCLAUGHLIN. A considerable increase in salaries, too, but the number of employees is 66 less than a year ago and the total salaries more than a year ago.

The CHAIRMAN. How is that?

Mr. MCLAUGHLIN. The estimates for salaries for the next year is more than for the year before, but there are 66 fewer employees so that those that remain must receive considerably larger salaries.

Dr. ALSBERG. Well, our force was not full. There wasn't any increase in salaries above the customary ones. We had a lot of positions filled for only part of the year and the money for salaries for the remainder of the year was not expended. There were a large number of chemists whom we could not get and we were carrying 60 or 70 vacancies in the technical force all during the period of the war, which accounts for the comparatively low expenditure for salaries for 1918. The difference in number of positions is due to transfers to the statutory roll. The salary estimates for 1920 are based on the supposition that all employees will be paid for the full year, while many of the employees in 1918 were paid only part of the year.

The CHAIRMAN. Doctor, on page 146 there, what does that star mean and that language "transferred to statutory roll in agricultural act for 1919"? Do those transfers come out of this $35,000? You say your actual increase is $50,000 while the apparent increase in only $31,000.

Dr. ALSBERG. Well, Mr. Chairman, the appropriation for 1919 is smaller than the expenditures for 1918. The appropriation for 1919 is stated in the brackets on page 145; it is $589,000; so that there is an apparent discrepancy, because the statement here compares the fiscal years 1918 and 1920, while the expenditures for 1919, the current year, are not stated.

The CHAIRMAN. Let me see if I can make my point clear. Your note reads "There is an apparent increase in this item of $31,140, but taking into consideration transfers to the statutory roll amounting to $18,860, the actual increase is $50,000." Now, the proposition is, if that increase is needed on account of the increased traveling expenses and cost of living, when you come to itemize it here we find only $15,000 of that amount.

Mr. HARRISON. Mr. Chairman, the right-hand column covers 1918. There were some transfers in the bill for 1919. The total expenditure for 1918 was $607,278.23.

The CHAIRMAN. So what is the increase?

Mr. HARRISON. I don't think there was any increase.

Mr. LINTON. There wasn't any increase in 1919. You will notice for 1918 the expenditure was $607,278.23, while the total appropriation for 1919 is only $589,081. The transfers to the statutory roll for this year represent the difference between the actual increase and the apparent increase.

The CHAIRMAN. Will that make up the difference between the $50,000 and the $31,140?

Mr. LINTON. This will make up the difference exactly. We were comparing the expenditures for 1918 with the estimates for 1920. The estimates for expenditures for the current fiscal year 1919 are not stated.

Mr. HAUGEN. On top of page 145 it says, "Chemists in charge—part time." Doesn't the chemist work the whole year?

Dr. ALSBERG. Yes, sir; but it means that he doesn't devote his whole time to this project, and his salary is pro rated.

Mr. HAUGEN. But he works all the time?

Dr. ALSBERG. Yes, sir.

Mr. HAUGEN. On page 147 does that apply?

Dr. ALSBERG. Yes, sir; that is the same thing. The chemist is Mr. Veitch, who not only handles the work on naval stores, but also does considerable work on leather and the like.

The CHAIRMAN. Do you employ people for part time?

Dr. ALSBERG. We do employ people part time, but not in the sense that these people were so employed. They are university professors, whom we employ on the day basis now and then.

The CHAIRMAN. Your next item, on page 147, item 96, "For investigating the grading, weighing, handling, transportation, and uses of naval stores." There is no change in that?

Dr. ALSBERG. No. The work is largely demonstrational—to put over in the field the results of research.

Mr. McLAUGHLIN. Will that work be permanent?

Dr. ALSBERG. It is like all research work, Mr. McLaughlin; it depends on how long you want to go on with it. On a small appropriation like $10,000 we can put in the field two parties consisting of two men each to go down into the turpentine sections and demonstrate improved methods of producing. It would take a long time for them to cover the territory. It is just a question of how long you want to keep at demonstrating; how completely you wish to reach every producer.

Mr. McLAUGHLIN. After you have gone all over the country and demonstrated these improved methods and processes, you would not need to go over that territory again until you have discovered some new method or process, would you?

Dr. ALSBERG. Unless you wanted to do some follow-up work, which might be advisable.

The CHAIRMAN. Anything further, gentlemen? We have two or three other items to take up. Now turn to page 148, item 98, about these dehydration processes.

Doctor, I would like to say to you and the committee before we begin on that that I have a very strong inclination, even before you start your testimony, that I have not much to give this item. It was put in purely as a war measure, as I understand it. We would like to hear you, however, on that.

Dr. ALSBERG. I have not very much to report on this item for the reason that the money became available very late in the season, after it was too late to do much of that work.

The CHAIRMAN. I think we can get along much more quickly if you answer a few questions. What is your judgment as to the soundness of this proposition as proposed under this item?

Mr. McLAUGHLIN. The second part of that paragraph ought to be eliminated undoubtedly, but let's hear the doctor on the proposition as to his judgment as to the value of this kind of work in the manner in which it appears in this bill here.

Dr. ALSBERG. It is my judgment, Mr. Lever, that the authorization might, with great advantage, be completely changed, and the manner of conducting the work very much modified. At the present time we are limited to cooperating with plants already in existence, and the language limits us very materially in what we can do. It is pretty hard to understand just exactly what Congress had in mind when they discussed cooperation with existing plants. Did Congress mean that we were to simply help those concerns already in operation, or did it mean we are to go into a plant and work experimentally, or that we were to assist in the production of the materials. It gave us no authority to purchase raw materials. I think, Mr. Chairman, that the language in this item might well be very materially changed and the method of conducting the work very materially improved.

The CHAIRMAN. Just what would be your method of conducting the work? I think it is important work, but doubt the wisdom of establishing three or four great big concerns here to be operated by the Government. I have always felt it was a wrong policy, but the House conferees were held up by the Senate and made to accept this proposition.

Dr. ALSBERG. Mr. Chairman, that is not what we are trying to do with this appropriation. We are not trying to establish three or four large plants.

Mr. CANDLER. I thought that was the intention of the Senate conferees.

Mr. HAUGEN. The Senate plan was that a number of small plants should be established.

Mr. CANDLER. That is what we tried to get them to accept.

The CHAIRMAN. That is what we tried to get them to accept.

Mr. CANDLER. We tried to get them to accept several small plants. They insisted on establishing a few large plants.

Dr. ALSBERG. The difficulty in this particular language is that it does not give us any authority to really establish a Government plant in the first place.

The CHAIRMAN. Let us see whether we can not get at the plan you propose. Would it be the establishment of a Government plant; would that be your plan?

Dr. ALSBERG. No; I should like to be able to establish somewhere, either independently, or in cooperation with some concern already existing, a plant, or at least facilities for testing out the various methods of dehydration. I should then like to have authority to assist any manufacturer, whether he had already a plant, or was going into the business, in learning how he could best operate. I would also like authority for what might be called a salesmanship campaign, to popularize these products. There are some very poor materials on the market which hinder the sale of the better products. A very necessary thing is to educate the people to use these products. Now, what we want is authority in the first place, to buy enough material, or manufacture enough material so that we can conduct an educational, or salesmanship, campaign, if you will, to popularize these products, and create a demand for them.

Next, we want enough authority so that we can assist the people in the industries to establish plants, and if we can not find the kind of products that we need in our educational campaign, we want authority to establish whatever plants are necessary to manufacture them.

The CHAIRMAN. Well, now, it seems to me, in view of the statement appearing in a copy of the Official Bulletin, which I have here, that up to the date of the signing of the armistice Gen. Pershing had ordered nearly 50,000,000 pounds of dehydrated vegetables for the use of the American Expeditionary Forces, and the further fact that there are already in this country some 15 or 20 very large dehydrating plants—there are now 15 dehydrating plants which have been supplying our overseas forces—that your problems are to investigate and determine upon the best methods of dehydration; and to go to work and put up a large plant at an enormous expenditure—$250,000—it seems to me, is absolutely absurd, in view of all these facts.

Dr. ALSBERG. Mr. Chairman, we have not done that, and we have not been proposing to do so.

The CHAIRMAN. I am glad you have not.

Dr. ALSBERG. What we have done is this: We have made a cooperative arrangement with one concern in Greenville, to help it go into the production of dehydrated sweet potatoes. The sweet-potato crop is a crop having an enormous amount of spoilage.

The CHAIRMAN. Greenville, S. C.?

Dr. ALSBERG. Greenville, S. C.; and we have contributed to that concern, which already had a plant that was making a breakfast food, some machinery that could be used. We have set up in that plant certain machinery that we have bought, which we own and control, to be able to make experimental runs on the production of dehydrated sweet potatoes, and particularly sweet-potato flour. In my judgment, sweet-potato flour is going to be a very important item of food. We have undertaken another experimental piece of work in Michigan, to see whether the processes for drying milk, which is a spray process, can not also be used for dehydrating certain watery types of vegetables like, let us say, the tomato.

Mr. McLaughlin. Do you know whether that is Webster?

Dr. Alsberg. It is not far from Detroit, is it?

Mr. McLaughlin. I do not know where Webster is.

Dr. Alsberg. I have forgotten.

Mr. Linton. Webberville is near Lansing in Michigan.

Dr. Alsberg. Mr. Linton tells me the place is Webberville, and that it is near Lansing, Mich. It is in connection with a milk-drying establishment. We wanted to use their machinery, the idea being that we might dry such things as tomatoes, fruit juice, and similar products by a system used in drying milk. We have negotiations under way for some cooperative arrangement with other concerns which have special processes for dehydrating.

The Chairman. It just occurred to me that one of the results that your educational campaign would have would be for the Government to put itself in position of advertising the goods of private manufacturers.

Dr. Alsberg. That is one of the things, Mr. Lever, that has been worrying me, particularly as to how far we should go. There is no use in undertaking an educational campaign unless the grocers have these products on their shelves. The women are not going to keep on asking for them until the grocer insists on getting them.

The Chairman. Let me ask you this question, Doctor. I think this is a very important proposition. Is not this true, that the people, as a rule, have been trained to eat fresh vegetables, and under normal conditions—not under the abnormal conditions that have existed since 1914—are there not sufficient fresh vegetables, fruits, and so on in this country to supply all the population, even though the cost of transportation on account of the bulk would add somewhat to its price? Aren't they willing to pay the difference in the price to get the fresh vegetables, or to satisfy their own prejudice in favor of fresh vegetables?

Dr. Alsberg. That is very true in season. It is not so, of course, out of season, when the price is very high; and then there is another factor to be considered, which is the convenience.

The flat dwellers in the city may prefer to use the dehydrated products over a portion of the year. Take potatoes, for instance. It is possible to dry sliced potatoes, from which French fried or ordinary fried or hashed brown potatoes can be made, possibly indistinguishable from the same article prepared from fresh potatoes. Paring potatoes and getting them ready is a mussy job, and they spoil. Moreover, city women have no storage facilities. It is a question whether there is not a market for some of these products in the cities just as a matter of convenience.

The Chairman. I can see how, if you could develop a plan of dehydrating sweet potatoes or Irish potatoes and vegetables of that kind, that it might be of some value, but I think it will be a long while before you can educate anybody to eat dehydrated onions. Here are some of them now [exhibiting samples]. These are carrots. Somebody gave them me—all kinds of things; this here is Brussels sprouts. Now, I am very fond of them, but I don't think I would enjoy them in that form very much.

Mr. Haugen. Why don't you cook it and try it?

The CHAIRMAN. I am afraid to. Here are some Irish potatoes.

Mr. McLAUGHLIN. The doctor says that dehydrated potatoes can not be distinguished, when prepared, from fresh potatoes. I am afraid there is a distinction between those and the natural product. I think they might be prepared so as to be palatable, wholesome, and nutritious, but I do not think they would have quite the natural flavor.

Mr. HAUGEN. Is it possible to make the product palatable and nutritious?

Dr. ALSBERG. It is entirely practicable, Mr. Haugen. What Mr. McLaughlin says is that they can be made palatable, but that the flavor would be different. There are some products that you can not handle at all, but the majority of them you can make in some cases with a flavor that is indistinguishable, and in some cases with a flavor that is a little modified. Of course we are already using an enormous quantity of dried fruits.

Mr. HAUGEN. You were speaking of the Army. Of course the Army had to eat whatever it was provided with; the Navy tried it out and would not use it, and then the idea was to force it on the Army.

Mr. McLAUGHLIN. That was on account of an unfortunate experience some years ago when the fleet went around the world.

Mr. HAUGEN. It was quite a few years ago. The department sent out circulars—what you call bulletins—appealing to the people to dry vegetables and fruits and various things, and your county agent appealed to them from the housetops, appealing to their patriotism, representing that this was such a superior quality, and by all means dry your fruit, and as a result the cellars are full of it and nobody eating it. I was out in the country when I was away asked about dried stuff and was informed that they had large quantities stored away, but they would not serve it. Now, can it be made equal to the preserved goods that are prepared in the ordinary manner?

Dr. ALSBERG. I will tell you, Mr. Haugen, you can not dry the ordinary vegetables on a small scale, such as the small-farm operations in the home, and get products that are merchantable. There are a few things that you can dry that way, but those are mostly fruits that are rich in sugar and acid, both of which act as a sort of preservative, and retain the flavor. You can in commercial plants dry a great variety of vegetables, such as potatoes and carrots, beets, and a variety of fruit, to make very palatable products. In some cases the products have not the identical flavor of the fresh material any more than the evaporated apple, with which you are familiar, has the same flavor as the fresh apple, but evaporated sliced apple is a perfectly satisfactory and palatable product. It makes a very good product. We all eat it and are fond of it.

Mr. HAUGEN. Provided you give it flavor by adding the sugar and things to it.

Dr. ALSBERG. It is used for pies and so on.

Mr. HAUGEN. The expense is greater than it would be to buy the preserved fruit, which is rich in flavor.

The CHAIRMAN. Let's see, Mr. Haugen, just one minute. I have never eaten any of this stuff here, and I don't think I shall want to. What do you think of the suggestion, that instead of erecting, as the Senate proposed, five or six of these plants at what they call "strategic points," in the country, and operating them and building up a pork-barrel proposition that would worry the life out of every Member of Congress and Senator in the United States, the investigation to determine the best methods of dehydration be conducted on the same general principle that obtains in the case of your experimental plant over here at Arlington? Let us give you a small plant in which to locate your laboratory——

Dr. ALSBERG (interposing). It would be very much better.

The CHAIRMAN (continuing). This to be on a sufficient scale to give information of commercial value; and instead of spending $250,000, you would probably get along with $50,000, or maybe less?

Dr. ALSBERG. I should prefer to do it that way.

Mr. HAUGEN. What do you think that would cost?

Dr. ALSBERG. I don't exactly know what it would cost. It would depend on whether we had to have a building and supply the boilers and power, or whether we could rent a place where we could get those facilities; but I suppose we might have to buy, first and last, of different types of machinery, $30,000 or $40,000 worth, which would probably not be a loss, because when we get through with it it would be sold again.

The CHAIRMAN. You think, then, Dr. Alsberg, it would be more satisfactory to have your laboratory in or near Washington, or to cooperate with some existing establishment?

Dr. ALSBERG. I think it would be more satisfactory to have one place.

Mr. McLAUGHLIN. I thought the bureau had worked out certain processes, and they were the processes that were, you might say, in dispute, or the failure to follow a correct process at certain stages had lead to bad results from private enterprises—that is, the bureau had worked out and shown wherein the private methods were wrong.

The CHAIRMAN. How much work have you done on dehydration, Doctor?

Dr. ALSBERG. We have worked for a year or two before this appropriation was made on dehydration. We have worked at it from a little different angle. We were particularly interested in the potato, in trying to see whether the dehydration of potatoes could not be used to salvage potatoes in times and places of overproduction by drying them so that they would not spoil, but could be used for stock food or for human food. In the main our work has been with potatoes. We have done some additional—in all, about two or three years—work, which has been relatively small. What Mr. McLaughlin says is in the main true. We thought we know what the processes were and we think we know how the best products can be made. What we have not done is to work them on any considerable commercial scale, so we have not got costs. As far as I know, no one can tell you exactly how much it costs to produce a pound of dehydrated potatoes if your raw potatoes cost you a given figure. That is one of the important things that is to be worked out.

Mr. McLAUGHLIN. For example, there is a hydrating plant, and you are not satisfied with the product. You investigate the processes in that plant and you discover wherein they make their mistake. You have worked out another process yourself that could be applied in that factory, and if it had been applied that mistake would have been overcome and the product would have been satisfactory. My idea was that you could go to the plant and point out to it its mistake, suggest changes of machinery, or a little different plan of operation. I gather that from some things that I have heard.

Dr. ALSBERG. I think that is true.

Mr. MCLAUGHLIN. If that is true, there is some opportunity for some kind of cooperation; but if you have got to start at the beginning and go all through it and devise your own machinery and your own processes, own methods, and carry it all out here, and wait until you have worked that all out before you can say anything to the manufacturers, it is a great deal different proposition, and different from what I thought it is.

Dr. ALSBERG. I think, Mr. McLaughlin, you have the situation very largely as we see it in the department. We do know what the processes are that should be followed. We do know how to proceed, and we have, since this appropriation was available and before it was available, been in various plants and helped them to improve their processes. One plant is now putting out a product that the Army is accepting as satisfactory which could not get its bid even considered by the Army eight months ago. We have been doing that, and I think we should continue to do that. What we do not know is what all the various processes that seem to be satisfactorily operated cost; and we do not know how to operate most economically and what it costs. Those are things we ought to know. They can be learned by going into some man's plant and getting him to agree to let us operate his plant for a while.

Mr. HAUGEN. I should not think it would be necessary to ascertain the cost of manufacturing if you have 15 large concerns in operation already.

Dr. ALSBERG. Practically none of them are making any considerable money, as far as I can make out at the present time. The question is, Do we want to create this industry? If we do want to create this industry, then one of the things that we can do is to show people how to operate economically, and that is where they are sticking at the present time.

Mr. MCLAUGHLIN. There is a factory in my district, or just across the county line. Most of the people live on our side of the street; that street is the county line, and previous to the war they had not operated profitably. There was a man named Whitney—you know him, I suppose—from New York or somewhere, who has been in the business. He went there and he leased that factory, or had some arrangement with its owners to operate it, and took a Government contract. The product was satisfactory, and the result was satisfactory to him from a financial standpoint. Now, there is something in the method of operation that is not known to everybody.

The CHAIRMAN. Do you know the method of operation, and only want to find out the cost of production?

Dr. ALSBERG. It is not merely that, though it is part of it. Also we want to find out the methods of the most economical operation. In some plants costs are so high they are prohibitive.

The CHAIRMAN. After all, it comes back to a proposition of finding out the most economical method of production and the cost of production, which is one and the same thing, after all.

Dr. ALSBERG. Yes.

The CHAIRMAN. It seems to me that, if you know everything else except that about the problem, you could easily cooperate with some existing concern which would be mighty glad to have your cooperation and get those facts.

Dr. ALSBERG. We can probably do that.

The CHAIRMAN. And not entail this enormous expenditure of money. I wish you would prepare a statement along that line.

Dr. ALSBERG. All right, sir. We have got to teach the public to use this stuff, because there is no use manufacturing it if they will not use it.

Mr. HAUGEN. If you make it palatable, the public will use it.

Dr. ALSBERG. There have been a great many millions lost in trying to put over a breakfast food which may be just as palatable a breakfast food as any on the market.

Mr. HAUGEN. Your intention is not to go on and advertise it?

Dr. ALSBERG. Not in that sense, of course.

Mr. HAUGEN. I presume each manufacturer will have to work out his own destiny.

The CHAIRMAN. Doctor, if you will try to get up an item covering the proposition of cooperation with dehydrating concerns, the proposition of a uniform product, and the proposition of the dissemination of intelligence about this business, we will talk it over when you come back before the committee again.

Mr. HAUGEN. Would it not be better to locate your plant here in Washington? If you don't get people to cooperate with you, you will never get rid of it if you start it elsewhere.

The CHAIRMAN. You had better not locate it here if you want to get rid of the product.

All right, Dr. Alsberg, I think we have a pretty general idea of your theory.

Now, take up item 99, on page 149, a new item of $10,000 for the investigation of rare chemicals.

Dr. ALSBERG. This is rather a new departure. The situation which led me to suggest to the Secretary of Agriculture the insertion of this item is something like this: There are a great many rare and unusual chemicals and reagents which are absolutely necessary in research that are not being made in the United States and for which we used to depend upon importations from Europe. When the embargo on importations came along an immense amount of research had to stop because the necessary chemicals with which to do it could not be obtained. These are rare materials that are produced in very small quantities and are not matters of ordinary manufacture, but are absolutely necessary if the country is to carry on any extensive chemical research. Now, if we are to hold our own in the chemical industries permanently I think there is nothing that can be done by the Federal Government that will add more to the development of chemical research and to establishment of a self-reliant chemical industry in the United States than to put some agency of the Government into the position of assisting in research by furnishing to investigators and to others doing research work these rare and unusual chemicals which can not be obtained in the markets.

Now, this item calls for authority for the Department of Agriculture, through the Bureau of Chemistry, to assist research outside the Government in that direction by enabling the bureau to procure or manufacture such rare substances. It does not involve establishing a plant; it is a matter that is done in a laboratory by a few men. The rare or unusual substances needed in research in the country, which are not obtainable now, which nobody wants to manufacture, and which, when we got them at all, we imported from Germany, we would be able to produce so far as the fund available permitted.

I don't know whether I have made the proposition clear. It is a rather new departure in Government activity, and I want it clearly understood just exactly what is involved.

Mr. McLaughlin. You say the required amount of some of these rare chemicals is small. You mean that you will require only small amounts of them if they were obtainable; a small amount would be sufficient for the entire country's use?

Dr. Alsberg. Yes. Take, for instance, these sensitizing dyes that we produced for the War Department. A few pounds of those dyes would probably keep the War Department going for six months or a year or longer for all the photographic work it had to do. Under ordinary circumstances a few ounces would supply the whole needs of the United States.

Mr. McLaughlin. A few ounces?

Dr. Alsberg. A few ounces, so small a quantity. The Bureau of Standards needed a dye which is known as dycyanine. It needed that dye in some of its special work. It had 1 gram—it takes 30 grams to make an ounce—it actually had 1 gram in stock. Ordinarily that is about a year's supply.

Now, that is a dye of which an ounce will cover the requirements of the United States. If the United States, or an investigator at Yale or Harvard, or Berkeley, or, say, some purely research institution should need a reagent which can not be bought on the markets, and if we have this appropriation, what we propose to do would be to gradually accumulate, partly by making, partly as a by-product of our other work, a large collection of these rare and unusual chemicals. There would never be more than a few pounds of any of them. We will accumulate a large collection of all kinds of rare and peculiar chemicals that might from time to time be necessary in research. Then if somebody in the United States doing a chemical research which will require some of this material can not procure it otherwise he can write to the Bureau of Chemistry and we can tell him whether we have got any of that material, or, if the matter is very important, possibly make some of the material, give him a little of it, put the rest in stock for future requirements, and enable him to complete his research where otherwise he might have to interrupt what he is doing for three months or a month or six weeks in order to obtain that material.

Now, it is in assisting the chemical research of the country in that way that we want to use this appropriation. It is a commendable thing for the Government to do. In this way the actual needs of the country could be met.

Mr. HAUGEN. Then, if you should work it out so that it would make a profit, then you can turn it over to others, who can go into the manufacture of it.

Dr. ALSBERG. That might happen. For instance, this is a thing we were asked to do some years ago: There was a physician who made an investigation and found that a certain chemical was valuable in testing whether and to what degree the kidney was functioning, and whether properly. It was a new substance he had made on a small scale, and wanted to know whether we could make it on a somewhat larger scale for him. We could not do it. We had no authority to do it. This was about six years ago. Now, if it seemed very important, we could, under this appropriation, make that material and let anybody have it who needed it. If in the process of making it we discovered a better method of making it, that, of course, would be published. We would not manufacture anything or make anything which any private concern was willing to do, but simply do those things which private agencies do not find profitable to undertake; as soon as they find them profitable to undertake, why, then, we would let them manufacture it.

Mr. McLAUGHLIN. You say if a new process should be discovered in the prosecution of your work you would let it be known and used. Does that mean you think you now know all the processes——

Dr. ALSBERG. No.

Mr. McLAUGHLIN (continuing). Necessary for the production of all these things that you have in mind?

Dr. ALSBERG. I hadn't in mind the production of anything new here. It might come up that there might be some demand for something new, but I hadn't that in mind; the processes are all in the books and you can duplicate them. It is rather a novel thing and in a sense a novel governmental function.

The CHAIRMAN. The next is item 100, for the investigation and development of methods of utilizing wool scouring waste, $9,000. Is that a transfer?

Dr. ALSBERG. That is a transfer from the food-production act.

Mr. HAUGEN. That comes from the emergency bill?

Dr. ALSBERG. Yes. The situation in this country with reference to wool scouring was this: That practically no wool grease was being recovered in any of the wool scouring plants—the loss of the fat and the potash that goes with it represented a very large loss. I have not the figures just at present, but it runs into the millions of pounnds. We were importing before the war very large quantities of wool fat, which is known in medicine as lanolin and which is the basis to-day of practically all pomades and ointments because it does not turn rancid like ordinary fats which were formerly used. Wool fat was used for this purpose.

Now, there was an immense loss of lanolin, which has great value, and of potash which should have been recovered out of these wool washings. The appropriation did not become available so that we did no work on it. In the meanwhile the situation has changed. It has changed because the War Department found it necessary—the chemical-warfare service found it necessary to go out and do in the industry, a part at least, of what we had planned. They found it necessary to secure very enormous quantities of lanolin in their protection against gas. Thus, in the meanwhile there has been developed a considerable industry producing lanolin. We do not know at the present time to what extent we want to utilize this particular appropriation. The appropriation became available here in the food-production bill in November.

What we are proposing to do at the present time is to have a chemical engineer make a survey of the wool-grease producing industry and see to what extent they are working efficiently, to what extent they are conserving all that they should conserve. We can not be in a position to say what should be done next year until that survey has been made.

Mr. McLaughlin. You spoke about the production of potash.

Dr. Alsberg. Yes.

Mr. McLaughlin. Do you look for a large quantity of it?

Dr. Alsberg. How much is there wasted, Mr. Veitch, do you remember?

Mr. Veitch. There is about 5 per cent carbonate of potash in unscoured wool. It makes a very large amount. It runs over 2,000,000 pounds of carbonate of potash which, at the present time, is selling around 38 cents a pound. In peace times it sells around 3 or 4 cents and is largely imported. It is a considerable item.

Mr. McLaughlin. Is that true as to the sheep's wool from all parts of the country?

Mr. Veitch. It varies considerably. Some is very low; some is very high; but that is considered a conservative figure.

Mr. McLaughlin. On the average, then, 5 pounds of unscoured wool will produce 1 pound of carbonate of potash?

Dr. Alsberg. No. One hundred pounds of wool will produce 5 pounds of carbonate of potash. It is 5 per cent.

Mr. McLaughlin. Five per cent?

Mr. Veitch. Yes.

The Chairman. What can you use potash for?

Dr. Alsberg. It is largely used in the manufacture of glass. It is in its most convenient form, for you can convert the carbonate into almost any other salt you want very easily.

The Chairman. Are any concerns doing this kind of work now, doctor?

Dr. Alsberg. That is what we do not know, and until we find out what they are doing we are in no position, Mr. Chairman, to say just what our plan will be. They were not doing it when we called for the original appropriation. The appropriation became available in November. Until the survey is made we are in no position to say just exactly whether we want to expend any of this money or not. So I would make the request that you let the appropriation stand and put us on our honor not to use it if it does not seem worth while.

The Chairman. I believe you told us what you got from this wool-scouring waste, but how much would that be worth?

Dr. Alsberg. I have not the figures. Do you recall that, Mr. Veitch?

Mr. Veitch. That is in there to the extent of 15 per cent. Ten per cent would be a fair figure, though. You recover 10 per cent on the basis of the wool; and in peace times it sells around 3 cents a pound. At the present time it is quoted at 16. It went as high as 28 cents during the war.

The CHAIRMAN. It would be a pretty good sum?

Mr. VEITCH. It is very profitable now, but the question about the matter is: Can it be used under peace conditions; and this stuff, you see, is very profitable now.

The CHAIRMAN. Somebody is making a mint of money on this oil, I presume?

Mr. VEITCH. Yes; it is very profitable.

Mr. HAUGEN. Have you any estimate as to the cost of extracting it? About 24 cents a gallon?

The CHAIRMAN. It would not pay largely on a peace basis?

Mr. VEITCH. It would not pay much on a peace basis.

The CHAIRMAN. Then, it would be a valuable by-product of the wool?

Mr. VEITCH. Not only that, but there is no more harmful material going into our rivers than wool-scouring waste, and it would eliminate this very largely.

The CHAIRMAN. You mean harmful to the fish?

Mr. VEITCH. Fish, water, and manufacturing enterprises.

The CHAIRMAN. Anything further on that, gentlemen? That is a very interesting statement.

Mr. HAUGEN. Have you any knowledge of the work being done in other countries?

Mr. VEITCH. It is an old industry in some other countries, sir. It has never been carried on in this country, however, as the conditions abroad are not similar to ours at all.

Dr. ALSBERG. Practically all of it came from Germany, Mr. Haugen. Am I right on that, Mr. Veitch?

Mr. VEITCH. Germany and England.

Dr. ALSBERG. And some from England.

Mr. MCLAUGHLIN. I understand that a man who has a flock of sheep and washes them just before shearing, in that process of washing them, takes out a lot of this stuff that you want to save?

Mr. VEITCH. He would take out only potash. I do not think it is a general practice to wash sheep before shearing.

Mr. HAUGEN. It is not in the district I come from.

The CHAIRMAN. Anything further, gentlemen?

Mr. HAUGEN. How much of the appropriations carried in the stimulation bill is merged in this one?

Dr. ALSBERG. What do you mean—this particular item?

Mr. HAUGEN. Not only this item, but all together—the aggregate.

Dr. ALSBERG. I will have to make a summary here.

Mr. HAUGEN. You have estimated on an increase in this bill here of $368,000.

Dr. ALSBERG. We ask for $368,180, which includes the item for drying.

Mr. HAUGEN. That is over 1918?

Dr. ALSBERG. That includes $250,000 for this dehydration work, which is merely transferred from another part of the bill.

Mr. HAUGEN. That started with that emergency bill, didn't it?

Dr. ALSBERG. No, sir; the drying work started before we went into the war, in 1915.

Mr. HAUGEN. I know it was recent.

Dr. ALSBERG. The total we have had from the stimulating agriculture appropriations is $161,000.

The CHAIRMAN. Anything further?

Mr. CANDLER. Mr. Harrison says this item, " dehydration," is transferred from the miscellaneous section of the bill.

Dr. ALSBERG. That was my point—that $250,000, or the bulk of that apparent increase, accounted for by the transfer of the dehydration item.

The CHAIRMAN. Doctor, you always make a very interesting statement. We are very much obliged to you.

(Thereupon, at 5.05 p. m., the committee took a recess until 10.30 a. m., January 8, 1919.)

AGRICULTURE APPROPRIATION BILL.

Committee on Agriculture,
House of Representatives,
Wednesday, January 8, 1919.

The committee met at 10.30 o'clock a. m., Hon. Asbury F. Lever (chairman), presiding.

Bureau of Soils.

STATEMENT OF MR. MILTON WHITNEY, CHIEF OF THE BUREAU OF SOILS, UNITED STATES DEPARTMENT OF AGRICULTURE.

The Chairman. Turn to page 151, Bureau of Soils. Dr. Whitney is here to present his recommendations.

Mr. Whitney, do you have any recommendations in your statutory roll for increases in salary above $2,500?

Mr. Whitney. No, sir.

The Chairman. Then turn to your lump-fund items, on page 153, for chemical investigations of soil types and so forth, $25,610. There is no change in that item at all?

Mr. Whitney. No, sir.

The Chairman. Will you tell us very briefly what you have been doing and what you propose to do under this item next year?

Mr. Whitney. This item covers all the chemical investigations that are going on and have been going on in the bureau for a number of years. It involves a considerable amount of routine chemical analysis. A great many samples are sent in by our soil survey parties and by other departments of the Government, a great many from the Interior Department and the Post Office Department, and it keeps us busy. We have always tried to keep two or three of our chemists on research work on fundamental principles of the constitution of soils. It is a very difficult work and, of course, very little progress is being made—only an occasional thing is discovered by the chemists who are working on this subject throughout the world.

The Chairman. Your next item, for physical investigation of the important properties of soil which determine productivity, and so forth, $12,225.

Mr. Whitney. Mr. Chairman, this has been an item of great importance during the past year. With the urgency of the war situation, it became necessary for us to throw every energy of the bureau on to the great questions of nitrogen fixation and other matters of that kind that had been going on for some time at the Arlington farm. When the press came we had to turn all of the energies of the physical laboratory, that is, of the machinists and some of the expert workers who were familiar with physical methods, over to assist in the work of erecting and operating the Haber process. It was an exceedingly difficult method, requiring a great deal of expert knowledge, and a great many of the questions were physical questions that had to be solved.

Mr. ANDERSON. Is that the coking process?

Mr. WHITNEY. No; this is the direct fixation of atmospheric nitrogen—the Haber process. Now we have had the benefit of the training of those men in the solution of this problem, and as this is not only a munitions problem in the past but is going to be a very important agriculture problem in the future, and has been so determined by Congress in their authorization in the Army bill for the erection of a factory out of the $20,000,000 appropriation, and as the product of this all may come and probably will come into agricultural use, we feel the necessity of continuing that work as rapidly and as energetically as we can. We are asking for an increase in the appropriation for the fertilizer resources which we will come to presently.

The CHAIRMAN. Let me see if I get what you are doing under this item. You have not finished your plant at Arlington, have you?

Mr. WHITNEY. No.

The CHAIRMAN. What condition is it in; how nearly finished is it?

Mr. WHITNEY. We have finished our installation; we are operating it.

The CHAIRMAN. You are operating?

Mr. WHITNEY. We are operating, yes; and with investigations that must go on for some time——

The CHAIRMAN. The investigations you are making at Arlington are scientific investigations?

Mr. WHITNEY. Scientific investigations.

The CHAIRMAN. With a view to see whether you can better the methods of nitrogen fixation?

Mr. WHITNEY. Yes.

The CHAIRMAN. What else are you doing?

Mr. WHITNEY. We will come to that under another heading.

Mr. ANDERSON. May I ask whether conclusions have been arrived at with any definiteness as to the relative efficiency of the different methods of obtaining nitrogen?

Mr. WHITNEY. Yes; but that comes under a different item. I am only explaining to the committee that the work of this particular item we have up now has been somewhat changed during this year, and we want to get it back to normal as soon as we can.

The CHAIRMAN. This item does not, on its face, carry a comprehensive idea of the work you are doing under it.

Mr. WHITNEY. Of course, it is physical investigations connected with soils.

The CHAIRMAN. I guess that word "physical" would cover it.

Mr. WHITNEY. Yes.

The CHAIRMAN. Turn to the item "For exploration and investigation within the United States to determine possible sources of supply of potash, nitrates, and other natural fertilizers." In this item you have an increase of $18,660.

Mr. WHITNEY. Yes; this is the item I spoke of where we have used the highest skill in the bureau to advance the work. This is the item under which we are studying and have been studying the fixation of atmospheric nitrogen to convert it into a form in which it is available for the plants and in which it can be used as fertilizer. We have been studying all kinds of nitrogen compounds, and also we developed the work of the utilization of potash from waste products.

The CHAIRMAN. How does your work under this item differ from the work under the item above?

Mr. WHITNEY. It is altogether different.

The CHAIRMAN. I wish you would make that plain.

Mr. WHITNEY. This is specific. This is something that has to be worked out; there are problems before us that we see perfectly well that should be worked out and that can be worked out if we have the men and the means. The physical investigations of soils have no specific, well-defined things to work on; it is something that the world has been exploring; it is something they have been working on since the earliest times—the physical properties of the soils. It is an exceedingly difficult, very deep, very intricate subject, and we keep our physicists measuring the physical properties in this way and in that way, attempting to show which are the significant physical properties.

The CHAIRMAN. Let us see if we get it; under item 40 you make your physical examinations of the soil.

Mr. WHITNEY. Yes.

The CHAIRMAN. You make your physical examinations of various types of machinery for nitrogen fixation?

Mr. WHITNEY. Yes.

The CHAIRMAN. I presume you also investigate the methods of precipitating potash at the cement factories—I mean, the machinery for doing that. Do I get that right?

Mr. WHITNEY. No; it merely meant we were equipped in the physical laboratories with machinery, with technical men who were expert in physical investigations, in physical methods, in physical measurements, in the construction of physical apparatus, and that we found it would be advisable to use them for a time in working out the physical side of nitrogen fixation. You understand it is not the same work; it is a different work, but it is attacked by the same methods and by the same men. If we had not had our physicists in our Bureau of Soils we would have had to employ physicists from the outside; if we had not had our own machinery for physical investigations in the bureau we would have had to install similar machinery for the study of the fertilizer problem.

The CHAIRMAN. That is under item 40?

Mr. WHITNEY. Yes.

The CHAIRMAN. Now, please make it a little clearer. What do you do under item 41?

Mr. WHITNEY. Under item 41 we have certain definite problems, we know specifically what we want to work out. We have phosphates in the rock unavailable to plants that have to be put into an available form; we have nitrogen in the air and we have nitrogen in vegetation that we want to convert into forms in which it is available to plants. We have potash in the rocks and potash in plants that is unavailable as fertilizer and which we want to convert into forms in which it will be available to plants. This is a specific and a narrow field of research of a few strikingly important things for agriculture.

The CHAIRMAN. I confess I dreamed last night that this item might be reduced instead of increased.

Mr. WHITNEY. The fertilizer item?

The CHAIRMAN. The exploration and investigation of fertilizers in this country. I got that idea on the theory that the Government has already adopted the plan of nitrogen fixation, so that we are going to get all the nitrogen we need from the air as soon as these plants are erected. And I assumed that we would have the cheapest possible source of supply as far as the farmers are concerned.

Mr. WHITNEY. Mr. Chairman, it is none too certain that we have methods for the production of nitrogenous matter.

Mr. MCLAUGHLIN. Is it possible we are spending all these millions of dollars for the erection of the plant while there remains serious doubt as to whether the process is satisfactory and practicable?

Mr. WHITNEY. I would not say that, but in the erection of the big plant it has been necessary to discover the proper catalyzers to use—proper methods.

Mr. MCLAUGHLIN. What is that word?

Mr. WHITNEY. Catalyzer. A catalyzer is an agent which has no sensible effect by itself but which induces changes in the gases which pass over it at certain temperatures and at certain pressures. Those catalyzers are exceedingly sensitive things, but the properties of the catalyzers are not understood by chemists or by physicists. The mere fact that they do these things is known, but how they do it is not known. The limiting conditions are very precise; that is, they are easily poisoned; they do not last long under certain usage. Now, these questions have all got to be studied, and notwithstanding the fact they have a big plant erected, but not yet in commercial operation, the War Department is using our plant for the investigation and testing of these catalyzers they propose to use in their big plant. The War Department is cooperating with us and while we lost some of our chemists to the war, the War Department has now replaced them. We now have from the War Department about 15 chemists who are working with the outfit we have.

The CHAIRMAN. This dream, which my friend from Alabama describes as a pipe dream, was predicated also on the further idea that, inasmuch as you had discovered your kelp as a possible source of potash and there had been a discovery of potash deposits at Searles Lake and a large deposit in Nebraska, the need for further investigation would be less acute. I understand the fertilizer companies are not using the deposits at Searles Lake and the Nebraska lakes. Do you know anything about that?

Mr. WHITNEY. Yes.

The CHAIRMAN. And, in view of the fact that we know all about the phosphates—know where they are—and that it is only a matter of digging them out, putting them on the market, and selling them; on account of this fact, I had this dream. What have you to say about that? What other source of potash, for instance, do you expect to discover in this country?

Mr. WHITNEY. The potash; of course, there is a special appropriation.

The CHAIRMAN. That is for the kelp?

Mr. WHITNEY. Yes.

The CHAIRMAN. What other deposits have you found?

Mr. WHITNEY. Of course, the great work we have done is on the cement possibilities.

The CHAIRMAN. Yes; I forgot about the cement.

Mr. WHITNEY. Then we are also working on the blast furnaces, where we are making a survey of the possibilities of potash recovery from the furnace flues. It has not gone far enough yet to make any definite statement, but our impression is that the possible amount of potash to be derived from the blast furnaces is larger than the amount that will be obtained from the cement mills.

The CHAIRMAN. What progress have you made in inducing manufacturers of cement to install your process of precipitation?

Mr. WHITNEY. They are installing it quite rapidly.

Mr. BROWN. About a dozen of them have installed apparatus for collecting potash and more are considering it right along.

The CHAIRMAN. What will be their output?

Mr. BROWN. Our estimate shows we could have an output of 100,000 tons if they would all put it in.

The CHAIRMAN. How much would those 12 produce?

Mr. BROWN. The actual figures of production for each mill are not available. These figures are collected annually by the Geological Survey, but with the understanding that only totals will be published and not individual-mill production. The figures for 1918 have not yet been completed by the survey.

On the basis of the Bureau of Soils' analyses, the 12 plants now collecting potash should recover about 13,500 tons K_2O. These figures, based on analyses, have invariably been found to approximate closely the figures for actual production in plants where comparison has been possible. It is probably safe to assume, therefore, that the 12 plants now collecting potash are recovering it at the rate of about 13,500 tons per annum.

Mr. McLAUGHLIN. How many have been added since you appeared before the committee last?

Mr. BROWN. Practically all of them. There were two about two years ago. The Riverside Portland Cement Co. was the first. They put it in for the purpose of eliminating their dust. And then the Security Cement and Lime Co. up here at Hagerstown was the second. And those were the only two a couple years ago.

Mr. McLAUGHLIN. You have been here within two years.

Mr. BROWN. These two were in actual operation, and the plant of the Alpha Portland Cement Co. on the Hudson was just beginning.

Mr. McLAUGHLIN. But you say there are a dozen actually doing it now?

Mr. BROWN. There are a dozen now actually in operation, I think.

The CHAIRMAN. As a direct result of your work?

Mr. BROWN. Yes; we feel it is a direct result of our work.

Mr. McLAUGHLIN. You spoke of a possible production of 100,000 tons?

Mr. BROWN. One hundred thousand tons of K_2O.

Mr. MCLAUGHLIN. Is that what is being produced by the entire operation?

Mr. BROWN. That is the possible potash output.

Mr. MCLAUGHLIN. How much is being produced by the entire dozen?

Mr. BROWN. Mr. Lever asked me and I said I would put it in the record.

The CHAIRMAN. You had some help from the War Department in your work at Arlington, did you not?

Mr. WHITNEY. Yes.

The CHAIRMAN. These estimates were made in October. I wonder whether this increase was not predicated on the idea that the war would continue and therefore you ought to speed up this work as rapidly as possible?

Mr. WHITNEY. No; the estimates were made with the understanding that it was uncertain how long the War Department would or could continue to cooperate with us. They have, of course, possibly their plans for putting in a testing plant themselves. I do not know.

The CHAIRMAN. If the War Department had continued with you during this next fiscal year, you would not have made the increase, would you?

Mr. WHITNEY. Yes; we would have made the increase because the part we are doing is more than we can bear under the appropriation we have had. In other words, I have had to call on the full resources of the bureau to get that work done.

The CHAIRMAN. In other words, you have shifted some men from other divisions to this work?

Mr. WHITNEY. I have called on their expert advice; yes.

Mr. ANDERSON. I may be confused, and probably am confused, between the nitrogen and potash propositions, but I had an impression there are several methods of procuring nitrogen; is that correct?

Mr. WHITNEY. Oh, yes.

Mr. ANDERSON. And that there has been a great deal of disagreement as to which is the most efficient and economical one. Is it now possible to say what method is the most efficient and economical?

Mr. WHITNEY. No; it is not possible; the investigations have not gone far enough. During this period of intense anxiety, England has been experimenting with these different methods and we have been experimenting not only with the Haber but with other methods, and France and Italy—you may say the world—has been trying to solve that very problem of which is the best method to use in any given set of conditions; which method is possible not only to give them the quickest returns for the needs of the war, but which will be the most commercially successful after the war. And it is impossible to answer that question at the present time.

Mr. ANDERSON. Is there any possibility that the project, for instance, for installation of a nitrogen plant at Muscle Shoals will prove to be uneconomical?

Mr. WHITNEY. The Muscle Shoals is a different proposition. There are two plants there in the same general locality. The one at Muscle Shoals is the cyanamid method. That has been used, there is no question, it can be used; that is all right if power can be secured cheaply enough. There are some difficulties connected with the use of the product, but the process fixes nitrogen and it is a commercial possibility; it has been used in other countries. It is a question of the cost of production; cost of production and the character of material you get. Now, with these other methods, leaving out of the question nitrate of soda and sulphate of ammonia, which are limited by commercial possibilities of production, we have the cyanamid process, the direct fixation by the Haber process, and then there are other methods. One that we have been working on ourselves is the high tension arc and the silent discharge.

Now, this whole matter is of vital importance to agriculture. It has come to the point and to the time where the amount of nitrate of soda we can get and the amount of sulphate of ammonia which comes entirely from the distillation of coal, is and always has been insufficient for our needs. There is little probability of great expansion beyond the present large production. The only other sources are of animal and vegetable origin, slaughter house products, the blood and scrap, fish scrap, and the cottonseed meal. Agriculture is calling upon them more and more for use as cattle feeds. An inquiry was made of me by a high official of the Government whether it would be possible to use all or most of the cottonseed meal for cattle feeds during the period of the war. There is something like a million tons of cottonseed meal used for fertilizer and it can not be withdrawn until a substitute is given to the farmer to apply to his fields.

The CHAIRMAN. What would be the relative value of cotton seed as a feed and cottonseed meal as a fertilizer?

Mr. WHITNEY. It is much more valuable as a feed.

The CHAIRMAN. I thought so.

Mr. WHITNEY. Oh, yes. But they want it and it is legitimate for them to use it. It is much more valuable to use fish scrap and dried blood and slaughter house products for feed than for fertilizer.

Mr. MCLAUGHLIN. In the sections of the country where legumes are grown successfully, has the farmer further need of nitrogen?

Mr. WHITNEY. Yes, sir.

Mr. MCLAUGHLIN. Why; tell us.

Mr. WHITNEY. In our modern system of agriculture, the rotation of crops and the introduction of legumes, which has been practiced since the old Roman and Greek writers wrote of agriculture, still needs to be supplemented by the commercial fertilizers.

The CHAIRMAN. As a matter of fact, the most direct and concrete answer to Mr. McLaughlin's question is that the great majority of farmers living in this section where you can grow these legumes successfully are not the best farmers, and the average farmer does not grow them at all. Is not that right, Mr. Lee?

Mr. LEE. I do not think so in my country.

The CHAIRMAN. Very few farmers in my country grow the velvet bean or the cowpea. Very few of them grow cowpeas, and if they do they cut it for hay. Of course, the best farmers do not. The other farmers buy their nitrogen.

Mr. MCLAUGHLIN. In our part of the country, I do not know of anyone who uses nitrogen except in gardening and intensive farming, and there almost without exception the farmers grow some legumes, largely clover.

The CHAIRMAN. That is not true in my section at all. It is being used more and more every year.

Mr. McLAUGHLIN. In general farming, not this gardening where they can not have rotation, but in other lines outside of these intensive farming lines, can not the ordinary farmer, who can grow legumes successfully, get all the nitrogen he needs?

Mr. WHITNEY. Practically it does not work. Practically they use the commercial fertilizer, even where they do that. It is a very difficult thing where you have a hundred acres in wheat or two or three hundred acres in wheat, to get the time, without waste of land, to grow legumes in rotation with your wheat as we grow wheat in this country.

Mr. McLAUGHLIN. There are writers on agricultural matters who tell the farmers that all the nitrogen that is needed can be had by turning under an occasional crop of clover and that the use of ready-mixed fertilized is not advisable and all that is necessary to be added after the clover is turned under is some ground rock phosphate or acid phosphate.

Mr. WHITNEY. Of course, in this country the use of commercial fertilizer has not been general. The use of fertilizer has not spread rapidly through the Central and North Central States. But your own experiment station is advocating their use and trying out fertilizers now, and they are advocating the more extensive use of commercial fertilizer in addition to the best practice they can maintain of rotation and green manure.

Mr. McLAUGHLIN. I have seen no suggestion of the use of nitrogen itself, because the price is so high there is hardly a farmer who is able to buy it.

Mr. WHITNEY. Still, there have been enormous quantities sold.

The CHAIRMAN. He means in his own country.

Mr. McLAUGHLIN. No ordinary farmer can buy it.

Mr. WHITNEY. They are paying $100 a ton for it now in the South, and you can get it in larger quantities now, I guess.

Mr. McLAUGHLIN. Yes; that is where clover is not grown, for the reason it is not fully understood or where it can not be successfully grown. I am speaking of sections of the country where the growing of clover is a general uniform practice.

The CHAIRMAN. The doctor is giving you his opinion about that.

Mr. McLAUGHLIN. I am very glad, indeed, to have his opinion.

Mr. WHITNEY. Commercial fertilizers have not been used under those conditions.

Mr. McLAUGHLIN. I do not speak of commercial fertilizer. A great deal of commercial fertilizers are used, with a little nitrogen, a little potash, and a little phosphate combined: but I am speaking of the use of nitrogen by itself.

Mr. WHITNEY. Oh, if that is what you mean, no.

Mr. McLAUGHLIN. It is used by itself—or as nitrate of soda by itself—in some sections where intensive cultivation is necessary or where the legumes can not be successfully grown?

Mr. WHITNEY. Yes. And there it is used largely as a top dressing in the spring. Mixed fertilizers are put on in the fall and a top dressing of additional nitrogen put on in the spring.

Mr. McLAUGHLIN. Something was said a day or two ago about the discovery in the Northwest of phosphates. Where is that?

Mr. WHITNEY. I do not know just what you refer to, but the occurrence of phosphates in the Northwest—in Idaho, Montana, Wyoming, and Utah—has been known for a long while. There are larger deposits there than there are in any other part of the United States.

Mr. McLAUGHLIN. I do not remember now who said it, but one of the gentlemen appearing now, as you do, before the committee, said, as I understood, there was some new supply or some new deposits which had been discovered in the Northwest.

Mr. WHITNEY. I have not heard of anything new; but there are large deposits there that have been known. Just a moment more in regard to phosphates. The treating of the phosphate rock by the use of sulphuric acid is limited. The ordinary way of making a superphosphate of lime is to apply about a ton of sulphuric acid to a ton of rock.

Now, they have to be careful of the kind of rock they use. They do not want to waste their sulphuric acid, and therefore they must have the rock that has very little of carbonate of lime and very little iron or aluminum, because the method is not commercially adapted to the use of phosphate rock that has much carbonate of lime or much iron or aluminum in it.

Now, we have been working for a number of years, as you know, with an electric furnace to distill off the phosphoric acid, whether it occurs in one form or another and regardless of the impurities that are contained. We demonstrated the method in connection with a commercial concern in Hoboken, N. J., and found we could produce the phosphoric acid, as I recall, for about 5 cents a pound. Still the cost was high; that is, a little high for phosphoric acid. Since then we have been working on a modification of the method; we have been working with crude oil. Instead of using electric heat we have been using crude oil. We think we have a method now, which is being tried out at Arlington on a semicommercial scale; that is, where we can use a hundred pounds of the rock, and run it continuously day and night smelting the rock by the use of oil burners, which gives us better results if we use the waste of the phosphate mines than if we use the pure rock; that is to say, if we use in this smelting process the rock that is used by the superphosphate manufacturers we have to add to it the sand, which the miners have rigorously excluded. So that the dumps in the phosphate field constitute how much?

Mr. BROWN. I do not know.

Mr. WHITNEY. They constitute a large per cent of the operation; 50 per cent or more of the rock is thrown away because it is unfit for treatment with the sulphuric acid.

Mr. BROWN. Two-thirds of the phosphorus acid that comes from the mine now goes to the dump and one-third goes to the market.

Mr. WHITNEY. That is about the figure. Now, we propose to use the mine run, to take it as it comes out and use this method of producing the phosphoric acid itself, with which we can treat the original phosphate rock and get a double superphosphate, which contains 50 per cent of soluble phosphoric acid instead of 16 per cent which comes from the use of sulphuric acid. Now, that, we think, is going to be a very valuable thing, particularly for the phosphate miners.

The CHAIRMAN. Take up your next item 42, for the investigation of soils in cooperation with other branches of the Department of Agriculture. What progress are you making in your soil surveys?

Mr. WHITNEY. We are going on very satisfactorily in spite of losses through the operation of the war in taking off our men. We have been able through the cooperation we have established with the States to keep up the record of the amount of area covered. We have surveyed about 38,000 square miles.

Mr. RUBEY. Doctor, I want to ask you about these publications descriptive of a soil survey. For instance, to give you an illustration, in one of my counties a survey was made, I think in 1905, and the supply of the publication of that soil survey is completely exhausted. What do you do in a case of that kind?

Mr. WHITNEY. It is a congressional publication. The edition is limited to 4,000 copies; 2,000 go to the Rerepresentative in whose district the area is, 500 go to each of the two Senators from the State, and 1,000 copies come to the Department of Agriculture.

Mr. RUBEY. The point I wanted to make was this, you go through the process and expense of making a soil survey of a county.

Mr. WHITNEY. Yes.

Mr. RUBEY. Now, after the lapse of 25 or 30 years the result of that expenditure is gone if it is impossible to get these publications.

Mr. WHITNEY. It is not impossible, but it has to be done through an act of Congress, which authorized it originally.

Mr. RUBEY. Could you give the relative expense of the publication of these results? Do you preserve the plates and things of that sort?

Mr. WHITNEY. No; the plates are not preserved. The engraving is done not by the Public Printer, but through contract, and copper has been so valuable that the plates have not been preserved except for a short time.

Mr. RUBEY. It would be very expensive then to have a republication of this?

Mr. WHITNEY. It amounts practically to what the original expense was.

Mr. RUBEY. How much would it cost to publish that?

Mr. WHITNEY. I think the average cost of publication of one of our soil survey reports is about $600.

Mr. RUBEY. That is to get these 4,000 copies?

Mr. WHITNEY. Yes; to get the original edition of 4,000 copies.

The CHAIRMAN. You have some new language, which you explain in your note is really not new language but merely a transfer?

Mr. WHITNEY. It is a transfer.

The CHAIRMAN. Is that transfer absolutely vital to the work of the bureau, or can you get along without it?

Mr. WHITNEY. It has come to the point where it is very difficult for us to proceed. The language of item 43 is specific to investigate and examine and classify agricultural lands in forest reserves in cooperation with the Forest Service. Now, they are getting along pretty well with that work. On the other hand there is more and more demand from the other Government departments, for example, the Land Office.

The CHAIRMAN. Why not change this language of item 43 so as to give you authority to cooperate with other branches of the Govern_ ment rather than to combine items 42 and 43? The policy of the committee is to segregate these items.

Mr. WHITNEY. That would be perfectly satisfactory.

The CHAIRMAN. I suggest you submit revised language to the committee, because I am unwilling, so far as I am concerned, to make this combination here.

Mr. WHITNEY. That would be perfectly satisfactory. But the point that we make is the demand for the same work is coming from the Reclamation Service, from the Post Office, and from all departments.

Mr. McLAUGHLIN. Why the Post Office?

Mr. WHITNEY. In connection with their land-fraud cases. There is a great deal of work there.

The CHAIRMAN. Take up item 44, which is the potash proposition, on page 156. Can you tell us what progress you are making there; what has been done and what you propose to do?

Mr. WHITNEY. The appropriation, as you know, came rather late in the fiscal year in which it was originally made and we took some time to examine the best available sites and to go through the legal process that was necessary to be sure we could establish certain rights and we proceeded with the erection of plant. The plant is in operation. We have harvested kelp with our harvester, brought it in and dried it and ashed it, and we have sold up to the present time about $50,000 worth of potash.

Mr. ANDERSON. Manufactured in what period?

Mr. WHITNEY. During the year.

The CHAIRMAN. At what price?

Mr. WHITNEY. I do not know what the average is, but I should say about $4.50 a unit on the average.

The CHAIRMAN. Put it in terms of tons. We folks do not know anything about a unit.

Mr. McLAUGHLIN. What is a unit?

Mr. BROWN. A unit is 20 pounds.

The CHAIRMAN. That would be about $80 a ton?

Mr. ANDERSON. It would be $450 a ton.

The CHAIRMAN. Is that right, Mr. Brown?

Mr. BROWN. Yes, sir.

Mr. WILSON. Where is this plant located?

Mr. BROWN. At Summerland, Cal. The language of the bill requires us to sell it at the market.

The CHAIRMAN. Yes; I know. The point I am interested in is whether or not you are going to be able to manufacture it on a commercial scale at a price which the farmers can afford to pay. This is a war price.

Mr. WHITNEY. It is pretty clear that we will not be able to manufacture it on a commercial scale to meet the prewar prices if we simply do as the kelp men have done—get the potash out alone. We have foreseen for a long while, and our original presentation to you gentlemen was that we would have to get out the waste products; we would have to save everything that it was possible to save in order to make it commercially possible.

The CHAIRMAN. What are some of those waste things?

Mr. WHITNEY. For example, the ammonia; there is 2 per cent of nitrogen in the kelp. The combustion of the dried kelp will give us ammonium sulphate, just in the same way that the coking of coal gives us ammonium sulphate from coal. We propose to get the ammonia. We propose also to utilize the charcoal that is obtained from the kelp under distillation methods that we have installed. My last report is that the absorbing properties of this charcoal indicate that it is of the very highest grade and is equal for industrial purposes to charcoal that normally sells for about $100 a ton.

The CHAIRMAN. What percentage of charcoal can you get? How large a quantity of charcoal can you get from a ton of kelp, or have you measured it?

Mr. WHITNEY. Of course, we get a rather large percentage of charcoal. I am not sure, without figuring it out, what it is, and I would not attempt to say offhand. But it is a considerable amount, because the kelp plant is a living organic product.

The CHAIRMAN. What else do you get?

Mr. WHITNEY. In addition to charcoal and ammonia we can certainly get iodine. We have prepared iodine from the kelp. It is a mere matter of taking care of the residue liquors after the salts have been crystallized out. Then in addition to that——

The CHAIRMAN. If you do not have them at hand, you can insert them in the record.

Mr. WHITNEY. I thought I had a list of the materials that were likely to be obtained. It is the tar products that come from the distillation of such materials—toluol.

The CHAIRMAN. Let me ask Mr. Brown, who is in direct charge of this work, what do you figure will be the value of these by-products or waste products from a ton of this kelp?

STATEMENT OF MR. FREDERICK W. BROWN, ASSISTANT IN CHARGE OF INVESTIGATIONS OF FERTILIZER RESOURCES, BUREAU OF SOILS, UNITED STATES DEPARTMENT OF AGRICULTURE.

Mr. BROWN. I am very glad to have an opportunity to say to the committee that the last report I had from Dr. Turrentine, in charge of the plant, was to the effect that he believed the charcoal we will get—that is, high-grade, high-temperature charcoal—and the iodine alone will cover the cost of operating the plant. Now, he is a very conservative gentleman, and he has never made a statement to me of that kind before, and I am very glad to have it and to give it to the committee. The last two weeks they have been producing charcoal with new retorts. Our first retorts broke; they buckled under the weight of the thing, and we had to take them out and had to put in stoneware retorts to stand the temperatures. At 2,000° F. we produce a high grade of charcoal that will sell, apparently, as near as we can come to it, for about $100 a ton. In addition, by leaching the char we get out potash salts, and by saving the mother liquors we get the iodine. And the man in charge of the plant says the latest evidence he has from the plant, and this is within a week, is that the iodine and charcoal alone will carry the expense of such a plant. I feel better than I have for a good while as a result of this last report. And those are just two of the products.

In addition to that, as Dr. Whitney has said, we have a whole line of products from the tar. You can crack that stuff exactly as you crack coal tars, and there is a whole chemistry of coal tar, and there probably will be a whole chemistry of kelp tar, which is very similar in many respects. We have already secured several oils which appear to have valuable properties for flotation purposes in mining. And there should be a good market for our charcoal with the sugar refineries in California. So, I feel very much encouraged about the potash-from-kelp plant, and I do feel we are in a way to prove this thing out within a very reasonable period.

The CHAIRMAN. Some of the powder companies have installed plants there during the year?

Mr. BROWN. The Hercules has a large $3,000,000 plant at San Diego. As you know, they were not there for potash; they went there for acetone for British munitions. Potash was purely a side issue with them. They are going out of business, I understand. With the end of the war they see no reason for continuing the plant for acetone, and they are closing up. I understand they have sold their harvesters and are going to close the plant out and quit.

The CHAIRMAN. I suppose they have made enough money during the war to do that.

Mr. BROWN. I suppose they have.

Mr. WILSON. Do you expect this to maintain itself, then?

Mr. BROWN. We have sold $50,000 worth this year.

Mr. WILSON. But you have expended $127,000.

Mr. BROWN. We have, but a good part of that was construction. I do confidently expect it to maintain itself. Of course, we turn this money into the Treasury.

The CHAIRMAN. What portion of this $127,600 do you propose to use for permanent improvements, if you want to call it that, and what portion for overhead expenses?

Mr. BROWN. There is for equipment and material an item of $166,000 that is provided. This is an experimental plant, as well as a commercial and demonstration plant, and it may become necessary to rip out this piece of machinery and put in something better. We have had two good, big items of that kind the past year. We had the retorts and also the leaching apparatus. The apparatus for leaching did not do the work and we have had to take that out and install one that will.

The CHAIRMAN. What is covered in a general way by miscellaneous items?

Mr. BROWN. Miscellaneous items—I do not know whether it is a comptroller's decision or a decision of the Secretary of the Treasury that we have to make them up in this way, but a miscellaneous item is any item that covers less than 1 per cent of our appropriation.

Mr. LEE. That item for rent; is that rent for building or land?

Mr. BROWN. That is rent of land. We do not own the land upon which the plant is built, and that item of rent is the actual figure we have to pay.

The CHAIRMAN. You do not seem to have any item there submitted for rent.

Mr. BROWN. Yes; for rent we have $3,500.

The CHAIRMAN. Freight and express?

Mr. BROWN. Freight and express we have taken out this year, because apparently we have the equipment out there.

Mr. WILSON. I notice equipment and material expense in 1918 of $74,000. You estimate you will spend $66,419 in 1920.

Mr. BROWN. Yes. In 1919 we expended somewhere in the neighborhood of $100,000 to complete the plant. There was a very small portion of the fund actually expended in 1918, because we started toward the middle of the fiscal year. In the following year we spent in the neighborhood of $100,000. Next year we calculate, as near as we can, that this $66,400 will cover actual equipment and materials we will have to have.

Mr. WILSON. The materials you will have to have; does that mean the materials in the equipment process?

Mr. BROWN. Yes; the ironwork, brick, lumber, cement, etc.

The CHAIRMAN. And the harvesters?

Mr. BROWN. That does not include the harvester. We already have a harvester.

The CHAIRMAN. The plant itself cost you about $100,000, as I understand?

Mr. BROWN. About $100,000.

The CHAIRMAN. And this added expense was largely for equipment, repairs, replacements, etc.?

Mr. BROWN. Replacements, repairs, etc.

Mr. WILSON. Next year do you expect to spend a lot of money for equipment also?

Mr. BROWN. The following year?

Mr. WILSON. Yes.

Mr. BROWN. I hope not. Of course, there is a certain depreciation on a plant of that kind, at least 10 per cent, probably, that will have to be replaced. But I hope we are going to get an installation there that will stand up, and stand the work, and will not have to be taken out for something better. Of course, this is absolutely a matter which never had been done before in this way, and we simply had to feel our way, and have done the best we could.

The CHAIRMAN. What is the life of the harvesting machine?

Mr. BROWN. The cutting apparatus will have to be renewed, and, of course, repairs to the hull, etc. The hull itself should be good for 20 years. The hull itself is nothing but a heavy barge.

The CHAIRMAN. But you do feel very much encouraged by the outlook?

Mr. BROWN. I do feel very much encouraged by the outlook.

The CHAIRMAN. Mr. Whitney, your next item down there is for general administration expenses. There is no change in that?

Mr. WHITNEY. No change.

AGRICULTURE APPROPRIATION BILL.

Committee on Agriculture,
House of Representatives,
Wednesday, January 8, 1919.

Bureau of Entomology.

STATEMENT OF DR. L. O. HOWARD, CHIEF OF THE BUREAU OF ENTOMOLOGY, UNITED STATES DEPARTMENT OF AGRICULTURE.

The Chairman. Turn to page 158, Bureau of Entomology. Dr. Howard, have you any increase of salaries in your statutory roll above $2,500?

Mr. Harrison. There is only one, and that is in connection with Dr. Howard's own salary. I presume the committee does not want to discuss that, but I would like to insert a memorandum in the record about it.

The Chairman. I had a letter from the Secretary on that yesterday.

Mr. Harrison. No; you have in mind another case. I would like to insert a brief statement in the record about Dr. Howard's promotion.

The Chairman. Very well.

(The statement referred to follows:)

Dr. L. O. Howard, present Chief of the Bureau of Entomology, graduated from Cornell University in 1877, and took one year's post-graduate work, specializing in entomology. In November, 1878, he was appointed assistant entomologist to the Department of Agriculture and held that position until June, 1894, when he was made chief of the division which was subsequently made a bureau. He has achieved eminence in the scientific world through the work which he has done for the department and has been given the degrees of Ph. D., M. D., and LL. D.; has been made honorary member of more than 20 foreign societies and academies, and is a member of the American Academy of Science and Arts, the American Philosophical Society, and the National Academy of Sciences, in addition to many other American societies. He has been permanent secretary of the American Association for the Advancement of Science for the past 20 years. His entire scientific effort has been devoted to economic entomology, and he has been a successful leader and administrator of the Bureau of Entomology, which is acknowledged to be the leading organization in the world in applied entomology. The value of his work and that of the bureau which he has directed to American agriculture is beyond estimate. In addition to agricultural entomology, he has paid special attention to medical entomology and has published two books and many bulletins and articles on this aspect of the subject. He has served continuously in the department since 1878, and entered his forty-first year of continuous service last November.

Since Dr. Howard's last promotion, July 1, 1911, the expenditures of the bureau have increased from $601,920 to $986,680. This increase has been distributed throughout 10 different sections of the bureau. The large growth in the activities of the bureau has added to Dr. Howard's administrative duties in directing the work of the numerous scientific employees who have been engaged during this period. Many new lines of investigation have been entered upon and the responsibilities of the office are constantly growing.

The list of Dr. Howard's published books, bulletins, and other scientific writings comprises more than 800 titles, not including more than 350 papers of which he was joint author.

Mr. McLaughlin. A man who has been in the service 40 years ought to have learned how to live on his salary.

Dr. Howard. He has.

The Chairman. You had to.

Dr. Howard. Obliged to; quite right, sir.

The Chairman. In your introductory paragraph under "general expenses" you propose some change in the language.

Dr. Howard. Inserting the words " and demonstrating." We have been doing a certain amount of demonstrating with the consent of the Secretary of Agriculture, and we simply wished to have the formal authority in the clause. We not only do a certain amount of research work but we are obliged to demonstrate the accuracy of the results we recommend. And this form of demonstration has been very successful, especially during the past year, and has met with ardent cooperation on the part of the different experiment stations, and so on, and we of course wish to continue it, and we wish to be authorized formally.

The Chairman. You have not been held up by the comptroller, have you?

Dr. Howard. Not at all, sir.

The Chairman. If you have been doing it and if you are authorized to do it, why is it necessary to put in this language here and have somebody inquire about it on the floor of the House?

Dr. Howard. If you think it is not essential, leave it out.

Mr. Anderson. Have you a demonstration in the bureau now?

Mr. Harrison. Under the research investigations results are secured which must be gotten out to the people, and the machinery used for this purpose is the extension service.

Mr. Anderson. If that is true, what does this demonstration language mean here, if it is all gotten out through the extension service?

Mr. Harrison. It is not absolutely essential.

Mr. Anderson. What is the character of this demonstration; is it demonstration to the general public, or demonstration to your county agents, or what is it?

Mr. Harrison. It is both demonstration to the county agents and to the farmers generally. The Bureau of Entomology will send experts into a State to work with the county agents for a while in putting on demonstrations for the control of various insects in the same way that Mr. Rawl explained the other day was done in connection with the work of his division, and as the other bureaus have explained.

Mr. Anderson. Are you asking for any more money?

Mr. Harrison. No; it is merely a change in language.

The Chairman. Page 163, item 66, for investigation of insects affecting deciduous fruits, orchards, nuts, and so forth; is there any increase there, Doctor?

Dr. Howard. There have been only three increases in the whole estimates. One of $5,000 in this special item for additional work on the Japanese beetle, which has been imported accidentally into New Jersey, and which we are working on intensively, not only to find out everything we can about it, but to prevent its spread. There is that item; and, then, two others.

The CHAIRMAN. Tell us a little about the Japanese beetle.

Dr. HOWARD. The Japanese beetle is a striking species, which does a great deal of damage to several different crops in Japan, which evidently was accidently introduced at Rivertown, N. J., by nurserymen, and probably came in around the roots of plants which they introduced from Japan. It is a species which feeds upon grapevines, and a number of economic plants, as well as a number of weeds, and which promises to do a great deal of damage to the garden crops, ornamental plants, and vineyards. We have the present area circumscribed for about 31 square miles. The State of New Jersey is cooperating with us and is appropriating funds, but it is increasing so rapidly that we think we should put more money into the project and endeavor to prevent a further spread.

The CHAIRMAN. You feel you have it surrounded?

Dr. HOWARD. No; we do not feel at all sure about that. It is a beetle of the nature of the May beetle or the June bug, which flies vigorously in the bright sunlight of the summer time, and it is very difficult to keep it from spreading.

The CHAIRMAN. How big is it?

Dr. HOWARD. It is somewhat smaller than the ordinary June beetle of your State. Perhaps, somewhat less than two-thirds the size. It is very striking looking in its oriental appearance. Its larva lives underground. We have found so far that it lives only in dry spots. There is a possibility that we may find a means of treatment of its preferred breeding places by irrigation.

Mr. MCLAUGHLIN. When was this brought in?

Dr. HOWARD. It was brought in about 1911. When it became numerous it was noticed almost at once on account of its striking appearance—different from anything we have in this country.

Mr. ANDERSON. How do these bugs get by the inspectors?

Dr. HOWARD. It came in, apparently, before the Federal horticultural board was started. It probably came in in the egg stage, attached to the roots of some oriental plant imported by the nurserymen, or in some way which could not easily be detected.

The CHAIRMAN. How much are you spending on this work now?

Dr. HOWARD. I think $10,000.

The CHAIRMAN. This would give you $15,000?

Dr. HOWARD. $15,000.

Mr. MCLAUGHLIN. How are you getting along with the pecan work?

Dr. HOWARD. It is getting along very well, indeed. We are studying all the different species of insects that affect the pecan tree, and a bulletin has recently been published.

Mr. MCLAUGHLIN. We were told that was only a temporary matter at the time the appropriation was made, and would be finished pretty soon.

Dr. HOWARD. I think so.

Mr. MCLAUGHLIN. How long will that probably continue?

Dr. HOWARD. I think probably in a year or two we will have reached results which will justify stopping the appropriation.

Mr. McLaughlin. I presume that is very important work, but I recall it was said at the time it would be only temporary..

The Chairman. You have only had this appropriation a year, haven't you?

Dr. Howard. Two years, possibly three; I am not quite sure.

The Chairman. Is there anything further on that item? If not. take up item 67, on page 164, for the investigations of insects affecting cereals and forage crops. You have an increase there of $25,000, and a recommendation that $10,000 of the total amount shall be immediately available.

Dr. Howard. That is on account of the new European corn borer. That is potentially one of the worst insects that ever got into the United States. It has been in this country about six or seven years, and probably came in before the Federal Horticultural Board was started, and the reason it was not discovered at an earlier time is that it was probably introduced in hemp coming from Europe to a rope walk near Boston. The rope walk was situated in a district where there were no cultivated gardens in the vicinity, and this insect probably escaped and on account of its resemblance to the native stalk borer, which does very little damage, was' not recognized until early last year, when it got into the gardens around Boston. We have conducted a survey during this past summer and find it has now spread to an area of about 300 square miles around Boston. It is a very difficult insect to control, for the reason it is not confined to corn, but breeds in the stalk of orchard grasses, ragweed, and dahlias, and almost every kind of annual plant which has a stalk large enough. The moth lays over 500 eggs, twice a year, in June and again in August. The area has been circumscribed, so far as we have been able to do it. The State has been working at it and has established a quarantine, and there has also been a quarantine by the Federal Horticultural Board, but it may be possible it is outside of that area to a very considerable degree. That we do not know. The danger of this insect getting into the corn belt of the country—Ohio, Indiana, Kansas, and the West—is a serious one. In Hungary this insect is a native and is said annually to reduce the corn crop by 25 per cent, and our experience with all these imported pests is that they breed more rapidly in this country and do greater damage than they do in their original home.

Mr. McLaughlin. Is there any parasite?

Dr. Howard. We do not know. There are none recorded. The insect lays its eggs on the stalk and the young caterpillar bores in at once so that it is difficult for the parasites to reach it. It is more or less protected in that way. The probabilities are that if we sent over there we could find parasites and import them but that would take a long time.

The Chairman. How does it navigate?

Dr. Howard. By flight. It is a moth and flies by night. The prevailing breeze at that time of the year there is toward the northwest and the insect is spreading in that direction.

The Chairman. How did it get into this country?

Dr. Howard. It came in probably in hemp imported from Europe. about six years ago, by a rope walk on the coast of Massachusetts.

The Chairman. Massachusetts has taken a great deal of interest in this matter, and I had a strong letter sent to me about this.

Mr. HARRISON. I may say that some effort is being made to secure an appropriation of half a million dollars. The department has received a number of letters on the subject. In a letter dated December 27, to the head of the department of agriculture of Maine, the Secretary discussed the situation very fully. If the committee desires, we can insert this letter in the record.

The CHAIRMAN. I would be glad to have it read.

(The letter referred to follows:)

DEPARTMENT OF AGRICULTURE,
Washington, December 24, 1918.

Hon. JOHN A. ROBERTS,
- *Commissioner of Agriculture, Augusta, Me.*

MY DEAR MR. ROBERTS: I have your letter of December 6, in which you urge the appropriation by the Federal Government of $500,000 for the eradication of the European corn borer in the State of Massachusetts.

The experts of the department, as you know, have been in close touch with the situation. They have given the matter very careful consideration, and they doubt the wisdom of recommending at this time the appropriation of more than $25,000, which has been included in the estimates. In addition to this item, there is available during the present fiscal year in the regular appropriations for the Bureau of Entomology of this department from $5,000 to $7,000, as well as a portion of the allotment under the food-production act for the control of cereal and forage insects.

The desirability of exterminating the corn borer, if such extermination is possible, is fully recognized. Unfortunately, the insect is one of a class which, when once firmly established over a considerable area, it is practically impossible to eradicate. Control measures, therefore, are limited to the determination of such field or other operations as will prevent, as far as possible, the losses to the crops involved and such steps as can be taken to retard the spread of the insect.

The experts of the Bureau of Entomology tell me that the habits of the European corn borer are such as to prevent an accurate determination of its present distribution. No quarantine, therefore, can be promulgated with any certainty of including all or even a considerable portion of the infested area. The insect breeds in corn and other cereals, wild grasses, all common weeds, truck crops, including such crops as spinach, tomato, and the like, and many ornamental and flowering plants of the dooryard or garden, and, in fact, in any plant of a succulent nature which has a stem or even a leaf with a fairly large midrib. Inasmuch as the insect is an internal feeder and gives no easy external means of determining its presence, infestation can be determined only by the closest inspection or, frequently, by actually splitting the stems of the plants. Manifestly, therefore, the area infested can be only roughly approximated. The examinations made so far have been of tracts of ground which are in corn or which have been recently planted to corn and their immediate surroundings. It would be exceedingly difficult, if not impossible, to make such minute examination over extended areas of all succulent annual and other plants capable of harboring this insect as would be necessary for the purpose of quarantine and eradication operations.

The known area of infestation includes Boston and its suburbs, involving upward of 30 towns and some 200,000 residences, most of which have yards and gardens, and includes also all the suburban towns and thousands of private estates in the immediate vicinity of Boston. The easy means of spread of the insect by flight or by transportation with host plants makes it very probable that it actually occurs much beyond the present-known infested areas and possibly at widely isolated points in the State of Massachusetts and in adjacent States. If in any way the actual extent of the distribution of the insect could be accurately determined, eradication could be effected within the area only by practically eliminating all low-growing vegetation other than woody perennials. It is a serious question whether the State of Massachusetts or the surrounding States would sanction such radical measures, particularly in view of the fact that no assurance could be given that the full extent of the distribution of the insect has been ascertained.

It is for these reasons that this department is forced to the conclusion that the insect, established as firmly and widely as is now known to be the case, can not be exterminated. This determination does not result from any failure to appreciate the possible future menace which the insect presents to agriculture but rather from a definite appraisement of the limitations on effective work due to the habits of the pest and the radical character of the exterminative measures that would be required.

The experts of the department believe that the funds already available or recommended will be sufficient to cover the work, which, at the present time, can be effectively prosecuted, in cooperation with the Massachusetts authorities, under existing conditions and limitations.

Very truly, yours,

D. F. HOUSTON, *Secretary.*

Mr. McLAUGHLIN. Have you told what you are doing—the kind of work you are doing?

Dr. HOWARD. We have studied the life history of the insect to find out exactly how it lives at all times of the year, and we find it is an insect which can be killed if you can destroy it in its hibernating quarters in the stems of these different plants during the wintertime. That is practically impossible in New England when the heavy snows are on, but there is a period in the autumn, and a longer period in the spring, when by burning over and destroying in some way or another all annual plants the insect can be reduced in numbers to a very considerable extent. We would practically kill 90 per cent or more of them in that way.

The CHAIRMAN. Is it as destructive as the boll weevil?

Dr. HOWARD. It is more destructive than the boll weevil when you consider there are so many crops liable to attack.

Mr. HEFLIN. It works in the ears of corn.

Dr. HOWARD. And also in the stalk and also underground in any plant that has a tap root.

Mr. HEFLIN. It is suggested you would have to make a desert of Massachusetts. Do you advocate that?

Dr. HOWARD. No. That is over strong, because the work can be done there only after the growing season.

Mr. HEFLIN. You would have to destroy a very large part of the ornamental plants?

Dr. HOWARD. Yes; those would have to be destroyed.

Mr. McLAUGHLIN. This is an answer to a letter from Maine?

Mr. HARRISON. Of course the people in the surrounding territory are interested in the problem.

Mr. McLAUGHLIN. Is there any evidence it has reached other States?

Dr. HOWARD. No; we have no information except that it has spread through this area around Boston for about 300 square miles and near the coast.

Mr. McLAUGHLIN. And how near is that area to the other States?

Dr. HOWARD. It has reached up near the New Hampshire line and relatively near the Maine line, and the New England States are very much exercised over the possibility of this insect getting into their territory, and the commissioners of all the States up there will probably send in letters on that line to the committee and to the Department of Agriculture.

The CHAIRMAN. Are you prepared to say now that the only hope of controlling the situation is to find its natural enemy?

Dr. HOWARD. No; I do not think that would be more than palliative.

The CHAIRMAN. I do not say exterminating; I say controlling.

Dr. HOWARD. We can control it there by extensive work in this area only by constantly scouting around to find places where it exists and burning over this area, but that would not exterminate it, because burning would not get down to the tap roots.

Mr. MCLAUGHLIN. Has the Legislature of Massachusetts made any appropriation?

Dr. HOWARD. The Legislature of Massachusetts expects to make an appropriation of $25,000 and the Legislature of New Hampshire expects to make an appropriation. We had a meeting at the department last Saturday and the commissioner of agriculture of Massachusetts was present, and also one of the gentlemen from the New Hampshire Experiment Station. They both largely favor a larger appropriation of $500,000, on the idea we know approximately the distribution of the insect, and they want to get to work with extermination measures at the border, working in for a certain distance as fast as they can until the money is expended.

The CHAIRMAN. How much do you propose to spend from funds appropriated under the food-production act during the present fiscal year for this purpose?

Dr. HOWARD. About $10,000.

Mr. WILSON. And you think you are asking for all you need for this purpose?

Dr. HOWARD. I think we can do a great deal of good work with that amount of money; we can settle all of the questions of the possible spread beyond the border, to a certain degree, and we can do as much work of the destruction of the insect as $25,000 will pay for labor.

Mr. MCLAUGHLIN. Will an appropriation made in New Hampshire be used outside of New Hampshire—can it be used outside of the State?

Dr. HOWARD. No, sir.

Mr. MCLAUGHLIN. And so far as you know there is no actual need of it in New Hampshire?

Dr. HOWARD. It is anticipatory; in case the insect occurs there, then the money can be used.

Mr. MCLAUGHLIN. I was trying to get an idea of the amount of money that will be available from all sources.

Dr. HOWARD. The New Hampshire money won't be available unless we find the insect in that State.

Mr. MCLAUGHLIN. And the same thing is true as to Maine?

Dr. HOWARD. Exactly, sir.

Mr. WILSON. Then you would have approximately $50,000?

Dr. HOWARD. Yes; approximately $50,000.

Mr. WILSON. In Massachusetts?

Dr. HOWARD. Yes; in Massachusetts. Of course, during the growing season last year there were large quantities of sweet corn shipped to New England summer resorts, to the Maine resorts, and on so, and we have had a certain amount of scouting work done and have not discovered that it has occurred in any of those places.

Mr. MCLAUGHLIN. That is only the matured product and by that time the thing should be very much in evidence, I should think?

Dr. HOWARD. Oh, yes. It is in evidence when it is full grown in the ears of corn; it would be very much in evidence.

Mr. McLaughlin. So that there would not be any difficulty of stopping its progress in the shipment of mature corn, if it might go in that kind of stuff?

Dr. Howard. Quite so. It would very probably be inspected, of course, but, of course, corn stalks are shipped around for bedding, etc., and it is not so observable in the stalk corn as it is in the ears of corn.

The Chairman. Is there anything further on that?

Dr. Howard. I do not care to take up the time of the committee, but we do not ask for the $500,000 appropriation unless you desire to give it, in which case, however, we would do our best to expend it as advantageously as possible.

The Chairman. Item 68. - There is no change in that item?

Dr. Howard. No change in that item.

The Chairman. I presume the work is of the same general character as heretofore?

Dr. Howard. Exactly. We have done a lot of cooperative work with the Federal Horticultural Board in the extermination of the pink bollworm in Texas, which Mr. Marlatt will tell you about. The cotton boll weevil investigations have practically culminated this year in the new poisoning method and we have made a great success with it.

The Chairman. It has been great.

Dr. Howard. Yes; we have tested it out on a large scale.

The Chairman. How much does it cost per acre?

Dr. Howard. A dollar per acre per treatment.

Mr. Lee. What about the red spiders?

Dr. Howard. That question has been solved, practically.

Mr. Lee. The reason I am asking is that it has been all over my district this year.

Dr. Howard. I had not heard of it there. We have measures of control of the red spider in cotton which your people can use, I think, to advantage.

The Chairman. Your next item is on page 165, item 69, for investigations of insects affecting forests.

Dr. Howard. We are not asking for any more money there. The work has been very successful in cooperation with the Forest Service and the Interior Department and with the different boards of the War and Navy Departments. Our advice in regard to insect damage to timber used in destructive implements used in war and in the wings of aeroplanes has been of value.

The Chairman. Your next one is on page 166, item 70, for investigations of insects affecting truck crops, etc. You have a little increase there?

Dr. Howard. The apparent increase of $20,000 is explained by the fact that we would like to have transferred to this paragraph from the miscellaneous appropriation of last year the item of $20,000 for the investigation and prevention of the spread of the sweet-potato weevil.

The Chairman. It is really not an increase?

Dr. Howard. It is really not an increase at all.

Mr. McLaughlin. You have been working on the sweet-potato business?

Dr. HOWARD. Yes, sir.

The CHAIRMAN. On what page will you find that, Doctor?

Dr. HOWARD. You will find it in the miscellaneous appropriations, at the end of the bill.

The CHAIRMAN. It is page 278. What progress are you making with the sweet-potato weevil work?

Dr. HOWARD. We have had a large force in the field visiting and locating the places where the weevil occurs and advising the owners as to the proper steps to take to prevent damage the following season. The subject is rather complicated by the fact of the very severe winter last year which destroyed the seed sweet potatoes in the northern portion of the sweet-potato belt. The result is that they will be obliged this year to get their seed from the southern belt, and there is very great danger of the spread there of the sweet-potato weevil. There are a number of different things the sweet-potato growers can do to prevent its increase during the growing season, and also measures must be taken to store the sweet potatoes in as dry a place as possible, because the weevil breeds only in the potatoes which are moist. And we have a large number of recommendations which the men are making to the individual planters.

The CHAIRMAN. Your next item is for investigations and demonstrations in bee culture.

Dr. HOWARD. For the bee-culture work we ask no increase next year. Our research work was largely interrupted, except in the case of bee diseases, but we employed a number of experienced men and sent them all over the country to interview the beekeepers and instruct them in measures looking forward to an increased supply of honey on account of the lack of sugar. The result of the season's work, as I understand, has been a great increase in the amount of the domestic consumption of honey and a great increase in the export of honey, the increase being made possible largely by this work of the bureau.

The CHAIRMAN. Could you give us the actual figures on that?

Mr. HEFLIN. What is the value of the honey crop?

Dr. HOWARD. The normal honey production is valued at $25,000,000, on a basis of 10 cents a pound. During the past year the price has risen two and a half times and is now 25 cents a pound. There was an export of 10,000,000 pounds during the past fiscal year and more than 4,000,000 pounds up to date in the present fiscal year. This is almost ten times the normal export. There has been an excessive demand for honey in this country, and the domestic consumption was increased very considerably. Looking over the whole field, the probabilities are that the production of honey in this country during the past year was increased over 50 per cent.

The CHAIRMAN. Item 72, page 167, for investigations of insects affecting tropical and subtropical fruits. There is no change there?

Dr. HOWARD. No change at all.

The CHAIRMAN. The same lines of work as in previous years, I assume?

Dr. HOWARD. The same line of work.

The CHAIRMAN. The next is item 73, "For investigations and control, in cooperation with the Federal Horticultural Board, of the Mediterranean and other fruit flies." There is no change in that?

Dr. HOWARD. No, sir; no change.

Mr. MCLAUGHLIN. How are you getting along with that work?

Dr. HOWARD. We are keeping the Mediterranean fruit fly out of the country and have practically completed the investigation of its life habits in Hawaii, and we are working on other fruit flies that are likely to be imported into this county if we are not careful.

Mr. MCLAUGHLIN. Has your money been used altogether in keeping the insect out of the country?

Dr. HOWARD. No, sir. It has been used in investigating the means by which it might be imported and methods of transportation, and that sort of thing. The question of actually keeping it out is done by the Federal Horticultural Board.

Mr. MCLAUGHLIN. That investigation, then, has been conducted in the original section of the world in which that thing is found?

Dr. HOWARD. No; but in Hawaii, the point from which we have the greatest danger of importing it, on account of the great quantity of fruit that comes from there. We are also studying other fruit flies that are likely to come in from Mexico and other parts of the world.

The CHAIRMAN. Your next item is on page 167, item 74, "For investigations, identification, and systematic classification of miscellaneous insects."

Dr. HOWARD. The work is the same as in previous years, and no increase is asked for.

The CHAIRMAN. Is not that a rather large amount for that kind of work?

Dr. HOWARD. It might appear to be a large sum to one not understanding the conditions. A certain amount of it is devoted to insects affecting man and animals. That is readily understood. But this work on the identification of insects is one that would not appeal to a man unless he understood the conditions thoroughly. We must actually know what is before us and what is known about it before we can intelligently start our work. Therefore we have seven or eight men who are among the foremost experts not only in this country but in the world on insects in their own special groups. Insects are sent to us from all the agricultural experiment stations, and every insect passes under their eye for the purpose of identifying it. By this identification we know the place of origin and everything we know about it up to the present time. I think Mr. Coville once before this committee, speaking of the identification of weeds in the same way, said you could parallel this identification work with the criminal procedure in courts at law—that first you have to identify your criminal.

The CHAIRMAN. I assume you work in cooperation with the Public Health Service in the inspection of insects affecting the health of man?

Dr. HOWARD. We do. We loaned them a man in their extra-cantonment work during the war, and are also helping on a new investigation they are conducting of the disposition of the human excrement.

The CHAIRMAN. Take the next item, page 168, item 75, "General administrative expenses." There is no change there?

Dr. HOWARD. There is no change there.

The CHAIRMAN. Your next is the gipsy and brown-tail moth proposition, on page 169, item 76. What progress are you making on that?

Dr. HOWARD. The work has been going on in the same manner. Neither the gipsy nor the brown-tail moth has made any marked spread from the territory which they occupied last year. The brown-tail moth has been very much reduced in numbers by imported parasites and is no longer such a danger as it was 10 years ago.

The gipsy moth we are holding on the outside border by very intensive work. When we find a colony of the gipsy moth on a hill top it has a very potential danger for the reason the young caterpillar soon after it is hatched spins a thread and is wafted in the direction of the prevailing wind. Therefore those hills are the most critical points from which the spread occurs. They are carefully watched and whenever they are found they are treated by spraying and banding the trees. There has been no essential spread toward the north and west during the year, but toward the east there was much trouble last year. The insect appeared in numbers on Cape Cod, and we found it had a new method of damage which had not been found before. It not only stripped the trees but it entered into the strawberry and truck gardens and stripped the leaves, showing it is not only essential to prevent the spread of this insect on account of the damage to the forest trees, but also to the gardens.

The CHAIRMAN. Do you have that under control?

Dr. HOWARD. At Cape Cod it is under control.

The CHAIRMAN. What about the parasitic bugs which you brought across?

Dr. HOWARD. They are increasing constantly. There is no doubt that in a large part of the area around Boston the imported parasites are killing off from 50 to 75 per cent of all the caterpillars that hatch out.

Mr. McLAUGHLIN. And there is no danger from the parasite?

Dr. HOWARD. Not the slightest. On the contrary, the same parasites kill off native insects in many instances.

The CHAIRMAN. All right, Dr. Howard, we are much obliged to you.

AGRICULTURE APPROPRIATION BILL.

COMMITTEE ON AGRICULTURE,
HOUSE OF REPRESENTATIVES,
Wednesday, January 8, 1919.

BUREAU OF BIOLOGICAL SURVEY.

STATEMENT OF MR. E. W. NELSON, CHIEF OF THE BUREAU OF BIOLOGICAL SURVEY, UNITED STATES DEPARTMENT OF AGRICULTURE.

The CHAIRMAN. On page 170 is the Bureau of Biological Survey, and Dr. Nelson, chief of the bureau, will present the items. There is no recommended increase in your statutory roll above the $2,500 limit, is there?

Mr. NELSON. Just the changes explained here in the book, certain transfers of employees from lump fund to the statutory roll, and the elimination of two positions at small salaries to be replaced by one at a higher rate.

The CHAIRMAN. But nothing above $2,500?

Mr. NELSON. No.

Mr. HARRISON. As you know, the Secretary has made a suggestion by letter regarding the salary of the Chief of the Biological Survey, which was inadvertently omitted from the estimates.

The CHAIRMAN. Yes; that can be inserted in the record.

(The letter referred to follows:)

DEPARTMENT OF AGRICULTURE,
OFFICE OF THE SECRETARY,
Washington, January 6, 1919.

Hon. A. F. LEVER,
Chairman Committee on Agriculture, House of Representatives.

DEAR MR. LEVER: I desire to recommend, for the consideration of the committee, that the salary of the Chief of the Bureau of Biological Survey be increased from $3,500 to $4,500 per annum. You will perhaps recall that a similar suggestion was made two or three years ago. In preparing the estimates for 1920 the matter was inadvertently overlooked.

Mr. Nelson, the present Chief of the Bureau of Biological Survey, has been in the service of the department since November 1, 1890, a period of 28 years. He served as chief field naturalist from 1907 to 1912, and as assistant in charge of biological investigations from 1913 to 1914. On August 16, 1914, he was appointed assistant chief of the bureau, and on December 1, 1916, he was made chief of the bureau. Mr. Nelson was president of the American Ornithological Unon 1908-9 and 1912-13, president of the Biological Society of Washington, 1912-13, was vice president of the Washington Academy of Sciences 1912-13, fellow of the American Association for the Advancement of Science, and corresponding member of the Society of Natural History of Mexico. He has participated in scientific explorations in Mexico and in other countries, and is the author of many publications.

The salary of the Chief of the Bureau of Biological Survey was fixed at $3,500 on July 1, 1911. Since that time the activities of the bureau have been extended in many directions and there has been a corresponding increase in the duties and responsibilities of the chief. I hope very much that the committee will take favorable action in this matter.

Very truly, yours,

D. F. HOUSTON, *Secretary*.

The CHAIRMAN. The first general expense item is on page 172. You have eliminated some language there, Doctor; what is that?

Mr. NELSON. The Lacey Act we desire to have united with the migratory bird act, that the two may be administered together. This elimination of the language here is for the purpose of transferring and combining it with the migratory-bird law.

The CHAIRMAN. Is that absolutely necessary?

Mr. NELSON. I think the Lacey Act appropriation should be continued but should appear under the same heading as the migratory-bird act in order to increase the efficiency of its administration. The migratory-bird act includes certain powers that existed in the Lacey Act and the same employees may be used to advantage in both services. The proposed change is merely for the purpose of increased efficiency and economy in the work; the administration of both laws will gain by the change.

The CHAIRMAN. As a matter of fact, you have not kept these items separate; you have combined them.

Mr. NELSON. They should have been kept separate. The $22,000 should be retained but placed under the same general paragraph. I think it would be a mistake to combine them otherwise.

The CHAIRMAN. I do not think the committee would have any objection to your transfer of the Lacey Act item to item 38 if you retain the sums at the proper place. You are spending $22,000 a year for the enforcement of the Lacey Act. My suggestion is to insert the appropriation for that work immediately after the language providing for the carrying of this Lacey Act into effect, so that the committee will know which is which.

Mr. NELSON. I think myself that should be done. I do not think the Lacey Act should be eliminated as an appropriation. It is merely a matter of placing it under the same paragraph with the migratory-bird law for administrative purposes.

The CHAIRMAN. Your language should read "including not to exceed $22,000 for the enforcement of the Lacey Act."

Mr. NELSON. That, I think, would be much the best way to put it.

The CHAIRMAN. I hope you will do that, then, and revise that language.

Your next is on page 173, for the maintenance of your bison range in Montana. You have no change there?

Mr. NELSON. There is no change there. I would like to explain to the committee that we are about to have rather a hard time this coming year in the administration of it, because the Audubon societies have been putting up from three to four thousand dollars a year, cooperatively, to help pay certain wardens and expenses. At the end of the present fiscal year, under the law providing that Government employees shall not receive compensation from certain outside sources, that contribution will be eliminated and we shall probably have to take over the resulting additional expense. We will undoubtedly manage to get along for the year on the appropriation, but we certainly could not get along on any less. As it is we have difficulty in properly caring for the reservations; there are so many of them and they are growing in importance.

The CHAIRMAN. How many reserves are you now maintaining?

Mr. NELSON. We have 74 reserves, of which 4 are for big game, 69 are bird reserves, and 1 is a combination of big game and birds. On these we have 310 buffalo, 274 elk, 55 antelope, and 21 deer. The game is doing finely and increasing rapidly. The Sully Hill Reserve, in North Dakota, is in great need of having some money spent to improve it. It is a popular resort for the people of that region. Thousands of them go there every year, especially on Sundays. People will often gather in from a hundred miles or more and spend Sunday in the shade of the trees. It is the only resort of that character in that region and money is much needed to make necessary improvements there to accommodate the people who visit the place.

The CHAIRMAN. Your next is on page 174, item 36, for investigating the food habits of North American birds, and so forth. There is no change in that amount?

Mr. NELSON. There is no change in that amount. That item covers our investigations into the relations of birds to agriculture, and also the investigations concerning our game birds and their food habits. The experts in this work are also used in determining the best methods of destroying birds that are injurious to agriculture, such as the blackbirds, which are really becoming a great pest, destroying enormous quantities of grain of various kinds in different parts of the country.

Mr. WILSON. What are you doing now to destroy them?

Mr. NELSON. We are trying to devise some method of poisoning. We have had fair success in poisoning these birds when they come into the cornfields.

Mr. WILSON. How much money are you spending, all told; can you tell?

Mr. NELSON. No; that would be difficult, offhand, but for the blackbird investigation perhaps $800. That is one item among a series of similar problems which we have.

The CHAIRMAN. What about your ground-squirrel work; are you getting along pretty well with that?

Mr. NELSON. We are getting along well with that work; I might say extremely well. We have regular rodent organizations in 14 States. In 12 States we are doing work sporadically as people ask for it, and 5 other States have asked us to create a regular rodent organization with a man in charge. Oklahoma is one of these States. This morning I received a letter from the county agent in Ellis County stating that the loss from jack rabbits in his county the past season had been at least $100,000 and asking us if we could not do something to help. We are sending a man there and to other points in Oklahoma to arrange for organized cooperation with the State extension service. We have had many reports of heavy losses from prairie dogs and other rodents in addition to those by jack rabbits. Our work in destroying rodents has been so successful that wherever we have initiated it there has been an immediate response by rapidly increasing cooperation, including both personal services and contributions of money. The money is from States, counties, and private individuals or organizations. The past season over $730,000 was contributed to that work in the Western States.

The CHAIRMAN. That looks like it is meeting with very great favor.

Mr. NELSON. The States are rapidly increasing this work. Wherever the rodent campaigns are being conducted each season shows a large increase in cooperation of the farmers over the last. One farmer writes he is convinced that for every dollar spent in that work there is $20 benefit to the farmer, and that opinion runs all over the West. There is very great chance for public benefit from this work, since the losses of crops and forage from rodents in this country are about $300,000,000 a year. Our work is showing that it is perfectly practicable to absolutely eliminate some of the worst rodent pests. This will require a number of years, of course, because they cover a tremendous territory.

The CHAIRMAN. What about your work on rabies?

Mr. NELSON. It may be interesting to the committee to know that since the rabies outbreak in the West 1,437 people have been bitten by rabid animals and treated by State officials. In addition, 47 people have died from the disease. Nearly every man who is bitten would die if not given the Pasteur treatment. In addition to those mentioned above, many people have been treated by private physicians; just how many is unknown.

The CHAIRMAN. What progress are you making?

Mr. NELSON. Coyotes are the most active animals in spreading rabies. We have reduced them so greatly in that territory that we are holding the disease down and preventing its spread. For instance, as soon as the man in charge hears of an outbreak, say in Nevada, he immediately concentrates into that locality a number of his best trappers and they at once exterminate as many coyotes and other predatory animals as possible. That procedure has again and again stamped out an outbreak of rabies and prevented its spread. If not promptly checked in this way the disease will be spread rapidly by wandering animals through a large area.

The CHAIRMAN. I understand you have had considerable receipts.

Mr. NELSON. We have, from the skins of predatory animals killed by our men. The skins taken by the Government hunters are Government property and have been sold by a large firm in St. Louis in their great fur sales. The money derived in that way from our skins has been turned into the Treasury. In 1918, $96,000 were turned in to the United States Treasury from this source, a by-product of our predatory-animal campaign.

Mr. WILSON. What animals, mostly?

Mr. NELSON. Coyotes, wolves, bobcats, and mountain lions. We have killed more than 200,000 of these predatory animals since we began the work, and have actually taken the skins of more than 80,000 and have poisoned others by the tens of thousands. Great poisoning campaigns are organized by dividing a region into districts, to each of which is allotted a skilled foreman with a gang of men to spread the poisoned bait out in all places frequented by the coyotes. The animals take the baits and are killed. As an outcome the coyotes almost all disappear from that section, and in the spring when the snow goes off hundreds of coyote carcasses are found. We had a record of 160 in one valley and have had reports of varying numbers from a few to more than a hundred in other localities, therefore we know positively we have killed them in enormous numbers. In Utah one of the sheep men on whose range we poisoned last winter told me that from the reports of his sheep herders he was satisfied we had killed a coyote for every section of land in his section of the State. Reports from other counties showed the same results. On that basis of a coyote to a section in the areas poisoned we had killed over 20,000 coyotes in Utah last winter.

We have another source of income from our mammal-pest work that is very interesting. Some years ago there were reports of serious damage to agriculture from a mole in Oregon. We sent a man out there who investigated the habits of the animal and devised a simple method of trapping it. The fur of these moles is very beautiful. We soon interested the fur dealers and thus created a market for it. As a result, last summer boys' and girls' mole trapping clubs organized by our representative, working with the county agents, sold $30,000 worth of skins.

The CHAIRMAN. How much do they sell for apiece?

Mr. NELSON. Up to 40 cents apiece; they are a much better quality of skin than the European mole. So our farmers in Oregon may get rid of their mole pest and make money at it.

The CHAIRMAN. Page 146, for biological investigations; there is no change in that?

Mr. NELSON. There is no change in that. This is fundamental work covering the scientific, technical investigations of the bureau. Through this work we learn the precise kind of bird or mammal we are dealing with and its distribution and habits.

The CHAIRMAN. Mr. McLaughlin offers the following resolution:

Resolved, That through respect to the memory of Ex-President Theodore Roosevelt, whose interment is to take place at 1.45 p. m., the committee do now adjourn until 2.30 p. m.

AFTER RECESS.

The committee reconvened at 2.30 p. m. pursuant to recess.

The CHAIRMAN. As I must be absent for a few minutes I will ask Mr. Lee to take the chair.

Mr. LEE (in the chair). The committee will come to order, and Dr. Nelson will continue his statement.

STATEMENT OF MR. E. W. NELSON, CHIEF OF THE BUREAU OF BIOLOGICAL SURVEY, UNITED STATES DEPARTMENT OF AGRICULTURE—Continued.

Mr. LEE. Dr. Nelson, what item were you on when we recessed?

Mr. NELSON. I think we had completed everything up to page 177.

Mr. LEE. That is where I understood we ceased examining you before lunch. Did you complete your statement in regard to item 38, on page 177?

Mr. NELSON. Except for a supplemental statement that I wish to make after I am through with the regular list here up to item 38.

Mr. THOMPSON. You had not made any statement on item 38, as I understood it?

Mr. NELSON. No; that is the one I am taking up now.

Mr. LEE. Yes; item 38, page 177.

Mr. NELSON. This is to cover the administration of the migratory bird act and it is agreed, as I understood this morning, to include under it the item of $22,000 to be appropriated for the Lacey Act, in order to make the administration of both more effective.

Mr. LEE. That is in connection with item 38. I think we agreed that you should furnish the committee a statement on that?

Mr. NELSON. Yes. I will do this later. The appropriation for the migratory bird work the present fiscal year is $50,000, the estimates here ask for an increase of $125,000 for the work. The situation at the present is——

Mr. LEE (interposing). Is that really an increase or a transfer?

Mr. NELSON. It is an increase. The situation under this law is now very difficult from the fact that we are able at the outside to employ only about 15 Federal game wardens for the entire United States. The State game officials are cooperating with us on the most friendly terms, but at the same time they ask that the Government place itself in a position to be able to do something in the States with them in helping to administer the Federal law. They all admit that it is a good thing. At first many were rather doubtful about it, but now perhaps one or two States are pulling back a little, but certainly 45 out of the 48 States are with us in this work and appreciate the benefits that are arising from the administration and enforcement of the migratory-bird act. It is increasing the game. A letter that I received this morning from the State game warden of Maryland says he was on the Susquehanna Flats early this season and found an enormous number of wild fowl there. Resident gunners of the State told him they had not seen anything like the number of wild fowl for years. There seems to have been a steady increase since the Federal Government enacted a law protecting wild fowl.

Mr. LEE. You think this legislation has brought that condition about?

Mr. NELSON. There is no question about it. Everybody admits it. We have received hundreds and hundreds of letters from State game wardens and others all over the country on the subject, and they are almost a unit in saying that the Federal law has caused the increase of wild fowl. When this law was passed the number of wild fowl was decreasing so rapidly that there was a general feeling in the country that it would be only a few years until we would have no wild fowl left unless something was done. The Federal law was enacted to try to effect a remedy, and that it has effected a remedy is evidenced by the reports.

Mr. ANDERSON. How do you expect to organize a force as provided for in this item?

Mr. NELSON. We now have a few Federal game wardens covering several States each. What we desire is to put Federal wardens in each of the important States, and then to pay in some cases a part of the salary of deputy State game wardens, who shall also be deputy United States game wardens, and let these men work for us and for their States at the same time. We will perhaps pay these men $300 a year who are already engaged in the States game service, and they will devote a part of their time to the Federal work. We do not ever expect to provide a warden service comparable in number with all the State game warden service. It would cost too much, and will not be needed, to provide such a large number of employees; but by utilizing the services of State game wardens, and paying a part of their salaries, and having one man in a State to direct the work, we can undoubtedly get most efficient service. The State game wardens in practically all States where the States laws will permit of this arrangement, approve of the plan.

Mr. ANDERSON. I had the impression that much of this work is seasonal in character; are these men employed the year round?

Mr. NELSON. They are employed the year round—that is, the regular men. In the first place it is not only for the open season for game, which is, of course, seasonal in character, but in the spring and summer, when the season is closed, it is necessary to protect the birds, especially in breeding areas. There is a prohibition against shooting birds in the spring, and more care is needed then than at any other time. We also have to protect our insectivorous birds, which are killed recklessly in a great many parts of the country.

Mr. ANDERSON. I take it that the protection of game birds is more or less seasonal and regional as well. I was wondering what these men did the year round?

Mr. NELSON. In addition to preventing the illegal killing of game and useful insectivorous birds they do educational work. They are organizing their districts and bringing the public to appreciate the need of protection; they are conservation missionaries, in other words. Under the present $50,000 appropriation an amazing amount of good has been accomplished simply in an educational way. We have changed sentiment in considerable areas of the country toward better game protection through a wider dissemination of the facts among sportsmen and other people. The permanent men will be usefully occupied throughout the year. Permanent employment is the only way in which you can get effective service—to have men continually in the work who are specialists. If you pick up men temporarily you can not get satisfactory service; for good men would have steady employment and it would be necessary to take on men whose usefulness would be decidedly doubtful.

Mr. McKINLEY. I am from Illinois, where we have a State game warden and other wardens, and the others are paid $900 a year. There is not one for every county, but one for a certain number of counties. What is your idea about cooperating there?

Mr. NELSON. If we have the funds we would ask the State game warden to recommend a few of his best men, who would be appointed deputy Federal game warden, and who would receive a part of their salary from the Government and a part from the State. In Illinois, however, the State constitution has been interpreted to prohibit such combined State and Federal employment, and we would have to pay full salaries to all our men there.

Mr. McKINLEY. I understand; but, for instance, I think I could safely say there are probably 50 of these men in Illinois. They cover certain districts—say they have two counties each. How would you cooperate in a case like that?

Mr. NELSON. We could not pay salaries to but a few men, but we could enlarge the number of cooperating wardens by making a large number of deputy wardens at $1 a month, who could keep us informed of conditions in their territory. We have now, I think, about 200 deputy State wardens that we are paying $1 a month as deputy Federal game wardens. They furnish us information as to violations of the Federal law, and, when necessary, we send a Federal warden to their district to investigate. In the case such as you mention we would do the same thing to a larger extent. These deputy State game wardens cover their States, and we would have the dollar-a-month men working as an intelligence service, assisting the regularly salaried wardens. The sharing of salaries by the Federal administration would enable the employment of more wardens and secure more effective conservation of our game and insectivorous bird resources.

Mr. RUBEY. Wouldn't you get better service if you paid them a dollar a year, or more especially, put them on a higher plane?

Mr. NELSON. As an example of the desirability of the dollar-a-month deputies, I may cite the situation in one of the Western States. The State game service there at first had been rather doubtful as to the value of the Federal law, but after the passage of the migratory-bird treaty act they became convinced of its usefulness, and have asked as a favor that we give them a considerably larger number of deputies at a dollar a month or even a dollar a year than we planned. This arrangement is serving well for the Federal and State administration.

Mr. LEE. Do you find that your regulations often conflict with the State law?

Mr. NELSON. In some States they do, but in a considerable number of the States they are practically the same.

Mr. THOMPSON. In this sum of money do you propose to use some of it to enforce the criminal laws of the United States with reference to destruction of migratory fowls?

Mr. NELSON. To see that the law is obeyed; and where a man disobeys it, of course, he becomes liable to prosecution in the Federal courts.

Mr. THOMPSON. What control does the Department of Justice have over the enforcement of this statute?

Mr. NELSON. When we find a case it is turned over to the Department of Justice for prosecution. The cases are handled by the United States attorneys before the Federal courts. Of course, our wardens have the power to make arrests and take offenders before United States courts for examination.

Mr. THOMPSON. You do all the investigating and ascertainment of the facts and then simply turn it over to the district attorney after the case is made?

Mr. NELSON. Yes; that is it.

Mr. THOMPSON. This migratory-bird act has been declared unconstitutional, has it not?

Mr. NELSON. No. The present migratory-bird treaty act, which was passed last year by Congress, repealed the old migratory-bird act, and the constitutionality of the old act was before the Supreme Court at the time. When the treaty act was passed by Congress and the old act was repealed the question of its constitutionality ceased to be of any particular interest. Therefore the Attorney General asked that that case be dismissed, because it was no longer a live issue.

Mr. THOMPSON. The Supreme Court has dismissed it?

Mr. NELSON. Yes; but it passed no judgment on the merits of the case.

Mr. THOMPSON. It had been held unconstitutional by the United States Court for the Western [Eastern?] District of Arkansas.

Mr. NELSON. Yes; but Judge Trieber, the author of that decision regarding the old law, has recently fined a man for violating the present migratory bird treaty act.

Mr. THOMPSON. I do not know whether you are a lawyer and will pass on it, that if by treaty you can do a thing you can do the same thing by statute?

Mr. NELSON. I am not a lawyer, but whether the old law was or was not constitutional remains undecided. The Constitution of the United States declares a treaty to be the supreme law of the land, and we are now acting under the treaty with Great Britain.

Mr. THOMPSON. It has been held unconstitutional by other courts besides the Arkansas Federal court, has it not?

Mr. NELSON. Not this new law.

Mr. THOMPSON. I mean the old law.

Mr. NELSON. The old law was upheld by several convictions under it, while a few courts held it unconstitutional.

Mr. THOMPSON. One attempts to do by treaty what the other did by statute?

Mr. NELSON. Practically yes.

Mr. RUBEY. How long had the case been in the Supreme Court?

Mr. NELSON. About two years, I think.

Mr. RUBEY. They waited and let us pass a new law before they passed upon it?

Mr. NELSON. I do not know what the reason was for the delay. The case was argued before the Supreme Court and later a new hearing was ordered.

(Mr. Lever resumes the chair.)

Mr. THOMPSON. A treaty would not have any more force than a statute, would it? You are asking this additional sum of $125,000, and the transfer of the $22,000 from another fund, to enforce the provisions of this treaty, which is similar to the statute that the court dismissed; that is, the case was dismissed under that particular act that came up from the western [eastern?] district of Arkansas seeking to enforce the provisions of that act?

Mr. NELSON. A treaty by the Constitution becomes the supreme law of the land. We still desire the $22,000 for the Lacey Act, but wish to have it transferred under the migratory bird appropriation in order that the two may be administered together; so that we can use a man and pay a part out of one fund and a part out of the other in cooperative service. We will still need $22,000 for the Lacey Act, but by this transfer we can get bigger results out of the $22,000. We now have five men under the Lacey Act, and by paying a part of the salaries out of this fund and a part of the salaries out of the other fund, we can get a larger number of employees covering a larger territory and will secure more effective results than ever before possible. That is the only object in having this transfer made—simply to unite the administration of the two funds for increased efficiency.

Mr. RUBEY. Just a question there on the matter of administration: It was stated here in committee the other day by some one that wild pigeons had returned and have been discovered here and there. Have you any information along that line?

Mr. NELSON. Yes; we are receiving correspondence on that subject all the time, and of course it is constantly coming up for discussion in the newspapers.

Mr. RUBEY. Are they really putting in an appearance?

Mr. NELSON. I do not think they are. The question constantly comes up, and well-meaning people honestly believe the birds have been seen. The band-tailed pigeon of the Rocky Mountains and Pacific Coast, a very different bird, is often seen and thereupon many people report wild pigeons have left the east and gone west. Others see the common mourning dove under peculiar circumstances and believe them to be the wild pigeon. So far there is no evidence that any competent person has reported to have seen a wild pigeon in recent years. For three years there was a standing reward of $1,000 for any one who would take a competent naturalist and show him a wild pigeon's nest. That reward was never called for, and I think that quite definitely disposes of the claim that there were any wild pigeons left.

Mr. HAUGEN. What is the object of the Federal Government paying a part of the salaries of State game wardens?

Mr. NELSON. Simply so that we can have the services of an increased number of wardens at a smaller outlay of money than would be possible if we had to pay full salary. We will employ those men who are already in the business, and who are expert in that business, and the Government will get the benefit thereof at a small rate.

Mr. HAUGEN. Isn't the Federal Government getting the benefit of the services of these people now?

Mr. NELSON. No.

Mr. HAUGEN. Why not?

Mr. NELSON. A State warden can not follow up Federal cases unless he is authorized by the secretary and his expenses are paid by the Federal Government. The object is to get that service.

Mr. HAUGEN. Aren't the States interested?

Mr. NELSON. They are interested; but the whole object of the Federal law was to more effectually conserve our game and insectivorous birds. In other words, the Federal law was enacted in order to supplement the work of the States, because of the fact that the individual States, through failure to act together, had failed in sufficiently protecting the migratory birds, as shown by the fact that the birds were decreasing alarmingly in numbers. The Federal law has been markedly influential in stopping the decrease in wild fowl and starting an increase, which has gone on ever since. So satisfactory has been the effect of the Federal law that State game wardens who at first were doubtful or critical as to the Federal law have become practically a unit in favor of it.

Mr. HAUGEN. Here is a proposition to employ people who have proven a failure, then?

Mr. NELSON. The failure to protect migratory birds properly by State laws was largely due to the local character of the laws and administration. The fact that a man can be taken into a Federal court and punished for illegally killing game or other birds is a powerful deterrent and will vastly increase the strength of the State game administration, as has already been demonstrated.

Mr. HAUGEN. If the violator is punished, it is not the employees of the Government, is it?

Mr. NELSON. No; but if the Federal wardens and deputies are scattered around in the various States it will have a wonderfully beneficial effect in conserving and increasing our bird life.

Mr. HAUGEN. They are already in the service of the States?

Mr. NELSON. Yes; but State funds can not well be spent to enforce a Federal law.

Mr. HAUGEN. They will help, just the same?

Mr. NELSON. In a way; but they have no authority to enforce the Federal law unless appointed by the Federal Government.

Mr. HAUGEN. Well, all of them are working with the one end in view—to enforce the laws, State and Federal?

Mr. NELSON. The game service everywhere needs all the men it can get in order to properly conserve our game, and the Federal Government will merely in the enforcement of this law use money to build up the game resources of the States.

Mr. RUBEY. It is a matter of economy?

Mr. NELSON. Yes.

Mr. HAUGEN. The statement is that the States need their services; and now you propose to take them away from the States and devote a part of their time to the Federal Government?

The CHAIRMAN. It is a matter of economy and efficiency, isn't it, Dr. Nelson?

Mr. NELSON. Yes.

The CHAIRMAN. We will simply get the advantage of their experience and services at an economical rate?

Mr. NELSON. Yes.

Mr. HAUGEN. I do not see why the Federal Government should step in and pay a part of their salaries?

Mr. NELSON. That will enable the States to employ more men, and the States are nearly all short of money.

Mr. HAUGEN. Isn't it safe to leave to the States to determine the number of men they shall have?

Mr. NELSON. You can, from that point of view, but the more thoroughly the States are policed in this regard the more your game resources will increase. Furthermore, practically every State game warden of the many I have consulted is heartily in favor of the plan.

Mr. HAUGEN. How much are you going to use for the employment of men?

Mr. NELSON. The most of this 125,000 will be used in the States in adding to our field force.

Mr. HAUGEN. The larger part of it will go to pay men by adding to their State salaries?

Mr. NELSON. No; we will put in a larger number of Federal wardens on full salary from the Government, as well as a number of men whose salaries will be paid in part. Only a minor part of this $125,000 will go to State wardens.

Mr. HAUGEN. How many have you now, and how many do you propose to have?

Mr. NELSON. We have about 200 State wardens that are getting a dollar a month.

Mr. HAUGEN. I mean men on the regular pay roll?

Mr. NELSON. I believe there are 15 men on the regular pay roll.
Mr. HAUGEN. How many do you propose to add?
Mr. NELSON. There will be nearly 50 regular wardens.
Mr. HAUGEN. Outside of the State wardens?
Mr. NELSON. Yes.
Mr. HAUGEN. How many in the States?
Mr. NELSON. There will be nearly 50 State wardens employed at small salaries.
Mr. HAUGEN. At about what salary?
Mr. NELSON. From $200 to $300 a year.
Mr. HAUGEN. Has the question of the constitutionality of this treaty act from that standpoint ever been questioned?
Mr. NELSON. No; no question has been raised. There have been a number of convictions under it, and the courts have supported it so far. Judge Trieber, as already stated has supported it.
Mr. THOMPSON. The question of constitutionality has been raised in all those cases?
Mr. NELSON. The question has not been raised.
Mr. THOMPSON. It has been raised in the trial court but not carried on up?
Mr. NELSON. It has not been raised so far as we know.
Mr. WILSON. In North and South Dakota it has been raised, has it not?
Mr. NELSON. Under this law?
Mr. WILSON. Under the old law?
Mr. NELSON. I am not sure about that.
Mr. THOMPSON. It has been raised in the trial court in some States, I know.
Mr. NELSON. It has been raised as to the old law, but so far as we are informed it has not been raised as to the new law.
Mr. THOMPSON. Then they may just as well plead guilty now?
Mr. NELSON. I think the question may possibly be raised in time.
The CHAIRMAN. How much does Canada spend in enforcing its treaty?
Mr. NELSON. I do not know.
The CHAIRMAN. Any further questions?
Mr. HAUGEN. In the opinion of your attorneys, is there any question of constitutionality in this matter?
Mr. NELSON. I think I can give you a very definite answer on that. Under the old law our solicitor in the Department of Agriculture and the assistant solicitor had doubts as to its constitutionality. But when we were preparing the migratory-bird treaty and the act for its enforcement they investigated the question thoroughly, going into all the law regarding the subject, and became absolutely convinced that it is constitutional, and that is the opinion of a great many lawyers we have heard from on the subject.
Mr. WILSON. I was absent when you made the statement, if you made it, and want to ask a question: How many new men are you asking for under this section for game wardens?
Mr. NELSON. All told, over the United States there will be, of the regular full-salaried game wardens, about 50.
Mr. WILSON. You have now how many?
Mr. NELSON. We now have 15.

Mr. WILSON. An increase of 35 men?
Mr. NELSON. Yes.
Mr. HAUGEN. You said a minute ago that you expected to add 50 men?
Mr. NELSON. That was an unintentional misstatement.
Mr. HAUGEN. You would add 50 men to the force?
Mr. NELSON. No; there will be about 50, all told, including the present force.
Mr. HAUGEN. Then you add 35? Let us get that straight.
Mr. NELSON. Yes; practically that.
Mr. WILSON. And you have provision for other men?
Mr. NELSON. That is to get the assistance of men—mainly deputy State game wardens.
Mr. WILSON. How many of them will you employ?
Mr. NELSON. About 50.
Mr. WILSON. How much will they get?
Mr. NELSON. Those 50 men from $200 to $300 a year.
Mr. WILSON. They will just be working in the hunting season?
Mr. NELSON. Some of them all through the year, at places where we feel we ought to have some one.
Mr. WILSON. They would be men on full pay?
Mr. NELSON. Oh, no; only $20 or $25 a month from the Federal Government.
Mr. WILSON. They will be men you will hire around in localities?
Mr. NELSON. They will be distributed to cover the States. In addition, we will have a considerable number at $1 a month, who will furnish information from territory where we have no regular deputies.
Mr. WILSON. Will these dollar-a-month men be anything like the dollar-a-year men we have had in Washington during the war?
Mr. NELSON. Not necessarily.
The CHAIRMAN. Is there anything further, gentlemen? If not, take up the next item, Dr. Nelson, on page 178, for general administrative expenses, $10,760. There is no change in that?
Mr. NELSON. No change except in the matter of transfer of men to the statutory roll.
The CHAIRMAN. Is there anything further that you wish to discuss, Dr. Nelson?
Mr. NELSON. Yes, Mr. Chairman, I would like now to call the attention of the committee to the matter of the emergency appropriation that we have this year. We have $225,000——
The CHAIRMAN. Have they been asked for in these estimates?
Mr. NELSON. No; they have not been estimated.
The CHAIRMAN. Well, we will not discuss that at all.

AGRICULTURE APPROPRIATION BILL.

Committee on Agriculture,
House of Representatives,
Thursday, January 9, 1919.

The committee met at 10.30 o'clock a. m., Hon. Asbury F. Lever (chairman) presiding.

DIVISION OF PUBLICATIONS.

The CHAIRMAN. The committee will come to order. Turn to page 182 of the Book of Estimates, and we will take up this morning the Division of Publications. Mr. Secretary Ousley is here to present the estimates of this division.

STATEMENT OF MR. CLARENCE OUSLEY, ASSISTANT SECRETARY, UNITED STATES DEPARTMENT OF AGRICULTURE.

The CHAIRMAN. Mr. Secretary, I believe you have some new places under this appropriation? In looking over your list I do not see any new places suggested.

Mr. OUSLEY. There are some new places suggested on page 185 in this book. You refer to page 182. That is where the Division of Publications begin. Then you will find, on page 185, mention of some new places which I would like to discuss for a few minutes.

The CHAIRMAN. All right; go ahead. You will notice that, gentlemen, about the middle of the page.

Mr. OUSLEY. To begin with, there is one chief editor, item 63, on page 185. We have been compelled to work out some reorganization of the Division of Publications under these war activities, and in recognition of the enlarged work of the division under normal circumstances and in anticipation of the continued enlarged work of the division, we have had heretofore a manuscript committee and still have that committee for counsel, consisting of representative men of the department, to pass upon the manuscripts that come from the various bureaus. It is impossible for a group of men of that kind to sit around a table and put a manuscript in shape. It is necessary to have an editor, and we have had an editor under these activities for the last year and a half in the person of Mr. Reid, who has since the beginning of the fiscal year been made Chief of the Division of Publications.

It is necessary now to find a man to take Mr. Reid's place, which pays $2,750. We have been trying very diligently for the last six months to get a man capable of doing that work, and we have failed so far.

Mr. MCLAUGHLIN. Was Mr. Reid formerly in the service and promoted from some other place in the department?

Mr. OUSLEY. Yes; he has been in the service quite a long while. He was made Chief of the Division of Publications at the beginning of this fiscal year. I am going to ask the committee to raise that item for chief editor to $3,000, because we can not get a man at $2,750.

The CHAIRMAN. You want to make that $3,000?

Mr. OUSLEY. Yes, sir. It takes an all-round, capable news editor with a knowledge of agriculture to handle the publications. I feel that I am warranted in asking that. In the last two years we have greatly improved the character of the publications of that kind by careful editing. It takes not only a man of fine discriminating judgment, but one who has a knowledge of agriculture, a very thorough knowledge of agriculture as well.

Mr. McLAUGHLIN. What was Mr. Reid's former work?

Mr. OUSLEY. He was chief editor on the Secretary's roll when he was promoted to this office of chief of the Division of Publications.

The CHAIRMAN. You have no editor for the Division of Publications?

Mr. OUSLEY. No, sir; we have not had one at all. The original office, you know, Mr. Chairman, was chief and editor.

The CHAIRMAN. Yes; I remember.

Mr. OUSLEY. But the talent for administrative work does not necessarily involve the talent for editing. That was sufficient while the business of the division was small, but it is not sufficient now. It is like a country newspaper where the one man is printer and editor. As his business grows he enlarges and finally has a printer and another editor and, when it gets still larger, he has to have a business manager as well; and then when it gets still larger he has to have a news editor. This work is expanded in this way in our Division of Publications, and the time has come when we must have a man as chief editor in the Department of Agriculture.

The CHAIRMAN. Is it the purpose of the Department of Agriculture to have these bulletins written in an easy, interesting way?

Mr. OUSLEY. That is precisely the object of this position.

The CHAIRMAN. Well considerable complaint has been made about most of the bulletins that have heretofore been issued because they have been written in such language that the average man does not understand them; they were not interesting; they were all right from the scientific standpoint but not for the average man.

Mr. OUSLEY. A great many of those scientific papers were prepared for scientific men, but the popular publications can be made much more interesting by having them written in an easy conversational style.

The CHAIRMAN. Item No. 64, superintendent of distribution; what is your idea on that?

Mr. OUSLEY. The work has expanded to the extent where it needs a general superintendent to oversee its activities, to select and direct the employees, and he should be a man specially qualified as an expert in distribution. The problem of distributing literature is a very serious one—to get it to the right place, to get it promptly dispatched. That requires a man of particular training, and we have found a man under the stimulating agriculture appropriation in the person of Mr. Cleary. We have made that position under the stimulating agriculture act.

Mr. McLaughlin. He has been in the service a long time?

Mr. Ousley. He was the head of the section in the division. This position we wish to make a statutory one. We have made this position under stimulating agriculture, and we want to retain it in our new organization.

Mr. Wilson. I guess every Member of Congress knows Mr. Cleary quite well, because he has appeared here on numerous occasions, and——

Mr. Ousley. I think so; yes.

Mr. Wilson (continuing). I expect, from the work he has done for all of us.

The Chairman. Then we come to the item which calls for three additional clerks of class 3.

Mr. Ousley. Yes, sir; those are simply to provide, Mr. Chairman, for the increase in responsibilities of that division by getting three men of a little higher class than class 2 for the responsible work. You would be interested if you spent a day there to see the large number of inquiries that come in for information on a subject, for instance, without naming the bulletin. Now, it takes something more than an ordinary clerk to find that particular bulletin. If he has not the intelligence to do it, he has got to refer the requests to various bureaus, and that involves a great deal of delay. For instance, suppose a man in Texas writes in for information about breeding sheep. He wents to get an answer quickly. If you have not a man of some intelligence, above the $1,200 clerk, he has to refer that to the Bureau of Animal Industry to find out what bulletin will fit. We need some man of larger intelligence who can acquaint himself with the general class of bulletins and furnish that information without having to refer the inquiries to the bureaus. I mention that as only one instance, but I could give you many of them.

The Chairman. I notice you have only one clerk in class 3 on the present statutory roll.

Mr. Ousley. Yes, sir.

The Chairman. That would give you four, would it not?

Mr. Ousley. That would give us four altogether. I would like to ask, Mr. Chairman, before we get away from this particular subject, that you insert an item for one machine foreman at the same price. We are using now, increasingly, a great many of these labor-saving machines, and men have developed great skill in the use of them. They have become almost as important in an office of this kind as the linotype machines, and we need to increase the salary in order to get a skilled man. We also need to increase, as we go on, these following positions here, some of the present positions, for the same purpose. We need at least a $1,600 man to act as foreman of the machines, as we can not get a man who is familiar with them for any less. It requires more or less mechanical knowledge and more or less business knowledge, and that same observation applies to that whole range of places following.

The Chairman. Mr. Secretary, as a matter of fact, item No. 65 does not provide for any new places exactly, but it represents the promotion of a few deserving employees, as I understand it; that is, you are dropping some of the low-grade places and taking on some higher-grade positions?

Mr. Ousley. Yes, sir.

The CHAIRMAN. So that, strictly speaking, they are not new places.

Mr. OUSLEY. Strictly speaking, they are not.

The CHAIRMAN. I notice on page 186 five machine operators at $1,200 each. Those are new places?

Mr. OUSLEY. The idea is to get proficient operators for these machines and to keep them. Heretofore we have been compelled to use low-salaried laborers, usually our messenger boys, and train them to run those machines. As soon as we get them trained they are in constant demand by the commercial concerns and other bureaus or other departments of the Government at a salary of $1,200 or more. We take a boy and teach him to run a mimeograph machine and only pay him $700 or $800, and very soon he is a very skilled multigraph or mimeograph operator, and some other fellow picks him up, or some other department, or some commercial concern picks him up at a much higher salary. It is therefore necessary for us to have a grade of machine operators and pay them higher in order to hold them.

Mr. THOMPSON. You answered, in response to Mr. Lever's question, that these were not promotions; they were the appointing of new men at a higher salary and stopping these lower-class men. What do you propose to do with them when you drop them?

Mr. OUSLEY. Some are going out because of the present wages, and we will get better men for them.

Mr. THOMPSON. You mean you are abolishing these places, and those men are not going out; you are just dropping them arbitrarily?

Mr. OUSLEY. As they go out.

The CHAIRMAN. You drop the place?

Mr. OUSLEY. Yes, sir; you see, there is a great demand for any people of skill along this line, and the Division of Publications has seemed to serve as a recruiting ground for other bureaus and other departments.

The CHAIRMAN. Anything further on that, gentlemen? I notice among the general expense items, on page 187, the item in which you have asked for a small increase of $1,500 for labor-saving machinery, including necessary supplies.

Mr. OUSLEY. Yes.

The CHAIRMAN. I presume that is on account of the increased work of the department?

Mr. OUSLEY. Not only that, Mr. Lever, but the improved machinery. There are some new devices that are available now on account of the demobilization of many of these war activities. We can substitute improved machines for some of the machines we now have, and we need some additional ones, and save a great deal of time and labor.

Mr. THOMPSON. You can not buy much machinery for $1,500.

Mr. OUSLEY. What do these machines cost, Mr. Reid?

Mr. REID. Because of the demobilization going on we can get them at much lower figures than formerly.

The CHAIRMAN. What kind of machines are they?

Mr. REID. Addressograph machines, folding machines, universal folding machines.

The CHAIRMAN. And mimeographs, too, I suppose?

Mr. REID. Mimeographs also. There has been an arrangement made with the General Supply Committee whereby departments will be able to buy these machines at a lower cost than the regular market price.

The CHAIRMAN. I see. Your next one, Mr. Secretary, is item 84, where you have asked for an increase of $5,000 for photographic equipment and materials and artist's tools and supplies.

Mr. OUSLEY. I will ask Mr. Reid to answer that question.

The CHAIRMAN. All right, Mr. Reid.

Mr. REID. This additional money would be used in the department's informational and other service. It is mostly photographic equipment. The cost of supplies has increased materially within the last two years, and it requires more money to buy the same amount of supplies.

Mr. OUSLEY. The demands of the newspapers for photographs, prints, and pictures to illustrate their own material and our material.

The CHAIRMAN. What receipts did you have from the sale of these things this past year, Mr. Reid?

Mr. REID. A little over $200.

The CHAIRMAN. How is your moving-picture work getting along?

Mr. OUSLEY. It is making progress, Mr. Chairman. We are going very carefully with it, and are asking for no substantial increase. My recollection is, Mr. Reid, that there is no substantial increase asked for that work under this item, is there?

Mr. REID. No, sir.

Mr. OUSLEY. We are feeling our way in that work and are very much gratified with the progress we are making. We are not planning for any great extension, because we feel it is a field in which we must be very careful lest we trespass on commercial concerns and also lest we go too far in the expenditure of public money. But there is a great demand among the farmers for motion pictures of agricultural operations. We could furnish to-day, if we had them, an almost unnumbered supply for the soldiers in Europe and in our own camps in the intensive training work.

Mr. THOMPSON. What do you mean by having an increased demand on the part of newspapers?

Mr. OUSLEY. The newspapers ask for photographs of the work we are doing in the States or in the department, illustrating the progress of demonstrations or the progress of experiments. We make a great many photographs for our own information and for our own records.

Mr. THOMPSON. You do not advertise or spend any money in advertising, do you?

Mr. OUSLEY. Oh, no; we do not advertise. I will give you an example: Here is a newspaper in my State interested in the suppression of the pink bollworm, or in Florida in the suppression of the citrus canker. They are vitally concerned in it. Our experts have made many photographs and obtained a complete line of information. The newspapers in those sections would welcome copies of those photographs.

Mr. McLAUGHLIN. Do you make a charge for these photographs which you furnish to newspapers?

Mr. OUSLEY. We do not make a charge for it. We ask them to return them. Sometimes they do and sometimes they do not.

Mr. THOMPSON. They make their own cuts?

Mr. OUSLEY. They make their own cuts. In the Office of Information we have lately furnished some composition rubberoid illustrations.

Mr. REID. Composition cuts.

Mr. OUSLEY. Illustrations on composition cuts. But that is a very small item.

Mr. MCLAUGHLIN. You sometimes get your cuts back?

Mr. OUSLEY. Sometimes we do and sometimes we do not. We lend them to the papers and ask them to return them; but some of them are very careless about it, and you can not pursue the matter, because it would involve too much expense.

The CHAIRMAN. All right. Your next item is 85, where you have a small increase for telephone and telegraph bills. I presume that is just a necessary increase due to the extension of the division's work.

Mr. OUSLEY. Just the result of the natural extension of the division.

The CHAIRMAN. And that is true of your next item—wagons, trucks, and so on?

Mr. OUSLEY. Yes, sir.

The CHAIRMAN. And your next item for fees for manuscripts, on page 187; you have an increase there of $1,000.

Mr. OUSLEY. Yes; that is just a sort of a catchall for some things that we anticipate may go beyond any possibility of estimating at the present time.

The CHAIRMAN. What kind of a manuscript could you purchase?

Mr. OUSLEY. Mr. Reid, will you answer that?

Mr. REID. Once in a while a good manuscript comes in which should be published as a Farmers' Bulletin, and unless we have a sufficient fund to pay for it we can not purchase it.

The CHAIRMAN. A manuscript coming from an outsider?

Mr. OUSLEY. From one of the State colleges, for instance, where it has involved some expense in gathering the data. That has been the case two or three times. I remember one very distinctly—a very good manuscript—Pugsley's "Home Drying Plants or Community Drying Plants." He went to considerable expense; and in a case of that kind we ought to reimburse the State college for the expense of collecting the data for our use.

Mr. MCLAUGHLIN. Well, why, in these land-grant colleges and these experiment stations for which the Government has contributed a great deal of money, is it necessary for you to pay for every writing which you get?

Mr. OUSLEY. Sometimes there are expenses involved in getting it out—typing the manuscript and things of that kind.

Mr. MCLAUGHLIN. Do you mean to say that you pay nothing for the brain work of the man who produces the manuscripts? You pay only the actual outlay in money that he has made or that the college has made in his behalf?

Mr. OUSLEY. No; in the instance of Mr. Pugsley in Nebraska—I don't know whether we have ever actually paid anything or not, but there are such cases where a member of the faculty or the extension service will write us a letter and say: "We have some interesting data, but our funds will not allow us to have it collated and digested and typed." They might say: "If you will take care of that expense I will be glad to furnish the data to you." He has it in his records, but he may want to make a trip to confirm some observation, or he may want to come to Washington to confer with us about it. We would not hesitate, if some independent scientist had a manuscript of great value for which he asked a fee of a reasonable amount, to purchase it. But I do not recall any such case as that. Do you know, Mr. Reid?

Mr. REID. There was a case, I think, in connection with some matter prepared in Columbia.

Mr. MCLAUGHLIN. What I was saying was not in any unfriendly criticism but just to get the facts.

Mr. OUSLEY. Most of that outlay will go for the actual expenses of these gentlemen. The men connected with the colleges do not make any charge for their work; they are already paid.

The CHAIRMAN. All right. Thank you, Mr. Secretary.

Mr. THOMPSON. Does the Division of Publication exercise any supervision over the periodical publications of the department—of the different bureaus?

Mr. OUSLEY. The Division of Publication does not any more.

Mr. ANDERSON. Can you say how many periodical publications are issued by the department and the different bureaus?

Mr. OUSLEY. I can get that for you.

Mr. ANDERSON. Well, I have asked Mr. Harrison for a statement and he will submit it.

The CHAIRMAN. I want to ask Mr. Reid whether there is any other point he wants to discuss?

Mr. REID. No, I thank you.

Mr. OUSLEY. Thank you, Mr. Chairman.

AGRICULTURE APPROPRIATION BILL.

COMMITTEE ON AGRICULTURE,
HOUSE OF REPRESENTATIVES,
Wednesday, January 8, 1919.

DIVISION OF ACCOUNTS AND DISBURSEMENTS.

The CHAIRMAN. We next come to the Division of Accounts. Is there any change in that?
Mr. HARRISON. No; except as to places below $2,500.
The CHAIRMAN. We will not consider that now.
Mr. HAUGEN. What are they; salaries?
The CHAIRMAN. There is no increase at all.
Mr. THOMPSON. Except below $2,500.
Mr. HAUGEN. Has there been any increase in salaries, Mr. Harrison?
Mr. HARRISON. There are none in the estimates.
Mr. HAUGEN. In the last year?
Mr. HARRISON. Promotions have been made, of course, as vacancies have occurred, but they have been relatively few.
Mr. HAUGEN. It runs along the same?
Mr. HARRISON. Generally speaking; yes.
Mr. MCKINLEY. Mr. Harrison, I notice, in running over this that there are some new places, are they actually additions to the force?
Mr. HARRISON. No; we insert some new places in the higher grades and drop some in the lower grades.
The CHAIRMAN. We will defer consideration of the Division of Publications until to-morrow inasmuch as the gentleman who will have to present it is out of the city to-day, and will now take up page 189, Bureau of Crop Estimates, in regard to which, I believe, Mr. Estabrook is prepared to speak. We will be glad to hear him.

BUREAU OF CROP ESTIMATES.

STATEMENT OF MR. LEON M. ESTABROOK, CHIEF OF THE BUREAU OF CROP ESTIMATES, UNITED STATES DEPARTMENT OF AGRICULTURE.

The CHAIRMAN. Dr. Estabrook, you have no recommendations for an increase above the $2,500 limit in your statutory roll, have you?
Mr. ESTABROOK. Not on the statutory roll, but in the lump-sum roll there are.
The CHAIRMAN. Let us go down to your general expense item, page 191, item 33.
Mr. ESTABROOK. Item 33?

The CHAIRMAN. Yes; "Salaries and employment of labor in the city of Washington and elsewhere, supplies, telegraph and telephone service, freight and express charges, and all other necessary miscellaneous administrative expenses, $25,980."

Mr. THOMPSON. There are general expenses just above that.

Mr. ESTERBROOK. This provides for lump-sum expenses in Washington, involving an increase of $1,750. As shown in note, $750 of it is for salary increase for three of the administrative officers of the bureau. One of these is Mr. Nat C. Murray, assistant chief of the bureau, and a statistician of recognized standing.

The CHAIRMAN. What is his present salary?

Mr. ESTABROOK. $3,500.

Mr. WILSON. And you want to give him how much?

Mr. ESTABROOK. $3,750. He is assistant chief of the bureau and acting chief of the bureau in the absence of the chief, and is undoubtedly one of the best statisticians in the United States. That is an extremely low salary for a man of his caliber, character, and reputation. He is unquestionably the most valuable man in the bureau. The second officer is Mr. Frank Andrews, chief of the bureau of crop records, which compiles all of the published statistics of foreign countries, and the published statistics, State reports, and private reports that are published in this country. He also is a man of fine ability and an experienced statistician.

Mr. WILSON. Who is the third one?

Mr. ESTABROOK. The third officer is the chief of the division of crop reports, which is the largest division in the bureau and has about 65 clerks, which tabulates and compiles all the scheduled reports which come direct to Washington from the voluntary crop-reporting service, amounting to several million reports during the year.

Mr. WILSON. Who is he?

Mr. ESTABROOK. Mr. Edward C. Crane is chief of the division, and has demonstrated administrative ability of a high order.

The CHAIRMAN. Then, you have $1,000 for stationery?

Mr. ESTABROOK. For additional supplies.

Mr. THOMPSON. What do they pay this last man now?

Mr. ESTABROOK. Mr. Andrews gets $2,500, and it is proposed to give him $2,750; and Mr. Crane gets $2,250, and it is proposed to give him $2,500.

The CHAIRMAN. What about your increase for stationery?

Mr. ESTABROOK. That is an increase of $1,000, which we regard as a very moderate increase in view of the increasing volume of work from year to year and the price conditions prevailing at this time.

The CHAIRMAN. Any other questions, gentlemen? If not, you may take the next item, No. 34, for "salaries, travel, and other necessary expenses of employees out of the city of Washington engaged in field investigations, $233,841."

Mr. ESTABROOK. This item relates to general expenses in the field, and provides for an increase of $42.279.

The CHAIRMAN. All right; explain that increase.

Mr. ESTABROOK. The reasons for this increase are set forth in the notes under the paragraph and are self-explanatory. I do not know that I could add anything to those notes.

Mr. ANDERSON. I want to inquire a little about this when we get around to it.

The CHAIRMAN. Go ahead.

Mr. ANDERSON. I notice one of the items explains that you want $3,600 for the appointment of two assistant truck-crop specialists, at $1,800 each. As I read the note, it looked to me like you were infringing a little on the province of the Bureau of Markets.

Mr. ESTABROOK. The line of demarkation between the Bureau of Crop Estimates and the Bureau of Markets is this: The Bureau of Crop Estimates pays attention only to things on the farm before they leave the farmer or the grower's hands. We estimate how much there is going to be marketed from the farms.

Mr. ANDERSON. The Bureau of Markets is doing that now?

Mr. ESTABROOK. It is not their province to do it.

Mr. ANDERSON. But they are doing it?

Mr. ESTABROOK. I know they are, and it is largely because the Bureau of Crop Estimates has not sufficient money to enable it to supply this information to the Bureau of Markets. But it is within the special province of the Bureau of Crop Estimates to estimate crop production on farms, and the Bureau of Markets is supposed to take up farm products after they leave the farmer's hands and are in the channels of trade.

The CHAIRMAN. Do you know how much the Bureau of Markets is spending now on this?

Mr. ESTABROOK. I do not know, but our work is fundamental to the work of the Bureau of Markets and constitutes an important fundamental relation to the Bureau of Markets, for the Bureau of Markets can not do its work properly unless it can know what the crop is going to be that is to be marketed. About the first thing a man in the Bureau of Markets does, and he can not do otherwise, is to try to obtain information of what the crops is going to be. Properly it is for us to supply this information, and it is for this reason we want the additional truck crop specialists and other increases mentioned in the estimates.

Mr. HAUGEN. Why can not the work be done under one bureau?

Mr. ESTABROOK. All crop-estimating work should be done under one head.

Mr. HAUGEN. Why not take it all over to your place?

Mr. ESTABROOK. It ought to be done.

Mr. HAUGEN. But a part of it is being done in the Bureau of Markets?

Mr. ESTABROOK. Yes; a part of it.

Mr. WILSON. Isn't the Bureau of Markets under the Department of Agriculture?

Mr. ESTABROOK. Yes.

Mr. WILSON. Couldn't that be arranged?

Mr. ESTABROOK. The point about it is this: The Bureau of Markets is doing very important work, and it is one of the most important and valuable branches of the Department of Agriculture to the farmers of this country. It is stronger and has had more money and more men to do these things than the relatively small Bureau of Crop Estimates with its inadequate appropriations.

Mr. WILSON. Why shouldn't they do it in the place of the Bureau of Crop Estimates?

Mr. ESTABROOK. It is not the proper bureau to do it, and for this reason: The Bureau of Markets men are necessarily in contact with sellers, buyers, and dealers, who are not the ones to be depended upon to estimate production, because they are financially interested and consciously or unconsciously are prone to overestimate or underestimate production; they are biased, and frequently get it wrong. It would be impossible for agents of the Bureau of Markets not to be influenced by the concensus of biased opinion with which they come in contact.

Mr. WILSON. You say they are biased?

Mr. ESTABROOK. I can cite a specific instance: The onion crop of Texas. It is a highly specialized crop and grown in a limited area. In 1916 the Bureau of Markets undertook to help the onion people of Texas market their crop, and very properly so; but they also undertook to estimate the production. Our truck-crop specialist had been there and estimated in March that the onion crop, based upon the best information he could get on the ground, would be about 5,100 cars, as I now recall the figures. The agents of the Bureau of Markets were on the ground also, and in close touch with the leading men of that onion organization. It was to their interest to minimize the size of the crop in order to hold up the price——

Mr. THOMPSON (interposing). To whose interests?

Mr. ESTABROOK. To the onion dealers' interest, and very much to their interest, as they thought, to minimize the size of the crop. And they talked that into the represenatives of the Bureau of Markets and got them to believe that the size of that crop would be 3,600 cars. The markets men came out and published that figure, and it was spread broadcast over the country on April 1 that the Department of Agriculture had reduced its estimate from 5,100 to 3,600 cars. Afterwards the shipments came up and up until they finally reached 4,900 cars. That is one way the market men are apt to be misled by interested people.

The CHAIRMAN. What was your estimate?

Mr. ESTABROOK. Five thousand one hundred cars, and theirs was 3,600 cars.

Mr. ANDERSON. You were about 104 per cent of the actual crop, and their estimate was just 73 per cent of the actual crop?

Mr. ESTABROOK. Yes; our estimate was within 5 per cent of final shipments, and their later estimate was more than 25 per cent wrong.

The CHAIRMAN. I notice you have $5,000 for additional traveling expenses for the truck-crop specialists, and then in the note following you have $18,450 for 41 field agents, at $450 each; you add, "The cost of traveling is increasing, and the more intensive inspection necessary requires the hiring of automobiles." How do you distinguish these two items? They look like the same thing to me.

Mr. ESTABROOK. No; the $18,450 is a subhead to the $20,650 for additional traveling expenses of the present field force. The first figure, $20,650, is followed by the subhead, (a) $18,450 for 41 field agents, at $450 each.

The CHAIRMAN. That item, together with $900 for one fruit-crop specialist and two assistants, and $1,300 for inspection trips by administrative officers, makes up the total of $20,650?

Mr. ESTABROOK. Yes.

The CHAIRMAN. I see.

Mr. HAUGEN. How much are you spending now for these truck-crop specialists on estimating work this year?

Mr. ESTABROOK. On truck crops?

Mr. HAUGEN. Yes.

Mr. ESTABROOK. I think approximately $35,000 altogether, including the weekly truck-crop news service.

Mr. HAUGEN. How much does the Bureau of Markets spend—have you any knowledge?

Mr. ESTABROOK. It is hard to say.

The CHAIRMAN. I have made a note to find out, Mr. Haugen.

Mr. ESTABROOK. I might mention another matter in this connection. The Bureau of Markets has had an appropriation of about $60,000 for the past two or three years for reporting on different classes and grades of marketable live stock, especially cattle, hogs, and sheep in the principal live-stock feeding districts and growing sections—that is, the number of stock feeders, and for other purposes. That means live stock on farms that have not gone to the packing centers at all. This phase of the work is crop estimating pure and simple. At the time that item was submitted in the estimates I immediately called attention to the fact that it was crop estimating work and should be in the Bureau of Crop Estimates. We were instructed by the Secretary to get together and cooperate. We did so and formed a cooperative project. Out of that fund the Bureau of Crop Estimates was allotted $500 one year and $1,300 another year, I think, for doing our part of it. We have been getting monthly reports on the increase or decrease of live stock in the principal States. That has been running something over a year, and now the information we are getting has become quite valuable. It shows the percentage of increase or decrease of each class of meat animals month by month during the year. It enables us to forecast pretty well what the probable total increase or decrease is for the whole country. So far as I know these are the principal results we have obtained out of that allotment.

Mr. ANDERSON. I was going to ask you, is the number of live stock on farms properly a part of your work?

Mr. ESTABROOK. Yes; all estimates of live stock and crop production on farms up to the time they are sold and enter the channels of trade.

Mr. ANDERSON. I know that I had a good deal of doubt about that item when it went into the bill for the Bureau of Markets, and my recollection is that we reduced the estimate somewhat. I thought we should have cut it out altogether, or put it under some other bureau.

Mr. ESTABROOK. The phase of the item I mentioned is clearly a crop estimating project.

Another item that has developed in the last year is the seed crop reporting item. Under the emergency appropriation the Bureau of Markets started a project of reporting seed stocks on hand with dealers, which was a very important project during the war because of its relation to the sufficiency of the seed supply. To supplement their reports of seed stocks they began to report on the estimated production of seeds, which was an out and out crop estimate matter. They realized, just as we did, that estimating seed production is a crop-estimating project, but we did not have the money to undertake it and they did. It was understood and agreed when the project was formulated and the work begun that so much of it as relates to estimating seed production should be transferred to the Bureau of Crop Estimates, where it properly belongs, as soon as the Bureau of Crop Estimates is supplied with funds to handle it.

Mr. ANDERSON. Well, I do not know how important that work is, but it struck me that much of it was getting down to a bird-seed proposition—the reporting of crops of relative unimportance, it seemed to me.

Mr. ESTABROOK. Most of these minor crops are of great importance to those who are engaged in the growing of them. While any one of these crops may seem relatively unimportant, they are of great importance in particular sections and in the aggregate their value is great.

The CHAIRMAN. Dr. Estabrook, can you put into the record the amounts expended in estimating each of the crops that your bureau covers—cotton, corn, wheat, oats, trucks, and so forth?

Mr. ESTABROOK. I will attempt to do so. It is a little difficult to do it, for we estimate on about 70 crops and different classes of live stock.

The CHAIRMAN. Take the big crops.

Mr. ESTABROOK. We can get at it approximately.

The CHAIRMAN. I realize that it is rather a difficult proposition but would like to have as near an approximation of the expense as possible.

Mr. ESTABROOK. I will be glad to attempt to do that.

(The statement referred to follows:)

Estimated distribution of cost of crop reporting service, 1918, by crops.

The expenditures from regular appropriations by the Bureau of Crop Estimates, 1918, were as follows:

Crop reporting and estimating	$247,900.87
Crop recording and abstracting	43,612.82
Administration	37,478.44
Total	328,992.13

(Including $10,257.59, 5 and 10 per cent increase of compensation.)

1. *Crop reporting and estimating.*—The crop reporting work is divided into three projects:

(a) General crops and live stock.
(b) Truck-crop investigatins.
(c) Fruit-crop investigations.

The distribution of cost under these projects is estimated as follows:

(a) General crops and live stock.

General crops:

Corn	$23,198
Wheat	22,814
Oats	13,125
Barley	3,878
Rye	6,015
Buckwheat	954
Flaxseed	451
Rice	5,047
Potatoes	9,766
Sweet potatoes	799
Hay	12,671
Tobacco	6,989
Cotton	18,511

General crops—Continued.

Sugar beets	$1,384	
Cane sugar	639	
Maple sugar	415	
Sorghum sirup	116	
Beans	2,424	
Peanuts	1,518	
Sorghums	4,880	
Onions	2,196	
Cabbages	2,461	
Hops	96	
Cranberries	398	
Apples	3,740	
Peaches	2,651	
Pears	2,514	
Oranges	315	
Clover seed	185	
		$150,150

Live stock:

Milch cattle	3,900	
Other cattle	3,900	
Horses and mules	3,900	
Swine	4,875	
Sheep	2,925	
		19,500

Total for regular inquiries		$169,650

Special inquiries:

General crops	24,500	
Live stock (in cooperation with Bureau of Markets)	5,000	
Total for special inquiries		29,500

Total for general crops and live stock		$199,150

(b) Truck-crop investigations.

This project deals with the commercial crop only:

Cabbages	5,400	
Onions	5,400	
Watermelons	1,790	
Cantaloupes	1,790	
Potatoes (early)	3,590	
Strawberries	1,790	
Tomatoes	3,590	
Canning crops	3,590	
Weekly news service	5,400	
Miscellaneous truck crops	3,635	
		35,975

(c) Fruit-crop investigations (commercial crop only):

Apples	9,580	
Peaches	3,195	
		12,775

Total for crop reporting and estimating	247,900

2. *Crop recording and abstracting.*—This item covers the maintenance of what is considered the largest library of agricultural statistics in the world—the collection, summarization, translation, analysis, and interpretation of world-wide data on agricultural production and consumption, exports and imports data. A very large amount of work was done under this project during the past year in supplying special information required by the Secretary of Agriculture, the Food Administration, and other governmental agencies concerned in the problem of food supplies.

The above figures represent the expenditures from the regular appropriation of the Bureau of Crop Estimates. These funds were augmented by an allotment of $61,397 from the appropriation for stimulating agricultural production, necessary to meet the increased cost of travel, the employment of clerks in Washington and in the offices of field agents, the purchase of modern office equipment for field agents, and for stationery used in special investigations. The extra funds so provided represented approximately 20 per cent of the total cost of the crop-reporting service during the fiscal year 1918 and enabled the bureau not only to increase by 56 per cent the number of schedules mailed over the number mailed the preceding year, but made possible a much greater degree of efficiency in getting important information quickly and disseminating it widely.

The total number of schedules mailed during the fiscal year 1918 was approximately 3,200,000.

Mr. WILSON. How long have you been estimating these crops?
Mr. ESTABROOK. The bureau?
Mr. WILSON. Yes.
Mr. ESTABROOK. The bureau has been estimating crop production since about 1865.
Mr. WILSON. How long have other branches of the service been estimating it?
Mr. ESTABROOK. The Bureau of Markets is a recent organization and has been in existence only five or six years.
Mr. WILSON. They did not start out estimating crops?
Mr. ESTABROOK. Yes; crop and live-stock estimates are such a fundamental and vital part of the information that they must have they began to do some estimating of production from the very beginning, but they have done less of it as time went on and as the proper functions of the two bureaus became better understood and recognized, especially by the newer employees of the Bureau of Markets.
The CHAIRMAN. I do not see why the Bureau of Markets should do estimating. You have the force and can do the work for them and can turn over the information to them. I do not see why they should have men for that work and duplicate your efforts.
Mr. ESTABROOK. We have felt that we have the best organization in the world to estimate crops, but have been greatly handicapped by inadequate funds.
The CHAIRMAN. Is there any friction between the two bureaus?
Mr. ESTABROOK. None in the world. The two bureaus are cooperating in many ways.
The CHAIRMAN. It would seem to me that there must be.
Mr. ESTABROOK. There was a little at first, before the new men in the Bureau of Markets learned that the Bureau of Crop Estimates had certain duties to perform and a certain field of activity prescribed by law.
The CHAIRMAN. Let us see if there isn't a conflict. I know if you encroach upon my work you will get me mad about it. How do you feel about the Bureau of Markets getting into your field?
Mr. ESTABROOK. There is no conflict between officials of the two bureaus in Washington. Naturally there is a little conflict in the field. There is more or less feeling among the field agents, the men out in the States, whose business it is to estimate crops and who are known and recognized as the crop estimators in those States. When they bump into an agent of the Bureau of Markets, who is attempting to do their work, of course there is a little conflict, but there is less of it as time goes on.
The CHAIRMAN. I thought that would be the natural consequence. You do not know how much the Bureau of Markets is spending on that duplication or work?

Mr. ESTABROOK. No.

The CHAIRMAN. Very well; we will find that out.

Mr. HAUGEN. Your information is from men on the farm and in the field, and you are better able to do it than the men in the Bureau of Markets?

Mr. ESTABROOK. Yes; unquestionably, because we are organized and our field agents are trained for that special purpose, and we have back of us half a century of experience.

Mr. HAUGEN. The Bureau of Markets people are coming in contact with the commercial end of it and are in better position to do that work than you are?

Mr. ESTABROOK. What was the question?

Mr. HAUGEN. I mean after it leaves the farm?

Mr. ESTABROOK. After farm products leave the farm the Bureau of Markets is unquestionably in a better position to follow the matter than we are, because they are organized and their men are trained for marketing work. They are specialists in marketing, just as we are specialists in crop estimating.

Mr. HAUGEN. There should be a line of demarcation?

Mr. ESTABROOK. There is a clear line of demarcation at the farm.

The CHAIRMAN. As soon as the products begin to move, the Bureau of Markets ought to take jurisdiction and not before?

Mr. ESTABROOK. Absolutely. We entirely disregard it from that time on. We stop after estimating production and after ascertaining the prices farmers get, we have nothing to do with marketing and the prices the middlemen get, or consumers other than farmers have to pay.

Mr. HAUGEN. As to estimating live stock, how is that done?

Mr. ESTABROOK. We start with the census, taking the number that is reported by the census on farms for a certain year, and the following year we ask our voluntary crop reporters to——

Mr. HAUGEN (interposing). How many have you in the field?

Mr. ESTABROOK. We have about 200,000 voluntary crop correspondents, about 60 for every county. In addition, we have a trained field agent who lives in the State, and who travels the State constantly and interviews the best-informed men he can find.

Mr. HAUGEN. You have 200,000 reporters?

Mr. ESTABROOK. Yes; the most of them farmers who have been in their locality for some time. We ask them to estimate what is the percentage of increase or decrease for live stock over last year. That is far easier to estimate than to attempt to estimate the actual numbers. We then apply that percentage of increase or decrease to the census number, and so on year after year. Then we check that up so far as we can with the live-stock receipts at the great markets, the movement that takes place each year; and also we check it up with the published State reports, with actual holdings on individual farms, and with the returns of the tax assessors in each State. Not that the returns of the tax assessors are regarded as absolutely accurate, because they are apt to be minimum numbers, but they do show the relation one year to another pretty well. And all those we use as checks on the information we get from our regular crop reporters.

Mr. HAUGEN. Do you check up the assessors' reports on stock?

Mr. ESTABROOK. We use the assessors' reports as a check on ours, not as to the actual number so much as for the changes they report from year to year, to show the relative increase or decrease.

Mr. ANDERSON. That is to say, if the assessors' reports taken as a whole show an increase in the number of head of cattle, or hogs, or whatever it is, and your estimate shows approximately the same thing, that is a reasonable check upon your estimates?

Mr. ESTABROOK. It tends to confirm the estimates. Now, there are some States where the tax assessors' returns are known to be quite accurate. It is our business to find out in which States these assessors' returns are most accurate, and how far they may be relied upon.

Mr. HEFLIN. How do you go about estimating the cotton crop?

Mr. ESTABROOK. Very much as we estimate all other crops. First we get the acreage planted in cotton in the spring, the percentage of increase or decrease as compared to the previous year, and then we get monthly estimates of the condition of the cotton during the season, and——

Mr. HEFLIN (interposing). At what time did you estimate the crop this year? At what time was your estimate published; in November, wasn't it?

Mr. ESTABROOK. The latest estimate in the year is always as of December 1. It is issued to the press about December 11 and published in the Monthly Crop Report for December.

Mr. HEFLIN. In Texas they put in more acreage than usual?

Mr. ESTABROOK. About the same; more than in 1917 but less than in 1916.

Mr. HEFLIN. And they had pretty fair prospects in June for a 4,500,000 or 5,000,000 bale crop?

Mr. ESTABROOK. The condition of cotton in Texas on June 25 was estimated as higher than on the same date the previous year.

Mr. HEFLIN. But the drouth in July cut the crop about 2,500,000 bales. Did you take that into consideration?

Mr. ESTABROOK. Surely. We have in each township in every county in Texas a voluntary crop reporter. We have in the county itself a county man who has several men reporting to him; and then we have our State field agent with his list of reporters in each county. In addition, we have some special cotton reporters and ginners in each county, all reporting on cotton. These men report conditions as they exist on the date of the report and take into consideration all essential factors.

Mr. HEFLIN. Do they report the condition of the crop with regard to the boll weevil and the red spider and every other insect that affects cotton injuriously.

Mr. ESTABROOK. They report on the condition of the crop, taking into consideration all those factors. The analytical report we get is from the field agent, who has been out into these counties and made a personal inspection and examination of the fields and interviewed the best-informed men. It has happened innumerable times that our field agent has been the first one to detect coming damage from the boll weevils. They have done that time after time. It is their business to see these things, and they often see them before the planter himself will see them.

Mr. HEFLIN. Your estimate this year is 11,700,000 bales?
Mr. ESTABROOK. Yes.
Mr. HEFLIN. I thought, and so stated in an interview, that you overestimated 500,000 bales.
Mr. ESTABROOK. Our experience has been that we have usually underestimated.
The CHAIRMAN. Mr. Heflin, what is the basis of your information?
Mr. HEFLIN. From correspondence with persons going through it and my own observation in going through it and seeing the injury done by the boll weevil and the red spider, and reports from Congressmen from Texas as to the injury done by the drouth. Last year, Mr. Estabrook, you began with about 10,000,000 bales and the crop was 11,249,000 bales, and this year it began with 9,500,000 bales. So you have estimated this year's crop at 500,000 bales more than last year, and reports show more had been ginned up to this time last year than has been ginned this year.
Mr. ESTABROOK. In 1917 we began with 11,633,000 bales and ended with an estimate of 10,949,000 bales in December. The census Bureau finally reported 11,302,000 bales. The proof comes with the final ginners' report.
The CHAIRMAN. Assuming that you are 500,000 bales out, what percentage of the crop would that be?
Mr. ESTABROOK. That is about 4 per cent. As a matter of fact, I can not agree to any such assumption. I do not think it will fall anything like that. Last year we underestimated the crop about 350,000 bales, as I recall it.
The CHAIRMAN. What percentage would that be?
Mr. ESTABROOK. About 3 per cent. But there was a reason for it. That great increase in cotton, picked after December, where they picked almost 200,000 or more bales along in February and March, was something that had never happened before, and something that the farmers themselves did not foresee. It was due to the high price of cotton in the early months of 1918 which made it worth while to pick the imperfect bolls which, in normal times, are not worth gathering.
The CHAIRMAN. As a matter of fact, isn't there a great deal of cotton in the field now?
Mr. ESTABROOK. Yes; the influenza and shortage of labor have delayed picking and ginning.
Mr. HEFLIN. Well, it will be destroyed by the weather, then?
Mr. ESTABROOK. Perhaps so.
The CHAIRMAN. That would not affect your estimate. You estimate what will be produced?
Mr. ESTABROOK. Yes. I think we can stand on our cotton record. In three years we came out within 1 per cent of the final ginnings. For four years in succession we have underestimated the cotton crop slightly.
Mr. HEFLIN. We will see how far you miss it this year. This is the second time that I have challenged the report. Before Mr. Wilson overestimated 450,000 bales, and I claim that you have overestimated this year 500,000 bales, or from 450,000 to 500,00 bales.
Mr. ESTABROOK. Very well; we stand by our report.

Mr. THOMPSON. These estimates, Dr. Estabrook, that you get of production—that information is always available for the Bureau of Markets, is it?

Mr. ESTABROOK. Yes.

Mr. THOMPSON. And, of course, you get those estimates out, and if the public accepts them the Bureau of Markets ought to accept them?

Mr. ESTABROOK. Yes, sir; and they do accept them.

Mr. THOMPSON. What is the use of their duplicating your work, then?

Mr. ESTABROOK. None; it is simply the natural tendency with market men always to be looking for information which they need; and, I presume, occasionally some of their new men lose sight of their own legitimate work and get onto ours. Besides, the language of their appropriation act and their field of action is very broad and they have ample funds with which to spread.

My statements regarding duplication of and encroachment upon the legitimate work of the Bureau of Crop Estimates by the Bureau of Markets are made in answer to your questions, as statements of fact, to emphasize the inadequacy of the appropriation for the Bureau of Crop Estimates and the necessity for strengthening this bureau, and are not in any sense intended as a criticism of the Bureau of Markets. I interpret the active participation of the Bureau of Markets and other agencies in some phases of crop-estimating work as evidence of the fundamental importance of crop and live-stock estimates to the success of their own work; and why, as a matter of economy and public interest, Congress should strengthen the Bureau of Crop Estimates so that it can supply the information needed by other important branches of the department. I know that the Secretary feels that, if the financial situation justifies it, additional provision should be made for more effective work by the Bureau of Crop Estimates.

Moreover, some of the information which the Bureau of Markets needs and ought to have can not be supplied by the Bureau of Crop Estimates, because of inadequate funds and force, although it is authorized by law and organized to get it; and if the Bureau of Crop Estimates had sufficient funds it could do the work more efficiently, more satisfactorily, and more economically than any other agency, because of its organization, its experience, its knowledge of methods and their limitations, and because its men have specialized on crop estimating.

However, we are all essential parts of one great department, and the public is not interested in knowing which branch of the department gets the information of value so long as the information is procured. For this reason the Bureau of Markets has undertaken certain work which is clearly crop-estimating work and clearly belongs to the Bureau of Crop Estimates, but which the Bureau of Crop Estimates can not undertaken because of lack of funds. Of this nature are the seed-production estimating project, the thrashers' project, and certain phases of live-stock estimating projects provided for in the present estimates. In all this work, however, there is the closest cooperation between the two bureaus.

Mr. WILSON. Do they get into all other branches of the work of the Department of Agriculture in the same way?

Mr. ESTABROOK. I do not know; but marketing covers a very broad field and there may be some overlapping.

The CHAIRMAN. I believe that is all the questions we desire to ask, Dr. Estabrook. We are much obliged to you.

LIBRARY, DEPARTMENT OF AGRICULTURE.

The next subject is the Library. There are no changes in this connection, and I suppose there is no necessity of getting Miss Barnett up here to discuss this appropriation.

AGRICULTURE APPROPRIATION BILL.

COMMITTEE ON AGRICULTURE,
HOUSE OF REPRESENTATIVES,
Monday, January 6, 1919.

AFTER RECESS.

The committee reassembled at 1.30 o'clock p. m., pursuant to the taking of recess.

The CHAIRMAN. The committee will come to order. Gentlemen, turn to page 199 of your Book of Estimates. We will take up this afternoon the States Relations Service. This is necessary to allow some of the gentlemen to attend a conference the latter part of the week.

STATES RELATIONS SERVICE.

STATEMENT OF DR. A. C. TRUE, DIRECTOR OF THE STATES RELATIONS SERVICE, UNITED STATES DEPARTMENT OF AGRICULTURE.

The CHAIRMAN. Dr. True, have you any recommendations for increases in salaries on your statutory roll above $2,500?

Dr. TRUE. No, sir.

The CHAIRMAN. That being the case, we will not discuss the statutory roll. Have you any outright new places except by way of transfer?

Dr. TRUE. Yes, sir; on page 201 there is a statement about new places with a note which is quite explantory.

The CHAIRMAN. These places involve promotions, do they not?

Dr. TRUE. Yes, sir.

The CHAIRMAN. We will not discuss them, because the other bill takes care of that. Turn to page 203, gentlemen. You have dropped an item there, "*Provided further*, That hereafter the Secretary of Agriculture be, and he is hereby, authorized and directed to certify to the Secretary of the Treasury," and so on, as that is permanent legislation.

Dr. TRUE. Yes, sir.

The CHAIRMAN. Your next item is: "To enable the Secretary of Agriculture to enforce the provisions of the above acts and the act approved May 8, 1914, $74,600." There is an actual increase of $10,000 in that item?

Dr. TRUE. Yes, sir.

The CHAIRMAN. Kindly explain to the committee, briefly, the purpose of that increase.

Dr. TRUE. That item provides for the general administrative expenses connected with carrying out the provisions of the experiment station and extension acts, and in the case of the extension act the fund has not yet reached its maximum, but is increasing at the rate of a million dollars a year, including both Federal and State contributions. That makes the administrative expense from year to year somewhat larger, and this $10,000 extra is asked for in order to meet the expenses of administration, particularly of the extension act.

The CHAIRMAN. Doctor, have you taken into consideration, with respect to this $10,000 increase asked for, the estimates that the Secretary is going to submit here for increases in this demonstration work?

Dr. TRUE. Yes, sir.

The CHAIRMAN. Any questions, gentlemen? If not, your next item is on page 205, No. 53, "For farmers' cooperative demonstration work outside of the cotton belt." There is no change in that, but it might be well to give the committee a brief summary of what you have been doing.

Dr. TRUE. It is for the work in 33 Northern and Western States, and includes, respectively, the county agent work, home demonstration work, the boys' and girls' club work, and a limited amount of work in the nature of farm management demonstrations. This is carried on in connection with and really forms part of the cooperative agricultural extension work which is projected under the Lever Act.

The CHAIRMAN. The Secretary of Agriculture has made certain recommendations in reference to these two items, the work outside of the cotton belt and the work within the cotton belt, and I will ask the clerk to read the Secretary's recommendations.

(The clerk read the recommendations referred to as follows:)

DEPARTMENT OF AGRICULTURE,
Washington, January 6, 1919.

The SECRETARY OF THE TREASURY.

SIR: I have the honor to transmit herewith, for submission to the Congress for inclusion in the agricultural appropriation bill for the fiscal year 1920, the following supplemental estimate:

Omit, under the heading "States Relations Service," the following items:

"For farmers' cooperative demonstration work outside of the cotton belt, including the employment of labor in the city of Washington and elsewhere, supplies, and all other necessary expenses, $551,280.

"For farmers' cooperative demonstrations and for the study and demonstration of the best methods of meeting the ravages of the cotton-boll weevil, including the employment of labor in the city of Washington and elsewhere, supplies, and all other necessary expenses, $645,040: *Provided,* That the expense of such service shall be defrayed from this appropriation and such cooperative funds as may be voluntarily contributed by State, county, and municipal agencies, associations of farmers, and individual farmers, universities, colleges, boards of trade, chambers of commerce, other local associations of business men, business organizations, and individuals within the State."

and insert in lieu thereof the following:

"For farmers' cooperative demonstration work through county, district, and urban agents and others, including the employment of labor in the city of Washington and elsewhere, supplies and all other necessary expenses, $5,670,000: *Provided,* That the expense of such service shall be defrayed from this appropriation and such cooperative funds as may be voluntarily contributed by State, county, and municipal agencies, associations of farmers, and individual farmers, universities, colleges, boards of trade, chambers of commerce, other local associations of business men, business organizations, and individuals within the State: *Provided further,* That 80 per cent of the sums appropriated in this act for farmers' cooperative demonstration work shall be allotted by the Secretary of Agriculture for use in the several States on the apportionment basis established in the act of Congress of May 8, 1914, entitled 'An act to provide for cooperative agricultural extension work between the agricultural colleges in the several States receiving the benefits of an act of Congress approved July 2, 1862, and of acts supplementary thereto, and the United States Department of Agriculture,' and that all sums herein appropriated which are used for demonstration or extension work within any State shall be used and expended in accordance with plans mutually agreed upon by the Secretary of Agriculture and the proper officials of the college in such State which receives the benefits of the said act of Congress of May 8, 1914."

Aside from the amounts accruing under the agricultural extension act of May 8, 1914, the agricultural appropriation act for 1919, and the estimate for 1920, which are now under consideration by the Congress, include the sum of $1,204,940 for the conduct of agricultural extension work in cooperation with the agricultural colleges of the various States. The food-production act of November 21, 1918, carries an additional appropriation of $6,100,000, making a total of $7,304,940 for the current fiscal year. The supplemental estimate, which has been prepared after very thorough consideration of the whole matter and consultation with the representatives of the agricultural colleges suggests a total appropriation for 1920 in addition to the amounts provided by the agricultural extension act of $5,670,000, a reduction of $1,634,940 below the amount available for cooperative extension work in 1919.

The agricultural extension act, passed three months before the outbreak of the European war, contemplated the gradual development throughout the country of a system of practical instruction in agriculture and home economics. It involved the location in the several counties of agricultural agents and home demonstration agents who, through close contact with the people and intimate relations with the agricultural colleges, experiment stations, and this department, would be able to acquaint themselves thoroughly with the needs of the rural communities and carry to the farmers and their families, on their own farms, the latest and best practical and scientific information regarding the agricultural problems confronting them. It involved also demonstration work among boys and girls, and the assignment of specialists in the various branches of agriculture and home economics, whose headquarters would ordinarily be at the agricultural colleges or the department, to supplement the activities of the extension agents.

All the States promptly accepted the provisions of this act, and the work under it proceeded rapidly. When the United States entered the war this great educational system was well established and had met with great favor in all sections of the Union. It was immediately recognized that it could be used as a very effective means for giving concrete aid to the farmers of the Nation in increasing the production of food, feeds, and live stock to meet the needs of the United States and of the nations associated with it in the war, as well as in carrying out the program of food conservation. The Congress, therefore, made provision in the food-production act for speeding up the development of the system. This has been done to such an extent that county agricultural agents are now employed in approximately 2,400 counties and home demonstration agents are working in about 1,400. These agents together with boy' and girls' club leaders, extension specialists, and administrative officers, constitute a force of over 6,000 persons engaged in demonstration and extension work. During the intensive campaigns for food production and conservation conducted under the severe war stress of the first half of 1919, approximately 1,000 additional workers were appointed as assistant country agents and specialists. These have since been withdrawn, so that the force now employed may be said to represent, in considerable measure, the development, somewhat earlier than originally anticipated, of the extension work as defined in and contemplated by the act of May 8, 1914. The expenses of living, travel, supplies, and the like, normally connected with such work have greatly increased since the passage of the act. The funds provided by it, therefore, are entirely insufficient for the maintenance throughout the country of such an extension system as the act had in view. Now that the work has been effectively organized and developed as a war measure, it seems to me that it would be highly desirable and wise to anticipate the funds that would accrue under the act by 1922 and to make adequate provisions for the continuance of the agents of proved efficiency already on the rolls. It would be a serious mistake, in my opinion, to dismantle this great organization and then build it up again through a series of years.

For the fiscal year 1919 the Federal appropriation under the extension act is $2,580,000, which, combined with the required offset from State sources of

$2,100,000, makes a total of $4,680,000. The States have, in addition, contributed nearly $4,000,00, and the regular and emergency appropriations to this department, as already indicated, amount to $7,304,940., In all, there is available for extension work this year about $16,000,000. To continue the work on its present basis, the following sums will be required:

Agricultural extension act:	
Federal	$3,080,000
State	2,600,000
Additional:	
Federal	5,670,000
State	4,650,000
Total	16,000,000

If the appropriation suggested in the supplemental estimate is made available, it is proposed, first, to provide for the maintenance of county agents in at least 2,400 counties, and to extend the work to such other counties as the funds accruing from State sources may permit; second, to maintain the present force of home demonstration agents; and, third, to use the remainder of the appropriation for the continuation and development of the boys' and girls' club activities.

The value of the extension work as a means of aiding the farmers and their families in crop and animal production, the marketing of products, the making of the home and its environment more comfortable and healthful, and the promotion of a broader and more satisfactory community life has been so fully demonstrated that it is not necessary to emphasize the importance of perpetuating the organization and providing for its reasonable expansion to more completely reach all the people in the rural communities.

During the past year a million farmers have associated themselves with the farm bureaus, county councils of agriculture, and other organizations supporting the work of the county agents, and about half of these farmers carried on demonstrations on their own farms. Through visits to farms, meetings, and otherwise, more than half the total number of farmers in the United States have been reached. At least 1,500,000 women have received instruction from the home demonstration agents, and 2,000,000 boys and girls have taken part in the club activities.

The increased production of the American farmers in 1917 and 1918 is sufficient evidence of the efficiency of the extension work.. By means of the extension organization, with its agencies reaching into 2,400 out of approximately 2,850 agricultural counties in the United States, the Government was able to present to the farmers of every neighborhood, by intimate personal contact, the Nation's needs. Unquestionably the farmers of the United States were governed in large degree by patriotism, but it is not too much to say that they could not possibly have produced so intelligently if there had not been this organized system of information and assistance. The same system is no less needed in the immediate future than it has been under war conditions.

Considering the rapidity with which the work has been extended during the past year, I think it may be said that the States and the counties have done well in supplementing the Federal appropriations. The problem now is to hold all that has been gained which is worthy of a permanent place in this system of popular practical education. It would be most unfortunate not to make permanent the results of the extraordinary efforts of the people and their extension agents during the war as far as these results will contribute to the prosperity of our agricultural and country life in times of peace. It is believed that this can be done with the aid of the appropriation recommended for the demonstration work and such additional funds as we may reasonably expect to be contributed from State sources.

The Federal appropriations under the extension act will increase by $500,000 annually until 1922-23. It may be found desirable to decrease the appropriations to this department after next year by a similar amount. If this were done and the States continued to supply funds over and above those necessary to meet the requirements of the act, the amounts available for demonstration work up to 1923 may be roughly approximated in the following table:

Funds for demonstration and extension work.

Years.	Lever funds. Federal.	Lever funds. State.	United States Department of Agriculture.	State, county, and other	Total.
1918–19	$2,580,000	$2,100,000	$7,304,940	$3,982,586	$15,967,526
1919–20	3,080,000	2,600,000	5,670,000	4,650,000	16,000,000
1920–21	3,580,000	3,100,000	5,170,000	[1] 4,650,000	[1] 16,500,000
1921–22	4,080,000	3,600,000	4,670,000	[1] 4,650,000	[1] 17,000,000
1922–23	4,580,000	4,100,000	4,170,000	[1] 4,650,000	[1] 17,500,000

[1] The interest of the farmers in the extension work is constantly increasing and it is probable that the amounts indicated under "State, county, and other," and consequently under "Total," for 1920–21, 1921–22, 1922–23 will continue to increase.

The supplemental estimate suggests that only 80 per cent of the appropriation be allotted for use in the States on the basis established in the extension act, in order that account may be taken of conditions in some States which may require special consideration and adjustment of allotments to make them most equitable. In addition to these adjustments, the unalloted 20 per cent would provide for the maintenance of the Washington extension office and the employment of a limited number of field agents, with headquarters in Washington, who will go into the States to assist in the organization and conduct of the extension work.

Very truly, yours,

D. F. HOUSTON, *Secretary.*

The CHAIRMAN. Dr. True, I would be glad if you would somewhat amplify that statement.

Dr. TRUE. That sets forth quite clearly, as it seems to me, the actual condition. We have used the emergency funds to supplement the other funds that were involved in the cooperative agricultural extension work throughout the country, and with great efforts on the part of all concerned, and with widely increased interest of the farming people and others associated with the work, we have been able to put this work on a more solid foundation than it otherwise could have been up to this time. That is perhaps especially true with reference to the women's demonstration work, because the emergency funds have been used for that purpose, especially in the Northern States, in a relatively large way, and the women are very much interested in this work.

As stated in this paper, we have directly reached during the past year, we estimate, at least a million and a half women, but that does not represent the total influence of this work, because, as you know, where such things are done they pass from lip to lip throughout the community, and then through publications and through the agricultural and other press a great deal of useful information has been given to the women of the country to help them in their household work and in every other home and community enterprise in which they are especially interested.

One great object of the women's work, as far as the country women are concerned, is to lighten their labors by giving them the best information that is available regarding the methods of household work, and also to bring to bear the influence of the family as a whole, the man of the family as well as the woman to improve household conveniences and the household surroundings with reference to their sanitation and in other ways, so that the country home may be made a more attractive and comfortable place in which to live and the labors of the farm women may be lightened. We think we have accomplished a good deal along that line, and it is our purpose, if the funds are continued, to work in that direction.

The CHAIRMAN. Doctor, I do not recall the figures, but for the benefit of Mr. Haugen, who is a little tardy, will you tell us how many county agents you have employed under your emergency fund?

Dr. TRUE. Under the regular and emergency funds, on the 1st of January, 1919, there was a total of 2,774 persons engaged in county-agent work. Of that number, 2,405 are located in individual counties, together with 148 local colored men who are working as local agents in counties having large colored populations, but who work in cooperation with the regular county agents. Then we have a certain number of district agents who work in a larger territory to supervise and supplement the county agents, and above them are the directors of extension, State agents, and assistant State leaders.

Mr. HAUGEN. How many district agents have you?

Dr. TRUE. The total force?

Mr. HAUGEN. You said you had a number of district agents. How many have you?

Dr. TRUE. The numbers that I am giving you now include all who are employed under both the regular and emergency funds, and these numbers are as follows: Directors and State leaders, 57; assistant State leaders, 99; district agents, 65; county agents (including assistant county agents), 2,405; and local agents, as they call them, who are colored men, 148, making a total of 2,774 persons engaged in county-agent work on the 1st of January, 1919.

Out of the emergency funds at present, for the same date, there were paid 18 directors or State leaders, 65 assistant State leaders, 14 district agents, 1,490 county agents, and 88 colored agents, making a total of 1,675 persons employed in county-agent work with the emergency funds.

The CHAIRMAN. Can you give us the home-economics workers in the same way?

Dr. TRUE. Yes, sir. Giving the total number of women employed with both regular and emergency funds, there are State leaders, 49; assistant State leaders, 66; district agents, 58; county home demonstration agents, 1,184; local agents (colored women), 134; city agents, 173 white and 15 colored women; making a total of 1,679 women engaged in home-demonstration work. Of these the following are paid from the emergency fund: State leaders, 27; assistant State leaders, 39; district agents, 38; county home-demonstration agents, 911; local agents (colored women), 97; city agents, white, 172, and colored, 15; making a total of 1,299 women employed in home-demonstration work.

Mr. HAUGEN. You ask for $5,670,000, outside of the annual permanent appropriation?

Dr. TRUE. Yes, sir.

Mr. McLAUGHLIN. Aside from the amount that would be available under the Lever Act?

Dr. TRUE. Yes, sir.

Mr. HAUGEN. That is, outside of the annual appropriation, is it not, the Lever Act and the rest of it?

Dr. TRUE. In addition to the Lever appropriation, Congress has been appropriating for a considerable number of years a sum directly to the Department of Agriculture for farmers' cooperative demonstration work.

Mr. HAUGEN. That amount is outside of the annual permanent appropriation. The Lever appropriation is a permanent annual appropriation?

Dr. TRUE. Yes sir.

Mr. HAUGEN. Now, you are asking for $5,670,000, outside of the annual permanent appropriation?

Dr. TRUE. Yes, sir.

Mr. HAUGEN. That is a reduction from last year of how much?

Dr. TRUE. About $1,600,000.

The CHAIRMAN. Doctor, you have combined in this supplemental estimate the two items in the bill carrying this work?

Dr. TRUE. Yes, sir.

The CHAIRMAN. What was the purpose in doing that?

Dr. TRUE. The object in doing that was to bring the appropriation for this work in the whole country under one general item, which is suggested as a substitute for the two items for work in the North and South which have been carried in the appropriation bills. The new item contains, as you will notice, two features stated in the provisos. The first is the one which has been carried for a considerable number of years in the item for the farmers' cooperative demonstration work in the Southern States, namely, a provision for voluntary contributions by the States, colleges, counties, or the people themselves immediately interested in the work. The second proviso is a new one and is intended to bring this appropriation, if it is made, more closely and definitely, as a matter of law, under the same general arrangements which are made in the Lever Act. That is, it is provided in this statement of the item that 80 per cent of the money thus appropriated shall be distributed for use in the States on the same apportionment basis as that set forth in the Lever Act.

The CHAIRMAN. Let me ask you this, because this is an important proviso here: The funds that you now carry in your current law are distributed along the same line as the extension act? In other words, you require a contribution from the States on a dollar for dollar basis, do you not?

Dr. TRUE. No; not absolutely on the dollar for dollar basis. We try to secure as much cooperation as we can, and there is a large offset for that extra fund above the offset required by the Lever Act; that is, this year, in addition to the offset which is required under the Lever Act, the States have contributed just about $4,000,000 to offset the funds for farmers' cooperative demonstration work carried in the appropriation for the Department of Agriculture and in the emergency food production act.

Mr. HAUGEN. To offset what amount? You said the department.

Dr. TRUE. To offset the regular and emergency funds given to the department for demonstration work.

Mr. HAUGEN. In the aggregate, $4,000,000 to offset what amount?

Dr. TRUE. To offset about $7,300,000. Now, considering the fact that this work in many places when we took it up under the emergency act, and that is particularly true of the women's work, was a new work, and we have pushed the matter very rapidly under the emergency that existed and the war needs of the Nation, it seems to me that we have met with a very considerable success in getting the States and local communities to offset that money so largely, but the indications are that in the future, as the interest in this work grows, those funds from the States, and particularly from the counties and local communities, will increase, so that within a reasonably short time we shall expect that it will be at least a fifty-fifty proposition.

The CHAIRMAN. Do you regard the second proviso here as absolutely necessary in carrying out the principle you have in mind? I do not wish to have the proposition antagonized, but I have a very grave fear that it would be subject to a point of order.

Mr. McLAUGHLIN. What is the second proviso?

The CHAIRMAN. The second proviso is this:

Provided further, That eighty per cent of the sums appropriated in this act for farmers' cooperative demonstration work shall be allotted by the Secretary of Agriculture for use in the several States on the apportionment basis established in the act of Congress of May 8, 1914, entitled "An act to provide for cooperative agricultural extension work between the agricultural colleges in the several States receiving the benefits of an act of Congress approved July second, eighteen hundred and sixty-two, and of acts supplementary thereto, and the United States Department of Agriculture," and that all sums herein appropriated which are used for demonstration or extension work within any State shall be used and expended in accordance with plans mutually agreed upon by the Secretary of Agriculture and the proper officials of the college in such State which receives the benefits of the said act of Congress of May 8, 1914.

I am satisfied that is legislation. Don't you think so? If it is, it is subject to a point of order and might go out, and if that proviso is not absolutely necessary for carrying out your plan I would suggest that it be dropped because I would not like to have the whole item go out on a point of order.

Dr. TRUE. I have no doubt, Mr. Chairman, that if this committee feels that that way of dividing the fund is an appropriate one the Secretary of Agriculture would be willing to undertake to divide it in that way, even if he had no express authority in the law. The reason for putting that in in brief is that there is a widespread feeling among the people in the States that we ought to have some pretty definite standard for the division of these funds among the separate States, and to meet that it would seem natural that we should take as the basic standard that which is set forth in the Lever Act.

The CHAIRMAN. I do not hesitate to say, Doctor, that I think your basis of apportionment is correct, but it is not a question of that so much in my mind as it is a question of getting this act through the House without having it cut to pieces by objections.

Mr. McLAUGHLIN. How large is that Lever fund this year, for the year that will end the 30th of June, 1919?

Dr. TRUE. I have the figures here.

Mr. McLAUGHLIN. It is $10.000 for each State, and then so much more each year as the years go by. How much is it this year? Ten thousand dollars for each State would be $480,000.

Dr. TRUE. I can give you the figures. For this year, 1918–19——

Mr. McLAUGHLIN. That is the year ending the 30th of June, 1919?

Dr. TRUE. Yes; the Federal contribution is $2,580,000 and the State offset is $2,100,000.

Mr. McLaughlin. That means that some States have not quite met their contribution?

Dr. True. No; the States are not obliged to meet the $480,000.

Mr. McLaughlin. That is right.

Mr. Haugen. Are there any others? That includes all the Federal aid, does it?

Dr. True. No. This is the amount under the Lever Act.

Mr. McLaughlin. Do you include any State contributions that come from the legislatures or any local contributing source?

Dr. True. Yes, sir; enough to make up the Lever Act offset.

Mr. McLaughlin. Yes; as mentioned in the proviso there.

Dr. True. The proviso relates to Federal funds outside of the Lever Act. For these we expect a large offset.

The Chairman. It is here in this statement, Mr. McLaughlin. Doctor, suppose you turn to page 4 of your memorandum there and read the last paragraph on the page. That will give Mr. McLaughlin what he is looking for.

Dr. True. I have not a copy of that memorandum in its present form.

Mr. Harrison (reading):

For the fiscal year 1919 the Federal appropriation under the extension act is $2,580,000, which, combined with the required offset from State sources of $2,100,000, makes a total of $4,680,000. The States have, in addition, contributed nearly $3,000,000, and the regular and emergency appropriations to this department, as already indicated, amount to $7,304,940. In all, there is available for extension work this year about $16,000,000. To continue the work on its present basis, the following sums will be required:

Agricultural extension act:
  Federal _____ $3,080,000
  State _____ 2,600,000
Additional:
  Federal _____ 5,670,000
  State _____ 4,650,000

  Total _____ 16,000,000

Mr. McLaughlin. The suggestion of the Secretary is something new. Before the Lever Act was passed Congress was making special appropriations for the work in the South, about $600,000, or $700,000, and just about the same for work in the North. The idea was—many of the committee had that idea, at least—that when the Lever Act matured, or the amount reached its highest point, that these special appropriations would not be continued. They were continued with the idea of anticipating the maturity of the Lever Act. Now, the idea is to go far in advance of the Lever Act and appropriate amounts far in advance of the Lever Act and these special appropriations besides.

The Chairman. The Secretary in his letter says that the Federal appropriation under the extension law will increase by $500,000 annually to 1922–23. It may be found desirable to decrease this appropriation to the department after next year by an equal amount. So he contemplates that by next year the Lever fund will have grown large enough to take care of the emergency fund we are providing here and to keep the machinery which has been built up during the war emergency from disintegrating.

Mr. Harrison. No; that is not correct. The fund arising under the Lever Act will not be sufficient next year. Answering Mr. Mc-

Laughlin, I may say that, so far as I am aware, the Secretary has never expressed the view that the direct appropriation to the department should be discontinued. I remember he stated before the committee two or three years ago, and also in his annual report that when the county-agent, the home-demonstration, and the boys and girls' club activities have been placed on a firm basis, the department should use the direct appropriation more and more for specialists to supplement the work of the extension agents. I think you will find that stated in the hearing a couple of years ago and also in the Secretary's annual report.

Mr. McLaughlin. Some members of the committee had a different idea.

Mr. Haugen. Mr. Chairman, if you will read the hearings, I think you will find the statement of the Secretary, and you will also find a sort of tacit understanding of the committee that as this Lever Act matured he would drop these annual appropriations. That was the explicit understanding we had to begin with, absolutely.

Mr. McLaughlin. We came very near taking that action in the committee two or three years ago, but the work was looked upon with favor. It is good work, and we wished to supply plenty of money for it; but when the Lever Act was passed it was stated that when it matured it would be the limit of the money to be furnished for that purpose.

The Chairman. I think that is true, Mr. McLaughlin, but I do not think you will find it stated by the Secretary anywhere. I know I had it very clearly in my own mind. Probably you will find it in my argument in favor of the bill that when it did accumulate we could very greatly reduce these appropriations carried in the annual bill, but I do not believe the department is on record, through the Secretary, as making that proposition.

Mr. Harrison. The Lever Act will not reach its full development until 1922. The war came on, and we had to build up this organization; and the question now is whether we are going to dismantle it and build it up again through a series of years or whether we are going to make provision for the retention of the greater part of that which has been gained during the emergency. At the same time, the expense of everything has increased, and we have had to revise our estimates.

Mr. McLaughlin. The Lever Act has not matured, but the idea of the committee was that each year enough should be appropriated so that with the amount the Lever Act itself provided, with the special appropriations, the two together would be sufficient for carrying on the work. Now, you are putting this amount away in advance. I am not opposed to that, because I am very strongly in favor of the work, but I think there ought to be a definite plan in the law of how that money should be used. I favored the way it is set forth in the Lever law that each State shall contribute as much as it receives, above the $10,000 a year. As this law matures, and a very large amount is available, I should favor the reduction of this amount that can be used in the discretion of the Secretary; and I should favor a proviso being put in that 80 per cent of it, or make it all, if necessary, should be available with that condition, that each State should make a like appropriation.

Mr. HARRISON. Mr. Christie and Dean Russell, who are here, can explain to you the difficulties that have been experienced in the States, and Dr. True will make a statement also.

Mr. HAUGEN. What will the Lever Act carry when it is fully matured?

Dr. TRUE. It will carry a Federal contribution of $4,580,000.

Mr. HAUGEN. How much does it carry at the present time?

Dr. TRUE. It carries this year $2,580,000 Federal contribution.

Mr. HAUGEN. Then it is short $2,000,000, is it?

Dr. TRUE. Yes, sir.

Mr. HAUGEN. How much are you asking for now, or estimating, outside of the permanent annual appropriations?

Dr. TRUE. We are estimating for $5,670,000.

Mr. HAUGEN. Then you are asking for $3,670,000 above what the bill will carry when it is matured?

Dr. TRUE. Yes, sir.

Mr. HAUGEN. Well, that is not cutting down, is it?

Dr. TRUE. No, sir; but I might say this, that at present——

Mr. McLAUGHLIN (interposing). I would like to hear what Dr. True has to say in regard to the use to be made of this money in the discretion of the Secretary, that is not tied up by the terms of the Lever Act.

The CHAIRMAN. The other 20 per cent?

Mr. McLAUGHLIN. The other 20 per cent.

Dr. TRUE. Shall I take up that point first, Mr. Chairman?

The CHAIRMAN. Yes; suppose you do. Would you rather have it now, or let him finish with this other first?

Mr. McLAUGHLIN. I am not particular about the way in which he does it.

The CHAIRMAN. Just reserve that question. Go ahead, Doctor.

Dr. TRUE. We have not taken into account, it seems to me, the actual conditions as they have arisen. When the Smith-Lever Act was passed, it was felt, without a knowledge of what would develop, that the appropriation made under that act would probably be ample for the cooperative extension work, but conditions have greatly changed in the course of four or five years since the passage of the Lever Act.

The CHAIRMAN. As I understand it, after the extension act has accumulated and completed its growth, if you maintain the organization which you have built up during the present fiscal year on its present basis, it will be necessary to make an appropriation for the fiscal year 1923, aside from the extension act, of something over $3,000,000; would it not?

Mr. HAUGEN. $3,670,000.

The CHAIRMAN. Is that right?

Dr. TRUE. Yes, sir.

The CHAIRMAN. And in order to cover your rural counties in the United States, that will be necessary to be done, will it?

Dr. TRUE. We will not cover all the rural counties.

The CHAIRMAN. Even at that?

Dr. TRUE. Even at that. This is the state of things at present. The county-agent work alone is using this year just about $8,000,000. When you add to that the work of the women and the boys' and girls' club work and the work of the extension specialists, you have a sum equal to that. That is, we double the $8,000,000 and make about $16,000,000 being used this year for extension work, whereas the Lever Act at its maximum will carry only $8,680,000. In other words, the enterprise, as it is developed under existing conditions, and taking into account the present value of the dollar, the extension system as it is developed will require more money to make it effective throughout the United States, on the plan on which it is projected in the Lever Act, than was contemplated when that act was passed, and so we are asking now for a sum of money which will enable us to hold what we have already obtained, and to seek more earnestly to get the States and counties and local communities to make larger contributions so that the relative amount put in by the Federal Government may be decreased rather than increased from this time on.

What we wish to prevent is the sudden cutting off of a large amount which would wipe out the work in a considerable number of counties, or which would destroy in a large measure, especially in the Northern States, the women's work.

Mr. McLAUGHLIN. I can see very well how the amount available under the Lever Act will be too small. The work has grown beyond the limits of that law, but is it not true now that you are employing men and women, both necessary during the emergency, but who will not be necessary or advisable during time of peace?

Dr. TRUE. No, sir; not as far as the funds we are asking for would cover. We did have on the 1st of last July over a thousand more people on our rolls than we have to-day.

Mr. McLAUGHLIN. You had a thousand more in this kind of work than you have now?

Dr. TRUE. Yes, sir. Actually, I think it was 1,318 at our last count. In other words, under the emergency we employed a considerable number of temporary agents to push the work. Now, we have allowed those to fall away, and what we have represents what we consider to be the permanent force which we need for this work.

Mr. HAUGEN. Mr. Chairman, in order that we may know where we are drifting, it was contemplated that at the maturity of the Lever Act the Government would expend $4,580,000.

Dr. TRUE. Yes, sir.

Mr. HAUGEN. We are already asking for that. You are asking for nearly $3,670,000 in addition to the $4,580,000. In other words, you have already doubled that, and at that rate, what may we expect in 1922? We are now expending $16,000,000, where it was contemplated to expend $8,000,000, and what may we expect if that is to continue?

The CHAIRMAN. We are now expending $16,000,000. That is the total of emergency and regular funds from both Federal and State sources. We are expending about $8,000,000.

Dr. TRUE. For the fiscal year 1919 there are the following Federal funds for extension work:

Under Lever Act	$2,580,000
Farmers' cooperative demonstration work	1,204,940
Emergency fund	6,100,000
	9,884,940

If the Secretary's recommendation is adopted by Congress there will be for the fiscal year 1920 for this work the following Federal funds:

Under Lever Act	$3, 080, 000
Farmers' cooperative demonstration work	5, 670, 000
	8, 750, 000

As far as the Secretary of Agriculture is concerned, I understand he does not at this time contemplate going beyond what we are asking for this year, but rather that in the years to come, up to the time when the Lever Act becomes fully effective, there will be a decrease.

Mr. HAUGEN. That years to come has been an old story. We have heard that old story every year, but instead of reducing it, we are jumping up by leaps and bounds, and there seems to be no limit to the thing.

The CHAIRMAN. Let me ask you this, Doctor. The Secretary suggests·here that after the next fiscal year it may be possible to reduce the appropriation carried in the Lever Act by $500,000?

Dr. TRUE. Yes.

The CHAIRMAN. How can you do that if you are going to maintain your present arrangement to cover all the rural counties in the United S a es? What economies can you work out by which that can be done?

Mr. MCLAUGHLIN. It will not permit of any extension.

The CHAIRMAN. The Secretary's answer to that question is this, Mr. McLaughlin: The interest of the farmer in the extension work is constantly increasing, and it is probable that the amount engaged in the States and counties will continue to increase. In other words, he thinks it may be possible, indeed probable, that the increasing interest in this work will influence the contribution of larger funds from other sources.

Mr. MCLAUGHLIN. It is only reasonable that the States will contribute what it is necessary for them to contribute in order to get the advantage of the Federal appropriation, and as the Federal appropriations increase the States must make larger appropriations to get the advantage of it.

The CHAIRMAN. Dr. True, if you have no further statement to make, I believe the committee would be interested in hearing from Dean Russell, who is in the field, and who is a member of the executive committee.

Dr. TRUE. I would just like to add this: If the emergency funds are withdrawn next year, a very serious situation will result. The farmers will lose the benefit of county agricultural agents in 1,000 counties, or over 40 per cent of the total number now in service. It will seem to many persons that the enterprise as a whole has failed, and even counties which might retain their agents will be inclined to withdraw their support. The efforts which many thousands of farmers have put forth to effect organization of the demonstration work in their communities will come to naught and they will hardly feel like engaging in such work again.

The work among the farm women will suffer a still greater disaster. It is estimated that over 60 per cent of the counties now having the services of home-demonstration agents would lose them if the emergency funds are withdrawn. In the Southern States, where it is most generally established, 400 home-demonstration agents will be withdrawn and the number of counties with women agents will go back to where it was when the United States entered the war. In the Northern and Western States practically all the work of women agents in the counties will come to an end. It has taken the period during which the emergency funds have been available to acquaint the farm women and their husbands with the character of the work of such agents, to demonstrate its value and to secure at least temporary organization of women through which the work might be done. Everything is now ready for a forward movement in this enterprise, which would bring multitudes of farm women within the circle of its influence and give them the benefit of practical instruction from trained women who will have an increasing understanding of their problems and will bring to them all available knowledge which will aid in their solution. This is a new undertaking—nothing like at has been attempted on so broad a scale. The women agents have received that experience during the past year which will enable them to render much more effective service in the years to come. It will be most unfortunate if this force is broken up and the work has to revert to an attempt to build it up again under discouraging conditions. Undoubtedly a number of years would elapse before it could be brought back where it is to-day.

The demonstration work in about 150 of the larger cities has been chiefly maintained with emergency funds. Much has been done toward acquainting large numbers of city women with actual food values, real economy in marketing, and a well-balanced expenditure of the family income. The relation of agriculture to the problems of city life has also been taught, and in many cases relations have been established between country and city people which have been mutually helpful. Considerable work has been done in acquainting women of foreign birth with American foods and the best ways of using them, and, incidentally, they have been helped toward a more complete Americanization.

If this work can be further developed it may easily become an effective means of securing a more intelligent and sympathetic attitude of city people toward the farming people, better relations between producers and consumers, and a larger degree of thrift in the urban population where it is especially needed. It would seem undesirable to cut off this work, now in an experimental stage, before its true value and significance have been sufficiently demonstrated.

Without the emergency funds the boys' and girls' club work would be put back to where it was two years ago; with the aid of the emergency funds the number of children enrolled in these clubs has been more than doubled, and has reached a total of at least 2,000,000. Even with this increase, less than 25 per cent of the farm children are yet reached. Here is a powerful agency for increasing the interest of country children in agricultural pursuits and holding them on the farm through their lives. It is also broadening their vision of the possibilities of agriculture and country life and stimulating them to seek such education as will best fit them for life in the country. Shall we now, at the close of this great war, when the problems of agriculture and the need of keeping intelligent people on our farms are greater than ever before, take action which will discourage the practical training of the farm boys and girls?

The accompanying table shows the number of extension agents at present employed in the several States and the number whose services would be discontinued after June 30, 1919, if provision for their maintenance is not made by Congress before that time.

I will insert them in the record.

(The tabular matter referred to follows:)

Statement showing number of agents employed in county-agent, home-demonstration, and club work, and number that would have to be discontinued upon withdrawal of emergency funds.

COUNTY-AGENT WORK.

States.	Regular.	Emergency.	Total.	Number that would be discontinued.
Alabama	53	37	90	32
Arizona	3	6	9	6
Arkansas	45	47	92	47
California	20	37	57	17
Colorado	2	31	33	20
Connecticut	5	7	12	
Delaware	2	3	5	
Florida	26	44	70	36
Georgia	47	71	118	75
Idaho	9	27	36	14
Illinois	18	46	64	31
Indiana	38	56	94	30
Iowa	30	78	108	50
Kansas	25	35	60	19
Kentucky	46	19	65	21
Louisiana	48	22	70	22
Maine	10	6	16	
Maryland	27	5	32	5
Massachusetts	4	13	17	
Michigan	15	59	74	30
Minnesota	15	81	96	60
Mississippi	69	24	93	28
Missouri	16	50	66	40
Montana	7	24	31	13
Nebraska	23	51	74	45
Nevada	3	2	5	
New Hampshire	6	10	16	
New Jersey	8	14	22	8
New Mexico	9	23	32	22
New York	30	51	81	
North Carolina	51	46	97	39
North Dakota	2	31	33	10
Ohio	17	59	76	33
Oklahoma	49	42	91	41
Oregon	10	16	26	9
Pennsylvania	2	50	52	15
Rhode Island	1	8	9	
South Carolina	27	28	55	19
South Dakota	21	30	51	16
Tennessee	55	34	89	24
Texas	77	111	188	103
Utah	13	16	29	8
Vermont	12	5	17	
Virginia	57	44	101	43
Washington	4	37	41	27
West Virginia	34	76	110	6
Wisconsin	5	54	59	27
Wyoming	3	9	12	5
Total	1,099	1,675	2,774	1,096

(b) HOME-DEMONSTRATION WORK.

States.	Regular.	Emergency.	Total.	Number that would be discontinued.
Alabama	19	47	66	47
Arizona	1	7	8	8
Arkansas	35	52	87	52
California	1	11	12	12
Colorado	1	11	12	12
Connecticut	1	18	19	18
Delaware		8	8	6
Florida	27	57	84	57
Georgia	41	86	127	86
Idaho		13	13	8
Illinois		32	32	16
Indiana	2	38	40	40
Iowa		49	49	49
Kansas	1	25	26	24
Kentucky	4	39	43	39
Louisiana	19	27	46	27
Maine	1	6	7	7
Maryland	1	34	35	34
Massachusetts	5	35	40	18
Michigan		31	31	31
Minnesota	1	20	21	21
Mississippi	16	53	69	53
Missouri		41	41	28
Montana		17	17	17
Nebraska	1	21	22	16
Nevada		4	4	4
New Hampshire	3	15	18	15
New Jersey	3	13	16	13
New Mexico	1	7	8	6
New York	6	39	45	36
North Carolina	14	51	65	51
North Dakota	1	12	13	7
Ohio		29	29	29
Oklahoma	23	35	58	35
Oregon		7	7	6
Pennsylvania		27	27	21
Rhode Island		7	7	7
South Carolina	34	32	66	36
South Dakota	1	12	13	13
Tennessee	44	50	94	50
Texas	39	28	67	28
Utah	2	15	17	15
Vermont		9	9	9
Virginia	20	84	104	84
Washington		15	15	15
West Virginia	12	4	16	4
Wisconsin		18	18	18
Wyoming		8	8	8
Total	380	1,299	1,679	1,236

BOYS' AND GIRLS' CLUB WORK.

Alabama	3		3	
Arizona	2	14	16	11
Arkansas	2	1	3	
California	5	17	22	17
Colorado	2	3	5	2
Connecticut	2	5	7	5
Delaware	1	1	2	
Florida	2		2	
Georgia	1		1	
Idaho	2	10	12	8
Illinois	1	16	17	12
Indiana		20	20	17
Iowa	1	9	10	6
Kansas	4	10	14	7
Kentucky	2	1	3	
Louisiana	6	1	7	
Maine		4	4	
Maryland	2	2	4	
Massachusetts	3	15	18	14
Michigan	5	7	12	4
Minnesota	3	32	35	29

BOYS' AND GIRLS' CLUB WORK—Continued.

States.	Number of agents now employed.			Number that would be discontinued.
	Regular.	Emergency.	Total.	
Mississippi	6	2	8	
Missouri	2	6	8	3
Montana	5	8	13	7
Nebraska	3	6	9	2
Nevada	4	6	10	5
New Hampshire		2	2	
New Jersey	2	8	10	6
New Mexico	4	2	6	2
New York	4	15	19	15
North Carolina	1		1	
North Dakota	3	9	12	9
Ohio	3	1	4	
Oklahoma	3	1	4	
Oregon	4	20	24	18
Pennsylvania				
Rhode Island	1	2	3	1
South Carolina	2		2	
South Dakota	1	7	8	4
Tennessee				
Texas	1	3	4	
Utah	5	18	18	10
Vermont	2	2	4	1
Virginia	2		2	
Washington	2	12	14	10
West Virginia	6	15	21	15
Wisconsin	1	5	6	1
Wyoming	5	11	16	11
Total	121	324	445	252

Mr. HAUGEN. Mr. Chairman, I would like to know something about the purposes for which the 20 per cent is to be used.

The CHAIRMAN. I think before we get to that we should ask Dean Russell to discuss the main features, and then we can take Dr. True again.

Mr. HAUGEN. Dean Russell is in charge of the work in the field, I assume?

STATEMENT OF DR. H. L. RUSSELL, DEAN OF THE WISCONSIN COLLEGE OF AGRICULTURE AND MEMBER OF THE EXECUTIVE COMMITTEE OF THE ASSOCIATION OF AMERICAN AGRICULTURAL COLLEGES AND EXPERIMENT STATIONS.

Dr. RUSSELL. I am a member of the executive committee of the Association of Agricultural Colleges, and, of course, they have a cooperative enterprise between the United States Department of Agriculture and the respective State colleges. When Secretary Houston had that matter under consideration he brought the subject to the attention of the executive committee and asked our advice as to what we thought ought to be done from the standpoint of the work as it is carried out in that manner; and the plan as proposed by Secretary Houston is the result of a joint consideration given by the executive committee and by the officials of the department.

It is our feeling that the success of this work has been shown by the results of the emergency work during the war and that these people ought to be retained, if an arrangement can be made which will permit that to be done, rather than to dismember this force, which has been built up as the result, of course, of the stress during the war.

The estimates, as indicated in the Secretary's statement there, are a reduction of about a million and a half dollars below that which is now being spent.

Now, a very important point was just brought out by Mr. McLaughlin in regard to this possible extension. I think it is only fair to say that the original conception of the Lever Act did not intend to have a woman demonstration agent in each county. No one knew at that time whether or not that work was going to be a success or not.

While the words "home economics" are added in this bill and are provided for in the Smith-Lever Act, it was the expectation—and I am speaking now from memory (I appeared before this committee at that time with Dr. Thompson, when that matter was under consideration) it was the expectation that the home-economics work at that time would be confined to people who went out from the colleges giving desultory service to a greater or less extent. So far as the work relates to the North, we had no women agents. Now, the war came on, and this women's work was called for in connection with all of their activities. It has been very successful during the last year, and the result has been that there has been an enormous development in reference to this interest, so far as the women's work is concerned, which was not projected at the time the Smith-Lever law went into effect. There is where there has been an expansion, a very material expansion, as I see it, over and above the original concept of the Smith-Lever law, so far as the women's work is concerned. It is the same also in regard to the boys' and girls' club work, which was provided for under a separate proposition.

Mr. HAUGEN. But the activity did not begin with the war.

Dr. RUSSELL. So far as the North is concerned, I do not think there were more than half a dozen women engaged as county agents.

Mr. HAUGEN. A considerable number were employed throughout the country.

Dr. RUSSELL. Not as county agents in any large measure.

Mr. HAUGEN. They have been employing women for some time in the South.

Dr. RUSSELL. But there was none of that work in the North until the war came on. In my own State, Wisconsin, we had none whatever. I do not think you had any in Michigan, Mr. McLaughlin, at the time the war broke out. I am speaking particularly of the northern end of the work.

Now, that work has taken such hold all through the North that a very considerable body of people have been gathered together with reference to these women's activities. This proposition is to see whether it is possible to hold that organization intact rather than to dissipate it, because in all probability the amount of organization under the terms of the Smith-Lever law will be required for the complete and full extension of the county-agent work in the main. Beyond the appropriation of $4,000,000 there will not be a sufficient amount to take care of these activities which the war has brought out and emphasized, and which have demonstrated their value beyond all peradventure. I think there is the point, Mr. McLaughlin, that bears on the question of the volume and magnitude of this work.

As this work has gone on and expanded in scope its significance is more appreciated. The States are coming forward rapidly at the present time, as indicated. The States are putting into this work about $4,000,000, is it not, altogether—even in advance in some instances. In my own State we are expending for extension work much more than the dollar for dollar which the Government requires us to put up. We get in Wisconsin at the present time something like $75,000 or $80,000.

The CHAIRMAN. The States are putting up $2,100,000 as an offset, and in addition to that they are putting up $4,000,000.

Dr. RUSSELL. In addition to the regular offset.

Dr. TRUE. At present the States are putting up in all something over $6,000,000.

The CHAIRMAN. As a matter of fact, the States are putting up, in all, $6,000,000. That is right.

Mr. HAUGEN. For current year?

The CHAIRMAN. For current year.

Mr. MCLAUGHLIN. Don't you think the States will cut off some of those emergency appropriations or contributions?

Dr. RUSSELL. Most of the emergency funds are provided for by the State commissions themselves from the county organizations, which are civic commercial organizations. In my own State, Wisconsin, we are considerably ahead of the national program at the present time. Of course, the emergency funds have been carried during the war entirely by the Government, but the value of the work has been so greatly appreciated that it is facilitating the development of the regular work.

The point Mr. McLaughlin raises there in regard to the 80 per cent proposition is a matter, I think, of very considerable importance, because the terms under which the present Smith-Lever law operates divides the moneys on the basis of rural population. If it can be arranged to take care of this supplemental work substantially on that basis, it is very much to be desired. The reason why this 80 and 20 per cent figure has been determined upon, in consultation with the Secretary, is that the Washington office, of course, has to be taken care of, and a certain amount of slack ought to be taken care of which can not be provided for on the basis of rural population alone. You take a State like Rhode Island or Massachusetts, which is so predominantly urban, in comparison, we will say, with a distinctly rural State. Take this garden work, which has been done in connection with the poorer regions in the city, where it is of very great importance. That would get no money whatever, you see, under the strict terms of the Smith-Lever Act, because the localities are so largely urban. If a small amount can be placed at the discretion of the Secretary in addition to this which goes to the Washington office, it would take care of those inequalities which are sure to develop here and there.

Mr. HAUGEN. They are not contemplating the expenditure of $203,840, estimated for the office here in Washington, outside of that?

Dr. RUSSELL. Dr. True can answer that question.

Mr. HAUGEN. Are we to understand that 20 per cent is to be used in Washington?

Dr. RUSSELL. Twenty per cent will be used for straightening out the inequalities which result from the fact that the States which have very large urban populations practically receive little or nothing. Take Rhode Island, for instance. It is only a few hundred dollars that they receive. I do not suppose they could put one man, for instance, to work on the garden work in Providence on the basis of what they get. The same thing is true in Massachusetts, which is so largely an urban State. There are some of those inequalities which ought to be straightened out.

Mr. HAUGEN. Do you have reference to the inequalities of the States contributing their share?

Dr. RUSSELL. No; on the basis of the Smith-Lever Act, Mr. Haugen.

Mr. HAUGEN. That is dollar for dollar?

Dr. RUSSELL. They do not receive anything, or, at least, only a very small amount. What does Rhode Island get, Dr. True? It can not be more than a very small amount.

Dr. TRUE. Rhode Island gets $800 this year, in addition to the $10,000.

Mr. HAUGEN. As I understand it, the proposition is this, that if a State or county fails to come up to the requirement of the law to contribute dollar for dollar, you propose to take the money out of the emergency fund to make up the amount that the State or county fails to put up?

Dr. RUSSELL. No; I do not understand that is the proposition.

Mr. HAUGEN. What is it to be used for, then?

Dr. RUSSELL. That is for Dr. True to answer.

STATEMENT OF DR. A. C. TRUE, DIRECTOR OF THE STATES RELATIONS SERVICE, UNITED STATES DEPARTMENT OF AGRICULTURE—Continued.

Dr. TRUE. The 20 per cent, as has already been indicated, is to be used for smoothing out some of the inequalities that have arisen in the States under the apportionment system of the Lever Act.

The CHAIRMAN. Will you just tell us what these inequalities are?

Dr. TRUE. In the New England States the amount which they can receive under the Lever Act is comparatively small, because of the peculiar organization of the towns in the New England States. We are going by the census, and the census makes a rough calculation of not over 2,500 inhabitants to a rural community. Now, New England has a very large number of towns which are rated as urban communities, but which are really relatively small communities that have considerable agriculture connected with them. As a result of that New England is unfairly treated under the Lever Act.

Mr. HAUGEN. Then the purpose is to do away with the dollar-for-dollar proposition?

Dr. TRUE. That is not the purpose of the 20 per cent proviso.

Mr. ANDERSON. Why?

Dr. TRUE. It is to smooth out these inequalities in the State allotments.

Mr. ANDERSON. I know, but why should not the States put up the dollar just the same? You are giving them more money for it. Why should not the States put up more money?

Dr. TRUE. Well, as far as that is concerned, the States are putting up more money than they are now required to do.

Mr. ANDERSON. If they put it up, what is the use of setting aside 20 per cent? If the States will put it up, and if they are putting it up, then there is no need for this legislation.

Dr. TRUE. They feel that under the Federal appropriation proposed they will have a fair deal, and they do not feel they are getting in all cases a really fair deal under the Smith-Lever Act, because of the inequality that arises out of that apportionment.

Mr. ANDERSON. What we are trying to get at is this. They have to put up dollar for dollar for the Federal money they get. It may be that the apportionment of the Federal money among the New England States is too small, but if that apportionment is made larger, what reason is there why they should not put up their dollar? That is what we are trying to get at.

Dr. TRUE. I do not think there is any good reason why they should not do it, if they can.

Mr. ANDERSON. Then why set aside 20 per cent for that purpose, if it is set aside for that purpose?

The CHAIRMAN. Let me see if I can make it clear. The extension act provides the basis of apportionment, and that basis is rural population. Rhode Island, under the definition of rural population by the census, has practically no rural population. She gets $10,000, which she does not have to match. In addition to that, on account of the basis of apportionment, she gets only $800 out of this fund.

Now, then, the 20 per cent here, as I understand it, is for the purpose of curing that unfortunate situation, so that Rhode Island, Massachusetts, and other States which have a great many communities which are practically rural, but under the definition are not, may not be discriminated against? Is that the idea you have in mind?

Dr. TRUE. That is the idea.

Mr. HAUGEN. But you just told us they were putting it up, and were willing to put it up in all the communities.

Dr. TRUE. The State of Rhode Island, in addition to the $10,000, under the Smith-Lever Act, is getting $800 this year. They could not get any more, under the Smith-Lever Act, because on account of this apportionment being based on rural population, they can not get any larger amount. You give them that amount on the basis of rural population. This would allow the Secretary of Agriculture to give them more money, but it does not do away with the provision in the Lever Act that they put up the dollar; it is just helping smooth out that inequality which they claim is an injustice.

Mr. HAUGEN. Your contention, then, is that they need more than they are getting?

Dr. TRUE. In some of the Western States, with small populations, the expense of the traveling and administrative work is relatively large, and those States are not getting, so far as their agricultural production is concerned, the same proportion as a State in the Central West like Indiana, Illinois, and some Southern States, with tremendous rural populations.

Mr. HAUGEN. I will ask the question, is not the purpose to use a great deal of this money to encourage the counties and States to take up this work?

The CHAIRMAN. That was the purpose of the $10,000, the initial appropriation, was it not, Dr. True?

Mr. HAUGEN. But here is $800,000 more.

Dr. TRUE. Yes; the original appropriation of $10,000 to each State, when we entered into this work, was made to encourage the States to undertake the work and see its value.

Mr. HAUGEN. Now, that is $10,000, and you want $800,000 more; is that the idea?

Dr. TRUE. Well, the proposition put up is practically this, that Congress continue to give the Secretary of Agriculture for this class of work just about what he has been getting for a number of years.

Mr. HAUGEN. But we are not getting anywhere, Doctor.

Dr. TRUE. That is to straighten out these difficulties that have arisen in the States, and also to employ here in Washington a certain number of field agents who go out and help the States in this work, carrying especially the new information from the department which is available for the country as a whole, and then for the administrative work that must be carried on here in Washington. There is nothing different in this proposition, as I understand it.

Mr. ANDERSON. There is not any difference in the proposition, but there is a great deal of difference between that proposition and the language which you propose here to carry it out. That is where the difference comes in.

Mr. HAUGEN. I would like to get one point cleared up. So far we have not cleared up anything. We are just where we started. Now, when we talk about difference, we started out on the policy of dollar for dollar. We started out on the policy of expending $4,680,000. Now, we have gotten up to $16,000,000. Now comes the proposition to set aside $4,800,000. What is that $800,000 to be used for? That is what we are trying to get at, but so far we have not gotten anywhere.

The CHAIRMAN. Let me ask Dr. True if this is not the fact, that in the appropriation for the demonstration work outside of the cotton belt you have $551,000, in round numbers. For this same kind of work in the cotton belt you have $645,000, which makes a total of $1,196,000, which the department is now using, and for which there is no law to compel the matching of dollars by the States, is that true?

Dr. TRUE. Yes, sir.

The CHAIRMAN. So that, as a matter of fact, under this provision which you suggest now, you are proposing to reduce that item to be expended without the matching of dollars from $1,196,000 to $800,000; you are reducing it by nearly $400,000. Is that true? Am I correct in my figures on that?

Dr. TRUE. I do not think you are exactly correct.

The CHAIRMAN. Let us get it correct.

Dr. TRUE. I do not quite see how you get $800,000.

Mr. HAUGEN. That is 20 per cent of $4,000,000, $200,000 to every million.

Dr. TRUE. We are asking for $5,670,000. One-fifth of that, of course, is somewhat over $1,000,000, which would be in the hands of the Secretary of Agriculture to distribute to the States as far as might seem desirable, to spend for field agents, with headquarters in Washington, and for the administration of this work. That, I say, is practically what we are doing now with the farmers' cooperative demonstration items.

Mr. McLaughlin. Mr. Chairman, could we meet the Secretary's wishes in this matter by granting the incerases that he asks, requiring him to distribute 80 per cent of it on the basis of rural population and having the money matched by the contributions of the States, leaving 20 per cent of it to be distributed as he pleases throughout the country, not on the basis of rural population, but requiring that each dollar be matched by an equal contribution by the States?

The Chairman. What do you think of that suggestion, Dr. True?

Dr. True. My judgment would be that it would be unfortunate to make that an absolute requirement for this next year because there may be some difficulty in reaching it fully. We hope that we will be able to reach it in large measure. That is for 1919–20, under the Lever Act, the Federal appropriation would be $3,080,000, and the States would then put up as an offset $2,600,000. In addition, the Department of Agriculture would have, if this proposed item goes through, $5,670,000. We have estimated that the States will be able to put up at least $4,650,000, which is $650,000 more than they are putting up this year, and that that will give us $16,000,000, which is equal for next year to the amount we have this year. In other words, we expect the States next year to do better than they have done this year, but we do not feel it would be possible, perhaps, for them to reach next year an absolutely 50-50 basis.

Mr. McLaughlin. This is all extension work, and Dean Russell has said it includes county work and home economics work, done largely by women, and the boys' and girls' club work, but it is all extension work, and it is all provided for in the Lever Act. The distribution of this money may not be entirely fair; the New England States may not get as large an amount of money as they need, because of the small amount of rural population. Evidently you wish to spend some money in the cities. It strikes me it would not be unjust to those cities to require that they meet the amount of money that they want by making an equal contribution. You propose to spend that money in the various places where money is most plentiful, and where the people are the best able to pay. You gentlemen, I guess, are all familiar with the growth of this idea of contribution by the States, and the demand of Congress for cooperation. In the past it has been very easy, indeed, for the States to come and ask for a Federal contribution. The easiest thing in the world, and the nicest thing in the world is to get money from the Federal treasury, but the Congress, whether wisely or not, has thought it just to give money only on the condition that the States contribute, that the States cooperate by putting up an equal amount, and I have favored that idea, and I favor the idea as embodied in the Lever Act.

I can see very well how some of this work ought to be carried on in cities or in communities that are not strictly rural, but at the present time I am of the opinion that when that money is paid out of the Federal Treasury contrary to the provisions of the Lever Act there still ought to be a way by which these communities into which it goes shall put up money themselves to meet it.

Dr. True. There is no difference of opinion between us, I think, except that we do not feel that next year it is likely that we can reach this fifty-fifty proposition. We have looked for that to be reached in about two years from now. We expect to use every effort to get it as near as we can, but we thought perhaps the committee and the Congress would be willing to leave that to the discretion of the Secretary of Agriculture for this next year at least.

Mr. McLaughlin. You admit that the principle is right, but the conditions will not make it entirely proper at this time; is that the idea?

Dr. True. That is the idea.

Mr. Haugen. My understanding is that a considerable amount of money is spent in soliciting funds and membership in this organization. Can you state the amount that is being expended for that purpose? Is it a fact that in many instances the cost of soliciting funds has exceeded the amounts that have been contributed by the counties?

Dr. True. I do not understand that to be so.

Mr. Haugen. Is it not your understanding and have you not knowledge of the fact that your people are soliciting for funds and membership and raising the funds necessary to match the Government dollar?

Dr. True. In the Northern States the common organization is to have what is called a farm bureau in the county. That is made up of some hundreds of farming people, and they decide themselves what contribution they want to make, whether it may be a dollar or $5 a head to aid this work. Of course they have to raise that money, and our instructions to our agents are not to raise that money themselves, but to let the farming people raise it—let the farm bureau raise the money.

Mr. Haugen. Well, that is not answering my question. I was asking you whether the department was using any of this money for soliciting funds and membership?

Dr. True. I do not understand that it is.

Mr. Haugen. I can say positively that they are doing it. I called your attention to it last year that they did it in my own county, and I met the people that were there representing the department, who were there soliciting for funds.

Dr. True. My understanding is that a farm bureau is doing the work.

Mr. Haugen. If you do not care to answer the question or if you have no knowledge of it, we will pass on.

Mr. Heflin. Mr. Haugen, do I understand you to say that they are spending Government dollars trying to get money to match Government dollars and are expending more Government dollars than they get in State funds to match in some instances?

Mr. Haugen. They expend Government funds. I could not state the amount, because we have not access to the record. How much money is expended to promote this political organization?

Dr. True. I do not understand that our agents engage in that sort of work at all.

Mr. Haugen. Is it not a fact that they are bringing about an organization, with a view to checking up Members of Congress with a view to enlightening the people and enlightening Members of Congress?

Dr. True. I do not understand that is the object of the organization.

Mr. Haugen. What is the object of it?

Dr. TRUE. The object of the organization is to interest farming people in this extension work and to lay out a program in a county which will be acceptable.

Mr. HAUGEN. I am talking about a political organization, about maintaining a lobby here in Washington, and checking up people and legislation.

Dr. TRUE. I know nothing about that.

Mr. HAUGEN. In connection with this extension work?

The CHAIRMAN. I think it would be fair to give the witness the names of the parties who are in this organization who are here, if you know them.

Mr. KNAPP. Mr. Haugen, I take it, is referring to this so-called Federated Farmers' Association, with which we have nothing to do.

Mr. HAUGEN. No; that is outside the Government. I have no reference to the Non-Partisan League or any organization of the kind.

Mr. KNAPP. I will say that the South has no organization of that kind. The Farmers' Union is entirely independent.

Mr. HAUGEN. I am not referring to these outside organizations. I am simply confining my remarks to our own Government organization within our own Government, and what I am trying to find out is what the expenditures are and what the object is. I know what these gentlemen tell me the object is.

The CHAIRMAN. In answer to that, Mr. Haugen, they deny your allegation. I do not think we can make a witness confess to a proposition which the witness says does not exist.

Mr. HAUGEN. If the doctor says he has no knowledge of it, that is all there is to it.

The CHAIRMAN. He has said it.

Dr. TRUE. That is all.

Mr. HAUGEN. I might bring in some of the publications, and then probably we might convince the doctor that something was going on.

Dr. TRUE. I do not hesitate to say I would like to see them. If such a thing is being done, we ought to know about it.

Mr. HAUGEN. I will bring them in.

The CHAIRMAN. Let us get back to this 20 per cent proposition. These two items carried in the regular appropriation bill, added together, taking into consideration the transfers to the statutory roll, amount to about $1,204,000. You may spend that without having the States match it dollar for dollar. Is that true?

Dr. TRUE. Yes, sir.

The CHAIRMAN. And 20 per cent of the total appropriation suggested by the Secretary's supplemental estimate of $5,760,000 amounts to $1,152,000, which is about $50,000 less than the amount carried in this bill now. That 20 per cent portion of it you propose to use without reference to the matching of dollars. Is that a clear statement of the situation?

Dr. TRUE. Yes; as a legal proposition. We expect, however, to continue our effort to get money from the States to match it, as far as we can; but we can not enforce it under this appropriation as a legal requirement.

The CHAIRMAN. In other words, you are just holding your present status, as it were, but are going to make an effort to have the States meet as much of the 20 per cent as possible, dollar for dollar, just as you are doing now?

Dr. TRUE. Yes, sir.

The CHAIRMAN. In other words, there is absolutely no change in your plans with reference to this amount of money?

Dr. TRUE. No.

The CHAIRMAN. There is no difference in it at all?

Dr. TRUE. Absolutely none.

The CHAIRMAN. Now, let me ask you about this 20 per cent proposition, this $1,152,000. How much of that will be expended in Washington?

Dr. TRUE. In Washington, I should say about $400,000.

The CHAIRMAN. Just what would be the character of the expenditure of that money; for what kind of service?

Dr. TRUE. We employ in the two extension offices a number of people as field agents, who go out into the States to assist in the organization and the conduct of this work. Then, we also prepare publications for use in this work, and we have, of course, the administration of the fund.

The CHAIRMAN. Personal expenses, I presume?

Dr. TRUE. Largely.

The CHAIRMAN. Have you got that worked out in detail, Doctor? If you have, I would like you to put it in the record. Can you give it for the current year?

Dr. TRUE. Yes, sir. For the current year the expenditures in Washington are estimated to be about $480,000 out of the $1,204,940 for demonstration work and the $6,100,000 emergency fund, or a total of $7,304,940.

On the basis of this year's expenditures it is estimated that the expenditures in Washington, out of the $1,152,000 included in the 20 per cent of the total $5,670,000 estimated for demonstration work in the fiscal year 1920, would be as follows:

For supervision, including personal services of administrative officers in Washington and agents going out from Washington to inspect the field work, clerical and subclerical force, preparation of publications for use in extension work, supplies, travel	$200,000
For services and travel of agents going out from Washington to collaborate in the county-agent, home-demonstration, and boys' and girls' club work in the States, and supplies used in field service	200,000
Total	400,000

Mr. LESHER. You use this money right before you appoint the county agent, do you not?

The CHAIRMAN. No; this money he is speaking of now, Mr. Lesher, is the money he is spending in Washington for the salaries of Dr. Smith, Dr. Knapp, and these other gentlemen who are connected with the extension service. The balance of this fund will be used just as it is now being used—in the field.

Dr. TRUE. Yes, sir.

Mr. MCLAUGHLIN. Yes, they might use it; because they are using it; because, as I understand it, that five hundred and odd thousand dollars for extension work in the North is used for paying the county agents, but no county agent is employed, or was not before the war, unless the said county in which the agent is to work put up a part of the money.

Dr. TRUE. We expect to continue that.

Mr. ANDERSON. Is not this the situation, when you are frank about it, that you have many counties in which you have reason to feel that the local authorities are not going to put the necessary dollar for dollar this next year?

Dr. TRUE. That is true if all the work is included, both agricultural agents and women agents.

Mr. ANDERSON. In those counties you want to keep up the agent organization, so you are proposing to put all of the money where you think it is necessary to put it?

Dr. TRUE. As much money as necessary to keep up the organization.

Mr. ANDERSON. Well, I think that answers the question. The only question remaining is whether we want to do that or not.

Dr. TRUE. Certainly.

Mr. HAUGEN. What are these 49 State leaders doing, what work?

Dr. TRUE. They are helping to make the organization in the States, supervising the work of the people under them, including the agents in the counties.

Mr. HAUGEN. With headquarters at the experiment stations or colleges?

Dr. TRUE. Their headquarters are at the colleges, where they also are preparing the publications they use in the work.

Mr. HAUGEN. They are employed by the colleges and you jointly. Is that the idea?

Dr. TRUE. Yes, sir.

Mr. HAUGEN. How about these assistants?

Dr. TRUE. They are doing similar work, only in more restricted areas in the States. If I might show this map, it may help you to get an idea of the situation in reference to the women's work.

Mr. HAUGEN. Let us not get away from this. These assistants, 66 of them; what are they doing in the States?

Dr. TRUE. They are aiding in the work of the county people.

Mr. HAUGEN. Aiding in what way?

Dr. TRUE. By going out and holding meetings. They prepare publications and send those out, and they instruct the agents in what they are to do.

Mr. HAUGEN. Do they have anything to do with the organization of the county in the soliciting of funds and membership?

Dr. TRUE. No, sir; I do not understand they do.

Mr. HAUGEN. What about the district agents?

Dr. TRUE. They are persons, like the assistant State leaders, who are working in areas of from 15 to 25 counties. You understand, Mr. Haugen, we have not filled up the whole United States with county agents.

Mr. HAUGEN. I understand that; but what are those district people doing?

Dr. TRUE. They are engaged in demonstration work, in instructions at meetings, preparation of publications, etc. They are all doing practically the same kind of work, except that these agents who have had quarters at the colleges and in the districts are aiding the work in the counties and in those portions of the State where there are no county agents.

Mr. HAUGEN. I called your attention last year to the two gentlemen who came to my county and spent a considerable time in organizing. Now, under what head would they be employed, if not under either of these heads?

Dr. TRUE. If we are to undertake the work in a new county the work has to be explained to the people, and the effort is made to gather together a considerable number of the farming people and have them organize a farm bureau.

Mr. HAUGEN. That is not the way it was done in my county. They were soliciting funds and membership.

Dr. TRUE. As I say, I did not understand that.

Mr. HAUGEN. Of course, if you have no knowledge of it we will not pursue it any further. I was trying to find out what head they were employed under and what the expense is for soliciting funds.

The CHAIRMAN. Dr. True has stated, not once, but half a dozen times, that they did not do that.

Mr. HAUGEN. I called the doctor's attention to it last year and I assumed that it was of enough importance at least to investigate it, and I naturally expected that in the expenditure of $16,000,000 one would have some knowledge of how that money is being expended. It might be that there is some one here who has knowledge. It is not expected that you should have knowledge of the details of each individual case of course.

STATEMENT OF MR. C. B. SMITH, CHIEF OF THE OFFICE OF EXTENSION WORK IN THE NORTHERN AND WESTERN STATES, STATES RELATIONS SERVICE, UNITED STATES DEPARTMENT OF AGRICULTURE.

Mr. SMITH. The man that goes down to organize the county goes from the college of agriculture. He is called a State leader or assistant State leader. He is the one that calls the people together. If they decide to organize a farm bureau it is a committee of that farm bureau that does the soliciting. If that is not true in Iowa it is the exception. It is the truth in 99 per cent of the cases in the United States. The members of the farm bureaus do the soliciting. If any agent has solicited funds we do not know of it.

Mr. HAUGEN. What would they do? Do I understand that they organize the bureau?

Mr. SMITH. Yes, sir.

Mr. HAUGEN. How is that organized? Are they organized at the expense of the Government?

Mr. SMITH. No, sir; they are organized at the expense of the people themselves. Let me show you how it is organized. The State leader from the college may go down to the county and present their interest in a farm bureau. He talks first with a few of the leading farmers. He may ask the banker who those leading farmers are. He explains the situation to these leading farmers, as to whether or not it will be desirable to organize a county bureau in the county and have a county agent. If those few farmers seem to be interested he suggests that they organize themselves into a temporary committee, and that group of people, thus organized, if they care to, invite in more farmers from about the county to consider the matter from every angle. They send out the literature over their own name.

If this little group of people decide to call together the farmers from the surrounding townships, and that is done, those farmers come together and it is explained to them again, all of them, by the State leader just what this farm bureau is and what it does, its purpose, its function, and if they decide then to organize the county, meetings are held by representatives of this temporary committee in each one of the communities, and representatives of this temporary committee, composed of farmers, solicit membership at that time, when the meeting is held in each one of the communities; but all the time it is a people's proposition.

Mr. HAUGEN. But the organizer—does he attend these meetings in the schoolhouse?

Mr. SMITH. He may attend them; the State leader may attend them, and it is desirable that he should attend them.

Mr. HAUGEN. That he assist them in every way?

Mr. SMITH. He attends to assist them; yes, sir.

Mr. HAUGEN. How long does it take to organize, and what is the expense of organizing?

Mr. SMITH. There would be that man's salary while he is down there and his traveling expenses.

Mr. HAUGEN. About how long would it take him?

Mr. SMITH. All told, it would take from a few days to a couple of weeks.

Mr. HAUGEN. And in some instances a few months?

Mr. SMITH. Rarely, unless the people themselves did all the work and in the absence of the agent worked more slowly.

Mr. HAUGEN. You have checked it up so that you are positive in your statement?

Mr. SMITH. Yes.

Mr. HAUGEN. What is the expense, the average?

Mr. SMITH. I could not tell you what the average expense of that would be, because the salaries of those State leaders vary all the way from $2,000 to $3,000 a year. The expense of a State leader in the county is not so very much because the farmers themselves take him around in their automobiles and there is not much expense for that.

Mr. HAUGEN. What is it, $2,500 to $3,000 and a per diem for subsistence, or do they pay their own expenses?

Mr. SMITH. They have their expenses paid.

Mr. HAUGEN. Subsistence; anything else?

Mr. SMITH. Subsistence; yes.

Mr. HAUGEN. Have you anyone here who is familiar with Iowa—how the organizations are made there?

Mr. SMITH. Yes, sir. The organizations are made practically the same way in Iowa as elsewhere.

Mr. HAUGEN. I mean who has a knowledge of the organization there; who had anything to do with it; who has personal knowledge of it?

Mr. SMITH. There is no one here who has been in the State to organize one of those counties.

Mr. HEFLIN. Do you know of any instance where any agent of the Federal Government has expended Federal funds in trying to get money to match the Government's part, except in the way you have explained?

Mr. SMITH. No, sir; I do not, except in the way I have explained.

Mr. HEFLIN. Have you heard of any such instance?

Mr. SMITH. The State people secure that fund.
Mr. HEFLIN. Have you heard of any instance?
Mr. SMITH. I have not; no, sir.
Mr. HAUGEN. If they explained it, it amounts practically to soliciting for the funds?
Mr. SMITH. No, sir.
Mr. HAUGEN. It is organizing each county?
Mr. SMITH. It is explaining to the county that if the county desires to organize a farm bureau there are some State funds and some Federal funds available that may be used to employ a demonstration agent providing the county organizes in a certain definite way and raises funds for cooperation. Usually the county contributes its part.
Mr. HAUGEN. That is soliciting support.
The CHAIRMAN. What objection could there be if they did?
Mr. HAUGEN. I am trying to find out if we are expending money in organizing and calling upon the people to pay $4,000,000.
Mr. ANDERSON. I want to ask you if you know of any cases in which the supervisor, the State agent, or whatever it is, who goes down to start this organization, has gone around, if I may use the expression, with the promoters of the farm bureau of the county to solicit the county's proportion of the fund?
Mr. SMITH. The county agent may go around with the committeeman of the farm bureau when that committeeman explains the necessity for funds or solicits membership in the farm bureau. The agent may go with him, but he himself solicits no funds.
Mr. HEFLIN. In other words, the Government agent explains the object of this work?
Mr. SMITH. He does.
Mr. HEFLIN. In the various counties?
Mr. SMITH. Yes, sir.
Mr. HEFLIN. And urges upon them the importance of taking advantage of this proposition and joining in so that they will get the benefit?
Mr. SMITH. Yes.
Mr. ANDERSON. In that case, you say the county promoter asks the candidate if he is willing to pay his share for that purpose ?
The CHAIRMAN. I see no objection to it.
Mr. ANDERSON. I am not objecting to it; I want to see what is done, that is all.
The CHAIRMAN. If you will permit me to say this, Dr. Smith: There is not a college in the United States that does not have solicitors or agents who go to the parents and explain the value of education, and this whole proposition is an educational proposition.
Mr. HAUGEN. If you are soliciting, that is the only point I am driving at, and I am trying to find out about the expense.
Mr. KNAPP. So far as the work in the South is concerned, neither representatives of the department nor representatives of the State extension services solicit funds from individuals for membership in the farm bureaus. In that territory in every State appropriations are made by the county courts, quorum courts, boards of supervisors, and other county officials, and the representatives of the State extension service, which represents both the department and the college, do exactly as we do here before Congress. They may, at the

request of officers in the State, appear before committees of their State legislature and tell what has been done and what the needs of the work are for the next year. They are also called before county courts, boards of supervisors, and other governing bodies to report regarding the work of the past year and to answer inquiries regarding the need of appropriations for the next year. This is the way the money is raised. In practically every instance the matter of raising local funds is in the hands of local organizations of business men and farmers, and the representatives of the department and the colleges are asked in simply to explain, but do not spend any time in soliciting from individuals.

STATEMENT OF DR. A. C. TRUE, DIRECTOR OF THE STATES RELATIONS SERVICE, UNITED STATES DEPARTMENT OF AGRICULTURE—Continued.

The CHAIRMAN. Take up your next item, page 208, item 55, your farmers' institute proposition. I have expressed some little doubt as to the value of that work, and you may explain that briefly. It has been explained several times, however.

Dr. TRUE. That work now consists very largely of helping the agricultural schools and the farmers' institutes which are separate organizations under the State Departments of Agriculture, get publications which are in good form for them to use in the institutes or in the schools. A good deal of that material, especially that which is prepared for the farmers' institutes, is also used by the extension agents. The coming of the Smith-Hughes vocational act has brought about a much greater demand on us for material which can be used in the agricultural schools and wherever agriculture is taught in the schools. We have a very good understanding with the Federal Board for Vocational Education as to cooperative arrangements in this work to avoid duplication, but we feel that this work is growing in usefulness and that it is reaching in this way, with the published information, a great many of the teachers and scholars who are engaged in teaching agriculture in the schools, as distinguished from the work carried on under the extension act.

The CHAIRMAN. I understand that the Smith-Hughes Act has very greatly increased the necessity for this kind of work; is that true?

Dr. TRUE. Yes, sir.

The CHAIRMAN. Take up your next item, 56, your experiment stations in the insular possessions. I see you have an increase there.

Dr. TRUE. Yes, sir. that is very fully explained in the long note on page 209.

The CHAIRMAN. I have read that note. Do you gentlemen want to ask any questions about that increase?

Mr. MCLAUGHLIN. There is money available there for Hawaii, but that is only in connection with the experiment station, isn't it?

Dr. TRUE. Yes, sir.

Mr. MCLAUGHLIN. Is there any money available for extension work in Hawaii?

Dr. TRUE. We are using now, in accordance with this item, of the sum appropriated for the experiment station in Hawaii, $7,500 for agricultural extension work in Hawaii.

Mr. McLaughlin. Where is that?
The Chairman. That was put in the bill last year, Dr. True?
Dr. True. Yes; that was put in the bill last year.
Mr. McLaughlin. Has that money been used?
Dr. True. Yes, sir.
Mr. McLaughlin. I was told that it had not been used. On what plan do you use it; do you require the Legislature of Hawaii or some of the people there to put up an equal amount?
Dr. True. No, sir; that is not done in that way.
Mr. McLaughlin. You are sure this money had been spent?
Dr. True. Yes, sir. Dr. Evans is here and can tell you in detail, if you would like to go into it.
Mr. McLaughlin. The people of Hawaii have been asking for more money.
Dr. True. They have been asking for more money, and the question has arisen as to whether we could use at least a little of the emergency fund for this purpose.
Mr. McLaughlin. The emergency money under this food-production act?
Dr. True. Yes. As I understand it, there is no legal objection to our using the money in Hawaii, but the Secretary has felt he ought not to do so without consulting this committee. He has, therefore, asked me to present the matter to you as to whether you think the department might spend some little sums out of the emergency appropriation this year for extension work in Alaska and our insular possessions.
Mr. McLaughlin. Under this plan that the Secretary suggests of adding this large amount of money to the Lever fund or on the plan you have given so much time to here would any of that money be available for Hawaii?
Dr. True. Under the terms of that item as we have presented it, there does not seem to be any legal objection to that. But we have so far held the emergency funds, and I think the Secretary would hold these funds strictly to the continental United States unless this committee think it would be a good plan to spend some of the money in Alaska and the islands.
The Chairman. If you did that, wouldn't you be up against the very same proposition you have been presenting to the committee with reference to the continental United States? If we start this work now, the argument next year will be that it can not be discontinued, since to do so would break up a going organization that you have built up. We might as well be frank with each other, and if you are going to use any emergency funds in the manner indicated we might as well make up our minds that we will have to continue that work. If the Hawaiian people need the extension work, this committee ought to give it to them.
Dr. True. I suppose it would be permanent work. They need that instruction out there just as much as it is needed in the United States; that is particularly true in Porto Rico, where we have a million people engaged almost wholly in agricultural pursuits.
The Chairman. What amount do we use for Porto Rico now—$5,000?

Dr. TRUE. Yes; about $5,000. Dr. Evans has charge of the work at the insular stations, and I would suggest that he be allowed to discuss the details.

The CHAIRMAN. All right, Dr. Evans. How much do we use in Alaska for this extension work?

STATEMENT OF DR. WALTER H. EVANS, CHIEF OF THE DIVISION OF INSULAR STATIONS, STATES RELATIONS SERVICE, UNITED STATES DEPARTMENT OF AGRICULTURE.

Dr. EVANS. There is no fund used specifically for that purpose, Mr. Chairman. The only extension work that has been done in Alaska was done this last summer or spring, when one of our men went over the Tanana Valley and urged the people to plant just as much as they possibly could, the station furnishing them the seed. The same thing was done in the Matanuska Valley before the time for the spring work. As a result of that effort, there was for the first time in the history of Alaska stations considerable production of food. In the Tanana Valley they raised 500 bushels of wheat, and probably outside of our station none was ever grown before. There were produced 5,000 bushels of oats, 12,500 bushels of potatoes, 350 tons of hay, 120 tons of cabbage and root crops, and 25 tons of other vegetables.

In the Matanuska Valley, where we recently established a station, a man spent the early part of the summer and spring on the same kind of work. The station furnished the seed—we sent 4 tons of seed grain from the Fairbanks station in there. There was produced 400 tons of grain hay this season, 500 tons of potatoes, and 400 tons of root crops, making a total of about 2,500 tons of food and feeds produced in those two valleys this last year. And that was all because of the extensison work, and that was done simply by these men taking their time from their other work on the late winter and early spring. There has never been any extensison work done aside from that in Alaska, although it is necessary there should be some done.

The CHAIRMAN. Why do you desire the $10,000 under the Alaska appropriation made immediately available?

Dr. EVANS. That is set forth in the note. It is to be used in livestock work and the erection of sanitary barns. We have a lot of cattle on the island of Kodiak, some of which are tubercular. They were tested for the third time this year and only six reacted. Every veterinarian sent there by the Bureau of Animal Industry condemns the barns, and says it will never be possible to do anything with the stock until the barns are more nearly sanitary. It has been estimated it will take $2,500 to complete the barns. We have made a beginning of live-stock work on Kodiak Island. In addition to that, the people of the Matanuska Valley are very anxious to have us do some work there, and that is probably a region that will develop into a dairy and stock country more quickly than any other part of Alaska.

The CHAIRMAN. How far are those two places separated?

Dr. EVANS. Only about 350 miles. The distances are very great up there. We have five stations in Alaska, and the nearest one to another is about 250 miles.

The CHAIRMAN. How do you get from place to place; by boat?

Dr. EVANS. We get from place to place by boat when we go. We seldom go.

The CHAIRMAN. Why don't you get some war airplanes?

Dr. EVANS. They might not be good cross-country flyers. There are said to be about 1,000 homesteaders along the line of the railroad in the Matanuska Valley. They have gone in there with some little stock, and in a letter a few days ago one of the settlers said he had two cows and another one had seven, and they were dry because there was not a bull in that valley. They want us to send some live stock in there, so they will have some breeding animals. So far as we can find, there is not a bull in that whole valley. And this man said that they needed breeding animals, and he hoped the station would take it up. What is proposed to do is not to repeat the mistake at Kodiak and get a lot of barns simply by building poles one on top of another, with a pole floor that fills with manure and dirt, with the result that presently the animals become tubercular. We had over 100 pure-bred cattle at Kodiak when it was found a lot of them had become tubercular, and we had to kill 56 of them. Those cattle had cost between $300 and $500 a piece. We want to start in the Matanuska Valley with a sanitary barn and probably some dual-purpose cattle to build up a herd, and as the herd increases to dispose of the increase by sale to the farmers. In this way there will be some breeding animals in there that can be used by the farmers at a nominal cost.

Mr. McLAUGHLIN. How much money do you propose to spend on the barn?

Dr. EVANS. The whole estimate of the enterprise will be about $7,500; that is, the barn and stock, clearing land, and getting ready for the cattle.

Mr. McLAUGHLIN. For the building—how much do you propose to spend?

Dr. EVANS. For the building the amount we will spend will probably not be over $2,500.

Mr. McLAUGHLIN. To accommodate how many animals?

Dr. EVANS. Probably in the beginning we will not have more than a dozen or so; but we want to build it large enough, so that we can take care of whatever increase there is.

Mr. HAUGEN. Those barns you refer to are Government-owned barns?

Dr. EVANS. Yes, sir.

Mr. HAUGEN. What is the object of sending up all this expensive high-grade cattle?

Dr. EVANS. We did not send up very many. We have been breeding them for about 12 years, and selling the increase as there was demand for them to the settlers.

Mr. HAUGEN. Are they being distributed now to the settlers?

Dr. EVANS. The station accumulated them until there were about a hundred head, when it was found a lot of them were tubercular, and quite a number were slaughtered.

Mr. HAUGEN. How do you dispose of them?

Dr. EVANS. The sound animals are sold and the proceeds turned into the Treasury.

Mr. HAUGEN. Then the furnishing of the cattle is simply for the shipping of them and the Government is reimbursed?

Dr. EVANS. Oh, yes.

Mr. HAUGEN. Are you buying the cattle and furnishing them free of charge?

Dr. EVANS. Oh, no. There are some people up there who want us to furnish them along with packages of seed.

Mr. HAUGEN. I was just asking for information.

Dr. EVANS. We have had a very similar proposition put up to us by the Railroad Commission.

The CHAIRMAN. One is just as justifiable as the other.

Dr. EVANS. I will leave that to the committee.

The CHAIRMAN. Take your next item—for Hawaii, $50,000—and tell us what you want with the increased appropriation.

Dr. EVANS. In Hawaii it is proposed to continue the extension work—$2,500 of it is to continue the extension work, bringing it up to $10,000. We have had a man since 1914—Mr. Krauss, on the island of Maui—who devotes his time entirely to extension work and demonstration work. He visits the other islands and holds meetings, and during the past year there were held in Hawaii about 181 meetings that were attended by 1,646 people. These were largely held by Mr. Krauss and other employees of our station, but in cooperation with the Territorial food administration, which has just gone out of existence, supplying some of the funds for carrying on the work. The men of the station furnished the expert advice and were usually present at those meetings to give addresses and to go into the field and conduct the experimental or demonstration work, such as spraying, planting, or caring for plants.

Mr. MCLAUGHLIN. This reads that of the sum herein appropriated for the experiment station in Hawaii $7,500 may be used in agricultural extension work in Hawaii. If you add $5,000 to the $45,000 above, you would do the same thing to this $7,500, wouldn't you?

Dr. EVANS. One-half of it is to be added to the $7,500.

Mr. MCLAUGHLIN. It would be necessary to make a change there; that would make that $10,000.

Dr. EVANS. That should probably be done in case the committee wishes to limit that amount.

Mr. MCLAUGHLIN. How many men will that provide for the employment of?

Dr. EVANS. There is now a county agent on the island of Maui. We want to put one on the island of Oahu; also one on Hawaii and possibly one on Kauai, although it is possible we will continue on Kauai the same plan as we have in operation—have one of the best farmers act as collaborator to carry out demonstration work and hold meetings under the auspices of the station.

Mr. MCLAUGHLIN. You have a station now at Maui?

Dr. EVANS. Yes. That is under Mr. Krauss.

Mr. MCLAUGHLIN. And then another one at Hilo?

Dr. EVANS. There is one at Hilo, and the contemplated plan is to put one in a new region near the Parker ranch that is going to be opened up for settlement within two years. That is to be provided for by the Territory's moneys.

Mr. MCLAUGHLIN. That is on the island of Hawaii?

Dr. EVANS. That is on the island of Hawaii. The money for the establishment of the station and land is set aside by the Territory. That proposition was brought up by the governor within the last two weeks, or at least a report on it was received within the past two weeks.

Mr. McLaughlin. If this $10,000 is set aside for extension work, will any considerable part of it be used for demonstration work at the experiment station?

Dr. Evans. Very little of it; practically none of it.

Mr. McLaughlin. Why shouldn't it all go to pay the salaries and expenses of men in the field, as county agents?

Dr. Evans. The salary of the man on Maui, the salary of the man at Hilo, and the collaborators on the island of Hawaii and the island of Maui are all paid from this fund.

Mr. McLaughlin. That is not strictly extension work. Some of those young men you have named you have located in buildings, and they are stationary; they are county agents.

Dr. Evans. They do not stay there all the time. They have to have local headquarters. The man at Hilo spends two days every week, and has for the past year, going around to other localities.

Mr. Haugen. Is the department doing anything to encourage the growing of tobacco? Are you making any progress over there?

Dr. Evans. We are not just at present, for the reason the tobacco business has been syndicated and while there is considerable being grown they have not asked the station's aid—in fact, we have been requested not to bother ourselves in their affairs, as they were competent to attend to them.

Mr. Haugen. What progress is being made? Is it grown to any extent over there?

Dr. Evans. This last year quite an area of tobacco was grown. For a few years before that the business had almost completely failed on account of the improper curing of their crop for a couple of years in succession, and it got so low in price they couldn't sell it.

Mr. Haugen. Is that due to a lack of skill?

Dr. Evans. We think it is due to a lack of skill.

Mr. Haugen. Is any considerable amount being grown there now?

Dr. Evans. I understand about 100 acres was being grown this last year.

Mr. Haugen. In all of the islands?

Dr. Evans. It is only grown in one island—on the island of Hawaii.

Mr. McLaughlin. You say this $10,000 for extension work will provide for the employment of how many men, what we call county agents?

Dr. Evans. Probably three county agents: One on Maui; that is Mr. Krauss, who has had the demonstration farm you saw, but he devotes a good deal of time to extension work and travels around the other islands. One on Hawaii and one on Oahu, the island on which Honolulu is situated.

Dr. True. In addition to that we might say we would like to spend a little of the emergency fund, if we could.

Dr. Evans. The plan is, if we could have some of the emergency fund, we would put this man on Oahu immediately. That is the island that has the largest population. They have a population on that island of probably 150,000. It is the most populous island, and we want to place a county agent on that island.

The Chairman. How much would you spend out of this emergency fund if the committee indicated to you that you should do so?

Dr. TRUE. I have the estimates here which we submitted to the Secretary's office for this: For Alaska, $7,500; Hawaii, $5,000; Porto Rico, $5,000; and the island of Guam, $2,000.

Mr. McLAUGHLIN. Has the expenditure of some of this money which you have wished to expend ever been refused to you by a ruling of the comptroller?

Dr. TRUE. The solicitor says we can do it.

Mr. McLAUGHLIN. I have been told the comptroller objected to some use of the money you proposed to make in Hawaii. Do you know of any such refusal?

Dr. TRUE. Mr. Harrison can probably tell you more definitely about it.

Mr. McLAUGHLIN. Mr. Harrison, has the comptroller forbidden the use of any money proposed to be used in Hawaii?

Mr. HARRISON. Not that I know of. Are you referring to the emergency money?

Mr. McLAUGHLIN. Any money.

Mr. HARRISON. Not that I know of; not in any case. Of course, we never contemplated the use of any of the Smith-Lever money in Hawaii, because that act related only to the States.

Mr. McLAUGHLIN. Are you afraid to use any money in paragraph 53 for Hawaii?

Mr. HARRISON. I do not think it has ever been considered.

Mr. McLAUGHLIN. Could you use it if you wished to do so?

Mr. HARRISON. I do not think there is any question about it. The solicitor has held that we could use the emergency money, and the appropriation to which you refer is practically on the same basis.

Mr. McLAUGHLIN. In the spending of this money in Hawaii for the extension work do you require cooperation and contribution by any local interests?

Dr. EVANS. In extenson work?

Mr. McLAUGHLIN. Yes.

Dr. EVANS. No, sir.

Mr. McLAUGHLIN. Then this work that is done there out of this money is all paid for by this money?

Dr. EVANS. Yes, sir.

Mr. McLAUGHLIN. Have you asked for contributions?

Dr. EVANS. We have not asked for contributions, as it was thought that if they wanted to come into the enterprise and help along they could make a contribution. The Territory did contribute for demonstration work for a while and they do contribute some toward the station which you mentioned as located near Hilo—a very little.

The CHAIRMAN. Is there anything further on that, Mr. McLaughlin?

Mr. McLAUGHLIN. That is all. I was told the department wished to do something over there and the comptroller would not let them.

The CHAIRMAN. Mr. Harrison said that is not true.

Mr. McLAUGHLIN. I do not know where they got that impression.

The CHAIRMAN. What are you going to do with the other $2,500?

Dr. EVANS. The other $2,500 in Hawaii will be used probably in some special investigations of a number of plant diseases. There has appeared quite recently a disease of the banana that threatens the banana industry of the island? There is an expert there now who has been working on the disease, and we want to send another pathologist. In addition to that, there is a question of some potato diseases that should be taken up.

The CHAIRMAN. What about this increase of $5,000 for Porto Rico? Didn't we give an increase to all these stations last year. That is my recollection of it.

Dr. EVANS. Congress gave increases to some of them. Without having the details, I couldn't say how much. One of the principal developments on Porto Rico would be in connection with extension work. We have no fund set aside definitely for extension work in Porto Rico, and never have had. We have been doing extension work particularly under the recent emergency in trying to increase food production. There are a million and a quarter people on the island of Porto Rico, and they were importing most of their food. We got started in on one item—they are great consumers of beans, and were importing beans amounting to $800,000 a year. They are now exporting beans. We have succeeded in getting them to grow considerable in excess of their own requirements.

Another article of great consumption is rice, of which almost none is grown in Porto Rico. A campaign in rice production was started in cooperation with the Office of Cereal Investigations of the Department under Mr. Chambliss. He went down and looked over the situation, and between 65 and 100 acres of rice were grown there this year. We want to continue this work through a number of years, to determine the varieties of rice to be grown, the possibilities of growing more than one crop, as is grown in Hawaii, the proper time and method of sowing, harvesting, and so on; and it is hoped we can have sufficient money not only to carry on the extension work we are doing, but to carry on investigation work in connection with rice, which looks to us as though it would prove to be a very excellent piece of work.

The CHAIRMAN. How much would you spend now for extension work?

Dr. EVANS. Probably about $5,000.

The CHAIRMAN. Tell us about Guam.

Dr. EVANS. The item in Guam is largely to repair the damages done by a typhoon of July 6, 1918. The island was swept by a typhoon and our buildings were badly damaged, and we are asking for the money there largely to repair those buildings.

The CHAIRMAN. You say largely; what proportion will you use for that purpose?

Dr. EVANS. The estimate just received a few days ago makes it $4,900 as the damage done to the buildings, poultry plant, and fences.

The CHAIRMAN. What are you going to do with the other $100?

Dr. EVANS. The high cost of living probably will take care of that.

Mr. MCLAUGHLIN. Couldn't you employ probably more than three county agents in Hawaii with $10,000?

Dr. EVANS. It might possibly be we could have four; but I do not believe we could have more than that, for they have to have their expenses paid. It is necessary to pay them fairly good salaries in order to get men that will stay, and if they travel from one island to the other or have consultations from time to time, it will be quite expensive. Traveling, as you know, is mostly by automobile, and the automobile bill, where they do use them, is generally $12 a day.

Mr. McLaughlin. Hawaii is a big island.

Dr. Evans. I know it; Hawaii is a big island; and the probabilities are that if the new station which is to be located near the Parker ranch is established, that that will be the headquarters for the extension men. That will probably cover one of the largest areas of agricultural homestead settlement. The man at Hilo will continue as a collaborator and devote probably two days a week on the east coast of Hawaii.

Mr. McLaughlin. I should think you would need two men on the island of Hawaii.

Dr. Evans. If we have some of the emergency money, we could put a man there on a full-time basis immediately.

Mr. McLaughlin. You could use some of that 20 per cent there, could you?

Dr. Evans. Yes, sir; if the committee is agreeable to that proposition.

Mr. McLaughlin. Do you need any direction from us to do it?

Dr. Evans. No direction; no.

The Chairman. Tell us what progress you have been making in the Virgin Islands. That is a new acquisition.

Dr. Evans. The Virgin Islands station has very little progress to report. The appropriation bill was very late in being passed, as you know. The matters of transfer, arranging the bonds, inventorying the property, and all that, are in progress.

The Chairman. You have some new language here, which I think the committee well understands; but you might explain it briefly.

Dr. Evans. Under the general law the employees assigned to duty in the Virgin Islands would only receive 15 days' annual leave, and this simply puts them on the same basis as the others, and allows them 30 days' leave.

The Chairman. They get no sick leave at all, do they?

Dr. Evans. Fifteen days' annual sick leave, under the general law.

The Chairman. This would give them 30 days' regular and 30 days' sick leave?

Dr. Evans. This would give them 30 days for each, the same as the other stations have. There is some additional language there, Mr. Chairman, in which we ask to have practically the provision that was inserted a year ago in the naval appropriation bill for the civil employees of the Navy outside of the continental United States; that is, permitting them to have cumulative leave for a period of four years. As it is now, in their isolated localities, the men have no place to go.

If they have only 30 days' leave it takes, coming from Hawaii to San Francisco, a week, going back another week; if they come East they could only about get here, and would have to take the next train back in order to return to Hawaii in 30 days. We simply ask that they be allowed to accumulate their leave not to exceed four years, and to take it at any time. That will have an additional advantage in that it will give these men a chance to get into a different climate than the tropics and to get reinvigorated; and also for some of the younger men, who have expressed a desire to do so, it will enable them to come back to some of our institutions and spend that two or three or four months in studying along the special lines they are investigating.

The CHAIRMAN. And give them a chance to get into a different atmosphere?

Dr. EVANS. Give them a chance to get into a different atmosphere. Some of our men, I might say, have not been off the islands in five years.

Mr. HAUGEN. Do you expect to give them credit now for what time they have not taken?

Dr. EVANS. No, sir. Credit will not begin until this law is passed.

STATEMENT OF DR. C. F. LANGWORTHY, CHIEF OF THE OFFICE OF HOME ECONOMICS, STATES RELATIONS SERVICE, UNITED STATES DEPARTMENT OF AGRICULTURE.

The CHAIRMAN. The next item is No. 57, on page 212, Dr. Langworthy's item. Have you found anything new to eat, Doctor, since you were here last?

Dr. LANGWORTHY. Yes, sir. We have worked with new foods and also found new uses for well-known ones. These have included potato flour, sweet potato flour, as well as soy-bean and peanut flours, fruits, and vegetables, dairy products, oils and fats. We have also given much attention to the use of corn, grain sorghums, rice, barley, and other cereals.

The CHAIRMAN. I notice there is an increase of $50,000 in this item.

Dr. LANGWORTHY. Mr. Chairman and gentlemen: Briefly put, we wish to develop and extend our work so that it may keep pace with the growth of extension work in home economics. A primary purpose is to collect subject matter for use in the extension work under the Lever Act. This would also be of value for the work carried on under the Federal Board for Vocational Education, and for other workers in home economics. The success of the efforts of home economics extension workers and others in helping housekeepers to meet the war emergency food situation is in large measure due to the fact that a fund of carefully tested information had been brought together, and a great deal of it by the Office of Home Economics. The ceasing of hostilities does not mean, I think, that our home problems will be those we knew during the war, or those we knew before the war, but rather new conditions and new problems. We want to do our part fully by bringing together information so that the housekeeper can meet and solve them. The interest in home economics has been growing for a number of years, and was greatly extended as a result of conditions growing out of the war. As a result housekeepers all over the country have turned to home-economics workers for help in solving the war emergency food problems and other home problems.

The Office of Home Economics has shaped its work as best it could to provide the information which was needed, and in all its efforts has had the hearty cooperation of the Office of Extension Work North and West, and the Office of Extension Work South. A feature of our work was the preparation of 20 war emergency food leaflets. The general plan of the leaflets was dtermined at a conference of home-economics workers from the agricultural colleges and other experts, and in carrying out the project the Food Administration cooperated. The leaflets were very popular, as is shown by the fact that a total of well over 20,000,000 copies was needed to supply the demand for them. It is interesting to note that in connection with its State food campaign Massachusetts translated these leaflets into eight or more foreign languages in order that the information they contained might be made available in localities where there was a large foreign-born population. We also prepared food cards, giving concise directions for preparing foods in accordance with the food regulations, circulars, and popular bulletins which dealt directly with war emergency food problems, and also prepared a great many articles which were used in the department's publicity work. That there was so much information on hand which could be made use of is due to the fact that the nutrition investigations and later the home-economics work has received the support of Congress. We now want to extend this work to meet the new situations that are coming and to develop all lines, laying special stress upon work pertaining to clothing, textiles, and household equipment, in order that we may secure a fund of information which will measure up to and keep pace with that we have for food.

The CHAIRMAN. You mentioned something about the Smith-Hughes Act a while ago. Did you publish those leaflets and pay for the publication out of those funds?

Dr. LANGWORTHY. No, sir; there was no work on the leaflets carried on under the Smith-Hughes Act. They were prepared as a joint project by the Department of Agriculture in cooperation with the Food Administration and, as I understand it, were published as a part of the publication work under the emergency funds.

The CHAIRMAN. That act is a thing of the past now, or will be the 1st of July, and you will pay for the publications out of these funds?

Dr. LANGWORTHY. No, sir; not out of those funds.

The CHAIRMAN. Out of what funds?

Dr. LANGWORTHY. I suppose the leaflets as they stand have about served their purpose. There will undoubtedly be many requests for them, but I think that the small stock which we have on hand will suffice for that purpose.

The CHAIRMAN. But you will issue other leaflets?

Dr. LANGWORTHY. Yes, sir; these brief, simple statements have proved very effective and we wish to prepare additional leaflets as needed as part of our regular work.

The CHAIRMAN. This $50,000 increase here is for the employment of additional experts?

Dr. LANGWORTHY. For the employment of additional workers and for laboratory expenses incidental thereto. It seems almost certain that for the next few months, and perhaps for a year or two afterwards, it will be necessary to stress thrift, and we are preparing publications on thrift which we hope will be as useful as those on food were during the war emergency situation.

The CHAIRMAN. Just what do you mean by issuing publications on thrift?

Dr. LANGWORTHY. I mean the writing of short summaries, which will make suggestions based on well-tested evidence, dealing with the effective use in the home of all the commodities which we use there—in other words, help the housekeeper to get the most out of everything she uses. These leaflets and other publications would take up a great variety of questions dealing with clothing, household equipment, and similar matters. That the interest in these subjects is very great is shown by the amount of attention paid to clothing and other home problems by extension workers. For instance, the extension workers in Michigan have brought together a large number of brief statements in multigraphed form on food, clothing, household equipment, and other home problems. These are prepared to suit local conditions. The same thing is done in connection with extension work in the other States. However, much more information is needed than is now available, and we want to do our part and provide this information, backed up by careful laboratory tests regarding clothing, textiles, and household equipment, as well as food.

The CHAIRMAN. Let me see whether I understand your plan: I suppose you mean the economical use of clothing?

Dr. LANGWORTHY. The plan includes the economical use of clothing. I mean, for instance, to provide information which will enable the housekeeper to select, use, and care for clothing in such a way that it will give the maximum satisfaction and service.

Mr. McLAUGHLIN. We propose to spend more money so that the people at home can spend less.

The CHAIRMAN. That is the purpose of this?

Dr. LANGWORTHY. Yes. I think that is very clearly put. That is exactly what we hope to do—make sure that the housekeeper spends her money wisely and gets a dollar's worth of value for every dollar she spends.

Mr. ANDERSON. What is the character of the work you do with respect to clothing?

Dr. LANGWORTHY. We wish to study problems which have to do with the wearing quality of textiles used for clothing and household equipment, their care and renovation, and other similar problems—the relative value of different materials and different weaves in protecting the body from head and cold. We are accustomed to think of woolen as the material which we used for warmth and of cotton as the material we select when we want to keep cool.

As a matter of fact the case is not so simple. We know that cotton wadding is commonly used in garments designed for warmth and that some woolen garments are particularly cool in summer. Keeping the body warm depends very largely upon the way the cloth is woven and the way in which it is used. We want to help provide housekeepers with information which will enable them to select wisely from the many good materials which our manufacturers provide. A great many studies have been made, I understand, of textiles needed for clothing, for blankets, and for other Army purposes, which have been of very great value. It is our hope to make similar studies which will be equally important from the home standpoint and help in the important matter of using wisely our available supplies. We also want to provide the housekeeper with data on the best way to care for, clean, and repair her household equipment and to do this in ways which will save time and strength. This means true thrift. As an illustration of the beginning we have made along this line I may mention our Farmers' Bulletin, " Spots and Stains and Their Removal," which has proved very popular. As a result of the work we want to do it will be easily possible to supply a great deal more information which will be equally useful. There are many things worth knowing, some of them very simple. For instance, hot water with a little oil and turpentine added is very satisfactory for cleaning furniture.

Mr. ANDERSON. Will that work on an automobile?

Dr. LANGWORTHY. I have not had experience, but I do not see why it would not be satisfactory.

Mr. MCLAUGHLIN. You haven't fixed up any new beverages?

Dr. LANGWORTHY. No, sir; but we have said a good deal about the great importance of milk as a beverage.

Mr. HAUGEN. Don't you think a bulletin on fashions would be more attractive than on the wearing qualities?

Dr. LANGWORTHY. Perhaps it would, and we will do our best to write good ones if the committee authorizes us to prepare them.

The CHAIRMAN. I think you would succeed with it.

Dr. TRUE. May I make just a brief statement about this item? It seems to me a very important matter.

The CHAIRMAN. When this nutrition investigation was started, I guess Mr. Haugen and I were the only two men on the committee. The work was the laughing stock of the committee and of Congress. But I think there is no man on this committee now who is not convinced of the usefulness of this work.

Dr. TRUE. Not only that, but if we are to put this work on its proper basis we must have considerable more money than we have at present. Now, it is an enterprise that is doing a very large work throughout the country, and when you take the spread of instruction in home economics in the colleges and schools and through the extension agencies you have a very great thing, and you can not carry that on successfully, in a permanent way, unless you are accumulating new information. In the case of agriculture, we have our agricultural experiment stations in every State, as well as large sums of money spent by the Department of Agriculture. But back of this home-economics movement there is as yet no organization which is doing any considerable amount of systematic investigating except this small Office of Home Economics in the Department of Agriculture, and it is entirely inadequate to meet the demands made upon it and the needs of investigation along those lines. The Secretary has gone into this matter thoroughly, I think, and is asking for this addition to put the work on a proper basis, so that we may give this great extension and teaching movement in home economics a proper scientific basis.

STATEMENT OF DR. A. C. TRUE, DIRECTOR OF THE STATES RELATIONS SERVICE, UNITED STATES DEPARTMENT OF AGRICULTURE—Continued.

The CHAIRMAN. Your next item is on page 214, item 56, which is your general administrative item, with a recommended increase of $10,000.

Dr. TRUE. That is simply an increase to provide for the enlarged work of the service.

The CHAIRMAN. That increase would be based, I take it, on the theory that the committee will allow this large increased appropriation for that extension work; is that true?

Dr. TRUE. That entered into the consideration in a general way.

Mr. HAUGEN. Wouldn't it be better to put all the administrative expenses in one item than to have a lot of items amounting to the same thing? You said you could use $400,000 out of that million for administrative expenses.

Dr. TRUE. This is the usual item.

Mr. HAUGEN. It is the usual item, and it is for the same purpose as the $400,000, as I understand it?

Dr. TRUE. This is not merely for extension work. This is the usual general item covering the more general administrative phases of the States Relations Service as a whole.

Mr. HAUGEN. Isn't it possible to put it all in one item?

Dr. TRUE. It might be; but this is in accordance with the general practice.

Mr. HAUGEN. I know, but we keep on doubling up. We make one appropriation and think we are through, and then we find half a dozen others covering the same thing, and in that way we multiply it several times; we might as well have them all under one head.

Dr. TRUE. If the same object could be gained by consolidation, there would be no objection to that; but this is in accordance with the general make-up of the appropriation act as we have had it for a number of years.

AGRICULTURE APPROPRIATION BILL.

COMMITTEE ON AGRICULTURE,
HOUSE OF REPRESENTATIVES,
Wednesday, January 8, 1919.

BUREAU OF PUBLIC ROADS.

STATEMENT OF MR. P. ST. J. WILSON, ACTING DIRECTOR, BUREAU OF PUBLIC ROADS, UNITED STATES DEPARTMENT OF AGRICULTURE.

The CHAIRMAN. The next is the Bureau of Public Roads, page 216. I regret to inform the committee that since our last hearing, the chief of this bureau, Dr. Page, has passed away. I think it is only fair to say that this entire bureau is a monument to his zeal and disinterested service.

Capt. Wilson, we will hear you.

The CHAIRMAN. Capt. Wilson, you have no increases to propose in your statutory salaries above the $2,500 limit, have you?

Mr. WILSON. There is one.

The CHAIRMAN. Where is that?

Mr. WILSON. In the salary of the director. I do not know whether you want to hear from me on that subject, or whether the Secretary will cover that. It is found on page 218 of the Book of Estimates.

The CHAIRMAN. We have a memorandum from the Secretary on that, and will insert it in the record.

(The memorandum referred to follows:)

Salary of the Director of the Bureau of Public Roads.

One director, who shall be a scientist, and have charge of all scientific and technical work, from $4,500 to $5,000, an increase of $500.

The salary of the Director of the Bureau of Public Roads was fixed at $4,500 in the agricultural appropriation act for the fiscal year ending June 30, 1915. The work of the bureau was very greatly enlarged when the irrigation and drainage investigations were transferred from the States Relations Service, and the investigations pertaining to rural engineering were inaugurated at the beginning of the fiscal year 1916. In addition, the regular activities of the bureau have developed very rapidly within the past few years, and more recently it has been charged with the administration of the Federal-aid road act, approved July 11, 1916. This act has imposed a very great burden upon the bureau, and the responsibilities of the director have correspondingly increased. Intimate contacts have been established with the highway commissions of the various States, and the machinery for the effective administration of this important measure has been developed. There are now pending in Congress many measures appropriating large sums for the extension of highway activities under the Federal-aid road act. Furthermore, the construction of roads was very greatly curtailed during the war, and it is highly important that the activities under the Federal-aid road act be resumed in full measure and prosecuted as vigorously as possible.

Since the estimates were submitted, the position of Director of the Bureau of Public Roads has become vacant through the death of Mr. Page. The department should be in a position to secure the best available man in the country to take charge of the work. The present salary is totally inadequate, especially when it is compared with the salaries received by some of the State highway engineers. For instance, the chief engineer in California, it is understood, receives a compensation of $12,000 per annum, and many others receive slightly smaller amounts.

The CHAIRMAN. Take up your lump-sum appropriation, item 70, on page 220, " for inquiries in regard to systems of road management," $38,240. There is no change in that item except by way of transfer?

Mr. WILSON. That is true.

The CHAIRMAN. Briefly, what do you do there?

Mr. WILSON. Just as it states, " for inquiries in regard to systems of road management throughout the United States, and for giving expert advice on this subject." We take up road management in the States so as to keep the department and the States, as well as individuals, posted as to these things; the delivery of lectures, and cooperating with the States in the matter of their laws. That has been one of the big items that we have covered in that; during the past few years quite a number of State highway departments have been formed, and we have been of incalculable value to the different States in helping them to formulate their laws. During the past year we have varied from this work, as a great many other branches of the Agricultural Department have done, and have helped out with war work. We have had several men at work and have done a good deal in helping the War Department to get information as to roads over which their transports were running.

The CHAIRMAN. Any questions on that, gentlemen? If not, you may take up the next item, Mr. Wilson, No. 71, " For investigations of the best methods of road making," $138,220. There is no change in that item?

Mr. WILSON. No change.

The CHAIRMAN. You are conducting the same character of investigation as in former years?

Mr. WILSON. Yes; these investigations are——

The CHAIRMAN (interposing). This is your field work?

Mr. WILSON. Yes; except for the necessary part of the work here, but practically all of it is in the field.

The CHAIRMAN. Any questions on that, gentlemen of the committee?

Mr. HAUGEN. You might give us a little idea of what is being done along that line, Mr. Wilson.

Mr. WILSON. Well, for the past year, and of course this matter is past but it may be of interest, we have been of considerable help, I think, to the War Department. We assigned a number of our engineers to supervise the construction of roads in their cantonments.

Mr. WILSON (of the committee). What are you going to do this year?

Mr. WILSON. This year we are going to take up the same line of work we have been doing in the past. That work slacked up during the past year on account of the urgency of war work. We will assist the States and counties in the construction of roads by way of furnishing engineers to look after the construction work in connection with object-lesson roads, and helping them to organize for their work. We have for the last two or three years, and probably will for the next year or two anyway, have a great deal of work to do with the State highway departments which have been recently formed. There are a number of State highway departments which are young yet, and we have been of considerable help to them. We are covering the territory where assistance is most needed.

The CHAIRMAN. I noticed in the newspapers or in the Official Bulletin that there will be a tremendous expenditure of money for road building during the current year. What is your opinion about that?

Mr. WILSON. Well, I think there will be an increase above normal. A great many States were unable to spend their appropriation or anything like all of it last year on account of labor conditions and inability to get material, and they still have a large proportion of their last year's appropriation as well as their current appropriation for expenditure this year. High costs, labor conditions, and disruption of contracting organizations may counterbalance this to some extent?

The CHAIRMAN. How much, do you know?

Mr. WILSON. No; but I think it has been estimated that normally about $300,000,000 would have been spent in the country during this year, and probably between $300,000,000 and $400,000,000 will be spent altogether by the Federal Government, the States, and the counties for the reasons above stated.

The CHAIRMAN. How much is the Federal road fund?

Mr. WILSON. Under the Federal road act there is the sum of $15,000,000 available for the present fiscal year; some for the previous fiscal year has not been actually expended, and after the 1st of July there will be $20,000,000 more, the fourth appropriation. So that in the next 18 months there will be available for expenditure of Federal funds—though of course some of it will run along into next year, the $20,000,000 available after July 1, and the $15,000,000, and practically all of the $10,000,000.

The CHAIRMAN. There will be $27,000,000 that the States will duplicate?

Mr. WILSON. Very nearly, excluding the $20,000,000 to become available July 1. They will more than duplicate the Federal funds. Up to the present time the Government has put in about 33⅓ per cent of the money on this cooperative work.

Mr. WILSON (of the committee). How much does a State have to put in?

Mr. WILSON. A State has to put in at least 50 per cent.

Mr. WILSON (of the committee). You estimate that there will be expended in the next 18 months on roads about $65,000,000?

Mr. WILSON. Yes; $65,000,000 to $75,000,000 under the Federal aid road law, without taking into account the $20,000,000 available July 1.

Mr. WILSON (of the committee). Under this item you give field advice and make demonstrations?

Mr. WILSON. Yes. We help the States in doing their own work. The Federal road act carries in it an allowance not to exceed 3 per cent of the funds appropriated for supervision of the Federal aid work. That is taken care of out of that appropriation.

Mr. WILSON (of the committee). This committee did not report that act, although it reported the first Federal road act that was ever reported. Does that mean 3 per cent of the total, or 3 per cent of what?

Mr. WILSON. It means 3 per cent of the Federal appropriation only.

Mr. WILSON (of the committee). For each year.

Mr. WILSON. Yes. And as our proportionate part has been something like 33⅓ per cent, it practically means about 1 per cent of the money expended; that is, our one-third and the States two-thirds would give about 1 per cent of the amount expended for that work, and it is pretty close sailing.

Mr. LEE. In Dade County, Ga., there is a road estimated to cost $50,000, and the engineers wanted to charge 7½ per cent for survey and supervision. It strikes me that that is a very heavy charge?

Mr. WILSON. I think it is a little heavy. My recollection is that in most counties in Georgia they are making arrangements with engineers for 5 per cent for surveys and supervision. I think that is rather a bad system.

Mr. LEE. I think that is an outrage?

Mr. WILSON. That is pretty heavy.

Mr. HEFLIN. In a State where a county is cooperating with the Federal Government and putting up its required amount of money, do you send a man down there to assist them in building the road, or in building a part of the road, to show them how?

Mr. WILSON. We have not done that under the Federal aid appropriation. The actual supervision of that work is, under the Federal aid law, placed under the State highway department; but under the old Bureau of Public Roads act, which was under discussion when we digressed, we were authorized to furnish engineers for that purpose, and have done it.

Mr. HEFLIN. At what expense does the man go? Does the State pay a part of his expense?

Mr. WILSON. We have worked all sorts of ways. We give a State or county a reasonable assistance in this respect from the Federal fund. If they want more than that we have furloughed a man and let him go on their pay roll. After he had been there a certain time and we thought we had reached our limit on the appropriation, and we did not think we could give more to any one county, we furloughed the man and let them pay his salary. But for a reasonable amount of assistance we pay the man's salary and expenses.

The CHAIRMAN. Any other questions, gentlemen?

Mr. HAUGEN. We got away from the question. I was anxious to know about the advice in building these sand roads and dirt roads, or mud roads, as they are sometimes called.

Mr. WILSON. We have a number of men who go into counties and build what we call object-lesson roads and stay on the job and see how it is put down.

Mr. ANDERSON. The best advice you can give on building mud and sand roads is not to build them, isn't it?

Mr. WILSON. Well, yes; but they are a great help in a great many cases.

Mr. HAUGEN. What is to be told to people about spreading sand?

Mr. WILSON. Well, the proportionate mixture is a thing that requires probably more expert information, and the class of sand that will mix best with clay, or whatever it is to be mixed with, as well as the proportions.

Mr. HAUGEN. You take whatever you have, don't you?

Mr. WILSON. Yes; but you may have sand banks half a mile apart and one is better than the other.

Mr. HAUGEN. Are you sending men over the country to locate these sand banks?

Mr. WILSON. No; but where a county wants its employees trained we send a man there long enough to teach the man they select to supervise the work how to select the better quality of materials— to make an investigation on the ground.

Mr. HAUGEN. What are you spending for that?

Mr. WILSON. The appropriation is $138,000.

Mr. HAUGEN. The finders of that sand—what is spent for that?

Mr. WILSON. I could not tell you offhand what is spent for that particular item.

Mr. HAUGEN. You said $15,000,000 was available, and then you said $5,000,000 is available; do we understand that $20,000,000 was available?

Mr. WILSON. The Federal-aid appropriation was $5,000,000 the first year and $10,000,000 the second year and $15,000,000 the third year. That makes a total of practically $30,000,000 available now.

Mr. HAUGEN. The first year's appropriation has been spent already?

Mr. WILSON. The first year's appropriation has been spent and a considerable proportion of the second year.

Mr. HAUGEN. Under that act how much is available this year?

Mr. WILSON. For which year?

Mr. HAUGEN. For the current year?

Mr. WILSON. For the current year there is $15,000,000 available.

Mr. HAUGEN. And $5,000,000 that was not expended before?

Mr. WILSON. Between $5,000,000 and $10,000,000. Some was under contract but not worked out last year.

Mr. HAUGEN. And $15,000,000 this year?

Mr. WILSON. Yes; and $20,000,000 more the 1st of July.

Mr. THOMPSON. Very little road work was done last year owing to the demands for war. You could not do much work?

Mr. WILSON. No; we had a big fight to get even enough material for maintenance, but we did finally get that through.

The CHAIRMAN. If you gentlemen of the committee will turn to page 49 of the Secretary's report you will find detailed figures on that proposition. Anything further on that matter? If not go ahead with item 72, " For investigations of the chemical and physical character of road material, $47,020." There is no change in that item, is there?

Mr. WILSON. That is for operation of our laboratory; for testing materials, both bituminous and sand, gravel, cement etc. It is one of the most important things that we have to do.

Mr. ANDERSON. Have we discovered anything new in connection with cement and bituminous binder for roads?

Mr. WILSON. Nothing very recently, but we are testing out new materials all the time. There is a great deal of importance attached to the matter of testing materials. It is the general rule of engineers to test all cement before it is used, and we have a great deal of time taken up in that kind of thing—assistance to States that have no laboratories and the smaller divisions which have none, and we make tests for them.

Mr. HAUGEN. Do you find any considerable amount of cement falling below the standard?

Mr. WILSON. Oh, yes; a sufficient amount to make it generally customary among all engineers using it to have it tested.

Mr. HAUGEN. Cement made by the larger manufacturers?

Mr. WILSON. Yes.

Mr. HAUGEN. Any considerable amount of it?

Mr. WILSON. Yes. That happens very often without one otherwise knowing it. A carload of cement may get damp, or wet, or something else may happen. There are a great many things that have to be watched pretty closely.

Mr. ANDERSON. Have any experiments been conducted about disintegration of roads on account of heavy trucks? Have you any definite experience along that line?

Mr. WILSON. We have made no extended investigations; no. But that is one of the things that we hope to get into this year.

Mr. ANDERSON. I think there are a good many people who have the idea that if the present heavy trucking conditions continue we will have to adopt an entirely new system of road construction. Have you any ideas about that?

Mr. WILSON. Yes. I think the average road as constructed up to the present time is not capable of carrying the very heavy traffic that it has recently been subjected to. Where there is much of that traffic the roads will have to be rebuilt, or reinforced certainly, and heavier construction will have to be had, or, what I think will likely come, a limitation on loads and speeds on these roads.

Mr. JACOWAY. Some years ago you built some roads adjacent to this city, that cost, Mr. Page told me, $900 a mile. Am I correct about that or do you know?

Mr. WILSON. That was possibly just for the surfacing of the road, not the entire building of the road.

Mr. JACOWAY. Then that was what it was?

Mr. WILSON. Yes.

Mr. JACOWAY. How did that experiment turn out?

Mr. WILSON. Very good roads, some of them; they turned out pretty well. Those roads were about Chevy Chase, as I recall, but that was before I came here.

Mr. JACOWAY. After a road has been properly surfaced and $900 a mile is spent on it, what is the life of it?

Mr. WILSON. Mr. Peirce, that $900 covered the work of reshaping the surface with bituminous material, didn't it?

Mr. PEIRCE. That was the cost of surface treatment only.

Mr. JACOWAY. What is the life of that road? That was four years ago, as I recall; what is the condition of the road to-day?

Mr. WILSON. Some of them are in very good condition, but we have been maintaining them at greater or less cost, according to the material used. That is one item contained in here.

Mr. JACOWAY. What is the average cost for maintenance per year?

Mr. WILSON. Mr. Peirce, what is that?

Mr. PEIRCE. I have a record of the cost in our report for experimental road work, and it varies with different sections.

Mr. WILSON. Between what prices?

Mr. PEIRCE. Between half a cent and 3 cents a square yard.

Mr. JACOWAY. And off to the side of the road you had a little house, and a man sat in it and made a record of every automobile traveling over the road?

Mr. Wilson. Yes; we kept a traffic census there every thirteenth day.

Mr. JACOWAY. Was the traffic on that road very severe or not? What I am trying to get at is, if this road can be built for $900 a mile, why not go at it?

Mr. WILSON. Oh, that is only the surface treatment after we had a waterbound surface road that had cost from $5,000 to $10,000 a mile, or at the present prices more than that. This is merely surface treatment on that road, to keep automobiles from tearing it up and having it blown away.

Mr. JACOWAY. I thought that was the cost of the road.

Mr. WILSON. Oh, no; that was just the cost of the bituminous surface on that road.

Mr. HEFLIN. What about the average cost of clay and sand roads in the rural districts?

Mr. WILSON. It depends so much on the local conditions that it is very hard to say, but I have seen them built for as low as $500 a mile and as high as $5,000 or $6,000 a mile, probably an average of from $1,000 to $2,000 a mile, or from $1,000 to $3,000 a mile would be nearer it. It depends on a great many things, and the $500 a mile road is very exceptional. At present prices you will not get any.

The CHAIRMAN. We build them in one county in my district at from $300 to $500 a mile?

Mr. WILSON. Yes; according to prewar prices.

Mr. HEFLIN. That is not a very hilly country?

The CHAIRMAN. No; it is a level country.

Mr. HAUGEN. What do you suggest about surfacing roads with gravel and sand; how heavy a coat do you surface with?

Mr. WILSON. With gravel I should say under present conditions, unless it is subject to exceptionally light traffic, where you will not have much automobile traffic and no truck traffic at all, 8 to 10 inches of compacted gravel, 10 to 12 inches placed loose. No gravel road will stand up under automobile travel unless it has a bituminous surface on it.

The CHAIRMAN. I thought a gravel road would stand very well?

Mr. WILSON. It does not break through always, but you will find such roads full of holes about the size of your hand or of this book, which will jolt you in traveling over it. The gravel that you take out of the earth is very seldom perfectly uniform. Sometimes you have more clay and sometimes less. It does not wear uniformly. If you have too much clay it forms mud and the mud will stick to the wheels and pick up. You can very seldom find gravel in its natural state that will make a road that will wear down uniformly.

Mr. HAUGEN. Do you suggest mixing gravel with clay?

Mr. WILSON. Yes; if it has not enough clay in it. The ordinary bed run of gravel, unless it comes out of a stream where it has been washed, usually has a certain amount of clay in it.

Mr. HAUGEN. There are sand beds that are free from clay?

Mr. WILSON. Yes. Where there is insufficient clay to make it bond there ought to be some clay mixed with it.

Mr. HAUGEN. Well, do you recommend mixing it?

Mr. WILSON. When conditions require it; yes.

Mr. HAUGEN. Well, ordinarily?

Mr. WILSON. With gravel?

Mr. HAUGEN. Yes.

Mr. WILSON. I say, if the gravel has enough clay in it you don't want any more put with it; if it has not enough clay in it you should mix some. That is as near as I can get at an answer to that question. Material is so variable in a bank that you can not know the factors without an examination.

Mr. HAUGEN. Well, with clean sand and gravel, do you need a little clay?

Mr. WILSON. Yes.

Mr. HAUGEN. Do you suggest a light coat?

Mr. WILSON. Of clay or gravel?

Mr. HAUGEN. No; in the case of sand and gravel. Do you suggest 10 inches instead of 6?

Mr. WILSON. Yes.

Mr. HAUGEN. Say 6 inches applied at two different times or 10 inches at one time?

Mr. WILSON. Put 6 inches on and let it pack, or if you are building the road with a roller, put on the lower 6 inches and roll it, and then put on another 6 inches and roll that. If you are going to let the traffic beat it down, put on a thinner coat of sand and let the traffic beat it down, then put on more and let that be beaten down, and so on until you have gotten enough to stand the traffic.

The CHAIRMAN. Take the next item, No. 73, "For conducting field experiments and various methods of road construction and maintenance, and investigations concerning various road materials and preparations, $60,000." Is there any change there?

Mr. WILSON. No.

The CHAIRMAN. I have had a great deal of difficulty in my experience with this committee on distinguishing item 71 from item 73. Explain the difference, Capt. Wilson.

Mr. WILSON. Item 71 is for the employment and furnishing of engineers for the supervision of the work, but does not include the cost of any of the materials that go into the work. Item 73 was included to furnish materials and actually construct the road at the cost of the department. The roads that we were just talking about near Chevy Chase were built under that item.

The CHAIRMAN. "For the purchase of materials and equipment"; that is, cost of materials and construction?

Mr. WILSON. Yes; that is the actual cost of construction.

The CHAIRMAN. These are your model roads?

Mr. WILSON. Yes.

The CHAIRMAN. Any other questions, gentlemen? If not, you may take the next item, Mr. Wilson.

Mr. HAUGEN. Can you give an estimate of the cost of maintenance of clay and gravel roads?

Mr. WILSON. That is variable, too, sir. Anywhere from $100 up to $600 or $700.

Mr. HAUGEN. $100 a mile?

Mr. WILSON. In some cases, yes:

Mr. HAUGEN. How low in others, or how high?

Mr. WILSON. Well, up as high as $400, $500, or $600 a mile some times. That is where your traffic is heavy.

Mr. HAUGEN. I am speaking of the average traffic in the country.

Mr. WILSON. From $100 to $300 a mile, together with cost of periodical resurfacing.

Mr. HAUGEN. They do not have to be resurfaced every year?

Mr. WILSON. No; I mean the cost of periodical resurfacing. Every five or six years perhaps.

Mr. HAUGEN. What is the average cost per year?

Mr. WILSON. That depends on how far you have to haul gravel, and so on. I would say from $100 to $300 or $400 a mile according to the varying conditions.

Mr. HAUGEN. What is the cost of maintaining these expensive hard-surface roads?

Mr. WILSON. They run as high as $1,000 or $1,200 a mile. Some of the roads in Massachusetts last year, I think, cost that much.

(Chairman Lever retires and Mr. Lee takes the chair.)

Mr. LEE (in the chair). Is there anything else under that item, gentlemen? If not, turn to item 74, page 223, Mr. Wilson, "For investigating and reporting upon the utilization of water in farm irrigation, including the best methods to apply in practice, $82,440."

Mr. WILSON. That is the same item we have had for a number of years and the work is the same that has been done heretofore.

Mr. LEE. Are there any changes?

Mr. WILSON. No changes. During the past year we have eliminated some of our work of a more investigative nature, which we will take up this year as soon as the season opens. The work will now be the same as it has been for a number of years past.

Mr. LEE. Any questions on that, gentlemen of the committee? If not, turn to the next item, Mr. Wilson, item 75, page 224, "For investigating and reporting upon farm drainage and upon the drainage of swamp and other wet lands which may be made available for agricultural purposes, and so forth, $73,760."

Mr. WILSON. I might say the same about that as about the irrigation. Irrigation is mostly in the arid regions, though we have some of that work in the East, and drainage is to take care of swamp lands and wet lands in the humid regions.

Mr. LEE. Is there any demand for that work?

Mr. WILSON. Yes; quite a good deal of it.

Mr. LEE. How much money are you spending for drainage?

Mr. WILSON. We are asking for $73,760, and will spend about that much this year.

Mr. LEE. How much in drainage? I presume it means giving advice as to drainage?

Mr. WILSON. Yes.

Mr. LEE. How much do you expend under that?

Mr. WILSON. Well, practically the bulk of the money is spent that way.

Mr. LEE. What are you doing? Do you go out on a farm and make a survey?

Mr. WILSON. Yes; we make surveys on small tracts and direct surveys on large tracts.

Mr. LEE. For tiling?

Mr. WILSON. Yes; and ditching.

Mr. LEE. Out on the farms?

Mr. WILSON. Yes; we do individual farm draining in localities where it is felt an object lesson would be generally profitable to a community. We try to do no more of this than is warranted for the use of an object lesson, and not to save the individual farm owner the expense of hiring an engineer except where it is thought proper to be used as an object lesson. We try to keep away from that.

Mr. LEE. Only where on an individual farm it may serve as an object lesson?

Mr. WILSON. Yes.

Mr. HAUGEN. Did you ever do any of that in the Northwest?

Mr. WILSON. Yes.

Mr. HAUGEN. In what State?

Mr. WILSON. Some in Iowa. We have two engineers now up on the Red River. I do not recall just what States are covered by that work, but I know Minnesota, North and South Dakota are included.

Mr. HAUGEN. Do you go out on a farm and make a survey for the owner?

Mr. McCRORY. We do in cases where it can serve as an object lesson for the surrounding people. If it is a small job and the survey will only take a small amount of time, possibly a day or two, or something like that. We do not make any extensive surveys except on large tracts, and then the local people generally furnish persons to do the detail work while our engineers just give the general directions.

Mr. HAUGEN. All of them have engineers, and that work could be done by them? We have always had to pay for our own surveying.

Mr. McCRORY. We have done some work in Iowa. But the bulk of the work is in the Southern States, where there is not much tile drainage. It is purely educational work, I might say, and people are not familiar with its value. We are developing a great deal of interest in drainage work in the South through the activities of the office.

Mr. HAUGEN. Do you furnish the tile, too?

Mr. McCRORY. No.

Mr. HAUGEN. Why don't you furnish the tile? Why go halfway and stop instead of furnishing everything?

Mr. McCRORY. In some instances in the preliminary work back in 1911 and 1912 some of the States bought the tile, for instance, Alabama, to put in experimental tracts to show the results that could be obtained. It was the very common belief that tile would not work in that country, and there had been a great deal of difficulty experienced in getting the work started, though, as a matter of fact, there was great need for it.

Mr. HAUGEN. Well, tiling is as old as the hills. Nobody remembers when the first tile was laid.

Mr. McCrory. But in the South there are a great many States where it is practically unknown at this time. We have a great deal of trouble educating men to do the work. We have to use men who have never seen tile and make tile layers out of them.

Mr. Haugen. Do you think it necessary to continue this appropriation?

Mr. McCrory. Yes.

Mr. Heflin. Where did you do drainage work in Alabama?

Mr. McCrory. The bulk of the preliminary work was done in the black belt in Alabama, near Montgomery, Pineapple, and Auburn Junction, and some other tracts whose location I can not name at this instant.

Mr. Thompson. Do you lay out drainage districts, too?

Mr. Wilson. Do we lay out drainage districts in a State, do you mean?

Mr. Thompson. You say you go out and survey a man's individual farm? There are drainage districts, aren't there?

Mr. Wilson. Yes; there are drainage districts, and we assist in organizing and making surveys for them, too.

Mr. Thompson. Do you furnish a man to superintend it and look after it?

Mr. Wilson. Well, to give it general direction but not to do the detail work. Local engineers are generally employed for that. Where there are competent local engineers, such as in Mr. Haugen's districts, where they have done so much of it, we do not have to go. We try to confine our work to object lessons, to do work in territory where people are not familiar with it, and where it will be of general instruction to the community.

Mr. Anderson. Where people help themselves you do not help them any?

Mr. Wilson. Yes; we help them where they help themselves, too. That is, people have to help themselves, but where people do not know or do not appreciate its value we try to give them an object lesson which will show them the value of it. It is important work.

Mr. Haugen. What are object lessons? Do you go and lay the tile for some farmer who is able to have the work done himself?

Mr. Wilson. No, sir; that is not the idea at all, but if a large tract of land or a number of counties, for instance, should be wet, if we could go into some section there and show them how to tile-drain it, or drain with open ditches, and that tract of land produced three or four times the amount of crop that all the land around it produces, you see other people would son get their lands drained.

Mr. Haugen. Have you not bulletins on drainage?

Mr. Wilson. Oh, yes.

Mr. Haugen. Would they not convey the same information?

Mr. Wilson. They will convey the same information, but I do not think they would make the same impression by any means. Lots of people sit up and read about things, and hear about things, but do not take them in as they do when they see them. That has been the case of the object-lesson road work, that this office did in years gone by; it has done as much to stir up sentiment as anything that could be done.

Mr. Heflin. After you drain a farm or place your system of drainage on a farm, then the people in that county or in adjoining counties could see how it was done and could go back and do the same thing?

Mr. WILSON. Yes; and if they want further assistance as to details, how to do it, we try to give them a reasonable amount of assistance.

(Mr. Lever resumed the chair.)

The CHAIRMAN. You do not commit yourself to the proposition that you do any actual drainage work?

Mr. WILSON. No; we only direct a man how to do it.

Mr. HAUGEN. It costs quite a good deal of money to have the work done.

Mr. LEE. If they want to drain a part of the land, you show them how to do it?

Mr. WILSON. Yes.

The CHAIRMAN. As a matter of fact, you go into a community which organizes itself, make a survey, and give these people in the community information as to the cost of drainage and plans for drainage; is that not all you do?

Mr. WILSON. Yes.

Mr. HAUGEN. Is there not anyone who can estimate the cost of drainage?

Mr. WILSON. Oh, yes.

Mr. HAUGEN. Do they have to have an expert from the department to tell them what the cost of drainage is, laying tile? That all depends on the cost of the tile and the cost of laying them, does it not?

Mr. WILSON. Yes; and the depth of the ditches and the amount of excavation to be done; and a great many other things that enter into it.

Mr. HAUGEN. It is only necessary to go to the tiler and find out what the excavation will cost and to the manufacturer of tile and he will tell you the price of tile, and a thousand tile will lay a little over 60 rods. I take it any schoolboy would be able to estimate the cost.

Mr. WILSON. Yes; if you give him the things that are to be used, the quantities, of course he can do the multiplying and adding and get the results.

Mr. HAUGEN. There is only the tile drain.

Mr. WILSON. There is the depth of the ditches, for instance.

Mr. HAUGEN. Of course, then, you have to get your estimate from the tiler?

Mr. WILSON. And how to run the tiles so as to make the water run and not try to make water run uphill.

Mr. HAUGEN. Is it necessary to tell them that water runs downhill and not uphill?

Mr. WILSON. No, sir; but most of those wet tracts are pretty flat, and the question of which is downhill is a right serious question sometimes; they look at a tract that is approximately level and do not know which is the downhill side of it.

The CHAIRMAN. Is there anything further, gentlemen, on that item? If not, the next is on page 226, administrative expenses; there is no change in that. On page 225, item 76, you have an increase in your rural-engineering work of $50,000?

Mr. WILSON. Yes; we have an increase there of $50,000, Mr. Chairman, and the note in the estimate gives a brief statement of what it is for. If you will allow me, I will ask Mr. McCormick, the chief of the Division of Rural Engineering, to answer any questions or to go into detail about that.

STATEMENT OF MR. E. B. McCORMICK, CHIEF OF THE DIVISION OF RURAL ENGINEERING, BUREAU OF PUBLIC ROADS, UNITED STATES DEPARTMENT OF AGRICULTURE.

The CHAIRMAN. Mr. McCormick, tell us in brief what you are doing and what you expect to do with this increase.

Mr. McCORMICK. The use we expect to make of that is to assist in the development and standardization of farm equipment of all kinds. That includes machinery and apparatus. We have had a very notable example of what can be done along that line in some of the activities of the War Industries Board here in the past year. For the sake of conservation it was necessary to cut out many of the less essential types of farm machinery and patterns, so that the equipment could be made from standard sizes—i. e., from standard-sized bars and standard-sized sheets of metal, and also to make use of the more available sizes of timber.

The War Industries Board, in cooperation with the Department of Agriculture, and also with the Farm Advisory Board, made quite a list of changes or eliminations. The most of them were arbitrary. They were based on the opinions of different persons and were made possible simply by the patriotic feeling among the manufacturers that they had to do anything that was suggested. I do not think the War Industries Board felt that they did the best that could be done. I know the rest of us did not, but they undoubtedly contributed a great deal toward conservation of materials in what they did do.

The CHAIRMAN. For example, how, why, when?

Mr. McCORMICK. Well, they cut out—this is several months ago and I do not know that my figures are accurate—but they cut out about 50 per cent of the shapes and varieties of disks. They eliminated probably 25 to 30 per cent of certain plow types. They cut out the left-hand plow altogether. There are a large number of shapes and sizes of machines that have grown up through personal prejudice on the part of the user, usually, however, started by the manufacturer in order to have something a little different from his competitor.

A few years ago the wagon manufacturers took up with our office some work in connection with wagon wheels. When they started out, they found they had about 1,200 different possible wagon wheels for farm wagons—not drays, but farm wagons. They have got that down now to about four different diameters of wagon wheels, with about an average of three or four different widths of tires; that is, they have cut it down from over 1,200 to probably less than 100 sizes, and sizes that anybody can make, and they are reducing the number still further. That action was based to a great extent on tests that had been made by our office.

The CHAIRMAN. What is your purpose here; of setting up your standards and then coming back to Congress later on and asking for an act and enforcing your standards?

Mr. McCORMICK. No, sir; we do not ask for that, because we do not consider that we need an act. If we, as the result of our tests and our experiments, decide that a certain machine has a certain power, or requires a certain power to operate it, it is our intention to authorize that rating, but we will not need any law to enforce it——

The CHAIRMAN (interposing). Common sense will do that?

Mr. McCORMICK. Yes.

The CHAIRMAN. But, as a matter of fact, are you not encroaching on the work of the Bureau of Standards?

Mr. McCORMICK. I do not think we are, Mr. Chairman. We are not trying to enforce a legal standard. It is merely assistance to the manufacturers and to the users of machines that have, as far as possible, interchangeability, and reducing a large number of superfluous sizes and makes. It is not establishing a legal standard, like a yardstick or a pound weight; it is not anything of that sort, and nothing that has any idea of legal enforcement to it. It is for the securing of information and making it available, both to the user and to the manufacturer.

Mr. LESHER. It is more in the line of suggestions and recommendations?

Mr. McCORMICK. Yes; and acting as a clearing house between the two, bringing them together. At the present time they consider, to a certain extent, their interests as antagonistic. We do not think they are. We think the last year of cooperation has shown they are not antagonistic.

The CHAIRMAN. Was this increase made on the basis of experience during time of war, or is this a peace time proposition?

Mr. McCORMICK. This is a peace time proposition. It has been requested, so far as I am concerned, for about three or four years now, and I believe it was presented to this committee before the declaration of war. It was presented last year.

The CHAIRMAN. As I recall it, when this item was originally suggested it had in it that language authorizing you to do this farm-machinery work, and my recollection is this committee cut that language out.

Mr. McCORMICK. They cut it out; yes, sir. That is, the committee cut the increase out; the authorization is already in the act.

Mr. HARRISON. There was no new language in the item proposed in the estimates of last year, Mr. Chairman, except a clause to make the appropriation immediately available.

Mr. HAUGEN. I think we cut out a little of the architecture, too, of the bill. I think the committee reached the conclusion that Sears & Roebuck and the rest of them were furnishing the people with blue prints and specifications, and the opinion was it was not necessary to continue the work.

Mr. McCORMICK. I was not present at that time. I did not hear any such discussion.

Mr. HAUGEN. I think there are hundreds of firms that are furnishing it, and furnishing it free of charge.

Mr. McCORMICK. We think we are furnishing designs better suited to farm conditions than are some who are interested solely from the commercial side.

Mr. ANDERSON. I should like to make an inquiry or two along that line. Is there any standard method now of determining the horsepower of a motor?

Mr. McCormick. No, sir. We have, I say, no standard method. There are several so-called standard methods. There are formulæ which take into consideration the length of the stroke and diameter of the cylinder and some constant factor, usually.

Mr. Anderson. That is a mere calculation?

Mr. McCormick. It is an arbitrary or empirical formula that is used. There are about five of them. We have worked out the horsepower for some of the more prominent engines, using the five different formulæ, and we find a variation of as much as 60 per cent, and we also find that the manufacturers' ratings are likely not to agree with any one of those five formulæ.

Mr. Anderson. I want to get at your purpose. Is it your purpose to establish a standard method of determining the horsepower of motors?

Mr. McCormick. Yes, sir; and actually determining the horsepower of any one type. For instance, we have designed a piece of apparatus by which we can test and calibrate the horsepower of any engine, and if any manufacturer desires, and if this money is made available, it is our intention to test and to calibrate that type. That is, the actual horsepower developed.

Mr. Anderson. I saw a recent article, I do not recall now whether in one of the motor magazines, or in the Scientific American, or somewhere, which indicated that the same general type of motor—as the result of adjustment, as the result of slight variation in the casting of the bearing metal, and dozens of other elements in the motor itself—would result in a very wide variation even in the same type of motor.

Mr. McCormick. There is always an accidental difference in various manufactured products that can never be avoided, but as the method of manufacture improves constantly and duplication in manufacturing is carried through, and there is less hand fitting of work, that accidental difference which formerly existed, is being reduced constantly. I do not suppose it will ever get to the point where two engines will be absolutely identical, but any manufacturer who has any expectation of continuing in business and any consideration for his reputation, will not attempt to rate an engine right up to its limit; that is, the most that it can possibly do under best conditions.

He makes an allowance. The allowance he makes should more than offset any accidental difference that will exist in the manufacturing or in the nature of the material.

Mr. Anderson. You lay a good deal of stress, I notice, in this note upon standardization of motors and of tractors, and the rating of horsepower, etc. Now, I suppose, that in the case of tractive effect of the tractor you have an entirely different problem than you would have in the case of determining the horsepower of the motor, because you have there, I assume, a matter of ratio, construction, and everything else. How can you arrive at any standard method there?

Mr. McCormick. The apparatus that we have in mind makes the actual test of the power at the drawbar, and in addition we take the power at the belt; that is, the belt power. We take both. In that way we can determine absolutely any loss between the two points.

Mr. ANDERSON. This matter of standardization or interchangeability of parts, or whatever you call it, that is a matter very largely of getting the trade together and getting men to agree to do certain things, is it not?

Mr. MCCORMICK. Provided we can show them those things have a foundation in fact for being done, yes; but if it is merely personal opinion, each manufacturer considers that his idea is fully as good as the other's, and he will not change. Somebody has to change if there is going to be a uniformity in construction.

Mr. ANDERSON. All of these manufacturers have engineers and designers, etc., and naturally all of them seek to make their product a little better than anybody else's, and there must, necessarily, be some leeway in design and engineering ability, somewhere.

Mr. MCCORMICK. A great many of the differences have grown up because of the separation of the manufacturing concerns from each other. That is, there may be a dozen different ways of doing one thing that are equally good. One man on the Pacific coast will adopt a certain plan; another man in Michigan something else. We have just recently taken up the question—they are apparently small items, and yet their effect is considerable—the question of mangers in dairy barns.

Mr. ANDERSON. You are getting away from the proposition. I want you to stick to tractors.

Mr. MCCORMICK. All right; what is the question.

Mr. ANDERSON. I want, if I can, to get some limitation upon what you are trying to do. I can see where it is possible to standardize for all tractors the sizes of rods, and perhaps the pinions and wheels. and one thing and another of that sort, but when you get into engines, motors, I do not see where you can get any standardization.

Mr. MCCORMICK. We are not trying to standardize to the extent that we shall attempt to destroy any individuality or invention, but throughout the entire machine, the transmission from the engine to the drawbar, and even from the gas tank, in the case of gas tractors, to the engine, there are large numbers of what are called accessories which should and can be made attachable to the same sized openings or fittings, so they are interchangeable one on the other. It is not being done at the present time. The question of attachment. for instance, of magnetos for the ignition system, the attachment of carburetors are entirely different; in fact, many ascceessories are located in different places relative to the engine.

Mr. ANDERSON. Do you think you can get any standard method of attaching a carburetor or magneto to the motor?

Mr. MCCORMICK. We can get a great deal more uniform method. Personally, I think the word "uniformity" in this case is as fully expressive for our purpose as standardization. Uniformity and interchangability, so far as we can get it.

But the question of the power rating is one that we get a great many inquiries about, and there are many others. One question that comes in is, "Why is one man's hitch for implements 6 inches or a foot higher off the ground than anothers?" "Why is it I can use one tractor in pulling certain implements, while, if I change tractors, I have to change implements?" "If there is a certain height that is as good as another, if not the best height for hitching. why does not everybody have that?"

The CHAIRMAN. Who makes these inquiries—manufacturers?

Mr. McCORMICK. No; farmers make these inquiries. It is from them that our inquiries and demands come. The manufacturers, many of them, say they would like to have some standard test to go by, something authoritative.

The CHAIRMAN. Are these inquiries very large in volume, or do you only have one now and then?

Mr. McCORMICK. They are coming in constantly, and are apt to be verbal. Whenever there are any farmers' gatherings here, or anything of that kind, they come into our office and ask about them, and when we are out in the field they ask, "Why don't you do this?" "So if we have a 10-horsepower sheller and a 10-horsepower engine," they say, "we know we can run the sheller with that engine; as it is we oftimes can not do it."

The CHAIRMAN. Have you made any inquiries of the Bureau of Standards to see whether they are not doing this class of work?

Mr. McCORMICK. I have made no inquiries, but I doubt very much if they are taking up the question of getting uniformity in agricultural implements and the parts of them.

The CHAIRMAN. I think you had better make inquiry and let us know something about it, because I have an idea, even if they are not doing this work, that it is in their field rather than yours.

Mr. McCORMICK. I know that two or three years ago there was some correspondence relating to standardization, or the adoption of uniform sizes of bolts and nuts on agricultural implements, which was referred to us from the Bureau of Standards, which indicated to me they were doing nothing in that line.

Mr. ANDERSON. They have done work as to uniform standards for screws and nuts on automobiles, have they not?

Mr. McCORMICK. There has been a standard established; yes; and there are three or four standards of threads, etc., in the country.

Mr. HAUGEN. They are testing engines and tractors, are they not?

Mr. McCORMICK. They are not testing tractors so far as I know. So far as I know, they are not doing any work at all on agricultural implements. They have been testing aeroplane engines, helping in the development of those. As far as I know, that is all the test work they are doing.

Mr. HAUGEN. What is the advantage in a high hitch?

Mr. McCORMICK. I do not know that there is any?

Mr. HAUGEN. A number of tractors are made with a high hitch, and they advertise that point as being far superior to the other.

Mr. McCORMICK. Usually the argument advanced in favor of the high hitch is that it gives a sort of a downward pull, which holds the traction wheels down; they claim that increases the tractive power.

Mr. HAUGEN. You can pull the plow with an engine of less weight?

Mr. McCORMICK. That is the claim; yes.

Mr. HAUGEN. Have you tested that out?

Mr. McCORMICK. We have not had any opportunity; no, sir.

Mr. HAUGEN. What is your idea about it? Is there a certain advantage in that?

Mr. McCORMICK. I do not know.

The CHAIRMAN. That is what you want this money for?

Mr. McCormick. Yes, sir; that is one of the things we want to get, whether that pull is enough to have an appreciable result; I do not know.

Mr. Haugen. You are aware of the fact that a number of them are made with the high hitch and some with a lower hitch, and they advertise that point very strongly, and contend that it saves putting so much material in the engine and requires less weight to pull the plow?

The Chairman. What do you mean by high hitch?

Mr. Haugen. Where you hitch the engine to the plow; the top of the plow.

The Chairman. Is there anything further, Mr. McCormick?

Mr. Haugen. Have you been testing out the various makes of tractors?

Mr. McCormick. No, sir; we have had no opportunity to do so.

Mr. Haugen. Has there not been any investigation made?

Mr. McCormick. There have been investigations in the sense of observations of the machines at work, and during the course of manufacture by individuals from the office whenever opportunity presented itself, but with the appropriation and the amount of ground to be covered, it has been absolutely impossible to do any more than what we can pick up.

Mr. Haugen. Have you any knowledge of the department carrying on any investigation of the kind?

Mr. McCormick. They have carried on no engineering investigations or mechanical investigations; they have carried on economic investigations as to the advisability of the tractor in the farm scheme, and the size of farm on which tractors have proven advisable. That has, however, been based on the experience of farmers themselves.

Mr. Haugen. I have been told the department had carried on some investigations as to testing out the various makes of tractors, and either had made reports or were about to make a report.

Mr. McCormick. I do not think any investigation has been made. We have been trying for three or four years to get that work started. Many of the manufacturers have known of it; in fact, have conferred with us, and our chief work——

Mr. Haugen (interposing). Some of the tractors turn turtle, do they not?

Mr. McCormick. Yes; some of them have done so.

Mr. Haugen. Have you investigated as to them?

Mr. McCormick. No, sir.

Mr. Haugen. As to the number of lives lost?

Mr. McCormick. No, sir; I have no authentic information at all in regard to that outside of just newspaper reports and rumors.

Mr. Haugen. After the investigation, what is your purpose, to certify as to the horsepower or what? What is the information that you propose to disseminate?

Mr. McCormick. Give the horsepower that that type of engine will develop.

Mr. Haugen. When you speak of type you mean that certain make of engine

Mr. McCormick. That certain make and size and type.

Mr. Haugen. Any manufacturer can send his engine here to have it tested out?

Mr. McCormick. Yes.
Mr. Haugen. And you certify as to the power?
Mr. McCormick. That that engine develops; yes, sir.
Mr. Haugen. And its good or bad qualities?
Mr. McCormick. We certify as to the power that it develops.
Mr. Haugen. And as to what besides the power?
Mr. McCormick. So far, we have not given that full consideration. I do not know how we can certify to any other feature until more uniformity has been secured.
Mr. Haugen. If you find one more practicable and serviceable than another, would you certify as to that?
Mr. McCormick. No, sir; I would not want to agree to do that in all cases.
Mr. Haugen. Then of what value, unless you feel free to give the information that you have at hand, is it?
Mr. McCormick. We can give the information that the farmer wants in knowing what power he can figure on from an engine. We would carry on tests also to determine what power is required for different operations, what power is required to pull so many plow bottoms.
Mr. Haugen. That does not get us anywhere. Any engine may be made with sufficient power; but I suppose what the farmer is interested in, or the operator is interested in, is the most economical tractor and the one that will use the least gasoline, and use the least oil—the materials that enter into the cost of the operation of the tractor. Now, if you are limited simply to the power, I do not see that it gives any information of any value whatever. They can all be made with sufficient power.
Mr. McCormick. They can, but they are not; and that is exactly the point the farmers are complaining about. They say, "We buy this engine, which is rated up 10-20. We can do a certain kind of work with it. We buy this engine, which is rated 12-25, and it will not do as much work as the 10-20. Now, how are we going to know how much power an engine has?" They can not tell.
Mr. Haugen. I take it, the expense of ascertaining the power is very small; that is, simply hitching it onto something and trying it out. If that is all, I should not think you would need any additional appropriation, if you have the equipment for it. All there is is fixing the engine onto something and testing its power.
Mr. McCormick. Well, it costs something to build that equipment to test that power.
Mr. Haugen. You have that equipment over in the Bureau of Standards?
Mr. McCormick. I do not think so; in fact, I know they have not; that is, not suitable for that work.
Mr. Haugen. Do you require a different equipment for testing a tractor than for an engine?
Mr. McCormick. Yes, sir; from a stationary engine; entirely different.
Mr. Haugen. Now, tell us what information you are going to give the people after you get through with this investigation.
Mr. McCormick. We hope to furnish the information from which the user and purchaser can go into the market and select an engine which he knows will give him a certain amount of horsepower at the

belt, if he wants to use it for belt work; at the drawbar, if he wants to use it for traction work; and in addition we expect to supply him with the information as to the power required to plow a certain depth in certain types of soil, pulling a certain number of bottoms; to operate a corn sheller, to operate an ensilage cutter, and similar work, which is being done by power on the farm.

Mr. HAUGEN. In other words, if he wants the power it is necessary for him to buy a large bore and a long stroke engine; is that not all?

Mr. McCORMICK. No, sir.

Mr. HAUGEN. Of the various types; you have different types?

Mr. McCORMICK. We hope to go a little further than that.

Mr. HAUGEN. You may point out where one type is superior to another, but after all it all depends upon the bore and the length of the stroke, does it not, and the quantity of gasoline that is used?

Mr. McCORMICK. No; not entirely; it depends also upon the compression in the cylinder and the number of revolutions that the engine will make.

Mr. HAUGEN. You can not get that without the gasoline and with the bore and length of stroke?

Mr. McCORMICK. You can have a given bore and length of stroke and yet have your revolutions vary anywhere from 100 to 1,500 or more. The mere fact that you have a certain stroke and a certain bore does not determine the power of the engine.

Mr. HAUGEN. The revolutions; of course, we understand that.

Mr. McCORMICK. And also the amount of compression that is in the cylinder.

Mr. HAUGEN. What besides that; what else?

Mr. McCORMICK. We hope to go further, so that after we have determined the power available and rated the power that can be secured from the types of engines, the power that is required for the different operations, we hope to go enough further so that the manufacturers of the driving machinery, in cooperation with the manufacturers of the driven machinery, will so construct their pulleys, their shafting, and their gearing, and the frames. the height of frames, so that those machines can be operated together as they should be, whether one of them is made in Colorado and the other in Maine or whether both are made in the same shop. The farmer and the user buys his machines of all types and of all manufacturers in any locality in the country. He needs badly a sufficient uniformity in styles, shapes, and auxiliaries, so that he can operate those machines together.

Mr. HAUGEN. The weight of the engine required to pull the load. would that be necessary?

Mr. McCORMICK. Yes, sir; the apparatus that we have designed tests, among other factors, the weight on the drive wheels. We not only get that portion of the weight that is on the drive wheels when the machine is at rest, but we get the portion of the weight, the distribution, on those drivewheels under varying loads. For instance, when an engine is working to its full capacity it is known that the portion of the weight on the drivewheels is far in excess of that when standing still. How much more we do not know, because it has never been tested, but one thing that makes it possible, sometimes, for a comparatively small looking engine, a light engine, to outpull a heavier one, is the fact that its weight is so proportioned that during its operation a large proportion of the weight is thrown on the rear wheel.

The CHAIRMAN. Is there anything further?

Mr. McCORMICK. No; I think not.

The CHAIRMAN. We are much obliged to you.

The only other item here, Mr. Wilson, is your general administrative expense item. There is no change in that?

Mr. WILSON. No change in that.

The CHAIRMAN. We will not discuss that. Let us turn to page 258, gentlemen, and take up the Insecticide Act.

AGRICULTURE APPROPRIATION BILL.

COMMITTEE ON AGRICULTURE,
HOUSE OF REPRESENTATIVES,
Thursday, January 9, 1919.

BUREAU OF MARKETS.

STATEMENT OF MR. CHARLES J. BRAND, CHIEF OF THE BUREAU OF MARKETS, UNITED STATES DEPARTMENT OF AGRICULTURE.

The CHAIRMAN. Now, gentlemen, we come to the very important Bureau of Markets, and while we do not want to limit the examination of the gentlemen who are here to present the estimate, at the same time I think we ought to keep in mind the fact that this is a short session of Congress and that it is very desirable to speed up the hearings as much as possible.

Turn to page 236, and we will take up the lump-fund appropriation.

Mr. THOMPSON. Are you going to skip page 227?

The CHAIRMAN. The salary proposition depends upon whether the Appropriations Committee allows the general increase or not.

Mr. Brand, your first general expense item, on page 236, is No. 118, for acquiring and diffusing useful information on subjects connected with the marketing of farm products, for which you ask $317,520, which is an actual increase of how much?

Mr. BRAND. An actual increase of $41,100.

The CHAIRMAN. Will you please tell the committee about that?

Mr. BRAND. The particular lines of work to be increased, Mr. Chairman, are the cooperative purchasing and marketing work, $15,000; the foreign marketing work, $12,000; and the cotton handling and marketing work, $14,100.

The committee is no doubt quite familiar with these lines of work. The cooperative work was one of the first lines that was started in the Bureau of Markets in 1913, and has grown greatly in importance and in the opportunity to accomplish results. We have now worked out methods of organization, the legal questions involved in organization—what organizations may do and the kind of activities they may engage in—and the cooperative work that should be done, considering the increase in the diversification of crops and the production of new crops in territories where they are not normally produced in large quantities. This work has grown very greatly. There are, roughly, 14,000 cooperative enterprises of one kind and another in the United States.

Mr. MCLAUGHLIN. How many?

Mr. BRAND. Fourteen thousand; and this work is calculated to reach and aid those who wish to organize into cooperative associations. We have worked out in cooperation with our solicitor's office the requirements which organizations should observe in order to comply with the Clayton amendment to the antitrust law, and we are encouraging that type of organization wherever we can.

The funds asked for will be used specifically in adding some men who are capable along this line and in bearing their expenses. It is a small amount and is a transfer from the food-production act appropriation rather than an outright increase of the regular appropriation.

Mr. McLaughlin. How much from the food-production act was available to you for this use?

Mr. Brand. My recollection, Mr. McLaughlin, is that we have available for such use this year $33,000; and when these estimates were prepared the war was still on and we expected that some part of that sum would still be available next year. Fortunately, the war is over, and consequently it will not be available. So this is really a reduction of about $17,000, as I recall it—those figures may not be absolutely accurate—from the funds available this year for the cooperative organization work.

Mr. Anderson. I would like to ask you a question, Mr. Brand, relating in a general way to your statutory roll, before you go any further with this lump-sum discussion. What percentage of increase is there?

Mr. Brand. There appears to be an increase in the lump-fund roll of nearly 100 per cent.

The Chairman. Mr. Anderson, don't you think we had better discuss this lump-fund portion first, for our disposition of that will determine whether we are going to grant these statutory increases? You can not determine very well what the statutory roll is going to be until you determine what these lump funds are going to be.

Mr. Anderson. If that is the understanding, of course we will not go into that now.

Mr. Haugen. Are you going to have these gentlemen here again to explain the statutory roll?

The Chairman. Yes.

Mr. Harrison. There is a suggestion regarding Mr. Brand's salary. I presume the committee does not wish to discuss that, but I would like to insert a memorandum in the record about it for consideration when the discussion of the statutory roll is taken up later.

Mr. Haugen. Let us have all these memoranda and discussion at the same time, so we can take them up together.

(The statement referred to follows:)

BUREAU OF MARKETS.

1 chief of bureau, from $4,500 to $5,000, increase of_____ $500

Mr. Brand, the present Chief of the Bureau of Markets, has personally directed the work in all phases of its development. With its rapid growth his duties and responsibilities have very greatly increased. It is proposed to increase Mr. Brand's compensation from $4,500 to $5,000 per annum, in recognition of his able and constructive efforts, as well as his untiring industry in developing and prosecuting the work of the Bureau of Markets. The suggested increase would merely bring his salary into line with the compensation received by the chiefs of other bureaus of similar size and importance. There has been no increase in the salary of the Chief of the Bureau of Markets since July 1, 1915, more than three and a half years ago.

The growth of the Bureau of Markets has been directed along sound and conservative lines, and the bureau to-day is an institution of direct and acknowledged usefulness to producers and others interested in the marketing and distribution of farm products. Its work inevitably affects deeply and directly the operations of large numbers of farmers and commercial interests.

When the Bureau of Markets was established very meager information was available on the subject of marketing and distributing farm products, and it was necessary to proceed with the utmost caution in developing the bureau and in formulating its policies. Under Mr. Brand's constructive guidance, important investigations were conducted, the results of which were fundamentally necessary in instituting marketing reforms. Before the outbreak of the war market news services had been instituted on fruits and vegetables and live stock and meats, and the bureau was charged with the enforcement of important regulatory measures, such as the grain-standards act, the cotton-futures act, and the warehouse acts. Mr. Brand also rendered a great deal of service to the committees of Congress engaged in formulating regulatory legislation, particularly the food-control and food-production acts.

The entry of this country into the war very greatly accentuated the need for the quick and intelligent solution of many problems connected with the marketing of farm products. Through the varied range of its previous activities, and on account of the comprehensive form of its organization, the Bureau of Markets was in position to render valuable service along these lines. On account of the war, the work of the bureau was largely expanded during the last year. The market news service on fruits and vegetables was enlarged until the framework for a national machine for the exchange of market information on such commodities was completed; the market news service on live stock and meats was much expanded and new features were instituted which added greatly to its usefulness and popularity; market news services on dairy and poultry products, hay, grain, feeds, and seeds were inaugurated; and a local market reporting service was developed to take care of the needs of the truck growers surrounding certain large cities and to supplement the telegraphic service on commodities which are shipped from a distance in car-lot quantities. The food-products inspection service was instituted to supply shippers of fruits and vegetables with certificates regarding the condition of their products on arrival at large central markets. All these activities have answered an evident need and their conduct has been uniformly satisfactory. Other large emergency projects have been successfully undertaken by this bureau in designing efficient refrigerator and heater cars, for the use of the Railroad Administration, and in conducting food surveys to determine the salient facts regarding the food supply of the Nation.

In addition to the great amount of work naturally falling within the field of this bureau, the Chief of the Bureau of Markets has had charge of the sale and distribution of nitrate of soda to farmers under the appropriation of $10,000,000 made by Congress for this purpose; has acted as chairman of the committee on cotton distribution of the War Industries Board; and has administered the regulation of stock yards instituted as a result of the President's proclamation of June 18, 1918. He was also a member of the wool section of the War Industries Board, and upon the dissolution of the board was made liquidating officer of this section.

The supervision of work conducted along so many different lines and touching vitally so many different interests calls for broad knowledge and unusual discretion and ability. Mr. Brand, with extraordinary energy and resourcefulness, has fully measured up to all the requirements of the difficult position, and has given his time and labor without stint to the solution of the problems involved.

Mr. Brand is a graduate of the University of Minnesota, and served as assistant curator of botany, Field Museum of Natural History, Chicago, 1902–3. He entered the service of the department in 1903 and had charge of its clover and alfalfa investigations until 1909, when he was placed in charge of the paper-plant investigations. In 1912 he took charge of the department's cotton handling and marketing investigations, and in May, 1913, was made chief of the Office of Markets, which was established at that time, and the name of which was later changed to Office of Markets and Rural Organization and still later to Bureau of Markets. He is a member of the committee on southwest cotton culture of the department; was a delegate to the Pan American Financial Congress in 1915; and was chairman of subsection 7, Marketing and Distribution of Agricultural Products, and of Section III,

Conservation of National Resources, Agriculture, Irrigation, and Forestry, of the Second Pan American Scientific Congress in 1915. He is the author of a large number of publications dealing with agronomic and marketing problems.

The CHAIRMAN. Go ahead, Mr. Brand.

Mr. BRAND. There is a $12,000 increase for the work on foreign marketing. Forty per cent of the total exports of the United States are agricultural products. We have, during the past 18 months on the very modest funds that we have had, had four different men working in the foreign field on special lines of work.

Mr. ANDERSON. You mean that has been before the war or just since the war?

Mr. BRAND. Since the war it would be more than that. But that is a rough average of past experience. Since the war I should imagine that the percentage is greater than that.

Mr. McLAUGHLIN. During the war?

Mr. ANDERSON. It is very much less than that.

The CHAIRMAN. You said, Mr. Brand, that you had four men doing special lines of work. Can you give us an example?

Mr. BRAND. We have one man in Europe in reference to cotton; one man in Australia with reference to grains and live stock; one man in Japan and China in reference to fruits, particularly our western fruits which are available for export to the Orient.

The CHAIRMAN. Just what do they do?

Mr. McLAUGHLIN (interposing). That is three; what is the fourth?

The CHAIRMAN. With what problems are they dealing?

Mr. McLAUGHLIN. You just named three.

Mr. BRAND. The fourth is a man who is now abroad on the question of farm and field seeds, that is the field crop and garden seeds.

Mr. McLAUGHLIN. To obtain them or to sell them?

Mr. BRAND. To find an outlet for those of which we have a surplus; and to prevent the exportation of those of which there is a shortage. There are certain seeds, particularly red clover, in which we are likely to find a very serious shortage, and we need to know the needs, as exactly as we can, of our associates in the war and the neutrals before we too generously part with our supplies. It is a protection to our own people.

The CHAIRMAN. Does the Bureau of Plant Industry have a man in Europe now?

Mr. BRAND. They are together, Mr. Chairman. They are in the field now.

The CHAIRMAN. Is their work any different?

Mr. BRAND. Yes; one of those gentlemen I think handles problems of production, and the other handles problems of surplus movements of crops beyond actual market needs.

The CHAIRMAN. Is there any duplication of this work by the Department of Commerce agent? They have these agents out in the field looking after markets and the like.

Mr. BRAND. Mr. Chairman, we have a very complete understanding with the Department of Commerce, and they do not cover any agricultural products except a very few manufactured products, products manufactured from farm products.

The CHAIRMAN. Your understanding, then, is that you handle agricultural products, and they handle manufactured goods?

Mr. ANDERSON. Is there any reason why they should not handle agricultural products?

Mr. BRAND. The only reason, Mr. Anderson, is that we have a complete organization dealing with those problems in the domestic field, and our men understand the work in the domestic field and are so thoroughly informed that it would seem a duplication and waste to have them practically have to put on a force and train them.

Mr. ANDERSON. Why should the bureau send out a man there if one man could do the work?

Mr. BRAND. As a matter of fact, the problems are so great that even with respect to one product it seems necessary at times to have more than one man in the field; and a man who is handling manufactured products is very very rarely indeed at all informed about. agricultural products.

The CHAIRMAN. I have always thought that our Government was very wea in the fact that it did not more generously make provision for that. k

Mr. BRAND. Mr. Chairman, other Governments have, I don't think it is overstating it, hundreds of men in this country on exactly this line of work and we have practically no one on agricultural products in other countries. I don't think it is a credit to this country and I don't think it is suitable protection to our producers who are so largely dependent upon foreign markets.

Mr. McLAUGHLIN. Are not those hundreds of men from foreign countries employed by private interests and not their Governments?

Mr. BRAND. No the men I refer to are commissioners and men employed by their Governments. There is not a week that we don't have one, two, three, or four come to us to get information from us on those lines.

Mr. HAUGEN. Is that now or more particularly before the war?

Mr. BRAND. The last few months.

The CHAIRMAN. Do you happen to know what the foreign Governments are doing in the South American field in this kind of work and whether or not they have stimulated their activities during the war?

Mr. BRAND. We understand that they have. We understand that particularly in South American and Oriental fields they were working very actively to gain back the markets they enjoyed before the war.

The CHAIRMAN. Well, we would be very foolish to sit down here idly and let them do it if we could help it.

Mr. ANDERSON. Have you any men in South America?

Mr. BRAND. We have not. We were planning to have a man go there and but for the war he would have gone.

Mr. ANDERSON. It won't be much to our advantage to send men to South America until we can get some passports so men can go down there and do business.

Mr. BRAND. I am not absolutely certain of that. I know a number of men who have gone there. I know there are some restrictions, but I do not think they are of the real iron-safe type.

Mr. WILSON. It is a very difficult matter to secure a passport to go to Mexico even now and they keep them waiting day after day and weeks at a time sometimes.

Mr. BRAND. I know that the War Trade Board has been trying to facilitate movements of crops from the west to the east coast and my understanding is that the Shipping Board has assigned a number of vessels to this trade and also some to the west coast trade.

Mr. WILSON. They may have done that, but they haven't got the passports.

Mr. HAUGEN. What is the character of the work these four men are doing over there?

Mr. BRAND. They are determining what the possibilities are of dealing with those countries—the business methods that it would be necessary to follow, the type of packages, packing, and standardization, and the things of that sort which must be adopted in order to meet the preferences of those countries; the type of banking arrangements that must be made—all of the things that are absolutely necessary to one desiring to start business in foreign countries.

Mr. HAUGEN. Do you have experts on banking, besides those supplied by the Department of Commerce?

Mr. BRAND. Our men are acquainting themselves as fast as they possibly can with all those matters which are very necessary to the specific performances of their tasks. They do not set themselves up as being experts on banking in any sense of the word.

Mr. HAUGEN. Do you need an expert on wheat to determine what can be done?

Mr. BRAND. That applies to every product, Mr. Haugen—every product has its distinct characteristics.

Mr. HAUGEN. So what you would have to have is an expert on every product that enters into exports.

Mr. BRAND. My feeling is that you can go too far in that direction in some cases.

Mr. HAUGEN. I think we have gone too far now in duplicating this work of another department.

Mr. BRAND. I do not think that is the case.

Mr. HAUGEN. We are sending people over, allowing large sums of money.

Mr. BRAND. Would it be duplication if a big hardware concern sent a man across and a glass manufacturing concern sent a man across?

Mr. HAUGEN. I think that is just about what the situation involves. A man engaged in agriculture and one in hardware, however, are engaged in different propositions.

Mr. BRAND. The problems are very distinct, Mr. Haugen. When you go to Liverpool with reference to grain you deal with a totally different crop and in a different way than when you go to Liverpool and deal with cotton.

Mr. HAUGEN. That is true.

The CHAIRMAN. Then, Mr. Brand, there is no duplication of anything except an ocean voyage?

Mr. MCLAUGHLIN. What do you have to pay men like that?

Mr. BRAND. They are worth a good deal more than they get.

Mr. MCLAUGHLIN. What have you been paying them?

Mr. BRAND. We pay those men about $3,000 to $3,500, and, of course, we can only allow them their regular per diem in the way of expenses, and expenses are very high. In one case we paid a man more than that, but the general run of salaries is about from $250 to $300 a month. It is an impossibility to get the class of men that are suitable representatives for less than that. Men are not around looking for jobs the way they used to be.

Mr. McLaughlin. I have some opinions about the matter, but I did not know what you were paying them.

Mr. Haugen. If everybody had been given a fat job, of course the supply won't be so great. I think if we go on at the rate we are going, there will be a greater shortage of help.

Mr. Brand. The industries have taken a very great number of our men. 'Mr. Bassett, a gentleman very well known to the committee—I don't hesitate to speak his name because you know him, as he has appeared before you—has left us within the last two weeks at a salary twice as great as we were paying him up to the 1st of November.

Mr. McLaughlin. What has he gone into?

Mr. Brand. Cooperative work on the outside. It is work connected with private enterprises, but it is conducted on the lines that the department has followed.

The Chairman. Do I understand you to say that under this appropriation you will have four men?

Mr. Brand. Those four men have gone, but they are not assigned to these funds. We think we can find the men to fill these places and put them in the field, but the sum is not very much for our purposes.

The Chairman. I agree with you.

Mr. Brand. It is pitiful. I want to say frankly to you gentlemen that it is a pitiful sum to put in for so important a matter.

Mr. McLaughlin. You spoke of Mr. Bassett going into cooperative work, employed by a private company. That means that he is out to organize dealers in farm products?

Mr. Brand. No; that means that he goes out to assist organizations that are on their feet and groups of men who wish to organize. His business is to get the tonnage of those organizations, in order that his exchange may make a profit out of the sale and disposition of those products.

Mr. McLaughlin. Formerly he was engaged, or some men were engaged, in effecting organizations of producers of agricultural products, and is it the fact that those organizations have become so effective that the purchasers and dealers in those products must organize against the producers? Now, has Mr. Bassett gone out to show them how to organize to overcome the work that he has been doing before?

Mr. Brand. No, indeed, Mr. McLaughlin; the distributors and dealers have had their organizations for a great many years, and the producer was the last man in the field. The distributor is coming in anew, except in a few very unusual cases.

Mr. Bassett will work with producers' organizations in soliciting their tonnage, consulting them, so that they can keep their membership going, work efficiently on the production end of the line, and turn their business over to this commercial exchange that will sell the products in the various cities.

Mr. McLaughlin. Practically, or to some extent, then, he is doing work for private interests that he was doing before for the department?

Mr. BRAND. Well, scarcely; because the Government in no case solicits business for anyone, and here he is actually soliciting business.

Mr. McLAUGHLIN. For the commercial organization?

Mr. BRAND. Yes; that is his duty, so that while there is a relation—he may, in some cases, deal with the same groups,—nevertheless, he deals with them on a totally different basis.

The CHAIRMAN. Anything further on this item, gentlemen?

Mr. HAUGEN. I would like to know something about the cooperative associations. What about them; what is being done?

The CHAIRMAN. Is not that carried under another item?

Mr. BRAND. No. We have just passed that before we took up the foreign-marketing item, but I would be very glad to return to it if the committee desires.

Mr. HAUGHEN. I think this item is $15,000, isn't it?

The CHAIRMAN. Yes.

Mr. BRAND. This $15,000 is for encouraging the promotion of co-operative associations in every line where we find there is a real need and a real desire, and where the groups affected make a sufficient showing of interest and importance to indicate that it is worth our while to assign a man to that section.

Mr. HAUGEN. What are the lines?

Mr. BRAND. Meats, vegetables, grains, dairy products, cotton, practically all fields of agricultural production are relatively unorganized and we have more requests for assistance than we can possibly fill with our present force and our present office.

Mr. HAUGEN. Now, then, what does the organization consist of what are the activities of these cooperative societies, and what do the organizations consist of; what is there to it; what do they do after they are organized?

Mr. BRAND. They buy and sell wheat, for instance, or buy and sell wheat primarily and deal in lumber, coal, or other products as side lines. They are engaged in furthering the interests of their producer members by getting their products for them at a reasonable saving, which makes it worth while to engage in the enterprise.

Mr. HAUGEN. It is substituting these cooperative societies for the middle man?

Mr. BRAND. It is another method of dealing. In some cases it results in a saving.

Mr. HAUGEN. It takes the place of the middle man?

Mr. BRAND. Yes; in some cases.

Mr. HAUGEN. It does away with the country merchants?

Mr. BRAND. It may in some cases.

Mr. HAUGEN. Let us have the facts.

Mr. BRAND. Take the case of the grain elevators: It has done away with thousands of old-line independently owned elevators and has substituted cooperatively owned elevators.

Mr. HAUGEN. Then, this appropriation is for the purpose of doing away with private enterprise or the middle man?

Mr. BRAND. No.

Mr. HAUGEN. Then, what is it for?

Mr. BRAND. It is for assisting citizens of the United States to be efficient in their legitimate occupations and enterprise by promoting cooperative action where it is needed. We also assist retailers who are operating independently. We try to assist all legitimate business and make it more efficient.

Mr. HAUGEN. The matter I am speaking about is this cooperative association. What is the purpose of it?

Mr. BRAND. I can not discuss one without discussing the other.

Mr. HAUGEN. Yes; you can, because each is different. I want to find out what this money is to be used for. My understanding is that it is to be used to put the other fellow out of business.

Mr. BRAND. That is an unwarranted statement.

Mr. HAUGEN. Just let me finish my statement, please; and at the same time to aid and assist the producer in disposing of his products to a better advantage.

Mr. BRAND. Would this thought cover what you have in mind? Suppose we say that we are not only trying to help the cooperative concerns but we are trying to help the grain dealer, the independent grain dealer——

Mr. HAUGEN (interposing). Not in connection with this cooperative proposition. Those are two different things. Let us dispose of one at a time.

Mr. BRAND. Well, I can not do it. I decline, in other words, to attempt that——

Mr. HAUGEN (interposing). Well, you decline to answer the question?

Mr. BRAND. I decline to try to dispose of these matters separately when they can not be segregated.

Mr. HAUGEN. Well, we can deal with each problem by itself. Do you mean to say that you organized cooperative associations for the purpose of benefiting the dealers or their associations?

Mr. BRAND. For the purpose of benefiting persons engaged in legitimate undertakings.

Mr. HAUGEN. That is your answer, is it?

Mr. BRAND. Yes.

Mr. HAUGEN. Then we will let it rest with that.

Mr. BRAND. We try in all cases, Mr. Chairman, to make it perfectly clear that we are not making invidious distinctions, and that we do not regard it is not a part of our business to put useful, efficient middle men out of business. The middle man renders a great service in some lines.

Mr. HAUGEN. You say to the farmers, "You cooperate, you take the place of the grain dealer in your town." If it is successful, you put him out of business. Your contention is, then, it would benefit him to go into another line of business?

Mr. BRAND. Upon the request of a group of men—producers—who may wish to organize, say, a cooperative grain elevator or a cooperative creamery, we send a man who is thoroughly versed to give them assistance and show them how to proceed. There are places in the country where the farmers are so well organized that it is not necessary to give them any assistance, but when groups of men who wish to organize and need assistance make requests upon us for help we assist them if we can.

Mr. HAUGEN. As far as cooperative associations are concerned, we have them in nearly every township in Iowa, and we have been able to organize them without the assistance of any Government department, and I think we have done just as well as those which were organized by your department. We have a very great number of them. They were started a great many years before we ever heard of the Bureau of Markets or any department here in Washington. Now, what I am getting at is the purpose. Is the purpose here to ultimately put the middleman out of business? That is what we were told some years ago, a lot of bunk from the street corners about putting the middleman out of business.

Mr. BRAND: The purpose is to help citizens who wish to engage in a legitimate line of business to be efficient in that line of business. As an incident of this work some middle man might be put out of business, but that is not the purpose nor the object of the work.

Mr. HAUGEN. The slogan is "From the farm to the kitchen."

Mr. BRAND. Yes, I have heard that slogan.

Mr. HAUGEN. What is your slogan?

Mr. BRAND. Our slogan is "Efficiency and the promotion of the type of distribution that best suits local needs."

Mr. ANDERSON. What are you doing in that direction? What is the situation with respect to cooperative packing establishments?

Mr. BRAND. Live stock and meat packing establishments?

Mr. ANDERSON. Yes.

Mr. BRAND. The situation with respect to them is not as satisfactory as we wish it, because of the technical problems involved in the operation of a packing plant. Several plants have been started and have made relative successes. One small plant in the South was quite a success. It was such a success that one of the big five bought it out. On the other hand four have not been successes, I think for the main reasons, because of inadequate management, and secondly, improper promotion. They, too frequently, are promoted by gentlemen who make a killing, as it were, out of the promotion expenses, and then leave the enterprise to sink or swim.

The purpose of this work could be stated in this way: This cooperative movement is to help both producer and consumer and to cut out not all, but all unnecessary middle men.

Mr. HAUGEN. Now, you want to kill them off gradually?

Mr. BRAND. Not necessarily, but just the ones that should be killed.

Mr. THOMPSON. There are some necessary middle men?

Mr. BRAND. Absolutely.

Mr. HAUGEN. In your extensive operations how many of these packing houses did you organize?

Mr. BRAND. We have not organized a single packing house. We have furnished information to a number in their efforts to keep on their feet, and to keep doing business successfully—four or five of them. We have tried to help a number of them in Wisconsin—as I recall it in North Dakota (Fargo), in South Carolina, and in Georgia—I think there are four or five.

Mr. HAUGEN. Those were established through your aid and assistance?

Mr. BRAND. We gave information to those who wanted to form them.

Mr. HAUGEN. Well, what of the one in Fargo, that is near home? How many head of cattle are you killing, and how many hogs?

Mr. BRAND. I don't think they ever got to the killing stage. I will state that I know they did not.

Mr. HAUGEN. How about the others?

Mr. BRAND. The Wisconsin one I think killed a good deal, but it has had an uncertain existence for several years.

Mr. HAUGEN. Did you assist in its organizing?

Mr. BRAND. It has not foreclosed, but it did not make a very great success.

Mr. HAUGEN. Did you organize it?

Mr. BRAND. No; we have given them suggestions and help that was calculated to keep them from going completely to pieces.

Mr. HAUGEN. When was it organized?

Mr. BRAND. That one has had a varied career. It was organized a number of years ago, and, I think, was closed and then opened.

Mr. HAUGEN. It was organized before your bureau was organized, wasn't it?

Mr. BRAND. I think the last organization is since our bureau was organized.

The CHAIRMAN. The one in South Carolina seems to be succeeding.

Mr. BRAND. I have not been in touch with it.

Mr. HAUGEN. Who organized that?

Mr. BRAND. We gave them assistance in the matter and furnished any information and suggestions we could as to how best to deal with the problem.

Mr. HAUGEN. Who were the stockholders?

Mr. BRAND. The farmers, the local producers, and the local business men, I believe, in that particular case subscribed the funds.

The CHAIRMAN. $250,000 was the capital, Mr. Haugen. Anything further on that item, gentlemen?

Mr. HAUGEN. Yes. Many of the activities of the Department of Agriculture were begun or just carried on primarily, it seems, for the benefit of the producers. That is, for the benefit of the farmers, planters, gardeners, and orchardists, and so on; but if you carry out your plans, Mr. Brand, of assisting anybody in every way, individually or in association, engaged in marketing on a large scale and in all agricultural products, it will not be long before you will get a long way from the primary object sought by a lot of these agricultural activities—the assistance of the farm. You go into the business of organizing and assisting men as far removed from farmers—well, I can hardly make a comparison, but you will get a long, long way from the farmer.

Mr. BRAND. Well, the foreigner seems a long way from the farmer, but the money he pays and the cost and profit is what the farmer finally receives.

Mr. HAUGEN. That is a long way in distance. I don't mean that. There is no limit to your activities. You could extend from local merchants and the local elevator up to the largest organizations for handling grain and farm products, and even up to a board of trade and chamber of commerce to advise it as to how it could best conduct its business for profit.

Mr. BRAND. I think that it is highly important that we should be thoroughly informed about boards of trade and chambers of commerce and exchanges.

Mr. McLaughlin. Then your idea is that it is the function of the Bureau of Markets of the Department of Agriculture to engage in all those activities?

Mr. Brand. In all those activities which is proper for a government to engage in.

Mr. McLaughlin. Pardon me; I don't like your use of the word "proper." Of course it is proper to do what is proper; but if you are going to engage in all these activities, in one line and another, don't you pretty soon get out of your proper sphere?

Mr. Brand. We have attempted not to, and I think we have not done so. I think we have each year disclosed to the committee all lines of work that we are attempting. We have tried to do so very completely; and I am prepared to say, from a daily contact with the work, that I know of no line of activity in which we are engaged that is not a proper activity. Some lines are emergency activities. For instance, I think our emergency work in distributing nitrate of soda would not be proper under normal conditions, but under emergency conditions I believe it is highly proper. That, however, is the only activity that we have undertaken, even as emergency work, that I do not think it would be proper for us to engage in at other times. I think conditions change so that ultimately it might be proper to do such work where there is a private or State monopoly of the entire stock of an important material.

Mr. McLaughlin. But you are organizing, advising and assisting men and people dealing in farm products who are supposed to be at least competitors in a way or antagonistic to the interests of those who are producing the farm products.

The Chairman. Now, let's see, Mr. McLaughlin. I think you raised a rather important question. Here is the situation in my own State. It happened to be in my own district, and I am therefore very familiar with it. I helped to promote it myself. I made a speech to a gathering there one day. Our country is not a hog country—it is not a cattle country. I think your view is that it ought to become a hog country and a cattle country to supplement our natural product down there, which is cotton.

Mr. McLaughlin. Yes.

The Chairman. Now, then, is it not important that these men who have expert advice to give as to the establishment of a packing plant—is it not important in the development of that industry to build a packing house and give us advice about it? Is that not in the interest of agriculture? Absolutely. In other words, it seems to me that the agriculture of this country has been awakened to the fact that it does not know its own business from the planting of the seed to the marketing of the crops and even to the sale of the manufacturers' products.

Mr. Brand. That has been the weakness of it.

The Chairman. And that is the fundamental of this whole work that we have been talking about.

Mr. Brand. I would like to say, Mr. Chairman, as a matter of assurance, that not only do we within the bureau scrutinize most carefully any project which is to be undertaken, but it is submitted to the Office of the Secretary. If it is not thoroughly sound, it falls by the wayside somewhere. It is subjected to very close scrutiny, and any unsound proposition has very little chance of being put on.

Mr. HAUGEN. Mr. Chairman, you were speaking about proper activities. Do you consider it fully proper, certainly highly important, that you should control or operate these exchanges—I presume them to be—and the board of trade—I presume they do more harm than all the rest of them together. What is your idea about these activities? How far are you going, and are these proper lines of demarkation?

Mr. BRAND. I do not want to be misunderstood in speaking about the future development of this thing?

Mr. HAUGEN. Your purpose is to build up?

Mr. BRAND. We try to assist, and correct, where we find them, the things which are not desirable and where methods have been injurious to production we do not hesitate to make suggestions as to changes.

Mr. HAUGEN. As to these exchanges what is your policy, do you consider that a proper line, to take over exchanges?

Mr. BRAND. No; I do not.

Mr. HAUGEN. Well, you organize and make cooperative associations, as you speak of, not only among farmers, but those who are not producers.

Mr. BRAND. We do not confine our activities absolutely to producers, though the greater part of our activities is confined to them. If I may illustrate the matter: Recently in the cotton market there was a determined attempt by some interests to beat the price down because of, I think, their ignorance of the fundamental conditions. We had no power over the matter, no direct legal power, but our influence, from our talk with them, was such that we are told that they ceased short selling upon our demand. We secured compliance with that request and in a period of less than 30 days, when the true fundamental conditions became known, the whole movement which, if it had gone on, might have resulted in millions upon millions of dollars of loss to the cotton producers, was averted.

Mr. HAUGEN. Yes; but you are getting away from the question—the cooperative part of it. Have you certain lines of demarkation, certain lines to pursue? Are you going to carry it into exchanges? Take these exchanges, for instance, the Chicago exchange, and all of these—some come under the head of boards of commerce and other exchanges—is the lending of assistance to them a proper function?

Mr. BRAND. I was answering your question; then, in saying that we have not assisted or encouraged the formation of that particular type of exchange, though we fairly believe that they are rendering a valuable service.

Mr. HAUGEN. Do you think that farmers could take it over, and operate it as a cooperative farmers' association?

Mr. BRAND. I am very doubtful about it.

Mr. HAUGEN. What I want to get at is your policy. To what extent are you going to carry it? Are you going to carry it further than the marketing of the products of the farm?

Mr. BRAND. We are trying to aid and assist those who are engaged in marketing in dealing more efficiently.

Mr. HAUGEN. Now, then, to what extent are you going to carry it? What is your policy? Do you know how many are going to be put out of business, and to what extent are these activities to be carried on?

Mr. Brand. Putting people out of business is not one of our functions.

Mr. Haugen. I think you will agree that when you take the place of the other man, he has been put out of business.

Mr. Brand. That depends upon whether his line of business is in position to make room for another.

Mr. Haugen. With what success have these cooperative associations met? Are they generally a success?

Mr. Brand. Mr. Haugen, I have a very distinct recollection of the time when a few line elevator companies controlled the main business along every line of railroads not only in Minnesota, but in North and South Dakota——

Mr. Haugen (interposing). We have knowledge of that.

Mr. Brand (continuing). And many of those line elevators were put out of business—the ones that used to have the big initials on them now have the name of a certain farmers' association. They were put out of business, and I have not any tears to shed over it at all.

Mr. Haugen. That is just exactly what I have been contending for, and you have admitted what I have been contending for.

Mr. Brand. We did not do that; the local farmers did that.

Mr. Haugen. It was through the associations you encouraged. Is that what this appropriation is for?

Mr. Brand. We are trying to help those who are in the business.

Mr. Haugen. And, as you say, trying to put them out of business?

Mr. Brand. No; we are trying to be of assistance to them.

Mr. Haugen. What put the elevators out of business if it was not the cooperative associations?

Mr. Brand. The cooperative associations did put those elevators out of business.

The Chairman. Is there any objection to putting them out of business?

Mr. Haugen. No objection.

The Chairman. He has answered your question.

Mr. Haugen. He took exception to my statement. Now, then, having succeeded in putting them out of business, with what success did they meet? Are these cooperative associations generally a success?

Mr. Brand. Well, when there are 14,000 of various kinds in existence you can judge for yourself that there has been some degree of success.

Mr. Haugen. Yes; and how many have failed?

Mr. Brand. A very large number. A very large number.

Mr. Haugen. You think the successes would be dependent upon the percentage of failures?

Mr. Brand. The failures are not so many as those in individual enterprises. The mortality of individual concerns, according to Dunn and Bradstreets, is very, very large. I do not exactly recall the percentage of failures of cooperative concerns, but the mortality is not so great.

Mr. Haugen. I am not speaking of Dunn and Bradstreet. I am trying to find out with what success these cooperative associations have met?

Mr. Brand. They have been very successful.

Mr. HAUGEN. Can you give us the percentage of failures that there have been?

Mr. BRAND. I can not give it. I do not think that there is any absolutely reliable data upon that subject.

Mr. HAUGEN. Well, there ought to be just as much data on that as there is to the number.

Mr. BRAND. We have a good deal of information, we have published bulletins on the subject, and we have, as to a certain period, the total quantity of their business, their division as to their types, and as to whether they are purely cooperative and nonstock, or whether they are cooperative and stock corporations but operating for the benefit of the producers who own stock. We have them classified in every possible way, but I don't know of any way in which we could show their percentage of failures without a national registration.

Mr. JACOWAY. How long have you been head of this bureau?

Mr. BRAND. Since it started, Mr. Jacoway, about the 15th of May, 1913.

Mr. JACOWAY. I want to qualify you as an expert witness on the stand. You are able to speak about the subject of these cooperative organizations. I want to ask you if these organizations have been helpful, in your view, to the producers?

Mr. BRAND. They generally have been.

Mr. JACOWAY. I want to ask you whether these cooperative organizations have been helpful to the consumer?

Mr. BRAND. They undodubtedly have, because they reduce in many cases the cost of distribution.

Mr. JACOWAY. I want to ask you whether one of the results of these cooperative organizations has not been to reduce overhead charges between the producer and the consumer.

Mr. BRAND. I think they have.

Mr. JACOWAY. I want to ask you whether these cooperative organizations do not get more for the man who produces the stuff and lay a larger quantity on the consumers table for less?

Mr. BRAND. That is true and especially so in the northwestern part of the United States, where cooperation has developed so that it almost outweighs in many respects individual enterprises.

Mr. JACOWAY. Another question: Mr. Haugen has asked you how many of these organizations have failed. Do you know what per cent?

Mr. BRAND. We are unable to tell, because there is no national registration from which we can tell. There has been a great mortality.

Mr. JACOWAY. Do you know how many men out of a hundred in the commercial world in commercial business have failed?

Mr. BRAND. No; it has been very large.

Mr. JACOWAY. It is 95 out of every 100. I want to ask you if the percentage of failures among cooperative organizations is as great?

Mr. BRAND. I seriously doubt whether any such high percentage of failures take place.

Mr. JACOWAY. I want to ask you as an expert whether or not in the handling of perishable foodstuffs this cooperative movement has not saved millions both to the producer and the consumer?

Mr. BRAND. These cooperative associations have enabled the farmer not only to produce more and better crops, but also to sell them to better advantage. They have rendered a service the result of which has effected the saving of many millions of dollars.

The CHAIRMAN. Any further questions, gentlemen?

Mr. THOMPSON. If I understand you, then, your system of marketing is very largely built on this foundation of cooperative associations? I understand, from a great deal that has been said here, or the substance of it, that your system of bringing the producer and the consumer together is founded and built very largely on the foundation of this cooperative system.

Mr. BRAND. No; that is merely one of the things that we are encouraging, and we are urging that very earnestly.

Mr. THOMPSON. Now, as you go along through a little, give us the other parts of it.

Mr. BRAND. Yes.

The CHAIRMAN. Are you through, Mr. Thompson?

Mr. JACOWAY. One other question, Mr. Brand. Now, just why is it in many districts all newspapers, from dailies to little weeklies with a circulation of 200 subscribers, there are appearing quarter-page advertisements from the packers showing the public how they are really doing them what is a great service? Now, can you state to the committee the reason of this propaganda, or why it is being done, or what is the cause of it?

Mr. BRAND. I am not sure that I can, but I think it is because of a desire upon the part of the packing houses to cultivate a feeling of friendliness among the producers and consumers on the farms.

Mr. JACOWAY. And the packers made more money out of the war than any other class of people?

Mr. BRAND. Their balance sheets have shown very large surpluses in the past two or three years especially.

The CHAIRMAN. Now, we come to this item, $14,100, for cotton handling and marketing.

Mr. BRAND. The item of $14,100 is for cotton handling and marketing work. This work is work which I have discussed before the committee before. We have done a great deal of work in many States this year demonstrating the value to the producer of the knowledge of the grade of his cotton in making his first sale; also to bring about improvements in ginning, in baling, and, I think, in sampling and marketing of cotton itself. The purpose of the very modest increase of $14,100 that is requested, is that we may extend the grading demonstration work to some additional States, and in order that we may give further attention to the questions of marketing cotton in the seed and, particularly, improve ginning, bailing, and handling methods.

Mr. ANDERSON. What is the character of the demonstration work you do? How is it done? Who does it?

Mr. BRAND. Each year we select certain places where a group of producers are going to form an association. Then we station a man there and, upon condition that the growers furnish samples, exact details as to their transactions, the price received, and so forth, we class that cotton and acquaint them with the class of it, in order that they may possess knowledge that will enable them to make better sales. We have found that this work has actually saved—we now have figures covering several hundred thousand bales—from $1 to $4 or $5 a bale.

Mr. ANDERSON. I suspected from the wording of the item that this demonstration work was designed to teach the farmers how to grade their own crops of cotton.

Mr. BRAND. It angles that way, but the possibilities of teaching so technical a subject to a large number of producers is rather remote, Mr. Anderson. I think you probably do not realize, because the grading of wheat is so well established that there is no such system whatsoever for cotton. There is not a single State in the United States where cotton is passed upon officially by a State organization such as those found, for instance, in Illinois and Minnesota and many of the other grain States. They are without that protection and this work is tending in the direction of giving it to them.

Mr. ANDERSON. This is an inquiry along the same line in another direction. I understand that the department had under contemplation at one time the demonstration of wheat standards to the general farming public. Was that work undertaken at county fairs?

Mr. BRAND. Yes. That comes under another project, but I am very glad to tell Mr. Anderson that that work was carried on with very efficient results.

Mr. ANDERSON. What item does that come under?

Mr. BRAND. Under the grain standards act.

The CHAIRMAN. Anything further, gentlemen?

Mr. HEFLIN. How many grades do you send out to the States, Mr. Brand?

Mr. BRAND. That is, how many grades of cotton, Mr. Heflin?

Mr. HEFLIN. Types of samples; yes.

Mr. BRAND. We have standardized 9 grades of white and the 11 grades of tinges, stains, and blues—3 each of the yellow stains and the blue stains and 5 of the yellow tinges.

Mr. YOUNG of Texas. Well, the act only names 9 grades, doesn't it?

Mr. BRAND. No; the act gives power to establish standards for all.

Mr. HEFLIN. I have here Market Report on Cotton, that is used in the spot markets throughout the South, and the following grades are named: Middling fair, strict good middling, good middling, strict middling, middling, strict low middling, low middling, strict good middling, good ordinary. Now, these are the only grades you ever see in the ordinary cotton markets. The producers and the cotton merchants, the cotton buyers, never see or know anything about your tinges—your blue tinges or any other sort of tinges and stains and shades of grades that you have.

The CHAIRMAN. If you ever sold any cotton, you would find out differently.

Mr. HEFLIN. I have seen cotton marketed.

Mr. THOMPSON. You mean local men who buy it?

Mr. HEFLIN. These grades are used only on exchanges, and I think it furnishes a field for the robbery of the producer, because from 80 to 90 per cent of the cotton crop is within these five grades that I have mentioned here to-day.

Mr. BRAND. That varies very greatly with the season, Mr. Heflin. The situation is about this: There is always to be found a certain amount of these tinges, stains, and blues wherever cotton is produced, and if you do not have any standards you do not have any suitable measure with which to judge the value.

Mr. HEFLIN. Take the case of the ordinary buyer. The producer comes to some place in town with his cotton. The buyer cuts into his bale and he pulls out a sample and he looks at it, and you never hear him say anything about tinges. He says that is "middling," or it is "good middling," or "strict middling," and he tells the man how much he will give for his bale. He uses the grades that are published in this paper. The producer and the local buyers never have any discussions about tinges and shades of grade.

Mr. BRAND. They ought to have.

Mr. HEFLIN. They do not.

The CHAIRMAN. I think you are mistaken about that. You take a bale of cotton to market and let a man cut into it and take a sample, and he will not say "this is middling cotton," but "it is middling cotton, with a good deal of stain to it, and I will cut your price on it."

Mr. HEFLIN. There are some low grades of cotton, of course, in every crop, but between these several grades there should not be these tinges and shades of grades that you have got running into twenty-odd. We destroyed the old exchange act because it had 28 grades and shades of grades and standardized and cut it down to the 9. Now you have made it so that there are 21 or 22.

Mr. BRAND. I have been in touch with the matter for 10 years, Mr. Heflin. The purpose for establishing standards was in order that the grader might have an official measure with which he could compare the products which he has to offer on the market. Now, in some years in some sections of the country as much as 60 per cent of the cotton will be tinged, stains or blues, or all.

Mr. HEFLIN. In some sections of the country.

Mr. BRAND. This year happens to be a very high-grade year in both Georgia and Alabama, but next year, if rains and frosts appear at a very unfavorable time, when the cotton is ripening, you will have a very large percentage of these very qualities, and unless you have standards you will not be able to tell very accurately within what grades the cotton should fall.

Mr. HEFLIN. Would not it be sufficient to place it under one of these grades: Good ordinary, strict good ordinary, low middling, strict low middling, and all those things? Why don't you grade cotton like you do grains—wheat?

Mr. BRAND. Mr. Heflin, we not only have the different grades with respect to wheat, but the grains are handled with respect to the hardness of the kernels, so you have a very considerable number of grades in grain.

Mr. HEFLIN. What are the grades in grain?

Mr. BRAND. In grain there are five grades, but there is winter wheat, spring wheat, red wheat, white wheat, and so on, and there are different grades in these classes.

Mr. HEFLIN. So you mean by No. 1 that that is the best grade of wheat?

Mr. BRAND. No. 1 would be the best grade.

Mr. HEFLIN. And No. 2 would be the next best?

Mr. BRAND. There may be a No. 1 of inferior quality. In other words, all the No. 1 are not of the same value. No. 1 white wheat may not be as good as No. 1 red wheat.

The CHAIRMAN. In other words, it may be tinged or stained.

Mr. JACOWAY. Is not this in order that the local buyer in the South can get the grade of the cotton?

Mr. BRAND. They have some general knowledge of grading, but they certainly do not grade very well. The good graders are largely employed by the cotton firms.

Mr. HEFLIN. Why would not all of these grades of cotton be covered by one of these: Middling, strict low middling, low middling?

Mr. BRAND. For the reason, Mr. Heflin, that those are only white cottons; and the colored cottons, we will say a stained cotton of middling grade, will be worth less than middling by perhaps 200 points. That is why you can not use that theory.

Mr. HEFLIN. That is a fine-spun theory, in my judgment, which is hurting the producer and used only to the advantage of the exchanges. That is the way I see it in either grain or cotton.

Mr. BRAND. It has resulted in hundreds of thousands of producers getting better value for their cotton.

Mr. HEFLIN. I think we will have to pass an act and define the whole thing. The local buyer who opens a bale of cotton would simply stick the grower on it; that is, he is not going to look at each market report for value as to each bale of cotton. If good cotton sells at a higher price your low grade of cotton is going to sell at a better price. It does not tend to pull the high grade down. Of course that is true in any market, grain or cotton.

Mr. BRAND. It is not true as to cotton, but under normal conditions it is always true of grain, because high grades are mixed with low grades in order to produce better milling qualities in low grades. There is no mixing in cotton.

Mr. HEFLIN. The low-grade cotton buyers take it to the cotton mill, they dye it red or blue or some other color, and then these tinges you talk about do not appear and the tensile strength is just as great as in the high-grade cotton. It is not affected by the stains.

Mr. BRAND. Absolutely; and our reason for making these different standards is to compel those people to pay for what they are getting. You are reasoning to a totally different conclusion than was the purpose in establishing standards.

Mr. HEFLIN. Well, I have got a letter here from a spinner who says he can not get delivered the grade of cotton he buys on the exchange.

Mr. BRAND. What is the spinner's name?

Mr. LEE. Comer.

Mr. HEFLIN. He is the biggest spinner in the South.

Mr. JACOWAY. Did Mr. Comer address an open letter to you?

Mr. BRAND. Yes; I received 30 or 40 open letters, which were also given to the newspapers.

Mr. JACOWAY. Did you answer them?

Mr. BRAND. Yes, sir; of course. I tried to be courteous.

Mr. HEFLIN. He says in this letter that you asked him to take the matter up with you and you would make investigations of the cause of the discrepancy between the exchange price and the price upon the open market. What is the reason for that?

Mr. BRAND. There are many reasons, but the most profound and substantial reason is this: The exchange practically permits the delivery of a range of qualities. In order that the activities of the exchange may mean the most, the quality of their deliveries must be a merchantable quality. In 100-bale consignments of prime you may receive a wide variety but always within those specific limits of merchantable cotton, whereas if you wanted to get 100 bales of middling cotton you might have to go through 1,000 bales to get that 100.

Mr. HAUGEN. How many grades are there?

Mr. BRAND. Nine white grades, five tinges, three blue stains, and three red stains.

Mr. HAUGEN. About 20 different grades?

Mr. BRAND. Twenty-one different grades.

Mr. HAUGEN. How many of those are deliverable on contracts?

Mr. BRAND. All of those are deliverable on contract.

Mr. HEFLIN. Sometimes the market value between the lowest grade and the highest is as large as $25 per bale, isn't it?

Mr. BRAND. It is more than that. The difference in value between good ordinary and middling is over $25.

Mr. HAUGEN. Your contention is that the grades should be limited and made less than 21?

Mr. BRAND. No; my contention is——

Mr. HEFLIN (interposing). That is my contention.

Mr. HAUGEN. I want to get his idea about it. That has been our contention for some time.

Mr. BRAND. My contention is that for the best protection of the producer you should have standards for at least all of those qualities of cotton which are produced in commercial quantities. The manifest purpose is to make possible accurate quotations so that the farmer can sell these grades as nearly as possible at their true value. Anything that results in the delivery of these lower qualities at an overvaluation—that is to say, at such a valuation as makes it impossible to turn around and sell the cotton received on a future contract at practically the same price in the spot market—depresses the value of basis middling on the contract.

The CHAIRMAN. The law fixes that. It is limited to merchantable cotton.

Mr. HAUGEN. I think it should be limited to less than half of the 21.

Mr. BRAND. You do the producer a very profound injustice as soon as you attempt to do that.

Mr. HEFLIN. Do you ever have any appeals now from people who are not satisfied with the cotton offered for delivery?

Mr. BRAND. Every month.

Mr. HEFLIN. Every month. They are not satisfied with the statement made by exchanges and appeal to your department?

Mr. BRAND. Yesterday I remember approving the findings in four disputes; and in two contracts, which were for 110 bales each, every bale in the two contracts was turned down as undeliverable.

Mr. HEFLIN. What was the contention made by the party appealing the case?

Mr. BRAND. I am not prepared to say in every case.

Mr. HEFLIN. Just one of them; give us one example.

Mr. BRAND. Generally speaking, it is because of the number of defects. In other words, the ginning, the trash, the unevenness of it compelled them to ask for protection. We compelled them to take three samples out of three different parts of the bale and forward them to us.

Mr. HEFLIN. In other words, they claim they had been offered unspinnable cotton.

Mr. JACOWAY. Did I understand you to say that if you didn't have these 21 grades you would be doing a great injustice to the producer; and so I want to ask you if between strict low middling and low middling there will be variations?

Mr. BRAND. Yes.

Mr. JACOWAY. Then if you do not have these variations in grades when the man brought his cotton to town to sell the buyer would give him a price that would insure his profit, which would be the lower grade; is that the idea?

Mr. BRAND. Yes.

Mr. JACOWAY. He would give him the lowest price he could?

Mr. BRAND. Without these grades there would be no standards established and to protect himself the buyer would give the producer the least he would accept.

Mr. JACOWAY. Then these grades would assist in getting him a standard price for his cotton?

Mr. BRAND. Yes; I have known cases in Texas where high-grade cotton has been discriminated against to such an extent as to lower the price by $25 a bale.

The CHAIRMAN. The clerk of this committee informs me that on the farm next to his there are 700 bales of unpicked cotton. That cotton is certain to be blues.

Mr. BRAND. Absolutely; blues or tinges and stains.

The CHAIRMAN. And the contention is that it ought not to be standardized.

Mr. HEFLIN. You ought to have a grade, then, such as low-grade blue cotton—cut out all these shades and tinges.

Mr. BRAND. It is middling blue stain, strict middling blue stain, and good middling blue stain.

Mr. HEFLIN. Those blue stains produce pretty blue market prices.

Mr. BRAND. The grower's pocketbook would be much bluer if you didn't have a standard at all to judge by.

Mr. HEFLIN. Standard grades have done a great deal of good, but I can not agree that these other tinges and shades help the producer. They help the speculator.

Mr. YOUNG of Texas. Mr. Brand, there is just one thing I have not been able to understand about the present season's cotton market. This is the fourth short cotton year in succession, the crops ranging from ten millions and a half up to eleven millions plus throughout the course of the last four years, but cotton down in my State has always been from 2 to 4 cents per pound on the actual spot market higher than the future quotations for the same grade of cotton. Say, for instance, take middling cotton, and we have had a great deal of middling cotton this year, worth 32 cents a pound on the market. Now, the spot quotation on that same cotton in New York would be 30 cents or 29 cents or as low as 28 cents on that same bale; that is a difference of 4 cents a pound. That has happened through this season and the rule has been all through the season that the actual spot sales were from 1 to 4 cents higher than the quotations on the New Orleans or New York Cotton Exchanges. Now what is the cause of that?

Mr. BRAND. Mr. Young, the situation in the cotton market, as you know, during the last 10 months has been a very extraordinary one. Whereas generally the future market is higher because of the carrying charges—the freight from production points to the point of delivery, and all that sort of thing—this year we have a reverse of the situation. We have the South sitting tight and holding its cotton. Considering the very fact that there have been four short crops, that is not a very high price. Indeed, careful and unbiased students of the matter are strongly of the opinion that if we had had those four short crops during times of peace the prices would have been much higher, and I am inclined to agree with them.

Mr. YOUNG of Texas. I do not think there is a doubt in the world about that. Take the State of Texas, which produces from one-quarter to one-third of the entire cotton crop of the South—I believe 28 per cent this year.

Mr. BRAND. Generally it is more than that. Generally it is about one-third.

Mr. YOUNG of Texas. Eighty-eight per cent of the Texas crop never finds a market in this country at all, but goes to the foreign spinners in England, France, in peace times to Germany and Japan. The war times resulted in lack of shipping, our docks have been congested, and we have had no way of getting it out at all, and we have been forced to hold our cotton, whether we wanted to or not, and it has locked the doors of all banking and business institutions in that country, because we could not get it out.

Mr. BRAND. The present freight rate, of course, on cotton is six or eight times what it usually is.

Mr. YOUNG of Texas. That is another thing. I understand that English bottoms that have carried cotton got $52 a bale to carry our cotton to Europe, 8 per cent of which was taken into their war treasury. In normal times it has only cost us about $5 to $8 a bale.

Mr. BRAND. To English ports the rate would be about $32 per bale. The figure you quote may be to Italian markets.

Mr. YOUNG of Texas. What has it been during the war?

Mr. BRAND. About $32 a bale.

Mr. YOUNG of Texas. I understood from information I got the other day that the English mills on last year's crops, for which we in this country got 27 cents, that the English mills bought that cotton, stood this heavy freight transportation, and declared a 34 per cent dividend on their stock, the largest in the history of the country, and yet they added to the price we got this heavy freight charge. If the English mills made that much profit, who can tell what the mills in this country made on cotton they got at those prices?

Mr. HEFLIN. They made their millions. I would like to mention. Mr. Chairman, there were 37,000,000 acres planted last year and about eleven and one-half million bales of cotton were harvested from it. Now, then, one other year we have harvested that much from 23,000,000 acres, so you can see how it turned out.

Mr. BRAND. It was the largest acreage that has ever been planted, so far as I recall.

Mr. HAUGEN. I understood you to say that practically no cotton is being delivered on contracts or has been since this law went into effect.

Mr. BRAND. I do not think that that law has stopped deliveries in the least. There are always some deliveries on contract. They are not great as to volume, but every month, I think, there are anywhere from ten to thirty thousand bales tendered on contracts. They are not always taken up.

Mr. HAUGEN. That has nothing to do with it. How many are delivered?

Mr. BRAND. I do not know absolutely. We can find those statistics for you.

Mr. HAUGEN. I think it is very important that we should have them. I think it is of some importance.

Mr. BRAND. The only thing we can know directly is the number of bales that are appealed to the Secretary of Agriculture when the receiver is dissatisfied.

Mr. HAUGEN. Have you no way of ascertaining the number of bales that are delivered?

Mr. BRAND. I think, if you were interested in that, I would be able and glad to send it to you.

Mr. HAUGEN. I am very much interested to know what this law has accomplished. It was the purpose of the law to accomplish the delivery on contracts of quantities of spinnable cotton.

The CHAIRMAN. As a matter of fact, the function of the exchange is not to promote delivery at all, is it?

Mr. BRAND. The object of the law was to enable the spinner to obtain cotton through exchanges.

Mr. HEFLIN. The purpose of the exchange is to serve to reflect prices that the law of supply and demand wants, isn't it?

Mr. BRAND. That is true.

Mr. HAUGEN. The contention of the spinners was that the system was so defective it was impossible to procure a single bale of cotton through these exchanges.

Mr. BRAND. The specific difficulty, Mr. Haugen, was that large stocks, relatively large stocks, of extremely low-grade and unmerchantable cottons were accumulated in the port of New York, which depressed the price of middling cotton because the receiver was in danger of receiving this low-grade stuff. The trouble was that he did not receive what he ordered. He would find upon the delivery of cotton that it was not spinnable cotton and that it was of no service—did not meet the requirements of a spinner. The object of the law was to compel the delivery of spinnable cotton or cotton that might be used in the mills.

Mr. HAUGEN. You have 21 grades, and, of course, I take it no mill is equipped to use all of the 21 grades and that it requires a certain grade or two, so we have made the law where it is practically inoperative and of no value. It is of no value to the spinner unless the cotton he gets is spinnable cotton.

Mr. BRAND. There are plenty of mills that use every one of the grades that have been standardized.

The CHAIRMAN. Anything further?

Mr. HEFLIN. All these grades are used, Mr. Haugen; they are used, but I take it not all of the mills will use all of the 21 grades. I agree with you that I do not think it is necessary to have the 21 grades.

Mr. HAUGEN. Mr. Brand says it is.

Mr. HEFLIN. I think there is no necessity for it.

The CHAIRMAN. The committee will stand in recess until 2 o'clock.

(Thereupon, at 12.30 o'clock p. m., the committee took a recess until 2 p. m.)

AFTER RECESS.

The committee reassembled at 2 o'clock p. m., pursuant to the taking of recess.

Mr. LEE. When we took a recess we had just reached item 119, on page 239, "For collecting and distributing, by telegraph. mail, and otherwise, timely information on the supply, commercial movement, disposition, and market prices of fruits and vegetables, $304,660."

Mr. BRAND. In order that this item might be adequately presented to the committee, Mr. Chairman, I have asked the officer in charge of this specific line of work to present the matter to the committee.

Mr. ANDERSON. May I ask what amount was carried in the stimulation act for this work?

Mr. BRAND. For this particular item, $500,000. That is for the present fiscal year, so that this increase represents less than half the amount carried in the stimulation act. I will ask Mr. Sherman to present this matter to the committee.

STATEMENT OF MR. WELLS A. SHERMAN, SPECIALIST IN CHARGE OF MARKET NEWS SERVICE ON FRUITS AND VEGETABLES, BUREAU OF MARKETS, UNITED STATES DEPARTMENT OF AGRICULTURE.

Mr. THOMPSON. What kind of information do the growers of fruits and melons get? In my State they do not get any; that is, the real producers do not get any.

Mr. SHERMAN. Which is your State?

Mr. THOMPSON. Oklahoma.

Mr. SHERMAN. We have an office in Oklahoma City.

Mr. THOMPSON. That is many miles away from the real producers.

Mr. SHERMAN. The producers on the Arkansas River, principally?

Mr. THOMPSON. No; the peach producers in the southwestern part of the State.

Mr. SHERMAN. The heaviest peach production is on the Midland Valley Railroad, between Muskogee and Fort Smith.

Mr. THOMPSON. I am talking about the south central part of the State.

Mr. SHERMAN. We had a temporary office at Chickasha for the distribution of information on watermelons. We had a man there temporarily, right on the ground, during the watermelon season a year ago. We did not have one there this summer because there was practically a failure there. In the summer of 1917 we had a temporary office at Chickasha during the entire watermelon movement. I have the figures as to the number of producers served there.

Mr. THOMPSON. In my particular part of the State, which is 55 miles south of Oklahoma City, that is a peach-producing country down there, and also a melon-producing country, and the farmers down there do not get anything at all. They do not get any of this service.

Mr. SHERMAN. Every man in Oklahoma with whom we can get into touch through our county agents has an opportunity to make an application for this service on one of these little application blanks, and our mailing list is made up entirely of the names of men who are interested enough to fill out an application and put a 3-cent stamp on it and mail it to us. We have no gratuitous mailing list.

Mr. THOMPSON. You send them this information from some central place?

Mr. SHERMAN. Yes.

Mr. THOMPSON. Then your agent there sends them the information daily?

Mr. SHERMAN. Yes; sends them daily reports. I have here a copy of the Washington report, which has on it quite a number of crops. Of course, at Chickasha there would be just one crop. This is the one issued at Washington, and it has reports on apples, then there is a report on cabbage, which occupies both sides of one sheet, then there is also a report on cauliflower, then there is a report on grapefruit, on oranges, and then also on spinach.

Mr. THOMPSON. You work in cooperation with the demonstration agent in the county if there is a farm agent there?

Mr. SHERMAN. The demonstration agent can help us with the applications, and help us get up a mailing list, and only to that extent.

Mr. THOMPSON. He is in touch with the producers. How do you reach them with that information?

Mr. SHERMAN. We reach them through the newspapers, through the association lists, and through the county papers. Of course, we realize that there are a great many people in the country who have not heard of our existence, but we have a mailing list of 123,000, of whom a large majority are actual producers.

Now, I would like to say a word briefly as to what composes the service. We have an arrangement by which every railroad superintendent in the United States sends us by wire every night a record of the number of carloads of perishables originating on his division during the day, and their destinations. That is our information on movement. We know just how many cars of peaches, for instance, originate all over the United States every day during the peach season. That is a most valuable part of our information which is given to the city distributors.

Then, we have our own men in each of the 32 principal cities, where we now have permanent branch offices, who are responsible for giving us accurate information as to the number of cars arriving in their markets, as secured from the railroads every morning. Those are secured by telephone, and they also go out and get the actual prices, and we will have on the report a statement covering the quantity and the prices, based on actual sales. Almost every one of our men can look at the sales slips, and thus find out exactly what the actual prices are, based on actual sales; and that is the basis of their reports. That is the way we get the information.

The two great sources of information are, first, the railroads, giving us an authoritative presentation of the shipments of the entire country, and second, our own men in the 32 principal markets, getting the arrivals, and the supply, and the prices on the market. They report the prices by commodities, and States of origin. For instance. the Philadelphia office will report how many Georgia peaches and how many South Carolina peaches, and then later on in the season there may be competition from other districts. We get those reports on the supplies, the State of origin, and the price for each variety.

Mr. ANDERSON. What proportion of the fruit movement is direct from the producers, not through associations or local buyers?

Mr. SHERMAN. From individual producers?

Mr. ANDERSON. Yes.

Mr. SHERMAN. No man can answer that question, because we do not know how much is handled in less-than-carload quantities and in express shipments. We get in New York City and Philadelphia and a few of the other larger eastern markets an estimate of the equivalent number of carloads which have come in by express and local freight and shipments of that sort, so that we can know what the total supply is on the market. When you consider the immense number of small markets in which we have no representation. which are supplied in much larger proportion by the small shippers than the larger markets, I think you will realize it is utterly impossible to answer that question.

But we have the actual records of shipments of almost two-thirds of a million cars of fruits and vegetables in a year, and our telegraphic market news service as it stands to-day, practically full sized, is covering a little over 500,000 cars of that movement. We are covering now with our telegraphic news service five-sixths of the entire carload movement of fruits and vegetables in the United States, and that includes some things we had not originally in mind. We have not yet taken up cowpeas, but we have included dry beans.

Mr. ANDERSON. In general grain shipments we have a proportion of farmers who ship direct to the market and who do not sell to the local buyers. I would like to find out approximately, if I can, what proportion of the fruit movement is a movement direct from the producer to the market.

Mr. SHERMAN. If you take the whole western part of the country from this line west [indicating on map], west of the mountain country, that produces one-third of the carload movement, you will find very little shipped by the individual producers, independent of any intervening marketing agency, unless it is through large producers operating on a scale way beyond what most of us have in mind in the East.

Mr. ANDERSON. In that case is the service which you render or the information that you furnish furnished to the associations or to the producers?

Mr. SHERMAN. It is furnished to everybody who will fill out one of these application blanks and send it to us, and we have producers and dealers separately listed, because we get a statement here as to the nature of their interest in the proposition, and we know approximately how many of each we are serving.

Mr. ANDERSON. Can you give those figures?

Mr. SHERMAN. Yes, sir. They are listed by stations. Take, for instance, our permanent city stations. Cincinnati has a mailing list of 2,000 bona fide producers and 800 are listed as distributors. That means that the 800 are presumably doing some buying or acting as agents for growers or some one else.

At the Spokane office we have a list of 4,200 producers and 1,800 distributors. At the Portland office we have a list of 3,500 producers and 1,000 distributors. At our Oklahoma City office we have a list of 100 producers and 200 distributors, which means that the service in Oklahoma City has been taken advantage of by the distributors in the smaller towns all over Oklahoma, and they have gotten on our mailing list before the producers. That is accounted for by the covering of the watermelon movement from Chickasha, which we covered from a temporary field station there during the season.

Mr. ANDERSON. To what extent is this service a seasonal service?

Mr. SHERMAN. It is just as seasonal as the crop is. In some places we have a large mailing list for a very short time, as in the case of strawberries. We have a man at Hammond, La., who may have a mailing list of a great many hundred men who are anxious to have the service during the short season. After the season is over they have no further interest in the service until the next year.

Mr. ANDERSON. Is your office maintained there all the time?

Mr. SHERMAN. No; offices like that are temporary offices. We had 90 temporary field stations open to serve for a particular crop during a specific season in the different parts of the country.

The CHAIRMAN. How many permanent stations have you?

Mr. SHERMAN. Thirty-two.

Mr. BRAND. We will be glad to insert in the record a list of the permanent stations and the field stations.

The CHAIRMAN. I wish you would do that.

(The statement referred to follows:)

List of permanent and temporary field stations of the Bureau of Markets, together with the number of persons to whom market reports were sent during 1918.

	Producers.	Distributors.		Producers.	Distributors.
BRANCH OFFICES.			BRANCH OFFICES—continued.		
Atlanta	2,500	500	Omaha	380	850
Baltimore		88	Philadelphia	900	800
Birmingham	1,200	600	Pittsburgh		750
Boston	1,000	900	Portland	3,500	1,000
Buffalo	400	500	St. Louis	160	400
Butte	50	230	San Francisco	650	400
Chicago	1,500	1,000	Spokane	4,200	800
Cincinnati	400	800	Washington	225	900
Cleveland	300	815			
Columbus	280	700	TEMPORARY FIELD STATIONS.		
Denver	3,500	1,300			
Des Moines	400	400	Albuquerque, N. Mex	250	
Detroit	2,400	1,100	Alexandria, La	475	
Fargo	700	200	Alliance, Nebr	1,800	
Fort Worth	1,600	1,000	Asherton, Tex	100	
Houston	400	225	Blackville, S. C	415	35
Indianapolis	450	500	Bowling Green, Ky	100	
Jacksonville	2,300	1,000	Brawley, Cal	300	
Kansas City	1,000	1,100	Chadbourn, N. C	450	50
Los Angeles	1,050	650	Charleston, Mo	460	40
Memphis	400	700	Chattanooga, Tenn	500	60
Minneapolis	1,000	900	Chickasha, Okla	500	
New Orleans	1,200	800	Council Bluffs, Iowa	375	
New York	1,200	1,800	Crystal City, Tex	580	
Oklahoma City	100	200	Crystal Springs, Mo	700	

List of permanent and temporary field stations of the Bureau of Markets—Con.

	Producers.	Distributors.		Producers.	Distributors.
TEMPORARY FIELD STATIONS—continued.			TEMPORARY FIELD STATIONS—continued.		
Cumberland, Md	1,100		Norfolk, Va	1,700	300
Dallas, Tex	550	63	Northampton, Mass	800	
Eagle Lake, Tex	310	40	Ocala, Fla	500	
Elizabeth City, N. C	1,000	100	Ogden, Utah	471	
Fitzgerald, Ga	400	70	Onley, Va	1,400	198
Fort Smith, Ark	365	35	Orlando, Fla	1,000	
Fort Valley, Ga	640	60	Palisade, Colo	885	
Freehold, N. J	2,150	150	Palmetto, Fla., or Plant City, Fla	1,000	
Fresno, Cal	300		Paonia, Colo	280	
Hammond, La	300	75	Pocomoke City, Md	500	
Hammonton, N. J	217		Port Clinton, Ohio	500	
Hartford, Conn	605		Presque Isle, Me	1,100	200
Hastings, Fla	1,100		Princeton, Ind	455	45
Hempstead, Tex	300		Racine, Wis	325	
Humboldt, Tenn	400	50	Rochester, N. Y	5,100	700
Grand Junction, Colo	1,400	200	Rocky Ford, Colo	250	50
Grand Rapids, Mich	2,100	250	Rogers, Ark	700	
Greeley, Colo	1,900		St. Joseph, Mo	302	
Idaho Falls, Idaho	3,000	250	St. Joseph and Benton Harbor, Mich	2,000	200
Jacksonville, Tex	725	75	Sacramento, Cal	340	
Judsonia, Ark	240		Sanford, Fla	700	
Kalamazoo, Mich	650		Seaford, Del	220	30
Kaw Valley, Kans	600		Selbyville, Del	600	125
Laredo, Tex	525		Starks, Fla	98	
Laurinburg, N. C	680	70	Swedesboro, N. J	320	
Leesburg, Fla	500		Turlock, Cal	270	30
Louisville, Ky	300	150	Valdosta, Ga., and Live Oak, Fla., and Thomasville	800	85
McGuffey, Ohio	250		Walkerton, Ind	645	
Macon, Ga	900		Waupaca, Wis	1,750	250
Meggett, S. C	380		Waynesville, N. C	280	
Mesa or Phoenix, Ariz	300	40	Westfield, N. Y	1,400	
Miami, Fla	550	50	Williston, S. C	400	
Mission, Tex	285		Winchester, Va	300	
Monett, Mo	500		Woodstown, N. J	580	
Monte Vista, Colo	750				
Muscatine, Iowa	91				
Muskogee, Okla	150				
Nashville, Ark	275				

Mr. SHERMAN. Mr. Chairman, my testimony before you three years ago closed with an informal discussion, and I want the privilege of refreshing your memory as to what occurred in the informal discussion. You asked whether we had formed any idea as to what this service would cost when it was a Nation-wide service, when it was extended all over the country in its scope and included all of the perishable commodities for which such a service would be useful. I said, as nearly as I could forecast it, that it would cost about half a million dollars to get the information, and you said, "If you do it for that amount, you will do it for half of what I think it will cost you." The facts show that the cost was about halfway between those two amounts. We can build the machine and keep the car in perfect running order on $500,000 a year, but that does not give us any gasoline.

The CHAIRMAN. So that I prophesied a little better than you did?

Mr. SHERMAN. Yes; you did. We are getting our leased telegraphic wires now at just half price. If we had to pay full prewar rates for the service, and transmitted the volume of the service we are transmitting over our leased wires, it would cost us a million dollars.

The CHAIRMAN. Am I right in the impression that you charge the receiver of your information the telegraphic tolls?

Mr. SHERMAN. Only when we wire it to him, and that is a small part of the service. These mailing lists comprise a total of over 120,000 names, and we mail the bulletins to them, giving the information free, but we have required a written application for that information, and every name we have on that list has come by means of one of those written applications, under a postage stamp. Some of those people pay as high as $12 a day for telegraphic reports.

The CHAIRMAN. Do they pay at the regular rates?

Mr. SHERMAN. They have to pay the full telegraphic rates.

The CHAIRMAN. What is the rate on the leased wires?

Mr. SHERMAN. We send no telegrams of information to anyone, except at his own expense.

The CHAIRMAN. But you get telegraphic information. What does that cost?

Mr. SHERMAN. Our own telegraphic information over our own leased wires costs us just half of what it would in normal times. In other words, the American Telegraph & Telephone Co. is leasing us the wires at a mileage rate, which is just half of the prewar rate. They said their facilities were being placed at the disposal of the Government during the war emergency, and because we were being financed in this proposition out of the war emergency fund they gave us the leased wires at one-half of the rate quoted us by the Western Union Telegraph Co.

Mr. HAUGEN. What is that rate?

Mr. SHERMAN. A little less than $9 a mile.

Mr. HAUGEN. How much per word?

Mr. SHERMAN. We have the wires 12 hours a day at that rate.

Mr. HAUGEN. What does it cost per word? Would it cost more than what you pay at the regular rate?

Mr. SHERMAN. It would cost possibly three times as much.

Mr. HAUGEN. That is rather indefinite.

Mr. SHERMAN. There is no rate per word over our leased wires.

Mr. HAUGEN. What is the Government rate per word?

Mr. SHERMAN. It is a minimum rate of 20 cents for a message not exceeding 20 words. We do not have that kind of a rate, because we pay rent and hire operators, and have an operator at the desk opposite a man who is using that information.

The CHAIRMAN. Mr. Haugen wants to get at the comparative price as between what you pay and what the commercial rate is.

Mr. SHERMAN. About one-third.

Mr. HAUGEN. The Government rate is about one-third of the regular rate?

Mr. BRAND. The Government rate is one-half of the regular rate. Our leased-wire cost is less than the Government rate.

Mr. HAUGEN. Can you not get it at so much a word? My understanding is that the Government pays 1 cent a word.

Mr. SHERMAN. We do not pay by the word.

Mr. HAUGEN. I know, but I want to find out whether you are paying more or less than the regular Government rate.

Mr. SHERMAN. The charge for our leased wires is about one-half as much.

Mr. HAUGEN. When they lease a line that is based upon the volume of business, is it not?

Mr. SHERMAN. No; that is based absolutely on the mileage.

Mr. HAUGEN. You have the exclusive use of the wire. If you pay $9 a mile and you send one message a day, it costs you $9 a mile for that message.

Mr. SHERMAN. We have the use of the leased wires from 6 o'clock in the morning until 6 o'clock at night.

Mr. HAUGEN. What would it cost you if you had to pay the regular Government rate?

Mr. SHERMAN. We have several statements as to what it would cost from the telegraphic section at the Government rate. The only basis for comparison is that we pay so much a mile per month for the wires. We hire all of the operators, which means that we have two operators at every one of the 32 branch offices, and their services cost us so much, and then the rent costs so much.

Mr. HAUGEN. When you send 5,000 words, of course, the cost is much less than when you send 500 words.

Mr. SHERMAN. What we actually do is to take off our messages simultaneously in all our offices as they go over the wire, and every word of that volume of messages is telegraphically transmitted information. We say that it has cost us the price of the leased wire and the salaries of our operators, and that cost is about one-half of what it would cost us to send it over the commercial wires at the Government rate.

Mr. HAUGEN. It would cost twice as much; is that the idea?

Mr. SHERMAN. In some months twice as much, and in other months four or five times as much.

Mr. HAUGEN. On the whole, what is the gain?

Mr. BRAND. We do not have the exact figures on that, but the gain seems to be about twice on the Government rate and three times on the commercial rate.

Mr. HAUGEN. Of the present cost?

Mr. BRAND. Roughly, if the cost for our leased wires was $50,000, the same volume of traffic handled over the commercial wires at Government rates would be $100,000, but at the regular commercial rates it would be $150,000.

Mr. HAUGEN. You have made a careful investigation and comparison?

Mr. BRAND. We keep an absolute account.

Mr. MCLAUGHLIN. You have two operators at each station?

Mr. SHERMAN. Yes, sir.

Mr. MCLAUGHLIN. What do you pay them?

Mr. SHERMAN. Most of the operators get between $1,200 and $1,400, and even at that rate of pay we have great difficulty in keeping them.

Mr. MCLAUGHLIN. Do you have to supply any equipment?

Mr. SHERMAN. The company furnishes the equipment.

Mr. MCLAUGHLIN. Do you have to build anything?

Mr. BRAND. No; that is all included in the lease. They put the instruments down ready to use.

Mr. MCLAUGHLIN. And they keep everything in repair?

Mr. BRAND. Absolutely.

Mr. HAUGEN. How do the salaries paid by the department compare with the wages paid by the telegraph companies?

Mr. BRAND. They are so very much lower than the salaries the companies are paying that we are losing our men.

Mr. HAUGEN. What do you pay?

Mr. SHERMAN. The operators get from $1,200 to $1,400.

Mr. BRAND. A supervising telegrapher gets $1,620 and the superintendent gets $2,000.

Mr. HAUGEN. Are the telegraph companies paying more than $100 a month?

Mr. BRAND. Yes; their average is about $1,600 per annum, and many of their men get $1,740.

Mr. HAUGEN. That is recently?

Mr. BRAND. Oh, no; for the last three years.

Mr. SHERMAN. Many of our men in the larger cities, whom we have permitted to work overtime for the telegraph companies after they have finished their day's work with us, go out and work in the evening a few hours and add 50 per cent to their income.

Mr. HAUGEN. They were getting less than that a few years ago?

Mr. SHERMAN. Yes; they were.

Mr. HAUGEN. Are the expenses of the grain market reports included in this item?

Mr. SHERMAN. No, sir. Fruits and vegetables.

Mr. HAUGEN. What item does that come under?

Mr. BRAND. Market reports on grains and seeds.

Mr. SHERMAN. We have these leased wires which go into each of the 32 branch offices divided into circuits, with not more than 7 on a circuit, which gives us only a sufficient number of stations on each circuit so that each one can transmit the information to Washington and get it in by the time we have to close the report. If you have more than 7 stations on the wire and each one has to report a long list of commodities, by the time you get to the eighth station, it is so near to the closing time, when we have to release the report, that if we had any more stations on the wire, the final compilation would be so delayed that the bulletin would not come out that day. We have had to split up the telegraphic work in that way.

The eastern circuit includes, Baltimore, Philadelphia, New York, Boston, Buffalo, Cleveland, Detroit. We have not put Cleveland and Detroit on that circuit particularly because they were eastern cities, but because they can be hitched up on the wire, and if you should put them on the central circuit you would overburden that circuit.

We are charged for these leased wires on the basis of the shortest railroad mileage between two points, but the company may not set up the wires between these offices in that way. As a matter of fact, we may communicate with Buffalo to-day by way of Pittsburgh, and to-morrow we may communicate with Buffalo by way of New York City. That is according to the convenience of the telephone company. They set up a circuit and they give us the exclusive use of that circuit for 12 hours, and during the other 12 hours they are using the wires for anything they please. We have a guarantee of the use of those wires during the 12 hour period on the basis of the shortest railroad mileage.

Our southern circuit includes our permanent offices at Atlanta, Birmingham, Memphis, New Orleans, and Jacksonville. It does not include Houston. Houston is now attached to another circuit, because by attaching it to another circuit and taking it off of the southern circuit we saved $80 a month, and we thought that was worth saving. So Houston is on the other circuit.

Then we have, temporarily, during the winter season, an extension of the leased wire to our field station at Orlando, Fla., and we send over the leased wire from Jacksonville to Orlando, Fla., all the reports to be published at Orlando. We did that because the amount of business going to Orlando every day makes it more economical to lease a wire to that point and put an operator down there than to transit that information by the Western Union wire with the risk of mistakes in coding and decoding.

The volume of business is so much more than possibly could be put over the wires in ordinary English that we have reduced everything to a code. Every word of these reports comes to Washington in code. At the same time Washington is reporting New York and every other station is on the circuit and is taking it off, and by the time the last station has reported the last station has the complete report from every other station and that is put on the stencils and sent out. The telegraph operator hands it, sheet by sheet, to the stenographer sitting next to him. It comes off of the telegraph wire in code and is decoded as it comes along, usually by the stenographer who cuts the stencil.

Our northern circuit, or central circuit, is composed of Pittsburgh, Columbus, Cincinnati, Indianapolis, Chicago, Minneapolis, and Fargo. That also includes a temporary station at Waupaca, Wis., where there is an important potato station for about six months in the year, and the leased wire only costs us the salary of an operator to have that information taken off there, because it is routed through that point.

Then, the central circuit is composed of St. Louis, Kansas City, Omaha, Des Moines, Oklahoma City, Fort Worth, Tex.; Houston, Tex.; and Denver, Colo.

Then there is the western circuit beyond that. We have no station in Utah, although the line is run that way. We have in that circuit Los Angeles, San Francisco, Portland, Spokane, and Butte, Mont. We have not a station at Seattle, although we ought to have one there. There are three or four places where we should have stations in order to absolutely complete the circuit.

Mr. HAUGEN. You have a leased wire into Fargo, N. Dak.?

Mr. SHERMAN. Yes, sir.

Mr. HAUGEN. Is the volume of business there such as to warrant the leasing of a wire? Is there a considerable amount of business there?

Mr. SHERMAN. Fargo is not such an important market as against all the others. It is a long way from anywhere else. It is also an inspection point for fruits and vegetables. That is a combination proposition. A good many of these offices are joint offices, between the market-news service and the inspection service, and the two together fully justify the expense of maintaining the station. As a matter of fact, they are an overnight run from Minneapolis, and it shortens the mailing time to everybody in that territory by one day by having a station at Fargo, and we have to have a station there particularly for the potato growers out in the Red River Valley.

Mr. HAUGEN. You pay $9 a mile for this leased wire?

Mr. SHERMAN. Yes.

Mr. HAUGEN. It cost, then, about $2,700 to maintain that service there?

Mr. BRAND. A little less than that; but it is a very important potato-producing section.

Mr. HAUGEN. You could send a great many messages for $2,700.
Mr. BRAND. You could not send as many as go over this leased wire.
Mr. MCLAUGHLIN. That does not include the pay of the operator.
Mr. HAUGEN. The pay of the operator would be another $1,200, so that the total would be about $4,000.
Mr. SHERMAN. We have got to close the Fargo office under the estimates as they stand, and when we close it, if we should dismiss every one there connected with the inspection and market-news service, we would save $5,960 on salaries, $780 on rent, about $2,400 on the telegraphic cost, $427.36 on the cost of bulletins (that is, the cost of actual material), and $200 on miscellaneous items. We would save in the aggregate for a year, by closing the Fargo office and dismissing its entire force, $9,767.36.
Mr. HAUGEN. This service now exists on the movement of the crops?
Mr. SHERMAN. And the prices.
Mr. HAUGEN. At Fargo?
Mr. SHERMAN. All over the country. Fargo gets its information from all over the United States. The news from all these various shippers in all parts of the United States is interchanged.
Mr. HAUGEN. Does Fargo report the shipments from a point 50 miles east?
Mr. SHERMAN. Fargo gets a record of every car of potatoes moving in the United States originating anywhere in the United States. They know about all those shipments for the whole country over.
Mr. HAUGEN. Every station in that vicinity?
Mr. SHERMAN. They get it for every station in the Union. The bulletin issued in Fargo to-day gives the carload movement of potatoes from every point in the United States for the preceding 24 hours, and they know what every competing district in the United States is shipping. They know also exactly how many cars have been received in every market in which they are interested.
Mr. HAUGEN. Do you get a daily report from every station?
Mr. SHERMAN. Absolutely; every market station reports to us by leased wire, and we take it off, and simultaneously every other station takes it off. It is a report in full of the arrivals and prices.
Mr. HAUGEN. But the shipments?
Mr. SHERMAN. We get a report of the shipments from every railroad division superintendent in the United States, and we put that on all the leased wires, and every man in the United States can, if he so chooses, get this information, and get a complete record of the movement and the prices every day as they are all over the United States.
Mr. HAUGEN. Nearly all those potatoes are put through the Twin Cities, and if you report the arrivals you get the same results, except what might be unloaded at the intermediate points. It does not seem necessary to get a report from every station of every car that is shipped. It seems to me that is quite an unnecessary expense.
Mr. SHERMAN. We get it from the station by mail; we get it from the division superintendent by wire for the daily news service.
Mr. HAUGEN. Then all the reports of the stations in a particular division would be reduced to just one report?
Mr. SHERMAN. One report; one published report. This paper shows every shipment of potatoes in the United States on yesterday.

Mr. HAUGEN. What I was getting at was the expense keeping up a station like that at Fargo, costing $6,000 or $7,000. It seems to me the report from the divisions can be sent to Minneapolis as easy as Fargo.

Mr. SHERMAN. How would you let the people in the Red River Valley get the information?

Mr. HAUGEN. They get the information from the same source.

Mr. SHERMAN. A station does not exist solely to distribute the information.

Mr. HAUGEN. The station at Detroit can telegraph to Minneapolis as easy as to Fargo, and you would have the same information, and the only object in maintaining the station would be for the purpose of reporting the few carloads that come to Fargo and are consumed, and that is a small amount.

Mr. SHERMAN. The object of maintaining the station is to help the distribution of the information; the shipment information comes from every division superintendent in the United States; the market information comes through every one of our 32 representatives, quoting the prices at various stations. The field stations also send us the prevailing f. o. b. prices.

Mr. HAUGEN. Fargo is an f. o. b. market?

Mr. SHERMAN. Yes; they may consign a good deal, but their prices are quoted f. o. b., and they sell a great deal in that way.

Mr. ANDERSON. Are you responsible for the new potato grading movement?

Mr. SHERMAN. No; I am not.

Mr. BRAND. If Mr. Anderson wishes to go into that, may I ask him to raise the question when Prof. Scott is discussing the market inspection of perishable products?

The CHAIRMAN. Most people can tell all they know in five minutes. You take five minutes, Mr. Sherman, and summarize the whole proposition without interruption from any members of the committee, and, then, if any members of the committee want to ask you questions, let them ask the questions after you have completed your statement.

Mr. SHERMAN. Telegrams received in Washington giving us the shipments of all perishables in carload quantities are received from every division superintendent in the United States. Reports of arrivals and prices from 32 markets; daily summaries prepared in Washington are transmitted over the leased wires to all of the 32 stations, from which the information is in turn distributed to thousands of producers and distributors, as is also the information received in Washington directly from temporary field stations, of which we establish and discontinue 90 in the course of a season; these wire us each night, giving f. o. b. prices at shipping points; these wires are also summarized by the night force in Washington, which has the f. o. b. information ready for transmittal in the morning at 6 o'clock, as soon as the wires are opened.

Every one of these 32 branch offices is informed as to all shipments of the day before and as to the prices prevailing and also important crop information from each of the 90 temporary branch offices, or such part of them as may be in operation at the moment.

As soon as the market opens in the morning the men at the various stations are at the market getting information as to prices and getting a record of the actual arrivals at the 32 points. They also receive in the summary of the shipments which we send notice of the number of cars originally destined to every important point; that is to say, Cincinnati gets a record of the number of cars of peaches shipped in the United States from every district and the number from each district destined to Cincinnati. Of course, those figures may be modified by diversions, which the men in the trade understand, and they understand what to expect.

As soon as our man comes in from the street he clicks in on the wire that his report is ready. Every operator has to be at his key. Philadelphia begins to send. Philadelphia is usually the first to begin to send. Detroit and everything east on that line begins to take it off. The stenographer is at the side of the telegrapher. As the telegrapher takes it down, he hands it sheet by sheet to the stenographer to decode, and as the work advances, step by step, as the information comes in, it is immediately decoded and written out and is put on the mimeograph in about 10 minutes after the information comes in on the wire.

Then, in turn, each station comes in on the wire, each awaiting its turn, so that we have a continuous use of the wire until the last report comes in. At the same time the same thing is going on in each of the other leased wires, every market on the circuit taking off the report of every other market on the circuit, as it comes in, and by the time they are all in, Washington clicks in and releases to Pittsburgh and every point that is interested on each of these other circuits the reports which we have received from the eastern circuit. The summarized report from the eastern circuit is put on each of the other circuits for their information, so that in a few minutes after the last market has reported every one of the 32 cities may have a complete report from all of the markets on all commodities. They utilize just as much of this information as the people on their mailing list are interested in.

Then the 90 temporary field stations, which are not shown on this map, receive, at the same time, reports from all the markets to which the products from their sections are shipped. For instance, this Chadbourn district happens to be shipping strawberries. We give Chadbourn the shipments of strawberries in the United States during the previous 24 hours, and we give them the shipments out of their own district in detail, showing the points to which they were distributed, so that every man shipping from there knows what part of the output has gone to the different markets. We also give them the prices at which the Carolina berries are selling wherever they are appearing, and we give them the prices at which the berries on competitive markets are selling. That is the information which goes to the field stations, and immediately the man at the field station has his stencils cut and gets that information on the mimeograph. Early in the afternoon his mail is ready to go out. The same thing obtains at each of the 90 temporary field stations at different periods of the year. Those field stations exist exclusively for the service of the producers. There are a few important centers of production that have not yet been served. We believe that this part of the service is most constructive, comes the closest home, and brings us the most heartfelt letters of commendation from the people from whom we like to receive that sort of thing.

The CHAIRMAN. Is that a fairly accurate description of the work?

Mr. SHERMAN. That is a fairly accurate description of the work. That is an outline of it. There are several points that could be made as to just what our men have accomplished in certain places. We have a distribution service that is not covered very well in what I have said. Our men located at a given point, especially where you have certain market conditions, can accomplish something which can not be accomplished very well without a disinterested agency.

We had a very unusual sort of a situation at Laredo, Tex., where we have a tremendous production of onions in a dry country under irrigation. There was a lot of competitive buying there, and the local situation was such that an unfortunate condition arose with many of the elements of the trade working at cross purposes. and the producer getting the worst of it. At the time when this territory is shipping, it has a monopoly of the market, except for a few old onions still in stock. After the bulletins had been issued a few days one of the dealers said: "We know the conditions pretty well from these bulletins, and we know what Texas onions were worth everywhere except here in Laredo. I sent a wire to Chicago and found that a competitor here in Laredo was selling onions for 10 cents less than anyone in Laredo was supposed to be asking." We said: "We will cure that situation if you will make us your agent. If every one of you men will sign an order giving our men the right to go to the Western Union Telegraph office and see every one of your outgoing and incoming telegrams and get a record of your confirmed sales, we will publish a report showing what the price of onions is f. o. b. Laredo." Every one of them came through and signed such an order.

We sent a man to the telegraph office and made a record of the confirmed sales and published the range on each grade of onions, the prices prevailing on the basis of sales f. o. b. Laredo, and we published that without regard to offers or quotations. It was an authentic record and every man who sold a carload of onions knew where within that range he had sold them, though his competitor did not know, and the result was that the range narrowed down, and then another thing happened. The market had been up to about $1 and had gone off to about 90 cents and was climbing. It had reached about 95 cents, and there was a bullish feeling, and somebody took a chance and quoted onions for delivery a week later at $1.15, about 20 cents a crate above what they were bringing. He found a buyer in the North, who ordered two carloads for shipment eight days later. There was a confirmed sale, and the next day we published it in the bulletin as a confirmed sale for shipment of two cars on Friday of the next week at $1.15.

The very next day prices went up 10 cents, and the next day 5 cents more, and it went on, and by the time those cars went out the market was above that price. Of course, that fellow made a good guess, but the result of publishing that fact was that everybody knew that thing actually had been done, and that it was not a case of somebody lying.

Consequently everybody advanced his price in accordance with what the situation permitted and the growers got an average of 10 cents a crate more for their onions than they would have gotten if the information had not been made public. That service has to be rendered in the producing section. We have to have an exchange of information on the spot, and we have to have a man on the ground to get that information. It leads to more uniform prices, getting the benefit right back to the producer.

The CHAIRMAN. The whole fundamental proposition is to find what the truth is and tell it.

Mr. SHERMAN. To find what the true is and tell it, and put every man who is interested in possession of the facts. The only criticism we have had from any responsible concern is from the man who formerly has had a very good line-up of the market situation. He thinks we have robbed him of his advantage.

Mr. BRAND. When these estimates were prepared the war was still going on, and necessarily we were expecting there would be an estimate under the food-production act. I think it is important to have Mr. Sherman bring out what it means to this service if we are to operate it on the reduced basis represented by this estimate.

The CHAIRMAN. What are you going to do with this $244,000 increase?

Mr. BRAND. Mr. Chairman, there is an apparent increase in this item of $108,000, but taking into consideration the transfers to the statutory roll of this bureau amounting to $135,700 ($27,060 from the regular and $108,640 from the emergency item) and the transfer of an electrical wireman at $1,100 to the statutory roll of the Secretary's office, the actual increase is $244,800. This increase represents the transfer of that amount from the emergency appropriation for a market news service on fruits and vegetables. This transfer of funds is less than is necessary in order to place the project on an adequate permanent basis. It is not an increase in work, and, unless the transfer of funds is effected and, in fact, the amount increased, it will, upon the withdrawal of funds now provided under the food-production act, be necessary for us to dismantle certain branch offices or to discontinue a large part of the service now rendered in producing localities. This would necessarily reduce materially the effectiveness of the service as a whole. That the work is greatly appreciated by growers and decidedly useful to them is clearly indicated by the many expressions coming to the department from the sections of the country directly affected.

When the news service on fruits and vegetables was expended under emergency funds, the work was enlarged in the only possible way. The bureau pushed through in one year arrangements for a service which, under normal conditions, might not have been so expanded for three or four years. Arrangements were made with the carriers, at a cost of much time, labor, and money, for furnishing reports to the bureau, necessary furniture and equipment were bought, quarters were leased, arrangements were made for the leased-wire service, and large numbers of workers were employed and specially trained to perform this work.

Mr. SHERMAN. We have this service almost up to what we consider its limit of size. We ought to open an office at Seattle, and we ought to have an office at San Antonio, Tex., in cooperation with the inspection service, and we ought to have one at Louisville, Ky. We have the equipment all ready and stored there. Then we ought to have an office also at Norfolk, Va., for inspection and to report the market, in order to serve this territory to which mail goes largely by boat. We ought to have those four additional stations, and if we had them we would feel that we were covering the country fairly adequately.

The CHAIRMAN. That would account for about $36,000 of this increase?

Mr. SHERMAN. That depends on the leased-wire mileage. The additional wire mileage would not be so much. At Norfolk it would be very little, and Louisville is practically on the way, so that would not add much to the wire cost.

We have now available for market news services on fruits and vegetables for the present fiscal year $696,660 in lump-sum appropriations. This, supplemented by the statutory salaries, makes the funds available for this work about $760,000. Under the emergency practically every man hired in the service as an investigator has been put on this work, and the strictly investigational work in this bill has been practically suspended for the last two years. For practical purposes we have treated our investigational allotment of about $25,000 as a part of our service fund. The total of all funds under which we are operating therefore amounts to about $785,000. If we spend that money this year, we could run this thing in full. We are almost up to our full size now.

The CHAIRMAN. Where do you get the figure $500,000? You are only estimating about $304,000.

Mr. SHERMAN. We now have under the food-production act $500,000. The estimates as they stand involve a reduction from the money we actually have available for the present fiscal year, although it is a big increase over the regular appropriation. As a matter of fact, we face, on the basis of this estimate, a reduction from the funds we had for this present fiscal year of $256,200.

Now, the question with which we are confronted is this, What are we going to cut out of this complete machine to save $256,200? You look at it on the records, and it seems to be an increase; the bureau has to face it as a decrease from the amount we are actually using this year, and the question is, What can we cut out?

The Pacific coast either is served or is not served. I believe there is nobody on this committee living west of this line [indicating north and south through Denver on map]. The territory west of that line (west of Denver) originates about one-third of the total carload shipment of perishable products in the United States. We either serve that territory or we do not. Either lease this wire or do not lease it. If we do not lease that wire and maintain these permanent branch offices we can not possibly transmit over the commercial wires at commercial rates enough information to justify the expense. That part of the service from Denver west [indicating on map] costs almost exactly $74,000 a year.

The CHAIRMAN. Let me ask you this question, and let us see whether we can not get at a practical understanding. Say a carload of potatoes is starting to move in Orlando, Fla. Is it necessary for you to telegraph that information to Washington and across the continent to San Francisco? Is there any real competition between a carload of potatoes here and a carload of potatoes in San Francisco?

Mr. SHERMAN. No, sir; we do not run the service to that foolish extreme. But with oranges we do. It is a vital matter, of course, for California to know what Florida is shipping in the way of oranges and what markets are receiving those shipments. When we are reporting potatoes in Florida it does not cost us any more to transmit it to all the points on the leased wire when we get it in, and we transmit it for the benefit of anybody who is interested in it.

The CHAIRMAN. In other words, your contention is that, unless this committee, over the estimates, shall give you the amount you now have, which is half a million dollars, you will have to cut off some of your service?

Mr. SHERMAN. Yes.

The CHAIRMAN. And that the estimates would not take care of the present situation?

Mr. SHERMAN. These estimates would not take care of the present situation. But, Mr. Chairman, frankly, I do not think it is necessary that we have for the next fiscal year quite as much as we have for the present fiscal year because of the economies we have worked out by cooperation. It will be brought out before you that in these various offices we have in some cases as high as six of the different projects, each of which has a separate appropriation item, occupying the same or an adjoining suite of rooms and pooling their mechanical and other equipment. In those respects we are able to save a little here and there of the operating expenses of the year before. Furthermore, we have bought all of our equipment for these offices. Last year we spent about $600,000.

Mr. ANDERSON. How much of that was equipment?

Mr. SHERMAN. I can not give you that figure offhand.

The CHAIRMAN. You can put that in the record.

Mr. SHERMAN. Yes, sir. It was not a big proportion of the whole. It was a good many thousands of dollars, but it was not a big proportion of the whole. The equipment is some hundred dollars in each office. We issued 10,000,000 bulletins and spent about $600,000.

The CHAIRMAN. 10,000,000 reports?

Mr. SHERMAN. Not printed bulletins. We issued 10,229,643 separate individual market reports on the different crops. That means that each report is separate because they go to different mailing lists. But with a total expenditure of $600,000 last year we have had an output of over 10,000,000 bulletins actually issued to people interested.

In the first six months of the present fiscal year, when the scale of expenditures is only about $150,000 higher than last year, we have issued already seventeen and one-quarter million. and we will, if we run to full size up to the 1st of July, on an added expenditure of from $100,000 to $150,000 over last year, give nearly three times the service.

The CHAIRMAN. Is it your belief that the increase of $244,000 will maintain the service in its present condition?

Mr. SHERMAN. Absolutely not. With the appropriation as it stands in these estimates, if we cut off the entire service from this point west [indicating Denver on map] we can not keep even.

Mr. BRAND. The estimate was originally made when we were still expecting that the war would continue and that there would be an emergency appropriation.

The CHAIRMAN. How much?

Mr. BRAND. We counted on the same figure.

The CHAIRMAN. What is that?

Mr. BRAND. It amounted to about $240,000 more than the present figure.

The CHAIRMAN. This estimate is $250,000 less than you think you ought to have?

Mr. SHERMAN. It is about that much less than it is this year, but we can get along on a little less than that this year.

The CHAIRMAN. Can you get along on the amount here estimated?

Mr. SHERMAN. No, sir; we can not carry the present service on that amount.

The CHAIRMAN. How much more do you need to make the service what it is now?

Mr. BRAND. We expected there was going to be a discussion of the emergency estimates, and we did not intend to inject that question into this hearing.

The CHAIRMAN. There will not be any emergency estimate.

Mr. BRAND. We rather expected that the memorandum which was sent to us prepared the way with respect to certain items for the possibility of some supplemental estimates. The situation is this: For about two years there has been practically no addition to the regular funds for conducting this work. Had there been no war our appropriations probably would have grown to the figures represented in these estimates. Under the emergency, however, this development has been going on, and we now have the question of cutting off this greater development. We are willing to cut it off, only we do not want to do it without having you realize that on the appropriations shown in these estimates it must be cut.

The CHAIRMAN. To maintain it, what additional recommendation in the way of an appropriation would you make?

Mr. BRAND. My own impression, point blank, is that we would have to have a sum of very nearly $200,000 in addition.

The CHAIRMAN. To what you have estimated here?

Mr. BRAND. Yes.

The CHAIRMAN. That would make a total appropriation of $744,000?

Mr. BRAND. That may be overstating it; but I have given you a rough impression, because we had not made any estimates.

Mr. HAUGEN. Would that include the four additional stations?

Mr. SHERMAN. I think we could do that, because we have the equipment for one of them, and the additional wire mileage is not great.

The CHAIRMAN. Mr. Sherman, can you put into the record the amount you spent for telegrams, equipment, and so on? I presume you have that.

Mr. SHERMAN. Yes.

Expenditures for telegraph tolls in connection with the market news service on fruits and vegetables during the fiscal year ending June 30, 1918.

Approximate cost.
Commercial messages relayed to field stations and f. o. b. reports from these stations; also daily reports of railroad superintendents_____ $15,000
Annual rental of leased wire circuits_____ 100,000

Total_____ 115,000

Expenditures for furniture, equipment, and miscellaneous items at branch offices of the Bureau of Markets in connection with the market news service on fruits and vegetables during the fiscal year ending June 30, 1918.

Atlanta	$1,307.93	Jacksonville	$1,628.68
Baltimore	101.50	Kansas City	451.05
Birmingham	1,424.77	Los Angeles	1,948.86
Boston	1,164.84	Memphis	921.33
Buffalo	1,045.40	Minneapolis	526.78
Butte	1,158.10	New Orleans	1,383.35
Chicago	1,829.03	New York	1,506.37
Cincinnati	551.96	Oklahoma City	1,136.72
Cleveland	1,211.80	Omaha	1,141.43
Columbus	1,164.33	Philadelphia	521.06
Denver	370.42	Pittsburgh	330.71
Des Moines	936.46	Portland	1,243.95
Detroit	1,562.98	St. Louis	151.53
Fargo	1,190.37	San Francisco	1,152.95
Fort Worth	1,592.00	Spokane	284.10
Houston	858.16		
Indianapolis	1,333.41	Total	33,132.33

Mr. HEFLIN. Mr. Sherman, any producer of perishable products, or anybody else in the United States who is interested and wants information as to markets, etc., can obtain that information by writing to you?

Mr. SHERMAN. Yes; we will put him on the mailing list, and the nearest station will furnish him the information free for as long a period as he has use for it. We ask him upon what basis he cares for it, because we do not want to waste paper.

Mr. HEFLIN. How frequently would he get that information?

Mr. SHERMAN. Daily, by mail; it would be put in the mail on the afternoon of the same day to which the information applies.

If this appropriation were continued in the neighborhood of $700,000 we have certain additional work we should do in producing sections, two of which happen to be in your State, Mr. Heflin. We have never had a man on the Mobile cabbage proposition, which varies in importance from year to year, and we hope this winter to put a man in this section. We hope also to have a man at Castleberry during the movement of strawberries.

Mr. HEFLIN. They claim they lose a good deal on cabbage?

Mr. SHERMAN. The price dropped off badly in the spring.

Mr. HEFLIN. This information you give to the producer tells him about the supply and demand in the various markets, and the price?

Mr. SHERMAN. It tells him specifically about that, in each market, by commodities and grades. We have a number of testimonials as to the usefulness of these reports.

Mr. JACOWAY. You give them the condition of the market, too, in this information? For instance, if Washington was the nearest big market, would not that information likely give them the condition of the market, as to whether it was glutted with supplies of stuff which they had for sale?

Mr. SHERMAN. We tell them how many cars have arrived, and whether the movement was brisk or slow, whether the prices were higher or lower than the day before, and whether home-grown receipts were heavy or light.

Mr. JACOWAY. Suppose a producer sent you a telegram, who would pay the expense of the message?

Mr. SHERMAN. If he wanted us to wire him?

Mr. JACOWAY. Yes.

Mr. SHERMAN. He would.

Mr. JACOWAY. I thought the department paid half and the man asking for the information paid half.

Mr. SHERMAN. Absolutely not.

Mr. HEFLIN. If he waits for the mail, it does not cost him anything except the cost of his telegram?

Mr. SHERMAN. That is right.

Mr. ANDERSON. Have you heard of any instances in which the information furnished under this service has been made the basis of price agreements?

Mr. SHERMAN. No.

Mr. ANDERSON. I have heard it said that this information given under this service—under the live-stock item—was used as a basis for price agreements in some markets.

Mr. SHERMAN. It could not very well be used as a basis for price agreements in the markets. It has had this effect, that we do not have the widespread difference in prices between nearby markets. That is one of the strong points in its favor. You do not have such irregular prices, because every shipper has the information at hand every day.

We had a grower out here in western Maryland, who wrote that he had shipped something less than 10 cars of peaches. He said he figured out how much he had made by using our service, and he said, "I watched your reports and I noticed that Boston was consistently paying for my grade of peaches a price which would enable me to pay the additional freight on all I sent there, so I made about $70 per car on the proposition."

Mr. ANDERSON. I have an impression that the service you are rendering is a commercial rather than a public service. I assume it is a valuable service. If it is, why should not the people who get it pay for it?

Mr. SHERMAN. That opens up the whole question as to how the thing shall be handled. I am willing to go into the whole matter any time anybody wants to go into it, as to whether it shall be a free or a pay service. I have my own opinion on that, but I am prepared to run this machine in either way.

Mr. BRAND. May I say, Mr. Chairman, in order to have that point clear, that we believe that when this service is established as a complete national service the Government will be fully warranted in asking the dealers who are benefited by it to pay a fair price for it. Many of them have said it is worth thousands of dollars to them.

and I think when the service is complete the Government will be in a position to say, now this service is complete and permanent; you can count on it from year to year; and it will be necessary for you to pay for it.

The CHAIRMAN. That opens up a field for speculation and argument. We are spending $500,000 a year for issuing the Farmers' Bulletins. We have come back to the principle of charging the farmer 5 or 10 cents for the bulletins.

Mr. BRAND. I do not think the farmer ought to be charged for this service.

The CHAIRMAN. Why not?

Mr. BRAND. Because the farmer can use it only on a single product for a very brief time, and it would be impracticable to charge him for it.

The CHAIRMAN. We have the meat-inspection service, costing several million dollars. The Government is paying for the service.

Mr. BRAND. I do generally favor people paying for the service. I think our inspection work, as rapidly as it can be developed, ought to be put on a self-sustaining basis.

The CHAIRMAN. I thoroughly disagree with you on that proposition. I think the Government ought to pay for it, if it is furnishing public information and let the whole country pay for it and not the enterprise that happens to receive the benefit it it.

Mr. BRAND. That illustrates how widely you can disagree.

Mr. HEFLIN. Is there not another reason, and that is that the Government should encourage the producer. This is under the Agricultural Department, and if anybody is to be encouraged it should be the producer.

Mr. BRAND. My thought was this: Many dealers and shippers formerly carried on their own news services, which cost them, in some cases we know of in connection with live stock and meats, possibly as much as $12,000 or $15,000 a year. This service is giving them more than they could ever get, because they have not the power to get the information that the Government has, and it is disposing of that expense. Of course, that should work itself out to the benefit of the producer and consumer by a slight raise in prices to the former and a more uniform supply and more stable price to the latter, so that perhaps Mr. Lever is wholly right.

The CHAIRMAN. But that is neither here nor there?

Mr. ANDERSON. So far as commercial concerns are affected by this proposition, who are using it for their own benefit to help them make a profit on their business, I agree with you absolutely as far as I am concerned, though I dislike to disagree with the chairman. I think this service ought eventually, to some extent at least, be a self-sustaining service; I would say so far as it is, in fact, a commercial service.

The CHAIRMAN. But you can not separate the two, Mr. Anderson.

Mr. ANDERSON. I think you can do it very easily.

Mr. BRAND. The stumbling block in my mind has been a discrimination between charging a dealer a price and not charging the farmer. I am convinced in my own mind that the farmer's situation is such that he ought not to be charged, and therefore the question of discrimination, which would arise, is the point I stumble on.

The CHAIRMAN. As a matter of fact, this service is to serve to the producer and not the distributor?

Mr. BRAND. That is the main idea, of course.

The CHAIRMAN. Every bit of service the distributor gets helps the producer in so far as it is handled in a general and public manner.

Mr. BRAND. You can not help the one without the other.

Mr. SHERMAN. Our service has this benefit, that it furnishes general information, producing open competition and doing away with lack of information and therefore unfair competition. If we give one distributor a line on a proposition we have given his competitor exactly the same line on that proposition. It has worked out so anyhow. That is the universal testimony of men in the producing sections which we have served.

Mr. HEFLIN. The producer wants to sell his produce and the consumer wants to buy it, and here you bring them together at the market place. It ought to be of service to both the producer and the consumer if it is not.

Mr. BRAND. The benefits are so widespread that it is a question whether you could fairly assess the cost against any particular class.

Mr. SHERMAN. May I for a moment answer Mr. Anderson's question about price agreements a little more fully?

The CHAIRMAN. Proceed.

Mr. SHERMAN. Don't you see, Mr. Anderson, in the case I outlined in Laredo, Tex., where the extremely desirable thing was accomplished, the effect upon the mind of the man in Kansas City who was trying to buy Texas onions? He found all those 30 men in Laredo were quoting a price within 5 cents of each other, whereas 30 days before there was a difference of 15 or 20 cents, and he thought the men had formed a combination. The fact is that it was simply a case of this kind: The prices were published and the men knew what they were. If there is only a range of 10 cents to-day, on to-morrow they can not get very far from it, not unless there are changed conditions which will be reflected in the crop movements, and about which the facts will be known to one shipper as well as to another.

The CHAIRMAN. This is exceedingly interesting, but we must hurry along.

Mr. ANDERSON. You have an estimate apparently in your statement in reference to what you would be required to do in case the appropriation is made at the figure carried in the estimates; that is, that you would cut off the entire service from one section of the country. I notice as I look over your report that you have a large range of products to report on, such as spinach, lettuce, etc.

Mr. SHERMAN. Those are the ones that happen to be on at the present moment.

Mr. ANDERSON. Isn't it possible to reduce your service by cutting off some of the products upon which you report?

Mr. SHERMAN. Absolutely. Let me look that up.

Mr. BRAND. It would save time if we could place these figures into the record, instead of discussing them at such length. I merely suggest that, with a view to save the time of the committee.

The CHAIRMAN. That would save time, and I think would serve the same purpose in furnishing the committee with desired information.

Mr. SHERMAN. I have it here.

AGRICULTURE APPROPRIATION BILL. 569

Some of the curtailments in Market News Service on fruits and vegetables which must be made if amount available for present year is reduced.

Five branch offices connected by leased wires have been opened in Los Angeles, San Francisco, Portland, Spokane, and Butte. An office at Seattle is necessary to complete the system.

The great distances covered necessitate treating all the work in the Western territory as a single leased-wire unit.

The cost of the Pacific coast system is as follows:

2,890 miles of leased wire		$27,915
9 telegraphers at $1,400	$12,600	
1 supervising telegrapher	1,620	
1 telegrapher	1,080	
		15,300
Personnel:		
1 clerk	900	
1 clerk	960	
6 clerks at $1,000	6,000	
1 mimeograph operator	720	
3 messenger boys at $480	1,440	
6 clerks at $1,200	7,200	
2 clerks at $1,100	2,200	
1 clerk	1,300	
		20,720
Cost of 1,675,000 bulletins		6,868
Rent		1,965
Miscellaneous		1,200
Total		[1] 73,968

After the elimination of the Pacific coast work must come the dismantling of offices at Houston, Birmingham, Jacksonville, Oklahoma City, Columbus, and Fargo, resulting in a saving as follows:

	Salaries.	Rent.	Telegraph.[1]	Cost of bulletins.	Miscellaneous.	Total.
Houston	$5,480.00	$1,080.00	$400.00	$1,849.93	$200.00	$9,009.93
Birmingham	7,020.00	450.00	30.00	1,958.94	200.00	9,658.94
Jacksonville	7,580.00	480.00	3,200.00	2,510.67	200.00	13,970.67
Oklahoma City	6,400.00	1,116.00	30.00	833.57	200.00	8,579.57
Columbus	5,240.00	450.00	30.00	889.49	200.00	6,809.49
Fargo	5,960.00	780.00	2,400.00	427.36	200.00	9,767.36
	37,680.00	4,356.00	6,090.00	8,469.96	1,200.00	57,795.96

[1] The offices listed are on leased wire, and the telegraphic cost varies in each case, according to the geographical location of each office.

Based on the crop movement, relative importance, degree of cooperation received, etc., it will then be necessary to abandon the temporary field offices at Bowling Green, Ky. (strawberries); Louisville, Ky. (potatoes and onions); Nashville, Ark. (cantaloupes, peaches, and watermelons); Shelbyville, Del. (strawberries); Rogers, Ark. (apples); Westfield, N. Y. (grapes); Waynesville, N. C. (apples); Kalamazoo, Mich. (celery); Albuquerque, N. Mex. (potatoes and beans); and Seaford, Del. (cantaloupes and watermelons). This would result in approximately the following saving:

Cost of telegrams	$2,248.42
Cost of bulletins	602.46
Travel, clerical hire, and miscellaneous expense	2,900.00
Total	5,750.88

This year there has been issued during the crop seasons reports on asparagus, strawberries, tomatoes, onions, white potatoes, watermelons, cantaloupes, peaches, sweet potatoes, apples, grapes, cabbage, dry beans, celery, eggplant, peppers, string beans, lettuce, oranges, grapefruit, tangerines, bunched vege-

---

[1] Does not include salaries of technical men in charge of these offices as they are paid by Food Products Inspection Service.

tables, cauliflower, spinach, pears, and prunes. To meet this reduction in appropriations we would have to proportionately reduce the number of crops reported. It is probable that the first crops to be eliminated would be asparagus, celery, cherries, eastern grapes, lettuce, fall onions, tangerines, string beans, eggplant, peppers, bunched vegetables, cauliflower, pears, prunes, and spinach. This would deprive of the service the growers of asparagus in South Carolina, New Jersey, California, and Illinois; celery producers in Florida, New York, Michigan, Colorado, and California; the cherry producers of Washington and Oregon; the grape producers of New York, Michigan, and Iowa; the lettuce producers of Florida, California, and Texas; the onion producers of Massachusetts, New York, Ohio, Indiana, Washington, Iowa, Minnesota, Colorado, California; the tangerine producers of Florida; the string bean, eggplant, and pepper producers of Florida; the bunched vegetable producers of Louisiana, Mississippi, and Texas; cauliflower producers of New York and California; pear producers of New York, Michigan, California, Oregon, and Washington; the prune producers of California, Oregon, and Washington; the spinach producers of Texas and Virginia.

This would result in the elimination of approximately 500,000 bulletins from branch offices and 250,000 from temporary field offices, effecting a total saving of about $4,000.

From this you will see how rapidly we reduce the service and how slowly you cut out $225,000 if you cut out a lot of stations. With all this service abandoned and all these stations closed we must find other means for saving over $100,000 more.

The CHAIRMAN. You have not answered Mr. Anderson's question. Why can not you withdraw some of these products? Take strawberries; that is a product that a very small number of people, especially poor folks like myself, can not pay for the cream needed?

Mr. SHERMAN. If we cut out asparagus, celery, cherries, eastern grapes, lettuce, fall onions, tangerines, string beans, eggplant, peppers, bunched vegetables, cauliflower, pears—and of pears alone 7,000 carloads move per year—prunes, and spinach, we would save only $4,000.

Mr. HAUGEN. Where does all this money go to?

Mr. HEFLIN. I am opposed to withdrawing the service from any of these people or from any of these products.

Mr. BRAND. The total carload shipments of strawberries is over 18,000.

The CHAIRMAN. Will you put into the record figures regarding the carload shipments of fruits and vegetables?

Mr. BRAND. We will do that, Mr. Chairman.

The statement referred to follows:

Summary of carload shipments reported to Bureau of Markets by mail during 1916.

[635,361 cars were reported from 8,789 billing stations.]

[NOTE.—The numbers in parentheses indicate the number of States from which the respective commodities were shipped or into which they were imported.]

Commodity.	Cars.	Commodity.	Cars.
Apples	87,544 (45)	Dried apples	868 (14)
Apricots	195 (2)	Dried apricots	27 (3)
Cherries	903 (15)	Dried figs	67 (3)
Grapes	12,046 (30)	Dried peaches	217 (5)
Peaches	25,069 (39)	Dried pears	1 (1)
Pears	7,444 (32)	Dried prunes	381 (7)
Plums	280 (12)	Raisins	2,860 (2)
Prunes	598 (8)	Dates	21 (2)
Quinces	16 (7)	Mixed dried fruit	298 (13)
Mixed fruit	19,367 (31)	Oranges	49,748 (15)

Summary of carload shipments reported to Bureau of Markets by mail during 1916—Continued.

[NOTE.—The number in parentheses indicate the number of States from which the respective commodities were shipped or into which they were imported.]

Commodity.	Cars.	Commodity.	Cars.
Lemons	7,482 (9)	Beets	843 (15)
Grapefruit	2,327 (8)	Carrots	741 (22)
Limes	10 (3)	Parsnips	35 (7)
Tangerines	19 (3)	Radishes	471 (12)
Bananas	16,501 (12)	Rutabagas	204 (8)
Fresh figs	2 (1)	Turnips	420 (28)
Pineapples	1,303 (7)	Broccoli	50 (2)
Pomegranates	7 (1)	Brussels sprouts	100 (1)
Blackberries	464 (13)	Cabbages	24,452 (43)
Cranberries	1,790 (8)	Cauliflower	2,872 (9)
Dewberries	210 (3)	Kale	2,579 (3)
Gooseberries	101 (5)	Celery	10,194 (16)
Huckleberries	122 (7)	Lettuce (including Romaine and Escarole)	4,703 (23)
Loganberries	62 (1)		
Raspberries	570 (10)	Parsley	18 (3)
Strawberries	17,869 (33)	Artichokes	307 (2)
Mixed berries	176 (13)	Asparagus	1,272 (10)
Currants	186 (3)	Rhubarb	270 (6)
Cantaloupes	17,071 (31)	Green lima beans	198 (4)
Casabas	371 (2)	String beans	2,706 (22)
Cucumbers	3,552 (25)	Green peas	935 (21)
Pumpkins	176 (11)	Dry beans	4,020 (22)
Squash	149 (18)	Dry peas	680 (20)
Watermelons	28,927 (40)	Green corn	922 (24)
Eggplant	293 (8)	Spinach	2,653 (11)
Peppers	1,066 (13)	Mixed vegetables	6,207 (44)
Tomatoes	19,294 (32)	Mixed fruit and vegetables	8,794 (31)
White potatoes	193,197 (48)		
Sweet potatoes	15,676 (29)	Total	635,361
Garlic	63 (4)		
Onions	21,909 (41)		

The CHAIRMAN. Is there anything further, gentlemen?

Mr. THOMPSON. There is some complaint among producers that when they use these cars to ship their products to distributing points, such as Kansas City, St. Joseph, Cincinnati, St. Louis, and Chicago, the dealers at these points, the commission merchants or whoever they send them to, play with them and hold them up and say they are injured and destroyed, and sometimes want to turn them back, and worry them, and in that way they suffer great loss. What supervision, if any, does your bureau exercise over these cars when they arrive at destination?

Mr. BRAND. That question brings up two outside questions that are not within the sphere of this service. Our inspection service handles these things as far as disputes as to physical condition are concerned. When you get beyond that question and get to regulation, there is a proposition that Congress will have to take up in its own way and settle. The Food Administration has been exercising some powers over dealers, but we can not do that. Mr. Scott will cover the inspection.

Mr. THOMPSON. I wanted to get what activities the department was exercising in an attempt to remove this trouble. The Food Administration did great work in protecting the producer, I think.

Mr. SHERMAN. The future of that work lies entirely in your hands. It all depends upon whether you want us to do it or not.

The CHAIRMAN. We are introducing a bill to license all cold-storage plants at distributing points and hope to cure the most of those evils.

Mr. HEFLIN. Haven't you a man in Chicago and at the other principal markets where these things are shipped who, if there is a dispute a on the condition of the produce when it arrives, can pass on it? b t

Mr. BRAND. Mr. Scott will discuss that.

Mr. HEFLIN. I understand they have saved thousands and thousands of dollars to shippers who have been the objects of these methods and would have been duped on the claim that their products had arrived in bad shape. Now, this Bureau of Markets has stopped that, hasn't it?

Mr. SHERMAN. I would not say they have stopped it.

Mr. HAUGEN. If they have, it is well worth the money. But, as I understand, it does not contend that that practice has been stopped?

Mr. BRAND. To some extent it has. We would not like to take credit for everything that has happened, but think we have helped conditions very much.

Mr. HEFLIN. My impression was that you have an agent that the shipper could wire to protect his products in event such a claim were made by the commission merchant, distributor, or other consignee?

Mr. SHERMAN. Yes.

Mr. HEFLIN. If he would report that your product was in good condition, it would enable the shipper to stand out against the buyer.

Mr. SHERMAN. Yes; but we have no authority to assess damage. The Food Administration has been passing upon whether a car should be accepted or not, but we have no such power.

Mr. ANDERSON. They haven't, either; but I suppose that was a war-emergency action.

Mr. THOMPSON. You say that your agent can do that on request from the shipper?

Mr. SHERMAN. He would inspect any shipment on request.

Mr. THOMPSON. The producers do not understand, certainly not generally, that they may avail themselves of that service.

Mr. SHERMAN. They ought to do that.

Mr. HAUGEN. To what extent has this service extended during the last year?

Mr. SHERMAN. If you are interested, gentlemen of the committee, I will explain the annual expansion of the service: During 1915 we reported on cantaloupes, peaches, pears, strawberries, and tomatoes for a short season. That was in its experimental stage. For 1916, the year for which you made your first appropriation of $136,600, we added to those 5 crops 10 more—apples, asparagus, cabbage, celery, grapes, lettuce, onions, prunes, watermelons, and white potatoes—making a total of 15. In 1917 we had war-emergency money, and we added 12 more—bunched vegetables, such as beets, carrots, escarole, and radishes; cherries; cranberries; dry beans; eggplant; grapefruit; honey—and I do not know whether you are going to pick me up on honey or not. We had a lot of demand for it. It is not a fruit or vegetable, but we added it—also oranges, peppers, string beans, sweet potatoes, and tangerines, making a total of 27. This year we added 5 more—cucumbers, green peas, mixed deciduous fruits, plums, and spinach.

Mr. HAUGEN. How much did you add to your expense?
Mr. SHERMAN. These are additional crops.
Mr. HAUGEN. But what about the additional expense?
Mr. SHERMAN. We have added to our field stations—I have not the record here giving the way our field stations expended the money—but the entire Pacific coast service has been put on within the last eight months.
Mr. HAUGEN. This is a war proposition, isn't it?
Mr. SHERMAN. It was done with the emergency fund.
Mr. HAUGEN. The expansion is due to the war, or to the emergency-fund proposition?
Mr. SHERMAN. I wouldn't say that, Mr. Haugen, because I believe, tacitly at least, this was decided to be made eventually a nation-wide service before any war was thought of.
Mr. HAUGEN. How much money have you appropriated out of the emergency fund?
Mr. SHERMAN. $500,000.
The CHAIRMAN. Yes; it is $500,000.
Mr. HAUGEN. How much of it is to be permanent?
Mr. BRAND. $244,800. That involves a cut of $255,200.
Mr. HAUGEN. That is not a cut, but an addition.
Mr. BRAND. Well, it is a cut from the total available this year—a cut from our present expenditure.
Mr. HAUGEN. It is an addition of $244,000 of the emergency fund to be carried into this bill.
Mr. BRAND. That is right.
The CHAIRMAN. And it is to be made permanent.
Mr. HAUGEN. Why discriminate against these Pacific coast growers you refer to? In speaking of the Pacific coast you mentioned that that section could be cut out, and so much money saved. The Pacific coast has no representative on this committee, but it ought to be taken care of along with other sections of the country.
The CHAIRMAN. Mr. Sherman is protesting against doing it. He does not want to cut it out.
Mr. HAUGEN. We have asked how this great emergency expenditure might be cut down, and he mentions that as a way to do it.
Mr. SHERMAN. There does not seem to be any way that you can scale it down. You must either serve that section or not.
Mr. HAUGEN. There are other sections that could be taken into consideration also?
Mr. SHERMAN. There is no other place where we could drop five stations and save $75,000.
Mr. HAUGEN. Why should one section of the country have a service over any other section of the country?
Mr. SHERMAN. I do not think it should.
Mr. HAUGEN. What is the reason for lopping off this particular section of the country and abandoning the service for it alone?
Mr. SHERMAN. We can answer that by saying we took it on recently under the emergency fund, and it was the last part of the service that was taken on. Acting on the same principle on which we dismiss first the employees last taken on, under the war emergency, we will have to drop first the last activities taken up under the war emergency.

Mr. HAUGEN. Is it of less importance than other sections?

Mr. SHERMAN. I do not think so. Those men are farther from their markets than anybody else, are more in danger of congesting certain markets in the East, and, I think, need our service just as much as producers in other sections of the country.

Mr. HAUGEN. Why not cut other sections?

Mr. SHERMAN. If you cut out twice as many in the East in an effort to save a considerable sum of money you will have no information to give producers; you would have no market report to give them. If you did not run a market list and give the merchants, say, in Cincinnati, the information, when a man comes around in the morning he will be politely told to go to some other place. We have no power to make these men give us information and give it to us accurately except the power of service rendered.

Mr. HAUGEN. The same rule applies to all sections of the country about the power you have to make anybody testify.

Mr. SHERMAN. Yes; and if you bring your power along to make a man testify you will get two or three statements a day whereas we want a good many hundreds of them.

Mr. HAUGEN. You must have market work in these centers to give service?

Mr. SHERMAN. No——

Mr. HAUGEN (interposing). I do not want it to go into the record that we are discriminating against any section of the country, because they have no representation on this committee.

Mr. SHERMAN. Certainly not.

The CHAIRMAN. That is the very contention that Mr. Sherman has been making.

Mr. HAUGEN. His contention was that we should cut this section off because it was an emergency appropriation, and that would result in cutting off the Pacific coast section.

Mr. MCLAUGHLIN. He said if any was to be cut off, that was the part that might be the more naturally and easily cut off.

The CHAIRMAN. The question before the committee when we come to write the bill will be whether we shall keep up the existing service or reduce it by $244,000 and dismantle a portion of the structure.

Mr. HAUGEN. It is whether we make $244,000 of the emergency appropriation permanent.

The CHAIRMAN. It will be more than that if we take all of it.

Mr. HAUGEN. Yes; but the proposition is to cut it in two.

SPECIFIC EXAMPLES OF BENEFITS OF MARKET NEWS SERVICE ON FRUITS AND VEGETABLES.

The following is an extract from a letter received from the agent of the Northern Pacific Railway Co. at Deerwood, Minn., dated July 19, 1918:

"You have done more to release cars and expedite the movement of necessities as well as to equalize prices than any agency that ever acted. It may take some time to get the retailer going, but when the full force of your work comes to a climax things will have been revolutionized, to everybody's benefit."

Mr. John Denney, of Denney & Co., one of the largest produce firms in Chicago, wrote as follows, under date of November 16, 1918:

"For your information it is our opinion that these market reports of shipments, inspections, etc., as handled by the Department of Agriculture are of greater benefit to the country as a whole—not only the dealers but to growers and consumers—than any other one thing that has been instituted by the Government in some time."

A letter, dated September 2, 1918, from J. A. Ward, a grower, of Brigham, Utah, contains the following:

" Will you kindly send to my address your Daily Apple Bulletin? Your Peach Bulletin has been very valuable to me in the marketing of my peach crop. I demanded a price consistent with your reports of market conditions and received it."

The Wenatchee-Beebe Orchard Co., whose head office is at Minneapolis, Minn., under date of October 14, 1918, wrote as follows:

" We may say that we find the reports of the very greatest value, and hope that we will not be omitted as to any one of them."

The following letter was received from Mr. Leslie R. Smith, superintendent of farm machinery, State Board of Agriculture, Boston, Mass., under date of July 26, 1918:

" I am in receipt of your communication in regard to the Onion Bulletin, and I certainly do want it, as per my inclosed blank. This is one of the greatest things that was ever done for the onion growers of the Connecticut Valley and saves thousands of dollars annually, I believe."

Mr. P. A. Rogers, general manager of the Ozark Fruit Growers' Association, from their branch at Humboldt, Tenn., wrote as follows, under date of July 18, 1918:

" We wish to advise you that your service in market reporting this year has been of very valuable service to us, and is coming to be regarded at this end of the line as indispensable in marketing the highly perishable crops which we handle."

R. H. Bryson, agricultural agent of Gulf & Ship Island Railroad Co., Mendenhall, Miss., in a letter dated June 13, 1918, states:

" Your office has been furnishing me report daily by wire, and it has been of considerable value to our growers, three shipping points combined saving $1,000 for the growers in one day; but the report is reaching me most too late for the best results."

The Wingrove-Austin Co., of Fort Worth, Tex,. wrote as follows, under date of April 10, 1918:

" When the Bureau of Markets office first opened in Fort Worth, not knowing anything about the methods, we were a little fearful that the office might interfere in some way with our business or that of our customers, and were not very enthusiastic. Now that we can see the very great advantages being derived from the information that goes out from your office to growers, shippers, dealers, and brokers, we are very glad of the opportunity to express ourselves as being quite favorable to the offices here being maintained, as it is our opinion that a great deal of good is being done and that the information that comes through your office is very beneficial to everyone, in addition to which your office goes a long way toward running down the broker, dealer, or shipper who is in the habit of making false statements for personal benefit."

Guy C. Porter, manager of the Aroostook Potato Growers' Association, Houlton, Me., states:

" I wish to take this opportunity to express to you my gratitude for the very complete market reports we are receiving from day to day. In my opinion there is nothing the Government could do for the farmers and shippers of potatoes which would be of any more benefit to them than this market-report system."

The CHAIRMAN. Anything else? If not, you may go ahead with your statement, Mr. Brand.

Mr. BRAND. The next item is 120, providing for market reports on live stock and meats.

The CHAIRMAN. You have an increase there estimated at how much?

Mr. BRAND. If I may, I will bring out the complete situation so that it may be before you. At the present time we have for this year a regular appropriation in the agricultural appropriation bill of $57,920. We also have $300,000 of emergency money. The proposal before you is to transfer $170,000 of emergency money to the permanent act, involving a reduction of $130,000 over the funds that are available for this year. I want that to be understood, because we have the same problem with respect to reduction in this service and I would like to have it before you.

Mr. HAUGEN. Available this year, including the emergency fund?
Mr. BRAND. Yes.
Mr. ANDERSON. Will you use the total emergency fund this year?
Mr. BRAND. Yes; we expect to use the total in that service. With reference to live stock and meats, we have had such an avalanche of demands for this work, you understand, that there is now under consideration in another committee a bill appropriating $500,000,000 to take over the stockyards. This work is tending toward a cure of the faults that lead to that sort of legislation.
The CHAIRMAN. Suppose you outline to us the machinery.
Mr. BRAND. There is so much of this that I have asked these gentlemen who are handling it more immediately to be present, and I will now ask Prof. Hall to make a statement on this proposition.
The CHAIRMAN. Now, gentlemen of the committee, suppose, in order to get this matter clearly before us, we give these division chiefs 5 or 10 minutes without interruption to set forth the machinery under which they operate, their plans, and needs. Without objection, that will be followed.
The committee will now be glad to hear Mr. Hall.

STATEMENT OF MR. L. D. HALL, SPECIALIST IN CHARGE OF MARKET NEWS SERVICE ON LIVE STOCK AND MEATS, BUREAU OF MARKETS, UNITED STATES DEPARTMENT OF AGRICULTURE.

Mr. HALL. Mr. Chairman and gentlemen of the committee, I want to tell you first what the service is; second, what it does; and third, some of the objects and results of the service.
It is not necessary, I take it, to say a great deal about what it is, because it has already been mentioned in connection with fruits and vegetables, and by a glance at the map here you will see in a general way the extent of the service. We have 17 branch offices, extending from Boston to Portland and Los Angeles, around down to Fort Worth, and have been upon the point of establishing an office at Jacksonville in order to stake down all four corners of the country. We are holding the latter office in abeyance, in view of the fact that the present estimate would not permit us to continue the office at Jacksonville if established, and we did not feel that it would be proper to establish it only to continue it for the balance of this year.
We issue reports on 13 commodities, as follows: Live stock, 5, being cattle and calves, horses, mules, sheep, and swine; meats, 5, being beef, lamb, mutton, pork, and veal; animal products, 3, being hair and mohair, hides and skins and wools. We call wools for the moment a by-product, but it is really a product itself.
We issue 10 different market reports, including two daily reports on the meat trade at five eastern and three far western meat-distributing centers, which include supply and demand and prices. We issue a live-stock loading report covering the entire United States on the same general principles as the fruit and vegetable report that Mr Sherman described so fully. We issue six daily telegraphic reports from the Chicago live-stock market. Since the 1st of June, 1918, we have conducted an exclusive live-stock market report service at Chicago, taking over all former services that were conducted there by

wire, including the telegraphic features of the "C. N. D.," as they call it—the commercial news department service—which supplies every hamlet in the United States almost, through the press associations. If you will pick up a Washington paper any evening you will notice the live-stock report from Chicago labeled "United States Bureau of Markets Report." The board of trade sends them out over the tickers just the same as the press associations send out the baseball report, so that one operator sends the report to thousands of other operators at various points.

We issue a weekly sheet, which we call the Weekly Live Stock and Meat Trade News, which is a catch-all for the various statistical information and particularly items regarding live-stock movements, in addition to our market report service which I have just mentioned. In this weekly bulletin we sum up the in-and-out movement of live stock in some of the principal feeding districts and grazing sections, where we have been conducting some field offices patterned after the fruit and vegetable offices that Mr. Sherman has described. That work has not been carried by us to nearly the point you have heard described in reference to fruits and vegetables, because the live-stock industry, as I will mention a little further along more in detail, is a highly concentrated industry and perhaps the most highly concentrated industry in the United States. A dozen large markets take care of about 80 per cent of the market receipts of live stock in this country, and a few distributing centers in the East handle a large part of the product of the animals slaughtered in the middle western stockyards. So that our service has followed the lines of least resistance, and we have tried to take points needing the information most, in a few large market centers, so that our service has not been as extensive nor as expensive for the same relative results as in the case of fruits and vegetables. Reports on stocks of wool and consumption of wool, and active and idle wool machinery, and stocks of frozen and cured meats in cold storage can scarcely be mentioned in connection with this market news service, since they are handled under other funds; but our project has worked very closely with those handling them and supplied schedules and technical information regarding service on these products.

We are serving 20,000 people by mail with our daily bulletins and our weekly bulletins, a large portion of which number are actual producers. Of course, a larger percentage of our subscribers are distributors than is true of fruits and vegetables, because, as I have said, our offices are in highly concentrated centers. I should say that half of our 20,000 mailing-list names represent distributors and meat packers, small and large, in the large market centers. Through the daily papers that use our Chicago live-stock wire service, served by the United Press, the Associated Press, and other news services, some of our statisticians have figured with their stub pencils that we reach about 5,000,000 people daily. That, of course, is more or less an approximation. We have distributed during the last fiscal year 4,000,000 separate reports of the 10 different series I mentioned a few minutes ago, which 10 different reports are:

1. Daily Report on Meat-trade Conditions.
2. Daily Report on Wholesale Prices of Fresh Beef, Lamb, and Mutton.

3. Weekly Review of Meat-trade Conditions.
4. Weekly Summary of Wholesale Prices of Fresh Beef, Lamb, and Mutton.
5. Weekly Live Stock and Meat Trade News.
6. Daily Live-stock Loadings.
7. Monthly Report on Live Stock at Stock Yards.
8. Monthly Wool Consumption Report.
9. Quarterly Report on Stocks of Wool.
10. Monthly Report on Active and Idle Wool Machinery.

If I had more than five minutes, I should like to tell you more in detail about one particular service.

The CHAIRMAN. You have 10 minutes.

Mr. HALL. I would especially like to tell you about our report on the Chicago live-stock market. I will try to limit myself to the 10 minutes, Mr. Chairman, since you have been so generous.

Chicago is the hub of the live-stock universe. Nearly every little stockyard in the country, and big stockyard, too—such as at Kansas City—waits in the morning until it hears from Chicago before beginning business. When you realize that the annual volume of business in live stock done at Chicago is $900,000,000, at Kansas City $600,000,000, and so on down through smaller stockyards at New Orleans, and Montgomery, Ala., and Billings, Mont., so that at 63 centralized stockyards the total annual live-stock business done is $5,000,000,000, you will realize the great volume of business waiting to hear from Chicago.

Until June 1, 1918, this country had gone along, strange to say, for 40 or 50 years without any official Government report on the live-stock market. At the requests of the American National Live Stock Association, various State and sectional live-stock associations, the National Live Stock Exchange, and others, the Bureau of Markets undertook to take over all telegraphic reports going out of Chicago. We abolished some features of the former reports. We found that two men were responsible for all the reports coming out of Chicago, and they were undertaking to tell in their telegram at 7 o'clock in the morning, and sometimes as early as 6 o'clock in the morning, the prospective market for that day, at a time before the stock was unloaded off the cars or even the trains were in in some instances, and before the demand in the East was known.

The message would read something like this: 20,000 cattle, prospects 10 higher. Thirty thousand hogs, prospects 10 lower, and so on down through sheep and calves. We decided to abolish that prospect feature of the message, because nobody has any business guessing at 7 o'clock in the morning what the market may be. We figured that we could tell a little closer than anybody else ever did before just as the Weather Bureau can tell closer than Dr. Hicks could tell what the weather will be. But we thought we should walk before we tried to run; so we have done away with that prospect feature of the old method of private reporting, and the opposition that naturally arose at first to such action has, since it has become understood, been overcome. Since we give the actual live-stock loading to arrive the following day, that takes the place of this other information, because it indicates quite definitely the prospective arrivals for the morrow's market.

We begin at 6 o'clock in the morning sending out a report by wire to all our branch offices of the receipts at the Chicago market for that day. At 7 o'clock it is followed by a second message, which sometimes varies a thousand or two head of cattle and hogs from the first message. I have copies of to-day's messages here if any member of the committee cares to see them. At 8.30 a. m. a message is sent giving the opening of the hog market. At 9.15 a. m. there is a flash wire which goes to the principal markets, and any market that wants it can have it. It is only subscribed for by a few markets, and those at which our branch offices are located. It gives a little further information on the opening. At 10.30 a. m. a message gives the prices on cattle, hogs, and sheep up to that time; and at 1 o'clock or whatever time the market closes a complete closing message is given, which is used by the afternoon newspapers throughout the country. As I say, that message not only goes to our own branch offices, but to the service conducted by the press associations and telegraph companies. That is a general picture of the service. I wish I had the time to fill in more details.

I want to say a word now about the objects and value of the service. The fluctuations in market prices at the stockyards especially Chicago, Kansas City, and Omaha, where hogs would fall a dollar or a dollar and a half in a day, and sometimes two or three dollars in two or three days, have been one of the greatest causes of dissatisfaction among stockmen, and one of the greatest causes of suspicion. Suspicion was natural, for no one knew the reasons therefor. No one was in a position to prove the reasons for those fluctuations. A great many people thought prices were manipulated, and a great many people think so yet. We do not know yet to just what extent it may have been manipulated, but we do know that the market at Chicago did not have information of what was going on in New York or Boston. Of course, the large packers, with their private wire systems, knew every hour what was going on at New York and Boston. The cattle buyers in Chicago knew what was the demand for beef in New York, but the commission men did not know, and the men who consigned to commission men did not know, and the men who consigned live stock to commission men were dependent upon the commission men. So that the selling side of the trade did not know the demand, while the buying side of the trade, or at least 98 per cent in volume of the buying trade, represented by a very few large packers, had all this information. They also had information regarding railroad movements of live stock throughout the United States more or less, but not nearly as completely as we are giving it now. The general public did not have access to reports on the sources of live-stock movement, and commission men had no way of getting it; so that it is not a matter of wonder that prices did vary up and down a great deal. Now, commission men who are selling cattle in Chicago know from our·Government reports whether there is a good demand for beef in New York or whether the demand is weak, and they know the same thing about Boston, Pittsburgh, Philadelphia, as well as San Francisco and Los Angeles. While, of course, Pacific coast points are not a real factor in the Chicago trade, in San Francisco it is of importance, and it makes a little bit of difference in Kansas City what the condition is on the Pacific coast, and more difference still on the Denver market.

So one purpose of this information was to iron out the ups and downs in prices at stockyards, which kept stockmen suspicious of the trade and guessing all the time. While the unusual market conditions during the past year or two have made it impossible to prove statistically to just what extent the service has ironed out these fluctuations, we have records of numerous instances in which individual markets or individual days of shipments have been very materially stabilized in price through the availability of this information.

Another and still more important difficulty with our live-stock markets is the absence of competition. You could not expect very much competition to grow up so long as very limited interests had access to all the information. You could not expect the small packer to launch into slaughtering beef cattle in Chicago with the idea of distributing it in New York or Boston without access to pretty complete information. And, of course, the small concern could not afford to put in a complete leased-wire system and the other facilities required in order to put it in a position to compete with the big institutions.

This complete-information service which I have described in 10 minutes or so has given to the small packer and the small butcher the same information, and more too, than the five packers—the Big Five, as we call them—had always enjoyed. It gives the retail meat dealer a better line on the market; and I have been told recently that there are movements on foot in different places among retail dealers to organize cooperative associations to build slaughterhouses and put their own buyers into the stockyards, and to slaughter their own cattle and distribute their own meat, instead of depending upon the large packers for it, and that it is partly the result of this information service. I will not say entirely so, for it is due partly to other forms of control; but we believe turning on the spotlight of information is one of two big factors in encouraging healthy competition. Two remedies are needed to correct concentration of control such as has always been exerted on this industry; one is information, and the other is regulation. There may be some others, but it seems to us these are the outstandingly important ones.

Then, even if we might correct these two conditions completely there is still another that would be troublesome. That is the shipper out in the western country, western Iowa we will say, not knowing what is due to arrive in Chicago 36 hours later when he is going to get there with his stock. He had not known that fact when he loaded his stock. And even the shipper near by, who is 24 hours closer to the market, was completely in the dark as to prospective arrivals at the time his cattle would arrive on the market. This has been met by a live-stock loading service, consisting of telegrams from every railroad division superintendent every night in the year, which data is summed up by our clerks during the night as it comes to our central office in Chicago, and is ready for distribution throughout the country, the same as the weather report, by daylight the next morning. That information is at hand at every distributing point, at every one of our market-news stations, where it is sent out by wire to anyone who is willing to pay for the telegram, or by mail, without charge, to anyone who wants the mail service; but particularly it reaches the little shipper or farmer out in the country in more instances through his commission man, upon whom he depends so largely for advice as to whether he shall or shall not ship. Commission men have the information available immediately upon its release in the morning, and a commission man will wire, say, to Bill Jones, at Podunk, Mo., whether the prospect is for a small or a large arrival the next day. Bill Jones will probably act as his commission man advises, or he won't. Commission men say Bill Jones usually does the opposite thing from what they advise him to do. But, be that as it may, the information is there to equalize these live-stock movements into the market, and this information has been made the basis of a zoning system at Chicago and Kansas City whereby the bunching of receipts on one or two days in the week has been very largely ironed out, so that we now have consummated the five-day market we talked about so much two or three years ago. Instead of 85 per cent of the receipts coming into Chicago on Mondays and Wednesdays one of our bulletins a week or two ago gave the information that only 47 per cent, or between 47 per cent and 48 per cent of the arrivals at Chicago came in on Mondays and Wednesdays. Even Saturday has got to be quite a market day, while formerly that was the day that commission men went out to play golf or indulge in other forms of recreation.

Then, another point, that means equalizing the movement over the seasonal period is the matter of reports of in-and-out movements in the feeding districts and grazing sections I spoke of a few minutes ago. We have only made a small beginning in that work, but we have an office at Lancaster, Pa., which is a prominent cattle-feeding county and in the center of 18 counties which feed about 75,000 cattle a year. Another office was located at Rocky Ford, Colo., in the Arkansas Valley cattle-feeding district. By this means we are able to know almost to the head the number of cattle and lambs in those districts. Formerly the best of authorities would disagree to the extent of 100 per cent on the number of cattle and lambs on feed in a number of districts. It was amazing to see the extent of the variation in what had always been regarded as reliable estimates. You may readily see that if we have information on 20 or 30 of the principal well concentrated feeding districts and well-defined grazing sections as to the stock moving in and out during the seasonal period, that any shipper or any feeder or grazer operating in one of those districts can tell from one to two or three months ahead, as the case may be, approximately when the stock would be ready to move out, and operators in one district can tell at a glance what the operators in another district are doing and regulate their shipments accordingly. I once asked Gov. Kendrick, now Senator Kendrick, of Wyoming, if a report of this sort would be of any benefit to him; that is, if he knew what was coming out of the Panhandle of Texas and as to the time, if it would affect the handling and marketing of his cattle in Montana or Wyoming. He said it might make a difference of from 30 to 40 days. While we are not yet in a position to give that information in those particular districts, we hope that with a continuation and an expansion of this service that such a service will be made possible in 30 or 40 of the leading grazing and feeding districts of the country.

So much for equalizing shipments to the markets, which will help to do away with this thing of farmers coming in to market and competing against themselves at one time, when they might just as well come in at different seasons of the year. The movement of lambs already has been spread over a period of six months, whereas formerly it came in during the period from September to November. Through concerted effort on the part of the National Wool Growers' Association, for years interested in bringing about an earlier lambing period, lambs now begin to come in to the market in June instead of in September, so that the marketing period is spread out over six months instead of only three months. This results in relieving problems of transportation, gives the consumer lamb over a longer period, and causes him to pay less extreme prices at any one time, and gives the producer a fairer and better regulated market.

Another general object and value of the service, as we see it, is the furnishing of authentic reports, particularly on live-stock prices and receipts, whereas formerly there were nothing but unofficial telegraphic reports available. I have already said something on that, but I now want to illustrate the point just a little: We found with the former reports, for instance, an elastic hog market at Chicago. Since the 1st of June, 1918, when we took over the live-stock market reporting at Chicago, we have found that our closing market has been about 10 or 15 cents higher, on a daily average, than the closing market reported by some of the newspaper market reporters. And we have had some complaints from packers who buy hogs shipped direct to their plants, and from local shippers who get into their Ford cars in the morning and go out and buy hogs from the farmers or who call up over the rural telephone and buy. They are complaining that our closing report at Chicago is higher than some of the market reports and higher than some of the daily newspaper reports. That is because the pacer who buys out in Iowa, for instance, has been in the habit of buying hogs to be shipped in to him on this basis: He takes the top of the Chicago market and the closing market and strikes an average of the two, and when the farmer's hogs arrive at the packing plant he marks up the price of the hogs according to that average, using that as the basis. Of course, the grade of the hogs would be considered usually, but that closing market has been a factor in forming the basis. And the country dealer or buyer who makes up a carload of hogs which he buys from a dozen or fifteen or twenty farmers uses the Chicago wires as his basis for buying from the farmer, and he, of course, always uses the lowest wire he gets during the day.

Now, when we came along and began reporting in the way that I have described, just as naturally as might have been expected it aroused some feeling on the part of these people who had been using the former system of reports as their basis for buying. And I might say right here that another one of our statisticians has figured out that with a difference of 10 cents a hundred pounds applied to live stock coming to Chicago, and figuring on the same basis for the principal stockyard centers, there has been the enormous sum of from $20,000,000 to $30,000,000 a year going into the pockets of intermediaries and which ought to have been going into the pockets of the farmers.

The live-stock situation in the United States has been retarded perhaps more largely by these four things—fluctuations in the market, lack of competition, irregular movement to the markets, and absence of authentic information—than by any other factors. I would like to show the committee a chart which I keep on my wall and which keeps me inspired all the time to put forth the best efforts within myself and my staff of assistants to help correct that situation. [Unfolding and holding up a chart.] Gentlemen, this is a picture of the live-stock situation as compared to population in the United States. From 1870 to 1900 the lines representing live stock ascended almost parallel to the population, but since that time the general tendency has been to remain about horizontal. Sheep have gone down hill, due to a number of factors, such as dogs, etc., and variation in the price of wool. Cattle and hogs have varied considerably and show fluctuations, not only in daily and weekly movements but annually. There seems to be some tendency upward now toward normal, but we are still in a period of discrepancy of about 30 degrees from the horizontal as compared to population. And that is the reason we have all heard so much about shortage of meat and high prices for beefsteak, and the taking over of stockyards and packing houses, etc.

There have been several committees appointed during the last several years to work on these matters, and we have been trying to put into effect from time to time the recommendations of these committees. The first one was in 1913, appointed by Secretary Houston, a committee on the meat situation. Another one was appointed by the President about a year ago. These committees reported their findings, and we have adopted several of the recommendations of both these committees. I think one of the outstanding recommendations among them all has been the need of accurate information, and this market news service is an effort to supply that information.

Gentlemen of the committee, I very seldom let an audience get away from me without making a stump speech on the importance of the live-stock industry, but your chairman has been so generous with me that I do not think I should attempt to hold you here for the presentation of statistics, and would like to put some of them in the record for the information of the committee?

The CHAIRMAN. Suppose you just put them into the record. Is there any further general statement?

Mr. HALL. I think that covers the salient points, Mr. Chairman.

(The statement referred to follows:)

EXTENT AND RELATIVE IMPORTANCE OF LIVE-STOCK AND MEAT INDUSTRIES IN THE UNITED STATES.

Value of live stock compared with all farm property.

[From Census Report, 1910.]

	Value.	Per cent.
Land	$28,475,674,169	69.5
Buildings	6,325,451,528	15.4
Live stock	4,925,173,610	12.0
Implements and machinery	1,265,149,783	3.1
Total	40,991,449,090	100.0

Estimated value of live stock on farms and ranges Jan. 1, for specified years.

[From reports of Bureau of Crop Estimates, United States Department of Agriculture.]

1912	$5,008,327,000
1917	6,735,621,000
1918	8,263,524,000

Sales of live stock compared with sale of other farm products.

[From Monthly Crop Report, Bureau of Crop Estimates, Department of Agriculture, 1915.]

	Per cent.
Live stock	36
Live-stock products	20
Crops	40
Miscellaneous	4
Total	100

Live stock compared with population in United States.

[From Reports of United States Census and Department of Agriculture.]

	Population.	Cattle.	Hogs.	Sheep.	Horses.
1870	39,000,000	24,000,000	25,000,000	28,000,000	7,000,000
1880	50,000,000	39,000,000	50,000,000	42,000,000	10,000,000
1890	63,000,000	58,000,000	57,000,000	41,000,000	15,000,000
1900	76,000,000	52,000,000	63,000,000	40,000,000	18,000,000
1910	92,000,000	54,000,000	58,000,000	40,000,000	20,000,000
1918	105,000,000	66,000,000	71,000,000	49,000,000	21,000,000

Live stock receipts for 1917 and 1918 at 63 stockyards.

[From reports of Bureau of Markets, Department of Agriculture.]

	1917	1918
Cattle	22,895,467	25,026,524
Hogs	37,982,216	44,323,080
Sheep	20,032,555	22,022,088
Horses and mules	1,430,737	1,158,602
Total	82,340,975	92,530,294

Estimated value of live stock sold in 1918 at 63 markets.

[Compiled by Bureau of Markets.]

Chicago	$900,000,000	Denver	$85,000,000
Kansas City	510,000,000	Other markets	2,910,000,000
Omaha	380,000,000		
St. Louis	210,000,000	Total for 63 markets	4,995,000,000

Slaughtering and meat packing compared with other manufacturing industries.

[From U. S. Census Bureau, census of manufacturers, 1914.]

Rank.	Industry.	Value of products.
1	Slaughtering and meat packing	$1,651,965,424
2	Iron and steel, steel works and rolling mills	918,664,565
3	Flour mill and grist mill products	877,679,709
4	Foundry and machine-shop products	866,544,677
5	Lumber and timber products	715,310,333
6	Cotton goods	676,569,115
7	Cars and general shop construction and repairs by steam railroad companies	514,041,225
8	Automobiles	503,230,130
9	Boots and shoes (leather)	501,760,458
10	Printing and publishing newspapers and periodicals	495,905,948

The CHAIRMAN. If the committee will permit me, I will ask the members to begin on my left and go around the table, each member cross-examining Mr. Hall as he may desire.

Mr. THOMPSON. Will you put in the record the number of different kinds of animals in the United States at this time?

Mr. HALL. Yes. That, of course, is furnished by the Bureau of Crop Estimates. The Bureau of Markets is not engaged in the collection of information regarding live stock on farms; we take it after it leaves the farms.

Estimated number of live stock on farms and ranges in the United States on Jan. 1, 1918.

[From Report of Bureau of Crop Estimates, Department of Agriculture.]

Horses	21,563,000
Mules	4,824,000
Cattle	66,830,000
Sheep	48,900,000
Swine	71,374,000
Total	213,491,000

Mr. HAUGEN. You said you had taken over the telegraphic reports. What has been added to the reports that was not given before? What change is there over the previous condition? Is any additional information furnished now?

Mr. HALL. There were never before any reports of supplies and prices of fresh meats.

Mr. HAUGEN. I mean as to live stock at Chicago?

Mr. HALL. We have changed the classification of live stock used in the telegraph companies wires and press association messages, so that they are of much more advantage than before. We began sending out a message at 9.15 a. m. on the hog market, and——

Mr. HAUGEN (interposing). What change have you made in the classification? What new information have you added?

Mr. HALL. I can not say that we have added new classes. I am not prepared to say off-hand just what the old schedule was, as it is not before me.

Mr. HAUGEN. You know what they are in a general way?

Mr. HALL. Formerly the message said: Medium to good steers, so and so. That meant nothing. "Medium to good" might mean either the twilight zone between medium and good or might mean all medium and all good, or it might mean almost anything.

Mr. HAUGEN. What terms do you use now?

Mr. HALL. Medium and good.

Mr. HAUGEN. Medium and good?

Mr. HALL. Yes; just on those grades.

Mr. HAUGEN. And the prices range between them?

Mr. HALL. Yes. We are not able to use as many terms as we would like to use, because the newspapers will only give limited space to the report.

Mr. HAUGEN. That is not of any importance as to classification. Do you classify stockers? They all come under one head, don't they?

Mr. HALL. Good, choice, and fancy select go in one range of prices, and inferior, common, and medium in another.

Mr. HAUGEN. That is not carried in the report by the press.

Mr. HALL. Well, the eastern papers use their scissors very freely on our reports. They claim the public in the East are not so much interested in live stock.

Mr. HAUGEN. And the public does not get the information because it is not disseminated through the press?

Mr. HALL. Anyone in Washington who wants the information can get it from our office.

Mr. HAUGEN. Does the press give any additional information over what was given before?

Mr. HALL. I think I can say that they give more complete information since our service was started than ever before.

Mr. HAUGEN. In the matter of classification?

Mr. HALL. Yes.

Mr. HAUGEN. Who pays the expense of the telegrams now? Before it was done by others—by the Associated Press itself.

Mr. HALL. We do not pay the expense of the telegrams.

Mr. HAUGEN. I mean for collecting the information. Who pays for that expense?

Mr. HALL. We pay for collecting the information.

Mr. HAUGEN. For the telegrams?

Mr. HALL. Yes; the information for the telegrams.

Mr. HAUGEN. You now pay the freight instead of the other fellow?

Mr. HALL. We furnish to the Western Union and to the Postal, and to the Associated Press, the United Press, and so on, the information which was formerly furnished by two gentlemen who were, in large part, paid by the packers in Chicago.

Mr. HAUGEN. Who paid it before?

Mr. HALL. The large packers, and the board of trade paid a part of it.

Mr. HAUGEN. The Government now pays it?

Mr. HALL. Yes.

Mr. HAUGEN. You pay the expense instead of the packers?

Mr. HALL. Yes.

Mr. HAUGEN. You are more reliable?

Mr. HALL. Yes.

Mr. HAUGEN. I take it that is correct. To what extent are your reports more reliable?

Mr. HALL. Because of the larger corps of men engaged in getting the information. For instance, we have four men reporting the cattle, hog, and sheep markets in Chicago, whereas the two men who formerly furnished this Western Union and Postal Telegraph and the Associated Press and United Press report merely went around to commission men and asked a few questions; and sometimes a boy in the telegraph office would go through their telegrams and make a rough estimate of the market.

Mr. HAUGEN. Every daily paper had its own representative engaged in gathering the information?

Mr. HALL. They still keep up that service. There is a daily market paper in Chicago that does it.

Mr. HAUGEN. Yes; and nearly all of the daily papers carry a market report.

Mr. HALL. They have their own market reports in Chicago, but no commercial telegraphic report is going out of Chicago except our own.

Mr. HAUGEN. Do they still furnish their own report?
Mr. HALL. Some do.
Mr. HAUGEN. They have the same report?
Mr. HALL. Yes; but they are obliged to keep fairly in line with the Government report or they would soon be discredited.
Mr. HAUGEN. Do they compare notes with you?
Mr. HALL. I am not definitely informed on that.
Mr. HAUGEN. My information is that this reporter for each paper goes to commission men and to packing houses and wherever he can get information, and makes up a report which is published. What changes have there been in that respect?
Mr. HALL. Our men get on horses and go up and down the cattle alleys instead of taking the second-hand information picked up at the Exchange Building.
Mr. HAUGEN. The farmer gets his daily report from his daily paper?
Mr. HALL. They get the press report and telegraphic news report that goes from our office.
Mr. HAUGEN. They do not get it in that way at all, as I understand, in Chicago. There are different concerns that they get it from, commission men, etc.
Mr. HALL. The C. N. D. service, or the Western Union service, or the board of trade service is information furnished by the United States Bureau of Markets.
Mr. HAUGEN. To what extent do you furnish it?
Mr. HALL. We furnish it exclusively.
Mr. HAUGEN. You said you furnished all press associations with the report, the Associated Press, United Press, etc. Do I understand that you furnish it to all newspapers?
Mr. HALL. Yes; except to some of the local papers at Chicago. There are local newspapers that have their own men at the market just as they did before. They have not seen fit to substitute our service for their own, and we have no authority to make them do it.
Mr. HAUGEN. Anybody looking for a report on the Chicago market would naturally go to a Chicago paper. The report in an eastern paper, say a Washington paper, is very limited as compared with the report in the Chicago papers, and naturally so, because the people here are not very much interested in it.
Mr. BRAND. Let me say that those papers use our reports.
Mr. HAUGEN. Here in Washington?
Mr. BRAND. No; the papers also in Chicago. That is the one they use in making up their own report.
Mr. HAUGEN. Mr. Hall told us they had their own reporters.
Mr. BRAND. They do not take our complete report and put it in as our report, no; but they use a part of it and add to it what their own reporters get.
Mr. HAUGEN. My information is that those reporters are sent to the stockyards, and I have been there when the reporters came in at 2 o'clock in the afternoon.
Mr. BRAND. If you will go there and talk to any one of those reporters you will find he has a copy of our report in his pocket, which saves him trouble, and he uses it.

Mr. HALL. Let me tell you how the afternoon reports are written. Copy has to be in by 10 o'clock in the morning, and, to be perfectly frank with you, it is mostly a fake. The man sits down in his office and writes up an imaginary report.

Mr. HAUGEN. I beg your pardon, for I have been in the office at 2 or 3 o'clock in the afternoon when the reporters brought in their reports, and I saw them.

Mr. HALL. That was for the next morning's paper.

Mr. HAUGEN. Well, for the afternoon paper it is the same?

Mr. HALL. The evening paper usually contains an imaginary report which is written before 10 or half-past 10 o'clock in the morning. Formerly they had until 10.30 a. m. to get up the report, but now they have only until 10 o'clock, and it is working the reporter's imagination pretty hard to get it in shape.

Mr. HAUGEN. How do you get your report in the morning before sales take place?

Mr. HALL. We do not give out an item on cattle, except as to receipts, until 10.30 a. m., and it is pretty hard to get information about sales until after 10.30.

Mr. HAUGEN. The information is not available for you earlier than for anybody else, is it?

Mr. HALL. Not until there are sales.

Mr. HAUGEN. A report of sales?

Mr. HALL. Yes. But the difference is that we do not give out our information until sales take place, and some other is given out in advance.

Mr. HAUGEN. Yours is not in advance?

Mr. HALL. No; but theirs is gathered earlier and goes off the press about 2.30 in the afternoon, while ours is gotten about 10.30 and is issued immediately.

Mr. HAUGEN. You wish to state that your service is a little slower and therefore more reliable?

Mr. HALL. No; our report is an hour or two ahead of them. I am speaking about the daily newspapers, and do not mean to include the daily live-stock market papers which are located at certain points, some of which are very efficient, and which we are glad to cooperate with. We are glad to have our information go throughout the country through their columns, because we believe that method is cheaper than any mail service we can build up.

Mr. RAINEY. The point you are trying to make is that the 5 o'clock daily Chicago newspaper reporter is out in the yard and gets in touch with various commission men and others in order to have a report in his newspaper at 5 o'clock, and that in order to be sure of that he must have his report at the newspaper office by 10.30 a. m., because the 5 o'clock newspaper is printed and on the street about 12 o'clock?

Mr. HALL. Yes.

Mr. RAINEY. Those reporters who cover this information and data get in touch with your office and collaborate as far as they can in the report and whatever estimates are off at that time?

Mr. HALL. Yes.

Mr. RAINEY. Because out there in the stockyards they start unloading cattle about 4 o'clock in the morning, and he can get some idea, but it is not as accurate as you get, because they continue unloading until 10 or 11 o'clock, or even 12 o'clock noon?

Mr. HALL. That is right.

Mr. RAINEY. The information that Mr. Haugen speaks of reporters gathering in the afternoon is for the morning newspapers?

Mr. HALL. Yes. And another thing, the newspapers undertake to do things that we do not undertake to do—to write up long descriptions of certain features of the market. We have not undertaken to conduct a complete descriptive market service.

Mr. HAUGEN. You are aware of the fact that some of these morning papers are printed in the afternoon?

Mr. HALL. Yes.

Mr. HAUGEN. Let us see about equalization of shipments; how have they been equalized?

Mr. HALL. Well, I stated that whereas two or three years ago 85 per cent of the receipts at Chicago came in on Mondays and Wednesdays, now only about 50 per cent come in on those days.

Mr. HAUGEN. How do you account for 42,000 received, I think it was, on the 9th of December? I am not so sure about the date, but 42,000 head of cattle came in on that day, and room could not be found for the cattle, even in the alleys.

Mr. HALL. I recall that day.

Mr. HAUGEN. So it does not seem that there was much equalization of shipments in that?

Mr. HALL. We are very far from complete equalization, but we are making headway.

Mr. HAUGEN. You are taking a great deal of credit for some things that have been accomplished. I have had some experience in these matters myself.

Mr. HALL. If you will compare the average receipts for five days of the week now with two years ago, you will see the difference. No man can stand here and explain all the causes of that, and I shouldn't wish to take for the Bureau of Markets all the credit. The Railroad Administration had an active part in the zoning system, which helped very largely to bring about that improvement, both at Chicago and at Kansas City, but the loading reports that I have described were the basis of the zoning system.

Mr. HAUGEN. Let us take the loading system: How about fluctuation in prices the first week in December? How do you account for prices going up about a dollar a hundred, and the next week dropping nearly $2 a hundred?

Mr. HALL. I do not have the causes of that particular phenomenon in mind, Mr. Haugen.

Mr. HAUGEN. I happen to know about it because I had cattle on the market, and supposed that you might have some information of it also.

Mr. HALL. There was a big liquidation of cattle at that time, and whether it was because of the curtailment in foreign shipments or whether it was arbitrary manipulation or what it was, I shouldn't like to undertake to say. I have not the information upon which to base a statement.

Mr. McLAUGHLIN. Then Mr. Haugen sent his cattle in at the wrong time?

Mr. HAUGEN. Do not supply and demand govern the price?

Mr. HALL. Yes; and we have had an artificial demand during the past year on account of the tremendous foreign shipments.

Mr. HAUGEN. You have nothing to do with fixing prices?
Mr. HALL. No.
Mr. HAUGEN. When you report large receipts that enables packers or buyers to purchase at lower prices?
Mr. HALL. That is right.
Mr. HAUGEN. They take advantage of it?
Mr. HALL. Yes; and vice versa. On the other hand, a report of smaller receipts would be of advantage to the seller. The net result is to iron out the ups and downs and bring about a more stable market.
Mr. HAUGEN. You spoke about the stockyards. What relief have you brought there?
Mr. HALL. I had reference entirely to the market news service in what I have said. What class of relief do you mean? I do not quite understand your question.
Mr. HAUGEN. You know there has been a good deal of complaint. Yesterday something was said about the stockyards buying hay and selling it at big profit.
Mr. BRAND. Mr. Chairman, Mr. Haugen raises a question that is an entirely different matter. While that is germane to his inquiry, that goes a great ways afield from this market news service work. We will be willing to discuss it at some time if you like, but it has no bearing on this particular item.
Mr. HAUGEN. Very well. What about fixing prices; have you any control over that?
Mr. HALL. No.
Mr. HAUGEN. Have you been able to help out the situation in that matter?
Mr. HALL. That is entirely outside of the authority of the Bureau of Markets.
The CHAIRMAN. That is a Food Administration matter.
Mr. HALL. Yes.
Mr. HAUGEN. Stockmen have had no benefit from your service along that line?
Mr. HALL. So far as fixing prices is concerned, we have had nothing directly to do with it.
Mr. ANDERSON. You referred to some work you were doing in collecting data touching the number of cattle or sheep being fed on the ranges?
Mr. HALL. I spoke of distribution over a longer season.
Mr. ANDERSON. Yes; but what I am getting at is this: I had the impression last year that in some one of these items there was carried an appropriation for getting information as to the number of animals on the farm about to move to local markets. Is that carried under this item?
Mr. HALL. No.
Mr. BRAND. I think, Mr. Hall, that Mr. Anderson has in mind the in-and-out work, such as we carry on at Lancaster and at Rocky Ford. There we determine how many head go in feed lots for finishing, and when they get ready for the market we give the figures on the date of the movement. I have an idea that that is what you are interested in, Mr. Anderson?

Mr. ANDERSON. I think that is it, although I am not certain.

Mr. HALL. That is not a separate item, if you will pardon me, Mr. Brand. It runs in my mind that there was a separate item for the expansion of work in the Bureau of Crop Estimates.

Mr. ANDERSON. To be entirely frank, the Crop Estimates people say that you people are encroaching upon their preserves in getting some information as to number of stock on farms. I would like to know what that is?

Mr. HALL. I would like to know what it is, too.

Mr. BRAND. The only thing we do of that character whatsoever is this in-and-out movement. I think there must be some misapprehension.

Mr. ANDERSON. What is that?

Mr. BRAND. Mr. Hall may better explain it, with reference to the Lancaster district, where cattle to the number of 75,000 are concentrated in a relatively small group of counties. They are practically finished in transit and move to the market. We do report on those cattle, in and out, but that is not an encroachment upon the work of the Bureau of Crop Estimates. I do not see how it could be so considered.

Mr. ANDERSON. If I am not mistaken, there was a proposition last year that there were some men in automobiles going out to gather up data as to stock about to move to market?

Mr. BRAND. In the feeding section of Rocky Ford, also where the pulp feeders are. We take it again of those that are going to move to market.

Mr. HALL. That work is done in cooperation with the Bureau of Crop Estimates.

Mr. ANDERSON. They say they have to concur with you because you have more money than they have, and more men, and that you are more influential, and that they do it on that account?

Mr. BRAND. I am sorry if we have that reputation. Everything we do is in perfect accord, and if some individual officer fails to observe that friendly spirit of cooperation which we all feel, and the case will be called to our attention, it will be immediately straightened out. But we do not cover the work of the Bureau of Crop Estimates. Mr. Hall has described the reports we issue, and I am sure you will recognize that they are reports that cover movement, and not reports of crop estimates. I will insert at this place a memorandum issued by the Secretary with regard to this matter:

MEMORANDUM 220.—*Re Coordination of crop and live-stock estimating work in the Department of Agriculture.*

DEPARTMENT OF AGRICULTURE,
Washington, October 6, 1917.

In order to avoid unnecessary duplication of work and expense in estimating acreages planted, condition during the growing season, yield per acre, and total production of crops, stocks on farms, numbers of different classes of live stock on farms, by States, it is directed that hereafter the facilities of the Bureau of Crop Estimates shall be utilized, so far as practicable, in collecting, tabulating, summarizing, and furnishing data bearing on the class of sujects mentioned when the information is desired for an entire State. The Bureau of Crop Estimates is constantly engaged in estimating crop and live-stock production in all States and before any State-wide survey or investigation is undertaken by other bureaus of the department relating to these subjects the Chief of the Bureau of Crop Estimates should be consulted with a view to utilize information already available in that bureau or the facilities of the bureau for collecting and summarizing such data or to coordinate the proposed investigation with the work of the bureau. Where the proposed investigation or survey relates to crop or live-stock production of a single county, or of several counties in a State, it is highly desirable that the field agent of the Bureau of Crop Estimates for that State should be furnished a copy of the results of the inquiry for his permanent file of county data. It is expected that the bureaus concerned in any survey or investigation relating to crop and live-stock production, or stocks on farms, in any State, will cooperate fully and, so far as practicable, keep each other advised of proposed work, methods employed, and results obtained.

D. F. HOUSTON, *Secretary.*

Mr. ANDERSON. But they are reports of the number of cattle on farms, or renewals for feeding purposes, in certain localities?

The CHAIRMAN. Stock about to move.

Mr. BRAND. Yes; practically feeding in transit. I think it would be a fair proposition for your committee to decide on the way it should be done. I think it would not tie in any better with the Bureau of Crop Estimates.

Mr. ANDERSON. We could only tell that by knowing what it is.

Mr. BRAND. The cattle move into these concentrated feeding areas and we report them in and out.

Mr. HALL. For the reason that we have close contact with the railroads, and arrangements of various kinds for getting information from the railroads, where it is very largely gotten.

Mr. ANDERSON. The cost of that service is borne under this appropriation?

Mr. HALL. Yes.

Mr. ANDERSON. We had a recent report from the Federal Trade Commission to the effect that the large packers controlled the price of cattle, and also prices of meat products. If that is true it would be somewhat cheaper to find out what they are going to pay than to go to all this expense getting information, wouldn't it?

Mr. HALL. That is what some commission men tell us. One of the officers of the commission men's organization told us there was no use of our trying to do anything with it, that the commission man had to work by the rule of thumb and take whatever the packer chose to pay him. But as soon as some of the efficient commission men began using our information, and using it advantageously, others had to use it. I have a number of letters before me substantiating the statement that the service has had a decided influence at times in increasing prices that the packer otherwise would have paid.

Mr. ANDERSON. Then you mean to say that at the present moment there is a considerable percentage of independent buying of cattle and hogs on the market?

Mr. HALL. That is very small, but we do say that we have increased the price that the packers had usually paid at certain times. As Mr. Haugen pointed out, if there is a big run our information tends doubtless to depress the extreme price that might have been realized on that day, but the information has a leveling influence, taken as a whole, and for that reason it is of distinct value.

The CHAIRMAN. Any other questions, gentlemen of the committee?

Mr. HALL. Pardon me for adding another word. Although I said I was through with the salient points, we have not said anything as to curtailment of the service.

The CHAIRMAN. I was about to ask you that. The emergency act for this purpose carries $300,000?

Mr. HALL. Yes.

The CHAIRMAN. And you propose to make it $170,000, so that you will be short $130,000. It will be a question for the committee to determine whether or not it is more economical in the long run to dismantle your existing organization and rebuild it as time goes on, as it will be rebuilt, or to maintain it now and take the chances of having the committee severely criticized on the floor of the House for doing something that it might be thought is not the wise thing to do. The committee will determine that later.

EXTRACTS FROM LETTERS REGARDING MARKET NEWS SERVICE ON LIVE STOCK AND MEATS.

Mr. C. H. Harin, representative of Clay, Robinson & Co. at the Kansas City market, says: "The information sent in through your Rocky Ford office has enabled us to keep in closer touch with the available supply in that district and when they will be moving to market better than we have ever been able to do before. The daily reports giving the condition of the dressed meat markets in the East are read with interest by shippers as well as by the commission men engaged in selling live stock here at the market."

Mr. J. W. Murphy, an independent hog trader on the Omaha live-stock market, said, with reference to the live-stock loading report: "I'm mighty glad to get that information, and I want to thank you for it. It keeps me posted on where the hogs are moving all over the country, and that means a lot of money to me."

Mr. F. M. Simpson, manager of the American Live Stock Commission Co. at the Denver yards, stated: "By knowing conditions of the wholesale meat trade in the East we were enabled on a recent market to get 50 cents per hundredweight more for cattle than we otherwise would have received."

Mr. Jonathan K. Rosson, president and general manager of the Campbell & Rosson Live Stock Commission Co. of Fort Worth, Tex., said: "I feel that this report should be of considerable benefit to the live-stock shippers and producers, through their commission firms, as it puts us in position to know the condition of the beef market in the East, and in consequence we are in position to know whether or not the reports we are getting from the packer buyers with reference to the eastern beef market are correct or not. On Monday they reported a demoralized veal market in the East, while your report showed in reality a firm, strong market, with light receipts and a good outlet."

Arthur Hill, of the W. M. Leitch Sheep Commission Co., Kansas City, Mo., says: "We would like to have you know that we appreciate the reports given us in regard to the sheep situation. We probably use the eastern dressed-meat report more than anything else. That gives us a line on the situation daily, and, of course, has an effect on the way we handle the selling end at the sheep house. We copy these reports very often in our market letter, which circulates through the Southwest, and we know it has been read with interest by our customers. The report of sheep on feed and conditions in the Arkansas Valley have been used in the same way, and we find them to be accurate."

Mr. A. E. Rogers, head salesman of the Omaha Live Stock Commission Co., made the following statement regarding the reports of the Bureau of Markets on eastern meat trade conditions: "The packers came out and tried to buy our cattle cheaper and would have got away with at least 10 or 15 cents cut if we hadn't had these reports that showed that meat was strong in the East. I told some of the other boys when I saw this bulletin that if we all kept a stiff upper lip we could hold the market up, and we did."

Elbert S. Brigham, commissioner of agriculture, State of Vermont, in speaking of the market reports furnished to him by the branch office of Boston, says: "The result is that our receipts from live stock sold will be four times the receipts of the year previous. I estimate that this service has been worth at least $12,000 to me as a State official. I hope that this service will be accordingly enlarged from time to time as Congress appropriates more money for this purpose. Ignorance on the part of the producer has enabled speculators to profit greatly at their expense, and your news service will, better than any other one thing, enable them to obtain a fair knowledge of current prices."

Prof. Rusk, of the University of Illinois, in speaking of the live-stock market reporting service of the Bureau of Markets at Chicago, said: "I have noticed a decided change for the better in the telegraphic reports of the Chicago live-stock market since the Bureau of Markets began supplying the information for these wires. Some of the papers published in Champaign, Ill., and surrounding towns have for a long time carried what purported to be local market quotations on live stock, supplied by a local buyer and shipper. As it suited his individual purposes best to have these quotations low, he never failed to see to it that the quotations he furnished the press were much lower than the market justified. When the papers started carrying Chicago quotations as furnished by the Bureau of Markets, however, the disparity between these quotations and his own local quotations was so wide as to prompt him to speedily revise his quotations radically upward. He no longer has the opportunity to depress the local market to such a marked extent as formerly. Producers in that section are the beneficiaries of these improved conditions, and the Bureau of Markets deserves the credit."

Mr. M. L. McCline, vice president of the Drumm Commission Co., of Kansas City, Mo., said: "Until your bureau furnished us this information, the producer and marketer of live stock were groping in the dark in regard to the prices and conditions of the eastern meat markets and supply and demand. Now, with this information, we feel that we are almost on an equal footing with the packer, as we find that your reports are reliable and can be depended upon. The fact that the commission man, who sells the live stock for the producer on the market, has this information in his possession prevents the buyers for the packers from jockeying the market. This service to the people is new, but it has passed the experimental stage and is now regarded as a necessity."

Mr. A. F. Stryker, secretary-traffic manager of the South Omaha Live Stock Exchange, stated: "I was very much interested yesterday to learn from one of our commission men they were using these bulletins. A sheep salesman said to me he was glad to have the bulletins giving the condition of the mutton market in Boston yesterday morning. One of the packers' buyers said there was no demand for mutton in the East. Your morning bulletin had shown an active demand and a good market. The sheep salesman was able to show the buyer he knew better."

Mr. W. P. Neff, vice president and editor of the Daily Drovers' Telegram, Kansas City, Mo., said: "The Drovers' Telegram believes the Bureau of Markets is rendering valuable aid to the live-stock interests through the market data compiled for their benefit, and I take this opportunity to commend those efforts. The daily reports of the eastern fresh-meat markets are particularly valuable to the stockmen and the feeder as well as to the commission men and salesmen. The data on stock loadings serves no purpose so far as the man on the farm is concerned, but it is valuable to the stockyards habitués, and would be very much more valuable to the commission men and salesmen if it were available the day preceding arrival at market. The main criticism on all Government information has been its tardy dissemination, but the Bureau of Markets is working along the right lines. Market information must be available on the minute or it is a waste of effort."

Mr. F. Witherspoon, jr., treasurer of the Witherspoon-McMullen Live Stock Commission Co., of Kansas City, says: "Although I have not had the pleasure of seeing you for the last year, I want to take this occasion to compliment your department for the very efficient service rendered here at this market. The bulletins issued have been of great benefit to our customers, and I have heard many expressions of appreciation from them."

Mr. Charles S. Michael, grain and live-stock editor of the Illinois Telegraph News Co., Chicago, writes: "After a careful investigation we take pleasure in submitting the following, which we will be glad to confirm to any Government official should they so desire, as it is based on facts as we know them: The Associated Press, Chicago, handles only the Bureau of Markets live-stock reports and serves about 1,135 papers, both morning and evening, of which about 400 get condensed reports. The Associated Press is furnished the report by the Illinois Telegraph News Co., via ticker, and sends out all flashes and the opening and closing markets. The opening at least goes out in full. The International News Service also uses the bureau's reports exclusively, serving approximately 200 papers, of which 125 papers get condensed market reports. The United Press serves approximately 650 papers, of which probably 500 secure condensed reports. These three press associations are the only ones of importance in Chicago, and it is safe to say that, with the exception of some of the leading papers in the very largest cities, practically all the live-stock reports used by the newspapers are made up from the Bureau of Markets returns. In this connection it must be noted that it frequently happens that the various papers may rewrite a press association 'lead' but use the prices as sent. As far as we can determine, the newspapers use practically exclusively the Bureau of Markets reports. There are two ticker services in Chicago which furnish the information on live stock for the big private wire houses which operate out of this market, of which the Illinois Telegraph News Co. is the largest. Through cooperation with the Bureau of Markets both these ticker companies send out exclusively the reports compiled by your bureau and handle no news on the livestock markets except such as you send out. The private-wire firms cover practically all the leading points in the grain belt, both west and northwest, and reach from coast to coast. As far as we have been able to find out, and this covers a period of some months, no report other than the Bureau of Markets is sent out over any private wire operated by a grain or stock firm. The branch offices of the various commission houses in the smaller towns disseminate the information as to the live-stock markets via phone, either calling up their customers or having them call up. I believe that some of the farmers' telephone systems make a practice of sending out this kind of information after having obtained it from the branch offices of the wire houses. In this manner there is no reason to believe that anyone interested in the live-stock markets can not secure the information sent out by your bureau without the slightest trouble. In sending out the live-stock reports the private-wire houses give the information the right of way, putting it ahead of grain-market news to many. This results in the quick distribution of the news and the papers are used by those interested to confirm the reports and also get the gossip as to any fresh news developments. It is safe to say that the only telegraphic news on the live-stock markets that gets to the country is furnished by your bureau. In this connection I might add the Illinois Telegraph News Co. furnishes practically exclusively all private wires, the Chicago Board of Brade, and the Associated Press with the report, and they depend on us to secure it for them. We wish to thank you and your assistants for the cooperation we have secured, for the excellent manner in which the live-stock report is relayed to us in order that it may receive the widest distribution. Mr. G. D. Rose, the manager of the Illinois Telegraph News Co., joins me in the thanks. Until the Bureau of Markets ceases business, which will probably never be, this company will use the bureau's reports only."

The CHAIRMAN. The next item is 121, " For collecting and distributing by telegraph, mail, and otherwise, timely information on the supply, demand, commercial movement, disposition, quality, and market prices of dairy and poultry products, $80,600."

Mr. BRAND. The appropriation embraced in item 121 is a transfer from the emergency fund. There was assigned to this work for the current fiscal year $164,000. The proposal is to transfer $110,000 of that $164,000 to the regular bill, involving a reduction of $54,000 in the amount available for that work.

I may say with respect to this particular line of work, being new work, that on account of the difficulty in getting men, and on account of the loss of men to the military service and to commercial occupations, that this service has not been developed to the point where it is expected we will expend quite all the funds set aside for it. We have therefore turned back to the Secretary some money, the amount of which I do not now recall, which it is not expected will be spent this year. Therefore we have not in such an acute form a reduction problem as we have in some other cases. I think the $110,000 provided for this item as it stands would enable us to carry on next year the same kind of work we are carrying on this year under emergency funds.

Prof. Potts is here and will explain briefly the character of the work. The principles involved are so similar that I think it might be quickly stated.

The CHAIRMAN. We will give Mr. Potts 10 minutes.

STATEMENT OF MR. R. C. POTTS, SPECIALIST IN DAIRY MARKETING, BUREAU OF MARKETS, UNITED STATES DEPARTMENT OF AGRICULTURE.

Mr. POTTS. I might say, generally speaking, that for the successful marketing of dairy and poultry products reliable and complete information is just as essential as in the case of fruits and vegetables or live stock and meats. In planning and developing our market news service on dairy and poultry products the effort has been to secure and furnish to those receiving our reports that fundamental information in regard to supply and demand, conditions, and prices that would enable them to carry on their business more efficiently and more economically.

In the large distributing markets for dairy and poultry products prices are established, those prices being reflected to the producing regions. This relation of prices makes it necessary that a market news service on dairy and poultry products be national in scope; that is, be of such scope that we are able to show conditions both in producing sections and in distributing markets.

The news service as now conducted by the Bureau of Markets differs from any commercial service existing before the Bureau of Markets undertook to conduct this work. Previous to this time there was conducted in local distributing markets a local reporting service. New York had such a service. It reported prices on dairy and poultry products in that market and reported receipts. The trade was not furnished, as the trade has admitted, with the essential information necessary for the most intelligent conduct of business, nor for the conduct of business in such way that prices would be most stable and would always reflect the supply and demand conditions. Therefore it was necessary for the Bureau of Markets in establishing this service, in order to provide the additional information necessary and fundamental for a proper understanding of supply and demand conditions, to secure additional information from those sources which would show supply and demand conditions.

Let us take, for instance, the New York butter market. To know supply and demand conditions in reference to butter on the New York market, you must have information in regard to receipts of butter on that market. Prior to the time when the Bureau of Markets undertook this work complete reports in regard to receipts were not issued. No reports were secured from the express companies, I am informed, and the New York Mercantile Exchange, which was one of the exchanges that previously issued incomplete reports on receipts, is now securing reports that are compiled by the Bureau of Markets with reference to express receipts in order that their reports, independent of the Bureau of Markets reports, may be accurate and reliable with reference to receipts of butter and eggs, as well as cheese and other dairy products on the New York market.

Information with reference to receipts must be supplemented by information regarding supplies of butter. We know that there are always stocks of butter on the market and that there are always stocks of butter in cold storage. Therefore you must know, in addition to the eggs received on the market, the movement of eggs in and out of cold storage. It is a fact, too, that the dealers engaged in the business, particularly in the wholesale trade, carry large stocks of butter in their own business houses. The stock that a dealer has on his floor in the morning is an important factor in order to determine whether or not he is going out on the market to pay more or less for butter on that particular day. Up until the time when the Bureau of Markets undertook to issue these reports the matter of local stocks in the wholesale trade was a matter of conjecture on any particular day, and no one phase of the work that has been undertaken by the Government is of more interest and perhaps of more value to the trade in determining the local supply and demand situation in the market than that regarding stocks in the hands of the wholesale trade. So, then, the Bureau of Markets report have assured more complete and accurate reports of receipts; they have furnished the trade with the in-and-out movement of eggs from cold storage and with reports regarding stocks in the hands of members of the wholesale trade.

The CHAIRMAN. Have you any further general statement to make, Mr. Potts? Have you pretty well covered the general idea?

Mr. POTTS. What I have said with reference to butter is also true of eggs and cheese and other dairy products.

I may say that we have a good many letters, a thousand or more, from the dealers themselves and from creameries testifying to the value of this service.

The CHAIRMAN. That is another case of getting the information and giving it to the public. Any questions, gentlemen?

Mr. ANDERSON. Has it been your experience that when the Government does something for people for nothing they usually appreciate it?

Mr. POTTS. We believe they do. If the letters in which they express their appreciation come from the heart—and we really believe they do—that must be true. We have met many of them personally, and from the way in which they speak of the service I believe they appreciate it.

Mr. ANDERSON. Do you believe they appreciate the service sufficiently that they would be willing to pay for it if it were not otherwise going to be continued?

Mr. POTTS. We received a letter from a man who said the service was worth at least $25 a year to him, but I do not know whether he would be willing to pay more or less. That was his statement.

The CHAIRMAN. Brand has explained that this was relatively a new proposition, and that this sum would be sufficient. You would not have to dismantle this organization.

Mr. BRAND. No; it is a newer service, and we would not have to dismantle it the same way as some others.

EXTRACTS FROM LETTERS PERTAINING TO THE MARKET NEWS SERVICE ON DAIRY AND POULTRY PRODUCTS.

We wish to register our decided commendation of the efforts of the Department of Agriculture to assist the merchants engaged in handling butter, eggs, cheese, etc., by supplying reliable market information, particularly giving daily wire service, which reflects the exact situation in the different large centers and gives to one who studies same the best kind of information on which to base the conduct of his business.

Case in point in our own business was through observing, five or six weeks ago, the reports of visible stocks of butter in the New York market, which showed a steady accumulation notwithstanding apparently healthy conditions and a liberal export movement. We saved a considerable amount of money for our shippers in the country by taking the selling side and keeping our floors cleaned up daily.

Shippers and dealers will also receive corresponding benefit when the strength in the market position is daily manifested and it is apparent that goods need not be pressed for sale but can be marketed as demand develops.—G. W. Bull & Co. (Inc.), by G. W. Bull, president, Chicago, Ill.

We commend your work very highly, as it gives us detailed information which we could secure from no other source. While your reports are valuable now, we believe they will become much more so when your bureau has been in operation for a year, so enabling you to secure comparisons of receipts in the various markets the same date in the year previous. Such a detail giving comparisons of receipts will show the tendency and condition of the markets and production very clearly.—Milton Dairy Co., by A. S. Gowen, St. Paul, Minn.

Regarding the weekly bulletin on butter and eggs, I wish to state that the same is of very much benefit to me in giving the actual conditions of the market, and the only fault I can find is that we did not have this service five or more years ago. The reference would be of great value at present. I doubt very much if I could improve on the report in any way.—George A. Petry, broker, butter, eggs, cheese, and poultry, New York, N. Y.

The daily reports which we receive from the Bureau of Markets each morning I consider invaluable, and we will be very pleased to continue receiving same. These reports are of the greatest benefit to the trade, and we certainly trust our Government will continue along the same lines and continue sending them to the people in our line, the same as they are now doing.—Marsh L. Brown & Co., Marsh L. Brown, president, Chicago, Ill.

We are glad to get your market reports on butter and eggs, as it gives us a better idea as to what is going on, and, too, it gives us something to check the commission houses on, as we can see what butter brought any day.—The Newton Creamery, by W. G. Adams, Newton, Kans.

We desire to say that we consider these as valuable to our business. It absolutely gives us a check on prices which we can depend on. We ship into most all of the eastern markets during certain periods of the year, and with these daily market bulletins coming in we know exactly what they are paying for the quality of butter which we ship. We certainly hope that you will see that these continue to come forward to us regularly.—The Hollywood Creamery Co., by G. A. Allebrand, secretary and treasurer, Colorado Springs, Colo.

The bulletins you are sending us are of great value to us, since they keep us better posted on the market and we can better tell how much we can expect to receive on butter shipped and what we can pay for cream.—Farmers' Mutual Cooperative Creamery, by A. Yonker, manager, Sioux Center, Iowa.

We find the daily butter bulletin of great help to us in paying right prices for butter fat, and we can also know for a certainty whether we receive right prices for our butter in the market. We hope the department will keep up the work.— Belle Plaine Cooperative Creamery Association, by N. O. Sorenson, manager, Belle Plaine, Minn.

I regard these bulletins as very valuable to our dairymen, and I hope before long that your butter-marketing service will be perfected so that your quotations will supersede those issued by the Boston Chamber of Commerce and other like bulletins. Butter produced by our creameries in Vermont has been sold at a premium above the highest Boston Chamber of Commerce quotation. For two or three months last winter the chamber of commerce did not quote on extras, but dropped to the next grade lower. This resulted in a loss of several thousand dollars to our butter producers, and I am anxious to see the quotation basis shifted to one which is more fair.—E. S. Brigham, commissioner of agricudture, department of agriculture, St. Albans, Vt.

I believe the certified reports of sales will at last answer a question that has baffled the trade for 25 years—how to arrive at a quotation. The trouble mainly was that most contracts, agreements, and even transactions in butter were based on the market quotations, not leaving enough transactions to form that base. It is the right move, and the middleman's compensation will adjust itself very quickly in a fair competitive way. My only suggestion is: Keep it up good and hard.—Jacob Jacobsen, Chicago, Ill.

We wish to say that we have been receiving the daily bulletins and we believe that they are O. K. Just the value in dollars and cents is hard to get at, as we have been receiving them only one month. It enables us to gauge our selling, also our buying price. They surely mean money to us. If the market is getting weak we begin to ease off on our buying price; if the bulletin indicates that the market is stronger, we raise a little. In place of buying a lot of stuff and then have the market go off the next day, we are able by following the bulletins to protect ourselves.—Blue Bell Creamery, per J. R. Congdon, Garnett, Kans.

The CHAIRMAN. The next item it 122, " For collecting information on grain, hay, and feeds, $41,560."

Mr. BRAND. Mr. Chairman, with respect to the grain, hay, and feeds service in this item, I have asked another officer to be present to explain it. With respect to the seed item, on account of the absence of Mr. Wheeler in Europe, I shall attempt to answer myself any questions the committee may wish to ask.

The CHAIRMAN. Your emergency fund for these two items is $100,160; is that right?

Mr. BRAND. The total emergency fund assigned this year is $150,000. The total requested to be transferred to the permanent act is $100,160.

The CHAIRMAN. That is made up of several items?

Mr. BRAND. That is made up of two items, and the two parts are grain, hay, and feeds, which is $53,160, and the remainder of the increase of $100,160 is $47,000 for the seed-reporting service.

If I may, I will say just a word about the seed-reporting service. That is a particular service——

The CHAIRMAN (interposing). What item is that?

Mr. BRAND. Item 123, I believe. I suggest that we ask Mr. Cole to discuss briefly the hay and feed work, and I will discuss the next item in regular order.

Mr. HAUGEN. Why are these items segregated?

Mr. BRAND. Because of the difference in their subject matter, and because they are handled by different people of different training.

Mr. HAUGEN. It comes on telegraphic information?

Mr. BRAND. The people who deal with seeds are seedsmen, and the men who deal in feed are feedmen, although sometimes they are one and the same man. Yet the subjects are so totally different that we can not deal with them together.

Mr. HAUGEN. The movement is practically the same?

Mr. BRAND. Seed reporting is not a telegraphic service except in a very small way; it is a mail service.

Mr. HAUGEN. It is collected information?

Mr. BRAND. The fundamental principles of handling it are relatively the same.

Mr. HAUGEN. Why couldn't you have all come under one head? They move in the same channels and in the same markets.

Mr. BRAND. When you say "come under one head," it is hard to interpret what you have in mind. They do fall in a similar field, but they must be tilled in smaller crops, and the people that deal in them are totally different.

Mr. HAUGEN. There is not much difference in dealing in grain and feed?

Mr. BRAND. Well, some crop men deal in hay and also deal in grains.
Mr. HAUGEN. And they deal in seeds, too, don't they?
Mr. BRAND. Only to a small or limited extent. The seed industry is practically concentrated in about 7,300 different enterprises in the United States.
Mr. HAUGEN. Practically every grain dealer handles seeds?
Mr. BRAND. To a very limited extent.
May I change the subject for just a moment and go back to something Mr. Anderson asked about? I find I have a memorandum here which perhaps would clarify just a little the question which he raised as to whether or not we are not duplicating reports of the Bureau of Crop Estimates.
The CHAIRMAN. I wish you would put it in the record at the proper place.
Mr. BRAND. Very well.
Mr. ANDERSON. You were cooperating in doing this work?
Mr. BRAND. Yes, sir; regarding those activities about which you raised a question. An assignment is made each year from the Bureau of Crop Estimates for that work.
Mr. ANDERSON. In other words, when there is a difference between you as to who shall do a piece of work, you compromise by both doing it?
Mr. BRAND. No, sir. We decide upon its merits whether it is a proper subject matter for them or for us, and to whichever one it properly pertains the work is assigned.
Mr. Cole, will you please present briefly the hay and feed matter?

STATEMENT OF MR. CHARLES S. COLE, SPECIALIST IN CHARGE OF HAY AND FEED REPORTING SERVICE, BUREAU OF MARKETS, UNITED STATES DEPARTMENT OF AGRICULTURE.

Mr. COLE. Mr. Chairman, we are giving our attention more particularly to hay and feed than to grain. We have the country divided into nine districts, with headquarters at Washington, Atlanta, Chicago, Minneapolis, Kansas City, Fort Worth, Denver, San Francisco, and Spokane.
Mr. THOMPSON. Do you have hay and feed reports?
Mr. COLE. Yes, sir. The report is issued weekly. It now goes out on Saturday afternoon, so as to get to the dealer and producer on Monday morning. It takes into account supply and demand, prices, and conditions governing the market. We have issued during the past year over 800,000 regular reports, and, taking into account the emergency reports, nearly 1,200,000. We report on all of the important markets surrounding each one of these central markets where the field office is located. The item of first importance is hay, and then feed; and then, too, we report prices on grains as a matter of information. We have done this because we feel reports are very much more needed on hay and feed than on grain. The grain trade is very much more highly organized than the hay and feed trade.
Mr. HAUGEN. What do you mean when you refer to feed?
Mr. COLE. Any kind of mill or ground feed, alfalfa, and cottonseed meal, beans——
Mr. ANDERSON. You don't refer to bran and millfeed?

Mr. COLE. No, sir. We have not dealt with that. There has not been a supply equal to the demand.

We have letters from the West, especially in the mountain districts and the Pacific coast, which state that this is the first report that they have had that seemed to be authentic to them. A hay dealers' association writes that this is the best report that they have received, especially on hay; that it is the first time they have had a satisfactory report which they can rely on.

We have had three emergency services during the past year, one at Fort Worth, one at Bozeman, Mont., and the soft-corn survey. In these emergency services we have issued a report three times a week instead of once a week, and have, in some places, received offers and bids; that is, we have taken the offers of the farmers and the bids of dealers and placed them before the public. That was a special emergency service in the drought area in Texas.

The mailing list to which our reports on hay, feeds, and grain is sent consists of about 16,360 names in the nine districts, and these mailing lists are made up of people who requested the reports. That is, we send out reports for several weeks and then we send a notice that if they do not wish the report it will be discontinued, so that the mailing list is a selected list.

As to the benefits of this service, we believe it has a tendency to even up the market. It is difficult to describe, but as to the monetary value of it we have letters from county agents and heads of farm organizations and little dealers out in the country, who claim that it has been of great monetary value to them. For instance, I have here a quotation from a letter from one county agent down in Texas who says that in 37 cars of feed they bought they saved $8,556. From another demonstration agent in Texas they claim on a thousand cars they have a saving, on an average, of $75 a car, $75,000.

At Spokane we discontinued the office for a period of about four months, and in one week we received 80 letters asking that the reports be sent out again. Those came largely from farmers, farmers' organizations, and county agents.

The Denver territory is being cared for now from the Kansas City office. We have the two mailing lists being covered by one office. That ought not to be so, and we hope if this appropriation is continued that we can put a man out there so he can cover that section.

The CHAIRMAN. This work, after all, is of the same character as that which has already been described here?

Mr. COLE. Yes, sir. I wish to say that we issue these reports weekly for this reason. Hay and feed are not subject to such fluctuations as meat products, which change by the hour or by the day.

Mr. THOMPSON. I judge here from this report that you have an agent at the different places. You say at nine different places in the United States. At my place I suppose Kansas City and Fort Worth would govern the hay and grain proposition. My State is a large producer of hay, particularly of hay, and grain, too, but they have got to make application to you to get these reports, and they are just a summary and issued once a week.

Mr. COLE. Issued once a week, on Saturday afternoon.

Mr. THOMPSON. And they don't go into details and give the prices, and so forth?

Mr. COLE. Yes, sir; they give prices.

Mr. THOMPSON. If this is a fair sample of it, it simply gives a synopsis of about what the amount placed on the market was and whether the demand was strong or weak.

Mr. COLE. The quotations are put in tabular form showing prices on each separate market in the district. For instance, in this report Chicago, Peoria, Grand Rapids, and so on, appear at the head of the table and on the stub is the product, the price being quoted under the city.

Mr. THOMPSON. I believe you said something in the general statement a moment ago about getting a bid offered by a dealer and the price that the producer offered to accept.

Mr. COLE. That was only an emergency service.

Mr. THOMPSON. Sometimes you did that?

Mr. COLE. That was only an emergency service.

Mr. THOMPSON. You don't do that generally?

Mr. COLE. No, sir.

Mr. THOMPSON. Do you furnish information in specific instances, if a dealer wants it?

Mr. COLE. If they request information we give them what information we have on the condition of the market.

Mr. THOMPSON. But you don't give them particular parties and particular places where they can get in touch with dealers?

Mr. COLE. Yes, sir. If they want to know about a certain product, where it can be sold, we will give them a list of names and tell them that we do not stand responsible for those people, but they are supposed to be reliable dealers.

Mr. HAUGEN. I am looking over this report, but I fail to find any quotation or price, for instance, of hay, except under the head of hay you quote the movements, the receipts, and so on. For instance, Chicago and different places, you quote the price at Indianapolis and Cincinnati.

Mr. COLE. Now, here: Timothy, clover, and alfalfa are quoted. We quote only those products that pertain to the district. For instance, the report we have in Chicago would not apply down in the South.

Mr. HAUGEN. In looking over some of your reports in the papers about two days ago in looking up the price on corn, to my surprise I found everything except what was desired. It did not give the cash price, but the future price.

Mr. BRAND. This is all on cash corn. None of this contains any future prices so far as I recall.

Mr. HAUGEN. The report I have reference to—I picked up one of the papers—I think it was the Star—about two days ago. I was anxious to see what the price of corn was.

Mr. BRAND. That is exactly an illustration of the thing we are trying to correct. The ordinary newspaper does not report the things that are of value to the shipper and dealer in the ordinary times.

Mr. HAUGEN. It purported to be a report from the United States Department of Agriculture.

Mr. BRAND. If it came from us, it gave spot prices and not future prices.

Mr. COLE. There has been a question as to whether we should quote future prices in our market letter, but we never have done it.

Mr. HAUGEN. I think that is perfectly proper, but as a general thing there is quite a range of difference between the future and the cash market price. What the seller and producer are interested in is to know the cash prices.

Mr. ANDERSON. Have you in contemplation any service on mill feeds?

Mr. COLE. We hope to get lined up on the situation for mill feed during the coming year.

Mr. ANDERSON. If you have refrained from reporting them heretofore on the theory that the price has been fixed, I think it has been very unfortunate, because in my part of the country within 100 miles of the largest milling district in the world, we are paying about $40, I think, in excess of what the so-called fixed price is. I don't know that the fixed price would do any good, but we are certainly in a bad way.

Mr. COLE. We have, as I remember it, in Minneapolis a report on the prices of mill feed going out to our mailing list.

Mr. BRAND. It has been very difficult to tell about any of the products for which prices have been fixed. The same is true of cotton seed.

Mr. McLAUGHLIN. Do the newspapers publish your reports?

Mr. COLE. Some of them are now publishing our reports on hay and feed.

Mr. McLAUGHLIN. With respect to the reports in the newspapers that are not correct, if they are furnished by you wouldn't it be your duty to see that they are correct or refuse to furnish them.

Mr. COLE. I think that the papers here in the city that get our report get it from the reports sent to them.

Mr. McLAUGHLIN. If what they give in the reports is misleading or incorrect, and they attribute it to you as based on your report, wouldn't it seem that you ought to have that corrected, have them publish correct reports, and not garbled or incorrect statements?

Mr. COLE. It would if the information had been given directly by the office. I don't know whether that was done or not.

Mr. McLAUGHLIN. If they put them in the papers under the heading "Reports of the Department of Agriculture" or anything to indicate to the reader that the reports were gotten up by your bureau, shouldn't you see that they are published correctly? It is a reflection on you, isn't it?

Mr. COLE. I don't know whether that should be taken as a reflection on the bureau. As fast as they are brought to our attention I think they should be taken into account.

Mr. McLAUGHLIN. If the people read these reports and attribute them to you, report it as the source, and they find they are incorrect, they blame you. Besides people are deceived and misled. They think you are doing it. Couldn't you refuse to give the papers data unless you find that they are uniformly publishing them correctly?

Mr. COLE. We could refuse to give them the information, but they could get the bulletins from other people. I think we could compel them not to put them under our name if they did not publish them correctly. I think we could do that.

The CHAIRMAN. You could do that now, couldn't you?

Mr. Cole. I don't know what the law is on that, but it seems that we could bring pressure on them to make them do it.

Mr. McLaughlin. So much has been said about the newspapers not being correct and still they come from you. In all probability it is that the impression is that they come from you, it seems that you ought to get in connection with that newspaper and if they attribute them to you, they should be correct.

Mr. Cole. I shall look this thing up. Mr. Haugen said last week, was it?

Mr. Haugen. About two or three days ago. I didn't say it was incorrect. I said they omitted the most important part that the producer wants to know. The producer is interested in knowing the cash price on grain and not the future. If you will take the paper to-day, I think you will find about 2 cents difference between May and cash. The shipper wants to know what he can get for his corn at time of selling it.

Mr. Cole. If they gave reports that were incorrect—that is, quotations of futures—we did not furnish those.

Mr. McLaughlin. About the character of newspaper reports purporting to come from your bureau.

Mr. Brand. I think Mr. McLaughlin is right. If our report is not published correctly, we should check up on them, and I shall issue instructions requiring that where a newspaper uses them it shall publish them correctly.

Mr. Haugen. How do mills dispose of their bran; the price is fixed on that, isn't it?

Mr. Cole. I can't tell you. They had to deal that out proportionately, I think.

Mr. Haugen. Is it not a fact that they sell it at an increased price?

Mr. Cole. I don't know.

EXTRACTS FROM LETTERS PERTAINING TO THE MARKET NEWS SERVICE ON HAY, FEEDS, AND GRAIN.

The Market Letter has enabled the farmers of this county to get feed at right prices at all times. They have handled 37 cars of feed, at a total saving of $8,556. Ninety-three additional cars were handled, the savings on which we have no record.—O. P. Griffin, emergency demonstration agent, Brownwood, Tex.

This is the first time we have been able to get a satisfactory market report on hay in the West.—Los Angeles Wholesale Hay Dealers' Association, Los Angeles, Cal.

The market reports gotten out by your office received by my 26 clubs through the year. There were 600 cars ordered from and through your lists. My 26 clubs shipped about 1,000 cars through all sources. The saving to our farmers ran from $30 to $200 per car, or about $75 on average per car on all.—Walter E. Davis, assistant emergency district agent, Austin, Tex.

We feel this report is very valuable to the trade and meets a long-felt want, and we hope these reports will be continued indefinitely.—Irwin & Co., by William Irwin, manager.

We have never been able to get satisfactory market reports on hay prices. Your Weekly Market Letter appears to be the first bright light upon the horizon to indicate to producers what the fair situation may be regarding deliveries and sales of hay and grain in the vicinities influencing the San Francisco market.—Huston Farms Co., San Francisco, Cal.

Mr. M. M. Williams, at Lowden, Wash., reports that this service was the best thing the Bureau of Markets had done for the farmers of the Northwest.—H. H. Boone, county agent, Walla Walla, Wash.

I am confident that when the final reports come in that they will show the saving of thousands of dollars over quotations made to the agents and farmers. In my opinion, however, this is a small portion of the saving effected. There is no doubt that the fact that the agent and the farmers through him were being kept posted as to actual values of feedstuffs has forced a very great reduction in the prices at which feeds would otherwise have been sold in these drought-stricken sections.—D. N. Barrow, emergency district agent, College Station, Tex.

The Weekly Market Letter sent out from your office is the best report we get from any scource on market conditions in California or elsewhere, and we want to be kept on your mailing list, for we appreciate your efforts very much.—Gorrie & Yeoman, Hayward, Cal.

Kindly send me your Weekly Market Letter, and will place it in a conspicuous place on our exchange.—Y. E. Booker, secretary-treasurer Richmond Grain Exchange, Richmond, Va.

Last winter we bought about 120 cars of feed, but very few cars, if any, were bought through your department; but one or two men in each community receiving your bulletins made it possible for me to organize these community organizations so the farmers could buy their feed cooperatively and save the large profit the feed men were making on stuff sold them. I think it would be out of the question to try to maintain these community organizations without the Bureau of Markets, even though they never bought anything through you; it keeps feed men straight and from profiteering on the farmers of this country.—E. T. Crozier, county agent, San Marcos, Tex.

Resolutions passed on June 11, 1918, by the Cattle Raisers' Association of Texas with regard to the work of the bureau follow:

"Whereas the Department of Agriculture has rendered a signal service to distressed Texas cattle and to the cattle industry of America during the summer and fall of 1917 by maintaining a cooperative movement and intelligent service, resulting in the saving of hundreds of thousands of breeding beef cattle of further productiveness: Therefore be it

"*Resolved*, That the executive committee of the Cattle Raisers' Association of Texas, in session at Fort Worth, Tex., June 11, 1918, does earnestly urge the Department of Agriculture to reestablish and make permanent a similar service and add to it at proper season a service for bringing the buyer and seller of foodstuffs together, as it was done for a brief time during the fall and winter of 1917, and resulting in great benefit to the cattle industry: And be it further

"*Resolved*, That the office of Cattle Raisers' Association at Fort Worth be offered, without charge, for the use of the Department of Agriculture and all facilities of the association be pledged in support and cooperation of such activities."

The CHAIRMAN. The next item is 123, on page 243.

Mr. HAUGEN. I should like to ask about this 123. Why is it necessary to have a $3,500 man to handle that matter? I can't understand that.

STATEMENT OF MR. CHARLES J. BRAND, CHIEF OF THE BUREAU OF MARKETS, UNITED STATES DEPARTMENT OF AGRICULTURE—Continued.

Mr. BRAND. Seed is a fundamental proposition, in all agricultural production, and up to now, we have had no authoritative seed report. There has been one commercial publication that claimed to give reliable information, in a very slight degree on the basis of what we are doing; but for that service they charged $100 per subscriber, and it probably did not cover one-twentieth of the ground that our seed-reporting service covers. It is absolutely impossible for a private firm to furnish the reliable information that we are able to obtain, and hence we may say that so far as this seed-reporting work is concerned, that it has not been covered at all adequately in the past. That is so true that the American Seed Trade Association, the war service committees of the various seed-producing organizations, and seed-distributing concerns have approved this work and are very desirous that an appropriation be made to continue it. I would like to insert in the record at this place, if I may, the resolutions and letters from the officers of those organizations requesting the continuation of this service.

REPORT OF ADVISORY COMMITTEE OF PRODUCERS.

The full report and recommendations of the Advisory Committee of agricultural and live-stock producers, consisting of 23 members from all parts of the United States, who were in consultation in Washington for a week with the Department of Agriculture and the Food Administration, is given in the issue of April 17, 1918, of the Weekly News Letter of the United States Department of Agriculture. The text of resolutions adopted and recommendations made by this committee pertaining to the seed activities of the department and to the need of increased production and careful conservation of certain seed crops follows:

1. We heartily indorse the action of the Secretary of Agriculture in the appointment of the committee on seed stocks, and the work that was assigned to this committee, since the results have been of inestimable value in securing better distribution of seed stocks and have aided in keeping prices within reasonable figures.

2. We heartily indorse the publication of the Seed Reporter as being a timely publication of great value in assisting the country in learning of the stocks of seeds and their commercial movements and prices throughout the country.

3. The national seed surveys conducted twice a year by the Bureau of Markets and the Seed Reporting Service are extremely valuable in making it possible for both the farmer and the local seedsman to gain accurate information as to actual available supplies of seed, thereby lessening the opportunity for profiteering, and we recommend that this service be made a permanent feature of the work of the Department of Agriculture.

4. The Department of Agriculture is to be congratulated on the successful efforts it has made to provide for good spring-wheat seed for the farmers of the United States, and it is suggested that similar efforts will be made by the department with regard to seed of winter wheat.

5. It is·urged that the field inspection of seed grains be extended as far as practicable, and that the various States be called upon to supplement the Federal appropriations that have been made for this purpose and to cooperate with the Federal agencies to the fullest extent possible.

6. In view of the increased cost of vegetable seeds and the consequent dissatisfaction existing among users of vegetable seed, the Department of Agriculture should be requested to investigate this condition with a view of ascertaining its cause and employing such means as are at its disposal to rectify it.

7. In view of the fact that the foreign supply of vegetable seeds is practically cut off by reason of war conditions, all growers of vegetables should be urged to save seed for themselves, as far as practicable, and to conserve such supplies of seed as may come into their possession.

8. We believe that the flax situation should receive special consideration by the Department of Agriculture and the several States in which it has been demonstrated that flax can be grown, and that serious considerations should be given to the possibilities of the utilization of this plant to the fullest extent possible this year, and especially that information should be obtained as to the stocks of flaxseed in the hands of crushers with a view of making the best possible use of these stocks under the present conditions.

9. Steps should be taken immediately to conserve supplies of buckwheat seed that are now in danger of being consumed as food, and the increased planting of this crop should be urged.

10. Recognizing the importance of millet as a late seeding crop, especially in the northern Great Plains region, recommendations should be made to the committee on seed stocks of the Department of Agriculture to take definite steps to supply necessary quantities of good stocks of millet seed for sowing for seed, feed, and forage purposes.

11. We recommend the accumulation of clean, moderate-priced alfalfa seed at convenient points in the Northwest, or that information be disseminated as to where such can be obtained, and that the local production of this crop be encouraged in places where it can be economically produced, with a view to producing home-grown seed.

AMERICAN SEED TRADE ASSOCIATION,
Washington, D. C., November 26, 1918.
Mr. W. A. WHEELER,
Chief of Seed Reporting Service, Bureau of Markets,
Department of Agriculture, Washington, D. C.

DEAR MR. WHEELER: Now, that the war seems to be over, as president of the American Seed Trade Association I wish to extend to you the congratulations of our association. At the same time request that if it is possible your bureau will continue its most valuable work; that is, giving the probable outcome of the crops to the Nation.

Your bureau has been a large force in maintaining stability as to food products. It has largely prevented unscrupulous speculation, and I know of no force in these troublesome times that has so much tended to stabilize values in seeds and farm products as has the information given out by your bureau to the general public.

Now, that the war is over and we are fast returning to our customary pursuits, your information, it seems to me, is more necessary than ever before. The world is short of feed. There is no one at present so well informed as the members of your staff as to where this food is and in what quantity. It is very necessary now to prevent speculation by the information your department can give, which, I feel certain, has prevented many products from obtaining unusual and prohibitive prices by this time. These prices would have been so made because of the lack of information.

To my mind your bureau is extremely essential to the proper adjustment of prices and the feeding of the world, which is now our part more than ever.

FRANK W. BOLGIANO, *President.*

WM. G. SCARLETT & CO.,
BALTIMORE, *December 2, 1918.*
Mr. W. A. WHEELER,
In Charge Seed Reporting Service, Bureau of Markets,
Department of Agriculture, Washington, D. C.

DEAR MR. WHEELER: In the course of conversation with you the other day it developed that in view of the fact that the seed reporting service of the Bureau of Markets was a war measure it was highly probable it would be discontinued in the near future. As seedsmen, we would very much regret this step, because we are convinced that it would be a distinct loss to the country at large and to the seed trade in particular.

As advised you on a previous occasion, the seed trade never knew the vast importance of a department such as you have developed until war conditions forced this department on us. Previous to the advent of the Seed Reporting Service the seed trade was one of more or less mystery and speculation in that sources of supply were known to but few and there was absolutely no equalization in distribution, with the natural result that one section of the country may have a feast and the other a famine. Your department, with its various publications, has changed this situation. We are now getting information through your department which greatly helps in the development of our business, and in our opinion we will need this help more during peace time than we did during war, for the reason that America will unquestionably largely expand its field of operation in the distribution of agricultural seeds. We will unquestionably operate all over the world, in which case it is highly important that we have all the reliable information that it is possible to obtain.

We sincerely trust that the Seed Reporting Service will be put on a permanent basis, and we shall be very glad indeed to render what assistance we can to this end.

We remain, very truly yours,

WM. G. SCARLETT & CO.

Mr. HAUGEN. It is not a question of the continuation of this service, but why all this overhead charge if it can be eliminated?

Mr. BRAND. It can not be eliminated. You can't do work without men, and you can't get them unless you pay them higher wages than the Government is paying. They are leaving the work every day and are going to leave more frequently.

Mr. HAUGEN. Oh, yes, yes, yes. I have heard too much about men leaving the Department, but what about this particular one?

Mr. BRAND. This particular man is one of the most highly trained men in the United States. I doubt if you could find his equal for this work, because for some time he was at the head of a large seed business and his education——

Mr. HAUGEN. Why do you need that sort of man?

Mr. BRAND. For this work you must have a man who knows the seed business and who knows the scientific fundamentals of plant breeding. He must possess the confidence of the seed industry in order to have charge of such important work.

Mr. HAUGEN. Collecting the information?

Mr. BRAND. Besides collecting this information and being responsible for its publication as a useful form he conducts general investigational work regarding seed marketing.

Mr. HAUGEN. You mean as to the quantity, or quality, or what?

Mr. BRAND. This particular work is largely inventory work. The copy of the Seed Reporter, which Mr. Anderson has in his hand, gives actual inventories of the most important seeds, information giving the actual weight, and the amount of the seed stocks in the United States. This is information which heretofore has been in the hands of possibly three, and not more than four, concerns. The big ones objected to it at first, but now they are glad to have it.

Mr. HAUGEN. Do you contend that a $3,500 man is required for that?

Mr. BRAND. Absolutely. You can't find such a man for a penny less than that. I would not ask him to serve for a penny less than that.

Mr. HAUGEN. Would you have it go in the record that it is necessary to employ a $3,500 man to measure and weigh seed?

Mr. BRAND. I think we can not get any man for less than that to handle the work I have described as it should be handled.

Mr. HAUGEN. What is the work?

Mr. MCLAUGHLIN. Doesn't he ask the dealers for the reports and accept their reports?

Mr. BRAND. That is one small feature of it, but when you stop at that that is the same as saying that a director of a corporation directs somebody to make pig iron and he makes pig iron. Yes, he does; but he has to have knowledge of the business to know how to do it.

Mr. MCLAUGHLIN. I want to pay men what they are worth, but for the life of me I can't see why a highly trained man is necessary to get these reports from the dealers.

Mr. BRAND. He has to arrange with these gentlemen who are doing business amounting to millions of dollars a year for securing these reports. He has that contact with them constantly.

Mr. MCLAUGHLIN. He gets those reports because he comes from a Government office, doesn't he?

Mr. BRAND. No, sir; but because he commands their respect. They know he knows his business. He has for 10 years been manager of an important seed distributing business. You can't send a messenger boy around to do that kind of work.

Mr. HAUGEN. To measure seed?

Mr. BRAND. You can't put it that way. This man entered the field from a plant-breeding angle. He was a professor in a college in Minnesota, and later in the Agricultural College of South Dakota, and then he organized a seed company, which he conducted for a number of years. His longing to do scientific work, however, called him back into this field.

Mr. HAUGEN. Can you tell us what he does outside of measuring these seeds?

Mr. BRAND. He does not do any measuring. He conducts investigations regarding the seed markets in the United States; he maps the areas of seed production. Very few people know the sources of seed. He passes on the question of price, he passes on whether there are methods of unfair practice, and what improved methods we can bring about—he takes these things up with the seed men and succeeds in improving many things without power to enforce improvements.

Mr. HAUGEN. About the cost of seed?

Mr. BRAND. No, sir. Not the cost of seed. About the various complex questions that arise in marketing and distributing our seed supply to the best advantage.

Mr. HAUGEN. After all, it is collecting and distributing information as to the quantity?

Mr. BRAND. Yes, sir; the quantity sometimes, including exports, imports, carry overs, and all those sort of things, as well as movement, prices, varieties, quality, etc.

(Thereupon, at 5.30 o'clock p. m., the committee took a recess until Friday, January 10, 1919, at 10.30 a. m.)

COMMITTEE ON AGRICULTURE,
HOUSE OF REPRESENTATIVES,
Friday, January 10, 1919.

The committee met at 10.30 o'clock a. m., Hon. A. F. Lever (chairman) presiding.

BUREAU OF MARKETS—Continued.

The CHAIRMAN. The committee will come to order. When the committee recessed last night, or yesterday afternoon, we were on page 243.

STATEMENT OF MR. CHARLES J. BRAND, CHIEF OF THE BUREAU OF MARKETS, UNITED STATES DEPARTMENT OF AGRICULTURE—Continued.

The CHAIRMAN. You had completed your general statement on item 123, Mr. Brand.

Mr. BRAND. I think, Mr. Chairman, we practically concluded the discussion of it. Mr. Haugen had asked some questions regarding the type of man who was necessary to handle that kind of work, and I think perhaps it is sufficient to say that with respect to this particular class of commodities, namely, seeds, the man handling it must be thoroughly capable of considering every economic and every practical question involved. Indeed, he must be practically capable of conducting a seed business himself, in order to understand the problems and to deal with them effectively.

Mr. ANDERSON. Is the information gotten under this item reported to trade organizations in any other way except through the seed bulletin, or whatever you call it?

Mr. BRAND. Seed Reporter?

Mr. ANDERSON. Seed Reporter.

Mr. BRAND. We also publish special reports; when they are required to be gotten out very quickly. We have been furnishing copies of the Seed Reporter to about 7,500 seed dealers, and to about 2,500 special growers of seeds, who grow seed under contract. It is of very great assistance to these people to know what seeds are really worth, the available supply, and all that sort of thing. This is the first time we have been able to have such information.

Mr. ANDERSON. This is rather essentially a trade service?

Mr. BRAND. More a trade service than most of the services, though it serves as a very great assistance to producers who either grow seed under contract or who sell a part of the seeds they produce in their regular operations.

Mr. ANDERSON. I don't want to philosophize about this particular proposition, but I have been trying to discover some limitation upon the extent of work of this character. So far I have not discovered any. When this sort of work is done, of course, as a commercial proposition, of course there is a limitation upon it, because there is no advantage in gathering information and disseminating it, except in so far as people are willing to pay for it. When you are gathering it and distributing it with public funds, that limitation does not apply. Where is your limit?

Mr. BRAND. Unfortunately, with most information of this kind, there is not a sufficient commercial stimulus for people to go into the business of preparing it. They haven't the sources of information. Seedsmen won't reveal the state of their business to commercial reporting agencies. They have revealed it very completely to the Department, so we are able to get absolutely reliable information. When you leave it to the commercial motive. the misfortune is that the man who gets it is the man who already has most of the information, and the poor fellow who really needs it is at even a greater disadvantage than he otherwise would be.

Mr. ANDERSON. I don't want to leave it to the commercial agency. I don't want to leave that impression. What I am trying to get at is this: All information has some value to somebody. It may be of some use to somebody to know how many inches it is around the world and how fast a railroad train would have to go to go around the world in a certain number of hours. Any sort of information has a value. Now, we have to put some limitation upon the activities of this bureau. We have got to find a line of demarcation, where we are going to quit. Can you offer anything on that proposition?

Mr. BRAND. With respect to this specific item, it is my impression that for a period of years the work that would have to be done need not cost to exceed $75,000, and that the returns from it would be very great indeed. In fact, buyers of seeds have been saved from profiteering and speculation, and things of that sort, to an extent never known of before. For instance, in the case of turnip seed, we found in one city over 90 per cent of the turnip seed in the hands of one firm, and it helped a lot to be able to deal with that situation rather than to let one firm profit, as it would undoubtedly have done. We found in the case of alfalfa seed, that a speculator, in a section of the country where alfalfa seed is scarcely ever grown, had cornered the major part of the alfalfa-seed supply. We have been able to cure a great many situations with that information, which could not be handled in any other way.

The CHAIRMAN. Anything further, Mr. Anderson?

Mr. ANDERSON. I don't seem to have gotten anywhere.

Mr. BRAND. Mr. Anderson, I am sorry I can not express myself any more clearly. For a service of this sort I think we can for many years do as much as necessary on an appropriation of not to exceed $75,000.

The CHAIRMAN. It is almost an impossible proposition to try to find a line of demarcation. When you are dealing with a product distributed through the trade, the information is valuable to the trade, the producer, and the consumer. Isn't that true?

Mr. BRAND. Yes.

The CHAIRMAN. In other words, if you did undertake to set up a line of distinction, you have a duplicated service. You would have one service dealing with the commercial end of it, getting the very same information you are getting for the producing end of it. Is that true?

Mr. BRAND. Yes; there is a great deal of truth in that. I'd like to give this assurance to the committee, Mr. Chairman, that we consider very carefully in every instance whether a piece of work is a service that the Government should render, or a service that private enterprise should render. We aim not to enter into a field where private enterprise can handle the matter; but in this matter of securing information and disseminating it, which involves going into the records of private enterprises, practically no one except the disinterested agency of the Government can do it.

The CHAIRMAN. Of course, you are careful not to duplicate any work of the Census Bureau.

Mr. BRAND. Absolutely. We are in close touch with them, and cooperate with them. Just at this time they are doing some work for us, because we haven't the facilities for doing it. We aim never to duplicate any other agency. Everything is taken up with any other agency that might possibly be concerned, not only with this department but the other branches of the Government.

Mr. ANDERSON. There might be a limitation, might there not, as to subjects upon which it was worth while to gather information and disseminate it?

The CHAIRMAN. Yes, Doctor, that is true?

Mr. BRAND. I do not think that is true. Of course, we exclude practically everything, except those things which are of specific utility, either to producers, consumers who buy seeds for planting, distributing agencies, who are responsible for seeing that the producers have seed, or for growers producing seed under contract or otherwise.

The CHAIRMAN. You are not doing work, for example, on canary-bird seed; that is an extreme illustration?

Mr. BRAND. I should perhaps say this. We have selected a list of seeds, of both field and garden crops, which includes those of the greatest commercial importance. We are reporting upon these seeds, which aggregate perhaps 90 per cent of the total seeds, and include only those that are of real importance.

Mr. MCLAUGHLIN. This may have been gone into; if so, the chairman can tell me, and I won't pursue it. I learned as to alfalfa seed, a lot of impure seed is on the market, and that a great deal of it that is sold is not true to name, in this: Grimm alfalfa seed is considered the most valuable. It is the highest priced. It is more suitable for Northern sowing than any other, and a great deal of seed sold as Grimm seed is not Grimm. Another thing, it is not considered advisable, as I understand it, to sow seed grown under irrigation—to sow that in sections of the country where irrigation is not used. A lot of the alfalfa seed, as I say, is not true to name; it is not Grimm, although the high price is charged for it. Alfalfa seed, as it is grown under irrigation, is sold improperly, and deceiving those who want seed for use in other sections of the country. Do any of your inquiries extend to learning these facts, and what do you do? Do you communicate with other branches of the department that perhaps would have that more directly in charge?

Mr. BRAND. With respect to that matter, Mr. McLaughlin, the temptation to misbrand Grimm alfalfa seed is perhaps the greatest single temptation we know of in the seed trade. That particular type of alfalfa seed looks exactly like any other type, for instance, Utah or California alfalfa. After a northern winter however, Grimm alfalfa may have perhaps 100 per cent of the stand, and many of those other varieties will be spoiled in the ground over winter. But the seed looks exactly the same. The temptation, hence, is very great. We have taken steps to bring about a truer marking of seed. We have enlisted the cooperation of most of the seedsmen in the better marking and branding of seeds, and we are inclined to believe that there should be something in the nature of seed-mark legislation, but we have not developed the matter to the point where we are prepared to submit it.

Mr. MCLAUGHLIN. How do you do that?

Mr. BRAND. By cooperation with the seedsmen. We get the American Seed Trade Association, for instance, to specify in their rules and regulations the trade practices that will be recognized by the Seed Trade Association.

Mr. MCLAUGHLIN. I suppose the result of your cooperation, as you call it, can be determined either by the scientific testing of the seed, or by actual use of it. Do you know whether by either of these ways of learning the real quality that your work has been effective, or not?

Mr. BRAND. Of course the practical testing may require a number of years. I personally handled all the red clover and alfalfa investigations of the Bureau of Plant Industry for many years, and know that you may have a period of two or three or four years in indirect tests in the open field, without disclosing any special difference. Then you may have an open winter, with 20 or 25° below zero, or even 38, as we had in our experiments in North Dakota, and in that event you will finally be able to determine the facts. But the grower is left under a false impression for years and years, thinking he has the real thing, and he has not. You can not tell by the tests in the seed laboratory as to hardiness. You can tell purity and things of that sort, and of course the seed laboratory carries on those tests. I suppose Dr. Brown has thousands of requests every season.

Mr. McLaughlin. Do you understand some of the scientific men of the department are able to distinguish one variety from another by close investigation, without actual planting?

Mr. Brand. If they are distinct enough. But you can not do that in the case, for instance, of alfalfa seed. The number of varieties within all of the strains are so great you could scarcely recognize them by the seeds themselves.

Mr. McLaughlin. If the distinction between the varieties is so great I should think they could distinguish them by investigation.

Mr. Brand. Frequently the seed looks exactly the same, and the grown plant looks very different. For instance, in the question of variegation in the color of plants, the seed may look exactly the same in a strain which is pure purple as in one which is yellow, blue, or other variegated colors.

Mr. McLaughlin. I don't like to take too much time, but does your work extend to making inquiry or investigation to learn the results in the field of the use of these different kinds of seeds?

Mr. Brand. Not at all; the Bureau of Plant Industry is charged with that work, and has a number of men assigned to it. We carry on the survey of seed stocks, after they are produced, and try to assist the producer who desires to better his strain to find growers or others who have suitable stocks for sale, but we do not take up the question of production at all.

Mr. McLaughlin. How do you cooperate with the proper bureau in the department so that they can know the results of your inquiries, and you can know the results of theirs?

Mr. Brand. This particular work is in charge of Dr. Taylor, and we have very close relationship with him. There is a joint interbureau committee that takes up many of these problems and deals with them.

Mr. McLaughlin. It is a very serious matter. Some alfalfa seed sells for $12 or $14 a bushel. Grimm is sold as high as a dollar a pound.

Mr. Brand. Yes; and there is a great deal of chicanery in its distribution. I think we have helped that situation. I think the department as a whole has done a very great deal to cure it.

The Chairman. Anything further, Mr. McLaughlin?

Mr. McLaughlin. No.

The Chairman. Take up the next item, No. 124, which is a new item, " For furnishing to producers, dealers, newspapers, and consumers accurate information regarding supplies of fruits," and so on. That seems to be rather a duplication of other lines of work that you have been covering.

Mr. BRAND. Mr. Chairman, I think it will become evident when it is described how very substantially different it is. It is, however, the last of the items which involve the news-service type of work, and, if I may, I'd like to say, with reference to all of these services, that their costs have gone up in the last three years very considerably, so that even with the same sum of money they could not do as much or as effective work. Traveling expenses, transportation, the cost of materials—cost of paper, for instance, particularly has more than doubled—ink, and everything that enters into these services, have gone up, so that we can not do with a dollar, as you gentlemen need not be told, what we used to do with a dollar. They are suffering from the high cost of living just as everything else is. There is a ray of hope on the other side, however. We lost about 280 of our men to the Army. These men are now gradually returning. They are all replaced in their positions, so that we are going to have more experienced and better men, and we will gain some of the efficiency through that channel that we are losing through other channels. This particular item, 124, is what we call our local market reporting service. The proposition involves an increase in statutory and lump of $50,000, $42,880 of which is lump and $7,120 statutory. I have asked Mr. Branch, who has developed this work from its very inception, to present the matter to the committee.

Mr. ANDERSON. Before you do that. There seems to be a very great disproportion in the amount of your lump-fund appropriation here and your statutory roll, if your statement is correct.

Mr. BRAND. In all these cases of transfers from emergency funds, Mr. Anderson, we have aimed to transfer to statutory the same proportion of clerical positions as the proportion of lump funds to be transferred bears to the total of the emergency fund in question. We have determined the ratio, not absolutely accurately, but relatively, and we have transferred in that proportion of statutory and lump.

The CHAIRMAN. What is that ratio?

Mr. BRAND. It is about one-sixth, I think. For instance, we have now about $350,000 statutory, something a little more than that, and our regular funds are about $2,000,000. Perhaps it is more than that. But it was very carefully—I didn't do it myself, so I don't know so much about it—but it was very carefully adjusted. I think that was observed, Mr. Harrison, in all of the other cases.

Mr. HARRISON. Yes; that is generally true, I think. We transferred the clerks and subclerical employees to the statutory roll, as we have done in previous years.

Mr. BRAND. The statute provides that persons engaged in certain work must be transferred to the statutory roll when the estimates are submitted to the committee.

Mr. CHAIRMAN. You follow the law and not the ratio.

Mr. BRAND. We follow the law. The ratio becomes established in operation.

Mr. ANDERSON. I don't want the matter to rest there. The statutory roll, under the present practice of the committee, has increased exactly in the ratio in which the department hires men under the lump sum fund, and afterwards we are asked to have them transferred and they are transferred.

Mr. BRAND. Yes; but it seems to work out as I have stated. That seems to be shown by the results over a period of years, in a practical way.

Mr. ANDERSON. Is that ratio one of money, or is it a ratio of a number of employees, or what?

Mr. BRAND. No; it would be money. It would be so much total lump sum.

Mr. ANDERSON. If that were true, the statutory roll in the different bureaus ought to bear a more or less relation to the lump-sum appropriations for that bureau. They don't bear any such relation at all.

Mr. BRAND. I think it will vary according to the type of work of the bureau. Bureaus like the Bureau of Markets that involve the collection of great amounts of information necessarily require a larger proportion of clerical workers than other bureaus. In bureaus like the Bureau of Plant Industry, for instance, where a larger proportion of the employees are scientific employees who are not transferred to the statutory roll, it is probable that a different situation will arise. So I think you will find a general standard—not an absolute standard—but depending upon the character of the work of the various bureaus. For instance, I imagine the Bureau of Crop Estimates shows a higher percentage of statutory roll than any other bureau in the department.

Mr. ANDERSON. I think you are wrong about that.

Mr. BRAND. You think I am wrong about it? I don't know. I haven't looked it up, but I should expect it to be true from the nature of its work. I am now merely judging from the character of the work, and what would naturally result under the statute.

Mr. MCLAUGHLIN. I have not gathered from the answer that your inquiry has been fully met, Mr. Chairman, as to the duplication involved here.

The CHAIRMAN. He is just about to explain this work.

Mr. BRAND. I am going to call on Mr. Branch to describe the work; that will indicate more truly its character.

Mr. MCLAUGHLIN. This looks to a rank outsider very, very similar to work provided for and carried on under other items.

The CHAIRMAN. Yes; it struck me that way.

STATEMENT OF G. V. BRANCH, SPECIALIST IN CITY MARKETING, BUREAU OF MARKETS, UNITED STATES DEPARTMENT OF AGRICULTURE.

Mr. BRANCH. Mr. Chairman and gentlemen of the committee, I anticipated that would be your viewpoint naturally from the reading of the estimate, so I will describe first just where our work differs, and how it really covers an entirely new and virgin field, and does not duplicate in any way the work previously described by Mr. Sherman, nor is it work which can best be carried on by his men. The City Market Reporting Service was started strictly as an emergency activity. Although we had seen the possibilities in such work, previous to the time of the emergency appropriation we had no money to start it. Mr. Sherman's work, or what we might term the National Telegraphic Market News Service, treats almost entirely on the leading products. It treats on those that are shipped from a distance in carload quantities to the large central markets. You can doubtless realize right away that there are many more shippers who ship in small quantities by express, for instance, and by other methods, to local commission dealers, than there are car-lot shippers, just as there are many more small farmers than large farmers. That is one of the main distinctions. Now, then, the little shipper, who has his small shipment to go to the commission merchant in his local market, or some market near him, does not want car-lot quotations at all. Those do him no good. He wants quotations showing the prices at which the commission man will sell his products in the local market. Now, we draw a distinction between such prices and the ones which Mr. Sherman reports on, rather roughly termed jobbing prices. As the car comes into the city it is broken up, and the car-lot receiver will sell say 25 or 50 packages out of that car, to the jobber, or possibly to a large retailer. That price is called the jobbing price. Now, you can readily see how that price is not of interest at all to this man who ships in a couple of crates by express to the commission man, nor is it of any interest to the very large number—the thousands of truck growers around our cities, our larger markets—who haul their products directly into the market. They come largely into farmers' markets, the big wholesale farmers' markets, or they haul the stuff in to the commission dealers and leave it there and go back to their farms. As I say, car-lot information and jobbing prices hardly interest them at all, except as they may present competitive quotations. So, we see there a very large field to cover. Furthermore, the information transmitted to growers by Mr. Sherman's service, or the service that he described, naturally goes to growers who ship from a distance. That would give the information, Mr. Chairman, to growers in your section shipping to the northern markets; growers in the West shipping to eastern markets; but there are thousands of truck growers surrounding our large cities like Philadelphia, Boston, New York, Baltimore, Washington, and many others, who have no service at all and never have had any kind of a market news service. Then there are the small farmers within the tributary territory to these big centers that depend almost entirely on shipping in their miscellaneous surpluses by express to the commission merchants.

The CHAIRMAN. What is your plan of reaching these folks?

Mr. BRANCH. That will involve just a very brief description of our service. I won't be long, because I realize you have listened to three or four other descriptions of market news services, and of course they all parallel each other in a general way.

Let us take a single market. For example, take Providence, R. I., where the work was initiated two years ago as the result of an experiment. We put a man up there to test this out, and it proved so valuable we took it up immediately, as one of the most efficient things we could do to help out in the emergency. A man is stationed at the Providence market. He goes out on the big wholesale farmers' market about 4 o'clock in the morning. Our men are all early workers. He gets the receipts on that market. There may be 300 growers come into the market. Many times, more than that on a summer's morning. He gets the receipts of the various products, and instead of treating on a few, as Mr. Sherman does, we reach as high as 50 or 60 products, because you know there is a big line of fruits and vegetables and other products that the farmers send in. He gets the receipts and gets accurate prices just as the other service does. He always secures the selling price, not the asking price, and then he gets also from Mr. Sherman's men, if we are in a joint office, or, if he is not, from the wholesale and commission men, the receipts and prices of locally grown produce which comes to them and which they sell. Therefore he has very definitely the receipts of all of this locally grown stuff tributary to that market, and the prices that it brought.

This information then is all made available through a bulletin issued daily in the summer time, or less frequently in the winter when the market days are mainly three a week. The distribution of the bulletin to the farmers is made in two ways. He can get it at the farmers' market, or at the wholesale district. Those who drive in regularly can get copies from boxes which we put in convenient places, so as to save the envelopes and the burden on the mails. To the farmers who don't come in regularly, and consequently can not get a satisfactory service in that way, we mail it. This will account for the fact that our own mailing lists are not as large as some of the others. Also they give but little idea as to how many farmers we reach, because while we can check up on the number of dealers and the number we distribute through boxes and in other ways, we find they pass them around a great deal. Further, a good many newspapers publish that report, and in certain cities some of these newspapers at least go very extensively into the near-by rural districts. Newspapers like the Providence Journal or the Springfield Republican go to a large proportion of the farm homes in the territory and many farmers can get the service quicker through the newspaper because of its special means of distribution.

What I have described probably forms the most important part of the service.

Mr. McLaughlin. Before you get away from that: In a city of the size of Providence there will be a large number of dealers. Is that true?

Mr. Branch. No; I wouldn't say a large number in a city the size of Providence. You mean wholesale and commission dealers?

Mr. McLaughlin. Those you would investigate.

Mr. Branch. Probably not to exceed, Mr. McLaughlin, 20 to 25. I take it you are referring now to wholesale commission dealers and not to retail grocers.

Mr. McLaughlin. The dealers to whom these small deliveries are made—sales are made—wouldn't there be a large number of them?

Mr. Branch. No; I think my estimate would be about right that there would not be to exceed probably 25 wholesale and commission firms in a city the size of Providence. Of course certain growers will sell their stuff and deliver it directly to retail grocers. I am not including them, of course. There are great numbers of retail grocers.

Mr. McLaughlin. Is your man able to see and investigate accurately the prices and quantities in each one of these 25 places?

Mr. Branch. Yes. You take the 25 dealers. I dare say there are not more than five or ten who do a commission business, that is who specialize on handling the locally grown products. May be less.

There is generally in a city of that size probably one or two large commission houses that specialize in handling that locally grown stuff, and the rest are more or less wholesalers who buy outright.

Mr. McLaughlin. When your man gets that information what does he do with it?

Mr. Branch. He gets the receipts, that is the amount the man has received, the accurate price at which he sells that stuff to the retail dealer, and then he publishes it.

Mr. McLaughlin. Does he send it by wire?

Mr. Branch. No, sir; he publishes it locally. That is why we call it our city or local market reporting service, because it covers that locality. It may spread over a State line, but it covers a territory tributary to that particular market.

Mr. McLaughlin. Then he has help and he has some printing apparatus.

The Chairman. He has a mimeograph there, doesn't he?

Mr. Branch. Yes. In a joint office, where our man is in the same city as the telegraphic market news service, the mimeographs and all machinery of that kind are pooled, so we don't have to have a new one. One will use it when the other is not using it, and that incurs no extra expense so far as machinery is concerned. In an office where the other services are not located, then we have a mimeograph of our own and a small addressograph.

Mr. McLaughlin. After these bulletins are printed, tell us a little more about how they reach those who are interested in them, particularly those who have to sell their products the next day, or subsequently to receiving the notice.

Mr. Branch. All right, sir. This morning's market is digested, so to speak, and put on this bulletin, and placed on the farmers' market and in the commission district in quantities in convenient receptacles so when the farmers drive in early the next morning they may get one. Many farmers come in in the evening and stay there all night and start selling next morning at three or four o'clock. Our bulletins are there when they get there, and they get from them a complete account of the previous day's market what the receipts of each different product was, and what that product sold for.

Mr. McLaughlin. Do you have a mailing list?

Mr. Branch. Then in addition, as I pointed out previously, to those who do not come in regularly so they can get satisfactory service by taking it out of the box, we mail a copy to such growers, and they get it in almost all cases the next morning.

Mr. McLaughlin. You have used Providence, R. I., as an example. Do you know how much of a mailing list you have there?

Mr. Branch. I have it here; approximately 400 growers and about 15 dealers. I guessed at the number of dealers, and said somewhere around 20 or 25. We have approximately 15 on our mailing list. I did not pick one of our largest markets. I picked the one we started this work in first. Our mailing list is always held to a minimum, because we try to serve growers in other ways if we can, to save the cost of mailing, but if information can not be satisfactorily served through the boxes, we mail it to them.

Mr. McLaughlin. That occurs, as I understood, every day?

Mr. Branch. Every day throughout the summer season. In the winter the markets are generally very heavy on three days and light on the other three days. When the markets are light enough, we reduce it to three days a week.

The CHAIRMAN. Mr. Branch, I notice in this bulletin here, "Daily market report at Fargo on apples," you say this: "No carload arrivals; demand moderate; no change in price." Then you go on and you report by bushels——

Mr. BRANCH. Mr. Chairman, may I interrupt to say that is not our report.

The CHAIRMAN. Let me finish my question. Then you report by bushels and barrels; then you report by boxes. Those farmers always bring in at least a box of apples, don't they?

Mr. BRANCH. Yes, but that is not a price on goods local farmers bring in at all, but on car-lot arrivals of different apples from different States shipped into that market. That is usually a highly standardized stock, like Northwestern box apples.

The CHAIRMAN. Have you this service here in Washington?

Mr. BRANCH. Yes.

The CHAIRMAN. Do you use the rural telephone in getting these prices out to the farmers around here?

Mr. BRANCH. No; we do not.

The CHAIRMAN. Would that be possible?

Mr. BRANCH. Yes, if the way we handle it did not serve them adequately. For those who come into the market on a certain morning the bulletin is there for them when they arrive and before they start selling; and those who do not come in are reached the same morning by mail. So if they come in the following morning they have read it, consequently, I think the distribution is pretty well covered in that way.

Mr. ANDERSON. Does this service relate entirely to wholesale sales?

Mr. BRANCH. No; that is another distinction between our service and the telegraphic service, in that our prices that we collect are largely prices that the grower receives on the wholesale farmers' market.

Mr. HAUGEN. Sells to who?

Mr. BRANCH. Retail dealers, hucksters, professional venders, and so on, who distribute it out over the city.

Mr. HAUGEN. The prices as quoted here, are they the prices the producer receives selling direct to the consumer?

Mr. BRANCH. No; to the retail dealer. On these large markets very little work is done direct to the consumer. The farmer comes into these farmers' markets and sells to the retail dealer.

Mr. HAUGEN. There is a good deal of it done here in the city.

Mr. BRANCH. Yes; there is considerable selling direct to the consumer in any city, but I am speaking about the part of it we cover. We could not attempt to collect the information in the various markets all over the town where the producer is selling direct to the consumer. That really after all forms such a small part of marketing it would not be worth the expense, so we work where the concentration is, on the wholesale markets, and we quote the prices to the grower that he gets by selling to the retail dealer, the huckster, and other retail distributors.

The CHAIRMAN. This information is available to the consumer?

Mr. BRANCH. Yes. That is the other half of our service, which I have not described.

Mr. ANDERSON. May I ask you if you have any service of this character on poultry products?

Mr. BRANCH. As fast as possible we are leaving fruits and vegetables—I don't mean "leaving them." I mean we are not confining ourselves to fruits and vegetables—but taking on eggs, poultry, dairy products, etc. We are aiming, in other words, to give to the farmers a report on practically all of the products they regularly bring in, or ship in, to the local market. The work is being expanded just as fast as we can do it. We find out what they want and as fast as we can get our lines out and get the information accurately we expand the service in that way.

The CHAIRMAN. If you don't have the figures I wish you would put into the record your mailing list for the city of Washington.

Mr. BRANCH. I can give you the figures right here. During the past summer our distribution here in Washington was about 600. We didn't start until August.

The CHAIRMAN. Six hundred?

Mr. BRANCH. That refers to the distribution of the bulletin.

The CHAIRMAN. The people who get it?

Mr. BRANCH. Yes.

The CHAIRMAN. Six hundred?

Mr. BRANCH. Yes.

The CHAIRMAN. And about 40 dealers?

Mr. BRANCH. Yes.

The CHAIRMAN. Does that include the consumers who use it, too?

Mr. BRANCH. No; that includes only the producers.

Mr. MCLAUGHLIN. Using Providence as an example again, have you any telegraphic service daily in relation to this work?

Mr. BRANCH. Practically speaking, no.

Mr. MCLAUGHLIN. What you have, what is it?

Mr. BRANCH. It is a local service, generally from men——

Mr. MCLAUGHLIN. Telegraphic service?

Mr. BRANCH. No, sir; men in these markets collect the information regarding the receipts and prices, compile it, and print it in their own offices, and distribute it from that office to the mailing list that they have, and to the farmers and dealers of that immediate city.

The CHAIRMAN. You did not get Mr. McLaughlin's question, I think. He asked you whether you use the telegraph at all in this business, and you said "practically no." He wants to know what you mean by "practically no." Do you use it at all; and, if so, to what extent?

Mr. BRANCH. At a place in New England, where the markets are rather close together, and where a farmer living between Boston and Providence and Worcester, Mass., may go to anyone of the three markets, we try to keep up communication between our three agents and they keep the farmers supplied on the bulletin with the prices on the main products in the Boston market, the Worcester market and the Providence market. That is done mainly by keeping in touch by phone, on just the main products, so that the grower may decide which one of the three towns, for instance, offers him the best price.

Mr. McLaughlin. How many men are necessary then to carry on this work you have spoken of in a city like Providence?

Mr. Branch. In the city of Providence we have only one man, with a stenographic assistant.

Mr. Lesher. In other words, then, if the commission merchants and these wholesale dealers would form an organization, they could practically fix the price, and then you would disseminate the price they fixed. Couldn't they do that?

Mr. Branch. Yes. Yes, I don't know of anything in any one of the services that would prevent a number of dealers from getting together and fixing a price if they could do it. All we know is that we get the actual price they sell the stuff at. We don't take their quotations. We get the actual prices they charged the man who bought from them, and we check those prices by getting them as often as we can from the men who bought the stuff, as well as from the men who sold it. If there was something back of that—if the wholesalers would get together and agree on prices—of course that is something we could not control, nor probably even ascertain.

Mr. Lesher. I say there are comparatively few of them, and they could do that if they wanted to do it?

Mr. Branch. Except for the difficulty of fixing prices on a highly perishable product that has to be sold quickly, and which must be sold according to the demand very largely. It is rather hard to fix prices on very highly perishable products like we cover.

The Chairman. I understand there is more speculation in eggs and butter than practically any other product known.

Mr. Branch. I really was thinking more of fruits and vegetables. We are just beginning to report on eggs and butter. There is a great deal of speculation, I know, on those products.

Mr. McLaughlin. How much is a man paid in a place like Providence?

Mr. Branch. $1,400 or $1,500. Salaries range from $1,400 to $1,920, according to the size market and the ability we have to have.

Mr. Rainey. You say they have to get up at 4 o'clock in the morning?

Mr. Branch. Yes; most of them have been working until 4 o'clock in the afternoon, too.

The part of the service I have not explained is the part which takes a different type of man, with different ability than the other news service.

Mr. McLaughlin. And he has to rent quarters?

Mr. Branch. Yes.

Mr. McLaughlin. Has to rent an office?

Mr. Branch. Our rental in many places in provided by the local farm bureau, or by the local chamber of commerce. We are asking for local cooperation, and in many places we use those offices, and pay no rental at all. In one market we paid around $900; that is the most expensive place; I think that is Boston. But the average for our 16 or 17 offices would not exceed $250 a year for rental.

The Chairman. Suppose you describe now the other end of the service.

Mr. Thompson. I want to ask him a question before he gets to that. I believe you said you usually had one man and a stenographic assistant.

Mr. BRANCH. In a market the size of Providence?

Mr. THOMPSON. Yes. If I understood you correctly, the work consists in this: He goes out, this man does, around town and finds out what different articles are being sold at—that is, celery, tomatoes, eggs, butter, and cabbage, and all these other articles. He takes that, gives it to his stenographer, and they put it on a sheet, and at the end of that day they mail it out to these producers, so they get it the next morning. Of course, you don't attempt in that to give the amount that there is on hand.

Mr. BRANCH. We attempt to give the amount, in most places, that is brought in.

Mr. THOMPSON. Do you go to every different dealer in town to get the amount he has on hand?

Mr. BRANCH. No, sir; to make it clear, we work on the wholesale farmers' market. It is a centralized market. The farmers all come in there, so possibly we have three or four hundred farmers in a restricted space.

Mr. THOMPSON. That don't represent everything that comes to town, by any means.

Mr. BRANCH. No; but it represents probably in most places ninety per cent, or more, of the local farm products brought into the city and sold at wholesale.

Mr. THOMPSON. That does not represent the amount on hand either, does it?

Mr. BRANCH. There is practically no amount on hand of the fruits and vegetables from day to day. It is almost a general practice to clean up every day.

Mr. THOMPSON. Apples, peaches, fruits—they sell them all out every day?

Mr. BRANCH. Yes. Not the storage stocks in the winter time, of late apples, of course.

Mr. THOMPSON. I am talking about the apples in the ordinary sense—if they have a practice of cleaning up those products every day.

Mr. BRANCH. That is the general practice. I would not say completely, but they approximate it as closely as they can.

Mr. THOMPSON. That is about the sum and substance of the service you render. Send that information out in a bulletin, and that reaches them the next morning.

Mr. BRANCH. May I inquire who has the copy of that bulletin I gave to Mr. Haugen, headed "City Market Reporting Service?"

Mr. HAUGEN. Here it is.

Mr. BRANCH. If I may outline what we do in that bulletin—we list the products and state the demand for each so the farmer will know what the greatest demand is for. In this case "active demand" for sweet potatoes, apples, and celery; "moderate demand" for oranges, grape fruit, bananas, etc.; "poor demand" for turnips, squash, cabbage, and so on. A man can see right away which products to push and which ones to hold back.

Mr. THOMPSON. What do you want to report on grape fruit at all?

Mr. BRANCH. I want to explain that. This covers a wide range of products. We get information from the telegraphic market news service, where we are associated together, of a number of shipped-in products too, for the benefit of the local dealer, and we just add those to our report, and it makes it of special value then to the dealer, who gets a full report, not only on the home-grown stuff, but on the shipped-in products, as well.

Mr. THOMPSON. Your man does not work up that. He took that from this other department.

Mr. BRANCH. Where we are in joint offices he takes it from the other department, so we don't have to use any time securing it. That just applies to joint offices. Where there are not joint offices, when our man is going around to get information from the commission men on the home grown stuff, he gets the prices at the same time on shipped-in products.

Mr. MCLAUGHLIN. You don't get any of that telegraphic stuff except you get it from one of your own men associated with you, one that does carry on this general telegraphic business?

Mr. BRANCH. That is correct; yes, sir.

Mr. THOMPSON. You have none of that yourself independent of any other office?

Mr. BRANCH. No, sir; absolutely none.

Mr. THOMPSON. That is true as to every city in which you carry on this work?

Mr. BRANCH. That is true. The next feature of the bulletin is to give a brief description of the market, bringing out the salient and interesting points about the market. We treat the farmers' market and the wholesale district separately, so if a grower is selling on the farmers' market he can look on the farmers' market report there and see the most important things about the market that morning, told in a kind of short story form. Next we give a table of the products. In some cities we give the accurate supplies, where they have taken it down on slips and know exactly the number of barrels, crates, and bushels of stuff that passes over the wholesale market. In other places, where that job is too large, our man gets a general estimate, a close estimate, and expresses it in terms of light, heavy, and moderate, opposite each different product, so that farmer knows whether apples are heavy, light, or moderate. He can judge in that way whether to sell then or hold. Then we give the prices that the farmers receive on the farmers' market, separately, and then the prices that the wholesale and commission dealers are receiving. If a farmer sells on the farmers' market, he looks in that column. If he leaves his stuff at the commission dealer's, he looks in this column and sees what the commission dealer is selling for, so when his account sales comes in from the commission man he can check each day exactly what his stuff ought to have brought.

The CHAIRMAN. Anything further on that?

Mr. BRANCH. I just want to add one thing. A letter we have from one of the growers who has received our report says, "As soon as I began getting your bulletin I changed my commission merchant."

The other phase of the service is the service to consumers. The consumers never before have had any kind of an accurate market news service given to them in a way they can understand it. What little has been given is given irregularly by newspapers, and we have found in all of our investigations that it has been very inaccurate, and mostly placed on the market page, where a housewife never would look, and she couldn't understand it if she read it, because of the technical signs that are used in market reports. So the consumers or the housewife, so to speak, have never had any market news service of any kind they could understand or use intelligently in their buying. Our man, of course, is in a position, with all of this information on the local market, to prepare something for the consumers' side which is very valuable. So the first thing in the morning after he gets this information he sits down and prepares what we call our Consumers' Press Report. That report is distributed almost entirely through the local city press. We have a very small mailing list—only to heads of organizations, labor unions, clubs, women that are carrying on home demonstration work, etc., but no general circulation by mail outside of such persons—the other is all through the local press. That report has to be gotten in early, of course, in the moring, by 10.30 or 11 o'clock, in order to be printed that same afternoon.

Mr. McLaughlin. You have to pay for any of these inserts in newspapers?

Mr. Branch. No. As a matter of fact, we are getting thousands and thousands of dollars worth of space in newspapers, even at a period when newspaper space was at a very great premium, which in effect advertises farm products to the people of the cities.

The Chairman. Do the Washington papers print that?

Mr. Branch. Here is a report right here from the Washington Star, "Marketing Guide for Washington Consumers." In general, the form is somewhat the same as the grower's report. We divide the products first into "abundant," "normal," and "scarce" classifications. Of course, that means to the housewife either cheap, medium, or high prices. Next, we put in text form a popular story of the conditions of the market, written in a simple way, without a single technical expression, so that she can understand it. In that text we aim to tell her every day the products in heavy supply. We always dwell on this, so as to throw the demand on to the products that are glutting the market. In that way we relieve that situation, and that is the most valuable part of this part of the service so far as the producer is concerned.

Mr. Thompson. How many papers in Washington print that?

Mr. Branch. Times, Star, and Herald.

Mr. Thompson. How often does that come out? I see it about once a month.

Mr. Branch. Unfortunately, the editor of the Times sees no value in this text comment telling housewives about what products are plentiful, when to buy for canning, etc., so he blue pencils that, and uses the abundant, normal, and scarce classification and the products and prices.

Mr. Thompson. Sometimes he doesn't even use that?

Mr. Branch. I couldn't say positively, for I don't follow it every night, but throughout the summer I think it was in practically every day; and now, when the season is lightening up, so far as home-grown stuff is concerned, it is occasionally left out, but it is in there pretty regularly, I believe. The Star, since the heavy casualty lists have been coming in in the last month or two, and because of the great difficulty in printing their paper on account of their big circulation, has not been running it regularly. It takes considerable time to set up and they have been pressed to the limit. Previous to that time it was run every day, from last August until along in November sometime. They have promised to take it up again, just as soon as they have space enough to devote to it.

Mr. THOMPSON. This is here in Washington, right under your nose. Away from here, do you know whether they publish it?

Mr. BRANCH. Yes; the Providence Journal, I think, for two years, has not missed a day in printing it and giving it two columns of space as large as that practically every day. The Springfield Republican, I may state, when the Government asked them to reduce the size of their paper, felt they could not devote so much space to it, so they said "We will take it once a week, but not oftener." In a week or two they were back, saying "We want it every day; our readers demand it;" and they are giving space to it every day of the week. I confess, in some of the cities, the problem of getting newspaper space in the big dailies is very difficult, but this condition is not general at all. One of the largest papers in Chicago which was pressed for space to the limit on account of restrictions in the size of paper, still decided to hold our feature, because of its value to consumers.

The CHAIRMAN. What is the population of Providence?

Mr. BRANCH. Between 250,000 and 300,000, I think.

The CHAIRMAN. Do you plan to put an agent in all cities of that size in the United States ultimately?

Mr. BRANCH. That brings up, of course, the point of expansion. In a way, there is no logical end to the value of this service, so far as the grower is concerned, but of course, viewing it from the standpoint of how far we could go in developing it, there is a logical end. We have been thinking of that very carefully and feel that it probably would not be advisable for us to go into cities of much less than 100,000 population.

Mr. THOMPSON. Why not? Why are not the people in cities of 50,000 entitled to it?

Mr. BRANCH. They are entitled, in a way. It is simply a matter of expense. We can put a man in a city of from 150,000 to 250,000, and handle the service with the same equipment it would take in a city of 25,000 or 50,000. In the larger city he might be serving from several hundred to a thousand growers tributary to that city, while in the smaller city he would be serving only a hundred or so. There hardly is a limit, however, to the good you could do in expanding the service.

The CHAIRMAN. Is there a possibility of organizing the truck growers adjacent to a city like Washington, so that, after you have demonstrated the value of this kind of work, they themselves might, through their organization, employ someone to do this work for them?

Mr. BRANCH. I have a record of a statement made by one of the officials of the Cook County Truck Growers' Association, at Chicago, comprising several thousand truck growers and farmers around there. In a comment that was sent in to our local representative, they say: "Our association has been trying to give a service of this kind for years, and has failed. This is the first time that we have ever been able to secure accurate market quotations." Another one said, "Since getting your report I have changed my commission man." Doubtless he found out he was not getting correct account sales. I have scores and scores of comments from growers, some of them I'd like the privilege of putting into the record.

The CHAIRMAN. By the way, gentlemen, Mr. Brand has suggested it might be interesting to the committee, after each of these news-service items, to insert in the record a few excerpts from memoranda and letters he has received of criticism and commendation. I think it would be advisable for the committee to have them.

Mr. ANDERSON. Of course; we know that people are glad to get any kind of service they get for nothing. There's nothing in that proposition.

The CHAIRMAN. That may be true. At the same time I'd like to see them myself.

Mr. HAUGEN. To what extent have the consumers of Washington been benefited by this service?

Mr. BRANCH. Mr. Haugen, the only way we can measure that, of course, has been comments that are sent in.

Mr. HAUGEN. Comments from whom?

Mr. BRANCH. From consumers, and consumers' organizations.

Mr. HAUGEN. Here in the city of Washington?

Mr. BRANCH. Yes.

Mr. HAUGEN. Can you name any of those consumers or organizations that are particularly pleased with this service and acknowledge the benefit?

Mr. BRANCH. I can not. I can in other cities. We have only recently established the service in Washington, and I am not in as close touch with the work right here as I am in other places where we have had it going longer.

Mr. HAUGEN. This is a fair sample of the market reports carried in the papers?

Mr. BRANCH. Yes.

Mr. HAUGEN. You call that a market report?

Mr. BRANCH. Call it what?

Mr. HAUGEN. A market report?

Mr. BRANCH. Yes.

Mr. HAUGEN. Where do you find the market report in this piece of paper? This seems to be entirely a Food Administration proposition.

Mr. BRANCH. We cooperate with the local Food Admisistrator in quoting fair retail prices to the consumer.

Mr. HAUGEN. You are not quoting prices as to the cost to the retailers. You say "Fair prices to the consumer to-day." You say "if consumers are charged on any day prices in excess of the prices published on that day in the fair-price-to-consumer column they should immediately bring the matter to the attention of the District Food Administrator's office?"

Mr. BRANCH. Yes, sir.

Mr. HAUGEN. Take, for instance, here is celery. It is quoted here, it costs 3½ to 8 cents, and the fair price 4½ to 11 cents. Do you contend that celery is sold at from 4½ to 11 cents?

Mr. BRANCH. Yes.

Mr. HAUGEN. Isn't it sold in excess of that?

Mr. BRANCH. Those were the fair prices on celery on that day.
Mr. HAUGEN. We are speaking of market prices.
Mr. BRANCH. I would say that probably 90 per cent of celery on that day sold within that range of prices. I did not describe many of the details of the service, of course. I didn't want to take your time. In Washington we have been cooperating with the District Food Administration.
Mr. HAUGEN. Is this the latest report you have here, marked September 25?
Mr. BRANCH. That is just one I selected at random from our files, to give an idea of what it looks like in print.
Mr. HAUGEN. Well, this is a matter that is entirely outside of your office, if it is enforced at all?
Mr. BRANCH. If the fair prices are enforced it is a matter for the local food administrator, with whom we are cooperating in this particular city.
Mr. HAUGEN. You were then cooperating with the Federal food administrator?
Mr. BRANCH. Yes.
Mr. HAUGEN. Through this food administrator?
Mr. BRANCH. Yes, through the District Food Administrator.
Mr. HAUGEN. Absolutely and entirely outside of your office?
Mr. BRANCH. That particular phase of the work on fair retail prices. The enforcement of that is up to the District Food Administrator.
Mr. HAUGEN. Who fixed these prices?
Mr. BRANCH. That is quite a long story, but I will be very glad to explain that.
Mr. HAUGEN. Was it fixed by you or the food admistration?
Mr. BRANCH. The routine work of arriving at the fair prices is done by our agent. That is done by having a committee of retailers sitting in with the Food Administrator and certain members of our office, in order to determine what we believe to be a fair percentage of gross profit to the retailer on each different product on which we quote. For instance, we find that potatoes can be handled by the average retailer at a gross profit say of from 18 to 20 perc cent on the selling price.
Mr. HAUGEN. I was asking by whom. I am not interested in that part of it.
Mr. BRANCH. When we arrive at a fair percentage of profit we apply that to the wholesale price of a product for that particular day.
Mr. HAUGEN. You say " we do." The question is, do you do it, or the other people do it?
Mr. BRANCH. We do it.
Mr. HAUGHEN. Well. This has been all over the country, hasn't it? Every little town in the whole country?
Mr. BRANCH. In 16 different cities.
Mr. HAUGEN. I am speaking about what has been done. The Food Administration has been doing this very thing in practically every little town in the United States?
Mr. BRANCH. On staple food products, but not on perishables. They haven't touched perishable products at all, and that is what we are mainly interested in.

Mr. HAUGEN. I will bring over some of my county papers, and I think I can convince you, if you will accept the evidence.

Mr. BRANCH. I would not say there isn't a city in the country that hasn't done it; but I am in close touch with what has been done and I feel sure that they have not handled fruits and vegetables.

Mr. HAUGEN. Tell us to what extent the consumers of Washington have been benefited by it.

Mr. BRANCH. There is no satisfactory way of measuring that.

Mr. HAUGEN. How do the prices in Washington compare with other cities—as stated here by Mr. Thompson, right under your nose? You are asking for $3,000,000 appropriation. We ought to have some results right here in the city of Washington, from this great bureau. And it is a great bureau. I am not finding fault with the bureau.

Mr. BRANCH. On July 23, we made a study of comparative retail prices in a number of the large cities of the country, and on the products that we got our quotations on Washington did not average any higher than other cities of comparable size, except on meats. The other products we got quotations on varied back and forth. Washington might be a cent higher on this, and a cent lower on something else. So we couldn't draw any conclusions on anything but on meats. They, as a class, were uniformly higher in Washington than in any other city in which we secured our prices, except Boston. Now, then, we weighted those products——

Mr. HAUGEN. You are speaking of meats. That is under the control of one corporation, and I take it they maintain a uniform price all through the country. How about the other foods, that you might have some control over?

Mr. BRANCH. The prices on fruits and vegetables, for instance, did not average higher in Washington than in many of the other cities.

Mr. HAUGEN. A report was given out some time ago, and the general contention is that prices in Washington are much higher than anywhere in the country.

Mr. BRANCH. I was just going to explain how that conclusion was reached. It means little to know that celery is higher in one place than another, when it cuts so little figure in a person's eating expenses. Proper weights were put on the different classes of food according to the amount of money the average family spends for that particular class of food. If beef, for instance, forms 10 per cent of the average expenditure of the average family, we give that a weight that would put it in its proper relation to the other products. Therefore, when we came to our final conclusions, the fact that meats in Washington were uniformly higher than in other cities, multiplied by the very heavy weights as a result of relative position meats hold in the average family's diet, it made the average of Washington prices way up, so Washington appeared higher, I think, with one exception, than any other place in the country.

Mr. HAUGEN. Your contention then is prices in Washington are very reasonable, and that they have been materially reduced by this service?

Mr. BRANCH. My contention is, that with the exception of meats, prices in Washington were so little different from other cities of comparable size in the country from which we got statistics that the variations were not worth considering.

Mr. HAUGEN. You claim to know the difference between the selling and the buying price. Speaking of meats, can you tell me the actual price received by the packer, and the price paid by the consumer, and who gets the difference?

Mr. BRANCH. No; that is entirely out——

Mr. HAUGEN. How many hands does it pass through, and how many profits are taken out, before it reaches the consumer?

Mr. BRANCH. That is out of my province entirely.

Mr. HAUGEN. You can investigate it.

The CHAIRMAN. He says he has not investigated it.

Mr. HAUGEN. I am asking about these other things. How does it come that no investigation is made as to the more important products, and so much attention is given to celery and a few little things?

Mr. BRANCH. Well, I think attention is being given——

Mr. HAUGEN. Attention is being paid to ascertaining the selling price of celery and a few things on the farm, but no attention seems to be given to the packers—large packers of meats and the prices paid.

Mr. BRANCH. That would have been a question to take up with Mr. Hall yesterday.

Mr. HAUGEN. Isn't that of as much importance to the consumer as the celery?

Mr. BRANCH. More importance.

Mr. HAUGEN. Why can not it be given some consideration and investigation?

Mr. BRAND. It is given a great deal of consideration.

Mr. HAUGEN. You seem to have no knowledge.

Mr. BRAND. His branch of the work does not relate to that particular topic.

Mr. HAUGEN. I presume you have to study it to investigate——

Mr. BRANCH. Other men in the bureau do that. That is not in my field at all.

Mr. HAUGEN. You are dealing with market reports?

Mr. BRANCH. Yes.

Mr. HAUGEN. Doesn't this deal with meats here?

Mr. BRANCH. No.

Mr. HAUGEN. Just perishable products?

Mr. BRANCH. Yes.

Mr. HAUGEN. Who deals with the others?

Mr. BRAND. Mr. Hall, who appeared yesterday, largely.

Mr. HAUGEN. Does he deal with the retail marketing of meats?

Mr. BRAND. Mr. Branch is aiming to expand his work to include that feature, poultry, butter, eggs, and those other very substantial foods, but in the local phases and not in the interstate phases.

Mr. HAUGEN. You are at the head of the bureau. How much attention has been given to the meat supply and the cost of production and the selling price and profits along that line?

Mr. BRAND. Mr. Chairman, that involves a discussion of an item which is not in this bill, but I'd like to answer that question.

The CHAIRMAN. It is not in this bill?

Mr. BRAND. It is not in this bill, but I'd be very glad to answer it. We have under license 2,440 live-stock commission merchants, stockyards, and other persons dealing in live stock in, and in connection with, stockyards. We have a complete system of supervision, under war-time power and emergency appropriations, and we are giving a very great deal of attention to the subjects Mr. Haugen mentions. They do not happen to be in connection with this item, or in this bill, in that particular supervisory sense; but much attention has been given to all of these questions under the items of work that Mr. Hall handles and which in part he discussed yesterday. At least, numerous phases of the work he discussed yesterday. As the result of that work we have cooperated with the Federal Trade Commission and with other agencies. We have assisted in the preparation of legislation at the request of the other end of the Capitol, and we have carried on a very great amount of work along that line. I would not like it to appear in the record, merely because Mr. Branch is not engaged in that work, that nothing is being done in that direction.

Mr. HAUGEN. When may we have the benefit of your investigations and your expert knowledge on this proposition?

Mr. BRAND. You are having the benefit of that every day.

Mr. HAUGEN. We have not had it so far.

Mr. BRAND. It appears every day. We have better practices in the market. We have a greater degree of cooperation with the stockmen than ever before.

Mr. HAUGEN. You are familiar with the Federal Trade Commission—its report. That report has been questioned. Now, then, you seem to have given a good deal of consideration to a number of things. You have had a good deal of money, and I presume it has been wisely expended, and I was in hopes you might throw light on those reports, and we might know something about it.

Mr. BRAND. A great deal has been accomplished.

Mr. HAUGEN. Well, if it has, we would like to know. Could you indicate——

Mr. BRAND. Would you like a specific example?

Mr. HAUGEN. Yes; if you have one.

Mr. BRAND. There is a certain stockyards in the United States, whose president has for many years enjoyed a salary of $25,000 a year, who probably has not given 30 days' service a year to that particular stockyards. When we began our investigations and supervisory work, we took it up with the gentleman, discussed it with him, pointed out the apparent unwisdom and unfairness of his participating in the profits of that concern to that extent, and he voluntarily renounced the salary of $25,000, which was coming out of the people utilizing the facilities of that stockyards. That is just a single instance of the economies effected. We are effecting economies, better service, better car movement, and all of the things that go to make up a better live stock industry.

Mr. HAUGEN. Now, you are drifting away from it, but that is an interesting question. To what extent have the shippers been benefited now, so far as that $25,000 salary——

The CHAIRMAN. I suggest that that is entirely apart from this item here. If the committee wants to investigate this whole question, we ought to do it in the proper way.

Mr. HAUGEN. Now, Mr. Chairman, we start to find out something and we get drifted away, and we never get to the point.

The CHAIRMAN. It is simply because members won't let these men get to the point.

Mr. HAUGEN. I am trying to get to the point. We are drifting in different directions. We started on the markets and meats, and we are now at the stockyards. I didn't start any stockyards discussion.

The CHAIRMAN. Who started it?

Mr. HAUGEN. Mr. Brand drifted into stockyards instead of marketing meats. If we could get a direct answer to a question, I think we might make better time.

Mr. BRAND. In the very next item some of these investigations have been touched upon, but I did not want it to appear in the record, and in fairness to the department it should not appear——

The CHAIRMAN. Anything further, Mr. Branch?

Mr. HAUGEN. I have been here all the time, and I haven't heard anything discussed about this proposition. Mr. Hall appeared here and took up a good deal of time, but I don't know that he threw any light on this.

Mr. MCLAUGHLIN. Do your records show, or are you able to tell us or give us anything like a correct estimate of the number of issues of the newspapers through the country in which the market reports, such as you have shown us here, appear daily?

Mr. BRANCH. We are putting in a system effective January 1st that will show that exactly, and I can give you that at the end of January. Because of the difficulties under which we organized this service—we have been handicapped to the limit in getting any men at all—it has prevented our developing certain refinements in the work to the extent we should like it to do. We have had to do certain things without keeping all the records and reports we should have under normal circumstances and which we are going to have from now on.

Mr. BRAND. Estimate it.

Mr. BRANCH. That would be almost impossible. It appears probably in an average of two to three large city dailies in practically all of the 16 cities in which we operate. They have circulations all the way from 50,000 to 500,000 a day. Of course I have reference to the consumers' press report and not the growers' bulletin.

Mr. MCLAUGHLIN. Just one more question. It was brought out yesterday that in many cases newspapers do not publish these matters as you give them, and that some of their statements are wrong and misleading, and deceive those who read them. Do you pay any attention so that you will know whether or not a newspaper publishes what you give it?

Mr. BRANCH. We certainly do, Mr. McLaughlin. We check the report over practically every day. I can give you a specific instance of how it happens that occasionally the papers publish reports that are inaccurate. In Cleveland, for instance, our man furnished the Cleveland paper not only with the consumers' report, but with a report for the financial page, a wholesale report on fruits and vegetables, and certain other products he got from one of the other bureau men in the joint office. The Cleveland paper put it under a headline of the Bureau of Markets, but threw in with it, as they were setting up the paper, reports on rabbits, geese, ducks, and a lot of other products they got from some commercial service, and it all appeared under the heading "Bureau of Markets" for a day or two, until we caught it up and asked them to change it. They do not always do exactly what we ask them to do, by the way, but generally their cooperation is quite cordial. So that is just one illustration of how it might happen, but it does not go on any longer than until we can catch it and have the paper change it.

The thought I wished to add, Mr. Chairman, was I think every man in the Bureau of Markets, who has had any thing to do with investigational work will agree that one of the most difficult tasks we have is to help the small farmer, who has a miscellaneous assortment of surpluses of various products to sell, who is not big enough to ship in carload lots, and who does not belong to a cooperative association. One of our hardest problems is to help that type of farmer to market his product to better advantage. The City Market Reporting Service caters especially to this type of grower.

The CHAIRMAN. I am sure I appreciate that. I think all the members of the committee do. I still have this in mind, however: How far we can go with this work——

Mr. BRANCH. I did not quite finish that. I said that the logical place to stop would be in cities of about 100,000 population. That does not mean every city in the county of that population. If it is not in a good agricultural district, and if we can not reach a large number of producers around it, if the food problems are not acute— I do not believe the work should be taken up. As a general idea, however, I think we should stop at cities of about that size.

EXTRACTS FROM LETTERS REGARDING THE LOCAL MARKET-REPORTING SERVICE.

These letters were received from growers, dealers, and consumers and are arranged by cities:

CHICAGO.

At a meeting of the board of directors of our association held on July 13, with 36 members present, and at which the work of the market reporting service was taken up, it was considered to be the most important and necessary move to improve the marketing conditions in the city of Chicago. It builds the foundation for more and better-regulated markets, notes the fluctuation of prices of vegetables and other perishable products, relieves the ignorance of the public at large as to the conditions, movements, and prices of these products, which is the main cause of the failure of regulating and establishing markets in Chicago.

The present report of the West Randolph Street Market has thus far worked with wonderful success, it assists the farmer or gardener to sell his produce quicker and prevents the scalper from getting the advantage of the ignorant producer regarding the market prices; it creates quick action with the buyer, as it keeps him posted of the value of the article that he buys; it will prevent a fair percentage of the unusual raise and drop in prices; it will encourage production, prevent waste. * * *

This market report, which has been hoped for by farmers and gardeners for a number of years, and which can not be satisfactorily issued by any other agency, is proving to be a great encouragement to the farmers and gardeners of this vicinity.—*The Cook County Truck Gardeners and Farmers Association (about 2,000 members).*

The daily market report bulletin inaugurated by the Department of Agriculture is, I am sure, the most satisfactory and beneficial service so far instituted for the market growers.—*John L. Johnson (grower).*

I am very well pleased with these market reports. I find them to be as nearly correct as possible, and hope you will continue this for the years to come.— *Fred C. Mahler & Sons (growers).*

I have received your marketing bulletins and appreciate them very much, as it keeps one posted on what things are worth. * * * Keep the good work moving. We will be there with the goods.—*Fred W. Holm, Worth, Ill. (grower)*.

Your daily reports are of so much value to us that we would not like to be without them again. We now have the necessary information to put the right price on our vegetables. Over 1,000 consumers are now buying from the farmers' wagons on Elston Avenue. It opens the road for the producer to the consumer and cuts down the waste. I believe the reports are more necessary and do more good in Chicago than in any other city. I hope you will continue the service.—*August Geweke, director, Illinois Farmers' Institute (grower)*.

We believe this to be a most praiseworthy work. From it will evolve the municipal market.—*Mrs. J. A. Armour, president Catholic Woman's Club of Rogers Park (consumer)*.

I desire to voice my appreciation of the careful and efficient manner evidently employed by your office in obtaining and disseminating this useful information.

Especially do I desire to approve of the information given to housewives pertaining to the abundance or scarcity of certain commodities, also of the advice pertaining to the proper time for canning fruit.

You are doing a great work meriting the fullest support of every patriotic distributor and it should result in benefiting the producer as well as the consumer.—*Sol Westerfeld, Secretary, National Retail Grocers' Association.*

The following are typical of the hundreds of written comments received:

"It is the greatest help the farmers ever had. It assists you in all lines of work."

"The report has been of assistance to me as it gives me the correct market prices and a number of times I was able to sell before going to the market, especially in the season when I was short of help."

"In numerous ways it has helped me. One day it saved me on cabbage alone $10.00."

"It is of great value to a person who does not go to the market every day."

"It keeps us posted on prices so that the scalpers can't get the best of us."

BOSTON.

No one would wish to have it discontinued here now, after one year's trial. The market gardeners are getting a more even price for their goods than formerly and are avoiding gluts through the publicity given by the market reports. We expect even better results this year than last year.—*I. W. Stone, President, Boston Market Gardeners, and Massachusetts State Vegetable Growers.*

"Find bulletins almost indispensable—papers' reports are not changed—farmers' papers too far behind."

"There is nothing issued that is any more beneficial to market gardeners than this bulletin."

"I think this has been the greatest help to the farmer that the Government has undertaken."

CLEVELAND.

"I value it very highly, could not be without it. It gives me the finest information on everything a farmer grows, and I know just what to sell and ask for everything I sell."

"Words can not express the value it has been to me. If I miss it a day I am lost."

DENVER.

"I find it of immense value because I know what to ask for my produce both on the market and on the farm. Heretofore, there were many growers who sold their produce at a loss early in the morning, not knowing the market price of the day previous. This is a movement I would like to see grow until it covers every agricultural product. Would like to see more power to the Marketing Division of the Department of Agriculture."

"The numerous ways the bulletin has been of help to me and my neighbors is beyond conception. I firmly believe it has a tendency to stabilize prices; and also to help sell produce when the market is very heavy."

"It downs the little stories that one gets from the buyers in regard to the different prices they are paying and the amount of produce on the market. I value it as an excellent aid to the grower."

"It greatly helps us in getting as much as our products are worth. Without it we are rather at the mercy of commission men."

SPRINGFIELD, MASS.

I take pleasure in saying that these reports have been an important and valuable feature and that their painstaking preparation by your representative has constituted, to my mind, a valuable service to the people in this community.—*Richard Hooker, editor and publisher, The Springfield Republican.*

I should like to express my appreciation of the local market reports which the United States Bureau of Markets furnishes. * * * I feel that whatever we are able to print under our caption: "The Market Basket" is comprehensive, up-to-the-minute, and helpful to our women readers.—*Eleanor Richards, editor, woman's page, The Springfield Daily News.*

PROVIDENCE, R. I.

You have no idea how our consumer-customers depend on it to see if we are giving them a square deal.—*H. W. Tinkham & Son, market gardeners, Warren, R. I.*

At the meeting of the Housewives League I spoke of the Providence Market Guide as prepared by you. * * * I asked how many of those present were in the habit of consulting it and found it a help in housekeeping. The response was immediate and general. * * *

I feel that the publication of these prices is of the greatest value, and it is something that as a league we have long wanted and now much appreciate.—*Rose C. Hilton, Providence, R. I., president of the Providence Housewives League.*

STATEMENT OF MR. CHARLES J. BRAND, CHIEF OF THE BUREAU OF MARKETS, UNITED STATES DEPARTMENT OF AGRICULTURE—Continued.

The CHAIRMAN. All right, Mr. Brand, your next item is on page 244, item 125, investigations relating to the production, transportation, storage, preparation, marketing, manufacture, and distribution of agricultural food products. Gentlemen, we are making very slow progress here with these hearings.

Mr. THOMPSON. Nearly all of these are new items.

Mr. BRAND. This is an old item, and there is no increase in that.

Mr. HAUGEN. If we are not to have any information, why have these hearings at all?

The CHAIRMAN. There is a limit. I believe two-thirds of our time has been spent in asking the same questions over.

Mr. HAUGEN. Well, you have to ask many of these questions a dozen times before you get an answer. That is the trouble. If we could get answers to our questions we could get along much better.

Mr. ANDERSON. If we can spend $3,000,000 getting information about canary-bird seed, spinach, and so on, we ought to spend a little time getting information about those $3,000,000.

The CHAIRMAN. Sure. We have spent a day and a half on this.

Mr. BRAND. Mr. Chairman, this particular investigation, as we have conducted it, is carried on in cooperation with the office of farm management and the Federal Trade Commission. The particular phases to which we give attention are the costs of marketing and distribution, and in connection with that work we have been following specific shipments of cattle from the ranches and the ranges and the farms through the market and through practically to the packing-house trade. At that point the investigations of the Trade

Commission come in, and are carried up to the point of distribution of the products. We have gotten marketing and distributing costs on nearly 3,000 head of cattle, on about 4,000 head of sheep, and on an average number—on nearly 30,000 head of hogs.

Mr. ANDERSON. Have these costs ever been published?

Mr. BRAND. No, because the investigation is not yet complete. It is very easy to go wrong in these fields of costs of production and costs of distribution and marketing, and we feel that the only wise way is to be thorough in our investigation, sound in the plans and policies that underlie the investigation, and not too hasty merely in order to secure publicity in the publication of conclusions. This work is rapidly approaching the point where we will expect to begin to publish such conclusions, however.

Mr. THOMPSON. How long have you been going over this?

Mr. BRAND. This is the second season.

Mr. THOMPSON. Been working at it two years and not published anything yet?

Mr. BRAND. We haven't published anything specifically on this particular matter, though we have published a bulletin covering the general field, which gives more information than was ever before brought together in a single cover. We have published information before, but not on these specific costs.

Mr. THOMPSON. Have you arrived at your conclusions and submitted them to the secretary's office on the cost of production?

Mr. BRAND. No. The cost of production work has been handled by the office of farm management. We have had an arrangement dividing the field, and the office of farm management handles certain phases within their province, we handle certain phases within our province, and the trade commission handles certain other phases.

Mr. McLAUGHLIN. Within your province, what have you to do with the matter of the production—that is the first of the words used here? Yours is a marketing proposition. Yours is the Bureau of Markets.

Mr. BRAND. Yes.

Mr. McLAUGHLIN. What has the Bureau of Markets to do with production?

The CHAIRMAN. This language was inserted on the floor of the House by Mr. Mann.

Mr. BRAND. Yes. We have nothing to do with production, and for that reason we have a cooperative arangement with the office of farm management, which has had certain investigational work proceeding in that field.

Mr. McLAUGHLIN. Shouldn't that word "production" then be stricken out?

Mr. BRAND. That is a question for you gentlemen to determine.

The CHAIRMAN. What character of work have you done under the word "production"?

Mr. BRAND. This bureau does none.

The CHAIRMAN. Then it has no place here at all?

Mr. BRAND. No so far as we——

The CHAIRMAN. Make a note, Mr. McLaughlin, to strike it out, so we won't have to take that up again.

Mr. McLaughlin. As to the "manufacture" and "preparation" of farm products, what has the Bureau of Markets to do with the preparation and manufacture of farm products?

Mr. Brand. We have to do with certain phases of manufacture. For instance, we study cotton spinning and testing, and things of that sort, under another item. In many other phases of manufacturing we are concerned, because manufacture relates so definitely to marketing and distribution. In still other phases we are not particularly interested.

Mr. McLaughlin. I remember very well the discussion we have had on that other item about cotton and the spinning and the tensile strength, and so on. We haven't been in entire agreement as to that, but that is another item. But under this item, what do you understand the Bureau of Markets has to do with the preparation and manufacture—they may be related—of farm products?

Mr. Brand. We are studying, for instance, in the case of certain products, canning and things of that sort. We confine ourselves to the cost of manufacture as it affects the cost of marketing. Sometimes the question of what is manufacturing is a pretty close question, and if the removal of the word is going to limit proper investigations I would suggest leaving it in. I haven't in mind a specific reason for striking it out.

The Chairman. The word "production"?

Mr. Brand. No; the word "manufacture."

Mr. McLaughlin. I am not saying you are wrong in pursuing these inquiries, but this is the Bureau of Markets, and the first thought that comes to me is that it would be your duty to study accurately conditions and methods of improving the marketing proposition, not go way back to study the feature of manufacturing and preparation, because if you pursue that to the limit, there would be no end. You could go back clear in the matter of preparation to every method pursued on the farms, in the preparation of the soil and the use of seed, and the cultivation of the crop and the harvest of it, and all that, which it strikes me is not a marketing proposition at all. If I am wrong, I'd be glad to be informed.

Mr. Brand. This much can certainly be said: We take up no phase of activity if another agency is responsible.

Mr. McLaughlin. Do you undertake to supply every deficiency in other bureaus?

Mr. Brand. No.

Mr. McLaughlin. If their line should be in a certain direction, and your line following it, is it up to you to take it up and follow it?

Mr. Brand. We do not.

Mr. McLaughlin. What about preparation. Where do you properly act in that respect?

Mr. Brand. Throughout the course of preparation for market. That is an essential part of marketing. The preparation of a product for marketing is an essential part of marketing.

Mr. McLaughlin. Be a little more specific. What do you do?

Mr. Brand. Take as an illustration the matter of fruit marketing. We take that up after the fruit is picked and goes to the packing house. We have advised many improved methods of packing, grading, branding, and things of that sort. We follow the product through from that point. All of those things are an essential part of the marketing process.

Mr. McLaughlin. Isn't that grading and packing done largely by the men who produce the article?

Mr. Brand. In many cases, yes; but in many more cases it is handled by the marketing organization, of which he is a member.

Mr. McLaughlin. Has your inquiry been of any benefit to the producer? Has it to the business man?

Mr. Brand. Decidedly so. In some cases he gets as much as 25 cents a box more for his apples than he would otherwise get.

Mr. McLaughlin. You don't take it up until after it leaves the hands of the producer?

Mr. Brand. No; we take it up while it is in the hands of the producer.

Mr. McLaughlin. My understanding of your former answer was you started in the packing houses and storage places.

Mr. Brand. Our interest in the matter starts with the harvesting of the material, in order that it may be prepared in such a manner as to reach the market in the condition that will bring to the producer the best possible return. We took up the question of handling oranges, for instance. The chairman and Mr. McLaughlin will probably recall the work done in that respect, which in its permanent effect probably saves annually to the California orange industry alone the sum of a million and a half to two millions of dollars. This results through the use of improved methods of handling oranges, lemons, and grape fruit in California.

Mr. McLaughlin. Is it necessary to make suggestions to an association like that every year?

Mr. Brand. No, no; but the field is vast. For instance, while California has put in great improvements and is working with us, I had a telegram from Mr. Powell this morning before I came to the hearing saying he wished to work with us still further. There are many improvements still to be worked out, under the leadership of the Government, in combination with the industry. In Florida they have not developed to the extent as in California, and there is great opportunity for assistance, and so on in many other cases.

Mr. McLaughlin. You are not interested in the manufacturing of farm products?

Mr. Brand. I am very much interested. Some people consider ginning cotton manufacturing. The reason I would like to leave the word in is that so many people give it such a wide meaning. Very many people contend strongly that ginning is the first process in the manufacture of cotton. I state that as an illustration.

Mr. McLaughlin. It seems to me there is danger of going too far in this line of work under the marketing proposition.

Mr. Brand. I think you can trust us not to go an inch farther than is necessary to secure the results for the people of the United States that you gentlemen desire. We always come back to you, too, and reveal to you what we are doing.

Mr. McLaughlin. I don't think the questioning of these matters indicates a lack of confidence in those doing the work. There is a duty devolving on Congress, though, and I think if we shift that, or shirk it, and say we will leave it to the discretion of an official, we are not doing our duty. I have noticed a great many times you put into the law, "This thing is to be done in the discretion of the head of the bureau." That is necessary a great many times; you can not do it in any other way; but in many respects or in many other matters it is the duty of Congress, if it has an opinion, to express it, and put it into the law. I don't wish anything I have said to show lack of confidence in the head of this bureau, but there are certain duties devolving on Congress, and it ought to perform every one of them.

The CHAIRMAN. Anything further?

Mr. RAINEY. I just want to ask a question which probably to you gentlemen may appear a little foreign to the matter at issue, but in the salaries suggested here I notice "Assistants at $1,800 and $1,860." Would you briefly tell us what kind of work those assistants perform? In other words, does it require any particular skill or study or experience?

Mr. BRAND. Decidedly. These are men trained along these specific lines. Mr. Rainey, I am sure, realizes just how foolish we would look in sending a man out to a big ranch to inaugurate the study of marketing of cattle on that ranch if we sent a bumpkin out who didn't know anything about the subject. We have got to send a man who not only knows the ranch end of marketing, but the Chicago, Kansas City, or Omaha end of the marketing game, and you can not hire that kind of a man at less than those salaries.

Mr. RAINEY. Are they practical men?

Mr. BRAND. We try in all cases to get men who know the practical as well as the economic phases of things.

Mr. RAINEY. But it does not require any particular college or university study for the information?

Mr. BRAND. Employees who have had university training in economics, covering a wide range of economic subjects, are more capable generally of dealing with the subjects than men who have not had that training. We do use a very large number of men, however, who have not had any college training.

Mr. RAINEY. I do not object to the salary at all. It is just a point of inquiry. For instance, take these men getting $1,800 a year in this particular department that are now on the pay roll. Have these men doing the active work made any preparatory study in order to fit them for this work?

Mr. BRAND. A great many of them have. In the live-stock work we have taken a very large number of men who have not had college training, but we do know the business from A to Z.

Mr. RAINEY. Is it difficult to get men of this kind, with information at hand as the result of practical experience and study, for $1,800 a year?

Mr. BRAND. It is exceedingly difficult to get the class of men we want at any price. We have got to content ourselves with what we can get in the end, and do the best we can with the material we have. These men are so valuable that they are constantly being offered higher salaries. One of them is just now leaving us. He so reported to me yesterday. He is to receive a salary of $2,000 a year more than we are paying. In other words, $5,000 a year. There is not a week when we do not lose from one to several of these men because some one else finds them so much more valuable to them.

Mr. HAUGEN. How many applications do you have for positions in the local service?

Mr. BRAND. We don't have a great volume of applications.
Mr. HAUGEN. How many have you on the list of applicants for positions?
Mr. BRAND. I can not say.
Hr. HAUGEN. You have no trouble in filling them?
Mr. BRAND. Yes; we have infinite difficulty.
A man was in to see me yesterday who is going back to his home in Texas, one of our warehousing experts. We were paying him $2,700, but he could not afford to stay here any longer at that figure. We have held several examinations, and are still without the men.
Mr. HAUGEN. Does this work include field work, shocking of grain, and so on?
Mr. BRAND. No. We do very little, if any, work on that phase of the matter. We do try to suggest methods of handling which will bring products to the market in better condition, but very little in the matter of threshing, stacking, shocking, or anything of that sort.
Mr. HAUGEN. Another bureau does that? It is being done.
Mr. BRAND. There is very little of that work being done.
Mr. HAUGEN. Done by another bureau, isn't it?
Mr. BRAND. I don't know specifically of anyone doing it. We have, in our earlier work, given some study to that matter, naturally.
Mr. HAUGEN. What do you suggest as to the handling of grain, and how much do you do with that?
Mr. BRAND. Very little. That was done in the past and is not being done at this present moment.
Mr. HAUGEN. Nothing being done as to grain, of that kind?
Mr. BRAND. Of that sort; as a rule.
Mr. HAUGEN. To what extent do you deal with grain?
Mr. BRAND. Throughout the process of marketing we deal with grain. That comes up under three items. We do some grain work that you may be interested in under this very project, but it does not bear upon that question.
The CHAIRMAN. Suppose, Mr. Brand, you outline briefly what you intend to do with this money.
Mr. HAUGEN. I am interested now in grain. This item reads, "To make investigations relating to the production, transportation, storage, preparation, marketing, manufacture," and so on. It covers everything.
Mr. McLAUGHLIN. "Production" is to be stricken from the bill.
Mr. HAUGEN. I am trying to find out what is being done.
Mr. BRAND. We have taken, from the books of over 400 elevators in North and South Dakota, Nebraska, Oklahoma, and Colorado, figures from which we arrive at the cost of marketing the grain they handle. We determine their operating costs, depreciation, and every factor entering into marketing. We have in our hands now, and in process of being worked up by the Bureau of the Census and the Trade Commission the most comprehensive figures on the cost of handling grain in the country that have ever been developed. We have also studied the practices of commission houses, so-called wire houses, and similar industries throughout the country that operate on a very large scale. We have also studied the practices of terminal elevators, and the effect of future trading upon prices. We are working on that whole broad question, and we have in hand a mass

of most valuable data, which is now being worked up. It is the first time that such comprehensive information will be available on certain phases of grain and live-stock marketing.

Mr. ANDERSON. Will this data ever be published?

Mr. BRAND. Yes.

Mr. HAUGEN. What about the elevators? Tell us something about that. You certainly know something about that, about the practice of the elevators and the cost. What do you suggest? What is the remedy? What has been accomplished?

Mr. BRAND. I don't know just what you mean.

Mr. HAUGEN. I know that this bureau is in its infancy; but, after all, I assume you have obtained some of the prices.

Mr. BRAND. What particular question do you ask?

Mr. HAUGEN. You were referring to the elevators. What have you accomplished in any of the lines indicated?

Mr. BRAND. We have accomplished a great deal in all of this various work. Your question is so broad it is impossible to reply to it.

Mr. HAUGEN. Confine it to elevators. Cost of handling grain. How it should be done. How the present method can be improved upon.

Mr. BRAND. We find a variation in cost of from about 15 cents per bushel down to 9 mills per bushel, varying according to the number of bushels handled by the house, the efficiency in handling, and the equipment, location, and all that sort of thing. We have determined what is probably—we should be able to say when all of the figures are in—what size of unit is probably the most efficient unit, as far as operating costs, and things of that sort are concerned, what is subtracted for services rendered from the market price which the producer is paid.

Mr. HAUGEN. What you have stated is a common knowledge, which any schoolboy knows.

Mr. BRAND. The men in the grain trade were very much interested when they found it out, Mr. Haugen. I presented it to them at their national meeting at Buffalo, at which there were about 300 or 400 present, and they were very much interested. I'd like to see the schoolboy who knows about it.

Mr. MCLAUGHLIN. Did you go at it in such a way as to show how this variation exists, and how it may be avoided?

Mr. BRAND. Yes; and these grain dealers are agreeing to adopt good methods.

Mr. MCLAUGHLIN. You have learned the reason, and are able to apply it?

Mr. BRAND. In some respects we are in the midst of the work, Mr. McLaughlin; but in some features of it we have already learned; things are being done.

Mr. HAUGEN. I take it that any elevator that employs a man, say at $1,000 a year, and handles only 2,000 bushels of wheat—I take it that anybody would understand that the cost of handling that grain would be greater than one man handling 50,000; and it wouldn't take a very big schoolboy to comprehend that. What do you propose to do? Do you propose to furnish them the required number of bushels to make it a paying proposition?

Mr. BRAND. I think that question itself calls for no answer, Mr. Haugen.

Mr. HAUGEN. What is your remedy?

Mr. BRAND. We own no wheat. We control no wheat. We certainly can not promote the business of any one elevator. So I don't think the question is susceptible to an answer on my part. I can say, however, that the efficient elevator will get the business.

Mr. HAUGEN. We know that too. What are we to get out of these investigations? How are you to reduce the cost and increase the efficiency?

Mr. BRAND. If the committee would like, I'd be glad to bring here the men who are handling the specific matters, to go at length into details as to just what sort of suggestions we probably would be able to make with regard to this work. It was not my understanding that you gentlemen would go into exact details of every bit of this thing. For instance, we have devised the system of accounting which is in use by 1,200 elevators. They have adopted that voluntarily, which indicates that it is valuable to them, and gives better results. In fact I have had them write me hundreds of letters, saying the systems we furnished them result in their being able to do their accounting accurately with half their former book-keeping expense. That is just an illustration.

Mr. HAUGEN. We had a man here a number of years ago, I think Spillman, who was the one that invented that.

Mr. BRAND. No; we devised the system of accounting, and it has grown every year, and it is now published by a large number of publishing concerns.

Mr. HAUGEN. What else could we tell the public?

Mr. BRAND. That is just a chapter——

Mr. HAUGEN. What else?

Mr. BRAND. I don't happen to have in mind just this moment any specific——

Mr. HAUGEN. That is the trouble. When we get into something, it has got to be referred to somebody else.

Mr. BRAND. Mr. Haugen, I am only one man. I'd like to invite you down to my office some day and let you see how many things I have to handle.

Mr. HAUGEN. After all you have to confess we are not getting very much information.

Mr. BRAND. I can not confess that.

Mr. HAUGEN. We are not finding fault with it, because it is a big bureau, and you are not expected to have an intimate knowledge of all of the details——

Mr. BRAND. We are very glad to give you all the information we can. I have tried to do so by giving examples of the kind of improvement we are bringing about.

Mr. HAUGEN. Mr. Chairman, I think we would do better if only one would talk at a time.

Mr. BRAND. Have you some specific question?

Mr. HAUGEN. I have asked a few questions.

Mr. BRAND. What is the question?

Mr. HAUGEN. What is the result of your investigation? You said you carried on extensive investigations.

Mr. BRAND. I have shown you about the movement of cars, and the number of elevator accounts audited, in order to determine operating expenses. I have recited the specific benefit which has come from the work. Now, if you have some further specific question I'd be glad to answer any.

Mr. HAUGEN. You have stated one, your bookkeeping. I take it the number of cars has nothing to do with it.

Mr. BRAND. That is the fundamental investigation; that leads to the improvement.

Mr. HAUGEN. The number of cars being moved?

Mr. BRAND. You have to have a sufficient number in order to arrive at accurate conclusions. You can not base your conclusions on two nor a dozen, or they will surely turn out wrong.

Mr. HAUGEN. How much have you spent getting that information?

Mr. BRAND. This particular item calls, I think, for $48,000; something in that neighborhood.

Mr. HAUGEN. Then we can tell Congress and the country you have prescribed bookkeeping and you are investigating as to the number of cars moving; and that is the extent of your work, is it?

Mr. BRAND. No; I will be very glad, if you like, to submit in the record at this point a detailed statement of the work under this particular item.

Mr. HAUGEN. Well, that does not give us the information just now.

The CHAIRMAN. Anything further, gentlemen?

FOOD SUPPLY INVESTIGATIONS.

SCOPE OF WORK.

1. These activities have been confined largely to live stock and meats, and to the principal grains entering into food and their products.
2. The Department of Agriculture has handled all the investigations concerning the cost of production of both live stock and grain, and the marketing of live stock and grain from the farm to the central and terminal markets. With reference to live stock the Federal Trade Commission handled that part of the investigation which related to the packing industry, and questions of ownership and control. With reference to grain the department and the commission worked cooperatively in the terminal markets.

COST OF PRODUCTION.

All work on the cost of producing grain was done by the office of farm management under cooperative agreement with the bureau of markets. Figures regarding the cost of producing live stock were obtained in the course of surveys made by the office of farm management, supplemented by figures obtained by employees of the bureau of markets.

COST OF MARKETING.

Live stock.—Figures were obtained on the cost of moving stock from the farms and ranches to shipping stations, of the cost of moving stock from the shipping stations direct to packing plants, and of the cost of moving stock to centralized markets and selling through public stockyards. These figures were obtained by representatives of the bureau who actually followed the stock through the various phases of marketing, reporting the data relative to each step in the marketing process. Records were also taken from the books of farmers, live-stock shippers, and managers of live-stock shipping associations concerning marketing data.

(1) *Territory covered.*—Range, country, and the corn belt.
(2) *Record of shipments.*—Four hundred and forty-four cars, containing 29,908 hogs; 129 cars, containing 2,959 cattle; 35 cars, containing 4,058 sheep.

GRAIN.

Country elevators.—1. Records have been taken from the books of over 400 elevators in North and South Dakota, Nebraska, Oklahoma, and Colorado, showing the cost per bushel of handling grain. These costs have been segregated into various factors such as operation, overhead, depreciation, labor, etc.

2. An intensive study has been made of 139 elevators in Illinois and Iowa. The study covers a 5-year period, and includes actual prices paid to farmers, purchases and sales of grain by months, the cost of handling grain per bushel, together with profits and losses. These figures disclose the actual buying average, together with the average spread by months and years.

TERMINAL ELEVATORS.

Figures have been taken from the books of several of the largest terminal elevators in Chicago. Their operations are typical of terminal elevator processes.

1. *Conditioning grain.*—An abstract has been prepared of the in and out weights by grades for five private elevators covering a period of five years. These figures include several hundred million bushels of grain and will give a clear and comprehensive idea of the results of mixing and conditioning.

2. *Sources of supply and distribution.*—Detailed purchases and sales of cash grain for a period of five-years have been taken from the original records of these firms and so classified as to show the source of grain supply, the price of heavy and light purchases, the type of dealer from whom the grain was purchased, the basis upon which it was bought, and the type of dealer to whom it was sold.

3. *Future operations.*—Abstracts have been made from the books of these companies showing in detail their operations in the future markets. These figures run into the billions of bushels, and afford an opportunity of studying the effect of futures on spot values.

WAREHOUSES.

A detailed study has been made of the operation of several large firms in Chicago. Financial statements have been examined which show profits and losses, costs of operation, and sources of income. An analysis has been made to show the occupation of the customers of and the mileage controlled by such houses, and the distribution of their branch offices and correspondents, together with the population they serve.

PIT SCALPERS.

A study has been made of "pit scalping," in order to obtain definite information regarding the actual operations of typical pit scalpers, the functions performed by such operators, and the costs of their operations.

CLEARING HOUSES.

A comparative study has been made of the methods of clearing houses in Chicago, Minneapolis, and Kansas City. In this study information has been obtained regarding the organization, membership, rules, and operations of the various commodities, with a view of ascertaining the reasons for their existence and the functions performed by each.

COMMISSION MERCHANTS.

An analysis has been made of the accounts of the largest grain commission firms in Chicago. Costs of operation have been segregated, sources of profit have been carefully analyzed, and a general study has been made to ascertain the economic function which commission merchants of this sort perform. Records were obtained from these firms regarding the purchase and sale of more than 250,000 cars of grain.

Mr. ANDERSON. I'd like to ask a question or two. What if anything is being done under the language "including the extent, manner and methods of any manipulation of the markets or control of the visible supply of such food products, or any of them?"

Mr. BRAND. In the arrangement that we made, in order that there might be no duplication in this work, Mr. Chairman, these phases of the work are handled by the Federal Trade Commission. We bring to their attention any specific cases that come to our notice in the markets where there appears to be either discrimination, unfair practices, deception, or any of those abuses which we are trying to root out.

Mr. ANDERSON. At the time that this item was put into the bill, on the floor of the House, there was pending a Congressional investigation of the methods used by packers, in connection with the stockyards, and their various other activities, and I think there was a distinct understanding that this item was put in with a view to securing to the Agricultural Department an investigation of the manipulation, or attempt to control, the markets on the part of the packers; and I have a very strong impression that the purposes of this item have been almost entirely subverted by the character of the work you have been doing under it.

Mr. BRAND. No; I think not, Mr. Anderson.

Mr. ANDERSON. I have a very distinct recollection of the purposes for which it was passed.

Mr. BRAND. My recollection is that the minority leader submitted this item, with the understanding that the work was to be jointly done with the Trade Commission, and they were given an appropriation of very much greater amount.

Mr. HARRISON. $250,000.

Mr. BRAND. $250,000. Because of the fact that their investigations covered that very difficult phase of the field involving combinations and restraints, and things of that sort.

Mr. ANDERSON. I sat next to the minority leader when this was acted upon. If there was any such understanding I did not know of it.

Mr. BRAND. I am guided wholly by the debate on the floor, which I read, and the discussion, which I have heard. As a consequence, I am unable to say, definitely, what was in his mind. However, we have called to the attention of the Federal Trade Commission many practices within the field of their investigation, under this activity, as well as under our other activities.

Mr. ANDERSON. I believe myself that the subsequent appropriation that was made for the Federal Trade Commission was based upon the theory that the Agricultural Department would not conduct the kind of investigation desired to be conducted under this item.

The CHAIRMAN. And that this item did not carry the full authority there.

Mr. ANDERSON. That is true, but that was due to a parliamentary limitation, and not to one of purpose.

The CHAIRMAN. This item as I recall it was passed before the Borland resolution was passed, wasn't it?

Mr. ANDERSON. It was passed while an investigation was pending, I think, touching the adoption of the Borland resolution.

Mr. BRAND. We have cooperated very fully and have carried out most of the investigational work, at least have it under way, that the gentlemen who are most interested in that matter were requiring. In fact, some of them have assisted us in the work.

Mr. ANDERSON. I do not wish to be understood as saying the work you are doing is not covered by the language of the appropriation, and I am simply saying I am personally disappointed in the work that is being done.

Mr. BRAND. I think the results of the next 12 months will tell much better whether there is reason for disappointment with regard to it. I think we have developed many things, Mr. Anderson, which will come to your attention later.

Mr. ANDERSON. In that connection I think it is very important that whatever information is available as to cost of production, cost of marketing, at this particular time, should be made public at the earliest possible moment.

Mr. BRAND. You would not suggest, Mr. Anderson, that if the investigators who are giving their whole attention to this believe that the results are not yet sufficiently complete to warrant it, that they should be published before they are completed?

Mr. ANDERSON. No. I only wish to say that the information ought, if possible, to be made public while it is useful, and not after its usefulness is relatively lost.

Mr. BRAND. We agree heartily with that, and I would like to have you gentlemen know that in the particular work under this item the men who have been working at the Chicago headquarters have put in all kinds of hours, day and night, and have worked like slaves. When you have to go over thousands of accounts and the books of hundreds of enterprises, in order to get the information you are after, you have to do a great deal of work, and in the end come out with a relatively small compass of information. It is not possible to do that kind of work in an offhand fashion. It is very involved and very difficult, and likewise we don't want to arrive at conclusions that are harmful to these big enterprises that are affected, and maybe do them an injustice.

Mr. HAUGEN. You were speaking about stockyards. To what extent have the abuses there been eliminated?

Mr. BRAND. There has been a very great improvement, Mr. Haugen, a very great improvement in feeding practices, in the matter of charging up feed that is not furnished, in the matter of keeping them clean and in a sanitary condition, and also in the matter of furnishing cars, and spotting cars, and all the things that make for efficient stockyards service.

Mr. HAUGEN. About spotting and furnishing cars. That has been under the control of another department.

Mr. BRAND. We are in cooperation with them. They take our suggestions for improvements.

Mr. HAUGEN. How about keeping them clean? Did you ever see the yards in the condition they are in now—as bad as they have been for the past year?

Mr. BRAND. I have recently returned from them, the one in Kansas City, at least.

Mr. HAUGEN. Take Chicago.

Mr. BRAND. I have not been to the Chicago yards for at least three months.

Mr. HAUGEN. I have not been in Kansas City, but I have in Chicago and St. Paul.

Mr. BRAND. With the volume of cattle that is moving to market there isn't the opportunity for conducting things as well as they ought to be conducted.

Mr. HAUGEN. The commission men and everybody agree they were never in such horrible condition as they are in now. The reason given is help can not be had. I suppose that is a good reason.

Mr. BRAND. Inability to secure labor in the stockyards is just as acute as anywhere. They have done everything they could do under the circumstances.

Mr. HAUGEN. It is due to the labor conditions.

Mr. BRAND. That is one of the important factors.

Mr. HAUGEN. How about the feeding? Aren't we paying more for hay than we ever did?

Mr. BRAND. I think, absolutely, yes; but the individual shipper is not being charged as much for hay by the stockyards companies. Indeed, I know that many commission firms have absolutely—and, so far as I actually know, all commission firms have stopped charging people for feed they never received.

Mr. HAUGEN. Well, assuming they are honest, and they are delivering it, what are they selling it for now?

Mr. BRAND. I don't know the price.

Mr. HAUGEN. They are selling it for two dollars a bale. A bale is how much?

Mr. BRAND. It varies greatly. About 70 pounds.

Mr. HAUGEN. Two dollars for 70 pounds. And what is the price of hay?

Mr. BRAND. About twenty dollars.

Mr. HAUGEN. Your quotation gives less than that. That is for this timothy hay?

Mr. BRAND. It is all together, and yet I am paying on my own place $22 and $23.

Mr. HAUGEN. We are speaking of stockyards. You are not running one,—a large place?

Mr. BRAND. What is the price per ton?

Mr. HAUGEN. According to your quotation "best timothy hay, $30,"—according to your quotation. Does best timothy hay go to stockyards?

Mr. BRAND. Prairie hay.

Mr. HAUGEN. What is that worth?

Mr. BRAND. Around $24 and $25, I should say.

Mr. HAUGEN. Good quality?

Mr. BRAND. Yes.

Mr. HAUGEN. Have you investigated so you can tell us the price paid for the hay they use in the stockyards?

Mr. BRAND. I can not tell you. The supervisor of the stockyards can tell you.

Mr. HAUGEN. Anyway, they pay probably not to exceed $20, or a cent a pound, and they sell it at three cents, don't they, close to three cents?

Mr. BRAND. I don't know what their selling price is. I know we have had no complaint recently from shippers as to unfair practices with reference to feed.

Mr. HAUGEN. You believe that buying hay for $140 a thousand, and selling it for $350 is a fair profit?

Mr. BRAND. None of the companies, under the rules and regulations, are aiming to make any profit out of their feed account.

Mr. HAUGEN. A committee is carrying on an investigation now, and the testimony was that hay was bought for $140 and sold at $350. Do you think that is a fair profit?

Mr. BRAND. It is not only a matter of delivering the hay itself. There is a great deal of labor cost, and things that go with it.

Mr. HAUGEN. You are satisfied that just a reasonable profit is all that is asked?

Mr. BRAND. We are carrying on at this time an investigation that involves the whole question, involving the fairness of yardage charges and commission rates, and other factors.

Mr. HAUGEN. You have taken over the stockyards?

Mr. BRAND. No, sir.

Mr. HAUGEN. When were they turned back?

Mr. BRAND. There is a bill pending in the House now to take them over.

Mr. HAUGEN. Were not the yards taken over in war time?

Mr. BRAND. They are conducted under license.

Mr. HAUGEN. That is practically taking them over.

Mr. BRAND. We prescribe the rules and regulations under which they operate.

Mr. HAUGEN. How much were the commissions reduced and the yardage reduced?

Mr. BRAND. Yard charges in most of the yards are the same as they have been for a period of years. In a few of the yards where the costs have gone up especially high, the yards companies have raised their charges. The justice of those increases are under investigation at this time, and similarly with respect to commission charges.

Mr. HAUGEN. Well, commission charges have been advanced also, haven't they?

Mr. BRAND. Yes; in a number of markets.

Mr. HAUGEN. Can you give us a single item that has been reduced?

Mr. BRAND. In a period of rising costs in war time I don't know just how they could be reduced. None of my costs have been reduced. I don't know about other people's.

Mr. HAUGEN. You know of none?

Mr. BRAND. I know we are getting much better service than ever, we have much less complaint, and we get action on complaints that we have never gotten in the past.

Mr. HAUGEN. How do you know we are getting better service?

Mr. BRAND. We have our men right there in all of the important markets, and the reports come to them from the people affected.

Mr. HAUGEN. My experience is entirely different, and I think you can find that practically every stock man will tell you the same thing, the service has not been improved upon, but that is neither here nor there. I don't suppose your man can stay in the yard and correct the service, or have much to say about the efficiency of the service. I take it the stockmen propose to run their own business in their own way, and there is very little you can do with it.

Mr. BRAND. The stockyards men have been very compliant to our regulations. They have put in better weighing facilities, and are handling stock generally more efficiently.

Mr. HAUGEN. Putting in additional scales?

Mr. BRAND. Yes.

Mr. HAUGEN. How many did you put in in Chicago?

Mr. BRAND. I don't know.

Mr. HAUGEN. Any at all?

Mr. BRAND. I don't know.

Mr. HAUGEN. Can you state you have put in a single scale——

Mr. BRAND. We haven't put in any. We have brought about improvements in those respects.

Mr. HAUGEN. They have been put in?

Mr. BRAND. Yes.

Mr. HAUGEN. In St. Paul?

Mr. BRAND. In Kansas City particularly the service has been improved greatly. We held a hearing there in order to arrive at those matters, and we succeeded in getting considerable improvements.

Mr. HAUGEN. In issuing these licenses, you assume that the charges paid all along the line were perfectly legitimate and reasonable?

Mr. BRAND. Mr. Chairman, we don't assume that, and we have in our possession at this time the complete records for the last 5 years of all the live stock commission men. We are taking those that can be safely used to arrive at a conclusion as to whether the commission men are entitled to increase those charges.

Mr. HAUGEN. How long have you been carrying on this investigation? How much money have you expended on it?

Mr. BRAND. It has been under way three months. I am unable to say how much money was expended on it.

Mr. HAUGEN. Weren't you doing some of it a year or two ago?

Mr. BRAND. No.

Mr. HAUGEN. You just told us you furnished the commission over here with information, been cooperating with them. Now, the report was made several months ago, wasn't it?

Mr. BRAND. That report resulted from certain investigations, which were carried on by a special attorney of the Federal Trade Commission.

Mr. HAUGEN. You didn't supply that information?

Mr. BRAND. That was the result of public hearings.

Mr. HAUGEN. The reports were made by the Federal Trade Commission?

Mr. BRAND. Yes.

Mr. HAUGEN. That is entirely outside of your office?

Mr. BRAND. Yes.

Mr. HAUGEN. What information have you been furnishing?

Mr. BRAND. On all of those lines you have been discussing.

Mr. HAUGEN. Anything that may be of value in the prosecution——

Mr. BRAND. Some of the cases might be made the basis for prosecution. In one case I had in mind a gentleman had taken, particularly from Iowa shippers, $32,000 simply by returning account sales that were from one to ten dollars lower than he sold the cattle for but which were within the range of the day's variations.

Mr. HAUGEN. You ran that down?

Mr. BRAND. Yes, and he has been restoring it to the shippers from whom he took it.

Mr. HAUGEN. Do you have access to the books of all the commission men?

Mr. BRAND. Yes.

Mr. HAUGEN. And the packers?

Mr. BRAND. No; I suppose we could have. I suppose if we had demanded access we could have.

Mr. HAUGEN. You could not except by order of court?

Mr. BRAND. Only with their consent, and thus far they have consented to what we have requested along those lines.

Mr. HAUGEN. Have you checked up the books of the commission men?

Mr. BRAND. Yes.

Mr. HAUGEN. Are the rakeoffs quite general?

Mr. BRAND. Not quite general, but we find a good deal of profit in the feed account.

Mr. HAUGEN. The feed account! Now, that is a very interesting question——

Mr. McLAUGHLIN. It is a big one, too. Some of us want to eat.

Mr. HAUGEN. All right. Can you tell us the difference in the price paid by the feeder and the seller? How many hands do they go through, and what are the profits?

Mr. BRAND. We are trying to bring about a more direct interchange instead of putting them through the yards; trying to bring about a direct distribution in the beginning.

Mr. HAUGEN. But you never accomplish it.

Mr. BRAND. Yes; we have accomplished quite an improvement.

Mr. HAUGEN. Ninety-nine per cent goes to the yards.

Mr. BRAND. Not that much, but a great deal.

Mr. HAUGEN. What I am interested in is the number of hands it goes through, and the rake-offs.

Mr. BRAND. It comes in to the commission man. A scalper may get hold of it, and a trader may get hold of it, it may get into the hands of the packers. It may go through four hands.

Mr. HAUGEN. Can you tell us what the scalper gets on an average, and the trader gets on an average, and the middleman?

Mr. BRAND. I think our records would show interesting information along those lines. I can not tell you off-hand.

Mr. HAUGEN. You are investigating it?

Mr. BRAND. Yes.

Mr. HAUGEN. Do you believe you will ever be able to give the committee and the country any information in regard to that?

Mr. BRAND. All of the information under those items are being handled in such a way that we hope we can allocate the expense to each of the various operations in marketing and distribution, and also indicate the hands through which they pass. It is not a simple matter by any means.

Mr. HAUGEN. What can you tell us about selling the feeders and stockers direct?

Mr. Brand. We have taken that up, and we are working with the county agents to bring about a direct interchange from one county, say in Iowa, to another county, instead of through Omaha, or through other centers. I should say several hundred thousand head have been marketed direct in that way.

Mr. Haugen. I have reference to the commission man selling directly to the feeder. A carload of cattle shipped to Chicago sold to the feeder in Kentucky. How many hands will it go through?

Mr. Brand. No reason for more than one.

Mr. Haugen. You don't know of any reason——

Mr. Brand. In many cases it only goes through one.

Mr. Haugen. Oh, no. Do you contend that a carload of cattle—that a commission man in the Chicago yards can sell a carload direct to the feeder in Kentucky?

Mr. Brand. They do in many cases. It was stated in our hearings that they do it in many cases. It has been charged that they do not, but in some markets that is quite a general practice. You can buy directly at first hand.

Mr. Haugen. I have it from the commission men themselves that it can not be done.

Mr. Brand. It varies in the different markets.

Mr. Haugen. We were discussing Chicago.

Mr. Brand. It can be done in many; and in many it is the general practice.

Mr. Haugen. There is one firm in St. Paul that does it.

Mr. Brand. There are many firms in other markets.

Mr. Haugen. What markets?

Mr. Brand. Omaha, Kansas City—I think the hearing there developed the same situation. I think a number of other markets.

Mr. Haugen. I don't want to take up any more of the time of the committee.

Mr. Rainey. All of the stockyards people show a willingness to cooperate with your bureau and give you all the information and data that might be helpful to you?

Mr. Brand. Yes.

Mr. Haugen. And isn't it true they have responded to any suggestions for improvement your bureau has suggested, and adopted them?

Mr. Brand. Very generally.

(Thereupon, at 12.50 o'clock p. m., the committee took a recess until 2.15 p. m.)

AFTER RECESS.

The Chairman. The next item, Mr. Brand, is page 245, item 147.

Mr. Brand. That is the food-products inspection work, Mr. Chairman.

The Chairman. There is an increase in that of how much?

Mr. Brand. There is an increase of $50,000, a transfer from the emergency funds. In connection with that work I wish to make a statement regarding joint offices. The bureau has a total of 171 projects or division offices in 107 branches and located in 56 different cities. 41 of the 107 offices are joint offices. In other words, we aim in every city where it can possibly be done efficiently to combine all of these units, not only under the same roof but, so far as possible, with the same general personnel to carry on their general work. That makes for a great deal of economy in the operation and makes it possible for Mr. Sherman's men and Mr. Branch's men, and each of these men to supplement each other's work without additional expense..

That has been particularly true under the item, page 145, item 126.

The CHAIRMAN. Tell the committee briefly just what your plan of operation is.

Mr. BRAND. If I may, I will ask Professor Scott to state that. I just wanted to bring out this important point concerning the joint operation of these offices for the sake of economy. Mr. Scott and Mr. Sherman operate 12 of their offices jointly, thus disposing of the necessity which would otherwise arise of employing 12 additional leaders in various cities. With that introduction I will ask Mr. Scott to present the subject.

The CHAIRMAN. All right. Mr. Scott, you may proceed.

STATEMENT OF MR. W. M. SCOTT, IN CHARGE OF MARKET INSPECTION OF PERISHABLE FOODS, BUREAU OF MARKETS, UNITED STATES DEPARTMENT OF AGRICULTURE.

Mr. SCOTT. Mr. Chairman, the food-products inspection service is so simple and its benefits are so obvious and direct that I shall require only a very few moments of time to explain it.

The law enables the Secretary of Agriculture to investigate and certify to shippers and other interested parties the quality and condition of fruits, vegetables, and other perishable farm products in the important central markets and provide for the charging of a fee.

Broadly speaking, the objects are to facilitate the distribution and marketing of farm products and prevent deterioration and waste by furnishing a medium through which shippers and receivers may settle their differences.

The certificates issued by the inspectors are received in the courts of the United States as prima facie evidence and are used as a basis for the settlement of disputes.

Mr. JACOWAY. What do you understand by the term "prima facie evidence" there? Do you mean when the certificate is issued the burden is on the other man to show the certificate is not true?

Mr. SCOTT. Yes, sir. The certificate furnishes a basis for the adjustment of controversies between the shipper and the receiver and for the settlement of loss and damage claims against the railroads. The shipper is furnished with an unbiased statement of the true condition and quality of his products upon arrival at the market so that he may be protected against unjustifiable rejections and unwarranted claims for allowances. On the other hand, the receiver is similarly benefited if the certificate shows that the quality and condition of the products are not as specified in the contract of sale, but even so the shipper is still benefited by such a certificate in that it prevents the receiver from misrepresenting the facts and claiming a greater allowance than is due him.

The Railroad Administration has recently indicated its intention of using the food products inspection certificates, when available, as a basis for adjustment of all claims. Heretofore they have had no adequate means of distinguishing between just and unjust claims. neither has the shipper had adequate evidence to support loss and damage claims against the railroads.

This service brings about a general improvement in marketing conditions from the producer through to the consumer. In the first place the producer is stimulated to the adoption of better methods of harvesting, grading, packing, and loading the products. The shipper knows that if his product is not properly graded and packed the inspection certificate at the other end will show this result.

In the market the operator who makes purchases for speculative purposes in the hope that the market will advance by the time the products arrive, and if it does not advance rejects the shipment, is practically removed by the inspection service. In other words, the temptation to make unjustifiable rejections and claims for allowances is greatly reduced.

The CHAIRMAN. Is that one of the bases of speculation—the amount of rejections that the commission merchant might make?

Mr. SCOTT. The operator will often purchase one or two or more cars of potatoes, for example, with the expectation, or rather on the gamble that when those cars arrive the market will have advanced sufficiently to make a profit. If, on the contrary, it declines, and he faces a loss he simply rejects the car and the shipper is at his mercy, then when he makes the rejection he claims an allowance. The rejection is made on the pretext that the stuff has arrived in poor condition or that it does not conform to the contract of sale—any pretext in order to make the rejection. The shipper may now call for an inspection which will reveal the true condition of the purchase.

I might cite one instance that occurred at Norfolk about a year ago. It was shortly after the inspection service was inaugurated, and shippers generally were not aware of the service. Four cars of potatoes stood on the track for 30 days while the shipper and receiver exchanged telegrams and letters trying to reach an agreement as to the allowance that should be made, the receiver having claimed that the stock was not according to the contract of sale. Finally the shipper agreed to make the allowance and settle the case. By that time the receiver had changed his mind and asked for a further allowance. This covered a period of 30 days. Four cars were tied up and put out of commission for that period of time, with consequent danger of freezing or other deterioration in the product. Finally the shipper heard an inspection service was available, wired to the Bureau of Markets and asked for an inspection. Although we had no office at Norfolk we sent a man there and made an inspection of these four cars and found they were No. 1 potatoes in first-class condition, and the receiver was forced to take them at the original sale price. That is the practical result of the inspection service.

Now, in answer to the chairman's question in regard to the markets covered. The service is in operation now in 45 markets.

The CHAIRMAN. Could you put in the record the names of the cities?

Mr. Scott. I shall be very glad to put that in the record.
(The statement referred to follows:)

1. List of markets in which food-products inspection offices are located: Atlanta, Ga.; Baltimore, Md.; Boston, Mass.; Buffalo, N. Y.; Butte, Mont.; Chicago, Ill.; Cincinnati, Ohio; Cleveland, Ohio; Denver, Colo; Des Moines, Iowa; Detroit, Mich.; Fargo, N. Dak.; Fort Worth, Tex.; Houston, Tex.; Indianapolis, Ind.; Jacksonville, Fla.; Los Angeles, Cal.; Memphis, Tenn.; Minneapolis, Minn.; New Orleans, La.; New York, N. Y.; Oklahoma City, Okla.; Omaha, Nebr.; Philadelphia, Pa.; Pittsburgh, Pa.; Portland, Oreg.; St. Louis, Mo.; San Francisco, Cal.; Spokane, Wash.; Washington, D. C.; Kansas City, Mo.

2. Additional markets served from offices in above list: Alexandria, Va., served from Washington, D. C.; Council Bluffs, Iowa, from Omaha, Nebr.; Dallas, Tex., from Fort Worth, Tex.; East St. Louis, Ill., from St. Louis, Mo.; Galveston, Tex., from Houston, Tex.; Jersey City, N. J., from New York, N. Y.; Kansas City, Kans., from Kansas City, Mo.; Lincoln, Nebr., from Omaha, Nebr.; Milwaukee, Wis., from Chicago, Ill.; Mobile, Ala., from New Orleans, La.; Newark, N. J., from New York, N. Y.; Providence, R. I., from Boston, Mass.; St. Paul, Minn., from Minneapolis, Minn.; Sacramento, Cal., from San Francisco, Cal.

It is proposed to establish the inspection service in as many of the following markets as the funds available, or to be available, will permit: Columbus, Ohio; San Antonio, Tex.; Louisville, Ky.; Toledo, Ohio; Wichita, Kans.; Seattle, Wash.; Montgomery, Ala.; Birmingham, Ala.; Richmond, Va.; Norfolk, Va.; Springfield, Mass.; Rochester, N. Y.; Albany, N. Y.

Mr. Scott. In each of 31 of these 45 markets where the service is now in operation an inspection office is maintained, while the remaining 14 markets are served from the nearest market in which an office is established.

Mr. McLaughlin. You do not send your men any considerable distance, do you, to make an inspection?

Mr. Scott. No. For example, Newark and Jersey City, N. J., are served from New York; Dallas, Tex., is served from Fort Worth.

Mr. McLaughlin. How far is that?

Mr. Scott. About an hour and 15 minutes, I believe, on the trolley.

The Chairman. What would it cost to extend this service to all cities that you think should have it, or have you about covered the field with this additional appropriation of $50,000 here?

Mr. Scott. We have not. Such cities as Columbus, Toledo, Louisville, Richmond, Norfolk, San Antonio should be supplied with the service. And there are a number of other cities of equal size and importance as markets that should have the service, but, of course, there is a limit to what can be done in this respect.

The Chairman. What, in your judgment, would be the total amount necessary to extend the service to the points where you think it ought to be given ultimately?

Mr. McLaughlin. Put that in the record and name the cities. That would make it complete, would it not?

The Chairman. Yes. I again repeat that I think you will have difficulty in the development of this work, very largely due to the discrimination as between cities. Take a place like Charleston, S. C., with about 75,000 inhabitants. You may establish this service there. Take Columbia, with probably 50,000, and Atlanta, Ga., with 200,000; would you establish it in those places also?

Mr. SCOTT. It is established at Atlanta and is in operation there.

The CHAIRMAN. I assume so; there is nothing going that Georgia does not get.

Mr. LEE. You mention Columbia——

Mr. SCOTT. It should be established in every market of a population of 100,000 or more, I should say.

The CHAIRMAN. I want to call to your attention, Mr. Brand, to this thought that has entered my mind. Take Columbia, in my own district. A great many small truckers live around Columbia. The land has risen in value from $2.50 to $250 an acre there in the last two years, because they have discovered it was a good trucking proposition. I recognize, of course, that it is almost impossible for the Federal Government to have its news service and its inspection service and all that kind of thing at each of these smaller place. At the same time, it seems to me, that there ought to be some demonstration, as it were, of the benefits of this kind of service in a campaign in the city of Columbia, let us say, for two months; then move your force to Columbus, Georgia, and put in a force there, with the hope that the organized truckers and the chamber of commerce of the city will get together and employ a man to do the very kind of work you are doing for these large communities.

Mr. BRAND. We have done some work of that character and expect to continue it, but aside from that it has brought about the permanent establishment of such services in several cities through our cooperation with the state commissions of marketing and state commissions of agriculture. I have enlisted their interests in this matter, and at their meeting in Baltimore this week they have taken up a number of them, and it is a question of development. We feel where it is wise for the Federal Government to stop we will be able, through our cooperations with the States, to get them to begin.

The CHAIRMAN. I hope you are right in that.

Mr. MCLAUGHLIN. The places you have named, though, and the condition you speak of would lead one to think that the products received at these large places come from nearby places and within the State.

The CHAIRMAN. I think there is a distinction here. Larger cities, of course, get the bulk of their products from distant points. The smaller cities get the bulk of their products, I assume, from nearby communities. Is that right, Mr. Brand?

Mr. BRAND. Yes; we consider all those factors. There are small markets. Oklahoma City is not a center of population, but it serves a very large back country, and that is included in the market. Fort Worth serves all of the country in northern Texas largely, much more so in that way than San Antonio. It has not, perhaps, over 70,000 population, but it serves a very large territory.

The CHAIRMAN. I should say in the city of New York they would not get one-tenth of one per cent of their perishable products from the immediate community?

Mr. BRAND. By no means as much as that?

The CHAIRMAN. And you have got to make up that difference somewhere?

Mr. SCOTT. The law provides for service in important central markets; so there is a question as to how small a market could be and be included within the scope of the provisions of the act.

The CHAIRMAN. I think you are following the spirit of the law absolutely, but I believe there is room for good work along the other line I suggest. It must be demonstration, and the actual work must be carried on by the local community.

Mr. McLAUGHLIN. But it would be advisable for that work to be limited to interstate commerce, and are we authorized to provide for the inspection of the products that are not in interstate commerce?

The CHAIRMAN. I think that raises a very interesting legal question, Mr. McLaughlin. I do not know.

Mr. SCOTT. I think this being a service which is not in any way regulatory that it would not have to be confined to interstate commerce. The inspector is there to serve the interested parties and when he is called on to make an inspection he makes that inspection and charges a fee for it.

Mr. McLAUGHLIN. But you go a little further than that. This inspection provides that certificate issued by the inspector shall be prima facie evidence in a court. Is it up to the Federal government to prescribe rules of evidence in State courts?

Mr. HARRISON. That is, in the courts of the United States, Mr. McLaughlin.

Mr. McLAUGHLIN. But I was going to follow that up by saying if you have this inspection of products moved from the garden country around a large city, all of it within a state, you are extending the federal activities a long ways and you are involving us in legal controversies in state courts.

The CHAIRMAN. Your certificate would have no bearing in the State courts except for its reputation and standing?

Mr. SCOTT. That is true; only in the United States courts.

Mr. McLAUGHLIN. But the inspector can be called on in controversies, and we will be getting into controversies between citizens of the state in the state courts. It may be all right: This thing properly carried out may be a good service.

The CHAIRMAN. What has been your experience with that? Would your inspector likely get into the State court on account of his intimate knowledge of the situation? Have you had any trouble in that regard?

Mr. SCOTT. No; we have not thus far.

The CHAIRMAN. I can see your point, Mr. McLaughlin.

Mr. SCOTT. But he could probably be subpœnaed.

Mr. HAUGEN. If it is a controverted question over a case of eggs has that got to be carried to the Supreme Court or the Federal courts? Does not that go to the state courts?

Mr. SCOTT. In which case our certificate would not be received as prima facie evidence.

Mr. McLAUGHLIN. The jurisdiction of the United States courts is limited to jurisdiction of a certain kind and largely limited to the amount involved.

Mr. HAUGEN. Certainly.

Mr. SCOTT. Of course, it must be the residence question anyway.

Mr. HAUGEN. But I take it that no Federal court assumes jurisdiction over a single case of eggs.

The CHAIRMAN. Mr. Jacoway suggests that about the only way you could get one of these certificates into the Federal court would be on account of citizenship or the amount of money involved.

Mr. McLaughlin. That is about the only way you could get the suit into the Federal courts.

The Chairman. I take it, as a matter of fact, Mr. Scott, that 99 per cent of all these disputes will arise between citizens of different States; is not that true?

Mr. Scott. I was just about to remark that most of the inspections are made on products in interstate commerce.

The Chairman. Will you tell us just what you are going to do with this $50,000 increase; I mean to what cities are you going to extend the service?

Mr. Scott. There are two things involved in the increase. The $50,000 could be very well used in extending the service to various cities like San Antonio, El Paso, Louisville, and other markets of that size, but it is desired to extend the service to butter, eggs, and poultry. Thus far the service has covered only fruits and vegetables. Plans are under way and organizations partly under way to undertake the inspection of butter.

The Chairman. That would have to do with its condition, I presume, would it?

Mr. Scott. Its quality and condition.

Mr. Anderson. That means grade?

Mr. Scott. Grade and score.

Mr. Jacoway. All of this inspection has to do with car-load lots?

Mr. Scott. Car load and less than car load—any quantity the inspector may be called upon to examine.

Mr. Haugen. Let us get this jurisdiction straightened out. Do you contend that the determining of the question of the value of a case of eggs shipped from Iowa to Chicago would have to be brought into the Federal courts?

Mr. Scott. Mr. Haugen, the inspection certificate would show the quality and condition of the product. After the inspection is made and the certificate issued the matter is out of our hands. How the courts would handle it I do not know.

Mr. Haugen. But what court would handle it?

Mr. Thompson. If it is an interstate shipment it is a Federal question, is it not, if criminal?

Mr. Haugen. This would not be criminal.

Mr. Thompson. If under interstate shipment?

Mr. Haugen. A case of eggs shipped from Iowa to another State?

Mr. Thompson. It is under the jurisdiction of the Federal Government.

Mr. Haugen. It is limited, is it not, to the amount?

Mr. Scott. Are there not some lawyers here who could answer that question?

The Chairman. I assume, gentlemen, the lawyers on the committee are more familiar with the law than Mr. Scott is.

Mr. Scott. It seems to me it is a question for the lawyers to decide.

Mr. Haugen. How many certificates have you issued under this act?

Mr. Scott. I am not able to give you the total number of certificates.

The Chairman. Just approximate them?

Mr. SCOTT. But since the new act went into effect, October 1, 1918, I can give it to you by months.

The CHAIRMAN. Yes; well, for a number of months?

Mr. SCOTT. October, for example, 2,025 inspections were made; in November, 1,671. The total number for December, can not be given at this time because they are all not in. The duplicates are sent to the Washington office.

Mr. HAUGEN. What are the fees charged?

Mr. SCOTT. $2.50 per car.

Mr. HAUGEN. I mean each inspection. How much for a part of a car?

Mr. SCOTT. $2.50 per lot in excess of one-half car, but not in excess of one maximum car, and $1.50 for less than one-half car.

Mr. HAUGEN. Is this service self-sustaining?

Mr. SCOTT. We do not know whether it is going to be self-sustaining on the basis of $2.50 per car or not—probably not.

Mr. HAUGEN. But that is the aim of the bureau?

Mr. SCOTT. Yes, sir.

Mr. HAUGEN. To make it self-sustaining?

Mr. SCOTT. Yes. It was placed on a fee basis October 1, so we have been running only three months on the fee basis. In the meanwhile we have been organizing and opening up new markets.

Mr. HAUGEN. That covers the overhead charges and all expenses connected, incidentals?

Mr. SCOTT. It will not be sufficient.

Mr. HAUGEN. What is the policy of the department, to make it self-supporting, to cover overhead charges?

Mr. SCOTT. To make it self-supporting ultimately. It is a new thing, and in the process of organization it is evident that it can not be made self-supporting for the first year.

Mr. HAUGEN. Speaking of making it self-supporting, does that include overhead charges?

Mr. SCOTT. It should include overhead charges.

Mr. HAUGEN. That is the policy of the bureau, to make it include overhead charges?

Mr. SCOTT. Ultimately.

Mr. HAUGEN. How close will it come to it now? Can you approximate it?

Mr. SCOTT. I should say that it is not paying over one-half of the expenses.

Mr. HAUGEN. You are expecting an increase so as to make it up?

Mr. SCOTT. We expect an increase in the demand for the inspections in the first place and a reduction in the expenditures. In other words, when we open up an office the office equipment has to be secured so that during the development period the expenses are heavier than they would be later.

Mr. HAUGEN. Due to the equipment?

Mr. SCOTT. Due to the equipment.

Mr. HAUGEN. In your estimation can it be made self-supporting, or, in other words, if you should fail to develop an increase what would you do then?

Mr. SCOTT. It can be made self-supporting in the large markets, but now if we extend this service to smaller markets where the salary of the inspector is practically the same as at a larger market and the inspections are only one-half, then it can not be made self-supporting without charging an unreasonable price for the service.

Mr. HAUGEN. Well the language would imply that it should be made self supporting. Would the policy then be to make a profit in the larger stations and make up the loss in the smaller?

Mr. SCOTT. That could possibly be worked out.

Mr. HAUGEN. Have you any definite policy as to that?

Mr. SCOTT. No.

Mr. MCLAUGHLIN. How do you find the charges you make strike the people that have to pay them?

Mr. SCOTT. There is no complaint whatever. We probably can increase the charges without an injustice to the shippers and receivers.

Mr. MCLAUGHLIN. How are the inspectors paid?

Mr. SCOTT. The inspectors are paid from $1,800 to $2,000. We have, I believe, one or two inspectors that are getting as low as $1,600, but the inspectors carry a very large responsibility. Each car that he inspects may involve a decision covering $500 or $1,000 in a matter of adjustment, and it is necessary to have men of mature judgment.

Mr. MCLAUGHLIN. These inspectors have offices, rent offices, do they?

Mr. SCOTT. Rent offices, yes.

Mr. MCLAUGHLIN. In all these places?

Mr. SCOTT. We have offices in 31 markets.

Mr. MCLAUGHLIN. Out of 45?

Mr. SCOTT. Out of the 45, and 12 of those are joint with the market news service.

Mr. MCLAUGHLIN. Do they have much if any apparatus, machines, or appliances of any kind to assist them with which they work to make these inspections?

Mr. SCOTT. Very little. It is necessary for them to have a thermometer and a hatchet and a hammer and a knife and a few things like that with which to open packages, and a kit to carry the instruments in.

Mr. HAUGEN. What would you have to say about extending it to hay, for instance?

Mr. SCOTT. This covers only perishable products.

Mr. HAUGEN. I know, but what would you think of extending it, the extension of the service?

Mr. BRAND. We have had a very great amount of requests from hay shippers, and particularly in Oklahoma, for hay inspection service. We have done nothing along that line except to assist the National Hay Association to draft a piece of legislation which I believe some member has introduced. Beyond that we have done nothing about it thus far. And there is a very important field and there is no product that is handled so carelessly in which the shipper and particularly the country shipper receives such a raw deal you may say, as hay.

Mr. HAUGEN. That is exactly what I was about to say. What do you say about extending this service to it?

Mr. BRAND. I think ultimately it will be extended to that unless you gentlemen feel we are spending too much money already, then we will not. We can not but feel there is a real need in that field.

Mr. McLaughlin. Does it not strike you when this service is new and you are trying it out to prove its worth that you would do better to limit it to kinds of work that one man can do instead of having a man there to inspect one kind of stuff and be not skilled in the inspection of another kind, and for that other kind of product you would have to have still another man and so on? Had you not better work along and see whether this is going to work as you are doing it?

Mr. Brand. That is the way we are doing. We are asking inspection on products that a single man, in the nature of things, would be familiar with rather than expecting him to cover perishables and non-perishables, which is very difficult to cover with one man.

Mr. Haugen. Could not one man do both, if it were extended to hay, could you not use the same inspector?

Mr. Brand. No, you could not especially in some of these markets. The men work all hours of the day and night as it is.

Mr. Haugen. I mean if his time was not fully occupied, could he not do it?

Mr. Brand. Very rarely. Possibly there might be an extraordiary case in which a fruit and vegetable inspector knew anything whatever about hay or grain, or anything of that sort. It would be a very unusual case in which he could inspect both lines.

Mr. Haugen. The abuses in perishable articles are small compared with that in hay. I agree with you there are more abuses in the sale of hay in the hay market than anything else. If a man gets enough to pay freight he is doing fairly well.

Mr. Thompson. Hay, you would not call that the most important market article, that is about the third most important article in the market, is it not.

Mr. Brand. I do not think as a shipping proposition it is.

Mr. Thompson. Wheat and corn produce more money.

Mr. Brand. I think live stock, and in the aggregate fruit and vegetables produce more, and dairy products in the shipping sense. I am only using it in the shipping sense.

Mr. Thompson. But you could not inspect hay unless you had grades for it, could you?

Mr. Brand. We have done some work under our investigational department with grain and hay and seeds looking to the establishment of grades.

Mr. Thompson. You have no grades on hay, have you, at all?

Mr. Brand. We have prepared tentative grades on hay. We have not enforced them, but used them for investigational purposes.

Mr. Thompson. Have you those grades so you could submit them to the committee?

Mr. Brand. We are scarcely ready to submit them. We have assisted in the preparation of a bill for the supervision and grading of hay.

Mr. Thompson. Does that imply the fixing of grades?

Mr. Brand. Yes.

Mr. Thompson. Has that been introduced?

Mr. Brand. No, it has not.

Mr. Thompson. You have not submitted it to anyone yet, have you?

Mr. Brand. No.

Mr. THOMPSON. The reason I ask you, that is a very important question down in my State, because hay is a very important product in Oklahoma.

Mr. BRAND. We found that to be true and we got more complaints, I think, from Oklahoma regarding hay than anywhere else. Shippers shipped to certain markets, as Mr. Haugen says, and do not get their freight back; some times they can not even get their letters. I have a case in mind. The bank at Enid repeatedly wrote to a commission merchant in Chicago, but could get no reply.

Mr. HAUGEN. That is a general complaint, and quite general all over the country. But speaking about eggs, you have no grade on perishable products, have you?

Mr. BRAND. Yes; we have on some of them.

Mr. HAUGEN. Official grades?

Mr. BRAND. Yes.

Mr. HAUGEN. Standardized by act of Congress?

Mr. BRAND. No; they are permissive grades; they are not compulsory.

Mr. HAUGEN. The same way with hay?

Mr. BRAND. Hay is graded by the various boards of trade and chambers of commerce.

Mr. HEFLIN. There is no hay exchange?

Mr. BRAND. Yes, there is a hay department in most of the prominent exchanges.

Mr. HEFLIN. Where they deal in future hay?

Mr. BRAND. No, they do not deal in future hay. They are more like the Montgomery exchange, for instance.

Mr. HAUGEN. What would you estimate the cost of hay inspection—inspection and certification?

Mr. BRAND. I am hardly prepared to say that.

Mr. HAUGEN. If the service is to be made self-sustaining it would not be compulsory; they would simply have to pay the fees.

Mr. BRAND. In all this work you can not expect it to be self-sustaining in the first year or two, because you have got an initial expense, you have got to educate the public as to their rights in the matter, in order to get the volume of work which makes it self-sustaining.

Mr. HAUGEN. I do not believe anybody would expect that, but somebody will be asking us questions.

Mr. BRAND. I think a beginning could be made on a very respectable hay inspection in the United States for $150,000.

Mr. HAUGEN. How many stations would it be necessary to establish?

Mr. BRAND. It would be necessary to have an inspection at practically all of the most important feed markets, and I suppose they would number in the neighborhood of 25.

Mr. HAUGEN. The most of it goes to certain central markets?

Mr. BRAND. Yes.

Mr. HAUGEN. It would not be necessary to establish it at all of them?

Mr. BRAND. No, sir.

The CHAIRMAN. Mr. Scott, I believe you said you would put into the record the names of the cities to which you intend to extend this service; and also that a portion of this money would be used for other purposes; what other purposes?

Mr. SCOTT. To other perishable products—butter, eggs, cheese, poultry.

Mr. SCOTT. May I make one more remark in regard to making the service self-sustaining?

The CHAIRMAN. Certainly.

Mr. SCOTT. One thing that operates against that is that the moment an inspection office is opened in a market the need for it in actual requests for inspection is greatly reduced. The operator who makes it a business to reject and go back on the shipper for an allowance is very much more careful about making such rejections, so that without making a single inspection the presence of the inspector in the market operates to reduce the number of rejections.

The CHAIRMAN. In other words, the greatest thing in this world to reduce crime is light?

Mr. SCOTT. Yes; and the inspector is there in the capacity of a policeman; he does not have to make an arrest or may not have to make many inspections, but his very presence there operates to bring about the remedy.

Mr. HEFLIN. His club and six-shooter have a very persuasive effect on settlements?

Mr. SCOTT. Yes.

The CHAIRMAN. Not so much his six-shooter as the fact that the culprit may be shown up in the daylight.

Mr. SCOTT. So this inspection service can not be measured in dollars and cents. In other words, we can not charge for that kind of service.

The CHAIRMAN. Let me ask you this question, and then I am through: Here you are charging these shippers and people who want inspection for the service. The policy of the Government has been that inspection service, such as the meat-inspection service, for instance, is to be charged to the Government. I think it is a very interesting matter of governmental policy as to whether or not we ought to expect these inspection services to be self-sustaining or whether the Government ought to take the burden of that in the interest of the general public. Personally, I adhere to the latter view and always have done so.

Mr. HAUGEN. Mr. Brand, how about the wheat-inspection service; on whom is the burden of proof?

Mr. BRAND. In all cases in which the finding is against the person who makes the complaint——

Mr. HAUGEN. We have the same rule of evidence.

Mr. BRAND. I ought to say, Mr. Chairman, that relatively very little revenue comes from that because it provides for the return of the fees in all cases in which the inspector is sustained, and he is more frequently sustained than not.

STATEMENT OF MR. CHARLES J. BRAND, CHIEF OF THE BUREAU OF MARKETS, UNITED STATES DEPARTMENT OF AGRICULTURE—Continued.

The CHAIRMAN. Mr. Brand, you may take up your next item on page 246. That is your cotton-grading work. There is no change in that item. I was wondering whether that work had not progressed far enough so that we might begin to cut down the appropriation a little.

Mr. BRAND. Mr. Chairman, there is still a great deal of work to be done under that paragraph. We are just at this moment about to issue the standards for length of staple from three-fourths to 1¼ inch, for which there has been almost universal demand; standards for sea island, standards for Arizona and California-Egyptian cotton are still to be issued and to be applied; also standards with reference to other qualities. I should regret to see any reduction in this item until we have done the work that still remains undone.

The CHAIRMAN. Can you hold out any hope that ultimately you will finish this work on cotton?

Mr. BRAND. Mr. Chairman, I do not know why we should hold out hope to finish a job while there is still so much to be done, and when we can not foresee the end. The improvement in the cotton industry depends upon continuance of this kind of work. We can not, in my opinion, at any point cease to do constructive work unless we are willing to cut the thing from its mooring and be content with retrogression instead of progression.

The CHAIRMAN. I quite understand that.

Mr. BRAND. Incidentally we are trying to get a universal and international adoption of our cotton standards. That applies to this item.

The CHAIRMAN. The only perpetual motion in the world is a scientific investigation, is it not?

Mr. BRAND. That is all right; that is where progress comes, Mr. Chairman.

Mr. LEE. What are you getting for these cotton standards?

Mr. BRAND. We have raised our price to $9. The price of everything has gone up; so we had to more than double our price.

The CHAIRMAN. What are you receiving for the sale of grades?

Mr. BRAND. That comes under another item.

Mr. MCLAUGHLIN. I see that in 1918 you employed 10 men; in 1920 you will employ 4, but you are going to pay those 4 men almost the same amount of money you paid the 10 before. There is some increase in salaries, evidently.

Mr. BRAND. Mr. McLaughlin, anyone that gets an increase in salary past the Office of the Secretary of Agriculture is a genius.

Mr. MCLAUGHLIN. The money goes out of the Federal treasury just the same, whether extracted by a genius or a novice, and I am observing there that four men are to get as much money as ten received a year ago.

Mr. BRAND. I do not quite see that point.

Mr. HARRISON. Ten were employed temporarily, a number of men went out on military leave and we employed people in their places a part of the time.

Mr. BRAND. That is true; some were employed temporarily in 1918. In no case have we reduced our employes from ten to four and given salary in the aggregate amount to the 4 that we have given to the 10, so I do not quite understand the point. On the cotton work I should say there has been a minimum of salary increases I do not recall any increase in excess of $250 per annum, and that was given to a very, very small number of employees, so small that within the as two weeks we have lost two of our employees in the cotton work. t

I do not think you gentlemen need worry about the salary business. If you are worrying about that I wish you would come down and see the difficulties I have in persuading men to undertake the work. This noon, when I went back to my office, one of our men who left us when getting a salary of $1,800, declined to return for less than $2,400. We need him exceedingly badly. That is our experience day after day.

Mr. McLaughlin. I do not think we are worrying about it very much, it is simply an inquiry and attempt to get information. It is our due, I think.

Mr. Brand. We try to be very careful with respect to those matters, Mr. McLaughlin. I myself recommend only the most meritorious cases, and I may say many of those that I think meritorious do not get by the Secretary's office. I am sorry to say that, but it is a fact.

The Chairman. You have a pretty strong censorship over that, have you not?

Mr. Brand. I never saw anything to equal it, gentlemen.

Mr. Anderson. They had a lot of practice the last year or so.

Mr. Haugen. Is it not a fact you start out with pretty good salaries which do not necessitate an increase?

Mr. Brand. We have never hired a man—I say this advisedly—and paid him a dollar more than was necessary. We force every man to communicate to us the absolute minimum that he will accept, and when he tells us the absolute minimum, half the time we go back and tell him we can not pay that much. We say "Won't you take $2,250?" where he is demanding $3,000.

Mr. Haugen. If you leave it to him he will make the minimum pretty high.

Mr. Brand. He goes by what he is receiving. We pay many and many a man a smaller salary than he was receiving in his other employment, because he thinks this work represents an opportunity for public service. You would be astonished to see how many people will work for the Government at a less salary than they are actually earning on the outside.

Mr. Harrison. We require him to state exactly what he was receiving on the outside.

Mr. Haugen. Of course, you understand there is quite a difference between working for the Government and on outside.

Mr. Brand. Why, Mr. Haugen?

Mr. Haugen. Because they have 30 days leave and have short hours.

Mr. Brand. I see Mr. Scott smile. You would have to take a microscope to find the leave Mr. Scott took the last few years.

Mr. Haugen. I am not talking about Mr. Scott in particular; I am talking about the employees generally.

Mr. Brand. I am merely taking that as an instance. I myself have not taken to exceed two weeks' leave in three years.

Mr. Haugen. And you probably work 10 hours a day. That is not required.

Mr. BRAND. That is true. There is never a night I do not carry a bundle of papers home and work after dinner; and the same is true of every one of these gentlemen.

Mr. HAUGEN. But that is not true of all Government employees.

Mr. BRAND. I have been around a great deal——

Mr. HAUGEN. I say there is a difference in service. One works a good many hours without leave, not even leave on account of sickness. Where the Government gives leave of absence with pay, I take it that is taken into consideration by these applicants.

Mr. BRAND. I have been in the service 15 years; and I have yet to take a day on sick leave.

The CHAIRMAN. You can not get it unless sick?

Mr. BRAND. You can not get it without a doctor's certificate.

Mr. HAUGEN. But anybody applying for a job would take that into consideration, and that makes the service more attractive?

Mr. McLAUGHLIN. I was asking about this place where it seemed four men appeared to receive as much as 10 did before. I thought an explanation was due, but it has not been made.

Mr. BRAND. In no case have we paid any four men the aggregate salaries of any 10 men who were previously in that work. In no case has there been any relationship whatsoever between the salaries of men who may have remained upon that work to those who were subsequently taken on the work, and in war times frequently we have had to actually close offices because of the number of men that have been lost. We have had to discontinue services, so that these figures which represent the salaries for even fractions of a year that a man may have been engaged in upon work do not represent the real status of the cases. For instance, it may show a man on a salary of $3,500 assigned to a certain task, but that may be only one of the tasks and his salary may be in that particular fund only, we will say, three months of the year.

Mr. McLAUGHLIN. But his time was charged to this particular work only such time as he put in?

Mr. BRAND. That is the idea.

Mr. McLAUGHLIN. And he was paid only for the work he did on this particular task?

Mr. BRAND. That is the idea.

Mr. McLAUGHLIN. Those men, then, were paid about nine or ten thousand dollars for that part time?

Mr. BRAND. No.

Mr. McLAUGHLIN. Following your answer that must be.

Mr. HARRISON. The table is on page 246.

Mr. McLAUGHLIN. I am talking about the table on page 246.

Mr. HARRISON. The salaries paid to employees in 1918 are indicated there.

Mr. BRAND. And it indicates they are part-time employees and temporary employees in every case on which that is true, in the fourth column. I have often thought, Mr. Chairman, that that sort of table leads to misapprehension, but investigation shows it is a part-time matter.

Mr. McLAUGHLIN. But they are paid and it is charged to this particular item only for the time employed?

Mr. BRAND. Mr. McLaughlin, if you will just run over those figures you will see that it shows a total of $9,000. If their whole time were put on the total would run nearly to $20,000.

The CHAIRMAN. In other words, Mr. McLaughlin, this one man here, the first number there, number one, is on part time at a salary of $3,000; that is the annual salary rate, but the man is not employed for a full year.

Mr. BRAND. That is the idea. The yearly rate is indicated, but the salaries are charged against that particular fund only for the number of weeks or months that the men worked on this particular job. With reference to the question of leave, both sick and annual, our field men do not receive 30 days' sick and 30 days' annual leave; they are entitled to only 15 days' sick and 15 days' annual leave.

The CHAIRMAN. If there is nothing further about that we will take up the next item, page 247, item 128, to enable the Secretary of Agriculture to make a study of cooperation among farmers, in the sum of $25,780. There is no change in that item.

Mr. BRAND. This is work with which the committee is perfectly familiar, unless there is some question about it.

Mr. HAUGEN. I should like to clear up a matter taken up the other day. I believe you or Mr. Sherman stated that you paid your telegraph operators $1,200.

Mr. BRAND. No; he stated that some of them received $1,200, some $1,400, and, I think he said two, possibly only one, received $1,620, and the supervising telegrapher received $2,000. That is my recollection.

Mr. HAUGEN. And that was, in fact, lower than the outside people were paid?

Mr. BRAND. Yes.

Mr. HAUGEN. Here I have a communication from the union. It refers to a 10 per cent increase they were granted, and it states in some cases the 10 per cent increase amounted to as much as $15; that would be $150 per month to an exceptionally high-salaried man. The average increase would be $8. I would infer from that that the average pay is $80 a month.

Mr. BRAND. Mr. Haugen, I am unable to speak with reference to the particular data you are furnishing.

Mr. HAUGEN. It just came in to-day's mail; it is dated January 4.

Mr. BRAND. The fact of the matter is we take up with the telegraph companies the employment of any of their employees before we offer positions to any telegraphers. In no case have we been bidding against them.

Mr. HAUGEN. Not bidding against them, but I take it that this comes direct from the organization.

Mr. BRAND. I presume your understanding is that they are getting $80 a month from the telegraph companies?

Mr. HAUGEN. Eight is 10 per cent of 80.

Mr. BRAND. Mr. Chairman, I am unable to say exactly what the rates of pay of telegraphers in the city of Washington are, but my impression is that, counting their bonuses and their average overtime, it runs a little over $1,700.

Mr. HAUGEN. Oh, the bonus has been cut off. They were asking for bonus?

Mr. BRAND. No.
Mr. HAUGEN. Here is their own statement.
Mr. BRAND. They still get that income.
Mr. HAUGEN. No; they do not, according to this statement. I will read it to you. It is here.
Mr. BRAND. I am under the impression that the statement Mr. Haugen is reading must refer to the thousands of telegraphers in the small villages all over the United States.
Mr. HAUGEN. This comes from the east part of Texas.
Mr. BRAND. And possibly even to other employees, even messenger boys and others in the employ of the telegraph service. It certainly does not apply to telegraph operators.
Mr. HAUGEN. It says they are required, first, to work eight hours, then two hours; then for over two hours they are allowed time and a half for overtime and double pay for Sundays.
Mr. BRAND. I shall be very glad to insert in the record at this place, if you wish, the facts established by the records. which we can get from the telegraph company.
Mr. HAUGEN. I think we would like to know. It seems as though every time a question is asked there is some doubt about the sincerity of the question.
Mr. BRAND. Not at all, Mr. Haugen. If you are able to state——
Mr. HAUGEN (interrupting). I am giving my authority. I will turn the letter over to you. It just came in to-day's mail. It speaks of the bonus and laying their grievances before Congress.
Mr. BRAND. This is dated El Paso, Tex., and unquestionably includes every telegrapher at small way stations.
Mr. HAUGEN. Gives 250,000 of them, I think.
Mr. HAUGEN. How many do you employ?
Mr. BRAND. We have 114, if I recall correctly.
Mr. LESHER. How many hours do your men work?
Mr. BRAND. The full Government hours, and they do clerical work between times. I may say they do not pull the union rules on us. The telegraphers we have are just as loyal in the service as any body of men could possibly be. Many of them do very much overtime. On some of the wires I should say they do 8 and 10 hours, purely voluntary, because they are interested in the service and are trying to help, just as the other employees are.
Mr. LESHER. That is what you stated the other day. and I was wondering how you got around the eight-hour law.
Mr. HARRISON. You work night shifts, too, Mr. Brand?
Mr. BRAND. Yes; we work night shifts.
Mr. HARRISON. The State Department has raised all their telegraphers, I understand, to $1,600.
Mr. BRAND. Yes; the State Department uniformly raised theirs, and that makes it difficult for us; because ours get restless.
Mr. HARRISON. I was going to say that I know our scale is lower, in every instance, than that paid by the local telegraph companies here. We got that information direct from the companies.
Mr. BRAND. There was a time last summer when I feared that any day we might have to cut off our whole service because of inability to employ the requisite number of telegraphers.
Mr. LESHER. I was wondering the other day how you were able to hold them.

Mr. BRAND. Due to the fact that they take a great deal of interest in their work. For instance, yesterday I had two applications from two of our best old men, who have been in the Army. They want to come back; they like the work, see possibilities in being connected with the work and think it a great service. One of them is an Irishman and has all the wit and ways of getting at things that Irishmen have. He helped us at the inception of the service, and he is willing to come back and work for less than he would get elsewhere, because he considers it constructive work.

The CHAIRMAN. It offers good educational facilities and all that sort of thing.

Mr. BRAND. Yes; all those factors weigh with them.

Mr. HAUGEN. Will you get the scale of wages paid by the telegraph company and put it in the record?

Mr. BRAND. Yes, sir.

(The statement referred to follows:)

Comparison of salaries paid to superintendents of telegraph, telegraph operators, etc., by Bureau of Markets (Washington D. C.), commercial telegraph companies, and private firms.

	Superintendents.	Division traffic supervisors.	Chief operator.	Morse telegraphers (first class).
Western Union Telegraph Co.[1]	$5,000–$7,000	$3,000	$2,800	Initial salary, $1,650 after 18 months, $1,920.
Postal Telegraph Co.	Unknown.	Unknown.	$2,000–2,400	$1,560.
Southern Ry. Co.	Unknown.	Unknown.	2,400	$1,815.
Commercial firms	[2] 6,000			$1,750 to $2,600.
Bureau of Markets	[3] 2,000		1,620	12, at $1,400; 3, at $1,500.

	Bonus for telegraphers.	Salary plus bonus.	Overtime.	Remarks.
Western Union Telegraph Co.[1]	$120 per annum	$1,770–$2,040	1½ regular time	Insurance, disability, and retirement.
Postal Telegraph Co.	Average piecework bonus, $640.	2,200	....do............	Do.
Southern Ry. Co.		1,815	....do............	Do.
Commercial firms	8 to 10 per cent	1,900–2,800	....do............	Do.
Bureau of Markets	$120 per annum if in service July 1, 1917.	1,520–1,620	None	No insurance, disability, or retirement.

[1] The Western Union Telegraph Co. employs about 50,000 Morse telegraphers, which is perhaps three times as many as that of all the other companies together. For this reason, the salaries paid by the Western Union may be taken as standard.
[2] Average salary.
[3] Exact salary.

The CHAIRMAN. There was something awhile ago that I overlooked. In your market news service you said your men began work usually about 4 o'clock in the morning. They must get their reports out for the afternoon papers by 10.30. During the balance of the day what are those people doing?

Mr. BRAND. They are carrying on investigational work. It is our local market reporters who are able to turn their information over in the early morning. The balance of the time they are working to determine the efficiency of various methods of retail distribution as between the regular grocery store, the cash and carry, the self-serve, and the other types of stores. We find, for instance, in the case of the self-serve stores that the question of thievery is the most important single factor to be considered in deciding whether or not such stores can be made a permanent feature of our distribution system. We found that not one of the great stores had an idea of the amount they lose in this way. We have collaborated with them in putting in an accounting system that will enable them to determine the amount of thievery, the amount of shrinkage. We found, for instance, in this particular matter, that the ordinary grocery store operates on a gross cost and profit basis of 19 to 21 per cent. Then, chain stores operate on from 5 to 6 per cent less; in other words, from 15 to 17 per cent. The cash and carry stores operate and make the same profit as the others on a basis of from 8 to 11 per cent, and they carry on that work all the time.

The CHAIRMAN. They are doing investigational work?

Mr. BRAND. Yes; and they do an amount of overtime that is simply astonishing. I go from time to time to our field offices and I find the clerks working there at 6 o'clock at night very frequently. One of our men happens to have been at our St. Louis office and he will substantiate that statement.

The CHAIRMAN. Take up this item 128 and tell us briefly what you are doing there. It is old work.

Mr. MCLAUGHLIN. As to this item, as you make your explanation, I wish you would have this in mind. This provides for investigation as to rural credits and other forms of cooperation and so forth. We have in the Government a bureau of rural credits, five very distinguished gentlemen, drawing pretty good salaries, whose duty it is to investigate certain lines. I would suppose all lines. In almost every bureau of the Government there are men who are looking after this question of cooperation in every line of work that the farmers engage in. I should like to know how you are justified in taking up this rural credit work at all, and wherein your work is different from the work the other officers are doing on this cooperative organization work.

The CHAIRMAN. All right, Mr. Brand, you may answer that.

Mr. BRAND. All right, Mr. Chairman; does Mr. McLaughlin wish me to specialize with reference to these particular employees?

Mr. MCLAUGHLIN. No; not the employees.

The CHAIRMAN. No; in a general way if you are duplicating the work of any other department of the Government in these investigations.

Mr. BRAND. Absolutely not. The only other agency engaged in this field at all is the Farm Loan Board, and they are engaged in the loaning of funds to farmers under the farm loan act.

Mr. MCLAUGHLIN. That applies to lands and does not apply to personal loans.

Mr. BRAND. It applies solely to long-time credit; and I may say this project, and the workers on this project, tried in the work on the farm loan act to accomplish certain results, and it is on the basis of the investigations in part provided for in this item that the act was framed. The investigations along these lines illustrate the outgrowth of the investigational work conducted by us. Our latter work has been on short time and personal credit, and not on long time credit. Where we touch that field at all, it is touched with the complete cooperation of the Farm Loan Board. They have called on us in numerous instances to send our men out to help them do work, to carry on educational work and so on, because they had no one available.

Mr. McLaughlin. I do not see why they should call on you. I do not see why they should not do it themselves and have it within their bureau instead of having this one kind of work scattered all through the different departments.

Mr. Harrison. Mr. McLaughlin, we were recently asked by the Farm Loan Board to send out special instructions to the county agents to help along their work.

Mr. McLaughlin. The county agents are not under the charge of the Bureau of Markets at all.

Mr. Harrison. But we are speaking about departments and what I have said shows how the Farm Loan Board does, in one instance, use the facilities of the Department of Agriculture.

Mr. Brand. It occurs to me that Mr. Thompson may answer your question a little better.

Mr. Thompson. As a matter of fact, this is an entirely new and different field—one that has never been exploited, as I understand it.

Mr. McLaughlin. What?

Mr. Thompson. This personal credit.

Mr. McLaughlin. It has all followed in the same manner in making loans to farmers.

Mr. Thompson. It never has been exploited.

Mr. McLaughlin. It has not been carried out, but it has been talked about, and it is all one big thing, the lending of Federal money to farmers on realty or personal property.

The Chairman. I happen to know personally, Mr. McLaughlin, that there was not any one mind that impressed itself on the rural credits act as the mind of Mr. Thompson, who will speak to you in a few minutes.

Mr. McLaughlin. If his work is big in that line, I think he ought to be connected with the Farm Loan Board.

Mr. Brand. No, Mr. McLaughlin; we need him in our own business.

The Chairman. This item has been in about four years?

Mr. Haugen. More than that.

The Chairman. The Bureau of Markets was established in 1913.

Mr. Brand. Just exactly four years, I think.

Mr. Haugen. We carried an appropriation for investigation of this work before that, did we not?

Mr. Brand. No, sir.

Mr. Haugen. When was the first appropriation made?

Mr. Brand. For the fiscal year 1915.

Mr. Haugen. It was carried about three years?

Mr. Brand. This is the fourth year now.

Mr. Haugen. And since that we have enacted the farm loan bill. It was suggested at the time it be carried for a short time. Now, it appears to me more ornamental than useful.

The Chairman. Let us see whether Mr. Thompson can enlighten the committee on that proposition.

Mr. HAUGEN. I do not mean to discredit the man in charge of it. I know something of his ability and his work.

The CHAIRMAN. Let us hear what he has to say.

STATEMENT OF MR. C. W. THOMPSON, SPECIALIST IN RURAL ORGANIZATION, BUREAU OF MARKETS, UNITED STATES DEPARTMENT OF AGRICULTURE.

Mr. THOMPSON. Several questions have been asked with reference to this particular item, one with reference to the relation between the work that has been done and the work of the Farm Loan Board. Speaking on that point, I may say that after the Farm Loan Board had begun its work and after the Federal land banks were being established, they called upon us for assistance with reference to the preparation of amortization tables, and one specific form of assistance we gave them was the working out of amortization tables, which were sent to them from the department. A farmers bulletin also was prepared (No. 792) entitled, "How the Federal farm loan act benefits the farmer."

I may say further that at their special request a representative went out to assist them in presenting matters publicly bearing on the farm loan act, especially in discussing the formation of farm loan associations. However. this was all done in the early months. following the establishment of the Federal land banks.

Mr. MCLAUGHLIN. Those men that were sent out from your bureau were experts in marketing?

Mr. THOMPSON. That happened to be the speaker, myself, who had given sufficient attention to the Federal farm loan act to be thoroughly familiar with the way in which a farm loan association is organized.

Mr. MCLAUGHLIN. When you were doing that work, did you have in mind that you were engaged in marketing work?

Mr. THOMPSON. No; I was working with them in the interest of rural credit improvement, under the item which is now being discussed, and that item, when it was included in the Agricultural bill, was placed with the Bureau of Markets, and that explains why the work was handled as it was.

The CHAIRMAN. I wonder if you would not relieve Mr. McLaughlin's mind of some dissatisfaction with this situation if you would explain to him that the original title of ths work was "Bureau of Markets and Rural Organization," and that, as a matter of convenience, the latter part of the title was dropped, and that this bureau does not confine its activities entirely to the matter of marketing. but also to rural organization?

Mr. THOMPSON. Yes.

The CHAIRMAN. That is what you had in your mind, was it not, Mr. McLaughlin—that this was not marketing work?

Mr. MCLAUGHLIN. I think it is not marketing work. We have a great big bureau with five great big men who have directly in charge the loaning proposition to farmers, and I think that there is enough of them to cover this entire field and that it is in no sense a marketing proposition.

Mr. THOMPSON. I may say, further, that in matters bearing on short-time farm credit, and questions bearing on improving relations between farmers and existing loan agencies for the purpose of short-time loans resting on personal credit or collateral credit, letters have repeatedly been referred to us by the Federal Farm Loan Board. Our investigations on that subject, in so far as they have been carried under this item (viz: Rural cooperation), have referred more particularly to short-time credit matters, and not to long-time mortgage loans, which, of course, come more particularly within the province of the Federal Farm Loan Board.

However, when it comes to the question of getting information as to the interest rates or charges paid by farmers, I may say, that this last year we have conducted an investigation to show what the interest rates are on both mortgage loans and short-time loans to farmers in different sections of the country, but before we included mortgage loans we took it up with the Federal Farm Loan Board, and they requested us to get that sort of information, stating that it would be of assistance to them. Likewise, we have recently furnished the Federal Reserve Board a statement bearing on a form of agricultural credit statement, another means of improving relations between farmers and banks.

The department receives many letters and communications bearing on farm credit which are referred to us for consideration.

I think a misconception is apt to arise in your minds, possibly from the assumption that this item is devoted solely to rural credits. As a matter of fact, and as a practical thing, only a portion of it is devoted to that.

Mr. McLaughlin. How much?

Mr. Thompson. Well, there is also the subject of agricultural insurance.

Mr. McLaughlin. How much of this credit business?

Mr. Brand. Ten or twelve thousand dollars is devoted annually to rural credit investigations.

Mr. Thompson. I should like to say this, that the work under this item is divided into two parts, one entirely rural credits, insurance, and communication, and the other rural, social, and educational activities, and that about two-thirds, roughly, would go under rural credits, insurance, and communication, and about one-third to the other.

The Chairman. What do you mean by " communication?"

Mr. Thompson. Telephone companies and so forth.

Mr. Anderson. You ought to be able to abandon that now since our friend Burleson has taken it over and is telling us how to manage.

Mr. Thompson. We have not been able recently to give very much attention to the rural telephone company inquiry. We have given quite a bit of attention to agricultural insurance the last year—to the study of farmers' mutual insurance companies and other companies that have to do with agricultural insurance. We have published bulletins, and we have prepared forms of records and accounts for local mutual insurance companies.

Mr. Anderson. What range does that cover? There are a great many kinds of rural insurance.

Mr. Thompson. There are 1,950 of the farmers' mutual fire insurance companies and for them we have in preparation a system of records and accounts.

The CHAIRMAN. Crop insurance—you attend to that, too, do you?
Mr. THOMPSON. We have given some attention to the matter of crop insurance and to existing facilities for that purpose.
The CHAIRMAN. And live-stock insurance?
Mr. THOMPSON. Live-stock insurance as well.
The CHAIRMAN. What else are you doing?
Mr. THOMPSON. I will say that the man we have who represents agricultural insurance is at this time, having been with us three years, in the unique position of having invaluable information on hand on the whole subject of agricultural insurance.
Mr. BRAND. With regard to the whole United States.
Mr. THOMPSON. If we were to lose him we would have no way of putting anyone in who could replace him.
The CHAIRMAN. You had better get his information on paper.
Mr. BRAND. He is getting it on paper right along.
Mr. THOMPSON. Yes; he is. We have manuscripts now in press, other manuscripts to be delivered, and several bulletins have already been published.
The CHAIRMAN. All right, doctor; what else have you?
Mr. THOMPSON. As I say, the major part of our attention has been given to these fields. However, we are also getting on hand considerable information regarding rural organizations generally.
I should like to add this point in reference to one question that I believe was asked yesterday. It was regarding the mortality in cooperative organizations. I think that, if you will give a moment's thought to the question, you will see that you could not give any very satisfactory answer for cooperative associations in general, because the mortality may be very high for certain kinds of cooperative associations, such as cooperative stores, and might be very, very low in the case of an association such as a farmer's mutual fire-insurance association. In other words, we have to consider the kind of cooperative association as such before your statement regarding the mortality rate would really have any significance.
Mr. HAUGEN. The insurance is all mutual by assessment plan?
Mr. THOMPSON. In the case of local farmers' mutual fire insurance companies, for instance, there would be a very small mortality rate. We have been checking up the information we have. We have a card catalogue of all the farmers' mutual fire insurance companies to see whether those that replied to us back three or four years ago are still with us, and we are surprised to find how consistently they stay on the records.
Mr. HAUGEN. The whole thing depends on the management, the efficiency of the management, does it not?
Mr. THOMPSON. I should mention that as one of the most important things.
Mr. HAUGEN. It is pretty much the whole thing, is it not?
Mr. THOMPSON. It is one of the most important things.
Mr. HAUGEN. Well, what else is there?
Mr. THOMPSON. There are many important questions that have a bearing on the efficiency of the local mutual fire insurance companies.
Mr. HAUGEN. I am speaking now about cooperative associations.
Mr. THOMPSON. Speaking of cooperative associations generally?
Mr. HAUGEN. Yes; put them all under one head.

Mr. THOMPSON. That is very difficult, but I can mention some things we have found which apply to a great many of them. One factor, of course, is management. One is the question of location; that is, is the enterprise properly located; is it in a field where there is any chance of success?

Mr. HAUGEN. Efficiency enters into that?

Mr. THOMPSON. Yes; it does; and the question of how to start it; was it promoted properly or not; was it started to advantage, or was it started with a handicap? In other words, did it have a millstone around its neck at its very inception, so that it had no chance to survive?

The CHAIRMAN. The spirit of cooperation that may have been developed in the community?

Mr. THOMPSON. Yes, sir. Then there is the question of accounts and audits for the organization.

Mr. HAUGEN. That depends on the good judgment of the organizer, does it not?

Mr. THOMPSON. Yes.

Mr. HAUGEN. It is all a question of efficiency?

Mr. THOMPSON. The question of the form or plan of the organization is very important, whether it is practically a cooperative association or not. Is it so constituted that after a while the members lose interest and fall away, or has it in it elements such that it will continue? There are very many important questions involved there.

Mr. HAUGEN. Well, with efficiency to make it a success, its success will largely depend upon the management.

Mr. MCLAUGHLIN. I guess, if the rates are reasonable and the company pays its losses, it continues to do business.

Mr. THOMPSON. We have found that improvement in these associations could be effected in a number of ways. For instance, in the classification of their risks and questions with reference to reinsurance of local risks are important questions that are being given attention at this time.

I think it would be interesting to take one example: In the State of Minnesota, represented by one of the members of the committee, you perhaps learned recently of a very devastating fire in the northeastern part of the State, which destroyed almost entirely the property of five or six of those local farmers' mutual insurance companies. In that particular case the State association has taken over not because it is legally required to do so, but voluntarily—it has taken over and acted in fact in the function of a reinsuring agency.

Mr. ANDERSON. They are very honest in Minnesota.

Mr. THOMPSON. And all the associations in Minnesota together jointly, are facing that hazard.

Mr. HAUGEN. The State did that?

Mr. THOMPSON. Not the State, but the State association of local farmers' mutual insurance companies.

Mr. MCLAUGHLIN. The state association took over the business of the local companies. It did not pay the local companies' losses, did it?

Mr. THOMPSON. It distributes the losses of that local mutual insurance company between that company and all the others of the State in such a way that the locals can face the losses.

Mr. McLaughlin. Then the losses that the local companies were not able to pay, these other companies paid those losses?

Mr. Thompson. Shared the losses, yes.

Mr. Haugen. How do you connect that with the department, what the State did in taking over the insurance? Is that a function of the department?

Mr. Thompson. It illustrates the importance of the reinsurance matter.

Mr. Haugen. What we are trying to find out is what this money is used for.

Mr. Thompson. Well, it is used not for service work in the sense such as you have been discussing heretofore, not in regulatory work, but in investigational work and demonstration work, bringing to the attention of all of these local mutual fire insurance companies information that will make them more efficient along these various lines.

Mr. McLaughlin. Now if you will tell us how any of this is a marketing proposition I shall be obliged to you.

Mr. Thompson. It is not marketing work.

Mr. Haugen. It was stated that you assisted in the framing of the land bank bill, the Federal land bank bill. What did you do or what assistance did you render? My understanding is that some one was employed to draft the bill and was paid a good fee for doing it.

The Chairman. How is that?

Mr. Haugen. My understanding is that some one, I believe in New York, was employed to draft the bill, and received a big fee for drafting it.

The Chairman. I never heard of it before, and it is not true.

Mr. Brand. Mr. Thompson and his associates prepared a complete draft of the bill, which was submitted and used as a basis.

The Chairman. He sat with me one night until 2 o'clock in the morning.

Mr. Brand. It was a composite of many, many ideas.

Mr. Haugen. Oh, well; there were thousands of ideas presented, of course; they were not all adopted.

Mr. Brand. No one worker in rural credits, I think Mr. Lever will agree with me, contributed as much, or certainly no more, than Mr. Thompson to the bill.

The Chairman. I think that is absolutely true, and all good, sound thought.

Mr. Haugen. Now we have the bill; what are we going to do with it; what is this appropriation for?

Mr. McLaughlin. He has nothing to do with the working of the bill, has he?

The Chairman. Not with the enforcement of the rural credits.

Mr. McLaughlin. That is what I thought.

The Chairman. He was about the only source of information we had under this item. Mr. Thompson had been studying the proposition, and there are those of us who framed the bill who thank him for his advice and suggestions, and I think Mr. Thompson and Senator Hollis, and Mr. Flannagan, secretary of the board, had as much to do with framing that legislation as anybody.

Mr. ANDERSON. There is one statement you made regarding investigations touching on interest rates. I am very much surprised to know that. I thought the Federal Reserve Board and the Farm Loan Board, through their branches throughout the country were getting information touching interest rates.

Mr. THOMPSON. I think possibly they have, but that is a matter we could do with very small expense. If you will look back in the records you will recall we presented data on that three years ago, showing the interest rates and costs, and it was the only data of the kind presented before the Congressional committees at the time the Federal farm-loan act was being discussed.

Mr. ANDERSON. I remember the comptroller, or the Secretary of the Treasury, within the last year or two made some very radical statements in regard to interest rates, particularly in the southern section of the country, evidently, I suppose, made after investigation; certainly they were made on authority, and it would seem as though institutions having this widespread ramification, such as the Federal Reserve Board and the Farm Loan Board, ought to have some information about interest rates, without making use of an organization which really ought not to have anything to do with that particular matter. If you can give any explanation of that, I should like to have it.

Mr. THOMPSON. I am just waiting to be sure that when I speak I speak to the point.

Mr. ANDERSON. What I was trying to get at is, what reason would there be for asking your particular organization to get this information, with the facilities which it would seem the Federal Reserve Board and the Farm Loan Board have of their own?

Mr. THOMPSON. When we made our investigation three years ago, our inquiry went not only to banks, but it went to farmers in all counties of the United States, and it also went, of course, to the other agencies that furnish loans, insurance companies, speaking on the mortgage loan side of the question. Of course, Federal land banks are only one of the many sources. We have insurance companies, life insurance companies; we have mortagage companies and other agencies that loan funds in that direction, and in the matter even of short-time loans the banks, of course, are one source and are a very important source, the important source, probably, yet there are short-time loans to farmers from other sources.

Mr. ANDERSON. Let me ask you there, did your investigation go to the extent of determining rates charged by local people—by farmers themselves—to loan money to their neighbors, and local money lenders?

Mr. THOMPSON. We were unable to line up our data in such a way as to generalize for, for instance, private lenders as such, but we did have the loans from banks separate from other sources, and our information from banks was shown separately from information from other sources.

Mr. HAUGEN. I recall John Skelton Williams furnishing the country with some very interesting information on the bank rates. Did you supply him with those?

Mr. THOMPSON. No, I did not. I will say further on the subject of the sources of information that we considered in conference with others the most efficient way of proceeding, and one of our methods adopted was utilizing the existing agencies of the Bureau of Crop Estimates to get the information from farmers all over the country, and we could do that very efficiently and very cheaply. That bureau has a list of correspondents ready to use in the matter of giving information.

Mr. HAUGEN. I notice that every division of this bureau takes considerable credit for this cooperative association work. You seem to have had a hand in it, and every other. Is there not some overlapping or duplication of work there?

Mr. THOMPSON. There is no overlapping of which I have any knowledge. In the Bureau of Markets itself there are certain projects that give attention to certain specialized lines of association; for instance, the cooperative purchasing and cooperative marketing comes under an item which has already been considered—the first item, I believe, before you. The matter of cooperative credit associations and farmers' mutual insurance companies comes under the particular item that is now being discussed, and under no other item. There is a clear differentiation between types of association considered under each project, so there is no duplication.

Mr. HAUGEN. And practically no cooperation in the department; it has to be handled by different men, each proposition by different men?

Mr. THOMPSON. There are illustrations I might cite to show how it is necessary for the projects within the bureau to cooperate as well as for the bureau to cooperate with other agencies. For instance, we have formulated a tentative model for a credit union law, a model State law, that was prepared in cooperation with the office of the solicitor. Then there was a model State law that has been published which was prepared by cooperation between officials of this project and officials of the cooperative purchasing and marketing project and other officials, and that is the so-called State cooperative law, which has been published and, I believe, has already been referred to in the proceedings.

Mr. HAUGEN. You send people in the field from your office over the country and advise them as to these things, as to how to organize insurance associations and others. Do you send field agents out?

Mr. THOMPSON. Our representative in insurance goes out to the insurance companies, to such local mutual insurance companies, and he is often present to advise with the officials in State and national associations of mutual insurance associations, and also has been called in conference by a committee of the National Association of Farmers' Mutual Insurance Associations to formulate with them a model State law for mutual insurance companies. A draft for such a law, by the way, had been prepared by the officials represented under this project, in cooperation with the office of the solicitor.

Mr. HAUGEN. Have nearly all the States passed laws now?

Mr. THOMPSON. We have laws in a number of States, but we also have some variation in those laws and we have many States where the laws are such that they are capable of considerable improvement.

Mr. HAUGEN. Now we are going into insurance. The object of this item is credits, is it not?

Mr. THOMPSON. That is one object, but there are several others that are also involved.

I may say that credits and insurance are two of the items. Now under this item we are also expected to and do furnish from time to time information regarding national associations of different sorts, rural organization of many kinds. We have a considerable amount of information on hand regarding a large number of national and State associations of different kinds, regarding which we are called upon to furnish information.

Mr. HAUGEN. It seems to me it more properly belongs to the other branch of the Government. I should think the bank would handle this and if necessary to do this work it could well be transferred over to the Federal Farm Loan Board.

The CHAIRMAN. The Federal Farm Loan Board would have no interest in mutual insurance companies, would it, or telephone companies. Mr. Thompson?

Mr. HAUGEN. I should think if it had any interest at all it would have just as much interest as any other department of the Government. What have you accomplished about short time credit mortgages or personal loans?

Mr. THOMPSON. We have formulated, as I stated a moment ago, a model State law for cooperative credit unions, which has been published as a service and regulatory announcement.

Mr. HAUGEN. Has it been enacted in any State?

Mr. THOMPSON. The law has been made the basis for enactment in States that now have cooperative credit-union laws.

Mr. HAUGEN. What States are they?

Mr. THOMPSON. In the State of North Carolina, and there has been suggested a modification in the law in other States.

Mr. HAUGEN. With what success? Are they doing a pretty good business?

Mr. THOMPSON. The credit unions, I should say, so far as they are farmers' credit unions, are most successful in the State of North Carolina. We have sixteen local credit unions there, organized entirely among farmers; the most successful examples, I should say, we have anywhere in the country. I think it would be interesting too to note that there has been organized, in the last year, a local cooperative credit association entirely among the colored people.

Mr. HAUGEN. Organized with capital?

Mr. THOMPSON. Under the laws of the State.

Mr. HAUGEN. How much capital do they carry?

Mr. THOMPSON. Just a small, nominal share capital that each man contributes; they have share capital, and they also put in deposits. The share capital is a small, nominal amount of $10.

Mr. HAUGEN. Pretty much on the same line as the land-bank real estate loans?

Mr. THOMPSON. The plan is quite different in many important respects.

STATEMENT OF MR. CHARLES J. BRAND, CHIEF OF THE BUREAU OF MARKETS, UNITED STATES DEPARTMENT OF AGRICULTURE—Continued.

The CHAIRMAN. Take up your next item, Mr. Brand, page 248, item 129, cooperative work with the States in marketing. There seems to be an increase there of $34,420. Tell us briefly about that.

Mr. BRAND. This is merely an extension of existing work. At the present moment cooperative field agents are employed by us in cooperation with State authorities in Arizona, Arkansas, Colorado, Connecticut, Georgia, Indiana, Iowa, Louisiana, Massachusetts, Michigan, Minnesota, Mississipi, Montana, Nebraska, New Mexico, North Carolina, North Dakota, Oregon, South Carolina, Tennessee, Texas, Utah, Vermont, Virginia and Washington. Those are the states in which we now have cooperative field agents.

The CHAIRMAN. To what States do you expect to extend that?

Mr. BRAND. We are anxious to extend the work and the States themselves very earnestly ask it and in many cases set aside a fund. According to our present plans we will take up work as soon as possible in Kansas, Missouri, Florida, Oklahoma, Kentucky and Idaho, and will extend the work in those States in which we are now working where advisable, particularly to perfect it somewhat in some of the newer States where we have only made a beginning.

The CHAIRMAN. This work has been going on about three years, has it, Mr. Brand?

Mr. BRAND. Yes.

Mr. MCLAUGHLIN. Did you have agents in those States cooperating with State authorities?

Mr. BRAND. Yes.

Mr. MCLAUGHLIN. What do they do?

Mr. BRAND. They are the points of contact within the State through which we coordinate all of our activities in marketing, and through which we bring about a uniformity of action with the States, in order that we may have some degree of national uniformity, which, as you know, is totally lacking in marketing matters. This work forms a very useful and successful method of bringing it about.

I may say that the States are devoting about twice as much money to the work as we are. We are devoting, all told, $75,000; and the States are devoting to the work $144,000; and other independent agencies are devoting, as I recall it, about $15,000 to this work.

Mr. ANDERSON. I think you said this is the item under which you are teaching the farmers to understand your wheat and corn grades?

Mr. BRAND. No; this is not that item. That will come up in connection with the Grain Standards act.

Mr. ANDERSON. Well, I have it marked down here (indicating).

Mr. MCLAUGHLIN. Have these State associations that you speak of been doing work at all similar to yours in gathering information about prices and quantities of different products in different parts of the country, and whether there is a glut or a scarcity in the market?

Mr. BRAND. More and more, Mr. McLaughlin, they are; and we are and have been furnishing leadership for that work in practically all of States. They look to us absolutely for the leadership and for suggestion, and for the outlining of what is sound and proper policy with respect to those matters.

We have drafted a so-called model law for the use of the States, as a suggestion of what they might enact in the way of a State law establishing State divisions of marketing. A number of them have followed our model—some literally—some have not been able to go as far as the suggestion; some have gone farther.

Mr. McLaughlin. Well, if such a State association was located at Detroit, Mich., for instance, and should get a report as to conditions and prices in Chicago, and you would get the same thing, there would certainly be a duplication of the work if the figures and facts are correct; if they are the real facts they will be the same.

Mr. Brand. No State marketing agency, excepting in the State of Oklahoma, provides for the securing of information in other States; and in Oklahoma that part of their law has not been followed, but they depend almost wholly upon the information we are furnishing them, from our national news service.

Mr. McLaughlin. My first question was, Is any State association doing work similar to yours, about getting information from the markets of the country?

Mr. Brand. No; none of the individual State organizations are; they depend upon us for that.

Mr. McLaughlin. They are gathering data as to matters within the respective States alone?

Mr. Brand. Yes. And I may say that officials in your State think they are warranted in supporting the Bureau of Markets because it carries on 90 per cent of its functions with respect to interstate markets. Michigan grows peaches; she grows apples, and she grows potatoes; and not one-tenth of them are consumed in Michigan. And the same is true as to other States. I only cite the case of Michigan because that State is a great producer of perishable products.

Mr. Haugen. Now, you have State agents on live stock; you have State agents on dairying and poultry; and you have them on grain, hay, and feed; and another item on seeds. It seems to me that you have run out of items. Why not consolidate all under one head and cut the appropriation—after making appropriations under separate heads for all of these items. What is there for these people to do? [Laughter.] They are doing about the same work, are they not? Could you not think of some other item you could put $100,000 under? [Laughter.]

Mr. McLaughlin. That is very amusing to the fellows who have been getting the money.

Mr. Haugen. How about dandelions? [Laughter.]

Mr. Brand. I want to respond to Mr. Haugen's question; it is a fair one. This particular item represents what has been decided to be the most efficient way of getting into the States through their own organizations and through their own citizens. Many of the lines of work are lines that we carry on on a national scale. It is an adoption, practically, of the principle that prevails with reference to agricultural extension work throughout the United States. It is a pure adoption of that principle.

Mr. Haugen. All of these other items are for the marketing of farm products, are they not? Now, in what respect does this differ from the other items?

Mr. Brand. This differs in its being a channel for placing in the several States, in the most effective way, the results of the whole work of the Bureau of Markets.

Mr. Haugen. What becomes of the other fellows then? They are lost sight of altogether.

Mr. Brand. When it comes to this particular matter they are lost sight of, because the work is carried on through this particular project in order that there may be coordination in our activities and in our dealings with each of the States. We can not have 15 or 20 projects dealing with each of the States; we have to carry it on through certain definite channels in order that we may carry out certain definite projects and know that they are being carried out; and in order that the States may know where to apply.

The CHAIRMAN. It is largely administrative work, is it not?

Mr. BRAND. It is largely administrative work, or bringing to them the information through administrative and educational channels.

Mr. HAUGEN. I agree with you—you can answer more questions than any man who ever appeared before this committee. [Laughter.]

Mr. McLAUGHLIN. I do not really see the need of this thing.

The CHAIRMAN. We have discussed it again and again.

Mr. McLAUGHLIN. This other information they get through their mailing lists; all of this information reaches everybody. The gentlemen were brought before the committee to tell about how widely they diffuse this information; everybody who wishes it, and needs it, gets it. Now, it appears that they have to have State organizations to which they must communicate this information, so that those associations may distribute it.

Mr. BRAND. Mr. Chairman, there are 6,000,000 farmers in the United States, and we are trying to get this information to just as many of those farmers as we can. We can not, as a national organization, bring it to more than a small fraction of them; but we realize that the 48 States, with their own agencies, can reach very many more; and this is the channel for putting it into their hands.

Mr. HAUGEN. You consider that they are ornamental, then?

Mr. BRAND. No; that they serve a broad national purpose rather than an intrastate purpose. For instance, take broom corn, in the State of Colorado; that was a State problem there. Another year it was a problem in Oklahoma.

Mr. McLAUGHLIN. If it was a State problem, why did you have anything to do with it?

Mr. BRAND. It was a State matter; but Colorado does not use her broom corn; New York does use it. So we make an effort to bring what information we can to Colorado with reference to marketing her broom-corn crop. I might say that in not a single case, have we inaugurated this work in coordination with a State without a very strong demand from the State that it be taken up. We have frequent requests for cooperation. Within the last five days I have had two communications from Kansas urging that we start this work there.

The CHAIRMAN. We will take up the next item, No. 130, on page 249; that is your investigational work on grain?

Mr. BRAND. That is for investigating the handling, grading, and transportation of grain and grain sorghums, $86,050. This work has been under way for a series of years. It is under this investigational project that the standards for corn were established and are now in force under the grain standards act. The investigational work which led to the establishment of the wheat standards is carried on under this project. Those standards are now in operation, and have been changed during the past year, to meet more adequately, we think, the existing situation with reference to the marketing of the wheat crop. It has been a very difficult situation, and we have tried to adapt our work to it.

The present activities are chiefly related to the standards for oats, the standards for rice, for barley, for rye, and for flax; the transportation and storage of grain; bulk handling, particularly in the Pacific northwest, where they handle their grain in bags and not in elevators, as we do in the primary grain country of the United States; control of smut and dust explosions, and things of that sort. Smut-control and dust-explosion work is carried on cooperatively with some of the other bureaus of the department.

Mr. HAUGEN. That is carried on by the Bureau of Chemistry, is it not?

Mr. BRAND. We have a joint project with the Bureau of Chemistry. There is not a penny of duplication in the matter. The Bureau of Plant Industry is also in the project with us.

Mr. HAUGEN. There are just two standards—those for corn and those for wheat?

Mr. BRAND. Yes, that are now being enforced.

Mr. HAUGEN. How many years has this work been going on?

Mr. BRAND. This work was originally established in the Bureau of Plant Industry in 1907, 11 years ago. It involves many other things besides the establishment of standards; it involves the storage of grain, the determination of the percentage of moisture that grain can bear in storage, and all of those questions.

Mr. HAUGEN. This takes in the stacking and shocking proposition, too, does it not?

Mr. BRAND. To a very large extent.

Mr. HAUGEN. Do you find that grain stands up better after shocking has been supervised by one of your representatives? [Laughter.]

Mr. BRAND. If it was subjected to this cross-examination for two days—yes, it would stand almost anything. [Laughter.]

The CHAIRMAN. If there are no other questions, we will proceed to the next item—131.

Mr. BRAND. The next item is very small and does not represent an increase, although it refers to a very important work. In the future we may suggest an amendment to the standard container act, which is the act that controls the manufacture, sale, use, and shipping of baskets, particularly the "snide" sizes of baskets.

The CHAIRMAN. What kind of baskets?

Mr. BRAND. "Snide," crooked baskets, that look like baskets of half bushels, for instance, but are short anywhere from an eighth to a quarter.

The CHAIRMAN. Made to deceive the public?

Mr. BRAND. Made to deceive the public. And we have a series of them that are simply wonderful. We have cured a little of that fraud, and we have now a couple of cases that we are recommending for prosecution. We have examined over 30 factories to determine if they are manufacturing the standard sizes of baskets, and we have the thing in fairly clean shape; but there are certain things that can not be reached under the legislation as it stands.

The CHAIRMAN. That act did not come from this committee, but originally came from the Committee on Coinage, Weights, and Measures.

Mr. BRAND. This act did not come from this committee and originally was not provided with any administrative machinery whatever; but upon the recommendation of the Secretary this committee provided a modest fund for it.

Mr. HEFLIN. There is no increase in the item?

Mr. BRAND. There is no increase.

The CHAIRMAN. Take up the next item—132. That is the flour mill project, and there is an increase there?

Mr. BRAND. Yes, sir; that is the item for an experimental flour mill. I have asked Mr. Marshall, our assistant chief, who has been handling this work for the past eight months, to present this particular question; he is much more familiar with it than I am.

The CHAIRMAN. All right. We will hear Mr. Marshall.

STATEMENT OF MR. HERBERT C. MARSHALL, ASSISTANT CHIEF OF THE BUREAU OF MARKETS, UNITED STATES DEPARTMENT OF AGRICULTURE.

Mr. MARSHALL. Mr. Chairman, I presume that all the committee is interested in is the reason for the change from the policy of renting a mill to that of constructing one. The increase in the appropriation refers to that.

Mr. HAUGEN. I am interested in this: We were told that $50,000 would be all that would be required; and now you are asking for $85,000.

Mr. MARSHALL. Because it seems desirable that the Government should build the mill, rather than rent it.

Mr. HAUGEN. The $50,000 included the building of the mill.

Mr. MARSHALL. No.

Mr. HAUGEN. Well, it did in the estimate.

The CHAIRMAN. No; this was never estimated for; this was put in as a Senate amendment.

Mr. HAUGEN. Exactly; we had it in conference for weeks.

Mr. MCLAUGHLIN. The word "install" was in the old law; that was supposed to cover the expense of building and equipping the mill, etc.

Mr. MARSHALL. The way the item reads makes it necessary for us to assume that we can only pay the rent of the building.

The CHAIRMAN. Well, I do not interpret the language in that way. I think that provision for payment of rent is the same kind of provision that is inserted in many of the other items in the bill as to the employment of people in Washington and outside of Washington; a great many of these items carry such provision.

Mr. MARSHALL. At any rate, in dealing with the matter, we felt that we had absolutely no power to build, even if the fund was sufficient.

Mr. BRAND. The fund was not sufficient, and the comptroller ruled that we had no power to build under the law.

Mr. MCLAUGHLIN. Did the comptroller say the authority of the Secretary of Agriculture to "install an experimental mill" gave him no authority to build one and buy machinery and equipment for it?

Mr. MARSHALL. Presumably, it would include buying the machinery, but not constructing the building. "Installing" would cover installing the machinery but not the construction of a building.

Mr. ANDERSON. Is he foolish enough to think that you could rent a mill in Washington?

Mr. MARSHALL. It was an error to use the word "install."

The CHAIRMAN. This committee never had any recommendation on this proposition; the Department has never made any recommendation; it was inserted by the Senate.

Mr. BRAND. We were recommending that such an item be included, I took it up with the Secretary, and the matter was included in the bill by the Senate committee. Under the statutes we are specifically prohibited from acquiring real estate without express authority.

The CHAIRMAN. That is true. But what I am trying to bring out is whatever fault there is is not an administrative fault, but a legislative fault; because you gentlemen made no suggestion or submitted no memorandum on it; the item was put in by the Senate; and the House conferees finally had to agree to it.

Mr. HAUGEN. I remember distinctly that the purpose of the item was to build the mill here in Washington; I remember conferring with Mr. Gardon as to the cost of the mill; and it was finally determined that $50,000 would build a small mill and carry on the experiment; and we concluded to give the $50,000 in the hope that the whole thing would be disposed of.

The CHAIRMAN. That is true.

Mr. HAUGEN. Now they come in and ask for $85,000 more.

The CHAIRMAN. Mr. Marshall, how much of that $50,000 have you expended?

Mr. MARSHALL. I can not tell you exactly how much has been expended; we have not expended all of it.

The CHAIRMAN. What have you expended any of it for?

Mr. MARSHALL. We have expended it for renting a small building and the installation of a small experimental mill, which will grind 10-pound samples. That machinery we have now installed, and with it we have a small baking establishment. The money has been entirely devoted to the equipment of this small mill and baking establishment, which is electrically heated, and to the payment of the salaries of four men who are the only persons who have been on this work this year.

Mr. ANDERSON. Is it necessary to go further than that in order to ascertain the milling value of wheat.

Mr. MARSHALL. That question was taken up, I think, to some extent, at a former hearing. There can be no question about the necessity of using a larger mill. We have conducted the mill as it is, a 10-pound sample mill, but the mill experts tell us that on these little samples you can not accomplish the results that are absolutely essential if definite and reliable conclusions are to be arrived at and do the work that it is necessary to carry out.

Mr. ANDERSON. That is very indefinite, when you say "the work that it is necessary to carry out." I asked you a specific question—whether it was necessary to go further than the experimental mill you have in order to determine the milling value of wheat.

Mr. MARSHALL. Perhaps I was wrong in saying the "experimental mill;" I should have said the "small mill."

Mr. ANDERSON. Can' I get an answer to that question, whether or not it is necessary to go further than the equipment which you have now, which, I understand, is a small experimental mill, in order to determine the milling value of wheat?

Mr. MARSHALL. Oh, yes. Nothing less than a 25-barrel mill would be of any value in determining the milling value of wheat—in practice.

Mr. HEFLIN. Have you consulted with experts in flour mills as to the size necessary?

Mr. MARSHALL. We have consulted with the best experts in the United States as to the unit that will give us the best comparable results. We are trying to shorten the rolls, and have opportunities for repeating on the rolls, so that we will have practically the same results we would get from a much larger unit, but our present equipment is not sufficient.

The CHAIRMAN. I do not like to break in on this line of questions; but I do not want the record to carry any incorrect statement of facts. I was under the impression, as I said before, that the department had submitted no memorandum on this question; that it was apparently a legislative act, rather than a department suggestion. I was correct in the statement that the proposal was not presented in the estimates; but I have here in my hand a letter, dated February 1, 1918, addressed to me by the Secretary of Agriculture, in which he points out the advisability of this work and suggests the very language that was put into this item. I will read the language:

To enable the Secretary of Agriculture to install an experimental flour mill, baking and other apparatus, in order to determine the milling and baking qualities of wheat and other grains, including the payment of rent in the city of Washington.

Mr. HAUGEN. What is the date of that letter?

The CHAIRMAN. February 1, 1918. So I was mistaken in saying that the department had submitted no memorandum on the subject.

Mr. MARSHALL. Whatever suggestion may have come from the department, I am sure everybody in the department is convinced that it would be an error to attempt to accomplish it by renting a building.

The CHAIRMAN. The department has changed its viewpoint, then.

Mr. MARSHALL. If that was the viewpoint.

Mr. BRAND. Mr. Chairman, I am sure that when the memorandum was prepared there was no such thought—my recollection is that a memorandum went to Mr. Young. I do not remember now the details of it, but I see that one went to you. The department's thought then was to do as it does in all other cases, to rent a building put up by some local man who wishes to invest in a building and then rent it to the Government.

The CHAIRMAN. I think the thought of the conferees in discussing this proposition was that you would put up on the Arlington farm a flour mill, at a cost of $50,000. Is that your recollection, Mr. Lee?

Mr. LEE. Yes; that is mine also.

Mr. BRAND. I remember the Arlington farm proposition.

The CHAIRMAN. Have you sufficient ground there on which you could erect a mill for such a purpose?

Mr. BRAND. There are some pretty strong objections to that location. The mill should be erected convenient to railroad facilities; and a very much better location can be obtained from that standpoint. The transportation of the wheat to the mill and of the flour away from the mill would be quite an item.

Mr. LEE. Then, it should be located where you could sell it when the Government gets through with it.

Mr. BRAND. Yes, that would be an object.

The CHAIRMAN. Let us see what we have here. You have an appropriation of $50,000, which will be available until the 1st of next July?

Mr. BRAND. Yes.

The CHAIRMAN (continuing). To build a flour mill. In addition to that, you desire $85,000 for the next fiscal year, which will make your flour mill of a daily capacity of 25 barrels. Is that right?

Mr. BRAND. Yes.

The CHAIRMAN. That gives you $135,000——

Mr. BRAND (interposing). Not quite that.

The CHAIRMAN (continuing). Taking out, of course, the salaries of the men employed, etc., which will be a negligible factor—probably $8,000 or $10,000 or $15,000.

Mr. BRAND. It is hoped that at least $10,000 of the present appropriation, as is suggested in the item here, can be devoted to the purchase of equipment for the mill, if it is provided for. As a matter of fact, the $85,000 will not of itself construct a mill, install the machinery, and take care of the work for the coming year. That $85,000 would not do it.

The CHAIRMAN. Well, if you start now, you will have $85,000 plus——

Mr. BRAND (interposing). I am sure we can not start on this $50,000. I am pretty sure the language of the present item would not authorize the construction of any building.

The CHAIRMAN. Is it your intention to stop expenditures out of this $50,000 with the renting of a little mill, with three or four employees on small salaries?

Mr. BRAND. If this $85,000, or a sufficient amount for building and installing the machinery is provided, then we would look forward to making some purchases in advanuce, just as the item before you indicates.

Mr. ANDERSON. Where did you get your estimates on the cost of construction?

Mr. MARSHALL. From builders. I did not myself get them. The man in charge of that project got them, and I cross-examined him on them, and went into it pretty thoroughly. I myself am not a milling man.

Mr. ANDERSON. It strikes me that $85,000 for a 25-barrel mill is an absolutely absurd figure.

Mr. MARSHALL. If you will notice, for construction there is $35,000; $4,000 for the purchase of land—and we are afraid that at present prices it will not do it.

Mr. MCLAUGHLIN. Is it necessary to buy land? The Government has land all over this District now.

Mr. MARSHALL. It is more important that the building should be located convenient to the railroads and the markets than that you should save a few thousand dollars on the purchase of the land. In the long run it would be quite an economy to purchase property correctly located.

The CHAIRMAN. I can see that.

Mr. ANDERSON. If that is true, why locate it in Washington?

Mr. MARSHALL. In order to have it under the Federal Government strictly. If it was located in North Dakota, Kansas, or Illinois, the results would not be accepted as readily by the rest of the country, we think, as if it were located in Washington.

The CHAIRMAN. That was the view we took, some of the conferees—that the department was already doing some cooperative work with that North Dakota experiment station——

Mr. ANDERSON (interposing). In other words, the farther you get your flour mill from the people who know about the milling business, the more likely they will be to accept the results?

Mr. BRAND. They have a large number of mills in the east.

Mr. MARSHALL. Yes; a number at Baltimore.

Mr. ANDERSON. They have some.

Mr. MARSHALL. Even with this 25-barrel mill it is certain that a large number of the investigations will be carried on in still other mills—mills of commercial size. It is not thought that a 25-barrel mill will be sufficient for all sorts of experiments; in fact, a 25-barrel mill is merely a minimum size.

Mr. MCLAUGHLIN. How many years do you think it would take you to do it?

Mr. MARSHALL. To construct the mill?

Mr. MCLAUGHLIN. No; you could construct the mill in 15 minutes. How many years to carry on the experiment?

Mr. BRAND. As long as the United States grades wheat.

Mr. MARSHALL. There are several objects in view—primarily the dealing with the grain standards. Those have been promulgated, but improvements, of course, will be made in them. They will have to be revised and changed as the situation warrants, and the principal purpose of the mill is to make investigations with that in view. Then there are other plans in prospect—questions of milling technology, and the efficiency of flour mills, can freely be dealt with in that mill.

The CHAIRMAN. You will have to change your language here [indicating] if you do that; you have no authority here to do that, under the language used.

Mr. MCLAUGHLIN. This does not say anything about the grades; this has nothing to do with the grades or with changing them.

Mr. BRAND. The grain standards act authorizes the changing of the grades—changing them after due notice.

The CHAIRMAN. That is a very big sum to spend on such a mill in the city of Washington. I can see that your overhead expenses would be much larger than if it was run by a private concern.

Mr. HAUGEN. It looks to me like perpetual motion—we were told that $50,000 would be sufficient, and now they want $85,000 more.

The CHAIRMAN. I will say that I never had any such thought. I knew this would be a large investigation. I thought $50,000 would start the plant; but I thought the investigation would run for a long period of time.

Mr. HAUGEN. I take it there is a limit to Uncle Sam's credit, and, of course, if it is absolutely necessary to bankrupt him at the start, all right; if not, it might be well to take a few of these expenditures into consideration.

The CHAIRMAN. Is there anything more as to this item?

Mr. MARSHALL. With regard to the amount of the appropriation, two of our men visited a large mill at Manhattan, Kans., and spent a week there, actually running the mill. The men who ran it were sick with the "flu," and our men ran the mill for a week, and they also made some further inquiries in Kansas City and also in Minneapolis, about costs; and when they came back I said, "What do you think of our estimate?" They said, "It is too low." And so I do not want to leave the impression that there is a possibility of that estimate being too high for building even the small mill that is contemplated.

Mr. HAUGEN. There are a number of mills now operated with 100-barrel capacity, having much less capital than even $50,000. Why should you need more money than they?

Mr. LEE. This is a very small mill.

Mr. MARSHALL. 25-barrel capacity.

Mr. HAUGEN. It does not take more money to operate a small mill than a large one, does it?

Mr. MARSHALL. I should suppose a very large proportion of the wheat of the country is ground in the large mills; so that we think it is very desirable that we come as near to that condition as we can, with reasonable expense.

Mr. HAUGEN. Is it the policy to compete with the Washburns?

Mr. MARSHALL. No; but to have a mill that will give us results that are in some way comparable with results in a large commercial mill.

Mr. HAUGEN. If a 100-barrel mill is not sufficient, how large a mill would you require—1,000 barrels?

Mr. MARSHALL. This is 25 barrels.

Mr. HAUGEN. But you say that is too small; would you want one of 50 or 100 barrel capacity?

Mr. MARSHALL. It would be better if the mill were larger.

Mr. HAUGEN. But I say those mills are operated with a capital of less than $50,000.

Mr. BRAND. I think there is a total misapprehension of this item.

Mr. HAUGEN. Go ahead.

Mr. BRAND. I think Mr. Anderson has in mind that this was only to grind wheat.

Mr. ANDERSON. That was the understanding when the item was put in.

Mr. BRAND. A corn mill is totally different from a wheat mill. A barley mill is so different that when a regular mill started to grind barley, it had to be reconstructed. I talked with Mr. Pillsbury on this subject——

Mr. ANDERSON (interposing). The Food Administrator's man says the contrary.

Mr. BRAND. The Food Administration man tells us so. He is the man who is looked up to by the millers as knowing more than anybody else; and he is the man who furnished us the plan, and he furnished our estimates. This mill is to include not only wheat, but corn, oats, barley, rye, and other products to which we must give attention.

Mr. ANDERSON. Let me ask you this question: Can you draw any language under which it will be possible to get down the particular thing that we had in mind to have done when this item was put in—which was an experimental mill to grind wheat?

Mr. BRAND. You have it in the plans that we are presenting to you—absolutely.

Mr. ANDERSON (continuing). And not including everything else that you, by the exercise of a very fertile imagination, can stick into it?

Mr. BRAND. That is not fair. The corn millers are just as anxiously demanding additional information so that they can improve their technology and have the same advantages the wheat people have; and we must think of all the other products. But it does include, specifically and most particularly, doing exactly the things, for instance, that the Northwestern States desire.

The CHAIRMAN. It says "the milling and baking qualities of wheat and other grains."

Mr. ANDERSON. Perhaps I did not know anything about it when the item went in; but this barley, oats and rye proposition is new to me.

Mr. BRAND. Would you suggest that it be limited to wheat? The corn crop amounts to 2¾ billion bushels.

Mr. ANDERSON. Could we defend such action? I do not know, but hardly think there is the same reason for an experimental mill in the case of oats as there is in the case of wheat.

Mr. BRAND. That is very true; and the money cost of making it adaptable for oats and these other grains represents a very small part of the cost.

Mr. HAUGEN. I was just going to ask you what was the cost of installing——

The CHAIRMAN (interposing). Before you do that, let me make another correction. I was mixed up on this item. The language, I said a moment ago, was suggested by the Department of Agriculture. That is not the fact. A careful reading of this memorandum shows that the Secretary only refers to the item as contained in the Senate amendment, and did not quote the amendment as a suggestion of the department; so that I come back to the original proposition that the Senate was responsible for it.

Mr. HAUGEN. My recollection is that it was incorporated in the Senate; and we fought it in conference. And now Mr. Brand says you ought to do so and so. I think it should be left to Congress as to what should be done.

Mr. BRAND. I heartily agree with you as to that.

Mr. HAUGEN. Now, it is a question whether the department shall determine what is to be done by Congress. Congress determined that it should be limited, and that the total expenditure should be limited to $50,000. And here you are asking for $85,000 more.

Mr. BRAND. I want to make it perfectly clear that we are only trying to present all of the facts and that we fully realize that we must and always do conform to the decisions of the committee. We are not trying to do more than present the facts; so that you will not include it or exclude it without having the facts before you. The other grains were included in the item as it stood.

Mr. HAUGEN. Well, if you are conforming with the committee's views, or the views of Congress, that means $50,000 for the experiment, that means the building of the mill, operating it, making your report, and that should be the end of it. That is my understanding.

Mr. BRAND. I have just refreshed my memory by consulting with Mr. Livingston, who assisted in passing upon the item when it was submitted to the department. He and Dr. Duvel considered it very carefully; and his recollection is very distinct indeed that they had no thought that it would be possible with the sum of money appropriated to build a flour mill in the city of Washington or its environs.

Mr. MCLAUGHLIN. Have you found any unwillingness or failure on the part of the millers of the country to make experiments and absorb improved machinery if they have discovered something good?

Mr. BRAND. The conduct of these tests, Mr. McLaughlin, will require the continual running time of any mill that is devoted to the question. I have followed the principle you have in mind in our cotton work very largely. We always work on the principle that where we can get the miller or commercial man to do the thing with his equipment we will not install the equipment.

The CHAIRMAN. This committee did not make the recommendation.

Mr. BRAND. I think Senator E. D. Smith did; I am not clear as to that. There was much argument in favor of it; but as long as we could get the cotton spinners to set aside parts of their mills; it seemed to us better to have them do so. So we never would have asked you for an appropriation of that character unless we thought it was necessary.

Mr. MCLAUGHLIN. Are your experts competent to tell Congress that they have found defective processes in the mills and that the flour is not made right, and other grain is not treated right, and that the baking is not done right, and all of those things, so that it is necessary for the Government to take this matter out of the hands of private interests, and it is necessary for the Government to devote a great deal of money to making these experiments over a great series of years?

Mr. BRAND. Mr. Chairman, the purpose of this item is more particularly to determine the importance of the various factors in the grading of grain, such as foreign matter, cracked and broken grain, weeds of various kinds, admixture of other grains, heat, or other forms of damage, and things of that character. The proposition rests primarily upon the needs of the Government for information in carrying out the grain-standards act. But in addition to that is the feature of improved milling technology.

The CHAIRMAN. Suppose you find out a good many things, for instance, that weeds in the grain will reduce its milling value and its grading; what are you going to do about it? You can not get rid of the weeds, can you?

Mr. BRAND. If it does not do any harm, we will immediately remove it as a grading factor, because there is no reason for a farmer to suffer from some factor that is now taken into account if it is not harmful or injurious.

The CHAIRMAN. That may be a point. Now, take your baking qualities of wheat and other grains. I take it that the matter of baking quality would be worked out by Dr. Langworthy in his laboratory.

Mr. BRAND. No; he determines the nutritive value and the physiological problems with reference to the various foods; but he does not carry on that kind of investigation. His work relates to the gluten content and those factors. Wheat is graded according to whether it is dark, hard, etc., and the reason why North Dakota and Minnesota Red are considered more valuable is that they are dark, hard, fibrous wheats which can be mixed with cheaper wheats and bring them up to the baking quality.

The CHAIRMAN. It seems to me that the logic of the situation is that a man who has studied the nutritive value could not escape determining the baking qualities of the wheat.

Mr. BRAND. The baking qualities of the wheat are a matter of the——

Mr. ANDERSON (interposing). Of the texture of the loaf.

Mr. BRAND. Yes; and Dr. Langworthy, I am free to say, would not have the smallest understanding of that, although he is the best-informed man on his subject in the world.

Mr. HARRISON. The Bureau of Chemistry has an interest in the matter.

Mr. BRAND. They have an interest in the matter, and they are going to cooperate in the work.

Mr. MARSHALL. There is one additional reason why it is not feasible to attempt this work in the ordinary commercial mill, and that is caused by the conditions under which the grinding is done. In ordinary grinding, the miller merely waits until his mill has been running an hour or so in the morning to ascertain the amount of flour that he obtains from the grain. If he does not get the amount of flour he ought to be getting, he adjusts his macinery accordingly. Now, it is felt to be perfectly certain that if we control the moisture in certain parts of the mill, that entire matter can be told with absolutely scientific certainty; and that is one of the very important considerations in having the mill so that we can have this moisture control and temperature control exactly as it is wanted. That, of course, you can not have in a commercial mill.

Mr. ANDERSON. When you say it can not be had in a commercial mill, you mean that it is not possible from a profit standpoint?

Mr. MARSHALL. The mills are not built for the purpose. To obtain such results it is practically essential that you build your building in a certain way—certainly that the equipment be all arranged according to a certain plan. And I understand that you can save from 1 to 3 per cent on the amount of flour; you can increase it from 1 to 3 per cent, if you have absolute control and know scientifically just how you should regulate the machinery.

Mr. ANDERSON. Well, is not from 1 to 3 per cent sufficient to warrant the creation of those conditions commercially?

Mr. MARSHALL. Probably it is; but just like many things that should be done commercially, the Government starts them. That certainly will justify this appropriation, and a very much larger appropriation would be justified, if some such improvement as that could be brought into the milling industry.

Mr. HAUGEN. It depends largely upon the cost of wheat, and also the selling prices of the by-products, does it not?

Mr. MARSHALL. Surely.

Mr. HAUGEN (continuing). Whether it would pay to put in additional machinery to save the 3 per cent or not.

Here is an item that started out to be $15,000——

The CHAIRMAN (interposing). What is that?

Mr. HAUGEN. Grain standards. This year we are asked to appropriate $598,000——

The CHAIRMAN (interposing). We have not come to that item yet

Mr. HAUGEN. The total has grown now to $598,600; and I take it that, at the rate we are going we will have a mill that will compete with the Washburns and other large mills in the milling cities. I was one of the conferees, and I know what the agreement was.

STATEMENT OF MR. CHARLES J. BRAND, CHIEF OF THE BUREAU OF MARKETS, UNITED STATES DEPARTMENT OF AGRICULTURE—Continued.

Mr. BRAND. I want to say, for the milling industry of the United States, that some of them are very anxious that we should carry on these investigations.

Mr. HAUGEN. Well, if we should repeal the Grain Standards Act, as some are in favor of doing, would you still need the mill?

Mr. BRAND. I should think you would need it much more; you would have removed one of the greatest protections to greater producers if the act were repealed. With this work you would still furnish some degree of protection.

Mr. HAUGEN. This is to aid in standardization, is it not?

Mr. BRAND. That is one of its functions.

Mr. HAUGEN. What other is there?

Mr. BRAND. I think the record clearly shows that we hope to obtain improvements in milling technology from the investigations.

Mr. HAUGEN. Well, this was given you to aid you in the standardization of wheat, was it not?

Mr. BRAND. I am sure the committee does not feel that when an instrumentality is provided it should be used only for the one specific matter, unless there is a prohibition to that effect—and especially where great benefit could come from it use for other purposes.

Mr. HAUGEN. I should suppose the committee means it should be used for just what it was appropriated for.

Mr. YOUNG of North Dakota. I regret that through illness I was not able to be here while you were testifying in respect to various matters connected with the Bureau of Markets, particularly in regard to the experimental flour mill for the testing of wheat, and laboratories for the testing of flour and other apparatus for baking tests, and so forth. Having introduced and put through the Legislature of North Dakota and having introduced the first bill upon that subject in Congress, you will understand my great interest in the subject.

Mr. BRAND. Yes, I appreciate that fact, Mr. Young.

Mr. YOUNG of North Dakota. From what I have heard from other members of the Committee in respect to your statement I am frank to say that I am disposed to support you in the proposal to have an experimental flour mill just as complete as you can make it. We can not know too much about the value of wheat for milling purposes, and the best way to get out of it the very best milling values. There is only one thing which causes me to hesitate, and that is I hope that the building of such a mill would not cause the grading of grain or the standards for the grading of grain to become more technical.

Mr. BRAND. Our thought, Mr. Young, with respect to that matter is that it may develop from these tests that some of the, you may say, refinements, that we now feel compelled to insert in the standards, may be obviated, for instance, if too much importance is being attached to a small amount of rye we should know it, and should know it positively in order that that factor may not be given the importance as a grading factor that now attaches to it, and similarly with other foreign materials, whether grains or weed seeds.

Mr. YOUNG of North Dakota. Do you think there is any possibility that any of the States now carrying on experiments may find it necessary to install a mill of similar cost in order to keep up with what is necessary simply in respect to the grading of grain.

Mr. BRAND. I would hope that that would be unnecessary, that with their small milling equipment they could carry out their preliminary tests, and then we would be glad to give them the use of our facilities and arrange cooperatively for them to make the somewhat larger test on our machinery.

Mr. YOUNG of North Dakota. In the past there has been conflict between the findings of the State-owned experimental mills and the commercially owned experimental mills, and that has naturally led to some confusion with the bureau officials, or at least added to the difficulties of the situation. Now, do I understand you correctly to say that in addition to what you might call the large experimental flour mill that you will also be able here in the department to conduct the smaller experiments with the smaller samples so as to be able to make comparisons with similar experiments made by State-owned experimental mills and commercially owned mills?

Mr. BRAND. The plans for the experimental mill include the small mill equipment which is now the customary experimental equipment of both the States and the commercial companies, so that we will be able to make tests and compare and determine disinterestingly which of any two disputants are probably right on any question.

Mr. YOUNG of North Dakota. So that in order to have a test made of wheat at Washington it will not be necessary to send a big sample, and the small sample can be handled with your small equipment.

Mr. BRAND. We will be able with the small equipment to test samples as low as 10 pounds each.

Mr. YOUNG of North Dakota. That ought to be satisfactory. How long do you think it will take to complete the mill you have in mind, the larger mill you have in mind?

Mr. BRAND. With the relative return to normal conditions of transportation and in the securing of materials, we believe it should be possible to begin to carry on milling experiments in September, shortly after the crop has begun to be harvested.

Mr. Young of North Dakota. That would practically then take care of the next crop?

Mr. Brand. Yes, it would.

Mr. Young of North Dakota. May I say again, Mr. Brand, I am very sorry I did not hear the main portion of your statement. I am frank to say that from what you have just said and from what I can learn about it, this committee ought not to quibble, and Congress ought not to quibble about the amount of money necessary to enable you to make the most complete and searching inquiries in respect to the milling of wheat. As you know, Mr. Brand, the shippers out through our section of the country have not been satisfied with the working of the Federal grades, and the feeling has gone to such an extent that many of the people want to go back to State grading systems. I am one of the northwestern Members who believes that the time has not yet come when we shall think of going back to State inspection systems and that we ought to try out this Federal plan further, and I will be glad to have you elaborate more fully perhaps than you have just how to proceed, just what character of mill you expect to install, the character generally of the apparatus that you expect to install, and just how you think it is going to work out in enabling you to make changes in the present system which will make it fit into the conditions of the grain producing and shipping and milling trade.

Mr. Brand. Mr. Young, being a northwestern man myself, and having the interests of the northwest very much at heart, it has been a source of regret to me that the standards under the conditions which have prevailed during their enforcement have produced a degree of dissatisfaction. We desire to do only that which will give to the farmer the full worth of his grain. I will be very glad to make a careful statement elaborating in slightly greater detail exactly the work to be done and the results we hope may be accomplished. The specific projects to be taken up are:

(1) Milling investigations for the purpose of establishing and revising grades for wheat and other grains.

This involves the investigation of the milling and baking qualities of the various classes and grades of wheat and other grains for the purpose of determining the relation of various factors such as the test weight per bushel, gluten content, color, texture, general appearance, different forms of damage including heat and frost damage, mixtures of different kinds and qualities of the same grain and different graints, admixtures of various impurities, various treatments to which grain is subjected in commercial handling, storing and milling to intrinsic values, for the purpose of establishing and revising grades for these grains.

The relative value of different lots of wheat is directly affected by their respective milling qualities, such as flour yielding capacity, baking quality of the floor when purchased, and the general condition of the grain affecting the cost of manufacture. The factors influencing these qualities are numerous and the extent of that influence is variable. To determine the extent to which each factor influences these qualities, and the relative importance of each as a grading factor is the function of the proposed experimental mill. It is particularly desired to determine whether undue importance is given in the standards to any factor to the detriment of the farmer. Tests of similar nature will be made on other cereal grains as well as wheat, and the plans for the plants call for the necessary incidental machines to make it possible to conduct like experiments with corn, rye, barley, oats and grain sorghums.

(2) Milling tests of new varieties of wheat.

Plant breeding and variety testing work, both of the Bureau of Plant Industry, and of the various experiment stations, result in the development of new varieties of the various grains having different or superior qualities, especially with respect, in the case of wheat, to flour strength and yield. The mill will be used when the supplies of these new varieties are still too small for commercial tests to determine accurately their values before they are recommended for general use by the farmer in planting his crops.

Cooperative work is planned with the Bureau of Chemistry as to important milling technology and baking tests.

The influence of various factors arising in the grading of wheat, such as wet or dry seasons and so forth, upon milling, and baking values will be investigated.

Also the influence of temperature and humidity control in mills upon flour yield, flour quality and grinding capacity.

This involves some special equipment for the control of atmospheric conditions in the experimental mill. Control of temperature and humidity has proven exceedingly beneficial in textile manufacturers, and it is possible that the practical application of this and other principles to flour milling may mean an increase in flour production of from one to several per cent or a saving of millions of bushels of wheat.

Different methods of conditioning wheat with respect to tempering and heating which relate themselves to grinding efficiency may play an important part in the stress that should be placed upon the various grade factors. Only by having such a mill can these tests be carried out as no commercial mill can afford to set aside its machinery which is operated in series for such experimental use.

In cooperation with the Bureau of Chemistry investigations of flour bleaching, aging and improving processes and their effects upon the food qualities of the same are planned.

Investigations of other processes, methods and operations of milling and mill management upon the efficiency of wheat and other cereal mills will be carried on.

All problems, as rapidly as we can get to them, connected with the handling, storing, and treatment of grain, in their effect upon milling and baking qualities will be studied.

The CHAIRMAN. All right; the next is the general expense item. I presume that is contingent upon these other increases?

Mr. BRAND. I hope it will not be contingent upon them, although part of the need for it arises from that. The Bureau of Markets has outgrown the very modest administrative fund which has been provided for it from time to time, and the sum is inadequate to provide for the needs of an organization such as ours.

The CHAIRMAN. All right; take your next item, 134, the enforcement of the cotton-futures act. That is an actual increase of $25,000?

Mr. BRAND. That is an actual increase of $25,000, necessitated by the increased cost of materials, particularly of cotton for the preparation of standards, and things of that character.

Mr. Chairman, yesterday you asked how much money has been collected this year?

The CHAIRMAN. Yes.

Mr. BRAND. The total collections for the determination of disputes was $2,202. The total receipts from the sales of cotton were $25,604, and the total receipts from the sale of standards $2,495; a sum of approximately $30,000 was returned to the Treasury out of the funds appropriated for that fiscal year.

The CHAIRMAN. So that the total cost of enforcing this act is about how much?

Mr. BRAND. A little less than $100,000. And I think that no act has been as great a protection to a group of producers as this act; and no act has given the Government a greater opportunity to be of service than this. The contact that we have enjoyed with the cotton industry from the enforcement of this act, the information that has come to us, and the respect that we have been able to gain from the interests dealing with the matter, have enabled us to be of great service to those involved.

The CHAIRMAN. Is there anything further, in a general way, about that item that you would like to talk about?

Mr. BRAND. Nothing occurs to me, Mr. Chairman. The situation has been a very difficult one to deal with this year. We have found many difficult problems—too many and too difficult to take your time to explain, although you personally happen to be familiar with some of them.

The CHAIRMAN. It has often occurred to me to ask this, but for some reason I did not do it: Under what authority did you act when you prohibted short-sale contracts?

Mr. BRAND. Under no authority.

The CHAIRMAN. That is what I thought.

Mr. BRAND. Under the authority we had from having the respect of the cotton industry; they were willing to do what we asked them to do.

The CHAIRMAN. That is a very high compliment to you.

Mr. BRAND. We try to deal with the industries in that way.

Mr. HEFLIN. The cotton-futures act requires that the differences in the grades named on contract on the exchange shall be settled according to the commercial difference in spot markets. I notice in section 6 that it says:

That for the purposes of section five of this act the differences above or below the contract price which the receiver shall pay for cotton of grades above or below the basis grade in the settlement of a contract of sale for the future delivery of cotton shall be determined by the actual commercial differences in value thereof upon the sixth business day prior to the day fixed, in accordance with the sixth subdivision of section five, for the delivery of cotton on the contract, established by the sale of spot cotton in the market where the future transaction involved occurs and is consummated if such market be a bona fide spot market.

Now, do I understand by that that on the New York Cotton Exchange the difference in grades is settled by them according to the price of spot cotton on the New York market?

Mr. BRAND. No; the New York market was not found to be a bona fide spot market within the meaning of the act. Therefore, the settlement is based on the average of the differences at Norfolk, Memphis, Montgomery, Houston, Little Rock, Galveston, and other markets. There are 10 markets.

Mr. HAUGEN. That is seven.

Mr. BRAND. There are 10 altogether.

Mr. HEFLIN. Are they really complying with that provision of the law?

Mr. BRAND. They really report telegraphically each day the differences that prevail in the market; and the New York settlement is forced by law to be based upon those differences, or they suffer a fine of about $10 a bale.

Mr. HEFLIN. Well, they did fix a spot price in New York until you forced them to comply with the law?

Mr. BRAND. They have a certain amount of spot cotton there.

Mr. HEFLIN. The act says as to what constitutes a spot market that the sales must be "only of such volume and under such conditions as customarily to reflect the actual price or value of middling upland cotton and the differences between the prices or values of middling cotton of other grades."

The CHAIRMAN. That was put in to exclude New York?

Mr. BRAND. That was the effect of the language, at any rate.

Mr. HEFLIN. New York, of course, is not a spot market.

The CHAIRMAN. Of course, not.

Mr. HEFLIN. But they get figures from there saying the spot prices there are so-and-so. Now, the difference between the spot price in New York—which is not a spot price at all—represents a difference from the future market of about $16 a bale.

The CHAIRMAN. But there is no authority to prevent that.

Mr. HEFLIN. You have no authority to prevent that, just so they do not settle on that basis.

Now, the price on the future market in New York on the 8th day of January was 28 cents a pound; and the spot market of Montgomery, Ala., was 31 cents, which is a difference of $15 a bale. Is there any way you can stop that discrepency? The future market ought really to be ahead of the spot market, when it is as far from the spot market as New York is, and there is freight, insurance, etc., to be paid.

Mr. BRAND. There is already a very pronounced narrowing of those conditions. We believe that with the return to normal conditions those quotations will resume their former parity. Under existing conditions, particularly because of the availability of shipping in New York, spot cotton has a greater value in the port of New York than it has in any interior part of the United States, because the ships are bringing troops in and there is opportunity to move cotton out into the export trade in New York that exists nowhere else in the United States.

Mr. HEFLIN. But when cotton reaches New York it has already been sold to the foreign factor?

Mr. BRAND. That is usually true; but New York now has cotton owned by cotton factors in the South—in order to keep them from losing a ship when one is available.

Mr. HEFLIN. So that that cotton sold in New York is called sales in the spot market?

Mr. BRAND. That is taken into account. The greatest use for spot cotton figured in New York is for banking loans, etc.

Mr. HEFLIN. The other day I asked you about the appeals taken from the action of exchange operators to the Secretary of Agriculture—you have had a good many of those?

Mr. BRAND. Yes; we took in about $2,200 this year as a result of the hearings. We charge a fee, as you understand, for that.

The CHAIRMAN. $2,200.

Mr. BRAND. Yes, $2,200.

Mr. HEFLIN. Where they changed grades and delivered cotton that the buyer said was not in accordance with the contract?

Mr. BRAND. The receiver was not satisfied, and he appealed to the Secretary of Agriculture to have the grade of the cotton determined. In many cases, of course, the figures are in behalf of the complainant, and in many other cases they are in behalf of the respondent.

Mr. HEFLIN. How many are presented in behalf of the respondent?

Mr. BRAND. I can not say off-hand; by consulting our records I can determine.

Mr. HEFLIN. I believe you said yesterday that if they could not figure as to the difference between the grades in settlement, the buyer had no remedy except to demand the actual thing contracted for?

Mr. BRAND. Yes; if he is demanding the actual cotton, that is the only case in which he has a remedy, except by such agreement as he may make with the tenderer.

Mr. HEFLIN. Now, there has been some complaint about the exchange not giving the differences that really exist between those grades named in the contract in the spot markets.

Mr. BRAND. That is not true. They are compelled to do so absolutely. The serious situation that has arisen has come from this fact: If you are receiving and I am delivering and I deliver you 100 bales and most of it is low grade, you can not turn around in the spot market and sell it at the price you were compelled to give on the average of these quotations from the ten spot markets, which is an indication that our commercial differences in the ten spot markets are not true commercial differences. We have investigated the matter and we have found that in too many cases the quotation committees of the spot exchanges and the spot markets have been giving asked instead of received prices; instead of actual transactions, they have been quoting the figures that people were holding their cotton for. Thus you have had a false figure to settle on; and when a man received his cotton he could not turn around in the spot market and sell it at the same prices.

Mr. HEFLIN. Suppose a man should buy 100 bales of cotton on the exchange and come up for settlement, and the man should show him the grades, and they should agree that those grades were in conformity to the contract. Then suppose the exchange man goes to settle with him as to the difference between the grades, and he objects and says, "You are not giving me the value of this cotton and the difference that obtains in these spot markets." What remedy has he?

Mr. BRAND. The arbitration committee of the exchange would force him to settle on those differences posted on the bulletin board; he could not go outside of those without losing his seat.

The CHAIRMAN. But, as a matter of fact, it is a question of having the Government have anything to do with the money transactions, which should be very cautiously avoided?

Mr. BRAND. Yes; and we do not handle the money feature of it. but the exchange does. That transaction has always been between two members of the exchange. The spot purchaser does not appear, although he is the principal, and the member is his agent.

Mr. HEFLIN. Suppose he should go into the courts, in New York, for instance?

Mr. BRAND. He does not need to do that; the exchange would force him to settle in that way or lose his seat.

Mr. HEFLIN. There has been some complaint that they do not give him the difference between grades.

Mr. BRAND. I can not understand that, because I am in touch with this matter constantly, and whenever these complaints come here we run them down. In every case we have found that they have forced not only compliance with the law but compliance with good business ethics.

Mr. HAUGEN. I understand you to say you have been instrumental in preventing future transactions?

Mr. BRAND. I issued an order prohibiting short selling.

Mr. LEE. Explain what you mean by "short selling."

Mr. HAUGEN. I understand it. If short selling is good, why stop it at this time?

Mr. BRAND. We were in possession of facts with reference to fundamental conditions of the cotton market that no private business enterprise could possibly have had. Therefore, in their ignorance of what the fundamental situation was, certain speculative groups, thinking that they divined the truth to be that the market was going down, started selling short very liberally. A large volume of that selling, by the way, came in the form of straddling from the Liverpool market, and much of it also came from our own people, who were fearful and thought they could take advantage of the situation in that way; but the greater part of it was in the completion of straddling operations between New York and Liverpool. Their mistaken idea was that the market was going down, due to their not knowing the fundamental conditions, such as the state of shipping, the state of stocks in other countries, and things of that character.

We had our fingers upon this information through all of the channels of the Government, and hence we thought it was only a proper protection to the cotton industry of the United States, and to the cotton farmer in particular, who was at that very moment at the height of his marketing season, to prevent what is really called a "bear raid"; and we forbade the short selling of cotton.

Mr. HAUGEN. What you did, then, was to protect the short seller—the speculator?

Mr. BRAND. No; we put him out of business.

Mr. HAUGEN. You put him out of business to protect him?

Mr. BRAND. No; we protected the cotton grower, the merchant of the South and the banks——

Mr. HEFLIN (interposing). Against the regular speculator.

Mr. BRAND. Against speculation which was due to their not knowing the fundamental conditions.

Mr. HAUGEN. They were speculators if they were operating in futures.

Mr. BRAND. No; among the heaviest sellers were the cotton mills.

Mr. HAUGEN. If they were selling cotton which they needed they were speculating.

Mr. BRAND. They were selling cotton against their goods and their spot cotton.

The CHAIRMAN. This order did not protect them.

Mr. BRAND. The short sellers? No; they have been put out of business. Most of them have agreed since that it was all right.

Mr. HAUGEN. They have been put out of business because it was bad business?

Mr. BRAND. No; under normal conditions the action they took would have been wholly warranted; because had there been no war and had they been in possession of the information which under the unusual conditions came only to the Government, they would not have taken the action they took. As it was, they maintained openly that they would put cotton down to 18 or 20 cents when it was 28.

Mr. HAUGEN. If they could in one instance should they not in others?

Mr. BRAND. It was an extreme case, due to the armistice. No one except agents of the Government could have been in a position to know what ships might be released to carry the product across the water under the new conditions.

Mr. HAUGEN. Under certain conditions it should be permissible, to a certain degree?

Mr. BRAND. I think under normal conditions short selling is one of the best things in the world; so that a man can go in and sell and thus hedge.

Mr. HAUGEN. A hedge is a different thing.

Mr. BRAND. You can not tell the difference.

Mr. HAUGEN. Well, one is defined as hedging and the other as speculating.

Mr. BRAND. Well, the transactions are identical.

Mr. HAUGEN. If I sell cloth and am going to use cotton next June, I have a perfect right to buy now, or, in other words, to hedge; but if I have no use for it I am simply speculating.

Mr. BRAND. The speculator serves some useful purposes: He is there in the market, and the spot merchant, the other holder of cotton, is not there in the market; so that if the spinner comes in and desires cotton for his future manufacture and the speculator stands there ready to take his chance and sell his cotton——

Mr. HAUGEN (interposing). I understand.

Mr. BRAND. And the producer is represented by him, in a confidential sort of way.

Mr. HAUGEN. If that was so, why was it not true more than a few weeks ago.

The CHAIRMAN. Mr. Brand has explained that two or three times. The question of transportation——

Mr. HAUGEN (interposing). Transportation does not enter into it.

The CHAIRMAN. Transportation does enter into it.

Mr. HEFLIN. Suppose 100,000 bales were accumulated in New York, and the speculator was due to deliver that inside of three months——

Mr. HAUGEN. Well, that does not eliminate the speculation.

Mr. BRAND. We eliminated the speculation for 30 days on the short side.

Mr. HAUGEN. If that was done on Monday, why not on Saturday?

Mr. BRAND. Ordinarily it is a good thing to have men willing to take that risk, because it makes a continuous market. We do not believe in their practices, but we believe they perform a good economic function.

Mr. HEFLIN. I think they do good if they are regulated.

Mr. BRAND. Yes; they do good if they are regulated. I suggested that another rule be put into effect which had a beneficial result. Fluctuations were limited to two cents. Previously they were 3 cents. I had suggested two cents, and they thought that was too radical and did not do it; but in the midst of the final crisis, upon request, they voluntarily put in a 2-cent limit; and that limit still prevails, although I had a letter yesterday asking if I would approve its reremoval. I can not approve of that yet, because I believe emergency conditions still prevail to such an extent that I think it would be unwise at this time.

The CHAIRMAN. I hope you will not.

Mr. HAUGEN. I think everyone who will think of it will say that the only safe and sane way would be to limit the things that may be delivered under contract. Of course, as long as you are allowed to deliver cats and dogs——

Mr. BRAND (interposing). That is not true at the present time.

Mr. HEFLIN. I have not been able to see yet that these variations of grades on shades and tinges are proper. I think that if the grades fixed by Congress are nine grades, they should be confined to those grades absolutely, instead of branching out to those variations of grades.

Mr. BRAND. I would like, if I can, to make clear to you the fundamental purpose in having the standards for middling and good middling blue, and for the yellow stains of the same grade, and the strict low middling yellow, and the grades below that.

Mr. ANDERSON. So that you can make it perfectly clear to me at the same time, I ask you whether there is any difference in commercial value between the middling blue and the middling yellow?

Mr. BRAND. There is a difference of from one to two cents between those, and a difference between middling blue and straight white middling of, possibly, at least five cents. At the present time I believe it is about six.

Mr. LEE. In other words, you want to give a market to those variations?

Mr. BRAND. We want to give them a market, and we want the producer to have a place where he can go and see how much off middling that cotton is worth. Is it not valuable to him to know that?

Mr. HEFLIN. It may be valuable to him to know it, but he never gets it.

Mr. BRAND. He gets it in a far greater degree than if there were no quotation on it.

Mr. HEFLIN. You take the local papers at New Orleans, Galveston, Memphis, Savannah, or any of those points; you never see any of these tinges quoted and sometimes they do not name but five grades.

Mr. BRAND. I went over 400 bales on Tuesday, and I am prepared to say that not 2 per cent of them were white cotton.

Mr. HEFLIN. Where did you find that—New York?

Mr. BRAND. They were sent to us from the New Orleans Cotton Exchange in the determination of disputes. The receipts at this time of the year are largely off color cottons, and that is what would apply—just yellow, red, and blue tinges.

Mr. HEFLIN. Eighty per cent and more are of the best grades of the crop?

Mr. ANDERSON. Suppose you have these yellows and blues, would that sort of cotton sell, as wheat does, on sample?

Mr. BRAND. It would, but it would not be deliverable, and there would be no quotations for it.

The CHAIRMAN. Mr. Brand, do I understand by your silence that you acquiesce in the statement that on an average 80 per cent of the crop would be of the best grades?

Mr. BRAND. No; I do not. Mr. Heflin, if you will come down to the department we will be glad to go over that with you. We have the report, by weeks, of the largest cotton farmers in the United States; so that we could tell you, to the fraction of a cent, what the crop has been developing.

Mr. HEFLIN. Do you not think 95 per cent of the crop is covered by your nine standard grades, without the changes or variations?

Mr. BRAND. In some seasons 90 per cent might be, but in the average up to the present it would not be true.

Mr. HEFLIN. Well, there is a market for the yellow tinges, and if the good grades are up high, of course, these other grades are lifted by that, because the lower the high-grade cotton is the lower the low-grade cotton is going to be; is that not true?

Mr. BRAND. Not this year. The excess demands for the high grades have depreciated them out of all proportion to the spinning value of those grades, and that has been due almost wholly to the paucity of transportation space. The 5 per cent waste in low-grade middling has resulted in their declining to give ocean space for low grades—and that is one reason for this disparity between spots and futures.

Mr. HEFLIN. You say that men pay a difference of 3 to 5 cents between one shade and white middling?

Mr. BRAND. Yes.

Mr. HEFLIN. When you buy that for weaving purposes there would be no difference, would there?

Mr. BRAND. Under another item of this bill which has been discussed, the cotton testing item, those experiments are carried on, and as a matter of fact those blue cottons will not take the dye in anything like the proportion of white cottons. That narrows the market to certain products, and hence the blues can not be considered nearly as valuable as the whites; and even as a dyeing proposition, difficulty of dyeing, mercerization, and nitration is such that you can not command the price for them because there is not the market.

Mr. HEFLIN. You take the blue; it will take it better than the white.

Mr. BRAND. Blue seems to be one of the most difficult kinds.

Mr. HEFLIN. It refuses to take any other color, does it?

Mr. BRAND. Yes.

The CHAIRMAN. I am glad to hear you make that statement, because there is a very widespread notion in my State that there is no spinning or commercial difference in these tinges of different grades.

Mr. BRAND. That statement is not true.

Mr. HEFLIN. There is no difference in the tensile strength, is there?

Mr. BRAND. There is no difference in the tent-making quality, where appearance. etc., have no bearing, and as a consequence we persuaded the War and Navy Departments to use those lower grades of cotton for that purpose. Unfortunately, the rather technical gentlemen who were put in charge of that matter were prescribing grades of cotton far better than was necessary, thinking that they were protecting the Government; but we succeeded in persuading them to adopt a more sensible course with reference to the matter; and that was one of the most important features in improving the cotton situation three months ago.

Mr. HEFLIN. But there is a great deal of cloth that could be made from this cotton for common use, and the consumer would never know or inquire as to the difference.

Mr. BRAND. Certain restricted kinds: denims, bagging, and things of that kind can be made from them.

The CHAIRMAN. I do not think the cotton grower will ever appreciate the debt of gratitude he owes to the Bureau of Markets; they will never know how much work, and valuable work, you gentlemen have done.

Mr. HEFLIN. They have done valuable work; there is no doubt about that. But I want to get Mr. Brand to see my views about tinges of cotton.

The CHAIRMAN. We will get together on that some time. The committee will now stand in recess until to-morrow at 10.30 o'clock.

(Thereupon, at 5.15 o'clock p. m., the committee took a recess until Saturday, January 11, 1919, at 10.30 o'clock a. m.)

HOUSE OF REPRESENTATIVES,
COMMITTEE ON AGRICULTURE,
Saturday, January 11, 1919.

The committee this day met, Hon. A. F. Lever (chairman) presiding.

The CHAIRMAN. Mr. Doolittle desired me to say to the committee that his absence from the hearings has been due to the fact that he has been seriously ill for ten days.

Bureau of Markets—Continued.

Mr. ANDERSON. On yesterday Mr. Brand made the statement that the proportion of the statutory roll to the lump-sum appropriation would probably be higher in the Bureau of Crop Estimates, owing to the character of their work. I expressed doubt as to the accuracy of that statement, but I find that he was entirely correct about it.

The CHAIRMAN. I do not want to open up this cotton question again, but after listening to the discussion on yesterday and thinking about it last night and this morning, it has occurred to me that there is probably something in some of the suggestions made, out of which the department by proper investigation and study might make some constructive suggestions that would relieve the situation and permanently help it. I would be very glad if your bureau, Mr. Brand, would set itself to work on that proposition. I feel that we ought not to do anything that would have a destructive tendency; yet, if there is anything constructive we can do, we ought to do it. I have some unbaked views of my own that are not really conclusions in my own mind, which I will discuss with you at some time.

Mr. BRAND. We will be very glad indeed, Mr. Chairman, to look into the matter and take it up with the view of seeing what we can suggest to you.

The CHAIRMAN. Before beginning your statement on the next item, have you discontinued any important line of work, or finished any line of work, so that it will be discontinued during the next fiscal year?

Mr. BRAND. Yes, particularly under the stimulation of agriculture we had intended to discontinue certain lines of work, and in connection with that we will probably be forced to discontinue some extensions of our present work.

We expect to cut the so-called food-survey work down to the bone. Under that appropriation we have been doing our monthly food stock reporting work, which we think should constitute a permanent part of our activities, and when we prepared our estimates we assumed that would be cared for elsewhere. That will have to be discontinued, as will also the motor transport work, and also our work on heater cars, storage for Irish and sweet potatoes and better car loading, and the traffic assistance that we have been giving during the past year and a half.

Mr. ANDERSON. Speaking about your car heater proposition, there has been a good deal of complaint in our part of the country that the administration is not furnishing heated cars.

Mr. BRAND. That is true. The railroads have not equipped themselves with heater cars. We have devised heaters and heater cars, and also improved methods of car ventilation, and if we can get these methods adopted we are going to save $10,000,000 worth of perishable products in a year. But that is a line of work we will not be able to continue. We had $175,000 of emergency funds for that work, and next year we will have but $23,000.

Mr. ANDERSON. It will be a demonstration proposition from now on?

Mr. BRAND. We have made haste and have gotten results. We got one of the biggest refrigerator car companies in the United States to permit us to use their cold-storage room, and we took our heater cars and put them in there and created winter temperature in the summer. We have made excellent progress, but we are confronted with the necessity of finishing that work.

The CHAIRMAN. Your next item is item 135 on page 253, the provision for the enforcement of the grain-standards act. You are asking for an increase of $175,500. Suppose you tell us how you are going to use that increase?

Mr. BRAND. Mr. Chairman, I have asked Mr. Livingston, who is in immediate charge of this work, to present it to the committee.

STATEMENT OF MR. GEORGE LIVINGSTON, SPECIALIST IN CHARGE OF FEDERAL GRAIN SUPERVISION, BUREAU OF MARKETS, UNITED STATES DEPARTMENT OF AGRICULTURE.

Mr. LIVINGSTON. Mr. Chairman, and gentlemen of the committee, I would like to ask if you desire to take up at the outset the way in which we propose to use the increase or whether you would like to have a general statement first?

The CHAIRMAN. I suspect the members of the committee know in a general way the lines of work you do under this appropriation, and it would be better, I think, if you would tell us how you are going to use the increase, unless some member of the committee desires you to make a general statement regarding this work.

Mr. LIVINGSTON. This work cost last year $519,140. This year it will cost the appropriation $456,580 plus $42,000 from the continuing appropriation of the act of 1917, making a total cost of $498,580 this year.

The estimate asked for this year involves an actual increase of $133,560 over the amount of money we expect to spend this year. I may say the total amount of money available this year from the current appropriation together with that which we have remaining from the continuing appropriation of 1917 is not going to be sufficient for us to carry on the work in the way we would like to carry it on, and it will be necessary to curtail some of our activities during the last two or three months of the present fiscal year.

The increase of $133,560 is made necessary primarily because of the enforcement of the oats standards next year. These will probably be promulgated in the near future, and will be made effective for the 1919 crop. The oats crop, when it comes under supervision, will increase our work from one-fourth to one-third. It probably will not increase it quite one-third, because we can use our present organization in the conduct of the work. Many of the overhead expenses are already provided for in the organization for supervising inspections of wheat and corn, but the oats standards will increase the work very materially.

We propose to spend $57,996 for new equipment for the field offices, for the purchase of such grain grading apparatus as moisture machines, weight per bushel testers, mixing devices, analytical balances, and equipment generally necessary for inspecting and grading oats. You may be interested to know what some of those things cost.

The CHAIRMAN. I think we would be.

Mr. LIVINGSTON. I brought down a few photographs showing some of this equipment. This moisture tester complete now costs $90. It formerly cost about $70. Seventy-five dollars was the price that prevailed at the time we made up the estimate, and it probably has advanced since that time. This weight-per bushel tester at the time we made up our estimates cost $60, and it now costs $74.25.

This sampling device at the time we made up the estimates cost $65, and now it costs $75. So our estimate is not going to be sufficient to buy all the equipment we had hoped to buy. All those things have gone up. This equipment is necessary in all the 35 field offices, as well as in our central office for the use of the Board of Review.

The CHAIRMAN. You have 35 field offices?

Mr. LIVINGSTON. We have 35 field offices; yes, sir. We expect to use $35,280——

The CHAIRMAN (interposing). How many of these instruments do you have in each office?

Mr. LIVINGSTON. That will depend upon the office. In some of the offices like Chicago, Minneapolis, Kansas City, and St. Louis we will require four or five. In other offices one may be sufficient to handle the work.

The CHAIRMAN. How much is the estimate for equipment?

Mr. LIVINGSTON. It is $57,996. I have only a portion of the equipment which is necessary.

The CHAIRMAN. What other equipment would you have?

Mr. LIVINGSTON. We would need platform scales and automatic analytical balances, which cost $125 for each balance at the time the estimate was made up, and I think they are a little higher now. Then we would need automatic dockage scales, which cost $125 each. We need additional corn sieves and wheat sieves and oat sieves, which cost $10 a set. We would need at least four or five sets in the large offices and one set in each of the small offices. We will need a large number of those sets because of the number of people using them. Then we need the large weight per bushel testers, and some small weight per bushel testers, which the men carry out to the cars and make examinations at the car rather than bring the samples in, which is desirable in many cases.

The CHAIRMAN. Do your records show an itemized statement as to how many scales you are going to buy and what you estimate the cost to be, and the same thing in reference to the other articles of equipment?

Mr. LIVINGSTON. Yes; I will be glad to put that in the record.

(The statement referred to follows:)

Laboratory apparatus, instruments, and supplies which must be purchased in order to supervise the inspection of shelled corn, wheat, and oats during the fiscal year 1920.

72 moisture testers, at $75	$5,400.00
72 moisture tester cabinets, at $59.39	4,276.08
36 platform scales for weighing bagged grain, at $12	432.00
36 automatic analytical balances, at $125	4,500.00
36 automatic dockage scales, at $125	4,500.00
180 grain probes, at $9	1,620.00
72 sets corn sieves, at $3	216.00

72 sets wheat sieves, at $12	$864.00
144 sets oat sieves, estimated $10	1,440.00
36 dockage machines (kickers), at $45	1,620.00
36 quarts weight per bushel testers, at $60	2,160.00
36 pint weight per bushel testers, at $60	2,160.00
72 analyses tables, at $40	2,880.00
72 sample filing cabinets, at $25	1,800.00
72 portable car-sample dividing devices, at $50	3,600.00
36 laboratory sample dividing devices, at $65	2,340.00
72 No. 5055 balances, analytical, at $55	3,960.00
36 No. 4000 moisture balances, at $20	720.00
36 No. 4050 torsion balances, at $25	900.00
23 smut testing machines, at $135	3,105.00
23 motors with controllers for smutters, at $50	1,150.00
72 dozen trays for illustrating types of wheat, corn, oats, and rice, at $12 per dozen	864.00
72 dozen triangular grain pans, at $6 per dozen	432.00
1,750 draw string individual sample bags, at $58 per thousand	101.50
500 1-peck composite sample bags, at $76 per thousand	36.00
500 1-bushel composite sample bags, at $179 per thousand	89.50
100 grain pans with funnels, at $1.40	140.00
840 Erlenmeyer flasks for sulphured oat detection (dozen in set), at $6.50 per dozen	455.00
Miscellaneous equipment	1,590.92
Equipment for moisture testers:	
180 dozen flasks, at $12 per dozen	2,160.00
72 dozen thermometers, at $12 per dozen	864.00
180 dozen graduates, at $9 per dozen	1,620.00
Total	57,996.00

NOTE.—Since the above estimate was made corn sieves have advanced from $3 to $4.25 per set; oat testers from $25 to $30 each; and quart weight per bushel testers from $60 to $70 each. Practically all equipment has advanced greatly in price.

The CHAIRMAN. It is a large sum for equipment.

Mr. LIVINGSTON. I realize it is, and yet the cost of equipment is unusually high. We had a telegram recently from the supervisor at Kansas City saying that some firms there wished to buy equipment themselves to see whether they were getting correct inspection. They made inquiry as to the cost of a weight per bushel tester of this sort, and the firm from whom they secured the quotation wanted $140 for it.

The CHAIRMAN. Is this process of increasing the prices on equipment due to some monopoly of manufacture of this equipment?

Mr. LIVINGSTON. These pieces of equipment are made by a relatively small number of manufacturing concerns. We have attempted to enlist the interest of some other manufacturers and get them to make a cheaper apparatus. The equipment is now made by only four or five concerns, and principally made by two or three firms.

The CHAIRMAN. Have you observed any facts which lead you to believe that there is any combination between these manufacturers?

Mr. LIVINGSTON. I do not know about that. I have reason to believe, however, that the cost of the various pieces of apparatus is unreasonable. For instance, a scale man employed by the Department of trade and commerce of the State of Illinois, in looking up the cost of this equipment for their office said that the equipment could be made, including the actual cost of material, for approximately one-half of what the manufacturers wanted for it.

The CHAIRMAN. I think that is a matter which might very well be brought to the attention of the Federal Trade Commission.

Mr. McLaughlin. They are all patented, I presume?

Mr. Livingston. This piece of apparatus was developed by one of the men in the Bureau, and I am not sure whether that has a patent on it or not. But this apparatus is covered by a public patent [indicating].

Mr. Anderson. What is that apparatus?

Mr. Livingston. That is a device for getting a representative sample.

The Chairman. What else do you propose to do with this increase?

Mr. Livingston. We expect to spend $35,280 for 14 new employees. Those employees will be necessary primarily because of the increased work in the application of the federal grades for oats.

Mr. McLaughlin. There is no difficulty in having the inspectors who have been doing work on one kind of grain carry on similar work for other kinds of grain?

Mr. Livingston. The same inspectors will undoubtedly do the work. They are now doing it, but not under our supervision.

Mr. McLaughlin. The inspectors are doing it under your supervision?

Mr. Livingston. Not on oats.

Mr. Anderson. You have a different set of supervisors to supervise oats?

Mr. Livingston. We have a supervisor in charge of each office. He has a certain number of assistants, depending upon the size of the markets and the amount of supervision required. The bringing of the oat standards under supervision will mean, in many places, that the force of assistants should be increased in order to help handle the work.

Mr. Anderson. That is you have more appeals and more samples to supervise and inspect, and consequently you have to have more men to do it, even though the same man supervise the inpection on wheat, oats and corn?

Mr. Livingston. Yes, sir. Our organization in any branch office supervises the inspection of all the grains for which standards have been fixed under the act.

The Chairman. Are these 14 men to be assistants or graders?

Mr. Livingston. Some of them are. We also need additional men for our Board of Review, who should be high grade men, because the Board of Review is the supreme court on technical grain grading matters, on matters relating to the handling and grading of grain under the standards.

Mr. Anderson. In how many places do you have boards of review?

Mr. Livingston. We expect to have only one, and that board of review is the final authority on matters of interpretation and classification.

Mr. Anderson. That is the one which practically takes the place of the Secretary in the final determination of the appeal?

Mr. Livingston. That board represents the Secretary on technical matters of grain grading. That board is now stationed in Washington, but we expect to move it to Chicago next week.

Mr. McLaughlin. Is that Board of Review a permanent body; all of the members permanent public officials?

Mr. LIVINGSTON. Yes. The members of the Board of Review are the best experts on grain we can get.

The CHAIRMAN. Let me ask you about the 14 new men. Their work is to be confined to the oats proposition?

Mr. LIVINGSTON. Not entirely, because we do not assign one man to wheat, one man to corn, and one man to oats. They will be additional assistants to the office force, and the force is used on the several grains without assignment to any one particular grain. We propose to add one man in Chicago, and one in Kansas City, two for administrative work in connection with inspection efficiency. We need one on inspection procedure. We have at the present time vacancies in the head position of grain supervisor at the Galveston, Oklahoma City, Fort Worth, Salt Lake City, Cincinnati and Cleveland offices. We may be able to fill those positions with some of the new appointees. If not, we will have to fill them by transferring some of our present employees, and then make appointments to fill the vacancies created by the transfers.

The CHAIRMAN. What are you going to do with the balance of the money?

Mr. LIVINGSTON. Our increase in rental is estimated at $13,700.55. At the time the offices were rented only shelled corn was under Federal supervision, and later the wheat standards were promulgated. At the outset we did not secure enough room to take care of oats. The present office space is small in some of the markets where oats are relatively important. Some of these markets are to become important markets after the oats standards are fixed.

The CHAIRMAN. What is your total expenditure for rent?

Mr. LIVINGSTON. It will be $57,022.84. Our expenditure this year is $43,322.29.

The CHAIRMAN. I assume, of course, that your rent charges are about in proportion to what private individuals pay?

Mr. LIVINGSTON. In some places we pay much less. In Chicago we have office space that is costing us 50 cents per square foot less than the regular charge to other tenants in that building.

The CHAIRMAN. Due to any overzealous patriotism, or what?

Mr. LIVINGSTON. Mr. Brand personally arranged for the rental of that space. I do not know whether it was his persuasive arguments, or whether they desired to have the Government offices in their building, or whether they considered the Government an unusually good tenant. At any rate, in all cases we make an extraordinary effort to get the rental at a minimum figure.

The CHAIRMAN. What else is included in this amount.

Mr. LIVINGSTON. That also includes $26,000 for miscellaneous items, which will include furniture for the additional officials, additional field station expenses for travel within each of the 35 supervision districts, for increased travel because of the oats standards on the part of the administrative officials, for increased travel in investigating complaints against inspectors, and charges of alleged violations of the act.

The CHAIRMAN. Have you a detailed statement covering all of the items?

Mr. LIVINGSTON. Yes, sir.

The CHAIRMAN. Suppose you put that in the record?

Mr. LIVINGSTON. I will do so.

There is also increased travel because of emergencies in handling the work for the Food Administration Grain Corporation.

(The statement referred to follows:)

Statement showing increased miscellaneous expenses for Federal grain supervision work occasioned by enforcement of standards for oats.

Desks, chairs, laboratory tables, and filing cabinets for laboratory analysis and appeal records for 35 offices and in Washington office at $138.88	$5,000.00
Miscellaneous equipment for 35 stations, including grain mailing envelopes, sample bags, sample cans, etc.; an increase of $83.71 per annum per station	3,000.00
Miscellaneous supplies, consisting of oil for moisture machines, moisture flasks, maintenance and, and operation expenses for automobile trucks used in securing samples, increase due to oats supervision, $45.00 for 35 stations	1,675.00
Freight, express, and drayage on furniture, laboratory tables, laboratory equipment, for supervision of oat inspections and for transmission of oat samples; an increase of $70 per annum for 35 stations	2,250.00
Miscellaneous services, to cover employment of skilled laborers, temporary clerks, and temporary samplers in Washington office and in 35 field stations; emergency periods involving immediate handling of grain work requires for brief intervals more help than economical to carry as permanent organization. The total increase for such services at 35 stations and Washington office is $85 per annum	3,000.00
Miscellaneous items not classified, to provide for emergency printing work, special inspection and supervision work for the Food Administration Grain Corporation, the War Department, and for similar unclassified items of expense: an increase of $85 per station for 35 stations	3,000.00
Increased travel from Washington, D. C., by officials engaged in investigation of violations, conduct of hearings relative to violations by officials doing the supervision work; by division supervisors and grain supervisors in charge of district, occasioned inauguration of supervision of oat inspections: Washington office $1,658.45; 35 field offices at $200	8,658.45
Total	26,583.45

The CHAIRMAN. That takes up your total increase?

Mr. LIVINGSTON. That takes up the total increase.

Mr. HAUGEN. How do the salaries paid by you compare with the salaries paid to people employed by the States' commissions?

Mr. LIVINGSTON. You ask for a comparative statement of salaries?

Mr. HAUGEN. A comparative statement of salaries paid by your bureau and the salaries paid by the States.

Mr. LIVINGSTON. They are about the same.

Mr. HAUGEN. About the same. Have you looked into it?

Mr. LIVINGSTON. Yes, sir. In some places the inspection departments pay higher salaries than we do, and in some cases our men get slightly higher salaries.

Mr. HAUGEN. You have 42 of them at salaries over $2,500, and you have six of them at $2,500, so that 48 of them are drawing salaries of $2,500 or more. How do those salaries compare with the salaries paid by the States?

Mr. LIVINGSTON. They are about on the same basis.

Mr. HAUGEN. What information have you? What do they pay in Chicago, or at any of these stations?

Mr. LIVINGSTON. In New York the chief inspector gets $12,000, and our supervisor gets $3,240.

Mr. HAUGEN. That is the chief.

Mr. LIVINGSTON. Our supervisor supervises the chief, and therefore it is not fair to compare his salary with that of the chief inspector. In Minneapolis the chief inspector gets $3,500 or $3,800 and our supervisor gets $2,760.

Mr. HAUGEN. What do the others get?

Mr. LIVINGSTON. The inspectors in Minneapolis?

Mr. HAUGEN. Yes.

Mr. LIVINGSTON. I believe some of them get $2,800.

Mr. HAUGEN. How many of them get any other sum?

Mr. LIVINGSTON. I do not know.

Mr. HAUGEN. Then you are not well enough informed to make any comparison?

Mr. LIVINGSTON. I do not know the exact number getting those salaries.

Mr. HAUGEN. You can approximate the number, can you not?

Mr. LIVINGSTON. No, I can not do that. I know their salaries range from $1,800 or $2,000 to $3,500.

Mr. HAUGEN. You do not know anything about the number of people employed at the various salaries?

Mr. LIVINGSTON. No, sir; I do not.

Hr. HAUGEN. You have not looked into it?

Mr. LIVINGSTON. No, sir; not as to the exact number of men getting any specific salary.

Mr. HAUGEN. You could not give an estimate, even?

Mr. LIVINGSTON. No, sir. I have a pretty hard job keeping exactly in mind the salaries of our men.

Mr. HAUGEN. That is an old story. It is unnecessary to repeat that.

Mr. LIVINGSTON. We do not employ the inspectors. They are employed by the inspection departments, and the salaries are not announced.

Mr. HAUGEN. You have 34 of them receiving more than $2,000—between $2,500 and $2,160?

Mr. LIVINGSTON. Yes, sir.

Mr. HAUGEN. How does that compare with the salaries paid by the States?

Mr. LIVINGSTON. I think it is on the same basis.

Mr. HAUGEN. You think so, but have you any information on the subject? The objection is that you are paying from 25 to 50 per cent above what the States pay and that you pick up the men from the States at an advanced salary. I want to know whether that is true?

Mr. LIVINGSTON. That is not true, because in no case have we employed a supervisor who was formerly an inspector at an unreasonable advance in salary.

Mr. HAUGEN. That does not answer the question. I am talking about the salaries.

Mr. LIVINGSTON. My remark was addressed to the salary question.

Mr. HAUGEN. It is stated positively that the States were employing these men and that you picked them up at an advanced salary. What do you know about that?

Mr. LIVINGSTON. Undoubtedly we did in some cases, but the increase was not unreasonable.

Mr. HAUGEN. That is a different answer again. To what extent was that done?

Mr. LIVINGSTON. I think in the case of almost every man we employed we have to pay some slight increase over the salary he is getting in order to get him to accept the position, because it involves the moving of his family, the expense of changing his home.

Mr. HAUGEN. At what increase have you employed them?

Mr. LIVINGSTON. At an increase very seldom over $240.

Mr. HAUGEN. In how many cases was it $240?

Mr. LIVINGSTON. I could not say what the exact figures are on that.

Mr. HAUGEN. How many $500 or other amounts?

Mr. LIVINGSTON. I think I am safe in saying that no one was appointed at an increase of $500.

Mr. HAUGEN. What was the highest increase?

Mr. LIVINGSTON. The highest increase?

Mr. HAUGEN. Do you state positively that no one was employed at more than a $500 increase?

Mr. LIVINGSTON. Not that I recall.

Mr. HAUGEN. You claim to have knowledge of the figures and the salaries paid?

Mr. LIVINGSTON. Yes, sir; but I do not carry all of the details in my mind.

Mr. HAUGEN. Could you say whether there were two or a hundred or two hundred?

Mr. LIVINGSTON. I say that is the normal increase.

Mr. HAUGEN. The normal increase is $240?

Mr. LIVINGSTON. Yes.

Mr. HAUGEN. Over what they were paid by the States?

Mr. LIVINGSTON. I would say that would be a very reasonable figure.

Mr. HAUGEN. You say a very reasonable figure. That is not what I want. How many were employed at an increased salary?

Mr. LIVINGSTON. I can not answer that question promptly offhand.

Mr. HAUGEN. Can you state whether there are ten, twenty or forty of them?

Mr. LIVINGSTON. No, sir.

Mr. HAUGEN. You do not know. Or five of them?

Mr. LIVINGSTON. I can say no one was employed at an unreasonable increase.

Mr. HAUGEN. That was not the question. I would like to get an answer to a question once in a while. The question is how many were employed at an increased salary?

Mr. LIVINGSTON. I can not answer your question with the facts at hand. I can put that in the record.

Mr. HAUGEN. If you do not care to answer the question, or if you have no knowledge about it, who, in your department has knowledge of it. I take it no department——

Mr. BRAND (interposing). Mr. Haugen, if you will let us know just what you want, we will be glad to get the information and put it in the record, or send it to you personally?

Mr. HAUGEN. Yes; you always say you will put it in the record.

Mr. BRAND. We will be glad to send it to you personally.

Mr. HAUGEN. The question is a simple one; how many men were employed at an increased salary over the salary paid by the States?

Mr. BRAND. Nearly every man we have gotten we have had to pay some increase in salary to or he would not leave his present occupation.

Mr. HAUGEN. How much of an increase?

Mr. BRAND. At an average increase possibly from $240 to $360.

Mr. HAUGEN. Then I will ask the question, What are the samplers paid by the states?

Mr. BRAND. We have no way of knowing except that the samplers tell us, or the licensed inspectors tell us. That is the business of other persons and we have no right to go into their records, and we know nothing about it except what we learn in the course of our work.

Mr. HAUGEN. You feel that it would not be fair to go to the records and ascertain what salaries are paid?

Mr. BRAND. Only in a few cases is it made public.

Mr. HAUGEN. I take it all of them have to make reports, and the reports are made public. There is nothing to conceal about it.

Mr. BRAND. They can be obtained at the State's capital. The reports issued by the inspection departments do not show the number of employees, nor their salaries.

Mr. HAUGEN. Your books are open to the public?

Mr. BRAND. We have a register which shows the salary of every employee of the United States.

Mr. HAUGEN. You did not think this was of enough importance to investigate as to the salaries paid by the States?

Mr. BRAND. We have told you that we know in sufficiently great detail so that we can not overpay. We try to employ every man at as reasonable a rate as we possibly can, so much so that we lose a great many men.

Mr. HAUGEN. Answer this question if you can. I am asking you about the increase of salaries. You state that you simply take the word of the man employed?

Mr. BRAND. It is under oath.

Mr. HAUGEN. It is under oath. Then, as shown in the statements under oath, what are the increases, and the number of them?

Mr. BRAND. We will have to go back over the civil service papers of the men we have taken to find out what they stated under oath on their civil service papers.

Mr. HAUGEN. What are the samplers paid? What are their statements under oath?

Mr. LIVINGSTON. From $1,000 to $1,620.

Mr. HAUGEN. You pay them how much?

Mr. LIVINGSTON. From $1,000 to $1,620.

Mr. HAUGEN. You have the samplers' salaries stated at $1,080; that is the lowest. But you have not any of them at that salary. You have one at $1,140. You said they ranged from $1,000 to $1,620. Do you not think it is a matter which ought to receive more serious consideration?

Mr. LIVINGSTON. I said our salaries ranged from $1,000 to $1,620.

Mr. HAUGEN. But here you have one at $1,140, 12 at $1,320, and 3 at $1,460, and they run up to $1,800.

The CHAIRMAN. That is not a contradiction of his statement.

Mr. HAUGEN. How many have you at $1,000?

Mr. LIVINGSTON. I think we have only one. We are not able to get them at that salary and can not keep them.

Mr. HAUGEN. Where is the man at $1,000 in the estimates? The book of estimates does not show that?

Mr. BRAND. He may not have been in the employ of the bureau at the time the estimate was prepared.

Mr. HAUGEN. When you talk about $1,000 and $1,600, they are two different things. I do not believe anything of that kind ought to go into that record.

Mr. LIVINGSTON. It is $1,080 instead of $1,000.

Mr. ANDERSON. He is not employed now. You had one at $1,080 in 1918, and the lowest employee you have now is the $1,140 man, and the highest one you have is $1,860.

Mr. LIVINGSTON. We have no samplers now getting $1,860. Those are assistant supervisors.

Mr. ANDERSON. It says sampler, $1,860.

Mr. BRAND. Some very capable men have taken the sampler's examination. At the outset they were appointed at the highest rates of salaries permitted under the sampler's examination, with the work of checking the grading of inspectors and acting as supervisory assistants. They were then moved into the higher classifications as to work, but they were not always moved as to title.

Mr. LIVINGSTON. Those are promotions of samplers.

Mr. ANDERSON. Then this statement you have here in the book of estimates does not accurately represent the situation?

Mr. BRAND. It accurately represented the situation at the time it was prepared.

Mr. ANDERSON. If that is true, then you have a sampler at $1,800.

Mr. BRAND. He is working as assistant supervisor, without the title.

Mr. LIVINGSTON. He has been designated as supervisor to assist in handling the appeals.

Mr. HAUGEN. Do you want to correct your answer as to the salaries?

Mr. LIVINGSTON. I started to say the range of salaries under the civil service announcement is from $1,000 to $1,620.

Mr. HAUGEN. We are talking about samplers.

Mr. LIVINGSTON. The salary range was from $1,000 to $1,620. Some of the men were employed at $1,200, $1,320, and $1,420.

Mr. HAUGEN. At the present time?

Mr. LIVINGSTON. That was on the first announcement from which we got our first supply of samplers. We announced a new examination, and when we selected men from that register we were obliged to pay from $1,440 to $1,620. We appointed some at $1,620. Then some of the men who came into the service at $1,200 and $1,320 have been promoted, and they have been put on the new basis.

Mr. HAUGEN. You took them at an advanced salary of $240, and you have been promoting them?

Mr. LIVINGSTON. No; the original list of samplers were brought in at the same salaries they were getting, many of them, and we took extraordinary precautions to get them at a low advance, and many of them were brought in at a salary lower than they said they would accept. After going back at them they finally agreed to accept at a lower figure than they first indicated they would accept.

Mr. HAUGEN. Are they given leave of absence with pay?

Mr. LIVINGSTON. Yes.

Mr. HAUGEN. Your contention is that a man who comes into your service and is given 72 days, if he takes it——

Mr. BRAND (interposing). These men get 15 days' annual leave and 15 days' sick leave, if they get sick.

Mr. HAUGEN. That is 30 days leave that they get, and, also, I suppose, the additional Saturday afternoons.

Mr. BRAND. Very few.

Mr. HAUGEN. Your contention is that when a man comes into your service and you give him 30 days' leave with pay you have to increase his salary $240. Is it necessary to do that?

Mr. LIVINGSTON. Let me clear up the record on this point. When I said $240 I was referring to the grain supervisors, and not the samplers.

Mr. HAUGEN. The question applies to the supervisors. Apply that to the supervisors.

Mr. LIVINGSTON. I made the statement also that it was necessary to pay some increase in salary to get the men. We have six or seven vacancies that we can not fill.

Mr. HAUGEN. Of course, there will always be vacancies, but I take it you have no trouble in filling them, if it is desired that they should be filled.

Mr. LIVINGSTON. There is not any doubt but that the places can be filled, but the question is to get the kind of men you want.

Mr. HAUGEN. You are all the time getting away from the question. If you do not care to answer the question, I do not care to discuss these things with you.

Mr. LIVINGSTON. I am perfectly willing to answer any question. What is the question?

Mr. HAUGEN. The question is, how do the salaries you pay compare with the salaries paid by the State, and the number of employees that have been taken over at an increase in salary?

Mr. LIVINGSTON. I will answer the first question by saying the salary range in our work is approximately the same as it is in the inspection departments. I think the limit of range is higher in the inspection department.

Mr. HAUGEN. You state that to be a fact?

Mr. LIVINGSTON. I stated the range in the supervision work is approximately the same as the range in the inspection departments. The limit in the inspection departments is much higher, the maximum limit is much higher than it is in our service, but the average employe in both services gets about the same salary. That answers the first question.

Mr. HAUGEN. We will make our comparison. What are the salaries paid in St. Paul, for instance?

Mr. LIVINGSTON. In St. Paul there are only two or three inspectors; most of them are in Minneapolis.

Mr. HAUGEN. Well, they are the twin cities and it is practically the same thing.

Mr. LIVINGSTON. The salaries range from $1,800 to $3,500. As to the question in regard to the exact number of inspectors getting certain, specific salaries, I am not prepared to answer because I do not know.

Mr. HAUGEN. Do you know how many there are at $3,500?

Mr. LIVINGSTON. There is one.

Mr. HAUGEN. What are the other salaries?

Mr. LIVINGSTON. I do not know. I think the chief deputy gets $3,000, and the second deputy gets about $2,800.

Mr. HAUGEN. How many of the others?

Mr. LIVINGSTON. I do not know.

Mr. HAUGEN. Or the salaries?

Mr. LIVINGSTON. I do not know. There are about 35 of them and I do not know what salaries they are getting.

Mr. HAUGEN. I take it you are interested in the salaries ouside of that of the chief and the top men?

Mr. LIVINGSTON. Yes; but I am not interested——

Mr. HAUGEN (interposing). So far we have three of them, the chief inspector and two deputies.

Mr. LIVINGSTON. Yes, sir.

Mr. HAUGEN. Now, about your samplers?

Mr. LIVINGSTON. I am not prepared to say what the range is for samplers, but I know of several cases of samplers employed in our Minneapolis office who have been offered higher salaries to go back to the inspection department.

Mr. HAUGEN. That is outside of the question. Can you tell me what they are paid? What do you pay them?

Mr. LIVINGSTON. They are paying approximately the same salaries that we are.

Mr. HAUGEN. What are they paid at St. Paul?

Mr. LIVINGSTON. I do not know.

Mr. HAUGEN. What are they paid at any other point?

Mr. LIVINGSTON. The samplers throughout the country are paid approximately the same salaries we are paying our men. I can not tell you the amounts and the number of men in the United States getting $1,000, or the number of men getting $1,200, or the number getting any other figure.

Mr. HAUGEN. According to the sworn statements of these men, what were they paid before?

Mr. LIVINGSTON. Just as I say, varying from $1,000 to $1,600.

Mr. HAUGEN. How many at $1,600 and how many at $1,200?

Mr. BRAND. We would be glad to send to the chief inspector at Minneapolis and ask him to send a statement of the salaries, and insert it in the record. I think he will furnish it to us. He is not compelled to do so, however.

Mr. HAUGEN. It seems to me that fact should have been ascertained before you hired the men.

Mr. BRAND. It is none of our business. We deal with the individual men whom we are trying to employ, and we try to get the men at the most reasonable salaries we can, considering the ability we require, and it is not incumbent upon us to investigate the ranges of salaries through an inspection department.

Mr. HAUGEN. I can not imagine that anybody would spend several hundred thousand dollars without ascertaining a few facts about the people they were employing and were going to pay out of that amount of money.

Mr. BRAND. The bookkeeping is perfectly clear.

Mr. ANDERSON. How many men have you employed at the Minneapolis office now?

Mr. LIVINGSTON. We have 2 supervisors, 3 assistant supervisors, 5 samplers, and 4 clerks, a total of 14.

Mr. ANDERSON. How many appeals were made to the supervisor at the Minneapolis office during the past year?

Mr. LIVINGSTON. I do not have that record with me; I do not know.

Mr. ANDERSON. Have you any record as to the number of inspections made, supervisor's inspections, that were not made on appeals?

Mr. LIVINGSTON. No, I do not have the number. Our men are getting samples every day. That is what the samplers are there for. I do not know how many they have taken in the Minneapolis office. I can get the number of appeals in the Minneapolis office. I do not think it was very large.

Mr. ANDERSON. I think it was 125 or 130 last year.

Mr. LIVINGSTON. I think that would be a reasonable estimate.

Mr. ANDERSON. You do know how many supervisory inspections that are made on appeal were made?

Mr. LIVINGSTON. That I would not be able to tell you without telegraphing to Minneapolis and getting the records. Our samplers go into the yards every day and sample as many cars as they can, and those samples are checked up in the office.

Mr. ANDERSON. Are they checked up with the inspections of the inspectors?

Mr. LIVINGSTON. Yes, sir; they talk that over informally with the inspectors.

Mr. ANDERSON. You did some work last year, I think, under this item in educating our farmers out there in your standards. Can you tell me about your work at the county fairs?

Mr. LIVINGSTON. The work there was done with the funds provided in the food production act.

Mr. ANDERSON. How much was spent for that work?

Mr. McLAUGHLIN. Although that was done under the emergency fund it was done by your office?

Mr. LIVINGSTON. Yes, sir.

Mr. ANDERSON. Do you intend to use any of this money for that purpose?

Mr. LIVINGSTON. For this purpose?

Mr. ANDERSON. Yes.

Mr. LIVINGSTON. Nothing, except traveling expenses. Previously that has all been carried under the emergency fund.

Mr. ANDERSON. These demonstrations consisted of showing the method of using the different instruments and that sort of thing?

Mr. LIVINGSTON. Yes, sir; there is a photograph of one of them (showing photograph).

Mr. ANDERSON. I do not want to go into the grading proposition at all. I confess I have to repress myself a good deal not to do it.

But do you consider it feasible for a farmer to have the machinery which is shown in this picture and test his own grain?

Mr. LIVINGSTON. No, sir; I do not.

Mr. MCLAUGHLIN. In organizing your forces have you found it necessary to employ a very large number of men who previously were employed by the State in their work?

Mr. BRAND. Most of our men have been employed either by the States or by the other agencies that supervised the grading of grain at the terminal markets. In Baltimore it is the Chamber of Commerce, in New York the Produce Exchange, and in Buffalo the Corn Exchange, and they have come largely from the grain trade and the majority of them come from the employment of the specific bodies that handle the grading and inspection work.

Mr. MCLAUGHLIN. When you employ a man and get him that way, you try to find out what he has been receiving?

Mr. BRAND. Always; we require him to state exactly what he has been receiving.

Mr. MCLAUGHLIN. And you take any other means of getting information as to his former salary?

Mr. BRAND. Yes, we make very careful inquiries and have our own men interview them before they make any tender of a position.

Mr. MCLAUGHLIN. They undertake to improve themselves?

Mr. BRAND. Yes; and the civil service papers, which are prepared under oath also give the information.

Mr. HARRISON. The secretary's office requires you to state in your recommendation the present salary the proposed appointee is receiving.

Mr. BRAND. Every recommendation is required to state the present salary.

Mr. MCLAUGHLIN. What inquiry, if any, do you make of the employers?

Mr. BRAND. If we have the slightest doubt as to the accuracy of the man's statement, we may ask the employers.

Mr. MCLAUGHLIN. In answering a question of Mr. Haugen a little while ago you said that was none of your business. It would seem to me it would be your business to know definitely just how much a man was getting, if you are trying to get him away from his former employers.

Mr. BRAND. My statement was in regard to the whole range of the officers of an inspection department. I do not conceive it to be our right to expect them, and we certainly have no legal authority to require them, to reveal to us the salaries of all their employees.

Mr. MCLAUGHLIN. But you have taken from these other employers a large number of men, practically your entire force.

Mr. BRAND. A great many of them do come from the employ of grain firms.

Mr. MCLAUGHLIN. Other employment of a similar kind?

Mr. BRAND. Necessarily, because only in this employment do men get training for this particular work.

Mr. MCLAUGHLIN. In nearly every case you have found it necessary to mak your employment in some way more attractive than was formerly the case?

Mr. BRAND. Yes.

Mr. MCLAUGHLIN. Largely by paying an increase in salary?

Mr. BRAND. Yes. For instance, I have in mind the specific case of one of a Minnesota man whom we employed, who was stationed at Duluth, and we wished to get him for our supervisor at Boston, and we necessarily had to pay him more than he was getting at Duluth, because not only did he have to move himself and his household furniture, but also his wife and children.

Mr. MCLAUGHLIN. In cases of that kind it is sometimes deemed advisable to consult the former employer as to whether he could conveniently let the man go and how much he is paying?

Mr. BRAND. In almost all cases, especially where it involves such a section——

Mr. MCLAUGHLIN (interposing). Then you learn the salary?

Mr. BRAND. Yes.

Mr. MCLAUGHLIN. From another source?

Mr. BRAND. I do not think there is a case in which we do not absolutely know the man's salary, and if we do not know it, it has been misrepresented; but there has never been such a case.

Mr. MCLAUGHLIN. Has there been any friction between you and those from whom you have obtained your men, because you take the men away?

Mr. BRAND. No. They are as sorry to lose their men as we are sorry to lose them when they take them back. I recall no case where there has been any friction.

Mr. LIVINGSTON. I think it ought to appear in the record that there are a number of men who are in the supervision service getting less salaries now than they got before they entered the service. One man whom we are paying $3,240 was earning $5,000 before he came with us. Another man who was getting $5,000 came in at $2,760, in order to be located at a certain point. He has since left the service. There are a number of supervisors in the service whose salaries at the present time are less than they were formerly receiving.

Mr. ANDERSON. Can you state how many inspectors you have licensed in Minnesota who are not licensed within the State?

Mr. LIVINGSTON. I can not. I believe there was only one, and I think his license has been canceled at his own request.

The CHAIRMAN. You have here a proviso which seems to be an amendment to the grain-standards act.

Mr. LIVINGSTON. I would like to answer Mr. Anderson's question a little more fully. He asked me whether the farmer was supposed to have the equipment. My reply was that he was not expected to do that. The farmer can not expect to be an expert grain grader The only thing he can do is to know when his grain is properly graded. The farmer can no more become an expert grain grader than he can become an expert along some other line which is really outside of his immediate field. His field is production, and does not enter far into the grain grading or grain marketing field.

Mr. ANDERSON. Then if he sells his grain at a local market he has got to take the buyer's word for what his grain is worth?

Mr. LIVINGSTON. In large measure. He should know enough about the grain to know whether the grade was determined before or after dockage is removed; the limits of the standards; and the general principles upon which the standards are based. He must know that in order to protect himself, but when it comes to a question such as damage grains, I do not think the farmer, speaking generally, will ever be in a position to grade grain according to any set of standards.

Mr. ANDERSON. I do not quite agree with you on that. If your statement is true, then practically all the grain that is sold at local markets must be sold without reference to the standards to any great extent, or any accurate application of the standards, because so far as my experience goes, I do not know of a local market in my district where a local buyer has the machinery to make the elaborate tests which seem to be required by the use of this machinery.

Mr. LIVINGSTON. All of that machinery is not necessary at the country elevator because the grain which comes into a country elevator runs fairly uniform, and it is not necessary to make a determination on all the grain received.

Mr. ANDERSON. I think that is true as to quality, in a general way, but, of course it is far from being true as to moisture, weed-seed content, damaged kernels and broken kernels.

Mr. LIVINGSTON. Those determinations are not difficult to make. The dockage determination is not difficult to make. I think almost every country elevator has the equipment to make a determination for that. It is very easy also to make a weight per bushel test.

Mr. ANDERSON. But it goes far beyond that. A man's grain may go one or two grades below number one, due to the presence of a small amount of other wheats, barley, or oats, the presence of inseparable matter, damaged kernels and all that sort of thing, so that a determination that does not take into consideration those elements is not very valuable.

Mr. LIVINGSTON. The equipment is used primarily to determine whether or not the sample is 1 or 2 or 3. The average elevator can tell by examining the sample whether it is good 1 or good 2. The difficulty comes in determining whether it is low 1 or high 2.

Mr. ANDERSON. Two or three cents' difference is just as important to a farmer if it is high 1 or low 2 as it would be if it was low 1 or high 2?

Mr. LIVINGSTON. That is true; but I don't think you can charge the standards with the fact that the farmer is docked 2 or 3 cents a bushel when his grain falls down a grade.

Mr. ANDERSON. I will not go into the standards proposition.

Mr. LIVINGSTON. I want to call your attention to the fact that 86 per cent of the wheat this year at Minneapolis is 2 or better.

Mr. ANDERSON. I will agree that the farmers raised an extraordinarily good class of wheat this year. That is what that statement means?

Mr. BRAND. They all agreed to that statement last year, too.

Mr. ANDERSON. That was true last year?

Mr. LIVINGSTON. Eighty-seven per cent was 2 or better.

Mr. McLAUGHLIN. That was the crop harvested in 1918?

Mr. LIVINGSTON. Yes, sir.

The CHAIRMAN. Suppose you discuss briefly what you propose in the matter of abolishing the notice of appeal.

Mr. LIVINGSTON. I would like to put a statement in the record regarding the number of appeals.
Mr. CHAIRMAN. We would like to have that statement.
(The statement referred to follows:)

APPEALS HANDLED AT MINNEAPOLIS OFFICE OF FEDERAL GRAIN SUPERVISION AND AT ALL SUPERVISION OFFICES DURING PERIOD DEC. 1, 1916, TO JUNE 30, 1918, AND JULY 1, 1918, TO JAN. 8, 1919.

Number of appeals received and handled at Minneapolis office.

To June 30, 1918_____ 169
Since July 1, 1918_____ 314

    Total _____ 483

Number of appeals received and handled at all points to January 8, 1919.

	Wheat.	Corn.	Total.
Handled by board of grain supervisors:			
To June 30, 1918	16	42	58
Since July 1, 1918	69	9	78
Total to Jan. 8, 1919	85	51	136
Handled by single supervisor:			
To June 30, 1918	350	1,050	1,400
Since July 1, 1918	1,987	809	2,796
Total since Jan. 8, 1919	2,337	1,859	4,196
Total filed:			
To June 30, 1918	366	1,092	1,458
Since July 1, 1918	2,056	818	2,874
Total to Jan. 8, 1919	2,422	1,910	4,332

Mr. ANDERSON. Will you also insert a statement showing the number of cases in which the appeals were sustained and the number in which they were not sustained?
Mr. BRAND. I will.
(The statement follows:)

Appeals sustained, not sustained, or dismissed.

Number of appeals sustained (grade changed)_____ 2,366
Number of appeals not sustained (grade not changed)_____ 1,854
Number of appeals dismissed_____ 112

    Total _____ 4,332

Mr. ANDERSON. Will you also furnish a comparative statement of the salaries of the supervisors, samplers, and other employees, all along the line? Suppose you take Minnesota and make a comparison of the salaries paid by the State inspection department of Minnesota and those paid by your own service?
Mr. LIVINGSTON. Yes, sir. Do you want the employees listed by name or by number?
Mr. ANDERSON. We want to get what a sampler is paid in Minnesota and what a sampler is paid by your bureau.
Mr. LIVINGSTON. Our range varies from $1,140 to $1,800.
Mr. HAUGEN. The statement should give the number in each class.
Mr. LIVINGSTON. It should be remembered in giving those that the supervisor in all offices compares with the chief inspector in Minnesota.
(The statement referred to follows:)

AGRICULTURE APPROPRIATION BILL. 721

Salaries paid to employees of the Grain Inspection Department at Minneapolis by the Minnesota Railroad and Warehouse Commission.

	Annual salary.	Overtime pay.	Total.	Grand total.
1 chief grain inspector	$3,800		$3,800	$3,800
1 chief deputy grain inspector	3,000		3,000	3,000
3 appeal board members	3,000		3,000	9,000
4 assistant deputy inspectors	2,110	$211	2,321	9,284
15 deputy inspectors	1,850	185	2,035	30,525
4 deputy inspectors	1,600	160	1,760	7,040
8 foremen of samplers [1]	1,440	144	1,584	12,672
19 grain samplers	1,320	132	1,452	27,588
18 grain samplers	1,200	120	1,320	23,760
51 grain samplers	1,080	108	1,188	60,588
Total				187,257

[1] A number of samplers and foremen of samplers employed by the Minnesota Railroad and Warehouse Commission are located at small markets outside of Minneapolis, and their living expenses are, therefore, lower than State and Federal employees living in Minneapolis.

Salaries paid to employees of the office of Federal Grain Supervision, Bureau of Markets, at Minneapolis.

	Annual salary.	Overtime pay.	Total.	Grand total.
1 grain supervisor (in charge)	[1] $2,760		$2,760	$2,760
1 grain supervisor	2,400		2,400	2,400
1 assistant in grain marketing	2,400		2,400	2,400
1 assistant grain supervisor	2,280		2,280	2,280
Do	1,800		1,800	1,800
2 grain samplers	1,620		1,620	3,240
1 grain sampler	1,500		1,500	1,500
Do	1,320		1,320	1,320
Do	1,200		1,200	1,200
Total				18,900

[1] This official supervises all inspection work performed by all the persons shown in these tables.

Mr. LIVINGSTON. I would like to put in the record the statement that we have handled on appeal this fiscal year approximately 15,000,000 bushels.

Mr. HAUGEN. Out of about how many bushels—out of about 500,000,000 bushels marketed?

Mr. LIVINGSTON. Five or six hundred million bushels; yes, sir.

The CHAIRMAN. Now, tell us the reason you want to repeal this notice proposition, or does it need any amplification?

Mr. LIVINGSTON. It is stated very clearly in the Book of Estimates, and I will have it reinserted at this point for the information of the committee:

REASONS FOR AMENDMENT REQUESTED.

(1) To permit the Secretary of Agriculture to entertain an appeal from the grade assigned by a licensed inspector to any lot of grain inspected and graded according to the official grain standards of the United States.

(2) To permit the Secretary of Agriculture to issue findings immediately after determining the appeal without serving notice on all interested parties.

The present language of section 6 permits the Secretary of Agriculture to entertain an appeal from the grading of a licensed inspector only when the grain is involved in interstate commerce. It is desirable to permit the Secretary of Agriculture to entertain appeals on intra as well as interstate grain for the following reasons:

(1) To maintain the integrity of the grain standards of the United States. Inspectors who grade intrastate grain under the Federal standards frequently

do not apply the standards correctly, thereby discrediting the standards and the Federal grain-supervision work.

(2) To protect those buyers and sellers who base transactions on Federal standards who do not now have the appeal privilege. Farmers and country elevator operators frequently are denied the right of appeal to the Secretary of Agriculture because their grain, although graded by a licensed inspector and according to the official grain standards of the United States, does not move interstate. Also, operators of public warehouses frequently must take into the house grain graded according to the official grain standards of the United States without the right of appeal, even though they believe the grading is incorrect.

(3) To meet criticism of the act by country shippers and other intrastate dealers in grain to the effect that the act is of little or no benefit to them. Such persons frequently express dissatisfaction with the law because they are obliged to accept the grading of an inspector without recourse.

The language of section 6 now requires that all parties interested in the transaction, other than those filing the appeal, be afforded an opportunity to be heard before the issuance of the findings of the Secretary of Agriculture. It is desirable to permit the Secretary of Agriculture to issue findings without opportunity for hearing, for the following reasons:

(1) To avoid delay in the handling of grain involved in an appeal.

(2) To avoid delay in the settlement of a transaction involving a appeal. To afford opportunity for hearing requires the serving of notice to interested parties, which involves a lapse of time—sometimes as much as two weeks—because of the distance from the point of appeal of other interested parties.

(3) Because an appeal is for the sole purpose of ascertaining the true grade of the grain in question, which is determined by an examination of the grain itself. The decision is not influenced in any way by statements of interested parties. Moreover, the true grade must be determined at once. Therefore, the opportunity for hearing serves no purpose in determining the question at issue. The opportunity for hearing has not been utilized by any party at interest in the 4,332 appeals thus far entertained by the Secretary of Agriculture.

(4) Because opportunity for hearing is contrary to trade practices and is considered "red tape" by the grain trade.

It is largely to do away with what the grain trade calls "red tape," the delay in closing up a transaction, and to facilitate handling the grain. Also considerable expense on the part of the office of Federal Grain Supervision in taking care of all these [indicating] records.

These papers must be made out in the field and passed on into Washington before an appeal can be closed up, and the grain men are not disposed to file appeals when they are obliged to fill out a complicated form of application. It looks rather formidable, although it is not when you analyze it. They are not accustomed to doing it that way.

Mr. ANDERSON. When you refer to an appeal, do you refer to an appeal prosecuted to your Board of Review, or to an appeal made to the supervisor?

Mr. LIVINGSTON. To the supervisor; and the way the regulations now stand, every appeal that is handled by a single supervisor goes to a Board of Review for final review.

Mr. ANDERSON. Let me be sure I understand you. Do I understand you to say that where an appeal is made from the original inspection, the appeal is made first to the local supervisor?

Mr. LIVINGSTON. Yes, sir.

Mr. ANDERSON. In every case is not the appeal prosecuted to the Board of Review?

Mr. LIVINGSTON. Yes, sir; on our instance, however, not on the instance of the shippers, or any other interested party. If any other interested party desires to have an opportunity to appeal from the decision of the supervisor he may call for a board appeal and have a quick determination. The appeal may be filed in Minneapolis and handled by the supervisor there. If either party in interest is not satisfied with the determination of the grade by the supervisor he may call for a board appeal. Then the grade is determined by a board of three supervisors, and a grade memorandum, signed by three supervisors, is issued to the parties in interest. In both cases the samples examined by the three supervisors and the single supervisor go to the Board of Review and are reviewed before the secretary's findings are issued.

Mr. ANDERSON. That seems to be a wholly unnecessary and cumbersome procedure.

Mr. LIVINGSTON. It is brought about by the requirement that the Secretary's findings have to be held up until every party in interest has had an opportunity to be heard.

Mr. ANDERSON. But there certainly must be a very large proportion of cases in which the parties in interest will be satisfied by the determination of an appeal by the appeal board rather than the board of review here. But as I understand you, in every one of those cases the appeal is prosecuted from the appeal board to the Secretary, or to the Board of Review here?

Mr. BRAND. I do not believe Mr. Livingston has in mind the point of the question. Will you answer this question, Mr. Livingston? How many board appeals have been passed on during the fiscal year?

Mr. LIVINGSTON. I think very few. This board of review represents the Secretary before he issues his findings.

Mr. ANDERSON. I want to get this machinery straight in my head. I want to know how much of it we have got.

Here is a carload of grain which comes into the terminal at Minneapolis. We will say it is examined by a State inspector and inspected by a State inspector, and from that inspection an appeal lies either to the Minnesota Grain Board of Appeals or to your supervisor?

Mr. LIVINGSTON. Or both.

Mr. ANDERSON. Or both. We will eliminate the State process and take up yours. From the supervisor, that is, the single supervisor, as I understand you, an appeal lies to a local board of review at the terminal point; is that correct?

Mr. LIVINGSTON. As soon as that appeal is filed with our Supervisor in Minneapolis, he determines the grade and issues the grade memorandum, which is used as a basis by the parties interested in closing up a transaction. If they are not satisfied with the grade placed upon the car of grain by the supervisor at Minneapolis, they may call for a board appeal, but very few of them have been called. This grade memorandum $m_u s_t$ be followed by the secretary's findings and his findings are taken as prima facie evidence in the United States courts in any controversy concerning the grade of the grain.

Mr. ANDERSON. I think ou are going too fast when you say that. I want to get what actually happens. We will say these people are not satisfied with the grade given by the supervisor. They appeal before a board of inspection, which consists of three men appointed by your office?

Mr. LIVINGSTON. Yes, sir.
Mr. ANDERSON. That appeal is final unless it is appealed from?
Mr. LIVINGSTON. Yes; it can not be appealed from; that is final.
Mr. ANDERSON. That is final?
Mr. LIVINGSTON. Yes.
Mr. ANDERSON. The board of appeals' findings at the local point is final?
Mr. LIVINGSTON. Yes.
Mr. ANDERSON. Then what is the purpose of the review by your Board of Review here in Washington?
Mr. LIVINGSTON. To see that the supervisors in the field have not gone astray.
Mr. ANDERSON. But that does not have any effect on the findings?
Mr. LIVINGSTON. Yes, sir.
Mr. ANDERSON. How would it if the finding is final?
Mr. BRAND. It has not been issued.
Mr. LIVINGSTON. This memorandum, and also a memorandum by a board of three supervisors is followed by the secretary's findings.
Mr. ANDERSON. Then in every case where there is an appeal to a local board before their determination can become final, it must be reviewed by the Board of Review here, and the finding approved by the secretary?
Mr. LIVINGSTON. That is our present administrative way of handling it. It is proposed to recommend a change in the regulations which will make the Board of Review the board that handles the second appeal. In other words, if the shippers——
Mr. ANDERSON (interposing). You mean the Board of Review here in Washington?
Mr. LIVINGSTON. It is located here now; we are going to place it in Chicago. If any party in interest is not satisfied with the determination by a single supervisor he calls for a board appeal, and that board will be the Board of Review.
Mr. ANDERSON. That will mean the appeal will be from the single inspector?
Mr. LIVINGSTON. Direct to the Board of Review.
Mr. ANDERSON. In Chicago.
Mr. LIVINGSTON. Yes, sir.
Mr. ANDERSON. And that means in every case there will be the delay incident to the sending of a sample to Chicago and the return of the finding to the point at which the original inspection was made?
Mr. LIVINGSTON. That will be handled by telegraph.
Mr. ANDERSON. You can not handle the sample by telegraph.
Mr. BRAND. That only occurs in the case of certain appeals, and for almost all purposes of trading what we know as the grade memorandum settles the case, but the law requires the issuing of the secretary's findings, which may be used in the courts.
Mr. ANDERSON. But the Secretary's findings does not do anything but give approval of the report made by the Board of Review?
Mr. BRAND. Three hundred and ninety-nine cases out of four hundred are settled on the grade memorandum.
Mr. ANDERSON. But even in that case, under your present arrangement, the sample must come to Washington and be passed upon by the Board of Review before you have any finality to your certificate?

Mr. BRAND. No; that is not the case. The purpose of that is to secure uniformity and correctness in the application of the standards. We have now reached a point where we have almost 90 per cent efficiency as between markets, so that the sending of these samples to the Board of Review relates to efficiency or inefficiency, but not to the conclusion of the transaction.

Mr. ANDERSON. If the Board of Review, in other words, at the local point issues a grade certificate, so far as the grading is concerned, that is final and can not be affected by the further review by the board here?

Mr. BRAND. If a supervisor has made an error the Board of Review will turn him down and issue the Secretary's findings on the basis of what they found to be the facts.

Mr. ANDERSON. Then there is not any finality until the Board of Review passes upon it?

Mr. BRAND. As a technical matter it is not final until the finding is issued; but as a practical matter, in 399 cases out of 400 it is final.

Mr. ANDERSON. That is true because an appeal is not prosecuted from the local board to the Board of Review?

Mr. LIVINGSTON. No; it is because the act requires the Secretary's findings to follow after all parties in interest have had an opportunity to be heard. The Secretary's findings could not be made in the field unless all parties in interest were notified and had an opportunity to be heard.

Mr. ANDERSON. Either one thing or the other is true, it seems to me. Either the certificate issued by the board of appeal, where the local inspection is had, is final, or it is not final. If in every case there is a review of the finding by the Board of Review here, and that finding is approved by the Secretary, then it is not final.

Mr. BRAND. The practical application of the matter is, that the inspector, to begin with, is usually right. In other words, the inspection is far more accurate than it ever has been, so that the complainant does not call for a board of supervisors to pass on an appeal, but he is satisfied with the appeal to a single supervisor. Then the Board of Review, which is an administrative agency to bring about uniformity and to apply correction, acts for the Secretary in the final preparation of the finding. But in the practical application of the case it is just the same as if the Minnesota State board of appeal had been called upon instead of the individual supervisor.

Mr. ANDERSON. Here is where I fall down on your proposition; where I do not understand it. Do I understand you now to say that if a board of inspection is applied for, that inspection is had and the certificate issued, and if the parties in interest are satisfied with the results it does not go any further?

Mr. BRAND. Absolutely no further.

Mr. ANDERSON. But if they are not satisfied, then the appeal comes to the Board of Review?

Mr. BRAND. That is the situation which will exist when the Board of Review has been constituted with the powers we intend to give it.

Mr. HAUGEN. The appeal from the State goes to one supervisor, and in 399 cases out of 400 that is satisfactory, and it is accepted and is final?

Mr. BRAND. Yes

Mr. HAUGEN. Then it goes to a board of three supervisors under the present practice?

Mr. LIVINGSTON. Yes.

Mr. BRAND. That has to be passed upon by the Board of Review before it is final.

Mr. LIVINGSTON. No, the Board of Review at the present time is an Administrative agency for bringing about uniformity of inspection and checking up accuracy, and it does not hold up the transaction for a single moment; the transaction proceeds.

Mr. HAUGEN. But the certificate must be issued and signed by the Secretary, and that after it has been reviewed?

Mr. LIVINGSTON. No, the grade memorandum settles the matter as a practical proposition.

Mr. ANDERSON. But that can not be true when an appeal is taken?

Mr. LIVINGSTON. That is true, except in these rare cases.

Mr. HAUGEN. Has not the Board of Review the power to review?

Mr. LIVINGSTON. Absolutely.

Mr. HAUGEN. Then it is not final until it has passed the Board of Review?

Mr. LIVINGSTON. In those few cases.

Mr. HAUGEN. The purpose is to eliminate the board of three supervisors and to go direct from the one man to the Board of Review?

Mr. LIVINGSTON. That is the idea, and also to eliminate the numerous papers which have to be made up and submitted in order that the parties may have a hearing under the terms of the act.

Mr. HAUGEN. Is not one a check upon the other?

Mr. LIVINGSTON. Yes.

Mr. HAUGEN. Why do you propose to set aside this board?

Mr. LIVINGSTON. Because we are placing upon this board men whom we believe will give it a faith and credence that could not be given to any board of three supervisors made up from three field supervisors.

Mr. HAUGEN. But the supervisors are on the spot?

Mr. LIVINGSTON. No, only in the largest markets are they on the spot.

Mr. HAUGEN. In a number of the important markets?

Mr. LIVINGSTON. In about six out of thirty-five.

Mr. HAUGEN. The purpose of the act was to expedite matters. The contention was that the appeals were to Washington, and that would necessarily delay matters, and that it was the purpose of the act to expedite the proceedings?

Mr. LIVINGSTON. That has not proven to be true, aside from this procedure, which we believe is very cumbersome.

Mr. ANDERSON. In view of what you have said, it seems to me in order to really understand what work is done by the Federal inspection service we would have to have inserted in the record the number of appeals taken to the single supervisors, and then the number taken from the supervisors to the boards, and so on up. Of course, under the system you have, the number of appeals prosecuted to the Secretary is no index at all of the situation.

Mr. BRAND. Of course, each State represents an independent volume of work.

Mr. ANDERSON. That is it exactly, and so if you simply state that there have been thirty or forty or one hundred appeals to the Secretary, that does not mean anything.

Mr. BRAND. I think we can very readily segregate it.

Mr. LIVINGSTON. Your point is that the forty-three hundred appeals include some duplications, because each appeal includes the appeal to the single supervisor originally, and then the appeal to the board of supervisors? I explained that in my original statement.

Mr. ANDERSON. I did not hear your original statement, and I did not know what that meant.

Mr. LIVINGSTON. Nobody carries an appeal to the Secretary under the present regulations.

Mr. ANDERSON. But they can?

Mr. LIVINGSTON. No, the present regulations close it off with the board of three supervisors, that is, so far as the grade is concerned.

Mr. HAUGEN. I understood you to say all of the findings of the board of three supervisors are reviewed by the Secretary?

Mr. LIVINGSTON. Yes; that is an administrative matter.

Mr. HAUGEN. Are all of them reviewed by the Board of Review?

Mr. LIVINGSTON. Yes.

Mr. HAUGEN. Then the number would be exactly the same?

Mr. LIVINGSTON. Yes; but the Board of Review does not count as a new body.

Mr. HAUGEN. No, but I am getting at the process. The number of reported appeals to the board would be the same as those passed upon by the Board of Review or the Secretary?

Mr. LIVINGSTON. Passed upon the Board of Review, which includes very few board appeals.

Mr. HAUGEN. It is simply a change of title, is it not?

Mr. LIVINGSTON. A change of title.

Mr. HAUGEN. The Board of Review is to take the place of the three supervisors?

Mr. LIVINGSTON. Yes, the three supervisors in the field.

Mr. HAUGEN. In the end, it is simply a change of title?

Mr. LIVINGSTON. Yes. It is consolidating under one board the authority now placed on boards that may be constituted in the field at various points.

Mr. HAUGEN. As I understand you the Board of Review simply passes upon the findings of the supervisors?

Mr. LIVINGSTON. At the present time——

Mr. HAUGEN (interposing). You propose to cut it out entirely?

Mr. LIVINGSTON. No, under the new plan the Board of Review will act——

Mr. HAUGEN (interposing). They take the place of the three supervisors?

Mr. LIVINGSTON. Yes sir.

Mr. HAUGEN. It is a change of titles is it not?

Mr. LIVINGSTON. Yes sir.

Mr. HAUGEN. What is the object of it?

Mr. LIVINGSTON. To expedite the handling of appeals.

Mr. HAUGEN. But at the present time you say you have these boards at six important markets, and now you propose to narrow it down to one at Chicago?

Mr. Livingston. Yes.

Mr. Haugen. What is the object in changing that? Can not the business be expedited more through the six boards established, especially when you have the machinery there?

Mr. Livingston. We would move the board out to Chicago to make it function as the board for all the surrounding markets. Nine-tenths of the appeals are handled within an overnight ride of Chicago.

Mr. Haugen. This board is to handle the business now handled by six?

Mr. Livingston. It becomes the board of appeals. There have only been a few such cases where appeals have been taken to a board of supervisors from the decision of a single supervisor.

Mr. Haugen. I know, but we will not discuss the number.

Mr. Livingston. Their real function is to interpret the standards and review the appeals that come along; to review the samples taken by the supervisors in the field; and to review the samples which the inspectors have graded.

Mr. Haugen. I think we understand that. What I am interested in is in expediting the inspection.

Mr. Livingston. Yes.

Mr. Haugen. You have set up the machinery at six points, and now you propose to narrow it down to one?

Mr. Livingston. Only in a few cases.

Mr. Haugen. Do you think that is the proper thing to do, inasmuch as you have the machinery? Will it involve additional expense?

Mr. Livingston. In many places we are obliged to call in a board where a superappeal is called. If a superappeal is called at Memphis we must either send the sample from Memphis to a market that has three supervisors or call to Memphis two additional supervisors. The real reason for taking the board away from the local market is that the trade object to having the man who originally passed upon the appeal——

Mr. Haugen (interposing). Serve on that board?

Mr. Livingston. Sit as a member of that board, and therefore it requires four supervisors, or else we have the situation where the man who originally handled the appeal sits as a member of the board.

Mr. Haugen. But you are all the time getting away from the point where the appeal is taken. They would have to go to Chicago before the appeal could be taken and disposed of——

Mr. Livingston (interposing). We propose to provide in the regulations for the handling of emergency appeals. On the Pacific coast, for instance, it will take a long time to get the samples to Chicago.

Mr. Haugen. One objection made to the service was on account of the delays involved in the appeals.

Mr. Brand. There has not been any delay, as a matter of fact.

Mr. Haugen. But you are now proposing to change it?

Mr. Livingston. The change relates to regulation 3 entitled "Appeals" which provided in detail for the method of taking an appeal. A complaint must be filed, signed by the complainant or his agent. Not only that, but a notice must be served upon every party in interest and sufficient time must be allowed for all of them to have received the notice and to have made answer to it. We have no means of telling, within a reasonable time, whether they are going to answer or not, and it may delay for 10 days or two weeks the technical settlement, which involves the issuance of the secretary's findings.

Mr. HAUGEN. Does that not account for the few appeals, because the procedure is known to be so cumbersome, and it is so expensive that it makes it impracticable?

Mr. LIVINGSTON. I think people will appeal more readily when the procedure is made more simple, but we had 8,500,000 bushels appeal recently at Chicago.

Mr. HAUGEN. We are discussing the boards, and particularly the Board of Review.

Mr. LIVINGSTON. Anything which simplifies the procedure will lead people to appeal more generally, but we have tried to discourage trivial appeals.

Mr. HAUGEN. Is that the object of removing the Board of Review from the point where the first findings are found?

Mr. LIVINGSTON. No; the purpose of utilizing the larger Board of Review is to give the greatest possible respect to their findings.

Mr. HAUGEN. But you are going to utilize the same board, are you not?

Mr. LIVINGSTON. No.

Mr. HAUGEN. That can be changed just the same?

Mr. LIVINGSTON. It will be a group of men to be permanently assigned to that work.

Mr. HAUGEN. You have men permanently assigned here to that work now?

Mr. LIVINGSTON. They do not pass in the same way as this particular body will pass upon the matter.

Mr. HAUGEN. In what respect? You said this board had the power to reverse the findings of the board of supervisors.

Mr. LIVINGSTON. The Board of Review will be located in Chicago and will act for the Secretary.

Mr. HAUGEN. You are changing them from Washington to Chicago; that is all?

Mr. LIVINGSTON. The present location is one thing that occasions delay in the issuing of the findings, and therefore the selection of the central location in Chicago, which expedites the matter, and the location of men in a market where an enormous volume of grain is passing all the time keeps them in contact with the problems involved.

Mr. HAUGEN. Anyway, the proposition is to centralize it in Chicago. Heretofore appeals could be taken and questions could be settled, definitely and finally, at St. Paul, whereas now they will have to go to Chicago?

Mr. LIVINGSTON. Only in the rarest case would they have to go to Chicago.

Would you think it wise to put in a provision for an opinion for the party in interest, that he may either appeal to the board of three supervisors on the ground, if there is a board present, or go to Chicago?

Mr. ANDERSON. In every case the appeal would be to the local board?

Mr. LIVINGSTON. Our experience is just the other way.

Mr. HAUGEN. Then your contention is that the service is defective in that respect?

Mr. BRAND. That is why we are suggesting that change, of course.

Mr. LIVINGSTON. They want to get it to the highest authority as quickly as possible, and so long as the Board of Review represents the Secretary of Agriculture in Washington, in the grading and lot of grain, that board is going to be the final authority, and the parties in interest want to get their sample there as quickly as possible.

Mr. HAUGEN. How many members are there of the Board of Review?

Mr. LIVINGSTON. We have five.

Mr. HAUGEN. How many cases?

Mr. BRAND. They pass on every appeal.

Mr. HAUGEN. How many appeals?

Mr. BRAND. Four thousand three hundred.

Mr. HAUGEN. You said one out of 400.

Mr. BRAND. The super appeal was called for only in about that number of cases, but the Board of Review passes on all appeals and sets up the correctness of the work to keep all the work of the supervisors uniform.

THE CHAIRMAN. Is that by regulation or by law?

Mr. BRAND. That is an administrative matter.

Mr. HAUGEN. You mean all appeals?

Mr. BRAND. Every one in the United States.

Mr. HAUGEN. Wherever they come from?

Mr. BRAND. Yes.

Mr. MCLAUGHLIN. Then, when they reverse the action of this board, it does not have any effect because the parties in interest have not followed it up?

Mr. LIVINGSTON. They have the Secretary's findings as a basis of the final settlement.

Mr. MCLAUGHLIN. But if this appeal was changed by the board of review——

Mr. BRAND (interposing). If a person received a grain order at a higher price, they would merely send him a check covering the difference.

Mr. HAUGEN. Are all the samples sent here to Washington?

Mr. LIVINGSTON. Yes; on all of the appeals.

Mr. HAUGEN. On all of those appeals?

Mr. LIVINGSTON. Yes.

Mr. HAUGEN. The samples are sent here?

Mr. LIVINGSTON. Yes.

Mr. HAUGEN. Of course, you could not pass upon them unless you had the samples?

Mr. LIVINGSTON. No.

Mr. HAUGEN. How much grain is there in each sample?

Mr. LIVINGSTON. About two quarts.

Mr. HAUGEN. That must net quite a revenue to the Government when you dispose of the samples?

Mr. LIVINGSTON. Yes; that is turned into the Treasury to the credit of "miscellaneous receipts." That amounts to quite a bit of grain in the aggregate.

Mr. HAUGEN. Two quarts of each of 1,000 cases would make 2,000 quarts, and that is quite a lot of grain.

Mr. LIVINGSTON. Yes.

Mr. ANDERSON. As near as I can understand it, an appeal is final when it is final, and when it is not final it is not final.

Mr. BRAND. Necessarily.

Mr. ANDERSON. And sometimes when it is final, it is not final if an appeal is taken to the Secretary; and although nobody had appealed, still, if the Secretary finds that the last board that examined the grain was wrong about it and the grade is changed, the fellow who originally had the transaction has got to give his check to the other fellow for the difference?

Mr. BRAND. Not at all. If there has been no appeal called for, so that the question is an open question, the settlement is on the original basis, but the original basis is corrected, so that he will not make the same error again.

Mr. ANDERSON. That is what Mr. McLaughlin asked you and you gave him an opposite answer.

Mr. BRAND. Then I did not understand the question.

Mr. HAUGEN. What occasion is there for this new language?

Mr. BRAND. That simplifies the procedure. By the change of language the procedure is simplified to a great extent.

Mr. McLAUGHLIN. In order to understand that, you would have to take the new language and have the original law at hand to see what difference it would make.

Mr. HAUGEN. Pretty nearly all of this is done by regulation in the department, and it is necessary to find what the regulations are. Is that the only purpose of this proposed change, to eliminate a supervisor?

Mr. LIVINGSTON. No; it is to simplify the appeal form. It is to enable us to make the decision of the supervisor out in the field final if we desire to do so, and thus to avoid delay in closing the transaction.

Mr. HAUGEN. That is, it shall be left to the descretion of the secretary whether all these findings shall be final or not?

Mr. LIVINGSTON. No, left to the discretion of the secretary whether the supervisor in the field station may issue the secretary's findings.

Mr. HAUGEN. That makes it final?

Mr. LIVINGSTON. Yes.

Mr. HAUGEN. Then it is left to the discretion of the secretary?

Mr. LIVINGSTON. Yes. But now the secretary may not issue the findings until every party in interest has had an opportunity to be heard.

Mr. HAUGEN. The idea or purpose of the law was that everybody should have the benefit of the findings of the Board of Review?

Mr. BRAND. They will have them, and have them promptly, without this unusual amount——

Mr. HAUGEN (interposing). But, Mr. Livingston says the Secretary shall have the power to make the findings of the supervisor final.

Mr. BRAND. Yes; it will be a matter of regulation.

Mr. HAUGEN. That eliminates the Board of Review?

Mr. BRAND. No; the point is this——

Mr. HAUGEN (interposing). If you issue an order, or the Board of Review issues an order making the findings of the supervisor final, you eliminate the Board of Review.

Mr. LIVINGSTON. But you still have a Board of Review. Let me tell you how it will operate. Say a car of grain has been graded by an inspector. You, as the shipper, are dissatisfied with the grade placed by the inspector. You appeal to the local supervisor——

Mr. HAUGEN. We have eliminated him.

Mr. LIVINGSTON. No.

Mr. HAUGEN. Under this law.

Mr. LIVINGSTON. No. You appeal to the local supervisor who grades the grain. The question is, are you satisfied with it?

Mr. HAUGEN. No, I am not. Go ahead.

Mr. LIVINGSTON. Suppose you are satisfied?

Mr. HAUGEN. That is the end of it.

Mr. LIVINGSTON. This change in the act will give the Secretary authority to make that determination final, if you are satisfied.

Mr. HAUGEN. If you are satisfied, and if I am satisfied, that ends it?

Mr. LIVINGSTON. Yes. If, however, within 24 hours after the supervisor grades the grain and makes a determination of the grade you say you are not satisfied, it will go to the Board of Review, and that will be final; but the local supervisor's grade will become, or may become final, if the Secretary desires, immediately after the time has elapsed during which you can call on the Board of Review.

Mr. HAUGEN. In other words, I have 24 hours to change my mind?

Mr. LIVINGSTON. Yes.

Mr. HAUGEN. How does this affect that? This law provides that you shall have a certain number of hours——

Mr. LIVINGSTON (interposing). To call for a board appeal? No; that is by regulation.

Mr. HAUGEN. If both parties have accepted, they have 24 hours in which to change their minds?

Mr. LIVINGSTON. The law does not say that. The law says every party in interest shall have had an opportunity to be heard.

Mr. HAUGEN. But if I say I am satisfied, I have been heard.

Mr. LIVINGSTON. But you are only one party in interest.

Mr. HAUGEN. But suppose the other fellow is also satisfied, and they both agree to it?

Mr. LIVINGSTON. Then the secretary's findings might be issued at once.

Mr. HAUGEN. Are they not now?

Mr. LIVINGSTON. No.

Mr. HAUGEN. Why?

Mr. LIVINGSTON. Because the parties in interest are not always in the same market. We have to follow a uniform procedure.

Mr. HAUGEN. But they have both agreed?

Mr. ANDERSON. Then there is not any appeal at all.

Mr. HAUGEN. That is what I am trying to get at. That is my understanding of it. He says they have twenty-four hours in which to change their minds. I want to find out what the object of the new language is. I can not see where it has anything to do with what we are discussing.

Mr. LIVINGSTON. It simplifies the procedure. It will enable the secretary to permit the supervisors in the various market to issue the findings, and those findings would be final.

Mr. HAUGEN. Issue the findings of the secretary?

Mr. LIVINGSTON. Yes, or he could designate the Board of Review to do it.

Mr. HAUGEN. He has the power now?

Mr. LIVINGSTON. He has the power, but this provision requiring an opportunity to be given for the parties in interest to be heard, delays it.

Mr. ANDERSON. Does the regulation require a written notice in case of an appeal to a supervisor?

Mr. LIVINGSTON. A written notice from whom?

Mr. ANDERSON. A notice to the parties in interest of an appeal to the supervisor.

Mr. LIVINGSTON. Yes; the supervisor, or the man calling for the appeal, must send notice to the interested parties.

Mr. ANDERSON. Under this law there must be a notice to the interested parties in the case of every appeal?

Mr. LIVINGSTON. Yes; but if one party is in San Francisco and one party is in New York——

Mr. ANDERSON (interposing). That results in delay incident to the sending of the notice to the place where the party in interest is located?

Mr. LIVINGSTON. That is it.

Mr. ANDERSON. Then all this amendment does is to remove the necessity for giving that notice?

Mr. LIVINGSTON. Yes, that is it.

Mr. ANDERSON. When a man appeals from the grade, it is on the question of the grade of the grain, as it has been determined. There never was any reason for this language, because the opportunity to be heard suggests at least that there shall be an opportunity for argument. There is not any question of argument in it. It is a determination of a fact by an application of jurgment. So that there is not and never was any reason for requiring notice to anybody.

Mr. LIVINGSTON. I think you have stated the case exactly right.

Mr. ANDERSON. All this does is to remove the necessity of giving this notice?

Mr. LIVINGSTON. Yes.

Mr. JACOWAY. As it is now you have this machinery that is cumberson, and it takes you a long time to reach a given result?

Mr. LIVINGSTON. Yes.

Mr. JACOWAY. And if this additional language is incorporated it will enable you to reach a result much more expeditiously?

Mr. LIVINGSTON. Yes; both to our satisfaction and the satisfaction of the trade.

The CHAIRMAN. The next item is for administration of the warehouse act. There is a request for an increase of $16,440, apparently, but taken together with certain transfers to the statutory roll, the actual increase is $20,000.

Mr. BRAND. Mr. Nixon is here, Mr. Chairman. He is in charge of this work, and I will ask him to present the matter to you very briefly.

STATEMENT OF MR. R. L. NIXON, SPECIALIST IN CHARGE OF COTTON MARKETING AND WAREHOUSING, BUREAU OF MARKETS, UNITED STATES DEPARTMENT OF AGRICULTURE.

Mr. NIXON. Mr. Chairman, I can give only a very general statement in regard to that increase. When the Warehouse act was passed it was impossible, because of the abnormal conditions for us to undertake the work with reference to the warehouses for the storage of the different agricultural products. The act authorizes the Secretary to license warehouses for the storage of cotton, grain, tobacco, and wool. It has been impossible to undertake the work with some of those products, primarily because it has not been possible to employ the men who are qualified to do the work.

We feel that it will be possible from now on to get men who are qualified to do the work, and the increase asked for would be used to extend the work to the products that have not been included so far.

The CHAIRMAN. You expended in 1918, $33,237.99?

Mr. NIXON. Our estimate there for the year was something like $60,000, and for the reason I have just stated we did not expend that entire amount. It was not possible to undertake all the work authorized and anticipated.

The CHAIRMAN. Just what was that expenditure for; salaries, largely, I suppose?

Mr. NIXON. Very largely for salaries, yes.

The CHAIRMAN. What are these men doing?

Mr. NIXON. They are engaged largely in cotton-warehousing investigations. We have three men who devote their time entirely to the cotton warehousing work, and we have three men at present in grain, and we have one tobacco man, and for a short time we had one wool man.

The CHAIRMAN. When did this item become effective?

Mr. NIXON. On August 11, 1916.

The CHAIRMAN. It has been in operation how long?

Mr. NIXON. For about two and one-half years.

The CHAIRMAN. What class of work have these men been engaged in; preparing regulations?

Mr. NIXON. That is part of the work. There was a great deal of investigational work necessary to be done before we were in a position intelligently to prepare regulations for warehouses.

The CHAIRMAN. For example, what kind of investigation did you undertake in reference to cotton?

Mr. NIXON. In regard to the preparation of regulations for cotton warehouses, we were doing some work before the act was passed, and in order to enable us to proceed intelligently the regulations must cover the duties of warehousemen under the act with respect to responsibility for insurance, the proper care of the warehouse, and the proper care of the products in the warehouse. Take a man who has been a successful warehouseman, very naturally he is not in a position to make regulations for warehouses that would apply to warehouses located in something like a dozen of the cotton States. He has to study the conditions in all those States and bring the results of the investigations together and make regulations that will be applicable to all conditions as nearly as possible.

The CHAIRMAN. Make them uniform?

Mr. NIXON. Yes; we have certain results that we want to accomplish, and we have quite a number of different State laws under which we have to operate, and very naturally it is rather difficult to make regulations that will not conflict with any of the State laws, and at the same time accomplish the purposes we desire to accomplish.

The CHAIRMAN. How do you expect to use this fund for the next fiscal year?

Mr. NIXON. Do you refer to the entire fund estimated for here?

The CHAIRMAN. Yes.

Mr. NIXON. There is the statement. You will see there is to be a specialist in charge, and then we provide for four investigators. You will recall that I stated previously that this act includes warehouses for four of the principal agricultural products, and we propose to divide our work into four divisions, one division for cotton, another for grain, another for tobacco, and another for wool.

The CHAIRMAN. I may say frankly that I have been greatly disapopinted that greater use has not been made of this act. I have felt all the time that some definite uniform system of warehouses of uniform receipts, would be one of the greatest things the Government could do for agriculture. Yet, for some reason or another, the farmer does not take very much advantage of this act. Is that true?

Mr. NIXON. Yes; I think it is. I think all of us have been disappointed in the results, but I think it has been due very largely to the abnormal times. For the last year, so far as cotton is concerned, the price has been very satisfactory, and the farmers have not been inclined to store so much of their cotton.

The CHAIRMAN. I expect to see a revival of interest in warehousing right now, because there is a big holding movement on cotton.

Mr. NIXON. The inquiries coming into our office indicate that there is going to be a revival in the interest in the act.

The CHAIRMAN. What about the interest of the wool growers? Are they doing anything along the lines contemplated by this act?

Mr. NIXON. This act includes wool, but we have had only one wool man, and he left the service shortly after he was appointed, so that we have not had an opportunity to do anything in wool.

The CHAIRMAN. Do you interpret the grain warehouse as an elevator?

Mr. NIXON. I think so; I, do not see how it can be interpreted otherwise.

The CHAIRMAN. Are any of the grain elevators seeking Federal licenses?

Mr. NIXON. Quite a number.

Mr. ANDERSON. How many?

Mr. NIXON. I do not know how many.

The CHAIRMAN. Have you issued any grain elevator licenses?

Mr. NIXON. The regulations for grain warehouses have not been issued. They are very nearly ready for promulgation, but public hearings will be held before they are promulgated.

The CHAIRMAN. So that, as a matter of fact, you expect to see warehouses for grain and cotton seeking Federal licenses and coming under your rules and regulations?

Mr. NIXON. I do. We have had a number of letters recently from cotton and grain men stating definitely that they were desirous of being licensed in the shortest possible time.

The CHAIRMAN. You have issued your cotton regulations?

Mr. NIXON. Yes.

The CHAIRMAN. And you have issued them in such a simple form that there will be no hesitancy on the part of the cotton growers to come under them?

Mr. NIXON. I will have to answer that in the negative, because it has not been possible to do so. The warehousemen themselves do not always understand the act and do not understand the regulations very well. We make every effort, however, to explain these matters to men who are desirous of becoming licensed and who do not understand the act and the regulations and do not understand how to operate under the act.

Mr. BRAND. They do not understand it because they do not read it, generally speaking.

The CHAIRMAN. Is there any national association of grain elevator and cotton warehousemen?

Mr. BRAND. There is the American Warehousemen's Association.

The CHAIRMAN. That includes cotton?

Mr. NIXON. The cotton warehouseman is eligible, but very few strictly cotton warehousemen belong to the association.

The CHAIRMAN. I had in mind to ask whether you had made it a point to bring these regulations and this act to the attention of that association.

Mr. NIXON. Yes; we have. There is not an association, however, of cotton warehousemen; so far as I know there is not any kind of an organization that is composed primarily of cotton warehousemen. The American Warehousemen's Association is composed very largely of general warehousemen who store general merchandise.

The CHAIRMAN. If this appropriation is to continue, I would say very frankly, without any criticism of the Department, that the Department ought, in some way or other, to set itself to work to impress upon the warehouses throughout the country the benefits of this act. I feel, and have felt for many years, that we ought to have something that the farmer can rely upon in the face of stress to take care of a bad situation, and this warehouse proposition is the only thing I see for it.

Mr. JACOWAY. How many States in the Union have a warehouse law?

Mr. NIXON. All the States have some kind of a warehouse law.

Mr. ANDERSON. How many States have a uniform warehouse law?

Mr. NIXON. About forty of the States have a law known as the uniform warehouse receipts act.

Mr. JACOWAY. Is it your judgment that, if all the States should cooperate with the Federal Government better results could be obtained than otherwise?

Mr. NIXON. Unquestionably. I think it is detrimental for some of the States to go along one line and other States to go along another line. That is what we have hoped to remedy and to bring about uniformity in State legislation governing warehousing generally.

Mr. JACOWAY. In my judgment, this is a bill which, if carried out will do great good, and I think the Department has been slow in enforcing it. Suppose a cause of action arises under the national warehouse law; how would you get service on the bonding house that bonds the warehouseman?

Mr. NIXON. You mean for some storage losses in a warehouse, who would suffer the loss? He could bring suit against the company.

Mr. JACOWAY. Would that be brought in a Federal court or in a State court?

Mr. BRAND. I think it would probably be brought in the Federal court, because the licenses are issued by the Secretary of Agriculture.

Mr. JACOWAY. Does not this law provide that service upon the secretary of each of the States shall be service upon the bonding company?

Mr. BRAND. No.

Mr. JACOWAY. Then, if you have to go into a Federal court to adjudicate all these differences, and you had to go down there to prosecute a cause of action, would you not lose even if you won?

Mr. NIXON. In other words, the expense would be too great?

Mr. JACOWAY. If that is so, what good can come of the law as it stands?

Mr. NIXON. You mean from the bonding provision of it?

Mr. JACOWAY. That is, if a man who brings suit has to go to a Federal court and eats up what he recovers in expenses he would be better off, would he not, if he did not bring a suit?

Mr. MCLAUGHLIN. Is not this true, where an outside bonding or insurance company is permitted to do business in your State: Your State law provides that that insurance company or that bonding company must have an agent in the State upon whom service can be made?

Mr. JACOWAY. That is the case in some States. Our law also provides that service upon the secretary of state is service upon the bonding company.

Mr. MCLAUGHLIN. But your statute provides that the service shall be service upon the bonding company?

Mr. JACOWAY. Yes; I thought when the law was passed service could be had in the State, and that any cause of action arising against the warehouses was to be brought in a State court.

Mr. BRAND. I think the law provides that the law of the States takes precedence.

Mr. HAUGEN. How many licenses have been issued?

Mr. NIXON. We have prepared regulations for cotton warehouses only, and three warehousemen's licenses have been issued; five for weighers and classifiers.

Mr. HAUGEN. What is that for, cotton?

Mr. NIXON. Yes. Regulations for grain, tobacco and wool have not been issued.

Mr. HAUGEN. None for grain?

Mr. NIXON. No.

Mr. HAUGEN. Not any for wool?

Mr. NIXON. No.

Mr. HAUGEN. Not any for tobacco?

Mr. NIXON. No.

Mr. HAUGEN. You have issued up to date three licenses?

Mr. NIXON. Three warehousemen's licenses.

Mr. HAUGEN. The storing of wheat would require inspection and determination of the grade?

Mr. NIXON. I think the inspection would be made in accordance with the grain-standards act.

Mr. HAUGEN. In order to certify, the grain would have to be inspected and graded?

Mr. NIXON. Yes.

Mr. HAUGEN. There are 181 grades in wheat?

Mr. BRAND. Five grades for each kind of wheat.

Mr. HAUGEN. In the aggregate 181 grades?

Mr. BRAND. I have never figured it out. I doubt very much whether there are. There are 30 classes and 5 grades in each class.

Mr. HAUGEN. In the aggregate 181 grades, as I understand it. That would require 181 bins, would it not?

Mr. BRAND. No.

Mr. HAUGEN. Are you not going to keep them separate, the different grades?

Mr. BRAND. Winter wheat is grown in winter wheat territory, and so there all you would need would be winter wheat binnage. Generally speaking, they have worked out the number of bins very carefully, and the elevator trade takes care of it successfully.

Mr. HAUGEN. Do you propose to have No. 4, No. 3, and No. 2, in one bin, of northern wheat?

Mr. BRAND. We would have nothing to do with it. That would be a question for the owner of the grain.

Mr. HAUGEN. The thought is that he may deposit his grain and call for the grain later. In order to deliver the grain you have to keep it separate, and you ought to keep it separate.

Mr. BRAND. That is what the elevator man does at the present time. It is required to be kept separate.

Mr. HAUGEN. Under the law, if it is to be kept separate there would have to be 181 bins. Can you imagine that any warehouse could be conducted along that line, providing for 181 bins?

Mr. BRAND. As a practical matter that problem does not arise.

Mr. HAUGEN. How are you going to overcome that, take them all together?

Mr. BRAND. Only a few kinds of grain are ever brought in a warehouse, and they are provided for with proper binnage.

Mr. HAUGEN. How many varieties are offered at Chicago?

Mr. BRAND. The Chicago market is the best developed in the world. They have binnage for every possible grade of grain.

Mr. HAUGEN. They have 181 bins?

Mr. BRAND. More than that. The New Orleans terminal has more bins than that, and all of the large terminal markets have a very generous supply of facilities.

Mr. HAUGEN. Do you mean they have a bin for each grade of wheat?

Mr. BRAND. Not only wheat, but other grains. They have binnage for all grains, and all grades.

Mr. HAUGEN. If we assume that there are 181 grades of wheat, they have 181 bins in a single warehouse?

Mr. BRAND. They have more than that in many warehouses.

Mr. HAUGEN. For wheat?

Mr. BRAND. They devote it to any kind of grain that is brought to them.

Mr. HAUGEN. Under their regulations they would have to have bins for each grade.

Mr. BRAND. No; we do not pass upon that subject. It is a question of whether a warehouseman has the facilities.

Mr. HAUGEN. In Minneapolis he would have northern wheat, and there would be a dozen grades of that, and he would have to keep each grade separate?

Mr. BRAND. That is required, as a matter of fact, under this act. As a matter of practical application they do mix the grain and deliver the grades according to what the warehouse receipt calls for.

Mr. HAUGEN. The shipper of No. 1 Northern would have to dump it into No. 4, and they would insist upon it being kept separate?

Mr. BRAND. Yes.

Mr. HAUGEN. We were told last year that we were making regulations, and so far we have had three warehouses who have applied for licenses, and you ask for an increase of $16,000. You had $53,000 last year, and now you ask for $69,000. Is that not pretty expensive for issuing three licenses?

Mr. NIXON. I do not think any of us would ask for a continuation of this appropriation or even of one-tenth of this amount if we did not expect to accomplish more than has been accomplished.

Mr. HAUGEN. How many applications have you on hand now?

Mr. NIXON. We have about 30 on hand, and about 400 written inquiries.

Mr. HAUGEN. You have 30 applications. What are they for; not for grain?

Mr. NIXON. We have not sent out any application blanks to grain warehousemen because the regulations have not been completed. The applications we have from grain people are informal, in the form of letters, and we have something like 30 or 40 of them.

Mr. HAUGEN. You estimate $13,640 for salaries and $13,000 for traveling expenses. That is about $4,500 for each elevator which has been licensed, in traveling expenses. That is rather large, is it not? Thirteen thousand expenses for traveling expenses to look after three licensed warehouses is rather large, and the inspection of the other 30?

Mr. BRAND. The expense of the work is involved in collecting information for preparing rules and regulations with reference to the crops, and expenses of making inspections of warehouse and classifications. I think single large elevator lines spend as much as this for their own individual line.

Mr. HAUGEN. This act went into effect August 11, 1916. That is over two years ago.

Mr. BRAND. The war has been on through that period. It has been practically impossible to develop the work as fully as it otherwise would have been developed. I am not here to say that it will be possible under the appropriation requested to get all we had hoped to get out of the act, but I am sure we will have an opportunity to go very much further than in the past, and I know from the inquiries that have been made, that we are likely to get a much larger number of applications for licenses under the new conditions.

Mr. HAUGEN. The war has been on; of course that has made an excuse for everything. But you have been expending all this money.

Mr. BRAND. No, we have returned some of it to the Treasury.

Mr. HAUGEN. How much have you returned?

Mr. BRAND. I can not tell you offhand.

Mr. HAUGEN. Can you approximate the amount?

Mr. NIXON. As I recall we have returned about $26,000 out of $59,000 last year.

Mr. HAUGEN. You spent $33,000?

Mr. NIXON. Yes.

Mr. JACOWAY. I would like to ask Mr. Thompson a question. Mr. Thompson, have you studied the provisions of this bill?

Mr. THOMPSON. Not the one before the Committee.

Mr. JACOWAY. I am talking about the old law.

Mr. THOMPSON. No.

Mr. JACOWAY. Insofar as it goes, is it your judgment that this comes nearer being a personal credit bill than anything you know of?

Mr. BRAND. I think it can be utilized to assist in that matter.

Mr. JACOWAY. In so far as it goes, does it not come nearer being a personal credit bill than anything you know of?

Mr. BRAND. Yes, in so far as it provides collateral upon which the farmer can raise money.

Mr. THOMPSON. Speaking to the point you raise, I would say it would have a very important bearing on the question of personal credit.

Mr. JACOWAY. If this bill is carried out, do you not think it will mean more for the benefit of the farmer than any other bill on the statute books?

Mr. THOMPSON. It ought to be a great benefit to all who can utilize that sort of collateral as a basis for loans.

Mr. BRAND. One of the important factors in preventing a freer use of the warehouse act has been the requirement that only the bonds of surety companies could be accepted. It seems quite important that that matter be changed so that personal sureties can be accepted. The bonding companies object to certain language which makes them responsible for fire insurance. They give that as their reason for not giving a more reasonable bond. That has been a great factor in restricting the use of the warehouse act up to the present time.

But now the insurance companies have reduced their rates by 25 per cent, and we hope to get the bonding companies to come around. I have here a full-page article from the New York Journal of Commerce, which says that the Manufacturers' Association is taking up the question and is bound to press a greater adoption of the warehouse system. Now, that they are turning their minds from the problems of war, they are going into the matters, and I have no doubt that next year there will be a much greater increase in the use of this act.

(Thereupon, at 1.15 o'clock p. m., the committee adjourned.)

AGRICULTURE APPROPRIATION BILL.

COMMITTEE ON AGRICULTURE,
HOUSE OF REPRESENTATIVES,
Wednesday, January 8, 1919.

ENFORCEMENT OF THE INSECTICIDE ACT.

STATEMENT OF DR. J. K. HAYWOOD, CHAIRMAN OF THE INSECTICIDE AND FUNGICIDE BOARD, UNITED STATES DEPARTMENT OF AGRICULTURE.

Dr. HAYWOOD. Gentlemen, I think I can very briefly tell you about this.

The CHAIRMAN. You will find that, Doctor, on page 260. You have an increase there of $1,500. Tell us about the increase.

Dr. HAYWOOD. The increase of $1,500 is asked because we have found that the cost of sending inspectors around the country has increased a great deal in the last year or two; their railroad fare and their fare for sleepers have increased. Not only is this so, but inspectors have to purchase samples on the open market. The samples of the materials which they purchase have also increased in price, and we have rather carefully estimated that $1,500 will cover the increased cost of this item.

The CHAIRMAN. How much are you going to use for travel and how much for increased work with insecticides?

Dr. HAYWOOD. I would say 50-50.

The CHAIRMAN. Are there any questions, gentlemen?

Mr. HAUGEN. In other words, this increase is due to the Government taking over the railroads, making travel more expensive?

The CHAIRMAN. Just half of it, Mr. Haugen.

Mr. HAUGEN. Very well, about half of it is due to that.

AGRICULTURE APPROPRIATION BILL.

COMMITTEE ON AGRICULTURE,
HOUSE OF REPRESENTATIVES,
Wednesday, January 8, 1919.

STATEMENT OF MR. C. L. MARLATT, CHAIRMAN OF THE FEDERAL HORTICULTURAL BOARD, UNITED STATES DEPARTMENT OF AGRICULTURE.

FEDERAL HORTICULTURAL BOARD.

The CHAIRMAN. Page, 263, gentlemen, general expenses, Federal Horticultural Board: "To enable the Secretary of Agriculture to carry into effect the provisions of the act of August 20, 1912," and so forth. That is the plant-quarantine act. Doctor, is there anything new in that line of work at all?

Mr. MARLATT. A number of new plant quarantines have been established during the year. We are now enforcing some 20 quarantines and restrictive orders against foreign plants and plant products, and 11 domestic quarantines. Seven of these are new since our last conference. There are several items that will probably come up in the near future for similar action. One is the potato wart in Pennsylvania, against which we have not yet taken quarantine action. A preliminary quarantine has been issued against the newly established European corn worm, but this quarantine will have to be extended.

The CHAIRMAN. You have several new propositions here which do not appear in the estimates. I recall the Secretary proposing a change in the plant-quarantine act so as to include the District of Columbia in the law. That seems not to have been included here.

Mr. MARLATT. The Secretary has submitted a letter to you embodying the proposed draft of an amendment to the plant-quarantine act, giving authority to do in the District of Columbia what every State practically is doing, namely, to regulate the movement in and out of plants and to control or stamp out any disease or insect pest which may become established. At the present time the District of Columbia is the only place in the United States where insect and plant diseases can be brought in with their host plants without hindrance and where no authority exists under law to prevent such entrance or to clean them up after they are here.

A notable illustration of the danger which comes from this situation is the Oriental peach moth which was brought into the District of Columbia some years ago with importations of Japanese cherry trees before the passage of the plant-quarantine act. You will recall there was a considerable interest aroused some years ago in the introduction of Japanese cherry trees to beautify the District drives.

Mr. ANDERSON. That is an ornamental tree?

Mr. MARLATT. That is an ornamental tree. The first shipment of these trees—I do not know whether you care to go into detail of that.

The CHAIRMAN. Not very extensively.

Mr. MARLATT. The first shipment was of large trees. Our inspectors examined them and found the trees palpably infested with a variety of borers and scale insects, so badly that in spite of the fact that they had been donated by the city of Tokyo we recommended that they be burned, and, with much "heart burning," they were burnt. Afterwards the city of Tokyo sent in a lot of very small trees, and they looked absolutely clean and in good condition to the inspectors of the department. At that time there was no Federal law by which we could control their entry. The first lot that was burned was burned by common consent. We said they were so ad they ought to be burned, and the officials allowed them to be burned.

This second sending, as I say, looked perfectly clean, but years afterwards these trees proved to be infested with a borer—the oriental peach moth. As now known, this insect, in hibernation, is so hidden as not to be possible of detection by inspection. The trees of this importation are now growing along the driveway by the river and are scattered throughout the city more or less. The insect brought in with this importation has spread from the District into Maryland and into Virginia. Similar cherry trees were imported into other parts of the United States at the same time and brought the insect into New York and other Eastern States. At this time in the District of Columbia this moth now infests these trees along the driveway, and practically every cherry, peach, and plum tree in the city and District, but we have no authority to clean them out. This insect is now being bred in the District and flying in every direction out of the District into Maryland and Virginia. This draft of an amendment to the plant quarantine act gives us that authority.

The CHAIRMAN. Put that letter in the record, will you, Doctor?

(The letter referred to follows:)

DECEMBER 31, 1918.

Hon. A. F. LEVER,
Chairman House Committee on Agriculture,
House of Representatives.

DEAR MR. LEVER. I have the honor to submit for your consideration, and if you approve it, for inclusion in the agricultural appropriation bill for the fiscal year ending June 30, 1920, in connection with the appropriations for the Federal Horticultural Board, draft of a proposed amendment to the plant-quarantine act of August 20, 1912, for the purpose of giving authority to regulate the movement of plants and plant products, including nursery stock, from or into the District of Columbia, and power to control injurious plant diseases and insect pests within said district. The proposed amendment is as follows:

That the plant-quarantine act approved August twentieth, nineteen hundred and twelve (Thirty-seventh Statutes, page three hundred and fifteen), is hereby amended by the addition of the following section:

SEC. 15. That in order further to control and eradicate and to prevent the dissemination of dangerous plant diseases and insect infections and infestations no plant or plant products for or capable of propagation, including nursery stock, hereinafter referred to as plants and plant products, shall be moved or allowed to be moved, shipped, transported, or carried by any means whatever into or out of the District of Columbia, except in compliance with such rules and regulations as shall be prescribed by the Secretary of Agriculture as hereinafter provided. Whenever the Secretary of Agriculture, after investigation, shall determine that any plants and plant products in the District of Columbia are infested or infected with insect pests and diseases and that any place, articles, and substances used or connected therewith are so infested or infected, written notice thereof shall be given by him to the owner or person in possession or control thereof, and such owner or person shall forthwith control or eradicate and prevent the dissemination of such insect pest or disease and shall remove, cut, or destroy such infested and infected plants, plant products, and articles and substances used or connected therewith, which are hereby declared to be nuisances, within the time and in the manner required in said notice or by the rules and regulations of the Secretary of Agriculture. Whenever such owner or person can not be found, or shall fail, neglect, or refuse to comply with the foregoing provisions of this section, the Secretary of Agriculture is hereby authorized and required to control and eradicate and prevent dissemination of such insect pest or disease and to remove, cut, or destroy infested or infected plants and plant products and articles and substances used or connected therewith, and the United States shall have an action of debt against such owner or persons for expenses incurred by the Secretary of Agriculture in that behalf. Employees of the Federal Horticultural Board are hereby authorized and required to inspect places, plants, and plant products and articles and substances used or connected therewith whenever the Secretary of Agriculture shall determine that such inspections are necessary for the purposes of this section. For the purpose of carrying out the provisions and requirements of this section and of the rules and regulations of the Secretary of Agriculture made hereunder, and the notices given pursuant thereto, employees of the Federal Horticultural Board shall have power with a warrant to enter into or upon any place and open any bundle, package, or other container of plants or plant products whenever they shall have cause to believe that infections or infestations of plant pests and diseases exist therein or thereon, and when such infections or infestations are found to exist, after notice by the Secretary of Agriculture to the owner or person in possession or control thereof and an opportunity by said owner or person to be heard, to destroy the infected or infested plants or plant products contained therein. The police court or the municipal court of the District of Columbia shall have power, upon information supported by oath or affirmation showing probable cause for believing that there exists in any place, bundle, package, or other container in the District of Columbia any plant or plant product which is infected or infested with plant pests or disease, to issue warrants for the search for and seizure of all such plants and plant products. It shall be the duty of the Secretary of Agriculture, and he is hereby required, from time to time, ot make and promulgate such rules and regulations as shall be necessary to carry out the purposes of this section, and any person who shall move or allow to be moved, or shall ship, transport, or carry, by any means whatever, any plant or plant products from or into the District of Columbia, except in compliance wtih the rules and regulations prescribed under this section, shall be punished as is provided in section 10 of this act.

There is at present no law under which the movement of diseased and insect-infected nursery stock and other plants and plant products into the District of Columbia from surrounding or other States or from the District of Columbia into surrounding or other States can be adequately controlled, nor is there statutory authority for control and extermination within the District of Columbia of plant pests and diseases. Such control is exercised under State laws in practically all the States in this country.

The immediate need of this legislation is evidenced by the fact that the oriental fruit moth, which threatens seriously to affect the fruit industry of the United States, gained entrance in large part through importations of ornamental stock into the District of Columbia, and there exist now within the District thousands of peach, cherry, plum, apple, and other trees infested with this insect, affording breeding sources from which the insect has spread to the adjacent States of Maryland and Virginia.

Verty truly, yours,

D. F. HOUSTON, *Secretary.*

Mr. ANDERSON. Is there now in effect a practical prohibition against any kind of ornamental fruit trees from other countries?

Mr. MARLATT. Such quarantine has been promulgated, effective June 1, 1919. Perhaps one of the most important items of work of the Federal Horticultural Board during the year has been the holding of the various conferences that the law requires prior to taking quarantine action and preparing a quarantine which will practically stop from the 1st of next June all miscellaneous plant importations into the United States.

The risk from such importations, even under any safeguard which could be placed about them as to foreign inspection and certification, or as to inspection and examination in this country, is so great, and has been so fully demonstrated, that we were forced to the step of declaring a practically complete embargo. The plants and plant products that will be permitted entry after June 1 are very limited in number. They include field, vegetable, and flower seeds, certain bulbs, rose stocks, and fruit stocks, cuttings, and scions. No ornamental stock will be allowed to come in and no ornamental trees or finished plants will be allowed to come in. The quarantine practically stops the trade in foreign ornamentals after June 1.

The CHAIRMAN. That is a new act, Doctor?

Mr. MARLATT. That is a new quarantine which has recently been promulgated by the Secretary of Agriculture.

I think most of the interests involved are pleased with the quarantine, although they have objected to it in years past rather strenuously. With the exception of a very few commercial importers—persons who bring in these goods because they can buy them cheaply in Europe and sell them at a good profit here—the horticultural interests of the country, including the main body of the nurserymen, are in favor of this quarantine.

The CHAIRMAN. These Japanese cherry trees, you say, are down here on the Mall?

Mr. MARLATT. Yes.

The CHAIRMAN. Do they bear fruit?

Mr. MARLATT. No; they are purely ornamental trees.

The CHAIRMAN. They do not bear fruit in Japan even?

Mr. MARLATT. No.

The CHAIRMAN. They are just ornamental, entirely?

Mr. MARLATT. They are like the rose; they have a double bloom. All the strength of the flower goes into the bloom and no fruit is formed.

The CHAIRMAN. You have a supplemental estimate of $50,000 for the eradication of the potato-wart disease. Let that estimate go into the record, too, will you, please, Doctor?

Mr. MARLATT. This estimate has been submitted in a communication from the Secretary of Agriculture to the Secretary of the Treasury. It has been transmitted to Congress by the Secretary of the Treasury.

The CHAIRMAN. All right; read it, please.

(The letter referred to follows:)

DEPARTMENT OF AGRICULTURE,
Washington, December 13, 1918.

The SECRETARY OF THE TREASURY.

SIR: I have the honor to submit herewith an estimate for a supplemental appropriation required by this department to meet the emergency caused by the existence in certain counties in the interior of Pennsylvania of the European potato-wart disease. For this item the following wording is suggested:

"To enable the Secretary of Agriculture to meet the emergency caused by the establishment of the potato wart in eastern Pennsylvania, and to provide means for the extermination of this disease in Pennsylvania or elsewhere in the United States in cooperation with the State or States concerned, including rent outside the District of Columbia, employment of labor in the city of Washington or elsewhere, and all other necessary expenses, $50,000, which shall be immediately available."

Several well-established cases of wart disease of potato were discovered in September of this year in gardens in 26 small mining towns in Luzerne, Schuylkill, and Carbon Counties, in eastern Pennsylvania. In most of these gardens it has been observed by the owners during the last two seasons; in many of them it has been severe for three years, while in a few instances it has done considerable damage for four years.

The source of the disease appears to be a shipment of several carloads of European potatoes of inferior quality, distributed in 1912, before the passage of the plant-quarantine act of August 20 of that year. This act permits an immediate quarantine against countries infested with the potato wart, and since its passage no importations of potatoes have been made from countries where the disease is known to exist.

The infested area is more or less isolated and the potatoes are grown in gardens for local use. There is no commercial production in the district, and it is unlikely that there will be any commercial or other shipments of potatoes to other sections. There is little danger, therefore, that the disease will spread rapidly to neighboring States, as the Pennsylvania State authorities, under the direction of Economic Zoologist J. G. Sanders, are cooperating in the making of a survey of the diseased area and will take the necessary restrictive measures to prevent infective material from moving out of the district.

It is not improbable, however, that other shipments of European potatoes, made prior to the quarantine, have carried the disease to other sections, and a country-wide examination of gardens of industrial and mining villages, which were the principal markets for foreign potatoes, is being made. The disease apparently has not developed in any of the important potato-producing sections of this country. Its effect is so marked that it would undoubtedly have been reported from regions where commercial potato growing is an industry of importance.

The conditions surrounding the outbreak of the potato wart in Pennsylvania are such as to make it probable that the disease can, by prompt and radical measures, be exterminated, thus freeing this country from a very serious source of future loss to one of its principal food crops. It is very important, therefore, that all possible means be taken to stamp out the disease in Pennsylvania in cooperation with the authorities of that State and that a thorough survey be made to locate other points of infestation, particularly in districts to which shipments of European potatoes in 1912, prior to the passage of the plant-quarantine act, have been or can be traced. It is contemplated that the study of the disease, including all research work, will be conducted by the Bureau of Plant Industry with funds available in its regular appropriations, and that the sum recommended herein will be utilized entirely for field surveys and for eradication work.

The potato wart is probably the most destructive of all potato diseases. Soil once impregnated with it remains a source of contagion to future crops of potatoes for a long period of years. It attacks the tubers and also the stems, causing irregular, warty upgrowth, beginning in the tender tissues near the eyes and enlarging until the entire potato may be changed into a black and worthless mass. The young galls are whitish or greenish, suggesting a cauliflower head. In the present outbreak the disease manifests itself in a very severe form, practically destroying the whole crop in many of the gardens affected.

There are attached photographs of diseased potatoes as well as photographs showing the actual effect on two typical hills of potatoes taken as a whole.

Very truly, yours,

D. F. HOUSTON,
Secretary.

The CHAIRMAN. Suppose you tell us about that.

Mr. MARLATT. The letter explains the situation.

The CHAIRMAN. Go ahead and tell us about it in your own way.

Mr. MARLATT. It will be recalled that the wart disease of the pototo was one of the three items which were specifically mentioned in the plant-quarantine act at the time of its passage in 1912. It is one of the diseases in Europe which this act was intended to exclude from the United States. Since the passage of that act on August 20, 1912, no potatoes have been allowed to come into the United States from any countries infested with potato wart. This fall (1918) the potato-wart disease was found in a few counties in eastern Pennsylvania, in a mining district. In this district potatoes are not grown commercially, the plantings of potatoes are purely garden plantings, in connection with the miners' houses. It appears that in the winter of 1911–12, prior to the passage of the plant-quarantine act——

The CHAIRMAN. I was wondering whether it was a result of the act or in spite of it?

Mr. MARLATT. Prior to the act we had a shortage of potatoes that year and considerable quantities of potatoes were imported from Europe. We have traced certain carloads of these potatoes to this particular region, and it is evident that this disease thus introduced has been there slowly incubating from that time. Potato growing not being a commercial factor in the district, the discovery of the disease was not easy. It is still limited to a fairly small district and to local gardens.

I have here photographs of the potatoes which show the working of the disease very graphically. Here are photographs of two potato plants showing every potato invaded by this disease. It looks like a mushroom growth, like a cancerous growth. Here are individual potatoes. I think these photographs illustrate better than anything I could say the dangerous character of the disease.

Mr. HEFLIN. What is the cause of that disease, Doctor?

Mr. MARLATT. It is a fungoid disease that, as far as we know, is limited to the potato with possibly a few other solanaceous plants, It infests not only the potato plant but it remains in the soil. I mean, if you get this disease once in the soil you can not plant potatoes in that particular soil again for certainly a considerable series of years without getting this result. The spores of this disease have wonderful vitality and persist in the soil for a long period.

The CHAIRMAN. What method of eradication do you propose?

Mr. MARLATT. The State of Pennsylvania is very much aroused over this disease. It is entirely within the State of Pennsylvania and will be quarantined by the State, the movement of potatoes out of the quarantined district will be prohibited, and steps to effect extermination will be taken. Our purpose is to cooperate with Pennsylvania very much as we are cooperating in Texas with the bollworm work. We have asked for $50,000 for this work because from the nature of the infestation and the extent of the territory invaded we believe that will be enough with what the State of Pennsylvania will expend to do all the work that is possible and practicable. There is no reason why this disease should not be exterminated if it is taken hold of promptly.

The CHAIRMAN. Are you asking that this amount be made immediately available?

Mr. MARLATT. We are asking that this be made immediately available so necessary work can be immediately begun.

Mr. LESHER. What counties in the State are infested?

Mr. MARLATT. Luzerne, Schuylkill, and Carbon Counties, in eastern Pennsylvania.

ERADICATION OF PINK BOLLWORM OF COTTON.

The CHAIRMAN. Kindly turn to page 275, and I will ask Mr. Marlatt in regard to the pink-bollworm matter. I notice you have increased the fund from $50,000 to $148,560 and ask that this sum be made immediately available. Kindly tell us about that.

Mr. MARLATT. One of the protective features of our work against the pink bollworm is the border-quarantine service, which controls the entry of all cars and freight from Mexico. We have that service established at all the ports of entry—some five—between El Paso and Brownsville. We have been conducting that service now for some two years. We have found it necessary to make the service more safe to build large fumigating sheds in which cars or even trains of cars may be fumigated as an entirety. The old method has been to liberate the disinfecting gas in the car and to spray or wash the outside of the car as well as could be done. This method is unsatisfactory, because the Mexican cars are pretty well battered up and do not retain the gas sufficiently long. We have had to paste them up with paper, and even then we have not overcome the risk of insects being on the outside. To accomplish a better system of disinfection we have been compelled to build these fumigating sheds. Some of these sheds will fumigate 15 cars at a time.

The fumigation of cars and freight heretofore has been done under our direction and guidance, but by private individuals, who charged what they thought was a reasonable fee. When we came to this more exact method of fumigation it was necessary to have it under our control. We could not get private persons to build these sheds and to undertake the work. They were not willing to make the investment, and we have therefore built these sheds and are now ready to undertake this work.

The CHAIRMAN. How many have you built, Doctor?

Mr. MARLATT. We have built five of these sheds.

The CHAIRMAN. Where are they located?

Mr. MARLATT. At Eagle Pass, El Paso, Laredo, Del Rio, and Brownsville.

The CHAIRMAN. As I recall it, the Secretary says you have had no reappearance of the pink bollworm in Texas.

Mr. MARLATT. That was true at the time the report was written. I will come to that subject in a moment.

I wish to say with regard to this $100,000 increase, that we have taken over this work of disinfection, and we propose that the freight shall pay the cost. In other words, the cost of fumigation, the cost of the chemicals we use, and the labor. We are making no charge for the department's investment or for supervision.

The CHAIRMAN. What do you mean by the freight paying the cost?

Mr. MARLATT. If it costs $10 to fumigate a car, the person owning that car or whose freight is carried in that car pays the $10. That money, under the act of last year, must be converted into the Treasury. We estimate that the annual expenditure, under the new arrangement, for chemicals and labor will be about $100,000. Our present appropriation of $50,000 for the border work is fully needed for the current expenses of our five stations, and about a dozen men employed as inspectors. The increase requested is simply to cover the fund that we will be turning back into the Treasury.

You will remember last year I asked for a revolving fund, and that was refused, but in lieu of that revolving fund it will be necessary to carry on this work to get this appropriation that will go back to the Treasury as received by us.

The CHAIRMAN. There is no real increase, then?

Mr. MARLATT. No.

Mr. HAUGEN. You are just asking for a loan of $100,000?

Mr. MARLATT. For a loan of $100,000 to pay for the chemicals and labor, and the charges covering these costs will be converted into the Treasury.

The CHAIRMAN. Suppose you tell us about the situation in a general way.

Mr. MARLATT. The most interesting feature is the situation in Texas, and particularly the fact that not a single pink bollworm has been found in the infested districts of last season since the clean-up of last winter. The committee will recall that last year the insect had appeared in two places in Texas; one was the large area surrounding Galveston Bay, involving a good many counties, and the other the very small area at Hearne, Tex., involving only a few acres of cotton.

You will recall also that the State of Texas passed an act in a special session of the legislature, giving authority to quarantine both infested areas and border areas and prohibit the growth of cotton in such areas.

Mr. HEFLIN. Did it establish a zone along the Rio Grande River?

Mr. MARLATT. It provided for the establishment of a zone along the Rio Grande River. Under that act the infested districts were quarantined, and the growth of cotton in these districts was prohibited by the State of Texas for three years, or for such a period as might be necessary. There was also established a limited zone including three counties along the Rio Grande opposite Eagle Pass, because the insect had been found in Mexican fields opposite that point. The law provides that such border zones shall be established in sections as it becomes necessary.

The most serious situation in Texas was the Galveston Bay region, where the insect when discovered had surrounded the bay and invaded plantings of hundreds of fields of cotton. The very successful work accomplished in this region has resulted from the active cooperation of the State of Texas with the Department of Agriculture and the hearty cooperation of thousands of planters.

Fully 95 per cent of the planters of this region have joined in the enforcement of that law and have planted no cotton and have persuaded their neighbors not to plant cotton. A small number, perhaps 5 per cent or less, of the planters refused to recognize the law and planted cotton. They were induced to this action largely by local lawyers, who saw a chance for fees and offered to defend such planters in the courts.

Mr. HEFLIN. Do you think you are going to be able by this work to get the pink worm out?

Mr. MARLATT. In spite of this small amount of violation of the State law the work has been very successful and would seem to indicate that the insect can be exterminated. We have had surveillance of this entire district, and every voluntary plant throughout has been destroyed. The illegally planted fields have also been taken care of. As stated at the outset, there has not been a single pink bollworm found in any of these old districts in Texas this year. This is much greater success than could have been anticipated. We thought we would be able to reduce them by 95 or 98 per cent. The clean-up last fall or winter, which I think has been reported to this committee, was thoroughgoing. The cotton was uprooted, the plants were put into piles, sprayed with oil, and burned, and afterwards negroes went over the fields and picked up every boll and leaf left. Nearly 9,000 acres of cotton lands were thus cleaned. The work was done throughout this entire district with such thoroughness that the insect, apparently, was utterly exterminated, at least in none of the fields in the district that were planted in violation of the Texas law, and in none of the cotton that grew up voluntarily from scattered seed was a single pink bollworm found. It is the most astonishing and remarkable experiment of the kind that we have a record of, and went far beyond our expectations. We doubtless were helped in this outcome by the fact that last winter, as you will recall, was a very severe one, and this probably helped in the elimination of any of the insects which may have been overlooked. The habits of this insect, however, lend itself very well to such control. It is an insect which apparently can only breed in the bolls or blossoms or squares of the cotton.

The CHAIRMAN. Is it in the boll or in the square that the insect breeds?

Mr. MARLATT. Both. That means a long period in the spring before these are available under normal conditions, and the mortality of the insect during that long period is very great. This point has been brought out in our research work which we are conducting in Mexico.

The CHAIRMAN. Have you any in Texas now?

Mr. MARLAT. Two new areas of infestation in Texas have been discovered within the last few weeks. In explanation of these discoveries, I will say we have not only examined the quarantined districts infested last year, but we have covered the whole State of Texas and particularly the regions about the cotton oil mills that had received seed from Mexico in 1916. We have carried our examination also to regions about cotton mills in other States where we knew from shipping records that cotton from Mexico had gone in former years. No outbreaks have been found in the vicinity of any of these mills.

In the course of these investigations, the Rio Grande was explored from Brownsville to El Paso, and a few weeks ago the insect was found in the Great Bend district. This is a region where no one thought cotton was grown but the high price of cotton has led to the establishment of a few fields in little bottoms at the base of the mountains that come down to the river in the Great Bend. Perhaps four hundred acres of cotton altogether were grown this year along the river in a distance of 150 miles. The seed, apparently, for some of this cotton was brought across from Mexico. Very slight infestation of pink bollworm was found in this district. It is not normally a cotton district at all; it is a wild, mountainous country, as you know, and cotton growing is a new venture. A little cotton had been grown on the Mexican side, in the river valley, and the Mexicans got their seed evidently from the Laguna, and brought with it the pink bollworm. Some of our people probably got seed from the Mexicans; in fact, the product of the Mexican fields has been smuggled across.

Along this Great Bend district, where there are no towns of importance, and the customs service is very limited if any, and there is little to prevent smuggling on a small scale. There is, therefore, little or no means of preventing a Mexican cotton grower from bringing his bags of cotton or cotton seed across. The river does not amount to much; he can wade it and sell his product to any willing purchaser on the American side. That is apparently the origin of the infestation along the Great Bend.

Immediate hold has been taken of the situation and the infested fields are being cleaned up just as we cleaned up the other district last year. So far as Great Bend is concerned, such clean up should be a simple matter.

The one other new point of infestation this year is at Barstow, Tex. in the Pecos Valley. In tracing the movement of the cotton grown in these various fields along the Great Bend and of cotton smuggled across from the Mexican side, it was found that this cotton went to an oil mill at Barstow, Tex. Some of this cotton of the 1917 crop went up there last winter and remained in the mill all summer and was not ginned until last September. This was seed cotton, cotton and seed together, and the insects had ample opportunity and did escape and infested near-by fields. This infestation seems to be confined to a few fields immediately adjacent to the mill and is very limited. The finding of the insect at Barstow is a much more serious matter, because here we are getting into an important cotton region.

The CHAIRMAN. What is the name of that new place?

Mr. MARLATT. Barstow. It is in the Pecos Valley in western Texas and in the midst of cotton culture on a fairly large scale. Staple cotton is grown here. We have practically the same situation here that we had last year at Hearne, Tex. We have now 12 men making a survey of that whole valley, but so far our records indicate that the insect is localized at Barstow.

This sort of survey and inspection and clean-up work we have got to keep up all the time, and that is the reason we are asking for the continuation of this appropriation. You will notice the large item is for just such work. It is in a sense an insurance item; we may not expend it, but if the need arises we can make good use of it.

The CHAIRMAN. What are the indications this year?

Mr. MARLATT. I doubt if we expend much more than two-thirds of the sum assigned to this item, but this will depend on the extent of the new infestations in western Texas.

The CHAIRMAN. You feel, however, that to be on the safe side we had better continue this large appropriation as an insurance fund?

Mr. MARLATT. I think that is fully justified, Mr. Chairman.

The CHAIRMAN. We shall just have to trust to your good sense.

Mr. MARLATT. We will not spend any money for the sake of spending it, you can rely on that.

The CHAIRMAN. Of course, your station in Mexico will be more or less of a permanent proposition?

Mr. MARLATT. I hope not, Mr. Chairman. We want to continue it another year. It is not a wholesome place. Our men do not want to be there any longer than absolutely necessary; but we ought to continue it another year to get the needed information. This station affords an opportunity to study this insect without risk to our cotton culture.

The CHAIRMAN. For your survey work in Mexico you estimate $25,000. How long will that continue?

Mr. MARLATT. That is work which should be continued every year, because we should keep informed as to what is happening across the border.

The CHAIRMAN. And your item of $148,000?

Mr. MARLATT. That is the border control and must be permanent.

The CHAIRMAN. But the only part you may be able to give up soon is the investigational work, that $25,000?

Mr. MARLATT. Yes. We hope next year to have obtained about all the information that can be obtained in Mexico as to the habits of the insect and methods of control.

The CHAIRMAN. You mean after next year?

Mr. MARLATT. Yes.

Mr. HEFLIN. The boll weevil has done a good deal of damage to this last crop throughout the cotton belt. Do you consider the pink worm more destructive than the boll weevil?

Mr. MARLATT. Yes; it is so considered, and I think there is no question about it.

Mr. LEE. Have you issued a publication, a pamphlet, on that?

Mr. MARLATT. Yes; we have published two or three papers on it.

Mr. LEE. I was thinking of the red spider.

Mr. MARLATT. Yes; we have issued a publication on that.

The CHAIRMAN. Is there anything further, gentlemen?

Mr. MARLATT. I should like to present another viewpoint on the pink-boll problem, Mr. Chairman.

The CHAIRMAN. All right.

Mr. MARLATT. In connection with this appropriation for the control of the pink bollworm we have presented to this committee before the situation that the real control of this insect is in cleaning it up in Mexico, and that if it were possible to get into Mexico and clean it up, we could save ourselves this $500,000 a year.

The CHAIRMAN. You would not save $500,000 a year, because you do not expend that much a year.

Mr. MARLATT. But it would save what we do expend.

The CHAIRMAN. Maybe you would save us from appropriating $500,000. How much would it cost to clean up Mexico?

Mr. MARLATT. If it were possible and we were permitted to do the work, the cost might not be more than our annual appropriation. Unfortunately, under present conditions, this work can not be undertaken. In the first place, we could not go into Mexico with a large force unless we took a protecting Army along, and, secondly, Mexico would expect to be reimbursed for crops that might be destroyed.

Mr. ANDERSON. Do you know how extensive it is in Mexico?

Mr. MARLATT. As far as we know now it occurs in what is known as the Laguna—a big valley up in the mountains entirely isolated from other cultivated districts.

Mr. ANDERSON. How large is the area?

Mr. MARLATT. About 50 miles across. It is not nearly as large as the area we cleaned up in Texas, for example. The cotton grown in the Laguna—and that is the important source of infestation in Mexico—is all under irrigation. It is easily found. If we could get authority under our law and the Mexican law to clean up the Laguna, without regard to losses to the planters, we could probably do it at less cost than the amount appropriated last year, and we might thus eliminate this danger from the American continent. As a practical proposition, the United States and Mexico should cooperate to accomplish this purpose.

The CHAIRMAN. You have an item for survey work to determine the infestation in Mexico. Have you determined that to your satisfaction?

Mr. MARLATT. We believe that we have determined it fairly accurately.

The CHAIRMAN. Why continue this appropriation?

Mr. MARLATT. Because there will be new points next year, just as we found these new points in Great Bend.

The CHAIRMAN. Did you ever take up with the Secretary of State entering into some sort of treaty arrangement with Mexico by which we might go down there and undertake that work?

Mr. MARLATT. We have not taken it up with the Secretary of State. We have taken it up directly with the Mexican authorities, including the Secretary of Agriculture of Mexico, who was here in Washington last summer.

The CHAIRMAN. Who controls that section down there, the Carranza government or the Villa government?

Mr. MARLATT. It alternates. In other words, the region is occasionally raided by Villa. I have photographs of our station at Lerdo in my office showing several of the Villistas decorating telegraph poles, and they stayed there until our men objected to the odor. During last summer in one of these raids there were killed 25 or 30 people within a few miles of our station.

The CHAIRMAN. Did not one of your men get killed a year or so ago?

Mr. MARLATT. Fortunately not. The men are taking some personal risk down there, however.

The CHAIRMAN. I think there is no question in the minds of the committee that, if you have located the points of infestation and if you can make some arrangement by which we can go in there and clean up, with the consent of the Mexican Government, it would be a saving of money to clean up.

Mr. MARLATT. The Laguna district is the chief source of cotton for Mexico. They grow some $25,000,000 to $30,000,000 worth of cotton in this district. Their view of the situation is that if the United States is willing to pay them the difference between what they would make on cotton as compared with corn or wheat, which they would have to grow in substitution for the cotton, they will be willing to stop the growth of cotton for the necessary period. That is about the proposition. If the American Government will pay the difference and agree at the same time to supply them with the cotton they need in their manufactures, then they will agree to the plan of extermination.

The CHAIRMAN. Where do they manufacture their cotton? You have got a complete quarantine against it.

Mr. MARLATT. There are factories in Mexico. The cotton production of Mexico has hitherto, that is, prior to the disturbed conditions there, been practically all consumed in Mexico.

Mr. HEFLIN. Does not this pink boll worm they have over there destroy their crop?

Mr. MARLATT. Yes; they lose probably 25 to 30 per cent of their crop. Their soil is, however, very productive under irrigation, and even with a loss of 25 to 30 per cent of the crop—they lose the second crop, which is quite an important one to them—they still get enough to make it well worth while to grow cotton.

(Thereupon, at 5.20 p. m., the committee took a recess until Thursday, January 9, 1919, at 10.30 a. m.)

AGRICULTURE APPROPRIATION BILL.

COMMITTEE ON AGRICULTURE,
HOUSE OF REPRESENTATIVES,
Saturday, January 11, 1919.

DEMONSTRATIONS ON RECLAMATION PROJECTS.

This work consists of demonstrations with individual farmers and farmers' organizations to encourage and aid in the general development of agriculture on the Government reclamation projects. The work is directed toward the promotion of the specific agricultural industries for which the conditions on the several projects are favorable. The isolated location of the irrigation projects necessitates the marketing of the products of the farms in concentrated forms, as these farm products can not generally bear the high cost of transportation long distances to the large marketing centers. For this reason the major portion of this work is being directed toward the establishment of live-stock industries. Some attention is also paid to the improvement of irrigation methods on certain projects where irrigation problems are acute and to the production of crops used to supplement alfalfa in live-stock feeding.

This work is now being conducted on 11 reclamation projects, as follows: North Platte, Nebraska-Wyoming; Truckee-Carson, Nevada; Huntley, Montana; Minidoka, Idaho; Yakima, Washington; Shoshone, Wyoming; Boise, Idaho-Oregon; Umatilla, Oregon; Uncompahgre, Colorado; Yuma, Arizona-California; and Belle Fourche, South Dakota.

The principal live-stock industries with which demonstration work has been conducted are dairying, and swine, beef, and sheep production. In connection with the dairy industry the settlers have been assisted in securing stock, improving their herds through breeding and cow testing, controlling diseases, planning and constructing barns and silos, and in improving their methods of feeding and marketing. Due largely to the efficient work which has been done by the department's field men engaged in this service, the farmers have obtained a better understanding of diseases affecting dairy cattle, and losses from these diseases have been materially reduced. The work of encouraging the construction and use of silos has made very satisfactory progress, and a large number of silos have been constructed. The farmers have also gained, through the educational work that has been done, a better appreciation of the necessity of using improved, high-producing cows.

The demonstration work in connection with swine production has had to do with the problems of breeding, feeding, housing, and marketing of swine and the control of diseases and pests affecting swine. The work in the control of diseases, particularly hog cholera, has been especially effective, and the settlers have been saved large sums of money as a result. They have come to appreciate the necessity of prompt action in reporting cases of sickness in their herds and the observation of quarantine measures to prevent the spread of contagious diseases among swine. Special attention has been paid to the production of irrigated field crops to be used as supplements to alfalfa for swine feeding, and a number of cooperative feeding tests have been conducted with excellent results.

In connection with the beef industry, the settlers have been assisted in securing improved breeding stock, in improving their methods of feeding, and in the control of diseases affecting beef cattle, particuarly anthrax. Special attention has been paid to the organization and conduct of farmers' organizations for the cooperative use of range lands adjacent to the projects, and cooperative grazing is now in progress on the Boise, Minidoka, Shoshone, and Yakima reclamation projects, with very satisfactory results.

The work in connection with sheep production has been directed toward the securing of breeding stock and to the cooperative marketing of lambs and wool. Cooperative grazing has been established on the Minidoka and Boise projects, and five bands of sheep are being grazed cooperatively on the national forests adjacent to these projects.

Demonstration work in crop production is being carried on in close cooperation with the Office of Western Irrigation Agriculture, chiefly on the Huntley, Truckee-Carson, Shoshone, Yuma, and Umatilla projects. Assistance has been rendered in the establishment of irrigated pastures for maintaining small bands of sheep and dairy cattle on farms, and these pastures are proving very successful.

EXPERIMENTS AND DEMONSTRATIONS IN LIVE-STOCK PRODUCTION IN CANE-SUGAR AND COTTON DISTRICTS OF THE UNITED STATES.

The amount provided in the estimates for this item is the same as that provided for the current year and for last year. This work involves two main projects: First, educational work with reference to live-stock production, for which last year $9,000 was applied; second, the maintenance of a live-stock station at New Iberia, for which last year $46,281.67 was applied.

The educational work is done by specialists in dairying, beef-cattle production, hog raising, poultry raising, and horse and mule production. These specialists introduce methods for promoting live-stock production that may be adapted and put into effect largely through the county agents. No other funds of the department are used in that State in work of this character. The amount from this appropriation used for extension work is being gradually reduced and the work taken over by the State extension department. As the funds for educational work have been decreased the funds for experimental work have been increased proportionately.

The station at New Iberia consists of a thousand acres of land provided by the State. During the past year it used $46,281.67 and returned to the United States Treasury for products sold the sum of $20,277.92.

The work at the station is divided into four separate projects, and the expenses of each last year were as follows:

Horse and mule project	$5,879.00
Hog project	6,651.32
Beef-cattle project	14,832.98
Dairy project	6,996.26
General expenses, including cost of office and all general equipment, machinery, etc., used in connection with the various projects	11,922.11
Total	46,281.67

During the fiscal year ending June 30, 1918, the following buildings were constructed:

2 small cottages	$5,072.18
96-foot extension to beef cattle barn	1,848.84
56-foot extension to machinery shed	1,043.54
Outhouse for one of the cottages	105.94
Total	7,070.50

Some additions were made during the year to the equipment of the place which is covered by the financial statement above.

Gradually, as the carrying capacity of the place is increased and the herds extended, it is believed that the returns will increase. While experimental work is always expensive and can not usually be done in such a manner as to make a plant self-supporting, every effort is made to utilize the products resulting from these experiments in a way so that the largest possible sum may be returned to the Treasury.

Results of experimental work.—All experimental work relates to the use of local feeds of various kinds, including sugar-cane tops, Japanese cane, sorghum, etc., and all grasses that grow in that region. Two projects with beef cattle are under way.

One project relates to the cost of raising steers under the conditions of that region. The results thus far indicate this to be approximately $14.72 a head for the first year and $11.15 per head for the second year, making a total of $25.87 for a steer two years of age.

The second project relates to the utilization of various local feeds in fattening cattle. Approximately 125 head of steers have been fed during the past year, and a similar number are now being fed, using these various forages in the form of silage with cottonseed meal. Some of these forages are used alone and others in combination. This work, notwithstanding the unfavorable conditions for experimental work for the past year or so, is making progress and in time will be of vital importance to beef-cattle production in the Gulf-coast region.

The hog project involves the problem of raising hogs on the various feeds that can be grown in the Gulf-coast region, including red clover, bur clover, rape, oats, cowpeas, soy beans, and sweet potatoes used as grazing crops. In some cases these crops are supplemented by some concentrated feed, such as rice polish, tankage, or corn; and in others they are not. The cost of producing hogs by these various methods is being established. Some of the results are proving very satisfactory and are contributing materially to hog production in that region.

The horse and mule project is devoted largely to the use of mares in comparison with mules for farm work. Mares are also used for mule breeding. The comparative cost of maintaining mares and mules and the comparative work done by each are recorded so as to determine the actual cost of raising mules in that region. It is desired also to determine the quality of mules produced there. The cost of raising the first lot of mule colts foaled in the spring of 1915 to the age of two and a half years was $156. Last year the mules that were worked averaged 243 days' work, with a feed cost of $228, while the mares averaged 160 days' work, with a feed cost of $238. The increased cost of the mares must, of course, be charged to the cost of raising mule colts. Costs last year, however, were abnormally high.

The dairy herd was assembled during the last fiscal year, and therefore is just getting under way. The herd consists of 13 pure-bred Jersey cows, 13 grades, and a pure-bred Jersey bull. Fourteen heifers have been born since the herd was assembled. This herd is being used for experimental work in feeding, again utilizing the products of the farm that may be grown in that region. It is also being used in conducting comprehensive breeding experiments. which include all dairy herds owned by the department.

Attention is given to the system of feeding that may be adapted in that region to the keeping of a very small number of cows.

On the whole, the work of this station has not progressed during the last year and a half as satisfactorily as it doubtless would had conditions been normal. Some of the men at the station were taken in the draft and others left the work for other reasons, but, on the whole, the work is progressing as well as could be expected under the circumstances and should go forward now in an efficient manner.

It is very desirable that the same appropriation for this work be made as heretofore.

EXPERIMENTS IN DAIRYING AND LIVE-STOCK PRODUCTION IN SEMIARID AND IRRIGATED DISTRICTS OF THE WESTERN UNITED STATES.

Of this appropriation, $11,000 has been applied to beef cattle, swine, and sheep work and $29,000 to dairy work.

The amounts expended on beef cattle, swine, and sheep projects are as follows:

Huntley (Mont.) reclamation project field station, $3,700; pork and mutton production on irrigated land: Extensive tests have been made to determine the values of different crops for pasturing hogs and the relative amounts of pasture and grain feed that should be used in producing pork at lowest cost. A small flock of sheep has been secured and is being used principally in the study of the kinds of irrigated pastures suitable for sheep and how they should be grazed and managed for best results.

Belle Fourche (S. Dak.) reclamation project field station, $2,700; pork and mutton production on irrigated farms: The work at this station has been similar to that at Huntley, Mont. Special attention has been given to pasturing of hogs and sheep on crops planted in regular rotations and in the use of pastures and various grains produced on the farm for finishing hogs for market.

Ardmore, S. Dak., dry-land agricultural field station, $3,500; beef production from native pastures and forage crops produced in dry-land farming: Small herds of steers have been used in fenced pastures to determine accurately the carrying capacity of pastures of the Great Plains region. Possibilities of improving pastures by different systems of management (deferred and rotated grazing, etc.) are also investigated. In winter feeding the relative value of various cured and siloed forage crops was taken up, as well as the suitability of concentrated feeds for supplementing the roughage ration.

North Platte reclamation project field station, Mitchell, Nebr., $1,000; por production: This work is similar to that shown for Montana and South Dakota, except that the crops and methods tested are such as are adaptable to the conditions existing on irrigated lands in western Nebraska.

Two dairy stations have been completed, one at Ardmore, S. Dak., in the dry-land area, and the other at Huntley, Mont., in an irrigated region. The buildings at each station include a dairy barn with attached shed, a concrete and a wooden hoop silo, a milk house, and a herdsman's cottage. Modern equipment was installed throughout.

The dairy herd at Ardmore consists of 7 pure-bred Holstein cows and 9 grade cows, 1 pure-bred bull, 6 heifers, and 3 young bulls. The average production for the 7 pure-bred cows last year was 11,206 pounds of milk and 360 pounds of butter fat.

The herd just established at Huntley consists of 12 pure-bred Holstein cows, 8 grade cows, 1 pure-bred Holstein bull, 4 calves, and a young bull.

The purpose of these stations is to investigate methods of establishing dairy farming on the irrigated and dry lands of the Great Plains area, in order to furnish a profitable means of disposing of the dry-land and irrigated crops produced in that region; to investigate methods of establishing and improving dairy herds by the use of pure-bred cows and sires and grade cows raised in that region; and to secure all possible information of value to present and prospective dairy farmers of the Great Plains and irrigated areas.

The herds on these stations are also being used in a comprehensive breeding investigation that involves all the herds owned by the Bureau of Animal Industry.

The expenditures on these farms for 1917–18 were as follows:

	Ardmore.	Huntley.	Total.
Salaries	$1,182.50	$1,130.01	$2,502.51
Wages (farm and dairy)	4,428.83	4,148.14	8,576.97
Travel	377.960	250.72	628.68
Equipment	506.71	210.78	717.49
Telegraph and telephone	41.46	1.30	42.76
Miscellaneous (feed, live stock, etc.)	4,121.04	3,235.12	7,356.16
Construction:			
Labor	1,566.00	3,133.12	4,699.12
Material	1,050.90	2,414.98	3,465.88
Total	13,275.40	14,714.17	27,989.57

The list of buildings to which construction items apply is shown in the estimates.

The increased cost of materials and labor has greatly increased the costs of equipping these stations. For this reason the original plan of extending this work to other stations as rapidly as possible has been abandoned for the present year. Therefore, all the funds provided for this item for the current year will not be used. It is desired, however, to go forward with the original plans as soon as conditions more nearly normal are restored.

CONTRIBUTIONS FROM OUTSIDE SOURCES TO SALARIES OF EMPLOYEES OF THE DEPARTMENT OF AGRICULTURE.

STATEMENT OF MR. CHESTER MORRILL, ASSISTANT TO THE SOLICITOR, UNITED STATES DEPARTMENT OF AGRICULTURE.

Mr. MORRILL. Item 15 in the miscellaneous section of the estimate is not designed to increase or extend the activities of the department beyond those already authorized by Congress, and which are found to be proper in carrying out the objects specified in the appropriations made by Congress. It is deemed necessary and is offered by reason of the provision contained in the act making appropriations for the legislative, executive, and judicial expenses of the Government for the fiscal year ending June 30, 1918, and for other purposes (39 Stat. L., p. 1106), which reads as follows:

Provided, That on and after July first, nineteen hundred and nineteen, no Government official or employee shall receive any salary in connection with his services as such an official or employee from any source other than the Government of the United States, except as may be contributed out of the treasury of any State, county, or municipality, and no person, association, or corporation shall make any contribution to or in any way supplement the salary of any Government official or employee for the services performed by him for the Government of the United States. Any person violating any of the terms of this proviso shall be deemed guilty of a misdemeanor, and upon conviction thereof shall be punished by a fine of not less than $1,000 or imprisonment for not less than six months, or by both such fine and imprisonment, as the court may determine.

The provision just quoted is the outgrowth of an amendment inserted by the Senate when the bill was pending, directed primarily at the use of money contributed by the General Education Board for carrying on activities of the Bureau of Education, but framed so as to apply also to the various executive departments. At that time this department presented its views as to the effect of the amendment to the Committee on Agriculture of the House and the Committee on Agriculture and Forestry of the Senate, and later the amendment was modified in conference and enacted in its present form, the effective date being postponed until July 1, 1919, so as to permit careful consideration during the intervening time of its probable effect and the necessity for modification, if any.

So far as the General Education Board is concerned, the Department of Agriculture has no cooperative agreement or understanding whatsoever, either direct or indirect with it, and does not propose to enter into any such arrangement. The facts with respect to such cooperation in the past, which commenced in 1906 and terminated in 1914, are set forth in a letter of April 3, 1914, to the President of the Senate from the Secretary of Agriculture, published as Senate Document No. 538, second session, Sixty-third Congress, and in letters dated February 9 and 10, 1917, to the chairman of your committee from the Secretary of Agriculture.

Under the authority conferred upon the Department of Agriculture by the acts making appropriations for its expenses, it conducts much investigational and demonstrational work through the means of cooperative activities in which State, county, and municipal agencies have no part or are not the sole outside parties.

In fact, Congress has provided expressly for such cooperative activities in connection with many of the items of appropriation for the Department of Agriculture, of which the following are illustrations:

In the act of May 8, 1914, providing for cooperative agricultural extension work with State agricultural colleges, certain funds are appropriated with the following proviso:

Provided further, That no payment out of the additional appropriations herein provided shall be made in any year to any State until an equal sum has been appropriated for that year by the legislature of such State, or provided by State, county, college, local authority, or individual contributions from within the State, for the maintenance of the cooperative agricultural extension work provided for in this act.

In the act making appropriations for the Department of Agriculture for the fiscal year ending June 30, 1919, under the heading "General expenses, States Relations Service," $650,140 is appropriated for farmers' cooperative demonstrations and for the study and demonstration of the best methods of meeting the ravages of the cotton-boll weevil, coupled with the following proviso:

Provided, That the expense of such service shall be defrayed from this appropriation and such cooperative funds as may be voluntarily contributed by State, county, and municipal agencies, associations of farmers, and individual farmers, universities, colleges, boards of trade, chambers of commerce, other local associations of business men, business organizations, and individuals within the State.

In the same act, under the heading "General expenses, Bureau of Markets," provision is made—

For acquiring and diffusing among the people of the United States useful information on subjects connected with the marketing and distributing of farm and nonmanufactured food products and the purchase of farm supplies, independently and in cooperation with other branches of the department, State agencies, purchasing and consuming organizations, and persons engaged in the transportation, marketing, and distributing of farm and food products.

Similarly, under the heading "General expenses, Bureau of Plant Industry," authority is given—

For conducting such investigations of the nature and means of communication of the diseases of citrus trees, known as citrus canker, and by applying such methods of eradication or control of the disease as in the judgment of the Secretary of Agriculture may be necessary, including the payment of such expenses and the employment of such persons and means, in the city of Washington and elsewhere, and cooperation with such authorities of the States concerned, organizations of growers, or individuals, as he may deem necessary to accomplish such purposes, $250,000, and, in the discretion of the Secretary of Agriculture, no expenditures shall be made for these purposes until a sum or sums at least equal to such expenditures shall have been appropriated, subscribed, or contributed by State, county, or local authorities, or by individuals or organizations for the accomplishment of such purposes.

Under the heading "General expenses, Forest Service," an appropriation is made for investigations of methods for wood distillation and for the preservative treatment of timber and other activities, and for commercial demonstrations of improved methods or processes, in cooperation with individuals and companies.

Provisions of this character have been carried for years in the acts making appropriations for this department, and other illustrations might be quoted if necessary.

It is manifest from these illustrations that Congress believed that cooperation by this department with individuals and agencies other than State, county, and municipal was not only desirable but in many cases essential.

Pursuant to such express provisions and acting upon the basis of what appeared to be the attitude of Congress generally, this department from time to time has entered into many different kinds of cooperative arrangements to which individuals, associations, and corporations, other than State, county, or municipal agencies, have been or are now parties. In some cases such cooperative arrangements have been found necessary in order properly to perform the duties imposed upon the department by Congress, even though cooperation was not expressly mentioned in the act making appropriation therefor. In fact, there are numerous items requiring the department to perform certain duties without expressly mentioning cooperation, but in general character similar to those in which cooperation is expressly provided for.

The most important activity in which the Forest Service is interested and in which persons are employed who may possibly come within the prohibition of the amendment is that of protection against forest fires. As far as it has been practical to do so, the Forest Service has brought together the fire-fighting services of the Federal Government, State authorities, and private interests for the common protection of the lands belonging to all. Obviously, it is impossible to determine in advance where or how often fires will originate in any particular region, and the lands of the Federal Government, State governments, and private interests frequently are so intermingled that it is absolutely essential that such work shall be carried on under a scheme which will give the protection desired without duplication of effort by the interests involved. Such agreements are participated in by private individuals, timberland owners, lumber companies, railroads, fire-protection associations, telephone companies, and others. While it is within the range of possibility that the Federal Government might pay the entire salaries and expenses of all persons employed by it for services rendered for its benefit, such divorcement would entail innumerable complications. In order properly to protect the national forests, the Federal Government might have to assume entirely the responsibilities which now attach to private owners and are now shared by them.

In some cases the parties to agreements provide for certain fire patrols, the share of each in the expense being determined by the amount of property of each to be protected and the actual expense for fire fighting is prorated. In the case of forest lands in the vicinity of railroads, it is particularly essential that the railroads should participate in the fire-protection service because the operations of the railroads frequently cause fires. If Government fire protection were segregated from that of private owners, it would be found that private owners would not and could not economically organize independent protection for their comparatively small areas. If they could not cooperate, they would probably leave the whole burden to the Forest Service either to prevent fires on their lands in order to protect Government lands or would allow the fires to burn until it became necessary for the Government to fight them in order to prevent their running over into Government property. Participation by private interests in such fire-protection work enhances their interest in the prevention and suppression of fires.

The Forest Service also has cooperative arrangements with lumber companies and timberland owners for the purpose of lessening the damage to timber by the cutting and treating of infested trees and the destruction of broods of insects through the services of employees paid by the department, but whose expenses are paid by the cooperators.

In carrying on its farmers' cooperative demonstration and other activities under the authority granted to the Department of Agriculture in the annual appropriations for the States Relations Service the department enters into numerous cooperative arrangements under which the salaries and expenses of agents and other employees of the department engaged in the work are paid partly by the department and partly by local soil and crop improvement associations, farm bureaus, agricultural committees, farmers' clubs and associations, fair associations, citizens' and business associations, chambers of commerce and boards of trade, banks, business men, railroads, and private subscriptions, aside from funds contributed from State, county, and municipal treasuries. Such contributions amount to several hundred thousand dollars per annum.

Other bureaus, such as the Bureau of Public Roads, Bureau of Biological Survey, and the Bureau of Animal Industry, are and have been engaged in important activities in which the accomplishment of the objects specified by Congress has been facilitated by cooperation with individuals, corporations, and associations, involving joint payment of traveling, subsistence, and other expenses, and frequently the joint payment of salaries of employees of the department required for the purpose.

While cooperative work of the character which the department conducts has resulted in a saving of expenditure, and compliance with the provision under discussion which becomes effective on July 1, 1919, may require that the department be furnished with largely increased appropriations in order to accomplish the same objects, the department does not rely upon the possible increase of expenditure as an argument against the application of the provision to its activities. Such cooperative work has brought to the department the moral support and the active assistance of those who provided the funds, when such support and assistance might not have been given otherwise. In many cases the carrying on of the work rendered necessary in order to accomplish objects of public interest results at the time in immediate benefit to the cooperators and it is believed that they should share in the expense for this reason. The department specifically retains and exercises full control over the employment and cooperative activities of persons engaged in such work.

In this connection there may arise differences of opinion as to the exact application in particular cases of the prohibitions contained in the provision which becomes effective July 1, 1919, and, as severe punishment is provided for the violation of any of its terms, the department would necessarily be compelled to refrain from entering into some apparently proper joint activities because of the fear that a very broad application might be made of such prohibitions.

In order to enable the department to carry out the express requirements which have been made by Congress in the past and in current appropriation bills and to accomplish the objects specified by Congress, where cooperation is not expressly mentioned, in the most efficient way and with the greatest benefit to both the public and the private interests involved, it is the belief of the department that express authority should be given for such cooperation as the committee may think proper, notwithstanding the item in the legislative, executive, and judicial appropriation bill, which becomes effective on July 1, 1919.

INDEX.

	Page.
Acetone production	375
Acetone production, Hercules munition plant	409

Accounts and Disbursement Division:
    Estimates and appropriations... 4
    Recommendations of committee... 18
Accounts Division, hearing... 445
Aeronautics, studies and stations.. 154–157
Agriculture appropriation bill, report of committee....................... 3–29
Agriculture Department:
    Miscellaneous expenses, estimates and appropriations................... 4
    Revenues, 1918.. 5–7
Agricultural extension, cooperative work, administration............... 459–486
Air studies, work and stations.. 153–157
Aircraft Production Bureau, cooperation of Chemistry Bureau.............. 375
Airplanes, production, work of Forest Service laboratory............... 336–338
Alabama, drainage work.. 512, 513
Alaska:
    Experiment stations, work.. 491–492
    Matanuska Valley, live-stock work................................... 491–492
Alfalfa seed:
    Market supply, quality, etc.. 612
    Supply and source... 291
Alkali, resistant crops, studies... 280
ALSBERG, Dr. CARL L., statement as chief of Chemistry Bureau............ 359–396
ANDERSON, Representative:
    Airplane use in forests.. 316–317
    Cattle-tick eradication.. 173
    Cost accounting... 132
    Crop Estimates Bureau work.................................. 446–450, 454
    Dairy marketing... 597, 600
    Enforcement of grain-standard act................... 707, 713, 716–733
    Estimates recommended... 66–67
    Experiment farms... 296, 299–304
    Experimental flour-mill project..................................... 683–690
    Farm labor.. 139
    Farm Management Office reorganization........................... 128–132
    Fertilizer use... 308
    Game wardens... 428, 429
    Horticultural Board work..................................... 742, 744, 752
    Insect-control demonstration.. 412
    Market news service on fruits and vegetables.. 550–551, 566–568, 576, 590–592, 597
    Markets Bureau.................................. 526–529, 540–541, 548
    Mileage rates for motor vehicles.................................. 352–354
    Nursery site.. 343
    Preparation and marketing food products...................... 635, 644–645
    Publications work.. 443
    Roads Bureau work........................... 506–508, 513, 516–519
    Secretary's Office.. 73–74, 80–82
    Seed-reporting service............................... 609–610, 614–615
    Soils Bureau work.. 398, 402, 407
    Solicitor's Office.. 95–99
    State's Relations Service................... 478–480, 485, 488, 500–501
    Timber sales.. 314
    Tuberculous cattle........................... 162–164, 166, 169–170
    Wood seasoning... 338

INDEX.

	Page
ANDREWS, FRANK, increase of salary	446
Animal diseases, control work and studies	207–219
Animal Industry Bureau:	
Appropriations recommended, proposed uses	10–14
Estimates and appropriations	4
Meat inspectors' salaries	231–259
Statement of chief and others	159–230
Animals, wild, killing, and use of skins	426–427
Appropriations:	
Emergency funds, discussion	336
Extension act	461–471
Forest, proposed changes	317–331
1920, increase over 1919	3–5
Arizona, school fund from forest receipts, 1918	6
Arlington farm, upkeep	288
Assessor's reports, live-stock checking	454–455
BAHNSEN, Dr. PETER F., statement on Veterinarian's salaries	248–250
Banana disease investigations	495
Barberry, eradication work	274–279
BARNES, WILL C., statement on grazing and stock poisoning in National Forests	338–341
Baskets, "snide," manufacture, investigations	681
BASSETT, Mr., work in Bureau of Markets	531
BAYARD, E. S., statement on meat inspection	244–248
Beans, velvet, feed value, investigations	367
Bee, culture investigations	419
Beetle, Japanese, introduction, and control	413
Beets, sugar, foreign-seed introduction, planting methods, etc	288–289
Biological Survey Bureau:	
Appropriations recommended, proposed uses	17–18
Committee recommendations	17–18
Estimates and appropriations	4
Hearings	423–435
Birds:	
Investigations	425
Protection	424–425, 427–432
Wild, increase under migratory bird act	428
Bison, American:	
Distribution by Agriculture Secretary	349–350
Loan or exchange, committee recommendation	28
Blackbird habits investigation	425
Blueberry, production, studies and experiments	281–283
Bollworm, pink:	
Appropriation recommended, and proposed use	28
Eradication—	
Estimates and appropriations	5
Hearing	748–754
Borer:	
Corn, European, introduction, spread, and control	414–418
Oriental peach moth, introduction on Japanese cherry trees	743
Bovovaccine, description, value, and source	207–213
BRANCH, G. V., statement on city market reporting service	615–634
BRAND, CHARLES J., Chief, Markets Bureau:	
Cooperative work with States in marketing	677–680
Cotton—	
Futures act, enforcement	694–702
Grading work	661–665
Marketing and warehousing	736–740
Dairy marketing	597–600
Experimental flour-mill project	682, 685–694
Food products marketing	634–651
Grain—	
Investigations by Markets Bureau	680–681
Standards act and enforcement	712–720, 724–731
Hay and feed reporting service	599–602

INDEX. 767

BRAND, CHARLES J., Chief, Markets Bureau—Continued.
Market— Page.
    Inspection of perishable foods... 654, 658–661
    New service on fruit supplies.. 613–615
    News service on fruits and vegetables................................... 551–576
    News service on live stock and meats.............................. 587, 590–595
    Rural credits work by Markets Bureau................................. 668–669
    Salary, discussion... 526–528
    Seed-reporting service.. 605–613
    Statements... 525–740
    Telegraph operators' pay.. 665–667
Bridges, improvement of national forests, 1918, 1919....................... 347–349
BRONSON, Mr., statements on auto and motorcycle service................... 353
BROWN, FREDERICK W., statements on fertilizer resources....... 401, 402, 405, 408–410
Brown-tail moth, control work... 421
Buildings, national forests, cost-limit increase.............................. 311–313
Bull clubs, necessity and value.. 182, 192–193
Bulls, breeds, selection, prices... 191–193
California, Summerland, kelp plant...................................... 407
Cane-sugar districts, live-stock production, experiments, statement on..... 756–758
Card indexes, sale receipts... 7
Carpenters, wages, discussion and recommendations...................... 112–122
Cars:
    Fumigation, in pink bollworm quarantine............................. 748–749
    Heater, for shipment of perishable products, need, work of Markets Bureau.. 703–704
Catalyzers, investigations.. 400
Cattle:
    Number on farms and ranges, 1918.................................... 585
    Raising in Gulf coast region.. 757–758
    Tuberculous, indemnity to owners, valuation, etc...................... 161–172
Chemicals, rare, investigations... 391–393
Chemistry Bureau, hearings.. 359–396
Cholera, hog, outbreaks in Iowa, 1918, by counties........................ 214–216
Citric acid manufacture, development.................................... 374
City market reporting service:
    Value, extracts from letters.. 632–634
    Work, statement of Mr. Branch...................................... 615–634
Clothing, economics.. 500–501
Clubs, boys' and girls', work................................. 460–469, 472–476, 481
Coconut oil, investigations... 367
COLE, CHARLES S., hay and seed reporting service....................... 600–605
Colors, measurement, work of Bureau of Standards........................ 380
Cooperative work, Chemistry Bureau, cost................................ 359–360
CANDLER, Representative:
    Chemistry Bureau work.. 385, 387, 396
    White pine.. 346
Cement, potash work.. 401–402
Cereal smut, eradication work.. 279
Cereals, production and disease control................................... 272–273
Charcoal, recovery from kelp.. 408
Cherry trees, Japanese, infestation with injurious insects............. 742–743, 745
Cheese, production, consumption, and prices............................. 174–193
Chemistry Bureau:
    Appropriations recommended, proposed uses......................... 15–16
    Committee recommendations.. 15–16
    Estimates and appropriations.. 4
Cholera, hog:
    Control and eradication, work of Animal Industry Bureau............. 213–219
    Losses, number and value, 1914, 1915, 1917.......................... 241–244
    (See also Hog cholera.)
CHRISTIE, G. I., Assistant Secretary, farm management, and farm labor...... 127–139
Clubs, mole-trapping, profits from skins sold.............................. 427
Colleges, agricultural, cooperation with Agriculture Department............ 475–478
Colored county agents... 464
Congressional seed distribution, packages for 1919......................... 309
Cooperation:
    Payment for work... 29
    With other departments, Soils Bureau................................ 406–407

INDEX.

	Page.
Cooperative work, department and outside agencies, discussion	760–764
Copra, preparation and use	367

Corn:
Borer, European, introduction, spread, and control	414–418
Seed selection for root-rot	273

Cotton:
Crop estimates	454–455
Destruction in Texas for bollworm control	749–751
Diseases, investigations	270–271
Districts, live-stock production, experiments, statement on	756–758
Futures act, inforcement, work of Markets Bureau	694–702
Grades	542–545
Importance in cotton marketing, discussion	695–702
Grading work, statement of Mr. Brand	661–665
Handling and marketing	540–548
Insects, control work	418
Loose, receipts, 1918	6–7
Marketing and warehousing, statement of Mr. Nixon	734–740
Pink bollworm eradication, hearing	748–754
Short selling, practices	698
Spot markets, prices, discussion	696–698
Transportation charges	546

Cotton-free zone, Texas, enforcement	7 9
Cotton-future disputes, receipts, 1918	6
Cotton-standards sales, receipts, 1918	6
Cottonseed oil, substitute for olive oil	366

County agents:
Discussion	60–469, 473, 476, 480–485
Functions and scope of work	135–136, 138–139
Solicitation of State funds, discussion	482–489
County organization methods	486–489
Cows, wintering for beef	136
Coyotes, extermination	426–427
CRANE, EDWARD C., increase of salary	446
Credits, rural, work of Markets Bureau, statement of Mr. Brand	668–669

Crop:
Correspondents, voluntary	453, 454

Estimates Bureau—
Appropriations recommended, proposed uses	19–20
Committee recommendations	19–20
Estimates and appropriations	4
Hearings	445–457
Production, estimating, date of work	452

Crops:
Alkali-and-drought-resistant, tests	280
Estimation, coordination of work in department, memorandum of Secretary	591–592
Losses from rodents	426
Reporting work, cost, by crops	450–452

Dairy:
Industry, scope and work	174–193
Marketing, statement of Mr. Potts	596–597
Products, Market News Service, extracts from letters	597–599

Dairying:
In semiarid and irrigated districts, experiments	758–760
Irrigated sections, estimates and appropriations	5
Dehydration processes	385–391, 395
Demonstration cooperative work	460–486

Demonstrations:
Insect control	412
On reclamation projects, statements on	755–756, 558–760
Animal control	207–219
Cotton, potato, truck crops, etc., investigations	270–271
Forest and ornamental trees and shrubs, investigations	268–270
Live stock, eradication work	232–234
Plant, survey work and appropriations	263–268

INDEX. 769

	Page.
District of Columbia, need of plant-quarantine law	742–744
Documents distribution, superintendent, statutory position	438–439
"Dollar-a-month" employees	430, 433, 435
Dourine, injuries to horses, distribution, eradication work, etc	218–219
Drainage, farm	511–514
Dropped places, by bureaus and offices	43–46
Dry farming, studies and experiments	283–285
Drying foods	385–391
Dry-land farming, statement of Dr. Taylor	283–284
Drug-plant diseases, investigations	270–271

Dyes:
- German formulas and patents ... 377–378
- Production, Chemistry Bureau work ... 374–380
- Sensitizing, production for War Department ... 375–376, 392

Dyestuffs, situation in United States ... 378–379
Editor, Chief, Publications Division ... 437–438
Education Board, General, contributions to departments, discussion ... 760

Emergency:
- Food leaflets ... 498–499
- Funds, use in extension work ... 463–476

Employees:
- Appointments and separations since November 11 ... 123
- Changes in titles ... 50–53
- Forest Service, depletion by war conditions ... 346
- New, Publications Division, discussions ... 437–440
- Transfers and salaries, discussion ... 261–263
- Weather Bureau, number and salary increases recommended ... 141–144

Engineering, rural, statement by E. B. McCormick, chief ... 515–523
Engines, horsepower, determination ... 516–523

Entomology Bureau:
- Appropriations recommended, proposed uses ... 16–17
- Committee recommendations ... 16–17
- Estimates and appropriations ... 4
- Hearings ... 411–421

Equipment:
- Expenses, Chemistry Bureau ... 383
- Form, standardization ... 515
- Household, care and repair, work of Home Economics Office ... 500
- Photographic, Publications Division ... 441

ESTABROOK, LEON M., statement on crop Estimates Bureau work ... 445–457
Estimates, summary and changes by bureaus and offices; statement by Mr. Harrison ... 31–72
EVANS, Dr. WALTER H., statement as Chief of Insular Stations Division ... 491–498
Experiment stations, insular, appropriations and work ... 491–498
Explosions, mill and thresher, work of Chemistry Bureau ... 360–363

Extension:
- Act, administration ... 459–485
- Work—
  - Insular experiment stations ... 489–491, 493–496
  - Northern and Western States, statement of C. B. Smith ... 486–489

Farm:
- Boys, proportion returning to farms from Army, inducements ... 136–138
- Bureaus, organization and work ... 462, 482–489
- Drainage ... 511–514
- Equipment, standardization ... 515
- Management, office—
  - Committee recommendations ... 9
  - Estimates and appropriations ... 4
  - Projects and proposed expenditures, 1919 ... 135
  - Proposed reorganization ... 127–136
  - Statement of Assistant Secretary G. I. Christie ... 127–139
  - Statutory-roll increases ... 127
- Products, insular stations, sale receipts, 1918 ... 7

Farmers, number in Army ... 136
Farm-help specialist, scope and value of work ... 138–139

106119—19——49

INDEX.

	Page.
Federal aid roads, expenditures	505, 506
Feed, Market News Service	599–605
Fertilizers, uses and value, experiments, etc	291–308
Fines, revenues for violation of statutes administered by department	91–92

Fire protection:
Cooperative, watersheds, estimated and appropriations	4
Forest Service cooperations with outside agencies	762–763
Various national forests, appropriation increases	331–334

Fires:
Forest, control work	334, 336
National forests, protection, cooperation of States with Forest Service	349
Prevention in mills and elevators	361–363
Fish, handling, packing, etc, Chemistry Bureau	364–367

Flax:
New Zealand, production experiments, proposed work	271–272
Straw, use and value for paper making, studies	279–280
Flies, fruit, investigations	419–420
Flour, sweet-potato, food value	386
Flouring mill, experimental, establishment, discussion	682–691

Food:
Administration, cooperation with Home Economics	499
And drugs act, enforcement	382
Investigations, biological	367–368
Products, production, marketing, etc., statement of Mr. Brand	634–651
Supply investigations, work of Bureau of Markets	642–643

Food-production act:
Appropriation transfer to agriculture appropriation	3
Work of Plant Industry Bureau	266, 270–271, 280–281, 285–286

Foods:
New, and new uses for old ones	498
Perishable, Market Inspection Service, statement of Mr. Scott	651–661

Foot-and-mouth disease, eradication:
Committee recommendations	28
Estimates and appropriations	3, 5

Forest:
Crops, diseases, investigations	270–271
Fires, fighting and protection	334, 336
Insects, control	418
Receipts, benefits to States, 1918	5–6
Receipts, school funds to Arizona and New Mexico, 1918	6

Service—
Appropriations recommended, proposed uses	14
Committee recommendations	14
Employees depletion by war, etc	346
Estimates and appropriations	4
Provisions for cooperative work	761–762
Statement of Assistant Forester	338–341
Statements of Forester	311–338, 341–358
Statutory-roll increases asked	311
Forester HENRY S. GRAVES, statement on Forest Service work	311–338, 341–358

Forest, National:
Annual receipts and expenditures	313–317
Appropriation changes proposed for each	317–331
Credit for resources furnished other departments	313–315
Fire protection appropriations, increase	331–334
Fire-law violations, rewards for evidence	313
Grazing investigations, fees, etc	338–343
Improvement by roads, trails, bridges, etc., 1918, 1919	347–349
Insect injuries and control work	335–336
Land classification	334
Receipts, 1918	5
Receipts and appropriations, 1909–1919, table	313–315
Receipts, 1918, and sources	313–315
Special uses, receipts, 1918	5

Fruit:
    And fruit trees, cooperative experiments and studies..................... 308
    Drying, estimates and appropriations.. 5
    Flies, investigations.. 419–420
    Sirups, manufacture... 381
    Supplies, news reporting service, statement of Mr. Brand.............. 613–615
    Carload shipments, 1916.. 570–571
    Market News Service... 548–576
Fumigating sheds for treatment of pink bollworm in cotton................. 748
Funds, State, solicitation by Federal employees, discussion................ 482–489
Fur, moles, value.. 427
Game:
    Protection.. 424–425
    Wardens, State and Federal... 427–435
Game-reserve regulations, arrests for violation............................... 354–358
Gins, cotton, fire prevention.. 362–363
Gipsy moth, control work... 421
Grain:
    Investigations, work of Markets Bureau, statement of Mr. Brand........ 680–681
    Market News Service... 599–604
    Market News Service, value, extracts from letters...................... 604–605
    Standards act, enforcement, work of Markets Bureau statement of Mr. Livingston... 704–733
    Supervision—
        Apparatus and equipment.. 704
        Equipment, items and cost... 705–706
        Statement of Mr. Livingston... 704–733
Grain-standards appeals, receipts, 1918....................................... 7
Gravel, use in road building.. 509–510
Graves, Henry S.:
    Forest Service Chief, statement on proposed appropriation changes for National Forests.. 317–331
    Statements as Forester... 311–338, 341–558
Grazing:
    Cooperative, on reclamation projects..................................... 756
    Forest permits, receipts, 1918... 5
    Permits, national forests, number of cattle and sheep, etc....... 338–343, 347–348
Guam Experiment Station, appropriation and work.......................... 496
Haber process of nitrogen fixation... 398, 402, 403
HALL, L. D., statement on Market News Service on Live Stock and Meats.. 576–596
HARRISON, FLOYD R., assistant to Secretary:
    Accounts Division work... 445
    Casein glue.. 181
    Chemistry Bureau work... 370–372, 380, 384
    Cotton-grading work.. 662–664
    Department transfers and reinstatements............................... 262–263
    Entomology Bureau work... 411, 412, 415
    Farm-management Office reorganization................................. 130–131
    Mileage for Government-owned machines................................ 357–358
    Mileage rates for motor vehicles.. 352
    Miscellaneous expenses... 123–126
    Overtime work for meat inspectors....................................... 221
    Roads Bureau appropriation.. 516
    Rural credits work by Markets Bureau................................... 669
    Salary increases.. 141
    Salary of Chief, Biological Survey.. 423
    Salary of Mr. Brand... 526–528
    States Relations Service.. 467, 468, 495
    Statutory roll and lump-sum appropriations............................ 127
    Summary of estimates and proposed changes, by bureaus and offices...... 31–72
    Supplemental estimates... 172
    Timber estimating and approving... 346
    Wages for mechanics.. 115
    Work of Secretary's Office... 73–82, 85–87

772 INDEX.

HAUGEN, Representative: Page.
Accounts Division... 445
Alkaline land... 280–281
Animal husbandry work... 189–206
Barberry eradication... 274–276
Cereal production and diseases... 272–276
Chemistry Bureau work... 366–396
Chestnut blight... 268–269
Citrus canker control... 266–268
City market reporting service... 619, 622, 626–631
Cost accounting... 134–135
County agents' work and appropriation uses... 135–136
Crop Estimates Bureau work... 447–449, 453
Dairy work... 178–186, 213
Dourine... 219
Dry-land farming... 285
Estimates recommended... 68–70, 72
Farm labor... 137–139
Farmers' living... 241–244
Federal and State salaries... 252–253, 255–259
Fertilizer experiments... 304–307
Flax straw... 279–280
Forest improvements... [1] 347–348
Game wardens... 432–435
Grain standardization... 681
Grazing fees and permits... 339–343
Hay and feed reporting service... 599–604
Heating orchards... 149–150
Hog cholera... 213–219
Hog-cholera losses... 242–244
Horticultural Board work... 749
Markets Bureau work... 526, 530–539, 544–547, 553–558, 572–576, 585–590, 634, 638–642, 645–650, 655–661, 663–664, 679–683, 691, 698–700, 709–716, 720, 725–733, 737–740
Meat inspectors... 246–248
Miscellaneous expenses... 123
New Zealand flax... 271–272
Plant-disease survey work... 264–268
Roads Bureau work... 504–522
Rural credits work by Markets Bureau... 669–679
Rural organizations... 673–677
Salaries... 144–147, 220–227
Secretary's office... 73–76, 81–87
Seed distribution... 308–310
Seed reporting service... 608–609
Sheep dipping... 255
Sheep slaughtering... 256–258
Solicitor's office... 111
States Relations Service... 464–471, 475–488, 492–494, 498–502
Statutory rolls, transfers and salaries... 261–263
Travel expense... 741
Tuberculous cattle... 161–163, 168, 170–171
Veterinarians' supply and demand... 249–250
Wages for mechanics... 116–117, 120–122
Weather forecasts... 151–152
Weather observation stations... 156–157
Weather reporting... 153–154
Wheat production cost... 133–134
White pine blister rust... 269–270
Wild plants and grasses... 281–282
Hawaii:
Experiment station—
Appropriation and work... 493–494
Work, proposed transfer. etc... 145–148
Extension work... 489–490, 493, 496–497
Hay, inspection service at markets, need... 658–660

INDEX. 773

	Page.
Hay, market news service	599–605
HAYWOOD, Dr. J. K., statement as chairman of Insecticide Board	741
Hearings, sole receipts	7
Heater cars, need for shipment of perishable products	703–704

HEFLIN, Representative:
 Cotton grades and marketing........................... 541–548
 Crop estimates work................................... 454–455
 Enforcement of cotton-futures act..................... 695–702
 Entomology Bureau work............................... 416, 419
 Grain production cost................................. 134
 Grazing permits and fees.............................. 341
 Horticultural Board work.............. 747, 749, 752, 753
 Roads Bureau work................................. 506, 509, 513
 States Relations Service.......................... 482, 487, 488
Hercules powder plant work, potash work, etc........... 409
Hog cholera:
 Control and eradication, work of Animal Industry Bureau........ 213–219
 Losses, number, and value, 1914, 1915, 1917............ 241–244
Hogs:
 Number on farms and ranges, 1918..................... 585
 Production, demonstrations on reclamation projects..... 755
HOLLADAY, H. H., statement on meat inspectors......... 254–256
Home economics:
 Office, statement of Dr. C. F. Langworthy............. 498–501
 Workers... 464, 476, 481
 Raising in Gulf Coast region.......................... 757
Honey prices... 419
Horsepower, motors, determination...................... 516–523
Horses:
 Army, breeding, methods and work..................... 203–206
 Breeding for military purposes........................ 203–206
 Dourine, studies and eradication work................. 218–219
 Number on farms and ranges, 1918..................... 585
 Raising, in Gulf Coast region......................... 758
Horticultural Board, Federal:
 Committee recommendations............................ 27
 Estimates and appropriations.......................... 4, 27
 Hearing... 742–754
HOSKINS, Dr. W. HORACE, statements on veterinarians' salaries........ 238–242, 253
Housing, department, outlook........................... 123–126
HOUSTON, D. F., secretary:
 Letter—
  On European corn borer.............................. 415–416
  On plant-quarantine law............................. 743–744
  On potato wart disease.............................. 745–746
  On States Relations Service appropriation........... 460–463
  Recommending increase of salary chief Biological Survey.......... 423–424
 Memorandum on crop and live-stock estimation work..... 591–592
HOWARD, Dr. L. O., statement as chief of Entomology Bureau........... 411–421
HUGHES, J. F., statement on lay meat inspectors........ 256–459
Incendiarism, National Forests, rewards for law violations................ 313
Insect, control demonstrations.......................... 412
Insecticide act, enforcement:
 Appropriations recommended, proposed uses............ 26–27
 Hearing.. 741
Insecticide and fungicide board, estimate, and appropriations............. 4
Insects:
 Classification, etc.................................. 420
 Control work... 412–421
 National forests, injuries and control work........... 335–336
Inspection Office, report of work....................... 86–87
Inspectors, perishable foods at markets, salaries, offices, etc......... 658–659
Insular experiment stations, appropriations and work... 491–498
Iowa, hog cholera outbreaks, May to October, 1918, table................ 214–216
Irrigation, farm....................................... 511

INDEX.

	Page.
JACOWAY, Representative:	
Cotton grades	545
Cotton marketing and warehousing	736–738, 740
Packers' advertisements	540
"Prima facie evidence"	651
Roads Bureau work	508, 509
JOHNS, Dr., promotion, discussion	369–373
KELLERMAN, Dr. Karl F., Assistant Chief, Plant Industry Bureau, statements	267–268, 273–279, 292–307
Kelp deposits, potash work	401, 407–410
KNAPP, Bradford, statements on extension work in the South	483, 488
KOEN, Dr., statements on State veterinarian salaries in Iowa	253–254
Laboratory work, Madison, Wis., saving to Government, etc	336–338
Lacey Act, enforcement	424–425
Land classification, National forest, cooperation of Soils Bureau with Forest Service	334
LANGWORTHY, Dr. C. F., statement as chief of Home Economics Office	498–501
Lanolin, from wool scouring, utilization	393–395
Law violations:	
Game-reserve regulations, arrests	354–358
National forests, rewards for evidence	313
Lawyers, salaries in Government departments	98–100
Leaflets, food	498–499
Leave of absence, cumulative, for men in insular service	497
LEE, Representative:	
Biological Survey Bureau	421–431
Chemistry Bureau work	361, 368, 374
Corn-root rot	273
Cotton insects	752
Farm machinery	295
Forest improvements	316
Forest receipts and expenditures	314
Game law violations	354–357
Grazing leases	340
Hog-cholera deaths	243
Lumber for forest buildings	312
Mount Weather station	156
Roads Bureau work	506, 511, 512
State experiment stations	296
Weather forecasting	151
Legumes as sources of nitrogen	403–404
LESHER, Representative:	
Bovovaccine	208
County agent funds	484
Dairying and cottage cheese	174, 189
Farm chickens	196
Farm labor	245
Hog-cholera quarantine	213
Meat inspectors	222
Messengers	145
Potato wart disease	747
Roads Bureau work	516
Salaries and bonuses	256, 257
Chestnut blight	269
Veterinarian scarcity	247, 249
Lever Act. (*See* Smith-Lever Act.)	
LEVER, Chairman:	
Aeronautics	154–157
Animal Industry Bureau	159–178, 181–182, 185–190, 193–200, 203, 206–207, 213–214, 218–221, 224–230
Biological Survey Bureau	423–427, 431–435
Bison distribution	349
Chemistry Bureau work	359–396
Cooperative fire protection	349

INDEX. 775

LEVER, Chairman—Continued. Page.
Cost limit for national forest buildings................................. 311–313
Crop Estimates Bureau work....................................... 445–457
Entomology Bureau work... 411–421
Farm labor.. 136–139
Farm-management reorganization............................ 127, 131–133, 135
Forest fires.. 331–334
Forest insects... 335
Forest nurseries.. 343–344
Frost protection.. 148–149
Government stock... 333–334
Horticultural board work... 742–753
Individual forest appropriations.................................... 317
Insecticide board work.. 741
Land classification... 334
Larkspur and loco control.. 338–339
Lump-sum appropriations... 127
Markets Bureau work.. 525–740
Market news service....................... 551–553, 560–576, 585, 592
Meat-inspectors' salaries.......... 231, 237–240, 243–246, 248, 251, 254, 255
Mileage rates for motor vehicles................................ 350–354, 358
Publications Division... 437–443
Plant Industry Bureau work............ 261–275, 279–303, 308–310
Receipts and expenses, national forests............................ 313–316
Rewards for law-violation evidence................................. 313
Roads, bridges, etc., for forests.................................. 347, 348
Roads Bureau work... 503–511, 514–523
Salaries and transfers... 141–148
Soils Bureau work.. 397–410
States Relations Service... 459–501
Statutory roll... 127, 311
Stock grazing.. 342–243
Timber estimating and appraising................................... 346–347
Travel expenses.. 152–153
War-time estimates... 345
Wood distillation... 336
Wood seasoning... 337–338
Work of farm-help specialists...................................... 138–139
Library:
 Estimates and appropriations...................................... 4
 No hearing.. 457
LINTON, F. B., statement on salaries, Chemistry Bureau............. 384
Live stock:
 Estimates cooperative... 449
 Estimating.. 453–454
 Estimation, coordination of work in department memorandum of Secretary... 591–592
 Industry, extent and importance................................... 583–585
 Market, Chicago, reports by market news service................... 578–579
 Market news service... 576–596
 Production—
  Estimates and appropriations..................................... 5
  In cane and cotton districts, experiments, statement............. 756–758
  In semiarid and irrigated districts, experiments................. 758–760
 Reporting and estimating, cost.................................... 451
 Work, Alaska.. 491–492
LIVINGSTON, GEORGE, statement on Federal grain supervision by Markets Bureau.. 704–733
Louisiana, New Iberia, live-stock production, experiments.......... 756–758
Lumber industry, production, markets, etc., national forests....... 345–346
Lump-fund:
 Appropriations, changes proposed.................................. 53–54
 Employees, transfer to statutory roll............................. 423
 Positions, salaries.. 369–370, 372, 383
Machinery, Publications Division................................... 440
Machines, Publications Division foreman............................ 439
Mail matter, chemical investigations............................... 360

INDEX.

	Page.
Manuscripts, purchasing, Publications Division	442
Market:	
Chicago, live-stock, reports by market news service	578–579
City, reporting service. statement of Mr. Branch	615–634
News service—	
Benefits, specific examples	574–575
Curtailments necessary for reduced appropriation	569–570
Expansion, stages	572–573
Expenditures for equipment at branch offices for fruits and Vegetables	585
On fruits and Vegetables, statement of Mr. Wells	548–576
On live stock and meats, statement of Mr. Hall	576–596
Work of employees, nature and hours	667–668
Telegraphic, rates use, and Value	552–560
Receipts, estimates and distribution of prices, city market reporting service	616–632
Reporting service, local, Value. extracts from letters	632–634
Marketing:	
Associations, cooperative, scope and purpose	532–540
Cooperation with States	677–680
Cooperative, growth and extension	525
Cotton, and warehousing, statement of Mr. Nixon	734–740
Foreign, studies by Markets Bureau	528–531
Markets:	
Bureau—	
Appropriations recommended, and proposed uses	22–26
Committee recommendations	22–26
Crop-estimate work duplication	447–448, 452–453, 456
Estimates and appropriations	4
Field stations, list, with number to whom reports are sent	551–552
Provisions for cooperative work	761
Work, statement of Mr. Brand	525–548.
	605–615, 629–651, 654–670, 677–704, 712–718, 724–733, 736–740
Inspection of perishable foods, list of cities	653
Marlatt, C. L., statement as chairman of Horticultural Board	742–754
Marshall, Herbert C., statement on experimental flour mill project	682
Marvin, Charles F., Chief, Weather Bureau, statement	141–157
McCrory, Mr., questions on Roads Bureau work	512, 513
Massachusetts corn borer, introduction, and control work	414, 416, 417
McKinley, Representative:	
Airplane cost	337
Forest buildings	312
Forest nurseries	344
Forest receipts and expenditures	316
Game wardens	429
McLaughlin, Representative:	
Army service of Weather Bureau air abservers	153–155
Beef boners' salaries	256
Breeding Army horses	204–206
Cattle increase	175
Cattle ticks	173
Cheese manufacture	177–180, 182–183
Chemistry Bureau work	360–364, 368–370, 376–395
City market reporting service	617–624, 631
Cooperative soil classification	334
Carriedale sheep	198–199, 202–203
Cottage cheese	190–191
Cotton-grading work	662–664
Cotton marketing and warehousing	737
Enforcement of grain-standards act	707. 717–719
Entomology Bureau	412–421
Experimental flour mill project	682, 685–686, 689
Experiment station work	296–299, 302–304
Fertilizer use	307, 308
Forest fire protection	331–334
Forest insects	335–336
Forest nurseries	344

INDEX. 777

McLaughlin, Representative—Continued. Page.
Frost protection in orchards... 149–150
Game-reserve arrests... 354–358
Glue making... 181
Grazing prices... 340–341
Hawaii experiment station.. 145–148
Hay and feed reporting service... 603–604
Holstein bulls... 193
Indemnity for tuberculous cattle... 162–172
Lump-sum salaries.. 127
Market inspection of perishable foods.................................... 653–659
Market news service on fruits and vegetables..................... 554, 557, 574
Marketing cooperation with States.. 678–680
Milk exports and imports... 174–175
Miscellaneous expenses... 123
Plywood.. 337
Preparation and marketing food products.......................... 635–639, 649
Price of alfalfa seed.. 310
Publications work.. 437–442
Resolution, memory of ex-President Roosevelt............................. 427
Rural organizations.. 670–674
Rural credits work in Markets Bureau..................................... 668–669
Salary increases... 144
Seed-reporting service... 612–615
Sheep inspection in Michigan... 255, 256
Sheep scabies.. 160–161
Sugar beets.. 288–291
Soils Bureau work.. 400–407
Solicitor's Office... 88, 95–99
States Relations Service.............................. 462–471, 477–484, 489–501
Woods suitable for paper... 345–346
Work of Bureau of Markets.. 525–536
Work of Secretary's Office.. 78–79, 83, 84
Meat:
    Industry, extent and importance...................................... 583–585
    Inspection—
        Appropriation increase.. 11, 231
        Employees' salaries, etc.. 219, 230
    Inspectors—
        Lay, description, and scope of work............................... 235
        Overtime payment, etc... 219–230
        Salary increases, letters urging.................................. 228–230
        Salaries, statements.. 231–259
Meat-inspection service, salaries and proposed salary increase, table...... 237–238
Meats, market news service.. 576–596
Mechanical-shop force, changes recommended by Mr. Reese................... 112–115
Mechanics, wages paid by Government and by private employers.............. 116
Mediterranean fruit fly, investigations................................... 419–440
Mexico:
    Conditions in the Laguna district.................................... 753
    Laguna Valley, pink bollworm infestation............................. 752–753
Michigan, sheep inspection.. 255, 256
Migratory-bird act:
    And treaty, discussion... 427–434
    Constitutionality, discussion................................... 430–431, 434
Milk drying... 387
Mildew-proofing methods, development...................................... 359
Mill:
    Experimental flouring, establishment, discussion..................... 682–694
    Explosions, investigations... 360–363
Miscellaneous expenses, statement of Mr. Reese............................ 122–126
Mohler, Dr. John R., Chief Animal Industry Bureau:
    Statements... 159–173, 207–230
        Meat-inspection service................... 239–240, 242–244, 251, 255
        Sheep and cattle scabies, etc..................................... 160–173
Moles, extermination, and use of fur...................................... 427
Montana, live-stock production experiments................................ 758, 759

INDEX.

	Page
MOORE, Dr. V. A., statement on veterinarians' salaries	250–254
MORRILL, CHESTER, statement as assistant to the solicitor	760–764
Moths, Brown-tail and gypsy, control work	421
Motor vehicles, mileage rates:	
Committee recommendation	29
In national forests	350–354
Motors, power, determination	516–523
Mules:	
Breeding project, in Gulf coast region	758
Number on farms and ranges, 1918	585
MUNCE, Mr., statements on State veterinarian salaries	253, 254
MURRAY, NAT C., increase of salary	446
NAGE, CHARLES F., statement on packers and packing-house employees	259
Naval stores, demonstration work	384–385
NELSON, E. W., statement as Chief of Biological Survey Bureau	423–435
Nematodes:	
Plant-infesting, studies	272
Sugar-beet, control work	280–281
New England States:	
European corn borer spread and control	414–417
Small proportion of Smith-Lever funds	478–479, 481
New Hampshire, corn borer control, appropriation	417
New Mexico, school fund from forest receipts, 1918	6
New places, estimates by bureau and offices	41–43
Nitrogen:	
Fixation, work of Soils Bureau	397–400, 402–403
Sources, legumes, etc	403–404, 407
NIXON, R. L., statement on cotton marketing and warehousing	734–740
Northern States, extension work, statement of C. B. Smith	486–489
Northwest, phosphate deposits	404–405
Nurseries, national forests, discussion	343–344
Oats, Federal supervision, equipment and expenses	709
Oil:	
Olive, shortage	366
Peach and apricot pits, new industry	366
Oils, substitutes for olive oil	366
Olive oil, shortage	366
Onions, crop estimating, Markets Bureau and Crop Estimates Bureau	448
Ordnance Bureau, use of Chemistry Bureau material	375–376
Ornamentals, foreign, quarantine	744–745
OUSLEY, CLARENCE, Assistant Secretary, statement on Publications Division	437–443
Oyster industry, supervision	367
Packers, profits during war	540
Paper, use of various woods, and sources	345–346
Patents, service, availability for public use	377
Pecan insects, work	413
Pennsylvania, potato wart disease and quarantine work	745–747
Periodical publications, supervision	443
Phosphates, deposits and sources	400, 404–405
Photo prints (and lantern slides) sale receipts	7
Photographic:	
Dyes, manufacture	375, 376, 392
Equipment, Publications Division	441
Photographs, furnishing to newspapers by Publications Division	441–442
Phraseology, changes, by bureaus and offices	63–66
PIERCE, Mr., statements on Roads Bureau work	508, 509
Pigeons, wild, return, question	431–432
Plant:	
Diseases, survey work and appropriations	263–268
Industry Bureau—	
Committee recommendations	12–14
Estimates and appropriations	4
Provisions for cooperative work	761
Statements of Chief and others	261–310
Quarantine act, enforcement	742–754

Plants: Page.
    Tropical importations, acclimatization work............................ 271
    Fibrous, paper-making experiments.................................. 279–280
Poi, origin and use... 368
Poisoning birds injurious to crops....................................... 425
Porto Rico:
    Experiment Station, appropriation and work......................... 496–497
    Extension work.. 490, 496
Potash:
    Carbonate, recovery from wool scouring............................. 394–395
    Deposits and sources....................................... 400, 401, 407
    Utilization from waste products..................................... 399, 401
Potato:
    Diseases, investigations... 270–271
    Shipments, value of market inspection service, instance................ 652
    Wart disease, spread, and quarantine work......................... 745–747
Potatoes, seed, improvement work, statement of Dr. Taylor................ 286–287
POTTS, R. C., statement on dairy marketing............................. 596–597
Poultry:
    Handling, etc., Chemistry Bureau.................................. 363–364
    Products, market news service, extracts from letters................. 597–599
Promotions, estimates by bureaus and offices............................. 34–41
Property, unserviceable, sale receipts.................................... 7
Publications Division:
    Appropriations recommended, proposed uses.......................... 18–19
    Committee recommendations....................................... 18–19
    Estimates and appropriations....................................... 4
    Hearings... 437–443
Public Roads Bureau. (See Roads Bureau.)
Quarantine:
    European corn borer... 414
    Live-stock diseases... 159–161
    Seeds and plants, importations.................................... 288–289
Quarantines, plant, enforcement.. 742–754
Rabbits, jack, extermination.. 425
Rabies, investigation and control work................................... 426
RAINEY, Representative:
    Meat-inspectors' salaries........................ 231–238, 240, 256, 257, 258, 259
    Income of veterinarians in private practice......................... 258
    Market news service on live stock and meats....................... 588–589
    Preparation and marketing of food products....................... 638, 650
RAWL, B. H., chief, Dairy Division, Animal Industry Bureau, statement... 174–193
Reclamation projects, demonstrations:
    Estimates and appropriations....................................... 4
    Statements on.. 755–756, 758–760
REESE, R. M., statement as chief clerk of department............ 73–87, 112–126
REID, EDWY B., statements on Publications Division work............... 440–443
Rent, District of Columbia, estimates and appropriations................. 4, 123
Revenues, Agriculture Department, 1918................................. 5–7
Rhode Island, funds under Smith-Lever act.......................... 477, 478, 479
Road:
    Building field work.. 504–505, 510
    Materials, selection and testing.................................... 507–508
Roads Bureau:
    Appropriations recommended, proposed uses...................... 4, 21–22
    Chief, salary increase... 503–504
    Committee recommendations..................................... 21–22
    Hearings... 503–523
    Construction in National forests, 1918, 1919......................... 347–349
    Federal aid, expenditures... 505–506
    Maintenance, cost.. 508–511
    Management, investigations....................................... 504
    Surfacing, cost... 508
    Traffic census.. 509
Rodents, extermination work.. 425–426
Rommel, George M., Animal Husbandry, chief, statement............... 193–206

INDEX.

RUBEY, Representative: Page.
    Forest receipts... 315–316
    Game wardens.. 430–433
    Lumber for forest use.. 313
    Soil surveys... 406
    Credits, work of Market Bureau, statement of Mr. Brand.............. 668–669
    Engineering, statement by E. B. McCormick, chief...................... 515–523
    Organizations, Market Bureau, statement of Mr. Thompson............. 670–677
RUSSELL, Dr. H. L., statement on work of agricultural colleges, etc........ 475–478
Rust, wheat, cause and control work....................................... 274–279

Salaries:
    Chemistry Bureau, changes, promotions, etc. 369–374, 383–384
    Crop Estimates Bureau increases.. 446
    Employees', contributions from outside, statement..................... 760–764
    Game wardens, discussion... 429–435
    New appointees, comparison with others, discussion................... 68–72
    Weather Bureau, discussion... 141–148
Salary:
    Chief of Entomology Bureau, statement by Mr. Harrison.............. 411, 412
    Increase—
        Chief, Biological Survey... 423–424
        Chief of Road Bureau... 503–504
Sand, use in road building.. 507, 509
Sardines, discussion... 365–367
Sargol tonic, drug case.. 360
Scabies, sheep and cattle, control progress.............................. 159–161
SCOTT, W. M., statement on market inspection of perishable foods......... 651–661
Secretary, office:
    Changes in bill... 8–9
    Estimates and appropriations.. 4
    Statement of chief clerk of department.................................. 73–87
Seed:
    Alfalfa, supply and source.. 291
    Clover, importation, and countries from whence received............... 290–291
    Crop estimates... 449
    Producers, advisory committee, report................................... 606–607
    Sugar-beet—
        American production, comparison with imported.................. 289–290
        Importation from Russia, and available supply..................... 289–290
Seed potato improvement work... 286–287
Seed-reporting service, statements of Mr. Brand........................... 605–613
Seeds:
    American production, growth of industry, quality, etc................. 289–291
    And plants, importations, quarantine restrictions, etc 288, 289, 291
    Congressional distribution... 14
    Prices, 1919, quota to farmers, etc...................................... 309–310
    Sale receipts.. 7
    Testing, selection, etc... 272–274
Serum, hog-cholera, manufacture, use, value, and price.................. 216–218
Sheds, fumigating, for treatment of pink bollworm in cotton............. 748
Sheep:
    Number on farms and ranges, 1918...................................... 585
    Production, investigations.. 193–203
SHERMAN, WELLS A., statement on market news service on fruits and vegetables.. 548–576
Sirup, table, manufacture... 380–382
Skins, wild animals, value.. 426
SMITH, C. B., statement on extension work, North and West.............. 486–489
Smith-Lever funds:
    Use in extension work... 460–486
    Use in insular stations, discussion...................................... 495
Smith-Hughes Vocational Act, effect on extension work................... 489, 499
Smut, cereal, eradication work.. 279
"Snide" baskets, use and purpose... 684

INDEX. 781

	Page.
Soda, nitrate, sale receipts	7

Soil:
    Surveys, publication, cost.. 406
    Types, investigations.. 397
Soils Bureau:
    Committee recommendations... 16
    Estimates and appropriations... 4
    Hearings... 397–410
    Land classification, cooperation...................................... 16
Solicitor:
    Department, statement... 87–112
    Office, work, nature, cases, etc...................................... 92–94
South Dakota, live stock and dairying, experiments..................... 758–759
Southern States, drainage work.. 512–513
Soy bean, food use, investigations..................................... 368
Standards, Bureau:
    duplicating work, discussion.. 5
    Duplication of work by Chemistry Bureau..................... 376, 379–380
States:
    Appropriations for cooperative extension work..................... 461–486
    Relations Service—
        Appropriations recommended, proposed uses.................. 20–21
        Committee recommendations................................. 20–21
        Employees in District of Columbia........................... 484–486
        Estimates and appropriations................................ 4
        Hearings.. 459–502
        Provisions for cooperative work............................. 761
    Road expenditures under Federal-aid act........................... 505
Statutory roll:
    Increase, Biological Survey Bureau................................. 423
    Positions, salaries.. 369–370, 383
    Transfers, States Relations Service................................. 483
Sugar-beet:
    Nematode, control work.. 280–281
    Seed, importation, planting methods, etc.......................... 288–289
Sulphuric acid, treatment of phosphate rock............................ 405
Superintendent of distribution, statutory position....................... 438–439
Survey, Mexico bollworm conditions.................................. 752–753
Surveys, road, costs... 506
Sweet potato, weevil control... 418–419
Sweet potatoes, drying.. 386
Swine, number on farms and ranges, 1918............................. 585
Tar, kelp, value.. 409
TAYLOR, Dr. WILLIAM A., chief, Plant Industry Bureau, statements...... 261–266,
                                                                                                        268–273, 279–291, 307–310
Telegrams, Weather Bureau lines, receipts, 1918........................ 6
Telegraphers:
    Salaries, discussion.. 665–667
    Scale of wages.. 667
Telegraphic market news, rates, use and value........................ 552–560
Testing road material.. 507–508
Texas:
    Barstow, pink bollworm infestation................................ 751
    Pink bollworm—
        Infestation... 749–751
        Quarantine work.. 749–751
Textiles, work of Home Economics Office............................. 500
Thrasher explosions, investigations................................. 360–363
THOMPSON, C. W., rural organizations, work of Markets Bureau....... 670–677
THOMPSON, Representative:
    Cheese use per capita, various countries............................ 179
    Chemistry Bureau work....................................... 369, 372
    City Market Reporting Service................................. 621–625
    Cooperative marketing.. 540
    Crop Estimates Bureau work......................... 446, 448, 456
    Dry farming.. 283, 285

782 INDEX.

THOMPSON, Representative—Continued. Page.
  Farm prices and farmers' wages and incomes............................ 240, 245
  Foreign cattle... 175–176
  Forest buildings... 312
  Game wardens... 430–434
  Goat milk.. 178–179
  Hay and Feed Reporting Service... 600–602
  Market inspection of hay... 659–660
  Market news service on fruits and vegetables.......................... 548–549, 571
  Preparation and marketing food products................................. 634–635
  Publications Division... 440–441
  Road Bureau work.. 507, 513
  Roquefort cheese.. 181
  Salary increases... 141–144, 263
  Solicitor's Office... 88–89, 100–111
  Transfer of meat inspectors.. 251
  Veterinary colleges... 247
  Work of Secretary's Office... 85–86
Tick, cattle, eradication.. 172–173
Tile drainage... 512–514
Timber:
  Forest, receipts, 1918.. 5
  Estimating and appraising, in National Forests, appropriation decrease... 346
  Insects, control... 418
Tobacco, production, handling, etc... 279
Tractors, horsepower determination.. 516–523
Traffic census.. 509
Transfers:
  From lump funds to statutory rolls.. 46–50
  Statutory rolls, by bureaus and offices................................... 50–52
Travel expenses:
  Crop Estimates Bureau... 446, 448
  Chemistry Bureau.. 382
  Increase, Insecticide Board.. 741
Treaty, migratory-bird, discussion.. 427–434
Trees, forest and ornamental (and shrubs), diseases, investigations......... 268–270
TRIEBER, Judge, decisions on migratory-bird law............................ 431, 434
Truck crop:
  Diseases, investigations... 270–271
  Specialists, Crop Estimates Bureau, cost.................................. 448, 449
TRUE, Dr. A. C., statements as Director of the States Relations Service.... 459–475,
                                                  478–486, 489–491, 494–495, 501–502
Tuberculosis:
  Animal, immunity studies and progress................................... 234, 241–242
  Eradication work, November, 1918, by States, table..................... 165
Vegetables:
  Carload shipments, 1916... 570–571
  Drying... 5, 386–388
  Market News Service... 548–576
Vehicles:
  Motor—
    Mileage rates, committee recommendation............................. 29
    Mileage rates, National Forests... 350–354
  Passenger-carrying, committee recommendations....................... 28
VEITCH, Mr., statements on wool-scouring wastes......................... 394, 395
Veterinarians:
  Importance of work to animal industry.................................... 241
  Scope of work, salaries, etc... 231–259
Virgin Islands, Experiment station organization, progress................. 497
Vocational Education, Federal Board, cooperation with................... 489, 498
Volcanic Research Association, title transfer................................ 145–147
War:
  Department, use of Soils Bureau nitrogen plant........................... 400
  Emergency work—
    Chemistry Bureau.. 360, 375, 376
    Entomology Bureau.. 418
    Soils Bureau... 398, 400

	Page
Wardens, game, State and Federal	427–435
Warehousing cotton and marketing, statement by Mr. Nixon	734–740
Wart disease, potato, spread and quarantine work	745–747

WASON, Representative:
Blueberry growing	282–283
Bovovaccine	207–213
Butter making	184–185
Chestnut blight	269
Cottage cheese	189–191
Department transfers	262–263
Frost protection for orchards	150, 152
Overtime pay for meat inspectors	227–228
Sheep raising	198–199, 202–203
Study of flora	282
Tuberculosis antitoxin	241, 242
Tuberculous cattle	163–164
Work of Secretary's Office	79–82

Waste:
Products, kelp	407–409
Wool-scouring, utilization	393–395
Waterproofing methods, development	359
WAY, CASSIUS, statement on veterinarians in private employ	259

Weather Bureau:
Aerial mail service	154–155
Committee recommendations	9–10
Estimates and appropriations	4
Frost-protection studies	148–149
Salaries and transfers	141–148
Statements of Charles F. Marvin, chief	141–157
Travel expenses	152–153
Weather observers, number, scope and work	153–154
Weather-observation stations, number and location	155–156

Weevil, sweet-potato:
Control	418–419
Eradication, estimates and appropriations	5
Western States, extension work, statement of Mr. C. B. Smith	486–489
Wheat, seed selection for root-rot control	273–274
WHITNEY, MILTON, Soils Bureau chief, statement	397–408
WILLIAMS, W. M., statement as Solicitor of department	87–112
WILSON, P. ST. J., Acting Director of Roads Bureau, statement	503–514

WILSON, Representative:
Biological Survey Bureau	425, 426, 434, 435
Crop Estimates Bureau work	446–448, 452, 456
Entomology Bureau work	417
Farm wages	246
Kelp	407
Madison (Wis.) laboratory	336–337
Passports to Mexico	529
Publications Division work	439
Women's demonstration work	460–476
Wood, distillation and preservative treatment, laboratory work	336–338
Wool scouring, by-products utilization	393–395
YOUNG, Representative, North Dakota, questions on experimental flour-mill project	691–693

YOUNG, Representative, Texas:
Butter making	175
Cotton marketing	543, 545–546
Estimates recommended	70–72
Secretary's Office	77–78, 85
Veterinarians	247
Wages, farm and city	245